Learning Disabilities

Selected
ACLD Papers

Learning Disabilities

Selected ACLD Papers

Edited by

SAMUEL A. KIRK
Professor of Special Education
The University of Arizona

JEANNE McRAE McCARTHY
Professor of Special Education
The University of Arizona

HOUGHTON MIFFLIN COMPANY • BOSTON
Atlanta • Dallas • Geneva, Illinois
Hopewell, New Jersey • Palo Alto
London

Library of Congress Catalog Card Number: 74–20857

ISBN: 0–395–20200–0

Contents

Preface

The purpose of this book is to provide students,
professionals, and parents who want to understand
the current concepts and controversies of the field
of learning disabilities with a collection of
selected articles from the *Proceedings* of the
ACLD Conferences, which began in 1963. This
unique and rich record reflects the thoughts of
those foremost in the field of learning disabilities
today.

The anthology is of particular value since the
Proceedings of the ACLD Conferences are not
always readily available; indeed, some are out of
print. These presentations will help to fill an
urgent need of many inservice training programs,
especially those that are hampered by a lack of
library facilities. This compilation should serve
as a supplementary text in any preservice or
inservice course in learning disabilities.

It is common knowledge that a selection of
articles from a vast number of excellent addresses
can be arbitrary and contingent on the interests
of the editors. To avoid such subjectivity, we
went through several stages in the selection of
the articles. First, we asked several graduate
students to review the papers in the published
Proceedings and to select the ones they felt were
important and interesting. We then reviewed
each of these and selected three or four articles
that were representative of each of the topics in
our volume. This compilation was sent to every
member of the Professional Advisory Board of
the ACLD with the request that they read the
volume and recommend additions or deletions.

Recommendations were made during the
ACLD conference held in Houston, Texas, in
February, 1974. Following this meeting, the
authors of the papers selected were asked to give
permission to reprint and to alter their
presentations if they so desired. Two asked that

their articles not be reprinted since they were now outdated; several made minor revisions.

The book is organized into ten sections. The first section is entitled "The Beginnings of ACLD" and includes four addresses by invited guests. These papers have been included for historical purposes and to explain to some extent why the term "learning disabilities" was chosen as part of the organization's title. The other sections are entitled "Overview," "Significant Issues," "Screening, Diagnosis, and Assessment," "Medical Practices," "Educational Practices," "Reading and Dyslexia," "Adolescence," "Parent Problems" and "Legislation." These topics appeared to be the major ones under discussion in the series of published *Proceedings*. Each of the sections includes an introduction by us with highlights from the presentations. Although the *Proceedings* of the 1972, 1973, and 1974 conferences have not been published, some addresses from these conferences have been included.

We appreciate the help given by the members of the Professional Advisory Board and the enthusiasm of the entire Association for Children with Learning Disabilities. The editors also wish to express their sincere appreciation to Marie Wittwer, graduate research assistant, for her untiring help in organizing and preparing this manuscript for publication.

ACLD does not yet have an official publication program. It is expected that this volume will be the first ACLD publication offered for sale by the national office and the state chapters, as well as by the publisher. We hope it will not be the last.

The Association for Children with Learning Disabilities receives all the royalties from the sale of this book so that the work of ACLD to help children with specific learning disabilities will continue undiminished.

Samuel A. Kirk
Jeanne McRae McCarthy

Learning Disabilities

Selected ACLD Papers

One

The Beginnings of ACLD

On April 6, 1963, representatives of the organizations listed below met in Chicago to participate in a symposium on perceptually handicapped children and to discuss the possibility of organizing a national association:

- Alabama Foundation to Aid Aphasoid Children
- Minnesota Association for the Brain-Injured Children
- Milwaukee Society for Brain-Injured Children, Inc.
- Tulsa Education Foundation and Oklahoma Council for Children with Learning Disabilities, Inc.
- Fund for Perceptually Handicapped Children, Louisville, Kentucky
- Fund for Perceptually Handicapped Children, Evanston, Illinois
- Hamilton County Committee for Crippled Children and Adults, Chattanooga, Tennessee
- The Memphis and Shelby County Association for Brain-Injured Children
- Maryland Association for Brain-Injured Children, Inc.
- Fund for Perceptually Handicapped Children of Central Kentucky, Inc.
- Michigan Children's Neurological Development Program
- Parent Teachers Council for Exceptional Children, Canada
- New Jersey Association for Brain-Injured Children
- New York Association for Brain-Injured Children
- National Association for Brain-Injured Children

This symposium was sponsored by the Fund for Perceptually Handicapped Children, Evanston, Illinois. Its stated purpose was "to obtain information, share ideas, and open channels of communication with all groups who are interested in the perceptually handicapped child . . . and to move toward investigation of the child who has average, or above average, intelligence but is not learning." The program was published as *The Proceedings of the Conference on Exploration into the Problems of the Perceptually Handicapped Child.*

One of the major decisions to be made at the conference was the determining of a name for the association. It will be noted above that many labels for perceptually handicapped children were used in the local and state associations, with "brain-injured" being the most common. After a discussion of the advantages of labeling and classification, Kirk suggested "learning disabilities" as the least objectionable term for this type of handicap. Myklebust also used the term "psychoneurological learning disorders."

After the symposium, a business meeting was held by the conference participants to discuss details of the formation of the national association. A summation of this meeting was reported by Walter Goodman, President of the Fund for Perceptually Handicapped Children, Inc., Evanston, Illinois, as follows:

Out of this meeting came the suggestion of a national association for children with learning disabilities. The meeting continued into the wee hours of the morning. A committee was formed with Walter Goodman as Chairman to proceed with the formation of such a national association.

We are happy that since the date of that meeting, most of the primary details have been worked out; contact has been made with the people who agreed to become the nucleus in the formation of a national association for children with learning disabilities, and by the time you read this, the nucleus of the association will be formed. At next year's seminar the first annual meeting of that association will be held.[1]

---

[1]The next meeting of the new association was held in Baltimore, Maryland, in 1964, but no Proceedings were

For further information about the progress of the association, please contact the Fund for Perceptually Handicapped Children, which has agreed to act until the new association can claim permanent quarters and a permanent staff and get into full operation."[2]

During the symposium each of the state and local associations gave a brief report of its activities. In addition, other speakers presented special reports. From these reports four addresses have been selected and are included here for historical purposes.

The paper by Samuel A. Kirk, "Behavioral Diagnosis and Remediation of Learning Disabilities" attempts to delineate the professional problems in the area of learning disabilities: classification and definition of etiological and behavioral terms used in the field; and the need for behavioral analysis of abilities and disabilities for remedial purposes. Of the many terms used for perceptual handicaps, he prefers "learning disabilities."

Helmer Myklebust discusses the meaning of learning disorders that affect the central nervous system, which he refers to as "psychoneurological learning disorders." These learning disorders are seen as the result of a brain that is not functioning normally in auditory, visual, or tactual spheres, or in the process of transducing information.

In his presentation, the late Newell C. Kephart discusses the perceptual process, the integrative

---

published. No national meeting was held in 1965. In 1966, Louise Meserow, of the Tulsa Education Foundation and Oklahoma Council for Children with Learning Disabilities, Inc., received permission from the Executive Board of ACLD to sponsor the Third International Conference of the Association for Children with Learning Disabilities, in Tulsa, Oklahoma, on March 3–6. This was a highly successful conference that established a precedent for the annual meetings which have been held since that date. The Proceedings have been published through the 1971 Eighth Annual Conference held in Chicago. The Proceedings have not been published since.

[2]Walter Goodman, "Summation of the Meeting to Form a National Organization," *Proceedings of the Conference on Exploration into the Problems of the Perceptually Handicapped Child,* vol. 1 (April 6, 1963), p. 92.

process, memory and memory traces, scanning, output, and feedback, as bases for inadequate learning experience. He explains his theory of the perceptual-motor process and outlines the essential elements for the training and practical management of these problems.

Laura Lehtinen presents some of her ideas in "Emphasis for the Future." She describes how, as a young teacher, she went to the Wayne County Training School in Michigan in the 1930s to work with Alfred Strauss and Hans Werner, newcomers to this country, and pioneers in the field of learning disabilities. She points out the continuing paucity of facilities and makes pleas for (1) more facilities and services; (2) improvement in diagnostic and remedial procedures, and (3) improvement in the training of personnel. In 1975 these improvements are still badly needed.

Behavioral Diagnosis and Remediation of Learning Disabilities

SAMUEL A. KIRK

Any group that meets to discuss the problems of children with developmental deficits of one kind or another is facing a formidable task. I say a formidable task because no one yet has been able to present us with a solution to the management and training of these children. If we had a foolproof solution to the management and training of deviations in children, this meeting would not be necessary. And the fact that there are so many diverse opinions and partial solutions should make this meeting highly interesting and hopefully challenging.

As I understand it, this meeting is not concerned with children who have sensory handicaps, such as the deaf or the blind, or with children who are mentally retarded, or with delinquent or emotionally disturbed children whose problems are caused by environmental factors. It is concerned primarily with children who can see and hear and who do not have marked general intellectual deficits, but who show deviations in behavior and in psychological development to such an extent that they are unable to adjust in the home or to learn by ordinary methods in school. The causes of these behavior deviations have been postulated as some sort of cerebral dysfunction.

There are two kinds of terms that have been applied to these children, either alone or in combination.

The first group of terms refer to causation or etiology. We try to label the child with a term that has biological significance. These terms are *brain injury, minimal brain damage, cerebral palsy, cerebral dysfunction, organic driven-ness, organic behavior disorders, psychoneurological disorders,* and a host of other terms. All of these terms refer to a disability of the brain in one form or another as an explanation of the deviant behavior of the child.

The second group of terms refers to the behavioral manifestations of the child, and includes a wide variety of deviant behavior. Terms such as *hyperkinetic behavior, perceptual disorders, conceptual disorders, Strauss syndrome, social dyspraxia, catastrophic behavior, disinhibition, learning disorders,* and the various forms of aphasia, apraxia, agnosia, dyslexia, and a host of other terms describe the specific behavior deficit of the child.

I know that one of your problems is to find a term that applies to every child. Last night, a friend of mine [at this meeting] accosted me with the statement, "We're going to ask you to give us a term." I didn't know how to answer his question, and I still do not believe I can answer it because the

---

From the *Proceedings of the First Annual Meeting of the ACLD Conference on Exploration into the Problems of the Perceptually Handicapped Child.* Chicago, Ill. (April 6, 1963), pp. 1–7.

term you select should be dependent on your specific aims. Is your purpose a research one, or is it a management and training problem?

Research workers have attempted to correlate the biological malfunctions with behavioral manifestations. Actually the job of the neurophysiologists and the physiological psychologist is to explain deviations of the brain and their effect on emotional, perceptual, and cognitive behavior, or vice versa, to explain the behavioral manifestations by finding the correlated brain dysfunction. This is a research task and of particular concern to the research neurophysiologist and physiological psychologist.

As I understand it, the task of the group meeting today, however, is not to conduct research on behavior and the brain, but to find effective methods of diagnosis, management, and training of the children. From this point of view, you will not be so concerned with the first category of concepts relating to etiology of brain injury or cerebral dysfunction, but with the behavioral manifestations themselves and with the methods of management and training of the deviations in children.

Actually, what does it mean to say that one of these children is brain-injured? It is actually saying that the overt behavior of a child, *hyperactivity* (which we can observe), *low intelligence* (which we can test), or perseveration, short attention span, or learning disability is caused by a *brain injury* or *cerebral dysfunction* for which we may or may not have adequate neurological evidence. But we have some brain-injured individuals, diagnosed as cerebral palsied, who have obtained M.D. or Ph.D. degrees. We have some definitely diagnosed brain-injured children who are severe mental defectives. We have some brain-injured children who are hyperkinetic (hyperactive) while others with brain injuries are extremely lethargic, underactive, and passive. If we can obtain diverse types of behavior, high intelligence or low intelligence, hyperactivity or hypoactivity, under the same label "brain injury," the label ceases to have diagnostic integrity from the point of view of management and training.

I have felt for some time that labels we give children are satisfying to us but of little help to the child himself. We seem to be satisfied if we can give a technical name to a condition. This gives us the satisfaction of closure. We think we know the answer if we can give the child a name or a label—brain-injured, schizophrenic, autistic, mentally retarded, aphasic, etc. As indicated before, the term "brain injury" has little meaning to me from a management or training point of view. It does not tell me whether the child is smart or dull, hyperactive or underactive. It does not give me any clues to management or training. The terms cerebral palsy, brain-injured, mentally retarded, aphasic, etc., are actually classification terms. In a sense they are not diagnostic, if by diagnostic we mean an assessment of a child in such a way that leads to some form of treatment, management, or remediation. In addition, it is not a basic cause, since the designation of a child as brain-injured does not really tell us why the child is brain-injured or how he got that way.

I often wonder why we tend to use technical and complex labels, when it is more accurate and meaningful to describe behavior. If we find a child who has not learned to talk, the most scientific description is that he has not yet learned to talk. The labels of aphasia or mentally retarded or emotionally disturbed are not as helpful as a description and may, in many instances, tend to confuse the issue. Instead of using the term hyperkinetic we would understand the child better if the observer states that he continually climbs walls or hangs on chandeliers.

I should like to caution you about being compulsively concerned about names and classification labels. Sometimes names block our thinking. I would prefer that people inform me that they have a child that does not talk instead of saying to me their child is dysphasic. People apparently like to use technical terms. I have received letters from doctors and psychologists telling me that "we are referring a child to you who has strephosymbolia." I would prefer that they tell me that "the boy has been in school two years, and he hasn't yet learned to read even though his intelligence is above average." This description of the problem is more scientific than the label "strephosymbolia," since the latter term itself has a specific meaning. It actually means the child has twisted symbols because of lack of cerebral dominance. But it is used by some people to designate a child who is retarded in reading, regardless of the cause.

Recently, I have used the term "learning disabilities" to describe a group of children who have disorders in development in language, speech, reading, and associated communication skills needed for social interaction. In this group I do not include children who have sensory handicaps such as blindness or deafness, because we have methods of managing and training the deaf and the blind. I also exclude from this group children who have generalized mental retardation. This approach has led me and my colleagues to develop methods of assessing children, or describing their communication skills in objective terms, in such a manner that gives us clues to management and training. A description of the development of a diagnostic test with illustrative cases follows. [Case descriptions deleted.]

This case illustrates a procedure for behavioral diagnosis and remedial education designed specifically for the deficits of an individual child. Since the child has not learned certain necessary functions during the developmental stages and since learning techniques were used in remediation, I have felt that the proper general designation for such children could be *learning disability*. The name, however, is not as important as the idea, namely the proper behavioral assessment of the child and the programming of learning materials that will ameliorate his basic areas of behavioral deficits.

In summary, I should like to state that the diagnosis of the child who shows deviant behavioral manifestations should first include a thorough medical examination. Some children labeled "brain-injured" have been found to have other physiological disturbances. I recall a child who was not manageable in a classroom because of extreme hyperkinetic activity. He tested borderline in intelligence, could not learn to read, had short attention span and demonstrated other behavior characteristics ascribed to brain-injured children. No neurological signs were found to confirm the diagnosis of cerebral dysfunction. At the age of ten, he was found to have hypoglycemia, a condition opposite to diabetes, in which the sugar was being burned up too fast. When this diagnosis was made and sugar added to his diet, he became a model boy behaviorally and learned in school at a rapid rate.

The second diagnosis should be that of the home and environment to determine whether factors in the home are contributing factors in his behavior.

And thirdly, he should have a behavior assessment, not just a general intelligence test, an M.A. and an I.Q. The assessment should be of the type described here. The major purpose of the psychological assessment should lead to methods of training deficits or conditioning social behavior. A classification and a label is not enough. We must analyze the factors involved so that the conditions of the environment can be programmed in such a way as to ameliorate deficits or to teach the child to control his behavior. A multidisciplinary approach to diagnosis can lead to medical management, social management, and remediation of behavioral disabilities. The most important treatment in most of these children, after medical attention when indicated, is the focusing of training on the behavioral deficits found in the child from a behavioral diagnosis.

What Do We Mean by Learning Disorders?

HELMER MYKLEBUST

You all know that a child is not born with the aspects that go to make up the adult human being. As a matter of fact, it takes the child almost a third of his lifetime to really achieve adulthood. It's a remarkable thing when you think about it; it takes the child longer to grow up than any other form of life known. Now, by virtue of the fact that it takes so long there are, of course, many vulnerabilities, many things can happen and, of course, all of us know that certainly many things do happen. Many children face obstacles in this process we call learning, in this process they must go through from the infant stage to the stage of adulthood. I think it's fair to say that there are three main types of obstacles that confront many children.

First of all, a child might, for any number of reasons (and I say it this way because certainly it is an oversimplification to say that it's always due to parents), encounter emotional trouble.

We here are not unaware that there are many children who have difficulties in developing the feelings that are commensurate with his age, the feelings that go along with the stage of development that he is in. If an individual reaches the age of eighteen, let us say, but has the feelings of those of five, six, eight, or even ten years of age, there can be real problems, real tragedy. So this is one kind of obstacle that faces every human being; that is, achieving the emotional maturity characteristic of his age.

This, however, is not the kind of learning problem we are talking about, although this kind of difficulty can affect learning. It can impede this process of acquiring the traditions, the kind of learning that we call scholarship, or education, which characterizes any given culture.

The second obstacle is referred to as involvements of the peripheral nervous system. We are referring to problems that arise in learning, in this process of growing up, as a result of some involvement of part of the organism, and that part which we refer to as peripheral nervous system. The two primary learning problems of this type, or conditions which cause learning problems, are deafness and blindness. Such involvements of a part of the organism plays a vital role in learning, a vital role in the individual's achieving the stage of grown-upness we call adulthood.

The third major kind of obstacle is the main one we are concerned with, that is, the one which entails and affects the central nervous system. This

From the *Proceedings of the First Annual Meeting of the ACLD Conference on Exploration into the Problems of the Perceptually Handicapped Child.* Chicago, Ill. (April 6, 1963), pp. 87–92.

one is the one that we refer to as causing psychoneurological learning disorders; that is, learning disabilities which have their base in brain disorders, the kind of learning problem which is inherent in the fact that the brain itself is not functioning normally. This is the basis of the condition which we refer to as "learning disorders." If the brain is very extensively involved, we have severe mental retardation. This problem, it would seem from the standpoint of the history of it, has been more readily recognized. If you study the evolution of understanding problems of people, you find that the ones that are the most debilitating, the most obvious in their effect on people, are the ones that have been recognized first. The one that we are talking about here is less obvious, although an involvement of the brain is entailed.

Now we shall spend just a moment on this brain of man. Man's brain is unique in that it is able to function in ways which are characteristic only of the human being. We don't have time to develop this in detail, so let me gist it like this: Man's brain is the only one that has at the higher levels of its development areas which serve the fundamental means by which man learns. There is an area that serves primarily for the purpose of dealing with that which we hear. Then there is an area in the brain of man that equally represents vision (unlike some lower animals, such as the dog). Both of these are very important in the understanding of learning disorders, and then may I say also, that in man's brain there is an area which is specifically for the purpose of integration, for making sense out of these things that come into it, an area which deals specifically with elaboration or with abstraction, with attaching significance and meaning to that which is coming in, in a manner which typifies learning in man, so that it is possible for man to foresee and foretell consequences. This is important because the way this brain is organized results in the many different types of learning problems.

However, let me spend most of our time on auditory learning disorders. Now notice what I have said. I have said that there are learning disorders which by their very nature are basically due to an involvement of the brain which affects that primarily which is coming in through the ears. Now how can we break this down? Well, if we are going to figure it out in a child, you have to break it down in lots of ways. If you are going to figure out what to do about it in the child, you have to figure it out, it seems, even more meticulously, more in detail than we are able to do at this time. But it may go something like this. It's possible for an auditory learning disorder to be of the type where the individual is unable normally, not in a 100 per cent way but in many instances, to differentiate between sounds; for example, like "cold" and "coal." This inability to get these straightened out certainly is going to cause trouble because what comes in is misunderstood; what comes in is not properly categorized and related to what it is supposed to be. This is one kind of problem, and another one is auditory memory.

Now auditory memory, difficulties in learning of the auditory memory type, also can be broken into different types. For example, a given child may have difficulty in learning a simple rote sequence such as days of the week, or months of the year. The average child of seven to eight is able to get most of this straightened out pretty well. After it comes in for a long enough period of time, he can relate it to what it's supposed to be related to, and it makes sense. However, we are seeing sixteen- and eighteen-year-olds, very mentally competent high-school students, who still can't do it. There is something wrong, you see, in a very simple rote sequence kind of learning.

Here is another kind of auditory memory difficulty, and it is fascinating, if perplexing, and it is a problem to the person, the individual, the child that has it! This is trouble with sequences of ideas. Days of the week is essentially one idea. But here is a child that when you, as a teacher, say to him, "Put your book over there, and then get your pencil, and then get your chair, and come over here by me," he is supposed to do it according to the sequence which you gave him. In this given example it may not be too important, but in certain situations, he'd better do it the way he's supposed to do it according to the one, two, three steps or, of course, the whole situation gets jammed up. This kind of break is very important and extremely difficult for some children; they are unable to follow the simple routines in the classroom because they're given in a certain order and expected to be fulfilled in this order.

Now there are other problems, for instance in remembering long sequences; you might read a long sentence, with the idea that the child is to be able to keep all of this in mind as a sentence, as one given bit of information on which to base his behavior. Now sometimes he just can't do this. The first part of it gets mixed up with the middle and the last part of it, and he is all confused in terms of what really was said. It breaks down on him.

We are talking about auditory involvement, we are talking about coming in auditorially and dealing with it just in the auditory sphere, in the auditory function. Now, it's possible to have the same kind of thing in the visual functions. We call this, just for our purposes for study and work with this, the intra-auditory and the intra-visual. But here I am going to leave the visual because what we would like to stress next is that we aren't just auditory; we are also visual, tactual, and so on. And the function of the brain is to take this auditory input and relate it to the others.

Let's take a couple of examples. What is the visual equivalent of "m-a?" Of course, you all know, it's "Ma." This is the auditory equivalent of what you see as "m-a." You all know this, but let me ask you, "How do you know?" Think about that. How do you do this? Now, let me give you this one—"p-a-p-a." What is the auditory equivalent? Or, if I say "Papa," what's the visual equivalent? Now this, of course, in engineering lingo, which is so important in the development of understanding so much of what goes on in the nervous system today, in this whole area of biomedical engineering, is what is called transducing, or the converting of energy into a different form. Now we are saying that the brain is doing this all the time; it's taking one kind of information, shifting it over to another kind, and back and forth constantly, because this is the process of everyday living; this is the process of everyday function and behavior. Well, this is where we run into very real problems in learning, very real problems. Many youngsters can function well within a given sensory area, the auditory or the visual, but they can't get these two going together.

Let us say for example that a child has difficulties in the auditory sphere. Now for very good basic reasons, which nature provided in the evolution of man, our language system is basically auditory—we don't first learn to read and write; we first learn to talk and understand and speak. We function very much in the auditory sphere. As we get to learning to read, especially to write and spell, we refer back to the auditory. But here's the individual who can't relate it, so this is one kind of reading problem. This individual breaks down. He learns what the letters sound like but he can't learn what they look like. He learns what they look like but he can't learn what they sound like. Take the case of W. J., who was sixteen when we saw him. I said, "W. J., spell *chair*, write *chair*." He said, "I can't write." I said, "Try it. Let's see what you can do." Of course, it was almost a hopeless affair. I said, "Can you do it if I spell it for you?" He said, "Yes." "Well," I said, "let's see." So I said, "*C*, write *C*," and he wrote it; I said, "*h*" and he wrote it, and so on. He wrote it perfectly. Now what did I do? I'm only trying to illustrate, you see, that in this particular instance, what we had to do was to provide an auditory aspect—he had the visual. It can be the reverse. In other words, this getting together of sensory information is really a very basic thing today in understanding learning problems in children, as far as we can tell.

Now, these problems aren't all verbal. There are the most baffling and intriguing problems that are nonverbal. Here's this youngster who can't get straightened out—although he has a good mind and is basically very sound in his learning capacities, but he can't get straightened out what's right and what's left. Right and left is broken down and confused. Then if you take him on to directions—North, South, East, West—he has a horrible time.

Here's this youngster who can't learn to abstract from maps, from blueprints or from a mechanical drawing. How does a youngster who can't abstract from maps do in your geography class? This youngster simply can't follow this kind of an abstraction or this kind of a symbolic representation of part of our experience. Then there's the youngster who does well with most things, but just breaks down on arithmetic, doesn't find any sense at all in what goes on in arithmetical functions. Now, there are many ways in which this can be off. It can be off in that he can't get the picture of the number in mind; it can be off in that he can't get the concept of the quantity of what is involved, and so on, and this has to be gone into very carefully.

Then, of course, there is the whole area of the problems generally referred to as the aphasias, the inability to understand the words as they come in, the inability to get the nervous system triggering off so the words can come out easily and readily, and the individual who finds it impossible to get the words to get to the point—he is always talking around it. He can't get the words to really hit the point of what he is trying to say. We say, "Now what do you like to do?" "Well," he says, "I like to build planes." We say, "Well, how do you do it?" "Well," he says, "you have to have clay." But it is very difficult for him to come to the point. This becomes a very basic problem in this area of learning disorders which we are talking about.

There is the problem of the inability to be able to normally sense the other person's feelings. I am not now talking about emotional disturbance. I am talking about the child who doesn't quite realize what the other child is doing in his play, and he simply can't relate himself to it. In a way this is an empathy problem, an inability to feel normally what the other person expects him to feel, which works havoc with games and play. Some parents repeatedly say to us, "When is he going to learn to play? He's doing well in the other things, but when is he going to learn to play?" Well, this is another part of it—the inability to realize that when these youngsters are doing this, he is supposed to come right in and play dead, or do something else that fits with the situation.

I want to say that as far as many of us in the science of this work are concerned, this is a new era. The new developments in teaching, the new developments in ability to analyze nervous systems—auditory systems, visual systems, tactile systems—will allow us to really enter a new era if we can get each of these spelled out and then figure out how they are breaking down and not working together normally. I think we are going to be able to do some things for some children that we have not been able to do in the past. There *are* learning disorders and these disorders *are* extremely important in people's lives, in many children's lives.

We have just been able to finish a laboratory which will use these new techniques, so that while a youngster is trying to figure out whether it is the visual that goes with the auditory, or the auditory that goes with the visual, we will simultaneously be able to get automatically by computer systems what he is doing—what he says, what he writes, and very importantly, what the nervous system is doing—mainly through automatic recording of his brain waves. So we hope to be able to see some of this new era relatively soon.

Perceptual-Motor Problems of Children

NEWELL C. KEPHART

Older theories in the field of psychology conceived of the perceptual process as a relatively simple event through which "sensory" information was received by the organism, certain "associations" took place, and a response occurred. The entire procedure was thought of as a straight-line process with only confined and restricted elaboration, as a quite circumscribed involvement of the total organism and as limited in temporal duration. Newer theories, on the other hand, consider the perceptual process as much more complex and much more dynamic than was formerly thought. These more recent theories go much further toward explaining the rather complex perceptual errors which we so frequently see in children who display the type of perceptual handicaps that we are discussing here.

The perceptual process begins with the stimulation of a sense organ. Some alteration occurs in the energy pattern which is impinging upon the sense organ. As a result of this alteration in energy pattern, certain sensitive cells discharge, sending to the cortex a pattern of neural impulses. This pattern of neural impulses, arriving at the cortex, is referred to as the *input* in Figure 1. It is to be noted that all that arrives at the cortex is a pattern of neural impulses. The pattern is determined by the number and location within the sense organ of the sensitive cells which discharged. The cortical pattern is similar to but not necessarily identical with the pattern of external energy which triggered the discharge.

This cortical pattern in itself conveys but little of the information which we are accustomed to consider as perceptual and upon the basis of which we are accustomed to respond. In the field of vision, for example, the cortical pattern contains no information regarding shape and contour, or figure ground relationships or spatial location or right-left distinctions. At best it tells us brightness, vague estimates of size, contrasts in brightness and perhaps color. It is, as Sherington has indicated, only a little "electrical storm" in the cortex of the brain. From this little electrical storm, the child must learn to extract all of the wealth of information about the world around him which you and I use to guide our daily responses.

When such an input pattern has been generated in the sensory projection areas of the cortex, its effects radiate out through internuncial neurones into the surrounding association areas. It is here that the *integrative process* takes place (see Figure 1).

From the *Proceedings of the First Annual Meeting of the ACLD Conference on Exploration into the Problem of the Perceptually Handicapped Child.* Chicago, Ill. (April 6, 1963), pp. 27–32.

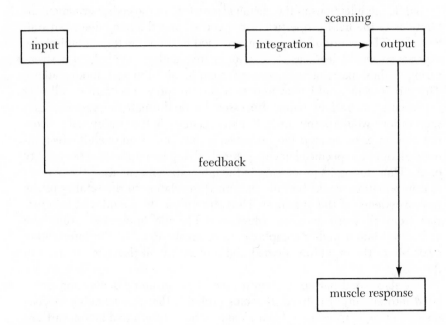

Figure 1

The integrative function involves two major aspects. First of all, it is here that the sensory impulses from all of the various sense organs are integrated together. Never, except in very rare laboratory situations, is a perceptual experience limited to one sense avenue alone. Normally, many sense avenues are sending in information simultaneously. The response of the organism is not to a single stimulus but to the total complex of stimuli being evoked at any given instant of time.

Into the association areas of the cortex where integration takes place, feed fibers from all the sensory projection areas. As a result of the integrative process, a complex pattern of neural activity is aroused in the cortex which encompasses the contributions of all the senses into one overall pattern. Our response is geared to this overall pattern, not to the pattern in any one sensory area. It is essential that such an integrated pattern be developed for use as a determiner of behavior, since only thus can we consider all sensory information at one time. Only then can we balance one sense field against another for more complete and more accurate information.

The second function of integration involves the coordination of past experiences with the present information. Involved here are the problems of memory and the memory trace. Many theories have been developed to account for the facts of memory and numerous hypotheses have been advanced. It seems probable that, at least one form of memory involves some sort of permanent alteration of the organism as a result of experience (synaptic modifications in the chemical structure of the cells, permanent alterations in the field properties of the cortex, and the like have been suggested). The continuous permanent modification of the organism by experience would lead, as it was summated and elaborated, to a structuring of those parts of the nervous system involved in such modifications. This structuring would then impose a certain form or pattern on all new experiential operations being processed by or through the system. Such speculations would permit us to think of memory in the perceptual process not as a series of isolated facts or specific data but as an overall effect, independent of its specific elements yet embodying by implication the totality of all. Thus during its processing in the integrative mechanism, the perceptual information would become patterned in relation to the totality of the past experience of the organism. Thus structured, the complex of information from all sense avenues, which was likewise integrated, would be elaborated into a highly complex pattern involving all of the information available to the organism, shaped and molded by all that has occurred in the past.

This elaborated pattern is then *scanned* by a scanning device and translated into an output pattern. It seems probable that this scanning mechanism is a simple translation from an association pattern to a motor pattern, without alteration and with a minimum of distortion. The nature of the scanning device is not fully known. However, it is thought to be related to the alpha rhythm of the cortex and thus to occur at the rate of ten to twelve cycles per second.

An *output* pattern has now been generated and we enter the output area of the diagram. This output pattern is again a pattern of neural impulses. However, at this point it is a pattern in the motor area of the cortex which can be sent down to muscle and will result in movement. The organism now has the possibility of response.

On the way to the muscle groups involved, however, a portion of the output pattern is drained off and is fed back into the system at the input end. The presence of such *feedback* in the perceptual process makes the system a servo-mechanism or closed system of control. Information from the output end of the system is oriented toward the input end where it is used for control. Control is then constant instead of sporadic and the system becomes its own control. Behavior can now be constantly monitored.

It will be seen that, on the first cycle of the process, an output pattern is generated, a part of which is returned to the input end through the feedback. This feedback output becomes a new input. As such, it alters the original input and, as a result of this alteration, triggers another cycle of the process. This second cycle results in a further alteration of the output pattern since, in the process of integration, new or different data were involved. This second output is again fed back to the input end where it creates another alteration of the input and triggers a third cycle. Thus at each cycle another cycle is triggered as a result of the process itself and independent of the external stimuli. This successive processing will continue until the input pattern and the output pattern are matched. When a match occurs, further feedback of the output pattern will not result in an alteration of the input and the process will stop since it is now in a state of equilibrium. Only when such equilibrium is attained will the perceptual process be completed and only then will the response fully represent the incoming data.

Perception, therefore, becomes, not a single act, but the termination of a process; it is not a limited procedure in time but continues over time. It is not a simple process but a very complex process involving large portions of the cortical tissue in simultaneous operation. Since the perceptual process is so complex and since it is so all pervading a function of the nervous system, it is not surprising that, if for any reason the organism finds it difficult to command simultaneous and continuous operation of any portion of the nervous system, perceptual disturbances would result. No longer, therefore, are we *surprised* to find perceptual disturbances accompanying problems of minimal brain damage, certain emotional problems and certain conditions of inadequate learning experience.

Since the perceptual process involves an input-output *match*, it is obvious that there must be stability at both ends of the system. We can only match two functions insofar as both are stable or vary in a stable relationship to each other. If either of the two functions is inconsistent, matching becomes very difficult or impossible. For the child, problems of consistency arise both at the output end and at the input end of the system.

The first problem with the perceptually handicapped child, therefore, frequently becomes one of giving him a consistent, dependable output or motor response. Note that the output pattern indicated in Figure 1 is a cortical pattern. It is a direction to muscles as to what to do. If the muscles, however, do not do what they are told or do it in an unpredictable fashion, the feedback reflects this inconsistency and therefore matching becomes difficult. A great deal of learning is required to achieve consistent motor performance. We have seen the young child learning how to coordinate muscles, how to integrate their actions, how to control the beginning, continuation and ending of their response. It is through this difficult learning process, emphasized so frequently by child development workers, that the child achieves consistency of motor response. It is only through such learning that the directions incorporated in the output pattern can be sent down through the lower levels of the nervous system to the muscles themselves with assurance that these muscles will obey orders completely and accurately. Only through such a stable response can the feedback information result in a match. It is for this reason that so much attention is being given today to the motor problems of the perceptually handicapped child. Motor response and perceptual response are inseparably knit together. Only the hyphenated term "perceptual-motor" describes the process.

Just as stability of output is necessary for the perceptual-motor match, so also is stability of input. The input function must be consistent just as the output function must be consistent. Consistency of input is achieved in part by control of the sense organ. The best illustration occurs in the field of vision. Here the control of the eyes and the head in relation to the object of stimulation determines what the input will be. Unless the eyes can be pointed at the object of regard, held there until all the necessary information is obtained and follow the object when it moves, the incoming information will vary. For the child, who at this stage cannot be aware of the nature of the difficulty, such variation can only be without rhyme or reason.

Notice that it is not control of the external eye muscles *per se* which is important, but their control *in relation to the sensory information*. The visual information itself must become the controlling factor in the muscle response. The coordination of the external ocular muscles itself is a neuromuscular learning process. A much more difficult learning process, however, is the establishment of a continuous, closed-system control such that the posture of the eyes is monitored by the information which results from this posture. It is only on the basis of such control, however, that continuous input can be achieved and the resulting perceptual-motor match can become stable. Hence the emphasis in training programs for perceptually handicapped children on ocular control and precise regulation of the eye movements.

Obviously, a stable perceptual process cannot be achieved unless the integrative function is adequate. Trouble in integration seems to take two forms. The first is quantitative in which the child appears to match only a portion of the input and output. Since he cannot achieve a match with all of the incoming stimuli, he neglects large numbers of them and achieves a limited match using only a small portion of the information. He then learns to live with this limited match, for in fact he can do nothing else, as though it were a stable equilibrium. The detail responses and much of the distractibility of the perceptually handicapped child can be seen as such lack of quantity in integration.

The second difficulty appears to arise from an integrative process which is disrupted or distorted. The integrative mechanism itself appears to be unstable (perhaps as a result of being based on unstable previous experiences). As a result, the elaboration of the input is unpredictable or incoherent. The bizarre responses and the form-perception problems of the perceptually handicapped child might be considered in this light.

Much attention has been given in the literature to the integrative aspects of perceptual problems. However, this integrative function is the one we know least about and is the one least accessible to experiment or training. It would seem that the only access we have to the integrative function is through the input-output match. If the situation can be maneuvered so that a stable perceptual-motor match is achieved, it would seem feasible that at least a partial stability of integration would also be achieved, even though limited to the immediate situation, through the process itself. By compounding such stable experiences, we might well contribute to the stability of the integrative function itself. In like manner, we might develop situations in which similar information is provided through many sense avenues at once and the child is encouraged to develop a match involving the totality of this stimulation. It might be possible through such "redundancy" of stimulation to induce more extensive elaboration in integration. It seems possible that such methods as Fernald's and the recent experiments of Myklebust are leading in this direction.

Inasmuch as we cannot approach the integrative function directly, it would seem more important for training and practical management of the perceptually handicapped child to concentrate more on the consistencies of input and output functions than to speculate further on the possible disturbances of the integrative function. Although the latter is important for theory and should not be neglected, the former may be more rewarding for our immediate problems in the education and training of these children.

It is obvious that disturbances in feedback can also occur. Here the speech problems of the deaf child provide an excellent example. Here again, two types of problems appear to exist: losses or reductions (as in the deaf child) and disruptions (as in the child who ceases to monitor, does not watch as he draws a form, etc.). In the former case, since the resulting distortion is constant, the stability of the process is not necessarily disturbed and the problem becomes one of teaching the child a constant correction which he can use in all matches and which will compensate for the distortion. In the case of a total loss, the child can be taught to use another sense avenue as a feedback source.

The second problem is more severe. Here again, feedback operations cannot be approached directly. We can only have access to them through the input-output process. It would seem probable that feedback would be stabilized whenever matching occurred. If we can maneuver the situation so that a match occurs and if we can direct the child's attention to the resulting feedback information, perhaps we can help him to learn to use this feedback to monitor his behavior. Training methods which appear to function on this principle would include all of the many eye-hand coordination activities, auditory-visual combinations, and the like.

In the perceptually handicapped child, it would appear that the perceptual process itself may be unstable. Attention might profitably be given, therefore, to training and management activities which would aid in stabilizing this process. Such activities would include:

1. attention to the development of a stable motor response system
2. attention to the control of the sense organs for the purpose of obtaining consistent input information
3. providing a large number of controlled situations in which a stable though limited match can be achieved by an individual child
4. extending both the number and extent of these stably matched experiences in order to contribute to an experiential "bank" of stable experiences, which can be used to structure integration
5. preventing insofar as possible experiences in which stability is not

achieved so that the experiential "bank" will be stability oriented. The isolation procedures of Strauss and Lehtinen may serve this purpose

6. setting the stage so that feedback information is emphasized and is used to achieve stability

7. presenting the same information simultaneously through a number of sense avenues so that the integrative elaboration is expanded and generalization is aided and so that extension of feedback control is encouraged.

Emphases for the Future

LAURA LEHTINEN

In thinking about the future, I feel as most of you feel, too, that the future doesn't begin today or tomorrow but it extends well into the past. As I meet here and talk with many old friends and professional associates, when I hear Dr. Chute recite a case history that goes back a good many years now, I feel a sense of the past that is very strongly with me today. I recall a suggestion that was made to me many, many years ago by a person who was prominent in the field of special education who suggested that I go out to Wayne County Training School in Northville, Michigan where, he said, two relative newcomers to our country—Dr. Alfred Strauss and Dr. Heinz Werner—were doing some interesting researches in the psychology and education of retarded children. The one who advised me was Dr. John Lee, himself a tireless worker in the cause of special education. He ventured the opinion at that time that the results of the Training School studies could well be highly significant to the development of the entire field. Being of a curious and investigative nature, his suggestion appealed to me and I went. I found that a teacher was, indeed, needed at the Training School. I applied for the position and was hired. So began my many years' association with Dr. Strauss and with the work of a lifetime which has never ceased to lose its fascination.

This early bud of new growth proved to be a remarkably hardy plant, as Dr. Lee prophesied. It has grown, spread to many new situational soils and adapted to a great many different environments. The attendance here today and the many questions raised attest to the vigorous interest and continuing need for exploration in this still growing area of human effort.

As you can see, bringing a desert to flower can be accomplished in many ways. Small groups working independently create their own oases of relative comfort or at least provide services for the fortunate ones who live in their environs. Representatives from these oases are here today to help, we hope, the ones living in the vast stretches between the oases which are still uncultivated, unserviced, and unstaffed.

Certainly everyone present today—not only the parents but the professional workers who must daily create plans with nonexistent services—would agree that the most pressing need is for more extensive facilities, and better services. While we may unconditionally agree on this ultimate goal, there is some diversity of opinion as to the routes to be taken toward it. We have heard some of these divergent viewpoints and tentative suggestions mentioned today. Viewing the picture from my own perspective point, I would like to comment on the several broad areas which can be

From the *Proceedings of the First Annual Meeting of the ACLD Conference on Exploration into the Problems of the Perceptually Handicapped Child.* Chicago, Ill. (April 6, 1963), pp. 81–86.

delineated. These are basic researches into brain function (Little has been said about this today, but I feel that it is certainly an important area; it will yield slow results, I am afraid, but it should not be overlooked in our thinking about the future.), applied efforts in screening, diagnostic testing, teaching, social and community participation, the question of clarification of terminology and the greater coming together in an interdisciplinary way of the various professions now working separately with each child.

The last point is the one I should like to elaborate first. In special education possibly to a greater extent than in the education of the normal child, educators have tried to apply in practice their theoretical commitment to the idea of the "whole child"—not because of their superior talents but because the nature of the material demands it. So to one degree or another, the child's medical, social, psychological, and educational status is considered in the treatment effort whenever the staff is available. The perceptually handicapped child's varying needs are there too, yet he is all too often being treated segmentally by the different disciplines involved without a coherent, overall treatment plan. The teacher works on a day-by-day basis, the psychologist evaluates the child usually once for diagnostic purposes, the social worker may or may not see the child and his parents with little opportunity to coordinate his impressions with other professionals. Rather remote from the action front is the physician who often prescribes medication with a "let's try it and see if it helps" attitude and little means of accurately checking on its effects, or he regards the learning problem as motivationally based. Fortunately in the larger urban areas at least it is becoming less common for the problem to be interpreted as the worried concern of an overanxious mother.

The most secure results have always been attained in these situations in which education, psychology, social work, and medicine, not to mention the parent, have recognized that this is a mutual problem and that while each can contribute from its unique competencies to the understanding of the whole, the most effective treatment develops from their integrated efforts. It is certainly an ideal for the future, but I trust one not impossible of realization, that part of the treatment plan for each perceptually handicapped child would include an evaluation by each one of these important specialties, a staff conference to integrate their thinking and a periodic review of the plan. This last, I want to emphasize because while a characteristic of all childhood is growth, the developmental course of the perceptually handicapped child is often more erratic or dramatic as significant life pattern changes must be made in response to his growth. At one age he may need to be sheltered in a small group or even a residential environment; as he changes, his environment must change—to a day setting, to a modified program or to regular class participation. Failure to assess the child's needs periodically can needlessly retard his growth. He may continue in a simple environment while already capable of a more complex one or he may muddle along with part-time help when more intensive help would be more beneficial. It is at these transition points that in addition to the permanent parental understanding he should have, his needs for such forms of help as medical and psychological support become intensified. Such help is easier to provide within the context of an ongoing integrated treatment plan. No suggestions were advanced today as to whether this could be in a centralized facility or traveling clinic.

Achieving such interdisciplinary communication is, of course, not only dependent upon the practical realities of time and space, which certainly must be considered, but on a mutual willingness to attempt real communication, and this will require not only greater appreciation of the competencies of one another (and in some instances recognition of one's own professional limitations as well) and a willingness to be open to the specialized knowledge accumulating in the other disciplines.

It is not only in the field of therapeutics but in research too, that interdisciplinary assaults on the problem hold promise of advancing our knowledge more rapidly than can isolated efforts. Why don't psychologists consult a teaching team in designing experiments with children? It might make them developmentally more appropriate. Or, why don't physicians work more closely together with psychologists and with teachers in some of the research on direct therapy?

One aspect of the whole problem of communication—not just between disciplines but within disciplines and between professionals and parents— is the distressing matter of the language we speak, the terminology we come to prefer. If the blind men viewing the elephant had been asked to give the creature a name, each would have chosen from his own point of view a label he thought was most descriptive of the object and doubtless, as he rejected the descriptions of the others, would have rejected their labeling also as inaccurate. In this field today we have a large number of labels, all of which seem to refer to one aspect of the problem and to carry with them their own limitations to understanding and hence communication. We now have the perceptually handicapped child, the child with cerebral dysfunction, the dysynchronous child, the child with central nervous system dysfunction, the brain-injured child with specified levels of intelligence, the Strauss syndrome, the special learning disorders, the nonachiever, the child with aphasia, the child with a language disorder, and many others. Do all of these terms actually refer to the same child? It hardly seems possible. If they do, perhaps the confusion could be reduced by having a single term as Dr. Kirk told us this morning, pointing toward the training in behavior and perception rather than etiology; if they do not, then a lexicon of terms and definitions might reduce some of the confusion. I suspect they do not. A clarification of terms and their referrents might even lead to a better delineation of the problem and to an improved dissemination of knowledge among the professions, which in turn would lead to better diagnostic services. I would like to underscore the importance of terminology, not only for communication, which is one of the functions of language, but for thinking. Language is a way of symbolizing experience and ideas; and our ideas, in fact our perceptions, are to a large extent determined by the language we adopt.

In the area of applied efforts at least three important shortcomings dominate. These are improving problem awareness and diagnostic instruments to make possible early identification, continuing to develop differential educational techniques according to the child's needs and the role of the general public in understanding the problem. I would like to add to this the collecting of normative data on the development of various perceptual, language, and conceptual skills at advancing age levels.

The importance of therapeutic efforts of early identification of the problem and accurate diagnosis can hardly be overstated. Not only does it make possible the institution of appropriate educational approaches at the time when the organism is probably most plastique in its response but it prevents the development of compounding negative social and emotional effects. We need alert and informed teachers to refer possible problems for study, or screening instruments to detect these problems which have escaped the teacher's eye. A valuable suggestion was made earlier for the revision of training curricula in schools of education and in the medical schools to bring to teachers and pediatricians an awareness of this problem so that they could be more effective in the early identification of the children.

Improved individual clinical diagnostic procedures are also a necessity, although perhaps of secondary importance to screening and early referral. Psychologists have tended to be neglectful of the powerful diagnostic tools already in their possession, perhaps because of the reluctance to regard intellectual testing as a refinement of the developmental neurological examination. It is difficult, too, to transcend the limiting confines of one's own training. For many years the psychological examination was intended to establish the level of performance and any qualitative variations in function were reported as peculiar or interesting individual differences. Gaps in understanding the "why" of the child's learning or adjustment failure were filled with a rejecting parent or rivalrous siblings. In respect to the medical aspects of the diagnosis, it is hoped that in time, a physical diagnostic study of the child with behavioral, emotional, or learning problems will not be considered complete unless a developmental neurological examination has been made.

Much study still needs to be done to improve the precision of differential diagnosis. One diagnostic differentiation I should like to comment on, which I heard little said about today, is that between the emotionally disturbed child and the child with an organic perceptual problem. The problem presents itself not only as a question of "Is he the one or is he the other?" In this case the fish can also be a fowl and treatment can only be intelligently planned if one assesses the balance of the factors in producing the symptomatology observed. A trend of the last few years has been to regard both groups as in need of the same educational and classroom management techniques with, I regret to state, sometimes unhappy consequences for the teacher, at least. Between the extremes of the child who can't learn because he has a disability in perceiving or organizing—the perceptually handicapped child—and the one who possesses normal learning processes but who can't learn because of his emotional conflicts is the long continuum of children who show both problems in varying degrees. Diagnostic differentiation of these problems should lead to differential treatment in the classroom. Clinically, I am convinced that the problems are quite different, and I think many an experienced teacher would agree. If we have no differential treatment in the classroom now, it is because we are not at the end point of our knowledge—in plain words we don't know how, either on the diagnostic or the educational level.

One of the difficulties faced by the clinician as well as by the teacher is to decide whether what he observed is a departure from the norm, and the norm of course is not the same for all ages. Perceptual development over the course of a child's growth is still only sketchily mapped out. Clearer statements of minimum perceptual skills required for given achievements as well as the effects of maturation on the development of such skills would be enormously helpful. Here, our normative studies need to be made. I know among my acquaintances many adults who have difficulty differentiating right from left. When one drives with them it is almost a hazard to say, "Turn left," because the driver wavers in his attempts to decide which way he should turn the vehicle. Yet, obviously these adults are operating on a high level of function, and while the right-left discrimination difficulty may have been a handicap, this individual somehow has been able to surmount it and to achieve considerable recognition as an adult in society. So, what is the cutoff point, or what are the interactions that make such a disability a crucial or a critical one? Is it always a disability? Or, can it be surmounted? What are the other factors that make this disability significant, and when is it not significant? I think our normative studies should, hopefully, shed some light on this problem.

These comments bring me now to the next large question of methods of specific or differential treatment for the individual child's needs. Efforts have been made toward this goal at the Cove Schools; and you have heard today from Dr. Kirk of the Illinois researches and Dr. Kephart of the work at Purdue. When we think of the unbelievable complexity of the nervous system with its multitudinous and interlocking circuits, it is hard to believe that our diagnostic procedures can ever become differentiated enough to provide specific recipes for the complex, interrelated difficulties encountered. I am convinced that greater precision than we have today can and will be achieved, but the rest will need to be left as it is today to the artful, ingenious, sensitive, perceptive teacher who carries the ultimate educational responsibility.

The most immediate and obvious need I have saved for the last—that of obtaining more well-trained teachers to staff programs on all levels. If we are not to drive prospective teachers away from the field, some of these other considerations, which may have seemed more remote as I mentioned them, assume more fundamental significance. No teacher will be willing for long to assume responsibility for an ill-assorted group of children with undiagnosed or vaguely defined "learning and behavior problems" nor to wrestle with them alone without the opportunity for consultation with other child specialists. A program will be only as good as the teacher, the administrator, and the screening staff make it. Its success will depend upon the coordinated efforts of all three.

The parents? Yes. Most of them are eager for knowledge in respect to specific planning in the home and guidance which will help them to dispel the anxiety, the frustration, the sense of isolation so destructive to their relationship with their child.

The emphases of tomorrow will arise from the shortcomings of today. I think this conference has made a long step toward looking critically and carefully at these shortcomings and a first step, hopefully, toward their correction.

Two

Overview

This section includes articles of a general nature that introduce the problem of learning disabilities as viewed by the respective authors.

In the first selection Sylvia Richardson summarizes (at one of the first meetings of ACLD) the problems from the viewpoints of physicians, psychologists, and teachers. Utilizing her interdisciplinary background in pediatrics, speech pathology, and education, she analyzes the problems of terminology, characteristics, behavior symptoms, etiology, and differential diagnosis. She points out quite clearly that we are dealing with a heterogenous group and that both the individual child and various methods for treating him must be studied. She expands this point of view by quoting from John Holt's *How Children Fail*. In her presentation Dr. Richardson places early emphasis on aptitude-treatment interaction, which has only recently gained importance as a research strategy in learning disabilities.

In the second article Samuel Kirk discusses the problem of labeling children. He states his reasons for wishing to de-emphasize the labeling of children as if it were a diagnostic procedure, and explains why he favors the use of intra-individual analysis of children's behavior and behavior modification techniques whereever applicable.

Harold McGrady in his selection describes the diagnostic-remedial approach that was prevalent at that time. He has added an evaluation of this report in a comment at the end of the article.

Jeanne M. McCarthy outlines in her paper the "Fifteen Ten Commandments" that were basic to an understanding of the field of learning disabilities. Her primary objective in delineating these principles was to infuse some common sense into a field beset by jargon, panaceas, and platitudes.

Learning Disabilities: An Introduction

SYLVIA O. RICHARDSON

When we speak about learning disabilities it is important to define our terms. In this meeting we are not discussing children who have difficulty in learning in general . . . we refer to children who have particular or specific difficulties in learning and/or those whose behavior is such that they cannot concentrate or attend when we try to teach them. The difficulties or disabilities in learning most commonly demonstrated by these youngsters are in the areas of language and/or mathematics.

Since the large majority of these children are not identified as having specific learning disabilities until they are placed in specific learning situations, they generally are not discovered or diagnosed until they have been in school for varying periods of time. Initially they may be described by their teachers as presenting behavior problems; they may be referred to by their kindergarten teachers as "immature" or "late bloomers"; they may be labeled as "emotionally disturbed."

When a child persists in atypical behavior and does not master the basic skills of the primary curriculum, or even attempt to do so, he may be called "a slow learner" (kindly), or "mentally retarded."

He is then submitted to a battery of psychological tests, the results of which do not add up to mental retardation; physical examinations and perhaps an EEG, both of which often are reported as within normal limits or "equivocal"; and his parents are questioned in depth with regard to all family interrelationships, which, of course, arouse suspicion and require further exploration. These procedures may continue for an extensive period of time. Meanwhile, the child may begin to feel like some kind of a freak, his parents undergo the tortures of guilt (now piled on top of the common guilt feelings that parents tend to have in relation to their child-rearing abilities), the teacher becomes increasingly frustrated as she prays that the "devil" in her class may soon be exorcised, and the physician may begin to think that he is dealing with a group neurosis, or he may simply feel that if everyone would just wait the child would "grow out of it."

Who is the child in the midst of the tumult? What do we know about him? We know that the child currently labeled "specific learning disability" is not intellectually subnormal, yet he has not been able to master the basic skills in the primary grades. On the basis of clinical observations, he shows evidence of some emotional disorder, but, as Eisenberg has stated, "it should be clear that emotional disorder is almost inevitably a consequence

From the *Proceedings* of the Third Annual International Conference of the ACLD, *An International Approach to Learning Disabilities of Children and Youth*. Tulsa, Okla. (March 3–5, 1966), pp. 11–19.

of the repeated frustration entailed in trying, but being unable, to learn to read."

"Unable to learn to read." Here, then, is something else we know about this child. The probability is greater that his "specific disability" is demonstrated in an inability to learn to read. In fact, most of the literature on "specific learning disabilities" actually discusses specific language disorders and/or specific behavior disorders. A language disorder is the inability of the child to use symbols for communication purposes and may be characterized by difficulties in speaking, reading, and/or writing. Thus, we know that this child probably has a specific impairment of symbolic learning. If he demonstrates just a reading disability we call it dyslexia or "specific" dyslexia, although this rose has had a multitude of names, e.g., . . . word blindness (Kussmaul, 1877); congenital symbolamblyopia; congenital typolexia; congenital alexia; congenital dyslexia (1909); amnesia visualis verbalis; developmental alexia; strephosymbolia (Orton); bradylexia; analfabetica partialis; constitutional dyslexia; specific dyslexia (Hallgren); specific reading disability; children who cannot read (Monroe, 1932).

Classroom teachers have provided much assistance in diagnosis through their descriptions of learning problems they have observed. Among the characteristics of the children with specific learning problems, teachers report the following:

1. poor visual discrimination and memory for words
2. poor auditory memory for words or for individual sounds in words
3. persistent reversals of words, syllables, or letters in reading, writing, and speech; rotation or inversion of letters; reversed sequence of letters and syllables; mirror-writing, or transposition of numbers
4. poor recall for reproduction of simple geometric forms
5. poor memory for auditory or visual sequence
6. weakly established handedness
7. clumsiness and poor hand control
8. immature articulation
9. hyperactivity and distractibility.

Clinical psychologists have discussed discrepancy demonstrated by these youngsters between the verbal and performance scores on the Wechsler Intelligence Scale for Children (WISC), pointing out that there may be from fifteen to thirty points difference in favor of the performance score. In fact, the findings on the WISC have been remarkably consistent, considering the different ways of defining these children. The most consistently reported low scores are on the Information and Arithmetic subtests. The Information subtest involves memory of information or facts presented both visually and auditorily. This finding supports the teachers' observations that the children tend to have poor auditory and visual memory. The low scores on the Arithmetic subtest may seem to conflict with the fact that the same children may have scored high on arithmetic achievement tests. However, the problems on the WISC Arithmetic subtest are presented orally and require auditory decoding, memory, and abstract reasoning, all of which involve symbolic or language skills; the achievement tests involve computational problems presented visually.

Psychologists have reported visual-motor and perceptual-motor problems in these children. Although it may be variously described, for the sake of simplicity, perceptual-motor impairment is the lack of normal functioning of either the perceptual processes (visual, auditory, or tactile), the motor processes (speaking, writing, manipulating, walking), or both. If the child's major difficulty is in correctly interpreting what he sees, the problem may be described as visual-perceptual. If the child's major difficulty is in correctly copying what he sees, it may be described as visual-motor. Again, the teachers have described these findings in the classroom, but in their own terminology.

Pediatricians, neurologists, and psychiatrists have described the following physical signs of difference between these children and those who learn the three R's:

1. mild tremor, especially on effort; mild choreiform or athetoid movements
2. hyper-reflexia
3. excessive clumsiness
4. monocular vision or minor ocular imbalance
5. disturbance of body image
   a. right-left confusion and absence of, or weakly established, laterality
   b. finger agnosia or impairment of finger-localizing ability
   c. impaired spatial concept
6. impaired form perception
7. immature articulation
8. hyperkinetic behavior with distractibility, short attention span, irritability, and emotional lability.

Acknowledging the risks of oversimplification and generalization, these children seem to exhibit signs of disorganization in the integrative perceptual-motor mechanisms of the brain. Any number of conditions—organic, environmental, or intra-psychic—may affect the way a child perceives sensory information; the result can be seen in his behavior, but the disorganization may not be appreciated by the observer until the child is of school age and fails to perform tasks that depend on perceptual-motor or behavioral organization which should have taken form earlier in development.

As stated earlier, kindergarten teachers tend to describe the behavior of some children as "immature." These same children often prove to have learning disabilities later in the primary grades. Twelve kindergarten and first grade teachers were asked to list what they believed to be the major characteristics of the "immature" child's behavior. In reviewing their descriptions, the most outstanding behavioral characteristics of the "immature" six-year-old appear to be inadequate language skills and insufficient attention span. His behavior was described most frequently as disorderly and disorganized rather than hyperkinetic. His vocal and motor output were thought to be excessive and without syntactical or contextual structure. Teachers reported that this child tends to speak and act without thinking, and when compared with normal peers the "immature" child requires much more auditory, visual, tactile, and kinesthetic reinforcement. He is described as clumsy and "closer to the ground," clinging and overly dependent on the teacher. The "immature" child, in general, seems to lag approximately one year behind his mature classmates in terms of performance in school activity, physical appearance, social and emotional interactions, and learning ability.

Now, if we re-view our child with "specific learning disability" as seen through the well-trained eyes of the physician, teacher, and psychologist his identifying characteristics include the following (at least in these the representatives of the three disciplines will agree):

1. poor auditory memory
2. poor auditory discrimination
3. poor sound blending
4. poor visual memory
5. poor visual discrimination
6. inadequate ability in visual and visual-motor sequencing
7. lack of, or weakly established, cerebral dominance
8. right-left confusion, with problems in laterality and directionality
9. fine motor incoordination
10. nonspecific awkwardness or clumsiness
11. ocular imbalance
12. attention defect and disordered or hyperkinetic behavior.

Although this child may show evidence of emotional maladjustment and immaturity, the relationship of cause and effect is not clear. The final observation, on which all agree, is that this youngster is of at least average intellectual capacity.

Those of us whose job is diagnosis tend to be "little old label-makers" searching for a cause. We sometimes create impressive labels and proceed with vigor to pin them on individuals rather indiscriminately. We create "syndromes" too; these are several signs and symptoms which tend to occur together, characterizing a particular disease. A syndrome is a bigger and better label.

Ever since Strauss described the behavior of children with a known history of brain damage, we have lumped together hyperactivity, short attention span, distractibility, irritability, and emotional lability into the "Straussian syndrome," or, more recently, "the hyperkinetic syndrome." Because children with learning disorders often show similar behavior at home and in school, the label "brain damage" fell into place. (For that matter, it has been noted that harried young mothers of preschool children also may show this kind of behavior!)

Many dislike using the term "brain damage" if there is no evidence of such. In fact, the Oxford International Study Group on Child Neurology in 1962 held a conference, the main achievement of which was the decision that the concept of "damage" be discarded.

Since the diagnosis of learning disabilities is made on the basis of symptoms of disordered function rather than on evidence of anatomical damage, the term "minimal cerebral dysfunction" is currently and justifiably more popular. Because of the heterogeneity of this group of children, it may be helpful to review T. T. S. Ingram's classification in which he defines three main categories within the concept of minimal cerebral dysfunction:

1. *Defined Clinical Syndromes with Constant Evidence of Abnormality.* In this group there is strong evidence of a *fairly constant association* between brain abnormality and particular symptoms and signs. In this category he includes the choreiform syndrome of Prechtl, the syndrome of overactive purposeless behavior known as the hyperkinetic syndrome, and the definite focal neurological abnormalities such as mild unsteadiness with intention tremor, mild ataxia, mild paresis of movement, and involuntary movements found in some clumsy children. The disorders included in this category form recognizable clinical syndromes in which the history or evidence of brain damage is fairly constant. For example, children with Prechtl's choreiform syndrome usually have a history of perinatal hypoxia. Evidence of temporal lobe damage may be found in a high proportion of children showing hyperkinetic behavior. In general, the same causal factors that are found in cerebral palsy may be found in most of these patients. Many, in fact, are regarded by some as having mild cerebral palsy, and the disorders are classified appropriately. For example, children with the so-called choreiform syndrome are appropriately classified as having mild dyskinesia or choreoathetosis.

Though there seems to be a relatively constant association between brain injury or abnormality and the disorders described in this category, it is important to remember that environmental factors may influence the symptoms. Hyperkinetic behavior, for example, seems almost self-perpetuating in some children whose parents themselves overreact to the child's unpredictable outbursts or apparently unprovoked tantrums. The magnitude of behavior abnormality depends greatly on the parents' reaction to the child's abnormal behavior (Prechtl, 1961; Pond, 1961).

2. *Defined Clinical Syndromes with Inconstant Evidence of Brain Abnormality.* Ingram's second category comprises those disorders of learning where, in some patients, but not in all, there is evidence of an association between the disorder and detectable brain injury or abnormality. In this category he includes specific retardation of speech development, which he calls developmental dysphasia, "specific developmental dyslexia" and

dysgraphia, and some cases of "clumsiness." Sometimes a history of brain injury can be found. For example, specific difficulties in reading and writing following measles encephalopathy are quite common (Meyer and Byers, 1952); but in a high proportion of patients with reading and writing difficulties there is a lack of other evidence suggesting that brain damage has occurred.

Before assuming that slow speech development, or clumsiness, or specific difficulties in writing or reading are the result of brain dysfunction, it is well to remember that there is a wide distribution of ability in children. For example, though the vast majority of children have IQ's between 90 and 110, a few normal children are well below average and a few are above average intelligence. Similarly, while some children are very dextrous others show less than average dexterity and may be called clumsy. Some apparently normal children say their first words before the age of nine months and others may not speak until over the age of two years.

Secondly, it must be remembered that many of these disorders can occur in generation after generation of apparently normal children. For example, slow speech development and specific difficulties in reading and writing often associated with ambidexterity or poor lateralization of handedness are relatively common in the families of Campbell and Maclean in Scotland. Are we then to assume that all Campbells and Macleans have brain abnormalities?

A major factor, which is often ignored, is the influence of environmental factors in producing specific clinical manifestations. A high proportion of children with retarded speech development, for example, have a history of being neglected by, or separated from, their parents in later infancy.

3. *Behavioral Symptoms in Which Brain Abnormality May Be an Inconstant Direct Cause or an Indirect Contributory Cause.* The third category includes disorders of behavior in which brain damage may be a contributory factor in a proportion of patients. There are a large number of these. Characteristics of the behavior of children with "brain damage" are said to be: unpredictable variability of behavior, hyperactivity, distractibility, impulsiveness, irritability, and difficulties in abstract thinking. Anxiety and emotional immaturity often may be found also. These symptoms include most of those for which children are referred to Child Guidance Clinics. Apart from hyperactivity of the characteristic type which has been described, all these disorders may occur in the absence of any suspicion of brain injury. Yet a significant proportion of the patients can be shown to have either a history highly suggestive of birth injury, or minor neurological signs which alone are of little importance, but which, in combination with these symptoms, may indicate that the brain is functioning abnormally.

Such a variety of symptoms and signs cannot be ascribed to the direct effect of brain injury, but abnormality of the brain in such patients may have contributed to the behavior abnormalities by damaging the infant's ability to adjust to the conditions in which he finds himself. These difficulties in adjustment are commonly reflected very early in the feeding situation, and this in turn may initiate maternal anxiety and a chain of events resulting in further disturbances in the mother/child relationship. There are some excellent studies that describe mothers' difficulties in making good relationships with abnormal babies (Oppe, 1960; Prechtl, 1961). However, it is necessary to differentiate between the normal child in an abnormal environment and the abnormal child in a normal environment; in either case behavior is disturbed.

It is almost impossible to assess the contribution made by brain abnormality to the emotional disturbances shown by children in this category. Certainly babies who have recovered from the effects of perinatal brain damage may continue to suffer in later life from the disturbances of mother/child relationship which have resulted from the original difficulty. In order to understand the behavior of a particular patient it may be helpful to know that there has been brain injury, but this discovery does not lessen in any way the need for adequate assessment of the environmental causes of emotional stress (Eisenbert, 1957; Pond, 1961).

The diagnosis of "minimal cerebral dysfunction" usually is made on the basis of clinical behavior, history, psychological evaluation, neurological signs, and EEG findings. The psychological evaluation includes tests of verbal and nonverbal intelligence, perceptual ability, language development (including comprehension, vocabulary, motor speech function, reading readiness, and reading skills) and behavioral characteristics. With regard to the EEG, in spite of the lack of agreement in this field, the high frequency of borderline records reported may be significant. For instance, the 6- and 14-per-second positive spiking pattern has clearly been found by Schwade and Geiger to be associated with outbursts of violent behavior. This is an important area for research. In general, however, it should be pointed out that the majority of neurological and neurologically oriented articles may not even refer to electroencephalographic findings, or may simply mention these in passing.

The accumulated weight of various signs and symptoms, or the singular specificity thereof (e.g., hyperactivity, dyslexic errors, large scatter or discrepancy between verbal and performance scores on the WISC), guide us in making a diagnosis. These must be evaluated carefully against a background of environmental and interpersonal determinants. At this stage of our knowledge it is logical to assume that any disorganization of brain function due to injury or to naturally occurring constitutional deviation places a hardship on the developing child. If, in addition, the interpersonal environment is unfavorable, the child is more likely to experience problems compounded of his original perceptual defect, his reactions to the attitudes of persons surrounding him, and to his own failures. These accidentally or naturally occurring deviations must exist in a scale from gross to subtle and to different degrees in the various functional and interlocking units within the brain.

Too often we have seen good parents who have a child who cannot learn to read, or who is a behavior problem, or who is impulsive and hyperactive, or whose speed of mentation is distinctly different from his siblings, for us to jump to the conclusion that the parents must have mishandled the child. The prevailing climate of opinion in both professional and "magazine" psychiatry is such as to create in these parents the convictions that somehow, by some magical aberration in their attitudes and behavior, they are to blame for the child's condition.

It is necessary to affirm again that we must take into account the full spectrum of causality from the unique genetic combination that every individual happens to be, to his gestation and birth experiences, to his interaction with significant persons, and finally to the stresses and emotional trauma of later life after his basic reaction patterns have been laid down. If at present we cannot measure, for instance, the contribution of the child's genes to his behavioral characteristics, then until we can, we should leave a large empty space in the formula of causality.

Possibly we have gone as far as we can, at this time, in our search for cause. We begin to sound too glib. Possibly now is the time to search more diligently for more suitable teaching techniques. It is highly doubtful that we are describing one condition. In fact, when these children are placed in various remedial settings, it becomes apparent that some begin to learn following psychotherapy with remediation, some with psychotherapy alone; some begin to learn when they are given visual-motor training; some show marked improvement when they are provided a corrective optical lens and orthoptic training. Some of these youngsters show remarkable improvement with specialized remedial reading such as the Fernald or Gillingham methods; some do well with remedial reading after they have received visual-motor training; and some seem to "grow out of it."

To return to a sentence stated earlier in this paper, since we are talking about a heterogeneous group we must turn our attention to closer and more detailed examination of each child, not just in the examining room but in the classroom. In every case where a child demonstrates an atypical approach to learning, there must be an adjustment in the ways the pupil is taught. An effort should be made to make as many adjustments as possible in the regular class, but wherever the severity of the learning disorder reaches certain proportions, class size must be reduced in order to maximize the individual interaction between the teacher and student. Kindergarten and primary teachers must be trained to utilize multisensorial techniques, to provide visual-motor training in the classroom, to search continuously for methods of instruction that will fit a child's needs rather than search for ways to make the child fit a particular method or curriculum.

Very often it is not until a child responds to a particular teaching technique that the underlying cause of his learning disability becomes apparent. Our teachers must receive appropriate training as well as every assistance from consulting psychologists and physicians; school programs of instruction must be flexible enough to permit a continuing search for new teaching methods; and the administrative leadership in the schools must not only allow but encourage experimentation, both with identification procedures and with adjustable methods of instruction.

I should like to close with a quotation from Mr. John Holt's new book, *How Children Fail:*

Some people say of nonreaders, "These children can't or don't read because of the way they use their minds." Others retort, "No; they don't read because of the kind of minds they have." The argument seems to me unreal as well as useless. The distinction between what our minds are and how we use them is one that exists only for purposes of talk; it does not exist at the level of reality. The mind is not a kind of thinking machine that someone or something inside of us uses, well or badly. It is: and it works, perhaps well; perhaps badly; and the way it works one time has much to do with the way it will work another time.

Religious mystics in India, so we are told, stand for many years with an arm raised, or a limb distorted or immobilized in some fashion. After a while the limb becomes unusable. What sense does it make to argue whether the cause of this is physical, or lies in the way the limb was used? It was the way it was used that made it the kind of a limb it was, a limb that could not be used in any other way. It is probably true of the mind, as well, that the way we use it determines how we can use it. If we use it badly long enough, it will become less and less possible to use it well. If we use it well, the possibility grows that we can use it even better. We must be wary, then, of assuming that because some learning difficulties seem to be caused by brain dysfunction they are therefore incurable. The brain, as an organ, may have far more flexibility and recuperative powers than we realize. What it cannot accomplish one way it may be able to do another. Conversely, we must be aware of the extent to which, in causing children to make poor use of their minds, we may be making their minds less and less useful to them.

From Labels to Action

SAMUEL A. KIRK

In the United States we have given a great deal of lip service to the education of "all the children of all the people." We have, as a result of this American ideal, established by law, under compulsory education, schools for all the children. To accommodate the volume of children who enrolled in the schools we attempted mass education—the education of all children by the same methods and materials. We of course differentiated the children into classes, with six-year-old children in the first grade, seven-year-old children in the second grade and so forth. For the majority of children this procedure has been successful, since the majority progressed in school because of, *or* in spite of, our mass education procedures.

But all the children of all of the people did not learn in the same way or at the same rate. Before we had compulsory education, these failures, for one reason or another, dropped out of school, often working on farms in rural America. It soon dawned upon authorities that children of the same age differed markedly in many respects. Some were slow learners, others very fast learners; some could not hear, and were either deaf or markedly hard of hearing; some were blind or very defective in vision; some were crippled; some were defective in speech; and some were emotionally disturbed. . . .

The totally deaf, the totally blind, and the severely crippled have always been recognized as different and treated accordingly. These children did not require differential diagnosis since their condition was obvious, and schools for the deaf and for the blind were organized in the early days. Public school classes for the education of exceptional children (the deaf, blind, mentally retarded, crippled, emotionally disturbed, and the gifted) were initiated at the beginning of this century, and have gradually grown to substantial numbers in all areas of the United States.

But there is one group of children who were not deaf but could not hear, or who were not blind but could not see, or who had difficulty in learning but were not mentally retarded. It was obvious that these children had difficulties—but their difficulties were hard to label as they were not deaf, or blind, or mentally retarded. As a matter of fact some of these children differed from each other so markedly that they could not be categorized. This situation became very frustrating to doctors, psychologists, social workers, teachers, and parents. We had no name that would encompass them all. But soon names were invented in order to decrease the frustration of professionals and parents. "Johnny is brain-injured—that is why he does not learn." "But how do you know he is brain-injured?" "Because he does

From the *Proceedings* of the Third Annual Conference of the ACLD, *An International Approach to Learning Disabilities of Children and Youth*. Tulsa, Okla. (March 3–5, 1966), pp. 36–44.

not learn although he is not deaf, blind, or mentally retarded." Few such children could be diagnosed neurologically as brain-damaged; but nevertheless it was a satisfying label. People believed that the word "brain-injured," even though not neurologically verified, actually explained the functional deficit. Also—because of the remnants of concern with family inheritance—it was better to tell a parent that he had a brain-injured child than that he had a mentally retarded child.

But attaching the term "brain-injury" did not solve the problem. Some children so labelled were hopelessly mentally retarded. Some with a label of brain-injury (cerebral palsy) were able to obtain M.D. or Ph.D. degrees. Thus the term "brain-injury" came to have little meaning since it applied to children with very different abilities. So we used other labels—brain-injury, brain-crippled, minimal brain damage, minimal cerebral dysfunction, cerebral palsy, just plain cerebral dysfunction, organic driveness, organic behavior disorders, psychoneurological disorders, and a host of others. Actually, all in this group of terms, regardless of which ones were used, attempted to establish an etiological basis for the behavior deviation of the child. It was a label that implied a biological cause.

Another group of labels dealt not with etiology but with behavior. I shall enumerate a few of them:

1. perceptual disorder, meaning that the child can hear and see, but does not see and hear like others; his perceptual processes, presumably due to a brain dysfunction, do not serve him effectively
2. hyperkinetic behavior, which describes the child who is always in motion
3. conceptual disorder, a disturbance of thinking, reasoning, generalizing, memory, or other cognitive functions
4. catastrophic behavior
5. impulsive behavior
6. disinhibited behavior.

Another group of labels deals primarily with communication disorders. And here we have evolved an extensive vocabulary of labels—aphasia, apraxia, agnosia, dyslexia, agraphia, acalculia, and many other terms. These are primarily neurological terms. Dyslexia could mean that the child has a problem in learning to read, but the term implies that the difficulty in learning to read is related to some brain dysfunction. I should like to read to you a hypothetical conversation between a psychologist and a sophisticated ten-year-old child who was having difficulty in learning to read.

PSYCHOLOGIST: You took a great number of tests yesterday. Did you like them?

BOY: No, because I couldn't read them so good.

PSYCHOLOGIST: Yes, that is why we have the tests—to find out why you haven't learned to read.

BOY: What did you find? What is wrong with me?

PSYCHOLOGIST: We have found that you have a severe problem in learning to read.

BOY:	Yes, that's what my teacher said. But why?
PSYCHOLOGIST:	You have dyslexia.
BOY:	Where did I pick that up?
PSYCHOLOGIST:	You didn't pick it up. You've probably had it all along.
BOY:	Is it catching?
PSYCHOLOGIST:	No, it's not contagious.
BOY:	Is it a bad disease?
PSYCHOLOGIST:	No, it's not a disease—it's a condition—a condition in the brain.
BOY:	A condition in the brain? Am I nuts?
PSYCHOLOGIST:	No. You're not sick.
BOY:	Will it get worse? Will I die?
PSYCHOLOGIST:	No. It's just a condition that makes it hard for you to learn to read.
BOY:	Oh, I see! That's what my teacher said—I can't read so good, huh?

The point I am trying to make is that labelling or classification of children into separate categories may be satisfying to us but not very helpful to the child. The Binet and Wechsler tests have been used primarily to determine whether a child is mentally retarded, dull, average, or superior, and have been used to place him into one or another program. Many psychologists have been concerned with the limited use of these instruments. They have become critical of an indiscriminate use of the IQ or MA and have sought a more differential diagnosis. Many have consequently fallen into the trap of differentiating some types of children and labelling them as brain-damaged even when there is no neurological evidence supporting the diagnosis—and even though the term includes children with widely different problems. In a small proportion of these cases, the diagnosis may lead to medication, but unless it does the diagnosis is of little value. From an etiological point of view it does not disclose any cause which can be removed; and from the point of view of treatment or management or training it gives no direction or purpose. Treatment advisable for one may be contraindicated for the next.

What we really want is not labels, but analysis of behavior. Such steps may be found to re-educate or re-orient or supply needed experiences on which improved functioning may be developed. At this meeting you will hear, or have heard, of the different approaches to diagnosing and treating learning disabilities. Most of the speakers are interested in diagnosis for treatment purposes, not for testing for classification.

Fortunately many are now becoming interested in organizing programs for those children—programs based on a behavioral and psychological assessment. These methods take many forms and deal with different problems. Diagnosis and treatment can work hand in hand to utilize our knowledge, understanding, and creative approaches in utilizing what we do know in order to alleviate conditions and remedy behavior.

One five-year-old child, for example, spent a great deal of time with her thumb in her mouth. We could label the child as neurotic, or we could say the child has a tic, or we could call the child by many other names. We could tell the mother she is rejecting the child, or the child did not have the right suckling experiences, or she is brain-damaged. But a more effective approach was found by observing the behavior and applying well-known psychological principles. It was noticed that when the child was playing she did not suck her thumb. But when she was watching her favorite shows on the television her thumb was always in her mouth. The question here was what to do about it. One method was to remove the television, but this would not stop thumbsucking, since it would occur in other situations. A simple procedure was devised whereby the mother pressed a button to turn off the television when the child's thumb went into her mouth, and then pressed the button to turn on the television when the thumb was out of the mouth. It did not take the child long to learn that if she wanted the television on, this would occur only when she was not sucking her thumb. This simple device was enough to break the habit of thumbsucking. This is what I mean by moving on from labels to action.

I think the best way to illustrate the variety of individuals who have different kinds of disabilities is to cite several case studies.

Some years ago a high-school graduate applied for admission to a college in which I was serving as selection officer. I refused admission because his grades in English in high school were very low and his scores on an intelligence test were below the lowest 25 per cent of high-school graduates. He then took courses in a junior college, repeated his English I three times before passing it with a grade of D, but obtained fairly good grades in mathematics and in drafting. After two years at the junior college he again applied to the college in which I was the selection officer, and again I rejected his application because of low scores on intelligence tests and his poor showing in rhetoric. But this time he was persistent. He appealed to the president for admission. At this point I was required to give adequate reasons for rejection, or at least look into his case further. Upon analysis of this individual based on a number of tests, I found that he was quite superior in spatial ability and in quantitative ability, but very inferior in verbal fluency. I admitted him into the college with the recommendation to the English department that he be given special tutoring in diction and in English.

Four years later this individual had not only completed his bachelor's degree in art, but also his master's degree. He was now art director in a very large city. He still had difficulty in English and diction but the supervision of art programs in schools did not require great verbal fluency. Here was an individual who had a learning disability in one area, who could have been denied an education had we not been forced to look into his situation a little more closely. His case made me wonder how many others were denied further education because of a learning disability in one area.

Some years ago a boy of ten years was brought to me by a school principal because of the child's inability to learn to read. On an individual intelligence test his IQ was 140. He was now in the fifth grade but was practically a nonreader. I found that he had two disabilities, one in auditorizing and one in visualizing. I recommended to the father that he have his eyes checked and that he obtain a good remedial teacher. I did not see this boy until he was twenty-two. He had graduated from high school, and had served in the Army for two years. He was also enrolled in a junior college. But his basic problem remained. On tests he now scored fifth and sixth grade in reading and spelling. He had completed high-school work because his mother read his lessons to him. He was admitted to a junior college and again succeeded partially with the aid of his mother. He now requested admission to a large university but was not accepted. After six months of special tutoring by a special tutor on his disability areas he now scored ninth and tenth grade. We asked that he be admitted into the university as an experimental case. Tutoring for one year in the university resulted in passing grades. Five years later this individual had passed all of the examinations and courses in animal science but had still failed his rhetoric exam because of a disability in spelling. It was necessary to waive the rhetoric examination which he had failed twice in order to award him a bachelor's degree in animal science.

Another interesting child was one who was committed to an institution for mental defectives at the age of two and a half years because of convulsions and severe mental retardation. At the age of four and a half he was given a series of examinations and scored around 50 and 60 IQ, but at that time he did not have any further convulsions. An EEG at this time, however, showed an abnormality. Here, according to our knowledge, was a child who was and could be labelled "feeble-minded." He was thus certified and labelled as such by physicians and psychologists. At this time we initiated an experiment on early training of mental defectives in the institution. Fifteen children, ages four to five, were taken out of the wards daily and offered intensive preschool education, while another group remained in the wards. This boy was a member of the fifteen experimental children. At this time his IQ was 50 to 60. His convulsions did not continue, although he still had an abnormal EEG. He made rapid progress in mental and social development in the preschool and was parolled from the institution to a foster home in the community. He was later adopted by a highly educated family. An EEG was repeated at the age of seven, and again it showed an abnormality. Much tutoring and care was given this boy in school, by his mother, and others. Today, at the age of nineteen he is a freshman in college, with an average grade of B. Where would this boy be today had he remained in the wards? How many more of these children have we labelled, without taking the time to do what should be done with children with problems?

Figure 1 represents a child who was diagnosed a number of times as mentally retarded, but who was probably a severe case of learning disabilities.

Here is a child who at the age of four and a half tested below 50 IQ except for tests that required no language, and on these she was low average. On certain tests she showed that she was able to understand

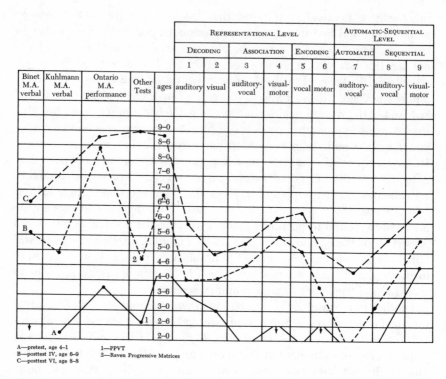

						REPRESENTATIONAL LEVEL						AUTOMATIC-SEQUENTIAL LEVEL		
						DECODING		ASSOCIATION		ENCODING		AUTOMATIC	SEQUENTIAL	
						1	2	3	4	5	6	7	8	9
Binet M.A. verbal	Kuhlmann M.A. verbal	Ontario M.A. performance	Other Tests	ages		auditory	visual	auditory-vocal	visual-motor	vocal	motor	auditory-vocal	auditory-vocal	visual-motor

A—pretest, age 4–1
B—posttest IV, age 6–9
C—posttest VI, age 8–8

1—PPVT
2—Raven Progressive Matrices

Figure 1. RESULTS OF REMEDIATION

and receive visual and auditory meanings, and was able to discriminate forms visually at an average age. She was defective in all other areas.

Intensive training with this child over a period of four years showed the following development:

She progressed mentally a year per year under remediation on psychological tests, whether they were performance or verbal intelligence tests. Although she was mentally about two years at the age of four, she now, at the age of eight is mentally six. She is still two years retarded but since the beginning of remediation she has progressed one year per year. The profile shows a more even development. In addition to this psychological profile, the child is doing second grade reading and arithmetic and is only slightly retarded in academic work.

The next child (see Figure 2) is one who is eight or nine years of age and who appears to be average in intelligence, and average in all abilities except the ability to express himself. It will be noticed from this chart that this is a child who cannot express himself vocally, or gesturally. Speech correction and counselling seemed not to help him. The treatment for this boy was by the use of programmed instruction in which the child filled in what he did not know on a typewriter and a tape recorder. It will be noticed from this profile that the boy made rapid progress in seven months of remedial instruction.

The reports of various types of disability at this conference show a major change in the approach to children with learning disabilities. Instead of

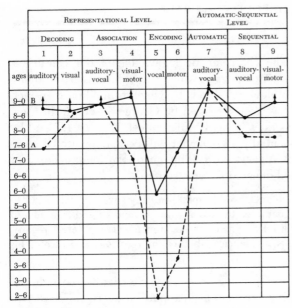

	Representational Level						Automatic-Sequential Level		
	Decoding		Association		Encoding		Automatic	Sequential	
	1	2	3	4	5	6	7	8	9
ages	auditory	visual	auditory-vocal	visual-motor	vocal	motor	auditory-vocal	auditory-vocal	visual-motor

A—pre-remediation CA 9–11
B—post-remediation CA 10–10

Figure 2. Comparison of Pre- and Post-Remediation Language Age Profiles

classifying children into categories, and instead of worrying about the etiological classifications, names, labels, and categories, the concentration of most workers at this conference—Kephart, Myklebust, Frostig, and many others—is an attempt to analyze the child's ability in such a way that remediation and training can follow. The philosophy of remediation does not deny a basic cerebral dysfunction. It implies, however, that in the growing stages children withdraw from areas that are uncomfortable, or are unsuccessful, and exaggerate the areas of response on which they are successful. If a biological defect causes a child to be unsuccessful in one area, that child will tend to avoid those areas and function in fields in which he is successful. At a later age when we test the child and find a marked behavior deficit, that deficit may be only partly the result of the biological defect, and partly the result of lack of development due to avoidance experience. An analogy can be made between the use of hands. If a cerebral dysfunction in the motor area makes the child's left hand uncoordinated, the child will avoid using the left hand, and over-use the right hand. As a result the growth of the use of the right hand is average or above, while the left hand grows in coordination more slowly. Remediation in this case would be special exercise of the left hand. Thus the philosophy of remediation of deficits asserts that the deficits are totally or partially environmentally caused, generally through avoidance of essential experience. Remediation then tends to reinstate this experience, even at a later date.

From Diagnosis to Remediation

HAROLD J. McGRADY

The characteristic knowledge of our century is psychological. We are living in an age in which many persons are studying behavior so that they may devise methods by which to modify it. In fact, the future of our world has been depicted by George Orwell in his now famous 1984,[1] by B. F. Skinner in his Utopian novel, *Walden II*,[2] and by others as a time when essentially all behavior will be manipulated or controlled. These predictions suggest the fulfillment of the fondest hopes of John B. Watson, the famed behaviorist, who stated:

Give me a dozen healthy infants, well-formed, and my own special world to bring them up in, and I'll guarantee to take any one at random and train him to become any type of specialist I might select—doctor, lawyer . . . (etc.) regardless of his talents, penchants, tendencies, abilities, or vocations and race of his ancestors.[3]

Psychologists interested in learning processes have tried for years to define "laws of learning." They have had little applicable success. Ernest Hilgard has, in fact, stated that "there are no laws of learning that can be taught with confidence."[4] Even more depressing is a statement by one psychologist who said "the sad truth is that, after fifty years of careful, honest, and occasionally brilliant research on the nature of learning, the only people who can be proved to have received any practical benefits from learning theory are the learning theorists themselves."[5] The application of learning principles to the modification of behavior has often met with failure.

B. R. Bugelski states: "Perhaps the whole effort to bring science to education is misguided."[6] Notwithstanding the success of teaching machines, not only is it difficult to develop techniques based on learning theory, but educators and psychologists are not even sure that the practice of teaching can be taught. We do not prefer to be so pessimistic. Progress is being made in the delineation of principles for teaching. In fact, we feel that the work with learning disabilities children is of great help in this dilemma. As more effective techniques are developed in our field they assist us in our understanding of the learning processes for all children. For this reason the work with learning disabilities children has important implications for the practice of education in this country.

Despite these recent advances in clinical teaching and the significant progress that has been made in identifying and evaluating such children, there seems to be a gulf between these two processes. There seems to be a

From the *Proceedings* of the Fourth Annual Conference of the ACLD, *Management of the Child with Learning Disabilities: An Interdisciplinary Challenge.* New York (March 9–11, 1967), pp. 37–41.

tremendous gap between our ability to analyze behavior and our ability to use this information to change behavior.

Thus, in our work with learning disabilities, there often is a noticeable gap between the diagnostic process (the analysis) and the prescription of procedures for remediation (the modification process). We might call this a "diagnosis-remediation gap." It represents a serious problem in dealing with children who have learning disabilities. Thousands of children each year are taught with little regard for intensive evaluations that have been completed, reported, filed, and forgotten. The severity of the gap depends on circumstances. In a university program such as ours where the diagnosis and remediation are done consecutively by persons with essentially the same background and training, and where communication between examiner and teacher continues, the diagnosis-remediation gap will be small.

In other circumstances where children are evaluated and then referred to other agencies for the remedial process, the degree of communication will vary. This is a situation common to any diagnostic referral clinic. The type of training or the professional disciplines of the involved individuals will determine the size of the diagnosis-remediation gap. In some instances the gap seems insurmountable—as some of you who have wrestled with diagnostic reports in an attempt to arrive at a remediation plan will attest.

Our comments today will be concerned with diagnosis and how it can contribute to better management of the child with learning disabilities. As we discuss this we shall try to keep as a guideline the notion that the purpose of diagnosis is to clarify—not to mystify.

What is diagnosis? It is, of course, the process through which information relative to a problem is gathered and analyzed. But if we define it only as such we have merely "evaluated," not diagnosed. If we truly diagnose we must determine two further characteristics, namely etiology and prognosis of the problem. As Robert I. Watson has stated "the diagnostic phase of the clinical method culminates in the formulation of a theory or hypothesis of causation. Once causation has been established, emphasis shifts to questions of what can be done and what corrective steps can be instituted."[7]

Diagnosis implies treatment or remediation. Otherwise it would be of no practical value. It is for this reason that some degree of ascertaining etiology (or cause) is necessary. The same basic presenting problem may be due to a number of causes. For example a child who does not read (the presenting problem) may be mentally retarded, deaf, blind, partially sighted, emotionally disturbed, aphasic, otherwise neurologically impaired, culturally deprived, just plain unmotivated, or the victim of poor teaching. The objective of diagnosis should be to determine which of these conditions is responsible for his disability. Merely to say that he does not read or reads at such and such a grade level, which is below his grade level, is not enough. If we assumed that all children with reading disorders were to receive the same training, then a diagnosis would not be necessary. We would need only to evaluate the child, that is, to determine the level of reading at which he is performing and proceed from there. The collective example of this would be called "descriptive diagnosis." In such an instance we would merely say that the child has this symptom plus that symptom, and another. Diagnosis which is only a cataloging of symptoms cannot be justified as diagnosis. Such a procedure represents only a complex evaluation resulting in a description of the problem.

The degree of specificity of the etiology is another matter. We feel that the initial diagnostician's role should be that of indicating the broad etiological category in which the child belongs. We operate under the general principle that learning can be disrupted for several basic reasons. A review of these factors may be pertinent at this time.

- Sensory deprivation consists of those conditions which are due to pathology of the peripheral nervous system. Deafness and blindness are the primary disorders.
- Disorders of emotional disorganization represent factors of individual psychodynamics which have interfered with learning. This might include a variety of psychoses and neuroses.
- Experience deprivation will also disrupt learning. This represents lack of opportunity to learn and includes a range of conditions such as "cultural deprivation" or lack of schooling and might be extended to include such circumstances as poor teaching. These represent social variables which have deprived the individual of normal experiences prerequisite to adequate learning.
- Neurological dysfunction represents a prominent etiological factor for consideration. There is perhaps a wider scope of subtypes of disorder and a higher incidence in the population than for any of the other etiological categories. Under this category we include mental retardation and lesser degrees of generalized intellectual incapacity. If other causative possibilities can be ruled out, the assumption is made that the central nervous system is implicated. Specific learning disabilities include perceptual disorders, language disorders, memory disorders, disorders of cognition, abstraction or thinking, and motor disorders.

A child who fails to learn, despite adequate sensory integrity, emotional stability, opportunity to learn, and mental capacity, is classified as a child with a specific learning disability. The assumption is that such disorders have neurogenic bases.

The individual who initially evaluates a child should determine which of these primary causative factors is responsible for the problem. It may not be necessary at this stage to be more specific about cause. For example, he need not determine whether the mental retardation is endogenous or exogenous to refer the child to a remedial program. (This information will be of benefit, however, in determining other problems to look for in the specifics of remediation.) The broad causative factor, however, should be sufficient for the initial post-diagnostic stage. Establishing such etiologies, however, implies a bringing together of information from a variety of disciplines in medicine, psychology, and education. Subsequent evaluations would be aimed at delineating the specifics of the child's learning problem by a professional from the area of special education which represents the established cause, whether it be deafness, emotional disturbance, or specific learning disabilities.

The learning disorders specialist will further delineate the behavioral disorders by means of sampling a variety of pertinent areas. We screen for vision and hearing defects and evaluate the child's perceptual abilities; we check his memory, his motor abilities, and his social maturity. These are in addition to the establishment of guidelines for levels of intelligence, language, and emotional behavior. In doing this we are looking for several contrasts:

1. between verbal and nonverbal abilities
2. between learning as it occurs through various sensory channels, particularly visual and auditory
3. between receptive comprehension and expressive functions, and
4. among types of cognitive functions, such as perception, memory, language, and conceptualization.

We attempt to evaluate the individual against himself—to establish that he has legitimate learning disabilities, that he is not mentally retarded, deaf, emotionally disturbed, etc. This kind of diagnosis and evaluation leads the teacher to a more thorough knowledge of the child's problem so that she may work with it.

Our concept of diagnosis is that it should be thorough; it is concerned with causes; it is concerned with prognosis; it is concerned with comprehensive behavioral assessment that allows the teacher to "know the problem" as the basis for her remediation. The resultant remediation is then an individualized matter for each child-therapist combination. It is based on a consideration of the child's assets against his deficits.

One question to be resolved is: "Who is responsible for diagnosis?" In many instances the diagnosis-remediation gap is large because of the psychologist-teacher gap, or the psychologist-physician gap, or other interdisciplinary combinations. In our communities and colleges we need to define the role of the psychologist (clinical or school), the classroom teacher, the remedial reading teacher, the social worker, the principal, the family doctor, the speech therapist, etc., in diagnosis and remediation. As one man asked at a conference some months ago: "How many people will it take to deal with one reading problem?" This is a question which we must all resolve.

It means to a certain degree that all teachers must be diagnosticians, that all school and medical personnel must be knowledgeable concerning learning disabilities, and that we must learn to cooperate and coordinate rather than to proliferate.

What is the solution to the diagnosis-remediation gap? My feeling is that it involves some degree of rethinking and restructuring of our training programs in education: for the regular classroom teacher, for special education teachers, and for other specialists such as school psychologists. Three suggestions are offered:

Regular teachers must receive some orientation to learning disabilities. One of our problems may be that the typically trained regular teacher in the classroom does not really have the background necessary even to sees. The classroom teacher needs to be sensitized to learning disabilities. recognize, let alone to deal with, learning disabilities children whom she She should be given more exposure to the theory and practice of utilizing learning processes as they apply specifically to learning disabilities children. In this way she would not only enhance her own general teaching by being able to deal more efficiently with individual differences in the classroom, but she would be able to work effectively with some types of learning disabilities children. This would include children who can succeed adequately with a minimum of structuring; restatement of instructions during teaching; slight changes in seating; use of materials, etc.

There are a significant number of students in our classrooms today who could be prevented from developing into full-blown learning-disabilities children if every classroom teacher had enough knowledge to identify such children and to deal with the more common and less severe problems in the classroom. Particularly she should know when to refer a child with possible learning problems.

We do not feel that the amount of training necessary to accomplish this would overburden the curriculum. It could, in fact, replace some of the stale repetitions, or outdated requirements we are all familiar with in teacher training. We feel that inclusion of this type of information in their programs is a must. It should make them better teachers for all children; and if we can believe the statistics regarding incidence of learning disabilities, every teacher who has twenty children in her classroom has one of these children to deal with. If this suggestion would be accepted, the diagnosis-remediation gap would be decreased because identification and remediation would begin in the classroom.

A second suggestion for closing the diagnosis-remediation gap is that the school psychologist's training must allow him to provide remediation suggestions or hypotheses after completing his evaluations. He needs to be able to translate psychological findings into educational prescriptions. A school psychologist who is only a psychometrician—not a psychologist—needs someone else to integrate the test information. In Britain all school psychologists (i.e., educational psychologists) work with remediation. They must have at least three years teaching experience, as I understand it, and must continue to work with remediation while working as psychologists. This, I believe, is a superior system to ours where, although many school psychologists do fit the above qualifications, it is not universal. The school psychologist's primary function will continue to be that of ruling out mental retardation or primary emotional disorders.

A third way of reducing the diagnosis-remediation gap would be to insure that every special teacher of children with learning disabilities has the proficiency to perform screening-level evaluations of such children. This person would be provided with training in psychoeducational testing. The learning-disabilities teacher should be thoroughly trained to give achievement tests, group intelligence tests, and pertinent special abilities tests. We are assuming, of course, that she is also a thoroughly trained teacher. We are also assuming that a complete program for training such a person cannot be accomplished in a regular undergraduate program alone; it will require some amount of graduate-level education. We feel that the teacher of children with learning disabilities is the one who can best serve to close the diagnosis-remediation gap. She will be a kind of unicorn who will be part psychologist, part teacher.

Thus, if this system were to work, the following would occur:

1. The regular classroom teacher would suggest or tentatively identify the child suspected of being learning disabled. The better her training and clinical acumen, the less false leads she would provide.
2. After tentative affirmation by the teacher of children with learning disabilities, the school psychologist would evaluate the child thoroughly to determine causation. That is, he would attempt to classify the child into the appropriate special-education category, utilizing his own testing together with that of other professionals in psychology, medicine, and education. If the child still classifies as learning disabled, then
3. the third step would be to have the learning disabilities teacher devise a remediation plan and begin.

A system such as this must be fluid and the various personnel must function cooperatively as a team. We feel that interdisciplinary effort is necessary. As more professionals learn to accept this and diminish the effect of territorial instincts, the diagnosis-remediation gap will be closed.

NOTES

1. George Orwell, *1984* (New York: Harcourt Brace, 1949).
2. B. F. Skinner, *Walden II* (New York: Macmillan, 1948).
3. John B. Watson, *Behaviorism* (Chicago: University of Chicago Press, 1958), p. 104.
4. Ernest R. Hilgard, *Theories of Learning*, 2d ed. (New York: Appleton-Century-Crofts, 1956), p. 457.
5. Donald Snygg, "Learning: An Aspect of Personality Development," in *Learning Theory, Personality Theory, and Clinical Research: The Kentucky Symposium* (New York: Wiley, 1954), p. 130.
6. B. R. Bugelski, *The Psychology of Learning Applied to Teaching* (New York: Bobbs-Merrill, 1964), p. 31.
7. Robert I. Watson, *The Clinical Method in Psychology* (New York: Harper & Brothers, 1951), p. 25.

Addendum*

When Drs. Kirk and McCarthy asked me for permission to reprint "From Diagnosis to Remediation" in this volume, I had several reactions:

1. I was flattered to have this speech printed for a third time. (It was originally given as an ACLD presentation in New York City during March, 1967, and published as part of the proceedings from that meeting; it was republished in 1971 as Chapter 12 of the book *Educational Perspectives in Learning Disabilities,* edited by Donald Hammill and Nettie Bartel.)
2. I was curious as to why such an article would be considered for reprinting after seven years without revision.
3. I wondered if I really believed what I said in New York City in 1967.

With these reactions in mind I stipulated that the article could be reprinted only if I could react to its contents through hindsight and utilization of my accumulations of seven more years of life and experience.

My reactions when re-reading the manuscript were mixed. In some instances I was surprised at how little my views have changed (although I thought before re-reading that the opposite would be true). In other cases I was surprised at how ignorant I had been at the time of the original writing. In some instances I was very proud of what I had written; in other cases I was abashed at what I read.

In any instance, as a result of these reactions, I would like to present the following comments, which may be entitled "From Diagnosis to Remediation Revisited."

There were several premises in regard to the nature of learning disabilities and the diagnostic-remedial process as represented by the 1967 speech. I might summarize them as follows:

1. Learning disabilities represent deficits or discrepancies in certain psychological processes, based on intra-individual differences.
2. There is an assumption of neurogeneity in children with specific learning disabilities.
3. Diagnosis must include some designation of "cause."
4. The diagnostic process must be accomplished cooperatively by a team of specialists, whose roles are carefully defined.

Looking at these four premises in light of current knowledge I have a paradoxical reaction, *viz.,* I both agree and disagree with each of them. Let me explain.

1. The "psychological processes" concept of children with specific learning disabilities (SLD) is currently under fire. Many studies show that so-called perceptual handicaps are really conceptual, or attentional, or motivational in derivation. Other studies show that training so-called

---

*Harold J. McGrady, "From Diagnosis to Remediation Revisited" (May, 1974). Written especially for this volume.

"underlying processes" such as auditory perception or visual-motor functions does not have direct effects on subsequent "higher functions," such as reading, conceptualizing, or mathematical performance. From these data it would appear that my stated premise about SLD as deficits or discrepancies in certain psychological processes is in error.

This concerns me, because it may be the one most basic premise underlying the field of learning disabilities. Carried to its fulfillment it supposes that such children can learn best only when we structure our teaching in such a way as to consider the uniqueness of their psychological processes.

I continue to believe this latter premise. We may not be able to presume that if we teach at one level or teach one type of process that it will automatically carry over into other learning (e.g., the premise that training in visual-motor areas yields improved reading performance), but I continue to believe that we can best teach a specific behavior if we have a thorough knowledge of the child's levels of ability in various psychological processes. A thorough analysis of assets and deficits tells us what to teach, where to start, and what integrities to use as a basis for comparison.

Our key problem in operationalizing this premise is how to define, describe, and quantify "psychological processes." Some individuals mean such functions as perception, memory, or thinking, for example. These are at best difficult to concretize into consistent, observationally reliable terms. Currently we attempt to do this by psychological or educational tests, which suffer from invalidity, unreliability, and general lack of applicability to disordered populations.

Our failure to adequately measure, describe, or quantify "psychological processes" does not negate the concepts. Certainly memory, perception, language, and conceptual thinking exist. Our problem is to find adequate ways to observe these behaviors.

Perhaps we have not even designated the proper psychological processes. But the fact still remains that there exist children who show dramatic intraindividual variations in their learning. We need but to describe these accurately to aid us in teaching them.

2. The assumption of neurogeneity seems passé today. The literature is loaded with references to negative findings for LD children when given full neurological examinations and EEG's. And the day has passed when we speak primarily of minimal brain damage (MBD) or brain damage (BD) and require neurological or EEG study to qualify for special classes in the schools. This premise is currently affected by the inclusion of many children with mild learning problems in the SLD category. If, on the other hand, we consider only the classic, clinical, hard-core variety of severe specific learning disability (the old clinical childhood aphasic, or dyslexic), the type really intended by early writers such as Strauss, Werner, and Orton, then the premise has more validity. By that I do *not* mean that all children must have demonstrable neurological deficits to be classified as SLD. Rather, I mean the converse: imbalances in learning so severe as to cause a child to be legitimately classified as a clinical, hard-core LD are

evidence enough to presume neurological deviance. For example, a child who talks late despite all other processes being proven intact has given evidence enough that his brain is not functioning normally. The terms "brain damage" and "brain dysfunction" are misrepresentations of such a condition. I prefer Mildred Berry's term "brain different." These children *are* brain different. Therefore, they must be taught differently. However, we do not change their brain; we learn how to structure their learning in ways uniquely necessary so that they can learn and adjust to the neurological mechanism and the process. Thus, holding to the assumption of "brain difference" does not imply mandatory medical treatment. It only states that certain children think differently because their neurological mechanisms are organized differently.

A critical point is that this finding is applicable to only a very small percentage of SLD children, perhaps less than 1 percent.

3. The incidence of SLD is closely related to our concern for the third premise, *viz.*, that "diagnosis must include some designation of cause."

In the field of learning disabilities we have drastically oversold the concept of LD so that virtually every child could conceivably qualify. Incidence figures range as high as 50 percent or more. By SLD we do *not* mean children with all of the exclusions (i.e., mental retardation (MR), emotional disturbances (ED), sensory deficits, environmental disadvantages, physical handicaps) as primary "causes." Neither do we mean the myriad of children whose learning failure is due to poor teaching or lack of educational and/or intellectual stimulation. Nor do we mean children who learn well, but merely differ in their "styles" of learning.

When we thus limit our designation of who shall be called LD and stress the "specific" in the term "specific learning disabilities," we are dealing with a much less sizable population and one which is more manageable administratively and economically. If we were to deal with only 1 percent of the school population, for example, as SLD, we could concentrate the efforts of our most skilled SLD specialists, thus achieving a greater overall academic effect at a lower cost.

The value to the total school population and to other teachers in the system would be:

1. intensive direct service to a few who otherwise disrupt the normal school learning process
2. models of exemplary teaching practice for other regular and/or special teachers to emulate whenever appropriate
3. the availability of consultative services to teachers and parents by the SLD specialists.

The foregoing model can only be implemented if and when we maintain our attempt in diagnosis to include some designation of cause. The words "cause" and "etiology" are the ones that tend to confuse and arouse persons in disagreement with this premise. I tend to feel that a slight shift in the semantics and connotation of these terms will allow this premise to be accepted more readily.

As I explained, in the 1967 presentation, by "cause" we mean a determination of which of the basic conditions leading to learning failure might be responsible for a given disability. If mental retardation, sensory deficit, emotional disturbance, physical handicap, cultural difference, lack of motivation, or poor teaching are primary factors in a child's failure to learn, any teaching must be done within that context. In a well-ordered and comprehensive system, it is advantageous to provide differentiated services to children, processing each of these different conditions as prime factors in their learning failure.

Thus, the term "cause" is interpreted now to mean "primary conditions responsible for learning failure." In this manner the child will be treated through services designed for that primary condition according to the organization of such services in his milieu. It also means that whenever multiple conditions exist, decisions must be made regarding which conditions are primary and/or which conditions need to be treated first and/or simultaneously. Our difficulties have really not been due to this concept of diagnosis; our difficulties have been due to our lack of technology in *operationalizing* the concept.

The term "etiology" has been confusing because it tends to stress the medical nature of the problem. It is often only of academic interest since the etiology cannot be negated (e.g., if the etiology is maternal rubella, an Rh incompatibility, there is no way to do anything about it). Medical etiology is only important in the few cases where a medical treatment might reverse or arrest the condition. In those cases, of course, it is extremely important. Therefore the entire diagnostic process should include a statement about etiology, or suspected etiology. In some instances this will only confirm that we cannot reverse the condition and must deal with it as it is.

Thus, my current feelings about determination of "cause" in diagnosis of cerebral dysfunction are that (1) we must continue to designate the primary condition(s) likely to be contributor(s) to the child's failure to learn; and (2) precise etiology should be sought in order to determine whether the primary condition(s) can be reversed or treated per se.

4.   Finally, let me address the fourth premise of my 1967 presentation, *viz.*, that the diagnostic process must be accomplished "cooperatively by a team of specialists whose roles are carefully defined." I still believe that the system can function as outlined at the conclusion of my original presentation. In fact, it *does* work, and it has been instituted in many school systems. During the past year, I have observed dozens of systems in schools throughout the United States in my role as a Program Associate with the Leadership Training Institute in Learning Disabilities. I am currently involved in a study of the wide variety of screening, identification, and diagnostic systems being used today. I was surprised to find how well this system is working, with slight variations in emphasis, and perhaps one major shift in roles.

I am convinced that classroom teachers must be our primary agents in suspecting children of having LD. They have the most intense contact with children in academic learning situations. Our job must be that of increasing their clinical acumen and helping to structure referrals. Their ability to identify children with potential LD is generally high; we must merely try to promote a finer and more specific calibration of teacher judgment.

Following suspicion of LD by teachers, I feel that the primary role in diagnosis should not be borne by learning-disabilities specialists, who of course are highly competent remedial diagnosticians. They should captain the team, but they must call on the myriad of other persons from whom information is to be gathered, including the psychologist, the physician, the parent, and other special educators, such as reading teachers, special therapists, etc. This represents some shift in my thinking, since I formerly placed this role in the hands of the psychologist. School psychologists, however, have not been well trained to accomplish this task. However, it reinforces my statement that "the teacher of children with learning disabilities is the one who can best serve to close the diagnosis-remediation gap"— if we can train that person in the necessary competencies.

The LD teacher has an advantage over the psychologist in that part of his/her diagnostic process can be diagnostic teaching. After the classroom teacher tentatively identifies a child as LD, the LD specialist can observe the child in the classroom and assess the interface of his characteristics with teaching methodologies and practice in his classroom; the specialist can then either make tentative teaching change suggestions or do trial teaching (a diagnostic teaching). This alone may save endless hours of testing, evaluation, and staffing. This affirmation of the child as a possible LD then will allow for psychologists, physicians, and other expensive, time-consuming specialists to be called upon only for more classical service cases. It also will allow the LD teacher to participate in the gathering of the most pertinent data for his/her ultimate role as special teacher for the children finally designated to receive his/her services.

In summary, I believe that children with SLD do, in fact, exist, and that their problems can be defined as deficits or discrepancies in certain psychological processes. It remains only for us to define the appropriate processes of concern and to operationalize these constructs into measurable entities, even if these functions may have different names from those traditionally in use today. Treatment of such children assumes that we designate the primary conditions responsible for learning failure, and, in cases of severe or chronic SLD (or what I prefer to call the "clinical SLD"), that we assume a variation from the norm in neurological organization. This does not imply, however, that we treat the neurological disorganization per se. Rather, we use that knowledge to devise optimum ways to structure the learning environment and our teaching strategies. Finally, I believe that a team of professionals, spearheaded by the SLD specialist, can bring together the comprehensive information necessary to reduce the diagnosis-remediation gap.

Since my original presentation appeared in 1967 a great many developments have occurred in the field of learning disabilities. They include:

1. a shift from the medical to the educational model
2. a shift from emphasis on diagnosis to remediation
3. a concern for labelling and categorization and
4. a concern about the validity of the "processing approach."

All of these, I think, represent advances in our professional thinking. However, let us not "throw out the baby with the bath" in our zeal for reform. Let us use the best from the past and build on it through modifications for the future. My comments above are presented to that objective.

Toward Dispelling the Mystique of Learning Disabilities

JEANNE M. McCARTHY

As learning disabilities have begun to emerge as a significant educational entity, concern has arisen in many circles over the mystique that has developed around these children and their disabilities. In the early years of the learning-disabilities movement, there was no legislation at the state or federal levels which authorized special education services for the child who does not learn. It was necessary in some states, in the 1950s and early 1960s, to concoct a diagnosis, perhaps as in Illinois, of multiple handicap—then services could be provided in the public school under the same reimbursement plan as for other handicaps. The usual route for the administrator who really cared was to have the psychologist test the child and declare him educationally handicapped and emotionally disturbed. Then, the parents would be referred to a selected pediatrician, or two, who would be willing to declare him possibly brain-damaged. Then, armed with this diagnosis of multiply handicapped, special teaching could be provided under the special education legislation of the state.

This lack of proper legislation, plus much professional jargon, has led to an aura of mystery developing around these children. Teachers began to think that these children constituted a "new" problem. They began to think that this child was so different that he did not belong in their classes. The mystique which has developed about this child has made teachers afraid to teach a child with an abnormal electroencephalogram with "fourteen- and six-spike seizure activity in the left parietal lobe." Teachers did not realize that these children and their problems are not new. They have always been in our classrooms. Teachers used to describe these children as having a "mental block." Now, in 1969, the children are the same, and their problems are the same. All we have done is to switch labels. In doing this, however, we have created a mystique which has proved to be a disservice to the child. I am convinced that the mystique is a mistake.

In an effort to dispel some of this mystique, one can turn for inspiration to one of the great literary masterpieces, the Holy Bible. In Exodus (20:2-7) are found the Ten Commandments, which can rather freely be translated into the fifteen Ten Commandments of learning disabilities. ... These fifteen Ten Commandments of Learning Disabilities are as follows:

- Thou art a member of a most honored profession charged with the responsibility of teaching all children. Thou shalt not put false gods

From the *Proceedings* of the Sixth Annual Conference of the ACLD, *Progress in Parent Information, Professional Growth, and Public Policy*. Fort Worth, Texas (March 6–8, 1969), pp. 39–40.

before thee, whether they be neurology, psychology, psychiatry, pharmacology, or electroencephalography, expecting them to assume your charge: to teach.

- Thou shalt not take my name in vain. I am a child who does not learn. Thou shalt not label me with such epithets as brain-damaged, dyslexic, hyperkinetic, or minimal brain dysfunctioned.
- Remember thou that I need to be taught how to learn what you want me to learn.
- Honor my abilities as well as my disabilities.
- Remember that children who do not learn do not do so for an infinite variety of reasons. The least likely and most difficult to document at this stage of knowledge in the science of neuroanatomy is that which attempts to relate the nonlearning to the condition of the brain itself.
- Thou shalt not overestimate nor underestimate the severity of my problem. Thee do not yet know the prevalence of learning disabilities in the public school population.
- Thou shalt not forget that severe learning disabilities are not a dichotomy. The child does not either have it, or not have it, like measles.
- Thou shalt not get bogged down in the organic—not-necessarily-organic controversy (the purist-pragmatist controversy).
- Thou shalt not engage in professional haggles over whether this child is emotionally disturbed or brain-damaged.
- Thou shalt never again list a set of characteristics of children with learning disabilities. Thee are now acutely aware of the fact that each child with a severe learning disability is idiosyncratic unto himself.
- Thou shalt remember that the diagnosis of severe learning disabilities is by its very nature temporary and ephemeral.
- Thou shalt not covet more research base to your educational practices than exists in fact.
- Thou shalt remember that it is very easy to tell parents what *not* to do, but very difficult to tell them what *to do*.
- Thou shalt not indulge capriciously in the referral game, but shall judiciously check each agency before referring parents to yet another source of help.
- Thou shalt remember that these children *do* belong in your classroom. They do belong in your school.

Three

Significant Issues

There are, of course, many issues in the field of learning disabilities. Many of the papers appearing later in this volume will address themselves to specific issues. The papers reported in this section, however, are those which are of more general significance. We have avoided reprinting some of the controversial papers from the Proceedings, for example those in the field of vision. We were unable to find articles that would provide a balanced presentation in this area.

In the first article James Gallagher (who at that time, 1968, was the Director of the Bureau of Education for the Handicapped in the U.S. Office of Education) outlines the program of the bureau. He raises some provocative questions. Areas focused on by Dr. Gallagher include curriculum reform, the controversial role of the clinical professor in training programs, information processing dysfunctions, the prevalence, prevention, and remediation of learning disabilities, and priorities for federal support.

The second paper, by Keith Conners, explains information-processing within a framework of systems analysis and describes the kinds of experiments that are conducted within this system. The issues involved in cognitive theory versus behavioral theory continue to be of concern to practitioners in the field.

The third selection deals with psychological aspects of learning disabilities. This brief, concise, and pertinent statement by Charles Strothers summarizes the state of psychological models in learning disabilities. He points out the danger of drawing inferences about "brain injury" from psychological analyses. He also points out the need for the identification of homogeneous subgroups in the ill-defined group of problems we call learning disabilities. He gives his views on the relationship between perceptual functions and learning.

The fourth article, written by Lowell Seymour and Barton Proger, addresses issues involved in the areas of performance contracting, accountability, and formal evaluation. Within the discussion of program-evaluation models, the authors present some highly specific guidelines for learning disabilities educators to follow. Although this presentation was made a few years ago, the fields of performance contracting and evaluation are still in their infancy.

William Cruickshank's article focuses on the inadequacies of training programs for teachers of children with learning disabilities. He points out that the field has developed so rapidly that universities have been unable to staff programs in learning disabilities with highly trained and experienced professors. He proposes a national training center for professors to update them on the various facets of the problem. He also outlines in-service training programs for teachers, supervisors, and administrators.

Unthinkable Thoughts

JAMES J. GALLAGHER

My first contact with youngsters who could be described as having special learning disabilities took place during my internship at Southbury Training School in Connecticut in 1948. At that time I discussed with Dr. Milton Cotzin a number of cases of mentally retarded children—at least at that time they were called "mentally retarded" children—who seemed to be unusual. They did not fit the pattern that one had come to expect of the educable mentally retarded child. They had dramatic strengths and weaknesses in their developing patterns of abilities. In some respects they appeared quite average. In other respects they were even more retarded than their general scores on tests would lead one to believe.

Many of these children were in an institution for the mentally retarded because society had no other way of dealing with their problems. Many youngsters came from families that were in trouble. Social agencies found that placing these children in institutions for the mentally retarded was a convenient way of dealing with a difficult situation.

In later contacts through my work in child-guidance clinics and other treatment centers, these unusual youngsters kept reappearing from time to time. In 1954, when I first joined the Institute for Research on Exceptional Children under the directorship of Dr. Samuel A. Kirk, I became involved in a three-year program to develop and evaluate a tutorial program for brain-injured retarded children. In many ways, the tutoring programs designed for each of the youngsters in this three-year study were the prototypes for the classroom planning that goes on today—although it is now at a much more sophisticated level. I am encouraged by the progress that has been made in research and program development with these children, but we still have a long way to go.

In spite of the fact that federal participation in programs to help the handicapped dates back more than 100 years, when Gallaudet College for the Deaf was first founded, the major impact of the federal government on educational programs for the handicapped is only a decade old. Starting from a small beginning in 1957 with the Cooperative Research Act which reserved less than one million dollars for research on mental retardation, there was, in fiscal year 1968, approximately 78 million dollars spent to help in the education of the handicapped.

Just a little over a year ago, legislation was passed through an amendment to the Elementary and Secondary Education Act which established a

From the *Proceedings* of the Fifth Annual International Conference of the ACLD, *Successful Programming—Many Points of View*. Boston, Mass. (Feb. 1–3, 1968), pp. 355–366.

Bureau of Education for the Handicapped to coordinate and administer programs for the handicapped within the United States Office of Education.

I would like to speak briefly about the new Bureau of Education for the Handicapped, its organization, and some of its goals. Discussions of organizational structure usually have the same excitement and sex appeal as campaign speeches for the office of local dogcatcher. But don't be deceived. I am discussing extraordinarily important matters, because complex long-range societal goals can only be achieved through organizations in our complex society.

There was a time not too long ago when organization and planning in our society were viewed as evil things. Our heroes were the Sam Spades, Tarzans, and Jack Armstrongs. All were antiorganization, they bucked the system, and through ingenuity and courage, they beat the faceless representatives or organizations bent on nefarious deeds. Our thinking today still contains elements of antiorganization or antiplanning, expressed in its most extreme form in the "hippies" and those who would rather "drop out" than become involved in the "system."

The job of all education—including special education—is to find the mechanisms through which we can trigger new knowledge into action at the instructional level. Only in this way can we improve our services beyond the craftsman or guild system, under which knowledge was accumulated and passed on from master to apprentice in each new generation.

From a geographic distance, it is difficult to appreciate the full impact of the change in the degree of interest in handicapped children within the United States Office of Education as a result of the establishment of the new Bureau of Education for the Handicapped.

One of the great advantages of the bureau is that it opens up new communication avenues with education policy-makers. I have found it disturbing for the future progress of education that the special knowledge which has been acquired about the exceptional child at such a high price is often unavailable to the general-education policy-maker. Yet the contributions of the exceptional child to society are easy to document. More than half a century ago, Binet's interest in the mentally retarded child stimulated important work on the measurement of intelligence. The study of and concern for the emotionally disturbed child and adult have provided us with insight into the personality development of the average child. Current work in developing a method for making more precise educational diagnoses of children with serious learning disabilities has the potential for providing us with a more thorough understanding of the developing intellectual abilities in all children.

In carrying out my responsibilities as director of the bureau, I have appeared and presented the position of our professional specialties to the association of school boards; to the staff members of the compact for states; to the chief state school officers; and I have testified before congressional committees. In addition, I have participated in weekly meetings on the policy level in the U.S. Office of Education. While it is difficult to measure the immediate results of our views at any of these meetings, it is reasonable to assume that the long-range consequences of this exchange of information will serve a constructive purpose on behalf of special education. These opportunities occur, not because of the nature of the job of the bureau chief, but because the office of education organization demanded such meetings.

The organization known as the Bureau of Education for the Handicapped was established January 12, 1967. It administers the funds for programs and projects relating to the education, training, and research of handicapped children and youth. These are children who come under the definition of federal legislation as "mentally retarded, hard-of-hearing, speech-impaired, visually handicapped, seriously emotionally disturbed, crippled, or are otherwise health impaired and [who] require special education." The bureau is composed of the Office of the Associate Commissioner and three divisions: Educational Services, Training Programs, and Research.

The Division of Educational Services is responsible for three programs specifically concerned with the education of handicapped persons. It provides the following:

- Grants to state departments of education under the Elementary and Secondary Education Act, Title VI-A, to aid them in initiating, expanding, and improving programs at the preschool, elementary, and secondary levels which advance the education of handicapped children. This amounted to 14.25 million dollars for the fiscal year of 1968.
- It also provides grants to state departments of education for projects designed to meet the educational needs of handicapped children in state-operated and supported schools. This support amounted to 24.7 million dollars in fiscal year 1968. The division directs a captioned-films-and-educational-media loan service on a nationwide scale for the educational, cultural, and vocational environment of deaf persons. Contracts are made for the production of captioned films, for research, development, and training in the use of media. This program is funded for 2.8 million dollars for this fiscal year.

The Division of Educational Services is headed by Dr. Frank B. Withrow. His background in media and his inventiveness and creativity provide important leadership in this important dimension.

The Division of Training Programs is responsible for making grants to public and private nonprofit institutions of higher learning, and to state departments of education. It supports training opportunities for teachers, supervisors, and other specialized personnel concerned with the education of handicapped children. Specialists in different types of handicaps review the applications and provide consultation to the field of special education. Grants are awarded for:

- junior- or senior-year traineeships or graduate fellowships for fulltime study
- special-study institutes
- summer-sessions fulltime traineeships
- development of new educational training programs for the handicapped at institutions of higher learning.

In 1968, this total program will involve more than 243 different institutions of higher education, 54 state educational agencies, and over 11,000 students. In fiscal year 1968 more than 24 million dollars was spent on this program. The division is headed by Dr. Leonard J. Lucito, who for many years has enjoyed a fine reputation as director of special education programs at the University of South Florida. Dr. Lucito joined the bureau staff about three months ago.

The Division of Research supports a wide variety of projects designed for improving the education of handicapped children. Within the broad definition of research or demonstration activities, the division supports three major categories of programs. These include projects involving research-facility construction, research and development centers, programmatic-research grants, departmental research developmental grants, and research projects grants. The division also provides support for a national network of fourteen instructional-materials centers, regional demonstration centers, demonstration projects, and conferences related to research. In addition, it provides support for projects related to the development and evolution of educational media and curriculum.

During fiscal year 1968, 11.1 million dollars was spent in this area. The director of this division, Dr. James W. Moss, is a very creative research administrator.

One year after the U.S. Office of Education put into effect the legislative mandate of the Congress to establish the Bureau of Education for the Handicapped, the Ninetieth Congress added new dimensions to the total programing for handicapped children and supplied the bureau with new and valuable legislative tools. Congress amended the Elementary and Secondary Education Act to authorize the following:

- The development of new resource centers to provide diagnostic and evaluative educational programing. Such centers, when operational, should become a great source of help to teachers concerned with special and unusual educational problems with handicapped children.
- Special diagnostic, evaluative, and educational centers for deaf-blind children. These children who have multiple handicaps—the victims of the rubella epidemics of 1964 and 1965—are a special problem. They need a concentration of the expert care which is now in such short supply.
- The expansion of a media program that has previously been specifically focused only in the area of deaf children. The new program will include children with other kinds of handicaps. This means that all children

coming under the general federal definition of handicapped children will now have the potential benefits of a tested program that will be designed to place in the hands of teachers as rapidly as possible the productive results of new media.

- A new information recruitment program that will hopefully stimulate and recruit young people to enter into an exciting and challenging teaching career, and which will also provide parents with information about where to obtain services to help their handicapped children.
- Fifteen percent of the money which will be expended for Title III of the Elementary and Secondary Education Act will be used primarily for innovative projects and supplementary centers which will be specifically designed for handicapped children. This will allow for a great increase in educational planning on a comprehensive basis for the handicapped child in the public schools.

Finally, a physical education and recreation program has been authorized, which will provide service for mentally retarded and other handicapped children. This new development represents an initial thrust into an area that has long been neglected in the total programing for handicapped children.

Now I would like to discuss a few unthinkable thoughts and leave you with a few unthinkable questions. These may evoke, on your own part, several unprintable responses. An unthinkable thought is a projection of a present problem to a probable future solution that is so different from what we know now, or so disturbing in its implications for change, that we don't even want to think about it.

In a dynamic and changing society we cannot confront our problems adequately unless we have the courage to peer at the horizon and see problems while they are still in the stage of a small cloud no bigger than your hand—and see them before they become mighty storms.

Here is unthinkable thought number one. *Is curriculum development for exceptional children too important to be left to the classroom teacher or, for that matter, to the special educator?* A little playlet may serve to illustrate the general problem. Miss Bravada, fresh from one of the university's teacher-training programs in special education, appears for her first job and asks about the special curriculum that will be applied to her exceptional children.

The administrator, a model of democratic correctness, says that he is determined not to impose his ideas on her; no siree. She is going to have that freedom that all professionals yearn for—the freedom to work out her own program.

Two weeks later, Miss Bravada is back in the supervisor's office begging —nay pleading—for him to take away her freedom, to dictatorially tell her what to do—to give her some program, some materials with which to operate. Ever sympathetic, the administrator proposes that a committee be formed to develop a curriculum for their school system, because if the truth be known, other special-education teachers have been asking for the same thing. So, after much hard work and hours of labor, they paste together an amalgamation of their own experience and knowledge. Meanwhile, in school systems all over the country, this little play is reproduced with variations, and innumerable little curriculum programs and pamphlets get mimeographed.

The huge curriculum-reform movement that struck the United States in the late fifties and early sixties, sponsored mainly by the National Science Foundation, was devoted to the proposition that local school systems simply did not have the expertise to write about mathematics or chemistry or history or biology. Furthermore, if biology was going to be a part of the curriculum, their position was that maybe a biologist ought to have a hand in the development of the program. Talk about your unthinkable thoughts.

Do we, in special education, have nothing to learn from these teams of curriculum developers who have operated in practically every content field and who have drawn from a wide background of knowledge and skills at the highest possible level to produce a consistent set of materials that was cognitively and pedagogically sound?

Are we destroying Miss Bravada's freedom? Or was her freedom, like so much of freedom in education, an illusion? We might as well go down to the corner garage and announce to the mechanics that they have the freedom to build a DC-8 jet. What we are giving her is the freedom to fail, and fail she will when she is given a task beyond her capabilities and resources.

Miss Bravada does have a role in total curriculum development. She has to take the proposed curriculum and field test it for her own class. She and her fellow teachers may have to make an intelligent choice between competing curricula. She certainly can provide important feedback to the curriculum developers on what works and what doesn't work in that all-important crucible—the classroom. It is one thing to learn how to play a sonata and quite a different one to compose one. Our teacher-training programs are in the business of training performers, not composers.

Henry Morgan once commented on what it took to start a modern newspaper. He said that it demanded intelligence, integrity, raw courage, and 10 million dollars. If the National Science Foundation experience is any criterion, we may have a similar price tag for some viable curriculum programs for the emotionally disturbed child or the child with special learning disabilities. We should not expect Miss Bravada, or a committee of Miss Bravadas, to come up with these programs.

Now for unthinkable thought number two. *Do our training programs for specialists who work with exceptional children have to be conducted exclusively within the halls of the college or university?* Let's consider what the best of current wisdom has created. The student attends college for three years. He takes a liberal arts background for the first two years, more technical courses the third year, and finally enters into his practicum year, as a senior, where he learns what teaching is all about. During this crucial year, his supervision is often handled by a faculty member who risks ptomaine and exhaustion or worse, racing from student to student—and often from town to town—spending a few brief hours with each, never really knowing what the student is doing.

After graduation, the former student is considered a professional and is on his own. If he returns to the university for further training, it is often in the summer where he sits in classrooms and learns more theory, which he finds very hard to apply to his situation. He may also attend in-service training programs, of which the most distinctive feature is likely to be a scalding cup of instant coffee which threatens at any moment to break through the fragile paper cup and cause grievous bodily injury. Here he may listen to a lecture by a visiting celebrity who talks about his research or special program. Is this the best that we have to offer? How can we break out of a system that we know is less than our best?

One approach is to substitute for this dim and overdrawn portrait a concept of continuous training, where the university plays a distinctive, but not the total, training role. In this view, the university can provide preservice training and special advanced training, but the practicum courses and supervision would take place within the school situation itself. One such new model, considered by many, is the concept of a clinical professor. He is a person who is extremely knowledgeable in the skills of his trade. He is on the university staff, but he is stationed in the school system, and his job is to supervise and conduct in-service training programs.

Where such training should be done is one issue, and how it is to be done is another. The key to the preparation of teachers lies in the need to show the teacher how to interact meaningfully with the learner. It is not enough to master a set of general principles about how children learn or the nature of the curriculum. If that were all there was to it, a quiet room and some clearly written textbooks would suffice. But teaching is like other skills that require a complex set of interactions with a changing environment, such as cooking, acting, flying an airplane, or playing golf. These skills cannot be learned solely through the written word. They must be mastered through observation, practice, and provisions for sufficient feedback about their own performances to allow the teachers or performers to analyze systematically their own behavior and modify it accordingly. It is this area which is the much-misunderstood province of the educator and which, when fully realized, will provide the basis for greatly improved professional preparations in all fields of education.

One trend, now in its infancy, but which promises improvement and change in specialist preparation in education, relies on a particular marriage of technology and educational theory. Feedback information about one's own performance as a teacher has not been easy to obtain. Ideally, one would like to have the means to study at leisure one's own performance and then to apply theories of instruction that would make such analysis maximally profitable.

The football coach, whose vulnerable status has, perhaps, made him more appreciative of the need for excellence in instruction, has been using such techniques for years. By replaying the game films in an atmosphere of quiet contemplation, it is possible to do extensive analysis of how the various interactions necessary to success were executed, what precise problems existed, and how such execution can be improved.

I would like now to present another unthinkable thought. This one is in the area of learning disabilities. It is an area in the field of the handicapped that has really been forced upon the attention of special and general educators. The history of classifying children who are in educational trouble, particularly when they are referred to as handicapped, generally has been described with medical terminology, based on the physical disability of the child. Thus, we have children referred to as deaf, blind, or cerebral palsied—all of which are expressions of a physical condition, but which have little meaning in educational usage.

As we have become more knowledgeable in the educational problems of these handicapped youngsters, we have begun to understand that it is not because a youngster cannot hear that he is essentially an educational problem. It is because his lack of hearing capacity interferes with his ability to receive communication with his developing internal conceptual structure of the world around him, and because of his inability to express his ideas to others.

To some observers, this may seem like professorial quibbling, but it really isn't. We sometimes tend to think about problems in terms of how we describe them in the first place. If we think about deafness as the inability to hear, then the major effort may be to utilize mechanical methods to aid youngsters to hear effectively. If we place the emphasis on communication, then we will direct our major effort toward devices and procedures by which we can improve communication. The important contribution in the area of learning disabilities has been to hasten the transfer of our thinking from physical aspects to a learning dysfunction, and in that transfer to make more effective and more comprehensive our educational programing.

Some variation of an information-processing system would seem to have maximum educational payoff. Such an information-processing system must encompass five major cognitive or thinking processes, and probably a number of others that we still do not fully comprehend. The first of these would be an orientation function. This involves the not-too-clearly-understood ability of the individual to focus attention on certain stimuli and, at the same time, to depress or disregard the effect of extraneous stimuli. This is one of the most important mental functions of humans. It occurs so naturally with those who function normally, that it is difficult to conceive of the world of the child who lacks such a function.

The second major function must involve intake of information. This means not merely the receiving of sound or visual stimuli, but the ability to effectively transmit this information to the central nervous system in a way that allows the person to directly interpret the stimuli.

The third major area is central processing of the information as it moves around the central nervous system itself. This occurs through the cognitive process of association, generalization, and through another process of importance—that of memory.

A fourth major area of mental function or information processing involves the ability to have information output, traditionally accomplished through speech or general motor performance.

A fifth major area of concern in an information-processing model involves the ability to develop feedback mechanisms. With this mechanism the individual is able to utilize information developing from his own behavior, so that he is able to interpret the impact that he makes on the surrounding environment.

All of these systems interact with one another. A defect in any one of them has substantial implications for the proper performance of all of the pieces of the overall system itself, just as a defect in a part of an automobile's function will show itself in decreased performance in other aspects of the car's overall performance.

A simple example of the interaction of these systems might be to imagine a youngster looking at a bird sitting in a tree singing. The bird suddenly flies away. The orientation function comes into play immediately, and the attention of the youngster would focus on the bird and his behavior. If all other stimuli in the environment had the same strength in attracting the child, he would not be able to focus his attention or to use the information that comes from such a focused attention.

This information about the bird sitting on a tree singing would come through visual and auditory channels. The information would be meaningful to the child in direct relationship to the central processing that the child is able to bring to the experience. First, he has to classify the stimuli as a bird on a tree and singing. The child might even go further and identify the stimuli as a particular kind of bird, or he might draw associations from the particular time of day, the weather, or other factors that would be favorable to such an event. Naturally he would have to depend on his effective memory to bring forth past associations and generalizations that bring meaning to an event.

The child's ability to communicate with others, either through gestures or drawings or through speech would be involved in any information output about the event itself. Finally, the feedback mechanism comes into contact if the youngster realizes what impact he is having on the total situation. For example, the child may move toward the bird, causing the bird to fly away. If the child does not see the connection between his action and the bird's behavior, he will never be able to study birds for any considerable length of time. In each of these five areas, it is obvious that a defect in any one of them will affect all of them. This is apparently what happens to a youngster who has special learning disabilities. However, thinking about the child in this context helps to identify the educational problem and to plan ways to remediate it.

One must understand that a child's lack of response is not due just to a physical defect, but one must see it in terms of the impact of the physical handicap on his information-processing abilities. With this recognition we can take a major step forward in planning educational remedial procedures by which these youngsters can be more effectively educated.

About ten years ago, I had an occasion to write a monograph resulting from some of our studies of brain-injured youngsters. From that time to now, I have had no new findings to justify changing what I had written regarding the need for defining youngsters in terms of their learning problems rather than their physical handicap. The words I wrote ten years ago are as follows:

Does the educator not gain more information from the fact that a child is perceptually disturbed rather than from the fact that he is brain-injured?

Brain injury is the proper province of the neurologist. However, the perceptual distortions, if disinhibition and problems of association sometimes occur in some brain-injured children, are the problems of the educator and the psychologist. It would seem only reasonable to expect the educator to make his own educational diagnosis of each child's perceptual development, personality skills, or language development, and to make his plan accordingly, whether or not a diagnosis of brain injury has been medically determined.

The educator is interested in function rather than in structure. It is in the function that we will find the clues for more effective educational remediation.

The new emphasis on children with learning disabilities has stimulated much activity and raised many questions. The answers to these questions— some of them unthinkable questions—will provide us with the basis for further advances in this field.

There are several questions being considered by policy-makers that I would like to share with you. *How many children are there who have serious disabilities?*

Our program has not been to get an answer to that question; rather, we get too many different answers. Do learning-disabled children constitute 1 percent or 20 percent or 30 percent of the school-age population, or somewhere in between? The difference in the number of children and the implications of these figures is profound. If the answer is 20 percent, meaning one out of every five school children, then this is a problem that transcends all of our other school problems put together. It transcends our problems of delinquency and cultural deprivation. It adds up to more school children than are to be found in the total school population of California, Pennsylvania, New York, and Texas. Training special personnel to meet this problem would be a monumental job. If, on the other hand, the percentage is 1 or 2 percent or less, we are dealing with a problem akin to mental retardation or, perhaps, blindness or serious societal and educational problems; but it becomes one in which some recognizable dimension can be charted.

To the knowledgeable policy-maker, the failure to arrive at an acceptable incidence figure meant that either the area is not clearly defined, the instrumentality used to identify the children is not adequate, or both. Therefore, careful attention needs to be given to these particular factors. *If we were to set about preventing this problem, what should we do?*

Notice that I am not now talking about educational treatment, but about how to eliminate the condition entirely. There is a world of difference here, just as with the prevention of deafness as opposed to the educational treatment of deafness. To plan preventive strategies, we have to think about the etiology or causes of the condition. Is it major brain injury or minimal brain injury that causes these defects in information processing? Is it emotional disturbance? Is the cause to be found somewhere in the culture or the environment? If so, what peculiar experience results in perceptual or motor problems for one child and not for another. If it is none of these, then what is it or what are they? Is it true, as some maintain, that this is merely a miscellaneous category made up of children that somehow did not fit any other category? *Is there a sound basis for educational treatment of learning disabilities, or is the treatment merely a collection of home-grown remedies, developed without evaluation or without relation to sound theory?*

The answer to this question is crucial to our support of research studies in this area, and central to the issue of the adequacy of undergraduate or graduate training programs which we are asked to support. Let me hasten to add that our decisions in such matters are the result not of our own staff deliberations but of the decisions of the most expert persons in the field, on whose sound judgments we can rely. Nor are we in the business of using federal funds to support one theoretical position and not another. We are quite content to let history and subsequent evaluations judge the adequacy of claims and counter-claims in this area—and a merciless judge it is. What our experts do insist upon—and we do too—is that there be some sound rationale presented for a training program or for a research project. Not "the" rationale; but "a" rationale. *Where should our priorities be placed in this field?*

Since there will never be enough money to do all that we would like to do, where should we act first? Should it be in a major effort for research to find the causes of this condition? Should it be in support of curriculum development or special remedial educational exercises? Should it be in teacher training in order to provide more professionals for this growing field? Or should it be in providing for the development of new educational models to solve this problem? Which should come first?

I have tried not to ask small questions—nor easy ones. Rather, I am asking those questions that trouble us, and which we believe must give you some periods of anxiety as well. In the past, I have talked at length about the importance of a partnership between all interested parties. It is only through cooperative local, state, and federal efforts, with the active participation and interest of lay citizens, that we can gain the knowledge, the resources, and the motivated and dedicated individuals to do the large jobs and attack the unthinkable problems that lie ahead of us.

Information Processing in Children with Learning Disabilities and Brain Damage: Some Experimental Approaches

C. KEITH CONNERS

I would like to outline the general manner of approach we have been taking towards the study of children, and to describe some of the specific experiments which we hope will eventually shed some light on the problems of children suffering from learning disabilities. It is our hope that the approach we are using will enable us to move away from the sterile typological approaches of the past, in which unitary concepts of "brain damage" or "learning disability" will be replaced by a more meaningful functional analysis of the complicated systems which make up the child's world of thinking, feeling, and action.

The approach we are taking by no means constitutes a complete theory, but might best be described as a point of view or orientation which helps to guide our experiments and the way we ask questions. This approach is sometimes referred to as a "systems analysis": that is, one may look at a machine whose inner workings are hidden from view and try to discover what it is like by examining what the machine does in its normal operation. By examining what instructions or commands the machine receives, and analyzing the operations it performs, one can infer what mechanisms it *must* have in order to do this particular job, or the set of all jobs that it can perform. In doing such an analysis, one tries to be economical and to use the least number of mechanisms which will adequately characterize the machine. Similarly, when it comes to the cognitive functioning of a child, we try to ask what functions the child must perform in, let us say, learning a set of numbers, or making a simple delayed response after some command has been issued; and by examining what is available to him, and what he must do, we can make some inferences about the mechanisms or functional processes that must intervene between the input and the output. Just as it is useful in analyzing a simple machine as a system in which information or commands flow through the machine to achieve some designated outcome, so we may think of the human organism as a system which transmits information from the external world towards some output which achieves various results.

This simple general model of behavior has, of course, in one sense, been the basic model for the study of behavior all along. Freud said that the

From the *Proceedings* of the Third Annual International Conference of the ACLD, *International Approach to Learning Disabilities of Children and Youth*. Tulsa, Okla. (March 3–5, 1966), pp. 206–222. This study was supported by funds from the National Institute of Mental Health Grant MH-02583.

basic model of all human mental life remains the simple reflex arc; behavior theory, derived from Pavlov and Hull, has made the elaboration of this concept the foundation of its psychology; and neurologists have always divided nervous-system functions into receptor, afferent, efferent, and effector functions. So in the sense of describing the basic design of behavior, some form of "systems analysis" has been with us for some time.

However, one of the difficulties inherent in these previous attempts is the use of narrow terms like "stimulus" and "response," which seem to be too limited to describe adequately higher-order human cognitive functioning. Moreover, they turn out to rely heavily on circular definitions; no independent definition of the "stimulus" can usually be given. To tell what constitutes a stimulus we usually have to observe change in a response pattern. These limitations have seriously hampered behavior theorists from adequately understanding higher-order mental functions.

Systems analysis (communications theory or information theory) has, on the other hand, emphasized that in a communication system the organism or machine does not function like a telephone switchboard or reflex chain in which response is governed by *specific* stimuli present in the environment, but rather response is always dependent on the total set of things or events which *might* occur. The set or class of events which might occur in a situation constitutes the *information* to which a child responds.

When we measure some simple function, such as the speed of reaction to a light, we must keep in mind, then, that the speed will depend not only on the occurrence of the light that is actually presented, but on *the amount of information* that the light conveys—that is, the speed will depend on how many lights could occur in this situation. Thus, it has been quite conclusively shown that people respond more slowly to a light when it is one of two or more possibilities, than when only one light may occur. In general, then, it is the information which events convey that must be measured on the input side of the child's behavior.

There is a mathematics developed within communications theory that enables us to quantify precisely the amount of information in any set of events, and this precise measurement allows us to make a much more meaningful analysis of behavior. For, among other things, we will be able to measure how much information from different parts of the environment is getting into the response of a child. I will illustrate this in a moment.

To summarize then, our general orientation is to ask what mechanisms must be present in a child to allow him to process information in a given task. We think of information as something which flows from a source through the organism and into response. Information theory allows us to measure precisely the information in the environment, and in the responses of the subject.

Let me now be more specific and show you one of the ways we can look at the general system of information processing in the human subject. Much available evidence with adults suggests that some general schema of the following sort is required to account for the simplest facts of learning and remembering (see Figure 1). Information arrives through the senses and is temporarily stored for a very short time. Much of this information dissipates very rapidly before it is selected for further processing. At this stage when it is selected, we are "attending" to part of the information, and there is a certain limit to the amount of information we can attend to at any time. As information is repeated, it must be stored for later retrieval; so a storage mechanism, or long-term memory, is required in the model. The diagram illustrates an important feature of these memories—that they condition what is selected in the future, determining to some extent what is selected for attention on other occasions. There must also be some mechanism to delay responding until appropriate information is obtained, either from our past knowledge or from the present inputs. The feedback from what we are attending to in the limited capacity channel is necessary to account for the common fact of being able to *rehearse* information. For instance, if you read a telephone number, you select it from all the other telephone numbers on the page and quickly begin rehearsing it while you walk to the telephone. When you get there, you hold the information long enough to complete dialing.

Now this simple flow chart of human information processing is by no means complete, but it does include some of the essential mechanisms that almost certainly must play a part in responding to our environment. It immediately suggests the possibility that disorders of functioning might be due to any number of possible breakdowns. Consider, for example, the oft-noted inability of some "brain-injured" children to ignore distractions. This

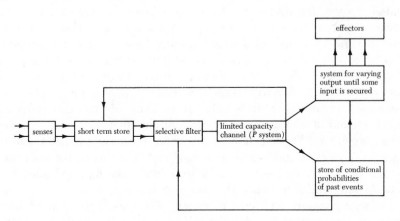

Figure 1. Model of Information Processing (After Broadbent, 1958). *The model indicates that information received by the senses is maintained in a short-term store before selection of relevant information is passed through a limited capacity system (perception). Stored information feeds back to determine what is selected. A mechanism is required to delay response for appropriate motor movements.*

deficit might correspond to some defect at the level of the selective filtering mechanism. In some children we have the impression that they are being overwhelmed by stimulation, not selectively responding to their environment at all. In other children the difficulty appears to be at a perceptual level in which the scanning mechanisms which operate to obtain information are either inefficient or defective. In still others, the children do not seem to learn from experience, and forget rules that would normally be retained for some time. In others we see the problem of impulsive responding or the inability to make appropriate delays between input and response. There are a variety of other attributes that appear in breakdowns of the normal information-processing sequences. It seems to us that a meaningful analysis of a child's functioning can be obtained by looking at the type of defect he has in information processing. Whether or not there are specific neuroanatomical lesions in certain cases which are affecting specific loci in this sequence, we do not know, and in one sense, do not care; for with our current knowledge it would make little difference in our ability to deal with the child or prescribe a course of instruction that is most suitable for his type of learning disorder.

Let me illustrate by some of our experiments the way in which some of these mechanisms operate:

Let us consider the level of information scanning. We assumed that the accuracy with which a child is able to preceive his environment might be strongly affected by the extent to which he initially samples or selects incoming information. To measure his information-sampling ability, we constructed several displays of increasing complexity or amount of information. In the first display we have combinations of two colors and two sizes—large-red, large-blue, small-red, and small-blue. This display has only four different kinds of figures and since there are just two dimensions of color and shape, there are two units of information—we call these units "bits," for "binary-digit." By combining three attributes—shape, color, and size—we get a display with three bits, and by making some hollow and some solid we have four bits of information. These displays then differ only in the amount of information they contain; note that they each contain 48 items. Now what happens if we ask a child to find all of the "small-red" figures in a display, and time him? According to our theory, the more information he has to deal with, the longer it will take him, provided he is actually sampling or scanning the information available.

The next illustration (Figure 2) shows the results of this part of the experiment: we see that the children do in fact take progressively longer as the display includes more information. Now, by taking the difference between a child's score on the low-information task and comparing it with the high-information task, we will have a measure of how much he was sampling the additional information. Is this sampling ability related to the accuracy with which he perceives his world? We tested this by having each child attempt to match a variable line with a standard line to see how accurately he could make size estimations. We also complicated the lines by

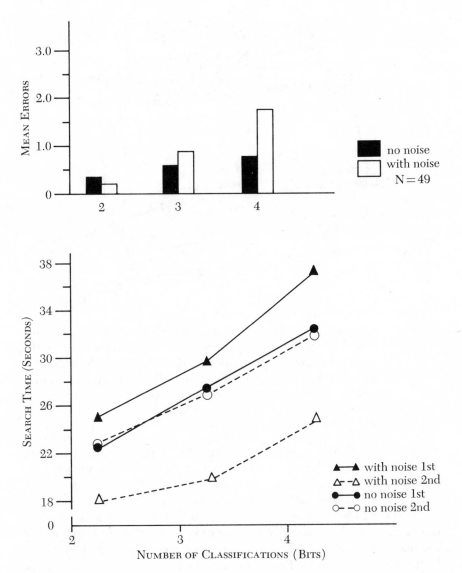

Figure 2

adding details that tend to give a distorted impression of length as in some of the familiar visual illusions. We find on several of these tasks that the accuracy of reproduction is highly related to information-sampling ability. Apparently, then, this first stage of information scanning is of considerable importance in making available accurate information for the child to work with; without adequate scanning the child is doomed to operate with a distorted input at the very beginning of the sequence.

We have pursued this question of the role of scanning mechanism and the ability of the child to attend selectively by devising a machine which

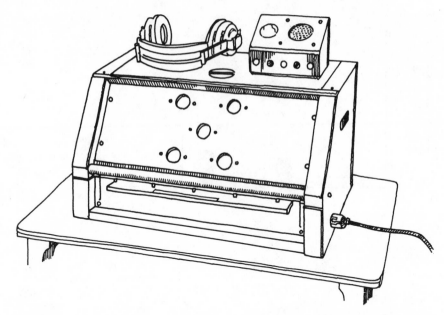

Figure 3. APPARATUS FOR PRESENTING INFORMATION TO A CHILD. *At each button a colored figure appears. The child pushes a figure in the outer four buttons which matches the figure in the inner button. He must match the shape but ignore the color. Auditing information may also be presented through earphones.*

presents the information sequentially, and which allows for a much more detailed analysis of the information processing sequence. In Figure 3 we see the apparatus used for this purpose. It presents the child with combinations of colors and patterns as in the previous experiment, and he is asked to search for a given item and respond to it as quickly as he can. The task is made slightly harder in that we can ask the child to match one of the shapes that comes up in the center with a shape in the periphery; but he must ignore the color. This is the paradigm for attention: selecting one type of information while simultaneously inhibiting irrelevant information. The stimuli are automatically presented by means of a punched paper tape and tape reader (Figure 4), and the reactions recorded on electronic apparatus (Figure 5). This apparatus records the child's errors and the response time for each signal and automatically punches this information onto IBM cards while the experiment progresses. From these data we will be able to answer a number of questions. For example, we are interested in long delays which occur every so often in performance known as blocks—when information processing breaks down momentarily. We will examine these "blocks" in attention as they are affected by therapeutic medications, by the passage of time in the course of the experiment (a measure of arousal or fatigability), and as they are related to the presence of pathology. Also, we will be able to calculate the amount of information from the irrelevant dimension which enters into the child's response; that is, how much information from color, for example, intrudes into responding to the dimension of shape. This, we hope, will be a sensitive measure of distractibility, or the extent to which the child analyzes incoming sensory input into its relevant and irrelevant dimensions, and separates these in his response. With such a measure we are hopeful that the effects of medications can be more sensitively judged and the optimal dosage levels studied in a quantitative manner.

Now this stage of the research is dealing primarily with the question of *intra*-sensory analysis—with the effects of one dimension in the visual world. But, as Sherrington, Birch and others have emphasized, one of the most important features of the development of information processing in the human is the elaboration of *inter*-sensory functions—the communication between one sense modality and another. In reading, for example, the child must learn to correlate information from the auditory and visual modalities. At the earliest stage the infant learns about his world through touch, taste and smell, and later must learn to integrate this information with the visual world. In terms of the model we presented earlier, we would have to add some mechanism that handles the task of integrating information from different sensory modalities. Again, I would like to illustrate the approach to this problem, using information theory. Birch has shown previously that an unselected group of brain-injured children were quite poor in their ability to integrate tactual and visual information, where the child had to feel behind a screen and try to tell by touch which of several forms before him he was feeling. Information theory allows us to ask this question in a slightly more sophisticated manner: *which* aspect of a form actually communicates information for the brain-injured child; for a geometric form has attributes of size, shape, angle, etc.

What we did was to take three shapes, each of three different sizes, and each of three different angles of orientation—for a total of $3 \times 3 \times 3$ or 27 figures—and display them before the child, who then reached under the display and actively felt a given form (Figure 6). He then had to point to the form that he thought he was touching. After presenting every form to the child three times—a total of 81 trials—we were able to use the mathematics of information theory to analyze how much of each of the dimensions of shape, size, and angle was entering into the child's visual recognition.

We were interested in the way the brain-injured, culturally deprived, normal, and emotionally disturbed children would perform on their task. Figure 7 shows the performance of some of these children. This gives the total amount of information transmitted, regardless of the type of information. We see that the brain-injured children do more poorly at most of the

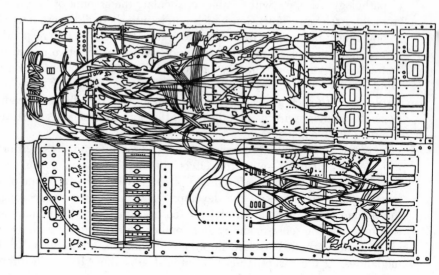

Figure 5

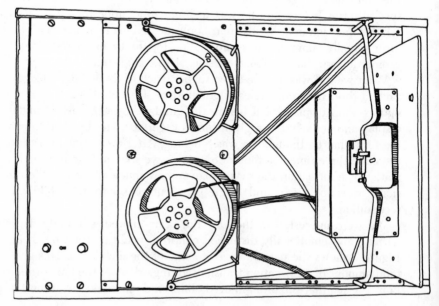

Figure 4

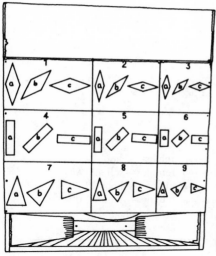

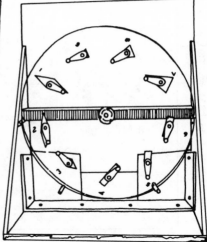

Figure 6a. Visual Display for Intersensory Movements. *A child reaches beneath the formboard and feels one of the forms he sees before him.*

Figure 6b. Rear View of the Formboard Apparatus. *Nine forms are attached to a disc which can be rotated. The particular angle of the form is adjusted separately. All 27 forms are presented to the child 3 times, for a total of 81 trials.*

age levels. Of interest, however, is the fact that some of these children do much more poorly on one dimension of intersensory communication than another (Figures 8 and 9). This confirms our expectation that tactual-visual communication of certain *attributes* is more difficult for *some children*. Two other findings are of interest. First, supposedly brain-injured children seem to have more difficulty in intrasensory analysis; i.e., in general, they tended to let information from shape or angle enter into their judgments about size, etc. And secondly, we note a large and highly significant tendency for the culturally deprived five-year-olds to be inferior on this task for all three attributes. The finding suggests that these children, for whatever reason, are about to enter school with a markedly inferior ability to translate their experience of the tactual world into visual terms. Is it possible that this deficit may underlie the serious gap in reading skills that later is to beset this group of children? They appear to catch up in this

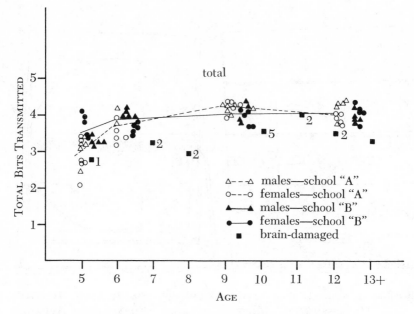

Figure 7. Total Information Transmitted in a $3 \times 3 \times 3$ Haptic-Visual Task. *School A = culturally deprived children. School B = middle-class children. The figure illustrates poor intersensory analysis in brain-damaged children and in lower-class five-year-olds. Effects of age are statistically significant.*

ability by age nine, but perhaps the early deficit comes after the critical period for developing reading skills has already passed.

What about short-term memory? Here we were interested in the question whether this type of memory is affected by the child's paying attention to interfering items, or whether this memory is essentially a fading trace that is easily disrupted by any kind of activity; and we wished to see whether children suspected of "brain injury" differed in the way their short-term memory functioned. Rather than use the conventional method of digit-span, or memory for words, which depends on the child's verbal ability, we showed him a series of pictures of common objects which he had to recall. In one group of children the list to be recalled was immediately followed by another list which was highly associated with the first one, interposed before recall for the first list. In a second condition the children saw a list which was also followed by another list, but this time of unrelated items. And in a third condition, the intervening activity consisted of a very different activity; namely, fitting some forms into a form-board. Thus, we had a recall task in which three types of activity could potentially cause disruption. The interesting outcome of this experiment was that, for normal and emotionally disturbed children, a loss of memory recall occurred when the intervening task consisted of other pictures; but

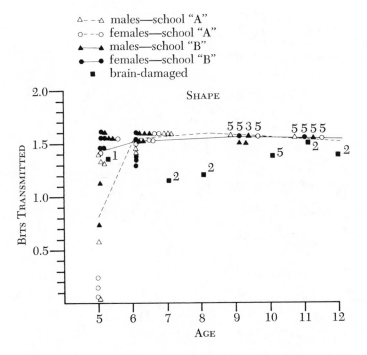

Figure 8. INFORMATION TRANSMITTED FROM SIZE AND SHAPE (TOUCHED)
TO SIZE AND SHAPE (VISUALLY PERCEIVED)

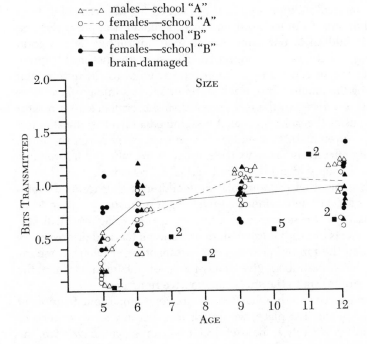

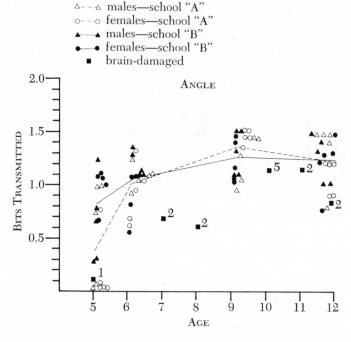

Figure 9. TRANSMISSION OF INFORMATION FROM ANGLE (TOUCHED) TO ANGLE (VISUALLY PERCEIVED)

for the brain-injured children, *any* kind of intervening task caused a sharp loss of recall ability. In other words, in this experiment it appears that the brain-injured children in our sample were easily disrupted by any form of intervening activity, even a formboard. This suggests that in this group there is indeed a susceptibility of short-term storage to disruption. But the passage of time alone, during which rehearsal was taking place, does not affect memory recall in these children; their performance after a short interval remains at the same level as it was immediately after the stimulus materials were presented. It is our guess that in these children the intervening activity effectively prevents the normal recirculation of information in the feedback loop which I described earlier as "rehearsal."

We are planning other experiments with children with learning disabilities of various sorts to determine what role long-term memory, or the "coding rules," plays in the sequence of information processing. We will also examine the effects of drugs on short-term memory, inter- and intra-sensory analysis, and on the inhibition of impulsive responding. Perhaps these experiments I have described give some flavor of the methods and the approach we are taking to the study of cognitive functions.

Let me summarize briefly what I think are some important features of this approach. In the first place, we do not feel that any series of tests of separate functions is likely to be useful in itself; for, as you have seen, the way we view information processing stresses the interrelationship among various mechanisms: the sensory input is affected by the child's coding strategies and previously acquired learnings; short-term memory is dependent on a feedback process, and this in turn on the efficiency of filtering operations; etc. In other words, simply because a child is unable to recall a series of items very well does *not* imply that the problem lies in his memory mechanism alone. Similarly, distractibility in a child needs to be defined quite precisely, for there are several stages of the sequence which might be responsible for apparent distractibility. It seems to us that what is required is a set of experiments with each child, carried out in such a way that one can systematically determine the stage or stages at which his processing of information breaks down. When a child performs poorly on the Bender-Gestalt test or the block-design test, it is not very helpful to conclude that he is "brain-damaged," or that he has a perceptual deficit. For such a poor performance might arise from several conditions: the child may not be adequately sampling the stimulus information; he may not have developed a classifying code which tells him, "This is a diamond touching a square"; he might not have adequate integration of the visual display with his proprioceptive and kinesthetic information while he is drawing; he might be experiencing momentary gaps in the intake of information which leaves him with a distorted input; etc. This much, I think, is obvious, and most good diagnosticians put together information from all available sources in arriving at conclusions about the child. But in addition to this, I think we must go beyond the conventional methods to more powerful techniques which refine measurement and quantify it in units which are meaningful. As we have seen, a geometrical form has different *kinds* of information which might pose problems to a child; and when we are able to quantify adequately some of the qualitative features of the child's world and his performance, we shall go much further towards adequate description of the type of function that is impaired in a given child.

Psychological Aspects
of Learning Disabilities

C. R. STROTHER

An examination of the current status of psychological knowledge concerning the nature and treatment of learning disabilities is likely to produce very mixed reactions. Hindsight, which is so much sharper than foresight, reveals the false leads which have been followed and the pitfalls which have trapped many investigators. On the other hand, there is evidence of considerable progress toward more sophisticated understanding of learning disabilities and strong promise of more effective methods of diagnosis and treatment.

Let us examine first some of the false trails which, unfortunately, are still being followed by many investigators, clinicians, and teachers. An understanding of the reasons why efforts have been diverted in these directions requires a brief glance at the history of the field. In the 1860s, medical interest in the consequences of brain injuries in adults led to the discovery of various disturbances in language—aphasias and alexias.[1] By the early 1900s, physicians working with children had reported somewhat similar difficulties in speech and reading, which they termed "congenital word blindness"[2, 3, 4] and "congenital auditory imperception,"[5, 6, 7] and which they attributed to some defect in the central nervous system. Later, studies of encephalitis and of cerebral palsy demonstrated that *known* brain damage in children resulted in a variety of disturbances in perceptual, emotional, linguistic, and other aspects of behavior.[8, 9, 10, 11] Pasamanick and others, through retrospective studies, revealed a sufficiently high incidence of abnormal pregnancies and deliveries among children exhibiting these problems of learning and behavior to warrant the inference that these disorders might be a consequence of brain injury even in the absence of clear-cut neurological signs of brain damage.[12, 13, 14, 15]

These and other studies left no doubt that various degrees of brain damage—from minimal to severe—occur with significant frequency in children and may result in a wide variety of disorders in perception, motor coordination, acquisition of spoken and written language, in hyperactivity and emotional lability. These studies were medically oriented. Attention was focused primarily on the diagnosis of brain damage. Little interest was aroused in the development of special educational programs for children exhibiting these problems of learning and behavior.

It remained for Werner and Strauss, in the 1940s, to excite this interest. The great influence which their work has had was due not only to their

From the *Proceedings* of the Second Western Regional Conference of the ACLD and the California Association for Neurologically Handicapped Children, *State of the Art: Where Are We in Learning Disabilities?* (February 3, 1973). ACLD and CANHC publications, copyright, 1974, pp. 29–36.

more precise analysis of specific disorders of perception, cognition, and motor and social behavior in presumably brain-injured children, but more importantly, to the facts that these disorders were considered to be remediable and that they, together with Lehtinen and Kephart, outlined specific educational techniques which might be used with these children.[16, 17] Their work led more or less directly to the formation of lay and professional organizations and to the passage of state and federal legislation providing funds for development of special educational programs for children with learning disabilities.

Unfortunately, Dr. Strauss chose to commit a deliberate logical error—an error which has led to a great deal of unproductive educational and psychological research. Strauss argued, in effect, that if brain-injured children exhibit certain characteristics, then all children exhibiting such characteristics should be considered to be brain-injured.[18] This, and other factors, have led many investigators to assume that children with learning disabilities ("brain-injured" children) must exhibit some common characteristics and that special learning procedures might be found that were applicable to this group of children. The research designs that have typically been employed involve the selection of a sample of children judged, usually by teachers, to have a learning disability. The investigator interested in diagnosis has then asked the question, "Do these children differ from a normal group with respect to figure-ground discrimination, visual-motor coordination, or some other specified characteristic?" The investigator interested in remediation has asked, "Is this particular method of training effective with this group of children?" While group differences might be found to exist, not all children in the learning-disabled group would exhibit the characteristic under investigation or benefit from the particular method of instruction which was used. Moreover, other investigators, using a different sample of children referred by other teachers for learning disabilities would fail to get the same results. After much wasted time and effort, it is now clear that children with learning disabilities ("brain-injured" children) are a very heterogeneous group.[19, 20] Definitive educational research is dependent on the identification of homogeneous subgroups in this ill-defined population. Then, given children who exhibit the same disabilities, the chances of developing effective educational techniques are greatly enhanced.

This problem is being attacked by psychologists who hold very different points of view. The views of contemporary behaviorists have been shaped, in large part, by Skinner and his colleagues. From this standpoint, adaptive behavior is instigated by its immediate antecedents and controlled by its consequences. While the focus of attention in much of this research has been on analysis of specific behaviors of individual children, it is beginning to result in a taxonomy of tasks, hierarchies of responses, and catalogs of procedures and materials that teachers may utilize with a wide range of learning difficulties and behavior problems.[21, 22] One important characteristic of this approach is the fact that it is directed toward an analysis of immediate learning tasks and to the modification of behaviors related as closely as possible to the behavior ultimately desired. Other approaches to be discussed are concerned with processes conceived to *underlie* the observed behavior. They seek to modify these processes by activities which may be remotely related to the desired behavior. An extreme example is the use of crawling exercises to develop patterns of neurological organization which are conceived to underlie reading behavior.

A second major point of view involved in current psychological research on learning disabilities is that of cognitive psychology.[23] This is directed toward an analysis of the cognitive processes—such as attention, perception, or memory—which are conceived to underlie overt behavior and toward the development of methods by which these processes may be made more effective. This type of research may proceed either from a very limited or from a more general model of cognition. It involves the application of psychometric, observational, or experimental techniques in the analysis of the processes of interest. Frostig's work may serve as an example of research based on a limited cognitive model.[24] Proceeding from a review of the literature on visual perception, a test battery was developed to assess four of the basic processes involved. A significant number of children with learning disabilities are found to be relatively deficient with respect to these processes when compared with children who are progressing normally in school tasks. While the heterogeneity of the population of children with learning disabilities is demonstrated by the fact that not all do poorly on the Frostig test, it is possible reliably to identify children who do and thus to sort out a group the members of which are homogeneous at least in this respect. Training materials and procedures have then been devised to improve the perceptual processes found to be deficient. At this point, a number of empirical questions may be raised, which should be possible to resolve by well-designed research—questions such as: Can these processes be improved by training; does improvement in these skills result in improvement on academic tasks; is any resulting academic improvement temporary or persistent? The evidence presently available is equivocal. The problems of experimental design involved in research on such questions are complex. Cruickshank, in a recent book, reviews the principal studies of perceptual-motor training. He comes to the conclusion that only seven of the forty-two studies reviewed meet acceptable standards of experimental design and that the results of these seven studies are contradictory.[25]

From my own review of research on the relationship between perceptual functions and learning, I have formed some tentative opinions—some more and some less well supported by evidence. For what they may be worth, these opinions are as follows:

1. Sensory-motor development and perceptual integration are important precursors of later cognitive development.
2. Perceptual abilities are specific rather than general and show con-

siderable variation in rate of development among normal children up to 6-8 years of age. The variation is greater among children with learning disabilities.

3. The relationship between perceptual-motor abilities and reading ability becomes rapidly less significant after the first grade.

4. Where specific perceptual-motor disabilities can be demonstrated in the young child, well-designed training programs can result in improvement in these skills.

5. Improvement in perceptual-motor skills is associated to some extent with improvement in reading skills. The degree of this association appears to be a function of the age of the child and the closeness of the relationship between the training tasks and the tasks involved in reading.

Another example of research based on a limited cognitive model is the work of Dr. Kirk and his associates.[26] His Illinois Test of Psycho-linguistic Abilities is widely used to identify children with specific disabilities in particular aspects of linguistic processes. As is the case with the Frostig test, remedial procedures may then be designed for each type of disability. The available evidence of the effectiveness of these programs is somewhat more convincing than is the case with perceptual-motor programs, probably because linguistic functions are more closely related to school tasks.

Some current research suggests that it would be fruitful to submit these specific cognitive functions to more detailed analysis. Let me illustrate what I mean by a very simple example. Suppose a child is unable to distinguish visually between a triangle and a diamond. One might conclude that he has a basic difficulty in form discrimination and might proceed to use remedial measures that had been reasonably successful in other cases in improving form perception. But a psychologist interested in the process of attention might discover, as did Zeaman and House, that the basic difficulty was not in learning to discriminate between the two forms but in learning to focus attention on relevant aspects of the task.[27] Given appropriate training for this problem, the child could learn to make the discrimination as well as children without a perceptual disability in form discrimination.

It is also possible, as Stott has shown with respect to errors in the discrimination of letters, that the difficulty may lie in impulsivity.[28] The child may simply make a response too quickly. If so, research has demonstrated the effectiveness of a variety of ways of teaching children to be less impulsive—procedures ranging from social reinforcement of delay, the use of specific instructions and modeling to the use of psychotropic drugs.

There are still other hypotheses which might be tenable but these examples may be sufficient to demonstrate that detailed analyses of specific cognitive functions may ultimately yield remedial procedures much more efficient than those which are now available.

Interest in cognition and cognitive disabilities extends beyond the specific functions which have been discussed. More comprehensive cognitive models present the possibility of identifying still other groups within the heterogeneous population of children with learning disabilities. Recently, Senf has suggested an information-theory model which might provide a framework for a broader search for types of learning disabilities.[29]

The research strategy which I have been discussing has involved the definition of a conceptual model of cognitive processes, the development of tests designed to assess components of this model and the identification of children showing specific disabilities with respect to these various functions. An alternative and more empirical approach involves the administration of a battery of psychological tests not selected on the basis of any explicit cognitive theory, and the use of various statistical techniques to identify children with similar patterns of test performance.[30, 31]

There are, then, various ways in which relatively homogeneous groups of children may be identified in the very heterogeneous population of children with learning disabilities—behavioral analysis, the assessment of specified cognitive functions, or empirical psychometric procedures. Much research remains to be done before the relative effectiveness of these methods of classifying children with learning disabilities can be evaluated. There is substantial agreement among investigators of all the disciplines concerned with this problem—education, psychology, biology, and medicine—that the problem of classification must be given high priority.[32] Until children with similar learning disabilities can be identified objectively and reliably, research on the etiology and remediation of these conditions will continue to be confused and inconclusive.

NOTES

1. H. Head, *Aphasia and kindred disorders of speech* (New York: Macmillan, 1926).
2. W. P. Morgan, A case of congenital word-blindness. *British Medical Journal* 2, (1896), 1378.
3. J. Kerr, School hygiene, in its mental, moral and physical aspects. *Royal Stat. Soc.* 60, (1897), 613-680.
4. J. Hinshelwood, *Letter-, word-, and mind-blindness* (London: H. K. Lewis & Co., 1900).
5. C. H. Town, Congenital aphasia. *Psychol. Clin.* 5 (1911), 167-179.
6. J. H. Claiborne, Types of congenital symbol amblyopia. *J. Am. Med. Ass'n* 47 (1906), 1813-1816.
7. A. W. G. Ewing, *Aphasia in children* (London: Humphrey Milford, 1930).
8. L. B. Hohman, Post-encephalitic behavior disorders in children. *Johns Hopkins Hospital Bulletin* 33 (1922), 372-375.
9. F. G. Ebaugh, Neuropsychiatric sequelae of acute epidemic encephalitis in children. *Am. J. Dis. Children* 25 (1923), 89-97.
10. R. H. Holden, A review of psychological studies of cerebral palsy. *Am. J. Ment. Def.* 57 (1952), 92-98.

11. M. L. J. Abercrombie, Perceptual and visuo-motor disorders in cerebral palsy. A survey of the literature. *Little Club Clinics in Developmental Medicine* 11 (1964), 1-136.

12. B. Pasamanick, M. Rogers, and A. M. Lilienfeld, Pregnancy experience and the development of behavior disorder in children. *Am. J. Psychiat.* 112 (1956), 613-617.

13. H. R. Knoblock, P. Rider, and B. Pasamanick, Neuropsychiatric sequelae of prematurity. *J. Am. Med. Assn.* 161 (1956), 679-690.

14. A. M. Lilienfeld and B. Pasamanick, The association of maternal and fetal factors with the development of cerebral palsy and epilepsy. *Am. J. Obstet. & Gynecol.* 70 (1955), 93-104.

15. A. M. Lilienfeld, B. Pasamanick, and M. Rogers, Relationship between pregnancy experience and certain neuropsychiatric disorders in childhood. *Am. J. Public Health* 45 (1955), 637-643.

16. A. A. Strauss and L. E. Lehtinen, *Psychopathology and education of the brain-injured child,* vol. 1 (New York: Grune & Stratton, 1948).

17. A. A. Strauss and N. C. Kephart, *Psychopathology and education of the brain-injured child,* vol 2 (New York: Grune & Stratton, 1948).

18. Strauss and Kephart, p. 42.

19. M. Bax and R. MacKeith (eds.). Minimal cerebral dysfunction. *Little Club Clinics in Developmental Medicine* 10 (1963), 1-104.

20. S. D. Clements, *Minimal brain dysfunction in children—terminology and identification* (Washington, D.C.: U.S. Public Health Service, Publication No. 1415, 1964).

21. R. H. Bradfield, *Behavior modification of learning disabilities* (San Raphael, California: Acad. Therapy Pub., 1971).

22. N. Haring and B. Bateman, *Teaching learning disabled children* (Englewood, New Jersey: Prentice-Hall, in press).

23. Ulric Nesser, *Cognitive psychology* (New York: Appleton-Century-Crofts, 1966).

24. M. Frostig, W. Le Fever, and J. Whittlesley, *Developmental test of visual perception,* 2nd ed. rev. (Palo Alto, California: Consulting Psychologist Press, 1964).

25. D. P. Hallahan and W. Cruickshank, *Psychoeducational foundations of learning disabilities* (Englewood, New Jersey: Prentice-Hall, 1973).

26. S. A. Kirk and W. D. Kirk, *Psycholinguistic learning disabilities: diagnosis and remediation* (Urbana, Illinois: University of Illinois Press, 1971).

27. D. Zeaman and B. J. House, The role of attention in retardate discrimination learning, In Ellis, N. R. (ed.). *Handbook of mental deficiency* (New York: McGraw-Hill, 1963), 159-223.

28. N. Marson and D. H. Stott, Inconsequence as a primary type of behavior disturbance in children. *Brit. J. Educ. Psychol.,* 40(1) (1970), 15-20.

29. Gerald M. Senf, An information-integration theory and its application to normal reading acquisition and reading disability. In *Leadership training institute in learning disabilities,* vol. 2 (Washington, D.C.: final report, U.S.O.E. contract, Bryant, N. D. (Director), U.S. Office of Education, 1972), 303-393.

30. C. K. Connors, Psychological assessment of children with minimal brain dysfunction. In *Minimal brain dysfunction.* De la Cruz, F.; Fox, B. H.; and Roberts, R. H. (eds.). Annals of the New York Acad. Sci. (1973), 205, 283-303.

31. Robert M. Knights, Problems of criteria in diagnosis: a profile similarity approach. In *Minimal brain dysfunction*. De la Cruz, F. F.; Fox, B. H.; and Roberts, R. H. (eds.). Annals of the New York Acad. Sci. (1973), 205, 124-132.

32. R. L. Masland, Epilogue. In *Minimal brain dysfunction*. De la Cruz, F.; Fox, B. H.; and Roberts, R. H. (eds.). Annals of the New York Acad. Sci. (1973), 205, 395-396.

Formal Evaluation of the Effectiveness of Performance Contracting Programs for Learning Disabilities

LOWELL A. SEYMOUR

BARTON B. PROGER

Contracts between publishers of educational materials and school systems that consume those materials are increasing in number and there is no let-up in sight.[1] Such contracts assume various forms: some merely provide materials and offer no insurance or guarantee that certain minimum achievement will be produced in the children who use them; others offer a comprehensive package of materials, personnel, consultation, and guarantees. However, no matter what arrangement is reached between the publisher and the school system, there is an implied or stated assumption that *accountability* will prevail. The concept of accountability has become so common among educators that no definitions need be given here.[2] Stated very simply, the term refers to an attempt to evaluate how well certain educational objectives are achieved. Another term that is receiving increased usage in the educational literature is *program evaluation*; indeed, one might consider this term synonymous with accountability.

We have outlined here some aspects of program evaluation that school systems should be aware of as they embark on more and more publisher-school contracts; such considerations are important if we are to insure that the taxpayers get their money's worth. A highly detailed account of program evaluation for the learning disabled has been issued elsewhere and will not be repeated here.[3] That publication also offers a comprehensive review of literature on accountability regardless of whether or not performance contracts are involved in the learning-disabled programs that it evaluates. This paper considers a model for program evaluation of performance-contracting setups for the learning disabled, and a series of operational problems that are associated with such a model. The model presented will have maximum utility in focusing immediately upon performance contracting itself rather than dwelling on a lot of peripheral, technical details. This model thusly becomes an "exportable" commodity that can be used in any performance-contracting operation for the learning disabled.

The word "performance" in the phrase, *performance contracting*, reflects what is to be measured: student achievement. If a commercial enterprise has guaranteed to raise the performance of each child by a specified

This paper was partially supported by PRISE, which is a Title III Project funded under the Elementary and Secondary Education Act of 1965. However, no endorsement on the part of PRISE or its funding agency, the U.S. Office of Education, is to be inferred. The opinions expressed herein are solely those of the two authors.

amount, which in turn determines how much reimbursement the company receives, then an evaluation model is needed. Unfortunately, while a "model" as such is easy to devise for measurement and research specialists, most people embarking on such a project are unaware of the many pitfalls they will encounter in the process of setting up an evaluation model.

Before the model can be presented, the terminology that is used in it must be clarified. When one talks about formal program evaluation for performance contracts, he is referring to measuring with acceptable testing procedures just how successful the performance contract program has been with *both* individual learning-disabled children and all children as a group. When one looks at the total group of children, he can gauge whether or not the program as a whole was successful in the goals it had set for itself; the changes in individual students allow one to qualify any generalizations from the total group that otherwise might be somewhat shaky with such a highly variegated population. Nonetheless, educators of exceptional children still manage to confuse formal program evaluation with other, more common types of evaluation, such as one that is made by the psychologist when an individual child has been referred for placement. Another mode of evaluation, that is somewhat less common, is a statistical placement strategy for ensuring maximum success for each learning-disabled child.[4]

Once the conceptual details are devised, we can describe existing formal program-evaluation models that are specifically designed for special education. First, however, some general features of formal program-evaluation models are presented in the sense that the original accountability movement intended. Finally, the performance-contracting evaluation model is presented. A concluding section will discuss some typical problems that are encountered by the serious learning-disabilities program evaluator.

The Conceptual Model for Accountability

Even though the accountability movement is still in its infancy, the general theoretical framework for the stream of formal program-evaluation models that has arisen in recent years can be traced to the Stufflebeam structure: Context, Input, Process, and Product (CIPP).[5] Rather than review some of the characteristics of the original CIPP model, let us look at one of the many modern adaptations of the model: the Randall Context, Design, Process, and Product (CDPP) model.[6] Describing the major steps in the CDPP evaluation process, Randall states:

Context evaluation consists of planning decisions and context information that serves them. . . . Design evaluation entails structuring decisions which depend on design information . . . the objectives need to be specified operationally if possible, and activities or means of attaining them need to be specified. . . . After a design has been structured and is put on trial, often called the pilot test, restructuring decisions are faced. Restructuring decisions are based on process information. . . . After components of a design have been tested, they can be put together in a program for a product or field test. Since this is the first full-cycle test, the major decisions faced are whether to recycle through another full-scale field test. The information needed, called product information, entails not only evidence about effectiveness in attaining short- and long-range goals, but also effectiveness . . . compared with that of another program or strategy.[7]

The model that is presented at the end of this paper illustrates in greater detail exactly what is meant by this general conceptual framework.

Special Education Program-Evaluation Models

Before presenting the detailed model that we recommend for performance contracts, we mention some existing guides to formal program evaluation. These guides do not dwell on models as such, but rather emphasize operational evaluation problems. In this sense, the existing guides should be highly beneficial to anyone who endeavors to engage in accountability. A. Ahr and H. Sims have provided special educators with an entire organizational setup for carrying out program evaluation on a large scale.[8] Many examples from different fields of exceptionality, including learning disabilities, are given. Those interested in organizational patterns of research offices in school systems should refer to E. Mosher.[9] A somewhat less ambitious guide to program evaluation in special education has been presented by W. Meierhenry,[10] and one of the earliest guides was issued by P. Annas and R. Dowd.[11] While not aiming specifically for special education, the Center for Instructional Research and Curriculum Evaluation, along with the Cooperative Educational Research Laboratory, Inc., has produced a similar guide,[12] and finally, another regular-education oriented guide was written by H. Grobman.[13]

A Formal Evaluation Model for Performance Contract Programs

The total evaluation process, including the planning stages, has already been described briefly in connection with the Randall CDPP conceptualization. However, most so-called formal program-evaluation models must of necessity be stated in very general terms so as to be applicable to a variety of different situations; the model usually loses meaning and fails to provide direct implications for the program administrator or teacher who is forced to resolve a host of specific problems.[14] Thus, our task now is to present some highly specific guidelines for learning-disabilities educators to follow in order to achieve several evaluation objectives.

First, the reader must be aware of some basic details of performance contracting.[15] If a guaranteed contract is signed by the school district and the commercial publisher, then somehow the company must be made accountable for backing up their guarantee. The school district must somehow arrive at some criterion level of performance to be reached by each child at the end of an academic year if the company is to be reimbursed a stated amount for each child that reaches such a level. Thus, before any thoughts can be given to a formal program-evaluation design, the school district must come up with realistic objectives of just how much achievement (or motor performance, or affective reactions) must be evidenced in a given child before the profit incentive is provided to the company. For example, perhaps for a normal child one might expect that his independent level of reading should be raised at least one whole grade level by the end of an academic year's effort by the company. This is fine for the normal child. However, the determination of reasonable objectives for the learning-disabled child is a sticky problem. If such a child has a severe or even moderate degree of specific reading disability, is it still reasonable to expect a year's growth in reading ability even after intensive remediation by the contracting company? Or should the objective be revised downward to 0.6 of a year's growth, or even 0.5? Here, then, is a major hurdle to the implementation of performance contracting for the learning-disabled child: the learning-disabilities field is in such a constant state of change and redefinition year by year, and data upon which to make rational decisions such as for determining realistic goals are so noticeably absent, that contract negotiations lose their "straightforwardness."

At any rate, once realistic objectives have been set, the student achievement, upon which the school district's reimbursement to the company depends, must be measured. The minimally acceptable design for measuring change would consist of the administration of both a pretest and a posttest. With this simple measurement paradigm, the evaluators can determine for each child whether or not the company should be reimbursed. Further the evaluators can gauge the progress of the program as a whole by averaging together the responses of all of the students. If one carries this logic one step more, he can extract additional valuable information if some meaningful classification system is built into the total pretest-posttest design. For example, perhaps the total group of students can be classified at the outset as to their degree of specific reading disability (from a mild through a moderate and into a severe disability) on the basis of some legitimate measure available or taken on all students. With this refinement in the design, the evaluator will be able to detect whether the performance contract package operates differentially for certain categories of children within the total program. For example, the contracting materials might work quite effectively for most children in the mild and moderate categories of specific reading disability but miserably with the severe disability group. These qualifications on the overall success of a contracted instructional program are often left to the "evidence" of heresay or opinion.

At this point in our discussion of evaluation models, the above design would be sufficient to gauge the progress of the program and to determine the extent of the reimbursement. A few words need to be said here about the methodological philosophy implied in the above designs. A very clear distinction must be made in formal program evaluation between judgmental evaluation and monitoring evaluation.[16] The above designs are of a monitoring type in that the success of the overall program can be determined only within the relativistic framework of the children themselves according to predetermined levels of criterion achievement. In this sense, the evaluation is criterion-referenced in nature.[17] The major *deficiency* is in the lack of data-based information on how well the contracted program functions in relation to different methods of instruction (such as traditional, teacher-directed reading activities, or other programed instruction approaches). This line of thought leads one to the final stage of sophistication in a formal program-evaluation design for performance contracts: the judgmental program-evaluation design.

The only way in which one can safely say that the performance contract succeeded in a general way (not in a relativistic way defined by one's own subjective criteria for success) is to compare it directly with some competing instructional approach. An evaluation design that embodies such comparisons would be judgmental in nature. One can literally make the value judgment of whether or not one approach was more successful than the other. That is, the monitoring evaluation designs that are described earlier in this section are descriptive in the sense that one is recording test data and the other records information for each child but only under *one* form of instruction: the performance-contracting approach. However, a judgmental design would collect exactly the *same* data on not only the performance-contracting type of instruction but also more traditional types of instruction and then would allow one to make judgmental inferences about the success of one instructional approach over a competing one. Naturally, the judgmental evaluation design assumes that the school district can allow more than just the performance-contracting type of instruction to operate within the same district but on different children. Such an assumption might be objectionable on the part of community groups that believe all children should be given the same instruction.

One point of confusion among teachers and administrators of learning-disabilities programs is that the only "legitimate" program-evaluation designs are of the judgmental type; that is, the monitoring or descriptive designs covered earlier in this section should really not be used. Such reasoning is totally wrong. First, one should not be confused by the use of the terms "monitoring (descriptive) evaluation" and "judgmental evaluation." In statistics, a distinction is usually made between descriptive statistics and inferential statistics, the latter somehow being more refined and useful than the former. When one speaks of monitoring or descriptive program evaluation, he is doing so in a global sense, not in a strict statistical fashion; statistical inferences are still possible with monitoring evaluation with regard to the classification categories embedded within the design. One should also note that when at least two monitoring evaluation designs are placed side by side, they become a judgmental program-evaluation design. There is a whole host of reasons why one would find a great deal of use for monitoring evaluation designs.[18] The one bias in reasoning against which one must be constantly on guard is the assumption that if an evaluator cannot carry out a judgmental design involving various control groups, then he should not even bother with a "mere" descriptive or monitoring design of a one-group-only paradigm. The basic philosophy behind any design is the gathering of data in as scientific a fashion as possible; one might even call this a data-bank type of activity.[19] In this regard, *both* the judgmental design and the monitoring design are ideally suited. The ultimate goal is to make cautious, intelligent decisions that are based upon carefully gathered data.

We have discussed two basic formal program-evaluation designs: monitoring and judgmental. In terms of the original conceptual CDPP model (context, design, process, and product), all but the "process" phase have been described. Process-evaluation feedback is crucial because of the flexibility it allows the evaluators and educational programers; this flexibility makes it possible for them to make necessary changes in the middle of a program (in-process) to improve the final educational product. One obvious way in which process feedback can be obtained is to institute the administration of a middle-of-the-year test that is equivalent to the pretests and posttests that are used. This midtesting can be incorporated into either the monitoring designs or the judgmental designs that have already been described.

Other types of in-process feedback can be incorporated. For example, the school district of Philadelphia has begun a computerized process-evaluation, data-collection procedure. Various types of key in-process information on the progress of each child throughout the academic year are collected from teachers on specially coded sheets. At fixed points throughout the year these data sheets can be processed by computer to yield various types of analyses; the results in turn can be fed back to administrators and teachers throughout the district. Here is a perfect example of the data-bank philosophy in special education: collect as much information as possible on the progress children make throughout the year at predetermined, uniform intervals. In connection with certain reading program packages bought from commercial publishers, the Philadelphia school district also considers it important to conduct in-process interviews of how teachers feel about the new programs and to conduct observational studies of how the programs *really* function in the classroom settings.

Operational Problems and Concluding Comments

We have attempted to present a realistic program-evaluation accountability model that can be used by any learning-disabilities program, or for that matter, any special education program in general, to gauge how successful their efforts were. The name of the rational educational game is decision-making on a logical information basis.

For judging success of perfect contracting, such decision-making with respect to keeping or changing an existing performance contract relies on change in student performance throughout the year. Various agencies have attempted to provide information background to the decision makers upon demand.[20] However, let us stop for a look at accountability and reality.

Most evaluators of programs agree that change in student performance is of primary interest. The model presented here has embodied the concept of change in a rather clear-cut fashion. However, be not deluded! *Regardless* of how one measures change, methodologists will attack his calculations from all angles. There are theoretical difficulties in any approach.[21] Nonetheless, let us assume your professional egos are sufficiently strong to withstand these assaults on your end-of-the-year evaluation reports on the status of the performance-contracting setup in your district. Your problems have just begun, if you are truly committed to accountability.

One of the worst pitfalls the administrative decision-maker could fall into is not to wait until the evaluation of performance contracting is complete. Put yourself in the position of the administrator who has bought a performance contract and is currently in the middle of the academic year. Pretesting has been completed and in-process monitoring is presently being completed. However, the real payoff criteria will not be available until the posttesting is completed at the end of the year. Yet you have just been asked by the district superintendent to make a decision one way or the other as to whether or not to keep the performance contract for next year. You will not have the complete evaluation picture until the end of the year. If you are the typical administrator, you will forget everything formal evaluation could tell you and rely on those old decision-making stand-bys: the number of smiles on the faces of children and the verbal praise from your favorite teachers and administrative aides. And here is the real tragedy in high-level decision-making: no one can, or perhaps wants to, wait for the verdict to come in. The decision for next year's program is made on a partial, sometimes faulty picture of what's happening now, and the final evaluation report, with all its wealth of implications, is completed at the close of the year and gathers dust on the administrator's bookshelf. Of course, most school districts do not have this problem. They simply don't bother to evaluate programs in a formal way at all; they base their decisions on opinions only. However, those few rare districts that do bother to evaluate at all run into the perennial time-lag problem between the decision and the evaluation. Will the biggest industry in the country always make decisions in this manner? Will the professional school evaluator-researcher always feel like a rather sophisticated but largely ignored professional? One could argue, of course, that even if the school district where a formal evaluation is conducted ignores such findings, at least the evaluation is done and will be available for other districts to examine in the future if they are faced with similar problems. This latter argument does hold some plausibility, but it seems a poor substitute indeed for a legitimate data-based decision-making process.

Let us go on to consider a few other frustrating problems that evaluators of performance contracts for learning-disabilities programs are likely to run into. The learning-disabled realm, or any area of special education, differs markedly from that of regular or normal education. In terms of implications for evaluation and testing, this means that the focus must be on the individual child. Group approaches are largely meaningless. Thus, part of the formal program evaluation of the effectiveness of any performance contract for the learning disabled must take individual testing into account in some way. For example, perhaps part of the evaluation design would include the administration of the *Peabody Individual Achievement Test* or the *Illinois Test of Psycholinguistic Abilities*. Fine! But now ask yourself this question, and make sure you provide an honest answer! Just who will administer all the individual achievement tests? One of these tests may well drag on for an hour or more per child. Make sure that time has been released from the usual time schedules of your psychologists or clinicians. Otherwise, as the year progresses, you may see an otherwise beautiful evaluation design falling apart before your eyes.

Another problem may arise that concerns any group measures of achievement that the evaluator feels might be appropriate for learning-disabled children. If one is involved with a large series of learning-disabilities classes, perhaps some type of group testing will become a necessity. (An alternative would be to draw a sample from the total population for intensive individual testing.) In turn, probably not enough testing personnel will be available. Thus, some fast and competent inservice training will be needed to prepare the teachers to carry out their testing legitimately. The main problem one runs into here is cooperation: getting the teachers together, finding enough time to go over all of the instructions, and enlisting the teachers' cooperation to agree to abide by whatever rules the total group comes up with. In the field of education, cooperation is often very difficult to obtain.

Finally, regardless of whether or not you decide to go into performance contracting for your learning-disabilities programs, the general issue of accountability should be examined rather closely before you embark on a full-fledged program evaluation. If you do not have a commitment to making rational decisions on the basis of data and past research, forget it! Formal program evaluation will merely be hypocrisy on your part. The really sad part of all this is that the vast majority of learning-disabilities programs do not engage in formal program evaluation.

At worst, the only testing the children get occurs during the initial psychological evaluation; at best, only once during the academic year. Very rarely is change measured. This reflects what has been termed "the failure of evaluation."[22] At present, only token lip-service is being paid to the concept of accountability as we have interpreted it here. Perhaps a few of you recall the huge Educational Research Training Program.[23] Where have all the graduates of this doctoral training gone? Professors of educational research who are working in colleges and doing isolated research studies and a little teaching are necessary, to be sure, but wouldn't it be nice to see a large number of these people enter the real world and try to rig the ongoing learning-disabilities machinery to keep a continuous program-evaluation system in operation to provide continuous data for decision-making. Clearly something has gone wrong with the whole educational-research movement. That movement, when viewed now in somewhat skeptical retrospect, could be interpreted as a rather vague embodiment of the accountability concept before it ever came into vogue. While isolated studies of both semibasic and applied types have increased in quantity and quality as generated out of universities, the real payoff for realistic classroom practice in the field is still rather shabby in appearance.

NOTES

1. R. Schwartz, "USOE and OEO Fund More than 30 New Projects: Performance Contracts Catch On," *Nations Schools* 86 (1970), 31-33; R. A. Ehrle, "National Priorities and Performance Contracting," *Educational Technology* 10, no. 7 (1970), 27-28; J. Morton, "Contract Learning in Texarkana," *Educational Screen and Audiovisual Instruction* 49, no. 2 (1970), 12-13.
2. S. Elam, "The Age of Accountability Dawns in Texarkana," *Phi Delta Kappan* 10 (1970), 509-514; Leon M. Lessinger, "Robbing Dr. Peter to 'Pay Paul': Accounting for Our Stewardship of Public Education," *Educational Technology* 11, no. 1 (1971), 11-14.
3. Barton B. Proger, "Program Evaluation: The Model-Building Game," *Journal of Learning Disabilities* (in press).
4. B. B. Proger, "Improving Evaluation Procedures in Physical Education Programs for the Learning Disabled: The Neglected Use of Multivariate Techniques." Paper presented at the 7th International ACLD Conference, Philadelphia, Pa.: February 12, 1970.
5. D. L. Stufflebeam, "The Use and Abuse of Title III," *Theory Into Practice* 6 (1967), 126-133; "Evaluation as Enlightenment for Decision Making," *Improving Educational Assessment and An Inventory of Measures of Affective Behavior*, ed. W. H. Beatty (Washington, D.C: Association for Supervision and Curriculum Development, NEA, 1969).
6. R. S. Randall, "An Operational Application of the CIPP Model for Evaluation," *Educational Technology* 9, no. 7 (1969), 40-44.
7. Randall, 40-42.
8. A. Edward Ahr and Howard D. Sims, *An Evaluation for Special Education* (Skokie, Ill.: Priority Innovations, Inc., 1970).
9. Edith K. Mosher, *What About the School Research Office? A Staff Report* (Berkeley, Calif.: Far West Laboratory for Educational Research and Development, 1968).
10. W. C. Meierhenry (ed.), *Planning for the Evaluation of Special Education Programs* (Lincoln, Neb.: Teachers College, The University of Nebraska, 1969).
11. P. A. Annas and R. A. Dowd (eds.), *Guide to Assessment and Evaluation Procedures: The New England Educational Assessment Project*, No. ED

012087 (Washington, D.C.: ERIC Document Reproduction Service, 1966).

12. Center for Instructional Research and Curriculum Evaluation (CIRCE), and the Cooperative Educational Research Laboratory, Inc. (CERLI), "Information Supplement No. 5: Evaluation Kit: Tools and Techniques," *Educational Product Report* 2 (1969).

13. Hulda Grobman, *Evaluating Activities of Curriculum Projects: A Starting Point* (Chicago, Ill.: Rand McNally, 1968).

14. Proger, "Program Evaluation: The Model-Building Game."

15. Albert V. Mayrhofer, "Factors to Consider in Preparing Performance Contracts for Instruction," *Educational Technology* 11, no. 1 (1971), 48-51; H. M. Harmes, "Specifying Objectives for Performance Contracts," Ibid., 52-56; George H. Voegel, "A Suggested Scheme for Faculty Commission Pay in Performance Contracting," Ibid., 57-59; W. Frank Johnson, "Performance Contracting with Existing Staff," Ibid., 59-61.

16. Lester Mann and Barton B. Proger, "Achievement Accounting and System Accountability: Their Roles in Urban and Suburban Special Education." Paper presented at the Convention for the Council for Exceptional Children, Miami, Fla., 1971.

17. W. James Popham and T. R. Husek, "Implications of Criterion-Referenced Measurement," *Journal of Educational Measurement* 6, no. 1 (1969), 1-9; George B. Simon, "Comments on Implications of Criterion-Referenced Measurements," *Journal of Educational Measurement* 6, no. 4 (1969), 259-260.

18. Donald T. Campbell and Julian C. Stanley, "Experimental and Quasi-Experimental Designs for Research on Teaching," *Handbook of Research on Teaching*, ed. N. L. Gage (Chicago, Ill.: Rand McNally, 1963).

19. Gilbert Austin, "State Directors Discussions: Test Scoring and Data Banking," *NCME Measurement News: Official Newsletter of the National Council on Measurements in Education* 13, no. 3 (1970), 9; John C. Flanagan et al., *The Project TALENT Data Bank for Research in Education and the Behavioral Sciences* (Pittsburgh, Pa.: Project TALENT, University of Pittsburgh and American Institutes for Research, 1965).

20. Proger et al., "Large-Scale, Personalized Information Retrieval of Psychological and Educational Research Findings for School District Decision-Making." Paper presented at the Seventh Annual National Information Retrieval Colloquium, Philadelphia, Pa., May 8, 1970.

21. Chester W. Harris (ed.), *Problems in Measuring Change* (Madison, Wis.: University of Wisconsin Press, 1963); Doris R. Entwisle, "Interactive Effects of Pretesting," *Educational and Psychological Measurement* 21 (1961), 607-620.

22. E. G. Guba, "The Failure of Educational Evaluation," *Educational Technology* 9, no. 5 (1969), 29-38.

23. Ken Walker, "Training Educational Researchers: For What?" *Educational Researcher* 20, no. 10 (1969), 1-2, 7.

Learning Disabilities:
A Charter for Excellence

WILLIAM M. CRUICKSHANK

In September of 1972 we wrote in the *Journal of Learning Disabilities* (Cruickshank, 1972) an article concerned with fundamental issues facing the education of children with specific learning disabilities. Therein we focused attention on the confusion in the field due to the lack of an appropriate educational definition of the problem. We noted that, since learning disability has become both a fad and a scapegoat of the decade, we see in public education almost everywhere programs functioning without direction and at a high level of mediocrity, the exceptions being startlingly few in number. We also focused attention on the quality of the corps of college and university professors which purports to function in this field.

It is indeed difficult to countenance what one sees in the education of children with specific learning disabilities in the schools of this nation today. In my opinion it is of unprecedented poor quality. But we are not writing today to grumble about the failures of the past decade or the ineffectiveness of learning disability education today. We wish rather to look at the stance we must assume in behalf of good education for these children in the years immediately ahead. Obviously, however, we would not be so concerned about futures if the present were in any way nearing a satisfactory state of affairs. This field of professional education is so lacking in anything which could merit the characterization of quality or excellence that we are faced with class action suits and court intervention. Against this backdrop, how can we move to serve children in terms of both quality and excellence?

Ten Phase Program

If the profession is going to accept seriously its responsibility, some rigorous stands are going to be required. We are not speaking of a mere motor tune-up; we are talking at the minimum of a complete overhaul if not the replacement of the old with a new motor. There are several components to the rigorous attack which we feel must be taken, and these, although interrelated, we propose to examine separately, thus highlighting each. Each one is important if quality education is to be achieved.

THE PROFESSOR AND TEACHER EDUCATION

In a very large measure the quality of public school programs is founded on and reflects the quality of teacher education and thus it reflects the quality of college or university professors. The total field of education of

Paper presented at the Tenth Annual International Conference of the ACLD, Detroit, Mich. (March 14–17, 1973).

children with specific learning disabilities is essentially a product of the last decade. Granted that research efforts on a very modest scale began in the latter part of the decade of the 1930s and that the interests of such people as Grace Fernald, Marion Monroe, Samuel Orton, and a few others then and earlier were concerned about children who could not learn, little was known or conceptualized about these children in an organized way. Facts nevertheless record that suddenly in 1963 the term "learning disabilities" burst on the scene and became the popular educational vehicle of the decade.

The demand of services by parents and the subsequent attempts by school superintendents to meet the parental demands brought a problem to colleges and to universities for which they were not at all prepared. The lack of definition of the problem, the research void, the lack of any content literature, perplexed educational faculties. A professional vacuum truly existed. Into this vacuum stepped young, often well-intended persons who possessed an absolute minimum of professional preparation and practical experience.

In 1963, at the time of the learning disability explosion, several persons were active in the field who had in a sense grown up with it. Among these persons can be noted such people as Samuel A. Kirk, Newell C. Kephart, Charles Strother, Helmer Myklebust, Sidney Bijou, this writer, and a few others who, often by happenstance, had been associated with multiply complex problems of brain-injured children and their concomitant perceptual pathologies. These people through association with Monroe, Strauss, Werner, the clinical work of Kurt Goldstein, Bruno Klopfer, Samuel Beck, through experiences with war-injured men who suffered neurological damage, and from fortuitous experience, accrued practical experiences, some research orientation, and excellent theoretical foundation. On these few persons, almost all of them psychologists, fell a responsibility of establishing educational training requirements. Relatively reputable but short-lived programs were developed at the University of Illinois, Northwestern University, Purdue University, and Syracuse University among the few universities which can be identified. Out of these universities has come another relatively small second generation of fine young psycho-educators who through personal contact with their professors have extracted most of what was known plus what was occurring to that date. Among these can be cited Barbara Bateman, James McCarthy, Norris G. Haring, and John Junkala. Samuel Clements and Sheldon Rappaport, again psychologists, joined this small group from other directions. The professional educators, other than Elizabeth Freidus, Jean Lukens, Laura Lehtinen, Mirian Tannhauser, and a few others who truly know this field, are almost completely unrepresented.

Into this demand-laden field, nearly void of personnel, stepped many unprepared persons who almost immediately, with little or no professional preparation or experience, became directors or professors of programs for teachers of learning disabilities. This unfortunate situation can be documented many many times over. The products of these programs, teachers accepted into service, unsuspectingly represented much less than the best preparation. This is obvious when one assesses classroom programs.

For some time this writer has been advocating a strong and aggressive stand to correct this situation. Let us examine it, and assess its implications. In the first place we must recognize that much of what is going on in the field of learning disabilities is exceedingly ineffective and of poor quality. We point to the unprepared college professor as the first point where logical criticism can be placed. With this in mind, we recommend that we move to correct this situation as rapidly as possible. Funds should be spent at once to provide the basis of one or two national training programs for professors in service. Of what would this consist?

1. First, there would be assembled into the training centers the national leadership, each on a maximum two-year leave of absence from his position, to serve as faculty members. This faculty would consist of those who have long been associated with this problem. The logistics of developing a faculty are difficult, but in no sense do they defy accomplishment. If there were two centers, the faculty could probably rotate between the two locations in order to make the core personnel available to both student groups.

2. Second, fifty or sixty college professors now in service would be selected by a review panel to become professor-students in this program. Each of these would be placed on a two-year leave of absence from his university or college. A written contract would exist between the funding agency and the university to the effect that the two years away would be considered in terms of promotions, salary increments, and that upon completion of his program the professor-student would be reinstated in his position at the university to undertake teacher education in the field of learning disabilities. These professor-students would be recruited from any age bracket and from any professorial rank. Proof of commitment to education, general or special, would be required. These would be people with a professional career already indicated in higher education teacher education. Their admission into the program would include full pay plus cost of living allowances, since often two homes would have to be maintained; in addition there would be allowances for travel, books, and secretarial assistance. The host universities or centers would receive their usual overhead costs as well as other reimbursements for direct costs. While it is probable that these programs would be housed in a major university, there is no reason why that is a mandatory factor.

3. What, in brief, might the programs be for the professor-student? It would not be a restating of what should have been learned earlier. This is not a remedial program for professors. The basic skills would be ascertained at the time of selection of the person into the program. The selection program would be rigorous and in depth. The actual

learning experience would consist of a number of significant things, some of which are detailed here. Some time ago authorities in the area under discussion made available an in-depth statement of the competencies needed on the part of teachers of these children (Cruickshank, shank, 1966). These competencies must be developed in teachers essentially through the medium of university instruction, hence they become even more critical as a statement of competencies of college and university professors. They are as valid today as they were a few years ago when they were initially published, and in some instances, as the result of certain social and economic factors, they have become even more essential. The professor-student, about whom we now speak, will be provided with learning experiences to help him develop his instructional competencies in the following areas:

a. He must know and understand the psychoeducational definition of his field. He will be able to define and defend these children from the point of view of perceptual definition, perceptual-motor definition, and motor definition; and he will understand the differences, subtle and gross, between these issues. He will understand the neurological and pseudo-neurological characteristics of these children as well as those characteristics which are developmental in nature. He will understand that the term learning disabilities per se is meaningless, and that it serves only for the gross identification of a large heterogeneous population.

b. The professor-student, as he presents deficiencies in his own background, will develop those competencies in areas of general teaching of reading, of mathematics, handwriting, spelling, and other areas of basic elementary education.

c. The professor-students will need specialized information on the development of cognition and cognitive structure. Specific attention must be given to the effects of neurological dysfunction on attentional processes, on memory formation, on ability to categorize experiences, on control of motor responses, and on the development of attention span.

d. These professor-students will receive input concerned with the development of visuomotor skills in relation to academic performance. The concepts of the perceptual-motor match of Kephart, prescriptive teaching developed by Peter, the education-perception match as we have discussed it, each and all, require a thorough understanding by the professor-student in order that implementation can be rationally undertaken.

e. The professor must have a basic understanding of perception, per se. He must know the difference between perception, perceptual-motor, and how attention and attention deficits modify both.

f. Although most of the work is theoretical and yet to be conclusively demonstrated, much of what goes on in the education of children with specific learning disabilities today involves motor training programs. The professor-student will be given training in these programs in sufficient depth that he can evaluate them carefully and thus to be able later to bring to his students rational concepts based on known evidence, theory, and practice.

g. In the same nondefinitive manner, issues of handedness, laterality, finger localization, and cerebral dominance still escape conclusive data. The professor-student must have what information there is well enough in hand, however, to deal with it logically in the face of frequent reference to these issues when presented as supposedly known fact and as supposedly the controlling elements in educational or psychological methodology.

h. The professor-student must become sufficiently expert in the use of some psychodiagnostic techniques that he can instruct teachers in their uses. Children of the categories about which we are concerned will require frequent albeit not necessarily in-depth assessments, of many aspects of their learning characteristics. Experience has demonstrated that teachers often can do this as well if not better than many school psychologists. They can certainly do it with the frequency which is required, something that psychologists can never hope to achieve so as to provide the basis of good daily instruction. Teachers need to have professors who understand this and who can provide the needed instruction.

i. Although the issues of the education of children with specific learning disabilities are essentially psychoeducational, the teacher needs some background to enable her to fit into a total professional experience. Several items stand out in this regard. The professor-student must have instruction in the area of neurology and neuropsychology in particular so as to understand the literature. He must have instruction in the area of clinical psychopharmacology, and understand the few positive and the many potential negative gains in reliance on medications. He must understand the payoffs for these children of education per se without medication. Most of these children will present themselves at the school door with emotional overlays; hence, teachers and professor-students must have a thorough background in the dynamics of emotion and emotional maldevelopment. Communication problems and communication disorders are a frequent characteristic of these children. The professor-student will receive background in this area of human growth and development in sufficient depth to know both what the teacher needs and how to deal with his colleagues in other disciplines so as to achieve this and all of the instructional inputs which others must teach to preservice teachers.

We have spent more time on this matter than we will on some other points because the lack of a corps of well-prepared teacher educators is so blatant, and because this is the group on whose shoulders the quality of education for these children will rest for the next several decades. It is an issue which cannot be further ignored. Poorly prepared professors must be bypassed, and must be replaced by those who know the field from the point of theory, practice, and organized knowledge and experience. The total cost of this program, while great for the two-year period and for a year of planning, would probably not exceed the sums invested by federal and state governments in traineeships for teachers attending inadequate programs of higher education and who later enter public practice as ill-prepared educators. Fifty or sixty professors, and a mechanism to provide a continuing supply, will not have the political visibility as do hundreds of teachers being given summer scholarships. But this is no time to be concerned with politics. The lives of thousands of children are in balance as are those of tens of thousands of their brothers, sisters, and parents whose life experiences are twisted because of the presence of the handi-capped children in their midst.

PROBLEM COMPLEXITY

In the reference to the aforementioned article (Cruickshank, 1972) in which we posed certain fundamental issues facing the field of learning disabilities, we once more stressed professional confusion in the absence of adequate definition. While we do not claim insight greater than those who have considered this problem before, we are prompted to examine the matter further, and hopefully to conceptualize both a definition and the basis for a definition.

The field of learning disabilities today is a conglomerate of different types of problems. It did not start out in this manner, but in more recent years problems of a widely diversified nature which appear unsolvable to general educators have been classified as learning disabilities and placed into special classes or programs under teachers generally ill-prepared to deal with the complex problems of most of the children. The issue of heterogeneity is with us, much as we may dislike and oppose it. The problem is to examine the issue and try to deal with its variations logically and in a more homogeneous manner. A crude and incomplete paradigm may be of assistance in clarifying the problem (see Figure 1).

There are three basic elements in conceptualizing the field of learning disabilities keeping in mind that we view this term as one which is broadly used to encompass a multiplicity of childhood problems. The three signi-ficant variables are (a) perception, (b) motor characteristics, and (c) intelligence. We present our thinking essentially from the orientation of the educational system thus consciously ignoring the psychological and medical systems which admittedly have a relation, but are not the central core insofar as long-term effort is concerned.

In the paradigm, perception is noted on a spectrum in degrees from normal to "severe" disability; motor characteristics likewise are noted on a separate axis from normal to "severe." Intelligence is noted on still a third axis, and is shown in a traditional quantitative scale from very low (zero measurement) to very high (infinity).

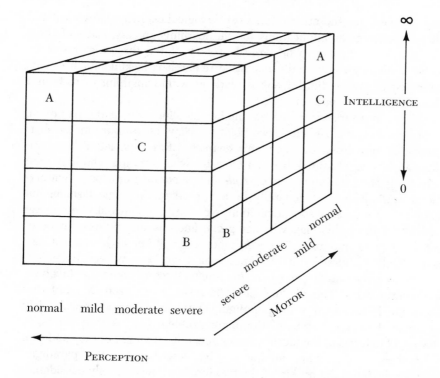

Figure 1

Perception is understood as a mental process through which the qualities or the nature of an object are recognized. We consider perception to be comprised of a multiplicity of characteristics which, through the relationship of memory with the special sensory systems of the body, brings the object to a conscious level. Perception, since it involves cells and sensory systems, is viewed as neurological. From the point of view of learning, it is recognized that numerous factors, some neurological (accident, disease, injury), some possibly developmental and others environmental, may distort or disturb both the cellular system and the normal function of one or more sensory systems. In the paradigm, complexity prevents the writer from noting that there are different perceptual systems relating to the several sensory modalities characteristic of humans, namely, vision, audition, taction, etc.

Due to any one or combination of factors, the sensory systems may be affected completely; partially, but each in different degrees; or not at all. Why this occurs is not fully understood. Differences occur between and among sensory systems to say nothing of between and among individuals and is a matter of fact. These deviations in neurological and sensory systems, however, are measurable—at least qualitatively—and to these measures are attached such labels as association or dissociation, memory, sequencing, discrimination, figure-ground differentiation, sensory and motoric hyperactivity, prolonged after effect of a stimulus (perseveration), closure problems, and other related psychological characteristics, each and all possessing great implications for the learning process. Each of these characteristics appears to be typical of each of the three major sensory systems, although admittedly definitive research is lacking. Each can be described on a paradigm if one is working with something more than a three dimensional cube concept.

Motor characteristics, noted on another baseline axis on the paradigm, must be conceptualized from two points of view, i.e., sensory-motor characteristics and gross- or fine-motor characteristics. The latter have traditionally been classified by neurologists when treating children with cerebral palsy, for example, as *normal, mild, moderate,* or *severe.* Sensory-motor activity has not generally been viewed in the same fashion, but here for the sake of our definition we view the uncontrolled motor activity of the individual, whether gross, fine, visual, auditory, to be of similar degrees and probably even more an inhibitor of learning. Characteristically children with these problems have been viewed by practitioners as hyperactive (or when gross-motor factors alone are involved, as hyperkinetic). The diagnostician, however, must keep in mind that the motor factor noted in the paradigm is very complex and varies widely in terms of degree, nature of the motor problem (i.e., sensory, gross, or fine), and in terms of the localization or generalized nature of the handicap.

Another factor cannot adequately be described on the paradigm, namely, the interrelationship of the two forces we have briefly considered. The impact of perceptual function or dysfunction on motor learning and activity is recognized, but not specifically understood. Thus the child in block "A" in the paradigm is a perfectly normal child of high intelligence, child "B" is a severely handicapped child, perceptually and motorically, and is of very low intelligence. Child "C" is moderately handicapped perceptually, of normal motor ability and of "normal" mental ability.

It is with the interrelations that the categories of perceptual-motor disabilities develop, i.e., eye-hand coordination, ear-hand coordination, tactual-motor activity, *ad infinitum.* In dictating a spelling lesson, for example, the teacher is requiring the child to employ both audiomotor and visuomotor systems simultaneously.

Intelligence has to be indicated on the paradigm, for it will be a controlling factor in the child's ability to learn to self-control his own problems, and it will be a factor in logical educational placement. There is nothing mystical about this statement. It is made by this writer in the full knowledge of the complexities of measuring intelligence in these children and of the fact that both perceptual and motor problems may affect intellectual function as measured. As a controlling factor, however, intelligence must be recognized.

A positive definition of this problem thus concerns itself with an individual (a) who is characterized by a quantitatively or qualitatively measurable deviation from the normal in total perceptual function or in any one or more of the sensory systems related to perception, (b) who is charac-

terized by a deviation in motor abilities in either gross- or fine-motor activities or in sensory activities related to perception, (c) who may be further handicapped by the abnormal interrelationship between perceptual and motor systems, and (d) whose intelligence may be of any quantitative level.

A diversified program is required. When one contemplates the tremendous variability possible in terms of the oversimplified paradigm, and much more pronounced in real life, it becomes obvious that no single educational solution can be applied within a community school program. The child's clinical needs, his educational program, and his placement will be determined essentially on the basis of qualitative assessments of a psychoeducational nature. On the basis of these data children will be provided a vital educational experience, not merely assigned to undifferentiated "learning disabilities class," a meaningless and unproductive term. The child will be placed in a clinical teaching situation, one of several types conceived as the most appropriate for a given child's needs. The educational perceptual match partially takes place at this point. Some of these children will be retained in the regular grades with understanding teachers where both teacher and child receive guidance and instruction from skilled itinerant teacher-clinicians. Other children, probably quantitatively in greater number, will spend varying amounts of time each day in a resource room where through one-to-one teaching situations, or in very small homogeneous groups, the deficits of the children will be treated. Still others whose perceptual-motor problems are pervading and severe will require a full-time clinical teaching station for long periods, perhaps years, until through training and/or maturation they are equipped to return to the regular grades fully or with resource or itinerant teacher supports. The mechanism we suggest is not new. The refinement in ascertaining the primary learning deficits, the educational placement in terms of severity of the problem, and the homogeneous groupings of children in terms of the type of perceptual-motor problem, although not a new concept either, is new in terms of what good practice requires. Implementation is a requisite now and in the immediate future.

QUALITY TEACHER EDUCATION

Qualified professors, prepared in depth to understand and implement the real issues in specific learning disabilities, will in all likelihood produce qualified educators. We have spoken and written so often on this problem that it is redundant to do so again. Certain conclusions from thirty years of work in this field are appropriate, however.

1. The field is so complicated that it cannot be treated in any satisfactory manner in three- to six-week summer courses. Were we again to undertake the organization of a bona fide teacher education program for resource, itinerant, or special class teacher-clinicians, it would be done on the basis of a sixty-hour master's degree program encompassing

eighteen to twenty-four months. The details of such a program have been delineated elsewhere (Cruickshank, Junkala, and Paul, 1968).

2. If retention of some of these children in the regular grade is a part of the policy, then *every elementary and every secondary teacher in the nation* must have a thorough orientation and understanding of the impact of specific learning disabilities on the learning process. If teachers do not understand and if they fail through ignorance to teach adequately, these children are hurt.

3. Every administrator as a part of his minimal certification requires a full understanding of the child with specific learning disabilities, the nature of programs of training, and the criteria for selective placement within a program.

4. The education of children with specific learning disabilities is not synonymous with remedial reading. Many children who need reading assistance may profit from methodology appropriate to that employed with some types of specific learning disabilities. Much of the failure of educators to deal appropriately with the learning disability issue is due to the administrative decision which suddenly assigned the learning disability program to the remedial reading program. The education of these children must go far beyond the best concepts of reading instruction.

Adequate Psychological and Diagnostic Services

The concept of the match between educational methodology and the specific learning disability must become the focus of assessment. Kephart speaks of the perceptual-motor match as a basis of his motor training program. We extend the idea of the match to education and perceptual-motor disabilities.

This concept is teachable to psychoeducational diagnosticians. The focus of diagnosis must be on those functions which are basic to learning the skills of reading, mathematics, handwriting, and spelling. The diagnostician seeks evidence of the intactness of such processes as have long been recognized as fundamental to perceptual-motor problems, namely the child's status relative to discrimination, attention span, memory span, selective attention, figure-ground relationships, and other crucial factors. From some quantitative instruments, but mostly from qualitative test situations and clinical skills, the next generation of diagnosticians must be taught how to build the perceptual blueprint of a child. From this, the qualified educator makes the educational match to child placement, learning environment, teaching method, and teaching materials.

Courageous Special Education Leadership

Special education has been much less effective that it could have been because it has too frequently bowed to the wishes of general educators and administrators regarding the placement of children. Special education has been used in a very indiscriminate manner to relieve the regular class of problems which the general educator could not solve. Special education leadership has aided and abetted these actions and has rarely refused to accept a child even though transfer was known to be inappropriate. As a result of this, because unteachable situations were created for teachers, special education is under attack. In the courts and in the community we hear these facts stated and restated.

Special education directors, supervisors, consultants, and departmental chairmen (1) must find for themselves large quantities of intestinal fortitude and use it appropriately in behalf of children; (2) must be prepared to seek court action if need be to protect children from unwise decisions regarding school placement; and (3) must match this in terms of its own appropriate action. Placement of a child in a clinical teaching situation is a serious matter, and the decision must be made thoughtfully and with all pertinent educational facts available.

RETURN TO THE REGULAR GRADES

We have often spoken of the care with which children should be placed into a special classroom and of the structured procedure which is helpful in organizing the special class group each fall. We have seen the value to both an individual child and the total group when the school administration adds one child at a time to a class, and carefully structures the total situation until the entire group of children is assembled.

Just as care must be taken in developing a special class or in assigning children to a resource room, so equal care must be taken in returning the child to the regular grades when it is felt he can cope with the less sheltered situation. It is indeed a major decision which now has been reached in considering return.

First, it must be agreed that upon return the child is able to compete at age in grade to the degree at least equal to the medium achievement level of the receiving group. Second, the decision must be reached early enough to permit the special class teacher, in cooperation with the regular class teacher, to undertake and accomplish an acquisition of the content material which the child will experience in the receiving classroom.

Third, care must be taken in selecting the regular grade room into which he will be assimilated. If there is a choice of multiple sections of a given grade level, our experience suggests that a general rule, would be to select the teacher among those available who is more comfortable than others with structure and who might be characterized as a traditional teacher—an adult accepting of children, but one who approaches the teaching situation with topic, class, and the individual child well in hand. The child in whom we now have an interest is one who generally finds difficulty in permissive situations and with a teacher or other adults who themselves operate in a very unstructured manner.

Fourth, the child must always know that in the event he needs to return to the special teaching situation, he may do so. There must always be an escape valve for the child, a prearranged procedure through which he may retreat with honor.

SUPPLIES, MATERIAL, AND TEACHER AIDES

It should be a truism that educators know how to select appropriate teaching materials. However, too often this is not so. Newell Kephart has written wisely regarding the perceptual-motor match. Peters (Peters, 1965) speaks of prescriptive teaching. We have stressed the importance of the educational and perceptual match. Each of these concepts strongly implies that the child's specific learning characteristics along with other considerations will be matched with specific teaching materials to complement one another. It is infrequent that sufficient care is taken in purchasing educational material, and too frequently mass purchasing leaves the teacher instructionally helpless and the child further vulnerable to poor teaching.

As we look forward to the future and to a degree of excellence yet to be attained in the education of children with specific learning disabilities, three issues remain to be discussed.

WELL-INFORMED PARENTS

Never before have parents so quickly become so well informed about the problems of their children as have parents of the children about whom we here write. Unfortunately, parents were often misled in assuming that professionals knew what needed to be done and that all that was lacking was a sufficient supply of dollars to provide the needed treatment and educational facilities. This is another story, but nevertheless is true. In the course of their efforts these parents became exceedingly knowledgeable, and subsequently exceedingly helpful in many communities in the development of educational facilities. But a well-informed parent group is not enough. Information alone is insufficient.

Our experience convinces us that the great majority of parents of children with specific learning disabilities come to a realization of the essence of the problem of their child with deep-seated frustrations, misunderstandings of guilt feelings of their own, and often unrealistic expectancies for the child. If this happens, the problems surrounding the child are often more than either he or the family together can handle. When counseling, often of an obligatory nature, has been included in the educational process for the family—parents and the siblings—the role of the learning disability in the dynamics of family living takes on a significantly different flavor, and the course of progress for the child is smoother. Psychiatrists, social workers, psychologists, guidance and counseling personnel, clergymen, and others, understanding both the counseling process and the learning disability problem, have been able to play unique and extraordinarily important roles in bringing family members to a new level of group integration. Residential facilities or private day schools which serve children with learning disabilities should profit from the experience of those which require this experience as a part of the acceptance of the child into the school program and which cover the costs of this additional professional activity within tuition and fee structures. The public schools, which will continue to serve the largest numbers of these children, must in cooperation with parent groups work out mechanisms whereby the same benefits can be accrued to families and children within the local communities. The issue of specific learning disability is so complex that a twenty-four hour approach is required. The impact of the disabilities is to be seen in dressing, eating, and general behavior in the home and neighborhood as well as in the school. Thus parents must be as well prepared to provide structured educational experiences in the home as teachers are to do the same in different areas in the school location. The future must include this consideration for a total program of educational service.

The Para-educational Support Team

The teacher of children with specific learning disabilities will require assistance depending upon the degree of severity of the child's problems. Support teams of specialist personnel have been used for many years in varying ways to assist the child and the teacher. Two factors are significant in re-emphasizing this important aspect of a total program. First, it is essential that all members of the support team have a common point of view regarding the learning of children with perceptual deficits. These children require structure; they cannot easily adjust to different approaches as they meet teacher, speech therapist, psychologist, or other professional person. Common points of view and common approaches to the problem must be practiced by all.

Second, a different way of utilizing support personnel may be required for many of these children. It is generally the practice to send a child from the classroom to the specialist. Many children cannot tolerate this movement, cannot adjust to new situations quickly, and become tense simply by reason of walking through school corridors. As a result, the time with the specialist is not utilized at an optimum, and time is required upon return to the home classroom to readjust from the tension of the earlier movement. Experience has demonstrated to us that with children possessing severe perceptual problems, it is better to have all or a major portion of the support personnel input made to the child via his teacher. The number of personalities to which the child has to learn to adjust is then minimized, and all inputs are assured of being presented in the same way and within the same theoretical structure. Administration has to provide opportunities for the teacher to meet with support personnel to receive their suggestions and directions for working with the child, and support specialists have to be provided with time to observe the child in the classroom so as to be able to provide the teacher with updated information and directions. Good programs logically conceived in terms of the child's limitations and needs, however, bring the skills of the specialists into the daily program in an appropriate way and at times when they are needed.

REVIEW BOARDS

As a final element in the development of a quality program of education for children with specific learning disabilities, I would like to discuss a technique on which we have written once before (Cruickshank, 1972), namely, the establishment and use of review committees. The quality of education for these children we have stated is poor. It is absolutely imperative that a program be conceptualized and made operational nationally in which we can have pride. Nothing should escape the spotlight of healthy scrutiny. The quality of the professorial corps and the teaching corps is not of a sufficient level of excellence to ensure to the child and his family the psychoeducational experiences the child requires to bring him to the level of community participation society expects. The issue of quality requires attack not only on the factors pertinent to the educational arena per se for children with specific learning disabilities, but also on both the total area of psychodiagnostics and psychological training and on general education as well.

As a drastic step toward the excellence we seek, we strongly recommend that at all levels of education there be established review committees to monitor the quality of excellence of the programs. Educators will object to this as being interference with traditional concepts of academic freedom. Academic freedom is indeed a right to be cherished. However, academic freedom does not give educational professionals the concommitant right to ignore their obligation to provide quality education to the very society which supports them. Medicine and dentistry, and to a much lesser extent psychology and some of the other disciplines, through their own professional mechanisms monitor and review the professional performance of their membership. This type of review is essential in those areas of service delivery where the general public cannot be authoritative. Society must rely on internal monitoring of the profession to guarantee high quality of personnel preparation, institutional efficiency, and service delivery.

There is, however, a problem with education and the schools. In these fields we are faced with the feeling that everyone is a specialist in both how schools should be run and how children should be taught. Everyone is an authority. That the schools are open to public inspection and education is a right reserved to the state and delegated to the local community. Intra-professional review is difficult to come by and to operate. This fact, however, does not minimize the need for professional standards and their constant monitoring. It only makes the problem a more challenging one.

Citizen or judicial review panels are upon us if the professions do not immediately move to establish their own monitoring systems. We have previously stated that education is often just as cruel to children as police are reported to be when on occasion they mishandle university students, members of minorities, and both those awaiting trial and those committed to prison terms. It is a difference of style, not fact. As citizens of many communities are taking a stance to demand review boards to monitor behavior of individuals and quality of programs for public protection, so citizens, joining with professionals, appear to be needed to establish review panels to monitor that which goes on in the name of education. It is essential that professional educators and psychologists move to assume this responsibility and establish quality programs before either citizen review boards or the courts of the nation assume that responsibility for educators.

REFERENCES

CRUICKSHANK, W. M. (ed.) *The Teacher of Brain-Injured Children: A Discussion of the Bases for Competency* (Syracuse, N.Y.: Syracuse University Press. 1966).

CRUICKSHANK, W. M., J. B. JUNKALA, and J. L. PAUL, *The Preparation of Teachers of Brain-Injured Children* (Syracuse, N.Y.: Syracuse University Press, 1968).

CRUICKSHANK, W. M., "Special education, the community, and constitutional issues," in *Special Education: Instrument of Change for the 70s,* ed. D. L. Walker and D. P. Howard (Charlottesville: University of Virginia, 1972), pp. 5–24.

CRUICKSHANK, W. M., "Some issues facing the field of learning disability," *Journal of Learning Disabilities* 5, no. 7 (1972), 380–388.

KEPHART, N. C., *The Slow Learning Child* (Columbus, Ohio: Charles E. Merrill, 1971).

PETERS, L. J., *Prescriptive Teaching* (New York: McGraw-Hill, 1965).

Four

Screening, Diagnosis, and Assessment

Screening, diagnosis, and assessment are the initial steps to be taken in any program for learning-diasabled children. Many procedures have been developed, especially in the psycho-educational field. Only a few representative approaches are presented here.

Marianne Frostig's classic description of the diagnostic process, although presented in 1966, is fresh and current today. Of particular interest are Dr. Frostig's emphases on curricular activities, visual-perceptual training programs, and the interdependence of sensory-motor functions, perception, language, and the development of thought processes. Dr. Frostig has made some minor adjustments in her 1966 article, which reflect her current thinking and practices.

Pearl Rosser, Carolyn Stewart, and Mitzi Parks discuss the problem of interdisciplinary diagnosis in their paper. The authors—pediatricians and educators—feel that effective communication between disciplines is necessary for progress. They present data showing the inter-relationship of the disciplines especially in the inner-cities among disadvantaged children, using case studies to illustrate their points. The importance of early intervention is highlighted.

In the third article, Charles Bartlett describes a model of educational evaluation that has been developed in a university-affiliated diagnostic clinic involving an Evaluation Division and an Education Division. The educational evaluation, described in detail, covers academic achievement, speech and linguistic competency, perception and perceptual integration, motor coordination and planning, and cognitive abilities.

The Relationship of Diagnosis to Remediation in Learning Problems*

MARIANNE FROSTIG

Learning problems arise from various causes and most often from a combination of causes. Therefore, the phrase "children with learning problems" does not refer to any specific etiology. The term may be applied to children with minimal neurological dysfunctions, or it may have reference to children who lack the experiential basis for learning or to children who are immature or emotionally disturbed. A high proportion of children in this group seem to have lags in specific developmental functions. Others show more general disturbances.

The specific lags, deficits, and disturbances shown by children with learning problems may be in sensory-motor functions, in language, in perception, in thought processes, or in emotional and social adjustment. The one characteristic common to all of these children is that their underlying deficiencies cause difficulty in learning.

Growing up requires continuous learning, of which school learning is but a part. The symptoms of the child with learning problems are therefore legion, and encompass all aspects of behavior—in school, at home, and in the community. His deficiencies involve him in many painful situations which irritate, antagonize, or make anxious the persons he encounters. Their negative reactions tend to compound his initial difficulties. Thus neurological disturbances, developmental delays, and noxious environmental influences reinforce each other in their detrimental effect on the child's learning and development.

A careful study of both the child's present environment and his life history usually shows that his difficulties are neither the result of organic deviations nor of environmental causes alone, but rather of an interplay of the child's environmental circumstances and his physical and psychological makeup. Efforts directed toward unravelling the causes of a child's learning difficulties will therefore need to be interdisciplinary in nature, and they will be most effective if they lead to recommendations for the multiple medical, educational, and psychological treatment procedures which are usually involved in the amelioration of the disorder.

During the latter 1960s about 25 percent of children with learning problems received psychotherapy, and about 25 percent of the parents received parent counseling. (If the child was in therapy, the parents were usually counseled also.) About 15 percent of the children took part in remedial

*Research basic to this paper has been supported in part by the Rosenburg Foundation.

From the *Proceedings* of the Third Annual International Conference of the ACLD, *International Approach to Learning Disabilities of Children and Youth.* Tulsa, Okla. (March 3–5, 1966), pp. 45–66. (Revised, 1974).

physical education programs or underwent speech therapy. The main approach, however, was educational in nature. Educational therapy was a part of the treatment program in all but a very few exceptional cases; in about 70 percent of the cases it was the only procedure used.

In deciding upon a child's educational program, it is necessary to take into account his ability in each of the six major psychological functions which develop during infancy and later childhood: sensory-motor functions, language, perception, thought processes, emotional development, and social adjustment. The child's performance in the four areas of sensory-motor development, perception, language, and higher cognitive functions largely determines the teaching strategy; his emotional development and social adjustment have the most important implications for classroom management.

A great variety of tests are used to explore the child's ability level in each of the developmental phases, but as a basis for establishing the curriculum at the Center[1] four tests are invariably used if the age levels are appropriate. They are the Frostig,[2] the Wepman,[3] the ITPA,[4] and the WISC.[5] Testing with these is repeated at regular intervals, preferably once each year, so as to gauge the child's progress.

Evaluation of Sensory-Motor Functions

A considerable amount of emphasis has recently been placed upon the importance of sensory-motor functions for the child's total development and learning.[6] Research in the two fields of human factor psychology and physical education has indicated that sensory-motor competence is highly differentiated.[7,8] The major attributes of movement that have been identified by previous factor analytic studies are strength, coordination, speed, agility, flexibility, and endurance.

Prior to 1972, the Frostig Center used a variety of assessment procedures to assist in the appraisal of the child's sensory-motor functions: for example, Kephart's scale,[9] the Purdue Perceptual-Motor Survey,[10] the Lincoln-Oseretsky Scale,[11] the Kraus-Weber Test,[12] and the appraisal of movement skills suggested by Florence Sutphin.[13] Since none of these adequately met our needs at the Center, it was therefore decided to develop two new instruments to facilitate the evaluation of sensory-motor functions. The Move-Grow-Learn Movement Skills Survey[14] was developed primarily as an observation guide to assist classroom teachers to evaluate selected aspects of the child's motor development. Eight broad areas are included: (1) coordination and rhythm, (2) agility, (3) flexibility, (4) strength, (5) speed, (6) balance, (7) endurance, and (8) body awareness. This instrument is intended to be used in conjunction with the Move-Grow-Learn[15] program.

The second sensory-motor assessment procedure developed at the Center was the Frostig Movement Skills Test Battery: Experimental Edition.[16] This test consists of twelve subtests and requires approximately twenty-five minutes to be administered to an individual child. Norms are provided for males and females separately for children of ages six through twelve. The factor analytic results for the seven different age groups provide evidence for the interpretation of five psychologically meaningful determinants: hand-eye coordination, balance, strength, flexibility, and visually guided movement. Since 1972, this test battery has become the major instrument at the Frostig Center for assessing the child's sensory-motor functions.

A recent survey of the population at the Frostig Center indicates a shift in symptoms and treatment procedures. Many more children show distinct neurological signs and disturbances in sensory-motor functions and in language abilities. There are now a greater number who need special physical education and speech therapy.

Evaluation of Auditory Perceptual Functions

The Wepman Test of Auditory Discrimination[17] tests the child's ability to discriminate sounds in words. It is easily administered, for the child merely indicates his ability to differentiate between sounds by stating whether the words presented to him in pairs are identical or different. The test explores a single auditory function only, but it is one which is most important for learning to read and spell. Additional evaluation of the child's ability to comprehend what he hears, to remember phrases and sentences, to differentiate the sounds in a word, to blend sounds, etc. are always needed.[18]

Evaluation of Visual Perceptual Functions

The Marianne Frostig Developmental Test of Visual Perception[19] (Table 1) was developed for the purpose of serving as a basis for the differential training of visual perceptual abilities, in either preventive or remedial programs. Although it was designed for children from preschool to eight or nine years of age, it can also be used at later ages with children with learning disturbances, when their lags or deficits in perception are sufficiently severe to keep their performance below the nine year level and so within the range of the tests.

Evaluation of Language Functions

Some language functions are evaluated in the process of testing for auditory perception, for the perception of language is the most important auditory task of human beings. But language involves more than perceptual abilities. It also involves expressive language, and association of language with movements and with visual stimuli, and memory skills. The authors of the Illinois Test of Psycholinguistic Abilities (ITPA)[20] (Table 2) were concerned with the broadest spectrum of behavior which could be measured. This test therefore gives clues concerning a wide range of developmental functions—motor and perceptual abilities, concept formation and memory, as well as language.

Table 1. Frostic Developmental Test of Visual Perception (Brief Summary)

Subtest Name	Example	Some Functions Covered	Some Suggested Training Procedures
eye-motor coordination	draw straight lines horizontally; stop and start on target	eye-hand coordination; necessary for handwriting, drawing, arts and crafts, manipulatory and self-help activities	eye movement training; arts and crafts; manipulatory exercises; handwriting exercises; physical education program
figure-ground	find a hidden figure; find one of two or several intersecting figures	ability to focus visually on relevant aspects of visual field and "tune out" irrelevant background	"finding" games; e. g., hidden figures included in many children's activity books; sorting exercises; unscrambling intersecting words
form constancy	find all the squares on a page regardless of color, background, tilt, size	ability to see sameness of essential form despite changes of image on retina; has implication for learning to identify letters presented in various prints	identifying objects or drawings at different distances or angles; drawing diagrams of 3-dimensional patterns; finding all objects of a certain shape in the room
position in space	find the form which is reversed or rotated	ability to discriminate position; to differentiate letters such as "d" and "b", "w" and "m"	exercises promoting awareness of body position in relation to objects–go under the table, over chair, around the desk, etc.; physical education program; learning directions in space: right, left.
spatial relations	duplicate a dot pattern by linking dots with a line	ability to see spatial relationships of objects to one another; related to ability to perceive the sequence of letters in a word	copying patterns with pegs, beads, marbles; puzzles.

Like the Frostig Test, the ITPA has been designed to serve as a basis for remedial programs. Training programs can be devised on the basis of the results of both these tests. The test results enable the teacher to focus on those abilities in which the child scores low, and at the same time to utilize the child's best abilities for the acquisition of subject matter and academic skills.

The ITPA has an upper limit of eight to nine years of age, as does the Frostig, but can also be used with older children who have learning disturbances.

Evaluation of Thought Processes

In children of six and a half years or older, higher cognitive functions, including memory, are evaluated routinely by the WISC, a test which is valuable in providing a rough measure of children's difficulties in language and perception as well as higher cognitive functions. Unlike the Frostig and the ITPA, however, the WISC was developed as a predictive test, not as a remedial test specifically developed to serve as a basis for preventive and remedial programs. Silverstein[21] and Cohen[22] have shown that commonality among the subtests in the WISC is great. It is therefore difficult to use the intratest differences as a basis for developing programs for educational intervention.

For children below six years of age, the WPPSI is used. We believe, however, that the ITPA and the Frostig explore all of the intellective factors found by Orpet and Meyers[23] and by McCartin and Meyers[24] in children six years of age, with the single exception of ESU (evaluation of symbolic units).[25] We therefore use at times only these, while we use the WISC for all older children. Table 3 shows the testing profile of a child which constitutes the basis for his training program.

Thus at any age level, our "basic tests" equip us to explore the abilities cited by Orpet and Meyers and McCartin and Meyers, except ESU.[26] They also include additional intellective abilities. For example, two of the subtests of the ITPA—motor encoding[27] and auditory decoding[28]—tap abilities which are not directly measured by the WISC.[29]

In Table 4 a comparison is made between Guilford's factors as explored in six-year-old children by Orpet and Meyers, and the range of intellectual abilities tapped by three of the four mentioned tests.

Training Programs

SENSORY-MOTOR TRAINING

Suggestions for sensory-motor training can be found in the Teacher's Guide of the Frostig Program for the Development of Visual Perception,[30] and in the Teachers' Guides to the three *Pictures and Patterns* workbooks which have been adapted from the original Program.[31]

Training in sensory-motor functions is concerned with four different areas:

1. Physical education (training in movement skills).
2. Development of body awareness (specific suggestions to help a child develop body concept, schema, and image).[32]
3. Training in manipulatory skills.
4. Training in eye movement (tracking).

The *physical education program* is based on factor analytic studies of movement (see Table 5). The attributes of movement with which the program is specifically concerned are motor coordination, balance, flexibility, agility, speed, strength, and endurance.

As the writings of many neurologists and psychiatrists attest, *body awareness* is of special importance for the child's undisturbed development. One aspect of body image which is most important is the awareness of the body in relation to the outside world, for this is basic to the development of the awareness of right and left and therefore of perception of position in space and of spatial relationships.

Manipulative activities, the third aspect of the program, should include work with construction toys and Montessori-type materials, arts and crafts activities, and self-help activities.

Tracking (eye movement) exercises are suggested because many children with learning difficulties have erratic eye movements. This type of training seems to be helpful, and it is not time-consuming.

A wide range of sensory-motor training exercises, including exercises for training eye movements, are included in Kephart's book, *The Slow Learner in the Classroom.*[33] *Movement Education: Theory and Practice*[34] and *Move-Grow-Learn*[35] have been published by this author.

VISUAL PERCEPTUAL TRAINING

As already mentioned, an adaptation of the Frostig Program has recently been published in workbook form. The new program, called *Pictures and Patterns,* is divided into three levels, Beginning, Intermediate, and Advanced, each with its Teacher's Guide. The original Program was presented in the form of about 350 worksheets, one set of worksheets for each perceptual area explored by the test. These five areas are visual-motor coordination, figure-ground perception, perceptual constancy, perception of position in space, and perception of spatial relationships.

The *Pictures and Patterns* exercises consist of approximately the same material, but they are presented in workbook form, and exercises from the appropriate level of *all* perceptual areas are included in each workbook.

But neither the worksheets nor the workbooks can provide effective training in visual perception if they are used without complementary training in both sensory-motor abilities and language. Sensory-motor training is required for the essential integration of perceptual and sensory-motor functions; language training is necessary for the development of concepts and thought processes. The development of sensory-motor functions, perception, and language are to a degree interdependent, and their development in turn affects the development of thought processes. Therefore no developmental area can be neglected in training, although one area may constitute the focus of the program.

Moreover, perceptual training can often be integrated with curricular activities, and this procedure becomes increasingly feasible as the child grows older. Writing, drawing (especially from nature), copying, making maps, plans, and diagrams (e.g., of a room, a building, or a playground), and shop work may all be used to develop children's perceptual abilities. Instruction in academic skills and much other subject matter can also contribute to perceptual training. Spatial perception, for example, can be promoted as the child is taught the position of one letter in respect to another in spelling, or when he studies the features of a map (geography), the lines, angles, and planes of a drawn figure (geometry), and the relative positions of the stars or drawings of constellations (astronomy).

TRAINING IN AUDITORY PERCEPTION

Training in auditory perception involves the ability to pay attention to both speech sounds and to sounds other than speech sounds. Speech sounds have to be discriminated in isolation as well as in the context of words and phrases. The child has to learn to identify natural sounds and to differentiate sounds of varying degrees of pitch and loudness. The child must also learn to discriminate relevant sounds from background noises. This latter skill may be termed auditory figure-ground perception.

The child must also learn to pay attention, to remember phrases and sentences and the main ideas in a story, to follow directions, to draw inferences, to see the relations between different statements, and so on.

The training in speech sounds leads to the teaching of phonics. The exercises and listening games specifically designed for auditory training can then be supplemented by the auditory training inherent in learning to spell, read, listen to stories, and learn foreign languages.[36]

LANGUAGE TRAINING

Several language training programs have been developed based on the Illinois Test of Psycholinguistic Abilities. Among them is one by Lloyd Dunn at Peabody,[37] another by N. S. W. Hart at the University of Queensland in Australia.[38] A third is the MWM Program.[39] Lloyd Dunn's program, which gives many excellent suggestions, is highly structured. It presents the exercises in the exact order in which the teacher should use them. Hart has a less structured program, which he used successfully with cerebral palsied children.

Another program based on the ITPA has been developed at the Frostig Center, where it has been in use for over two years. The feedback from a number of schools where it has been used experimentally is helping in the current reshaping of the program. Bush and Giles's textbook[40] gives many excellent suggestions for training the abilities tested with the ITPA.

TRAINING IN THOUGHT PROCESSES

The various programs for training children in the functions tested with the ITPA also develop conceptual abilities. Programs for improving higher cognitive functions specifically also exist, and are most helpful in the development of curricula and instructional procedures.

Jerome Bruner[41] has given many excellent suggestions concerning the development of thought processes through educational measures.

Both E. A. Peel[42] and Aurelia Levi[43] base training approaches on the theories of Piaget. Aurelia Levi diagnoses the needs of the children with the help of the WISC; but her teaching approaches constitute variations on the single theme of developing the child's ability to solve problems by using strategies he has previously acquired. In Harlow's terminology, the child is helped to develop a learning set.[44]

Comprehensive training in higher cognitive functions involves training in the ability to visualize, to remember, to classify, to arrange in series, to develop concepts, to manipulate thoughts, to keep a thought in mind while working toward a goal (in solving an arithmetic problem, for example), to work with symbols, and to perceive relationships, thereby being able to infer and to judge.

EMOTIONAL AND SOCIAL DEVELOPMENT

Not only evaluation and training of the developmental skills of movement, perception, language, and thinking are basic to the educational program of the handicapped child; but, above all, emphasis must be given to helping the child in his emotional and social adjustment. Follow-up studies on retarded children have demonstrated that it is the ability to adjust to the exigencies of the environment in a smooth and friendly way which is decisive in regard to a child's chances for employment, marriage, and social integration. The clinical experiences of this writer and her colleagues have also shown that the youngster who is well liked will be able to lead a satisfactory life, while the child who is rebellious, aggressive, unfriendly, impulsive, and lacking in social skills will not succeed, even if his other deficiencies are minor.

A child's improvements in sensory-motor functions, language, perception, and higher cognitive functions will tend to benefit his emotional and social adjustment, but it is often not sufficient to ensure smooth adjustment at home, at school, and in the community. The teacher who wants the children to reach their optimum potential will therefore try to influence their adjustment through wise classroom management and direct personal contact.

In certain school systems behavior rating scales, the results of sociometric tests, or even projective testing, are used to indicate the level of adjustment of a given child. Most commonly, however, such scales and tests are reserved for research purposes, for evaluating a child for placement, or for assessing a disturbed child's improvement. Fortunately, they are not indispensible for conducting an educational program. Usually the teacher can judge the child's adjustment by observing his behavior.

The organization of the classroom, the emphasis on friendliness, helpfulness, and order, the amelioration of anxiety and tension through reassurance, support, and firm guidance; the development of inhibition through reinforcement of controlled behavior, and the use of social reinforcers wherever possible are some of the measures through which a teacher can help a child's emotional and social growth.

Summary

The development of a child's educational program on the basis of a careful evaluation of his assets and disabilities has been discussed. It has been suggested that certain tests should be used for the evaluation of the child's specific educational needs in the areas of sensory-motor functions, language, perception, and higher cognitive processes. Reference has been made to programs and techniques for the development of each of these functions. Emphasis has been given to the necessity for careful classroom management and individual attention to aid the child's emotional and social growth.

NOTES

1. The Marianne Frostig Center of Educational Therapy, 7257 Melrose Avenue, Los Angeles, California 90046, operated by the Foundation of Educational Therapy for Children. It is a non-profit institution combining educational, psychiatric, and psychological services.
2. M. Frostig, D. W. Lefever, and J. R. B. Whittlesey, *The Marianne Frostig Development Test of Visual Perception* (Palo Alto, Calif.: Consulting Psychologists Press, 1964).
3. Joseph M. Wepman, *Wepman Test of Auditory Discrimination* (Chicago: Language Research Associates), 1958.
4. Samuel A. Kirk and James J. McCarthy, *Illinois Test for Psycholinguistic Abilities* (Urbana, Illinois: University of Illinois Press, 1961).
5. *Wechsler Intelligence Scale for Children* (New York: The Psychological Corporation, 1949).
6. J. Piaget, *The Psychology of Intelligence* (Totowa, N.J.: Littlefield, Adams and Company, 1966).
7. J. P. Guilford, "A System of Psychomotor Abilities," *American Journal of Psychology* 71 (1958), 164-174.
8. D. C. Nicks and E. A. Fleishman, *What Do Physical Fitness Tests Measure: A Review of Factor Analytic Studies* (New Haven: Yale University Press, 1960).
9. N. C. Kephart, "Perceptual Rating Survey Scale," *Slow Learner in the Classroom* (Columbus, Ohio: Merrill, 1960).

10. Eugene G. Roach and N. C. Kephart, *The Purdue Perceptual-Motor Survey,* (Columbus, Ohio: Merrill, 1966).
11. *Lincoln-Oseretsky Motor Development Scale,* ed. Wm. Sloane (Chicago: C. H. Stoelting, 1955).
12. Hans Kraus, "Kraus-Weber Test for Minimum Muscular Fitness," *Therapeutic Exercises* (Springfield, Ill.: Charles C. Thomas, 1963), pp. 125–126.
13. Florence E. Sutphin, *A Perceptual Testing and Training Handbook for First Grade Teachers* (Winter Haven, Florida: Lions' Research Foundation, 1964).
14. R. E. Orpet and T. Heustis, *Move-Grow-Learn Movement Skills Survey* (Chicago: Follett Educational Corporation, 1972).
15. M. Frostig (in assoc. with P. Maslow), *Move-Grow-Learn* (Chicago: Follett, 1969).
16. R. E. Orpet, *Frostig Movement Skills Test Battery: Experimental Edition* (Palo Alto, California: Consulting Psychologists Press, 1972).
17. Wepman, *op. cit.*
18. Helmer R. Myklebust, "Learning Disorders: Psychoneurological Disturbances in Childhood," *Rehabilitation Literature* 25, no. 12 (December 1964).
19. M. Frostig, D. W. Lefever, and J. R. B. Whittlesey, *op. cit.*
20. Samuel A. Kirk and James McCarthy, *op. cit.*
21. A. B. Silverstein, "Variance Components in the Developmental Test of Visual Perception," *Perceptual and Motor Skills* 20 (1965), 973-976.
22. J. Cohen, "Factorial Structure of the WISC at Ages 7-6, 10-6, and 13-6," *J. Consulting Psychology* 23 (1959), 285-299.
23. R. E. Orpet and C. E. Meyers, "A Study of Eight Structure-of-Intellect Hypotheses in Six Year Old Children," Draft Report NIMH, Grant No. MH 08666-01, June 9, 1965.
24. R. A. McCartin, Sr. and C. E. Meyers, "An Exploration of Six Semantic Factors at First Grade," *Multivariate Behavioral Research* 1 (January 1966), 74-94.
25. Guilford used a visual task to test for this factor. The child was required to match identical letters and numbers by inspection.
26. It is hoped that a cluster analytic study which we are currently conducting will confirm this contention.
27. Motor encoding, which means the expression of an idea by movement, involves imagery and presupposes experience with the concepts involved.
28. Auditory decoding refers to understanding the spoken word.
29. Auditory decoding is involved in several WISC subtests, as the directions and questions are given verbally.
30. M. Frostig and D. Horne, *The Frostig Program for the Development of Visual Perception* (Chicago: Follett Publishing Company, 1964).
31. M. Frostig, A. Miller, and D. Horne, *Teacher's Guide* to *Beginning Pictures and Patterns* (Chicago: Follett Publishing Company, 1966). M. Frostig and D. Horne, *Teacher's Guide* to *Intermediate Pictures and Patterns* and to *Advanced Pictures and Patterns* (Chicago: Follett Publishing Company, 1967).
32. These terms are defined in the *Teacher's Guide* to the *Frostig Program, op. cit.,* 1964, pp. 17-18.
33. Kephart, 1960, *op. cit.*

34. M. Frostig (in assoc. with P. Maslow), *Movement Education: Theory and Practice* (Chicago: Follett, 1970).
35. Frostig, 1969, *op. cit.*
36. An introduction to auditory training can be found in H. Barry, *The Young Aphasic Child* (Washington, D.C.: Alexander Graham Bell Assoc., 1961).
37. Lloyd Dunn and James O. Smith, *Peabody Language Development Kit* (Minneapolis, Minn.: American Guidance Service, Inc., 1965).
38. N. S. W. Hart, "Experimental Language Development Programme, Based on Osgood's Language Theory and ITPA Profiles," mimeographed, available from the author, Dept. of Education, University of Queensland, Brisbane, Australia. See also the same author's "The Differential Diagnosis of the Psycholinguistic Abilities of the Cerebral Palsied Child and Effective Remedial Procedure," *Special School Bulletin*, no. 2, Brisbane, Australia (1963).
39. E. H. Minskoff, D. E. Wiseman, and J. G. Minskoff, *The MWM Program for Developing Language Abilities* (Ridgefield, N.J.: Educational Performance Associates, 1972).
40. W. J. Bush and M. T. Giles, *Aids to Psycholinguistic Teaching* (Columbus, Ohio: Merrill, 1969).
41. See, for example, his *Toward a Theory of Instruction* (Cambridge, Mass.: The Belknap Press, 1966).
42. E. A. Peel, *The Pupil's Thinking* (London: Oldbourne, 1960).
43. Aurelia Levi, "Treatment of a Disorder of Perception and Concept Formation in a Case of School Failure," *Journal of Consulting Psychology* 29, no. 4 (1965), 189-295. See also Aurelia Levi, "Remedial Techniques in Disorders of Concept Formation," *Journal of Special Education* 1, no. 1, (1966), 3-8.
44. H. F. Harlow, "The Formation of Learning Sets," *Psychol. Rev.* 56 (1949), 51-65.

Table 2. Summary of ITPA * Subtests Taken From *Learning Problems in the Classroom*†

	Test Description‡	Examples of Classroom Observations
auditory reception	The child indicates "yes" or "no" to such questions as "Do babies drink?" "Do barometers congratulate?"	Does the child understand what is said? Can he follow written directions but not verbal ones? Can he take down dictated sentences? Can he identify common animal sounds? musical instruments? classroom noises?
visual reception	The child must select from a group of pictures the one of an object that is used in a same or similar way as a stimulus picture.	Can the child get specific requested information from pictures or films? Does he have a wide acquaintance with everyday objects, such as tools?
manual expression	The child must show through gesture how an object (e.g., a phone, a toothbrush) is used.	Can the child express action through movement? Can the child play charades? Is he hesitant and awkward when the class does creative movement?
verbal expression	The child is asked to describe a familiar object, such as a ball.	How well does the child express himself? How many different concepts does he use? Is he creative and imaginative?
auditory association	The child is required to make analogies in completing sentences: e.g., "Cotton is soft; stones are (hard)."	Does the child understand the concepts of "same" and "different?" Can he understand math relationships? Does he have difficulty in classifying?
visual association	The child must associate pictures on the basis of relationships such as functional usage (sock and shoe) and conceptual categories (horse and cow, both animals; bread and cheese, both foods).	How large is the child's store of concepts? Does he make logical connections between ideas? Does he understand that the same object can be classified in different ways?
grammatic closure	The child is asked to complete sentences using the correct inflection: e.g., "Here is a dog; here are two (dogs)." "The man is painting. He is a (painter)."	Does the child speak correctly?

auditory sequential memory	The child is requested to repeat a series of digits presented rapidly.	Can the child, after hearing a spoken sentence or number fact or a word spelled orally, repeat the information?
visual sequential memory	The child is shown a sequence of geometric forms; it is removed, and the child is asked to reproduce the sequence by placing chips in proper order.	Can the child focus his attention? Can he discriminate among similar geometric forms? Can he copy a pattern? Can he reproduce it from memory?
visual closure	The child is asked to identify all the partially obscured pictures of common objects against a distracting background; he must do so in 30 seconds.	Does he scan pictures? Can he work rapidly? Is he easily distracted? Can he locate specific information on a printed page? Does he have special difficulty in reading hyphenated words or blurry ditto copies?
auditory closure (optional)	The child is asked to repeat words or phrases in which certain sounds have been omitted: e.g., "Easter unny" (Easter bunny).	Does the child understand a speaker with a different accent? Does he understand phone conversations? Can he understand speech in a noisy room? Does he leave off word endings?
sound blending (optional)	Sounds are spoken at half-second intervals, and the child must blend them into a word: e.g., "f-oo-t, f-u-n, wh-e-n."	Can the child decode unfamiliar words in reading if he can associate the sound with the individual letter? Can he blend sounds into words, as in the test?

° S. Kirk, J. McCarthy, and W. Kirk, *Illinois Test of Psycholinguistic Abilities* (Examiner's manual), rev. ed. (Champaign, Ill.: University of Illinois Press, 1968).

†M. Frostig and P. Maslow, *Learning Problems in the Classroom* (New York: Grune and Stratton, 1973).

‡ The questions used as examples are not those actually used in the ITPA.

Table 3. Basic Test Results

1973
Perceptual Quotient – 108
Verbal I.Q. – 115
Performance I.Q. – 103
Full Scale I.Q. – 110
I.T.P.A. Lang. Age –

Achievement Testing

3/13/73 WRA I

	Date	Test	Lev.		Date	Test	Lev.
RDG.	Vocab. 5.0			RDG.			
SPL.	3.9			SPL.			
ARI.	Fund. 2.2			ARI.			

©MARIANNE FROSTIG, PH.D – 1971

CODE # _____ NAME _MCT IM_ B.D. _11/15/65_ C.A. _____ P.S. Grade _____ DATE _____

TEST	SUB-TESTS CATEGORY		
	SENSORY MOTOR & MOVEMENT SKILLS		
I	BEAD STRINGING		
II	FIST EDGE PALM		
III	BLOCK TRANSFER		
IV	BEAN BAG THROW		
V	SIT-BEND-REACH		
VI	BROAD JUMP		
VII	SHUTTLE RUN		
VIII	LYING TO STANDING		
IX	SIT-UPS		
X	WALKING BOARD		
XI	ONE FOOT BALANCE		
XII	CHAIR PUSH-UPS		
	VISUAL PERCEPTION		
I	EYE MOTOR COORDINATION		
II	FIGURE GROUND		
III	FORM CONSTANCY		
IV	POSITION IN SPACE		
V	SPATIAL RELATIONS		
	WECHSLER INTELLIGENCE SCALE FOR CHILDREN		
I	INFORMATION		
II	COMPREHENSION		
III	ARITHMETIC		
IV	SIMILARITIES		
V	VOCABULARY		
VI	DIGIT SPAN (forward - backward)		
VII	PICTURE COMPLETION		
VIII	PICTURE ARRANGEMENT		
IX	BLOCK DESIGN		
X	OBJECT ASSEMBLY		
XI	CODING		
	I.T.P.A.		
I	AUDITORY RECEPTION		
II	VISUAL RECEPTION		
III	VISUAL SEQUENTIAL MEMORY		
IV	AUDITORY ASSOCIATION		
V	AUDITORY SEQUENTIAL MEMORY		
VI	VISUAL ASSOCIATION		
VII	VISUAL CLOSURE		
VIII	VERBAL EXPRESSION		
IX	GRAMMATIC CLOSURE		
X	MANUAL EXPRESSION		
XI	AUDITORY CLOSURE		
XII	SOUND BLENDING		
	WEPMAN AUDITORY DISCR.		

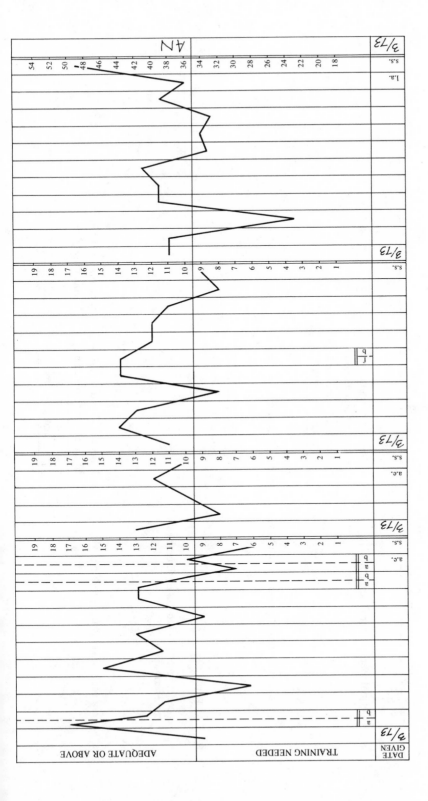

Table 4. Comparison of Factors of the Structure of the Intellect at Chronological Age Six with the Abilities Tapped by the ITPA, Frostig, and WISC

Guilford's Factors	ITPA	WISC	Frostig
I. M.F.S. (visual memory for figure units)	visual-motor sequencing (visual-motor association) remedial exercises: language program		
II. M.S.S. (auditory memory for symbolic units)	auditory-vocal sequencing remedial exercises: language program	digit span (forward and backward)	
III. M.F.T. (convergent production of figural transformation)			figure-ground perception remedial exercises: Frostig program for the development of visual perception
IV. N.M. (convergent semantic production)	auditory vocal automatic auditory vocal association remedial exercises: language program	comprehension vocabulary	

V. D.M.U.

(divergent production of semantic units)

VI. D.M.C.

(divergent production of semantic classes)   vocal encoding

remedial exercises:
language program

VII. E.F.U.

(evaluation of figural units)   visual decoding
visual-motor association

evaluation of figural units on conceptual level (subtests figure-ground and spatial relations, mainly)

remedial exercises:
language program

remedial exercises:
Frostig program for the development of visual perception

Guilford's E.F.U. speed of perception plays a role   (speed of perception does not play a role in the ITPA or the Frostig material)

VIII. E.S.U.

(evaluation of symbolic units)
(no counterparts in Guilford's structure of intellect factors)   motor encoding
auditory decoding

(no subtest in the "four basic tests"; no remedial exercises)

remedial exercises:
language program

Thanks to Dr. Charles Meyers and Dr. Russell Orpet for their advice concerning this table.

Table 5. Factors in Human Movement and Physical Education Programs

Area	Guilford*	Summary of 78 Studies Reviewed by Nicks and Fleishman†	Mosston‡	Kephart§	Frostig
Coordination	coordination –gross body	coordination area –gross body –multiple limb			coordination –across body axis of different muscle groups simultaneously; especially in directions –dissociative movements –laterality and dominance rhythm –jerky versus smooth movements –synchrony prerequisite (see Doll‖)
Flexibility	flexibility –trunk	flexibility— speed area –flexibility –extension flexibility –dynamic flex	flexibility –spine & pelvis –shoulder girdle –bending forward and sideways		flexibility –maximum extension in trunk and limbs –rotation of joints
Speed	speed –e.g., arm movement	speed –speed of limb movement –running speed –speed of change of direction (agility)		receipt and propulsion	speed –continuous movement in space –running
Speed and Agility	impulsion –general		agility –take-off	contact –reaching,	agility –initiation of movement

	[*]	[†]	[‡]	[§]	[||]
	—limb thrust —finger-tapping speed		change of posture in air —touch and go	grasping, & releasing —manipulation to obtain information	change of direction
STRENGTH	strength —general —trunk —limbs endurance	strength —explosive —dynamic —static endurance	strength —shoulder girdle and arms, back, abdomen —legs		strength —general and specific muscle groups endurance —sustained movement over time (see Cureton#)
BALANCE	static precision —static balance —steadiness —hand aiming dynamic precision —aiming —finger and hand dexterity	balance —static balance —dynamic balance —balance of objects	balance	balance —maintenance locomotion —dynamic relationship to gravity	static balance —standing on toes dynamic balance —tightrope walking

* J. P. Guilford, "A System of Psychomotor Abilities," *Amer. J. Psychology* 71 (1958), 164-174.
† Delmer C. Nicks and Edwin A. Fleishman, *What Do Physical Tests Measure—A Review of Factor Analytic Studies.* Technical Report I prepared for the Office of Naval Research by the Departments of Industrial Administration and Psychology. (New Haven: Yale University Press, 1960).
‡ Muska Mosston, *Developmental Movement* (Columbus, Ohio: Charles E. Merrill, 1965).
§ N. C. Kephart, *The Slow Learner in the Classroom* (Columbus, Ohio: Charles E. Merrill, 1960).
|| Edgar A. Doll, *Neurophrenia.* Devereux School Publication, reprinted from the *American Journal of Psychiatry* (July 1951).
Thomas Cureton, "18-Item Motor Fitness Test," *Physical Fitness Workbook* (Champaign, Illinois: University of Illinois, 1952).

The Importance of Differential Diagnosis to the Learning-Disabled Child

PEARL L. ROSSER
CAROLYN H. STEWART
MITZI A. PARKS

Recalcitrance and ignorance are too often attributed to children who, despite otherwise normal and perhaps even above normal intelligence, are unable to master certain educational skills commensurate with their general ability. Many have been labeled as behavior problems and placed in "social adjustment" classes; others have been labeled as mentally retarded and placed in classes for the retarded. Unquestionably many such children have simply remained in the classroom, functioning minimally, with some awareness, which is crucial to their sense of adequacy, that they just don't seem to understand like other children do.

In recent years these children have been brought in increasing numbers to the pediatrician and family doctor because they "can't learn." Many of these children suffer from what we term "learning disabilities." The high incidence of learning disorders among school children, which is based on perceptual abnormalities with concomitant behavioral-emotional problems, places a grave responsibility on the educational and medical professions and the community.

If we are to meet the needs of these children, it is essential and fundamental that effective communication, cooperation, and coordination be established between pediatricians and educators. Between the extremes of unrealistic expectations on the one hand and contempt and total lack of communication on the other, there must be a middle ground wherein these disciplines effectively complement each other.[1] This is even more urgent in the case of the inner-city black child since these two disciplines may well represent the only continuous professional relationships that this child and his family are likely to know.

In an effort to identify earlier the inner-city child who has minimal faulty neurologic integration, a high index of suspicion is primary. It is essential that efforts be made to differentially assess the disadvantaged child so that "cultural deprivation" ceases to be a "lumping" category. It is appalling that three-fourths of those persons identified as mentally retarded are to be found in the isolated and impoverished urban and rural slums. We submit

From the *Proceedings* of the Seventh Annual International Conference of the ACLD, *Meeting Total Needs of Learning-Disabled Children: A Forward Look.* Philadelphia, Pa. (February 12–14, 1970), pp. 47–54.

that this is more a label of convenience than of actuality and that a large percentage of these children are "learning disabled" rather than mentally retarded. We have seen too many discrepancies between labels and achievement potential.

A report by M. M. Kappelman, E. Kaplan, and R. L. Ganter indicates that efforts have recently been initiated in this direction.[2] Their study describes the spectrum of learning disorders encountered in 306 affected disadvantaged urban children. Most significant was the finding that neurologic handicaps of varying degrees were the causative factor in over 50 percent of those inner-city children with learning disorders. When the facts of inner-city life are viewed in perspective, this finding is not surprising. Significantly, those conditions cited as contributing to or eventuating in learning disorders are conditions that are seen in abnormally high incidence in ghetto and urban populations. Affecting the unborn fetus and the growing young child are the following disabling factors of poverty:

- poor maternal nutrition
- lack of prenatal care
- toxemia of pregnancy
- prematurity
- extremes in maternal age, especially the young teenage mother
- lack of childhood immunizations with subsequent preventable childhood infections
- lack of general health supervision
- high and low level exposure to lead via paint, plaster, etc.
- high incidence of accidents
- emotional deprivation and inappropriate stimulation

The conclusion of a review of studies made in the past is that there is a higher incidence, in lower income groups, of abnormalities of pregnancy resulting in "behavioral disorders."[3] It would be of interest to investigate these findings further in an effort to determine what percentage of the behavioral disorders (such as hyperactivity, short attention span, distractibility) can be attributed to minimal faulty neurologic integration.

Because of the complexity of the problem, the need for a multidisciplinary evaluation cannot be overemphasized. In the Child Development Center (CDC), Howard University, Washington, D.C., all children admitted to the program participate in a complete multidisciplinary diagnostic evaluation. This evaluation includes detailed medical and neurological evaluations with supportive laboratory studies as well as psychological, nutritional, social, speech, language, auditory, and educational assessments. The child is also observed in the home and school environments before any conclusions or prescriptions for remediation are offered. The aim is to move away from medically oriented diagnostic labeling; the method preferred is that of referring to both the child and the program of remediation in terms that are understandable to the parent, usable by the teacher, and commensurate with the function of the school.

Analysis of CDC Population

An analysis of the population of the center over the four and one-half years since its inception shows an increase in the number of children who are referred with the diagnosis of "mental retardation with hyperactivity." After evaluation by the multidisciplinary staff of the center it is frequently found that, although underperforming, these children usually have average, or indeed higher, potential with evidence of minimal faulty neurologic integration with learning disabilities. Some of the findings of that analysis are shown in Table 1.

In 1968 and 1969 almost half the new children seen for evaluation were diagnosed as having minimal faulty neurologic integration. The ratio of boys to girls in the general population of the center is approximately two to one. Among the reasons for this ratio, one possibility is that both teachers and parents are more apt to show concern about the boy who is not achieving or who is a behavior problem. It should be noted, however, that the ratio of boys to girls among those who are diagnosed as having minimal faulty neurologic integration with perceptual disorders is much greater than two to one. This is extremely significant when we consider the high dropout and school failure rates in inner-city schools. At the root of this problem is there a combined physical/social cause? This certainly bears further investigation, for if this is indeed a fact, a whole new approach to school-community-police relations should be developed.

Another finding of interest and significance is the high incidence of known identifiable complications in the perinatal period. The most frequently seen complications were prematurity and toxemia of pregnancy. Many of these mothers of children who are diagnosed at the center received no perinatal care. Three of the mothers were sixteen years of age or younger. These findings are important because, for the most part, the conditions cited are preventable.

Three cases are discussed below in an effort to illustrate more vividly the kinds of problems seen at the center. In the first case, there were no known perinatal complications; in the latter two, there were. We are acutely sensitive to the limitations inherent in using standard psychological test instruments to assess children who are in the lower socioeconomic groups. The results that were obtained in our multidisciplinary evaluation represent only one facet of the comprehensive study. As is the case with all children who are admitted to the center for diagnostic study, these three children received detailed medical and neurological evaluations with supportive laboratory studies and were also given speech, hearing, language, social, psychological, and educational assessments. Only the positive findings are discussed.

Table 1. Selected Findings on Review of Case Records in the CDC from 1966 to Early 1969

Year	New Cases Seen	MFNI*	Boys	Girls	Known Perinatal Complications	Area of Disability†			
						VP/M	SLA-R/E	G & F Motor	M
1966	34	5	5	0	3	2	—	—	3
1967	57	10	10	0	3	1	3	—	6
1968	85	40	32	8	23	11	8	3	18
1969 (Jan.–June)	50	22	16	6	11	12	1	—	9

*Minimal faulty neurologic integration. †VP/M = Visual Perceptual and/or Visual Motor; SLA-R/E = Speech-Language-Audition: Receptive and/or Expressive; G & F Motor = Gross and Fine Motor; M = Any combination of the above

Martin

Martin was referred to the center by a psychiatrist. He had never been in any kind of school setting. The mother had sought help because she could not understand why the child did not speak spontaneously. Evaluation using various items from numerous tests was undertaken. Although Martin did not speak spontaneously, he did use speech in response to pictures that were presented to him. It soon became obvious that Martin possessed a great deal of receptive and inner language, which appeared to be average, if not superior, for his age.

Martin was able to comprehend, and he carried out verbal directions quite well. Despite his lack of formal schooling, he was able to express himself through writing. He not only had an excellent memory for symbols previously seen, but in response to words that were suggested by the examiner, he also possessed basic word attack skills through transfer of learning, which is essential for writing unfamiliar and complex words.

The fine-motor skills necessary for writing and drawing were adequately developed and he was hyperperceptive. However, utilization of these skills was handicapped by hyperactivity, short attention span, and distractibility. Elements of his behavior suggested impulsivity and disinhibition. Formal achievement testing was not accomplished, but intelligence testing indicated the potential for average functioning with a present score of 77.

Performance on large muscle tasks disclosed poor coordination and balance, with difficulty in making spatial judgments. Testing evidenced a severe lag of about three and one-half years in the area of gross motor development. Behavior during the test period was often erratic and apparently nondirected with frequent bizarre movements. Assessment of Martin's level of social functioning indicated another area in which he showed a serious lag of three years.

A visit to the home and conversations with the mother added significantly to our picture of Martin. A small, inadequate house set in the midst of a small woods offered little in terms of basic comforts (such as plumbing), aesthetics, or freedom to explore and develop physically or socially. Martin had no interaction with children other than a younger sister. Activities were generally confined to the home since the family's one car was used by the father for work from early morning to late at night. There was considerable evidence of emotional stress in the home from innumerable factors, including those mentioned here, as well as economic instability and the father's diagnosed mental illness.

Andy

At the age of five and one-half years, Andy was already in public school and already in trouble. He was hyperactive with a short attention span, distractible, and perseverative. He was unable to get along with his peers at school. His father was unable to get along with the staff at school. His mother was considered too incompetent, subsequent to brain surgery, to be permitted to have a close relationship with the child. Pressures and indications of rejection were feeding in from all sides.

Andy's intellectual functioning and social adaptivity were both normal, and he was singularly aware of the problems impinging upon him but unable to do anything about them. In moments of frustration, the initially shy but friendly, cooperative child could no longer control his feelings and would strike out aggressively. At the time that we saw Andy initially, he was on probation at school, and the father appealed to us to find another school for him.

Further evaluation showed that not only was Andy functioning normally in the areas of intelligence and social adaptation but that he had no problems in language or verbal skills. Auditory ability appeared intact. He spontaneously corrected errors that were made on visual-perceptual tasks, and this was considered to be probably age-appropriate. He had some difficulty in describing similarities and differences but had quite adequate skills in distinguishing the essential from the nonessential, in defining words, in memory, and in general knowledge.

Andy's weakest skills were in all areas of motor functioning. Gross motor development was less adequate than fine motor. On all tasks there was a serious inability to control responses, to coordinate movements, and to maintain equilibrium.

The combined factors of awareness of inadequacies and the inability to control either self or the environment joined to present a most unhappy child. Subsequently, Andy was placed in a special school that is geared to the needs of the learning-disabled child. Recent reports from the school indicate a radical change in his classroom behavior. Based on data received from the center, the teacher was able to initiate an appropriate program for Andy.

John

John came to the center at the age of eleven years with a ready-made set of labels. He had been passed along to the fifth grade, where the teacher suggested placement, which was based on the quality of his work in the classroom, in a class for the severely mentally retarded.

Standardized achievement tests were administered at the center and it was found that John, academically, was functioning barely at grade one level in all subjects. With this criterion, alone, one might tend to support the teacher's recommendation for severely mentally retarded placement. However, it was interesting to note that John's responses during verbal testing were significantly better than his written test scores, leaving the question of retardation open to suspicion.

This same discrepancy was noted on John's intelligence test results, which showed performance to be less competent than verbal skills. If, however, placement in a class setting were to be made that was specifically based on the full scale test score, John, with an IQ of 72, would still be fair game for a class of educable children. Further investigation of his test behavior indicated that John had the potential for average functioning, with good verbal abstract abilities.

At all times during examinations it was apparent that John was ill at ease. He had difficulty in relating, was tense and constricted in his responses, and gave evidence of feeling helpless and inadequate. These behavioral manifestations gave rise to the hypothesis that John might well function more optimally if he were seen in a more comfortable, supportive environment and had the opportunity to develop a more positive self-image.

Reports received from previous neurological examinations stated that John suffered from mixed dominance since he used his left hand, and wrote "upside-down and backward." At the time of his examination at the center, he was checked for eye, hand, and foot laterality. It was found that rather than having mixed dominance, John showed left side preference in all areas. There was little evidence of strephosymbolia at this time. He had now apparently compensated for whatever "upside-down and backward" writing had been previously manifest. This ability in itself was an additional indication of better than retarded intelligence.

Performance on fine motor tasks showed a marked lack of skill in the use of small muscles. Detailed evaluation of both the auditory and visual-perceptual areas not only revealed weakness in perception but pointed to an actual hearing loss in his left (dominant) ear.

Test responses indicated that John had a severe deficiency in the ability to relate symbols as meaningful material, thus affecting his performance in sequencing, memory, reproduction, and comprehension of written words and numbers. Thus he was unable to achieve in any of the Three R's without special help and was diagnosed as having dysphasia, agraphia, dyscalculia, and agnosia.

Continued failure in the academic setting contributed to John's own feelings of frustration, incompetency, and poor self-image. Reports from the home and school stated that he expressed his dissatisfaction with himself through an alternating pattern of withdrawal and aggression. His behavior led to nonacceptance by the adults in his life, and finally, rejection by his peers. John felt little motivation to expand his horizons either intellectually or socially and often became "too tired" to do anything. His social age, although superior to academic achievement, was that of an eight-year-old.

It is obvious that for too many years only the most cursory evaluation of John's problems had been made and that little had been done in the way of programing for his needs.

Reappraisal of Approach

There is need for a realistic reappraisal of the approach to the problems of the socioeconomically disadvantaged child. In our concentration on his social and economic difficulties, it is important to remember that even prior to his birth as a social and economic being, all of the forces of poverty and the anxieties of economic constriction were having their effect upon him.

Early identification and remediation should be immediate goals for teachers, physicians, and parents alike. Primary prevention is the ultimate goal. Early identification and diagnosis is possible even at the preschool level, but parents, educators, and physicians must be aware that such a phenomenon as the learning-disabled child exists. As stated before, a high index of suspicion is of utmost importance. During infancy and the preschool periods, awareness of hyper- or hypokinesis, awkwardness, delayed speech and language development, perceptual disorders, fluctuating auditory responses, etc., can lead to early treatment and remediation.

Perhaps nature has presented the best argument for the importance of early identification by providing an optimal growth period in children. The child's natural processes work with us to achieve maximal results in his habilitation and education.

Our work with children at the center indicates that there are some basic concepts that are valid and at least worthy of mention.

The first requirement in the consideration of the education of the child with learning disabilities is that the teacher should recognize that this child has special needs and should not just classify him with a general concept of human failure. His needs must be delineated and separated from those of other children who may also be having problems in school. If he is mislabeled and misgrouped or not recognized at all in terms of special needs, he is being deprived of his right to an optimum education.

Primary consideration of the child's problem must not only be in terms of defining achievement but also in defining the deficits and integrities, such as perception, memory, cognition, speech, language, audition, motor characteristics, etc., in particular functioning areas. Only then can the team plan logical programs for the child, which he would otherwise lack, that are appropriate and that will offer him the opportunities to develop. Because of the complexity of the problem and nature's own dynamic neurophysiological change that is occurring in the growing child, ongoing evaluation and reevaluation is obviously needed. These in turn must be incorporated into the child's daily program of habilitation and education in an integrated and holistic approach to his ongoing development.

There is no single cause for learning disorders and there is no single way of diagnosing children's learning problems; consequently, there is no single way of teaching the learning-disabled child. Therefore, the multidisciplinary team must be included in his habilitation and education. It requires only humility to acknowledge that any one professional discipline is less than omnipotent. Such realization enhances the possibility for effective diagnosis and remediation for the learning-disabled child.

The problems of diagnosis, habilitation, and education of the neurophysiologically impaired child do not lend themselves to simplistic solutions. In the best of all possible situations, given our present knowledge and skills, our responsibilities would require the time it takes a child to grow from conception to productive, independent adulthood. Having much less than this, we must applaud our gains without losing sight of their limitations. The organization of parents and professionals, the primary multidisciplinary team, in the Association for Children with Learning Disabilities is such a gain. The sensitivity training we receive in such meetings as these, the passage of legislation to assure a national pooling of our resources, and the growing public awareness of the existence of these problems are all gains to be counted. If knowledge is power, our united efforts are the mechanism to give that power direction and force until, hopefully, we have worked ourselves out of our jobs.

NOTES

1. R. L. Clemmens and J. Davis, "Complementary Roles of the Pediatrician and Educator in School Planning for Handicapped Children," *Journal of Learning Disabilities* 2, (October 1969).
2. M. M. Kappelman, E. Kaplan, and R. L. Ganter, "A Study of Learning Disorders Among Disadvantaged Children," *Journal of Learning Disabilities* 2, (May 1969).
3. B. Pasamanick and H. Knoblock, "Epidemiologic Studies on the Complications of Pregnancy and the Birth Process," *Prevention of Mental Disorders in Children*, ed. Gerald Caplan (New York: Basic Books, 1961).

The Educational Evaluation in an Interdisciplinary Setting: A Developing Concept

CHARLES H. BARTLETT

There is increasing reference in the literature to-day to the need for and importance of a thorough educational evaluation for the child suspected of having a learning disability, a learning disorder, minimal cerebral dysfunction, dyslexia, etc.[1] For several years there has been general agreement that the overall diagnosis of such a disability itself is a complex and involved undertaking that requires the services of several disciplines.[2]

The contribution of the educator is one component in the diagnostic procedure and the overall evaluation. The information contributed by the educational evaluation is of significance when considering appropriate educational placement and programing. Other members of the diagnostic team who have important contributions pertinent to final recommendations are generally from psychology, the medical field (neurology, pediatrics, and psychiatry), audiology and speech pathology, and the social services.

The reasons for this choice of disciplines are evident from the nature of the child's dysfunctions. Most frequently he demonstrates dysfunctions in one or more of the areas with which these disciplines concern themselves; for example, motor coordination, sensory losses, perceptual deficits, emotional problems, articulation difficulties, language disorders, and psychological aberrations are all manifest within various social matrices (the home school, and community). Efforts are made by members of the team to determine the relative importance or weights to give to the findings.

The data seen as pertinent, and therefore worthy of being gathered by the educator or any of the other members of the diagnostic team, will be determined to some extent by the background and bent of the professional who is collecting it. That is, his knowledge and acceptance of various theoretical models for learning and behavior will partly affect this collection of data. However, it is my contention that the educator should concern himself primarily with the collection of data that is directly applicable to the educational program of a given child. In addition, he should be able at a later time to interpret, in terms that are meaningful to the classroom teacher, the findings of the other disciplines. He should also be able to assist in the incorporation of certain aspects of these other findings into the educational prescription.

The data collected by any one person will also be dependent to a degree

From the *Proceedings* of the Seventh Annual Conference of the ACLD, *Meeting Total Needs of Learning-Disabled Children: A Forward Look*. Philadelphia (February 12–14, 1970), pp. 27-46.

upon the unique setting in which it is being gathered and the presence or absence of other professional personnel; for example, children referred to a speech and hearing clinic are more likely to have a hearing loss, an articulation problem, or a language disorder as a component of their problem or disability, while children referred through a clinic for mental retardation are more likely to require a diagnosis that differentiates between mental retardation and other handicaps. If personnel in psychology or audiology and speech pathology are present, the educator will be less likely to collect as detailed and standardized information in these two areas. The same can be said when other combinations of professional personnel are either on a team or are available for consultation within the community.

The Setting

The setting in which this model of an educational evaluation is being developed is an interdisciplinary or multidisciplinary (these two terms will be used more or less synonymously hereafter) evaluation program for children with mental retardation and related developmental disabilities that was founded in 1957 and that today consists of staff and programs in the areas of mental retardation, children's neuromuscular disorders, birth defects, children with severe learning disabilities, a metabolic disorder treatment program, and an adolescent program. The setting of the Hamilton County Diagnostic Clinics, Cincinnati, Ohio, is one of several university-affiliated programs across the country where, in addition to services rendered to children, stress is placed upon the interdisciplinary training of professional personnel from many fields relative to working with children who give evidence of having such handicaps, disorders, and disabilities.

- For the most part, children are brought to the clinics by their parents, and in some instances they must come a distance of several miles.
- The physical facilities are in an urban area bordering on a large hospital complex.
- There is, at times, a waiting period of several weeks before the evaluational procedure is initiated.
- Due to the demands placed upon such facilities today, the evaluational procedure, once it is initiated, may last for several months before coming to completion.
- During this time, the parents must make and keep many appointments.
- Children must be seen several times during evaluation; this often disrupts their daily school attendance or other appointments.
- Educational evaluations and appointments with other professional personnel most frequently take place on school days, and therefore children are released from school for this purpose.
- Frequently there is an urgency for the educational evaluation to be completed to aid in school or other placement and programing.

- The educational evaluation is carried out on a one-to-one basis (child and educator) and is, as a rule, accomplished in from one to two hours.

The overall evaluational procedure is best explained by Figure 1.

The Learning Disabilities Program

The Learning Disabilities Program consists of two divisions: (1) The Evaluation Division, which is headed by a pediatrician with background in audiology, speech pathology, and special and preschool education; and (2) The Education Division, which is funded by the Junior League of Cincinnati Incorporated and has been operational since September 1968, is headed by an educator whose background is in special education and communication disorders and whose work for many years has been with children demonstrating serious learning dysfunctions thought to be the result of minimal organic impairment. Figure 2 explains graphically the organization of the program.

Working in conjunction with the Department of Special Education at the University of Cincinnati, the Education Division functions as a training facility for graduate students in special education and includes a laboratory class in which children can be seen for extended periods of time for additional observation and assessment. Pertinent information is passed on to the school system or other appropriate agency upon the completion of the child's stay in the classroom.

Principles

The educator's primary objective during the educational evaluation is to gather as much information pertinent to the child's learning processes, behavior, and academic achievement as he can.

- He wants to observe the child's competencies as well as his difficulties; therefore, the session must be arranged in such a manner that the child will have every opportunity to demonstrate both his social and academic abilities. Premature or undue channeling or restriction of the child's actions and performance will not allow him to do this. The modification of evaluation materials, including the manner in which they are presented, is introduced along the way, only when a need to do so is indicated, and only to the extent required to direct the child while maintaining his attention. Some details may be missed following this procedure but it does save valuable time because it concentrates on pertinent information. As a rule, the child will be glad to demonstrate his competencies. Many times he will also indicate his weaknesses, either by stating them quite frankly or by attempting to cope with problems in various ways. Such coping mechanisms are frequently of importance later in program planning when considering the degree of preferential treatment, structure, etc., that may be required.

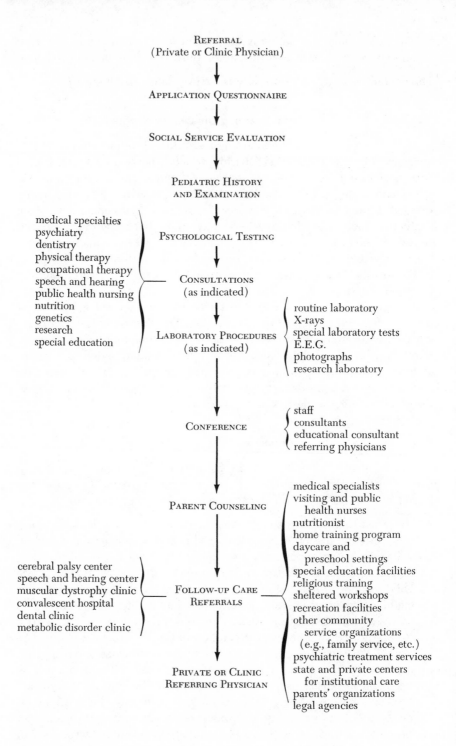

Figure 1. OUTLINE OF THE PLAN FOR PATIENT EVALUATION AND FOLLOW-UP CARE

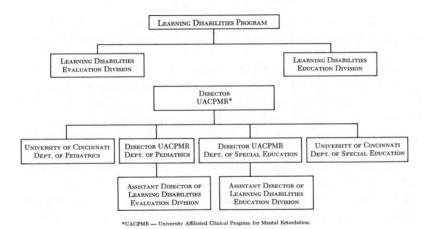

Figure 2. STAFF AND PROGRAM ORGANIZATION

- The child cannot function at his best if he feels threatened in any way. He must be as relaxed and receptive as possible. If he perceives the procedure as something undesirable or by his behavior makes it necessary to terminate the evaluation, any combination of the following may result: the representativeness of the data already collected may be questioned; it may be inconvenient to have the child return for another session; valuable time may be lost in the overall evaluation efforts; and any feelings (negativity, disinterest, etc.) that are engendered by the procedure may well carry over into the next session to further complicate it. Therefore, the educator must give thought to not only the materials he will present but to the order or sequence of presentation and to the manner of presentation; for example, if the child can read few if any of the word lists presented, the examiner will present easier contextual reading materials. Also, because it is usually less threatening, the educator might well consider the collection of some factual information from the child before working into the more academic materials, and of course the whole procedure should be conducted in a pleasant and friendly manner. When this can be accomplished, the educator is in a better position to note whether tension or any changes in attitude occur during the presentation of specific materials. Again, such observations are of value later when plans are made to meet the child's needs.
- Throughout the educational evaluation, the educator must be alert to the child's responses to himself, to the materials and activities, and to the setting. In addition to collecting data pertaining to academic achievement, the educator addresses himself to the appropriateness and dynamics of the child's behavior, not only so that the session will run smoothly and so that he can continue to collect data, but also to make a more comprehensive evaluation of the "whole" child. The child is

treated at all times with respect, dignity, and understanding. For one thing, the educator wants to note the child's response to such treatment and determine whether the child is able to reciprocate or whether he attempts to take advantage of the situation. In other words, what is his response to the offer of such a relationship? Does he respond in a mature fashion, or is he distrustful, etc.? Again, it is of importance to note how the child interacts under such circumstances, whether or not his behavior appears adequate, and if not, how this will conceivably direct recommendations later.

- The educational evaluation should not collect overlapping information without good cause. For one thing, to do so is to use precious time inefficiently. The child may well become fatigued part way through the session and cease to function optimally, forcing the educator to terminate his efforts earlier than anticipated. If this occurs, and the educator has collected information that can largely be obtained from other sources but has failed to collect information that is unique to the educational evaluation, the session will not be as productive as would otherwise be the case. The child may need to be rescheduled for another session to finish gathering needed information. It would seem best, at least within the setting being described, for the educator to focus his attention upon the collection of data directly useful to the educational planning of the child.

- Many techniques can be used to maintain the child's interest; for example, the educator can be alert to indications of perseveration or restlessness and be prepared to shift occasionally to a manipulative activity or to engage the child in brief conversation before going on with tasks that make greater demands upon him. Distractibility and hyperactivity may also be lessened by having the child's desk face the wall and by removing superfluous materials from the child's view.[3] Also, it is usually advisable to place any active or gross motor items at, or near to, the end of the session. Thus, if the child is so overstimulated that he is unable to settle down again, little other information is lost.

The educator, then, is seeking to ascertain the nature of the child's academic strengths and weaknesses and his behavioral responses when confronted with certain specific academic activities, as well as his response to the setting and the educator himself. He checks the differentials that exist in the child's performance under the many and varied input, output, and associational demands that are placed upon him, as well as noting the degree of complexity that the child can cope with adequately.

In large part, the determination of such specific differentials and the degree of complexity that the child can cope with successfully are the crux of the educational evaluation, and they furnish the sources for our initial educational programing.

This is true because psychological testing does not give us all the necessary information, and also because we cannot assume that the child has a standard educational background by his age or grade level. That is, it may be that the educator is evaluating a child with a learning disability, but on the other hand, it may be that the school system may not have taught a given skill as yet. Therefore, the educator seeks clinical impressions of the child's functioning when he is faced with the same materials that cause the learning problems within the classroom—reading, writing, spelling, and arithmetic. To get this information, he presents these materials initially in much the same manner as they would be presented in the classroom. Then, dependent upon the child's ability to handle them satisfactorily, they are presented in a number of ways in order to locate the specific learning problems that they present to the child. The way in which this is done is comparable to the methods used with the preschool cerebral-palsied child as described by Else Haeussermann.[4] It is a clinical procedure and one in which the educator quite thoroughly probes and observes analytically the child's responses to materials and activities. It is a procedure that requires a well-trained, experienced, and flexible examiner if it is to achieve its goals.

If the educator feels the need to do so, he can supplement the information gathered during the educational evaluation by visiting the school to observe the child's functioning within the classroom setting. This also gives him the opportunity to discuss various findings with the teacher.

The Educational Evaluation

There are really two kinds of evaluations spoken of in relation to the child with a learning disability. One is the initial educational evaluation and the other is the ongoing educational evaluation. Each has a different purpose, and each is conducted in a different manner. There is also the need for a periodic reassessment (reevaluation) of the child's progress, both in the schools and in the clinic.

The information gathered at the initial educational evaluation is meant to be a descriptive picture of the child's functioning in all areas of learning. It can be of assistance in establishing guidelines for the beginnings of remediation. These guidelines are attempts to determine at what point or level and in what manner the child may be introduced to various remedial efforts so that he will begin to experience academic success.

The ongoing educational evaluation is generally carried out by the teacher conducting the educational program once it is under way. It is accomplished both on a daily basis and at periodic intervals to help achieve short-range and intermediate goals.

Every effort is made during the initial educational evaluation to have the child become involved in the activities in a relaxed but interested and cooperative fashion. This initial educational evaluation attempts to collect information that is relevant to behavioral and academic competency under the following seven headings.

- the initial and continuing observation of behavior
- the child's ability to supply factual information of a general nature

- the exploration of academic achievement and competency
- the child's speech and language competency
- the exploration of perception (visual, auditory, tactile, and their motor components) and the perceptual integrations required for academic achievement
- motor coordination and planning
- cognitive abilities

Summary statements are then made concerning the findings with preliminary recommendations following such statements. I will now describe each of the above seven headings in more detail.

The Initial and Continuing Observation of Behavior

This is akin to Haeussermann's "controlled" or "educated" observation.[5] Observation of the child's behavior begins with his arrival, accompanied by an adult, and continues until he leaves with the adult. The educator will take note of such things as:

- The parent-child relationship. Is there independence, dependence, hostility, testing behavior, etc.? How best might the prevailing situation be described?
- The child's general behavior. Is the child's behavior organized and goal-directed? Is it aimless, perseverating, hyperactive, etc.? Again, how does it appear and how might it best be typified?
- The child's linguistic competency. Does it appear adequate for his age? If not, how is it to be described specifically? Is he talkative? Does his linguistic production reflect good reasoning? Is he easily directed by language? Does he use complete statements, fragments, or single words?
- The child's speech production. Are there articulation errors? Does he talk rapidly, slowly, slovenly? Is the speech production effected in noticeable ways by the presentation of various activities or materials? Do stimulation techniques improve his articulation? How are the errors to be described?
- The child's behavior during the evaluation. How does the child behave in the classroom with the educator when he is faced with academic materials? Is there a differential response when he is presented various materials and activities? How does he hold up during the evaluation as it proceeds? Does he fatigue, lose interest, become irritable, hyperactive, require increasing structure and channeling? Does he demonstrate negative feelings towards the school work in general, towards one particular subject or skill, towards the examiner? Are there avoidance or acting out responses, testing, controlling, manipulating behavior, etc.? Is such behavior general, or is it related to specific activities?
- Other observations. Here the educator will note anything that seems to

be outstanding; for example, if the child is wearing glasses, does he take them off when he leaves his parents or refuse to wear them during the evaluation? If he has several cuts and bruises, can he tell how they were incurred? (These children fall frequently.) We also take note of the child's response to any needed efforts to channel, direct, or limit his actions during the session, and whether or not, and to what degree, they were successful.

All such observations are valuable and they may be indicative of the need for helpful procedure within the appropriate setting.

Ability to Supply Factual Information

The session is planned to work from the initial gathering of general information towards the gathering of specific information, especially that of academic subject material. The attempt to gather identifying information provides the educator with an inventory of the child's ability to retrieve information and formulate statements about himself and his surroundings. As a rule, he finds such a procedure less threatening than if he were asked initially to perform in the more academic areas. Of importance is the specific information that he has for his given age, the availability of such information upon request, and the way in which he relates it (specific detail, organization, etc.). He can be asked such things as:

- his name, address, and telephone number
- his age and birth date
- his siblings' names, ages, and perhaps their birth dates
- the names of any pets in the home; this frequently stimulates discussion and helps the educator to acquire a corpus of the child's linguistic competency
- the name of his school, his grade, and his teacher's name
- the date (day of week, month, date, and year)
- his mother's and father's first names: he is sometimes reluctant to answer this

This area can be investigated as thoroughly as desired and as the child's capabilities allow. It may include questions concerned with telling time, the monetary system, seasons, etc. Competency here is indicative of general performance and is of assistance to the educator in his considerations regarding placement and programing for the management of the child and presentation of suitable materials. The educator wants to know how available the information is to the child and how well he can organize and communicate it to another person. He also wants to determine how detailed and specific it is and whether or not the child updates current information, such as the date, or whether he relies mainly upon overlearned and rote information, such as his address and telephone number. The way in which the child responds in such a situation is also of importance. Does he do so with confidence? Does he give name, address, and telephone number rapidly but fail to do so with other factual questions? Is he slow and labored in his responses? Does he eventually recall the required information, or does he fail to do so?

The examiner will also begin to gather information regarding the child's speech and language performance during this initial part of the evaluation, and these efforts will continue throughout the session. He will take note of articulation errors and whether or not they are consistent for certain sounds or whether they are erratic. He will note morphological and syntactic errors. There may be errors in flowing speech that do not appear in isolated sound production. This should be noted. This information may also be collected while the child is being asked to produce sounds in connection with reading. There may also be sequencing errors, sound and syllable omissions and substitutions, in words or within sentences. The child may be echolalic or have other noticeable language disorders requiring description and comment. The evaluation is arranged so that the child will have several opportunities to express himself, sometimes in a general manner and at other times in relation to specific materials and activities.

Exploration of Academic Achievement and Competency

Important here is the way in which the child approaches these subjects as well as whether or not, and to what extent, he is successful. His phonics skills are inventories as is his ability to apply them to reading and spelling, both written and oral. When writing, the child may do one or more of the following things.

- misform letters
- reverse or invert certain manuscript letters
- have difficulty staying on the line
- not be able to transfer from manuscript to cursive writing.

If he writes in both cursive and manuscript, he may:

- not be able to read one or the other
- form cursive symbols incorrectly
- copy manuscript or cursive writing exactly, including any errors in the example
- have difficulty determining word boundaries
- leave out letters or words when writing
- write letters or words out of sequence
- fail to dot his *i*'s and cross his *t*'s
- have difficulty connecting another letter to the lower case cursive letters *b, v, w,* and *o*
- place supernumerary humps and peaks in the letters *m, n, u, v, w,* and *i*

When spelling, he may:

- make an effort to spell phonetically but omit certain vowels, omit a silent letter, or omit consonants from consonant blends
- guess at the spelling—sometimes wildly
- drop prefixes or suffixes from words
- omit unstressed elements in words
- omit unvoiced elements in words
- be erratic in his spelling from one instance to another.[6] In an education program this would appear also as being inconsistent in his spelling from day to day

What is sought here are the differentials that may exist in the child's success with these activities, depending upon how they are presented. He may be asked to write the symbols for phonemes that are presented auditorially, particularly those that are customarily reversed or inverted: *b-d-p-q, s, n-u-v, f-t,* and *m-w.* This will allow the examiner to collect not only information relative to his knowledge of these sounds, but also his reversals and the copying attempts and confusions that occur when he writes them. He may then be asked to give the sounds for other letters, which the examiner writes for him. This will provide the examiner with information on his ability to identify vowel qualities, to blend initial and final consonant clusters and initial consonants with phonograms, his knowledge of digraphs, suffixes, prefixes, etc., as well as his ability to attack whole words by such means.

He is also asked to spell and to read words that are likely to produce reversals and other errors or that will demonstrate his ability to apply phonic skills. Important to the assessment is the need to ascertain the child's ability to apply the skills that he does possess. The inability to integrate given skills with others will result in specific learning disabilities. The analysis of such disorganized or poorly integrated functioning gives direction to initial teaching efforts that are aimed at improving the child's academic abilities. He may therefore be asked to spell some words aloud and to spell others by writing them. There may be a differential in his performance on the two different tasks. The act of spelling, when coupled with writing, may be too involved for him to manage successfully.

He may have negative feelings about writing because of unresolved problems with reversals or because he is left-handed and has not compensated for it adequately in terms of manipulating the paper and pencil successfully. He may turn the paper around a good deal and thus see letters that are reversed or rotated much of the time. These things must all be noted to make preparations for remediation. Spelling words may be presented visually on cards and turned down before he is asked to spell them. His ability to revisualize such materials is also an important consideration in planning remediation. He is asked to read from word lists of various kinds (see Figure 3).

Such lists may contain words that are easily reversed: *saw-was, on-no,*

Figure 3

Digraphs and Consonant Clusters

th	ch	sh	wh	ph
sc	st	sm	sp	sl
sn	tr	bl	gr	dr
fl	scr	str	spr	scl
nt	ng	mp	nd	nk

Phonograms

ay	at	ar	ip	ag
im	an	en	in	it
ig	un	ink	ank	unk
ing	ang	ung	ate	ite
old	ong	ill	ell	all
ight		oung	aught	

Words for the Child to Read

this	these	that	then	them
they	those	than	there	the
what	why	where	when	white
which	while	wheel	want	went
ash	oar	too	arm	sea
raw	tea	aim	air	toe
ask	eat	zoo	oil	eye
bad	fit	dip	fun	hit

and *bad-dab*. Sometimes reversals are found when he writes but not when he reads, or vice versa, and at other times reversals will be found in both activities.

Graded lists of words may be given as a means of checking the contrast between his ability to read isolated words and his ability to read contextual materials. Word lists containing silent letters or unusual pronunciations may be used at times to determine his competency with printed materials. Oral reading is checked for fluency and his ability to perceive and use punctuation markings. Note is taken of whether he reads word-by-word or by phrases, and whether he reads with good, fair, or poor comprehension, even though he may be fluent. It is also noted whether or not he loses his place on the page, dropping at times from one line to another, rereading or omitting words, and if using a line marker or his finger seems to help him in this respect. The examiner attempts to determine whether making other changes in the format leads to noticeable changes in his ability to cope with the material—changes such as larger type or greater spaces between the words or the lines. Silent reading may be contrasted with oral reading for speed and comprehension.

The way in which any of this is done must remain flexible and of course will be determined by the amount of skill the child possesses. There may be indications that, although his comprehension is good, the child is subvocalizing his silent reading in a laborious fashion that is slowing him down. There may be indications that his comprehension diminishes when he cannot hear himself read. Using materials on various grade levels, the educator may read to the child to determine his listening comprehension. These assessments are made to determine what is causing, and how materials may be presented to overcome, the child's disabilities. It is possible that the child is "up to grade" in reading but not in other academic areas or that the reading disability is contributing to the child's problems in arithmetic. This is especially true at the higher grade levels where success with arithmetic is dependent upon reading the arithmetic problems from a text rather than upon the basic computational skills required in the lower grades.[7]

The child's writing is also investigated. Note is taken of which hand the child uses for writing and also of how he manages the activity as a whole. How does he maneuver the paper and pencil? Does he hold the paper down with one hand? How does he grip the pencil? Some children approach the act of writing in a very tentative and inefficient manner. Some do not make attempts to hold down the paper but let it slip and slide around on the desk while keeping one hand in their lap. In all such instances the educator will attempt some initial teaching efforts to note the child's response to them; for example, he may show the child how to hold down his paper when writing and observe if he continues to do so or fails to see the significance of doing so. Some children turn the paper excessively or continually so that, in actuality, they are perceiving rotated or inverted symbols much of the time. Some cover their writing, especially left-handed children, and they either do not look underneath their hand to see what they are producing or they look underneath frequently, but in so doing lose continuity in their writing and may leave out words. The examiner checks the child's ability to write upper and lower case symbols in manuscript and cursive. Some children first produce cursive symbols and then printed capitals in efforts to mask or to keep from having reversal problems. The examiner notes how skillfully the child makes his symbols, whether or not they are small and neat or large and uncontrolled. It is noted whether or not he is able to hold a line, is guided by lines when writing, or requests lined paper, and whether he manages writing on unlined paper. His ability in this area is checked further as he does arithmetic problems. There may be reversals of number symbols as well. The child's eye-hand coordination will be noted when he uses such materials as pegs and pegboards, blocks of various kinds, form boards, and jigsaw puzzles.

For children in the six to ten year age range, arithmetic is explored primarily in the basic number skills and the child's understanding of the basic processes of addition, subtraction, multiplication and division. Again, how far such a procedure will go or how detailed it will be depends upon the given child. Most of the children who are evaluated in our program are in the elementary grades.

The assessment of the child's basic arithmetic skills will include: his understanding of larger and smaller; the serial order of numbers (this investigation will include his understanding of the number system to the base of ten and place values); his flexibility in handling numbers (his ability to count backwards, give the number before, after, and between one, two, and three-place numbers); his ability to count by two, three, four, five, ten, and perhaps twenty; his ability to identify numbers in isolation and to write given numbers from dictation, etc.

His knowledge of the numerical processes is checked in oral and written computation and also by means of word problems. He is taken as far as he can go. The addition and subtraction of one, two, and three-place numbers, simple multiplication and division, carrying and borrowing, long division and multiplication, fractions and decimals, telling time and the monetary system are checked as indicated.

At times the child is given simple equations, ratios, and number patterns to note his ability to handle the same processes under other than usual conditions. Occasionally such presentation will take the child's interest, especially if he has a good grasp of arithmetic, and he will, by contrast with the more common presentation, make a better showing. When this occurs, it has implications for planning the academic program.

The educator must be alert to the differences between an understanding of numbers and numerical processes, and rote work. Frequently, if the child is accomplishing such work by rote means, he will not be able to contend with a new or different presentation of the same materials that he has been using. Therefore, he will be given both vertical and horizontal problem forms and problems with missing numbers that require him to manipulate numbers in a somewhat flexible manner. The examiner will also take note of whether or not the child counts on his fingers, uses little marks next to the problems, counts under his breath, partially counts, etc. Some children, because of their lack of understanding of the number system and their inflexibility in using it, refer everything that they do back to number one; for example, in giving a number out of context they must first count up from one each time until they reach it. To count backwards from ten to one, they must in fact count up each time to the next smaller number before starting it. This is often done subvocally. Therefore, the educator must be alert and make every effort to determine how the child is arriving at his answers and whether or not they are meaningful or simply rote responses.

The child's memory for digits or digit span, his memory for sentences, and his spelling are checked for instances of sequencing errors and lack of ability to reauditorize. Indications of such problems may show up in the child's speech, either within words, or in the way that words are placed within sentences, or both. He may also leave out unvoiced or unstressed sounds in words and find it difficult to pronounce polysyllabic words, thus reordering the syllables or simplifying the pronunciation and dropping words out of sentences, etc. Such errors will also frequently appear in his written work.

The examiner may find it necessary to repeat instructions or to reword them in various ways, stressing certain elements or simplifying them. In other words, there may well be communication difficulties to be considered when conducting the evaluation. The nature of such difficulties must be noted as well as their severity and the success or failure of specific techniques used in dealing with them. It is important to note how well the child handles verbal input in following directions.[8]

Visualization and revisualization are checked to determine how meaningful graphic materials are to the child and how able he is to recall wholes and parts upon request. He can be asked to interpret pictures by identifying simple and central objects within pictures, by identifying and recalling several objects, or by giving their function and by describing the event depicted. He may also be asked to project his thinking into the past or the future on the basis of the situation seen in a picture.

Speech and Linguistic Competency

The mechanics of the child's speech production are noted. This is done to determine whether or not there are specific articulation errors, whether or not they are consistent, and to what extent they are determined by a given sound environment, that is, by the preceding and following sounds. The educator takes note of any differentials between sounds produced in isolation and those same sounds produced in context or flowing speech. In general, he wants to determine the characteristics of the child's speech. Does the speech mechanism seem to be mobile and adequate? Is there a sufficient column of air for sound production? Does the child coordinate parts of the speech mechanism adequately or is the need for some speech therapy indicated? The mobility and strength of the speech mechanism and the ability to sustain diadokokinetic patterns (reciprocal movements) and their rates are checked. The child may be referred to a speech and hearing center for more intensive study.

Phonemic, morphologic, and syntactic features of the child's language are also noted throughout the evaluation for various immaturities and specific errors in the use of: verb tense, suffixes, prefixes, infixes, negation, interrogative rulings, auxiliary verb placement, etc., as well as for omissions and sequencing errors.

In addition, the amount of speech production is noted. Is the child a chatterbox, is he reticent about talking, has he obtained a good speech corpus? His semantics are also checked. What is his ability to apply language to the situation at hand or to carry on a discussion in a reasonable and meaningful manner for his age?

Perception and Perceptual Integration

The child's ability to be directed by verbal means is noted. He is also asked to identify gross environmental sounds. (Digit span and memory for sentences have been mentioned.) Auditory discrimination may also be checked in various ways. However, if personnel from a speech and hearing department are going to see the child, the educator may simply note the presence of various errors in production and await further clarification through a consultation with the speech and hearing department.

Visual perception is frequently checked by means of various manipulative activities using cubes, pegboards, parquetry blocks, form boards, and jigsaw puzzles. The educator takes note of the child's ability to organize discrete units such as pegs and puzzle pieces into larger wholes—designs, pictures, and forms. He notes the manner in which the child proceeds. The child may turn the puzzle pieces over in an impulsive way without looking first to see what he is expected to do. Can he be led to inspect the task prior to attempting it? Can he upon inspection do a better job? Does he profit from some guidance or efforts to teach him? In other words, do suggestions and the help offered by the educator bring about a better performance? Such materials are frequently used in programs for children with learning disabilities as well as in preschool programs to help them organize close space. They also are applied in the teaching of basic arithmetic skills; for example, the Sterns and Cuisenaire materials and the colorful and manipulative Montessori materials are used for this purpose.

The child's ability to integrate perceptual data or his intersensory facilitation is also checked. This is largely done while he is involved with the academic materials and activities. How much complexity can he manage? Can he produce written spelling and handle contextual reading with good comprehension? Can he handle written arithmetic processes independently and with good understanding? How much adaptation or modification must be applied to materials and their presentation for him to be successful with them? How much of his skill remains isolated in given areas and is therefore inoperable in the regular academic setting? These variations in the way that such activities are presented are used to determine the best initial approach when planning for remediation. That is, the child may have phonic skills that he is not applying to reading or spelling; he may be able to spell words that are dictated to him orally if the component of writing is eliminated; he may be able to comprehend numerical functions and processes when and if he is allowed to manipulate materials—if he can see and handle them, he may be directed by speech and language that relates to things directly at hand or is concrete; he may be able to direct his hand meaningfully when given a copy to trace but not when expected to initiate his own patterns or to recall a pattern.

The disabilities of some of these children may be compared to those of adult brain-injured patients, where there are numerous breakdowns in perceptual integration. Therapy with such adult patients stresses the analysis of the task with subsequent simplification in presentation, in which the task must be overlearned and then gradually reintegrated into greater complexity.

It is the educator's place to determine the nature of poorly integrated functioning in the academic areas and to begin to make the necessary plans for correction. Once a program is underway, there is then the need for a continuous and ongoing evaluation. The teacher must check the child's successes and failures every day, task for task, and determine how and if activities will be changed the following day or whether or not they will be eliminated. He must plan to sequence the activities in a manner that will lead at some future date to the child's success with the complete and complex tasks that are required within the regular classroom.[9]

Motor Coordination and Planning

Motor planning ability, or the ability to execute common gross, fine, dynamic, and static coordinations, is checked, at least in a cursory way, during the initial educational evaluation. Fine motor inco-ordinations are checked mainly in the areas of speech production, writing, and the child's visual-motor management of the printed page when reading. Difficulties in these areas are, at times, indicative of the need for specific therapy and also give information for directives in planning and designing materials for a successful academic program.

Difficulties in gross motor ability will frequently show themselves by awkwardness in the production of or by absence of various movement patterns typically associated with childhood: skipping, jumping, hopping, galloping, etc. The child frequently demonstrates clumsiness and insecurity when ascending and descending stairs. He may lead with one foot, bringing the other foot to the same tread, long after he has reached an age when this should no longer be the case. He will also seek the support of a railing and show insecurity in other ways.

In addition, the child may not be able to initiate gross motor patterns upon request but may need to have them demonstrated for him first. He may then omit the patterns after one or two repetitions on his own. He is often not able to change flexibly from one pattern to another but will perseverate an action. He is in all likelihood stiff and awkward in his production of such patterns, if he does accomplish them, and will fall easily or stumble and make excuses for his actions. He may be better able to maintain static balance than dynamic balance. Not being flexible in the production of these movement patterns, he may not be able to reverse them and walk, hop, jump, or skip backwards or sidewards without difficulty or failure. (Here we are reminded of the way in which this child handles arithmetic on a rote, overlearned basis.)

Motor problems such as these have far-reaching effects throughout the child's day. Buttoning, zipping, tying knots and bows, managing eating utensils, bicycles, swings, teeter-totters, and other recreational equipment and playground games all present him with various degrees of failure and frustration. At times he is literally earth-bound, not having the coordination necessary to lift both feet from the ground at once. Frequently, he stands at the sidelines in childhood games, or if he still attempts to play, he gets into trouble with his peers. A skilled occupational therapist or physio-therapist can often make good gains in this area.

When these many things are found in the various areas being checked, it is the educator's place to evaluate the nature and seriousness of such breakdowns in skill and, at times, devise a plan for correcting them as would the occupational therapist, the speech therapist, etc. In actuality, this is an ongoing and continuous process, as the teacher in such a class begins her program and checks her progress each day in planning for the activities of the next day.

Cognitive Abilities

Although the psychologist will make a thorough assessment of such abilities, the educator must also check the child's cognitive functioning at first hand. The child is asked to identify objects in pictures, describe the events taking place, and make projections into the past and future that are based on these events. He is also asked to identify the use of several common objects and to state the logical consequences of several common events. His auditory-vocal-associative abilities may be checked, though the psychologist will undoubtedly explore this in greater detail. Here again, the examiner is checking the child's ability in order to see how he manages himself, and to determine whether or not noticeable deviations, idiosyncracies, immaturities, or specific confusions and tangential thinking appear, and if so, what they portend for remediation. If severe or generalized deviations appear in this area, the child may require placement in a self-contained classroom or a residential setting. Less severe problems may be handled by individual tutoring in a given academic area, perhaps, while the child remains within the regular classroom.

The approach to the overall evaluation of such learning disabilities is a positive one. It admits to a present-day lack of understanding regarding human mental functioning, but it is also one that, despite these gaps in our own knowledge, does make every effort to collect the information that is pertinent to our attempts to increase our understanding of such disabilities and that can effect desirable changes in the child's performance, both academically and socially. The educator continuously seeks methods and techniques that will make it possible for the child to function in a more acceptable manner in his peer group.

The evaluational items given in this paper are planned to collect as much information as possible in a period of approximately one to two hours. If more is necessary, the child may need to be seen a second time; the educator may seek more information by classroom observations, or, as is the case in our particular setting, the child may be enrolled in a laboratory classroom program for extended observation. The educator's purpose in doing these many things is to help him in making the best possible decisions relative to educational placement and programing. When the educator's findings are brought together with the findings of other disciplines at the interdisciplinary conference, the child may be recommended for one of the following:

- referral to other personnel for further evaluation or therapy
- placement in readiness program
- placement in the regular grade with some preferential treatment
- supplementary tutoring in one or more of the academic areas
- placement in a self-contained classroom for children with learning disabilities
- placement in a homebound program
- residential placement

There are many remedial methods and programs available today for the child with a learning disability. This is in contrast to the situation just a very few years ago. The educator must be aware of and conversant with the many programs that exist, realizing that none "solve" the problem, mainly because there is not a single problem, but instead a multitude of factors operating to form different constellations in each instance.

Such methods and programs are more than likely helpful in part, and some in greater part than others for any given child. For this reason the educator must decide when, how, and if he should recommend the application of one or more methods or programs, and what direction to take from there. Examples of such methods and programs are:

- the Montessori Method, with efforts directed today towards adapting it to use with children having learning disabilities
- the Optometric Extension Program, which perceives that much benefit can be derived from exercises aimed at developing visual-motor competency
- the Marianne Frostig Program of Visual Perception, a series of activities that stress various aspects of visual perception
- the Winter Haven Program of Visual Perception, which includes motor based programs such as those of Newell Kephart, Ray Barsch, and A. Jean Ayres
- neurophysiologically based programs such as that of Glenn Doman and Carl Delacato
- auditory based programs such as those of Helmar Myklebust, Barry and Dorothy McGinnis
- the work done by Alfred Strauss and his co-workers, stressing stimulus reduction and structure of the educational materials and the environment
- academically based programs such as those of Anna Gillingham, Romalda Spalding, Grace Fernald, and Laura Lehtinen
- various remedial reading programs such as the one by Samuel Orton and ones by others using the Initial Teaching Alphabet, color cuing, phonics, visual methods of other kinds, and syllable methods of other kinds[10]

What has just been said about reading programs can also be said about methods in other school subjects such as the work done by Myklebust and Spalding in writing and the methods of Stern and Cuisenaire in arithmetic.[11] The decision to recommend specific techniques, activities, and materials will be made by the educator based upon his findings in the educational evaluation plus the additional contributions of the evaluational team at conferences, of the schools, of the parents, and any other valid sources.

NOTES

1. Katrina De Hirsch, Jeanette Jefferson Jansky, and William S. Langford, *Predicting Reading Failure: A Preliminary Study* (New York: Harper and Row, 1966); F. E. Lord and R. M. Isenberg, "Cooperative Programs in Special Education," The Council for Exceptional Children and the Department of Special Education, National Education Association (1964); Mary Nacol Meeker, *The Structure of Intellect: Its Interpretation and Uses* (Columbus, Ohio: Charles E. Merrill, 1969); Mary Pannebacker, "A Speech Pathologist Looks at Learning Disabilities," *Journal of Learning Disabilities* 1, no. 7 (July 1968), 403-409.
2. Morton Bortner, *Evaluation and Education of Children with Brain Damage* (Springfield, Ill.: Charles C. Thomas, 1968); Bessie Burgemeister, *Psychological Techniques in Neurological Diagnosis* (New York: Harper and Row, 1962); William M. Cruickshank, et al., *A Teaching Method for Brain Injured and Hyperactive Children* (Syracuse, N.Y.: Syracuse University Press, 1961), p. 256; R. R. Holt, *Diagnostic Psychological Testing*, rev. ed. (New York: International Universities Press, 1968).
3. Else Haeussermann, *Developmental Potential of Preschool Children: An Evaluation of Intellectual, Sensory, and Emotional Functioning* (New York: Grune and Stratton, 1958).
4. Ibid.
5. Ibid.
6. John I. Arena (ed.), *Building Spelling Skills in Dyslexic Children* (San Rafael, Calif.: Academic Therapy Publications, 1968).
7. Hirsch, Jansky, and Langford, *op. cit.;* Lydia A. Duggins, *Developing Children's Perceptual Skills in Reading* (Wilton, Conn.: Mediax, 1968).
8. Clark H. Millikan and Frederic L. Darley (eds.), *Brain Mechanisms Underlying Speech and Language* (New York: Grune and Stratton, 1967).
9. Laurence Peter, *Prescriptive Teaching* (New York: McGraw-Hill, 1965); Robert M. Smith, *Clinical Teaching: Methods of Instruction for the Retarded* (New York: McGraw-Hill, 1968).
10. Richard B. Adams, "Dyslexia: A Discussion of Its Definition," *Journal of Learning Disabilities*, no. 12 (December 1969), 616-633; MacDonald Critchley, *Developmental Dyslexia* (Springfield, Ill.: Charles C Thomas, Publisher, 1968); R. M. N. Crosby, with Robert A. Liston, *The Waysiders* (New York: Delacorte Press, Dell Publishing Co., 1968), pp. 11, 15; James L. McCarthy and Joan F. McCarthy, *Learning Disabilities* (Boston:

Allyn and Bacon, 1969); John Money (ed.), *The Disabled Reader: Education of the Dyslexic Child* (Baltimore: The Johns Hopkins Press, 1966); Patricia I. Myers and Donald D. Hammill, *Methods for Learning Disorders* (New York: John Wiley & Sons, 1969), Ch. 7.

11. Cuisenaire Company of America Incorporated, 9 Elm Ave., Mt. Vernon, New York; John Money, *op. cit.*; Helmar Myklebust, *Development and Disorders of Written Language*, Vol. II (New York: Grune and Stratton, 1967); Catherine Stern, *Structural Arithmetic* (Boston: Houghton Mifflin, 1965).

Five

Medical Practices

Medicine, although a very broad field, has certain facets that have a direct bearing on learning disabilities; those specialties having the most influence are, perhaps, neurology, pediatrics, and psychopharmacology. The role of the medical profession as related to the field of learning disabilities is to diagnose correlated organic factors that are treatable; the articles selected for inclusion here discuss the role of drugs and prevention and point out that the bulk of the treatment for children with learning disabilities is educational remediation.

Sylvia Richardson, physician and educator, brings her uncommon "common sense" to the discussion of the relationships between specific learning disabilities and neurological damage. She dispels the myth that all children with learning disabilities have brain damage. Instead she points out that some of them have known neurological problems, others have environmental, social, and emotional problems, and some have developmental lags without brain damage. She pleads with educators to emphasize direct teaching of basic language skills rather than substituting perceptual-motor and other nonlanguage programs. She points out interestingly that this field is not new, that psychologists Bronner in 1917 and Hollingworth in 1923 discussed the behavioral aspects of children with abilities vs. those with disabilities. Dr. Richardson makes a plea to educators that they emphasize in a frontal attack the remediation of basic language skills and be less concerned with etiology. Their job is to reclaim the children as their responsibility, not to define them into the realm of medicine.

Parents and others have become concerned about the excessive use of drugs in treating children with learning disabilities. A report on this topic, by Roger Freeman, is reproduced here. He has on several occasions reviewed and reported on studies of the effects of drugs on learning in children; his first review was published in the *Proceedings* of the Sixth Annual ACLD Conference, held in 1969 in Fort Worth, Texas. A later report at the 1974 Houston meeting is the one reprinted here.

The use of the neurological examination in the early diagnosis of "neurologically immature" children is discussed by Mark Ozer. The use of a screening scale designed for large scale use, requiring a total of fifteen minutes, is advocated and detailed. Dr. Ozer points out that the purpose of the neurological examination is to assess brain functions, including speed of learning, so that remediation can maximize the child's performance.

In the final paper in this section Richard Masland discusses some medical aspects of learning disabilities. He summarizes the literature on causation, showing some psychological differences between brain involvement and possible genetic disabilities. He also points out some areas of early identification and prevention.

Neurophysiological Management
of Children with Learning Disabilities

SYLVIA O. RICHARDSON

As a physician and as an educator, I have become deeply distressed by the widespread acceptance of the myth that a specific learning disability is actual evidence of neurological damage or disorder. Educators and psychologists today use medical terminology with abandon, and psychologists may even be heard discussing the "site of the lesion." Neurologists, on the other hand, may now be heard often discussing a child's particular behavior.

In diagnostic clinics, we see many children whose school difficulties are not always specific and not clearly related to neurologic impairment. They are unable to achieve in basic school skills in a regular classroom of thirty-five children with standard teaching techniques, yet they are of normal intelligence and have no organic problems. These youngsters are too often provided with labels, which vary according to geographic location, such as brain damage, minimal brain injury, minimal brain dysfunction, perceptual handicap, neurological handicap, aphasia, dyslexia, educational handicap, etc. The majority of these terms are of medical derivation, but the problem is pedagogical. A relatively small percentage of the children demonstrate clear evidence of neuropathology.

In many states physicians are required to certify that a normally intelligent but underachieving child has some neuropathology so that the schools can admit him to a special class. An electroencephalogram as well may be required by the Department of Special Education, despite the fact that most physicians do not consider this to be a particularly useful diagnostic tool in relation to learning. For educators to require a medical referral for special education, particularly when in the large majority of cases there is no palpable medical problem, is as incongruous as for physicians to require an educational referral for surgery.

Children who are unable to achieve in school, despite adequate sensory, motor, and intellectual capacities, are an extremely heterogeneous group. To label them all brain-damaged, dyslexic, minimal brain dysfunction, etc., furthers the overwhelming current confusion. If we must place a child in a diagnostic category, we should try to use a term that does not imply a specific etiology—especially not a medical term (unless, of course, it applies in a particular case).

In his book, *Brain Damage in Children,* Herbert Birch writes:

. . . the category [brain damage] is entirely behavioral and implies that any of a number of kinds of cerebral damage will result in a common pattern of behav-

From the *Proceedings* of the Sixth Annual Conference of the ACLD, *Progress in Parent Information, Professional Growth, and Public Policy.* Fort Worth, Texas (March 6–8, 1969), pp. 27–31.

ioral disturbance. Locus of injury, nature of the lesion, and the temporal course of the illness are usually not considered in the designation, and the nonbehavioral, neurologic confirmation of the fact of anatomic insult has been conspicuous by its absence. These considerations make it clear that the term brain damaged refers to a behavior syndrome and not to the fact of brain damage as such.[1]

With regard to the easy equating of neurological insults and inability to learn, there are quite a few reported case studies which can hardly be ignored. In 1943, for example, R. K. Byers and E. E. Lord followed fifteen children of normal intelligence who had acquired lead poisoning in their school years.[2] Although thirteen of these brain-injured children were failing in school, there was no positive correlation between IQ and school success. One child with an IQ of 109, the highest of the group, was failing; another child with an IQ of 82 was doing very well. Although marked behavior and attention deficits were noted along with problems in visual perception and visual-motor coordination, Byers and Lord reported that they found adequate reading skills in these brain-damaged children.

In 1947, S. S. Ackerly and A. L. Benton reported an individual who had been considered to be an emotionally disturbed child and who presented many behavior problems in and out of school, yet who had no difficulty with reading and had average intelligence.[3] When this patient was twenty years of age, pneumoencephalography, followed by intracranial surgery, showed that he had absence of both frontal lobes and probably some temporal lobe damage as well. Of particular note, electroencephalographic findings were within normal limits. These are but two examples. Many similar ones are available.

On the other hand, as Birch reminds us in his book, we must not "throw the baby out with the bath water," and the problem must not be minimized because of current lack of diagnostic clarity. At present, the term "specific learning disabilities" seems to cover at least three groups of children:

- Those with known, or frank, brain injury, who show clear-cut neurologic deficits. The history usually reveals the cause of the injury, such as prenatal toxicity, birth trauma, anoxia, encephalitis, or head injury, etc.
- Children with exogenous problems, such as severe environmental, social, and emotional difficulties which interfere with learning.
- Those with what may be termed a developmental or maturational lag, which in itself may be accompanied by other signs of immaturity, in "soft" neurological signs, and in a peculiar configuration of psychological test findings. A lag does not imply that, if left to himself and nature, a child will either catch up or just continue to lag along. Such a deviation or unripeness will necessitate special help in the early school years to assist the child to acquire the preacademic and then the basic skills, as he goes along. (Optimally, all children should be allowed time plus flexible teaching via multisensorial avenues in the primary grades).

That a developmental or maturational lag may have an hereditary anlage or predisposition is quite possible. That minimal insults to the brain during the prenatal or neonatal periods might complicate, or even create, such developmental problems is equally possible. Such questions, however, are academic. The child and his educational needs are the reality which educators must accept.

Regardless of why or how a child got where he is (or is not) educationally, the teacher must work with him at his level, at his pace, and with specific techniques to which the child can respond, via the sensory modalities through which he best learns.

This presentation embodies two pleas. First, we must stop using medical terminology and medical thinking in education. The physician is trained to think in terms of etiology and pathology. He cannot treat his patients adequately unless he knows the cause of the disease, the site, and the nature of the pathology. Symptomatic treatment in medicine is temporary and palliative, at best. The teacher, on the other hand, must help the child where he is today—she cannot wait until someone, or some team, arrives at a cause, which may still be only hypothetical. Symptomatic treatment in education can be therapeutic. Teaching is in itself ongoing diagnosis along with treatment. Parenthetically, if a teacher is told that a child's electroencephalogram shows paroxysmal dysrhythmia, non-focal, how will this influence her choice of teaching methods or her approach to the child?

This is not to say that there is no value in the etiologic or medical approach. However, it must be kept in mind that *the purpose of medical evaluation is to determine the presence or absence of organic factors which can be treated medically or ameliorated.* The multidisciplinary teams established to evaluate children with learning disabilities can provide medical evaluation and behavioral assessment—which includes psychological, language, and educational evaluation—but it is still the classroom teacher's responsibility to teach the child. Hopefully, the results of the diagnostic evaluation will add to her understanding of the child and will assist her in teaching him.

Physicians, psychologists, and educators must continue to be concerned with, and active in, research, which moves slowly. Also, they must convey their results in useful form to teachers. Meanwhile, teachers must not stop teaching children, and every child should be provided with a thorough medical and educational evaluation prior to school entry in order to rule out any organic problem and to try to determine his particular style of learning, his particular stage of ripeness for undertaking the academic program provided in the primary grades.

My second plea is for education to resume the standard frontal attack on the academic deficiencies of children with specific learning disabilities. The many perceptual-motor programs now in vogue are good, but they must not be used as substitutes for the careful educational diagnosis and direct teaching of basic language skills (listening, speaking, reading, writing, and arithmetic). They could in fact be added to the regular curriculum for all primary-grade pupils and should be considered as specific additions for children of any age who demonstrate serious deficiencies in school skills or the general behavioral skills necessary for success in school.

In relation to this, we must not delude ourselves by believing that we have come up with a lot of new teaching techniques and new ideas in education. If we would read our *old* literature it would become embarrassingly evident that we simply have added new packaging. In 1917, for example, Augusta Bronner, a child psychologist, published the *Psychology of Special Abilities and Disabilities,* in which she stated:

It may be said that analysis of the reading process shows that there are involved (a) perception of form and sound, and discrimination of forms and sounds; (b) association of sounds with visually perceived letters, of names with groups of symbols, and of meanings with groups of words; (c) memory, motor, visual, and auditory factors, and (d) the motor processes as used in inner speech and in reading aloud. Reviewing the whole process, we see that in the actual performance of reading there must be finally some synthetic process uniting all the separate elements. This is a point that has been little emphasized by students of the psychology of reading, but its validity and importance seem clearly established throughout analysis of cases of special difficulty in reading. Analysis of the mental processes involved in reading has never been applied to individual cases of inability to learn to read, so far as we know. The fact that some individuals have a pronounced disability in this field has been observed, it is true. It is exceedingly interesting to find that neurologists and even ophthalmologists have dealt with this question far more than psychologists.[4]

In 1923, Leta Hollingworth, an educational psychologist, stated in her book, *Special Talents and Defects:*

We see, therefore, that nonreaders, of general intelligence much above the minimum level required for reading, do learn to read when special training is given. This training may stress phonics (Schmitt), it may stress the motor and kinaesthetic avenues of approach (Fernald and Keller), or it may stress visual perception (Gates). It may or may not proceed by use of the old "alphabet" method (Hinshelwood). . . . In fact, no investigator has established his or her method as the only successful approach to particular cases, by excluding other methods through experimental teaching. . . . For nonreaders such as have been described under the criteria laid down by the investigators quoted, it seems highly probable that the best method would be that wherein all avenues of approach are fully utilized.[5]

Prior to Bronner and Hollingworth, there were many others who provided the broad matrix of teaching techniques from which our current "package plans" or "cookbooks" in remedial education have derived: Itard; Sequin; Montessori; even Comenius in 1657; Quintillian in 90 A.D., who taught the Roman soldiers to write using grooved wax tablets with a stylus; and many others.

Education must reclaim the children called specific learning disabilities, etc., instead of defining them out of the realm of education into the realm of medicine. Although the number of teachers especially trained to work with these children in a self-contained classroom is relatively small, there is a wealth of information, techniques, and material available to all teachers. Our task for the future must include appropriate revisions of both general and special education by way of such facilities as the ungraded primary, transitional classes, resource teachers—such as tutors and diagnostic-remedial specialists—liaison educators, resource rooms, language laboratories, and both preschool and parent-education programs designed to prepare our children for the academic process.

If we insist that every child must start school at the age of six years, it is the schools' responsibility to see that every child learns the basic skills—the tools with which he learns to learn—in the way which is best for him and at his own pace. Until we achieve this goal, until we hold ourselves responsible for appropriate teaching, we have no right to place the entire burden on the child. Is the child not learning, or is he simply unable to learn what the teacher wants him to learn, in the way that she teaches him and in the standard amount of time the curriculum provides? Do all of these children have "learning disabilities"? Many of them may have "teaching disabilities." Perhaps we should concentrate less on the child's disabilities and focus our concerted attention on his readiness for school and possible revisions of the current lockstep system of primary education.

As a postscript, perhaps those of us who are parents should concentrate more on our child's abilities and his total development as a self-respecting, productive human being. Although he may have difficulty learning school subjects, he is nevertheless constantly learning in other respects. Parents should strive, not to tutor and nag, but to provide a nourishing, nurturing emotional climate in which the child can enjoy learning and living.

NOTES

1. Herbert C. Birch, *Brain Damage in Children: The Biological and Social Aspects* (Baltimore: Williams and Wilkins, 1964).
2. R. K. Byers and E. E. Lord, "Late Effects of Lead Poisoning on Development," *American Journal of Diseases of Children* 66 (1943), 471-493.
3. S. S. Ackerly and A. L. Benton, "Report of a Case of Bilateral Frontal Lobe Defect," *Proceedings, Association for Research on Nervous and Mental Diseases* 27 (1947), 479-504.
4. Augusta Bronner, *Psychology of Special Abilities and Disabilities* (New York: Columbia Teachers College Press, 1917).
5. Leta Hollingworth, *Special Talents and Defects* (New York: Columbia Teachers College Press, 1923).

Medical Management and the Politics of Learning Disabilities

ROGER FREEMAN

A few words are necessary first to spell out certain assumptions about the causes and assessment of children with learning disabilities.

The *causes* of learning disorders are many, and attempts to arrive at consensus about which are most important have failed. Learning itself is a process which is obviously complex and difficult to define. Many erudite papers and books have been written which have also been subjected to erudite and sometimes emotional criticism. The problem of definition and causes has also been complicated by the fact that the child is a developing organism exquisitely sensitive to its family and social matrix. Another less-frequently discussed factor is the preference of some workers for a particular theory, perhaps based upon their training or special experience: it is not too difficult to select data which will support a wide variety of theories of causation.

I will assume that generally *we do not know the cause* in any true sense of having a full explanation. We must manage the problem despite uncertainty. This is an unpopular view.

The *assessment* of learning disorders is also quite varied, depending upon one's preference and experience. Obviously there are many models to choose from, none of them so clearly superior as to wipe out the competition. It could be quite amusing to watch us "experts" arrive at some kind of conclusion about a child, were the results not so often deleterious.

Here I assume that one needs to look at many different areas of a child's functioning, but that no one has arrived at an accepted minimum or maximum in the number and variety of professionals and tests to be applied. This situation permits us all to have endless discussions and debates, but may often be quite confusing to the parents who are less concerned with academic points.

One must, however, give professionals credit for imagination. There are some of us who believe that the symbolic shape of certain letters sets off emotional conflicts which impede the reading process. There are others who can find indications in the history, description of behavior, and physical functioning to invoke a mystical notion of "minimal brain dysfunction," beloved of pharmaceutical manufacturers, since the term can be nicely shortened to "MBD" which is an almost automatic reminder to try a drug. Others test children's vision and suggest exercises, finding reason to do so

Presented at the Tenth International Conference of the ACLD, Detroit, Mich. (March 14–17, 1973).

in the majority of cases they evaluate. We even hear of subclinical epilepsy, subclinical low blood sugar ("hypoglycemia"), and subclinical vitamin deficiencies and allergies as major causes with their appropriate therapeutic regimens. And so it goes. Of course, each of us is well-trained, well-intentioned, rational, and anxious to help!

I must confess that I almost hesitate to teach students about learning disabilities, because the situation is so confused that to give them any "facts" which they desire to pass their exams would require falsification. And what of parents? Do they suffer from this rather ludicrous mess? I believe many of them do. Those whose children do well under whatever system of management will be grateful and may even advise it for others. But what about those not so fortunate? Don't they go from one system to another, hoping each will have the answer? Don't some of them become "true believers" despite *lack* of much success? Perhaps this is just self-protection, for otherwise they would have to doubt our helpfulness, and feel hopeless.

If you look hard enough at a child and family, you can probably find something to label "an emotional problem." This has been done for years with infantile autism, for example. And probably such children *do* have a higher incidence of problems than average children. But what does that really mean? If you then look at a child's lateral preference, or balance, or eye muscles, or "soft signs," or EEG, or psychological test patterns, you may also find all sorts of things. In some cases you may be able to show a statistically significant excess of such findings in the learning disability group, as compared with the general population. But what does *this* really mean? *What is the learning disability group?* It isn't really a group with much in common among its members. And generally there is much overlap when this "group" is compared with another, so that the "statistically significant findings" may not help a lot when dealing with an individual case.

You may think I have set up a straw man or exaggerated the situation. You may also think I am simply a nihilist who is overly critical of the realities of science and practice, and unappreciative of the efforts of many workers in the field. And all of this may be true. But I think somehow you have to keep a sense of humor on the one hand, and a sense of outrage on the other, mixed with occasional respect and great flexibility in the face of great uncertainty. If you start taking too much very seriously at this time in our development of knowledge and services, I think you're in trouble.

One assumption I think needs to be challenged again and again. Test and examination conditions which are "standard" are employed to enable us to state that the observed findings, deviations, etc., are *within the subject.* This is convenient, and much of clinical practice is based upon this belief. But I don't really believe it. An excellent book which discusses this point in detail is available (Friedman, 1967). Furthermore, I have to extend my cynical remarks even further to state that I have doubts about much of the published clinical research. I have participated in research projects both as an assistant, an observer, a subject, and a principal investigator, as well as a critic. And I don't like very much of what I have seen. I find rather little in the published results which indicates how sloppy the research was, yet that degree of sloppiness is the very thing which makes the findings (no matter how elegant the methodology and statistics) highly questionable.

I readily confess that these points are nasty, for they suggest I have little faith in my fellow professional; but being a gentleman is less important to me than reality.

I am saying that much more of science is corrupt than we like to admit, and that it is corrupt because it is performed by humans. It is strange that everyone expects politicians to be corrupt . . . but not scientists. And why not? Don't scientists have to get grants, render reports, impress others as well as themselves, make money, climb the professional or academic ladder, and feel well-intentioned despite all the corners they have to cut to do these things? The scientific method unfortunately cannot prevent these factors from having some effect.

As a consultant to the U.S. Food and Drug Administration I had a number of enlightening experiences which have added to my cynicism.[2] These experiences will undoubtedly put me in opposition to other writers, but this is probably a good thing.

Well, what *is* the physician's role in the management of learning disorders? Given the uncertainties described above, the physician can:

- Use his power and authority to take an adequate history, perform a physical examination, and obtain other components of an assessment. In doing this, he will have to make sure that he doesn't depend upon information from *one* teacher, *one* parent, or *one* setting.
- In sorting out this information, he will have to keep in mind that unrecognized sensory (visual, auditory) deficits and medical conditions (such as chronic kidney disease, anemia, etc.) could cause or contribute to the learning difficulty. This should be one major area of application for his expertise.
- He will have to be aware that no one type of problem excludes the possibility that another, still unrecognized, may be more important. Thus, finding indications of "emotional problems" or "brain dysfunction" might be fine, but not necessarily the whole story.
- He will do better if he gains the child's, family's, and school's confidence and rapport. He then may learn something of great value in understanding the case, which was not provided in a report or in a first interview.
- He will recognize that ongoing situations, such as school, may provide a much better setting for assessment than his office or the psychologist's one-shot tests.
- He can find out the family members' attitudes and fears about the

problem which might not be a cause but could be a contributing factor. What they have done about it is also of importance. He may have to recognize, however, that he has neither the time nor the expertise to accomplish this.

- Somehow he must find out which professionals in his community are helpful, rather than depending upon paper qualifications. This is tricky, but realistic. It would probably be wise to avoid "true believers" who always use the same methods and claim wonderful results from them. Gradually he will confirm or disconfirm his view of a particular professional's helpfulness.

- As a picture of the problem in its various temporal and geographical settings emerges, the physician will have to decide how extensive to make the assessment and how large the "team" should be; naturally, this decision may not be his to make, since other disciplines may have the primary role. He may consider specialist evaluations in the area of neurology and psychiatry as well as psychoeducational work which is probably of more general usefulness.

- He should avoid blaming parents for their errors, but can help them see where a shift in management might possibly be useful. Most parents can tolerate quite a bit of uncertainty, and do not need false labels, provided they feel supported and engaged in constructive help.

- Psychopharmacologic agents are of some use, although how much will require individual trials. Drugs should *not* be used as short-cuts, although this assertion is somewhat controversial. The indications for *stimulant* drug use are probably: child is not psychotic, does not have need to engage in the undesirable behavior for psychodynamic reasons, has certain "target symptoms" which may be modified by drug use—overactivity, short attention span, or distractibility; singly, or in combination. The presence of "organic" signs is probably *Not* of great importance. *Major tranquilizers* are often more predictable in reducing psychomotor overactivity, but may not favorably affect attention span and distractibility; they are preferred for psychotic children.

The physician is inevitably left with the reality that he himself may not have a great role to play in the long-term management of most children with learning disabilities. But he can still do a great deal to facilitate an adequate assessment, obtain better services in his community, and help the family in certain types of crisis. He can also, by virtue of his position, *prevent* these things from happening and cause much trouble. In a sense, the problem of the learning-disabled child and the physician is the problem of medical training and practice in the face of any chronic disability: he has to know his limits, the assets and liabilities of his colleagues, and the controversies in etiology, assessment, and management. As soon as he retreats from his responsibilities in remaining humble yet helpful, he violates the basic medical axiom *"primum non nocere"* (above all, do no harm).

REFERENCES

FREEMAN, R. D. "Drug Research: Out of Sight, Out of Mind," *J. Spec. Educ.* 7 (1973), 223-228.

FRIEDMAN, N. *The Social Nature of Psychological Research: The Psychological Experiment as a Social Interaction* (New York: Basic Books, 1967).

Early Diagnosis of Children with Neurological Problems Relating to Learning Disabilities

MARK N. OZER

The neurological examination has been developed over the past one hundred years as a means of identifying asymmetries of function. The focus has been on identifying differences between the two sides of the body as clues for localization of abnormalities. The presence of weakness and sensory deficits, and the particular patterns of such dysfunction, serve to indicate both the side affected and the level of the nervous system which is affected. The examination has primarily served as an instrument for the diagnosis of acute neurological disease. Originally developed for use in adult neurology, it has been adapted for the diagnosis of the fortunately less common acute neurological problems of children such as tumors and vascular disease.

It is in the delineation of the large number of children with developmental lags that the traditional neurological examination has been less useful. The child differs in that injury, albeit frequently conjectural, had occurred at some point early in its development. Perinatal experience has been considered as a major opportunity for injury. However, opportunities for injury must, of course, have come about at any point during gestation and from the very process of fertilization. The results of such injury must be considered in a continuum of time to a greater degree than in the adult. It is a function of both the degree of insult to the organism and the repair possible as a function of growth and maturation.

The effects of such injury are frequently bilateral rather than focal. They may be evident in organization of several different aspects of development. They are displayed primarily in the context of time by the lags shown in meeting the milestones of life.

The aim has been to delineate those children who are functioning considerably below age level. The so-called "immature child" should be identified early in his school career. The usual procedure has been to provide him with a "trial of school," comparable to the trial of labor in obstetrics. Only after several years of failure would he be identified and placed in classes more specifically designed for his needs. Several years of failure with attendant emotional disturbance would have become superimposed by then. The development of a neurological examination should focus on identifying these "neurologically immature" children early in their school career by means of a screening examination to be done on a large scale.

From the *Proceedings* of the Fourth Annual Conference of the ACLD, *Management of the Child with Learning Disabilities: An Interdisciplinary Challenge*. New York (March 9–11, 1967), pp. 27–29.

The examination of motor performance has been the traditional measure of brain function in the child. The usual motor milestones of sitting, walking, etc., are well known. More recently, emphasis has been placed upon the time of cessation of the normal neonatal automatisms as a measure of the degree of organization and integration of the nervous system. These methods are quite useful in delineating those whose injuries have been more gross. The range of normal which is permitted may, however, vary within a rather wide range. The child approaching school age may have met these early milestones. In contrast, the range of behaviors required in a school setting may be relatively narrow. Manipulating a pencil for writing, for example, requires relatively fine movements. Progressively more integrated motor activity is expected with increasing maturation of the nervous system. There has been no easily administered standardized examination for the identification of the child with significant motor clumsiness.

The neurological examination for the identification of children with lags in development must then provide for the sampling of the more subtle but relevant motor disabilities. To this end, a standardized, scorable motor examination has been developed and norms established for age groups from four and one-half to eight. It focuses on testing for coordination of finer movements. Items from the Oseretsky scale have been selected that are most applicable to the age groups considered to be at risk.[1] The motor examination also includes items which have been useful in the general neurologic examination but have been made standardized and more easily scorable.

The motor examination is a relevant and frequently used measure of brain function. It is not, however, necessarily the most relevant measure of potential learning problems. The child with significant motor clumsiness may be considered to be at risk but the relationship need not be one to one. There are many relatively clumsy people who do quite well in learning school materials. There are also, of course, many relatively adept people who have considerable difficulty in their school performance.

Our feeling was that a neurological examination should not limit itself to the motor testing alone. It was necessary for this screening-type instrument to be more reflective of the actual behaviors to be sought in the school. It also might provide an opportunity for delineating the strengths and weaknesses in a fashion directly translatable to the channels available for instruction.

One such task then would be measures of the child's ability to organize his spatial environment. Tests of right-left orientation have been used for this purpose. Our concern was to identify those children whose performance was inconsistent. It appeared that large numbers of normal children below six were inaccurate in their identification of the right and left portions of their body according to the usual convention. However, they were consistent in their application of a particular label, be it right or left, to a particular side of the body. A much smaller percentage, felt to be at greater risk, were those who were inconsistent in their application of these labels.

They might identify a particular side as their right side and then again their left. The relative randomness of their performance was felt to be potentially reflective of disability in the school setting.

Other tasks involve the following of directions involving crossing the midline. This is intrinsically a more difficult performance than identification of body parts. It involves the clear-cut discrimination of both right and left and the concept of crossing over. It is, to a considerable degree, a measure of listening behavior which might have considerable relevance to the child's readiness to follow verbal instruction in the school setting. The scoring does not penalize errors in identifying the correct sides of the body but rather the failure to get the idea that differential labels are applied and to discriminate between them. There is an opportunity for the child to learn the requirements of the task by some instructions which, by their very nature, involve crossing over. An example would be "cross your left leg over your right knee." His ability to use these cues then raises his score above the level which is considered to be evidence of "immaturity."

Other tasks deal with the ability to separate visual materials where there is a problem of visual figure-ground confusion. The H-R-R pseudo-isochromatic plates have been used for this purpose. Initially designed for color-blindness studies, they have served as measures of visual confusion. The procedure is to teach the child the simple act of tracing these figures on the initial cards. He is then required to identify, by tracing, the same geometric forms which had been previously taught. He is not penalized by failure to draw the form with complete accuracy. We are concerned primarily with the fact that he sees the form as distinct from its background. This is felt to be relevant to the ability to organize visual perceptions in a fashion appropriate to the needs of the school. As before, we have provided an opportunity for the child to learn the requirements of the task prior to testing him.

Along with the auditory and visual channels we test the child's performance when utilizing more complex tactile cues. In this task he is required to write the same simple geometric forms previously utilized in the visual testing. They are now traced on the palm of his hand. A series of three trials is provided for each. They include a straight line, circle, cross, and triangle. The scoring involves the number of trials required for each of these forms to be done accurately. An opportunity is provided for the learning of the requirements of the task and the rate of learning is then measured as the score.

The rate of learning is perhaps the most relevant measure of brain function. The clinical examination must then provide opportunities for learning to occur for that is also what school is very much about. Other tasks have been used for this purpose. The face-hand test is one such measure. In this, the child is required to pick up two stimuli simultaneously. A series of learning trials are provided to learn the set of pointing to the site touched and the two stimuli are provided simultaneously. This is done with touch applied to the dorsum of both hands in full view of the child. Following this, touch is applied to the cheek and hand in a random series with the eyes closed. Repetition of the initial cues is provided if he fails to learn within the first series of trials. If he has not learned within ten trials, touch is applied with his eyes open. The scoring reflects the number of trials required for learning.

Still another task attempts to simulate still further the conditions under which learning must occur in the school setting. This deals with the ability to tune out an irrelevant stimulus as a measure of distractibility. In this sound-touch test, sound is applied to the ear in the form of snapping fingers along with touch applied to the hand. He is instructed to point to the place touched. Cues are provided and the inability to tune out the irrelevant sound stimulus is reflected in the scoring.

All these items are done simply without any elaborate apparatus. The testing requires a total of fifteen minutes and can be done on a large scale. Instructions are provided both for administration and scoring. The aim is to measure performance in the child as related to those functions which might have greatest relevance to the conditions one would be predicting. Whenever possible, the child is provided an opportunity for learning the set required. The neurological examination thus is an attempt to simulate in the clinical setting that which school is about. The child who does not have the behavior consistent with his age level may be considered as "immature." He lacks the requisite behaviors which are present in his contemporaries of school age. One must delineate those children who are at risk so that programs can be more specifically designed to make up the behaviors they now lack. Moreover, the attempt is made to identify those behaviors which are immature and the channels by which performance may be enhanced. The diagnosis of "immaturity" does not, however, permit the process of "maturation" to be considered a passive one. One does not mature by the very fact that one grows older. Considerable teaching goes on, albeit implicitly, in the home as well as the school. One may speed up the process by being explicitly aware of the needs of the children who are at risk and programing to their level, doing so via the channels most readily available. One has then avoided the trial of school with its attendant frustrations.

The aim, then, of the neurological examination is to provide a measure to be done on a large scale. It provides a more dynamic assessment of brain function in a way that leads to the process by which the child's present level of performance may be maximized.

NOTE

1. N. Oseretsky and William Sloan, *Lincoln-Oseretsky Motor Development Scale* (Chicago, Ill.: C. H. Stoetling, 1948).

Learning Disabilities: Medical Aspects

RICHARD L. MASLAND

It always makes me uncomfortable to participate in a multidisciplinary symposium where I feel called upon to defend one or another approach to the complex problems of the learning disabilities, for I feel that each of us should be concerned with the total child and his spectrum of problems. Yet I must recognize that each discipline has its own emphasis. Thus, the educator, faced with the immediate practical problem of helping the disabled child, is not so much interested in how he got that way. His concern is for how he is now—what are his actual performance strengths and deficits, and how can they be remedied. The physician on the other hand can afford a more detached and possibly long-term view. He is more inclined to ask "what disease is responsible for this picture?" In addition, he will be preoccupied with the chemical and structural basis of the disorder and the chemical and physical means of remediation rather than the educational ones.

What have we learned about causation? Let me cite just one study of many which may throw light on this question (see Table 1).

Table 1. CHARACTERISTICS OF CHILDREN REFERRED BECAUSE OF LEARNING DISABILITIES

STUDY OF 164 "FAILING" CHILDREN AGE 7+

not failing	54
retarded	19
psychological	9
true reading failure	82
(reading only)	63
(reading and arithmetic)	22

Adapted from T. T. S. Ingram, "The Nature of Dyslexia." In *Early Experience and Visual Information Processing in Perceptual and Reading Disorders* (Washington, D.C.: National Academy of Sciences, 1970).

This table summarizes the results of a study of 164 children referred to Dr. T. T. S. Ingram for school failure. Of this group, 73 suffered from mental retardation or specific sensory deficit, and were not properly categorized as LD. Nine were failing because of a primary emotional problem.

From the *Proceedings* of the Second Western Regional Conference of the ACLD and The California Association for Neurologically Handicapped Children, *State of the Art: Where Are We in Learning Disabilities?* (February 3, 1973). ACLD and CANHC publications, copyright © 1974, pp. 9-22.

Only 82 of this group were actually LD. Dr. Ingram divided this group into two categories—those whose only failure was in reading and spelling, and those who had a more general failure, including arithmetic. When he compared these two groups (Figure 1), he found significant differences

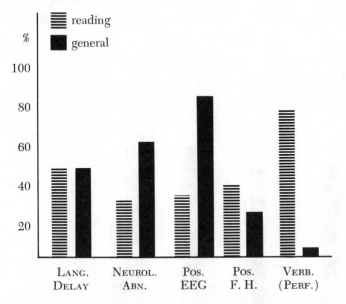

Figure 1. COMPARISON OF CHARACTERISTICS OF CHILDREN WITH READING DISABILITY ONLY AND THOSE WITH A "GENERAL" DISABILITY IN-CLUDING READING AND ARITHMETIC

Adapted from T. T. S. Ingram, "The Nature of Dyslexia." In *Early Experience and Visual Information Processing in Perceptual and Reading Disorders* (Washington, D. C.: National Academy of Sciences, 1970).

in their characteristics. Among those with reading disability only, there was a higher proportion with positive family history. Those with a more general deficit were more likely to have a history and finding suggestive of previous insult to the brain. Those with the pure reading disability had, on the average, a higher performance than verbal IQ, those with the more general deficit had, on the average, a higher verbal score. Finally, those with pure reading disability were inclined to have particular difficulty with establishing verbal associations, the "general" group showed greater difficulty in perceptual-motor skills. It is of note that over half the children in each group had previously exhibited a delay in learning to talk.

Ingram's study is only a beginning effort to establish and characterize subtypes of learning disability—there are other studies too numerous to mention with other approaches and other subtypes, yet Ingram's is of special importance in that it documents the existence of a genetic factor and of an injury factor, and that there may be demonstrable differences in the performance pattern which they produce. But this is only a statistical analysis, and these are wide areas of overlap. Probably more often than not, the child's performance today results from the interaction of his inherited constitution—more or less modified by disease or injury, and the social environment—his lifetime of training and experience.

There is plenty of evidence that each of these elements is important (Figure 2). Studies of twins (Shields, 1962) reveal the remarkable

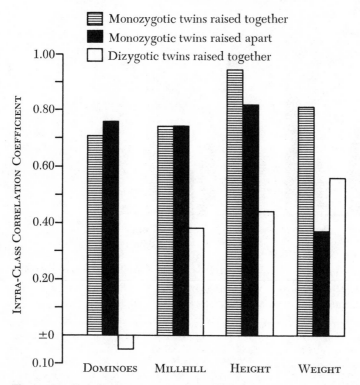

Figure 2. Resemblances between Twins

From James Shields, *Monozygotic Twins* (New York: Oxford University Press, 1962).

similarities of the intellectual abilities of those with identical inheritance. Retrospective studies (Figure 3) show that within a population of children with LD, there has been an increased frequency of those perinatal conditions known to be associated with impairment of development. The EEG (Figure 4) also suggests some subtle deviation of brain function in a significant proportion of those with LD, although this test must be recognized as an indicator of brain function, not necessarily a reflection of deviant brain structure or anatomy.

It is encouraging that for some of these conditions, medical science has found a means for prevention. The impairments due to neonatal jaundice are now largely preventable. Those due to maternal rubella need never

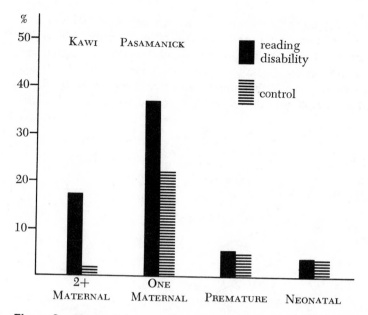

Figure 3. Frequency of Perinatal Complications in the History of Children with Reading Disabilities and Controls

From A. A. Kawi and B. Pasamanick, "Association of Factors of Pregnancy with Reading Disorders of Childhood," *Journal of American Medical Association* 166 (1958), 1420–1423.

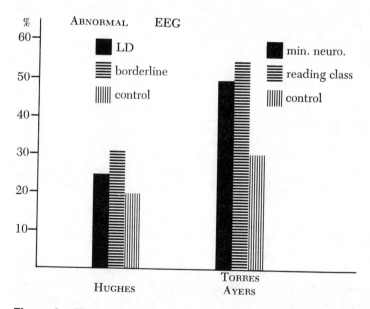

Figure 4. Frequency of Abnormal EEG in Children with Learning Disability

Adapted from J. R. Hughes, in Helmar Myklebust, *Progress in Learning Disabilities*, vol. 2. (New York: Grune and Stratton, 1971); and F. Torres and F. W. Ayres, "Evaluation of the EEG of Dyslexic Children," *Journal of Electroencephalography and Clinical Neurophysiology* 24 (1968), 287.

recur, that is if people take the trouble to be vaccinated. Probably one of our most significant remaining problems is that of prematurity (Figure 5). It is of interest that in this study, the small babies showed a significant impairment of the Bender Gestalt—a test which Jansky and de Hirsch (1972) have shown to be highly predictive of reading disability. Some prematurity, for example that due to smoking, could be prevented. Gross

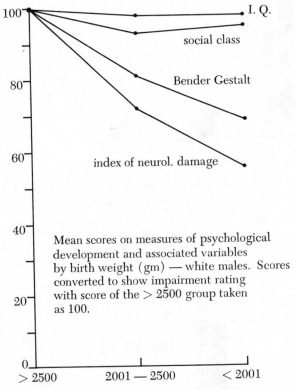

Mean scores on measures of psychological development and associated variables by birth weight (gm) — white males. Scores converted to show impairment rating with score of the > 2500 group taken as 100.

Figure 5. Effects of Low Birth Weight on Test Scores at Age Four

From G. Wiener, R. V. Rider, W. C. Oppel, L. C. Fischer, and P. A. Harper, "Correlates of Low Birth Weight: Psychological Status at Six to Seven Years of Age," *Pediatrics* 35 (1965), 434–444.

malnutrition, both prenatal and postnatal, is clearly related to stunting of growth, and the brain is especially vulnerable (Figure 6). Even in the U.S.A., a relation between physical growth and intellectual ability is evident (Figure 7). How much does this account for the vast differences of intellectual performance that separate the underprivileged and the undereducated from those more favored?

I am aware that in the above examples I have made little distinction between the problems of overall mental retardation and the specific limited deficits which characterize the child with LD. I suspect, however, that in

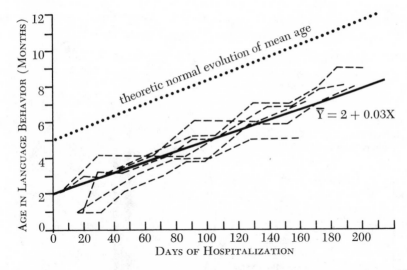

Figure 6. IMPAIRMENT OF INTELLECTUAL DEVELOPMENT AFTER NUTRITIONAL DEPRIVATION DURING FIRST SIX MONTHS OF LIFE. *Graph shows failure of language behavior to approach normal evolution during 200 days of hospital treatment.*

From H. G. Birch and J. D. Gussow, *Disadvantaged Children* (New York: Grune and Stratton, 1970).

general, the causative factors are similar—the symptomatology depending upon whether the developmental or environmental factor has been localized or general in its action on the brain. It would appear from Ingram's data, that, especially in the area of reading disability, we are dealing more with a hereditary developmental factor than with one of brain injury per se. Recent research on brain function, combined with more precise analysis of the nature of the reading task now provides an opportunity for a better understanding of what some of these limited deficits or "idiosyncracies" may be.

Of particular interest is recently acquired information regarding the differences of function of the two halves of the cerebrum of the brain (Figure 8). It has long been known that the language function resides in the left hemisphere (Figure 9). It has only recently been appreciated the extent to which recognition of form and spatial relationships is a specialty of the right hemisphere (Nebes, 1972). It is my suspicion that the left hemisphere specializes in the analysis of the temporal sequence of events. The right is concerned with the static display of parallel events. The latter are exemplified by the spatial array of the visual fields as projected to the occipital cortex, and by the similar array of the somesthetic sensations in the parietal region. In each instance, the cortex appears to serve as a map representing the appropriate projected pattern. The recognition and analysis of such spatial arrays is most effectively mediated by the right hemisphere (Sperling, 1970). Thus, although most people are right

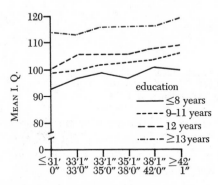

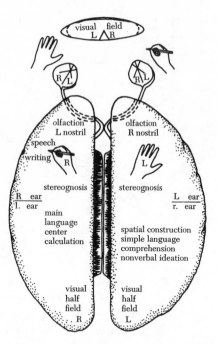

Figure 7. RELATION BETWEEN BODY
WEIGHT AND IQ AT AGE
FOUR, ACCORDING TO MA-
TERNAL EDUCATION

From R. L. Masland, "Mental Retardation
in Relation to Post-Natal Events," *Trans.
XII International Congress of Pediatrics* 1
(1968), 566–587.

Figure 8. REPRESENTATION OF COG-
NITIVE FUNCTIONS IN THE
CEREBRAL CORTEX OF
MAN

From R. W. Sperry, "Cerebral Dominance
in Perception." In *Early Experience and
Visual Information Processing in Perceptual
and Reading Disorders* (Washington, D. C.:
National Academy of Sciences, 1970).

handed, it is not generally appreciated that for activities requiring tactile
discrimination, the *left* hand is best (Rudel and Denckla, in press). The
distinction between right and left hemisphere functions is possibly best
exemplified by the carpenter. With his left hand he holds the nail—a static
event requiring tactile discrimination; with his right hand he performs the
complex sequence of movements of the hammer.

It is possible that a similar, but even more complex dichotomy exists
within the single area of audition. The comprehension of *pitch* is dependent
upon a spatial array on the cerebral cortex—the sense organ in the ear
having almost a point-to-point projection to the brain comparable to that
of the skin. The appreciation of *tone*, thus, depends upon the area of the
sense organ of the ear which is stimulated, and in this sense is dependent
upon a spatial and not a temporal analysis. This analysis is primarily accomplished in the right hemisphere (Figure 10). Removal of the right
temporal lobe leads to a greater impairment of analysis of timber and of
tonal memory than does removal of the left.

On the other hand, the interpretation of speech sounds is unquestionably most effectively mediated within the left hemisphere. This has been interpreted to mean that when sounds have symbolic meaning (presumably requiring wide intersensory associations) the left hemisphere is

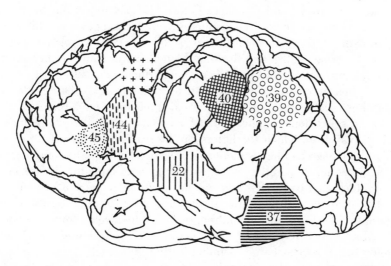

Figure 9. REPRESENTATION OF LANGUAGE FUNCTION IN THE LEFT HEMISPHERE OF MAN. *45–44: Broca's area; 22: auditory association area; 40–39: angular and supramarginal gyrus verbal association area; 37: visual auditory association area.*

From E. C. Crosby, T. Humphrey, and E. W. Lauer, *Correlative Anatomy of the Nervous System* (New York: Macmillan, 1962).

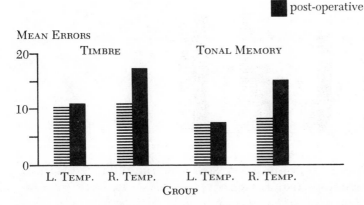

Figure 10. COMPARATIVE EFFECTS OF RIGHT AND LEFT TEMPORAL LOBECTOMY ON SEASHORE TESTS OF TIMBRE AND TONAL MEMORY

From B. Milner, "Laterality Effects in Audition." In V. B. Mountcastle, *Interhemispheric Relations and Cerebral Dominance* (Baltimore: Johns Hopkins Press, 1962).

involved. However, speech sounds played backwards—and thus presumably without symbolic significance, are also most effectively recognized in the right ear (left hemisphere) (Kimura, 1968). Here again, it may be that it is because there is a sequence of events involved that the left hemisphere is dominant.

A study by Rudel and Denckla (Figure 11) may reflect this interesting difference between the two hemispheres. Individuals showing evidences of impairment of the left hemisphere (right side) show relative impairment of verbal skills, and have a higher performance rating on the WISC. Those with right hemisphere "impairment" do better with verbal skills. When asked to do a digit span test (Figure 12), those with right hemisphere (left sided) deficit show an interesting impairment of digit backward repetition. It appears that for reverse recall, there is required a digit display from which the letters can be read off backward.

This high degree of hemisphere specialization has important implications for the learning to read process. Spoken language is a naturally sequential event interpreted by the left hemisphere. Written language is presented in parallel array as a display—the sequencing must be done by the reader (Sperling, 1970). For many children, this must involve a complex cooperative effort between left and right hemispheres—structures which may heretofore have been barely communicating with each other. It may be that some instances of reading disability may stem from constitutional or environmentally determined idiosyncracies of the relative dominance of

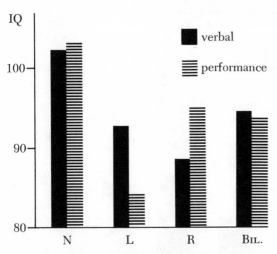

Figure 11. Verbal to Performance Scores of the WISC in Children with Learning Disabilities according to Laterality of Neurological Signs. *V = verbal; P = performance; N = normal; L = left sided signs; R = right sided signs; Bil = bilateral signs.*

R. G. Rudel, M. B. Denckla, and E. Spalton, "The Functional Asymmetry of Braille Letter Learning in Normal, Sighted Children." In press, 1973.

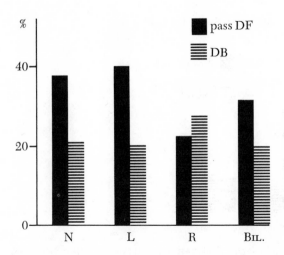

%

40—

20—

0—

          N   L   R   BIL.

■ pass DF

≣ DB

Figure 12. ABILITY OF CHILDREN WITH LEARNING DISABILITY TO DO DIGIT FORWARD AND DIGIT BACKWARD MEMORY TEST ACCORDING TO LATERALITY OF NEUROLOGICAL SIGNS

R. G. Rudel, M. B. Denckla, and E. Spalton, "The Functional Asymmetry of Braille Letter Learning in Normal, Sighted Children." In press, 1973.

one or the other hemisphere for these specific functions—or their complex functional interrelationships. (Note, in passing, that perceptive motor skills, so often impaired in LD children also require a similar translation from a static, special display, to a sequence of movements required to reproduce it.)

It is probable that the group of children with such disabilities also represents a relatively small subgroup of the dyslexic, for disturbance of language skill per se appears to be an element in many instances of reading failure. Prospective studies of Ingram (Figure 13) reveal the high failure rate of slow talkers. Evans and Bangs (Figure 14) show the significant gains that can be accomplished by preschool remediation in a group of such children.

At this point, I would like to get the M.D. back into the picture. The studies which I have just cited demonstrate that susceptibility to reading failure can be recognized early in the pre-kindergarten years, and that proper remediation can prevent school failure. Who is to recognize the susceptible child? In a large proportion of instances, it is the family doctor to whom the parents turn for guidance regarding their slow talking child, and it is he who has the background of the history to help him in an overall evaluation. But I regret that all too often he fails in his responsibility to recognize the significance of the problem, and especially to make the proper referrals for preschool remediation. It could be an important program of the Association to bring to the attention of all pediatricians the simple screening tests which have been developed for preschool prediction of LD, (Asbed et al., 1970, Jansky and deHirsch, 1972, Evans and

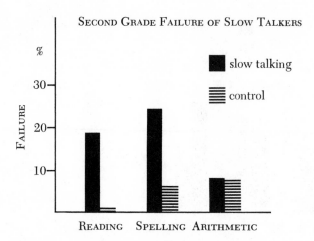

SECOND GRADE FAILURE OF SLOW TALKERS

Figure 13. FREQUENCY OF SUBSEQUENT LEARNING DISABILITY OF CHILDREN WITH DELAYED SPOKEN LANGUAGE AND CONTROLS

T. T. S. Ingram, "The Nature of Dyslexia." In *Early Experience and Visual Information Processing in Perceptual and Reading Disorders* (Washington, D. C.: National Academy of Sciences, 1970).

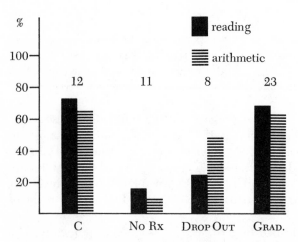

Figure 14. EFFECTS OF PRESCHOOL REMEDIATION IN PREVENTING READING FAILURE. *Percent succeeding in reading and arithmetic after preschool remedial program: C = normal control; No Rx. = refused preschool remediation; Drop out = failed to complete preschool remediation; Grad. = complete remediation.*

J. S. Evans and T. Bangs, "Effects of Preschool Language Training on Later Academic Achievement of Children with Language and Learning Disabilities," *Journal of Learning Disorders* 5 (1972), 585–591.

Bangs, 1972, Frankenburg et al, 1971), and within each community, to keep him advised regarding the remedial programs available to his patients. Only by making him to some extent a partner in the remedial education team can you provide him with the orientation which will make him effective in the early recognition and referral of the child predisposed to LD.

One final word about the medical treatment of learning disabilities. There is now unequivocal evidence that the appropriate use of stimulant or tranquilizing drugs is an important facet of the management of certain types of children with learning disabilities (Office of Child Development). Drugs are no panacea. In addition, their use is justifiable only when this therapy is coordinated with an overall remedial program of social and educational readjustment. The unfortunate abuse of drugs (like many other good things) in our society necessitates tight control of drug therapy, and this must rest in the hands of the physician. Once again, I urge the physician and the educator to join hands in the cooperative effort required to provide for the LD child the full contribution which each can offer.

REFERENCES

ASBED, R.; MASLAND, M. W.; SEVER, J.; WEINBERGER, M.: Early Case Finding of Children with Communication Problems, *Volta Review*, 72:23-48, 1970.

BIRCH, H. G.; GUSSOW, J. D.: *Disadvantaged Children*, Grune and Stratton, New York, 1970.

CROSBY, E. C.; HUMPHREY, T.; LAUER, E. W.: *Correlative Anatomy of the Nervous System*, Macmillan, New York, 1962.

EVANS, J. S.; BANGS, T.: Effects of Preschool Language Training on Later Academic Achievement of Children with Language and Learning Disabilities, *Journal of Learning Disorders*, 5:585-591, 1972.

FRANKENBURG, W. K.; GOLDSTEIN, A. D.; CAMP, B. W.: The Revised Denver Developmental Screening Test: Its Accuracy as a Screening Instrument, *Journal of Pediatrics*, 79:988-995, 1971.

HUGHES, J. R.: In: HELMER MYKELBUST. *Progress in Learning Disabilities*, volume II, Grune and Stratton, New York, 1971.

INGRAM, T. T. S.: The Nature of Dyslexia. In: *Early Experience and Visual Information Processing in Perceptual and Reading Disorders*, National Academy of Sciences, Washington, D.C., 1970.

JANSKY, J.; DEHIRSCH, K.: *Preventing Reading Failure*, Harper and Row, New York, 1972.

KAWI, A. A.; PASAMANICK, B.: Association of Factors of Pregnancy with Reading Disorders of Childhood, *Journal of American Medical Association*, 166: 1420-1423, 1958.

KIMURA, D.: Neural Processing of Backward Speech Sounds, *Science*, 161: 395-396, 1968.

MASLAND, R. L.: Mental Retardation in Relation to Post-Natal Events, *Trans. XII International Congress of Pediatrics*, 1:566-587, 1968.

MILNER, B.: Laterality Effects in Audition. In V. B. Mountcastle. *Interhemispheric Relations and Cerebral Dominance*, Johns Hopkins Press, Baltimore, 1962.

NEBES, R. D.: Dominance of the Minor Hemisphere in Commissurotomized Man on a Test of Figural Unification, *Brain*, 95:633-638, 1972.

OFFICE OF CHILD DEVELOPMENT: Report of the Conference on the Use of Stimulant Drugs in the Treatment of Behaviorally Disturbed Young School Children, Office of Child Development, Department of Health, Education and Welfare, Washington, D.C., January 11-12, 1971.

RUDEL, R. G.; DENCKLA, M. B.: Relation of Forward and Backward Digit Repetitions to Neurologic Impairment in Children with Learning Disabilities, in press, 1973.

RUDEL, R. G.; DENCKLA, M. B.; SPALTON, E.: The Functional Asymmetry of Braille Letter Learning in Normal, Sighted Children, in press, 1973.

SHIELDS, JAMES: *Monozygotic Twins,* Oxford University Press, 1962.

SPERLING, G.: Short Term Memory, Long Term Memory, and Scanning in the Processing of Visual Information. In: *Early Experience and Visual Information Processing in Perceptual and Reading Disorders,* National Academy of Sciences, Washington, D.C., 1970.

SPERRY, R. W.: Cerebral Dominance in Perception. In: *Early Experience and Visual Information Processing in Perceptual and Reading Disorders,* National Academy of Sciences, Washington, D.C., 1970.

TORRES, F.; AYERS, F. W.: Evaluation of the E.E.G. of Dyslexic Children, *Journal of Electroencephalography and Clinical Neurophysiology,* 24:287, 1968.

WIENER, G.; RIDER, R. V.; OPPEL, W. C.; FISCHER, L. C.; HARPER, P. A.: Correlates of Low Birth Weight: Psychological Status at Six to Seven Years of Age, *Pediatrics,* 35:434-444, 1965.

Six

Educational Practices

The most critical area in the field of learning disabilities is that of educational and psychological practices. A large proportion of lectures at ACLD meetings deal with some aspect of educational practice; only a representative few of these lectures are reproduced here. Many of the topics attempt to answer the question, "Once we have found the children, diagnosed them, and categorized them, what do we do with them?"

Doris Johnson contrasts training and education, relating these concepts to clinical teaching— which incorporates work on content with work on specific disabilities in the psychological processes that underlie learning. Her discussion of curriculum design alternatives underscores the relationship between disabilities and subject matter, and between language and learning processes, in an effort to improve the quality of education for learning disabled children.

Sister Mary Consilia explores in some depth the perceptual development and classroom behaviors of the child who has auditory learning disabilities, as opposed to visual or motor problems. The child's subsequent difficulties with comprehension, abstraction, and expressive and interpretive language are explored. Her specific suggestions for remediation extend to a detailed description of teaching techniques for sound-blending and spelling through word families.

Since early identification and prevention of learning disabilities continues to be of significant interest in the field, the description of the Developmental First Grade by Jeanne McCarthy and the staff from Schaumburg, Illinois, has been included. The importance of careful screening at this level, of providing a program before the child has failed, and of providing the services of a speech clinician, a school nurse, a psychoeducational diagnostician, a social worker and a psychologist are discussed.

Two articles by Frank Taylor are included, one having evolved from the other. The discussion of the Engineered Classroom model provides an example of the application of behavioral modification principles, to a greater or lesser extent, to a public school setting. He describes the classroom setting, the "checkmark" system, and various intervention settings. This procedure, used with emotionally disturbed children, was later applied to a noncategorical program based on specific learning deficits, rather than the traditional categories of the handicapped. These classes included children previously labeled as educable mentally retarded, educationally handicapped, learning disabled, visually impaired, and auditorially impaired.

Operant conditioning is a term that has been equally accepted and rejected. Thomas Lovitt feels that esoteric terms used in operant conditioning have tended to frighten teachers, or to remind them of the boring introductory psychology class in which they were drilled on the concept of dogs salivating to meat powder. He has attempted to explain the basic principles of operant conditioning in teachers' terminology rather than that of psychologists, and to show how these can be applied to a classroom environment.

The original purpose of the last article, by Edwin Martin, was to inform ACLD of the cooperation of the Bureau of Education for the Handicapped (a division of the U.S. Office of Education), of which he is director. He shares with the group some of the desperate letters he has received from parents. He also projects his view of the future development of programs at the state level.

Clinical Teaching of Children with Learning Disabilities

DORIS J. JOHNSON

Three hundred and twenty-six years ago, in the state of Massachusetts, an important law was passed. This law of 1642, passed by the Massachusetts legislature, is remarkable for it was the first time in the English-speaking world that a legislative body representing the state ordered that all children be taught to read. In a sense, we met in Boston in February 1968 to assist in carrying out part of this law. We are concerned with a substantial group of children who cannot read, speak, write, or calculate because they have learning disabilities. Although these children have at least average mental ability, sensory integrity, and emotional adjustment, they are unable to learn normally. Because our country is committed to public education for all children, provisions for this group must be made in our schools.

The current interest in this population is indeed gratifying. Throughout the country new legislation is being passed, programs are being established, teachers are being prepared, and materials for both diagnosis and remediation are being developed. All of these things are necessary, but in our haste to "do something" I hope that we do not fail to examine broad objectives. It is critical that we do not become absorbed in the details of teaching techniques and materials without formulating overall educational plans. In this connection, I wonder how many of you, at some time, have been asked whether you were a perceptually handicapped teacher. Usually, when addressed in this manner, we smile in understanding, knowing that the speaker meant to say—a teacher of *children* with perceptual or learning handicaps. Occasionally, however, after observing some hastily planned programs and an undue emphasis on isolated skills, one wonders whether we are not indeed perceptually handicapped. Excessive attention to the details of teaching techniques per se, without regard for the total educational process, certainly smacks of a perceptual disturbance in part-whole relationships.

Although teaching techniques and instructional materials are basic to good education, they should not form the basis of education. The architect selects his materials on the basis of the blueprint and so must we. Yet even before the architect begins his drawing, he must inquire about the purposes of the building. He asks, "Who is to live in it? How will they live? What will they do there?" I am suggesting that we look carefully at the criteria by which we select our materials and procedures, not only in relation to the individual child, but to the overall objectives of education.

From the *Proceedings* of the Fifth Annual International Conference of the ACLD, *Successful Programming—Many Points of View.* Boston, Mass. (February 1-3, 1968), pp. 386-398.

Without a blueprint, the direction is vague and our growth will be haphazard, somewhat like Topsy. Stating this point somewhat differently, I think, at this point in learning disabilities history, we cannot afford to overlook broad educational objectives lest we place ourselves in the bizarre position of teaching children without educating them. The two are not synonymous. Children can be taught many things, but that does not necessarily constitute good education. Our concern is for the best education possible. Thus, as we select materials and techniques for our daily plans we must make some judgment as to the rationale and ultimate value for the student.

In our planning we might consider the four classes of goals outlined by the Educational Policies Commission.[1] They are referred to as the objectives of (1) self realization, (2) human relationship, (3) economic efficiency, and (4) civic responsibility. A study of these objectives shows that they may be classified under the four broad headings of knowledges and understandings, attitudes and appreciations, skills and abilities, and behaviors. When planning programs for children with learning disabilities, we must try to maintain a balance among these various areas. The dyslexic child who is able to acquire concepts auditorially should also be taught to read. The child who can communicate orally should also be taught to write. Children who can function in a one-to-one relationship also should be helped to live and work in a group.

H. S. Broudy, O. Smith, and J. Burnett stress the importance of general education for all children.[2] They define general education as those central skills, ideas, and evaluations which can be most significantly and widely used in order to deal with life in our times. These same authors are concerned that our current educational system tends to relegate the underprivileged child (and we might add, many exceptional children) to a vocational education which rapidly approaches obsolescence. Thus we take the potential school dropout, give him training rather than education, and in so doing we prepare him to be a society dropout. Many of the technical jobs for which we prepare these young people may well be eaten up by mechanization and automation tomorrow. Therefore, the school should provide opportunities out of which student changes or learnings occur in the form of cognitive maps, associative meanings, intellectual operations, attitudes and values, and skills of manipulative and executive operations.

Making these objectives more concrete and converting them into action is more difficult than stating the goals, particularly for exceptional children. In order to do so, it is necessary to have a framework or model into which we can write the behaviors to be learned. We need a system which will permit us to view both the whole and the parts. A useful tool for making the translation from objectives to instruction is shown in Figure 1. This guide was suggested by G. Beauchamp for the elementary curriculum, but it has considerable merit for educational planning in learning disabilities.[3] The headings of the five-point notation system include the following:

Figure 1. Instructional Guide

Subject or Unit _____   Grade _____

Subject Matter Breakdowns in Topics	Suggested Activities for Children	Expected Outcomes in Changed Pupil Behavior		
		Concepts, Facts or Generalizations to be Learned	Skill Performances to be Developed	Developmental Values to be Acquired

Instructional Guide Worksheet (Wilmette, Ill.: The Kogg Press).

- subject-matter breakdown in topics or units
- suggested activities for children to perform
- concepts, facts, or generalizations to be learned
- skill performances to be learned
- developmental values to be acquired.

Beauchamp feels that this type of notation sheet causes the educator to relate the activity to the expected outcomes, thereby deliberately forcing a relationship between them. In learning disabilities, it provides a means of planning a comprehensive program that does not overemphasize skills. Moreover, it provides us with an opportunity to examine the areas of behavior in which the child deviates most.

The implication is that the clinical teacher of children with learning disabilities must look at more than the "peaks and valleys" on test profiles. The instruction should be related to broad educational objectives. Through careful planning, the work on specific deficits can be coordinated with information which is presented in the classroom. We need to begin designing units of instruction which facilitate the integration of content, processes, and skills. For example, a unit on transportation would contain suggestions for the presentation of content, but also would have exercises or worksheets for specific disturbances in auditory or visual perception, memory, sequencing, visual-motor functions, language, etc. Conceivably, these units could be made available through instructional materials centers in the various states. By using the Instructional Guide shown in Figure 1 the teacher can coordinate content and processes. Note the following examples:

EXAMPLE NO. 1. LANGUAGE ARTS

Column 1   Language arts—listening skills
Column 2   Ask children to close their eyes and listen for specific sounds such as the crumpling of paper, opening and closing the door, bouncing a ball.
Column 3   Identification of social sounds
Column 4   Ability to hear similarities and differences in social environmental sounds
Column 5   Importance of listening carefully.

EXAMPLE NO. 2. MATHEMATICS

Column 1   Mathematics—sets
Column 2   Go around the room and point out things that are placed in groups (bunches of flowers, collections of coins or insects). Discuss groups of things that are not in the room (a nest of eggs or a bed of flowers).
Column 3   Develop concept of set and empty set
Column 4   Identify sets
Column 5   Begin to understand that we can gain and also remember more information when we group things.

EXAMPLE No. 3. PHYSICAL SCIENCE

Column 1 Matter and energy

Column 2 Demonstrate the nature of different matters

        Solids: Move blocks from place to place and show that the shape does not change.

        Liquids: Let children run fingers through water, noting that they cannot do so with blocks. See how water fits into tall glasses, flat bowls, etc.

        Gases: Fill balloon or basketball with air. Show air as gas that can escape. Discuss use of gas in home. Discuss harmful effects of gas and the care that must be taken with gas heating units.

Column 3 Matter exists in different forms. Matter exists in nature in three basic states. Gases can be harmful.

Column 4 Ability to differentiate solids, liquids, and gases. Ability to take care with gas stoves, etc. Ability to identify smell of certain gases.

Column 5 Develop critical observation powers. Appreciation for certain gases in helping at home and in the environment.

These examples show how the clinical teacher might incorporate work on content with specific disabilities in perception, comprehension, language, etc. However, it is evident that the teacher must have well-defined objectives and a thorough understanding of the children and their problems. In recent years we have seen great progress in the development of procedures for child study and evaluation. Now we need extensive, longitudinal studies in regard to education. For example, more emphasis should be given to the development of curricula for self-contained classrooms. What type of curriculum design is most appropriate for classrooms in learning disabilities? What should be the scope and sequence—that is, what should be taught, and in what order should the material be taught? How can we maintain a balance between content and work on disabilities? All of these questions are relevant, but few, if any, have specific answers.

Consider the type of curriculum design. Generally, design refers to the way in which we organize the material to be taught. The type used most frequently in schools today is the subject-centered plan which includes the areas shown below, with the exception of the first item.

Areas of Study in Subject-Centered Curriculum

- experience
- language arts
  - listening (auditory verbal comprehension)
  - oral expression
  - reading
  - writing

- science
- social studies
- mathematics
- health and physical education
- the fine arts.

Here I have added "experience" because the teacher of children with learning disabilities cannot assume all students have integrated their past experiences normally. For example, many hyperactive children have been "on the go" so much that they never truly assimilated sensory experiences. They have not compared things that were rough or smooth nor things that were sweet and sour. In addition, many children have nonverbal learning disorders which interfere with the acquisition of concepts. Hence, when they are taught to read, write, or calculate, the symbols are lacking in meaning. Therefore, it often is necessary to provide structured experiences which serve as the core for learning in language, reading, science, mathematics, and other subjects. Field trips, special projects, and film strips are particularly beneficial. From the core experience and the various subjects we would attempt to integrate work on specific deficits. For example, a child with visual-perceptual problems might have special assignments in science which would help him with part-whole relationships (e.g., simplified diagrams showing body parts of animals, etc.). Students with a disturbance in social perception might be helped through well-planned social studies units, including role playing. Those with visual-motor problems can be assisted through carefully planned sequences in art.

Some workers in the field of curriculum prefer the fusion plan to the subject-matter approach. With this type of design the focus is on basic human processes; the individual subjects lose their identity. A fundamental assumption of the subject-oriented design is that transfer of training will occur, and that the subjects provide a base for future learning. Advocates of fusion planning postulate that the immature mind is not capable of making this transfer; hence, the course of study is arranged according to human needs. If their criticism of the subject-matter approach is valid for normal children, then it follows that we, who have students with more than the usual problems of abstraction, might consider a fusion curriculum. An example of such a design is below. Instead of planning the instruction around reading, mathematics, etc., the emphasis is on the following processes.

Areas of Study in a Fusion Curriculum

- observation of the environment—reacting to the world around us
- communicating ideas and feelings
- protecting and conserving human and natural resources and property
- producing, exchanging, distributing, and consuming food, clothing, and shelter

- transporting people and goods
- organizing and governing
- creating tools, techniques, and social arrangements
- providing recreation
- expressing and satisfying aesthetic and spiritual impulses.

The above list is but one way of organizing the curriculum. Perhaps educations in the field of learning disabilities would select different processes which would focus on deficits in perception or conceptualization. Irrespective of the design that is chosen, it seems critical to coordinate broad educational objectives with work on specific disabilities.

If the clinical teacher has a resource room rather than a self-contained class, we strongly recommend a careful study of the school curriculum guide. Examination of these guides helps the teacher gain a perspective of what is expected at various grade levels. In addition, she can, perhaps, anticipate some of the difficulties children will have as new material is introduced. Whenever possible, the remediation is integrated with the media from the regular class. In this way the child has a greater opportunity for success in the group. Furthermore, his total educational plan is less fragmented. We also find it beneficial to go over the curriculum guide with the classroom teacher, noting the areas of study which might be most troublesome for the learning-disabled child. When the classroom teacher is alerted to these areas, she often can modify assignments.

We also suggest that the clinical teacher take a physical walk through the child's school day noting how and when he deviates. She observes him in various classes, noting whether he comprehends instructions, whether he knows the names of various pieces of equipment or utensils, whether he is ever called upon in class, and whether he ever volunteers. She also observes the child on the playground or in the lunchroom to determine whether problems of perception, memory, language, orientation, or motor function interfere with the performance. Every effort is made to help the student perform more adequately at home and school. This is not to suggest that the clinical teacher merely tutors the child in school subjects or assists him with daily assignments. Rather, relevant material from the environment is selected as media for work on disabilities.

We need to help classroom teachers so they become more aware of learning processes and the interrelationship between disabilities and subject matter. Often they see only a failure in a particular subject such as social studies, biology, or mathematics. For example, take the hypothetical case of Miss Jones. She has a small group of third-grade boys who reportedly did poorly in mathematics. Although all of these boys are failing certain aspects of their arithmetic assignments, they have unique problems which require far more than tutoring in number concepts. Note the differences:

Johnny has an auditory-comprehension problem. He has trouble understanding certain words, especially those words with multiple meanings.

Many of these words are used in mathematics, so there are times when he has not the vaguest idea what the teacher means. Words such as "set," "carry," "times" all have meanings in other contexts, but he cannot shift nor comprehend the meanings in relation to arithmetic.

Bill has a reading problem. Therefore, he cannot read many of the words in the story problems, but when he practices the arithmetic facts orally and when the problems are read for him he has no difficulty. Yet on his written assignments in class he must leave some answers blank because he cannot read the words.

Jim has a visual-perceptual problem so he often confuses the 8's and the 3's or the 6's and 9's. As a result he gets some problems right, but others wrong. He also has difficulty with spatial relationships so he never knows whether he should start figuring from the right or the left.

Ted is one of the best readers in the class and always contributes to class discussion, but because of visual-motor problems, he cannot form some of the numbers to be written on his worksheet. Yet, he knows the answers.

Bob fails his assignments because he does indeed have a disturbance in quantitative thinking. He does not understand the principles of either addition or subtraction. At times one would question whether he even has a one-to-one correspondence.

Although all of these boys performed poorly in mathematics, only one had serious problems in quantitative thinking. However, unless learning processes are considered, there might be a tendency to tutor them in mathematics or to reduce the level of instruction. Neither plan is appropriate. If a child can conceptualize but cannot write, the teacher should not hold down the level of mathematics instruction. Rather, until the student improves in his visual-motor performance the classroom teacher might give him worksheets on which the answer could be circled or she might give him a rubber stamp set so he could print the numbers. In the meantime, the clinical teacher will work on specific deficits. The disability is not avoided, but temporary modifications of assignments are made until the student can function more normally.

Educators must become more aware of the interrelationship of language and learning processes. In normal children all functions seem to be interrelated. Information and learning of one type is spontaneously converted or translated into other types. If a child hears, we expect him to understand; if he understands, we expect him to speak; if he spells orally, we expect him to write from dictation. These same assumptions cannot be made in regard to children with learning disabilities. Their deficits in processing information result in unusual learning patterns. For example, consider the acquisition of the concept of "three" and the symbols used to represent the quantity (see Figure 2). On the far left side of the diagram several figures indicate the nonverbal concept of "threeness." In reality this might be three objects, three pictures, three sounds, etc. Next the word "three" is written in quotation marks to indicate the spoken word. The child learns to respond to oral commands such as, "Give me three pencils." This is fol-

Figure 2

Experience	Spoken Symbol	Numeral	Printed Word
⊙ ⊙ ⊙	"three"	3	three
– – –			THREE
0			
0 0			

lowed by the numeral and, finally, the printed word in both lower- and upper-case type. The normal child is able to make the proper associations between all of these figures after he has had instruction. Children with learning disabilities, however, may have a variety of problems which interfere with the integration of these symbols. For instance, a student with an auditory-comprehension disorder often learns to associate quantity with the numeral, but not with the spoken word. In contrast, dyslexic children often associate quantity with the spoken word and with the numeral but not the printed word. Some dyslexics can read the word in lower case but not capital letters. This example is only a simple illustration to demonstrate the need for analyzing learning processes in relation to subject matter.

In order to help teachers understand the dynamics of a learning disability we have often given them a guide for analyzing tasks. The purpose is to look at assignments that are given to children from the standpoint of learning systems and processes. By analyzing tasks and relating them to the child's pattern of success or failure, it is possible to determine which learning "circuits" are operative or inoperative. Each assignment given to a student is studied according to the areas outlined below:

Input
Sensory channels involved (auditory, visual, etc.)
Number of sensory channels involved (intrasensory, intersensory, etc.)
Meaningful or nonmeaningful
Verbal or nonverbal

Output
Gesture, marking, recognition, manipulation
Oral (spoken)
Written

When utilizing this model we first look at the nature of the input and the sensory channel or channels being tapped by the task. Is it intrasensory or intersensory? That is, does the child need to integrate information from one or more sensory modalities? Consider the different processing required for reading tasks. When a child is asked to match printed words with pictures the task is intrasensory-visual. In contrast, if he is asked to respond to the oral command, "Mark the word 'cat,'" the task is intersensory because the child must integrate auditory and visual symbols. Many children with learning disabilities can complete the former task but not the latter.

The next area on the model is concerned with meaning. We need to know whether a task is meaningful or nonmeaningful. Some children are totally confused when asked to work with isolated sounds or nonsense syllables. If taught according to a synthetic phonics approach in reading, they may ask, "What's a *g*?" or "What does *h* mean?" On the other hand, some children cannot interpret meaningful material. They learn the names of letters or numerals, but they do not learn to read or calculate.

We also note whether the task is verbal or nonverbal. Certain children can deal with nonverbal information (sounds, pictures, etc.), but not with the verbal (spoken words, reading, etc.). Others show the reverse pattern; they are poor in nonverbal functions. Some can read well, but they cannot interpret gesture, pantomime, or facial expressions.

Finally, the mode of response or output is examined. Here, for purposes of simplification, the responses are categorized into three major types. The first involves pointing, manipulation, pantomime, or gesture; the second is spoken; and the third is visual-motor or written. The teacher needs to know which systems for output are intact and which are impaired. By analyzing tasks according to this systems approach and by noting a child's performance, it is possible to learn more about the nature of a disability and to modify assignments so the students can perform more successfully.

Note the countless modifications which can be made with a simple word card (Figure 3) if the teacher is oriented to learning processes.

Figure 3

boat	hat	sand	bat	band
man	hand	gun	lamp	sun
cat	cup	train	nut	cap
ship	cake	dog	lake	pen
ring	rug	fish	dish	string

- Hold up a card on which the letter "b" is printed and say, "Put a mark on all of the words that start with this letter." In this instance, the task involves predominantly visual-perceptual processes; the student matches the letter on the card with those on the larger word card. No memory or interpretation is required.
- Contrast the above task with this: "Cover all of the words that start with 'b' (bee)" or "Cover all of the words that start with 'buh' (the letter sound)." Now both auditory and visual processes must be integrated.
- Observe the integrities necessary for completing the following assignment. "Put a mark on the one that rhymes with the word 'coat.'" Here, many processes are required, including auditory perception of a unit

within a word (i.e. rhyming), verbal comprehension, visual perception, and memory.

- Note the difference if one were to hold up a card on which the word "coat" was printed; then say, "Put a mark on the one that rhymes with this word." Certain children who have no rhyming ability could succeed because only visual processes are necessary (except for understanding the oral directions). In this instance, the teacher might be helping the children to perform successfully in a group, but further work in auditory perception would be necessary.
- Again, note the difference if one were to hold up a picture of a coat with no printed word and say, "Put a mark on the one that rhymes with this." Although this task might appear simpler than some of those above because of the use of pictures, in some respects it is more difficult, particularly for children with severe auditory-perceptual disorders.
- Observe the nature of the input and the expected mode of response with the following: "Mark the word 'hand.'" Here we have a conversion from an auditory to a visual symbol. In contrast, ask the child to "Read the first word in the bottom row." Aside from the fact that the child must comprehend the verbal instruction, the primary requirement is the conversion of a visual symbol to an auditory-verbal (spoken) response. Children who can point to words on command may not be able to say them because of reauditorization or motor-processing difficulties. In another instance the teacher might hold up a picture of a coat and say, "Mark the word that goes with this picture." Now the task is intrasensory-visual. The child associates a visual, nonverbal stimulus with a visual, verbal pattern. The form of response is matching.
- The same card could be used for lessons in language. To illustrate, one might say, "Mark the one that is a part of your body," or "Mark all of the ones you eat," or "Mark all of the foods," or "Yesterday we went swimming in the _____."

These examples are meant to emphasize the importance of analyzing assignments we give children to ascertain more about the nature of the disturbance and to modify activities in the classroom. The clinical teacher must learn how to manipulate activities in order for children to perform most successfully.

Many of you will ask how we can implement this—how we can provide for broad educational objectives and specific deficits. There is no single solution; however, we need to orient teachers and other professional workers to the concept of learning disabilities and the importance of studying learning processes. I believe we will need the coordinated efforts of many professional persons to increase the effectiveness of programing. I believe we need educational teams, just as we have medical teams or athletic coaching teams. On the team we need educators, administrators, psychologists, social workers, and professionals such as programers, artists, writers, and photographers to assist in the development of materials. The head of the team might be comparable to an athletic director. This person would be highly trained in educational diagnostics and programing. Provisions would be made for both group and individual instruction, with every attempt being made to coordinate processes and content. If we were to visualize this operation in a school we might see modules of rooms—some devoted to group work, others to the individual. In the group area, we might see a teacher conducting a science lesson, perhaps performing an experiment to illustrate the concepts. Smaller areas would be devoted to specific-learning processes, such as visual perception, visual-motor integration, language, etc. Conceivably the educational director would observe the students in the group, noting their special needs. Children would be assigned to individual instruction based on the deficit, but whenever possible the work on deficits would be coordinated with the content. The student with a visual-perceptual disorder might receive help on part-whole relationships by working with diagrams. Some might have special instruction in measurement. For example, children with visual-spatial disorders could be taught many concepts in relation to the science lesson. Those with language disorders might work on the names of products or the pieces of equipment. Those with problems of abstraction would be helped to see how things are alike or different. The reading vocabularies for dyslexic children would be drawn from the basic assignment in science. Students with auditory-memory problems might listen to tape recordings of the initial lecture by the teacher. These are but a few examples from a host of possibilities for coordinating work on processes and content. With dynamic planning, effective organization, and the utilization of creative resources, I believe we can and must improve the quality of education for children with learning disabilities.

NOTES

1. National Education Association (Washington, D.C., 1959).
2. *Democracy and Excellence in American Secondary Education* (Chicago: Rand-McNally, 1964).
3. Curriculum in the Elementary School (Boston: Allyn and Bacon, 1964).

REFERENCE

JOHNSON, D. J., and MYKLEBUST, H. R., *Learning Disabilities: Educational Principles and Practices* (New York: Grune and Stratton, 1967).

Meeting the Needs of the Auditorially Impaired Child

SISTER MARY CONSILIA

As director of the Center for Developmental Learning and Reading, Newburgh, New York, it is a major concern of mine to attempt to identify and provide help for the disabled child. The children who are referred to the center are described in the following seven categories:

- Those who manifest specific neurological signs—seldom gross, often "soft" signs—those with high incidence of left laterality and mixed laterality and confused perception of laterality; those with poor spatial awareness and a distorted sense of body image and directionality.
- Those who appear to have been poorly taught, or who frequently appear to have been untaught (the workbook experts at filling in blanks). The child whose teacher says, "Write a book report," but doesn't show him how; whose teacher says, "Write a paragraph," but gives no directions in structure; whose teacher says, "Write a story," but doesn't tell how to plan such a piece of writing.
- Those who word-call in reading but who are impaired in concept-formation. They see and say words, but they have no idea what meaning belongs with those words in that context. The words might just as well be written in a vertical column.
- Those who lack interest and motivation, who demonstrate frustration and an attitude of "Don't bother me, I've done all that before."
- Those who have basic language dysfunction, for whom language is communicated by single words that are frequently muttered, half swallowed, poorly enunciated, often mispronounced. These children communicate with spartan simplicity, expecting and getting the adults in their environment to supply the full meaning to their limited use of language. One hears "un-huh," "yep," "nope," or "yeah" in response to sentences directed their way. "How old are you?" elicits a single word response: "Eight." "When is your birthday?" gets "dunno" or maybe just a shrug. These near-aphasic children are unable to write an account of a simple experience such as "The Kind of Fun We Have in Winter," with correct paragraph form, spelling, the use of whole sentences, or even an approximation to the proper use of punctuation. Children of this category spread out and overflow into all the other classes I describe.
- Those who present disorders of thinking, of abstract reasoning, of generalization, of memory and association; those who show no ability to

From the *Proceedings* of the Seventh Annual Conference of the ACLD, *Meeting Total Needs of Learning-Disabled Children: A Forward Look.* Philadelphia (February 12-14, 1970), pp. 63-81.

arouse images in response to spoken or read concepts. These are children who fail in comprehension of reading, in learning in the content subjects, and in symbolic learning in general.

- Those who come with a roadblock to learning apparently involving the input channels of learning. At times, the blocks are difficult to pinpoint and the problems seem insuperable. Time runs out on these children, and by the time they get to junior high they are labeled "nonreaders," "underachievers," or "slow learners," and they are put on the G track. G means "General Course" for the administrators; for the children, G stands for "Goner," which means "Quit," and all-too-frequently they do. The unwilling, the unable, and the slow (but able) often find themselves grouped together, and when they do, you know what happens all-too-frequently.

Anyone who has worked for any reasonable period of time with the "blocked" learner knows that for these children with impaired avenues of learning, ways can be found to help them and, therefore, save a sizeable segment for responsible society. The right teacher, at the right time for the right child, *can* save him from the near-illiteracy that might otherwise be his.

The foregoing categories can be reduced to two: (1) those children who word-call, who cannot get to the meaning of the ideas expressed in written language; and (2) those who have impairments in the channels of learning involved in language, and specifically, in reading. The other categories form clusters of concomitant attitudes and disabilities, which delay, at times, even the attainment of the earliest prerequisites to learning.

I will spend no time describing the behavioral characteristics of hypertension, distractibility, and disinhibition, which are almost universally demonstrated by the learning-impaired child.

Lack of motivation, gnawing frustration, language dysfunction, poor teaching, and unreadiness in neurological and motor areas are not *causes* of nonlearning; they are, rather, guaranteed preventives of the acquisition of the skills required for learning. These factors can affect all areas of learning, though it is not uncommon to find a child who is impeded only in language but not in math or science. There is no guarantee, however, that the elements could not or indeed, do not, affect generalized learning.

Let us turn our attention to perceptual impairment as background for the understanding of the auditorially impaired child, which is our main concern in this paper. Perceptual impairment involves the central nervous system. The blocks to learning which I will treat lie somewhere along the extensive mileage of this system. The impairment may be (1) in the conducting nerve axons that bring information in to the brain, (2) in the synapses or junctions where the incoming messages are transmitted to other tracks enroute to the specified brain areas of reception, (3) in the reception areas of the brain itself, or (4) in the association and integrating areas deep within the brain.

As a very simple illustration of this last named function, consider the technique used by the primary teacher to connect, as it were, the concept of mother with a picture of a mother, with the printed symbol MOTHER, and with the spoken term "mother." When she actually achieves this with a child, she has employed a natural ability of the child to make associations between experiences and the symbol for experience. She has employed visual and auditory memory, since the child can associate the spoken word with the printed symbol. She has also employed the integrative processes of transducing information from one sense modality over to another. The involvement becomes greater when the child is asked to write the word from memory. It is in this intricate, complex interlocking activity of association and integration that deep-seated types of learning disability may be found. These four steps might be considered the stimulus-response circuit of learning—in more contemporary terminology, the input and output channels, the associative and integrative functions.

To understand the auditorily impaired child (or the visually), one must be able to distinguish between sensation and perception, and between perception and conception. The input channels bring information in from the external senses: eyes, ears, nose, taste buds, skin, etc. Each external sense organ has its appropriate stimulus; each receives its "image" or "trace" from the environment. When the proper stimulus acts upon the sense organ and the organ reacts appropriately, the activity is termed *sensation*. Let us concentrate on sight and hearing. The stimuli picked up by the eye or ear (sensation) are conducted along well-laid traffic routes and are deposited in, that is, received by, the brain in specific areas organized to interpret that particular kind of information. So there are visual areas, auditory areas, and language areas, and even in these there are breakdowns to specific types of visual interpretation of incoming information. When the brain in its perceptual function gives meaning to the information brought in by ocular pathways, the act of *vision* takes place. (Remember, sight had already taken place in the eye.)

So it is with auditory neural tracks, which travel from the external ear to the temporal lobe of the brain, conveying there for interpretation and association, for integration and memory-storage, the sounds of our environment, both verbal and nonverbal. This is auditory perception, intact or impaired, depending upon the many physiological factors involved in the pickup and delivery processes, and the reception accorded the material.

The excellence of output will depend upon the excellence of input and the processes of giving it meaning. Dysfunction is possible anywhere along the neural trails as well as in the control center. The impairment may be so minor as not to evidence itself at all. It may be major so as to disable a child severely, or it may be any degree of crippling in between. Often it remains undetected until the challenges of learning, particularly of language, reading, writing, and spelling, in fact, any form of symbolic learning, are undertaken.

Before proceeding, I should say a few words about memory, a faculty that is sadly wanting in too many children today. Memory involves the recall of information previously possessed for either short term or long term. Rote memory would be the automatic recall of auditory input. Memory span is the period of time over which a person has retained information. These are generally known facts. However, the processes that are not that well known, or not included in the extension of the term memory, are *visual* memory, *kinesthetic* memory, and *motor* memory, that is, the memory of specific powers to recall previously experienced visual images, muscular movements, and gross and fine motor activities. I do not have adequate time to develop the roles of the various memories, nor of the associative and integrative powers, but let me liken them to bridges between the incoming information and the outgoing responses. But they are not bridges that are used simply for passage; they connect activities that change, absorb, unify, and store a vast flood of incoming material into readiness for responsible reaction in the present or the future.

Simple? Not really; my presentation just makes it seem so. The process is intricate, complex, difficult to grasp. What we know about these things today is far beyond the understanding that the classroom teacher had a decade ago. The difference between our current understanding and what will be known by teachers a decade hence might reasonably be compared to the difference between what the Wright brothers knew at Kitty Hawk and what the astronauts knew on the moon.

Perception, then, is reception in the brain of external stimuli, with interpretation, integration, and evaluation of that information. Children with problems of perception are externally in contact with their environment, but the reception in the brain might be thought of as scrambled, garbled, or distorted; therefore, it is not matching or related to reality. A visual scramble might be likened to a child's mistaking a *d* for a *b,* or a *p* for a *q.* An auditory scramble might be likened to a child's mistaking the sound *th* for *f,* or his inability to distinguish the short *a* sound from the short *e* sound. The dysfunction generally produces a constellation of scrambles, distortions, and associated unrealities.

The motor-impaired child is clumsy. He stumbles, falls more than the average child. He walks into furniture because he has no real concept of space and of himself in relation to space and the objects in space. He draws poorly, writes poorly, has a difficult time copying from the chalkboard.

The visually impaired child loses his place in books, reverses or inverts letters and words; his writing is disproportionate in size. He cannot put items down in neat columns (words, money amounts, decimal points, organization of an outline). And more, much more detrimental is his failure to develop a sight vocabulary.

The auditorially impaired child, our concern from this point on, is in a sense the opposite of the visually impaired child. He can and does develop a sight vocabulary. He can perform better in structural analysis since the visual aspects of words undergoing structural changes are more easily worked with; they come in small bits and are more closely related to his sight vocabulary. While he tips the scales in his own favor in these few things, he has serious and complex difficulties along his route to learning.

He cannot rhyme. He cannot discriminate isolated sounds, particularly the short vowel sounds. He may also be very deficient in auditory memory, an instance of which would be the number of times that the teacher has to tell him the sound represented by a letter; for example, that short *a*, as in *apple*, is distinct from short *e*, heard in *egg*. He may even pronounce it *aig*. It may be that he cannot discriminate the sounds, and when the teacher says one and asks him to repeat it, she may find him pronouncing a different sound altogether, one that may not even be in our language. If he does achieve the discrimination of short *a* from short *e*, will he remember the individual sounds with or without the key word? That depends upon how short his memory is and how little association he was able to form between the sound and the key word. Will he have it at noontime, at three in the afternoon; will he have it tomorrow? For a seriously impaired child in this area, each *new* meeting of the sound, isolated or embedded in a word, is a new experience; he has to learn it over again, as if he had never heard it before.

Be sure of the distinctions here. Parents are often confused. They fail to discriminate between *sensation* at the outer organ and *perception* in the brain. The child hears sounds, since he responds to spoken language. He is not deaf. The difficulty is internal, between the going-in and coming-out-again over the auditory-vocal and visual-motor systems. Something has gone wrong with the heard sound. His problem is interpretation, and it lies in his inability to sort out one sound from another, or to associate an isolated sound he now hears with the same sound he has often heard and said when it was embedded in words.

The auditorially impaired child has poor enunciation and pronunciation habits. He has poor lip and tongue movement; he chews his words, mumbles his speech, and misses the opportunity to learn from correct monitoring or auding of his own spoken words. Also, and this may be more our fault than his, he fails to receive correction of his inferior speech because "teacher has to hurry on."

When this child watches a speaker, some degree of anxiety is manifested in his expression. He listens to directions but cannot process the series so as to perform as directed. Simple messages to the principal, to another teacher, or his parents, become garbled when relayed by him, if not forgotten almost immediately. (I find this even in older boys who can relate the latest batting averages, players on league teams, last year's victories, and even exchanges of players among various teams.) A favorite expression of this child is "I forgot; I forgot what you said," and this can be an immediate reaction when you ask him to repeat the message. Did he "forget" or did he "not get"? Two different things are involved.

The child is frequently overwhelmed by the talkative teacher, the one whose action-reaction rating is 90 percent teacher-talk, 10 percent child-talk. If a teacher would demand sentence-use in oral responses, the children's portion of the speaking time would be raised considerably and the teacher's time diminished to mutual advantage.

One frequently sees the auditorially impaired child in a classroom cupping his hands over both ears. His eyes are saying, "Too much, too much. Let things get quiet for a minute. Can't we ever be quiet?" By way of contrast, let me ask if you have noticed a visually overloaded child's reaction? He makes circles with his thumbs and index fingers and holds them to his eyes, thereby diminishing the field of vision. Whereas the auditorially impaired child is asking for more quiet in his environment, for aloneness, the visually impaired child is asking for fewer sights and more sounds—maybe singing, marching, beating rhythms. Each type of impaired child seems to have his own way of reacting to overloading. The teacher should be aware of the signs. Doris Johnson and H. R. Myklebust warn us concerning the observance of tolerance levels and the dangers of overloading.[1] In certain children, incoming signals from two or three channels, for example, the auditory and the visual or other channels, may obliterate one another. Here lies the possibility of lack of success for a really concerned teacher who may fail to observe whether each learning disabled child can benefit from multisensory or unisensory approaches.

An observant teacher knows the signs. She learns the reasons. She gives the children the relief they ask for. Alternating the activities helps. She can change from a visual activity such as silent reading or a quiet study period, to auditory tasks as in listening comprehension or instruction in a content subject. She can move from auditory to auditory-vocal where the child reads orally or recites poetry. She can go to visual-motor activities such as penmanship, art, copying, and to auditory-motor as in dictation, written spelling, and following oral directions.

These auditorially impaired children like to draw, paint, and employ themselves in creative activities. They engage in model making and they like physical exercise (unless, of course, they have motor involvement as well). They involve themselves in activities of the visual, tactile, and kinesthetic faculties to compensate for the auditory disability they recognize in themselves. Thank God for the instinct to compensate! They are like us: if we don't make a good pie, we make cake *instead.*

There are games to play with this kind of child to improve his auditory awareness. Stand him with his back to the class. A second child, at a distance, makes a noise: he knocks, drops, stamps, rolls a pencil, taps a pattern, calls, whispers, tinkles a bell, crinkles paper, etc. The child should respond: "You dropped a ruler ... you knocked on the window ... you turned the pages of a book," etc. These drills in nonverbal matter develop in a child attentive listening, effort, interpretation, identification, and improved memory in auditory matters.

Give exercises to develop awareness of *soft, loud,* or *very loud,* through use of a bell, of clapping, jumping, noises overhead, a spoken word, the falling of a paper clip, of a scissors, of a flowerpot. At the center we play an auditory game during reading. I do the reading or we play a favorite record such as "Winnie-the-Pooh." Each child is supplied with four small index cards, each bearing a number from one to four. It is determined that card number two represents the normal tone of voice we would use in speaking or reading. Number one is a quieter tone, soft, even a whisper. Number three is loud, firm, calls for attention. Number four is exciting, very loud, a tone to demand immediate attention. The game starts with the cards spread out before the children. As the reading proceeds, the children hold up the appropriate number cards as they listen to the tones. If a dispute arises, we stop and demonstrate the tones and decide which child held up the more appropriate card. This can call for fine discriminations of meaning and interpretation.

The auditorially impaired child frequently is unable to comprehend that a word is made up of a series of sounds. He is unable to hear the sequence of sounds which enunciate the word. He may hear wholes but not parts. He says whole words, but he cannot break the whole into its sound parts. Many of them never thought of a whole word as being a series of sounds. It is like opening a door for them when they learn this. Do not confuse sound parts with letter parts. We are speaking of hearing sounds, not spelling the letters of a word. There is a vast difference between these two tasks, which sometimes is not considered by teachers who think that because a child can read, he also should be able to spell.

Let us take the case of Johnny, who can say the word *hat* and can read it as a sight word. What he cannot do is hear in isolation the three sounds that make up the word. There is no way of putting sounds *as sounds* on paper, and I hesitate to write the letters that spell the sounds in the word *hat* since that would require that Johnny be spelling, not sounding. In attempting to help Johnny isolate the sounds, I would say the three sounds of *hat* and try to individualize them as distinct sounds but without stopping between them. We call this *taffy* when we stretch out the sounds of a word to enable the child to hear them individually. We take an overly long time to say the sound of *h* and blend in the short *a* and stretch over a bit more to blend in the *t* sound. For each of these sounds, the teacher will need to change the position of her mouth. She should practice it first with a mirror and then ask the children to watch her mouth and tell the number of positions they observe. For each sound there is a position; hence, in observing the positions they should be able to tell the number of sounds. Not letters, mind you! Sounds. English has digraphs that have one sound but are spelled by two letters. *Fish* is an example of this. It has the sounds represented by *f*, by short *i*, and by the *sh* combination. It has three sounds, yet not three letters.

When the children have learned that sounds are represented by letters, I have them listen to my *taffy* words and see if they can put down the corresponding letters as they hear the sounds. At first I use only those words that have an equal number of sounds and letters. When the children learn both how to sound and how to spell digraphs, I then employ the digraphs too.

Much can be done to help the auditorially impaired child if the teacher is well aware of these matters herself and incorporates them into her presentations. I would say that about 80 percent of the hundreds of children we see each year do not function as if they knew the difference between sounds and letters, and for the auditorially impaired child there is enough confusion already, especially when he has difficulty in reacting to the visual symbol with the appropriate sound or vice versa. I have heard teachers say, "Write the sound you hear first in the word *house*." The children hear a sound, but they cannot write the sound. They can write only the graphic representation of sound, that is, the letter *h*. (Pardon my stress on this. Experience has shown me it is not misplaced.)

The use of poetry helps also, especially if it is rhymed, since the auditorially impaired child has great difficulty in rhyming; he has less, but still considerable trouble, with substituting initial consonants. Many of these children also have difficulty in understanding directions, such as "at the beginning" and "at the end" of the word. If they learn the skill of stripping down a word to isolate the medial vowel, and they are asked to put *t* before or in front of the vowel, they will often put it at the end and will manifest great confusion over what you are asking them to do.

Frequently these children have difficulty with abstraction. The younger ones cannot classify such things as toys, foods, and people; the older ones have difficulty in grammar. Most of them find any kind of generalization very difficult. They cannot understand the multimeanings of words. In language development they find it difficult to evoke descriptive words expressing moods of feelings; hence, when telling or writing a story or in interpretive analysis of a story, these children fail to include colorful, descriptive words and cannot grasp their significance when they read such words. They are unable to state even their own reactions, much less the reactions of characters in stories. Try such questions as these in developing or interpreting the closing sentence of a paragraph: "What words would be good to describe how you feel on a summer morning ... after a fall into a cold lake ... when biting into a hot frank ... getting a good mark in school?" The children overwork the words *good, sad, happy*. That seems to be the extent of their descriptive vocabulary. Picture study can be effective in this.

In cooperative compositions, this type of child finds it difficult to suggest substitutes for words in a sentence. For instance, we start with the sentence: *The train ran down the track* and we try to supply more vivid words for *ran*. Children with adequate language can supply, even at third-grade level, such substitutes as: *zoomed, clattered, sped, dashed, lumbered, chugged, slid, rumbled, raced, zipped, crawled, shot*, etc. The auditorially impaired child seems to be satisfied to settle for less imaginative language. It may be because the effort to get substitute meanings is just too taxing for him, or the end product does not seem any better for the effort. "After all," he would think, "the train ran, didn't it?" He is not one to appreciate the implications in word selection.

Such difficulties with expressive and interpretive languages seem to be a factor in the child's failure to develop adequate comprehension by the ordinary recommended methods of developing it. Comprehension becomes a relatively poor attempt to remember facts and details rather than interpret meanings and evaluate situations. The child may remember that visually his eye picked up the word *red* before the word *engine*, but if you asked him if it made any difference in the story whether the color was red, the child might be unable to relate to the question; he might even wonder why on earth you ever asked that question.

Effective picture study can develop the insight that is required for comprehension. From a picture one can judge relationships and significant details, study moods, and identify the main idea suggested by the picture. It develops language skill to engage the child in efforts to express the main idea of a picture in the form of a topic sentence.

A very tantalizing problem of the auditorially impaired child is the association of sound with symbol and with a picture of the real object that has been graphically represented. One of the earliest phases of developing the child's ability to comprehend is to show him how things are related to spoken sounds, then to the written symbol as well as to day-by-day experiences. Pictures can be useful in studying the relationship of speech to thing, of thing to words. A picture of an ice cream cone is not an ice cream cone; it *pictures* one; that is, it represents it concretely. The letters i-c-e-c-r-e-a-m-c-o-n-e are not the ice cream cone nor the picture of one. They are the language equivalents. They express in written symbolic form what we see on the picture or hold in our hand, while the letters present to the eyes what we intend to communicate when we *say* the sounds of "ice cream cone."

Children can be helped to associate all these aspects together if the teacher goes about the task with a variety of interesting means, with patience, and without confusing *symbol* with *sound* with *reality*. Sooner or later most children receiving training in sound-symbol-reality association will respond to these mutual equivalents of communication. Sometimes it will be necessary to ask a child to draw a ball, to stand the picture beside the ball, and then to sound the name *ball*. It helps to get the child to write the word as well.

An exercise we find especially helpful in developing understanding of the spoken or read word, in encouraging arousal of the imagination, and in stimulating interest and assisting the memory, is to read a brief selection such as the following with the indicated interruptions of the reading for the purposes suggested. The selection is from Book B, *New Practice Readers* and is entitled "The House Eaters."[2]

Termites are little insects. (Stop.) To the children: "What are you thinking of, John. . .Mary. . .Linda?" If the response is negative, probably because no one is reacting to the thoughts conveyed by the words, I then say, "Do you know what I am thinking? I wonder how little they are. I wonder also if they look like a bee. . .or a ladybug. I am also thinking, 'Did I ever see a termite?' . . .Let us continue."

They may not be large, but they can do much harm. (Stop.) To the children: "What are you thinking, Linda. . .Joe. . .Jerry?" In the early stages of this development, do not expect too much. You have to show the way by expressing yourself out loud. "Do you know what I am thinking? I wonder what kind of harm they do. I would also like to know how they can do much harm if they are little. So I really would like to know how small they are. What do they compare to? Maybe the rest of the selection will answer some of my questions, so we will resume."

They eat paper, cloth, and wood. (Stop.) "Linda?. . .Joe?. . .Andre?. . . No reactions? I think they must be goats because goats eat things like that. Does anyone else have ideas about the termites, or questions you would like to have answered?"

They eat right through a book from cover to cover. (Stop.) "Any comments? Good, Jerry. . .Bill? I am thinking of how far it must be to eat right through a book from cover to cover. It is hard enough sometimes to read a book from cover to cover. What do you think we now know about termites which we did not know before?" and so on to the end.

There is great satisfaction in seeing how the children pick up the questioning habit and react to the information after the second or third such session. We call this game "Reaction, Please!" and believe me, we do not stop at literal comprehension (a misnomer anyway), but the technique moves us right up the comprehension skills ladder to critical thinking, and at times, recourse to resource materials.

The auditorially impaired child needs much training in listening to commands and performing them. A simple start should be made with one-unit commands such as "Please put your books on the nearest windowsill." Then proceed as soon as feasible to two-, three-, and four-unit commands. The child takes in the directions via sound vibrations in his auditory channel. After hearing the sounds, he must pass them along to the brain where they are interpreted. That gets him as far as perception. However, he must also remember not only the words of the directions but the number of the items and their sequence. He cannot close the window before he gets to it; he cannot look out the door until he remembers where it is and goes there. Hence, auditory and perhaps even visual memory is involved. The child may employ inner language to help him both remember the sequence and distinguish the meanings. He would have to integrate channels so as to transduce the auditory input into motor output. It is also demanded that he use his visual powers to direct his motor activity; hence, a visual-motor coordination is required; again, this demands a coupling of systems. He needs also to differentiate left from right, before from behind, and to manage himself in space.

These are the very specifics at which the child with learning disabilities can least achieve success. Training is long, requires patience, but in the long pull it can become successful with varying degrees of performance and self-satisfaction.

In a sense, the auditorially impaired child has a harder time than the visually impaired child. Suppose you were reading a book and you missed an important clue. Your eye could travel back over the preceding words, sentences, or even pages to pick up what you had missed. This regression is precisely what the child with impaired auditory powers cannot do. His is the road of no return, unless, of course, he has an empathetic tutor who will patiently repeat for him without encouraging careless listening. Even the ordinary flow of speech is too fast for him to absorb, and this child will habitually say "Pardon me?" with a question mark in his voice. It is the way you react when someone speaks a foreign language in your presence, and though you hear all the sounds, you cannot distinguish them into words and meaningful phrases, much less sentences. Therefore, the thought content is lost.

In spelling, the auditorially disabled child most reveals his difficulties. This child cannot spell the words he uses and understands. He has difficulty in building up written words and he is no more successful breaking whole words into parts—without structured help, that is.

Why? For one thing, he may have sequencing trouble, so that even if he did know the right letters for a word, he is very likely to disorder them. To disorder letters in a word is to misspell them. The most seriously impaired child may put down any letter his visual memory or his motor memory might dictate, without regard at all to the sounds of the word. This is an unusually bad exhibition of misspelling. It is difficult to know what the child is trying to write. It is far more difficult than it is to discover what the less disabled child wants to say when he writes *gril* for *girl*.

Another reason why this child cannot spell is that he cannot blend, which is a simple process for most children of putting two congenial sounds together, such as *b* and *l*, which, when fused, are heard at the beginning of the word *black*. Some will find it an even more difficult task to blend initial or final consonants to phonograms; they will be unable, for instance, to take *hat* and change it by substitution to *mat* or *fat*.

Since so many of our English words start with two- and three-letter blends, as in *track*, *bleach*, and *splash*, this child is at a serious disadvantage, since he is blocked at the very threshold of words. Imagine how difficult it is for him to spell words with two- and three-consonant blends in the final position, as in wea*lth*, stre*tch*, and su*ng*.

We at the center use the following technique to help children with problems of this kind. The technique covers many skills in addition to blending. We start with sight vocabulary, since this child usually has a fair one. We use his strength to reduce his weaknesses. There are about sixteen structured, repetitive, sequential steps, which a teacher soon masters, and, almost without fail, helps a child to develop. I shall interpret the stages as we go along. During the regular class periods, a child can accomplish in one or two sessions of one-half hour each, all the steps I shall demonstrate. This includes word meanings and all the other "goodies" the technique employs. The children love this technique and ask for it should we skip it on occasion.

Step One. Start with the sight word *top* (or, *mop, hop, stop*, whichever is known). Ask the child to say it, aud it (listen with care!), discriminate its sounds as he monitors it, recall the look of the letters which represent those sounds, and visualize the whole word. Lastly, have the word written.

Step Two. Write the *op* part of the word *top*. (Usually the first round is done at the blackboard to guide the child.) This second step may be difficult for some children who cannot hear what is happening to the word *top* to get *op*. If the child cannot hear that the initial consonant is dropped, show it to him visually: *top — op.* Return then to the auditory equivalent. The aim is to train his ears, not his eyes. For more drill, the teacher may use *mop, hop,* and *stop* to exercise the auditory skill of stripping down a word. Excellent drill in the auditory modality is provided for this child in stripping, especially when it is exercised not only initially on a word but also on the final sounds. When it is mastered, it gives the child another key for unlocking words: *brush — rush,* and *rush — rut.* So long as the exercises are not monotonous, the more discrimination drills the child has, the more he is likely to advance (other things being equal, of course).

The teacher will see some children who can say *top* correctly, who can aud it and write it, but who will then write *up* for *op* at this stage of the drill. The discrimination necessary to distinguish the two sounds is not available to some children, even with the prior experience with *top*.

Give a little exercise at this point to help the children to hear the differences. Let the teacher say slowly, carefully, *top.* Have it repeated. Say *op.* Have it repeated with very special care so that the short sound of *o,* not of *u,* is said. The teacher should demonstrate by showing the wide-open position of the mouth for short *o* in comparison with the relatively narrow opening for short *u.* Embed the two sounds in words: *not — nut.* Note the position of the mouth for each. Have the child listen for the sounds which issue as a result of the two positions. Place the child before the mirror, if needed, so he may look as well as listen. Try the same procedure on *top — cup.* One must not get discouraged. It is quite impossible at first for a child to hear the differences, especially if his enunciation is poor and he is not accustomed to opening his mouth in the production of clear sounds. Eventually, daily discrimination drill, coupled with enunciation exercises, works wonders.

Let us backtrack for a moment. In step one, we started with *top:* spoken, auded, re-auded, and written. In step two, we stripped the word *top* down to *op.* This syllable we hold in reserve.

Step Three. Here we select a new sight word: *her.* It should be said, auded, stripped of the initial consonant down to *er.* The child should be encouraged to attend to the sounds he hears so that he can improve in associating it with the correct visual symbol. If he has trouble with the visual production of words, encourage him to think how *er* looked when it was part of *her.* He will then have a second syllable in reserve for the word he will be asked to synthesize.

Step Four. Introduce the next sight word: *ate.* This will be the third component part the child will use in his construction of a whole word. A slight digression here may be helpful to teachers who have children like mine. These children will produce the word *eat* when asked for *ate*. Since it involves an added opportunity to clear up auditory indiscrimination, we repeat the word *eat* and ask the children to repeat it. Then we note that it started with a sound they might be able to identify as one of the letters of the alphabet. This does produce an answer quite often: *e*. Then the teacher points out that the word they were asked to aud was *ate*. We work on this until they can give us the symbol *a* for the sound they hear first in the word. But that is not all. Many such children will go on to write *ate* as *aet*. Not much time need be spent on this last error because so few words in the English dictionary put the two vowels together in that sequence. I do not tell the children that I spent a whole evening with a dictionary to determine how often that combination of *ae* sounds like long *a*. I discovered that it occurs in very few words. The ones I found were mostly foreign words, from the Greek, the Celtic (for example, the word *Gaelic*), Old English. So we just teach the children that the general use of the two vowels where the sound is of long *a* are in words spelled with a consonant between them, as in *wage*, *same*, and *rate*. The word *ate*, they are told, is like that.

The teacher might even show the difference it makes in saying and spelling words when we use or do not use the *e*: *at* — *ate*. No great delay is called for. The primary concern at this point is to help the children sequence word elements, which they can hear, spell, and write into real words. It is something they cannot do initially on their own.

Step Five. We now have three word elements which, when properly sequenced, will spell a word: *op er ate*. The child should say the word in parts, repeat it as a whole, beat the syllables with his hands, counting the number of syllables as he does so. The first beat should be intensified. He should listen to the stronger beat on the first syllable. Explanations should be given. Once again, have the child say it, beat it, aud it, spell it orally in parts, write it in parts, and write it as a whole word. I have done this hundreds of times with children and can testify that it takes this much directed, sequenced drill to produce the first writing of the first word, but the fruits of the patient efforts are worthwhile. The best fruit is the child's own reaction to his success.

When the child has assimilated the processes, discuss the meaning of the word *operate*. Tell the child that it is borrowed from a LATIN word which means to put to work or to work on something, as when a man operates a tractor. We could say that he drives it. A bus driver operates the bus. The elevator is operated by a man or woman. Each machine does its own job: it operates. The one who runs the machine is the *operator*. At this point we have the base word, upon which we will assist the child to build its variations in form.

Step Six. Select another sight word, for this is the child's area of strength. The teacher can choose *give*. Ask the child if he can make *gives* from *give*. Do not provide him with visual help at first. Let him listen to what happens when *give* is now said as *gives*. Then confirm his answers by visual means; for example, write both *give* and *gives* on the blackboard, while carefully pronouncing the words. For reinforcement, because we are trying to obtain a generalization from him, do the same with *take, drive,* or any other word ending in silent *e.* Explain that adding the *s* indicates that someone is doing that in the present time. Some children will want to add *es* because somewhere along the line the two endings were not adequately discriminated. It is sufficient to point out that since the silent *e* is already on the word, it is necessary to add only the *s.* When they don't accept that, I show them what it looks like to have the two *e*'s there and I try to get them to say it. They give up and accept adding *s* only. (Some poorly instructed children will tell you one must drop the *e* and add *es* or *ed.*)

The next word, then, is very easily performed by the child. We say, simply, "If you can make *give* say *gives,* and *take* say *takes,* why can't you make *operate* say *operates?*" He responds with smiles and he proceeds to do it. The steps must be observed: say it; beat it; hear it; spell it orally; write it as a whole; and mark the accent.

Step Seven. Use the sight word *bake.* Discuss what it means, how it is sounded, what sounds are heard, and how it is spelled. Have it written so that the child can see visually the presence of the *e* at the end. Ask how we would change the sounds and the spelling of the word to indicate that "Mother did that to cakes yesterday." Elicit the word *baked.* Say it; aud it; spell it; and write it. For reinforcement, repeat the process with *rake* and *save.* Involve only regular verbs with the silent *e* ending. Review now the meaning of the word *operated.* Refer again to the tractor, the bus, the elevator. Ask the child what each driver might be called. Say the word. Aud it; beat it; re-aud it; beat it again to have him listen for the stress. Ask him if the stress changed. Next say, "Since you can write *baked* (very carefully saying it with a good strong sound of *d*) and *raked* and *saved,* why can't you write *operated?*" Again you will see that joyous reaction, the eagerness to do it because he feels secure in the act. Security! That's what these children need to feel. Success and the teacher's attitude contribute greatly to it. Engaging all avenues of learning in the task, including also the direction given in sequencing the word parts, makes for success.

Step Eight. Start with the sight word that was used in step six: *give.* Say it carefully, stretching out the sounds like taffy, then compressing it to normal pronunciation. Ask the child to say it, aud it, re-aud it, and then to spell it orally and write it on paper or the board. Then ask, "Who can tell me how I use the word *give* when I want to say I am doing that now? I am _____ you a lesson now. What is the word? *Giving.* Say it. Beat it. Aud it. How many syllables does it have? See if you can close your eyes and remember how it is written. Do we change any part of the word?" Call for the spelling and the writing of it. Ask for a generalization of the rule where one drops the final *e* before a syllable starting with *i.* (That's sufficient generalization for them.) I laughingly tell the children, "*E* goes out when *I* come in!" They get it. Take time to visualize the generalizations for the child. Now introduce the word *live.* It is this careful step-by-step teaching and reinforcing that pays the dividends.

$$\text{give} - \text{giv}\cancel{e} + \text{ing} = \text{giving}$$
$$\text{live} - \text{liv}\cancel{e} + \text{ing} = \text{living}$$

Always provide support to your presentation by requiring the child to write whole words. Do not permit short cuts or patching of any kind. The child must not only see the parts but he must sequence them into wholes.

Reinforce again by saying, "If you can make *give* into *giving* and *live* into *living*, you can also make *operate* into *operating*." Again, have him say it, aud it, beat it, re-aud it, spell it orally, count the syllables, listen for the stress, and finally, write it as before.

If a child gets lost midway, have him repeat the auditory monitoring, and when he can say the parts in sequence, the teacher should dictate each part for him until he gets the whole. Let him then do it by himself in parts, and finally without parts.

Step Nine. From *give* and *live*, strip down to *ive*, just as you did to get *op* from *top*. Now again go through the auditory processes of listening to the whole in normal enunciation: *operative*; to the whole pulled out like taffy; to the word broken into syllables: *op er a tive*; to clapping it while listening for the number of syllables, the stress, and whether the accent has moved to another syllable. When the auditory and kinesthetic processes are successfully completed, have the word written in syllables while the child repeats them to himself. He then writes the word as a whole word, repeating the word before and after writing it.

This word building, when directed initially by the teacher, will assist the child in the reverse process (word recognition) when reading. He comes to recognize many word elements that recur in general vocabulary: *per, an, ter, ing, op, pre, en, tion, re, d, ed, ive, ment, able,* etc. The knowledge obtained in synthesizing exercises makes its contribution to skill in analyzing words that a child has never seen before:

com pen sate	in sti tu tion
in su late	re cip ro cate
at ten tive	en ter ing

Step Ten. Take time to teach a syllable that occurs at the end of many words the child meets, for example, on words such as recrea*tion*, vaca*tion*, examina*tion*. We write such a syllable in colored chalk with a box around it at the upper corner of a chalkboard. We call it "Our Practice Box." Whenever we get a difficult part of a word, we put it in the practice box and keep it visually available until the child has mastered it. *Tion* is one of the difficult syllables that we often use. After the child sees how its spelling is different from its sound, he is encouraged to look to the practice box for help in spelling it. After a relatively short time, the spelling is mastered, and by then another word-part is put into the box. The word-part *ble* stays there a longer time. Have the child at this point listen to words ending with *-tion*. These words are for saying, not for reading. Aud them carefully.

| vacation | rotation | dictation | examination |
| implementation | modification | notification | meditation |

Step Eleven. Now the child is ready to attack the word *operation.* Say it normally, then as taffy, slowly, pulled out so the sounds can be well auded and the new sound heard clearly. Say it; aud it; and clap it. Have him listen for the stress. Ask him if it has changed place. Have him count the syllables, write the word in syllables, then as a whole. Discuss the meaning of *operation.* Let it not be limited to the meaning of the word as it is used in hospitals. Relate it to projectors, elevators, tractors, busses, etc.

In normal classroom instruction, is there such stress on enunciation, pronunciation, meaning, spelling, syllabication, and accenting? We find that our auditorially impaired children end up better off in these skills than other children. All children need some degree of this deliberate, elaborate presentation of a word with all the trimmings.

Step Twelve. We use another sight word now: *coke.* The children see this word often and we can depend upon it that some of them will have it well fixed visually. Call for the careful pronunciation of the word. Listen for the sounds. Ask for the first sound. Ask what letters could spell that first sound. If they do not know, then tell the children that in this word the letter *c* spells the *k*-sound. We strip the word to *co* and have a new word part with which to build.

Ask if anyone knows the word we use when we say that people work well with the teacher. Get it or give it: *co op er ate.* Say it; beat it; and aud it. Have them listen for the change in stress. Repeat it. Aud it. Spell it orally in syllables. Write it in syllables. Write it as a whole word. Discuss further meaning if necessary.

Let us see how many new words the children now know as words; that is, words they can understand the meaning of, can spell and can write, words which we have derived from half a dozen sight words:

op er ate -s -ed -ing -tive -tion

Now we can add six more, using the *co-* prefix.

Step Thirteen. Set up another practice box. It will contain a small syllable, one that is heard very often. The syllable is pronounced *er*, and it can be spelled *er* or *or*. It also has other spellings, which can be studied another time. Here are some words using the *er* sound (no visualization should be given to the child when saying *er* because of its several spellings). The teacher can say and the child can repeat:

| farmer | actor | teacher | painter | sailor | trailer |
| player | worker | visitor | doctor | hunter | tractor |

The teacher may help develop the meaning of the syllable by asking, "What do we call someone who farms ... who teaches ... who acts ... who sails ... paints?" Get the generalization that the *er* syllable tells *who, the name we give to* those who farm, teach, hunt, work, paint, sail, etc.

At this point, visualization may be introduced. The teacher should put the syllables *er* and *or* in the practice box and explain that some of these words get the *er* ending and some of them the *or* ending. There is no real reason for one or the other, except that words have been formed that way. Ask if the child can visualize the word *sailor* and recall how the last syllable is spelled. Repeat with the words *work, farm,* and *visit.* The teacher cannot generalize here. She must just strive for the visual image of the word with its appropriate ending. Then, simply, we say, "The ending which goes on *operate* is the same one as is used on *sailor, actor,* and *doctor.* What is it?" The teacher must be sure that no distortion of the sound is made to indicate the *er* or the *or* spelling. If she wishes to, she may mention the schwa and indicate that the vowel in both the *er* and the *or* spelling sounds alike.

To prevent the child from making a mistake (by leaving the *e* on *operate*), we here dictate the syllables one by one after the usual saying, clapping, auding, etc.: *op er a tor.* (Otherwise, with some children it may turn out *op er ateor.*)

Step Fourteen. Start with the sight word *fun.* Say it. Aud it. Then strip it down to *un.* Explain that when *un* is placed before *cooperative* it tells us that the person is *not* cooperative. So now if the child can spell *cooperative,* he can also spell *uncooperative* and *uncooperating.*

Step Fifteen. The last ending we want to build on the word *operate* is the syllable *-ble.* The teacher should put it in the practice box. The children should pronounce it *b'l* and explain that it has a very hidden vowel sound between the two consonants. With mirrors or careful watching of the teacher's lips and mouth, the child should see and hear the difference in sounds between *b'l* and the *bl* we hear at the beginning of the word *black.* The *b'l* does have a vowel sound even though it is obscure, but the first two letters in *black* are closely blended with no other sound heard.

The teacher should pronounce the word *op er a ble.* Explain its meaning: the broken tractor has been repaired and now it is *op er a ble* once more. It can now perform; it can be put to work by the operator. Have the child listen carefully to the parts and to the sound of *a,* which was long in most of the other forms of the word. This time the *a* sound will be less clear. Tell him it will be sounded like the *a* we use when we say, "I want *a* book, *a* pencil, or *a* cookie." The teacher should have the child say *a* that way. Actually, it is the schwa and it is heard at the beginning and the end of *America.* With some attention to the hearing and then to the vowel, which at this time and in this word is spelled with an *a,* the child will be able to write, after the usual steps of saying, auding, beating, re-auding, etc., the word *op er a ble.*

If the teacher will refer back to the syllable *un,* which she put before the word *cooperate,* and if she will explain to the child that the syllable *in* also is used to say *not,* then the child knows the word for a machine that cannot be operated. It is *in op er a ble.*

Step Sixteen. This step will gather up the words the children have learned to say, to identify the sounds of, to know the syllables and the accent of, to know how to spell orally, and to write:

op er ate /s/ /ed/ /ting/ /tive/ /tion/ /tor/ /ble/

Combining these with the prefix *co-* we have:

co op er ate /s/ /ed/ /ting/ /tive/ /tion/ /ble/

Combining *un* with the root word and *in* where appropriate, we have these:

in op er a ble   un op er a tive   un co op er a tive   un co op er a ting

Showing the children how to add *ly* brings us to *co op er a tive ly* and *un co op er a tive ly*. Now that's a week's supply of words for a child!

The average child in the average classroom gets twenty new words a week. Because he is not auditorially impaired, the average child can master, through visual memory, anywhere from ten to twenty of them and get anywhere from 50 to 100 percent correct on his spelling for the week. Do you teachers find that those 50-to-100-percent children have these words available for utilization weeks or months later, when they need them?

By using the procedure we have just completed, the teacher of impaired children teaches a whole word *family*; the root; the variant meanings derived from inflectional endings; the meanings; the discrimination of spelling among words that sound as if they should be spelled alike; syllabication and the function of accents; phonetic skills and ear training; and above all, a sense of achievement.

There is less challenge for the unimpaired child who receives twenty dissimilar words each Monday. He usually finds some he already knows. He treats his list as a chore to be gone through, with memory as the chief functioning faculty. If he can hold the list in memory till Friday, and if he writes them carefully, he may get 100 percent. Many lose the look of the word, and poor penmanship further decreases the chance of a good mark. It is my opinion, from long experience, that the average student who studies spelling by the Monday-to-Friday list does not build up a reservoir of words for later retrieval when doing homework, when writing reports in content subject areas, or for employment in composition writing.

May we not give the auditorially impaired child a break? Get a list of phonetically regular root words and work with the children, not just in learning to spell them, nor in exploring their structural analysis; not just in phonetic development nor in learning syllabication and accent. Use the exercise to provide the child with the key that will open many more reading words to him, words he can identify and of which he knows the meanings. Make reading for him a joy to engage in, not a chore to be avoided.

You may say: But what of the unphonetic words? Yes, what of them? They constitute about 25 or 30 percent of our words. Some will be sight words. We shall have to work to build up that category. As for the phonetic words, the auditorially impaired child would not achieve them without the structured, careful, bit-by-bit technique explained above. By repetition of many elements, the child makes sight words, as it were, of the syllables. It remains for him to hear them in sequence and to aud them as he writes them. Whether he becomes fully successful is a moot question. He will, if our experience is any indication, be in a better position to synthesize and to analyze more words than he would ever achieve by the twenty word, Monday-to-Friday list.

By increasing the child's sight vocabulary, you will be giving him a broader base upon which to draw for word-parts when you employ them in synthesis. He has a better eye and ear understanding of words when he has put them together so that they will be usable to him when he meets them in reading.

Remember, they too, can conquer. Will you contribute your strengths to theirs?

NOTES

1. D. Johnson and H. Myklebust, *Learning Disabilities* (New York: Grune and Stratton, Inc., 1967).
2. Stone and Burton, *New Practice Readers, Book B* (New York: Webster Division, McGraw-Hill, 1962).

Identifying and Helping Learning-Disabled Children In Kindergarten

JEANNE M. McCARTHY
SONYA PETERSEN
BARBARA H. SOMMER
JOAN E. JOHNSTON

The focus on children with specific learning disabilities engendered by the research and demonstration project in Schaumburg District 54 funded by the Bureau of Education for the Handicapped led quite naturally to a concern with early identification and a program of prevention. Our presentation will describe a derivative of the learning disabilities project, the developmental first grade program, and will include the philosophy of early education, the selection process, the treatment plan, the cognitive and perceptual characteristics of children selected as being not ready for first grade, and the effects of the treatment plan on these cognitive and perceptual processes.

One of the most common, and yet most questionable practices in education is the practice of placing children who are not ready to succeed in an academic program in first grade. The other alternatives—repeating kindergarten or remaining out of school until readiness for success in first grade develops—are equally unsound and lacking a base in either research or theory.

Although readiness, especially for reading and academic learning, has been a controversial subject, current thinking accepts the fact that maturation unfolds in continuous interactions with environmental stimulation. If this is true, the educator cannot afford to wait passively for maturation to occur, especially in those children who have not responded in a normal way to their preschool and kindergarten environments. Nor should the child be exposed to a kind of instruction that is clearly inappropriate to his particular stage of growth. It becomes incumbent upon the schools to match teaching methods to the child's specific developmental needs.

Admitting very immature youngsters into the first grade, where their chances to succeed are slim, and where, at the very beginning of their school careers, they are exposed to the damaging experience of failure, is highly undesirable. The psychological stresses experienced by children who are not ready for the educational demands of first grade have been described by many researchers. Allowing non-ready children to enter first grade in the belief that they will outgrow their difficulties is a procedure fraught with hazards. Immature first-graders do not necessarily catch up; indeed they tend to fall further behind.

From the *Proceedings* of the Fifth Annual Conference of the ACLD, *Successful Planning: Many Points of View.* Boston, Mass. (February 1–3, 1968), pp. 169–188.

The developmental timing of immature children is usually atypical. At kindergarten age they may be unable to benefit from a formal reading readiness program. Repeating kindergarten would give them an additional year in which to mature and might thus have certain advantages, but it would not provide the intensive and specific training they need. Promotion into first grade, on the other hand, does not solve their problem either, since the pace in first grade is usually too fast for those youngsters who are ready to learn but as yet unable to cope with organized reading and writing instruction at the conventional age.

After four years' experience with children with special learning disabilities in Schaumburg District 54, it became apparent to us that non-ready children do not need a reduced program such as that received by repeating kindergarten. They are desperately in need of an intensified program if they are to overcome the disabilities that have already impeded their academic progress.

Such an intensified program, involving identification of children with learning problems at the kindergarten level followed by specific remediation the next year, was provided in the developmental first grade program in Schaumberg Elementary District 54.

In the spring of 1967, sixty children were selected who met the criteria for admission to the new classes. The treatment plan proposed as part of this program consisted of three variables:

1. reduced class size, with fifteen children per teacher
2. careful teacher selection
3. a specially modified curriculum, with heavy emphasis on language development.

It was administratively and financially feasible to cut normal first-grade enrollment in half because the developmental first-grade program met the criteria established by the Office of the Superintendent of Public Instruction for Socially Maladjusted Classes, Section 7.01A of the Illinois School Code. This section defines the socially maladjusted as children with "poor social adjustment associated with such factors as cultural deprivation, educational retardation, population mobility, socioeconomic considerations, and inadequate school opportunities." The children were considered to be educationally retarded. The State Office reimbursed the school district at the rate of $4000 per professional worker.

The possible outcomes that were foreseen ranged from extremely optimistic to extremely pessimistic:

1. immediate placement in a regular first grade for those children who, in September, did not seem to need such a program (It was anticipated that some children would change dramatically over the summer, or that the screening process would have identified some children who seemed not to need the special program.)
2. placement in a regular first grade during the year if success with the normal academic curriculum could reasonably be predicted

3. promotion to a regular second grade the following year if the problem areas could be sufficiently remediated in the developmental first grade
4. placement in a regular first grade the following year, where success rather than failure could be predicted (Thus, for those children who could be expected to repeat first grade, the two years of success would replace the usual one year of failure followed by one year of dubious success.)
5. special class placement in one of the existing programs for children with special learning disabilities.

Because of the numbers of children involved in the kindergarten program (1200) and the limited special education staff available, screening devices were used by classroom teachers, a procedure that resulted in a minimal amount of involvement on the part of psychologists, social workers, or psychoeducational diagnosticians. A five-step screening procedure was devised which provided samples of various kinds of behavior:

1. a measure of the child's behavior in a group situation over an extended period of time
2. a measure of the child's behavior in a one-to-one situation
3. a measure of the child's ability to function on a paper-and-pencil task
4. a measure of speech and language development
5. a full staff conference in which all variables, including other alternatives to special class placement, could be weighed.

Using this procedure, those children judged by their teachers to be not ready to succeed in an academic first grade program were placed in one of four developmental first grades.

At the initial orientation meeting, held in early Spring, the program was described in detail, and copies of the Teacher Estimate were distributed to each teacher, along with the "Guidelines for Estimating Pupils' Abilities," developed by Winifred Kirk in 1966. This one-page instrument was filled out for all students about whom the kindergarten teacher had reservations concerning ability to succeed in first grade. These rating scales were graded by the psychoeducational diagnosticians, and the scores adjusted for chronological age differences. This checklist was devised by Winifred Kirk and tested for validity in the Urbana, Illinois, schools and appeared in the December, 1966 issue of *Exceptional Child*. This teacher checklist contains nine variables on which the child is rated by the teacher on a five-point scale. It correlates as high as .70 with individually administered Binets. Each teacher was given a copy of the guidelines explaining each variable and enough copies of the Teacher Estimate for the lower 25 percent of her class. We anticipated that approximately 300 children would be referred, out of 1200, as a result of this initial step of the screening procedure.

Those children who scored below 40 were then tested individually by their kindergarten teacher, who used a modification of the Behavior and Development Screening Scale developed by Haring and Ridgeway in 1967. This test samples the child's performance on a variety of tasks, including speech, language, auditory discrimination, auditory perception, auditory memory for meaningful and nonmeaningful material, visual discrimination, visual-motor integration, laterality, and eye-hand coordination. All children scoring below 80 on this scale were considered potential candidates for placement in the class.

The third step in the screening procedure involved the Metropolitan Reading Readiness Test routinely given to all kindergarten children in the spring of the kindergarten year. Only those children scoring below the 20th percentile were considered to be in need of placement in the developmental first grade.

In addition, the Speech Correction Department in District 54 devised a speech and language evaluation which included some items similar to those included in the School Readiness Test, an articulation test, and the Peabody Picture Vocabulary Test. The child was seen individually by the speech correctionist who administered this screening scale.

From the group of children considered eligible on these four screening measures, final selection of the sixty children to be placed in the classes was made at a staff conference attended by the principal, kindergarten teacher, special class teacher, the psychologist, the psychoeducational diagnostician, the social worker, the nurse, and the speech correctionist. All available information concerning the child, including the health history, the social history, and reports from other agencies were considered in the final selection process. With those children who could conceivably adjust to the regular curriculum, the deciding factor in some cases was the availability of a very strong first-grade teacher. Those children selected for the special classes met the following criteria in addition to that outlined above:

1. existence of a problem in adjusting to the demands of the regular curriculum, primarily associated with educational retardation
2. the presence of at least one of the following characteristics in association with the academic, emotional and/or social adjustment problem:
   a. slow social and/or physical maturation
   b. poor motivation for attendance or participation in kindergarten program
   c. poor communication ability
   d. inability to comprehend or follow directions
   e. problem with socialization with peers
   f. poor familial-cultural background
   g. poor familial relationships and attitudes toward child or school
3. the ability to profit from and learn in the developmental first grade.

At this point, the speech correctionists began a program which was three-fold. Their role in this program was first to aid in the diagnosis, appraisal, and screening of the children who were placed in the developmental first-grade classes; second, to develop a language program for those children who had language difficulties other than those of a maturational nature; and third, to work directly with all the developmental-first-grade children in the classroom setting.

It was not the purpose of the speech correctionist to give speech-improvement lessons for the purpose of correcting maturational articulation errors, but rather to focus on listening skills, language activities, speech improvement, and the creation of an awareness that speech and communication can be fun. These goals, of course, could not be realized by a once-a-week lesson presentation, so it was necessary for the speech correctionist to work closely with the classroom teacher.

The development of listening skills provided a useful base on which to increase attention span since many of the children found it difficult to sit for even short periods. Identification and discrimination of gross sounds like bells, drums, sanders, gongs, etc., were initially presented. These were followed by finer auditory-discrimination tasks such as identification of school sounds, home sounds, and animal sounds, which enhanced listening ability to the point where most of the children were able to identify many of the sounds of speech.

Early in September, the psychoeducational diagnosticians completed a battery of diagnostic tests on each child, including psycholinguistic abilities, visual-perceptual abilities, auditory discrimination, and visual-motor integration. The test results, together with diagnostic observations and data gathered during diagnostic teaching sessions, were discussed at length with the teacher of the developmental first grade.

After the testing was completed, the diagnosticians made plans to work with some of the children in the classes. Schedules were arranged to meet the needs of the individuals in the classes. Children were seen in small groups and on an individual basis.

As part of the diagnostic procedure, the Wechsler Preschool and Primary Scale of Intelligence was administered by the school psychologists.

The WPPSI is a new test, having been in general use for less than a year. For those who are not familiar with WPPSI, it differs from the Wechsler Intelligence Scale for Children (WISC) in several ways. In place of the standard coding of the WISC there is a coding test that requires the child to match colors and animals. The motor development required by this subtest is more in keeping with the motor abilities of young children than the paper and pencil coding of the WISC. In the WPPSI, the maze subtest is not optional, as it is in the WISC; the mazes are easier and there are more of them. Also, there are neither object-assembly nor picture-arrangement subtests. Instead, there is a geometric-design subtest with ten designs to be copied by the child, including a circle, a square, and other simple figures. An optional verbal test replaces digit span. This test requires the child to repeat sentences rather than digits. We were generally pleased with the WPPSI and felt that it provided much insight into behavioral problems.

Full scale IQ scores on the children have ranged from retarded to superior. The sample is skewed to the left, with 85 percent of the scores below 100. The cluster is in the 90 to 100 range. The lowest scores have generally been in the areas of arithmetic and block design and the highest in the area of vocabulary.

Many of the behavioral patterns observed during testing would place these children at a disadvantage in a regular first grade. The first area is general testability, which was consistently poor. The children were eager and happy, but getting them to finish a subtest was sometimes difficult. Frequently we had to make games out of subtests; we had to scold, place children on our laps, and really work for attention. Some of the tests took a long time to administer, especially when we had to take time out to answer questions and listen to stories associated with the stimuli of the subtests. Then again, some children, when asked a question, would sit and stare straight ahead with seemingly no response at all.

Several subtests required answers in the form of phrases or sentences, and some of these children—more than would be found in a typical first-grade class—had trouble giving more than single-word associations.

Many of these little ones showed some of the individual differences that make it difficult for children to "get along" in first grade. Sometimes these problems were compounded with various physical problems and learning disabilities. We did have two cerebral palsied children, several perceptually handicapped children, and some children with rather complicated motor problems.

In addition to the cognitive and intellectual characteristics of the developmental first-grade children, emotional and social problems were also apparent and of concern to the social workers in District 54.

The emotional characteristics or problems seen most often in the children in developmental first grade this year can best be described under the general heading of emotional immaturity. Their immaturity is evidenced by numerous reports of short attention span, infantile speech patterns and language development, poor internal control resulting in poor behavior, and an excessive amount of dependency. The great majority of these children were not oriented to completing assigned tasks, nor did they appear to feel a sense of responsibility for doing their work. From the beginning, many responded well to the teacher's undivided attention, but showed only a minimal ability to function in a class-group situation.

Of course, immaturity, depending upon the degree and possible pathology in the home environment, can be a severe emotional problem in itself. This year we have seen a few children manifesting beginning neurotic disorders. However, it appears that the majority of youngsters, with this more individualized attention coupled with their physical maturation, are maturing with no indication of serious emotional disturbance. This matter of physical maturation is of extreme importance, as almost all of these children show some limitation in their gross- and fine-motor coordination.

We have seen a trend in family patterning. Slightly over 50 percent of the children are from large families (classified as four or more for the purpose of this study). Also, the majority are in the middle of the family constellation with both older and younger siblings close in age. This finding does suggest the possibility that, because of their middle or close-to-middle position in a large family, they may often have lacked the quantity and quality of parental interest afforded their siblings.

One area handled by the social worker is that of referrals to agencies outside the school. When families have problems severe enough to warrant help, we can refer them to public and private services in our area. We usually provide a list of several possibilities and offer to cooperate with the agency of the family's choice. This may involve staffings, phone calls, reports, or whatever is requested. Sometimes while parents are working with outside agencies, we may continue to work with the child at school.

Another service we provide is to collect a social history of the family whenever it would seem to be of value in programing for the child. Often family situations give us much insight into the causes for certain functional patterns of a child. Also, we can sometimes spot the areas that must be dealt with if a child is to be allowed to work up to his capacities. These services are not only for our developmental first-graders, but because they are part of our program, they get them, too.

All of the first-graders in our district are screened for vision and hearing by the school nurses. The developmental first-graders went through this, too. As we have consistently noticed, testability has been poor. Screening for these children was done on a one-to-one basis. In order to get valid results we invented response tasks to maintain interest and attention. For example, for the audiometer we might say, "Drop the block in the box when you hear the sound." When using the Snellen E Chart for acuity, the instruction might be, "Make your cardboard E look like that E." Fewer games had to be made up for developmental first-graders screened recently than for those screened at the beginning of the year.

While the children are in school, the nurse provides the kinds of services that we provide for all the children in our program. When we pick up problems in the vision and hearing screening, we check and recheck, and then we make suggestions to teachers and parents for following up the problem. This may involve special seating in the classroom and referrals to physicians. At the request of parents and other members of the team, we communicate directly with physicians and other professionals in order to collect information and suggestions for the individual programming of each child.

In each school we serve, we see every first-grader, whether through screening, accidents, or illness. Sometimes a scratch or bruise is only an excuse to see us. We like the idea that children see us as "friends" rather than disciplinarians. This makes it easier for us to help children and their families. We are available at certain times, and many of the children know that. Often we get a real feeling for a child and can share our impressions with the other members of the team.

For special-education placements and whenever it is requested, we make home visits and collect health histories to add to the information of the other members of the team. At the end of the health-history form, we like to attach a sheet with a couple of paragraphs, giving our impressions of the total family situation, significant health problems or patterns, or anything we feel is important for the educational planning for the child.

In implementing an effective learning-disabilities program, it was felt important to include the parents. This was begun through a meeting held in June of last year. It was an evening meeting so that both the fathers and mothers of the children could be present. The two school psychologists, and two developmental first-grade teachers, conducted a discussion to explain the purposes of the program and answer the many questions we knew the parents would have.

Some of the materials which we would use were displayed in order to explain more clearly what kinds of perceptual and linguistic deficits were present and what kind of remediation was planned. Because of the newness of the program, there was much interest and many questions. Some parents felt we had singled out their child unfairly, others were grateful that the school showed concern.

In the fall, we were anxious to meet with the parents to inform them further of the activities that would be provided during the year for their children. During the month of September, we had open house so that the parents could visit the classroom and meet with us. At this time we were able to explain more thoroughly the curriculum that would be followed.

The first formal parent-teacher conferences were held at the time of the regular reporting period in November. Since the regular first grades do not use a written report, we were not obliged to use one either.

In order to explain to the parents what progress the child was making, we set up a list of goals. These were based partially on the kindergarten expectancies and on experiences we considered necessary for first-grade readiness.

The children were rated in the following areas: proficiency in language, readiness for reading and arithmetic, gross- and fine-motor coordination, self-expression in art and music, social skills, personal habits, and work habits. Parents were given suggestions on how to help the child to improve some of these areas.

One of the activities in which the parents could assume a teaching role is in the routine of daily living. For example, setting the dinner table could involve oral directions such as, "Put the fork next to the plate." Number concepts, in counting the correct amount of silverware, can also be practiced. In addition to this type of help, parents were requested to avoid trying to teach specific academic subjects.

The curriculum basically developed around the goals which we wanted the children to achieve. Specific subject areas, which may be part of the regular first-grade program, are not included as such, but are taught as part of the total language program as concept development.

The lowest scores on the ITPA were in the automatic sequential areas. Skill in these areas is desirable, as it is necessary to have these abilities in order to count, learn the alphabet, spell, or read. There are many activities we can use to teach this.

Use of beads for stringing and the color chips from the Peabody Kit are semiconcrete aids which the child can manipulate to learn sequential order. Examples of activities in the area of sequencing include:

- Starting with three color chips in a chain, the child copies, in proper sequence, with a chain of his own.
- Stepping stones are useful in teaching the sequence of numbers, as a child can involve his whole self in progressing from numeral to numeral.
- Sequencing in stories can be taught through simple pictorial representations of an activity or process.

As shown by the scores on the Wepman Auditory Discrimination Test, most of the children have inadequate ability to discriminate; therefore, much training in this area is necessary.

With the aid of the two levels of the Peabody Kit, duplicate pictures of animals can be obtained. Each child is given a picture of an animal while the teacher holds the duplicates. I use a tape recorder to increase interest and lessen the use of visual "cues" often obtained through watching the movements of the teacher's lips. You can have the child turn his back to you if a tape recorder is unavailable. A typical lesson might be like this: "Look at your pictures. If you have the animal that makes this sound, bring your picture to me. We'll see if they match." Another similar technique is to have one child at a time wear headphones to increase attention to the stimulus and decrease distractibility. Have at least three pictures of animals in front of the child. Say, "Point to the 'moo-moo.'" Additional activities can be done with musical instruments or noisemaker toys with which the child has become familiar. These activities can then be incorporated into a music and rhythm program.

Many of the children have difficulty in learning to identify and write the letters of the alphabet. It is necessary to involve as many sensory modalities as possible so that each child can learn through his own strongest channel. Let's use the letter "K" as an example. Following are several techniques which I use to impress upon the child the image of the letter "K":

- Trace the letter on dotted lines.
- Write with a stylus on a board covered with clay.
- Mold the letter out of clay.
- Make it out of scribble stix.

- Trace it on the beaded kinesthetic cards.
- Match two halves in the correct way.
- Write the letter by itself.

The child can retain the image of the letter by hearing me say the name of the letter as I write it, seeing me write it correctly, and saying it to himself as he writes it.

Adequate visual perception often depends upon the child's image of himself and others. To develop awareness of the body, we utilize activities which employ pictures of parts of the body, as well as the body itself. For example, using a picture of a face which has no identifying characteristics, such as sex, I say, "Here is a face. Let's name the parts as I point to them. Show me on your face where these are." I might then tell the student to close his eyes; I remove a part from the face picture, then say, "Can you tell me what part is missing? Good. Can you put it where it belongs?" These instructions are repeated as often as necessary.

There are many other activities and techniques which can be used to remediate special problems. I hope that those outlined above will give others some ideas which can be adapted for their own use.

Changes in diagnostic test scores indicate that the rate of development of the psycholinguistic abilities which underlie learning can be changed significantly with the modified first-grade program. It would appear to provide a vehicle for effectively remediating specific deficits found in these children. It is possible that modifications of the goals of the kindergarten, and of the curriculum, could facilitate this clinical approach to young children with learning disabilities.

The Santa Monica Project:
An Engineered Classroom
FRANK D. TAYLOR*

For several years the Santa Monica Unified School District has been concerned about the increasing number of inattentive, failure-prone, hyperactive children who are average, or above average, in intelligence but who cannot be contained within the usual classroom structure.

The school district recognized that these students had the potential to achieve in school if some appropriate program could be developed for them. It was obvious that the assignment of children to home teachers was not an effective way to meet the problem. At the same time it was not feasible to leave the students in the regular classroom.

Recently a model called "behavior modification" has demonstrated its usefulness with exceptional children. Rather than viewing the educationally handicapped child as a victim of psychic conflicts or cerebral dysfunction, this approach concentrates on bringing the nonstudent behavior of the child into line with standards required for learning.

This model, as developed for application in the classroom by Dr. Frank M. Hewett, Head of the Neuropsychiatric Institute School at University of California in Los Angeles, is known as the Engineered Classroom. The goals of the Engineered Classroom are to lengthen attention span, promote successful accomplishment of carefully graded tasks, and to provide a learning environment with rewards and structure for the child in accord with the principles of learning theory.

Dr. Alfred A. Artuso, superintendent, and Dr. Frank D. Taylor, director of special services of the Santa Monica Unified School District, envisioned the Engineered Classroom design as a possible solution to the problems described earlier.

The classrooms for educationally handicapped students as developed in Santa Monica assign to the teacher the role of behavioral engineer. The design attempts to define appropriate task assignments for students, to provide meaningful rewards for learning, and to maintain well-defined limits in order to reduce, and hopefully eliminate, the occurrence of maladaptive behavior in school.

*Co-investigators with Dr. Taylor on this cooperative project between the University of California and the Los Angeles and Santa Monica School Districts were Dr. Frank Hewett, University of California at Los Angeles, and Dr. Alfred Artuso, superintendent of the Santa Monica Unified School District.

From the *Proceedings* of the Fourth Annual Conference of the ACLD, *Management of the Child with Learning Disabilities: An Interdisciplinary Challenge.* New York (March 9-11, 1967), pp. 197-199.

The Engineered Classroom model attempts to translate behavior-modification principles and theories, not rigidly but pragmatically, to a public-school setting. Behavior-modification principles such as immediate feedback of results, building secondary reinforcement through initial use of primary reinforcement, scheduling of reinforcement, shaping behavior through successive approximation, and focus on observable events, are utilized in this design. The design provides four important elements of structure for the classroom teacher.

Hierarchy of Educational Tasks

The hierarchy postulates seven educational task levels: attention, response, order, exploratory, social, mastery, and achievement, and describes the educationally handicapped or emotionally disturbed child with respect to deficits at each level. Each level is considered in terms of three ingredients which are thought to be essential in all learning situations: a suitable educational task, provision for meaningful learner reward, and maintenance of a degree of teacher structure or control.

While the ultimate goal of the teacher is to engage the student at the mastery and achievement levels, children must first be considered in terms of their development at lower levels and assignments in school must take this into account. In helping an educationally handicapped child get ready for intellectual training the teacher can profitably use the behavior-modification principle of shaping and, rather than hold out for the ultimate goal (for example, student achievement approximating the intellectual level), foster successive approximations of that goal (for example, functioning at attention, response, acceptance, order, exploratory, and social levels). The Engineered Classroom design attempts to do just that.

Classroom Arrangement

The physical environment can be described according to three major centers, paralleling levels on the hierarchy of educational tasks. The Mastery and Achievement Center consists of the student desk area where academic assignments are undertaken. Adjacent to, and part of, this center are two study booths or "offices" where academic work may be done without visual distraction. Ideally these are carpeted and outfitted with desks and upholstered easy chairs. An Exploratory Center is set up near the windows and sink facilities. Here equipment for simple science experiments, arts, crafts, music, and communication activities are provided. Social skills are fostered in the communication area of the Exploratory Center. The Order Center is in an opposite corner of the classroom and consists of two double desks and a storage cabinet where games, puzzles, exercises, and activities emphasizing attention, orderly response, and routine are kept.

The Checkmark System

Mounted by the door is a work-record-card holder, much like a time-card rack near the time clock in a factory. An individual work-record card for each student is in the holder. As each student enters the room in the morning he picks up his individual work-record card which is ruled with two hundred squares. As he moves through the day the teacher and aide recognize his efficiency to function as a student by giving checkmarks on the work-record card. Checkmarks are given on a fixed interval, fixed ratio basis, with a possible ten checkmarks for each fifteen minutes.

This system attempts to provide rewards on a concrete, immediate basis for children who have not been responsive to the more typical kinds of rewards provided by school (for example, long-range grades, praise, parental recognition, and competition). Students save completed work-record cards and they are exchanged on a weekly basis for candy, small toys, and trinkets.

Classroom Interventions

Nine specific interventions have been developed which encompass the seven levels on the hierarchy of educational tasks.

As long as the child is able to stabilize himself during any of the student interventions, he continues to earn checkmarks on a par with those students successfully pursuing mastery level assignments. He is in no way penalized for the shift in assignments made by the teacher.

Each student starts his class day in either reading or writing language activity. If, at any time, he begins to display signs of maladaptive learning behavior (for example, inattention, daydreaming, boredom, or disruption) his assignments are quickly altered. The teacher may select any intervention she sees as being appropriate for a given student or she may try the student at each intervention level until his behavior improves.

It is unrealistic to assume that the hierarchy of educational tasks, classroom organization, checkmark system, and interventions represent a foolproof formula for success with all educationally handicapped children. The guidelines do however offer sound educational, psychological, and developmental principles for training more effective teachers and establishing more adequate classrooms for disturbed children than is now possible through reliance on subjective judgment, intuition, and "cafeteria" approaches.

Madison School Plan

FRANK D. TAYLOR[*]

The decade of the sixties has left special education in ferment. Dissatisfaction with the traditional disability categories as a basis for educational programming is widespread. The specialist approach that has emerged, with reference to teacher training, credentialing, legislation, curriculum, and organization of special classes in the public school, may be contributing to an unnecessary preoccupation with labels. Past efforts to classify, describe, and provide separate educational programs for handicapped students need to be reappraised.

Concern about possible limited effectiveness of traditional curriculum, instructional methods, doubts about the cost-effectiveness and the social-psychological impact of traditional special classes have reached major proportions.[1]

I and my co-investigators have felt that students could be grouped according to their learning deficits, with resource room or a type of learning center remediation and maximum regular classroom integration rather than separated into discrete categories of exceptionality and isolated in separate, self-contained rooms. With this in mind an educational model, the Madison School Plan, was developed and made operational. It provides an instructional program for exceptional children based on their specific learning deficits rather than traditional categories for the handicapped. These efforts were made possible through a California State Department of Education Title VI-B Grant.

The project was directed toward the demonstration and evaluation of a plan for the education of a group of handicapped children who would traditionally be labeled educable mentally retarded, educationally handicapped, learning disabled, visually impaired, and auditorily impaired.

This plan, to be described in detail below, provides for the education of these children in a setting that allows free flow of children between the regular classes and the specialized facility (learning center). It permits the elimination of traditional disability grouping for all but administrative purposes and provides an instructional program that is linked to a continuous assessment of those educational variables that operated to hinder the performance of the exceptional child in the regular classroom.

The grouping framework utilized in the Madison School Plan was organized on four levels: Pre-Academic I, Pre-Academic II, Academic I, and Academic II.

[*]Dr. Taylor has coauthored a related discussion of the Madison School Plan. See F. M. Hewett, F. D. Taylor, A. A. Artuso, and H. C. Quay, "The Learning Center Concept," Behavior Modification of Learning Disabilities, ed. Robert H. Bradfield (San Rafael, Calif.: Academic Therapy Publications, 1971).

From the Proceedings of the Eighth Annual Conference of the ACLD, The Child with Learning Disabilities: His Right to Learn. Chicago (March 18-20, 1971), pp 85-89.

Pre-Academic I

The first level is conceived as a largely self-contained class grouping of six to twelve children with behavioral problems that overshadow academic deficits. The students learn to sit still, pay attention, respond appropriately, take turns, follow simple directions, get along with others, and develop the ability to function in a small group. Initially, these students would have been unable to spend any length of productive time in a regular classroom. This setting is designed to bring the overt behavior of the children into line with minimum standards required for learning. Lengthening attention span, encouraging appropriate responses, and developing student-like behavior represent the main focus. In many ways, it is similar to the Engineered Classroom.[2]

Pre-Academic II

The second level is a small teacher-group setting for four to eight children having readiness academic problems that overshadow academic problems. These students need to receive intense remediation in specific academic areas. Severe deficits in reading or arithmetic are typical of the factors that make it difficult for these students to function in a typical large group setting or a regular classroom. This small group setting provides opportunities to concentrate on primary academic remediation, developing a readiness for participation in larger group settings in terms of oral participation and language emphasis. Flexible assignment between settings within the learning center is stressed, with continuous daily and hourly student assessment emphasized. Students in Pre-Academic II are still on a systematic immediate and frequent reinforcement schedule similar to Pre-Academic I.

Academic I

The third level is a simulated regular classroom setting within the learning center for twelve to twenty-five children who have primary academic problems that can be dealt with in a large teacher-class setting. Students in this setting have the ability to spend increasing amounts of time in the regular classroom and have a readiness for the more traditional system of grading in terms of effort, quality of work, and citizenship. The teacher leads large class type discussions and presents large group lessons in reading, arithmetic, spelling, social studies, and English. Students are grouped within this large setting in the same manner expected by a regular classroom teacher; opportunities for silent, independent study are present. Emphasis is also placed on helping each student with the specific skills needed to increase the amount of time spent in a regular classroom.

Academic II

This setting is the regular classroom in the school, with from twenty-eight to thirty-five students, and it follows the typical public school program. All handicapped students in the program are assigned to one of the Pre-Academic I, Pre-Academic II, or Academic I settings, with those in the latter two groups integrated for varying periods of time in Academic II (the regular classroom).

A daily schedule for all three settings within the learning center is carefully planned to provide individual, independent, and group lessons dependent on student needs. Commercially available materials are utilized, programmed instructional techniques employed, and teacher preparation time is kept to a minimum. One of the specific learning center daily schedules is shown in Figure 1.

Assessment

The model implies, in essence, that first you assign children to a grouping category, and once this assignment has been made, you zero in on a detailed assessment over a period of time, rather than stopping with just an initial full-scale preplacement assessment, as is often the case in traditional programs.

In order to maintain a continuous assessment of each child's progress and provide data for reassignment to different groupings, two types of procedures are utilized. A checkmark system in Pre-Academic I and II, and a numerical rating system in Academic I and II. The checkmark system involves giving each child a possible ten checkmarks, in the form of alphabet letters, every twenty minutes during the morning.

This system makes it possible to determine the percentage of rating points earned by each student over the week in relation to his readiness for regular class functioning, as well as a profile of pre-academic or academic areas in which he needs to improve. In the Academic I rating system, the teacher gives each student a one-to-five rating in three areas every twenty minutes: effort, quality of work, and citizenship. Weekly percentages reflect the child's functioning in these traditional grading areas. Each regular classroom teacher who has contact with a project child also is asked to provide a weekly rating in these areas for each child. When they consider reassignment for a given child, his progress, or lack of it, as shown in their evaluation data, is carefully reviewed.

Regular Class Integration

At the beginning of the school year, as many of the educationally handicapped children with learning disabilities as possible are assigned to regular classrooms. As students are referred out to the special program because they cannot handle the behavioral and

	ACADEMIC I	PRE-ACADEMIC II	PRE-ACADEMIC I
8:45	TYPICAL CLASS OPENING EXERCISES DIRECTION-FOLLOWING TASK		
9:00	**READING** typical large class reading program; group and individual reading; basal readers, SRA, etc.	**READING** remedial-reading instruction or motivation for story writing	**READING** individual reading
		story writing or remedial follow-up task	word study
		word study; individual reading, programed material	skill reading
10:00	·····recess ·············· recess ················recess···········		
10:15	**ARITHMETIC** typical class program; discussions; group and independent work	**ARITHMETIC** arithmetic instruction; specific follow-up tasks; remedial opportunities	**ARITHMETIC** arithmetic drill
			instruction
			follow-up
10:55	spelling	language development and/or spelling	language skills
11:25	····· lunch ·············· lunch················· lunch ·········		
12:25	read to class	pre-academic II students join ←——either——→ group according to their individual needs	**EXPLORATORY** art
12:40	social studies English art		science order communication
1:50	·····recess ·············· recess ················recess ··········		
2:00	physical education		opportunities for individualized remedial instruction
2:30	individual tutoring		
3:00			

Figure 1. DAILY SCHEDULE OF ACTIVITIES IN THE LEARNING CENTER

academic demands of the class, an attempt is made to preserve some link with the regular class by having the child return for morning exercises, physical education, music, etc. As they demonstrate academic and/or behavioral improvement, an effort is made to increase their time in the regular class until optimum placement is reached. The evaluation procedures presented in the preceding selection aid in determining this reassignment. The educable mentally retarded children start in the special program, but early in the school year efforts are made to establish a regular classroom link for them. During the year their progress on the evaluation ratings is noted, and integration is increased whenever possible.

In summary, the Madison School Plan, developed over a four-year period, attempts to combine traditional categories of exceptionality along a dimension of readiness for regular classroom functioning and provide education for special types of exceptional children in Pre-Academic I, Pre-Academic II, and Academic I groupings. Assessment and evaluation of the children is based on academic and behavioral functioning, and a major goal of the plan is to increase the amount of time the exceptional child participates in a regular classroom program.

NOTES

1. L. M. Dunn, "Special Education for the Mildly Retarded—Is Much of it Justifiable?" *Exceptional Children* 35 (1968), 5-22; L. Blackman, "The Dimensions of a Science of Special Education," *Mental Retardation* 5 (1967), 7-11; L. Connor, "The Heart of the Matter," *Exceptional Children* 34 (1968), 579; H. C. Quay, "The Facets of Educational Exceptionality: A Conceptual Framework for Assessment Grouping, and Instruction," *Exceptional Children* 35 (1968), 25.
2. F. M. Hewett, "Educational Engineering with Emotionally Disturbed Children," *Exceptional Children* (March 1967), 459-467.

Operant Conditioning Techniques for Children with Learning Disabilities

THOMAS C. LOVITT

Often when the advantages of operant techniques are explained in detail to public school teachers, their reply, in effect, is, "Fine. I can see that in your experimental class with six pupils, one teacher, several observers, an aide, a supporting staff, elaborate measurement and recording devices, one-way mirrors, programmed materials, and a short school day, these procedures might get results. But how can I be expected to record the behaviors of thirty children when I have no help, am limited to the material provided by the district, see the school psychologist only about an IQ test or some grave issue, have children whose parents couldn't care less about academic improvement, and have to cope with all the other endless demands on my time during the school day?"

Criticisms such as these often block the use of operant procedures in the public schools, but there are other reasons as well for the schools' reluctance to adopt behavioral principles in their programs.

Undoubtedly, the main reason many teachers balk at applying operant procedures in the classroom is that often those who have sought to translate procedures for classroom use have used too many terms that are meaningless to the teachers. Terms such as S^D, S *Delta*, *positive reinforcement*, or *extinction* are not commonly taught in educational methods classes. Furthermore, the very term *operant conditioning*, particularly *conditioning*, has ringing connotations of bells, saliva, and dogs to many teachers who have been bored to tears in educational psychology classes.

No one would argue that if teaching is to become more a science and less a folksy art, a standard basis for communication must be established, but a science of teaching can quickly put itself out of business if its terms are so complex and esoteric that it is more difficult to master the jargon than to practice the method itself.

Another reason for resistance to operant techniques may be that much of the evidence on its effectiveness relates only to severe behavior problems studied in laboratory settings. Many of the problems and situations described in current studies are not those with which the public school teacher will deal. Studies, for example, demonstrating the control of violent temper tantrums, thumbsucking, teaching the cerebral palsied to walk, the mute to talk, or the severely retarded to attend to their sanitary needs do not seem immediately applicable in a public school setting. There are only

From the *Proceedings* of the Fourth Annual Conference of the ACLD, *Management of the Child with Learning Disabilities: An Interdisciplinary Challenge.* New York (March 9-11, 1967), pp. 183-189. Revised and published in *The Journal of Special Education*, vol. 2, no. 3, pp. 283-289. Addendum added for publication in this volume.

a few studies referring to the modification of academic behaviors in such areas as reading or arithmetic, and even fewer citing the use of operant procedures in modifying complex social and verbal behaviors.

Perhaps a final blow to the use of operant or behavioral principles in the classroom is dealt when proponents of the operant method talk of the apparatus and gear they use to collect their data. Pulse formers, timers, digital printout systems, cumulative recorders, voice-operated relays, and computer-based instructional systems are hardly standard equipment in most classrooms. The operant technician who criticizes the casual observational tactics of the teacher does little to foster the adoption of operant procedures in the public schools if he insists upon school-alien measurement techniques.

Operant practices, however, are not based on mystical principles nor do they require expensive equipment or highly trained clinicians. They may be adopted by anyone concerned with behavioral modification—including the modification of school-related behaviors. Operant principles and procedures offer such a sound framework for classroom management and have such immediate utility in the classroom that they must be seriously considered as valuable adjuncts to teaching. Further, the operant methodology encompasses many of the optimal characteristics of educational therapy.

Principles of Operant Methodology

The basic characteristics of operant methodology applicable to the classroom appear to be: *operational, objective, continuous, systematic, functional,* and *general.* They can be defined as follows:

Operational. To insure reliable communication among teachers or between home and school, behavior must be defined and specified. Such terms as *hyperactivity* or *slow learning* must be described in behavioral terms and their rate of occurrence noted if observations are to be reliable and useful.

Objective. The accurate transmission of behavioral information depends not upon speculation, but upon data. The quantification of behavioral data eliminates the either/or aspect of behavior and places events sequentially along a continuum. Reporting that a child has learned three new arithmetic facts in two days and can compute arithmetic problems at a specified rate can describe his functioning more effectively than noting simply that he is failing or passing in arithmetic.

Continuous. Continuous assessment of behavior enables a teacher to make instant evaluation of a child's progress in any program as well as of her own efficiency as a programmer. Continuous assessment is more sensitive to a child's academic progress than is periodic testing at the end of a unit, after six weeks, or at the end of a semester.

Systematic. Not only do curricular materials or teacher instructions affect children's learning rate; other environmental variables do so as well. Therefore, the teacher must constantly discover variables in the environment, following as well as preceding a child's behavior, that might affect the occurrence of some academic behavior.

Functional. By manipulating one variable or environmental component at a time, the teacher is able to evaluate the relative effects of her total programming efforts. For example, if she wants to increase a child's oral reading rate, there are a number of variables with which she might be concerned. Reading material may be altered, instructions made more explicit, or comments following the child's reading changed. However, to assess the function of any one of these environmental variables, only one at a time should be modified and its function assessed before another is changed. Otherwise, the teacher may not know which variable or combination of variables effected the behavioral change.

General. There is enough existing evidence to demonstrate that operant procedures may be used in a school not only by teachers but by all school personnel coming in contact with the child, e.g., speech therapists, school nurses, and remedial reading instructors.

Immediate Application

For immediate and effective use of behavioral principles, the teacher first describes the specific behaviors that each child in her classroom should acquire or manifest at the end of a specific period of education. What are the general educational and behavioral objectives for each child? At present, the behavioral objectives generally used to describe expectancies of pupils as they pass from one teacher, or one grade, to another are rather gross and vague. Often, for example, the yearly objective for a fourth-grader is that at the end of a school year he should be ready to perform as a fifth-grader, or for a student in special education that at the end of a training sequence he should be economically self-sufficient and socially adjusted.

The behaviorally oriented teacher must be more specific—she must describe in detail the behaviors or skills that each of her pupils is to acquire by the end of the school year. Many of these objectives will be academic; others will be social. Some typical goals for a first-grader might be to count to 100, to add and subtract certain combinations, to have a sight vocabulary of so many words, to be able to use certain facets of structural analysis, context cues, and phonemic analysis in analyzing new words, to be able to recite certain geographic facts, to be able to spell certain words, and to raise his hand before asking a question. In specifying these objectives, the teacher must also describe the conditions under which the child will perform these activities as well as the criteria for acceptable performance.

Finally, when each goal has been detailed, a uniform procedure must be established for measuring and recording the behaviors' *rate* of occurrence —the basic unit of a scientific analysis. Since behavior is temporal, developing along a time dimension, with both a beginning and an end, it is vitally important to record data about behavior in terms of *rate*. To do this, the teacher must define her units of measurement (dependent variables) consistent with each objective, units that can be specific in terms of rate of response. Specifically, these units might be rate of hand raising, reciting sight words, oral spelling, or computing arithmetic problems.

Once behaviors are described and related dependent variables specified, the classroom must be so structured that as many of these behaviors as possible can be recorded. First, work areas must be established to facilitate observation, with the classroom arranged wholly for this purpose, not for the enhancement of interior design. Second, both to maximize observations and insure their reliability, the teacher must establish a stable environment. Constant shifting and manipulation of bulletin boards, learning centers, etc., may produce undesirable and unreliable behavioral variability in pupil response. To obtain continuous, reliable behavioral data, there must be a certain degree of system, organization, and constancy in the classroom.

After educational objectives have been determined and structured within measurable rate dimensions, and the room modified to provide the best possible environment for observation, the teacher must develop effective tactics to record as many significant behaviors of each child as possible.

TEACHER RECORDING

The most logical person in any classroom to record behaviors is, of course, the teacher herself, and although she cannot be expected to gather continuous data on each behavior for thirty children, there are certain procedural tactics that she may put into practice. For example, she may record each student's daily rate of work by counting each written response at the close of each day. Certain social or verbal behaviors may be recorded throughout the school day by a time sampling technique. If a child, or for that matter several children, are being programmed toward a higher rate of compliance skills, better articulation, or more complicated verbal responses, they can be grouped and a situation arranged to expedite the recording of these behaviors during a segment of the school day. To record these behaviors a teacher might use a pencil and a pad of paper, a wrist counter, a stop watch; or, if the verbal behaviors are multiple and complex, she might use a tape recorder. These are techniques readily adaptable to the classroom. Other groupings may be used in a rather traditional context to permit the recording of certain academic behaviors in reading or arithmetic. Traditional grouping procedures may be used as children with similar skill levels and educational objectives are brought together, and rate measures taken of oral reading, word recognition, or computation.

A teacher may use a tutorial period for the observation of a single child. For example, one teacher in a suburban Seattle school set aside a fifteen-minute period three days a week to record one student's performance on three target behaviors. During this time she presented systematic, structured programs to the boy to assess his performance rate on word and number recognition and his rate of speed and accuracy on a writing program.

Another teacher in the school scheduled a segment of her school day to assess a particular child's rate of clearly articulated speech. The child's speech varied from precise articulation to garbled sounds; initial observations in a structured setting provided evidence as to the rate of articulate speech. After the initial assessment, modification procedures were introduced which decreased the child's rate of misarticulated speech.

PUPIL RECORDING

A strain on the teacher's ingenuity and time, however, is readily apparent when recording is solely her responsibility. Several school classrooms have allowed the children themselves to record their behaviors. Many children not only tabulate the number of problems performed, words read, sentences written, or pictures drawn, but note their own beginning and ending time for each task, thus furnishing the teacher the necessary data to calculate their work rate.

An attempt to extend the data-gathering skills of a single subject in the Experimental Education Unit at the University of Washington is now underway. A boy is presented at the beginning of each day with his full complement of work, which he may distribute as he sees fit. When a unit of work is completed, he corrects his own performance. At present his record of response is plotted daily by the teacher, but in the future he will be expected to plot his own frequency and rate.

Self-recording may be used not only for obtaining continuous data on academic response rates, but in some instances may be adopted for social behaviors as well. In one junior high school class, this procedure proved to be effective in decelerating the interrupting behaviors of two boys. Having identified as a target behavior *leaving the desk without permission,* the teacher recorded its occurrence in both boys, and showed the boys the graphs depicting their rate of moving about without permission. Noting, however, that this had but slight effect on their behavior, she instituted self-recording procedures, and as a result, the occurrence of the inappropriate behavior of both boys was reduced to near zero.

Self-recording was also used in decelerating lateness in a child attending a Seattle school. Initially the teacher attempted to decelerate this behavior by showing the child her two-week record of late arrivals, giving her a bus schedule, and explaining the benefits of punctuality. None of these procedures worked. Then the child was provided with a graph, helped to record her own rate of late arrivals, and placed on a "contract" of two cents per day for prompt attendance. In five days the child's rate of punctuality increased dramatically. However, it must be noted that the teacher violated a basic dictum of the operant paradigm by simultaneously manipulating several variables. It was not established whether behavioral control was a result of the contract, the self-graphing, or a combination of the two.

Self-recording as a decelerating tactic has been used on a much broader scale in another Seattle school. It was initially used with one boy who had frequent tantrums. Not only did the tactic bring about rapid improvement in the boy, but other children in the class asked to use the same procedure. This use of a particular managerial tactic with one child often raises the question, "How do you justify a certain procedure for one child when you have twenty-nine others to consider?" Here the answer is provided by the teacher's using the interest of other children to advantage by inaugurating a self-improvement plan for the entire class. Each child specified a behavior that he wished to attenuate and kept individual recordings of the number of times the target behavior occurred. No baseline calculations were obtained, but according to the children's records, many inappropriate behaviors have apparently dropped out.

Supportive Personnel Recording

Although self-recording produces a maximum amount of pupil data and approaches the goal of planned self-management and self-control, there are many instances in which data must be obtained from other sources. The teacher can supplement her own efforts by using the data-gathering potential of supportive personnel.

If teachers can justify accurate data gathering as a first step toward educational objectives, it is often possible to enlist the assistance of school psychologists, school nurses, social workers, school secretaries, counsellors, music and art teachers, speech therapists, janitors, lunchroom attendants, and parents.

Recently, in a Seattle school, a school secretary assisted in the management of a special class. In this particular class each student had been assigned certain quality criteria and time limitations for his work papers. If the work was not completed or did not meet certain requirements of spelling and legibility before recess, the student took his work to the secretary's office. There, he finished the work and evaluated his efforts himself. If they were satisfactory, the child asked for an admission slip from the secretary; when he presented the slip to his teacher, he was allowed to participate in recess for the time remaining.

There are several instances in which parents have also been involved in a common effort to attain behavioral objectives for their children. One study in progress concerns a situation common in many special education classes where the child wants to be given homework "just like other kids" (or perhaps it is the parent who wants his child to have such work). Often these attempts have met with little success. Because children in special classes are not generally given grades or an equally powerful incentive, interest in homework soon wanes. In this study, a boy was given math problems to do at home and was told not only to bring the work to school the next day to be evaluated but to record the time it took him to do the work. Initially, the child's rate of returning work with a recorded time was quite low. Procedures are now in effect that systematically utilize a sequence of contingencies. If the child's response rate at school reaches a certain point, he is allowed homework. Contingent upon his bringing the work home, he is allowed to watch television for a certain period of time.

The parents correct his work, note the time, and record the child's rate of responding. The next day, if his homework fulfills the specified rate requirements, he begins a new contract. This procedure has served to place the homework responsibility on the child and parents and has increased the boy's rate of returning the homework and his response rate at school.

Conclusion

This paper has attempted to illustrate how operant procedures may be put into practice in public school classes. Although the teacher may not have the elaborate response recording gear and the latest curricular innovations that are the tools of scientific operant conditioning, it is the procedure and not the tools that are of primary concern. Certain principles are inherent in the operant system, and a gross error is made by those who select and use some principles but not others. Confusion, rather than progress, may stem from a teacher's attempt to combine some operant procedures with other managerial and educative processes. Some features of the operant methodology are not harmonious with those of other educational systems. Explicit behavioral analysis is not compatible with inferential measures; continuous assessment is not compatible with pretests and posttests; the measurement of overt responses is not compatible with speculation about mediating processes; and, finally, the belief that rate of behavior is a product of environmental variables is not compatible with the belief that behavior is symptomatic of an inner mental or physiological activity. Operant principles are eclectic only insofar as they represent a dynamic experimental system designed to discover all the variables that affect the probability of response.

Operant procedures can provide the special educator with powerful tools to maintain or modify the behaviors of exceptional children. By functionally assessing behavior, designing explicit goals, initiating systematic procedures to reach these goals, and continuously measuring performance, a teacher is constantly made aware of each child's abilities as well as of her own competence in programming.

Addendum

In this article, it was suggested that one way to increase the amount of data obtained from a classroom is to train pupils to count their own responses. This technique has since been used in many classes.

In the past few years there have been numerous studies reported where pupils managed other aspects of their teaching process. Pupils have been allowed to self-schedule, specify contingencies, evaluate, and select their own remediation techniques. Invariably, pupils have been reinforced by these responsibilities. Research in regard to pupil-management should continue to be a high priority area.

The Right to Learn

EDWIN W. MARTIN

I want to begin by congratulating you (ACLD) on your existence. This is something of an existential comment that is related to the concept that "being" is the ultimate reality.

I see your existence as being tremendously important for a number of reasons. First, as a parent's organization, you are dedicated to providing your children with the "right to learn." Secondly, from the earliest days of the Association for Children with Learning Disabilities, you have made your allegiances with professionals who are also dedicated to your goal, and so, today, you have an organization that combines into useful effort these two important segments of our population. The third reason, and perhaps this is the most important one, is that your existence and your successes exemplify a characteristic of our American system that is vital to our *survival* as people.

You are a minority group that has identified a need—equal educational opportunity for your children. You are now in the process of rearranging national, state, and local priorities towards the end of meeting this need. I think your progress has been exceptional.

The Congress of the United States has recognized this need and has created a special section under the Education of the Handicapped Act, which will develop increased educational opportunities for your children. The National Advisory Committee on Handicapped Children, stimulated by such men as Samuel Kirk, Charles Strother, Jack Irwin, and others who have served on this committee, has attempted to provide a definition or description of children with learning disabilities, and this has facilitated the development of federal statutes and of federal programing. In many states and localities, the results have been even more impressive in terms of the number of children who are now being served and in the establishment of new priorities at the local governmental level.

With the assistance of the Bureau of Education for the Handicapped programs, a number of colleges and universities are developing new programs or modifying older programs so that the teachers who are being trained will be able to offer assistance to an even greater number of children with learning disabilities.

These are impressive accomplishments that are attested to by the thousands of people who attend this convention and by the tens of thousands of children who are now in special education programing. The forces that have caused the system to change and to modify in the past are the forces that must be multiplied and expanded in the future, if the "right to learn" is to become a reality rather than rhetoric.

From the *Proceedings* of the Eighth Annual Conference of the ACLD, *The Child with Learning Disabilities: His Right to Learn*. Chicago (March 18-20, 1971), pp. 11-17.

Children with learning disabilities now find themselves included in a group of approximately six million school-age children and perhaps another million preschool-age children who are identified as educationally handicapped. All of these children require a special response from the schools if they are to succeed. Our estimate is that about 40 percent of these children are now receiving some special education services, although we know that in some cases, these services may not be of the highest quality. For example, only about 50 percent of the 120,000 teachers who are employed in the states are certified, and an estimated one-half of the noncertified teachers are no longer operating on valid temporary certificates. This does not automatically mean that the services to those children who are being taught by noncertified teachers are less adequate than the services offered by certified teachers. In fact, each of us knows of examples to the contrary. It does suggest, however, the magnitude of the problem that we have in relation to feeling some minimal assurance that our handicapped children will be reasonably well educated.

Each day I receive letters from across the country. In addition to the letters that I receive and those that the bureau staff receives, 25,000 letters have come in to *Closer Look*, which is our computerized service that provides a list of schools that offer special education classes. These letters that I receive are important, and I want to share a few excerpts of some of them with you. Some of us do not know about such letters, and I believe that we should continue to keep them visible, and that we should continue to try and open ourselves to the feelings of these parents who write them so that our level of motivation toward responding to them is kept at a maximum high.

A mother wrote that she had a young child who had a physical handicap in addition to being deaf. During the first years of the child's life, the mother had been able to get some services for her youngster by visiting the university hospital school in her state. When the child was older and required daily instruction, the hospital school could not provide this service because they had no teacher for deaf children. The state school for the deaf, which was located in another city, did not accept physically handicapped deaf children, and there was no place for her to turn.

Kurt Vonnegut presents a powerful statement on the destructiveness of mankind, particularly relating this destructiveness to the fire bombing of Dresden, in *Slaughterhouse Five, Or the Children's Crusade: A Duty Dance with Death.*[1] In an ironic refrain, each time death is mentioned in the book he adds the phrase, "so it goes," and I think that this is society's response to this lady who had no place to take her deaf and physically handicapped child for instruction ... so it goes. I received the following letter this week:

I am hoping you can direct my efforts in seeking education for my handicapped son, age sixteen. He is brain-damaged with some emotional problems stemming from the brain damage. First, he is excluded from public school education. Our state allows a parent $2,000 toward tuition in a private school. We purchased a privately published directory and wrote to every school in the U.S. which is listed as accepting this type of child. There is not one residential facility with a tuition of $2,000. Most cost at least $6,200 and one as much as $22,000 per year. If my son is to have a chance to live in society and not be institutionalized the rest of his life (can you imagine being doomed at sixteen years of age?) then he must be in a proper educational setting. I have written or gone to see many resources in the state in which I live, but none have any constructive advice.

So It Goes

While both of these letters are from parents who have children with multiple handicaps, they probably represent our most critical need in terms of nonavailability of services. It is no less a fundamental violation for a child with a mild handicapping condition to be deprived of a full educational opportunity.

I have tried to understand what the reasons are for our present failure to provide special education for handicapped children. A number of possibilities come to mind. The most commonly verbalized problem is that there is not enough money, but an analysis of school budgeting suggests that this is probably not true. There are many items in the school budget that support parts of the educational program that may be desirable but which may not be critical; for example, my son receives instruction in such subjects as music, art, and physical education. I am happy that these courses of study are provided in our schools and that my children have a chance to participate in them. At the same time, it does not seem to me that extras for the normal child have a higher priority than reading, writing, and other basic educational essentials for the handicapped child. And what about the provision of transportation? We make transportation available to and from school for nonhandicapped children, but not for handicapped children. The problem of not having enough money is really the problem of insufficient priorities. And this problem is probably not based on the fact that school officials, or school board members, are heartless and cruel. There must be other reasons.

The first possible reason is that most people in this nation do not understand that education for handicapped children really works, and that the overwhelming majority of the handicapped children can be educated. With appropriate vocational education and training, handicapped children can fit into the job stream as well as into society in general.

Patterns of isolating handicapped children from the majority of the citizenry have resulted, I think, in stereotypes of what handicapped people are. The picture that comes to mind is only of the most severely retarded, the most severely emotionally ill, the most severely physically disabled child. With this picture in mind, the average man probably sees education for the handicapped as being a "kind" thing to do, a kind of charitable babysitting, but not truly cost-beneficial to society, and this average man also imagines that there are very few handicapped children. I have had instances reported to me of school officials who honestly felt that there were no handicapped children in their areas, and that all handicapped children were being well served because there was a state school for the blind, deaf, and retarded.

Society's Prejudices

It is also possible to speculate that there are deeper psychological barriers to the provision of services to handicapped children; and this includes not only education, but some of the other problems that handicapped people face, such as being denied job opportunities, access to public buildings, and access to transportation. The fact that people do have handicaps may suggest to us the fact that injury, crippling conditions, and ultimately death, are part of human life, and a part of our own experience. The desire to repress and not focus on this aspect of our finite human existence causes us to hide our heads in the sand. When these feelings are strong enough, they may make us wish to deny the presence of handicapped children, to deny the reality of their circumstances, and to focus, instead, on areas that are more reassuring, and more comforting.

In discussing these issues, Robert Lewis Shayon of the *Saturday Review* has called them funds, fatalism, and fear, which helped us focus our attention upon them. I am sure that many of you can offer additional hypotheses concerning societal attitudes, or additional parameters of the problem— and we should strive to do just that so that we understand the nature of our opposition, and how to develop the best possible constructive answers to these problems.

Labeling Learning Disabilities

A number of years ago, Wendell Johnson, the great speech pathologist and semanticist at the University of Iowa, wrote a little piece called, "The Indians Have No Word for It."[2] Johnson's premise, as it was developed in that article and in other articles, was that the problem of stuttering was caused, in good part, by the actual labeling and identification of the disorder itself. He proposed that normal hesitations and disfluencies in speech for many children, at least, were received with an overresponse from the parents and teachers in the child's environment. This overreaction sets up a circular process in which the child, himself, begins to become fearful of hesitations, begins attempting to avoid them, and begins to struggle. This succession of self-conscious awareness creates the pattern of stuttering.

Whether one agrees fully with Johnson on the etiology of stuttering, it seems clear to me that he understood at least part of the process, and we recognize a phenomenon that is part of our everyday human experience as we struggle with self-consciousness with various kinds of fears.

There is a self-fulfilling prophecy dimension to much of human experience. In a conversely analogous way, Robert Rosenthal's studies, published in recent years, suggested that the positive prophecies of teachers with regard to the ability of children very much influenced not only their perceptions of these children, but the children's actual achievements in school.[3] Additional research is necessary to substantiate this theory, but for the sake of argument, let's accept the premise that behavior can be shaped, at least in part, by the label we give to it and by the assumptions we have about it.

I think we need to keep these principles in mind as we think about the future development of programing for children with learning disabilities, and for children with all kinds of handicapping conditions. Identifying and labeling the learning problems of children by their individual handicaps has been useful to us in a variety of ways. Labeling may help us to focus attention on the problems, to communicate the seriousness of the educational needs of our children, and it allows for the development of specific programs to meet those needs. We are a great society for categorizing and labeling, and to a certain point such methods of classification are useful.

A basic premise in the development of programing for learning-disabled children, however, has been an attempt to avoid strict etiological labels, such as brain-injured and dyslexic. Instead, we have attempted to focus on the specific learning tasks that are necessary for the child to succeed in school. Extending this reasoning a little, I think all of us should consider carefully what our future strategy will be as we approach the general education system on behalf of these children.

In what may be seen by some as a kind of Swiftian "modest proposal," I think that we should consider an amicable divorce of learning-disabled children from the ranks of the handicapped, and expand the ranks of the normal student to include many children with the kind of variations and learning styles that are displayed by the majority of children who are called learning disabled. I think this approach is worth considering for the following reasons:

- The question of the self-fulfilling prophecy of the label "handicapped," a premise we are accepting positively for the sake of argument, which is that behavior can be shaped by the label we give to it and by the assumptions we have about it.
- A careful analysis of the distribution of educational resources suggests that nowhere in the United States are handicapped children receiving full educational opportunities. While this pattern is changing and improving, I am dedicating myself to bringing about a full commitment across the nation, to equal educational opportunity for every handicapped child by the end of this decade. It is nevertheless true that in many instances special education is a separate and segregated school

system, and that it suffers from the inequality that segregated systems are recognized to have.

A New Direction for Education

I think we should challenge the general educator with his own responsibility for increasing the flexibility within every school, as well as within every classroom, so that a broader segment of the normal population of children may be served. This is the direction of innovation in education. This is the direction of flexibility of programing and scheduling. This is the direction of individualization. It should not be necessary to separate the child, to identify him as handicapped, and to provide him with separate programing in order to meet his individual learning needs.

Do not misunderstand my meaning. A number of years ago I made a similar suggestion to the people who were then interested in the development of this association, and I think that some of them interpreted my remarks as an attempt to close them out of the handicapped camp. That is not what I am saying. We have a substantial commitment to learning-disabled children in the special education field and in the Bureau of Education for the Handicapped, and we will be expanding that commitment as rapidly as we are able.

Essentially, I see the development of programing for learning-disabled children moving down the paths of increased programing under special education laws. Here, the ultimate success of services for children depends on the development of new national attitudes and making a national commitment to each child that will afford him an appropriate educational opportunity. In many states, we are well along the way in this direction and this may be the best and fastest route to travel. In other states and localities we are just beginning. And here I think we ought to consider, carefully, whether our children's needs can be met through reform of the general education system.

Future Plans

As most of you know, we now support programs for training teachers of children with learning disabilities, under our training authority. As this program develops, through our own authorities and through the authorities of the Bureau of Educational Personnel Development, we will be encouraging the training of specialists who can fit into either model. There will be teachers who are better able to help children with learning disabilities participate in regular educational programs and specialists who will work intensively with children for whom regular education is not the answer. Similarly, in our research program, we will continue to emphasize research in a variety of approaches towards solving this educational problem. One of the ways we propose to implement the learning-disabilities portion of the Education of the Handicapped Act is through a special institute of national leaders in the learning-disabilities field for the purpose of developing a careful plan for future research and training activities. With such a plan, we will then go about funding the kind of projects that will bring us the information that is critically needed in this field. At the same time, we will make grants available to a number of states in conjunction with local school systems, colleges, and universities, and private agencies for the expansion of the best current practices in the treatment of learning-disabled youngsters. Our efforts in this program will be directed towards having a maximum catalytic or multiplier effect on the use of federal funds by providing support to the agencies that are now established in several states, which can do the most to bring about the expansion of educational opportunity for learning-disabled children.

We must move out of the charity era; we must move out of the era of just enough programing to ease the conscience of the citizenry and which does not offer educational opportunities for the learning disabled and the handicapped. We must establish that the right to an education is an intrinsic right and that it is not something to be given by the "haves" to the "have nots" in the spirit of generosity. We are in an era in the United States in which there is a new sensitivity to the concept of equality, and we know that equality does not mean sameness. Instead, it means appropriateness, so that equality of opportunity for one child may be quite different from equality of opportunity for another child.

On many occasions I have said that this is an important work that we do, not just for the handicapped children that we serve, or their parents, and not just for the teachers who will participate in it. But it is an important work for all of the United States because, at least in part, it helps to promote this understanding of equality. It helps all citizens to understand the intrinsic nature of man and that his worth is not dependent on whether his arms and legs work the same as those of a nonhandicapped person, or whether he is able to grasp reading or arithmetic as quickly as a "normal" child, or whether his skin is black or white.

What is important is that he is a human being and that under our system it is his humanity to which we must respond. Your efforts to bring the right to learn to your children are the efforts that will strengthen the character of our nation. Do not hesitate to claim that right. Do not feel that your purposes are selfish. They serve every man. I pledge my support to you in your endeavors.

NOTES

1. Kurt Vonnegut, *Slaughterhouse Five, Or the Children's Crusade: A Duty Dance with Death* (Boston: Delacorte Press, 1969).
2. Wendell Johnson, "The Indians Have No Word for It," *Quarterly Journal of Speech* 30 (1944), 330-337.
3. Robert Rosenthal, *Pygmalion in the Classroom: Teachers' Expectations and Children's Intellectual Development* (New York: Holt, Rinehart, and Winston, 1968).

Seven

Reading
and
Dyslexia

The term "dyslexia" is primarily a medical term
signifying the inability to learn to read. To some
specialists it implies minimal brain dysfunction.
To others it does not imply a brain lesion, but
rather a congenital condition, a maturational lag.
To others the term is meaningless since it has
never been operationally defined.

In the first article reprinted here Macdonald
Critchley, a noted British neurologist, defines
dyslexia as "a disorder manifested by difficulty
in learning to read, despite conventional instruction, despite adequate intelligence, and despite
sociocultural opportunity." He relates disabilities
in the acquisition of speech and language to
developmental dyslexia which is dependent upon
"cognitive disabilities," frequently of a constitutional order. He also points out the relationship
between difficulties in reading and difficulties in
spelling and writing.

In the second article, Janet Lerner discusses
the purported differences between reading disabilities and learning disabilities. Her original
paper, published in the ACLD *Proceedings* in
1969 as "Dyslexia or Reading Disability—a
Thorn by Any Other Name," was updated and delivered at the Houston ACLD convention in 1974.
In this article she points out the major differences
between learning disabilities and "reading problems," "dyslexia," and "reading disabilities" and
the differing approaches used by the reading
specialist and the learning disability specialist.
This is a provocative article and likely to open a
lively controversy.

In the third article, John McLeod discusses
research that has been conducted primarily in
the British Isles and Australia. He presents experiments showing relationships between the WISC,

the ITPA, and the Dyslexia Schedule, a questionnaire that uses parents as informants. He found
that the Dyslexia Schedule misdiagnosed only 4
out of 46, the ITPA misdiagnosed 9, while the
WISC misdiagnosed 18 out of 46. The Dyslexia
Schedule developed by Dr. McLeod is included
for those who wish to use it.

These three articles are, of course, hardly a
representation of the 20,000 books and articles
that exist on the subject of dyslexia, but they
present three viewpoints on treating the problem.

Language Acquisition in Developmental Dyslexics

MACDONALD CRITCHLEY

The acquisition of language skills by the developing child is one of the most striking adventures within the field of perception. In the first place, there is the steady growth of an ability to communicate by way of articulated verbal symbols. This is a process of learning that is in many ways unusual—if not, indeed, unique—when compared with other accomplishments. Though a linguistic environment is obligatory, for no child can possibly attain language if reared in an acoustic vacuum, the learning takes place without the active intervention of a preceptor. From out of the booming, buzzing confusion of auditory signals that surround him, the child gradually derives meaning, and by an elaborate process of selection, reception, imitation, and exteriorization, he gradually succeeds in coding and decoding the auditory symbols.

Those who are interested in what is currently dubbed "psycholinguistics" are apt to take for granted the veritable miracle that goes on every day under our noses: namely, the facile and seemingly effortless acquirement of speech by a normal child. How often do we pause to consider the sheer magnitude of this learning process? This might be especially appreciated by those who experience the laborious acquisition of a second language later in life. In this connection, some pertinent questions have been put forward by Jesperson, the famous linguist of the last century who, though himself a Dane, wrote and spoke in the most perfect English:

How did it happen that children, in general, learn their mother tongue so well? That this is a problem becomes clear when we contrast a child's first acquisition of its mother tongue with the later acquisition of any foreign language. The contrast is indeed striking and manifold. Here, we have quite a little child without experience or prepossessions. There, a bigger child, or it may be a grown-up person with all sorts of knowledge and powers. Here, a haphazard method of procedure. There, the whole task laid out in a system, for even in the school books that don't follow the old grammatical system, there is a certain definite order of progress from more elementary to more difficult material. Here, no professional teachers, but the child's parents, brothers and sisters, nursery maids, and playmates. There, teachers trained for many years specially to teach language. Here, only oral instruction. There, not only that, but reading

From the *Proceedings* of the Eighth Annual Conference of the ACLD, *The Child with Learning Disabilities: His Right to Learn. Chicago* (March 18-20, 1971), pp. 3-9. Portions of this paper are based on Dr. Critchley's presentation, "Developmental Dyslexia: A Constitutional Disorder of Symbolic Perception," given at the symposium of the Association for Research in Nervous and Mental Diseases, entitled *Perception and Its Disorders* (December 6-7, 1968).

books, dictionaries, and other assistance. And yet, this is the result. Here, complete and exact command of the language as a native speaks it, however stupid the children. There, in most cases, even with people otherwise highly gifted, a defective and inexact command of language.[1]

The acquisition of language skills depends, as a matter of fact, upon a constellation of influences, some of them extrinsic, others intrinsic. Sociocultural factors are as important, perhaps, as questions of innate intellectual level and the degree of ego strength. G. A. Miller, a linguist, provides a concise summary of the factors that influence the acquisition of spoken speech: "If we tried to picture the most precocious child orator, we should think of a blind girl, the only daughter of wealthy parents. The child with the greatest handicap would be a hard-of-hearing boy, one of a pair of twins, born into a large family with poor parents who speak two or three languages."[2] These two formulae describe succinctly the diversity of the circumstances that influence the rate of speech acquirement. At a later age and by dint of a process of indoctrination and learning, a child ordinarily achieves mastery over the graphic symbols with which he is confronted so that he can not only discern meaning within the lines and shapes before him, but, in turn he can transmit his ideas into a set of graphic symbols that can be stored for an indefinite period. This aspect of the acquisition of language comprises, in plain terms, the art of reading and of writing.

Charles Dickens must have come across many, many children who had difficulties with learning and reading. In *Great Expectations* he wrote, "I struggled through the alphabet as if it had been a bramble bush, getting considerably worried and scratched by every letter. After that, I fell among thieves, the nine figures, who seemed every evening to do something new to disguise themselves and baffle recognition. But at last, I began, in a purblind, groping way to read, write, and cipher on the very smallest scale."

Neurologists and others are aware that this communicative faculty is highly sensitive and vulnerable. It can readily become impaired and even destroyed by dint of disease processes within the brain, particularly when the lesion is located within certain regions that seem to possess peculiar significance in the specialization of linguistic function. Nor is that all. The developing child does not always attain expertise in the facility that is common to the average child. In the acquisition of spoken speech, he may lag behind, not by dint of a congenital deafness, which is understandable, nor by reason of intellectual inadequacy. The problem may be essentially one of delayed development of articulate utterance, occurring in vacuo, as it were. We have no adequate term for this state of affairs, the usual expression, *congenital aphasia*, being wholly unacceptable to neuropsychological purists.

Pursuing this problem more deeply, we can also discern cases where the processes of decoding are at fault; that is, where the perception of linguistic information does not keep pace with the child's ability to transmit data. There are two chief examples of this kind of perceptual difficulty; one of them very rare, one comparatively common. The more unusual of these constitutional deficits comprises an inability on the part of the child to comprehend the meaning of auditory speech—in other words, congenital word deafness, or better, congenital auditory imperception. The current habit of referring to this syndrome as *childhood aphasia* cannot be too strongly deplored by neurologists.

The more common instance of an innate difficulty in the realm of language comprehension occurs in cases of specific reading retardation, a topic which I will consider in a little more detail. Reading skill, together with its allied faculty of correct writing, is less easily attained than articulate utterance and the correct interpretation of speech and sounds. Many circumstances may cause the school child to lag behind his age group in reading and writing. Some of these are intrinsic—others, environmental. There is, however, a condition whereby—and for constitutional and genetically determined reasons—the youngster falls behind others, not only in his own age group but also those in his intellectual bracket, when it comes to the task of mastering the mystery of verbal symbols in print or in script. This is not a psychologically occasioned difficulty, nor a consequence of inadequate teaching techniques, nor the outcome of intellectual insufficiency, nor the byproduct of imperfect vision or hearing. This particular difficulty represents to neurologists an isolated entity, which is currently spoken of as *specific developmental dyslexia*. Somerset Maugham probably stumbled on this in his short story, "The Verger." He said, "The cook in my first place tried to teach me to read, but I didn't seem to get the knack of it. I couldn't seem able to get the letters in the head when I was a nipper."

Neurologists have often been criticized for neglecting to define clearly what they mean by the expression, *developmental dyslexia*. The definition that has been promulgated by the World Federation of Neurology is as follows: "A disorder manifested by difficulty in learning to read, despite conventional instruction, despite adequate intelligence, and despite sociocultural opportunity. It is dependent upon fundamental cognitive disabilities which are frequently of constitutional origin." That is the agreed definition.

It is perhaps desirable to recreate the negative features of this particular type of difficulty in learning to read. The child with developmental dyslexia is not emotionally disturbed—primarily, at any rate—although, understandably, he may become frustrated later with the ideas of inferiority or with reactive aggression, and it is important to note here that he has no disorders in the visual sphere. This includes such less obvious defects as ocular-motor imbalance or incoordinate eye movements. It was concluded at a recent symposium in the United States that an increasing number of parents are being bilked out of large sums of money by charlatans who have made a travesty of the eye's role in reading. Much of this activity has centered around the phenomenon of eye dominance. The belief that this can be at the root of so profound and broad a human problem as a reading or learning disability is naive, simplistic, and unsupported by scientific data.

With these children, no impairment has been discovered in the auditory field, not even any confusion in the interpretation of phonemes of somewhat similar nature. The blame cannot be laid upon such pedagogic shortcomings as unduly frequent changes of schools, nor to either premature or belated attempts at teaching, nor even to inappropriate techniques of instruction. The grotesque illogicality of the spelling of the queen's English cannot be blamed either, for we now realize that dyslexia is encountered in children throughout the world, whatever the basic linguistic structure of the mother tongue.

This difficulty in learning to read is also not aligned with any obvious cerebral pathology. It is perhaps necessary to emphasize this side of the problem, for there has been a tendency in some circles to correlate developmental dyslexia with minimal brain damage. This latter, in itself, is an entity of dubious validity. Some physicians have laid stress upon the presence of subtle, tenuous, or miniscule neurological signs. Regrettably, they are spoken of as "soft" neurological signs. But, with greater experience with this problem, one realizes that these "soft" physical disabilities disappear as a child grows older, and one is tempted to look upon them as marks of an associated maturational lag, rather than of a structural lesion.

In the normal child, reading entails two separate, albeit coordinated, processes. The child not only learns to attach meaning to a graphic symbol, but also to associate the visual appearance of that symbol with its acoustic properties. In the Indo-European group of tongues, this double task is facilitated by the fact that each constituent word is phonetic, being made up of a combination of phonemic signs, that is to say, letters. Expressed differently, it can be said that such words can be spelled out and synthesized along phonetic pathways.

Japanese is different in that there is a combination of two types of script, neither of which is literal. One is syllabic, and the other is ideographic. Chinese, however, is an extreme example of a total linguistic dissociation between appearance, sound, and meaning. The task of aligning these three activities must be one of unusual difficulty, and it would not be surprising if we were to learn that reading retardation is unusually common in China. This, of course, would not have any real bearing upon the problem of developmental dyslexia, which we regard as independent of the inherent structure of the language concerned.

A child with developmental dyslexia has no problem when it comes to identifying and distinguishing straightforward signs and symbols and signals, even though they are instances of nonverbal communication. Thus, the developmental dyslexic has no trouble at all in understanding traffic signs. He can, like anyone else, pick out, sort, and name various makes of automobiles or aircraft, postage stamps, dogs, birds, butterflies, flowers—

indeed anything except verbal symbols. Usually, he can identify numerals, and his powers of calculation are intact until his school grade brings him up against the task of interpreting mathematical problems as set out in writing or print. Musical notation may or may not be beyond the competency of a dyslexic. There is no rule here.

By way of specialized skill and intensive training, the dyslexic gradually overcomes much of his predicament with reading. Indeed, some fortunate dyslexics, even without special tuition, learn eventually to read through a process of sheer intellectual effort, coupled with drive and assisted by sympathetic parental and scholastic encouragement. However, such "ex-dyslexics," as I like to call them, may confess that even after their school days are behind them, they do not read for pleasure. Or, if they do, they may read slowly. They skip long and unfamiliar words. Or, in an obsessional fashion, they endeavor to look up puzzling terms in the dictionary. These ex-dyslexics confess that they continue to feel embarrassed when called upon to read aloud, for they find particularly bothersome the duplex task of enunciation and interpretation. The former problem is well shown by the manner in which, confronted with a polysyllabic word, they may put the stress upon the wrong syllable. The performance of these ex-dyslexics is sensitive to stressful situations. Thus, called to the witness stand in a law court, an ex-dyslexic adult may experience unusual perplexity in reading aloud the letters and documents handed to him by the attorney. Such an individual may also undergo a temporary deterioration in reading skills as the result of an intercurrent anxiety state or a depressive illness.

Difficulty in writing is the natural consequence of difficulty in reading. Copying usually presents no burden, although the dyslexic child may have great difficulty in copying from a blackboard because the words are exposed far too short a time. The dyslexic who is an "uncertain speller, a seldom reader," as Harper Lee put it in her novel, *To Kill a Mocking-Bird,* or a reluctant reader, an erratic speller, as I prefer to say it, is unable to express himself freely and easily on paper, or even to take down a text that is dictated to him. The principal hardship, however, lies in the correct spelling of the words that he wishes to write. So extreme are the errors perpetrated by the dyslexic that it is possible to diagnose the nature of the disability from the mere perusal of the text. In other words, the dyslexic's mode of writing transcends that which one might ascribe to mere educational inadequacy, or intellectual subnormality, or sheer idiosyncratic poor spelling. It would take too long to do justice to the great diversity of defects that may be discerned in the spontaneous writing executed by a dyslexic. The following are a few, broad types of defects:

• Overall untidy penmanship, with badly formed letters. Indeed, some of the words are so distorted that they are barely identifiable. Not infrequently, one letter may fuse with the next so as to form an unorthodox scriptorial amalgam. Capital letters are often interpolated within the middle of the word, or one word may be linked with the next in an odd way by means of smooth or interlacing strokes.

- Rotations of letters. These are not infrequent, and confusion commonly occurs between such mirror-opposite letters as *d* and *b, h* and *y.*
- Reversal of syllables or words, for example, *was* instead of *saw.*
- Abnormal arrangement of the constituent letters of a word, the correct letters being used but in the wrong order. Thus, instead of *not,* the dyslexic may write *tno,* and instead of *evening,* he might write down something like *enevgni.*
- Gross errors of spelling, other than the above. Some are explicable as phonetic substitutions like *laf* for *laugh.* Others are quite bizarre in character to the extent that the word may be wholly unintelligible to the reader. On the whole, the dyslexic errs by putting down too few letters, resulting in a misspelled word that is shorter than it should be. Occasionally, the dyslexic puts in too many letters, and here again, Charles Dickens must have stumbled upon this phenomenon in the boys around him, because in *Bleak House* he says, "If he were not so anxious about his spelling and took less pains to make it clear, he'd do better, but he puts so many unnecessary letters into short words that they sometimes quite lose their English appearance."
- An overall impairment of a semantic rather than syntactic or orthographic character may at times be identified. The victim of dyslexia, particularly in adolescence or adulthood, may obviously find graphic exposition an uphill job. In other words, he cannot express himself on paper very well. The superficial impression is that of an acquired language disorder, though it would not be correct to speak of congenital dysgraphia in this context, as some have done.

Many of the foregoing spelling mistakes can be interpreted as resulting from an inherent disorder in the conception of serial arrangement. This is especially so when the dyslexic sets down on paper the right letters but in the wrong order. Older dyslexics often admit to considerable difficulty in checking their spelling when referring to a dictionary. Their automatic recall of the letters of the alphabet in their correct sequence is too vague. For the same reason, these dyslexics are perplexed when it comes to tracing a number in a telephone directory. This confusion as to serial order may well extend beyond the alphabet, for many dyslexics are somewhat confused as to the correct succession of the months of the year, or, occasionally, the days of the week. More understandably, they may be unable to correctly align historical events. For example, the dyslexic may be quite at a loss to say whether William McKinley preceded or followed James Abram Garfield as President of the United States and where in that same connection stood Chester Alan Arthur.

In conclusion, we should take a sympathetic view of the plight of the adolescent who is undiagnosed and untreated, the dyslexic in a contemporary sociological setting. He is in many ways an alien in a world where the written language is quite foreign to him. Although the vernacular is familiar, the environment is strange, almost hostile. Symbols surround him, but to him they are nonsymbolic, for they are devoid of reference, function, or meaning. And yet, they have menacing overtones. In his view, they are angry hieroglyphs. He does not know whether they indicate "In" or "Out," "This Way" or "Keep Off." Another quote from Dickens' *Bleak House* indicates the dilemma: "To shuffle through the streets in utter darkness, to see people read and not to have the least idea of all that language."

The crusade for the due recognition of learning disorders in general, and developmental dyslexia in particular, has been long and arduous. Many doubters have to be convinced, and many prejudices overcome. I believe the goal is in sight when these unfortunate and misunderstood children will soon be recognized for what they are, and soon they will be screened adequately and at an even earlier age. Fads and faddists claiming to cure reading retardation by strange techniques will be deservedly forgotten. It is a public responsibility to take in hand these appropriate scientific and rational remedial instructions so as to fit them into the community which their basic intelligence warrants. In the nineteenth century, the philosopher, Herbert Spencer, described the three phases through which human opinion passes—the unanimity of the ignorant, the disagreement of the inquiring, and then the unanimity of the wise. It is manifest that the second is the parent of the third, and this is the phase we are witnessing today.

NOTES

1. O. Jesperson, *Language, Its Nature, Development and Origin* (London: George Allen & Unwin, Ltd., 1934).
2. G. A. Miller, *Language and Communication* (New York: McGraw-Hill, 1951).

Two Perspectives:
Reading and Learning Disabilities

JANET W. LERNER

The child who cannot learn to read or learns the skills of reading only with considerable difficulty has long puzzled educators, parents, physicians, psychologists, and others involved with children. Literature reporting and analyzing the problem has been appearing for many years under a variety of labels including simple descriptions such as reading retardation and reading disorders and more esoteric terms such as wordblindness, strephosymbolia, receptive written language disorders, and the highly controversial term, dyslexia.

There is general agreement among those concerned that many children have severe reading problems, but there are basic and sometimes highly emotional disagreements among authorities about the nature of the problem, the label to be given to the phenomenon, the diagnostic procedures required, and the proposed treatment for the disorder. In analyzing the controversy we find there are two frameworks with which to view reading problems and problem readers. The two frameworks represent on-going work in two important areas of study: the field of reading and the field of learning disabilities. Because there are many issues, theories, and approaches about which these two disciplines represent contrasting points of view, it seems essential to first analyze the existing differences between these perspectives of the failing reader. Once these differences are clearly discerned, we can attempt to recast both fields by searching for a higher framework that can encompass these discrepancies. Indeed, the building of higher and more encompassing frameworks is considered the essence of theory building.

The purpose of this paper, then, is to examine from two perspectives, the nature of the controversy and debate concerning children who are disabled readers; the two perspectives are those of reading and of learning disabilities.

Two Fields of Study

The two fields of reading and of learning disabilities are concerned with children who have difficulty in learning to read. Each is a discipline in its own right. Each has a full course of study in universities, leading to degrees from the undergraduate to the doctoral levels and to specific types of certification. Each has its own scholars, journals, and affiliated professional organizations. Each has its own history of development, philosophy, approaches, and assumptions. In spite of their

Paper presented at the Eleventh Annual International Conference of the ACLD, February 27–March 2, 1974.

independence from each other, the two fields have something in common: a deep concern for the child who has manifested a difficulty in learning to read. A brief examination of the two fields may serve to clarify their differences and similarities.

The field called reading includes all aspects of reading: normal reading development (developmental reading), methods and materials to teach reading, evaluation of reading, organization of reading programs, analysis of the reading process, adult reading, as well as an area that began developing in the 1920s called "remedial reading." The term remedial reading designates programs for individuals who are not learning to read for a variety of reasons. Remedial reading, which combines aspects of psychology, education, and reading, is but one part of the field called reading.

The beginning of the field called learning disabilities can be traced to the 1950s with a developing interest in an area of special education specifically concerned with the brain-injured child. The focus in this field is children of normal intelligence who may be failing in any of a number of learning areas, including arithmetic, language skills, writing, motor development, and social skills, as well as reading. Unlike the field of reading, however, the cause of the learning disability is *not* considered to be primarily due to emotional disturbance, mental retardation, sensory handicaps, or educational deprivation. Thus, while the reading specialist seeks pluralistic causes of the reading problem, the learning disabilities specialist attempts to rule out these causes as primary contributing factors. Further, it is speculated that the learning problem for these children is related to a central nervous system dysfunction. Concern for the child with reading problems is but one portion of the field of learning disabilities.

Figure 1 shows the relationship of the two fields. While each field has a broader area of total concern, their areas of interest overlap in the shaded portion of the figure.

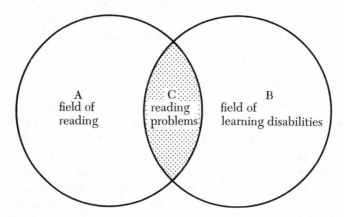

Figure 1. Relationship between the Field of Reading and the Field of Learning Disabilities

In the field of reading, the shaded area is called remedial reading, reading disability, reading retardation. For learning disabilities, the shaded area refers only to those disabilities that are specific to reading and may be referred to as reading disabilities, dyslexia, or receptive written language disorders.

In spite of these seeming conceptual separations, operationally the two fields may be quite similar. In spite of the broad range of interests that the field of reading encompasses, most reading specialists in schools report that the greatest portion of their time is spent in dealing with children's reading problems. Similarly, learning disabilities specialists report that among school-age children with learning disabilities, reading problems are the most frequently encountered.

In addition to the different labels and definitions used by professionals in the two fields, they differ in certain underlying conceptual frameworks which guide both diagnosis and teaching. Four of these differences are discussed below.

MENTAL PROCESSING VERSUS THE DEVELOPMENTAL SKILLS APPROACH

Learning disabilities can be characterized as a field which seeks to analyze children's learning problems by examining underlying abilities and sub-abilities needed for learning. These abilities, referred to as mental processing or cognitive functioning, give clues to the nature of the child's learning problems. The child's reading problems within this frame of reference are analyzed by assessing strengths and weaknesses in the underlying processing abilities. For example, the learning disabilities specialist will assess the child's auditory and visual processing abilities, perceptual and motor abilities, language facility, and memory abilities, etc. Such information both leads to a diagnosis of the problem and guides the plan for remedial treatment. Teaching will depend upon assessment of the child's strengths and weaknesses in the abilities and sub-abilities. The process has been called a psychoeducational approach, and a diagnostic prescriptive treatment (Mann, 1971) as well as an analysis of intra-individual differences (Kirk and Kirk, 1971).

Within the learning disabilities framework, some authors suggest that to diagnose and thereby treat problems in children with learning disabilities it is important to first assess specific and discrete underlying psychological functions and then to build up those functions that are found to be deficit areas. Other authorities suggest that following assessment in areas of deficits and strengths in mental processing that treatment procedures utilize the areas of strength. Still other authorities suggest that treatment involves building up areas of deficit processing while at the same time teaching through areas of processing strength. In a review of research on learning disabilities for the National Institute of Neurological Diseases and Stroke, Chalfant and Scheffelin (1969) stress the mental processing approach by titling their monograph, "Central Processing Dysfunctions in

Children." In this work the authors review the following underlying dysfunctions or abilities:

1. dysfunctions of analysis of sensory information (auditory, visual, and haptic processing)
2. dysfunctions of the synthesis of sensory information (multiple stimulus integration, and short-term memory
3. dysfunctions in symbolic operations (auditory language, decoding written language, encoding written language, quantitative language).

In contrast, the reading specialist in analyzing the reading problem is likely to focus on the level of reading skills development or the lack of skill development shown by the child. Using a postulated hierarchy of reading skills the reading specialist will attempt to diagnose how far the child has gone along the reading skills hierarchy, what he does not know within the hierarchy, and where in the hierarchy the teaching of reading should begin. Thus, in analyzing a child's reading problem the reading specialist might concentrate on the word analysis skills the child does not know in the hierarchy of word recognition skills: initial consonants, vowels, blends, syllables, prefixes, or suffixes. For example, in the *Wisconsin Design for Reading Skills Development*, it is suggested that children will master the skill of reading by mastering the contributing subskills. Forty-five subskills of word attack skills are listed in this design. In all, six major skills of reading are presented with their accompanying subskills: word attack skills, study skills, comprehension skills, self-directed reading skills, interpretative reading skills, and creative reading skills (Otto and Ashkov, 1972).

Cohn (1969) reflects the view that emphasis should be on the reading skills per se, rather than on underlying abilities and disabilities when he comments that we should teach children to read, not crawl, cross pattern, or draw triangles. The inability to perform such tasks, of course, reflects poor underlying mental processing abilities. Essentially, an understanding of normal growth or developmental reading is the thrust of the diagnostic approach within reading. Reading growth proceeds through a sequence of phases and skills. Such developmental growth is likened to climbing the rungs on a ladder. Each rung must be touched in climbing to the top; if the learner misses some rungs, he may fall off altogether.

Thus, the reading specialist tends to focus on the child's break or blockage in the developmental reading hierarchy; the learning disabilities specialist tends to focus on the underlying mental abilities contributing to reading achievement. This focus, in turn, colors both the diagnosis and treatment procedures.

REMEDIAL READING VERSUS PSYCHOEDUCATIONAL TREATMENT

Another difference between the two fields, reading and learning disabilities, is the nature of the treatment procedures. The reading specialist, while acknowledging that a child with a reading problem needs *remedial reading*, does not view remedial reading as something essentially different from *developmental reading*. Developmental reading refers to the continuous reading progress and assimilation of reading skills that occur within the child who is progressing in a satisfactory manner. Developmental reading also refers to those techniques and materials that are used in a good classroom setting to facilitate normal reading progress. Harris (1970) professes such a belief:

In many ways remedial instruction resembles good classroom instruction. Both are aiming toward the same desired outcomes regarding reading skills and interests. Both try to apply or induce effective motivation. Both attempt to suit the nature and pace of instruction to learners. Both utilize many materials in common. Both involve applications of the basic principles of learning. The distinction between remedial teaching and classroom teaching has become less sharp because superior teachers have incorporated into their daily procedures the principles which are fundamental in good remedial work (Harris, 1970, p. 281).

Similarly Karlin (1971) perceives no basic difference between remedial reading and developmental reading:

Insofar as methodology is concerned, there are not real basic differences between them. Programs that are suitable for pupils who are progressing satisfactorily are equally suitable for those who are not achieving to the extent of which they are capable ... there are not basic differences between developmental and remedial reading. If any differences do exist, they are not of kind but degree.

Another reading specialist, Heilman (1967), indicates what he believes remedial reading is not:

1. Remedial reading is *not* a subject matter that is different in principles and practices from developmental reading.
2. Remedial reading is *not* composed of a number of highly specialized techniques which only the initiated can practice.
3. Remedial reading is *not* something that must be done outside of the regular classroom.

Thus, the reading specialist sees little, if any, difference between the principles or the practices followed in remedial reading and the everyday instructional activities of a conscientious, creative classroom teacher.

In contrast, the specialist in learning disabilities is more likely to view the child's reading problem as a highly specialized and unique phenomenon requiring a specific and differentiated technique and procedure to diagnose and treat the problem. Adelman (1971) contrasts remedial and classroom teaching in that remedial instruction must be very specific, using specialized circumstances and a particular pupil's assimilated schemata. Regular instruction, on the other hand, can be broad in scope. The child who has a learning problem requires "narrow band" teaching practices, which consist of specific adaptations of general broad approaches and special systems techniques and materials developed specifically for problem pupils.

Bryant (1964) warns that remediation for dyslexia is almost doomed to failure if it merely repeats the classroom procedures. Brown and Botel (1972), advise that the developmental program must be vastly altered in terms of instructional processes for severely disabled readers.

There is often a mystique-like condition surrounding certain approaches to reading, particularly those that are related to medical and neurological contructs. A number of these specific methods of teaching have evolved as a result of the developer's affiliation with a medical theory. For example, the Gillingham approach (Gillingham and Stillman, 1966) evolved from work with the neurologist Orton, who is associated with the cerebral dominance theory of reading disorders (Orton, 1937). The Lehtinen approach to education is associated with the neurological theories of Strauss on brain-injury (Strauss and Lehtinen, 1947).

Upon investigation of the specialist treatment procedures, however, one often discovers that the techniques suggested are identical to those used for children with a variety of reading problems and are similar to approaches used in developmental reading programs that have been used throughout the years.

For example, a professional who works in a dyslexia-oriented institution recently told me of a new treatment that they were using for dyslexia—a new multisensory approach to learning letters and their sound equivalents. The method was a multisensory reinforcement approach. The child not only used his visual, auditory, tactile, and kinesthetic modalities to learn the letters by seeing, hearing, touching, and feeling them, but the reinforcement was introduced through the gustatory pathway with a cookie topped with a frosting shaped into a letter, thus enabling the child to actually taste the letter with his tongue.

A quick check into the history of American reading instruction reveals that this new approach to curing dyslexia had been used in the early colonial period to teach developmental reading. Gingerbread cookies were formed into the shape of the letters of the alphabet and as the child learned a letter he was permitted to eat it (Cooper, 1968). Going back still further in the history of teaching reading, in 54 B.C. there are reports of coaxing children to learn their letters by using tidbits of pastry made in the form of the letters to be learned (Fernald, 1943, p. 27).

Thus, the reading specialist tends to perceive remedial reading methods as similar to those used in good developmental reading programs, while the learning disabilities specialist sees the need for highly specialized, specific, and differentiated approaches to children who have failed in reading.

DYSLEXIA OR READING DISABILITY

Another area of controversy between the field of reading and the field of learning disabilities can be seen in the opposing views toward dyslexia. While one group vehemently denies the existence of the entity called dyslexia, another group of scholars is busily engaged in conducting research, publishing books, and holding conferences on the condition. In the past few years interest in the problem has not abated, but increased, both within the lay public and among professionals.

As an example of the increased lay interest in dyslexia, the recent theater production *Forty Carats* portrays a rather disreputable character who decides to change his ways and settle down to live the life of a typical American. His plans and dreams include getting married, buying a house with a white picket fence in the suburbs, and having a son who is being treated for dyslexia. Two professional examples of the continuing and expanding interest in dyslexia are the reports published by the National Advisory Committee on Dyslexia and Related Disorders (1969) and by the ERIC/CRIER Reading Review Series entitled, *Dyslexia: Definition or Treatment* (Brown and Botel, 1972).

PROBLEM OF DEFINITION

One of the basic problems that has plagued this issue is that of finding a definition of dyslexia that is acceptable and useful, at least to all who use the term. Definitions run the gamut from highly technical definitions such as a "lesion in the posterior end of the corpus callosum which prevents visual stimuli from being conveyed from the right visual region to the speech area where they could arouse auditory associations" (Geschwind, 1968) to the rather cynical definition of "a label in search of a disease" (Cohen, 1972). A review of the literature reveals that the word dyslexia is currently being used in a variety of ways by different authors. The diverse definitions include (1) evidence of an etiology of brain damage, (2) the observation of behavioral manifestations of central nervous system dysfunction, (3) the indication of a genetic or inherited reading problem, (4) the inclusion of a general language disability along with the reading problem, (5) the presence of a syndrome of maturational lag, (6) a synonym for reading retardation, (7) the description of a child who has been unable to learn to read through regular classroom methods, and, to make the circle complete (8) the child with a reading disability who does *not* exhibit brain damage (Rawson, 1971).

Upon examining this diverse range of definitions and views of dyslexia, it becomes readily evident that they can be grouped within two wholly separate modes of thinking. One framework is found in the literature that developed from the fields of medicine, including psychiatry, neurology, ophthalmology, and speech pathology. Much of this literature originated in Europe. This medical framework is closely associated with the field of learning disabilities.

The other framework concerning dyslexia is found in the writing of educators, psychologists, and reading specialists. This work originated largely in the United States. This educational perspective of dyslexia is closely allied with the field of reading. A brief review of the historic development of these two frameworks highlights the nature of the differences between these two perspectives of dyslexia.

The Medical Perspective: A Learning Disabilities Specialist's View

As early as 1896, an English physician published a description of a case described as congenital word blindness; that of a fourteen-year-old boy who could not read in spite of the fact that he appeared to be intelligent (Morgan, 1896). A few years later another English physician, Hinshelwood, defined word blindness as a pathological condition due to a disorder of the visual centers of the brain, which produces difficulty in interpreting written language (Hinshelwood, 1917). An American physician who contributed to the medical literature was Samuel T. Orton (1937), who studied language disorders including reading. His theoretical framework suggests that the cause of language and reading difficulty is the lack of establishment of cerebral dominance. Orton preferred the term strephosymbolia, meaning twisted symbols, to describe the child under concern here.

A number of European physicians have contributed to the medical literature in more recent years. In Sweden, Hallgren (1950) concluded from his study that the dyslexia pattern is inherited and the condition is genetic in nature. Hermann (1959), a Danish neurologist, attempted to establish a medical explanation for dyslexia; and an English neurologist. Critchley (1964), searched for common symptoms of children he called developmental dyslexics. Johnson and Myklebust (1967) view dyslexia as a type of psychoneurological learning disability which is caused by a dysfunction of the brain.

Finally, a medical dictionary (*Dorland's Illustrated Medical Dictionary,* 1957) reflects the medical perspective by defining dyslexia as an inability to read understandably due to a central lesion.

Within the medical framework the term is related to the term "alexia," which is a medical term describing the loss of ability to read because of an injury to or disease of the brain, such as cerebral stroke. The condition of alexia, also called "acquired word blindness" occurs in an adult who has already learned to read. Children who did not learn to read normally were presumed to have a brain lesion similar to those cases of *alexia* in adults. Since the condition of adults who lose the ability to read is called *acquired alexia,* children who fail to learn to read are assumed to have *developmental alexia* or *dyslexia.* In the close to eighty years of study about dyslexia, over 20,000 books, articles, and papers have been published on the subject seeking evidence of medical symptomology and a neurological etiology.

The Educational Perspective: A Reading Specialist's View

The alternative perspective of the condition called dyslexia evolves from the writing of scholars in the disciplines of education, psychology, and reading. Although these scholars have been aware of views of dyslexia for a long time, they question the etiological basis and the operational value of this view.

While workers associated with the educational perspective may note characteristics in children with reading problems similar to the behavioral dysfunctions described by the dyslexia-oriented group, they are unwilling to attribute the cause of the problem to a single factor—neurological damage. The educator is unwilling to assume that damage to the neurological system does, in fact, exist. Since opportunities to perform autopsies on children suffering from dyslexia are fortunately very rare, the educator stresses that one can never be certain of a diagnosis of brain injury. Moreover, the educator is likely to perceive several factors that are contributing to the reading problem; he is not likely to diagnose that any one factor is *the* single cause of the problem. The Disabled Reading Committee of the International Reading Association recently reaffirmed the concept of a multiplicity of factors in the etiology of severe reading disability (International Reading Association, 1972). Finally, reading specialists see the label of dyslexia as confusing, adding little or no knowledge of diagnostic or therapeutic value.

The neurological factor was noted in the early studies of reading failure conducted by two early reading researchers, Monroe (1932) and Robinson (1946); but these researchers concluded at that time that the neurological factors had not been strongly established within the research. According to Robinson, the neurologists who reported cases of alexia or word blindness noted certain symptoms and ruled out all other causes when making a diagnosis of alexia or word blindness.

Harris (1970), a reading authority, notes that the dyslexia hypothesis has little value for the reading clinician. He defines the term dyslexia as simply meaning there is something wrong with the person's reading. Vernon (1968), a psychologist and noted student of the causes of reading disability, states that she cannot accept the dyslexia hypothesis and therefore does not use the term, dyslexic, in her book.

Bond and Tinker (1967), in their text on reading disability, conclude that since it is practically impossible to distinguish "specific dyslexia" from other cases of severe reading disability, the clinical worker may question the value of the term.

In contrast to the definition from the medical dictionary, a glossary of terminology for reading problems compiled by the Center for Applied Linguistics presents the following definition of dyslexia (Gunderson, 1969):

A disorder of children who, despite conventional classroom experience, fail to attain the language skills of reading, writing, and spelling, commensurate with their intellectual abilities. Comment: This term is best used as a synonym for reading disability. It may be qualified as specific or congenital when the criteria for specific reading disability are met. Unfortunately, this term has been used in many contexts and as such has caused confusion. The term, dyslexic, then, is not a specific neurological disease. It is a symptom, just as reading disability is a symptom, the cause of which must be determined in any individual case (pp. 538-539).

In summary, the educational reading perspective suggests that it is difficult to accept the term dyslexia as a diagnostic entity. They reason that brain damage or neurological dysfunction as an explanation for reading failure is a presumption made without empirical evidence. Educators and reading specialists tend to favor a pluralistic theory of causation, emphasizing the wide range of contributing handicaps and the continuity of problems from mild to severe. Moreover, this group cannot accept the argument that the child who is unable to learn to read is like the adult who has lost his ability to read because of cortical damage.

Recent Developments

The debate continues in intensity. The National Advisory Committee on Dyslexia and Related Reading Disorders was created by the Secretary of Health, Education, and Welfare to investigate, clarify, and resolve the controversial issues surrounding dyslexia. The committee report, released by HEW in August, 1969, concluded: "In view of these divergencies of opinion the Committee believes that the use of the term dyslexia serves no useful purpose" (National Advisory Committee on Dyslexia and Related Disorders, 1969). Since there was no prospect among committee members of reaching a definition of dyslexia that could be accorded general acceptance, the committee resolved the conflict by renaming the final report, *Reading Disorders in the United States.*

Dissatisfaction with the committee's conclusion was evidenced by many medically-oriented specialists. For example, Bateman (1971) responded to this report by retorting that "Discussion about the value of the term dyslexia certainly will not cease with the opinion of the Health, Education and Welfare Committee that it serves no useful purpose."

In a recent monograph on dyslexia, Brown and Botel (1971) wisely acknowledge that the charge of formulating a precise definition of dyslexia is professionally impossible at this time and find the controversy nonproductive. Instead they focus on the issue of educational treatment. Even with the focus on treatment, however, the controversy does not cease. Those who advocate the diagnosis of dyslexia stress that it is important to identify the dyslexic child from among others to provide appropriate therapy, therapy that differs significantly from other reading approaches. Often investigation reveals, however, that the method used to treat dyslexia is similar to the treatment for teaching other kinds of reading disabilities and to approaches used in developmental reading programs that have been used throughout the years.

Perhaps the confusion of the definition is best summarized by Adams, who after a vain attempt to find similarities in definitions of dyslexia, concluded:

But sometimes a word gets born which, rather than live like a servant to man, moves out in life like a Frankenstein monster wrecking havoc in the discourse of sensible man. *Dyslexia is such a word.* Its meaning is obscure and it has divided the effort of professional men when collaboration would have been the better course (Adams, 1969, p. 618).

Task Analysis

The interpretation of the concept of task analysis provides yet another difference between the field of reading and that of learning disabilities. In general, task analysis is a method that is used to provide further diagnostic information; it is an approach to evaluation. In the field of learning disabilities, task analysis is used to evaluate and analyze the processing abilities required of the child to understand and perform the task; in the field of reading, task analysis is used to analyze and evaluate what is to be learned—the task itself.

A comprehensive presentation of task analysis as it is used in learning disabilities is presented by Johnson (1967), who points out that such analysis shifts the orientation from the subject matter to the process. Two aspects of the task are analyzed: the manner of presentation of the task and the expected mode of response. These modes may also be considered as the necessary input and output required to understand the task and to perform the task. One might also ask what mediating or associative processes must occur between the input and output.

Johnson (1967) suggests that each of these modes can be analyzed in a number of ways. Each can provide diagnostic and evaluative information about the child and his processing abilities. The teacher can ask: (1) What *perceptual channels* are required in order to receive the presentation and perform the task? These channels could be auditory, visual, kinesthetic, or tactile in nature; (2) Is a single sensory perceptual system needed, or is a cross-modal shifting from one sensory system to another required? That is, to perform the task must the child shift from the visual modality to the auditory modality? (3) Is the task primarily verbal or nonverbal in nature? What role do language and meaning play in this task? (4) Does the task require social or nonsocial judgment? (5) What skills and levels of involvement (perception, memory, symbolization, conceptualization) are required?

If a child fails a task, then the teacher analyzes whether failure is due to the manner of presentation or to the mode of response expected, and the teacher probes for the underlying processing abilities or disabilities that account for this failure.

The other approach to task analysis, one that is representative of the field of reading, is oriented toward an analysis of the task itself so that learning experiences can be designed to direct a child to reach these objectives. The focus is on the subject matter rather than on assumed underlying processes. Bateman (1967) describes this approach as one that places relatively little emphasis on discovering abilities or disabilities within the child, while it places major emphasis on the specific educational tasks to be taught. The important questions behind curriculum planning with this approach are: (1) What specific educational tasks are important for the child to learn? (2) What are the sequential steps in learning this task? and (3) What specific behaviors does the child need to perform this task?

In other words, an educational objective is operationally determined. For example, reading may be the objective which is operationally defined as being composed of a certain hierarchy of subskill components. A specific subskill is set as the objective. The task is analyzed in terms of component skills and the hierarchy of subskills needed to accomplish the task. The desired educational task is broken up into small component parts or sequential steps. Finally the specific desired behavior of the child is determined for each step. In analyzing the task of reading skill development, Otto and Ashkov (1972) indicate that teachers must decide the following: (1) exactly what they want children to learn, (2) who already knows it, (3) how they can teach it to those who do not, and (4) how to decide when it has been learned.

Further, these authors suggest that the tasks are to be analyzed in terms of these elements: identification of essential skills, statement of objectives, assessment, identification of appropriate teaching/learning activities, and evaluation.

In summary there are several implications of task analysis as a tool of evaluation. For the learning disabilities specialist the most important question to be answered in part by task analysis is what are the underlying processing abilities and disabilities of the child as revealed through his performance of a task. In contrast, the reading specialist sees task analysis as an analysis of the subject matter in terms of its sequence and skill development. Harris (1970, p. 139), a noted authority on remedial reading, states that the most important question to ask about a child's reading is, "How difficult a book can this child read?" The most important question for the learning disabilities specialist is, "How does this child process information?"

Summary

A comparison has been drawn between two fields of study—reading and learning disabilities—in order to emphasize their contrasts and to clearly differentiate the two approaches. The following differences were noted:

Reading problems—one component of each. Remedial reading is but one portion of the field of reading, while the teaching of reading to children with learning disabilities is but one portion of that field of endeavor.

Pluralistic causes vs. exclusion clause. Reading specialists seek pluralistic causes of the reading problem, including emotional, educational, language, and cultural factors. Learning disabilities specialists, on the other hand, define the learning disabilities population as children who do not have emotional, cultural, intellectual, and physical factors as the primary cause of their learning problem.

Views of dyslexia. Whereas the reading specialist tends to prefer the term reading disabilities to dyslexia, the learning disabilities specialist is likely to utilize the dyslexia syndrome in both diagnosis and treatment.

Mental processing vs. skills development. The two fields can be contrasted in their emphasis on mental processing or on skills development. While the reading specialist puts more emphasis on the hierarchy of reading skills, the learning disabilities specialist tends to concentrate on underlying mental processing abilities and disabilities assumed to contribute to learning.

Remedial/developmental reading vs. specialized reading methods. While the reading specialist sees little difference between developmental reading and remedial reading in terms of methods, materials, and techniques, the learning disabilities specialist tends to seek a unique treatment procedure that is differentiated from developmental reading.

Task analysis. The implications of task analysis differs in the two fields. In learning disabilities the orientation is to analyze the task in order to determine the underlying abilities and disabilities within the child. The orientation in reading is to analyze the task by studying the content and the skills to be learned.

Organizational setting. Finally, while the reading specialist is associated with the general program of the school, the learning disabilities specialist is associated with special education. This not only provides tremendous differences between the background and training of the teachers, but it also gives them different supportive and administrative personnel within the school organization.

The fields of reading and learning disabilities seem to be clearly separated by basic differences in theoretical constructs, perspectives toward etiology, diagnosis, treatment, and nomenclature. Yet the two fields represent professionals most concerned with reading problems and problem readers.

We must note that in spite of these conceptual differences, in the real world the demarcation is not so clear. We should also note that both fields consider many other elements of learning—the child's feelings and emotional status, his home environment, his interest and motivation, his language development, and his previous educational experiences. Nevertheless, it is important to first clearly discern the differences between these two fields. Once the full significance of these differences are fully perceived, it seems important to recast both fields by searching for a higher framework—one that takes into account these two systems of studying and treating reading problems.

Disciplines mature by creating frameworks that can accommodate seeming contradictions and discrepancies. To fully perceive all aspects of the disabled reader, it becomes necessary for those trained as learning disabilities specialists to recast their views to take into account the knowledge, skills, competencies, and insights that have evolved in the field of reading. At the same time, it is important for the reading specialist to recast his view to take into account the significant findings within the field of learning disabilities.

By forging these two contrasting approaches to reading problems into one that enfolds both fields of endeavor, perhaps they can become co-operative, not competitive, and engage in collaboration, not disputation. In this way reading instruction can be improved and children with reading problems can be helped.

REFERENCES

ADAMS, RICHARD B. "Dyslexia: A Discussion of its Definition," *Journal of Learning Disabilities*, vol. 2, December 1969, pp. 616-633.

ADELMAN, HOWARD S. "Remedial Classroom Instruction Revisited," *Journal of Special Education*, vol. 5, no. 4, Winter 1971, pp. 311-322.

BATEMAN, BARBARA, ed. "Diagnosis and Remediation: Medical and Educational Views," *Learning Disorders*, Seattle: Special Child Publications, 1971.

_____."Three Approaches to Diagnosis and Educational Planning for Children with Learning Disabilities," *Academic Therapy Quarterly*, vol. 2, 1967, pp. 215-222.

BOND, GUY and MILES TINKER. *Reading Difficulties: Their Diagnosis and Correction*. New York: Appleton-Century-Crofts, 1967.

BROWN, VIRGINIA L. and MORTON BOTEL. *Dyslexia: Definition or Treatment*. ERIC/CRIER Reading Review Series, 1972, Bloomington Indiana University.

BRYANT, N. DALE. "Characteristics of Dyslexia and Their Remedial Implications," *Exceptional Children*, vol.. 31, December 1964, pp. 195-197.

CHALFANT, JAMES C. and MARGARET A. SCHEFFELIN. *Central Processing Dysfunctions in Children: A Review of Research*. NINDS Monograph No. 9, Bethesda, Maryland, U.S. Dept. of Health, Education, and Welfare, 1969.

COHEN, S. ALAN. "Review of Specific Reading Disability: Advances in Theory and Method," ed. Dirk J. Bakker and Paul Satz in *The Reading Teacher*, vol. 25, April 1972, pp. 691-693.

_____. "Studies in Visual Perception and Reading in Disadvantaged Children," *Journal of Learning Disabilities*, vol. 2, 1969, pp. 6-14.

COOPER, WILLIAM H. "Common Denominations of Reading Instruction," *College Reading Association: Proceedings*, ed. Clay A. Ketcham, Fall 1968.

CRITCHLEY, MACDONALD. *Developmental Dyslexia*. Springfield, Ill.: Charles C Thomas, 1964.

Dorland's Illustrated Medical Dictionary, 23rd ed. Philadelphia: W. B. Saunders, 1957, p. 419.

FERNALD, GRACE M. *Remedial Techniques in Basic School Subjects*. New York: McGraw-Hill, 1943.

GESHWIND, NORMAN. "Neurological Foundations of Language," *Progress in Learning Disabilities*. New York: Grune and Stratton, 1968, p. 194.

GILLINGHAM, ANNA and BESSIE W. STILLMAN. *Remedial Training for Children with Specific Disability in Reading, Spelling, and Penmanship*, 7th ed. Cambridge, Mass.: Educators Publishing Service, 1966.

GUNDERSON, DORIS V. "Reading Problems: Glossary of Terminology," *Reading Research Quarterly*, vol. 4, Summer 1969, pp. 534-547.

HALLGREN, B. "Specific Dyslexia: A Clinical and Genetic Study," *Acta Psychiat. Neurol.* (Supp. 65), 1950, pp. 1-287.

HARRIS, ALBERT. *How to Increase Reading Ability*, 5th ed. New York: David McKay, 1970.

HEILMAN, ARTHUR W. *Principles and Practices of Reading*, 2nd ed. Columbus, Ohio: Charles E. Merrill, 1967.

HINSHELWOOD, JAMES. *Congenital Word-Blindness*. London: H. K. Lewis, 1917.

JOHNSON, DORIS J. "Educational Principles for Children with Learning Disabilities," *Rehabilitation Literature*, vol. 28, 1967, pp. 317-322.

JOHNSON, DORIS and H. MYKLEBUST. *Learning Disabilities: Educational Principles and Practices*. New York: Grune and Stratton, 1967.

KARLIN, ROBERT. *Teaching Elementary Reading: Principles and Strategies*. New York: Harcourt Brace Jovanovich, 1971.

KIRK, SAMUEL A. and WINIFRED D. KIRK. *Psycholinguistic Learning Disabilities: Diagnosis and Remediation*. Urbana, Ill.: University of Illinois Press, 1971.

LERNER, JANET W. *Children with Learning Disabilities: Theories, Diagnosis, and Teaching Strategies*. Boston: Houghton Mifflin, 1971.

_____. "A Thorn by Any Other Name: Dyslexia or Reading Disability," *Elementary English*, vol. 48, January 1971, pp. 75-81.

MANN, LESTER. "Psychometric Phrenology and the New Faculty Psychology: The Case Against Ability Assessment and Training," *Journal of Special Education*, vol. 5, no. 1, Winter-Spring 1971.

MONROE, MARION. *Children Who Cannot Read*. Chicago: University of Chicago Press, 1932.

MORGAN, W. P. "A Case of Congenital Word Blindness," *British Medical Journal*, November 1896.

National Advisory Committee on Dyslexia and Related Reading Disorders. *Reading Disorders in the United States*. Washington, August 1969.

ORTON, SAMUEL T. *Reading, Writing, and Speech Problems in Children*. New York: W. W. Norton, 1937.

OTTO, WAYNE and EUNICE ASHKOV. "Wisconsin Design for Reading Skill Development," *The Quest for Competency in Teaching Reading*, ed. Howard A. Klein. Newark, Del.: International Reading Association, 1972, pp. 106-118.

RAWSON, MARGARET R. "Teaching Children with Language Disabilities in Small Groups," *Journal of Learning Disabilities*, vol. 4, January 1971, pp. 17-30.

ROBINSON, HELEN M. *Why Pupils Fail in Reading*. Chicago: University of Chicago Press, 1946.

STRAUSS, ALFRED and LAURA LEHTINEN. *Psychopathology and Education of the Brain-Injured Child*. New York: Grune and Stratton, 1947.

VERNON, M. D. *Backwardness in Reading: A Study of its Nature and Origin*. London: Cambridge University Press, 1958.

Wisconsin Design for Reading Skill Improvement: Interpretive Scoring Systems. A division of National Computer Systems, Inc., 4401 W. 76th Street. Minneapolis, Minnesota.

Psychological and Psycholinguistic Aspects of Severe Reading Disability in Children: Some Experimental Studies

JOHN McLEOD

A word which I shall be using from time to time during the course of this paper is "redundancy" and so I think we might as well know what it means before we begin. A certain amount of a written or spoken message is redundant insofar as the message is still understandable, even when the redundant parts have been left out. That is why we are able to send telegrams and save money by omitting words that are not necessary and the telegram is still, hopefully, meaningful. Sometimes you have total redundancy, when the message is still completely intact even though part of it has been omitted. If you omit something which is partially redundant, then your message is likely to be not quite as clear as it was before.

Redundancy is not the same as superfluousness. Redundancy is not useless. In fact it is very useful indeed. It is the redundancy of language that enables us to communicate with each other, because if you miss part of the message, you are able to fill in from the rest of the message. It helps to emphasize a particular point and to make sure that the message is truly communicated.

The Remedial Education Centre in Brisbane, where I work, was established by Fred J. Schonell, who is an Australian by birth and who established his reputation in England, returning to Australia in the 1950s. You will appreciate, therefore, that our thinking about reading disability—I am English by birth too—has been influenced by British experience more than by developments in the United States. Hence, if I appear to protest too much about the existence of a subgroup of disabled readers whom I shall label as dyslexic, please bear in mind that as recently as 1965 Professor Magdalen D. Vernon of Reading University has stated that educational psychologists in England are still engaged in a controversy as to whether dyslexia exists at all.

Holmes and Singer (1964) have recently expressed the view that:

A field of study is generally headed for a spurt of creative productivity when theory construction and experimental research become closely interdependent and mutually directed. All signs indicate that the psychology of reading is on the threshold of just such a forward thrust and that both stimulating and dis-

From the *Proceedings* of the Third Annual International Conference of the ACLD, *An International Approach to Learning Disabilities of Children and Youth.* Tulsa, Okla. (March 3-5, 1966), pp. 186-205.

turbing days lie immediately ahead. In this new atmosphere, cherished ideas are bound to be challenged and new ones will contend for their places when the old ones fall.

The considerable shift in approaches to reading research on the contemporary scene can be discerned in the titles of the predominant sections of the American Educational Research Associations triennial *Review of Educational Research* which is devoted to Language Arts and Fine Arts.

The contents of the 1955 *Review* represent, in a sense, the passing of a conventional, complacent, consolidated era. In that year, the first four chapters were headed: Reading (Psychology), Reading (instruction), Oral and Written Language, and Auding. Infatuation with the promise of communication theory (or information theory) was at its zenith three years later, as is evidenced by the pride of place accorded to communication theory in the 1958 *Review*, but by 1961, something of an agonizing reappraisal of the potential value of information theory seems to have been made, reference to communication theory having been replaced by the more conservative "Psychology of Language." Yet in the most recent *Review*—that of 1964—linguistics, if not information theory, appears to have consolidated its position, while sections devoted to theoretical models and to interdisciplinary activities have appeared for the first time.

Linguistics, information theory, the development of theoretical models and the growth of interdisciplinary approaches to reading disability are not independent, but interrelated.

Psycholinguistics is a new branch of science whose origins date back only to 1951 when an inter-University seminar was convened at Cornell University in this country, and it represents a fusion of the study of linguistics and of the psychology of communication, which is itself involved with the application of information theory to psychology (Osgood and Sebok, 1964). When we come to theoretical models, we encounter such names as Wepman, and Kirk and McCarthy, who are concerned with communication and the breakdown of communication in children. And the *Illinois Test of Psycholinguistic Abilities* of Kirk and McCarthy is based on the theoretical model of Osgood, who has himself been, and is, one of the leading figures in the development of the science of psycholinguistics.

These movements have been in a predominantly psychological framework, but there has been, in addition, a broadening and enrichment of perspective through contributions from other disciplines, one of the most significant examples of which was the 1961 symposium on reading disability at Johns Hopkins to which several members of the advisory board of this Association made such distinguished contributions.

In Brisbane, I feel that we are being carried along by the eddies of what Boring has referred to so many times in his *History of Experimental Psychology* as the *Zeitgeist*. Over the past decade or so, there does appear to have been a complex of orientation towards neuropsychology, information theory and psycholinguistics that is perhaps moulding the habits of psychological thinking in the area of reading disability. My own assessment of the current trend in the field of severe reading disability is that dyslexia is being reexamined as a concept and re-interpreted as a breakdown in psycholinguistic functioning or communication process. It is largely within this frame of reference that our experimental research activities in Brisbane have been designed and carried out. It is really remarkable that language should have been so neglected in the study of reading disability over the years, in comparison with intelligence, personality, and emotional factors. Perhaps this comparative neglect has in part been because intelligence and personality have been more easily quantifiable and measurable—or rather it has been relatively easy to construct tests of what we have been pleased to call "intelligence," "anxiety," "need," "achievement" and other intangibles and so have enjoyed the illusion that we have been able to measure these things. On the other hand, it has not seemed to be as feasible to measure "language." And if it *were* possible to devise a metric, would not the physical task of measuring language be prohibitive, requiring sophisticated equipment and technical skill? How can the seemingly boundless cacophony of utterances and writings be reduced to some sort of order?

It is in answer to questions such as these that the communication engineers have made a contribution, through information theory, in that they have provided us with a means of quantification. Perhaps appropriately, the concept which they have qualified is that of "uncertainty." Language *does* possess some remarkably stable properties, for example, the relative frequencies of letters and words and the pattern of letter sequences, or, in spoken language, the pattern of phonemes and phoneme sequences. One piece of research on which we have been engaged at the Remedial Education Centre has been to use the concept of uncertainty, or more correctly, the concept of the redundancy of language in order to assess the readability level of children's books. We believe that we can now do this with far greater sensitivity and validity than can be achieved through the usual readability formulae and with at least three times the reliability. This research is beyond the terms of reference of today's paper, but I should like to show you one slide which demonstrates quite vividly, to my mind, the precision and stability of observable and measurable characteristics of language. Figures 1 and 2 show the relationship between the redundancies of two different sets of English prose, as estimated by randomly selected, independent groups of children at different ages (McLeod and Anderson 1966).

A psychologist who has made one of the most notable contributions to psycholinguistics is G. A. Miller of Harvard. And one of Miller's major contributions has been to construct words and word sequences which approximate in different degrees to the structure of English. For nearly a century, psychologists have made use of nonsense syllables, particularly in learning experiments, and what Miller has succeeded in doing is to control

log $_{10}$ (Estimated Redundancy of Standard Passages)

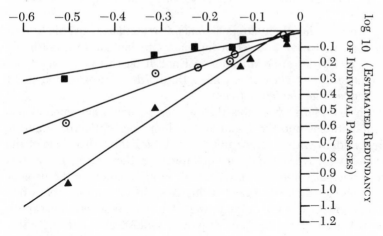

Figure 1

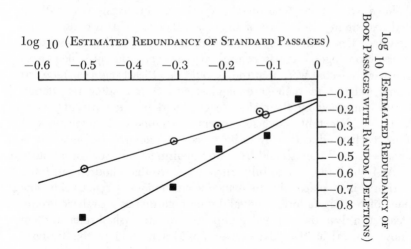

Figure 2

the amount of nonsense. I do not propose to go into the methods by which this is done, but I think that you will be able to appreciate intuitively, from a few examples, that what are termed the higher order approximations do resemble English more closely than do the lower order approximations. For example, taking letters as our basic element, zero-order approximations might include such pseudo words as *eqgm, ptbkg, hhokjb*. First order approximations might be: *mhtt, bdyef, leogtr*, while third order approximations are becoming quite like ordinary words, for example: *tast, manci, mitted.*

Taking words rather than letters as units, it is similarly possible to construct contexts that have a lower or higher approximation to English. An example of first order approximation to English on this basis might be: *Have a he just this an trained law,* while a third order approximation might be: *most I hoped that she felt as free.*

It is with material such as this that we have carried out some of our experimental studies into the visual and auditory perception of linguistic signals by children with severe reading disability. I think that some of the results which we have obtained are of interest in themselves, but at this stage, the principal value that has accrued, in my opinion, is the demonstration of the fact that experiments using this sort of material are in fact feasible and practical with quite young children. Whereas the experiments of Miller and his colleagues employed sophisticated university students, we have experienced no practical difficulties with children of six and a half to seven years of age who have reading problems.

Most of the results which I shall present were obtained in what I hope and believe was a well-controlled experiment involving twenty-three retarded readers in Grade Two of Brisbane schools. (This is really equivalent to Grade One in the United States—or at any rate in Illinois—schools, as far as chronological age is concerned). The criteria by which these children were selected were that they should be at least one year retarded in reading, relative to their chronological age, their reading retardation should be confirmed by their class teacher and by their parents, there should be no detectable adverse exogenous factors such as changes of school or teacher, education by radio or correspondence, bilingualism in the home, etc., and they should have no impairment of visual or auditory acuity. As I shall argue more fully later, I believe that children satisfying such criteria in a place like Brisbane, which enjoys a remarkably low incidence of reading failure, may validly be regarded as a dyslexic group, or at least as a dyslexia-enriched group. At any rate, I shall refer to them from now onward as the "dyslexic group." Each child in this dyslexic group was matched by selecting at random a child of the same sex from the same school class.

I shall discuss the results of an experiment involving tachistoscopic presentation of printed letter sequences of different orders of approximation to English. The performances of the dyslexic group and the controls are illustrated in Figure 3. The controls were superior at all three levels of approximation, and their superiority was consistent, i.e. it became neither more nor less marked as the letter sequences became more nearly like real words. Another finding that might be worth following up in future research is that, for both groups, performance was significantly better with letter sequence at a higher order of approximation (and for the statistically

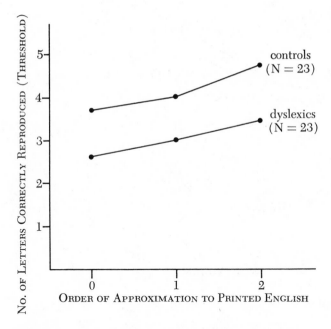

Figure 3. Thresholds for Tachistoscopically-presented Letter Sequences (Grade 2)

minded, all significant differences in this experiment were significant at the .001 level). In other words, even the children who had virtually no measurable reading ability were able to reproduce letter sequences that resembled words better than sequences that did not resemble words.

The results of this experiment with Grade Two children can be compared with the results of a similar type of experiment which I carried out some time previously with children in Grade Four. In the Grade Four experiment, the children were not necessarily dyslexic. I simply administered group tests of reading and spelling to about 450 children, from whom were selected four groups, one of which was above the median in both reading and spelling, another was below the median on both tests, while the other two groups consisted of children who were above the median in one skill and below the median on the other. I have tried to show the results of the statistical analysis in a more straightforward manner in Figures 4 and 5. Figure 3 shows what happens when we classify the children into good readers and poor readers. The results are very similar to those obtained with Grade Two dyslexics. That is, the good readers are significantly better than the poor readers, and their superiority is consistent for all levels of approximation to English.

When the children are classified according to spelling ability however, we get a rather different picture. The good spellers are again superior, but their superiority increases as the letter sequences approximate more closely

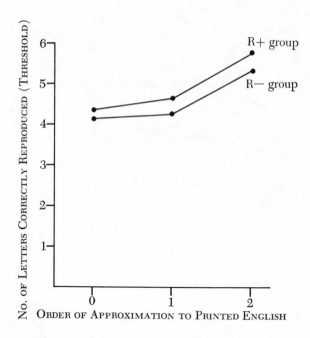

Figure 4. THRESHOLDS FOR TACHISTOSCOPICALLY-PRESENTED LETTER SE-
QUENCES (GRADE 4—GOOD AND POOR READERS)

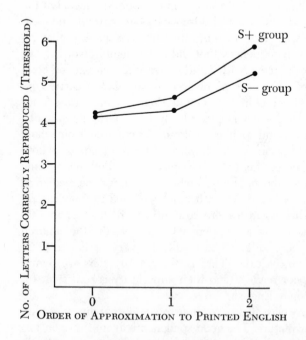

Figure 5. THRESHOLDS FOR TACHISTOSCOPICALLY-PRESENTED LETTER SE-
QUENCES (GRADE 4—GOOD AND POOR SPELLERS)

to ordinary English words. In other words, the poor spellers do not appear to take as much advantage of the redundancy of printed English in reproducing letter sequences.

Bizarre spelling is a frequently quoted characteristic of dyslexic children, so that I suspect that if we follow up our Grade Two dyslexics, we shall find that, as they get older, their performance on this kind of task deteriorates relative to the control group with the more highly redundant letter sequences. Indeed, failure to read could be interpreted as a failure to process redundant visual linguistic signals—the dyslexics are unable to distinguish what to the competent reader are familiar and meaningful letter sequences from jibberish; or, in the language of the communication engineer, they are unable to discriminate the message from noise.

If the dyslexic child is unable to make use of redundancy in printed English, how does he fare with spoken English? To examine this question, two experiments were carried out with the twenty-three dyslexic children from Grade Two. One experiment examined the children's ability to reproduce words which were preceded by spoken contexts of different degrees of approximation to English, some examples of which I gave earlier. This ability was expressed in terms of the sound level at which the stimulus word had to be presented for the child to be just able to reproduce it. The results are expressed graphically in Figure 6(a).

It can be seen that the control group is again superior to the dyslexic group, but that with spoken English, the dyslexic's inferiority is less marked when the preceding context approximates more closely to normal English. That is, with spoken English, the dyslexics appear to make more

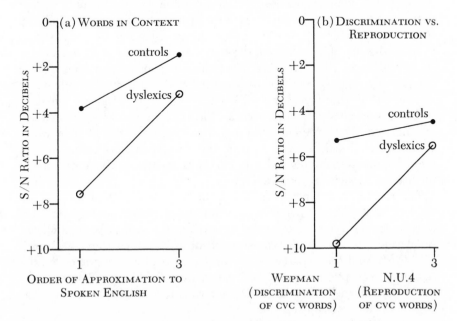

Figure 6. Sound/Noise Thresholds (Grade 2)

use of the word redundancy, or conversely, the more uncertainty there is in spoken English context, the more inadequate are dyslexics to cope with it.

The dyslexics experienced even greater difficulties when they had to cope with uncertainty *within* words. The method we employed was to compare the ability of the twenty-three Grade Two dyslexics to *reproduce* a consonant-vowel-consonant word (presented in isolation) with their ability to *discriminate* between two similar consonant-vowel-consonant words whose frequency of occurrence is comparable. There is generally less uncertainty involved in reproducing a word. For example, if the stimulus word *soon* were presented at a sound level such that the *n* is just indistinguishable from an *m* (but the other features of the word were perceptible) then the child would almost certainly reproduce the presented word, because the most probable alternative—*soom*—is not a real word. However, if the child were presented with the words *dim* and *din* under similar conditions and asked to judge whether they were the same or different, there would be only a 50 percent chance that he would make a correct judgment.

Using the N.U.4 Test of Tillman, Carhart and Wilber (1963) to assess word reproduction and the Wepman Test word pairs to measure discrimination, the performance of the dyslexics was very significantly poorer (p. = .001) on the discrimination task, whereas there was no significant difference between them and the controls when it came to word reproduction, as is illustrated in Figure 6(b).

In information theory terms, the results of these experiments suggest that dyslexic children might, with some validity, be thought of as communication channels whose capacities are unusually limited for both auditory and visual language signals. Maybe as a result of their exposure to auditory signals necessarily preceding their exposure to visual signals, the dyslexics have by the age of six or seven, through massive overlearning, achieved a relative efficiency in exploiting the redundancy of spoken language—a competency that has perhaps to some extent been partially built up to compensate for the fact that their capacity for visual language signals is still so limited that they have been unable to make use of the redundancy of language signals presented through this sensory mode; or, in a word, they can't read. But let us turn from this theoretical speculation—and I should want to carry out a bit more research before I ventured much further out on such a theoretical limb.

The finding is not new that discrimination between words—or more correctly that ability to perceive phonemes within words—is important for learning to read. Wepman himself considered the skill to be of sufficient significance to warrant the construction of a test to measure it. Durrell (1954) stressed the importance in learning to read of what he called the "auditory perception of sounds in spoken words" while the Soviet educational psychologist El'konin (1961) referred to the importance of what he termed the "developed phonemic ear."

The possibility is suggested by another inquiry we carried out at the

Remedial Centre that poor phonemic discrimination might be a characteristic of dyslexic children which is carried over to their reading and which is reflected in their errors. The oral responses of twenty-four consecutive referrals to a diagnostic reading test (McLeod and Atkinson, 1972) which consisted of printed consonant-vowel-consonant words were analyzed. And although other factors undoubtedly influenced the responses, in most instances, the most frequently occurring substitution errors were often in closest "phonemic proximity" to the phoneme being misread, in the case of both vowels and consonants (see Tables 1 and 2).

We can get some sort of support for this notion of the importance of phonemic discrimination if we look at the family *b-d, m-n, p-t.* The *b-d* confusion is a perennial bogy in reading and the phenomenon is usually explained away in terms of visual directional confusion, i.e. that *b* and *d* are mirror images of each other, which leads us into the realms of cerebral dominance and all that. But *b* is a relatively easy letter to read when it comes at the beginning of a word (where it occurs fairly frequently) but a very difficult letter to read when it comes at the end of a word (where it occurs very infrequently indeed). Similarly, a final *d* (which is a common word ending) is easy but an initial *d* (which does not occur so commonly) is more often misread.

A final *b* is most commonly misread as a *d*, while a final *m* is most commonly misread as an *n*, again from the less frequently occurring to the more frequent. With some trepidation I followed this pattern through to

Table 1. MOST FREQUENT VOWEL SUBSTITUTIONS

VOWEL PRESENTED	"IMMEDIATELY ADJACENT" VOWEL	MOST FREQUENT VOWEL SUBSTITUTION
a	e and u	e and u
e	a and i	a and i
i	e	e
o	u	u
u	a and o	a and i

Table 2. MOST FREQUENT CONSONANT SUBSTITUTION IN CVC READING TEST

PRESENTED CONSONANT	"IMMEDIATELY ADJACENT" CONSONANT	MOST FREQUENT SUBSTITUTION
b	d and p	d
d	b and t	t
g	k and j	ng
m	n	n
n	m	m
p	b and t	t
s	z and th (Θ)	sh
t	d	d

Table 3. ARTICULATION* †

MANNER	PLACE	
	LABIAL	DENTAL
voiced plosive	b	d
nasal	m	n
unvoiced plosive	p	t

* Most frequent substitutions: −b ♦ −d; −m ♦ −n.

† Frequency per 1000 words: −b : 1; −d : 111; −m : 20; −n : 68; −p : 6; −t : 98.

find out what happened in the case of a final p. Of course p does not resemble t at all visually, but it does bear the same relationship phonemically to t, as does b to d or as does m to n. Further, p is an infrequent word ending, whereas t is one of the most common (Table 3). Although a final p was not misread to anything like the same extent as a final b in this inquiry, it can be observed in Table 2 that the most common substitution for a terminal p was in fact the predicted t.

The skills involved in the experiments I have been describing thus far are at what the *Illinois Test of Psycholinguistic Abilities* would term the Automatic-Sequential level rather than at the Representational level. There have been several studies using the ITPA which have reported consistent findings of weakness on the sub-tests at the Automatic-Sequential level by children with learning disabilities and the study of Grade Two dyslexics was no exception.

Perhaps my own orientation towards a psycholinguistic approach to the understanding of reading disability was cemented when the advent of the ITPA followed almost immediately on the derivation of what were, to me at the time, some very puzzling results which I had obtained from an analysis of WISC sub-test scores of children with reading disability. The puzzling aspect had been that two of the sub-tests—Coding and Digit Span—discriminated between the retarded readers and the controls, yet for neither group was performance on either of these two sub-tests significantly correlated with IQ (McLeod, 1965). It is now clear that both of these tests are operating at the Automatic-Sequential level—indeed Digit Span is one of the Automatic-Sequential sub-tests of the ITPA—whereas measured intelligence, and in particular, Vocabulary, Arithmetic and Information (the other discriminating sub-tests) require representational mediating processes. This hypothesis is confirmed by a factor analysis of the data which I have made since I came to Illinois (McLeod, 1966a).

Perhaps the demonstration of the importance for reading of automatic skills is the most significant contribution which psycholinguistic research has made to the understanding of reading disability. We have long been accustomed to differentiating the child who cannot read "because of low intelligence" from the child who cannot read "in spite of adequate intelligence." With the dyslexic child, we have honored in theory rather than in practice the idea that measured intelligence is an index of the expectancy and potentiality of reading achievement. As Rabinovitch has observed, it is often a very creditable achievement if we can get a dyslexic child to fourth or fifth grade level in reading, even though this falls short of his measured intelligence level. Might it not be that the child who fails to read satisfactorily "in spite of an adequate IQ" is perhaps deficient in automatic level psycholinguistic skills which are necessary for reading and which have until recently tended to be either taken for granted or ignored, and which are not measured adequately by IQ tests?

And there are grounds for cautious optimism that if these skills have been stunted, they might be capable of rehabilitation. Very promising results have been obtained at Peabody and at Illinois (Smith, 1962; Wiseman, 1965) in this country and by Hart in Australia (Hart, 1963) which suggest that remediation based on the ITPA model not only produces improvement in performance on the ITPA—there would be nothing very remarkable in that—but also that there is definite positive transfer which leads to improved reading skill.

Remediation of learning disabilities is, of course, the overriding and prepotent reason for research in this field. If, as a by-product, we can achieve a more adequate psychological theory of human behavior, so much the better. One stage better than the remediation of reading disability is its prevention, and for the remainder of this paper I should like briefly to describe a screening instrument which we have developed at the Remedial Centre and what for the want of a better term we call our Dyslexia Schedule (McLeod, 1966).

Hermann (1959) has spoken of the fundamental nature of dyslexia as "this wilderness of contradictions" and Rabinovitch has ascribed to children with what he terms primary reading retardation a "characteristic pattern with much variability from patient to patient." This expresses in a nutshell the paradox that has bedevilled, and maybe befuddled, some educational psychologists—particularly in the United Kingdom—who would demand, if the concept of dyslexia is to serve any useful purpose, that children described as dyslexic must be "demonstrably different *in a significant respect*" from other backward readers (Davis and Cashdan, 1963). This requires that the correlates of dyslexia be unidimensional and invariant. Why? This restriction does not appear to be a prerequisite for such concepts as scholastic aptitude, or even intelligence, to be meaningful and useful. Money (1962) reminds us that:

It is not at all rare in psychological medicine, nor in other branches of medicine, that a disease should have no unique identifying sign, the uniqueness being in the pattern of signs that appear in contiguity

—and that this applies also to dyslexia.

It might well be that the existence of dyslexia is more obvious clinically than semantically. It might well be that dyslexia has become an abused and an emotionally charged word. It might well be that some clinicians have asserted the existence of dyslexia with a dogmatism that has sometimes tended to vary inversely with the experimental rigor with which they have gathered their data, but they are not all fools.

Bender, Critchley, de Hirsch, Hermann, Ingram, Money, Myklebust, Orton, Rabinovitch and many others have described cases of severe reading disability, the "characteristic pattern" of which can be sensed, even though it might be blurred by "much variability from patient to patient." The English parents who almost literally jammed the doors of the 1962 London Conference which culminated in the establishment of Dr. Bannatyne's Word Blind Centre were not all fools (Franklin, 1962). Many of them knew their children to be neither unintelligent nor from adverse home environments, whether the English educational psychologists had resolved their disputations or not.

In an attempt to evaluate the alleged symptoms or developmental correlates of childhood dyslexia, we constructed an instrument which, in its original form, was used as the nucleus of a parent-social worker interview, but which has since been employed many times as a straight parent questionnaire form. Its ninety items included references to symptoms which some twenty-seven workers in the field had variously asserted to be associated with dyslexia.

To validate the instrument, we wanted to apply it to a dyslexic group and to a control group, and see which, if any, of the items discriminated significantly. The problem was to find a group that could be described as dyslexic. But does this not bring us back full circle to where we started? Where is there to be found a pure group of clinically accepted dyslexics?

At this juncture, we must exercise a little patience. Arguments about dyslexia have been raging for half a century. We should not expect a final answer overnight. It seems to me that one—maybe the only—feasible approach to the identification of dyslexia is to follow a procedure analogous to the chemists' fractional distillation. That is, first of all find a group of children which is likely to be "dyslexia enriched" and use this group for a first validation of the diagnostic instrument. The instrument can then be progressively sharpened by using it to predict further cases of dyslexia and observing its adequacy to do so. There is inevitably involved some circularity of argument, but remember that circles can also spiral and therefore make linear progress.

Fortuitously, Brisbane appears to be an eminently suitable location to initiate a plan along these lines, for it has a remarkably low incidence of reading retardation. My subjective opinion, formed over a period of five years in Australia after ten years experience in England, was confirmed by two surveys we carried out in 1965. The first of these showed that out of a random sample of some 400 children in Grade Four only about 3¼ percent had Reading Quotients lower than 80, compared with at least 21 to 25 percent in Britain, according to the latest Ministry of Education survey there (Ministry of Education, 1957). More striking evidence of the low incidence of reading failure in Brisbane came from the second survey, which compared the reading achievement of Brisbane children with that of the children in the English i.t.a. experiment. We gave exactly the same test, under exactly the same conditions, to a representative sample of about 400 children after they had been in school one and a half years.

It can be seen in Figure 7 that whereas 38.95 percent of the English control group and 14.45 percent of the English i.t.a. group failed to score at all, *every* Brisbane child scored. Moreover, the respective proportions who achieved a score of 10 or lower on the test were: English control group 67.35 percent, English i.t.a. group 32.25 percent, Brisbane 5.7 percent.

If dyslexia is a function, or a partial function, of neurological or genetic factors, it would be reasonable to expect that its incidence is reasonably constant from culture to culture—unless the same recessive genes that predispose a person to dyslexia also tend to inhibit emigration to Queensland. On the basis of probability alone, the chances of a case of reading failure in Brisbane being dyslexic would be greater than would a case of reading failure in places where the incidence of reading retardation is several times greater. When, in addition, we are dealing with cases of reading failure in Brisbane that have been brought to the attention of the Remedial Centre—often the end of the line—I think we have reasonable grounds for

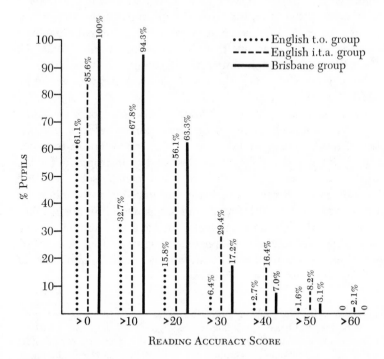

Figure 7. READING ACCURACY AS MEASURED BY THE NEALE ANAYLSIS OF READING ABILITY (FORM A)

believing that we have at least what I have termed a "dyslexia enriched" sample.*

Accordingly, we first compared the number of adverse responses to each individual item on our Dyslexia Schedule in respect of twenty-four consecutive cases referred to the Centre with those from an equal number of controls. Adverse responses were generally self-evident—for example, "Yes" to "Is he overactive?" or "Does he jumble letters in writing his name?" Seventeen items were found to discriminate between the twenty-three Centre cases and controls at the required level of confidence.

These seventeen items discriminated between the Grade Two dyslexics and their control group at the .001 level (t being 7.87 for 44 degrees of freedom) and when the data from the second inquiry was analyzed, the number of items which discriminated significantly increased to twenty-three. (Currently, the pooled data from the two inquiries are being analyzed, and it is anticipated that one or two more items will achieve significance). However, the items that have already been shown to discriminate are set out in the appendix to this paper [not in this volume].

As an indication of the diagnostic value of this instrument, let us assume for the moment that the twenty-three nonreaders in the Grade Two experiment *were* in fact dyslexic and that the controls were not. If we count up for each child the number of adverse responses to the discriminating items (which I shall call the child's AR score) we can see what would happen if we were to diagnose dyslexia on the basis of a given AR score. In particular, we can vary the critical AR score until we achieve optimal diagnostic accuracy—that is, we can determine the AR score which would reduce the number of misdiagnoses to a minimum. Misdiagnoses consist of dyslexics who would be diagnosed as non-dyslexic and non-dyslexics who would be diagnosed as dyslexic.

Table 4 indicates that if we had taken an AR score of 6 or more, then we should have missed three out of twenty-three dyslexics, and the total number of misdiagnoses would have been only four out of forty-six.

Neither the ITPA nor the WISC were designed as instruments for the diagnosis of dyslexia, of course, but for the sake of comparison, the cutoff scores on each of these instruments which would have given the minimum number of misdiagnoses was also found, and are shown in Figure 7. ITPA and the WISC Verbal Scale do quite well, but have a minimum of nine misdiagnoses while—as might be expected—diagnosis from the WISC Performance Scale is hardly better than chance, with a minimum of eighteen misdiagnoses out of forty-six cases.

---

*Several people asked after the presentation of this paper why Brisbane is apparently so blessed with the low incidence of reading disability cases. In the present author's opinion, the most likely factors are: (1) a very comprehensive program of screenings and treatment of speech problems in Grade One, and (2) maybe the beginning of formal reading teaching at an optimal age. (The average child is five and a half years old when formal reading is started.)

Table 4. Distributions of Dyslexics and Controls on WISC, ITPA and Critical Items of Dyslexia Schedule

WISC Performance IQ

IQs	74–81	82–89	90–97	98–105	106–113	114–121	122–129	130–138
DYSLEXICS	1	2	5	7	4	2	2	
CONTROLS		2	1	9	4	3	3	1

WISC Full Scale IQ

IQs	82–89	90–97	98–105	106–113	114–121	122–129	130–138
DYSLEXICS	4	7	6	4	2	3	
CONTROLS	1	1	3	7	6		2

WISC Verbal IQ

IQs	75–82	83–90	91–98	99–106	107–114	115–122	123–130	131+
DYSLEXICS	1	4	8	7	1	2	2	3
CONTROLS		1	0	5	5	7	2	3

ITPA Raw Score

SCORES	139–149	150–160	161–171	172–182	183–193	192–204	205–215	216–226
DYSLEXICS	2	7	7	4	1	2	3	2
CONTROLS		1	3	2	6	6	3	

Dyslexia Schedule: Adverse Responses to Critical Items

AR	13	11–12	9–10	7–8	5–6	3–4	1–2	0
DYSLEXICS	1	1	6	8	4	2	1	0
CONTROLS			1	0	0	10	6	6

AR scores on the Dyslexia Schedule were correlated with ITPA Language Ages and WISC Full Scale and Verbal Scale IQs, for both dyslexics and for controls. Only the correlation between ITPA and AR scores for the control group reached significance, and that only at the 5 percent level.

The validation studies carried out to date have been concerned with children who have already experienced some reading failure. However, as the items that have been found to discriminate require for the most part only a parental report on their child's pre-school experience and history, there is reason to hope that they will also *predict* children who might be expected to experience severe difficulties in learning to read. A pilot study is currently in progress in Brisbane and, if we can find the necessary financial resources, we hope to carry out a more ambitious investigation to examine the effectiveness of the Schedule as a screening device. Although it was originally designed to be used in an interview situation, the complete Schedule has already been completed by scores of parents who have been in contact with the Remedial Centre, so there is no reason to anticipate any difficulties in having parents complete a truncated version of the Schedule at the time of their children's first entry to school.

Of course, the identification of children who are likely to become cases of childhood dyslexia is not a final answer—but it would be a big help. It still remains to initiate preventive measures, but there are grounds for hope from the generally optimistic results of language development programs which have been generated from the *Illinois Test of Psycholinguistic Abilities* and its underlying rationale, that deficiencies in necessary skills can be ameliorated.

The position that I think we have reached, as far as research is concerned, is that the science of psycholinguistics has opened up a new perspective for the understanding of reading disability, and what I hope our experiments up to now have demonstrated is that certain research methodologies are practicable and sensitive with children, so that not only has psycholinguistics provided us with a new perspective, but also with a vast, uncharted—but chartable—field of research. Meanwhile, our Dyslexia Schedule will provide us with an operational means of defining the sort of children about whom we will be accumulating psycholinguistic data and—hopefully—about whom we will be increasing our understanding.

REFERENCES

DAVIS, D. B. and CASHDAN, A. Critical Note: Specific Dyslexia. *British Journal of Educational Psychology,* 1963, 33, 1, 80-82
DURRELL, D. D. Learning Difficulties among Children of Normal Intelligence. *Elementary School Journal,* 1954, 55, 201-208.
EL'KONIN, D. B. Psychological Study of the Learning Process in the Elementary School. *Sovetskaia Pedagogika,* 1961, 9. (Translation in *Soviet Education,* 1962, 4, 36-44.)

FRANKLIN, A. W. (ed.) *Word-Blindness or Specific Developmental Dyslexia.* London, Pitman, 1962.

HART, N. W. M. The Differential Diagnosis of the Psycholinguistic Abilities of the Cerebral Palsied Child and Effective Remedial Procedures. *Queensland Education Department, Special Schools Bulletin,* 1963, August, 3-20.

HOLMES, J. A. and SINGER, H. Theoretical Models and Trends Towards More Basic Research in Reading. *Review Educational Research,* 1964, 34, 127-155.

McLEOD, J. A. Comparison of WISC Sub-test Scores of Pre-adolescent Successful and Unsuccessful Readers. *Australian Journal of Psychology,* 1965, 17, 220-228.

————. Prediction of childhood dyslexia. *Slow Learning Child,* 1966, 12, 143-154. (Reprinted in *Bulletin of Orton Society,* 1966, 16, 14-23.)

————. Dyslexia in young children. A factorial study with special reference to the *Illinois Test of Psycholinguistic Abilities.* Urbana, University of Illinois, IREC Papers in Education (in press) 1966a.

————. Dyslexia schedule and school entrance check list. Cambridge Educators Publishing Series, 1969.

McLEOD, J. and ANDERSON, J. Readability assessment and word redundancy of printed English. *Psychology Reports,* 1966, 18, 35-38.

McLEOD, J. and ATKINSON, J. K. *Domain phonic test-kit.* Edinburgh, Oliver and Boyd, 1972.

MINISTRY OF EDUCATION. *Standards of reading 1948-1956.* London, H.M.S.O.; 1957.

MONEY, J. (ed.) *Reading Disability; Progress and Research Needs in Dyslexia.* Baltimore, Johns Hopkins Press, 1962.

OSGOOD, C. E. and SEBEOK. *Psycholinguistics.* Bloomington, Indiana University Press, 1965.

SMITH, J. O. Group language development for educable mental retardates. *Exceptional Children,* 1962, 29, 2, 95-101.

TILLMAN, T., CARHART, R., and WILBER, LAURA. *A Test for Speech Discrimination Composed of CNC Monosyllabic Words (N.U. Auditory Test No. 4)* U.S. Department of Commerce, Office of Technical Services, 1963.

VERNON, MAGDALEN D. Specific dyslexia. *British Journal of Educational Psychology,* 1962, 32, 143-150.

WISEMAN, D. E. *The effects of an individualised remedial program on mentally retarded children with psycholinguistic disabilities.* Unpublished doctoral thesis, University of Illinois, 1965.

School Entrance Check List

Name of child . . . .

Address . . . . Phone . . . .

School . . . . Grade . . . . . Date of birth . . . .

1. (a) Have you ever suspected that your child may have defective eyesight? . . . .*Yes/No*

   (b) If so, has he ever been seen by an optometrist or by an eye specialist? . . . .*Yes/No*

   (c) If so, what was the result of the examination? . . . .

2. (a) Have you ever suspected that he may have defective hearing? . . . .*Yes/No*

   (b) If so, has he ever had his hearing tested? . . . .*Yes/No*

   (c) If so, what was the result of the examination? . . . .

3. Was he in the hospital *at all* before he was three years old? . . . .*Yes/No*

4. If he has been separated at all from one or both parents, did he seem different in any way after separation? (e.g., more clinging, affectionate, indifferent to parents) . . . .*Yes/No*

5. Has he any nervous tendencies?
   (a) bedwetting . . . .*Yes/No*

   (b) excessive story telling (lies or fantasy) . . . .*Yes/No*

   (c) fear of dark or nightmares . . . .*Yes/No*

   (d) fear of making mistakes . . . .*Yes/No*

6. Does he show anxiety and/or depression? . . . .*Yes/No*

7. Is he over-active? . . . .*Yes/No*

8. Was he over-active in infancy? . . . .*Yes/No*

9. Was he over-active before he was born? . . . .*Yes/No*

10. At what age did he speak (apart from "da" and "ma")? . . . . *years* . . . . .*months*

11. At what age was his speech (i.e., two or more continuous words) intelligible to persons *other than mother?* . . . .*years* . . . . .*months*

12. Was his talk still immature at age four or five, i.e., at or just prior to starting school? (e.g., "fink" for "think," "dat" for "that," reference to himself by name rather than by "I" or "me") . . . .*Yes/No*

13. Has he ever tended to mix up the order of words in a sentence or to mix up parts of words? (e.g., "flutterby" for "butterfly," "hopgrasser" for

"grasshopper," or "Did you lawn the mow?" for "Did you mow the lawn?", etc.) . . . .*Yes/No*

14. By the age of 3½ or so onwards, did he tend to omit words? (e.g., "I going school.") . . . .*Yes/No*

15. As an infant, did he constantly ask you to repeat what you had said so that the procedure became more or less automatic? . . . .*Yes/No*

16. Can he remember a short message word for word, or a telephone number, for instance? . . . .*Yes/No/Don't know*

17. Has he had any difficulty in distinguishing right from left? (e.g., in following directions, performing actions involving turning handles to the right or left, etc.) . . . .*Yes/No*

18. Have any members of his family experienced difficulties with reading and/or spelling? (i.e., parents, grandparents, brothers, or sisters) . . . .*Yes/No*

Signature of person who has completed the check list . . . .

Relationship to child . . . .

Date . . . .

Comments:

Eight

Adolescence

Secondary school programs for the learning-disabled continue to present unique problems, as unresolved problems become compounded—academically, socially, and emotionally.

There are relatively few programs in secondary schools as compared to the number in elementary schools. Nevertheless, the percentage is increasing, as the secondary school recognizes the existence of the problem of learning disabilities.

A research study by Bruce Bell, Franklin Lewis, and Robert Anderson, conducted in the public school system of Beaumont, Texas, provides some interesting data on reading adequacy as related to race and various personality dimensions. Retarded readers were characterized as venturesome and undisciplined, regardless of race. The personality characteristics they displayed on personality tests were consistent with those noted by parents, teachers, and physicians. The need for emotional support as well as academic remediation at the junior high school level is emphasized in this study.

The current emphasis on career education for the handicapped, particularly for adolescents and young adults, is reflected by Milton Brutten in his description of the vocational education program in a private school that applies the concept of programmed experiences in a simulation laboratory. The rapidly changing social structure within our rising economy, together with modern technology and automation, is going to require new methodologies of education for adolescents with learning disabilities.

Personality and Reading Retardation in Junior High School Students*

D. BRUCE BELL
FRANKLIN D. LEWIS
ROBERT P. ANDERSON

Since it is generally agreed that learning disorders are *symptoms*,[1] diagnosis of underlying conditions usually precedes any remediation effort. For example, R. Rabinovitch postulated that reading deficits could be explained by deficiencies in one or more of the following areas:[2]

- general intelligence
- specific capacities
- developmental readiness
- emotional freedom to learn
- motivation
- past opportunities for learning.

D. B. Bell and F. D. Lewis studied selected variables in five of these six areas to determine which types of problems most reliably differentiated between adequate and inadequate readers in the junior high school age group.[3] No measures of developmental readiness were used because of the students' ages.

The findings regarding the effects of intelligence, motor skills, and social status have been reported previously.[4] In reporting data on motivation and personality, Bell, Lewis, and R. P. Anderson employed Rabinovitch's definition of reading deficiency, which holds intelligence constant.[5] However, the data have not been previously analyzed in terms of the relationship between the child's reading performance and his age or grade placement. The purpose of the present study was to examine the personality data in this practical context.

Procedures

The sample of 100 students, which has been described in detail in previous reports,[6] consisted of apparently normal junior high school boys, selected to meet the requirements of a 2 × 2 analysis of variance design; 50 percent were black (drawn from one junior

*The cooperation of the Beaumont Independent School District, Beaumont, Texas, in furnishing the facilities and students for this research, is gratefully acknowledged by the authors.

From the *Proceedings* of the Eighth Annual Conference of the ACLD, *The Child with Learning Disabilities: His Right to Learn*. Chicago (March 18–20, 1971), pp. 203–208.

high), and 50 percent were white (drawn from a second school). Half were reading within six months of what was expected for their ages (the average readers), and half were two or more years below that level (the inadequate readers). Thus each of the four groups consisted of twenty-five students.

The measure of personality was the *Jr.-Sr. High School Personality Questionnaire* (HSPQ), by R. B. Cattell and H. Beloff,[7] which yields fourteen personality "factors." It was group administered, and the items were read to the students so as not to penalize those students whose reading level was below that demanded by the test. The reading criterion was computed as an average of the Reading Comprehension and Vocabulary subtests of the *Iowa Tests of Basic Skills*. These scores were taken from the students' school records.

Results and Discussions

Table 1 shows the results of the 2×2 analysis of variance: the mean sten scores obtained by each of the four groups, and the levels of significance between the means.

RACIAL GROUP DIFFERENCES

Significant racial differences occurred on five of the fourteen HSPQ measures: Factors B, F, I, J, and O. On the basis of these findings, the black students, as a group, appear to be (1) more concrete in their thinking, (2) more sober, (3) more tender-minded, (4) more doubting, and (5) more placid than the white students.

The fact that the black students obtained significantly lower scores on Factor B (Concrete vs. Abstract) might seem to indicate that the black students were less intelligent. However, this was not the case. The scores of the two groups on the *Wechsler Intelligence Scale for Children* (WISC) were not significantly different; moreover, Factor B failed to correlate significantly with any of WISC scales. Among the alternative explanations that might be suggested for the differences among the races on this variable, D. H. Ecroyd's observation seems the most pertinent.[8] He found that blacks who are living in ghettos communicate in a language substantially different from standard English. Therefore, the blacks may have done poorly on the items in Factor B because of linguistic rather than intellectual difficulties.

The black students appeared more sober on the HSPQ, as represented by lower scores on Factor F (Sober vs. Happy-Go-Lucky), and in their behavior in the presence of the examiners. According to R. B. Cattell and M. Cattell,[9] Factor F measures a fixed trait that represents, in this study, a stable difference, which may be associated with the relatively higher

Table 1. Mean HSPQ Scores for the Two Races and the Two Reading Groups (N = 100) and the Level of Significance Associated with the Analysis of Variance

Variable	Racial Group			Reading Group		
	Caucasian	Negro	Level	Adequate	Inadequate	Level
reserved vs. outgoing (Factor A)	5.44*	5.18		4.98	5.64	
concrete vs. abstract (B)	5.26	4.52	.05	5.14	4.64	
easily upset vs. calm (C)	4.80	5.42		4.84	5.38	
phlegmatic vs. excitable (D)	6.04	5.56		6.18	5.42	
obedient vs. assertive (E)	5.70	5.64		5.70	5.64	
sober vs. happy-go-lucky (F)	5.56	4.54	.05	4.90	5.20	
expedient vs. conscientious (G)	5.36	5.94		6.02	5.28	
shy vs. venturesome (H)	5.14	5.06		4.74	5.46	.05
tough vs. tender-minded (I)	5.98	7.10	.01	6.32	6.76	
vigorous vs. doubting (J)	5.28	6.26	.05	5.80	5.74	
placid vs. apprehensive (O)	5.94	4.96	.05	5.82	5.08	
group dependent vs. self-sufficient (Q_2)	5.66	6.26		6.02	5.90	
undisciplined vs. controlled (Q_3)	5.24	5.72		5.96	5.00	.01
relaxed vs. tense (Q_4)	5.78	5.06		5.68	5.16	

*Low scores are associated with the verbal description on the left end of the continuum, whereas high scores are associated with the verbal description on the right.

standing of the black students within their school.* However, the seriousness may also be, in part, a function of the use of white examiners.[10]

The black readers had a higher mean score on Factor I (Tough vs. Tender-minded), which suggests that they tend to be independent, overprotected, sensitive, and to have somatic complaints.[11] Since the black students were achieving at or above school norms despite cultural and environmental handicaps, the finding of indications of "stress" may suggest that the black readers are paying a "price" for their academic success.

As a group, the black readers tended to be somewhat more individualistic (higher mean scores on Factor J—Vigorous vs. Doubting). Individuals with lower scores on this continuum tend to participate vigorously in group activities; those with higher scores do not.

Another significant racial difference became evident in Factor O (Placid vs. Apprehensive). Although both groups appear within the average range on this scale, the black students seem to be slightly more placid, self-assured, or confident in their relationships with others, while the white students tend to be more apprehensive or worried.

The picture emerges of the black student who is concrete, very serious, somewhat anxious, and a "loner." He appears to be somewhat more self-assured in his position than his white counterparts. Although none of the racial differences were related to reading when measured against national norms, they may be in part a function of differences in the relative academic achievement of the two groups. The relationship could be more fully understood if the study were replicated drawing samples from all three levels (high, middle, and low) of both local schools.

READING GROUP DIFFERENCES

Table 1 also reveals two significant differences between the reading groups (Factors H and Q_3). There were no significant interactions between reading and racial groups on any of the fourteen variables.

Factor H (Shy vs. Venturesome) is analogous to the introversion-extroversion concept. The venturesome end of the continuum, which characterized the retarded readers, is associated with activity, overt interest in the opposite sex, impulsiveness, and frivolousness. Since Cattell believes that Factor H is constitutionally determined,[12] the impulsiveness seen in this measure may be the same impulsiveness which S. D. Clements and J. E. Peters observed in minimally brain-damaged retarded readers.[13] Such

---

*In order to test whether differences in "past opportunities to learn" were important to reading (see Rabinovitch, "Dyslexia: Psychiatric Considerations," in Notes), the two schools chosen for the study were quite different in the average achievement of their students. That is, whereas the predominantly Caucasian school had a building norm indistinguishable from the national one, the predominantly Negro school was producing students who read, on the average, two years below national norm. Consequently, the black students who were only reading on an "average" level nationally were in the top 10 percent of their classes locally. Likewise, the inadequately reading blacks were achieving what was expected in a school two years below national norms.

children may be unable to inhibit hyperkinetic behavior and to assume the quiet, passive behavior which M. D. Jenkinson believes is necessary for the development of reading skills.[14] The association between venturesomeness and inadequate reading could also be the result of an interaction between the hyperkinetic, driven behavior and the social consequences of such behavior. That is, the children may find that such actions have an attention-getting payoff, and inadvertent reinforcement may make the behavior even more enduring. Regardless of its origin, distractable behavior reduces the opportunity for learning and practicing reading skills.

The retarded readers also obtained lower scores on Factor Q_3 (Undisciplined vs. Controlled). Such scores have been found to be associated with a lack of discipline and self-regard, uncontrolled emotionality, excitability, a rejection of cultural demands, acting out behavior, and juvenile delinquency.[15] Low self-concept among white retarded readers has been observed by others,[16] as has rejection of cultural demands.[17] Again, it is difficult to ascertain whether lack of discipline is responsible for the reading difficulty,[18] as is a reactive adjustment to it.[19]

The significant point is that retarded readers manifest the same personality characteristics on the HSPQ that have been noted by parents, teachers, and physicians. Therefore, this test might be used in conjunction with remediation efforts. Children who have abnormally high scores on Factors H and Q_3 might require psychological as well as educational intervention for improvement of their reading skills. The prevalence of these two characteristics in the group of retarded readers in the present study seems to indicate that they are common in most retarded readers. Practitioners would thus do well to avoid reinforcing these self-defeating traits in their students.

NOTES

1. B. Bateman, "Learning Disorders," *Journal of Educational Research* 36 (1966), 93-119.
2. R. Rabinovitch, "Dyslexia: Psychiatric Considerations," *Reading Disability: Progress and Research Needs in Dyslexia*, ed. J. Money (Baltimore, Md.: Johns Hopkins Press, 1962).
3. D. B. Bell, "The Motivational and Personality Factors in Reading Retardation Among Two Racial Groups of Adolescent Males," unpublished doctoral dissertation (Lubbock, Tex.: Texas Technological University, 1969); F. D. Lewis, "Motor Abilities as Related to Reading Retardation in Two Male Racial Groups of Adolescents," unpublished doctoral dissertation (Lubbock, Tex.: Texas Technological University, 1969).
4. F. D. Lewis, D. B. Bell, and R. P. Anderson, "Relationship of Motor Proficiency and Reading Retardation," *Perceptual and Motor Skills* 31 (1970), 395-401; idem, "Reading Retardation: A Bi-racial Comparison," *Journal of Reading* 13 (1970), 433-436, and 474-478.

5. D. B. Bell, F. D. Lewis, and R. P. Anderson, "Personality, Motivation, and Reading: A Factor Analytic Study." Paper presented at Southwestern Psychological Association Annual Meeting, St. Louis, Mo., April, 1970; R. Rabinovitch, "Reading and Learning Disabilities," *American Handbook of Psychiatry*, ed. S. Arieti (New York: Basic Books: 1959).

6. F. D. Lewis, D. B. Bell, and R. P. Anderson, "Relationship of Motor Proficiency and Reading Retardation"; idem, "Reading Retardation: A Bi-racial Comparison"; Bell, Lewis, and Anderson, "Personality, Motivation, and Reading."

7. For sources of tests mentioned in this article, see Appendix to the *Proceedings of the Eighth Annual ACLD Conference*.

8. D. H. Ecroyd, "Negro Children and Language Arts," *Reading Teacher* 21 (1968), 624-629.

9. R. B. Cattell, and M. Cattell, *Handbook for the Jr.-Sr. High School Personality Questionnaire*, (Champaign, Ill.: Institute of Personality and Ability Testing, 1969).

10. O. Klienberg "Negro-White Differences in Intelligence Test Performances: A New Look at an Old Problem," *Education and Social Crisis*, eds. E. T. Leach, R. Fulton, and W. E. Gardner (New York: John Wiley and Sons, 1967).

11. Cattell and Cattell, *Handbook for the HSPQ*.

12. R. B. Cattell, *Personality and Motivation Structure and Measurement* (Yonkers-on-Hudson, N.Y.: World Book Company, 1957).

13. S. D. Clements and J. E. Peters, "Minimal Brain Dysfunctions in the School-Age Child," *Archives of General Psychiatry* 6 (1962), 17-29.

14. M. D. Jenkinson, "The Roles of Motivation in Reading," *Meeting Individual Differences in Reading*, ed. H. A. Robinson (Chicago, Ill.: University of Chicago, 1964).

15. R. B. Cattell, and H. Beloff, *Jr.-Sr. High School Personality Questionnaire* (Champaign, Ill.: Institute of Personality and Ability Testing, 1962).

16. R. F. Spincola, "An Investigation into Seven Correlates of Reading Achievement Including the Self-Concept." Unpublished doctoral dissertation (Tallahassee, Fla.: Florida State University, 1960); J. M. Paulo, "Character and Causes of Retardation and Reading Among Pupils of the 7th and 8th Grades," *Elementary School Journal* (1963), 35-43.

17. G. D. Spache, "Personality Patterns of Retarded Readers," *Journal of Educational Research* 50 (1957), 461-469; R M. Stang, "The Relation of Guidance to Teaching of Reading," *Personnel and Guidance Journal* 44 (1966), 831-836.

18. A. A. Fabian, "Reading Disability: An Index of Pathology," *American Journal of Orthopsychiatry* 25 (1955), 319-329.

19. R. P. Anderson, "The Basis of Underachievement, Neurological or Psychological?" *Elementary School Guidance and Counseling* 2 (1968), 212-221.

Vocational Education for the Brain-Injured Adolescent and Young Adult at the Vanguard School

MILTON BRUTTEN

Perhaps the most challenging development in American special education has been the recognition of the special character and the requirements of neurologically impaired children. This has been accompanied by strenuous efforts to extend to them the specialized educational services which take cognizance of their distinct character and are designed to advance them maturationally and promote their ultimate adaptation to open society. Provision of such services necessitates a dynamic, unfolding diagnostic process which highlights, at various stages of each child's development, the particular spectrum of liabilities that confronts him and the positive attributes or compensatory resources available to him. A pivotal consideration in the commitment to ongoing evaluation of children who make deviant response to learning requirements is a comprehensive and detailed functional or skill analysis which need not and should not be pegged to any preconceptions as to what may constitute the obstacles in the way of the child's optimal development. For example, perceptual handicap does not in every case characterize the child with minimal brain dysfunction, for some youngsters with indisputable evidence of brain damage may be quite intact in terms of perceptual organization. Their pivotal disorder, blocking the way to educational advance and social fulfillment, may be a significant derangement of language development or cognitive process. A clear-eyed, pragmatic approach requires a thorough investigation of all of the barriers and resources for dealing with them that confront the child as he moves ahead, and inspection of how these shift and take on a new balance of force in the course of time. We are essentially interested in determining where the child stands in relation to significant skill development, how certain deficits have blocked or deterred him, in realistically appraising a valid destination towards which he is headed, and in the establishment of a plan of action towards circumventing and reducing malfunctioning in order that he may arrive at his worthwhile objectives most rapidly and most efficiently.

Although the special educator is concerned with the youngster's movement towards successful adaptation to social reality and suitable career choice, he has set his sights primarily on the provision of appropriate remedial methodology for the young school age child. He is concerned primarily with the reduction or obviation of developmental discontinuities and "skill discrepancies" that stand in the way of optimal realization of

From the *Proceedings* of the Third Annual International Conference of the ACLD, *An International Approach to Learning Disabilities of Children and Youth*, Tulsa, Okla. (March 3-5, 1966), pp. 154-163.

available potential towards valid social and vocational objectives. However, most special educational facilities accommodating the learning-disabled child dwindle markedly or fade to nothingness in relation to the evolving needs and developing resources of the adolescent child with neurologic dysfunction, the child who has grown beyond the purview of the special educator whose exclusive concern is the primary age child. One probable reason for the diminution in professional engagement on behalf of the teenager and young adult consists in the hope that the learning-disabled youngster can return to the educational mainstream by early adolescence and can from that point move forward in the company of his peers. While there is not significant evidence to show the extent to which this optimistic view is supported by experience, it is probable that a significant proportion of the neurologically impaired adolescent population cannot proceed and achieve with comfort or security in the conventional school setting. Many display residual achievement lags that make requisite special provision throughout their secondary school career.

Perhaps the child's early educational program requires so much individual enhancement in relation to specific skill development (as in perception, co-ordinative function or linguistic attainment) that the child's total pace of achievement is necessarily slowed in relation to conventional curricular demands. Also, the conventional secondary program steps up its demands in a markedly accelerated fashion and makes little provision for teenagers who display residual skill discrepancies. The Vanguard Upper School, which now accommodates about 150 teenagers, receives a substantial number of its referrals from excellent specialized educational facilities which have not been able to move their graduates into the conventional educational structure by twelve or thirteen years of age, at which point their programs terminate. But not all of the learning-disabled adolescents in our program come to us out of other specialized facilities (or have moved up from our own primary and intermediate programs); we are, in addition, receiving referrals of students who have been able to cope with the challenges of a regular school program through the intermediate level, often with the support of substantial individual remedial work, psychotherapy, parent counseling and other services.

However, these boys and girls have found the transition to the less protected secondary program difficult to negotiate, or, indeed, devastating in its impact. They have found it hard to organize themselves in relation to an intensified reality constituting a stepped-up curriculum, a change from self-contained classes to a departmental format, a more complex and depersonalized set of circumstances and other features that make overwhelming demands upon their limited adaptive and integrative capacities. This necessitates the establishment or expansion of sophisticated special educational programs reaching well up into the teen years and encompassing the total secondary curriculum. We are confronted in the establishment of such programs with the fact that there is relatively little scientific information available about the psychopathology and learning characteristics experienced by the adolescent perceptually handicapped or learning-disabled student, though Laufer, Gordon, Anderson and others have contributed to our expanding awareness of the teenager's life experience and his response to it. The brain-damaged adolescent characteristically is erratic or spotty in his preparation for formal secondary work and may have developed hostility to the learning process and school situation itself, tied in with his lack of self-confidence and impaired self-image and sense of identity. The youngster may feel himself damaged, inadequate or incomplete and therefore ill-equipped to face mounting biological needs welling up from within as well as the stresses impinging upon him from without. The child may feel that his poor school achievement is but one evidence of his inability to establish a satisfactory sense of identity and is concrete evidence of his inability to cope, and to attain mastery over essential "tools for living."

We have come around to the thinking that our exclusive concern at bolstering deficit function in the early school age learning-disabled child requires considerable modification when we approach the problems of the teenager. We feel, in other words, that a special school continues to have the responsibility to provide skill enhancement in relation to deficit areas but must also encourage the teenager's ego development by undergirding and advancing those talents, aptitudes and skills which are intact or unimpaired. In our experience, virtually every learning-disabled teenager of average intellectual endowment is capable along some line of endeavor, and it is incumbent upon the special educator to locate, identify and nurture this unimpeded capability and help the teenager to bring it to fruition. Contrary to expectations, many of our boys demonstrate remarkable ability in relation to skills whose acute development we would not anticipate in the light of their initial spatial disorganization, visual-motor impairment and coordinative skill deficits. Many of our boys, for instance, show unusual ingenuity in relation to various skilled mechanical and electrical operations. Many of our boys understand very well how engines work or how motors may be modified to accomplish specific objectives, although they may not be able to express these operating principles in abstract terms. Apparently these processes tap some inherent source of intense interest and motivation of such magnitude that the child is spontaneously spurred to push through the barriers initially imposed by foreground-background disruption or impaired spatial awareness. I think it was Francis Bacon who said, "The best way to combat nature is to ally yourself with her." Therefore, we are placing ourselves more and more on the side of aptitude, interest and high-level motivation and attempting to resolve underlying deficits, not by direct assault upon residual skill discrepancies through deficit training, but more and more by encouraging the youngsters to exploit their intact abilities and innate potentials through projects and tasks which make sense to them in terms of their unfolding life experience and are of inherent high interest value. In this way we think we can approach some of the straightforward learning deficiencies in a way alternate to specific remedial measures, which have by the adolescent years become very tedious and irritating.

We find, for example, that the "dyslexic" child may not find himself so hopelessly enmeshed in the mechanics of reading when he is looking through a parts and operations manual as he attempts to figure out the "bugs" in a defective Chevy or VW engine. The boy may be a functional illiterate, or be able on formal tests to manifest skills at perhaps a third grade level, but somehow he's going to make sense of a manual at least at a sixth grade level and take out of it what he needs in order to accomplish the day to day, concrete operations that are so vitally important to him. I think that more and more we have to tie in our formal academic preparation in meaningful and concrete operations with the adolescent who has nagging doubt as to whether reading, writing and arithmetic are "for the birds" or may have some worthwhile contribution to make toward his pursuit of realizable gratifications and life objectives, and his construction of a solid feeling of competence and worthwhileness. Immature as he may be in some ways, the adolescent learning-disabled boy shares many of the values of the normal peer group, he has many of the same needs and wants the same kinds of assurances in relation to these needs. If the curriculum for the adolescent can be organized in such a way that it minimizes the frustration and discouragement he has experienced in relation to conventional school demand, but on the other hand advances his notion of how the school can directly and concretely contribute to the gratification of his needs, we are allying our educative efforts with what we know about the healthy ego aspirations of both "normal" and learning-disabled teenagers.

Our concern with the impinging social and occupational requirements in the teenager's life leads us to emphasize skill development which is likely to shade over into direct work application and to bridge the traditional domains of special education on the one hand and vocational preparation on the other. At the Vanguard Upper School, the vocational rehabilitation and guidance services form an integral part of the program of scholastic preparation, for we feel that the student is more comfortable and assured and that society's needs are best served if we blend academic pursuit and vocational preparation in the direction of helping the student develop marketable skills. These enhance the child's sense of identity and his fundamental connectedness with the realities of the external world. We have observed that the majority of our teenage students who are accomplishing these tentative steps towards vocational and social adaptation tend to be persistent, undeviating, responsible and, indeed, compulsively meticulous. Although this meticulousness may have its dynamic origin as a defense against inherent disorganization, it can be capitalized to serve useful vocational objectives and will be seen by a prospective employer as an indication of reliability. Similarly, the child's intentness upon the restricted objective may from one point of view reflect shallowness, unimaginativeness or lack of capacity for refined judgment and decision making. On the other hand, the formation of these traits can have useful vocational application, for society is more and more in need of individuals that carry out essential and skilled, though perhaps fairly routine, procedures at technical and pre-professional levels.

There is overwhelming evidence that the changing realities of our society are providing ever widening opportunities at these levels. Industrial sources forcefully document the growing need for trained, but narrow-scope, technical personnel in subordinate positions to free the college-trained engineer for tasks that require creative flair, abstract judgment of the highest order and decision making. The ratio of trained technical personnel to high-level creative personnel is invariably of the order of five-to-one or seven-to-one. Industry appears to be vitally concerned with the recruiting and training of this indispensable class of back-up technicians. For example, in the field of data processing, Dr. John W. Sullivan of Remington Rand Corporation has recently pointed out that the data processing industries will create 500,000 jobs at the technical level during the next ten years. The operation of computers requires maintenance personnel, operators, technicians and clerical assistants, and Dr. Sullivan has pointed out that high school graduates with a few years of specialized training can qualify for positions at these levels. Most of the opportunities in the data processing industries, in point of fact, will concentrate at the lower technical levels which are methodical and repetitive in nature rather than creative and abstract. For most of the positions that will be available, industries will not wish to hire college level personnel, for their academic achievements will exceed those required of the average computer operator or maintenance man. The vocational guidance counselor is charged with the responsibility of determining whether a student's intact abilities and burgeoning aptitudes match the job requirements of a particular occupational niche and this involves a matching process based upon the ongoing diagnostic appraisal of the individual's aptitude spectrum in terms of the known requirements for various job clusters. Each major occupation, or cluster of occupations, is divided into dozens of sub-occupations, and each echelon within the major groupings requires different levels of skills, aptitudes and responsibilities.

One other pre-professional field which holds outstanding promise for the occupational fulfillment of learning-disabled individuals may well be that of library clerical training. There appears to be a growing need for young people to work in libraries in a nonprofessional capacity and under the direct supervision of the college-trained, professional librarian. Librarians have a most interesting and valuable position in our society, and the growing demand for more extensive library facilities of various kinds has made the need for trained personnel acute. The professional librarian is now trained at the level of a master's degree, but it is necessary that he have available to him the services of librarian clerks and aides, whose major utility will be in the area of technical services. These include the organizing, arranging, and indexing of materials so that they may be readily located, the filing and organization of the card catalog, the correct placement of materials in accordance with the classification scheme, and such necessary rudimentary tasks as preparation of books for shelving, the preparation of corresponding card listing, the weatherproofing and repair of materials, etc. It is estimated that in most libraries the professional librarian will require the assistance of four or five qualified library aides and clerical assistants.

The U.S. Office of Education in its recent publication "Vocational Education in the Next Decade" indicates that changes in our economy and our new scientific developments are creating opportunities within a wide range of technical and pre-professional occupations. There will certainly be a considerable growth in the health service occupations because of the large increase in population and the higher standards of medical care. Some day training opportunities for the learning-disabled young adult must be made available in the preparation of practical nurses, medical and dental technicians, laboratory aides and research assistants, and others who will function within a great variety of community mental health services. Entry of America into the space age is creating thousands of new jobs for technically trained, skilled craftsmen who will be required for the manufacturing, installation, operation, and maintenance of many kinds of equipment.

Realizing that the labor market is undergoing revolutionary changes due to the influences of technological improvements and automation, we are developing the basis of our evaluation and testing program from information secured from existing business, government and industrial practices. Effective vocational guidance anticipates the nature of job trends and provides this data to the youngster as he surveys the various occupational possibilities that relate to his interest, emotional needs, skill development and other proclivities. The Vanguard Career Guidance Center, developed by Watson Klincewicz, has already created certain prototype testing models which simulate realistic work demands and conditions, and those models are being consolidated into a formalized job evaluation battery according to the accepted procedures of sound test development. We aspire to broaden our evaluation facilities so that they will encompass the full range of training and placement possibilities from the simplest service areas through those requiring college and technical study. This requires the integrated school-vocational training program and makes possible the young person's smooth transition from school setting through ultimate placement. These functions will include vocational evaluation, a program to develop an individual's understanding of self in relation to the assumption of a worker role, actual practice in work activities, development of better social habits and insights, the individual's realistic self-appraisal of endowments and skill potentials, guidance in discovering the locations and levels of various job opportunities and eventual assistance in the actual placement process. In this total plan, school activities are synchronized with each student's tentative occupational objective; thus the classroom teacher will begin to work in concert with the vocational program towards equipping the youngster with the academic background prerequisite to his ultimate training objectives. Such experience at Vanguard School, consisting of classroom activities pre-vocational evaluation, job exploration, pre-training opportunities and others, are clearly defined and arranged in a chronological order according to a natural sequence. The student's progress through this system is controlled on an individual basis so that optimal success, motivation, self-understanding and ego development are achieved.

This objective can perhaps best be attained through the establishment of a system termed Programmed Experience which interrelates all aspects of our comprehensive program towards the creation of optimal conditions which will facilitate the formulation of a sound vocational plan for each student. Programmed Experience is in essence a control apparatus which enables us to afford each youngster an opportunity to advance through carefully graduated life experiences without the possibility of suffering failures that trigger frustration reactions. It presents a systematic progression which does not permit an individual to be exposed to a concentrated segment of a higher echelon of experience till he has successfully negotiated one of lesser complexity. In essence the Programmed Experience concept determines each minute step of the total program in accordance with concepts evolving from cybernetics theory and the communication sciences, computerization, and other elements of our exploding technology. Programmed instruction, of course, is becoming an accepted technique in education due to its extremely rigorous promotion through research and application by recognized authorities, and Vanguard School relies in part upon programmed instruction as an effective teaching adjunct. But the Programmed Experience concept, its natural outgrowth, allows for a continuing, unfolding and realistic appraisal of aptitudes and skills in relation to a given sequence ranging from the various phases of formal learning experience, vocational evaluation, personal adjustment training, exposure to part-time work activities, regular training and ultimate job placement. Each step in a student's progression of achievement is followed closely and criteria developed which describe his next appropriate move in the progression. In this way the student with learning disorders responds to an approach which controls the environmental conditions by reducing requirements to small and manageable units through which he can be guided towards an ever-expanding success pattern.

It is possible to select activities in the school, in the pre-vocational setting or in a workshop and place them on a scale of ever increasing difficulty. This will ensure that each youngster will experience success, will achieve the satisfaction of having completed a concrete assignment, the accompanying surge of self-confidence and enhanced motivation to go on to progressively more demanding responsibilities and challenges.

A second step is the establishment of a simulation laboratory within the vocational evaluation center in which we further the Programmed Experience concept by controlling the variables that characterize a particular job category. Behavioral scientists at Princeton University describe simulation as follows: "By simulation we mean a technique of substituting a synthetic environment for a real one—so that it is possible to work under laboratory conditions of control." The individual with learning disorders experiences frustration and emotional blocking under minimal stress, and more quickly and deeply than does "the average" individual. If we place our students in a real life situation, they may be prone to suffer failure and intense frustration due to other factors than those we are presumably measuring. For a population like ours at Vanguard School, a simulation technique becomes an integral part of the Programmed Experience progression and serves as both a useful diagnostic and training tool. One of the early examples of simulators was the famous Link Trainer of World War II. A mock-up of an actual airplane instrument panel was put into a land-based device whose motion was synchronized with the pilot's control movements. Inside the cockpit the pilot experienced almost all of the events of actual flight. This not only afforded an inexpensive means of testing the pilot's skills, but also provided an actual graphic record of his "flight" for further evaluation and improvement. We have developed parallel instrumentation which "stage" a number of vocationally-oriented situations. As an example: if an individual expresses a vocational preference for a retail selling job, he might undergo a simulated experience of the following sort. In a large booth, closing off the immediate environment and isolating the testee, he faces a motion picture screen within a mocked-up setting of a department store counter. Recorded instructions are fed into a loudspeaker placed in the booth. A programmed sequence of filmed customers approach the screen toward the synthetic counter and request items. The student has before him a reference list of prices and on the counter before him samples of actual goods. He places the requested goods into receptacle and obtains "money" from another receptacle, making correct change, placing it in turn into a money changer machine adapted for automatic use. The equipment will make it possible to produce simulations of other occupational events, such as inspection, quality control testing, machine tending, watching gauges, or making appropriate adjustments, etc.

The ability to control each facet of a constellation of job-connected tasks in a laboratory setting becomes an invaluable adjunct of the Vanguard Vocational Evaluation and Training process. It provides us with an objective picture of the patterns of difficulty which an individual may experience and will suggest areas for remedial action. Simulation is an economical and trouble-free process for testing the individual's available response repertoire and predicting what will happen in the reality situation under comparable conditions; it also allows remedial action through graduated exposure to pre-set steps so that breakdown in relation to the challenge that each step presents the individual can be evaluated and treated. A battery of simulations representing broad occupational families and their subordinate requirements is being developed. These will involve man-machine interactions, the use of videotape, closed circuit television and specialized instrumentation. "Gaming" involving the reaction of certain events associated with life and work situations yields information concerning the individual's capacity for handling interpersonal relationships, especially with authority figures. Gaming will also employ videotape and two-way closed circuit television. Situations involving the taking of directions from a "boss figure" in a work situation are videotaped and played back to the individual. He will be required to progress through a series of directions on the television screen and to activate certain response mechanisms. Professional actors portray the authority figures. Once they have been videotaped a standardized "test" is available for the acquisition of normative data. The objectives are to explore the variety of suitable work-related situations which produce meaningful response and to determine if they help to produce self-insight and bring about a modification in undesirable behavioral patterns and an enlargement of available response repertoires.

The rehabilitation setting, employing the modalities of Programmed Experience, simulation and gaming, occupies the spectrum from formal school experience through actual job placement. Our aim is to concentrate the key rehabilitation activities within the Vanguard Career Guidance Center, which in many respects resembles the traditional workshop where clients engage in performing various tasks subcontracted from industry. However, it takes on a greatly expanded function in the Vanguard program, for classrooms or "learning laboratories" situated just off the assembly lines attempt to provide relevant interaction between the concrete job task and the abstract related academic skill enhancement. Remedial teaching is coordinated with the techniques borrowed from space and military sciences such as programmed instruction, simulation, computerization, closed circuit television and videotape presentation. The overall objective is to demonstrate that the workshop setting can serve as a major strategic step towards advancing the rehabilitation program of the disabled youngster in a rapidly changing society. Workshops have traditionally emphasized semiskilled production areas whose utility is rapidly diminishing in a technological society of increasing complexity. The individual's preparation for highly skilled, though narrow-gauged, requirements involves the Programmed Experience approach, the fusion of academic, remedial and rehabilitative modalities and the utilization of every available technical resource. These objectives are carried out through a work orientation and personal adjustment training center, through realistic tryout opportunities employing simulation and gaming for students who lack the understanding of real life situations. The emphasis is upon building personal and social qualities and offering guidance in helping students to reconcile their attitudes towards their choice of occupation and their subsequent adjustment to the world of work.

All of this is intended to investigate the individual's capability to occupy those vocational areas which hold promise for entry-level jobs. Whereas traditional workshops have emphasized semiskilled production areas that are diminishing under the impact of automation, we are attempting in these ways to prepare our students for fields which show considerable growth potential and where they can be expected to show a maximum of transfer of training. In addition, the workshop facility provides training in occupational core areas such as electronics, graphic arts and reproduction, metal working and lathe operation and others whose description is beyond the scope of this presentation.

The central notion contained in the foregoing material is that an increasingly complex social structure in a swiftly changing economy influenced by technology and automation is creating an urgent need to investigate new methodologies in the education, training and rehabilitation of the learning-disabled individual. Our knowledge is believed to double every seven years and unquestionably personal flexibility will become a well sought commodity by business and industry. Adaptability and ready transfer of previously mastered skills will increasingly become desirable characteristics of the new labor force. We can anticipate the academic preparation and skills required to achieve job entry levels in relation to these altered and new work opportunities and these must be taken into consideration in the total rehabilitation program. New forms of counseling and guidance will emerge to assist individuals in mastering essential skills and in acquiring the qualities of flexibility and adaptiveness which our changing economy will reward with increasing degree. As Lloyd Berhner, a leading scientist, has stated, "The educational objective imposed by the technological revolution of today must be the advancement of each individual of the community to the limits of his intellectual capacity." This dictum applies in full measure to the learning-disabled individual for whose ultimate welfare and self-fulfillment we are responsible.

Nine

Parents' Problems

This series of articles is for parents, about parents, and by parents. ACLD is basically an organization for parents. Its highly professional conferences have always attracted specialists in the field; its focus, however, is on parents, since they are the ones most concerned about their children.

The first selection is a transcription of a tape recording of a question and answer period. Three pediatricians, Drs. Richardson, Kloss, and Timmons, kindly subject themselves to questioning by parents and provide frank answers to questions concerning diagnosis and remediation. Most of the parents have previously been frustrated in their attempts to obtain these services for their children.

Kenneth and Janice Beers, who have three sons with learning disabilities, are the authors of the second selection. They describe their own experience and outline the progress the children have made in school and under remediation. They describe lucidly the stages of shock, fright, grief, and guilt they experienced and what they did about each. Since their article was published several years ago, they have written an Addendum for this volume.

The article by Alice Thompson deals with some of the problems of working with parents. She cites principles that can aid in dealing with parents and their children.

In the final paper of this section, Dr. Leo Buscaglia gives us his philosophy of returning to one's own self, abolishing superficiality, and helping to decrease the tendency to be a plastic society. He ends by quoting Joseph Zinker:

I must face my own shortcomings, my own mistakes, and my transgressions. . . But tomorrow is another day, and I must decide to leave my bed and live again. And if I fail, I don't have the comfort of blaming you or life or God.

The Parents Talk to Doctors

SYLVIA O. RICHARDSON
JOSEPH L. KLOSS
DEAN TIMMONS

The following dialogue is a tape-recorded transcription of a unique panel that was held at the 1971 ACLD conference.

DR. RICHARDSON: It is often said about medical people that you can't ever talk to us or we don't ever listen to you, or some such thing. Now you have the opportunity to talk to some physicians who are also quite remarkable men because they are two of the rare breed that you usually don't see very often at meetings, since they are too busy seeing patients. They practice medicine. This group is probably the least represented at most meetings.

Dr. Joseph Kloss is a pediatrician who received his medical training at St. Louis University and trained in pediatrics at Children's Hospital in Akron, Ohio. Probably more important than the fact that he has been practicing pediatrics for ten years is the fact that Dr. Kloss has five children, four boys and one girl.

Dr. Dean Timmons is a pediatric neurologist who is practicing in Akron. He received his medical training at Indiana Medical School and his subsequent training in pediatrics, pediatric neurology, and neurology in Indiana. Dr. Timmons is also a father. He has three girls.

Both of these men are certified members of their respective boards, which is a very important fact. Each man is going to speak, briefly, about his point of view, and then we are going to ask for questions from the floor.

There are a couple of ground rules we are going to ask you to observe: speakers from the floor are asked to limit their talks and questions to five minutes; otherwise things can get out of hand. Please try to keep the questions general and avoid personal case histories; it is very difficult to make a diagnosis on the telephone and most of us don't try to do this. You can direct the questions to whomever you like, and then we can argue up here and question each other if necessary. First, Dr. Kloss is going to tell us about some problems he sees in his office, and give us a general idea of how he looks at children with learning disabilities.

DR. KLOSS: I want to make some general comments on the role of the pediatrician in handling learning-disabled children. There are two possible situations that should be considered. The first situation is one where you

From the *Proceedings* of the Eighth Annual Conference of the ACLD, *The Child with Learning Disabilities: His Right to Learn.* Chicago (March 18-20, 1971), pp. 41-55.

have taken care of this child from the time of birth. The second situation is one where you are seeing this child for an initial evaluation, although the child has already been diagnosed as having a problem. It is helpful if you have taken care of a family from the time the child was born. You have a knowledge of things that we might talk about later, what you would call high-risk children, or high-risk infants because of certain problems. As doctors, we like to see the children in the hospital after delivery for initial examination, if at all possible, and then we follow-up with regular visits. If you see the child in the hospital after delivery, you immediately have the information concerning the child's delivery, pregnancy, how the child acted at birth, and various things that might be significant. You then have the opportunity to follow the child with regular checkups, noting his developmental milestones, how he performs in relation to other children his age, and hopefully, to see if there are signs of problems or difficulties that will help the family, prewarn them, if possible, that something significant might be coming.

If you are performing an initial evaluation on an older child who is having problems already, then the situation and approach are a little different. You are familiar with the health background of the child whom you have followed regularly; you know his past medical history. But in the case of the child you are seeing initially, your first function is to perform a good physical examination to rule out the possibility that there might be anything physically wrong with the child that might impair his school performance. You might consider whether there are types of metabolic or glandular problems that would be significant. Is the child anemic? Is he malnourished? Does he have allergies? If you screen this child and find that, medically speaking, he is in good health, and there is no obvious reason why he should be having problems in this regard, then you will consider his school background, educational background, home environment, and so on. You consider the behavioral aspects of this child in the home setting versus what the child does in the school setting. When this type of evaluation is completed, then there are three possible considerations left for the practicing pediatrician: does the child qualify for and would he benefit from some type of drug therapy? Counsel the family regarding the child's problem, as much as possible. Refer the child to other qualified people for further evaluation and further testing, if you feel that more information is necessary to make a true evaluation. Some of the children you have problems with are then referred to a pediatric neurologist, such as Dr. Timmons.

DR. TIMMONS: The child, by the time he gets to me, has been diagnosed quite adequately in the general pediatric mode. At this point, there are several things that have to be considered. Most of the time, I see a child for one of two basic reasons—one is to give support to what the parent has already been told because the child may very well have been adequately diagnosed; however, the diagnosis may not have been acceptable to the parent, and it may have to be reinforced by a second, sometimes a third, fourth, fifth, sixth, and seventh party. The other function is to find further diagnostic avenues of approach, and as a pediatric neurologist, obviously, I am interested in the functioning of the nervous system, and I am interested in the functioning of the nervous system in regard to the child's intellectual development, motor development, verbal development, and social development. Obviously, you are quite limited in a single hour as to how much you can do, so you try to define the primary aspects and from there consider further diagnostic avenues of approach. Further referral to the speech and language therapist may be indicated, or to the physical therapist, to an orthopedic surgeon, and so forth. The point is, though, that at this time, I attempt to define what appears to be the primary problem. I feel it is very important to emphasize the primary problem because the child may have a number of different problems, and if you attempted to attack all of them at once, you would overwhelm the youngster to such an extent that he would certainly not function. At this point, too, since we're talking about the school-age child, a high number of these children certainly have significant educational problems, which have to be identified in conjunction with the educator and the school psychologist, and then attempts must be made to get such a child into the correct educational program. As you are all aware, programs certainly vary from one school system to another and from one state to another, depending on what facilities are available, and what tag has to be placed on the child so that he can qualify for placement in a certain educational program.

PARENT: *I would like to know what exactly are "soft signs" in a neurological examination?*

DR. TIMMONS: This depends on the person with whom you are talking, but the most important thing is to recognize that this is a type of neurological sign, and that it is not one of the classical "hard signs" like the Babinski, or increased reflexes, paralysis of the limbs, and so forth. This may be a mild overflow of movement, such as opening the hand, back and forth, and not being able to check it correctly. You can have the same type of thing with the tongue, or it may be a mild difficulty in opposing the finger to the thumb. It may be mild difficulty in the development of motor criteria. The child may be four years old and not be able to perform three-year-old level motor tasks yet. These are within the realm of the "soft signs."

DR. RICHARDSON: (repeating a question from the audience) This question was very nicely and very politely put: *If only 40 percent of the children who are handicapped are getting special education services, couldn't we doctors provide, in addition to our practice in medicine, psychological and diagnostic services of other types?*

DR. KLOSS: One of the problems we have on something like this is, in a way, beyond our control. All of the children aren't in proper placement because there are not enough classes. There aren't enough classes because there are not enough qualified teachers to handle them, and there is not enough money in the budget to set up more classes. In Ohio, we use the term, "neurologically handicapped." We have long waiting lists of children who need to get into neurologically handicapped classes. In the city of Akron alone, we probably could handle double the number of classes. Some of this backlog is taken up with part-time tutoring of some of these children for an hour or two a day, and there are some who could benefit from full-day special classes, but we are unable to do anything with them because of placement. This is frustrating to the physician, and it is even more frustrating to the parents when you tell them they have a child who has a problem and there is no place for them to go to solve it. I think this is an area in which the ACLD chapters and local lobbying in your state congress are helpful for initiating funds for more classes. Of course, we still have an inadequate number of teachers for the classes. There is not much that we can do about this right away, except hope that more and more teachers are being trained who can handle this type of problem.

DR. TIMMONS: As I heard the question, in essence, we are being asked if the physician could have some ancillary personnel working out of his office. Some do. As a matter of fact, in my office I have a girl with a master's degree in speech and hearing, and I have a part-time psychologist. We attempt to do this, but we are limited. You know it takes a lot of money to continually pay for private tutorial services and this type of thing, and I grant you that much more can be done along this line. I'm sure that many avenues can be investigated that we are not touching on at the present time. However, I think this is sort of a stop-gap solution; the real thing to do is to identify the problem where it exists and try to fund it so that all children in the community can benefit from the help they need, not just the ones whose parents can afford it.

DR. RICHARDSON: I think one of the most difficult things pertaining to what you are asking, is early identification of children with possible learning disabilities, which of all the problems is probably closest to home for the pediatricians because we see the child develop gradually. There have been many feelings about the effectiveness of early identification of children with possible problems. One approach has been suggested in some areas. We know that if an infant had a difficult birth, and had a little difficulty in the neonatal period, this may indicate a possible high risk. The question that arises is this: does the physician tell the mother at that time that the child may have a problem? Many of us don't like this idea because we know about something called a self-fulfilling prophecy. You know if you look for trouble you'll get it in any area. If you look for a "terrible two," you'll get one, no matter what else you have. Most professional people dislike the notion of warning that there may be a problem. On the other hand it is possible for the physician to put a star on the chart or have some way of noting to himself to closely watch the manner in which this child develops. Some of the areas that are the toughest for pediatricians are now gradually being overcome. For example, Dr. Kloss, Dr. Timmons, and I did not see any normal kids when we were in our medical training. We saw sick children, we saw problem children. We didn't really get to know about the normal child's growth and development sequence. This is changing. Today our pediatric students, residents, and interns are beginning to get this kind of training built into their program.

PARENT: *I would like to know who you recommend if you examine the child and he does not have brain damage but he is perceptually handicapped, but the psychologist hasn't been able to pinpoint the extent of the child's perceptual handicap.*

DR. TIMMONS: I think this opens up a whole bag of worms, really. In the first place, we get into our definitions of terms, and, unfortunately, the term *brain damage*, even when we put a qualifier of *minimal* in front of it, carries a connotation to a neurologist of a child who has had some anatomical destruction of the neuron. This means that those nerve cells are dead. As a consequence, this presents great problems, and even when we put qualifying terms and adjectives in front of it, *brain damage* runs parents right up the wall and makes them feel that there are great problems that this child is going to develop in the future. I don't know where you are from or what terms are used in your locale, but in the child that you are talking about, there may very definitely *not* be any true anatomical destruction or disruption of the nervous system. However, he may be quite impaired in his perceptual abilities. It makes no difference, really, whether this child is functioning well one day and poorly the next day. We know that some days he is going to be functioning poorly and, as a consequence, he has to get some type of special educational approach or program that is defined primarily for the days he is doing poorest. The training should build from that point. I care not what term you put on it, I care not where you are or who is the local "god" in your area. However, it is very important that this child's problems should be defined, and that some kind of program be outlined for him—one that is not dependent upon who you happen to be reading at the time, and one that is specifically suitable for the child.

DR. KLOSS: I would like to comment on the term. From a pediatric standpoint we would prefer, at least in our own usage, to either drop the aspect of the brain altogether and just say "the child with learning disabilities," or if you need to bring the brain or nervous system into it, perhaps use the term "cerebral dysfunction," which at least doesn't imply damage or specific anatomical problems. You're saying then that things don't function the way they should. This may be to some extent a maturational lag. We know that many of these children do improve with time. I am not advocating that you wait for this to occur because there are things that need to be done in the meantime. The idea that they'll grow out of it is partly true. I don't advocate relying on this exclusively because by the time they do outgrow it, they encounter so many educational and psychological problems that they may never catch up, but I think this term has a little less connotation as a definition of actual neurological problems.

PARENT: *As a parent, I find that in most areas pediatric neurologists are rare birds. They just don't exist. We have pediatricians who are very good. Even in a large town the size of Houston, if you can find this rare bird, he works only with diagnosticians. We have become so specialized in medicine that we are in a mess again. You take your child to a doctor because he walks funny, and the doctor prescribes special shoes because he has difficulty with his feet. He doesn't see too well, so you take him to an eye specialist, and you put glasses on him. He is so accident-prone that you decide he has crisp bones and take him to a bone specialist. How do we tie all of these things together?*

DR. RICHARDSON: The pediatrician is paralyzed when he gets all these reports from all these different doctors and he has to correlate them. There are training centers to relate these findings. There is one at the University of Cincinnati. Its primary purpose is to provide interdisciplinary training using representatives from many different viewpoints. We have a department of pediatrics, a department of special education, social service, psychology, nursing, speech, and hearing. Each of the separate departments has its own trainees, but they all attend lectures in all the departments, and at the case conferences on the children when the trainees are present, they are uniquely able in each setting to say to any one of us, "What are you talking about?" Someone in education can say to a doctor, "I don't understand a word of what you just said. Rephrase it." We're beginning to learn the gobbledygook of the different disciplines. It's a place where people in training can learn about how other professional people think, and move, and have their meanings. This is good. Scholarships are being offered. There is a lot of post-graduate training available now. There are many medical schools that have post-graduate courses just like those offered in the field of education.

DR. KLOSS: Dr. Timmons and I are in separate practices, although we do work together quite a bit. I am sure the day is coming when there will be pediatricians who will do nothing but specialize in learning disabilities. I think that this is probably a coming thing. They may do this on their own, or they may work with a pediatric neurologist directly in the same office. There are enough fellowships now in developmental pediatrics and in learning disabilities, and handicapped children, in the medical schools that some of these fellows are going to filter out into practice. They are not all going to stay in the university, which unfortunately happens too often.

DR. TIMMONS: There is quite a bit being done, in addition to what Dr. Richardson said. In our Children's Hospital we have approximately ten to fifteen residents a year in pediatrics, and these boys all have to go through clinics, which are staffed by educators, speech and hearing people, psychologists, physical therapists, occupational therapists, and so forth. All of these children have been evaluated by separate people and then reports are given and then following this, the decision is made as to what the priorities are concerning the approach to each youngster. In addition to this, Ohio has recently recognized some of these problems. There is now a joint committee between the state medical association and the state's special education section. We are in the very first aspects of looking very hard at the qualifications for various special educational programs and we just started the first pilot program this month.

PARENT: *I would like to expand on that question a little bit. In our town, this multidisciplinary concept just hasn't worked at all. The parents may have the diagnosis of their child and have an idea what is there, but at a certain point they need a further prescription about what to do. How does a parent know where to turn, where to go, other than Cincinnati or something like that. Where do we get the straight talk on whom to see?*

DR. RICHARDSON: Medically, you should be getting this from your pediatrician, and educationally, you should be getting it from the school. One thing I would like to point out, too, is that the physician's primary responsibility is to determine the health or lack of health in a child. Our job is to keep people well, basically. The medical follow-up should be through your physician. He knows the child.

PARENT: *They don't do it, this is the point. Where in the profession can we get some straight answers on who is qualified to give answers, and if it isn't in your town then recommend some other town. This is what we're saying. Where do you get the straight answers on which person to see?*

PARENT: *Who's responsible? I'd like to talk further on this. When you go from place to place and you get an answer from this one and that one, and you finally go to one whom you think is the authority, your state medical school, or something else, then you may also get the statement that we got from a pediatric psychiatrist, "This child is the victim of a fat folder syndrome." He's been seen all over the place and nobody has given anybody any answers.*

DR. RICHARDSON: By one token, you may have an answer very early in the game from a physician whom you couldn't hear. Don't forget this: you will hear when you're ready to hear. In our setup and almost every UAF (University Affiliated Facility for Children with Developmental Defects), when the child is seen by the different specialists that are required in conference, then you go back for counseling to the pediatrician who has been following this and who wraps up the whole thing for you, because we recognize that the parents can't put medical information together and come up with an understandable picture of what has been said. But when you ask who's responsible, the physician who is taking care of the child really holds that responsibility and I'll stop on that.

DR. KLOSS: You have to remember that doctors are people and they have different interests. There are some pediatricians who have no interest whatsoever in school problems or learning disabilities; they couldn't care less about it and they aren't about to change. There are others who do have some interest, and they try, but they also have a busy practice of pediatrics and can't do everything. I have a family at home, and to try to space out my time to do this and do that becomes increasingly difficult. If someone calls the office and has a child with a school problem, it might be a long wait before I am able to see him. This is a simple mechanical problem when you have a busy schedule. This is distressing to us, too. I'm sorry there is nothing you can do about it. You're going to encounter a number of people who have no interest in the problem whatsoever, and to get you out of their hair they send you to somebody else. You have to accept this for what it is. Hopefully, the people who are coming up, the so-called new breed, are being trained differently and will have different interests. Of course, this doesn't help your immediate problem.

PARENT: *Will you please tell me whether you have found an increase in adopted children with learning disabilities and what your feelings are about this?*

DR. TIMMONS: I will address myself to that, because I was very impressed with the number of adopted children who were coming to my office that were having problems. I was asked last spring to participate in a meeting at Ohio University, and since I have such interest in this, I thought I would use this as my address. Unfortunately, it is difficult to find the basic figures concerning adopted children in the general population, and the only good figures that I was able to find were from Canada. But for the United States or anywhere else, I haven't been able to find any good figures. What really surprised me and shocked me and almost panicked me, because it shot little pieces out of my address when I finally came up with it, was that the incidence of adopted children who were in the special educational program in the city of Akron, Ohio, was exactly the same as the number of adopted children in the general population of Canada.

PARENT: *What do you think accounts for this? Why?*

DR. KLOSS: There was an article published recently and I really can't remember if it was from Canada or not. This article stated that in a number of surveys, an increased number of adopted children were found to have learning disabilities of one type or another. Some of the hypotheses that were put forth were that all of these children were unwanted children in the first place. We see mothers of twelve, thirteen, and fourteen years of age not infrequently. You have a number of factors here. Many of these mothers have no prenatal care whatsoever. They show up in the hospital at the time of delivery and say, "I'm going to have a baby." No one has taken care of them during their whole pregnancy. A lot of them walk into a hospital with eclampsia or toxemia. They have had no care for this. A lot of them are very young and this is their first pregnancy. They often have difficult deliveries. The mother may or may not have an adequate pelvis for delivering children, and I think in general a fair number of these children probably have a more traumatic birth situation both prenatally and postnatally than the average population.

DR. RICHARDSON: We don't have any evidence, and I don't know of any way of getting any evidence as to how many of these young mothers try, but without success to abort themselves. This also is a factor that needs to be considered.

PARENT: *What do you feel about medication?*

DR. TIMMONS: You'll probably find three different opinions up here in that regard. I must admit that my experience has been that medication can be quite effective for modifying the behavior activities of these youngsters. The physician has to be willing to work with the family, with the school, and with the child. He must see to it that the dosage of medication is adequate for helping this youngster. I think that one of the big hang-ups we get, though, is people who expect that this pill is going to magically solve all their problems. This certainly is not the case. The only thing that I attempt to do is try to modify the behavior, to relate and structure the environment of this child. If you can take the edge off just a little bit, you get through to the parents much easier in regard to working with the child. For example, if Mama has a kiddy who is getting up at 3:00 A.M. every morning and wandering downstairs and taking all the pots and pans out and spilling flour and sugar around on the kitchen floor, she is not very nice to him the next morning when he gets up, and she is a little grouchy to Daddy and everyone else. If you can establish a good sleep pattern for this child through medication, then mother is in a much better situation to deal with the problem in a very structured program the next day. Likewise, if you can slow down the child so that his attention span, instead of being five seconds, becomes fifteen minutes, he can begin to be reached by the educator. It is awfully nice to be able to sit at least fifteen minutes at the dinner table without having this kid kick it over or jump up to run into the other room and so forth. I feel that you certainly can do a lot with behavior modification, but these are not magic answers. There are many other problems that have to be identified and worked with at the same time, and unless you do this you are going to fall flat on your face as far as the medication is concerned.

DR. KLOSS: I would rank with Dr. Timmons as a "pill pusher." I give medication frequently and have no hesitation about using it if I think it is indicated. I don't think there is any problem related to using it as far as habituation or addiction or anything like this. You may remember that there was a flurry last year out in Kansas, I believe, about all the children taking pills. There have been several reports recently, one by a study through the AMA and another report just last week through Senator Gallager's committee, and there didn't appear to be any problems related to using medication with these children. Medication should be used if you think it is really needed. If you have a child who, in your opinion, really doesn't need medication, then don't use it. It should be individualized. There are various types of medication, and I don't know how deeply you want to get into this, but I can tell you the general types we use. The two most popular types would fall into what is called the stimulant or psychic-energizer group. First, there are the amphetamines, such as Dexedrine, which I use quite frequently, and which often is spectacular in its effect in the appropriate child. In one or two days, the mother will call my office and say that he is a completely different child. You have to remember that this is a trial-and-error type of thing. What works beautifully for one child may have no effect whatsoever on another. It may show just the opposite effect and set the child off even more, so the parents have to realize from the start that if we are going to use some kind of medication that we think is appropriate in a situation, we can't expect immediate results. We may have to adjust the dosage; we may have to stop it altogether and try different medications. Second to Dexedrine, another common type is Ritalin. After this, you go into a "tranquilizing" type of medication. In our area, the medication that we use most in this category is Mellaril. Children can tolerate quite large doses of this without any difficulty. We use Thorazine on some children, and Benadryl at times on others. These are some of the medications, and there are others that can be used also, but this is a representative amount. I have not encountered any problems up to the present time with the use of medication. It has been my finding, personally, that as these children get older, they don't want to take medication anymore, and they tell the parents, "I don't want these pills, I don't need them now." And I say, "Fine, if you don't need them, let's try it without them." I have not encountered children who wanted to stay on medication. To the contrary, most of them are more than happy to stop taking the pills as they approach adolescence. If we still encounter problems, we may want to start them again. I have no hesitation about using medication in appropriate circumstances.

DR. TIMMONS: Could I give a couple of personal biases about this? As a physician I feel very strongly that when you treat, you treat. You can't cast a broken leg on weekends and uncast it during the week. Likewise, you don't treat a little diabetes nor do you treat a little congestive heart failure. You decide on the appropriate program to follow, and then you treat it. You treat seven days a week, fifty-two weeks a year. The child does not cease learning just because he is not in a formal educational system. The fact of the matter is that he is learning more outside his formal educational system than he is learning in school. This is one of the things that disturbs me personally. I recognize that a number of patients whom I see have been counseled otherwise and that there are many others that feel quite differently about this. However, I still feel that once you have decided to treat, you should treat.

DR. RICHARDSON: I surely agree with that. One handicap that we face, if a child is on medication, is that we have to count on the reliability of the parent. If the doctor has prescribed medication seven days a week, then give it to him seven days a week. A mother called me two weeks ago and said, "Well, I just wanted to find out if that stuff was really needed, so we took her off it. Then we put her back on." When you try these home experiments, it really doesn't help anybody, and there is no way for the physician to gauge the accuracy of the treatment.

PARENT: *I am a physician in a family practice and I am interested in the problem because I have six children, two of whom have learning problems. In our area, we have encountered difficulties because of a number of reasons. We don't have any physicians who are interested in the problem;*

it's a new science to us—nobody trained us. I became interested only because my immediate family is involved. There aren't many physicians who have had formal training. Secondly, some of us have problems on the school district level. I think that ACLD chapters are a very good source for experts in all the disciplines, and by urging parents to go through ACLD, you can actually set up family protocols and projects.

DR. RICHARDSON: That's very good and useful.

DR. KLOSS: I would like to comment on one thing that the doctor mentioned. I am sure you are aware of this yourself: just as there are differences in physicians who are interested in the problem, there are differences in school principals who are interested in the problem. I have had encounters with people who say, "Well, there is no such thing as a hyperactive child. They're all just spoiled brats. There is no such thing as a learning disability." You can't convince them otherwise.

PARENT: *I have always heard about medication for children who are hypoactive. Could you explain?*

DR. KLOSS: This depends. We treat children who are hyperactive because they don't function well in any setting. They can't sit still long enough to concentrate on anything or accomplish anything constructively, and to temper them down, we treat these children. We don't usually hear too much about the hypoactive children because they don't bother anybody, and the parents usually don't come to us because these children are so nice, quiet, and cooperative. Occasionally, we will get a situation where we may treat an extremely hypoactive child. The type of medication that works here is again, difficult to say. If you were to just take a number of average people and put them on Dexedrine or Ritalin, they would be stimulated. For some reason hyperactive children get a paradoxical effect: they are calmed. If you want to treat hypoactive children, you might try this type of medication to see if you would get the normal, stimulated response.

DR. TIMMONS: This is the child, probably, that one has to feel the sorriest for, simply because this child goes the longest without being recognized either by the educator or the parent. One of the great problems we have here is that the child who is excessively hypoactive has given up many times, and although we occasionally can get some help with medication, the big secret here is to try to work with this child in successful reinforcement, and this is where the educator must really come in and dig in with this youngster. My experience in treating hypoactive children with any kind of medication has been dismal.

PARENT: *I have a comment and a question. If parents are having difficulty getting appropriate programs for their children, we have them go right to the very top state level because every state has mandatory legislation and does have somebody in charge. We suggest that if you get brushed off, you have your lawyer talk to them the next time.*

PARENT: *I think as parents we waste too much time running back and forth between doctors and school principals, and we must realize that our child's problem is really in the classroom and not in the doctor's office. My question is this: I am wondering what will be the future effect of drugs that are now being taken by our high school and college kids, and what effects do these drugs have on learning disabilities, and what effects will they have on future babies?*

DR. TIMMONS: I don't think that either Dr. Kloss or I tend to try to put ourselves forward as experts on drug ingestion, drug culture, and all of this. We do know that, particularly, LSD has shown some chromosomal breaks as such. Whether these other medications will also show some problems along this line, I don't know. One has to be impressed with what happens to a newborn infant whose mother is a heroin addict, as the infant is convulsing, coming out of the withdrawal situation after it is born. In essence, are these youngsters who are taking the various forms of medication at the present time going to harm their unborn babies, or perhaps their unfertilized babies at the present time? I don't know. The problem is, you see, that you name just a few drugs, and what some of these kids put into their veins is fantastic. Many times when you ask them, they really don't know. They will have a mixer party where they dump everything they have and stir it up and some of the problems that they get from it are fantastic!

DR. KLOSS: I would agree with Dr. Timmons. I have no comments, except that in some studies with the use of LSD there have been chromosome breaks in the infants, and this, of course, will increase the possibilities that there might be some difficulties. I think we should be concerned, also, with what happens to these children after they are born. This would be a significant thing to consider in caring for these children in a family type setting or whatever it might be: what happens to them then?

PARENT: *I found that by organizing small groups of parents, you might be able to talk things over with someone else who has the same problem that you have. I think that sometimes when you're able to talk with another parent this helps to generate your understanding as well as that of the group.*

DR. RICHARDSON: You mean groups like the ACLD chapters?

PARENT: *Yes, like breaking them down into smaller groups.*

DR. RICHARDSON: Small groups of ACLD chapters, groups of parents who have children with learning disabilities who could work together and study together and talk together about their various problems. And what do we do about that one?

DR. KLOSS: I think this would be an excellent idea because when you talk to parents who have children with these problems it is surprising to hear some of the solutions and answers that they come up with that you never thought of yourself. I think we could all benefit from each other's experiences, and this is really the best way, to sit down, and talk about it, and if you have an active ACLD group, there is no reason why you can't have a meeting, or several meetings a year when you have nothing but a gab session.

DR. RICHARDSON: If you do this you could bring in local people.

DR. KLOSS: You could decide on a certain facet of behavior that you are going to talk about and people could bring in their suggestions or comments.

DR. RICHARDSON: It's also nice to find out that somebody else has a kid that's worse than yours.

DR. TIMMONS: We have experienced this in such things as myelodysplasia, epilepsy, and so forth. We find that a parent can say to another parent the same thing that a physician has said to the parent, and the parent may not hear the physician but he will hear another parent. We also find that the psychological support that members of a subcategory group like this can give to one another is fantastic. It is much more than any medical individual can do.

PARENT: *What about the Doman-Delacato method?*

DR. TIMMONS: My experience has not been good with this. My personal bias is not in favor of it. I recognize that there is a lot of enthusiasm for this and that there are a lot of programs for this throughout. I think that they have done one very good thing, though. They have made everyone who works with handicapped children recognize the importance of involving the parents in the actual day-to-day handling of the child's problem, whether the handicap is a learning one or a physical one. My personal experience has been that many times the results are less than what the parents have been led to believe they would get from this. In addition, on many occasions it requires the localization of a rather large number of the adult population where you live to follow through with the total program. I recognize, as I said, that there is a lot of popular enthusiasm and that many people in this audience probably have their children in this program or a program based on this, but my personal bias is that I do not recommend it.

DR. KLOSS: Yes. Results with the few patients that I have had who were involved in such programs have not at all been satisfactory as far as the way things have worked out. The thing you have to remember is that the Doman-Delacato method is a theory. There are lots of theories in the world, and this is an individual theory from the group in Philadelphia at The Institutes for the Achievement of Human Potential. There are many physicians and neurologists who do not support this whatsoever. They have found no basis for the theory that has been proposed. In fact, last year the American Academy of Pediatrics, The American Academy of Neurology and United Cerebral Palsy, and about eight other groups came out with a formal statement saying that they found this method to be of no proven value. One thing that I personally have noted is that it took an enormous amount of the parent's time to carry out the programs as recommended. Often this was to the detriment of the other people in the family. The other children, the father, and the mother are all relegated to a secondary position and everything is focused on this one child; getting the patterning done and getting this done and that done at the right time. On two different occasions I had families whom I knew well, and they had done their best to do things as recommended, and when they went back for reevaluation they were told that their child was not progressing well because they weren't doing their part. This was an enormous emotional problem for these families. They were devoting great amounts of time trying to do their part, and they were told that their children were not getting better because they were not working. This gave me a very bad opinion. Several studies have been done, one by Dr. Robbins, in which these same theories were tried in a formal program, and another was done on the Doman-Delacato method, with problem readers. These studies showed that the theory had no particular value as had been predicted.

DR. RICHARDSON: There are portions of the theory that are perfectly legitimate. If you look at some of the ideas of the Doman-Delacato method, you will see that we utilize a lot of the visual-motor techniques. Occupational therapists use some of these techniques, and other disciplines use many of the techniques. It's the packaging that is disturbing and very distractive to many. I have often thought that mothers should take some training into tutorial assistance for children and start working on their school systems, not as, you know, "Sit down and read with me Johnny" type of tutors, but as real tutors of various types, utilizing all different kinds of techniques. I would like to see these mothers do that kind of work instead of working as patterners and using so much of their time to pattern a patient of mine, while all the time I am thinking, "My golly, if I would have had those seventy-seven mothers tutoring kids in school." It would have been a greater blessing for a large number of children. I feel strongly about the use of time in this regard.

PARENT: *It took us ten years in New York to get the medical profession to recognize this, and it has only been within the last five years that some have accepted. This is a question of expecting and demanding clinical services, diagnostic services, and treatment. I must admire the strength of the three on the panel because here we are discussing the problem that you are undertaking and trying to solve, and no one has said one word about the obstetricians. The fact is that many of these children have prenatal and paranatal problems. Nothing has been said about practices of the obstetrician, the induced labor, the long labor, the medication or lack of medication, the overdoses of medication, whatever it may be. Now I know that this is a very touchy subject because I'm asking one field of medicine to be critical of another field of medicine. The only reason I'm mentioning this is because they deliver the child, walk away, and this is the end of it, and yet I think there is a lot to be demanded of this particular field of medicine. I don't know how the other areas of medicine can help us in this, but we certainly do care.*

DR. KLOSS: This is a question that is difficult to generalize because there is no question that most of the obstetricians I'm familiar with are very conscientious, good physicians. As in any field, there are differences in individuals. Some things are done for convenience, some patients are over-medicated before delivery and they get a very sleepy baby, and we know we can expect this from certain obstetricians. You can tell them about it but there is not a whole lot else you can do to get them to change their practice. They say, "Well, my mothers love it because they are very comfortable and don't have any pain." And we say, "Well, the babies don't love it." But it isn't until they get involved in a serious problem situation where the baby doesn't breathe or doesn't survive that they then sometimes think twice about how things are approached. The comment on prenatal care isn't always the fault of an obstetrician; there are some mothers who just don't show up until just before delivery, and we can't blame the physicians for that.

Dr. Timmons: I don't think this is a simple problem. We're talking about society. Where do you have the high incidence of prematurity? You have it around your poverty areas. Where do you have your high incidence of lack of prenatal care? Again, it is in your poverty areas. Where do you have your high incidence of young mothers much more so than in another place? Again, it is in your poverty areas. I grant you that not every obstetrician is a shining knight, and there is no question that mistakes are made. However, I think that there is much of the problem that they cannot always control, such as the dietary problems of the mother during the time of pregnancy, whether or not she lives in an area where the incidence of TB or other diseases is very high. Rather than just pointing a finger at obstetricians, we also have to point a finger back at ourselves and really ask if we are willing to extend the monies, and the time, and the effort to try to assure the right of every child to be born without complications. We haven't accepted this challenge yet, and until we get to the point that we are willing to accept this, we are going to continue to have a fantastic number of children who, by the time they are one hour old, are already predestined to have a significant number of problems.

Parent: *Is there anything for the laymen to read so that they can understand the problem better?*

Dr. Richardson: I think that the nicest things for parents to read are good common-sense books on normal child growth and development. One thing that scares me about parents reading a lot of books is that we get an awful lot of parents that come in with a diagnosis. I have one father who literally came in and handed me a *Pageant Magazine* and said, "That's my son." It was a psychopathic child. It's very hard to differentiate when you read something whether it is real or it is not. I use the example that I had a brain tumor in medical school while my roommate had tuberculosis. So you have to watch what you read. There are some books written for parents that are good books, if you read them intelligently. There are quite a few books about things you can do. I think that one of the best books on the problem of learning disabilities is *Waysiders,* by R. Liston, a neurologist, and R. M. Crosby, a layman. I think that this is an excellent book to read about learning disabilities in children. There are many books, one of which is written by Joanne Beck, *How to Raise a Brighter Child,* which has all kinds of practical advice on what to do, what you can do, how a normal child grows up, and how to apply this kind of information in this particular setting. Then there are other nice books about how to avoid having your children run you around. Rudolf Dreikurs and Vici Stoltz wrote a book entitled *Children, the Challenge,* which is a very nice book to have and is helpful for parents who are interested in child management. You know, in times of stress, I think that there is one book that is better than any other that I know of on child care and that's the Bible, and I'm serious about that—the more you read it, the more you find out.

Parents, Professionals, and Public Policy

KENNETH N. BEERS

JANICE I. BEERS

We are the parents of four children—three sons who have serious learning disabilities and one daughter who seems unaffected. Each of our boys started eagerly to school. Our highest expectations went with each one. Three times we have had the devastating experience of having their eagerness and hopes dashed and our expectations flounder on the reefs of learning disabilities. It is only through helping other children that we can turn this tragedy into something useful.

Our entire educational background and personal experience taught us the importance of the four R's in this technological age: reading, 'riting, 'rithmetic, and reasoning. We took it for granted that our children would be successful in school, acceptable in play, ambitious, and independent. We took too much for granted. Parents so often do. So today we speak as parents who hope we can help other children and other parents.

We are proud of all of our children. They are handsome, healthy, and happy, and they are so normal that we challenge you to pick them out of any school classroom. They all have high-average or superior intelligence. The boys all got through the early grades without serious difficulties; their real disabilities became apparent as they progressed through school. By the sixth grade they were ready for total failure. Some people may think that we were lucky they didn't fail sooner. Perhaps, but by doing well in the first few grades we expected them to continue to do well. When their disabilities overwhelmed them, they got no sympathy, no specialized help, no concessions from their parents or their teachers. If they had had crippled arms people would have had some sympathy and understanding. Instead, we were disappointed with them, teachers were disgusted, and everyone thought that they were lazy and irresponsible. They were invisibly handicapped. Our three boys are typical of a large proportion of the school population—those children whose learning disabilities are unrecognized in the early grades and are incapacitating, or partially disabling, in later grades.

When a child has learning disabilities, nobody is more involved than the child himself. He may be a problem to many people, but most of all, he is a problem to himself. He is a child, a human being, a person with feelings.

From the *Proceedings* of the Sixth Annual Conference of the ACLD, *Progress in Parent Information, Professional Growth, and Public Policy.* Fort Worth, Texas (March 6-8, 1969), pp. 3-19.

Only three people are unwillingly involved when a child can't learn: the child and his parents. Teachers choose to be teachers, and they know some children will have trouble in their classes. Doctors choose to be doctors. Psychologists choose to be psychologists. We were not only untrained to be parents, we didn't elect to be parents of children with learning disabilities. Our family and our world were quite unexpectedly and unintentionally turned upside down by the children we love so much.

Kenny, our oldest, was born in 1956. Daddy was in medical college, so we followed Kenny's progress in pediatric textbooks. Our only concern was with the fact that he was awake so much—twenty hours out of twenty-four by actual count—and that he cried endlessly, and for no known reason. Our pediatrician was not concerned, so we decided that some babies were just like this. After a few months he stopped crying; then he lay awake as much as before, but he was an active, alert, happy delight. He crawled, talked, and walked when we expected him to. He was very intelligent. He memorized a book of Mother Goose poems when he was two and one-half years old, turning the pages—people asked in amazement if he could read. Kenny was active and unpredictable. We called him our *little tornado* and put a harness on him when we shopped. He couldn't keep his hands off anything in the house, and many things were quite accidentally demolished. Now we know enough to describe him as hyperactive, distractible, and impulsive. Discipline had no lasting effect.

We moved to Alaska, and Kenny was indoors so much that we decided he needed to meet other children. He was three and one-half years old when we started him in a nursery school. The nursery school was located in a cramped room, and the children were expected to sit at their desks most of the time. We can't imagine how Kenny managed, but we got no complaints about his behavior. The first hint of trouble came in the third week: The school didn't have enough crayons, so Kenny was given one blue-green crayon to color an entire picture—sun, tree, sky, and grass. He started, but then asked for a different crayon. The teacher stood him in the corner for talking and colored his picture for him while he was in the corner. Mother let him color a similar picture at home the way he wanted to do it. A week later the teacher met her with a curt, "He was supposed to color three bluebirds." On the way home Kenny said eagerly, "I colored a canary, a bluebird, and a cardinal." The teacher saw that he didn't follow directions. Mother saw that he was intelligent and original. When he was given a picture from a regular coloring book, he scribbled on it—it was too detailed and far beyond his ability. When he colored simple pictures, he tried to stay within the lines, but day by day he came home with red frogs and many pictures in the wrong colors. Kenny was upset each time. We suspected that the teacher was giving him the wrong colors. When he came home with a brown elephant, copied from a sample that was colored gray, we were furious and did not take him back to that school again.

We found another school across town; the class was small, there was a piano, and lots of space. Most important, all the children adored the teacher. The teacher said that Kenny was "active" without a hint of reproach. We knew that Kenny was a handful. From this wonderful woman, he learned to sit still when he was supposed to, to get along with other children, to say poems, to sing songs, and to do folk dances. He was seldom given pictures and told how to color them; instead he was often given paper and crayons and turned loose to produce his own four-year-old masterpieces. He went through an airplane period, then a whirlwind period. Since whirlwinds looked like scribbling, I would suggest other subjects for his drawings, but back would come more whirlwinds. Then he started a long period of "explosions"—more scribbling—very colorful. We began to wonder if something was wrong with Kenny. A psychiatrist sent Mother packing after the first visit: The boy is just fine. We now know that this concentration on one subject for overlong periods is called perseveration. Kenny got in a rut and stayed in it—not like most children do from time to time during kite season or during yo-yo season. Kenny's ruts were deeper and longer. They bordered on an obsession with whatever his current interest was.

Kenny stayed in that wonderful nursery school for two years. At home he learned to recognize letters and he learned phonics. He also practiced recognizing and understanding numbers. Kenny learned easily. We had no hint that six years later he would be close to total failure. When he was five years and nine months old, the public school wouldn't take him. He entered a private first grade. We knew he was *immature*, but he learned so effortlessly, and he was so eager and bright.

Kenny learned to read with only slight difficulty. His teacher sent books home and night after night we listened to him. We can remember being impatient and telling him that he wasn't trying very hard. Sometimes he would know a word in one line and then not recognize it several lines further on. Or, he wouldn't know it if *-ing* or *-ed* was added to it. He struggled along and became a good reader. He was in the best reading class.

His printing started out wiggly, and he had a very hard time staying within the guidelines, but this improved. The most obvious thing about his writing papers was his horrible spacing. He crammed letters together and forgot spaces between words. Very occasionally he reversed letters, as ᒑ for *j*, *q* for *p*, and ᴎ for *n*. Sometimes he got letters out of order, as *raed* for *read*. An astonishing number of papers came home marked "Not Finished." He learned to do arithmetic. His main problem was his lack of proper spacing so that arithmetic problems were against each other or any place on the page—disastrous if the teacher stresses neatness and order, as well as accuracy.

It was six more years before we discovered that Kenny had visual-perception problems and a very confused concept of space. He was a bright-eyed, eager dynamo. He was not a discipline problem. We were lulled by almost straight A's on his report card; he did well in relation to the other children. Neither we nor his teacher recognized the significance of his *minor* problems. At the end of the year his teacher wrote, "Kenneth is doing good work, but he must be 'prodded' to finish." We were astonished and annoyed. We now know that it is as important how a child does his work as it is that he does it. How he does it is diagnostic.

We moved to California where Kenny entered the second grade in a public school. He complained that the children couldn't read very well. On teacher-parent conference day, I found out why: It was school policy to put all new children into the slowest reading group until they proved their ability. The teacher had moved Kenny into a faster reading group one quarter of the way through the school year, the day before conference day. Kenny's report card contained all B's and C's, though his work was beautiful and neat compared to the first grade. Kenny was completely unable to satisfy that teacher. Beautiful papers came home with a big red "Untidy" on the top.

Kenny's teacher was cold and overdemanding; Kenny lost his interest and momentum. We still have his second-grade work and the notes from his teacher; we are willing to let others judge the situation if they think we are being unfair to the teacher. She set out to prove to us that Kenny wasn't as bright as we thought. We received a succession of notes of which the following is typical: "On checking the workbooks of Kenny's group last night at home, I discovered Kenneth's assurances that he had finished all incomplete pages the other morning when he came early was inaccurate. He has done the pages from 60 on, but failed to notice others further back. Today he hurried to get some done that are incomplete, but would you kindly have him do the following pages: 44, 45, 48, 50, and 51." On his report card she wrote, "Kenny could do a lot better if he would listen and not dream so much. He needs continual reminding to apply himself to the task at hand." Before each report card day, she sent home a big stack of unfinished work.

We went to the principal and were informed, "she is one of my best teachers." We didn't know the answer to that then. Now we know the answer is: "She may be one of the best teachers for some children; she is one of the worst for Kenny and others with learning disabilities." Some good teachers demand that children be unusually neat and responsible—in the first and second grades. Some good teachers demand that children work independently in the early grades. The fact that a teacher is most competent does not mean that that teacher can successfully teach every child. Different children react differently to a teacher. A teacher reacts differently to different children. Sometimes teachers and administrators forget that group teaching is successful only to the extent that it facilitates individual learning. Kenny needed a structured situation in order to learn. He needed some recognition for his successes and he needed encouragement. Kenny learned some things from that teacher, but she collided with his learning disabilities head-on. The price was too great. It was to be five years before we would recognize that his daydreaming was his response to intolerable pressure, and that his lack of attention to the task at hand was due to auditory- and visual-perception problems and distractibility. He began to suck his thumb in the second grade.

To our horror his only friends were a mentally retarded child and younger twins with severe speech-articulation problems. Kenny and his dad joined Indian Guides. Kenny's behavior during this time was inexplicable, especially since he obeyed at home. He'd grab all the brownies; he'd shake his soda so that it would spray the room; he'd rush around the room on all fours barking like a dog. The other boys and fathers just looked at him. Daddy took him to a couple more meetings under protest. Finally, he found excuses to miss the rest of the meetings. We moved again, fortunately. In fact, we moved again three more times, once each summer. These moves were especially hard on Kenny; he had such a hard time making friends. They did have one advantage: They kept his reputation from preceding him.

Each year Kenny's work became worse and messier. In the first and second grades, his answers were usually correct. Characteristically, the work was unfinished or horribly spaced when he printed words or copied arithmetic problems. Everything ran together. In the third grade no letters were reversed; cursive writing does not lend itself to reversals as much as printing. Spacing improved, since cursive writing flows together and any space between words is acceptable. Space problems were still evident on arithmetic papers. Kenny's learning disabilities did not lessen above the third grade; they were manifested in different ways. His spelling was atrocious. Oh, he got 100 percent on most spelling tests, but he spelled horribly on written work. Capital letters were put in unlikely places in sentences, though he knew the rules of punctuation. Sentences were incomplete or without quality, though he spoke with perfect grammar. His spelling, capitalization, and punctuation were defective whether he wrote a composition himself, copied from the blackboard, or copied from a book. After the fourth grade much of his work was almost illegible. His grades on report cards were mostly C's and D's, daily grades were A's or F's.

His teachers described him: he didn't use his time wisely, he didn't follow directions, he didn't work well independently, he didn't complete assigned tasks, he was not neat in his work habits, and he didn't work well with others. We were told these things in conference after conference. We had no idea what we were supposed to do about Kenny. Teacher after teacher had listed the symptoms of Kenny's learning disabilities and not recognized them as symptoms. Teacher after teacher said, "He could do the work if he'd only try."

The first and most important professional in a position to recognize the normal child with learning disabilities is the teacher. Teachers must be taught to recognize the daily clues to learning disabilities. Once a teacher recognizes the clues she can adapt her teaching to the child's needs. Many teachers have intuitively done this for years. This can explain why a child performs well some years and performs poorly other years. The responsibility for recognizing learning disabilities should not be thrown on the parents when a child cannot learn.

We scolded, we pressured, we threatened, we removed privileges—nothing made Kenny *responsible*, nothing kept him from being *lazy*. We were disappointed and frantic.

Let his sixth-grade teachers describe him:

Assignments are either not turned in or are incomplete. Work that is turned in is rarely readable and sentences are incomplete or lack quality. When Kenny is asked questions in class, a perplexed look crosses his face and he is unable to answer the simplest of questions . . . He comes to class unprepared for work. He rarely ever has a pencil or pen with which to do his work. He seems totally unaware of the materials around him—bulletin boards, blackboards, etc. His power of observation in class is nil . . . The time Kenny spends in my class is a complete waste of time . . . Kenneth Beers has exhibited little interest in classroom activities, participated very little in classroom discussions, and expended minimum effort on written assignments since the beginning of school. He is not a disrupting factor—he reads often—but his achievement is shackled by his indifference to school . . . He spent much of the time daydreaming . . . and desk work was always messy and disorganized. He was not accepted by his peer group, and his friends were few.

One teacher told us, "He just isn't with us." The principal said, "She is one of my best teachers."

Kenny had an IQ of 141 on the *California Mental Maturity Scale* in the third grade. He had an IQ of 132, as measured by the *Otis Quick-Scoring Mental Ability Test, Beta, Form Fm,* in the fifth grade. In the *Stanford Reading Achievement* test (SRA), his composite score placed him in the 98th percentile of those taking the test nationally. In the sixth grade, his SRA composite score was in the 96th percentile. Group IQ scores and SRA test results by themselves cannot predict ability to succeed in school. If children are selected for premium classes on the basis of high IQ and SRA scores, some, like Kenny, will fail because of learning disabilities. It is not fair to assume that such intelligent failures are just lazy. In the sixth grade, Kenny had an IQ of 135 on the *Wechsler Intelligence Scale for Children* (WISC): 126 verbal and 138 performance.

Mother set out to tutor Kenny. She got his homework assignments herself, and she and Kenny worked for hours each night. Kenny was patient with his mother, but his classwork did not improve. It became obvious that Kenny could learn single-word answers by rote, but he couldn't answer discussion questions. He could learn facts, but he couldn't form concepts. When he knew an answer he couldn't get it down on paper adequately. Our nightly sessions went on for one month.

Daddy said Mother was making Kenny too dependent on her. Mother rejected the charge. Kenny was too dependent on her, of course, but she began to help him in response to his need, and besides, she had not ruined the other children. When Daddy, or some other professional, decides the child is too dependent on the mother, he'd better offer some more acceptable solution than letting the child fail completely on his own. Nobody would kick the crutches out from under a child with withered legs and tell him, "Get up and walk—you can do it if you would only try." How long would the mother stand by and watch the child struggle on the floor? Too many neighbors and professionals are quick to tell a mother to stop helping a child. "Make him work for himself or fail." The implication is that he deserves to fail. It behooves professionals to determine carefully if a child *can* succeed as they expect him to. Don't knock away his crutch until he's able to stand alone. Neither a mother nor a child can achieve emotional stability until someone identifies the child's learning disabilities and teaches him to compensate for them.

In the sixth grade, Kenny had a perpetual "put-upon" look. (He had one friend, a third grader, as silly and hyperactive as he.) Kenny perseverated on armadillos. Then he perseverated on quail. He spent a year reading about ducks, drawing ducks, sculpturing ducks, writing about ducks, starting duck clubs, and quacking greetings to people. He was musically and artistically talented. He took prizes for his ability to play the piano and he took prizes for his art work. But Kenny was a failure in his own eyes.

How did Daddy react to each new crisis Kenny went through in school? He reacted as most fathers do. A father is not intimately involved with the child day to day as the mother is; a father has outside interests while a mother stays home and worries. Daddy had Kenny (and each of our boys, in turn) tested very reluctantly. Each testing was done to indulge an over-concerned and frantic mother. Daddy was amazed to find the boys had real disabilities. At first, a father doesn't think the child has a problem. Once he knows the child has a problem, he doesn't think it's as bad as it is. Once he knows how bad it is, he doesn't think the treatment will work.

Mother refused to accept all the blame for Kenny's problems and we set out to find a psychologist who could tell us why Kenny acted as he did. Then a remarkable thing happened. Daddy called a local pediatrician and asked to be referred to a psychologist. He told her why, and she asked several questions, beginning with, "Is he overactive and sometimes hard to control? Does he persist overlong at tasks sometimes and at other times leave in the middle of a task due to seemingly mild distractions?" The answer to all the questions was "yes." Then she said she didn't think we needed a psychologist. She thought the boy was minimally brain-injured and she recommended a pediatric neurologist. The doctor in Dr. Beers sputtered some, but her recommendation was made. Physicians just don't very often make a diagnosis over the phone for a child they've never seen, but see how easy it is to make a diagnosis on our children when the diagnostician knows what to look for?

We went to a Houston pediatrician who limits her practice to child neurology. She could explain, logically, that the things Kenny did were symptoms of his learning disabilities, true handicaps. She examined him thoroughly, studied his school work, and read reports from his teachers. He had poor auditory discrimination, poor auditory perception, poor auditory memory. Of course he didn't listen in class, couldn't answer questions, and forgot his homework. He could hear well and not understand or re-member what he heard. He had poor visual perception, poor sequential memory, and poor eye-hand coordination. Of course he couldn't spell, capi-talize, punctuate, or even copy his work correctly though his eyesight was 20/20. He had trouble understanding abstractions and forming concepts. Of course he couldn't organize work or answer discussion questions. He had no sense of time, so he didn't get started on his work, he wasted time once he did, he didn't like to wear a watch, and he almost never arrived at home at the preset deadline. He had a poor concept of space and where he was in space, so his work showed poor spacing and lacked form, and he was terri-fied when he first climbed a tree. He had poor eye-hand coordination, so with his other disabilities he couldn't compete successfully with his peers in ball games. His peers had him pegged. They called him "mouse," and that fit him. He was colorless and scampered out of their way.

Kenny is invisibly handicapped. In Texas such children are medically diagnosed as "minimally brain-injured." Don't misunderstand. We can't know that Kenny is brain-injured at all. Minimally brain-injured is a cur-rent descriptive medical diagnosis based on "soft neurological signs"— circumstantial evidence. Kenny has learning disabilities and minor be-havioral problems similar to some children with known brain damage. A more commonly used term today is "minimal brain dysfunction." The emphasis is not on the minimal; it implies inapparent, not minor, mani-festations. Depending on geography, the diagnosis could have been neuro-logically handicapped or perceptually impaired or a number of other labels. Depending on who made the diagnosis, the label could have been emo-tionally disturbed, dyslexic, hyperkinetic, or low achiever. The terms are numerous. Kenny was put on medication so that his hyperactivity de-creased and his schoolwork improved.

We went into shock upon hearing "minimally brain-injured." We were also relieved—at least Kenny wasn't just lazy and contrary. After we parents came home with the diagnosis, Kenny swung around and said, "Am I crazy?" We reacted in horror and said we had never suspected such a thing. He demanded, "Am I retarded?" We said of course he wasn't. He was very intelligent. Where did he get such an idea? "The other kids say I'm retarded." At least he asked and didn't just keep wondering. Several days later, when we could manage to talk to him, we told him he was mini-mally brain-injured. He was relieved, visibly relieved. Mother said to him, "We're sorry we pushed you so hard, Kenny; we thought you just weren't trying." Kenny answered, "Mommy, I thought I wasn't trying, too, but I didn't know what to do about it."

Several months later, Dr. Robert L. Tips, Houston pediatrician, spoke at a Council for Exceptional Children workshop in Galveston. He listed stages parents go through when they are told their child has a genetically transmitted disease. We were fascinated, for these were the same stages that we went through when we were told Kenny was minimally brain-injured.

Stage One: Shock

Utter disbelief. Numbness. Horror. Depression. Surely the diagnosis was wrong. The grandparents said it was nonsense. We couldn't concentrate on normal tasks and Mother cried easily. We couldn't even decide what to do for Kenny. Shock lasted for weeks.

Stage Two: Flight

Our first reaction was, "We must get Kenny back east where there are good doctors." (You can tell where we are from.) When we phoned back east, we were advised to stay in Texas. We decided to find out for ourselves if the diagnosis was correct. Some people rush from professional to professional; we read every book we could lay our hands on. The diagnosis was right. We were lucky: for us flight lasted only three weeks; for some parents it lasts for years.

Stage Three: Grief and Guilt

We knew that we were not to blame for Kenny's disabilities; he had been hyperactive from birth. But we wondered if we had put him in the playpen too much, or if Mother hadn't stuck closely enough to her low-salt diet before he was born. Silly? Parents are in no condition to be calm and rational. They'll feel guilt when they deserve none. On the other hand, they will resent being blamed if they feel they aren't to blame. In desperation and resignation we reached:

Stage Four: What Do We Do About It?

When the pediatric neurologist made the diagnosis, she outlined a program to help Kenny. Once we could think again, we knew that she had said for us to take Kenny out of the sixth grade immediately, on an emergency basis, and send him to a special residential school she recommended. Our glance showed that we were instantly agreed: we would never put Kenny in an institution. We didn't put Kenny in an institution as we had pictured having to do. We did put Kenny in this school which is specifically for the educational retraining of children with learning disabilities. Our two youngest sons are there now.

The school required a battery of educational tests and evaluations by specialists: a psychologist, pediatrician, neuropsychiatrist, optometrist, and developmentalist. All these tests confirmed the diagnosis. We visited the school. Daddy was interested in symptoms and methods; mother looked over the children. Kenny entered the school in September, 1967. By Christmas his whole personality had changed. He was relaxed and quiet. His put-upon frown was seldom seen and his negative attitude was disappearing. He talked with adults with confidence. The boy was noticeably changed.

In May, after eight months at the school, he had gained two years and four months in reading vocabulary, four years and nine months in reading comprehension, two years in spelling, five years and seven months in arithmetic reasoning, and three years and seven months in arithmetic fundamentals. His score was equivalent to the tenth, eleventh, or twelfth grade on each item. The final report said, "Kenny is a happy, dependable, well-liked boy whose attitude toward his work, other people, and himself has improved remarkably. Kenny can organize his material now and get it down on a piece of paper in the time limit usually given to a class. He can now do his work and still have time for his wonderful creative work."

This year Kenny is in a public-school seventh grade. After three weeks of school, he was moved to premium classes. For the first quarter of the year his grades were three A's, one A—, and two B+'s. Most significant, Kenny's teachers report that he is enthusiastic and an asset to his classes. He gets his work done and almost always finishes his homework before class is over. We've discovered that those nights he does have homework, he has often finished it after school before we thought to ask if he had any. He has undertaken several special-project assignments early and finished them comfortably before the deadlines. Kenny accepts his limitations. We drive him to school to avoid the noise and excitement on the school bus; he rides home on the bus since this provides an opportunity for him to make arrangements for playing with his friends. To avoid noise, competition, and confusion he does not take physical education. These bring about hyper-activity, causing him to be at his worst with his peers and decreasing his ability to settle down for learning in later classes. He voluntarily quit Boy Scouts for the same reason. TV and movies bother him, so he avoids them.

Kenny's eyes are alert and he smiles readily. He has a number of friends. It is no longer a novelty when the phone rings for him. He fishes and reads. He's taught himself to play the guitar. He enjoys success. What a joy he is to us—now.

Ricky, our second boy, was always a charmer with bright eyes, orange hair, and a big grin. He was not noticeably hyperactive and always had lots of friends. When he went to the public-school kindergarten he had a terrible time recognizing letters and learning phonics. His teacher sent work home and Mother spent hours, happy hours for Ricky, teaching him. We spent an unbelievable amount of time getting Ricky to put the numbers from one to ten in sequence and proper orientation. He could count to one hundred but was not able to manipulate numbers from one to ten. We feared he was retarded. Worst of all, Ricky would learn something until we were sure he knew it, and then when we would ask him a question about it, he would give us a big grin and not have any idea what the answer was. Sometimes he would remember something for a while, and then he would act like he had never heard it before. He loved kindergarten; he had no idea how badly he had done.

We sent him to the first grade and he had a master teacher. To our amazement he learned to read and write effortlessly. He was a model pupil. He loved school and his teacher; unlike Kenny, all his work habits were satisfactory. As we look at his work now, we can see a few reversed letters and a few letters out of sequence. His work was good, however, better than Kenny's.

When his grades began to slip we weren't very concerned. After his disastrous kindergarten year, we didn't expect as much of Ricky as we did of Kenny. Ricky learned cursive writing in the second grade, and it was fluid by the third grade. He could not remember how to borrow or carry in arithmetic and still needed to be reminded how to do borrowing and carrying in the fifth grade. Along through the years his work became worse and messier. By the fifth grade, he needed much attention and developed severe asthma attacks which we believe were largely emotional.

His teacher helped him at school; Mother undertook a remedial program at home. Kenny was in the residential school, so Mother had the time. Ricky's grades went up and his motivation zoomed. His old friends dropped him and he made intelligent new friends. The asthma attacks stopped.

Good motivation took Ricky far, but he couldn't sustain the gain. This year in the sixth grade, he had hysterical frustration tantrums over his homework. It became apparent to us that he couldn't read his geography book. Standard tests showed him reading just at grade level, but he didn't even try to figure out words like precipitation or distillation. His spelling was horrible. He would begin to spell a word and end it any old way. In October, we told him to bring his geography book home the next night. He was agreeable. Why? Mother told him she wanted him to read for the doctor. His gasp was audible, and the words poured out, "No, don't make me bring my geography book, let me bring my science book. No, I don't know the words in it either. Let me bring something easier." Ricky was eager and his bright eyes and attentive manner misled most of his teachers. His WISC IQ was 120: verbal 116; performance 118. His scores on subtests varied by 33 points. Ricky had auditory-perception problems, he had trouble with visual sequencing, he had trouble with abstraction and reasoning, and his memory was unreliable. He went blank on tests. He went blank under pressure. He forgot items he had learned perfectly a short while before. He gave us all the clues in kindergarten. Nobody recognized them as symptoms until the sixth grade. Now we knew why Ricky so often said, "The teacher didn't explain it," or, "She didn't explain it very well," or, "I was sure I knew it but I got a 66 on the test." Since October, Ricky has been making good progress at the residential school for children with learning disabilities.

Jeffrey, our youngest boy, follows still a different pattern. He has always been slow, and he slept far too much as a baby. When he was awake, he was alert but we worried about him. He has a slight speech-articulation problem that was cute when he was little; it is still audible today. He frequently wanders off or gets left behind when we go someplace. He has no friends. Jeff moves slowly where Kenny is hyperactive. Jeff is compulsively neat where Kenny is unbelievably messy. We had no idea he had learning disabilities, for we had come to associate learning disabilities with Kenny's symptoms.

Jeff loved nursery school and kindergarten. His teachers described him as mature for his age, sensitive to art and music, quick to learn, and a pleasure to be with. In the first grade he had no enthusiasm for school at all. He printed well enough but he was so very slow. He learned to read but without enthusiasm. He was very independent and conscientious. The second grade went by effortlessly and we were preoccupied with Kenny's problems. We asked several times why he was so slow, but it wasn't a real issue, and we got no answer.

Jeff had a wonderful third-grade teacher and for the first time was eager to go to school. The year went well until the last month. Jeff began to walk in the door after school and burst into tears, "I'm so slow." The teacher was letting Jeff stay in from music and recess period to finish his work. She let him bring classwork home to finish, so he had almost straight A's on his report card and he kept his A's. If she had said, "Turn in your papers," and then marked the unfinished work wrong as so many teachers do, Jeff would have been close to failing. But finally he was crying at the dinner table and at night. Mother went to see the teacher two weeks before school was out. The teacher assured her that Jeff did fine, he was just slow. She told of an instance when Jeff had been at the blackboard that week. She said, "That's fine, Jeff. Now you may sit down." Jeff looked at her. He didn't sit down until she said again, "Jeff, sit down." She was puzzled. She had spotted one of Jeff's worst problems. His auditory perception and auditory sequencing are very poor. He often says, "What did you say?" His visual sequencing is poor and abstraction and reasoning are deficient. His left side is very weak, and he is compensating remarkably well for motor problems we didn't realize he had.

Jeff was miserable last Labor Day weekend. He was afraid to start school because he was so slow. In the fourth grade his classwork was painstakingly done, but it showed the now familiar atrocious spelling, random capitalization, meaningless punctuation. Reports Jeff wrote listed minor details and omitted major facts. We noticed he could not spell words on his spelling list orally. When he took a written test he would get 100 percent. His auditory sequencing was impossible; visually he could tell if he was spelling the words correctly. Jeff's IQ on the WISC was 128: verbal 124; performance 127. He had a 51-point spread on the various subtests. His true IQ is believed to be much higher than his scores would indicate. Jeff has been at the residential school with Ricky since October.

Slow is the one word parents and teachers seem to use more often than any other to describe children with learning disabilities. The child is *slow* at his work. If a child must overcome multiple handicaps, it is quite understandable that he will be slow. Pressure to hurry is likely to compound his problem. How would you feel if day after day you were sent to a boss who determined what kind of work you would do that day and gave you more work than you could possibly finish? How would you feel if he graded you all day on what you couldn't do and couldn't finish and then sent the grades to your relatives? Lazy and irresponsible are favorite descriptions for children like Kenny. Too often the teacher who decides a child is lazy and irresponsible sics frustrated and desperate parents onto an already frustrated and desperate child. Too often the teacher tries to force the child to be responsible. Responsibility cannot be taught by letting the child get hopelessly behind and giving him an F. Children learn by reinforcing their successes. If a child has a brain dysfunction causing memory failure as severe as Kenny's and Ricky's, it is futile and cruel to know a child will forget a project, let the child forget the project, and then jump on him once he has forgotten the project. Teachers complain that they must keep reminding the child. Yes, and they will need to keep reminding him if he is to succeed in the classroom. Slow and lazy and irresponsible are descriptions of behavior. They are not explanations in themselves. Our message is this: If a child is slow or lazy or irresponsible, find out why. Don't believe that he is just immature or disinterested. If children cannot learn in present classes by present methods, let's not say that they are immature and wait for some obscure development that may or may not occur in the child. Let's change methods and teach the child in his present state of development.

Some say that it is easy to pick out the children who need help. True, it is easy to pick out the disaster cases. The fact is that nobody really knows how many children need help. Most teachers cannot even pick out the children who need to be tested. This conclusion is based on the experiences of parents we know in Texas and in states as far away as Pennsylvania and Alaska. The first children they recommend for testing are the hyperactive or aggressive children who bother them or disturb the class. They also recommend for testing poor oral readers and children who don't speak clearly. They overlook more often the quiet child who perhaps daydreams and is a problem mostly to himself. They overlook the very intelligent child who is easily regarded as just lazy. Once a child gets past the first or second grade, his chances of being sent for diagnosis and help decrease. No teacher at any time suggested that we have any of our boys tested. Teachers were skeptical when we said that there might be something wrong with Ricky and Jeffrey. Some weren't convinced even when we had test results that revealed physical disabilities. Nobody knows how many *average* children are working far below their capacity. Children are so different and their disabilities are so varied that teachers need special training to help them recognize learning disabilities before the child reaches the stage when he seems to no longer care, and seems to no longer try.

We can't let students fail before we offer them special help. Many people think failing means F on report cards. Those who are getting F's on their report cards are indeed failing. Kenny and Ricky, however, are examples of a more common type of child, the one who continually gets A's and F's, B's and zeros on daily work. Often these grades average out to C's and D's on report cards. For years we blamed the C's and D's on everything but learning disabilities. Where were the A's? In workbooks, on mimeographed pages, on tests with one-word answers, on multiple-choice tests that jogged their memories. The already structured form of the work let the child concentrate on the answers. Where were the F's? On book reports, on original compositions, on tests with discussion questions, on experiments written up in poor form, and on timed tests where the child was under pressure. If teachers want to spot learning disabilities, let them give more in-school book reports and in-school compositions. We're recommending these as diagnostic tools. Grading them would embarrass or fail children with learning disabilities.

We say that these children who are getting A's and F's, B's and zeros are already failing. The child is either failing to understand instructions, failing to perceive the intent of the instructions, failing to remember the instructions, failing to get started, failing to comprehend what he is reading, failing to comprehend what a question asks or implies, failing to form concepts, failing to structure his answer, or failing to get it on paper legibly and acceptably. He's failing somehow. The child can fail in so many ways.

When do we help these failing-but-note-quite-F students? We've heard so often, "Let's spot learning disabilities in kindergarten." Some educators would like to have children tested at age three years or some other early age. Why? So that the children can be taught to compensate for their disabilities early, before they fail in school and academic remediation and emotional rehabilitation are also necessary. Ricky's memory problems should have been identified in kindergarten. Kenny's hyperactivity and multiple problems would have helped spot him. We don't know if Jeff could have been spotted. None of the boys were given diagnostic tests before they began school. None of the standard tests given in school disclosed their disabilities. All three boys were overwhelmed when abstract reasoning and concept formation were demanded in grades four, five, and six. If such trouble is not apparent until the fourth or fifth grade, let's not say to the child, "Too bad, we can't help you; you did not fail soon enough." Children with learning disabilities, who start to read and write well enough to get by in the first grade, face progressive failure—failure in slow, tortuous steps. Yet nobody is sympathetic or helpful, for after all, most people think if they could work well once, all they need do is buckle down to keep working well. Not so.

As a student, were you ever sick for several weeks? Did you ever have to catch up and keep up? Children with learning disabilities fall behind their classmates. They get discouraged, some faster than others. Motivation may never have been strong or it decreases when discouragement lasts for years. These children have no assurance of competency to encourage them. They have never succeeded; or if they seemed to succeed early in school, they eventually conclude their self-confidence was unwarranted. They often work hard and long with poor results, while other students get along better with less apparent effort. Daily homework, frequent tests, and an ever-present teacher keep children from hiding the fact that they are falling behind. They haven't been sick, so they have no excuse to fall behind. Without sympathy, the children with learning disabilities spend years trying to catch up and keep up. Is it any wonder they develop emotional and behavioral problems?

When we mention something our children do as a symptom of their learning disabilities, we often hear, "but normal children do that." Of course normal children do many of the same things, but they don't do them as long or as much or as hard. How can we compare our children with normal children? They themselves are so normal that we and their teachers didn't recognize their disabilities until nine or ten years had passed. The trouble is that children are judged against normal children and their work is judged against average work. They are compared with other children and not compared with their own capabilities. We've been asked over and over, "What makes you think he *should* be doing better than he is?" The things Ricky did and the things he did wrong were explained by the simple fact that he was an average little boy. It was easier to believe we were pushy, overconcerned parents than it was to believe Ricky had auditory and memory disabilities. Kenny, Ricky, and Jeffrey struggled along. They are among the children Ray Barsch calls the *walking wounded* gamely competing.

We are not unwilling to accept our children's limitations. We are not trying to push our children to get all A's. We are eager to give these three very different individuals a chance to overcome real disabilities, a chance to develop to their fullest potential.

When talking about learning disabilities, several teachers and administrators have said in one form or another, "This is something extra parents are asking teachers to take on," "This attitude is defensive." Teachers themselves will seek information about learning disabilities once it occurs to them that learning disabilities are the basis for many of their most puzzling and difficult classroom problems. Yes, parents are asking. But, parents shouldn't *have* to ask. And parents are not asking anything new. For years parents asked that the schools educate their underachievers or their low achievers. Today parents ask schools to educate their children with learning disabilities. Only the name changed. The children are the same. More and more parents and teachers know that children are often low achievers because of learning disabilities. That information has reached far too few regular classroom teachers in local schools. Just as teachers need to keep up with modern subject matter, they need to keep up with new information about how children learn and why children don't learn. Up-to-date understanding of the learning process should improve teachers' abilities to teach all students. Parents won't have to ask once public schools take the initiative themselves.

We have found teachers sympathetic and anxious to help our children when they were told about their handicaps. We have found most teachers interested in learning disabilities. Once teachers recognize these learning disabilities, however, they are frustrated unless they know what to do about them. They'll help once they know how. Over and over they ask, what can we do about learning disabilities in the classroom? Educators will have to answer their questions. Since teachers aren't getting enough answers now, public school systems should assume the responsibility for preparing them to teach the otherwise normal child with learning disabilities.

We are discovering that education and special education are too separate in teacher-training institutions. Teachers have the separation firmly in mind. We are not suggesting that all teachers be given a survey of special education. New classroom teachers should come out of teacher-training institutions able to recognize learning disabilities and informed on how to cope with them.

Not all the burden for teaching children with learning disabilities can be carried by the regular-classroom teacher. Educators and legislators need to plan for extra diagnostic and supporting personnel. We can never expect to have special classes for one-fifth to one-third of the public-school population. Many educators are questioning whether special classes serve the purpose for which they were intended. Children with learning disabilities have diverse problems. Whatever the plan for educating these children, it will need to begin by teaching them how to learn. Don't let them plod along on watered-down versions of the regular curriculum. Teach them how to compensate for their disabilities. Teach them how they can learn. Once our children are able to learn, they can acquire facts and grasp the regular curriculum. The goals and methods of education should not be determined by parents. However, if professionals determine the goals and methods, then parents have a right to expect that the goals will be worthy and the methods effective.

At present there are too few solutions for the child who doesn't learn and can't be bundled off for special education. School personnel say that parents refuse to believe that their children have disabilities. They also say that parents refuse to take their children to a physician or to permit the schools to provide special services for their children. Parents, we know, would be more willing to admit that their children have problems if the schools had more acceptable solutions for these problems. Our schools offer limited testing, some remedial reading, and some speech therapy. If the child does not receive these, or these are not sufficient, parents have only three options:

- They can take the child to a physician, have him labeled minimally brain-injured, and put him in special education.
- The child can remain unsuccessful and frustrated in regular classes.
- He can be removed from the public schools and educated in private facilities.

Parents may follow the school recommendation and take their child to their family doctor or pediatrician. The diagnosis of a child with learning disabilities is a function of present knowledge about the structure and function of the brain and nervous system and the sophistication of present techniques available to study them. It is also a function of the knowledge, training, and experience of each individual physician. Physicians who completed training before 1963 are likely to be unaware of the concept of learning disabilities. If the family pediatrician is aware of the existence of learning disabilities and the work being done with children with learning disabilities, he is often not convinced of its validity. One physician commented on the subject, "Aren't kids just stupid anymore?" The physician may believe that there is a problem, but certain experts physicians respect are still telling them that nothing can be done. The physician may pat the child on the head and say, "He's a fine boy. He'll outgrow it."

Can physicians wait to help children with learning disabilities until the causes of learning disabilities are unequivocally established by methods not yet devised? Medical opinion on treatment of learning disabilities is in a stage equivalent to medical opinion throughout the Sister Kenny period of treating paralytic polio. Physicians cannot put off helping as effectively as possible the large number of children who suffer from learning disabilities believed to be organic in nature.

Physicians who can and will diagnose children with learning disabilities have a vital role to play in the multidisciplinary management of these children. The physician fills a need by prescribing medication to control hyperactivity and other behavioral manifestations and to increase the ability of the child to concentrate on his school work. Other professionals must write the educational prescription for the child. Physicians will have an even larger role in the future when research on the brain and nervous system, physiology of learning, genetics, biochemistry, and diet reveal concrete avenues for medical management. As psychotherapy is being supplanted by drug therapy, possibly present treatment of children with learning disabilities will be supplanted by radical new medical management.

The least justifiable function of the physician today is labeling children for educational purposes. A physician should not have to label a child as minimally brain-injured, neurologically handicapped, emotionally disturbed or with some other specific label in order for that child to receive educational help in the public schools. If the physician is unable or unwilling to make the required diagnosis, the parents must shop until they find a doctor willing to place such a subjective label on the child. If quasi-ethical use of the medical profession is to be avoided, legislators will have to change restrictive laws and officials will have to change outmoded policies.

Teachers will tell you that discipline problems in school are the result of poor discipline at home. This may be true in some cases. At least as early as 1947, an anticonvulsive medication was successfully used to modify behavioral problems in otherwise normal, nonconvulsive children. Early investigators reported improvements in school work but didn't emphasize this unexpected aspect of the medical management of behavior. Nobody knows how often poor discipline at home is being blamed for what is really impulsiveness, hyperactivity, and lack of foresight—inability of the child to control himself. Some children are driven from within, and no form of management which attempts to control behavior solely by modifying the environment or interpersonal relationships can succeed. Teachers and neighbors are quick to notice that *undisciplined children* often run in families. They cite these families as certain proof that the parents have allowed the children to run wild. They also note that such families are often in turmoil much of the time. More and more families today have two or more children with *diagnosed* learning disabilities. We can cite six families where two to five children have been so diagnosed. More commonly parents concentrate so much on the worst-afflicted or hyperactive child, as we did, that they don't notice less-obvious problems in their other children. More investigation should be made into the genetic familial aspects of learning disabilities. If children are organically involved, are discipline problems the result of abdication of parental responsibilities or does the organic defect make the children difficult to control at home as well as at school? Are these discipline problems because the family is in turmoil or do the discipline problems contribute to the turmoil?

Knowledgeable professionals of various disciplines do not agree on diagnosis, let alone suitable management of children with learning disabilities. There are advocates of tutoring, drug therapy, gross-motor programs, visual training, patterning, language development, psychotherapy, speech therapy, prescriptive education, and those who claim maturation will solve the problem. A multidisciplinary approach is obviously best, but it is too seldom available to parents. Parents are buffeted from theory to theory and from expert to expert. Unable to obtain adequate professional guidance, parents are forced to become instant experts. The fact is that no parents are experts. Every parent we know feels profound insecurity, a desperate sense of "What *shall* we do?" "*Are* we doing the best thing?" Driven by frustration and necessity and lacking multidisciplinary leadership, they must make professional decisions. They fear gaps or overlap in their treatment programs for their children, sure they may never know the *right* answers.

We all know children who are receiving long hours of tutoring or specialized training, all in addition to their long, frustrating hours at school. We're not condemning it; many children are being helped in this way. However, when the child or parents rebel, then the treatment has become worse than the original problems. Mothers have suffered acute psychotic breakdowns where early anxieties were caused by their children with learning disabilities. Divorces and separations have occurred over disagreements about these children and their management. We don't know of all the unhappy families struggling along as best they can, not only failing to get help but actually misled when they sought help. Some parents are suspicious and lethargic since they were misdirected in the past and saw much money paid for ineffectual therapy. Some are misguided, unwilling to spend money now, saving it for college when their progeny are unlikely to finish high school.

What is to become of the vast majority of children whose parents are without the knowledge, money, or inclination to help them overcome learning disabilities? The only place to educate such children is in the public schools. Let us change whatever laws need to be changed to allow public-school personnel properly to evaluate these children. Let's change whatever policy needs to be changed to let public schools teach these children under the best possible circumstances. Let's erase the line between education and special education. Let's have school services which will permit children with the fewest disabilities to remain in the regular classroom and receive part-time help with their specific disabilities. Let's have classes where otherwise normal children with more severe learning disabilities can be educated for a time in separate classrooms without unnecessary special labels. Let's have more consideration for the feelings and needs of children and their parents and less compromise for political expediency.

Schools exist to make children literate. To function in our technologically oriented society children must be able to read and understand what they read, able to think rationally, and able to express themselves orally and in writing. It is fine for schools to set out to produce citizens who are adjusted, productive members of society. But let's not minimize the importance of academic achievement. Our children have normal, potentially normal, often above-normal intelligence. Our children can learn. Once the public schools assume the responsibility for teaching them, parents will not need to be as involved as they are now.

Addendum*

As we review our presentation in 1974, we believe it is as valid as when we prepared it in 1969. Much progress is being made in the field of learning disabilities, but the benefits are unevenly available to the students who need help.

All three of our boys adapted readily when they returned to public school regular classes. Four years ago we moved from Texas and enrolled them in their new schools without reference to their learning disabilities or the special help they had received. We wanted to see if they could succeed on their own, and they could. They thrived. All three are now in college preparatory courses in high school. They have no special restrictions.

Ken, our oldest, will be graduated in June. He is a National Merit Commended Scholar who has been accepted at the private liberal arts college of his choice. Throughout high school he has played guitar and bass in several youth musical groups which give concerts and play at dances. He has played ice hockey in a local amateur hockey association for the last three years.

---

*Written for this volume, May, 1974.

Rick has almost straight A's with outstanding effort reported in many of his courses. He's taking French III, chemistry, algebra II, social studies and English—a full schedule. He has played baseball with a local league each summer, played ice hockey in the amateur hockey association each winter, and won a position on the high school varsity tennis team this spring.

Jeff, our youngest, has straight A's with outstanding reports from his teachers. He completes his work in the allotted times. He plays baseball and ice hockey. In spring, he runs the mile for the school track team and in fall he runs on the cross country team—with outstanding success.

We credit these boys' great success in overcoming their problems to the multidisciplinary program which was developed for each. Their deficiencies were diagnosed in great detail by a number of professionals who then cooperated to develop the boys' strengths and to help them compensate for their weaknesses. Now our boys are happy and successful academically, athletically, and socially. We hope their progress will be an inspiration to students and to parents who are struggling as we were a few years ago.

Working with Parents of Children with Learning Disabilities

ALICE C. THOMPSON

It has been recognized for many years that work done with children who manifest various kinds of problems should optimally be accompanied by work done with their parents. Service has been traditionally focused on psychotherapeutic aid, but several influences have arisen to widen the scope of our efforts. These influences include the sparsity of therapy available, growth of medical knowledge, recognition of the importance of constitutional and biochemical factors, improvement of educational services, and the avid interest and indefatigable energy on the part of the parents themselves.

Society has taken remarkably little responsibility for training for parenthood, even among supposedly normal families. Parenthood has always been one of the human conditions whose major requirements appeared to be obvious and natural. The formula seemed simple: do what comes naturally; give every child love and opportunity to do things other children do, have things other children have; send him to school; provide him with the right food and physical care; and maintain solicitude for his welfare. If he should not obey or conform, punish him in time-honored ways: spank, scold, deprive of privileges.

No provision was made in the formula for deviations in either parents or children. While considerable attention has been given to the individual differences and needs of target children, not much has been directed toward those of the parents themselves. This oversight is in part deliberate and self-conscious. It has been a contribution of the parents to acknowledge that parents of unusual children are themselves statistically more likely to be unusual. This circumstance has often influenced their friends and protectors to ignore it, and their detractors to exaggerate it through criticism and innuendo. Once the moral judgment is removed, awareness of the influence of familial factors contributes positively to the situation, both in better understanding and management of the child, and in communication, ease, and cooperation with the parents. Sometimes special conditions are better interpreted as statistically unusual genetic or mutative features than as pathologies of interpersonal origin.

The fact that many difficult children have not responded favorably to standard methods of attempted control has not so much convinced parents of the inapplicability of the methods as it has confused and upset them. The plight of parents has not as much generated help and compassion for

From the *Proceedings* of the Fourth Annual Conference of the ACLD, *Management of the Child with Learning Disabilities: An Interdisciplinary Challenge.* New York (March 9-11, 1967), pp. 101-103. Revised for this volume.

them as it has focused criticism upon them. Many parents have sought help in one center after another without conclusive results; and many of them harbor resentment and bitterness against persons and agencies for real or imagined slights and ills. Certainly there has been no clear voice of authority to answer their questions.

In line with the thinking of clinical psychologists, the general assumption had been that since the personalities of parents exert significant influence on the personalities of children, the major aim must be to assist parents in solving their own personal problems. In this way, parents would provide a healthy, reclaiming environment for the children.

Although there is no reason to question the beneficial effect upon children of healthy parents, it began to be evident that not only were there not enough therapists to go around, but also that, except in relatively isolated instances, the expected changes were not taking place in either the parents or the children. Clearly, measures more available and more effective had to be added.

The discovery that many children with learning difficulties may be influenced by more than willful disinterest in learning or by "emotional blocks" has opened the way to new directions of educational and medical inquiry, many of which can be participated in by parents, and all of which are of interest to them. Emphasis is being laid upon the learning problem as a learning problem rather than primarily as a spinoff from underlying emotional conditions; and distorted emotional life begins to be regarded as itself a learning problem. Many people, young and old alike, have not learned how to feel, how to enjoy themselves and others, how to judge their own qualities and circumstances accurately, how to direct themselves wisely. The development of these capabilities must become an increasing part of the learning program for both parents and children.

A major contribution of medical progress has been to demonstrate that most children manifesting severe learning difficulties are handicapped by more than the deleterious qualities of their parents—i.e., by physiological factors, innate or acquired, permanent or modifiable, and deriving from multiple sources: biochemical, cellular, neural, metabolic, genetic. Another important contribution is the growing refinement in the prescription of medications used to tide over the rough spots and to increase neural organization and efficiency. ·

The mushrooming of parent organizations strikingly shows how desperate parents are for information and aid for their children's conditions, for themselves, and for social action. Parents have exerted tremendous influence upon legislation and upon their own communities. It seems certain that educational effort alone could not have accomplished so much. They have been instrumental in launching research, distributing pertinent literature, organizing conferences, encouraging workshops, generating interest and activity, and comforting one another. They want to know about practices and tenets of those who are their children's teachers and helpers. They want to know what the teacher is doing and why certain methods are selected over others. They want to know how their children are progressing, whether they should help them at home with their school work, and how they might be able to extend into the home the major benefits of the school. A growing practice among private schools and cooperative groups is to involve the parents in the training process so that they may understand thoroughly what is being attempted and how they may adapt the ideas within their own situations.

They seek information to allay their anxieties over whether their children are "brain-damaged," and to comprehend what this terrifying term means. They have often been led to believe that if the problem is "emotional" it is potentially curable, and that it stems primarily from their own behavior toward their children. On the other hand if the problem is "organic," they have supposed it to be irreversible, but not of their making. It is a brutal experience to be caught between such alternatives, and it is particularly regrettable because these are not true alternatives.

It seems clear that human beings tend to feel safe and benign when they can count on certain important features of their lives: biological sufficiency, a place to belong where they are welcomed and wanted, opportunity to explore and to satisfy curiosity without fear, a wide range of sensory experience and stimulation, pleasant social interaction with several others. While such anchor points are important for everyone, they are doubly important for individuals whose learning modes are unusual and virtually unknown. Complicating the matter with children is that their behavior is so unpredictable that the principal authority figures of their world do not themselves know what to count on, unless it is that they cannot count on very much except continued turmoil and unpredictability.

Because of this double jeopardy, the child with learning disability is even more handicapped. He needs an unusually consistent environment in which to live, but his own failure to learn as others do not only makes the most consistent environment difficult to internalize, but also injects irregularity into any situation. His parents are so distraught by the threatening features of their joint lives that they move frantically from one mode of management to another in response to his behavior, continually seeking some better ways of getting favorable results. Thus the child lives in an even less reliable environment, and gains even less security because he does not learn easily and because he generates inconsistency toward himself.

Caught by continuing frustration and conviction of inadequacy, parents find little firm footing. Every expectation they had of parenthood is foiled. Every new attempt at correction and guidance is a failure. They are bewildered and discouraged by vague concepts of personality improvement, or guilt-inducing assurances that their children need love and affection, especially when these children are at times very difficult to love.

Perhaps nothing can ever atone for the burdens of guilt which have been willfully or implicitly laid upon multitudes of parents in the mistaken assumption that their children's predicaments derived directly and solely from parents' mismanagement, neurotic example, and lack of love for each other and for their children. Parents have been admonished to love their children or blamed for not doing so, as if the experience of cherishing another human being could be achieved by command or effort.

At the same time there tended to be neglect of education to develop conscientious concern for other aspects of children's development: their physical welfare, social opportunities, recreation, variety, environmental stability. Education does not insure implementation of learning, but parents have proved to be generally amenable to new ideas and grateful for information. In fact, it may be that the most beneficial thing that we who work with problem children have had to offer their parents is sharing with them our information, our hopes, our thinking, even our own problems and failures. If people cannot by taking thought open and close the flow of love for others, we still can learn techniques of support and aid that can be of lasting benefit.

One obstacle that has often stood in the way of improved parental procedures is the difficulty of applying large generalizations to specific instances. It is one thing, for example, to accept the principle that consistency is desirable, but quite another to know what constitutes consistent management at choice points. Parents can usually, however, identify a few key areas of conflict and select a number of examples of behaviors on their own part which they can use as targets for change. To achieve consistency in a few matters is to take a big step toward stabilizing the expectations to which even erratic children can adapt.

Each generalization or principle which could be of value to parents is most helpful when accompanied by a multitude of detailed illustrations, some of which will be close enough to the family's own practices to provide incentive and a sense of familiarity. A volume could be compiled listing these principles with specific illustrations, and made available to those who are interested.

Examples of principles which could be cited, amplified, and made pertinent include the following:

- Children tend to repeat behaviors which have yielded gratification.
- Attention spans tend to lengthen when tasks are short and successful.
- Children are more likely to be comfortable with expected things than unexpected things even when the expected things are less than optimal.
- Constant reminding of children increases their dependency upon being reminded.
- Communication should be couched in positive rather than negative terms.
- Children tend to return to interests and activities from which they have been emphatically turned away.
- Doing an act increases the probability of doing it again unless the consequences are aversive.
- It is easier to bring about compliance and cooperation when requests are tied to desirable events immediately to follow.

- Be the one to whom the child reacts rather than the one who always reacts to the child.
- Learning is facilitated in atmospheres of pleasantness, joy, and humor.

We have learned a great deal from the parents themselves about what can be done to help them. The chief problem now is to put these things into workable form, to disseminate information, to provide support, to be ourselves open and well informed, and to continue the educational trend toward greater learning efficiency.

Parents Need to Know:
Parents and Teachers Work Together

LEO F. BUSCAGLIA

It is a tremendous, exciting thing for me to discuss some of my ideas about parent conferencing, about parents and teachers working together. My students always tell me that even though my classes have different labels, they all end up being Love 1A and Love 1B and Love 1C, and that's probably how this paper will end up. But I do have an enormous love for parents, and the sum of what I am going to say is this: as far as I am concerned, it is about time that professionals began to look at parents as warm, pulsating, beautiful, tender, fantastic, unbelievable, intelligent, incredible human beings. And then I want to discuss how parents and professionals can work together, for as long as parents are trapped with professionals, and professionals are trapped with parents, we are going to have to find a way to reach one another.

First, some ideas I have about things like change—and things like hope —and things like growth—because I believe fervently that counseling is education. When I am talking about counseling, I'm not talking about psychotherapy. It is of little or no interest to me to find out about parents' sex life. This won't help me to help their child. But there are ways in which the two of us can get together and really help the child. The focus will be on the child and the people who will be working around him. Counseling is education, growth, and change.

In connection with this, I recommend that readers become familiar with the work of Herbert Otto, who is one of the people involved in a wonderful thing called the Institute for the Development of the Human Person. I hope that some day I'll be there, and perhaps some of you will end up there, too. It's a place where they are trying to find out how to help people *Become,* and I can't think of a more wonderful undertaking. Herbert Otto says this: "Change and personal growth take place when a person has risked himself and dared to become involved in experimenting with his own life."[1] Isn't that fantastic? It's true—growth is a risk—and after risk, it is an experiment. You never know what is going to be happening next in this process of becoming. It's beautiful! Everything is new, everything is exciting. It's also fearful because you can't be certain about what is around the corner. I tell my students all the time that probably the greatest trip you take in the world is the trip you take in becoming you.

From the *Proceedings* of the Eighth Annual Conference of the ACLD, *The Child with Learning Disabilities: His Right to Learn.* Chicago (March 18-20, 1971), pp. 27-39.

Change is inevitable. Everything is changing. It is going to occur with or without you. De Chardin, in *The Phenomenon of Man,* makes a wonderful statement: "Change is occuring so quickly today that you can no longer stand still, for if you are, you are moving backwards."[2] That's exactly what is happening, and we have got to keep up with change. One way to do this is to be curious about what is happening out there and to be wondrous about all the things that are in yourself that you haven't yet realized but that are waiting to be let out. That is what I believe to be the essence of counseling—a voyage, so to speak, into the world of you to find out about yourself, to discover yourself, the process of growth.

Saint Exupery, in a beautiful book called *Wind, Sand and Stars,* says, "Love is perhaps a process of my leading you gently back to yourself."[3] And maybe teaching is a process of my leading you gently back to yourself. And certainly counseling is a process of my leading you gently back to yourself. Not to *me* but to *who you are* because, of all things, you are the best you. One of the most beautiful things in the world—and probably the greatest hope I have—is that we can change you back to believing that you are the best you—and not try to make you anyone else. One of the things that I tell my students in love class all the time is that the game we don't want to play is "follow the guru." If you try to be me, you are always going to be like oleomargarine—the second-best spread. I'm the best spread if I'm the best me. But you are the best you. And so counseling is the process of leading you gently back to yourself, leading the children gently back to themselves, leading the parents back to themselves.

So I am talking about a process that I call educational counseling, which is not psychotherapy, which is not encounter groups. I am really kind of uptight about encounter groups. I recently saw the film, *Diary of a Mad Housewife.* That film really got to me, and I recommend it to you wholeheartedly. But I warn you, if you are the kind of person who attends a film and is up and halfway out the door the minute the last shot is on, you are going to miss the most significant part because the film ends with an encounter group. For two hours we've been face to face with the life of this incredible woman, a housewife, who runs around baking pies and taking her husband's shirts to the cleaners and taking care of two little kids and walking the dog in the park, and so on. We've been very intimate with this woman. We've been allowed to get into her head, and we feel—at least I feel—a tremendous empathy with her. I couldn't help but weep over her life, her beautiful, incredible life. There should have been more than just what she was having to experience here—walking the dog and cleaning the kids' noses. She was also an individual. The final shot, which occurs behind the credits for director, producer, writer, etc., is the face of this woman while you hear the people in her encounter group saying such things as, "You're lucky, you don't know how lucky you are, what are you sitting there crying about? You have a husband, and you live in a ten-room apartment. . . ." And you can just see on her face, "My God! Nobody sees me. Nobody knows really what I'm up against. Nobody knows really who

I am. Nobody understands my real needs." But it is very easy for these people to sit there and attack her.

I have a very essential philosophy, very simple indeed, and that is that most of us are extremely vulnerable, most of us are very easily hurt, most of us are very close to tears. God knows there is enough of this kind of thing going on without having to sit around and attack each other. Now that may offend some people, and it may be that that's your bag—and if so, attack. But as far as I am concerned, people are very puncturable, I am really afraid to stick my fingers through them, to make interpretations of them. I don't know you. I don't know what loneliness you are feeling, what joy you are feeling, what makes you cry, what makes you happy. I don't know what will turn you on and what will turn you off. I can only see you as essentially a human being and identify with you as a human being. I know what I feel, for instance, when someone attacks me. And so I believe that counseling should be a very gentle process.

The counseling I am talking about is essentially a learning process. I believe that emotions are learned, and I believe that anything we have learned, we can unlearn, and we can relearn. It is a process of trying out your new learning behavior and seeing if it is right for you, not for the counselor, but for *you*, and then behaving accordingly. That's essentially it. So when I talk about educational counseling, I am talking about helping the counselee to desire to change and to have hope that change is possible, then to volitionally try out new behavior that will lead him to new adjustments.

For six years of my life as director of special education in a large community in California, I did little more than sit down with parents of children who were exceptional, who had impairments, everything from severe cerebral palsy to one woman who had three blind children—and I rapped with them. There is nothing in the world that annoys me more than either a counselor or a teacher who says that a parent must accept his exceptional child. The best response I ever heard to that in my life was from a beautiful woman, and I almost burst through a one-way mirror and hugged her. A counselor said to her in a teaching situation, "You must accept your exceptional child or I can't help you." And she said, "Why the hell must I?" And I thought, "Good for you, honey!"

It becomes a process of education and reeducation; it becomes a process of becoming ready. Another thing that is always ludicrous to me is when professionals turn parents away, saying that they are uncooperative. You know what that usually means? "They don't see things the way I do. They're uncooperative. They don't accept their children. They don't really understand the problem. They are unrealistic." How many times have you heard that? Let's put ourselves in the place of this parent and let's look at the dynamics involved in being a parent of an exceptional child. In fact, let's look at the dynamics involved in being the parents of "normal" children.

The role of the individual within the family is a very unique and wondrous thing with an enormous responsibility, because it is essentially within the family that a person learns to love or hate, that a person learns how to accept or how to spend his life fearing, learns how to kill or create, learns how to live with life or live without life, how to relate or how to be lonely.

In the family you learn who you are, you learn what the world is all about, you learn what is expected of you and what you can expect. In other words, you learn how to perceive yourself and your world. These things all happen in the family, and that is why the early years of life are tremendously important. Many of us were raised in a time that told us once these years were set, there was nothing we could do about it, we were stuck with our hangups for the rest of our lives. I essentially do not believe this. I believe that there comes a time in your life when you can take your life in your hands, and you can do with it what you will. That is why if you wanted to put a philosophy around me, you would not only say I was a humanist, I hope, but an existential humanist because I truly believe that you make your own scene. I have said before that you write your own play, paint your backdrop, surround yourself with actors, play your background music, and if you don't like the show, then get the hell off the stage and write a new one. Don't sit there and wallow in your own loneliness. Ask yourself, "What can I do?"

I am always telling people who go around saying how lonely they are, that maybe if they removed the wall and let people in, they would be less lonely. Maybe if we expected less from people in terms of their coming to us and saying, "May I help you?"—it would be beautiful but that's not what life is all about—maybe we should reach the point where we can turn to people and say, "I need you." I had a beautiful girl in love class who, when someone asked, "What do you do if there is a wall around someone," said, "I ignore it." Think about that. "I ignore it."

Now let's look at the family that has an exceptional child. There is a very interesting study now going on at UCLA. Many of you are acquainted with the literature and are, as I am, following it eagerly. They are trying to find out what is the difference in the hospital atmosphere when an exceptional child is born. What happens when a child is born, let's say, without an arm, or when a child is born blind or with cerebral palsy? What happens in that hospital? They have found some very, very interesting things. First, there is a delay from the time that the child is born to the time that the child is taken to its mother. Mothers are human, too, and they sense this: "What's wrong? Is something wrong? How come everyone else has their child, and I don't have mine?" A delay in time. There is also a contest as to who will be the nurse that will bring this child, who will be the person who will tell this mother. What does this say to the mother right from the beginning? "My child is different, my child is unique, there is something not quite right with my child." Rejection.

We are also in a culture that stresses perfection. Our idea of perfection amuses me. It's the Rock Hudson-Doris Day perfection syndrome. It always amuses me that in this country we are in the Audrey Hepburn all-bone syndrome—and then I go to Italy where it is the Sophia Loren all-flesh syndrome. Notions of perfection change. We have this conflict about what is perfection, and we are a little bit afraid of what is imperfect. The whole phenomenon of birth is a miracle. You can't take it lightly. A child is a gift, and nobody wants to give an imperfect gift. And so immediately what happens? Different dynamics! You are dealing with a different kind of human being, not only with the hangups of every family—for no family is perfect and all have their essential loneliness and fears—but on top of this you have *new* dynamics at work.

First, there is fear, real honest-to-God fear. The parents wonder, "What's going to happen to this child? If he is different, will I be able to educate him? Is he going to be able to find work? What are my friends going to say?" Old wives' tales are conjured up. My beautiful mother used to tell my sisters when they were pregnant that they shouldn't go out during an eclipse, and she really believed it. I am sure that if my sisters had gone out —they were just as superstitious as Mama—and something had happened, they would have blamed it on the eclipse. There are real fears, fears that the child will be rejected later on. There are real guilt feelings—"What did I do?" I have never worked with the parents of an exceptional child who didn't wonder, "Was it something I did? Did I do something wrong? Did I not take care of myself? Did we not get the right doctors? Could I have done more?" What I am trying to do is create for you how unique these people are with whom we are working and how impossible it is to say to them, "You must accept your exceptional child. Rid yourself of all these things overnight." How unrealistic this is—we forget that we are still dealing with human beings.

And then there is shame. It wasn't too long ago that any kind of exceptionality was associated with filth, with disease, and we are not altogether through with this. When an exceptional child walks down the street, you still see people turn around and gawk and say, "Look Mabel." You know that, and I know that. There is still fear. I require that every single one of my students who wants to do anything in terms of teaching children and understanding people must work in a situation with exceptional children. Every time we bring them into a hospital setting, an institutional setting, a school setting, they all admit how fearful they are until they get down to working with these kids. Then all of a sudden they recognize human beings, and the fear vanishes, and they even forget. One of my students who was working with blind children was horrified because one day she had said, "What's the matter with you, Johnny, can't you see?" And you know he giggled! He was human, too.

I have never sat down with a parent of an exceptional child without finding out that these poor people have been to 150 pediatricians, 150 neurologists, 150 educators, all with great hope in their hearts that they could find an answer, a miracle cure. These are the things we are going to have to deal with because parents don't just get over it. We are going to have to look at them. We are going to have to face them, and we are going to have to realize that they are not superhumans. They are only human beings, and of course, that is their greatest strength—as it is ours. But not only do they have all of the problems and handicaps that all families have,

they have a special complex problem. We have to recognize their uniqueness and try to get into their heads and see the problem from their side of
the fence. So no more talking about "you must accept your exceptional
child."

The first step in educational counseling is to help the parent get over
this period that Solnit and Stark call—and I like this—"a period of mourn-
ing,"[4] a period of loneliness, a period of isolation, a period of confusion, a
period of fear, a period of misunderstanding, a period of guilt, a period of
depreciation of self, a period of shame. In doing so, several things can
happen. One is that they can hide away in confusion or, secondly, they can
overreact, and you get the very aggressive parent who breaks the door
down and says, "This isn't enough; I've got to have more." We need this
kind of parent, for they are the ones who keep us moving.

How can we help parents to get over these initial feelings? First of all,
we have to have some empathy, we have to be able to relate to them as
people. I always start this by saying that parents are people—just like
you. It always amused me when I was working in the schools when open
house came, and all the teachers were reacting, "My God! The parents are
coming!" They overlooked the fact that they, too, were parents. On the
other hand, I have a psychiatrist friend who is scared to death of teachers!
He's got three kids, and when he goes to school for a conference, I am sure
that the teacher looks at the records, sees that he is a psychiatrist, and is
scared to death of him. So here comes a man scared to death of the teacher,
and she's afraid to open her mouth because he might interpret it, and they
are supposed to try to relate about his kids, and they don't get anywhere.
It's hysterical! We must believe that parents are people, too, and give them
credit for having intelligence. In California, before we passed laws, we
never allowed parents to look at any of the children's records—*their kids*,
yet all records were secret. We would only tell them what we thought they
should know. That's absolutely brilliant. "It's your kid but I'm not going
to tell you anything about him; I have secrets about him." We couldn't
imagine that parents could possibly understand what we big teachers and
psychologists understand! Anything you know, they can know, too, but you
have to take the time to let them know it.

When I was director of special education, I decided that I would solve
all the parent conferencing in one big fell swoop. This was my first or
second year, and I had about 300 parents at a parent education seminar.
Isn't that exciting? Poor things, they worked all day and then had to get
dressed up and come to this damned seminar! I had neurologists and
psychologists and fantastic teachers, and I was never so brilliant in my
life—lectures that lasted two hours in which I told them everything they
had to know! Then at the end I made an incredible mistake. I gave them
an evaluation form which asked, "What is the one most important thing
that you got from this seminar?" Of course, I was sure it would be something brilliant that I had said. Do you know what it was? More than 70
percent of them said, "The greatest value I got from this seminar was to

find that there are other parents like me who have exceptional children." Boy, did that make me humble—and I stopped having mass meetings.

It is the same ludicrous kind of thing, for instance, that we assume when we take third graders and put them together in one room and believe we can teach them all in the same way. Every parent is unique, every parent is an individual. You are not and can never be me, and I can never be you. I can never really understand you 100 percent, even though I might believe I can, nor can you ever understand me 100 percent, even though you might believe you can. All you have to do is read some of the things that psychologists write about parents, and you can see how far away they are. The same parent I interview is not the parent that she interviews nor the parent that you interview. Everybody perceives through their own eyes and their own hangups.

You can't ignore this frozen period of inability to go beyond the emotions. I know some programs, for instance, that start parents immediately when strong feelings still exist, and then they are wondering why parents are resisting. It is because they still have these very real feelings, and they have to deal with these first before they can become really involved in this process. That doesn't mean that they have to become self-actualized. They only have to become aware that those feelings are there, and then they can do something.

The second aspect of educational counseling is to help the parent to bring himself to the point where he can accept himself, love himself, be able to say, "I am not responsible. I am not guilty. There are things I can do. I am also alive. I have a responsibility to me as well as to my children, because as I grow, so can they grow. If I stand still in this frozen position, so will they be frozen in their position." Mama plays the largest role in adjustment and in learning in children. One of the professors at the University of Southern California has just finished a study of deprived children in which he showed that the attitude of the mother toward learning was the most important factor in the child's ability to learn, regardless of how poor they were, how deprived they were, and so mother's attitude is tremendously important.

Now we have to take parents in and let them become part of a team, and I don't mean a team in words but an actual team in the process of initiating change. The mother must be asked how much she can do in this process and then become really involved. *The Siege* is a beautiful book by a woman who had an emotionally disturbed child,[5] and her thoughts are highly pertinent here. She put her finger right on it. She took her little child to a neurologist and a psychologist and educators. Weeks and months and thousands of dollars later they sat this mother down, and she writes:

This is what they had to say. It is not a summary of what they said. It is *all* they said, although the psychiatrist, a hesitant, rather inarticulate, elderly man took considerably more time to say it than it takes to write it here.
1. Ellie needs therapy.

2. She has performed above her age level on that part of the IQ test she could do. It was, therefore, believed that she had no mental deficiency.
3. She has many fears.

That's it. That is what they had to say of all that information and of all our time, energies, and money.

Her reaction to this is not unfamiliar to many parents:

We wanted information, we wanted techniques, we wanted sympathy, not the soapy kind, we were grown up adults, but some evidence of feeling that ordinary doctors seem to have. Was it so unreasonable to ask for this? We wanted a little reassurance, a little recognition of our own needs, and a little praise. It never occurred to us that these expectations were naive, that the gulf between the parent and the professional must deliberately be kept unabridged by any ordinary techniques of interpersonal relationships.

Does this sound familiar?

It should have been easy, after all, to say, 'Look, you're a professional, I need references, I need to know how to do for Ellie. I need to know all I can do and all I can learn about my child because whoever else may or may not work with her, I, her parent, shall always be her main psychotherapist.'

So—parents need help, but not the current kind of idea h-e-l-p. She continues:

I feel a breakdown or separation between the parents and professionals. At present it is common practice for a child to receive education or therapy for months and sometimes years without the mother or the father having any direct conversation with that child's therapist or teacher. This is especially true of the large clinic where the social worker acts as a sort of mediator or buffer between the therapist, teacher and the parent. It is thought best that the parents of a small child know nothing of what goes on in these privileged sessions, and the only way she may hear of what the therapist actually thinks of her child's case is if she happens to meet him accidentally in the hall, and he is nice enough to tell her a thing or two.

She ends up with this paragraph, and if I had any sense, I'd end this paper here—but I don't have any sense:

The answer must be in training parents as nonprofessionals unless there is to be no answer at all. Above all, we must train parents to do with skill and effectiveness what they have to do anyway. Mothers will make ready pupils as people do when they are learning what they have immediate need for.

How do we help people to change? This is something that recently I have questioned very, very strongly. I have read as much of the literature on change as I could possibly get my fingers on, and I think I have a few ideas. First of all, I think we have to help people see the dissonance between what they are seeing and what they are doing, and to see what is "reality," the reality of the situation. This is a very difficult thing to do because we don't see things actually as they are. We see them as we must see them. You know this is true. You see a tree uniquely your way, and this may not at all be the tree.

If you really want to go back and get some exciting mind trips, read the works of Virginia Woolf. Get her books—they are all in paperback—and sit down and read this remarkable woman, a woman who, like so many women today, was wasted—and it really freaks me when I see this happen. You know, intelligent women have a hard time surviving in our culture. I don't know how women do it—I mean, who wants an intelligent woman? Men seem to want some of the little freaky gigglers—that's the kind they marry. They have discussion groups with the others. Virginia Woolf struggled and struggled to communicate. Recently an incredible volume of her letters has been published. Read them, for they are unbelievable. She struck up a tremendous letter-writing situation with a minister who was inferior mentally to Virgina Woolf, but he was aware emotionally of her needs to be recognized and to be realized. Even though she sent him tremendously deep, profound, unbelievable letters, he would write to her about trout fishing and so forth. She kept exposing herself in these letters, and he really kept her alive longer even than he thought. Eventually she committed suicide, throwing herself into the Thames, drowning herself in that muddy river, which is again one of the great tragedies.

Sometimes when we look at the works of these great sensitive people, we find definitions that the great scientists can't give us. When I look for a definition of *perception*, how we see things, I always turn to the works of Virginia Woolf, for here is a sensitive, beautiful woman talking about perception as I have never been able to read about it in any book. This is what she says simply in one of her letters:

We are constantly endeavoring to give meaning and order to our lives, the past, the present, and in the future, meaning to our surroundings and the world we live in, with the result that our lives appear to be a total entity in our own conception which, to be sure, is constantly changing more or less radically, more or less rapidly depending on the extent to which we are obliged, inclined or able to assimilate the onrush of different experiences.[6]

That is an amazing thing to say about reality and the constant change of reality.

Like a teacher, the greatest counselor is a person who is aware. I cannot handle techniques of counseling—you know, for example, the ten rules of greeting people. "How do you do, Mrs. Jones," is number one. "Oh, hello, Mrs. Jones," is number two. "Please, Mrs. Jones, won't you sit down . . . ." That's nonsense! What I am trying to do is to help people return to themselves, and we are doing wonderful little things that I call renewing our awareness. Some people call it sensitivity. I don't care what you call it. We're learning to taste again, we're learning to smell again, we're learning to feel again, we're learning how little we do these things. I brought in fresh spinach, and I put a leaf of fresh spinach in front of each of the students, and I said, "Eat it." They picked it up and started munching like, "Oh, God, here goes Buscaglia again." They started eating it, and they started lighting up and saying, "Wow!" Do you know there were people there who had never tasted fresh spinach? One man said, "My God, why do we cook it to death and put vinegar on it when it tastes so good?" But we're learning again to taste, we're learning again to smell, we're learning to put linguistic structures around the things we are experiencing so that we can express ourselves to other people because, like it or not, the only things we have to deal with are symbols. Yet symbols don't serve us because those are the symbols that someone has taught us, not what we truly feel.

Recently Buckminster Fuller said an incredible thing: "I've gone through my life dealing with my environment in terms of words people have given me, and I found myself using other people's words to describe my experiences and my feelings, and they weren't adequate, and so I moved away to a little ghetto."[7] He did—for two years when he was twenty-two he lived in a little ghetto in Chicago. He got a tiny room, and he said, "In these years I spent my time clearing my mind of old concepts of words and finding out what words can mean. What did this word mean to me? Not what did it mean to all those people who had taught it to me. . . . I'm having a ball with language because every time I speak, I say what I mean and not what other people mean."

My students and I made a dictionary of what we called "bummer" words, and we made a long list of words we were not going to use— words that were prejudicial, words that were full of fear, words that were full of hate. In another dictionary with an enormous number of pages, we wrote down positive words, happy words, joyous words, and we decided that these were the words we were going to use just for an experiment for about a week. It changed people's lives! All of a sudden things really happened. They started looking at things in a more positive way. People were responding to them in a more positive way just because they had changed the words they were using.

I am very concerned about this process of change and this process of growth, and I think that all change involves a disintegration of where you are at and a reintegration of something new, a breaking down of what you are presently believing and a re-creation, an allowing in, of new things. And so we are doing things like tasting and touching and feeling. Another thing—I'm giving people mirrors, and I say, "Look at yourself, but I mean really *look* at yourself." For five minutes they stare into that mirror and, of course, there is an awful lot of giggling. People don't know how to look at themselves—so they titter and laugh. And then I say, "Put your mirror down and tell me what you saw." They start describing themselves, and it's amazing how little they see. Then I go round the group, and I say, "Let's add and tell them what else there is." And people start saying,

"There are little lines by your eyes that are so beautiful . . . . I love the curve of your lips . . . . You have beautiful hands . . . ." All of a sudden you find out how little you do see. This is a growing process, a becoming process, and as you grow and become, then will those in your environment grow and become because you can give them all the things that you see and touch and feel and smell and know, the new world you have become aware of.

The phenomenon of change, then, occurs only when we get out of our mind, the way we are now, and move into raw experience. If I don't say anything else, that's the one thing I feel the most strongly about. Change will occur when we get out of our minds and into raw experience. You can talk about it forever; you can lie on the analyst's couch until you are blue in the face, but until you get out and *do* something, you will not know who you are. And so to be is to do, and that's one of the most important things. That may mean all kinds of things. It may mean, for instance, getting parents involved in a good course in learning theory. How does a child learn? Why not teach parents learning theory? If this is what you are going to be doing in the classroom, why not let the parent know what you are doing, how you are doing it, what are the best techniques, and then teach them what *they* should be doing—instead of this great gap, this mystery between school and the home. Teach the parent how to teach the child. I would love it if we could train parents as paraprofessional personnel and bring them into the schools. Let them see what they can do. Help them learn techniques and then work together really as a team. But this can only be done if we don't judge, if we recognize the need of all individuals, and if we remember that we are not gods. We are guides—we are not gods. And we must realize that even a maladjustment is an adjustment, so we don't condemn people for maladjustment. We help them. I remember one mother—and I shall never get her face out of my mind—who came into the office and said, "Now I know why I was given three blind children. That is because God was sure that I was the one who would be able to take it and help them. Of all the mothers in the world, God chose me to have three blind children because I would be able to help them." If she believed that and if she could function and bring up three beautiful kids, get off it, man, if you have the urge to say to her, "What nonsense! God didn't choose you. Let's be realistic, Mrs. Jones." She did a damned good job with those three kids. All three of them are in a university right now.

We must act on our belief, then, that each person has dignity—and start to treat parents as if they are human beings with dignity—knowing that each person has to find his own path. Your way is not my way, and there have never been two parents who have had exactly the same way to go. They must find their own way, and then you must guide them along that way. Give them reinforcement. Help them.

Castaneda's book, *Teachings According to Don Juan,* has a beautiful quotation about paths. The book is about an old Yaqui Indian of great wisdom who says:

Each path is only one of a million paths. Therefore, you must always keep in mind that a path is only a path. If you feel that you must not follow it, you need not stay with it under any circumstances. Any path is only a path. There is no affront to yourself or others in dropping it if that is what your heart tells you to do. But your decision to keep on the path or leave it must be free of fear or ambition or hate. I warn you: look at every path closely and deliberately. Try it as many times as you think necessary. Then ask yourself and yourself alone one question. It is this: Does this path have heart? All paths are the same. They all lead nowhere. They are paths going through the brush or over the brush or under the brush. Does this path have a heart is the only question. If it does, then the path is good. If it doesn't, it is of no use. Both paths lead nowhere but one has heart and the other doesn't. One makes for a joyful, productive journey. As long as you follow it, you are one with it, but the other will make you curse your life and die of loneliness.[8]

Working with parents involves the following things: the cognitive, certainly, the head, and the manipulation of knowledge. Parents need facts, and we are the only ones who can give them. And, secondly, the psychomotor—they need to be put into action. They are productive, exciting, intelligent human beings, and we need to use them in this way. And, thirdly, we need to be concerned about the affective, and that is the emotional reaction all along the way.

I am ending this paper with another man's thoughts on changing our existence. Written by Joseph Zinker, it is one of those precious things I've found in the past few years. He is at the Gestalt Institute in Cleveland, and he ends his paper, "On Public Knowledge and Personal Relevance,"[9] in this way:

If the man in the street were to pursue personal knowledge, what kind of guiding thoughts would he come up with about changing his existence? He would perhaps discover that his brain is not yet dead and that his body has not dried up and that no matter where he is right now, he is still the creator of his own destiny. And he can change this destiny by taking his one decision to change seriously, by fighting his petty resistance against change, by learning more about his mind, by trying out behavior which fits his real needs, by carrying out concrete acts rather than conceptualizing and talking about them, by practicing to hear and see and feel as if he has never known these senses before, by creating something with his own hands without demanding perfection, by picking out ways in which he behaves in a self-defeating manner, by listening to the words that he utters to his wife and his kids, by listening to the words and looking into the eyes of those who speak to him, by learning to respect the process of his own creative endeavors, and by having faith that they will get him there some day, and by engaging in collective activities with his neighbors and his friends which are designed to build both their mutual efforts. He must remind himself, however, that no change takes place without getting your hands dirty, and no change takes place without suffering, and no change takes place without some conflict. But he is not afraid. There are no formulae and no books to memorize for this process.

I only know this. I exist. I am. I am here. I am becoming. I make my life, and nobody else makes it for me. I must face my own shortcomings, my own mistakes, and my own transgressions. No one can suffer my own non-being as I do. But tomorrow is another day, and I must decide to leave my bed and live again. And if I fail, I don't have the comfort of blaming you or life or God.

NOTES

1. Herbert Otto, *Explorations in Human Potentialities* (Springfield, Ill.: Charles C. Thomas, 1966); Herbert Otto and John Mann (eds.), *Ways of Growth: Approaches to Expanding Awareness* (New York: Viking, 1969); Herbert Otto, *Guide to Developing Your Potential* (New York: Charles Scribner's Sons, 1967).

2. Pierre Teilhard de Chardin, *The Phenomenon of Man* (New York: Harper & Row, 1959).

3. Antoine de Saint Exupery, *Wind, Sand and Stars* (New York: Harcourt, Brace & World, 1940).

4. Albert J. Solnit and Mary H. Stark, "Learning with Teachers," *Children* 14, no. 1 (January-February 1967), 19-24; Albert J. Solnit and Morris Green, "The Pediatric Management of the Dying Child, Part II: The Child's Reaction to the Fear of Dying," *Perspectives in Child Development*, eds. Albert J. Solnit and Sally Provence (New York: International Universities Press, 1963), 217-228; Albert J. Solnit, "Psychologic Considerations in the Management of Deaths in Pediatric Hospital Services, I. The Doctor and the Child's Family," *Pediatrics* 24 (1959), 106-112.

5. Clara Claiborn Park, *The Siege* (New York: Harcourt, Brace, Jovanovich, 1967).

6. Virginia Woolf, *Flush: A Biography* (New York: Harcourt Brace Jovanovich, 1933).

7. Buckminster Fuller, *Ideas and Integrities* (New York: Prentice-Hall, 1963).

8. Carlos Castaneda, *Teachings of Don Juan: A Yaqui Way of Knowledge* (Berkeley: University of California Press, 1968).

9. Joseph Zinker, "On Public Knowledge and Personal Revelation," *Explorations* (April 1968).

Ten

Legislation

When Public Law 88-164 was signed by President Kennedy in 1963, the term "learning disabilities" was not included in the definition of the handicapped. The closest reference to it was "crippled and other health impaired that require special education." As a result no allotment in the federal appropriations was made for learning disabilities; however, the U.S. Office of Education allotted some funds for research and personnel training under the authorization for "crippled and other health impaired."

1969 was a historic year in the field of learning disabilities. It was in that year that Congress enacted the Learning Disabilities Act. The major sponsor of the bill was Senator Ralph Yarborough of Texas. His report at the ACLD Conference in 1969, reprinted here, was quite influential; in it he presents the history of congressional support for handicapped children as well as some of his own philosophy.

In the second selection, Willeta Silva, Chairman of the Legislative Committee of ACLD, John Forsythe, legal council to Senator Yarborough, and Frederick J. Weintraub of the Council for Exceptional Children present their points of view on legislation and on the implementation of programs for children with learning disabilities. These two presentations are actually historical documents since they present the beginnings of federal legislation for learning-disabled children.

The Measure of a Society

RALPH YARBOROUGH

It is an honor to have this opportunity to speak to the Sixth Annual International Conference of the Association for Children with Learning Disabilities (ACLD). I did not accept the invitation with any delusions that I could bring any expertise to this problem. I came, rather, to talk of ways that we can work together to obtain the federal appropriations so necessary for full treatment of this problem.

In those rare instances when we have time to think of our civilization, we ask ourselves: What are we building here? There is a story concerning some future anthropologist returning to search through the artifacts of our civilization to try and figure out what it was all about. If this anthropologist, in the distant future, while sifting through the ruins of our civilization, picks up a Coke bottle, an electric razor, a can of spray deodorant, and a videotape of last Tuesday's television shows, what would he really know about us? What is the mark of our civilization? I am sure we all agree that we need to define this civilization as more than just the admitted material success of our society. One important way to do this is to define our progress in terms of how we treat people, or how we behave toward people who are in trouble and in need of assistance. How do we treat them in our society? Do we disdain and mock them? Do we, with some embarrassment, turn our backs and pretend that their pain and sorrow do not exist or are not our concern? Do we face these problems and accept them as our own and set up means to solve them?

Most of us in this audience probably can recall experiences in which youngsters who did not learn in school, for whatever reason, were treated badly and were almost outcasts, receiving no special assistance or help. The degree to which we have advanced as a civilization is that we see less and less of that type of treatment of our fellow man, and we do indeed make a genuine effort to help.

Recently I had the pleasure and honor of being a host for the second birthday party of the Bureau of Education for the Handicapped. The bureau was established in the Office of Education by Congress—despite the opposition of the Secretary of Health, Education, and Welfare—to administer and to give leadership to programs to help handicapped children. I am proud to be one of the original sponsors and supporters of the bureau and of the programs it administers. One of the reasons that the problems of children with learning disabilities have received increased attention recently is because of the priority placed on this area by the first annual report of the National Advisory Committee on Handicapped

From the *Proceedings* of the Sixth Annual Conference of the ACLD, *Progress in Parent Information, Professional Growth, and Public Policy*. Fort Worth, Texas (March 6–8, 1969), pp. 33–38.

Children. The Advisory Committee recommended that the problems of children with learning disabilities were so important that they justified special attention and special consideration by Congress. As you well know, these children are often hard to define as a group, and the Advisory Committee itself went to great lengths to suggest a definition. I have used the definition of this group of experts in developing the *Children with Learning Disability Act of 1969*, which I introduced February 28, 1969.

It has been possible for children with learning disabilities to participate to some extent in the federal programs designed in the last few years to increase educational opportunity for handicapped children, but these efforts are not comprehensive enough to provide a full-scale attack on the problem. It might surprise you to know, however, that it is not only children with learning disabilities who find themselves in this position. For example, less than one-half the nation's school districts offer special services for retarded children. As I pointed out on the floor of the Senate early this month, there are between five and six million American children, not including those with learning disabilities, who require special classes, treatment for speech and hearing disorders, or other special-education approaches to their handicapping conditions. In the most recent statistics available to us from the state education agencies, how many children, of this 5.5 million children, do we find who are receiving the special education they need—five million? four million? three million? You are too optimistic. The answer is two million, or under 40 percent. When we add to the 5.5 million children included in the present definition of handicapped the millions of children with learning disabilities, we realize that perhaps 20 percent of our school children need special education, but that only about 4 percent are receiving any special assistance. In 1966, Congress created the National Advisory Committee on Handicapped Children in the Bureau of Education for the Handicapped. At the same time, Congress passed a program which would give grants to the states for the initiation, expansion, and improvement of educational programs designed to meet the special needs of handicapped children. These three features became Title VI of the Elementary and Secondary Education Act. This title, also called the Education for the Handicapped Act, was more than a collection of several new programs—it was a symbol of a national concern for handicapped children. It was a statement of policy. In effect, Congress said: "We recognize that the handicapped child and his parents have not been getting the full benefit of our educational system, and we feel that it is a national priority to do something about it. We must aid the local schools and the states in meeting this challenge."

In the time that has passed since November 1966, there has been a tremendous surge of interest within the national government, in both the legislative and the executive branches, in developing educational programs for handicapped children. In 1967, we extended and expanded the authority under which the Bureau of Education for the Handicapped makes grants for fellowships, institutes, and other training activities designed to provide teachers and other specialists to work with handicapped children. In 1969, $30 million will be used to support these training activities. Over $1 million of this sum, including $60,000 at the University of Texas, will be spent on pilot-training projects in the area of learning disabilities. We have also extended and expanded the basic-research authority for education of the handicapped, which will provide some $14 million this year. Again, as a specific example, Dr. Empress Zedler, at Southwest Texas State College, and Dr. John Carter, at the University of Houston, will be conducting research supported by this program, on the learning behavior of neurologically impaired children.

In addition to these programs, Congress passed legislation creating new programs to develop regional resource centers, centers and services for deaf-blind children, and authorized two new programs—one for recruiting young people into the worthwhile activity of teaching handicapped children, and the other for providing information to parents about services available for their children. Another new program, which I know has had an impact on the lives of children with learning disabilities, is the provision of Title III of the Elementary and Secondary Education Act which specifies that at least 15 percent of the funds available to the states under that program must be spent on special projects and programs for handicapped children. This new provision has provided over $20 million this year for such programs, and a number of these projects have been designed to meet the needs of children with learning disabilities.

I can't tell you how wise I think it is to begin programs at the preschool level. As you may know, I co-sponsored the Handicapped Children's Early Education Assistance Act last fall, so that we could really provide an impetus to this developing preschool activity. With this new program we will be able to support about twenty-five model programs this year, using the $1 million which has been appropriated primarily for planning activities. In the next few years we hope to bring this up to one hundred model programs so that school districts all over the country will be able to see first-rate preschool programs which they can use as models for developing their own efforts.

To get back to Title III of the Elementary and Secondary Education Act, almost every state is either moving ahead or planning a project in the learning-disabilities area. In Bay City, Texas, there is a project in which children with learning difficulties will receive diagnostic and evaluative services, and in which a number of in-service training programs will be conducted for their teachers. A number of other examples could be mentioned—including a project of the independent school district in Greenville, Texas, where five school districts are establishing a program for children with language disabilities—but perhaps this is enough to give you a flavor of what is going on in the use of these new federal-program funds. Similar innovative projects are being carried on under Title VI, where children with learning disabilities have been served if they meet the criteria of the "other health impaired" definition in that legislation. For example, Okmulgee County, Oklahoma, has had a highly rated in-service training program for the teachers in that district. Local resources have been well used—pediatricians, neurologists, psychiatrists, the staff at Central State College, and the local council of your ACLD organization, which arranged transportation for children with learning problems so that actual materials and methods could be demonstrated, rather than just talking about "how to do it."

So, you can see that there has been some progress toward fulfilling our commitment to the nation's handicapped children, and next year yet another new resource will be employed. In the recent revision of the Vocational Education Act, we specified that 10 percent of the funds under that act must be spent for special projects to benefit the handicapped child. As you know, special education has been concentrated on the elementary program, and now, with this preschool program being developed, and junior- and senior-high-school programs being strengthened by the Vocational Education Program, there is hope for a full-range educational program for all children—those with handicaps as well as the majority who are not handicapped.

These steps, however, are not enough; they are only samples to whet the appetite of those of us who wish to provide more effective and more comprehensive services to youngsters with learning disabilities and to their parents. One of the great satisfactions—in fact, the greatest of all satisfactions—of being a senator is that the position often gives a unique opportunity, a chance to act for the common good and to see to it that things are accomplished that could not have otherwise been accomplished. I had the beginnings of that feeling on February 28 when I introduced the *Children with Learning Disabilities Act of 1969*, which was designed to provide for special programs for children with learning disabilities. Now I want you to help me pass it, so that we will feel together that we have done something worthwhile.

This bill will provide the Commissioner of Education, and through him, the Bureau of Education for the Handicapped, with three new authorities:

- resources which will enable him to make grants and contracts to carry out programs of research and related activities, surveys, and demonstrations specifically related to the education of children with learning disabilities
- support for professionals or advanced training for educational personnel who are teaching or preparing to be teachers of children with learning disabilities, or to support the training for persons who are preparing to be supervisors of teachers for such personnel
- resources for support for developing and operating model centers for improvement of education of children with learning disabilities

The centers I see developing will:

- provide testing and educational evaluation to identify children with learning disabilities who have been referred to such centers
- develop and conduct model programs designed to meet the special educational needs of such children
- assist the appropriate educational agencies or professional organizations and institutions in making such model programs available to other children with learning disabilities.

It is my belief that through expanded research efforts we can find more effective methods and materials that will improve the education of these children. Through supporting training we can provide that supply of trained personnel without which all educational programs are impossible, and by establishing model centers we can demonstrate the best of current practice and provide the means by which others can emulate these good practices.

These three programs, taken together—*research, personnel training,* and *service*—will pave the way for bringing the area of learning disabilities into full partnership with other special-education programs. To accomplish these goals, I am asking Congress to authorize $12 million dollars for the fiscal year ending June 30, 1971; $10 million dollars for the fiscal year ending June 30, 1972; and $31 million dollars for each of the succeeding fiscal years, and prior to July 1, 1975.

I believe that such a bill is necessary to provide that degree of focused attention and concern from the federal government that will allow us to develop a meaningful educational breakthrough in this area. It is something I think you who are parents of these children deserve—you who may have suffered feelings of self-incrimination, worry, remorse, and guilt, even though you have worked so hard and sacrificed so much. Above all, it will help the children become more effective citizens of the future, because it will help them to get their fair chance.

This new bill will add to our increasing resources for handicapped children. The gradual growth of federal support in the area of education of the handicapped from 1958—when the first teacher-training support bill was passed, providing less than $1 million—through 1965—when about $30 million was available—has been accelerated into rapid gains in funding in the last two years. Adding together the sums from the new Vocational Education Bill; the 15 percent of Title III of the Elementary and Secondary Education Act; the grants to state-operated schools for the handicapped under Title I of the Elementary and Secondary Education Act; plus the training and research programs and the new smaller programs, such as the deaf-blind and the early education bill; with the $29.25 million for Title VI; we come to approximately $150 million, which will be available to the colleges, universities, and state- and local-education agencies in the fiscal year 1970, which will begin July 1. This has been growth for which all can be thankful, but in closer analysis we can see that there is much more to be done.

History of Authorization and Appropriation of Title VI Grants

The basic support program of the Title VI grants to the states has the following funding history.

In 1967, although $50 million was authorized, only about $2.5 million for planning and developing the state plans was appropriated; in 1968, the appropriation increased to $14.25 million for actual services, although $150 million was authorized; and in 1969, $29.25 million was appropriated, although $162,500,000 was authorized. This year, there is no increase in the administration's budget request, although the authorization for this program now is $200 million. The gap between that $29 million requested and $200 million authorized may help you focus on the difference between the congressional authorization process, the development of the president's budget, and, finally, the congressional-appropriation process. The authorizing committees provide the skeletons, the appropriation process fleshes out the bones. With over five million handicapped children, not counting the special class with learning disabilities, the basic national support program is providing only five dollars per child. If we consider all the types of funding I have mentioned together, we are still talking about only twenty-five dollars per child. As a man climbs a mountain, he looks at the peak ahead, and he may be overcome by looking at how far he has to go. He must also pause and look back to see how far he has come for some psychic nourishment. That is where we are; we can be justifiably proud of the increasing national commitment to education for the handicapped, and at the same time, somewhat awed by what is ahead. And we should be humiliated by how little has been appropriated to do what Congress has already authorized to be done. Every one of us must take an active part in this climb. You have some friends in Washington and that is a good beginning, but we cannot legislate and urge more funds unless it is clear that those of you back home, in every community across the nation, will help us. Demand that the government be as concerned with the future of six to ten million handicapped children in America as it is with burning down villages in Viet Nam. This is a time when funds are scarce, yet we will spend our dollars on what our society demands—we will have money for what is important enough.

Perhaps in thinking about our anthropologist again you can see he will have a more complete evidence for the nature of our civilization, if he can come upon a picture of teachers working with children on their learning disabilities, or researchers trying to unlock the secrets of more effective learning, or a teacher trying to learn more about her craft and profession. If he sees these things, he will truly have a better portrait of what we are all about, he will see a compassionate, pragmatic society.

What do politicians really esteem most? The answer is, what they accomplish. We pose for pictures, put plaques on the wall, receive awards, eat at appreciation banquets, make speeches, brag on others and are bragged on, and, to the public, that may seem to be our life, or a big part of it. But that is the froth or foam, as transitory as the foam on a river in flood. The real measure of our lives is what we have done in office to improve the lot of our fellow man, to improve the quality of our civilization. To me, acts such as these to aid the handicapped are the real reason for our arduous exertions to grasp and retain the offices we hold. Without these goals, the legislative offices are better unfilled.

Legislation—Initiation and Implementation

WILLETTA SILVA
JOHN S. FORSYTHE
FREDERICK J. WEINTRAUB

Part I (Willetta Silva)

Billions for bombs and pennies for people. Senator Yarborough has eloquently identified the plight of the handicapped in this country and the need to enact legislation which will meet the needs of our children. The senator's words also underscore the concerns of the Association for Children with Learning Disabilities (ACLD)—the urgency to move ahead, service for that vast group of kindergarten children who flunk the sandbox curriculum, or who become the romper-room rejects. These children enter public schools with their birth certificates but without their birthrights.

The bill which the senator introduced on February 28, 1969, marks a milestone in ACLD legislative history and promises to serve children, for example, who are brain-injured and yet who cannot qualify for services because their disability cannot be proven. The intent of the bill is to provide for those children in the various states who begin their school years with the misdiagnosis of "immature" and then acquire in the secondary school, a different label—the slow learner. Many of our children somehow manage to move through the public schools, only to graduate ill-prepared and cheated of the opportunity to participate meaningfully in a democracy, which has inherent in its very structure, the mandate that every child shall be educated to his fullest capacity.

In order to spell out these concerns, our panel will attempt to present an analysis of the bill S.1190, explain the legislative processes which lead to the creation of a law, and highlight guidelines for effective state and local action in initiating state legislation.

Two events of 1968 pointed to the need to introduce specific legislation for children with learning disabilities: One was the adoption of a definition by the National Advisory Committee on Handicapped Children, and two was the priority recognition given by this committee for the need to secure funds for research and training for learning-disability children. *The First Annual Report of the National Advisory Committee on Handicapped Children* (January 31, 1968) recommended that:

Funds appropriated for research and training programs be substantially increased. Such additional funds, necessary to define and explore this new area,

From the *Proceedings* of the Sixth Annual Conference of the ACLD, *Progress in Parent Information, Professional Growth, and Public Policy.* Fort Worth, Texas (March 6–8, 1969), pp. 43–45.

should not be allocated at the expense of the pressing program needs in established areas.

When the legislative committee analyzed the limited amount of monies that previously have been spent in the areas of research and training, it became apparent that means must be secured whereby funds and services could be provided in proportion to the need. The procedures for accomplishing this goal have been the central issue of the legislative committee for the past months. Consideration has been given to the possibility of amending the statutes to include the term learning disabilities. However, this position would result in ACLD securing services at the "expense of the pressing program needs in established areas."

In consideration of this problem, the legislative strategy which would enable our children to enjoy a measure of the services now enjoyed by other categories of handicapped children is the creation of a separate authority. This authority would provide funds for training, research, and the establishment of model centers. The following is a description of the provisions contained in the proposed bill.

Section 1 provides that the Act may be cited as the "Children with Learning Disabilities Act of 1969."

Section 2 amends Title VI of the Elementary and Secondary Education Act of 1965 (which title may also be cited as the Education of the Handicapped Act) by redesignating Part E thereof (General Provisions) as Part F and inserting a new Part E, being section 611.

Subsection (a) of section 611 authorizes the Commissioner of Education to make grants to institutions of higher education, state education agencies, local educational agencies, and other public and private nonprofit educational and research agencies and organizations and to make contracts with any of such agencies and organizations in order to carry out special programs for children with special learning disabilities.

Three types of such programs are authorized:

1. He may make grants and contracts to support projects for research and related activities, surveys, and demonstrations relating to the education of children with learning disabilities.
2. He may make grants and contracts to provide professional or advanced training to teachers of children with learning disabilities and to educational personnel who are supervisors and teachers of such teachers or who are preparing to become supervisors and teachers of such teachers.
3. He may make grants and contracts to assist in the establishment and operation of model centers designed to improve the education of children with learning disabilities; such centers shall provide testing and educational evaluation services to children who have been referred to them, develop and conduct model educational programs designed to meet the needs of children with learning disabilities, and assist such

other educational agencies, organizations, and institutions as may be appropriate in establishing model programs for children with learning disabilities and in making the services of those programs available to such children.

Subsection (a) requires the commissioner to give special emphasis to projects designed to promote the adoption of new or improved educational ideas, practices, and techniques in dealing with, and creative approaches in meeting, the special educational needs of children with learning disabilities.

Subsection (b) requires the commissioner to seek to achieve an equitable geographical distribution, throughout the nation, of programs to train educational personnel to meet the needs of children with learning disabilities and of personnel trained to meet the needs of such children. Subsection (b) further requires the commissioner to encourage the establishment of a model center for children with learning disabilities in each of the states.

Subsection (c) provides that payments under the section will be made in accordance with regulations.

Subsection (d) defines the term "children with learning disabilities" as meaning those children who have a disorder in one or more of the basic psychological processes involved in understanding or using written or spoken language. Such disorder may manifest itself in imperfect ability to listen, think, speak, read, write, spell, or do arithmetic. Such disorder includes such conditions as perceptual handicaps, brain injury, minimal brain dysfunction, dyslexia, and developmental aphasia. The term does not include learning disabilities arising primarily from visual, hearing, or motor handicaps, from mental retardation, from emotional disturbance, or from environmental disadvantage.

Subsection (e) authorizes appropriations for fiscal years 1971 through 1975. For fiscal year 1971, $12 million is authorized; for fiscal year 1972, $20 million is authorized; and for each of the fiscal years 1973, 1974, and 1975, $31 million is authorized.

Part II (John S. Forsythe)

The United States Congress is composed of two bodies, the Senate and the House of Representatives. They have equal legislative functions and powers, except that only the House of Representatives may initiate revenue bills. The Senate is composed of one hundred members, two from each state, without regard to its population or area. The term of office of senators is six years, and one-third of the total Senate is elected every second year. The House of Representatives is composed of 435 members, who are elected every two years. The congressmen are elected from congressional districts which are roughly based on population.

There are about four main sources of ideas for the context of legislation.

- Most education legislation originates with the "executive communication." This is usually in the form of a letter from a member of the cabinet, the head of an independent agency, or even from the president himself, transmitting a draft of a proposed bill to the Speaker of the House and the president of the Senate. Many of these communications follow upon the president's state-of-the-union message which is delivered early in the congressional year.
- Another source is the congressional members themselves—through personal experience, election campaign promises, etc.
- A member's constituents—either as individuals or in groups—may transmit proposals to him in letters or petitions.
- A "draft bill" may be the result of a study made by a commission or committee of Congress or of the executive branch.

A member, or the staff, of a committee may obtain the services of the legislative counsel of the body involved in preparing a proposed bill. Any member of the House or Senate may introduce a bill, although the exact procedure varies somewhat in the House and Senate. The real work of Congress is done in the committees. It is in committee that the most intensive consideration is given to proposed legislation, and this is where the people are given an opportunity to be heard.

There are, at present, twenty standing committees in the House of Representatives and sixteen in the Senate. In addition, there are several standing joint committees of the two houses; the only one which may report legislation, however, is the Joint Committee on Atomic Energy, which reports identical bills to each body simultaneously. Each committee has jurisdiction over certain subject areas of legislation, and all bills affecting that area are referred to that committee. In the educational field, the most important committees are the Senate Labor and Public Welfare Committee, the House Education and Labor Committee, and the appropriations committees. The latter have separate jurisdiction over the matter of providing the necessary funds for all types of programs. Members rank in seniority on committees in accordance with the order of their appointment. The ranking majority member is automatically elected chairman. Most of the committees have several subcommittees which specialize in considering particular classifications of bills, depending on the subject matter involved.

Many bills are simply referred to committees and never receive any further attention. For major bills, though, the subcommittee will usually set dates for public hearings. The subcommittee will invite specified persons to testify, but others who are interested in testifying may write to the committee and request permission to testify. Permission is generally granted. Many witnesses submit prepared statements and then are available for questioning from members of the subcommittee. All these records are printed in the printed volumes of the committee hearings. After the conclusion of the hearings, the subcommittee meets in executive session, which is commonly known as "marking up" the bill. Here the various amendments are proposed and voted on. The subcommittee may decide to report the bill favorably to the full committee—with or without amendment—or unfavorably; or it may suggest that the bill be tabled. The bill is then taken up by the full committee, generally in its regular meeting, and the full committee can again vote to report out the bill, with or without amendment, or to table it. A committee report is prepared by the committee staff when the bill is reported out. This gives explanatory information concerning the legislation and contributes to the legislative history by establishing the intent of the committee on questions of definition and interpretation.

So far, I have talked in general terms about the congressional establishment. Now I think it might be interesting to take a typical bill and follow it through the process. Let us assume that we are working with an education bill and that it was proposed by the administration as a part of the president's education message. It was introduced in both houses by the chairmen of the respective committees and was referred to these committees for action. The House acted first, holding its subcommittee hearings, adding amendments, and reporting the bill out for floor consideration.

In the House of Representatives, there are many more bills reported out of committee than can be brought to active consideration before the House. In order to provide a "traffic cop," the House has established its Committee on Rules as the body which generally decides which legislation is to be considered, when it is to be considered, and under what terms. The best way, and the normal way, to reach the floor of the House is for the Committee on Rules to grant a special resolution or "rule" for its consideration. The Rules Committee establishes the time limitations for the House debate, and may limit floor amendments and waive points of order against the bill.

There are a great many technicalities involved in the consideration of a bill on the House floor which time will not permit us to cover here. Basically, the House can operate in two general styles—as the Committee of the Whole House, in which it has to have only a quorum of 100 members, instead of the normally required 218. Most of the detailed legislative work on the House floor is done while in the Committee of the Whole House. In this situation, debate is limited—as may have been prescribed by the Rules Committee—and the chairman and the ranking minority member of the committee which reported the measure divide this time up among their respective members.

Let's assume, then, that our bill has been given a rule by the Rules Committee, has been considered in the Committee of the Whole House, and finally has been approved with amendments by the House. At this point, technically, it becomes an "act," rather than a bill. It is then sent to the Senate for consideration.

In the Senate, the bill is referred to the appropriate standing committee, and it generally receives the same kind of consideration it did in the House —public hearings by the subcommittee, executive sessions by the subcommittee, and consideration by the full committee. In the Senate, the Majority Policy Committee has the right to decide the time at which a bill will be called up for debate, but in actuality, the procedure in the Senate in bringing a bill to the floor is much less formal and less complicated than it is in the House. Time will not permit me to describe in detail the Senate procedure, but it is generally arranged so as to give the senators a maximum of individual choice and authority.

Let us assume our bill has suffered some additional amendments and has now passed the Senate. Since the form in which it passed the Senate is not exactly the same as that in which it passed the House, it is necessary either for the House to agree to the Senate version or for the two houses to appoint a Conference Committee to iron out the differences. It is generally the custom to appoint as conferees on a particular bill the members of the subcommittees which handled it in the two houses. The conferees attempt to reach compromises which will be acceptable to both houses. Sometimes they find this impossible and must report back to their respective houses for further instructions. Usually, they do reach compromises, and generally these compromises are then accepted by both houses in final votes on the measure. It is then on its way to the president for his signature, which makes it into a law.

Part III (Frederick J. Weintraub)

Senator Ralph Yarborough of Texas has, at this conference, initiated a major federal attack on the problems of the learning-disabled child throughout the nation. While this moment is historic and should definitely assume our attention and support, we must remember to maintain the direction of our energies to that source of public enterprise having the prime responsibility for the education of children—state government.

In order to guide our work with state legislatures in the development of effective state legislation, there are four basic principles that we should keep in mind. The first is that legislation is the means by which the people establish basic public policy. The purpose of government in a democratic society is to reflect the will of the people. The people express their will in a republican manner (and I don't mean party) through their elected representatives in a system of balance of power between the legislative and administrative departments of the government. The legislature expresses the will of the people to the executive branch through legislation. For this reason legislation—whether it concerns itself with welfare, hospital benefits, farm produce, or special education—defines the boundaries of governmental responsibility in any particular area.

Since education in this country is a matter of public concern, it is defined through public policy or legislation. Therefore, whether we educators and parents like it or not, education is a political phenomenon. Perhaps we ought to define more clearly what we mean by the term "political phenomenon." I mean political in the sense that no matter what the question concerning education, there is always more than one correct answer; and when there is more than one alternative to select from we have a debatable issue. Any debatable issue must be resolved through compromise, or through the power of one side of the issue to suppress the other side of the issue. The process of determining public policy on issues where there is mixed sentiment is called politics. Learning disabilities is a very clear issue in this regard. All too often, groups coming before state legislatures advocating programs for the learning-disabled child disagree over whether the state legislation should create training programs for reading teachers, develop programs for learning-disabilities specialists, or provide for tuition for the learning-disabled child in private schools. And while this debate is going on, there are people who are suggesting that public funds could be better served by providing hot school lunches, lights on football stadiums, etc. Legislators are thus put in a position of sorting through these various issues to determine what best represents the will of the people.

This leads us to the third principle. In a democratic society public policy generally tends to represent the will of the majority. This becomes a reality when we realize that legislators are elected officials, who represent a constituency, and in order to maintain their positions, they must be responsible to their constituents. In such a system there is an inherent tendency for the minority always to suffer. One need only look at the long history of civil rights conflicts in this nation to see the difficulty that the democratic system has in coming to grips with these hard issues. Parallels can be drawn to the problems of the handicapped. To what degree can we convince the majority that it ought to extend substantial portions of its resources to help the minority?

One final principle offers us a solution to the previous one of the minority versus the majority, as handicapped children are one of the great American phenomenon along with motherhood, God, and apple pie. Special education and the problems of the handicapped are good politics. I've had legislators on the state and national level tell me repeatedly that they like the idea of supporting the handicapped because it offers good publicity and very little negative reaction. For this reason there has been a substantial increase in the last several years in the amount of legislation improving programs for the education of handicapped children. However, I think we need to make a distinction between expressions of public policy and the provision of financial resources to implement the programs. Most state and federal legislators have been willing to join forces in an area of partisan activity to seek authorizing support for programs for handicapped children. But, often these same friends cannot be found when it is time to vote for the dollar and the increased taxes necessary to support these programs.

In 1966 the Council for Exceptional Children, under a grant from the

United States Office of Education, undertook an analytic study of state legislation for handicapped children to gather all of the state laws concerning special education and to assess the relationship between laws and program development. While the final report of the study is not presently available, I would like to share with you four major findings regarding legislation, which our study uncovered, and which I think particularly relate to learning disabilities.

The first finding is that legislation must be designed to meet the uniquenesses of the state and local communities which it is to serve. All too often we develop sophisticated models in our wealthy suburban communities and then attempt to apply them to other sections of the country. Perhaps we can use the following as an example.

Recently it was estimated that if Glasgow, Montana, was selected as a central point, and a ring was drawn around that community, with a 100-mile radius (an area of 31,000 square miles), you would find a student population of approximately thirty thousand, or less than one pupil per square mile. Most of the people in that region are farmers, many of whom are Indians. On January 26, 1969, the temperature in that area was thirty-eight degrees below zero. If we are to provide services to learning-disabled children in this area, it is questionable whether a program model established in Montgomery County, Maryland, would have much success. First, we could predict that you would not be able to find one of the suggested members of the diagnostic team—you might need to travel three hundred miles over several mountain ranges to find a psychologist. Secondly, school districts would have difficulty hiring a reading specialist, or a learning-disability specialist, or whatever name we might use for that position, since it is doubtful whether such a person could be recruited to work in that area. Also, the cost of hiring such a person might be prohibitive for a small school district.

I'm afraid that the fact of the matter is that over half of the twenty thousand school districts in this country have a student population of less than five thousand and thus are representative of Glasgow. Sophisticated models, therefore, are not designed to meet the needs of the majority of students which we must serve. Also, we need to look not only at the rural question, but at the urban problem to see what relevance our designs for programs have to the urban sector. If we look at the great emphasis in learning disabilities on providing services through private facilities, one needs to ask about the relevance of such a private facility to the urban-ghetto core and the reality of whether this approach will ever provide effective services to ghetto children.

In addition, we need to ask about the sociological impact of the etiology aura of the program which we wish to provide. I think it is apparent that the learning-disabled concept and the concern which has been manifest is a middle-class phenomenon, and that most of our descriptions of adequate ameliorative services tend to reflect the criteria established by middle-class demands for upward mobility. I'm afraid that our concept of the normal and above-average child, who for some reason is having difficulty learning to read and therefore needs the services of a dozen or more highly skilled professionals, is foreign to many sectors of our nation.

Many may ask what relevance these different perspectives have to legislation. Well, it has relevance in regard to our original premise that legislation is the expression of public policy and is reflective of the demands of the people. We need to ask ourselves what the people are demanding and what kinds of services are appropriate under the circumstances in which the people live. Certainly we can see that legislation providing transportation to the learning-disabled in Rhode Island may be irrelevant to the transportation needs of learning-disabled children in Wyoming. I have seen cases where states have tried to adapt the legislation of another state to their own state, only to meet with disastrous results.

The second point I would like to make is that legislation must consider broader issues than just the psychoeducational needs of the child. All too often the great debates among professionals, and others, concerning the merits of various pieces of legislation center around what we should call the child. How shall we define him? Who shall provide the service? It is my feeling that these approaches tend to muddle the issue behind all legislation; in this case, it is the services we wish to provide for the child and the elements necessary to guarantee the development of such services. The debate on whether the child is brain injured, dyslexic, or learning disabled is not going to provide bus transportation to get him to the program, whatever the program may be. The fact of the matter is that these programs in most cases are going to be developed, housed, and administered in educational facilities. Thus, it is my bias that the more closely consistent the legislation is with the needs of the education community, the better chance we will have for effective program operation.

This leads us to the third point, which is that legislation must be designed to be administrable. We must find ways to write into our legislation those program elements and the other elements that are necessary to guarantee the effective administration of the program. This may mean the provision of transportation, construction, teacher training, etc. It also demands a factor which we often overlook, and that is visibility in program administration. In this sense, we go back to our earlier concern about the problems of the minority. Although public policy is achieved, often programs are severely neglected because they are not a priority to an overburdened administration. We need to consider whether competent administration is provided at the state level for our program and whether such administration has the viability and authority to present adequately its needs to the legislature.

Finally, legislation must be in tune with political and financial realities. We must remember that we live in a complex world, a world that has many priorities, and although the problem of the learning-disabled may be a foremost priority in our minds, it is not a major concern of our nation. Thus, at this time when strife is facing our cities, when other activities are demanding great sums of the public resource, and when the taxpayer is raising his arms and saying that there's a limit to what he can pay, we need to consider how we can develop our programs in a manner that will take into account these political and financial realities.

I don't mention this to discourage you, but I do believe that when we come before a legislature with a proposal to provide a 1 to 8 teacher-pupil ratio for 25 percent of the school population, and place a figure in the multimillion-dollar category, we're being unrealistic. The chance of getting approval is questionable. Yet, experience has shown that if we can establish clear-cut priorities on a graduated basis, we can achieve tomorrow the program which we are building today. This is difficult because it speaks to you of parent delay. It says, provide a program for my neighbor's child so that my child may have one tomorrow, or that my child's child may have a program in the future. But this is the reality of change within our society, and it is one which I think we must deal with in order to achieve adequate programs for the learning-disabled child.

STUDIES IN BRITISH ART

RICHARD NORMAN SHAW

ANDREW SAINT

Published for the Paul Mellon Centre
for Studies in British Art (London) Ltd
by
Yale University Press
New Haven and London
1976

Library of Congress catalog card number: 75-4333

International standard book number: 0-300-01955-6

Designed by John Nicoll and set in Monophoto Baskerville

Filmset and printed in Great Britain by
BAS Printers Limited, Wallop, Hampshire

Published in Great Britain, Europe, Africa, the Middle East,
India and South-east Asia by
Yale University Press, Ltd., London.
Distributed in Latin America by Kaiman & Polon, Inc., New York City;
in Australasia by Book & Film Services, Artarmon, N.S.W., Australia
in Japan by John Weatherhill, Inc., Tokyo.

PREFACE

'IN a few years they will be saying "What on earth were these old fogies up to?" ' Thus did Norman Shaw predict future reaction to his memory, when towards the end of his lifetime Richard Phené Spiers tried to prepare a book about his architectural work. 'Spiers worked hard upon the project,' says Hector Bolitho, 'but Shaw's realism discouraged him and the project was dropped.'[1] It is a humbling reminder to a biographer if his subject would have thought little about it. This book, therefore, is meant to inform and entertain rather than to pretend to profundities. This is certainly what Shaw would have wished; his comment to Spiers should rightly stand as its subtitle.

Because Shaw was so self-effacing, the full memoir of his life which many close contemporaries might have written never appeared. After the obituaries, there was nothing for nearly thirty years. It was left to the aged but energetic Sir Reginald Blomfield to fill the gap with a short biography published in 1940, when the 'old fogey' was almost forgotten.

Much of the stock of Blomfield's book was destroyed during the war, so it has long been hard to find. Rather like Lethaby's fine life of Philip Webb, it attempted to blend personal recollection with an objective assessment of Shaw's stature as an architect, but of the two books it looked out of date the sooner. Indeed Nikolaus Pevsner, a young German art historian of the new school and an admirer of the *Modernismus* against which Blomfield had often fought, immediately wrote a long review arguing for Shaw's achievement as a precursor of modernity in his earlier domestic works, and not, as Blomfield conceived him, as a great classicist *manqué*.[2] By now, this attitude in turn is looking a little out of date. If the reader of this book feels obliged to choose between these interpretations, he will find that Shaw's own sentiments, at least over his last twenty-five years, tended towards Blomfield's view of the matter. But he need not make such a choice; this is meant to be firstly a work of biography, and only secondarily one of art history.

The true deficiency of Blomfield's book is not its interpretation, but its lack of original personal information on Shaw. This stems from the way it came to be written. In the late 1930s, Shaw's son Robert sent his long set of invaluable but disconnected notes on his father's life to Sir Reginald, asking for advice and help in their publication. Eventually this turned into Blomfield's own project, Robert Shaw generously agreeing to let him make free use of the family notes. As a result, the book gives the impression that Blomfield knew and understood Shaw better than he really did; in fact he was not among Shaw's intimate friends. The best chapters discuss Blomfield's contemporaries, the Shaw pupils, whereas he makes mistakes, some out of bigotry, about Shaw's earlier achievements and ideas. Still, Blomfield committed to paper what others had only intended, and did so with all his customary clarity, trenchancy and Latinity.

My own emphasis is naturally different. I have tried most of all to see Shaw as his contemporaries saw him, in fact to fit him into his complicated and changing architectural context. Therefore I have quoted as freely as I have been able to do (with slight changes in punctuation) from his letters, which more than anything give the flavour of the man and his attitudes towards his work. Some may think that I have dwelt too little upon Shaw's wide but undefined architectural influence. There are several reasons for this. First is the simple one of length; secondly, in default of biographies of other late Victorian architects, it is not yet easy to write about this influence accurately; lastly, an architect as fertile, personal, and engaging as Shaw should surely be judged as far as possible by the best contemporary lights, not according to the morals and achievements of succeeding generations. Wren was an only briefly influential architect until the late Victorian 'Wrenaissance', but we do not think the worse of him because Palladianism supplanted his school.

The debts I owe for help are so extensive that I have felt it best to acknowledge many people in the list of works, under the individual buildings for which they have given information or assistance. Of the many others who have helped generally I must pick out first Miss Marjorie Campbell Shaw and Mr Bryan Shaw for their unfailing help, and for letting me borrow and use Robert Shaw's manuscript notes and abstract of his father's account books, together with other material and photographs in their possession; and Peter Howell, who first taught me, as he has many others, to appreciate Victorian architecture properly, for his unflagging encouragement and his suggestions at every stage. Jules Lubbock read most of the manuscript and made many sage comments. Of others who improved parts of it I must mention Jill Allibone, Peter Bezodis, Alan Crawford, Jill Franklin, Tom Greeves, Anthony Quiney and Clive Wainwright, who all assisted in other ways as well. Thanks for their help must go to Gordon Barnes, Susan Beattie, Sir John Betjeman, John Brandon-Jones, Helen Brooks, Stephen Croad of the National Monuments Record, Michael Darby, Roger Dixon, Margaret Floyd, Mark Girouard, John Greenacombe, Martin Harrison, Ted Hubbard, Paul Joyce, David Low, Christopher Monkhouse, Christine Harding and Constance Parker of the R.A. Library, Brian and Dorothy Payne, Leo Plendello, John O'Callaghan, Margaret Richardson and Joanna Symonds of the R.I.B.A. Drawings Collection, Godfrey Rubens, Peter Silsby, Gavin Stamp, Anthony Symondson, Nicholas Taylor, Robert Thorne, and last but far from least Lynne Walker. The University of Essex kindly supplied me with a couple of small grants while I was in their employ; I must thank all in the Department of Art there for their humour and help. The plans have been drawn by John Sambrook, Alan Fagan and Roy Bowles, for whose time and care I am most grateful. I must also acknowledge special permission from the Chairman of the Liverpool Cathedral Building Committee to use and quote from their archives, and the kindness of Lord Inchiquin of Richards Castle and Mr Edward Holland-Martin of Overbury Court for letting me borrow the Shaw letters in their possession. For access to and use of private diaries and papers I am grateful to Mrs Nancy Strode (J. C. Horsley), John Munday of the National Maritime Museum (E. W. Cooke) and Mrs Claire Ridley (Lutyens letters).

Finally, two special acknowledgments must be made. One is to Mark Girouard and Paul Thompson, whose respective books on the Victorian Country House and on William

Butterfield have transformed our understanding of the period's architecture and have served me throughout as models. The other is to the Mellon Centre, without whose financial aid the publication of this book would have been, in these hard times, impossible.

Andrew Saint,
July 1975.

CONTENTS

ix

LIST OF ILLUSTRATIONS

PHOTOGRAPHIC ACKNOWLEDGMENTS

Gordon Barnes 41, 212, 227, 236, 237. Mrs J. E. Benson 244, 245. Philip Binns 40. Bromley Public Library 15, 112. Miss Helen Brooks 132, 133. Convent of Bethany 130, 131. Cookridge Hospital 43. Country Life 21, 23, 33, 64, 84, 158, 159, 161, 162. Greater London Council 116, 120, 126, 257, 285, 286. Mrs Greenleaves 239, 242. Martin Harrison 31, 101, 102, 103, 104, 105, 106, 108, 109, 255 (and photographs of R.A. drawings). St Margaret's Church Ilkley 226. Lord Inchiquin 231. A. F. Kersting 280, 287. All Saints' Church, Leek 232. Leek Public Library 61. Liverpool University 69. National Monuments Record 35, 42, 45, 46, 48, 49, 50, 77, 78, 98, 114, 140, 147, 156, 157, 165, 174, 175, 180, 182, 194, 197, 199, 200, 209, 210, 218, 220, 221, 228, 234, 240, 243, 256, 261, 267, 268, 269, 270, 271, 284, 290. National Portrait Gallery 4. Mrs Magnus Osborn 95. Lord Ponsonby 59. Mrs G. L. Y. Radcliffe 248, 249. Royal Academy 18 (and for permission to publish other R.A. drawings). Royal Geographical Society 118, 119. R.I.B.A. 12, 13, 60, 97, 115, 217. Donald Scougall 214. Bryan Shaw 1, 2, 3, 80, 81, 96, 138, 141, 143, 167, 168, 176, 177, 184, 186, 187, 188, 190, 191, 192, 193, 211, 238, 246, 262, 272, 274, 288, 289, 291. Mrs Nancy Strode 20, 22, 94. Victoria & Albert Museum 11, 136, 171, 204, 224, 229. Revd. M. Vonberg 254. Barry Woodcock 5, 195.

KEY TO PLANS

B	Bedroom		bp	Butler's Pantry
Bal	Ballroom		bu	Butler's Room
Bf	Breakfast Room		c	Cupboard
Bil	Billiard Room		ck	Cook's Room
Bou	Boudoir		cl	Cloakroom
Bs	Business Room		d	Dressing Room
D	Dining Room		dr	Drying Room
Dr	Drawing Room		dy	Dairy
Dre	Dressing Room		g	Gun Room
G	Gallery		h	Hoist
H	Hall		hk	Housekeeper's Room
L	Library		k	Kitchen
M	Morning Room		l	Larder
S	Studio		li	Lift
Sal	Saloon		ms	Men Servants' Rooms
Sch	Schoolroom		org	Organ
Sit	Sitting Room		p	Pantry
Sm	Smoking Room		s	Store
St	Study		sc	Scullery
T	Tea Room		sh	Servants' Hall
To	Tower		si	Silver Room
a	Area		sr	Strong Room or Safe
b	Bathroom		sy	Servery
bo	Boots		ws	Women Servants' Rooms

LIST OF ABBREVIATIONS

A	*The Architect*
A.A.	Architectural Association
AAJ	*Architectural Association Journal*
ABJ, ABN	*Architect and Builders' Journal/News*
AR	*Architectural Review*
B	*The Builder*
BA	*The British Architect*
BJ (AE/AR)	*Builders' Journal (and Architectural Engineer/Record)*
BN	*Building News*
CEAJ	*Civil Engineer and Architect's Journal*
CEO	Crown Estates Office
CL	*Country Life*
DEB	H. Muthesius, *Die Englische Baukunst in der Gegenwart* (1900)
DEH	H. Muthesius, *Das Englische Haus* (3 vols., 1904–5)
DNB	*Dictionary of National Biography*
E	*The Ecclesiologist*
Eccl. Comms	Ecclesiastical Commissioners (now Church Commissioners)
Fabs	Foreign Architectural Book Society
FG	*Furniture Gazette*
HBB	Heaton, Butler & Bayne
HO	Home Office files in P.R.O.
ICBS	Incorporated Church Building Society
L.C.C.	London County Council
MBW	Metropolitan Board of Works
MEPOL	Metropolitan Police files in P.R.O.
P.R.O.	Public Record Office
R.A.	Royal Academy
R.I.B.A.	Royal Institute of British Architects
RIBAJ	*Journal of Royal Institute of British Architects*
R.I.J.	Rolled iron joist
RNS	Richard Norman Shaw
V & A	Victoria & Albert Museum

acc.bk.	account book (Robert Shaw's abstract)
ack	acknowledgment due to
attrib.	attributed
c	cost
cl	client(s)
ctr(s)	contractor(s)
c/w	clerk of works
d	date
des.	designed
dr	drawings (provenance of)
exec.	executed
exh.	exhibited
ill.	illustrated
insc.	inscribed
m	materials
r	references
reprd.	reproduced
st/drs	stone dressings
t	tender
t/h	tile-hanging
$\frac{1}{2}$tmb	half-timbering

Apprenticeship

The Pencil Speaks the Tongue of Every Land

Motto, *Architectural Sketches from the Continent*

DEDICATION AND PUPILLAGE

WITH the burial of Welby Pugin at Ramsgate on 21st September 1852, one phase of the Gothic Revival in England came to a close. For the mourners who witnessed the interment in Pugin's own church of St Augustine, the only building for which funds and time sufficed to see his principles perfectly applied, there was much that was pathetic about the occasion. In life he had been ridiculed and pilloried; now, out of it, his death was overshadowed by the Duke of Wellington's. Pugin's style of work, emotionally ennervating and physically strenuous, had been admired but also feared by his contemporaries. His fanatical Catholic evangelism had seen his belief in Gothic as the only true style for architecture through to triumph; but it brought hostility to his career, and indifference to his troubles, illness and madness. Towards the end there was a little relenting. During his last year, Pugin was granted a government pension, the poor recompense of a public that had appropriated his ideas and skills while shunning the man and his religion. When he died, the injustice was laid bare. 'I have passed my life', Pugin had declared, 'in thinking of fine things, studying fine things, designing fine things, and realizing very poor ones.'[1] A great architect was being laid to rest in a fine building: should not many more works of like quality have followed from his pencil?

So much was in the minds of those who attended Pugin to his vault. It was known to Sir Charles Barry, representative of older modes of belief and design, incongruously carrying a candle in homage to the decorator on whom he had relied to the last at the new Houses of Parliament. It was known to Hardman, Crace, Bury, Myers, and Lambert, subordinates in the guild of church builders that Pugin built up from nothing, artisans and apprentices once, but now original craftsmen and leaders of the new ecclesiological profession. It was known, too, to two students of architecture, who having come to see Pugin's masterpiece on this very day, became witnesses to his funeral and memory. He had had few architectural pupils, and they were of modest talent; his true pupils were the whole rising generation of English architects. There, as its unconscious representatives, stood a young, unnoticed pair, William Eden Nesfield and Richard Norman Shaw.[2]

To look at, they offered an instructive comparison. A stocky youth of merely seventeen, Eden Nesfield had close-cropped fair hair, a fleshy face, and distinctive liquid eyes that in later years were to stop the quick thickening of his features from degenerating

I

into an appearance of mere flabbiness. Confidence and impetuosity of character already lent him dynamism, charm, and the independence of early maturity. His companion, Richard Shaw, was four years older, a wide gap at that age in close friendship, and testimony to Nesfield's assurance. He stood over six feet, and possibly had more to grow: a tall, mild-featured creature with ample hair brushed off the forehead and round the ears (ill. 1). His relaxation of limb might have passed for foppishness but more probably arose from a boyish unselfconsciousness. With Nesfield, Shaw shared a merriment of eye. Style, wit, and elegance they had in common; in observing and intuiting they were both fast. In other respects, their friendship was founded upon temperamental differences.

Compared to Nesfield's, the family background from which Shaw emerges is opaque, to say the least.[3] In his mixed Irish and Scottish ancestry, one can see his particular blend of buoyant wit with discipline, and of creativity with organization. The businesses of his two grandfathers, on his mother's side an Edinburgh notary, on his father's a Dublin coachbuilder, permit traditional diagnoses such as these. But beyond that it is hard to go. The Dublin grandfather, William Shaw, was an Irish Protestant who had been in the army as an officer; his wife, Jane Norman, came from County Meath and may have had Huguenot blood. They had two sons: Richard, the elder, became a Captain in the 27th Enniskillen, but of the other son, William, born in 1780, scarcely anything is known. He too may have been in the services, possibly the navy; he was certainly restless and unsuccessful. Eventually he came to Edinburgh, set up there as a lace merchant and married Elizabeth Brown, who presented him with six children. Then in 1833, only two years after the birth of the youngest, Richard Norman Shaw, he died. At his death, William Shaw was heavily in debt and intestate, so his widow was left to struggle on with the four surviving children.[4] In 1839 came a further loss when the eldest son, William George Shaw, who had entered the Mercantile Marine Service, died in Sierra Leone at the age of twenty. This left Janet, then aged twenty-one, Robert, aged sixteen, and the eight-year-old Richard. The spacing of ages probably meant a lonely childhood, and serious impoverishment of the boy's education in circumstances of shabby gentility.

Elizabeth Shaw, fortunately, was a matron of consequence. Eldest child of a large legal family, she was 'upright, clearheaded and severe', with the tart piety and determination of the Scottish Presbyterian.[5] Thirty-one when she married, she was forty-six when she gave birth to Richard, and died in 1883 at the age of ninety-eight, when her son was renowned. She had ruled her family imperiously but wisely, and was rewarded for her achievement.

The family house at Edinburgh was first in Annandale Street and then in Haddington Place. Richard went until at least 1842 to an academy for languages at 3 & 5 Hill Street, winning the odd prize but showing no real distinction. Linguistic aptitude was not his forte; 'there is something in him but it is not Greek' is the only judgment recalled from his schooling. A year at a school in Newcastle followed, probably made possible through the mother's careful savings. But more than any school, it was his sister Jessie who gave him his real education.[6] Meanwhile Robert Shaw, who may also have had a curtailed upbringing and begun work after his brother's death, had found a job in London, most likely through the aid of his young cousin J. W. Temple, with Messrs Willis

1. Richard Norman Shaw as a young man.

2. Janet Shaw.

3. Robert Ewart Shaw shortly before his death in 1864.

Gann of Crosby Square, a large firm of shipping agents. To London, therefore, Elizabeth Shaw brought her other two children in about 1846, settling at first in Middleton Road, Dalston. So far as is known, Richard went to an unknown architect's office almost immediately.[7] We do not know what he learnt there or how he developed, but he liked the profession and showed enough aptitude to be articled to William Burn in or before 1849.[8] Burn perhaps was struck with the boy's remarkable facility in draughtsmanship, and felt sympathy and affinity for a fellow Scot. He had come down from Edinburgh to open a London office only a few years before, so the Shaws may have had introductions to him. For them, the choice augured well; Burn was a well-known architect with a smart practice, who would see Richard safely through his articles and into the solid, steady business of architecture.

But the turmoil in English architecture was intensifying annually. No bright young man wanted to be articled to Burn, a sixty-year-old eclectic who had been nurtured in the Greek Revival but now traded in debased modern classic or in Scottish baronial, which he had imported with him across the border.[9] In Burn's capable hands, architecture was never plain bad, but it was usually prosaic, for with all his practical skills he was not an outstanding designer. What he could do and others could not was to plan large country houses for the rituals of upper-class life. In this taxing task, Shaw's five-year-long apprenticeship was an essential lesson. Burn and his friend Anthony Salvin had alone taken the full advantages for a freer lay-out that accrued when the old classic, symmetrical plans were broken up after 1820 in favour of picturesqueness. Indisputably, the lay-out of a Burn country house was the best then available. But Burn was by no means technically perfect. He would design stairs up which no one could walk, and his clerks had to alter the plans, Shaw told his son. Indeed, Shaw's own interest in drainage and sewage was first aroused by Burn's inadequate plumbing. Altogether, the stolid succession of mansions for the duller Tory aristocrats must have been trying for a young man whose brain was teeming with Gothic churches and all the showmanship of exterior design and ornament.

However, Shaw showed patience. During the day he learnt the business of architecture in Burn's Stratton Street office; and on some evenings, at the R.A. Architecture School, he imbibed the dignified but now-despised teaching of Professor Cockerell, then withstanding the buffetings of the Gothic tide. It was valuable experience, at least in part digested. In his last years of practice, Norman Shaw openly wished to stand for all that was great in the contradictory geniuses of Cockerell and Pugin: in Pugin, a selfless, consuming dedication to the craft of architecture; in Cockerell, the steadfastness, the polish, and the maturity of aim which late Victorian buildings so regularly lacked. But at this time, though Shaw and his contemporaries at the R.A. School like E. M. Barry and James Brooks absorbed Cockerell's academic lectures, they yearned for the spirit of Pugin.

There can be no doubt who introduced Shaw to this brave new world: Eden Nesfield. Nesfield had been born in 1835 to a tradition of artistic talent, money, and adventure which four years at Eton in the company of madcaps like Simeon Solomon had done nothing to curb. Of his many-talented father William Andrews Nesfield, successively soldier, watercolourist and landscape gardener, we know less than we might.[10] Only the last of these professions can concern us here. In 1826 his sister had married her cousin, Anthony Salvin, a pupil of Nash who was then getting a reputation for country house design. Salvin built the two families a pair of villas at Finchley which his brother-in-law landscaped.[11] At this time, architecture was beginning to wrest from landscape much of its hold over educated enthusiasm. There was something of a gap in the profession. So Lieutenant Nesfield, picturesque artist and genial organizer of men, stepped in and started properly upon the business. Soon, he was expanding the formal garden which Repton had restored to the immediate environs of the country house, to meet the scale of Charles Barry's Italianate palaces. His success brought copious orders for laying out or reorganizing grounds along similar lines.[12] He then moved forward upon London's parks, altering St James's Park, remodelling the gardens at Kew with avenues and vistas, and lastly, with his sons' help, rearranging the Broad Walk in Regent's Park.[13]

When Eden Nesfield decided to be an architect in 1850, his uncle Salvin was the obvious choice of master. He was one of the few architects who had safely made the transition from the picturesque to the scholarly Gothic Revival, to which young men were now leaning. True, Salvin's welcome by those guardians of Gothic purity who wrote *The Ecclesiologist* was reserved. But he knew more than they did about mediaeval secular architecture, and from a patron's point of view could restore an old castle brilliantly if you had one or build you a new one cleverly if you hadn't. What really placated the ecclesiologists was that Salvin could also build and restore churches competently enough. In fact he was a modest but very successful architect with a wide clientèle and a foot in both camps.

Yet it was not to Salvin that Lieutenant Nesfield sent his son after a brief period with a tutor in Berne, but to Salvin's friend William Burn.[14] Articles were not signed to start with; the boy was still very young and had had only an odd drawing lesson or two from J. D. Harding in 1848. He needed to learn to draw architecture better and could afford to

4

4. William Eden Nesfield aged twenty-four, drawn by Édouard Brandon.

pay, so Burn passed him on to J. K. Colling, who often took pupils for this purpose. Though in weak health and therefore unequal and unprolific, Colling was an architect of some originality and skill. Draughtsmanship was his chief strength, architectural foliage his obsessive interest, and of this he could turn out magnificent drawings with wonderful rapidity. In the front window of his offices there stood an indiarubber plant, and Colling was reputedly 'never tired of gazing upon its broadly-treated foliage.'[15] For the young Nesfield, Colling proved an enthusiastic teacher who visited churches with him, and instilled in him the elements of fine architectural draughtsmanship. At about this time Nesfield first met Richard Shaw at his father's house in Windsor, and when in 1851 he was formally articled to Burn, a close friendship ensued.[16]

Burn personally was a kindly man, but dry, gruff, and ageing. The young Scots in his office, James Donaldson, J. Macvicar Anderson, David Macgibbon and Shaw, could take the sobriety, but Eden Nesfield could not. In 1853 he broke his articles and went off to the more cheerful atmosphere of his uncle Salvin's office in Argyll Street, where there was more personal responsibility for him and a more varied practice. Churches were what young men wanted to design, and of these Salvin had his share. Shaw was left with Burn and the rough and ready evening classes at the R.A. In spirit, Nesfield and Shaw were now more pupils of Pugin than of any living architect. It was hard to know where else to look. Butterfield was only just establishing himself, and never easy of access. Scott's office was in tremendous demand, and Street, whose perceptive lectures might be read in *The*

5

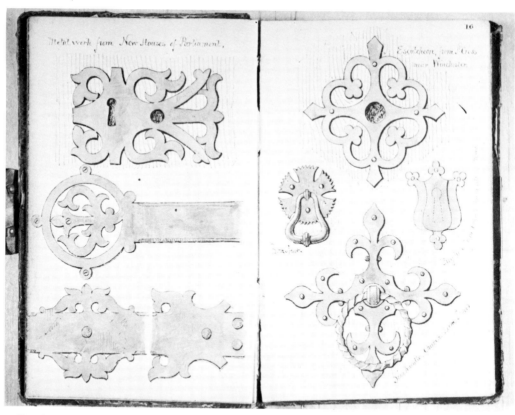

5. Sketches of Pugin details from the Palace of Westminster, 1852–3.

Ecclesiologist, had yet to arrive in London. Before Butterfield's first London churches were finished, there were already calls to widen the scope of the Gothic Revival from mere imitation of precedent, but only a few hints as to the right way forward. Pugin and the mediaeval monuments were still the only sources of real value for an aspiring Goth.

The beginnings of a better acquaintance with the methods and designs of the great reviver followed fast upon their melancholy visit to Ramsgate. Through Nesfield's father, the pair obtained Barry's permission to clamber over the scaffolding of the unfinished Houses of Parliament, and to sketch Pugin's decorative work there, which they did in the winter of 1852–3.[17] Both men's drawings survive; Nesfield's in a scrapbook of his early sketches at the R.I.B.A., Shaw's in a small sketchbook at the R.A. (ill. 5). They are virtually identical sheets, and it would be foolish to say who was copying whom. They show bosses, keyholes, bell handles and door handles, panelling and cresting, all carefully drawn out and sometimes embellished with wash in blue or red or gold. They are in Pugin's strict two-dimensional idiom, but finished to a higher point than the master's time allowed; they are both the first and the finest drawings of the new building. In Shaw's more compact sketchbook are interspersed other decorative details that caught his eye, mostly Gothic, either ancient or modern. Scoles' Farm Street church, Pugin's St Peter's Woolwich, Ferrey's St Stephen's Rochester Row, and other London churches of the revival

6

are scoured for attractive Gothic detail by the hard-worked clerk with neither time nor money to travel. There is a positive trail of sketches on the route back from the office to St John's Wood, where the family had now settled.[18] But only the details drawn from St Mary Magdalene, Munster Square are of lasting significance.

It was this church, built by R. C. Carpenter in 1849–51, which enabled Shaw to establish parity between his ambitions and hopes as a designer, and his own beliefs. Here, under the Reverend Edward Stuart's tutelage, took place the transition of Richard Shaw from God-fearing and prudent Presbyterian to committed Tractarian, an event necessary for the strengthening of his personality, vital for his architectural future. When Shaw's own generation matured, many were anxious, even though they were Pugin's disciples, to untie the links with which he (and in a different way, Ruskin also) had bound religion and art, and to assert art's autonomy. Burges was one, Philip Webb another, even Nesfield, in the habits of his practice, another. William Morris was to spend the last part of his life in an endeavour to expand and deepen Ruskin's social philosophy, and to plug the dark and depressing hole which gaped when religion had dropped out. Had Shaw's own convictions been merely received and at no point adjusted, they might have been shaken by the Darwinism whose claims he left for experts to decide;[19] or they might have degenerated into a fanaticism destructive of his freedom and confidence in his own artistic ability. Those of his architectural contemporaries who shared his views, such as Bodley and Sedding, often found their faith more intensive and committing than Shaw ever did, and it limited their scope. Among the doubters and sceptics, the one man able to preserve his integrity of approach absolutely intact through fifty years of service to the ideals of the Gothic Revival was Philip Webb, who only did so by means of a personal brand of self-denial and courage of intellect, resulting in similar limitation. To Shaw, a believer in 'the perfectibility of all things',[20] the sacrifices Webb made of his talent were unfortunate. For himself, there was no need to regret being 'a house man not a church man', no need to regret building for the rich and not the poor, when God required only the perfecting of your best talents and their lavishing upon the world.

This was the philosophy that Shaw built up, perhaps incomplete, yet happier and sweeter than that of the first generation of Tractarian architects. Meanwhile, he was also quietly deciding what a church should look like, for Carpenter's St Mary Magdalene satisfied his version then and thereafter. 'It is the *beau idéal* of a town church,' he wrote fifty years later. 'In general aspect it is very restful, and is entirely free from all affectation in design.'[21] Particularly he admired the display of plain ashlar walling and the floor, then an unbroken expanse of red tiling. For forty-two years, Shaw was a regular worshipper at St Mary Magdalene, and its spirit is everywhere at work in his church designs. Whether they are large or small, French or English, recollections of the all-over quarry tiles and blank wall surfaces of Carpenter's noble church recur.

In default of opportunities to take longer journeys, the job of learning mediaeval architecture had to be pursued at Westminster Abbey, until the summer holidays came round. In December 1852 came a first triumph when Shaw was awarded the R.A. Silver Medal for a finished drawing of the Cloisters at Westminster, as they were before Scott's drastic restoration. The unique citation says: 'In consideration of the great excellence of the drawings, in addition to the Medal the Academy gave Pugin's "Specimens and

6. Design for a military college in honour of the Duke of Wellington, awarded the R.A. Gold Medal, 1853.

Examples of Gothic Architecture" in three volumes quarto handsomely bound and suitably inscribed.'[22] There may therefore be some truth in the tradition that Cockerell saw Shaw as a favourite 'pupil', though their relationship can only have been remote. Next year, Shaw carried off the Gold Medal with a classical design for a military college in honour of Wellington. Oddly, it is the only one of his three prize-winning projects to survive, through a press illustration (ill. 6);[23] it looks clumsy enough in that, but no doubt the judges were seduced by the original drawing, perhaps too by the planning, of which we know nothing.

The clean sweep was completed when in 1854 the R.A. Travelling Studentship fell to Shaw for a late-Gothic palace design, close in style to the Houses of Parliament, connected by cloistered courts and dominated by a large apsidal chapel.[24] He was only the sixth architect since the Academy's foundation to win this studentship, his significant predecessors being Soane (1777) and Lewis Vulliamy (1818). His destinations would be very different from theirs.

TRAVELS

By now Shaw was twenty-three and had travelled little compared to Nesfield. His first proper tour had probably been the fortnight in the previous summer which Nesfield and he had spent travelling to Worcester, Great Malvern, Tewkesbury, Gloucester, Salisbury and Winchester, studying and sketching in the abbeys and cathedrals during the day, and then exchanging drawings in the evening in order to copy and learn from each other.[25] They had the advantage of seeing many of these buildings in their naïve state before the visitations of the 'earnest band who spoilt half the churches in the land'[26] and the assurance that they were still among the pioneers, noting features of decoration which nobody had yet recorded. On return, Shaw had ground through his final year of 'grubbing at Stratton Street',[27] and his articles were now complete. The R.A. Studentship fell exactly right.

8

Mrs Shaw now determined to accompany her son abroad and to bring Jessie. She was no Mrs Ruskin, and Richard was certainly spared the neurotic delicacy of that famous offspring. She may, however, have guessed that this would be her only chance for foreign travel (perhaps, too, her daughter's). Two whole years abroad without a fixed base might be unhappy ones for an innocent young man who as yet had little maturity to accompany his bewildering, unexpected talent. He was not physically strong, being already prone to a mysterious 'ague' that plagued him at intervals for the rest of his life; and though no word of it occurs in the letters to his mother, his son says that much of his work abroad was intermixed with pain. The adventure must have bitten deep into the family savings. Had Robert Ewart Shaw, now about to marry, not risen to command the freight department at Willis Gann, the uncertainties of the future might have deterred them. But instead, Elizabeth Shaw decided at whatever cost to see the great cities of Europe, and then to settle for the remainder of Richard's time abroad in a cheap pension at a German spa. Duly therefore, at the end of July 1854, Elizabeth and Janet Shaw betook themselves to Brussels. The autumn they spent in Paris, the winter in Florence, and then after a visit to Rome, in Spring 1855 Mrs Shaw and her daughter settled at Cannstatt near Stuttgart, whither Richard made periodic but brief forays. The arrangement seems to have suited all parties.[28]

Shaw himself started a little earlier in the company of Nesfield, who agreed to spend the few weeks of his summer holidays with him looking at the cathedrals of Normandy. At the end of July, having visited Rouen, Evreux, Beauvais, Gisors and Amiens, they parted for nearly two years, and Shaw hastened north to his family in Brussels. The pattern of a tour partly with friends and partly alone had begun.[29] In his own mind, this extended tour was purely educational; we know of no immediate plans for publication on his own account, and the sketches he did eventually publish are often unrepresentative of what he chose to draw. To start with, he made many perspectives and detail drawings, nearly always of churches, but as he moved on out of France into Italy and then Germany, he began more consistently to record plans, measured elevations, and sections. Perhaps this was because French Gothic material was more readily available for study in England, and therefore it was better to concentrate elsewhere. There was in fact a publication in question, not his own, but Thomas Henry King's *Study Book of Mediaeval Architecture and Art*, an enormous source book of foreign Gothic church plans and details, the first of the four volumes of which finally appeared in 1858. King is a mystery figure, an English architect of good education who converted to Roman Catholicism, for some reason migrated to Belgium, and there translated Pugin into French. He lived in Bruges (which Shaw visited in August 1854) and had some kind of architectural practice, but he spent much of his time scouring Europe in preparation for his great publication. Though Shaw is acknowledged only once in the book, he knew King well, was often noting details for him, and indeed planned to help him with an entry King projected for the Lille Cathedral competition of 1855.[30] Three years later his first architectural commissions seem to have come through King.[31]

Did Shaw, at the outset of his trip, grasp the role which continental Gothic, through books like King's, was about to play in English architecture? One suspects not. The continental movement was yet in its infancy. Ruskin's *Seven Lamps* were still only

9

glimmering in the darkness, and the applicability of his newer (and very variously reviewed) book on Venice was yet more obscure. Even his accurate, poetic sketches of detail had still to commend themselves fully to educated architects. Italian Gothic, for instance, still needed the boost of Street's *Brick and Marble in the Middle Ages* (published in 1855 while Shaw was abroad) to gain general acceptance. Shaw was little impressed by Italy and its architecture (Venice detained him ten days but he did no work there), more by Germany, but most of all by France, national preferences which remained with him even when his tastes changed. His selections of subject for drawing and his conclusions had to be made on his own judgment and initiative. There were few aids to help him along his route, except the highly erratic *Murray's Guide*, with which he was in frequent disagreement. In Germany he went with expectation to Merseburg, Halle and Altenburg in succession, only to be disappointed at each through false commendations in Murray.[32] By now, an English architectural traveller's obsession with Gothic could be as myopic as the blind neglect of previous generations. At Vicenza, Shaw noted 'a great many classic palaces by Cockerell's friend Palladio—but little or nothing in my way'; at Rome, where he also found little to draw, he was 'a good deal more pleased with St Peters than I expected, though I still hold my old opinion that it is a beast after St Pauls'.[33] He found himself a surprised admirer of Schinkel's Museum at Berlin, but he teased his mother neatly over von Klenze's masterpiece, the Valhalla for Ludwig II near Regensburg: 'it is exactly what would please you to a t—an exact copy of the Parthenon on the side of a hill and up an unlimited number of steps, inside it is all marble, gilding, and paint, and is filled with rows of busts—terribly flash place.' This narrowness of aim helped him to concentrate upon the great Gothic monuments of France and Germany.

The survivors of the long letters that Shaw wrote to his family while on tour give the first graphic evidence for his character. They are jolly and whimsical, and affect the Dickensian slang of the contemporary architectural student, an incongruous *argot* which the ardent mediaevalists made especially their own. Its derivation was acknowledged. 'Our conversation is decidedly Pickwickian,' reports Shaw from Lucca while travelling with J. T. Christopher, 'and we have determined on buying a cheap copy at Leghorn as the surest way of keeping off all *ennui*.' An exciting church or house to draw was 'pork'; trousers were 'continuations'; for food there was no end of special vocabulary, 'busters' and 'blow-outs', 'wittals' and 'flare-ups'. From first to last a continual theme of anxiety was the standard of the Cannstatt puddings, for Mrs Shaw and Jessie could not afford luxurious fare between their imbibings of spa-water and were much dependent on the favours of their dinner-women. All this brisk vulgarity, when tempered, would later make Shaw and Nesfield among the most charming of correspondents of the period. Topsy (Morris), Ned (Burne-Jones) and their circle of course affected it too, and with both groups it stuck into the 1860s and to some extent beyond. Burne-Jones, said Shaw when he died, 'was a devoted student of Dickens generally, and knew most of his works pretty well off by heart. Somehow Burne-Jones and Pickwick did not seem to go well together.'[34]

To his family he gives a brisk narrative of his travels and doings, omitting most architectural information for fear of boring them; instead, outline descriptions of the towns that he visits and their inhabitants are as much as they normally get. Here is a typical passage in a letter to Jessie from Le Mans.

It is a nice enough old place. I was assured by the architect at Chartres, that it was quite a little Paris, very unlike Chartres which as he said was dreadfully dull, and so it is I should think and no mistake. I must say however, for the old lady's consolation, that I can see no resemblance. I think the likeness ends in there being a very high block of houses and a chocolate making machine. It is as dull as possible, but there are several good looking shops, too. I can't make out where the people live. The cathedral is fine, the choir magnificent, quite knocks one down to see it . . . There is also another church here, which I must be content with looking at. It's well enough, but not excruciating. The great square, where the Vendean army was massacred, that we read about in that French book with the hard Greek name, is a very seedy place, containing the hotels (also seedy), caffés and cabarets, ill paved and muddy with a large round tub in the middle intended for a cornmarket. So much for Le Mans.

In the middle of 1856, nearly two years after setting out, Shaw rejoined his family at Heidelberg and accompanied them back to England. In his portfolio, besides the perspectives and details, were invaluable measured drawings of the cathedrals and churches at Lucca, Nuremberg, Regensburg, Erfurt, Lübeck, Halberstadt, Verona, Ulm, Braisne, Strasbourg, Metz, Toul, Chalons, Le Mans, Tours, Bourges and many others. By July 1856 he was settled with Nesfield in Salvin's office, setting out churches to his heart's content. The sketches were submitted to the R.A. and they recommended publication. Architects might have preferred the plans and sections, but the clarity of Shaw's pencil drawings made the details and picturesque perspectives far from useless, so that these sketches, doubtless more appetizing for the academicians, gained the day when he decided what to omit. Shaw could now have rested on his laurels and turned the drawings over to Day and Sons' lithographers. Instead, he spent the next two years acquiring lithographic techniques, and putting nearly every one of his hundred plates upon stone. Conceivably, he was taught by J. D. Harding, Nesfield's earliest drawing master, for the results have something of that able lithographer's own manner. Nesfield too was learning engraving and lithography at this time, and himself put a minority of the plates in his later *Specimens of Mediaeval Architecture* upon stone.[35]

Duly, *Architectural Sketches from the Continent* appeared in the summer of 1858, rather over a year after it was announced. According to common practice, it was issued first in fascicles and then in complete bound form. It was well if briefly noticed in *The Builder*, but made no huge impression. Its timing, coinciding with a burst of continentally-inclined building, was excellent but to a degree fortunate. In a brief, stilted preface, Shaw admits as much.

A fine frontispiece introduces the collection (ill. 7). Inset is a tinted lithograph of the Tiergarten Tower at Nuremberg, Shaw's favourite city, within a taut Puginian border of sinuous patterns. These frame vignettes of the mediaeval crafts drawn by John Clayton, Shaw's lifelong friend.[36] The plates that follow compromise between old picturesque techniques of drawing and the new requirements for accuracy of structure, scale and detail (ills. 8, 9). The outline is blurred only slightly by the shading and stippling of the lithographic crayon, to create texture. Though good drawings, in many ways they are immature. The detail is often crude and exaggerated, and for all the elegance of surface

7. Architectural Sketches from the Continent (1858), frontispiece.

Shaw has yet to learn to convey or indeed really see the spaces and volumes of Gothic. The low viewpoint he often uses for his perspective constructions creates scale well, but needs the perfection this technique acquired in Nesfield's *Specimens* before Shaw can handle it with the brio of his later drawings.

Foreknowledge of Shaw's career attracts one to the few scattered drawings of vernacular town houses; in France at Angers (ill. 9), Beaune, Beauvais and Le Mans; in Germany at Erfurt, Halberstadt and Hildesheim. One must be careful here. It was natural for him to study Jacques Coeur's house at Bourges, one of the few Gothic town houses that were big enough, fine enough, and in plan complex enough to warrant a revivalist's attention. Good, authentic models were in demand to get the domestic revival of Gothic off the ground, a subject freely debated in the mid-1850s.[37] Jacques Coeur's house was ammunition for the followers of Pugin who believed that symmetry counted for little in mediaeval houses, and therefore its inclusion among the sketches was topical. On the other hand, the pretty French timber-framed houses and the jettied-out street fronts of Germany were the kind of thing that any English sketching traveller of the '40s and

8. Erfurt Cathedral, east end, from *Architectural Sketches from the Continent*.

9. Angers, timber-framed houses, from *Architectural Sketches from the Continent*.

13

'50s might have drawn, albeit with less care. If Shaw thought they had any 'suggestive tendency', to use the words of his preface, it may have been unspecific. Obviously, though, they engaged his interest, allowed him to study timber construction and its forms of ornament, and would enable him to grasp more firmly what was particularly English about his own country's lively tradition of farmhouse, cottage, and townhouse. Already in England attempts were in train to graft the vernacular on the revived Gothic; Shaw, in his sketches, just gave himself and his public a more disciplined idea of what was meant by continental vernacular. Hardly a motif in the book has close counterparts in the early practice of Nesfield and Shaw. And when Nesfield issued his *Specimens*, at the very time their domestic style was evolving, the proportion of secular work was much reduced from Shaw's own book.

Two years in the Salvin office were enough for Shaw. Though Salvin was a more charming and sympathetic architect than Burn, he too was ageing and his style of work not really so different. Often he was away at his most exacting job, the refashioning of Alnwick Castle in his native north-east, and for a period in 1857 he was seriously ill following a stroke. The churches that Salvin built were only competent, and began to look more than a little old-fashioned and 'starved'. In the office Richard Shaw no doubt had a privileged position and respect from the junior clerks. But Nesfield could take advantage of kinship as Shaw could not, and as Anthony Salvin junior, the third senior assistant, had not the skill to do. In the head's absence, Nesfield ran the office and probably did some of the designing too. His first work, the Puginian canopied tomb of Lord Crewe in Barthomley Church, Cheshire, was up in 1856 when Shaw still had nothing to show.[38] Next year, on the strength of £300 inherited on his coming of age, he relinquished his post and was off on a series of rollicking continental tours which put the measured progress of his friend in the shade. They began with an extended visit to France, including a week or two in Viollet-le-Duc's atelier.[39] Of the great *Dictionnaires*, the early volumes of the *Architecture* were now out, the first of the *Mobilier* in preparation, and one would guess that the news and hints that Nesfield brought back from this meeting were of vital value not just to himself and to Shaw, but to the whole circle of advanced Goths in England. By the end of 1857, Nesfield had reached Italy, where he travelled with John Hebb, and next year he went on with James Donaldson to Athens, Salonica, Athos and Constantinople. These were not serious sketching tours, it seems; their finest product is the beautiful pastel portrait of Nesfield, drawn at Rome by Edouard Brandon in the style of Holbein (ill. 4). It was only on his return that Day and Son commissioned from Nesfield a sequel to *Architectural Sketches*, which had evidently done well. The material for this book was mainly collected on a series of special shorter journeys which Nesfield made to France in the summers of 1859-61, and issued as *Specimens of Mediaeval Architecture* in 1862.[40]

When Nesfield came home at the end of 1858, he set up a little office for himself in Bedford Row, though his practice was only notional till 1860 or 1861. This must have made his friend, now twenty-seven, restless to do the same, but he lacked the money and contacts needed by a beginner. Shaw was in fact effectively debarred from many opportunities his richer friends had. In 1859, he was invited to join a new and in the event very successful élite society, the Foreign Architectural Book Society (Fabs for short), but had to decline: 'I have several good reasons to prevent me. I have no dibs to spare (have not paid my tailor for ever so long), and I live such a long way off, it makes it so very troublesome. However you will without doubt easily find a dozen fellows ready to join you and stump up their guineas like bricks.'[41] A letter recently found at the RIBA shows that as late as 1861 he was still sufficiently hard up to apply for the curatorship of the Soane Museum, a job for which he had neither particular qualifications nor the appropriate scholarly cast of mind. However, from 1858, when Shaw's brother branched out on his own, the family situation began to ease and to provide hope for the future. Robert Ewart Shaw's intelligence and magnetism had won him friends throughout the shipping business, but enemies among his superiors at Willis Gann, who disliked his expansionist policies for the firm. Clumsily, they reduced his salary, so he, his assistant Walter Savill, and a host of juniors resigned to set up their own business of chartering steamers for the New Zealand trade. While Robert Shaw looked after the finances, Savill, who must have provided the capital, had responsibility for shipping and cargoes. Shaw Savill and Company set up in Billiter Street a few doors away from the office of James William Temple & Co., shipping agents and store merchants. Temple already had several years' experience of independence in the business, and appears now to have thrown in his lot with his cousin. The business soon prospered.[42]

STREET'S OFFICE

When therefore in early 1859 an offer came to Shaw to prolong his apprenticeship into his thirties, he was in a better position to consider it on its merits. Wisely he accepted, for how many others had the great George Edmund Street asked to be his principal assistant? Only one, Philip Webb. Now Webb was leaving, to try his own hand at practice and help Morris and Burne-Jones set up their firm. Shaw and Webb will have already met, at the Architectural Association Class of Design, which both attended and where both contributed work for exhibition in 1858.[43] For a few weeks, as they overlapped in Street's Montague Place office, they had the chance of closer acquaintance. It never ripened into real friendship. Both modest men, they came to admire each other's work with reservations, but they had strangely little ground to meet on. Webb's 'liking for the ugly' and the strict limitation of his practice became a puzzle to Shaw, who outgrew his own puritanism in different ways; while Webb, though his only recorded remarks on Shaw are words of praise, would have seen faults in the extravagance and imperfections of the other's designs. Through Webb, Shaw must at least have met the junior Pre-Raphaelites. Morris he came to mistrust and owned no allegiance to him; Burne-Jones he admired unreservedly to his dying day. Two other talented pupils to welcome the newcomer into the fold of advanced ecclesiology and to become fast friends with him, were the Sedding brothers: John Sedding, a pious, sensitive and nervously bumptious Cornishman, and his elder brother Edmund (nicknamed 'Jagbag' or 'Jaggybaggy'), an early Street pupil. Edmund left soon after Shaw arrived to start his own practice, but was already ill; there was physical weakness in John too, belied by his antics in the office, from which he had sometimes to be restrained for fear of Street's wrath. P. B. Hayward, another assistant, was later recalled for his stutter, an excuse for mutual banter in song rather than speech, Shaw playing his role in a pleasant, unpractised tenor. Shaw himself soon

15

acquired a nickname, 'Corporal Bullfoot', because he turned up at the office for a period with his foot in plaster.[44].

The larking in Street's office was intense compared to that in the establishments of Burn or Salvin because the tasks were intense. Work was unremitting, Street himself sober and preoccupied with his labours, and the atmosphere in all probability physically chilly. The clerks badly needed a let-out when Street was away on his endless travels. It would have been intolerable had their dedication to Street and to his vision not sustained them and turned drudgery into vocation. We know nothing of Shaw's feelings, but he was probably content with his modest salary. He was working on church architecture with the man who during those years bade fair to be Europe's greatest architect; what more could be wanted? He was learning all the time: how to draw yet better, how to conceive of volume and space in architecture, and how 'to engraft on our national style many beauties and peculiarities hitherto confined to the continent', to borrow the words of his own book's preface. Street in fact helped him outgrow Pugin. Shaw expressed his debt later by maintaining that he learnt all he knew about architecture that was worth knowing in this period.[45]

In 1858–62, Street was indeed the unrivalled leader of the Ecclesiological Movement.[46] Although he only arrived in London from Oxford in 1856, already the inventiveness of his churches and his sheer industry reduced others into followers. In terms of designing ability, two architects could claim equality with him: Butterfield, living in a private world where he worked out his own original form of ecclesiology, and Burges, Street's equal as a scholar but neither prolific nor committed to the Tractarian movement. Gilbert Scott alone could cope as well as Street with the administrative side of architecture, but young men of discernment knew, after he had consented to design the Foreign Office in the Italian style, that his integrity was less certain. What Street had over and above these qualities was the ability to turn his drawings into compositions that had movement, force and volume. At All Saints' Margaret Street, Butterfield had revealed the magic of a high and static space enclosed by flickering, jewelled surfaces. Street was now busy transforming all this to his own ends: subordinating colour to the stronger rhythms of his structures, separating the elements of arcade, clerestory, chancel arch and chancel, flattening the profiles of walls to enforce the direction of their mass, and then engineering collisions between the parts. Sculpture, colour of brick and stone, black mastic and mosaic, go to emphasize, not (as with Butterfield they sometimes do) to diminish these structural encounters. Above all, Street opened men's eyes as no architect had done since Soane to the drama of interior volume, of gaping voids between blunt arcades, and to a sense of containment within imprisoning walls. The first masterpieces in this manner were building as Shaw entered the office, St James the Less Westminster, Denstone in Staffordshire and the earliest of Street's Yorkshire churches, at Howsham and Whitwell; their great successors, his churches at Oxford and Clifton, were evolving while Shaw was still there. The lessons were not lost. After his time with Street, Shaw drew with a grasp of architectonic reality and weight, and in all his subsequent designs the quality is firmly implanted; he is never a two-dimensional architect. Arguably, in Holy Trinity Bingley, Shaw built the finest church of all in this manner.

Not long after Shaw left Street, the dynamism of his churches starts perceptibly to fall off. It is the saddest story of the Gothic Revival because so entirely avoidable; the Law Courts saga which actually caused Street's death is almost a postscript. His over-exertions amazed and appalled his pupils. The feats of design as Shaw recalled them were astonishing.

> The rapidity and precision with which he drew were marvellous. I have never seen anyone not merely to equal, but to approach him, and he was as accurate as he was rapid. I well remember a little *tour de force* that fairly took our breath away. He told us one morning that he was just off to measure an old Church—I think in Buckinghamshire—and he left by a ten o'clock train. About half-past four he came back and into the office for some drawing paper. He then went into his own room, reappearing in about an hour's time with the whole church carefully drawn to scale, with his proposed additions to it, all ready to ink and finish. Surely this was a sufficiently good day's work—two journeys, a whole church measured, plotted to scale, and new parts designed in about seven hours and a half.[47]

But the strain was immense. Shaw vowed never to try and practise on Street's absurd scale, accepting every little job in the name of the Gothic crusade. Sometimes he came near it, but he avoided the most ridiculous excesses of overwork. Street, in Shaw's famous phrase, would never even let his pupils design a keyhole;[48] and Shaw, in letting his assistants go a good way beyond keyholes, well recollected the more trying times of his training.

Shaw's post with Street allowed him to be constantly on the move, taking drawings to one job, instructions to another, superintending points at a third. On these days he paid swift visits to other churches in the area. Time off, scanty as it was, he spent in more leisurely visits to further churches: in 1859, for instance, to Bedfordshire, Northampton-shire, and the cathedrals of Ely, Lincoln, St Albans, and Rochester. Next year we know of only a single but significant visit to Haddon Hall.[49] By the summer of 1861, Nesfield had ended his continental wanderings and was becoming engrossed in his practice. But he still had time to spend some of July combing the Yorkshire dales for mediaeval detail with Shaw, who was in the north for nearly the whole month. This is the first of two tours for which both men's drawings survive in the R.I.B.A., recorded in octavo sketchbooks (that is, a size bigger than those normally used) of a kind of creamy 'strawpaper' most likely suggested by Harding's experiments with tinted sketching paper.[50] So short a time before the Nesfield–Shaw partnership begins, their sketches are still emphatically ecclesiastical. In 144 pages recording Shaw's Yorkshire observations, a mere five subjects are secular, and only two, an old house at Hull and a cottage at Howden, vernacular; he was still steeping himself in minsters and abbeys. But minsters, abbeys or even parish churches were not the way to start a career, as Shaw was by now anxious to do. Street battened upon church restorations which Scott might have passed over entirely to one of his young men. The way ahead was hard, the means to get secular commissions uncertain. Besides, what style should houses be built in?

It was Nesfield who had to tackle this vexing problem first, and to do so he looked for guidance not so much to Street as to Burges, who at this time had built little but suggested much. There is no record of friendship between Burges and Nesfield, but it must have existed, for they had everything in common. Both were rich, mercurial, jovial young egotists, fascinated by decoration, ornament and heraldry. Both made free of their money and talent in designing little things and big things. Both enjoyed the masculine company of their peers in painting, such as Rossetti, Solomon, Albert Moore and Whistler, and both took part in the 1860s in the hearty architectural tours of the Fabs.[51]

In 1860, Burges's architectural style, a stumpy, rounded form of early French Gothic counted for less than his decorative work and furniture.[52] He had inherited Pugin's talent for fast, inventive detailing in any material, wood, iron, or stone, but he cared little for precise stylistic propriety in ornament. Now, he was busy injecting a current of alien motifs into the pure bloodstream of the revival. Burges invites comparison with Viollet-le-Duc, with whom he shared enormous scholarship in Gothic such as Nesfield and Shaw never attained, and a willingness to look for ideas in historical precedent of any kind. But what absorbed the Frenchman were structural techniques and precedents to assimilate, publicize and reapply, whereas Burges thought little of such matters—decoration was his perpetual quarry. Classic scenes on a Gothic cabinet, for instance, had no impropriety for him. Japanese ornament too was already a subject of study in his circle well before the 1862 Exhibition, thanks to the initial enthusiasm of Rossetti, and the frequent parallels of its geometrical patterns with mediaeval details were well noted. Two different schools of design that sprang from Gothic and by degrees moved away in the 1860s benefited from Burges's enthusiasm for *disegno*. On one side, his encouragement of classical and Renaissance figurative techniques among the artists who painted his furniture led directly on to the decorative work of the Morris firm, especially in stained glass. On another, his own abstract and architectural ornament, both Gothic and Japanese, offered ideas for the detailing of the early architectural designs of Nesfield and Shaw.

Between the variable, volatile styles of Nesfield's earliest buildings, before he had taken to the vernacular revival, the common factor is Burges.[53] The derelict farm buildings at Shipley Hall (1860–1) are a good example (ill. 30). They amount to a medley of the most up-to-date tricks of the High Victorians in secular architecture: separated parts, display of roofing with half-hips, polychrome brickwork, and tiling prettily diapered. But the actual style is Burges's, and so too is the verve, the disregard of expense and the decorative brilliance of the ironwork. For the dairy ceiling, Nesfield for the first time called in young Albert Moore, who at about this time was one of the painters to work on the big Burges bookcase now at the V & A. Likewise at Combe Abbey, where he spent the first year of his work (1861–2) remodelling the kitchens, Nesfield provided a delightful set of Burgesian roasting jacks and culinary paraphernalia. There is fertility and invention in all this, but little consistency, and few hints of the future until the new wing at Combe began to rise in 1863.

FIRST DESIGNS

There is inconsistency, too, in what little Shaw himself, eking out the evening and holiday hours, was able to produce over the four years in Street's office. There were two courses open to him, exhibition and competition; too extensive a use of the second alternative would be time-consuming and probably frowned upon by Street. Exhibition,

10. Organ design, 1858.

therefore, was his main policy. For the time being, Shaw made no attempt to send in drawings for display at the R.A., whose shows of architecture were in the doldrums. He concentrated instead upon the annual 'Architectural Exhibition', a body then in its brief prime, with good, capacious galleries. It prominently featured the latest works of the established Goths, but their pupils also found a place upon its walls. Shaw's first success came in 1857 when the palace design which had won him the Travelling Studentship was shown there; in the following eight years he exhibited there annually, with the exception of 1862–3. The entries he sent in 1859–61 are our main clue to his activities, especially the two delightful fantasy projects for organs shown in 1859, which by good luck have survived (ill. 10).

'Have you sent anything to the Exhibition?' Shaw asked C. F. Hayward, the Fabs secretary, that year. 'I have—something too Rampagenous (you see I require it spelt with a capital R).' No word could be more apt for these first extant designs of his. Dating from March 1858, they show him at the point he had reached when he transferred from Salvin to Street. In some ways they even hint forward to his new master. Street was much occupied with organs at precisely this time, having collaborated in 1856 with the Reverend John Baron, to produce a decent, small instrument on the strictest Gothic principles, called the Scudamore organ. There, however, the similarity ends. Instead of the neat, rough chastity of the Scudamore design, Shaw has gone over heart and soul to that 'mischievous extravagance in organs, which, in many cases, seems connected with the Babel-like spirit which aspires after monsters of all kinds—such as a Transatlantic telegraph, a Leviathan ship etc.'[54] To the practical Father Baron such designs were anathema, but Shaw can be forgiven for not being so mundane. He was, after all, a natural designer still baulked of an outlet. Here in fun he is fooling with the structural and decorative capabilities of this mightiest of church fittings, creating crazy visions from an almost overheated imagination. These in fact are fantasies after the manner and cult of Burges, who had designed such an organ for Lille Cathedral, however little they follow his own preferred forms. For the source of Shaw's own ideas, the *Building News* shrewdly quoted the proverb 'Nürnbergs Hand geht durch alle Land'.[55] But sources matter not at all compared to the spirit of activity, complexity, and glorious riot. A year or two later, Shaw produced a third such design, for an organ boldly arranged under a circular transept window. This time, the lack of sculptural detail and the charming 'Japanese' inlay patterns on the casework showed he had by then thoroughly digested the ideas of Burges and the lessons of Street. Still, this design has something also of the wild 'Rampagenous' exuberance of the 1858 drawings, done in the flush of first enthusiasm for continental Gothic.

1859 was the year of the competition for the Manchester Assize Courts, won by Alfred Waterhouse on the merits of his planning. For this, Nesfield and Shaw entered a lost design which is probably their only entirely joint work. It won high commendation, for the drawing and details as much as the conception, and after a showing with the other designs in Manchester, was displayed in London at next year's Architectural Exhibition. As in Shaw's later Bradford Exchange design, over the principal entrance there was a tower of unrelieved wall surface rising to an ornamented summit, and beyond, a public hall conspicuous from the outside and surrounded by offices arcaded along the exterior. The style was the inevitable foreign Gothic, supported by excellent sculptural and detail work, reported the *Building News*.[56] To accompany these drawings in 1860, Shaw showed, in striking deal frames, two further very puzzling projects, which were less well received. One was an elaborate jewelled design flavouring strongly of Street for a Priest's House 'about to be executed' in the small village of Drogenbos, just outside Brussels, and with it went drawings for tombs in Bruges Cemetery. What do these locations mean? The Drogenbos presbytery may never have been built; the Bruges tombs are unidentifiable.[57] The elusive T. H. King of Bruges must have helped Shaw to these jobs, but why he should have done so and what was their fate we shall probably never know. If executed, they constitute a strange start to his *oeuvre*.

20

Last of the exhibits to appear before Shaw left Street's office was the great bookcase now at the Victoria and Albert Museum (ill. 11). This sole, tangible relic of young Richard Shaw's flamboyant mediaevalism is so hard to connect with its author's later history that it too easily appears merely curious, a token piece of early playfulness. Shaw himself was certainly to think it so. Having shown it in 1861 and again in the Mediaeval Court of the 1862 International Exhibition, after its several years' service in his home or office, he tired decisively of his bookcase and gave it to his daughter's convent, where it reappeared, long forgotten, in 1962.

The 'reform' tradition of sturdy, gawky Gothic furniture to which the bookcase belongs was initiated by Burges, Morris and Webb in the late 1850s, when they were still living out a naïve life of jest and fantasy in an Arthurian dream world. The style was never intended for wide dissemination or mass production. The early pieces they showed in the 1862 Exhibition, where the Morris firm scored its first successes, were the private playthings of the architects and artists who created them, esoteric painted cabinets and cupboards destined for the chambers, studios, or offices of themselves and their friends. Into this pattern Shaw's bookcase fits, but with salient differences. It is a stray member of another school of early reform furniture which by bad luck has scarcely survived. Nesfield, we know, designed much furniture, but all the movable pieces seem lost; and likewise, of Street's rare secular furniture we have only a fine sober bookcase of 1865, and none of his exotic painted pieces.

Ironically, Shaw's craftsman stood on a surer social footing with his designer than any of Morris's at the time. Nesfield and Shaw had known James Forsyth since the days with Salvin, for whom he had worked at Wells Cathedral.[58] A fellow Scot from Roxburghshire, he was a virtuoso carver in stone or wood, able to attempt Gothic, classic, or any of the freer styles of the '60s and '70s. His was the undisputed place of sculptor and carver to the friends in the years of their early successes, though he was more intimate with Nesfield. He could also design, it seems, if he was really both author and craftsman of the Japanese screen he gave Shaw as a wedding present in 1867. Forsyth first became well known in 1859, when he worked the elder Nesfield's vast and vigorous Perseus and Andromeda fountain at Witley Court; the bookcase, so different in manner and materials, followed two years later.

In this earliest of their collaborations, techniques of jointing, dowelling and inlay have been thought right through between Shaw and Forsyth to achieve the most deftly made and craftsmanlike piece of early reform furniture. In subtlety of ornamental method and colour, it excels anything of the kind previously made. Busy flush patterns in light patinas of rosewood, satinwood and bird's eye maple adorn the non-structural surfaces, leaving the shafts, drawers and shelves to the darker textures of the different, unpolished oaks. The little veneering allowed is the least happy part; otherwise, the decoration is 'honestly' contrived, by means of exposed dowels, punched and gouged quatrefoils, and proper, painstaking marquetry. The actual ornamental forms themselves, overlapping suns, flowers, peacock tails and part circles or 'pies', derive partly from the abstracted whorls of Rossetti's picture frames, partly from similar incised shapes on mediaeval church chests. Japan has already arrived, but delicately integrated with the Gothic in the flat, unobtrusive forms of inlay.

Shaw in fact is acknowledging a debt to Burges, but voicing a criticism as well. Burges's early, slaphappy pieces were ill-made vehicles intended for the display of painting, and the same is true of the early Morris pieces before Webb took diligent hold of their production. Shaw, on the other hand, still under Street's discipline, expresses 'honest' construction nearly everywhere, not least in the techniques of colouring. Only the top storey of the bookcase, which is the least successful part, directly recalls Burges, and only this section is painted, apart from the shaft rings. Shaw also manages to eschew much of the iron binding which disfigures many of the poorly jointed pieces of early furniture. Such bands as the bookcase has, and the great lock to the desk, are beautifully wrought by James Leaver, Street's smith.[59] Further, Shaw and Forsyth have experimented more ambitiously than either Burges or Morris had done at that point with difficulties of form and function in furniture, witness their coalition of different parts with different uses, and the play with profile and taper between them.

From another aspect of structure, the bookcase was as open to criticism as its predecessors or indeed its ultimate mediaeval models; in fact, it was so criticized.[60] For all its display of joints, tenons and dowels, the structures imitated are those not of wood but of stone. Architectural and lapidary too were the few mediaeval counterparts to which Burges and his followers looked, the *armoires* of Bayeux and Noyon. For them, these precedents sufficiently excused the designing of cupboards apeing little houses and castles, with arches, cresting, finials, and, on Burges's Yatman cabinet, even painted imitation of roof-tiling. Shaw's more modest roof gables and arcading were no more popular with the purists, but in his case there is a personal reason for looking beyond the fault. The designers of the other pieces were mostly rich young men, launched on their careers and with art collections of their own. The cupboards were for their clothes, their treasures and their drawings; the surfaces, when they came from the cabinetmaker, were coloured by scenes from Chaucer or Malory; the shelves supported their rare folios or their exclusive bargains in blue and white Nanking porcelain. But Shaw, now thirty years of age, is still poor when he designs his bookcase, without clients, without practice, without the money to build more largely for himself. Ten feet are enough for the tall Richard Shaw and all his possessions. Under the top gables, he keeps perhaps a pair of precious pots of his own, below that his two rows of books, further below a few hidden treasures, in the drawers his correspondence which he answers at the desk; at his feet, his rolls of drawings are stacked in a thin cupboard. All that he has fits neatly within this substitute-house, his most precious object and, as yet, his only creation. What is now needed is an office to which to remove bookcase and designer, and a job of work on which to start. Richard Norman Shaw will then be off on his fifty-year career. It is a late beginning, but he will not regret that.

11. (left) Bookcase, 1861.

CHAPTER 2

South and North

All are Architects of Fate
Working on these walls of time
Some with massive deeds and great
Some with ornaments of rhyme

Nothing useless is or low
Each thing in its place is best
And what seems but idle show
Strengthens and supports the rest.

Inscription from Longfellow, on the screen given by James Forsyth
to Richard and Agnes Shaw as a wedding present

ORIGINS OF OLD ENGLISH

NORMAN Shaw's long training had been poised between two separate traditions of architecture—the picturesque and the ecclesiological. Such strands in the art of mid-Victorian England can constantly be parted: on the one hand, the Pre-Raphaelite painter or the Gothic Revival architect, the moralists; on the other, the genre scene painter or the picturesque architect, the aesthetes. This helpful distinction becomes glib, if it is merely used as an instrument to denigrate the second tradition. In ecclesiology, we can easily see a new ideal of architecture vigorously explained and explored by its proponents, and identify a well-formed body of work and thought. But there are ideological roots too to the older and laxer concepts of the picturesque. In domestic architecture at least, life and the will to growth were still strong in them; by degrees, by broad-minded development, their adherents would grasp the new stock, entwine themselves around it, and begin to constrain and choke the quick-spent strength of Puginian Gothic.

In architecture, the difference between the traditions was never as complete as Pugin managed to suggest in his writings. His passion for serious, scholarly Gothic, and his strictures upon the levity of the picturesque and classic schools of design distort the situation and indeed the nature of much of his own best secular architecture. His propaganda, however, was victorious. Once Ruskin had endorsed so many of his views, no serious architectural critic could have truck with the stucco and jerry-building of Nash, or the Gothick solecisms of the Wyatts. Yet the antithesis must have seemed superficial to intelligent architects such as Salvin. In painting, it never existed to the same degree. When Ruskin reviews pictures, he can commend Prout and Mulready with Brown and Rossetti in the same breath. His contemporaries did not question this. But our own century, presuming outright preferences and distinctions, until recently has scorned the coherent school of genre scene painting that was all the while continuing. It is through these painters, who were to be among Shaw's foremost clients, that we have to seek an understanding of his vernacular style.

24

In the early years of the nineteenth century, William Wells, a retired partner from a shipbuilding firm, took up residence at Redleaf outside the village of Penshurst in Kent. Wells was a shrewd collector of paintings, possessing amongst others Van Dyck's *Three Heads of Charles I* and Claude's *Enchanted Castle*.[1] He was also one of three remarkable patrons of contemporary English genre and landscape painting, surpassing his rivals Robert Vernon and John Sheepshanks in hospitality if not in taste. Farington records frequent visits to Redleaf in the 1810s and comments on the beauty of the grounds.[2] The halcyon days came a little later, when the next generation of artists, followers of Wilkie, Mulready and Constable, came down to Redleaf to paint. These were painters not of the city but of the village, forced to dwell mainly in London by the exigencies of the market. Selectors and interpreters of passages from English country habits, life and scenery, already vanishing before the advances of industry and the improvements of transport, they felt impelled to give new meaning to the old subjects of the Dutch tradition, and record before their devastation the rural landscapes and cottages, and the cheerier, more sentimental scenes of village life. Up to his death in 1847, Wells held prolonged house parties for such painters at Redleaf. Cooke, Cooper, Frith, Goodall, Horsley, Landseer, Lee, Patrick Nasmyth, Richard Redgrave, Turner, and Webster were all among his friends; of these, five in later life were to be among Shaw's patrons. They stayed at their ease, met Wells's distinguished neighbours and guests, and went shooting and sketching.[3] Some of the painters also helped Wells and his gardener transform the grounds of Redleaf into a notable picturesque landscape with evergreens, rocky boulders, outcrop dramatically uncovered, and the earliest known experiments in crazy paving. Wells himself designed at least one remarkable vernacular estate cottage of 1826, characterized by the admiring Loudon as 'Cyclopean'.[4] It is not yet an authentic Kentish cottage such as George Devey was to build for the next generation, but it forecasts what was to come.

From Penshurst, the painters could travel to any pretty house or village that caught their fancy. The several unrestored mansions of the area were much frequented. Ightham Mote was the quaintest, prized for its old-world textures and patinas, and ripe for the mellow plates of Joseph Nash's *Mansions of England in the Olden Time*, the contemporary bible of the picturesque. Knole was the most accessible and fashionable; Burne-Jones was to paint there in 1860, and the Fabs visited it a little later. But Hever and Penshurst itself had the choicest associations: Astrophel and Stella, and the Boleyns. This was true Tudor saga, the stuff for the pretty style of English history painting now being commissioned for the walls of the Palace of Westminster—the 'island story' perceived through the distorting lens of Walter Scott.

Into this story fit fragments of information about the architectural connections of the Penshurst set. Not so far away at Scotney Castle, Salvin and his client Edward Hussey were busy in 1837–44 upon one of the subtlest interrelations of house and landscape of the whole picturesque movement; at Penshurst itself, Salvin rebuilt South Park for Wells's neighbour Lord Hardinge in 1848. So all that was going on in the district will have been known to Salvin and his friends. Among these was Decimus Burton, who had dabbled in estate development at Tunbridge Wells, built one or two things near Penshurst, and kept up a lively interest in local architecture.[5] But the central, still mysterious figure is George Devey. Behind Devey stand painters; his uncle Augustus Egg, John Sell Cotman to whom

he had been apprenticed, and, more significantly, his second master J. D. Harding, the teacher and intimate of the Nesfield family circle. Devey was the first to transform his predecessors' idle interest in the Kentish cottages into an active enquiry into the methods and materials of their construction, and Penshurst was the first place to see that knowledge, stimulated no doubt by Pugin's remarks upon structural honesty and tradition in architecture, put into practice. He began as Lord Hardinge's architect for farm buildings at South Park, but was soon employed by Lord De L'Isle of Penshurst Place. In 1850 he extended and added most skilfully to the Leicester Square cottages in front of the church, the first of a long series of estate works. Soon after, he was turning another local house, Culver Hill, a cottage built by the painter F. R. Lee, into Hammerfield, the first more largely articulated house of the Old English style.[6]

Salvin, Burton, and Devey: surely then young Shaw and Nesfield? Nesfield had visited Penshurst as a boy, and his father may have worked at South Park.[7] And August 1862 saw Shaw down there, drawing Penshurst Place and the back of the Leicester Square cottages. A month later he and his friend were off together for a week's sketching in Sussex, intent upon wealden vernacular subjects.[8] It is a sudden shift of interest, unrecorded before Shaw left Street in May or June of that year and set up his plate at home, 8 Albion

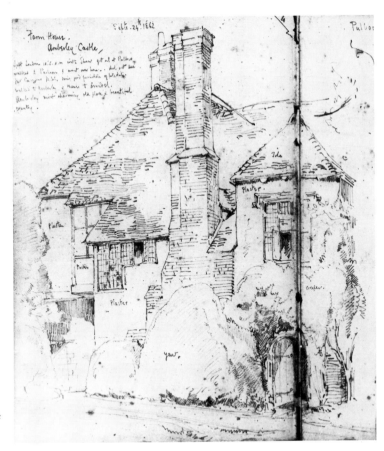

12. (left) Amberley Castle farmhouse, sketch by Shaw, 1862.

13. (right) Amberley Castle farmhouse, sketch by Nesfield, 1862.

Road, St. John's Wood. There was a dearth of jobs to start with, but plenty of time to renew travel. On Nesfield's experience so far, future commissions were likely to be secular. The forms of domestic architecture were still as uncertain as ever, but Devey's achievements were much in the air.

The Sussex journey of September 1862 was their last of length together, and brought the Nesfield and Shaw tours to a climax. Happily, both sketchbooks survive, Shaw's more austerely confined to drawing, Nesfield's accompanied by a concise diary that reflects their rollicking mood. Now, churches and cottages are equally valued. At Pulborough church where they begin, the main attraction for both is the seventeenth-century gallery; against Nesfield's misdrawing of the balusters Shaw writes 'This is not right, you old rascal, there is no deniging of it.' At Amberley, they sketch a tile-hung farmhouse from the same aspect; Nesfield's drawing has greater prettiness, Shaw's a shade more verve (ills. 12, 13). The architectural jokes and slang are still in force. They visit Arundel, passing 'old Burn's very ugly entrance', Angmering Church 'which turned out an awful sell as it was totally restored by Teulon in his best manner', and Broadwater, 'a most abominable church done by a twelfth-century Habershon no doubt'. At Tortington, Nesfield observes 'two sows lying back to back head to tail for mutual support against the combined efforts

14. Beechwood, front elevation of cottage, 1862.

of their respective litters of about 13 sucking pigs each. Good dodge.' Tossing up at the end of the week for a single bed at Devils Dyke, Shaw wins—an omen of their future fortunes.[9]

Manors, farmhouses, cottages and old town houses henceforward carry the day in what little we know of either man's itineraries. In June 1863, Nesfield was down at Tunbridge Wells and Speldhurst, getting a further feel of the wealden style, and in September 1864 Shaw and he spent a day together at the big half-timbered Ockwells in Berkshire, this time dutifully noting plan as well as elevation. By 1870, the sketchbooks of every architect would abound with such familiar, well-loved buildings of the countryside.

Immediately, the 'Old English' style emerges. In August 1862, the month he visited Penshurst, Shaw designed a small, brick-built gardener's cottage for an unidentified estate called Beechwood (ill. 14); in November, Eagle Wharf, a tall warehouse building in Shadwell; and the following May, the first of a series of estate buildings for Bromley Palace in Kent. Two things are clear straight away. Firstly, this is a homogeneous style, destined at the start with some variation to cope with a broad area of building types. Secondly (and this is a point to be looked at in the next chapter), a methodical selection has been undertaken from the vernacular originals; where they fail him, Shaw has borrowed from the domestic architecture of Street and Butterfield. In this sense, the new style is superficial. All three buildings boast the obvious apparatus of the old wealden houses: massive chimneys, tile-hung upper storeys, mullioned windows with leaded lights, and a complex enveloping roof grasping the whole composition. But they also possess rigid structures of stone or brick, not of timber, and where half-timbering occurs, whether constructional or not, it is just a charming appurtenance.

Nothing could drive home the limitations of the new style more forcibly than Eagle Wharf, Shaw's first major building. It is the ultimate test of the vernacular's flexibility, and it ends up being hardly vernacular at all. The commission came from his cousin James Temple's firm, but the storage space provided was probably used by the Shaw Savill line. Since 1859, when Robert Shaw and Walter Savill had begun chartering ships, trade had

15. Bromley Palace, Bailiff's Cottage.

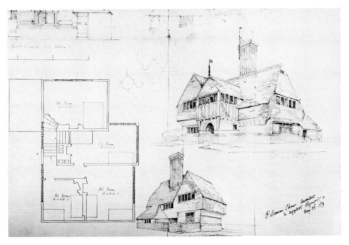

16. Bromley Palace, Bailiff's Cottage, drawings, 1863.

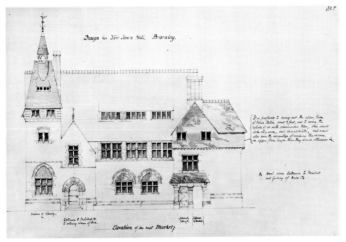

17. Bromley Town Hall, unexecuted design, 1863.

fast expanded, and now the partners were hoping for a contract, duly awarded in 1863, to carry emigrants to Otago. As yet they probably had no vessels of their own, which will have increased their storage problems. The Savills, who had building and brewing interests in the East End, may also have needed wharfage and warehouse space. Temple accordingly found a thin plot on either side of Narrow Street behind Ratcliffe Highway, and asked Richard to provide a tall warehouse, an office and housing for the wharfinger. By chance, Shaw had already built a warehouse. The first work he appears to have acquired on leaving Street was a warehouse with vaults for a city wine merchant, on an awkward site in Coopers Row. It was in Gothic of a kind, but very likely hulking and incoherent. That was designed in June 1862 before his visits to the weald; in Narrow Street, he hankered for something prettier. But for Old England to come to the insalubrious London dockland, Shaw had to make sacrifices and mix styles quite freely, rather as Nesfield was beginning to do at Combe Abbey. Though therefore there is still much of Street and Burges in the design, there is much else of startling originality. Though long ago demolished without remark, Eagle Wharf is known from a set of smart contract drawings and an ebullient water-colour perspective (ills. 18, 19). A sheer brick block rises from the river, the corners unencumbered, the top tile-hung beneath the gable, and capped with a crisp roof crowned by ship finials. Rough derricks and spars punctuate the sides of the hatches, which run straight from top to bottom, splitting the centre. To Narrow Street, the upper storeys are corbelled out over stumpy stone piers at the ends of the ground floor office. On this side of the street, the planning and construction are orthodox; the vaults have iron ties, the upper floors cast iron pillars to obtain the maximum superficial footage. It seems likely that this Thames-side part of the project alone was built. But the drawings (ill. 19) show the scheme extended to carry the internal railway used for haulage at first floor level across the street on a flap which could be let down at will, to a smaller building opposite incorporating storage space and housing.[10]

Of the Bailiff's Cottage at Bromley Palace (1863–4), now also demolished, we have a photograph, enough to recognize a masterpiece *in parvo* (ill. 15). The house clasps itself tight around the central stack, as though the whole top storey cannot break free from the walls and is bound by the contradictory tendency of its members to slip in different directions. The planning, too, is taut (ill. 16). On this small scale, good lighting and generous spacing are hard to effect. Shaw manages it, by means of tricks such as bringing up the flues over the stairs to the stack, or preferring to lose space at the stairhead and divide the steps left and right at that point, in order to get more room below.

Slightly later, Shaw ran off some cottage designs for the brickyard workmen of this estate. One semi-detached example survives at Widmore, poorly detailed and perhaps built without supervision, but still markedly original for its date (1866) and again possessed of the same self-contained will to movement. However, his most enterprising scheme for Bromley was never built. Coles Child, his client, who had recently bought Bromley Palace, wished to secure his status as lord of the manor by presenting Bromley with a new Town Hall. In 1863 Shaw produced designs, again mixing wealden vernacular with the Gothic of Street and Burges (ill. 17). Police station, market and assembly rooms were to be piled with gay abandon upon an irregular and closely bounded site, in the same unprecedented style he had used for Child's bailiff. No better illustration

18. Eagle Wharf, watercolour perspective of riverside front of warehouse, c.1862–3.

19. Eagle Wharf, long section, showing warehouse and proposed premises across Narrow Street, 1863.

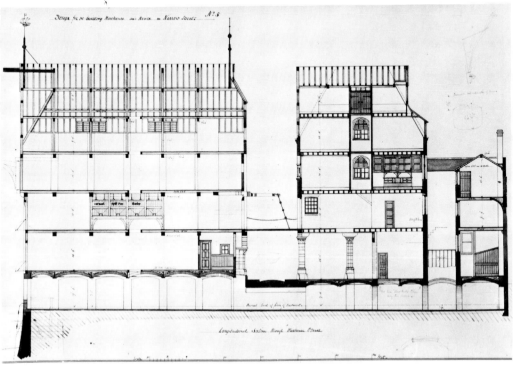

exists of the apparent effortlessness and natural power of his early work; as with the 1858 organs, the genius of this medley defies discussion as it defied imitation. It is fun, but it would also have been expensive, and the project was passed over.[11]

Projects like this were good practice, but they did not pay the rent. Nesfield was now beginning to make headway in his work, and Shaw sorely needed to do the same. 1864 looked like being a bad year. The church he was hoping to build in Yorkshire was put off for lack of funds, and he fared no better in the competitions he entered. Further, to find his feet in the Old English style, Shaw really needed to apply it in the context from which it was derived, that is, to land a lucrative domestic job in the southern counties. He must therefore have been thankful when, late in the year, the painter and academician J. C. Horsley asked him to extend his farmhouse near Cranbrook in Kent. This commission turned out to be not just Shaw's saving but his making. Almost at once, Horsley found him another job nearby, with others to follow.

see p 25

John Callcott Horsley had been one of the Redleaf painters and was now, in common with others, continuing that tradition. After the death of William Wells, the association of artists at Penshurst continued for a while. Several local families, the Hardinges at South Park, their stepson Walter James (who took Redleaf for a time), and Lord De L'Isle himself at Penshurst Place still exercised a modest form of Wells' hospitality. And the railway, inimical to the country ways the painters wished to record, but a boon to their own movements and independence, was opening up the home counties. This encouraged one or two of them, notably Academicians, and artists of life rather than landscape, to rent vernacular farmhouses or cottages where they might lay the scenes for their reconstructions of country customs, and yet be only an hour or two from the Academy and the events of the season. Painters were thus among the earliest commuters and weekenders. Some chose Surrey. Abinger became an early artistic haunt, after Richard Redgrave took a farmhouse there in 1851. In 1853 he was joined by James Hook, who afterwards moved to Churt and designed and built himself a tile-hung home there in 1865–6. And in 1861, Birket Foster settled at Witley, building a half-timbered house with some help from Decimus Burton.[12]

But the main choice fell upon the sleepy Kentish town of Cranbrook, as yet not reached by the railway, but with nearby connections. The pioneer was Thomas Webster of the old Redleaf group, who in the early 1850s began to spend his summers there with his pupil Frederic Hardy, painting cottage interiors. When C. W. Cope visited them in 1857 they were in residence for much of the year, and by the early 1860s, a homogeneous group of artists was painting there regularly: Webster, Hardy, G. B. O'Neill, A. E. Mulready and Horsley. These were the nucleus of the Cranbrook Colony, with the American G. H. Boughton a more occasional visitor.[13]

Of these men, Horsley was the most powerful and talented character. A puritanical, stubborn and emotional figure, he by turns amused and exasperated his fellow Academicians with his vagaries; now a hitherto-unknown form of greeting called a 'Christmas Card' for Henry Cole, now an angry campaign against nude modelling. Music, art and medicine all turn up regularly in the talented Horsley strain, whose connections, even for the Victorian period, were remarkable. Mendelssohn, for instance, had regularly graced the soirées of the 1840s at their Kensington town house, while I. K.

20. Willesley, entrance front, with Shaw's additions of 1864–5.

21. Willesley, view of back, showing rear of the 1864–5 additions, with studio (1869) to left, and old house to right.

Brunel had married Horsley's sister. Horsley himself had seemed something of a prodigy in youth. His precocious *Rent Day at Haddon Hall in the time of Queen Elizabeth* (1836) showed historical genre painting at its best: an exact colourful recreation of Tudor custom, conceived by the nineteen-year-old Horsley over a series of lingering visits to the Derbyshire house. Since then he had progressed little, but was accepted as a charming painter of the second rank and a good teacher at the Government School of Design. The death of his first wife had been a great blow, so when he was remarried, to the sister of the pioneer etcher and surgeon Seymour Haden, he was content to seek a quiet country life. The Cranbrook experiment gave him his chance. He found a comfortable farmhouse half a mile north of the town at Willesley, and soon bought it. Now he was applying to Shaw for an extension to it.[14]

Later, Shaw must have shaken his head at the way in which he approached this job. He had before him not an old, rambling half-timbered yeoman's house like Old Wilsley over the road where G. B. O'Neill had his *pied-à-terre*. Here instead was a neat, five-bayed brick box of the earliest years of the eighteenth century, with a high hipped roof and a tall ash before the door. Shaw's response was to stick on an extra unit at one end, a long hall with a wide-mullioned projecting bay at the other, dormers above, and at the back of the roof, a cheeky square belvedere (ill. 20). At a stroke, the neatness plunges into an additive chaos, saved from dissolution only by clever extension of the planes of the old roofing, and adroit placing of the chimneys. There is certainly control here, of a strange sort. Behind, in the back yard, come the fireworks (ill. 21): a very broadly hipped gable united with the stack of Shaw's first inglenook, casements under the eaves, fishscale tile-hanging, pink brickwork with the 'headers' toned in blue, and unprecedented Japanese-style patterns incised in plasterwork and crowned with green bottle bases (ill. 63). As a climax, Shaw had a peacock incised in the gable head, with each of the eyes of its tail feathers made of the same green glass.

Within is the first of the long series of Shaw's halls, and at the same time the one most integral to family life (ill. 22). Since the Horsleys consciously strove to ape the old communal customs and hospitality, it blends roughness and refinement in an anticipation by thirty years and more of the mood of Baillie Scott. The hall is single-storey still, but appears high after the farmhouse ceilings elsewhere. Oak panelling (originally unstained) procured locally with great difficulty lines the walls, yet at one end it was flanked by a rich embroidered curtain. In the inglenook, contemporary with Nesfield's first at Farnham Park, heavy settles framed a bluntly protruding chimneypiece, yet above and round the whole room ran a frieze of French stamped leather. Bell pulls, casement fasteners and gas brackets are all fashioned in the manner of old wealden ironwork, and Shaw designed deliberately crude rush-seated angle chairs for the room (ill. 139). But again, the plasterwork takes pride of place. Upon the white ceiling floats a bevy of incised circles and ellipses in simple sun and moon patterns (ill. 64). They, like the external plastering, were executed by Crump the builder and his two assistants, after Shaw himself had drawn the first lines upon the soft plaster.[15] Here is the spirit of Ruskin asserting itself: equality of craftsman and architect, involvement of the workman in decorative design. Indeed, the incised ceiling patterns became a Cranbrook speciality, recurring in the ceiling of Webster's studio a decade later, and in the additions made to Willesley in 1886. By then,

Shaw had himself extended the house, for in 1869 he made it even more lopsided by adding a galleried studio next to the hall, with a wagon ceiling in panels and some rare structural half-timbering to the back.

How much John Horsley's friendship meant to Shaw may be seen from the many commissions he won from the artist's friends and clients. There is another telling test. Through Shaw's office in the 1870s and '80s passed three children of the Cranbrook painters, Edwin Hardy, Frederick O'Neill, and Gerald Horsley, and a fourth pupil from the district, W. West Neve, of the same social circle. It is a significant shift of profession. As the domestic revival waxed, a whole generation of artists fledged among the cottages found their passion in architecture rather than in the gradually dying picturesque school of painting. In architecture alone was the rural, romantic tradition really alive at the turn of the century, when literature had turned elsewhere and English painting was uncertain of its course.

That Horsley could set up Norman Shaw's career is something of a surprise. It shows

22. Willesley, a corner of the living room.

how much we underrate the power of the Victorian establishment painters. They were rich men, commanding high prices at the galleries and assured of a steady income through reproduction rights. Often enough they owned two large studio houses, one in the country and another in London. The pictures they sold were painted for a market in which the same clients and dealers would feature, so their patrons would sometimes form friendships with them, quite different from the stiffer, more exacting social role entailed between architect and client. A painter, too, had qualifications to decide on matters of taste which might easily lead him to be asked advice on the choice of an architect. Thus a millowner like Hugh Sleigh of Leek or a powerful industrialist and inventor like Sir William Armstrong could follow Horsley's lead and employ Shaw. More important were the evidence of Willesley itself and an introduction to its architect. Lady Armstrong, visiting Cranbrook in 1868 when Shaw was there, must have taken glowing reports back to Newcastle. And local society, as at Penshurst, quickly welcomed the artistic interlopers; the Steuarts and D'Aguilars of Hawkhurst and the Houstons of Sissinghurst were all soon keeping Shaw busy with jobs of greater or lesser import. A little further afield, he was in 1868 designing a small suburban house at Beckenham for the successful novelist Dinah Mulock and her husband George Lillie Craik, friends again of the Horsleys.[16]

The painters themselves are a different case. They had their own judgment, could be expected to make a personal choice of architect, and often wished to participate in the making of the design. The first after Horsley to go to Shaw was the marine painter Edward Cooke, the second Frederick Goodall, both old companions from Redleaf days. It is now Cooke, born in Pentonville without property or prospects, but by this time rich and secure in a talent of a higher order than Horsley's, who plays his part in the furtherance of Norman Shaw's country house career. His surviving diary breathes the resolution and romance of the self-made man building his own house in the country.

Cooke from his youth had great vitality and diffuse interests: gardening, geology and art. Each of these had to be catered for in the house he dreamed of for his old age. He was already familiar with the skills of architecture, having been one of Augustus Pugin's draughtsmen for a short while.[17] In 1864 he added to his London house under the supervision of Decimus Burton, an old friend, and soon after, he began to think seriously of selling up in town and building for himself in the country. He started by consulting another architectural friend, Anthony Salvin. The difficulty was not finding a designer, nor was it style or manner of building. Redgrave's Abinger farmhouse, the projects of Foster and Hook, and Horsley's additions to Willesley must have been the talk of this small set, and on top of this, Salvin himself had acquired a farmhouse at Fernhurst in the country beyond Haslemere, with scenic views and a rocky glen, where the Donaldsons, Nesfields and Cooke spent a pleasant weekend in 1865. The second half of that year was taken up for Cooke in a determined enquiry into the availability, cost and appearance of different dramatic, picturesque sites. Here was the problem. In September, he inspected land at Reigate, in October at Haywards Heath; in November, Salvin suggested a farm at Fernhurst. But in December, friends drew his attention to some superb land belonging to the Goldsmiths' Company, five miles from Penshurst on the Kent and Sussex border at Groombridge.[18]

From Groombridge to the north-east runs a series of sharp, irregular valleys bearing the minor Medway tributaries. Upon their sides starts out spasmodically a sandstone outcrop, best known from the boulders on the commons at Tunbridge Wells, and unexpectedly brusque and powerful in this warm, wealden environment. It gave a tang to the jaded palates of the Victorian urban middle classes seeking the medicinal comforts of the spa at Tunbridge Wells. A mere thirty miles from London, they found in the bare outcrop and harsher vegetation of these slopes, token reminders of Scotland or the Alps, acceptably watered down to English taste. Ruskin, in a lecture given there in 1858, recollected how in boyhood 'Tunbridge Wells was my Switzerland, and I used to be brought down here in the summer, a sufficiently active child, rejoicing in the hope of clambering sandstone cliffs of stupendous height above the common.'[19] Three miles further south and west, Groombridge had all these delights, more splendid and unspoilt. On the flat land by the infant Grom stood Groombridge Place, most exquisite of moated houses. Across the stream in Sussex began the huge Hamsell Estate of the Goldsmiths' Company, till lately ruinous as a result of a long chancery suit, and now ripe for improvement. A Tunbridge Wells to Uckfield railway was in the offing, and at Groombridge, where an important junction with other lines was contemplated, the Goldsmiths had astutely secured the promise of a station.[20] Once that was open, in 1867, they were ready with the bait of large estates on long building leases; E. W. Cooke was their first fish. Round the small village, Shaw was to build three houses, a school and a church.

Wanting to fix the best possible site for his house on this uncrowded terrain, Cooke considered and sketched several. The problem was the railway, essential for access; a coupling junction to avoid Groombridge was intended, threatening some of the best land, and involving Cooke in negotiations with the railway company and frequent visits. On April 18th, 1866, Cooke fixed a site and christened it Rockhurst, then drove on to Redleaf to tell his old friends of his decision. Two days later, the 55-year-old Academician was back on the overgrown ground, felling trees and removing hollies and shrubs with his own hands, like any do-it-yourself improver of today. From then on he was constantly at the site, directing workmen in the clearing work, excavation, and rock blasting necessary to make space for the foundations and reveal the outcrop more boldly. The site had the contours customary for many country houses: level on the entrance side for easy access, but dropping quickly from the back to give a good view from where the reception rooms were to be. In spare moments, Cooke prepared plans for his house. As early as January, Burton was giving him hints on how to improve the design. Then suddenly in early May he put himself into the hands of Norman Shaw. No doubt Salvin had tipped him off, but Shaw's startling work for Horsley (whom Cooke considered an ass in other respects) must have been the decisive factor.[21]

As Shaw was to do on other occasions when people approached him with ideas of their own, he quietly took Cooke's plans over until they became entirely his. But the plan and style of the house must to a degree have been Cooke's choice, and in that he was important. Nesfield and Shaw had both built vernacular cottages, and Shaw had already produced one warehouse and a town hall design in the style. But when preparing an abortive design for the Farnham Market Hall competition of 1864, where Old English would have been at least as suitable as at Bromley, he reverted to Gothic. So there was still stylistic prevarication in Shaw's mind, and at this date no reason why his country houses might not have gone in a wholly different direction. Nesfield, already as we shall see the architect of country houses big and small, used Old English for his additions to Farnham Park, just as Shaw had done at Willesley, but avoided it in his new large jobs; the first country houses in which he opts entirely for Old English do not occur until the early 1870s. Devey too, after Hammerfield, was cautious about letting too much of the vernacular obtrude into his larger buildings and tended to restrict it to his cottages. But ten years after Hammerfield, the style recurs revitalized in two larger houses for rival marine painters: 'Hooksville' and 'Cookesville'.[22] At Churt, J. C. Hook's Silverbeck showed what an artist might build for himself, a crude pioneering house with Gothic detail and tile-hanging loosely mixed. At Groombridge, in going to Shaw for Glen Andred (as the house came soon to be called) and insisting upon the wealden style, Cooke was laying a path which nearly a hundred years of housing in the south of England would tread in one form or another. For transferring the style from cottage to country house, the painters themselves are in large part responsible.

Glen Andred shares its niche in history with two other houses at Groombridge, the one more modest, the other more magnificent. At the end of 1866, Cooke and Shaw made the journey half a mile up the lane to a high rocky site overlooking Glen Andred, again on Goldsmiths' ground. Here they fixed the position of Leyswood, a larger country mansion intended for James Temple, the rich cousin of Shaw's who by now directed the Shaw Savill line. And on 10th May 1870, they helped lay out and toast the success of Hillside, a new house on the other side of Groombridge for Cooke's friend, the explorer William Oswell, who had witnessed Cooke's own ceremony nearly four years before. These three houses lie at the heart of Shaw's country house career. In creating Glen Andred and Leyswood, he welded and tested the elements of his domestic 'Old English' style. They are explorations of a new vocabulary up to the very limit, to fit the spectacular sites and personal tastes of his clients. Neither the planning nor the details of these two bask yet in the calm authority of the third house, Hillside. There, on the mellower Kentish slopes beyond the outcrop, Shaw can by 1870–1 casually sling together the well-known mélange of brickwork, tile-hanging, half-timbering, pointed porch, high chimneys and blunt gables, into a happy, four-square whole. In Glen Andred and Leyswood this was yet to be done. Glen Andred, the first of the group, lies flanking the top of the escarpment, its basement exposed and battered against the incline over which it perches (ill. 24). It has a leanness and tautness; no bargeboards encumber the gables, there is no half-timbering, the tall stacks are crisp and abnormally thin, all windows are held sharply in under the eaves line, and even the capping of the polygonal bay, a standard item in Shaw's merchandise of the 1870s, adheres to the main roofline. At Leyswood the selections are different: a looser, conglomerate composition for the site, a half-timbered entrance front, a proliferation of variable gables, only the smallest of angle bays, and above all, ranks of tough, thickly ribbed chimneys of a new and stronger profile, which *The Builder* found 'excessively ugly and indefensible upon any but archaeological grounds'.[23] On both houses, the fetching decorative motifs of Willesley beat a retreat. Only the finials at Glen Andred are Japanese, and the plasterwork is confined to the three 'date' gables over the door (ill. 23). For Leyswood, Shaw borrowed many points of planning and of the

23. (above) Glen Andred, entrance front.

24. (left) Glen Andred, perspective of garden side, *c.* 1868.

25. Leyswood, revised bird's eye perspective showing court, 1870.

26. Leyswood, perspective of garden side, 1870.

27. Leyswood, entrance front.

28. Leyswood, stables and gate tower.

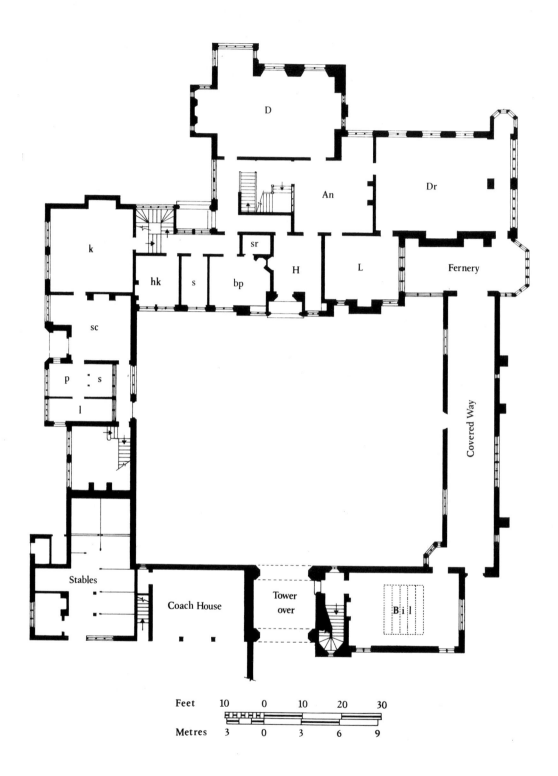

29. Leyswood, reconstruction of ground floor plan as completed.

handling of brickwork from Nesfield's masterpiece, Cloverley Hall. But the effect of the changes he made between his two perspectives of the house, the first of 1868 and the second of 1870 (ill. 25), was to omit most of the surface ornament that Nesfield would have loved and to strengthen and simplify the main lines of the house, as Shaw's sense of style matured and the dark tone of the site had its influence upon his thought.[24]

Even now, the mood of Leyswood can be partly caught from its ruins. It was the queen of the Groombridge houses, dominant upon the very highest rocks that could be found (ill. 26). Approached from below up a sinuous ascending drive, it started up from the crag like a sort of citadel in a romantic burst of dull-red brickwork and tilework, dark windows, and fierce oversailing chimneys. Skirting the side of this arrogant front, a short gorge driven through the outcrop (here Shaw intended a footbridge over from house to gardens) led the traveller to a kinder, level court, bounded by hedges of clipped privet. To the left, a gate in the walled garden still beckons to the longlost orchard, hothouses, little gooseberry pavilion, and thatched dairy. Straight on was the stable yard, hidden behind another high wall. But to the right still stands the only memorial to the departed severity of Leyswood, a high tower guarding the entrance, crowned with a tile-hung hutch (ill. 28). It is a deft adaptation of Nesfield's stable tower at Cloverley (ill. 34) to the confines of the weald, but it embodies too, perhaps, a rare reminiscence of Shaw's travels—a hint back to the city gateways of Nuremberg. Within, the setting dissolved into something warmer and more homely. Here lay a square, sixty-foot yard, a full recreation of the old manorial garth, such as Scott had lately commended for his ideal house, such too as Shaw must have known well from Ightham and Haddon.[25] And the house itself, on the further side of the court (ill. 27), was markedly small and intimate after the dour foreshadowings from below—certainly smaller than Shaw's own perspectives suggest. Its centre was compact, with a mere three reception rooms. The offices and outhouses rambled along one side of the garth to the stable and coachhouse by the tower, while a covered passage along the other led, after 1871, to the billiard room (ill. 29). In another sense, the perspectives do reveal the truth: Old English good cheer in the heart of sternness and drama.

One further word on Glen Andred and Leyswood, and by implication on many of Shaw's buildings: the sea. Unprompted, people without knowledge of Shaw or his architecture will frequently liken his buildings to ships. It is the mark of certain fine buildings to convey, when most firmly anchored upon their site, some sense of their direction. A pure intuition of volumes and proportions permits us to grasp this, mainly from the outsides of buildings, but sometimes within as well; the name of 'nave' cannot have been given to the spaces of early churches on grounds of shape or function alone, without some added sense of analogy with the loveliest of hollow bodies known to man. With Shaw at his best, this intuition constantly recurs. The Bingley Church, the Bournemouth Convent, even the massive fortress of New Scotland Yard, attain it. But at Groombridge it has a significance that was conceivably conscious. For Cooke, the marine painter, engaged, in Ruskin's words, in 'hunting quarries across the foam', Shaw designs a house recalling a long, trim vessel athwart the escarpment's edge; for his own cousin, director of a shipping line, he creates the mighty stranded ark of Leyswood, whose proud finials, had the contract drawings been exactly followed, would have been crowned with

43

schooners like those of Eagle Wharf. The sea was in Shaw's veins, whether he knew it or not. More than any other great English architect, he spent a lifetime designing ships upon land.

NESFIELD AND SHAW

Early in 1863, shortly after the first of the Old English works were begun, Eden Nesfield and Norman Shaw took the remainder of Salvin's lease for the ground floor at 30 Argyll Street, close to Oxford Circus, and set up office together. They were not yet partners even in name; that was an arrangement which existed for only three years, 1866–9. But they could now exchange ideas and assist each other without interruption, and immediately the question arises of who originated what. What, in particular, was Nesfield's role at the time?

Blomfield repeats Shaw's son, whose memoir assumes that Nesfield was his father's follower in everything he did. That is far from the truth, but so too is a view which has had more recent credit, that Nesfield was the innovator and Shaw came after him and stole his glory. The position is this. Nesfield's earliest buildings are all Gothic in style, however variable they may be. His Croxteth Hall estate cottages, for instance, of 1861–2, and his small country house of 1863, Sproughton Manor, still conform to the brickwork traditions of Street and Butterfield, however strenuous and excellent they may be. The first real sign of genius was the sumptuous, stone-built wing at Combe Abbey (1863–5).[26] Here, after experiment, Nesfield decided on a personal method of articulating Burges's idiosyncratic style of Gothic, several years before Burges had built Castell Coch or Cardiff Castle. But if Burges had encouraged eclecticism of detail, Nesfield now applied it triumphantly to architecture proper (ill. 33). In style, the Combe Abbey wing passed from Norman to Gothic to Tudor with perfect ease; in composition, its facility foreshadowed Shaw at his most masterly. It was the boldest step yet among Gothic revivalists away from stylistic purity. It provides the kernel of an understanding of Nesfield without Shaw, of the point of departure he had reached when they began working together. But though Combe Abbey was of inestimable value for Shaw's development, it offered limited hints for Old English.

For Nesfield, the move towards eclecticism was decisive. Though the leaded parapets, cannon chimneys and queer roof shapes of Combe recur later in his career, they become just some of the appurtenances of a handful of fast-changing domestic styles. Of these, Old English was certainly one of the most important. After the Sussex tour of 1862 with Shaw and his further visit to the Tunbridge Wells area, Nesfield evolved his own variant of the new vernacular. But to his agile mind, it was another style to add to the gamut, charmingly effective for small cottages, but of doubtful relevance to larger houses. So with the exception of an early addition at Farnham Park (1864–5), not unlike Willesley, Nesfield at first kept Old English for the little jobs he so much liked, estate improvement works for old clients and friends of his father and himself. The Regent's Park lodge (1864), his first essay in the manner, also gave London its introduction to the revived vernacular.[27] It was paid for by William Cowper, the Commissioner of Works, as part of a campaign of improvements to the London parks undertaken in collaboration with the Nesfields.[28] Promenaders along the Broad Walk, as reorganized by Eden's brother Markham Nesfield, noted the stout young man, now bearded and wearing the French artisan's smock, energetically sticking the bottoms of green bottles into the cement coving of the quaint new lodge.[29]

These broken glass pieces imposed upon incised cement work occur in both men's jobs of the mid-1860s. Nesfield used them again in the lodge at Bradfield Combust (1865) and in his pretty cottages at Crewe Hall (1865–7, but sometimes misdated as earlier); Shaw at Bromley and at Willesley. They are one of many signs of a frank interchange of all ideas between the two; their Old English vocabulary is one and the same. So there is no serious question of priority. The friends invented the style together in 1862–4. Yet a contrast between Nesfield's and Shaw's cottages of the 1860s does highlight their differences of character. Nesfield, we know, was 'a man of strong impulses, equally actuated by strong likes and dislikes'. Accordingly at Regent's Park and Crewe Hall, almost every cottage seems bulky, squat and blunt, half-hipped and cut back jerkily to the ridge, the work of a stubborn and impetuous temperament. In Gothic the result would be fierce, but Nesfield lovingly adorns his designs with a riot of wilful detail in any manner from the Japanese to the vernacular: incised work, carved bargeboards, tongue-shaped wall tiling, turned balusters, heraldry, monograms and dates. It was for this multiplicity of enthusiasms that his chosen intimates loved him. Shaw's vernacular is less busy and extravagant than this. His buildings, big or small, seem longer, leaner, taller and milder, mirroring the difference in physical height and proportion between the friends. Gables may be subdivided, windows may be unequally spaced, but all is tied together with a conviction that Nesfield sometimes lacks.

The 1860s were Nesfield's architectural heyday.[30] While they shared offices, Shaw took freely from the wealth of innovation that Nesfield lavished upon each of his early compositions. He had perceived early on that Old English would not offer as many answers as Shaw, initially perhaps, hoped. Other domestic architects also took refuge in eclecticism, but Nesfield outshone all at fusing disparate elements into coherent new styles. While his powers lasted, they were of prodigious range. Cloverley Hall, for instance, designed in 1864 and built in 1866–8, enlarges upon and refines the ideas of Combe Abbey. Here there was a plethora of original ideas for Shaw to mull over and integrate with his own thinking; two-inch brickwork, split-level planning, massive use of concealed structural ironwork, slate-hanging (on one of the lodges), and the stable tower with penthouse which we have seen Shaw reworking at Leyswood (ill. 34). Elsewhere Nesfield was pioneering something quite different. The Kew Gardens Lodge of 1867 (ill. 31) and the reconstruction of Kinmel Park (ill. 35), also designed in the late 1860s, were among the first recognizably Queen Anne buildings, the rubbed brickwork of the one inspired in part by the Dutch House at Kew, while the other borrows from Wren's Quadrangle at Hampton Court. But though they had their effect upon Shaw, these buildings were not published and do not strictly belong to the Queen Anne style soon to emerge in the 1870s. Here, the differences of approach between the two men are illuminating. For Shaw, Queen Anne was to be a distinctively urban style. Twice in the 1860s he used such a manner outside London, but both times for altering existing houses;[31] for new domestic works in the country, Old English was his preferred choice.

45

30. Shipley Hall, farm buildings (Nesfield, 1860–1).

31. Kew Gardens, Temperate House lodge (Nesfield, 1867).

32. Broadlands, Romsey, main lodge (Nesfield, 1870).

33. (above) Combe Abbey, Nesfield's wing, 1863–5.

34. (right) Cloverley Hall, Nesfield's stable tower, 1866–8.

35. Kinmel Park, Nesfield's remodelling of the entrance front, 1871–4.

When Shaw went more gradually through the stylistic transitions that Nesfield made so fast, he was always searching for something more appropriate for each building type. But for Nesfield, style was a delight pure and simple, to be decided upon almost whimsically. After 1870, the invention began to run out, though the cleverness continued to the end of his career. There are high points: the reconstruction of Bodrhyddan, the bank at Saffron Walden and the library at Bank Hall. But he began availing himself of Shaw's ideas, just as Shaw had been glad to use his earlier on, and started to build more largely in Old English. By this time his pupils were looking as much to Shaw as to him. Nesfield could not create a school, because his eclecticism required such formidable ability. The same has been said of Shaw, but it applies more acutely to Nesfield.

The first three years in Argyll Street, from 1863, were halcyon. Nesfield, 'the stout party in the other room' (as Shaw describes him to Cooke),[32] set the tone from the start by importing an office parrot. It did not take to the atmosphere, soon died, and was drawn by Nesfield lying in state on a special catafalque.[33] His office became more accurately a studio, a treasure-house of exotic oddments, furniture of all types, Japanese prints, and drawings by artist friends.[34] Shaw's room was less flamboyant, but contained whatever he could afford to collect and display. Never an obsessive collector, he confined himself to one main interest at a time; later it was to be clocks, but in the 1860s it was 'pots'. By this was meant the blue and white Nanking porcelain soon to become so fashionable. It was already avidly sought by the smart artistic set, among whom the orient was the current novelty.

The history of 'blue and white' in England follows the pattern of dissemination of Japanese print and book designs.[35] Not long after the first systematic plunderings of the Far East by Europeans, its fine wares began to appear in western markets. Both were first noticed in France, taken up by Rossetti and then by Whistler, and introduced to a wider public by the 1862 Exhibition. The first regular importer of Chinese porcelain into England was the young Arthur Liberty, but the trade was soon identified with Murray Marks. Shaw was a friend of both. He gave help when Liberty set up his own shop, and was to be thankful for Liberty's loyalty during the final chapter of his own career.[36] For Murray Marks he designed a famous Oxford Street shopfront for the display of 'pots' (1875–6), helped lay out an exhibition of Sir Henry Thompson's blue and white in 1878, and took over, on Marks' recommendation, the redecoration of F. R. Leyland's house after the historic quarrel with Whistler over the Peacock Room and the death of its architect, Thomas Jeckyll.[37] From both men Shaw had what seemed afterwards bargains which adorned the office and the rooms at Albion Road. When his eldest son Robert was born, his father's first reaction was 'we have an heir to the blue pots'.[38] But Shaw may have parted with much of his blue and white towards the end of his life, as did many collectors, tempted by inflation and bored by later enthusiasts. Rossetti gave away much of his to pay off debts; Shaw probably sold pots to buy clocks instead.

The effect of these oriental discoveries upon Victorian architecture and furniture should not be exaggerated. In architecture proper it was naturally small. Certainly, the freedom of some of the best buildings associated with the Japanese taste, notably E. W. Godwin's studio houses in Chelsea, is the counterpart of the sense of liberation that swept a whole school of painters in the wake of Rossetti and Whistler. Men knew suddenly that they could now look beyond Europe, break out of the classical and Dutch traditions, shake off even the new mediaevalizing bonds, and use each of them when and as they wished. But the actual Japanese motifs of decoration that bedeck the works of Nesfield, Shaw, Godwin and their rivals between 1865 and 1880 are symptom, not cause; they symbolize the claim to a wider freedom of stylistic choice. This is what the 'Aesthetic Movement' signifies as a meaningful term: neither a mere oriental craze, nor a coherent philosophy aimed at liberating art from ethical values.[39] And architects could not contribute as much to the orientalizing movement as painters did, because of the non-stylistic norms in western building which could not be easily overthrown.

Shaw himself assimilated Japanese ornament slowly and used it sparingly. In the 1850s, Rossetti began to adorn his picture frames with small whorl decorations derived from the sun and petal patterns upon his eastern pots and prints. They foreshadow the painted whorls upon the early furniture of Burges and Morris, the roundels or 'pies' of Nesfield and Shaw's practice of the 1860s, and the sunflowers which became the badge of 'Aesthetic' architecture. But what they did at first was to open architects' eyes to the existence of such formalized circular patterns in mediaeval work: the Cosmati pavements in Westminster Abbey, the marble discs shown in Ruskin's illustrations of the Venetian palaces, and, most remarkably, the gouged roundels of English mediaeval woodwork which embellish the sides of many old church chests and bench ends.[40] Thus in the inlay of the 1861 bookcase, Shaw is bent on reinterpreting mediaeval ornament in the light of Japan. So too, when Nesfield and Shaw incise the cement-plasterwork of their early cottages, they are again resurrecting and varying an old tradition, this time the pargetting of East Anglia. More literal borrowings they at first avoided. The very 'pies' were field enough for the invention of an infinity of patterns; they could be liberally and asymmetrically dotted round in differing materials and contexts: ceilings, bargeboards, gateposts, grates, dados and even the background patterns of church fittings.

However, they could be overworked. Nesfield, who was the more fascinated by Japan and appears to have introduced the name 'pies', definitely overdid the effect on some of his buildings. He was probably the first to employ overlapping and free-floating pies, a charming but sometimes heavy hallmark. Shaw, who followed suit on the bargeboards of the Farnham Bank, afterwards shrank from such liberality. Sometimes they are shown on his drawings, and they continue in his repertoire into the 1870's, but he avoids the mistake of depending too much upon this kind of ornament. It is the mark of a gradual loss of interest. The patterns of the early bookcase, or the plastering of the Willesley ceiling contribute to an integrated scheme of decoration; the occasional sunflower plaques of his Queen Anne houses do not.

After three years of sharing an office, in 1866 Nesfield and Shaw made the mistake of setting up a partnership together. Of this much discussed and misdated partnership, one thing has been frequently and correctly stated, that Nesfield and Shaw never did a joint work together. This is confirmed by the authority of J. M. Brydon, who was in the office at the time, working as clerk to both men.[41] All surviving drawings, letters and statements unite in showing that they designed their own jobs separately. Not even with the working drawings (which of course prove nothing about authorship) is it definitely possible to identify the other partner's hand, though it is tempting to ascribe one or two sheets for Cloverley Hall to Shaw, and for the Farnham Bank to Nesfield. All official reports were written in the formal plural, but can again be allotted to one of the two. They certainly supervised each other's jobs; Nesfield went more than once to Glen Andred, and Shaw managed important matters and made decisions over Cloverley and the Kew Lodge, so each knew his partner's work intimately.[42] But payments during this period seem to have been made to Nesfield, and the trained assistants who helped in the office, Brydon and Richard Creed, though they worked for both, owed their loyalties to Nesfield rather than Shaw, who did not take his first pupil until 1870.

Alongside all this one must put Robert Shaw's remark, reflecting (as normally) his father's retrospective opinion: 'The trouble was that Nesfield was always wanting to do everything and wished Mr Shaw to leave it all to him. Then nothing got done owing to Nesfield's habitual laziness. So the partnership came to an end.' This judgement, accepted by Blomfield, seems contrary to the evidence I have given. But there is an easy explanation. At the end of 1865 Shaw had little income still; his prospects perked up only in 1866–7 when the partnership was already operating. Probably, they rearranged their financial affairs so that Nesfield's capital was more involved and he paid the assistants, while Shaw earned extra money by helping Nesfield with administrative and perfunctory matters. That is confirmed by the case of Kew Lodge; though it was entirely Nesfield's design, three out of four surviving letters about it come from Shaw, not Nesfield.[43] Certainly, Nesfield delegated correspondence as Shaw never did, and probably in all good faith and enthusiasm concentrated too much on the designing part of the job. In any case, Shaw plainly found the arrangement disillusioning and tiring. By 1868, the volume of his own work made its continuation unnecessary, so next year they reverted, amicably but more distantly, to separate practice.

There were difficulties, too, in Nesfield's personality. John Hebb puts the matter with a splendid vagueness: Nesfield had 'an imperfect sympathy with conventional society'.[44] A little detail emerges here and there. Simeon Solomon, casting about for scurrilous 'swishing' stories with which to regale Swinburne, lights upon the Etonian experiences of Eden Nesfield, 'one of our very best architects, a man of great knowledge, invention, and consummate amiability. He is a fat, jolly hearty fellow, genuinely good natured, very fond of smoking, and I deeply grieve to say of women.' Solomon goes on to qualify; Nesfield, 'although doubtless bearing the marks of the many Etonian rods I mentioned, feels no more the *real* merit and meaning of that instrument of delight than my pen does; I should unhesitatingly pronounce him to be not at all of a sensual temperament in your and my conception of the term'.[45] Whatever this amounts to (and it may really be very little), there were other weaknesses later on at least. Robert Shaw says he 'tended to drink more than wise'; certainly he aged in appearance prematurely, and died from cirrhosis of the liver. Nesfield's notebooks and letters betray exclusive notions of honour and lineage, and abound with high spirits and literary wit. Yet underneath runs a current of melancholia and morbidity, a strain which deepened with the years and drew him into reclusiveness.[46] Thus he writes to a client in 1877:

> Personal work is very difficult, and I think becomes more so in one's sear and yellow. It used to be so nice:
> Tell zeal it lacks devotion
> Tell love it is but lust
> Tell time it is but motion
> Tell flesh it is but dust.[47]

It is unlikely that any one of these characteristics caused a rift. Shaw was chaste but not a prude, and he was known for his kindness; the two continued to share offices until 1876 without rupture. Further, twenty years of extensive practice are enough to scotch the idea that drinking and idleness got the better of Nesfield until 1880, when he gave up his practice, aged only forty-five. Five years later he married a divorcee, Mary Annetta Gwilt, daughter of the architect J. S. Gwilt. They retired to Brighton, where Nesfield died his sad and premature death in 1888. It was a pathetic demise for an architect of genius.

What may have hastened the drifting apart of the two friends was Shaw's own marriage. During the bachelor days in the office, while Nesfield was still convivial, Shaw's social life must have been intensive enough, yet little is known of how he spent his time or who his friends were. He had after all been through the R.A. and A.A. Schools and three distinguished offices, so he must have been on terms with most of the prominent architects of the reformed Gothic school, and with many artists, academic and Pre-Raphaelite. Yet only Nesfield seems to have been a real intimate. After him, John Clayton, John Sedding and Aldam Heaton (to whom we shall soon come) were the closest; Alfred Waterhouse, if the cradle Shaw designed for his infant son is a guide, may also have been a good friend. But none of these four moved freely in the more abandoned circles of Burges, Morris and Nesfield. The lack of means which excluded Shaw from the Fabs had not been relieved by the success of the Shaw Savill line. For in November 1864 Robert Ewart Shaw died suddenly of a heart attack, aged only forty-two. It was a dark moment in his brother's career. He was offered the partnership with Savill but declined it, so this lucrative post went instead to James Temple;[48] henceforward Shaw's links with the firm were to be professional. He had to console himself by designing a dour Gothic tomb for the family in Hampstead churchyard (ill. 288). What money there was went to Robert's young widow Augusta, while Shaw himself had to take on the role as head of the family. The time had come to think of matrimony.

John Horsley to his wife, on 30th November 1866:
Agnes is the Xian name of Shaw's *feehongsay*, her other cognomen I did not catch. She is decidedly pretty and intelligent looking, dark with an uncommon face somewhat. She is Australian! No mother I believe, and the Father not particularly referred to (all this was Nesfield's information walking home). She has been brought up by an uncle and aunt, commonish folk but looking highly respectable, near neighbours of the Shaws by whom they have been known (Agnes included) for years. Nesfield says S did not "spoon the girl" at all, but quickly made up his mind and proposed as recently as Tuesday week! Last night was his first introduction, as well as that of S's old friends the Pages, the eldest brother of the Page "over the way". As it was therefore a bit of a party and as I was the last comer I did not have much to say to Miss Agnes, but I was specially introduced in the evening, and was favourably impressed in the few words that passed. It is however impossible to form any particular opinion at such an interview. It is quite a love match, not a farthing of money being involved according to Nesfield.[49]

Agnes Wood was almost twenty at the time, the second daughter of James Wood, a colourful East Anglian who had emigrated to Australia, taking a favourite racehorse and a pregnant wife with him, and quelling a mutiny on shipboard *en route*. In the 1860s he brought his copious brood on a visit back to England, and Agnes was left there to finish her education under an aunt's care in Albion Road. Family tradition has it that she was about to return when Shaw stepped in and proposed to 'the girl next door'.[50]

They were married on 16th July 1867 in Hampstead Parish Church. Looking back on 'that eventful morning', Shaw recalled 'such a desire to jump over the churchyard wall into Mr Airey's garden! What a good thing I didn't, for they have been 18 years of unalloyed happiness, chiefly owing to having you alongside of me you dear old thing.'[51] They settled at 10 Albion Road. The Woods were at 14, Mrs Shaw and Jessie at 8, so this little street of plain modern houses near the Swiss Cottage became quite a family colony. To remove any doubts about his taste, Shaw had his drawing room painted white, his bedroom yellow with hangings, and special black furniture installed, probably to his own designs.[52] 'In 1870 these arrangements took people's breath away', says his son.

Agnes Shaw accorded with the serious side of her husband's temperament. Her upbringing had made her slightly prim and gave her a sense of religious proprieties which became a little overwhelming after Shaw's death. During his lifetime it was his custom to keep her good-humoured and cheerful by teasing her. But her shyness and preference for privacy must have increased his disinclination towards the Bohemianism of Nesfield and his coterie. Possibly Agnes and Nesfield did not get on. Though he was a frequent visitor to Albion Road in the early days of the marriage, Nesfield's appearances there decreased in the 1870s, and eventually the Shaws almost entirely lost touch with him.

From the start of the marriage, Shaw's practice began to 'take off', and the newly-weds were much on the move. The honeymoon at Canterbury was cut short by an attack of the recurrent malady that punctuated Shaw's career. There was some anxiety, but the trouble passed. In October they went off to Paris, partly no doubt to see the 1867 Exhibition, partly because it was on the way to Lyons, where the British consul Charles Haden had asked Shaw to design an English Church. From Lyons he wrote Agnes the first of a small but enlightening group of surviving family letters. At the beginning of his marriage, a Victorian husband might hardly know his wife, and there was here the added factor of an age gap of almost sixteen years. So at first he is a shade stiff, but speedily he warms into a rattle of endearments, absurdities and regrets. After the first child, Elizabeth Helen, was born in May 1868, Agnes was frequently left at home or went to stay either at Sissinghurst, to be near the Cranbrook friends, or with the Heatons in Yorkshire. From different points of the compass Shaw indited hard-pressed letters to her such as this:

10 Albion Road St J[ohns] W[ood]   Friday evening [July 1869]

My duck o'diamonds pussy cat,
    All serene, I got here this afternoon a little after 4, and found your tiny little letter a waiting for me. I am so glad to hear that you are well and enjoying yourself, and hope poor little Duckie is better, and getting on nicely with her teeth, poor little dear. I do miss you both so much you can't tell. It is as dull as ditchwater not having a ittle wife to tuddle, and with Baba to pet. I left that filthy Stockport on Thursday morning and did Meerbrook in the morning, and Calton in the afternoon. I find they want to build a chancel at Calton and have only got about £2 10 to spend, so I shall have 5 per cent on that which will amount to 2/6d good pay ain't it? Jessie says you write to say you are enjoying yourself very much. I hope you are ducky, and that you are getting on nicely with Mr and Mrs Heaton. The old lady is quite well, at least very fairly well—and Jessie do. Katie and she have just gone off to Mr Baumer's Concert, full fig in low bodies and short sleeves and with somebody elses curls in their hair. I have to go down to that hideous old D'Aguilar's tomorrow. If all is well I hope to be with you on Wednesday afternoon, and to stay as long as they will keep us. I remember now I went away and never left you any money—wot a beast? I hope you have some, and if you want any be sure you borrow. I ain't got a mortal thing to say, not one word. The house is all serene, nothing run away. All the chimbleys have been swept, and some of the carpeats beat, and the rug has come home from Duggins and looks cleaner, and the house is in generally a squashy state. Mrs Street called and left her and George Edmund's cards, and your aunt is staying with the Meadmores. I don't know where they live in Clarendon Terrace, but will be sure to see your aunt somehow. No more at present from
                                                    ever your most affectionate husband
                                                            Richard N. Shaw.

P.S. I have got David Copperfield for you.

In a pretty house called Woodbank, a mile out of the Yorkshire mill town of Bingley, lived in the 1860s a manufacturer of furnishings and stuffs called John Aldam Heaton. At heart he was an unwilling businessman, but he had got himself into an awkward position. His father had been a not so successful stuff merchant in Leeds, and when his sister Fanny married, confusingly enough, Dr John Deakin Heaton, the eminent and forceful physician of the Leeds Infirmary, the doctor rather than his homonymous father-in-law became head of the whole family. Into this family, Dr Heaton brought with him his redoubtable sister, Miss Ellen Heaton. Ellen was a professional celebrity chaser, firstly of Browning and then more doggedly of Ruskin, who took polite pains with her and soon had her collecting Rossetti's drawings. But she proved quite an ally for Aldam when he needed one; for in 1855, to imprecations on the part of his father, of Dr Heaton, and of a malicious aunt, he married the governess of the Heatons' highly respected neighbour Sir Peter Fairbairn. This was not an easy thing to live down in the closed social circles of Leeds, so Aldam Heaton and his bride betook themselves to nearby Bradford. There, from apparently little capital, he built up a series of interests in the stuffs trade. In 1861, he rented Woodbank, and began to take a larger interest in local affairs.[53]

Really, however, Aldam Heaton was a frustrated textile designer. At sixteen, he had produced a damask design for a Halifax firm.[54] On the basis of its success he had designed other fabrics, but such commissions gave him neither the artistic freedom nor the livelihood he wanted. To fulfil his ambitions, he fell in with his sister-in-law Ellen Heaton, and in about 1860 one must presume an extensive visit on his part to London, and introductions to Ruskin, Rossetti, Burges and Norman Shaw. His experiences had stiffened him; he was no longer, as when he courted his wife, uncertain of his future or his faith, but had developed a head for business, a sympathy for Ruskin's paternalistic socialism, a loyalty to the High Church Movement, and a passion for Advanced Gothic. Bradford and Bingley were not yet outposts of this last creed, but Heaton returned north ready to propagandize and convert his friends and neighbours. His ally in the campaign was a wealthy landowner, Alfred Harris of Ryshworth Hall.

Their success was spectacular. Very soon Ruskin, ever intuiting the sensitivities of his locality and audience, was giving the revolutionary doctrines of *Unto This Last* an application to art and manufacturing in a lecture at Bradford, and the Heatons were beseeching him to appear again.[55] In 1861, Rossetti's first stained glass went up in Aldam Heaton's home, three small panels, of which one showed his wife as the 'Lady of Woodbank'. Next year, before the 1862 Exhibition made their name, Heaton's neighbour Walter Dunlop commissioned the Morris firm to make panels for his house at Harden Grange. In 1864–5, Burges and Morris were doing work at Oakwood on the north side of Bingley. Lastly, in Bingley itself, Alfred Waterhouse designed the Mechanics Institute, and in March 1864 Norman Shaw was producing the contract drawings for the church of Holy Trinity, where Aldam Heaton was to be churchwarden.[56]

The campaign culminated in a magnificent failure, the Bradford Exchange Competition of 1864. Though it has been forgotten, it has a claim to be among the most illustrious and bizarre of the many bungled Victorian architectural competitions. The evident aim of Harris and Heaton was to foist Advanced Gothic upon the merchants and manufacturers of Bradford. Harris was Secretary of the Exchange Committee and could pull strings from there, while Heaton lobbied publicly from outside. Their strategy was at first wholly successful. The competition was to be limited to ten architects. No doubt most of the committee, who knew little about architecture (and were, as usual, not advised by a professional referee), cared only as long as the local men were well represented. They therefore put up Paul and Ayliffe (Bradford), Brodrick (Leeds), Lockwood and Mawson (Bradford), W. & G. Audsley (outsiders from Liverpool), and Milnes and France (Bradford), mostly classicists; while Harris procured invitations to Burges, Shaw, Philip Webb, Street and Waterhouse. The plotters must have been well content. Lockwood and Mawson, and Brodrick were the only men to fear, while on their side, nobody knew much about Burges, anything about Shaw or Webb—the only names conceivably familiar to the locals would have been Street and Waterhouse.

During the preparation of the designs, which despite very short notice had to be in by May 1864, Aldam Heaton pulled off what seemed to be the master stroke. John Ruskin was bidden by a special committee to lecture on 21 April in the Mechanics Institute on 'The Relation of the Architecture of Public Buildings to Daily Life'. He stayed at Woodbank beforehand, and was tipped off to say quite straightforwardly what kind of style he thought should be followed in the new Exchange. A packed audience on the evening eagerly waited for the great prophet, then at the height of his rhetorical powers, to deliver his answer.

Here things went awry. Ruskin's lecture was none other than *Traffic*, the most violent and thrilling of his whole career. It was an occasion when the best wined-and-dined bourgeois, anticipating a vague performance on the colours of the Venetian lagoon, must have felt his self-confidence plummet under the weight of Ruskin's invective. He told them straight: firstly, that he had been asked there to advise on their Exchange, secondly, that he did not care about their Exchange because they did not, and that the best they could have in the circumstances was an appropriately ugly temple to Commerce, the Great Goddess of Getting-On. Proceeding, he read them a lengthy lesson on the unpleasantness of their city and the immorality of their life style, and with this the audience went away, variously chastened or offended. That at least is how the published version of the lecture runs. It is intriguing to note that this omits a sentence or two of practical advice which he did include to mollify his hosts a little. Gothic, he said, was better, not just for churches but for all styles of building; if the burghers of Bradford really wanted a model for their Exchange, they could not do better than consider Mr Waterhouse's Manchester Assize Courts, in which he found the 'hall of exquisite proportions, beautifully lighted, the roof full of playful fancy, and the corridors and staircases thoroughly attractive and charming'.[57] But the tenor of his onslaught on local mercantilism had done the Advanced Gothic cause little good.

Luckily perhaps, in view of these remarks, Waterhouse had now withdrawn from the Exchange competition because of lack of time. So too had Street, and when it came to the deadline Philip Webb and Cuthbert Brodrick failed to complete.[58] The Goths were thus depleted, so that when it came to the judgment it was a fight between Burges, Shaw, and the locals. In the event, the other directors of the Exchange flattened Harris. They knew

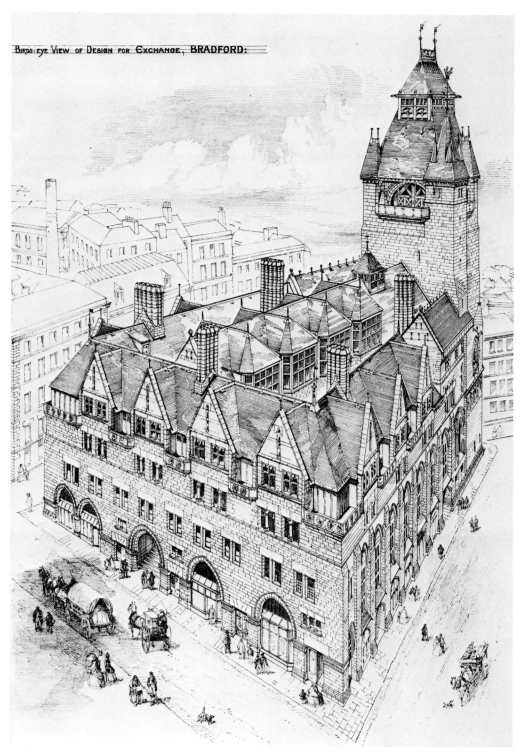

BIRDS-EYE VIEW OF DESIGN FOR EXCHANGE, BRADFORD:

36. Bradford Exchange, bird's eye perspective of competition design, 1864.

well that Burges had been staying at his house, so when Harris voted for him, the others to a man chose Lockwood and Mawson, who also had their contacts well organized. The anonymity of the designs and their mottoes fooled nobody; they all knew that No. 1, *With all my heart*, was Burges, No. 2, *Experientia*, was Lockwood and Mawson, and No. 6, *Rien n'est beau que le vrai*, was Shaw. Where Lockwood and Mawson scored was in unexpectedly and not too incompetently switching from classic to Ruskinian Gothic, thus taking wind from their opponents' sails and leaving themselves open aesthetically only to the charges of 'façadism' and poverty of detail.

There were plenty of other charges, though, and Heaton leapt into print to put them. Costing, and lack of professional arbitration were his main lines of assault. The winners had given a disingenuously low estimate to meet the condition. Shaw's designs, on the other hand, were over the cost limit but offered an extra floor for rental. Only Burges was strictly eligible on these grounds, as Waterhouse had conveniently found when he assessed the six submissions on this point. But Waterhouse was acting without the Directors' official permission, so his advice was not heeded. Heaton was all for regularizing the point of assessorship by referring the designs to an extraordinary committee of five architects, Scott, Street, Butterfield, Waterhouse, and Bodley, and five laymen, Ruskin, Beresford Hope, E. B. Denison (Lord Grimthorpe), J. H. Parker, and Acland, but nobody can have been blind to the particular prejudices of this talented assemblage. The correspondence in the *Bradford Observer* soon degenerated into mud-slinging, but not before the publicity-shy Nesfield had bestirred himself to write and announce his decision to forsake competitions without professional referees, and a new ally, the more experienced competitor E. W. Godwin, had also dissociated himself from Bradford's absurd proceedings.[59] Lockwood and Mawson however triumphed, to the city's ultimate loss, and five years later won the Town Hall competition with equal sleight of hand. *Experientia docet*. But if Shaw was dashed, he had a curious revenge forty years later, with the Town Hall Extensions.

Every architect treasures one early, unfulfilled scheme; *Rien n'est beau que le vrai* was Shaw's (ill. 36). The site was triangular, narrow and inconvenient, with little interior space, and this favoured Shaw's talent. The design therefore became the first of many object lessons in layout and the interrelation of irregular elements in façade design. Waterhouse was as clever in planning, but what he and Scott's other followers never attempted, what even Burges refrained from doing quite so blandly, was to articulate storeys in opposing yet interlocking rhythms. Street had this capacity, but Nesfield had already taken it far further than anyone else in his extensions to Combe Abbey, which is the clear inspiration for the leaded and stamped parapets, cannon chimneys and squat arches. Shaw's elevations appear more lucid than those of Combe, but one must remember that if in the bird's eye view the recessed roof holds everything in check and overall symmetry, it would have been obscured at street level; and the massive tower, in itself impressive from far and near, would have dwarfed the whole of Old Market. Thus we have an early warning to deal cautiously with these brilliant perspectives, high and low level, which are rarely good guides to the real appearance of Shaw's buildings.

But Shaw cared less for scale here than for 'Truth', and this the tower and the exchange itself were designed to express. It is amusing to read the clumsy special pleading which a still rather inarticulate Advanced Goth put into his report to extenuate his

DESIGN: FOR: ENLARGING: THE: CH
OF S:MARY: Cheltenham:
B

V iew shewing the old west front re-built exactly as it stands
at present - with the addition of a new south aisle:-

37. (left) Cheltenham Parish Church, perspective of competition scheme for proposed enlargement, 1863.

38. (right) Church project of *c*.1864, exterior perspective.

39. (over page) Church project of *c*.1864, interior perspective.

inventiveness. Gothic was suggested both by Shaw's own 'predilections in favour of a style whose history has been marked by instances of a devotion, which the severe monotony of Classic art has failed to awaken', and by the antiquity of Bradford as a centre for the woollen trade.[60] If this was sentiment, why not sentiment when it was allied with truth? Other sympathizers with the eternal verities might have wondered why in a blatantly commercial building, an architect did not use iron and glass for the exchange itself, instead of vaulting and high clerestory bays. To them, Shaw replied that stone was more monumental, durable, and insusceptible to breakage and leakage. Further, such a structure was more expressive. Round the tower over the entrance was to run a relief frieze showing the episodes of the wool trade: washing, combing, dyeing, weaving, and so forth. Here was a kind of expression of function; for the plain expression of material he also still had time. At the top of the tower, he intended the rough wooden cage for the clock to be visible, and to expose the iron cramps holding the ashlar blocks of the parapet. In all the complex sections, not a single girder is to be seen. Truth was not yet quite so elastic.

After Bradford came Holy Trinity, Bingley, the great church which Shaw had been ambitious to build for over a decade. He had been making his preparations for such a work for some time. At the 1864 Architectural Exhibition, when the perceptive editor of the *Building News* considered already that 'Nesfield, Shaw, Webb, and Power bid fair to establish a school of their own, which will differ from anything that has gone before', Street allowed Shaw to exhibit a masterly set of pen and ink drawings of his Clifton church, afterwards slightly revised in design and built in 1864–5 as a forceful tunnel-vaulted chamber with passage aisles and a strongly separated chancel.[61] These set him thinking and assimilating Street anew. In 1863, he entered the abortive competition for extending the parish church at Cheltenham (ill. 37), and at about this date he produced what may pass for his finest architectural perspectives—two superbly finished drawings for a large church with a north-west tower (ills. 38, 39). They could be either pure fantasy, or an early, highly imaginative design for Bingley. The structure and articulation lean heavily upon Street, the details more heavily still upon Ruskin's pleas for rich, impassioned variety: piers and capitals of different shape, veneered wall surfaces, and a complex, rugged timber roof to the nave.

58

But Bingley was poor, and the new church needed in its poorest, most industrial district. It was the old northern story: 'The manufacturers are nearly all dissenters and compel the children working in their mills to attend their day-schools. The principal resident landed proprietor has hitherto refused to contribute towards the new church, but one gentleman, merely resident and without landed property in the parish, contributes a thousand pounds.'[62] He was, of course, Alfred Harris. Even in 1866 when building began, they only had £1400 more promised. Simplicity and construction by stages was therefore demanded; already, too, the High Victorian tide was ebbing, and strong colours and contrasts of rhythm in church architecture were a thing of yesterday. Ruskin cared less and less for architecture, as *Traffic* betrays, and Bodley and Pearson were pioneering quieter churches.

'No modern church I know is finer', said Goodhart-Rendel, of Holy Trinity, Bingley.[63] It is a judgment hard to dispute for those who made the pilgrimage before the tragic demolition of 1974. It was not a big building; an abrupt, square-ended sanctuary, steepled tower over the choir, and three bays to the nave round which aisles and a western narthex pitted high, lean-to roofs (ill. 40). The lights were of unusual simplicity; single lancets in the aisles, clerestory and east window, and even in the west window Shaw dallied with the idea of changing the rose that was built into pairs of coupled lancets like those he later used at St Michael's Bournemouth. That is almost the last of the High Victorian details left from the first design of 1864; for then, the inconsonant rhythm of clerestory and arcade had been stronger, and a squatter, more bulbous French tower was intended to complement the rose. Redesigned to a more daring height only in 1869, and built as late as 1880-1, the tower turned out one of Shaw's few constructional failures, too weighty for the crossing; the damage this glorious crown wrought upon the body of the church became the cause of its own destruction.[64]

The form of the church is a simple borrowing from Street's St Philip and St James's Oxford, with hints from Street's own model, St Matthias's Stoke Newington, by Butterfield. For the exterior, Shaw was content mainly to correct Street's awkwardnesses and to update and reapply the design to the locality and materials. The dark millstone and dirty air of Bingley gave little hope to colouring. Therefore the external concentration was upon outline alone, the crisp edge of body, roof, tower and steeple against a sunless sky. Within, where the same dark stone walls and piers themselves contained the space, the points of lancet light offered no such natural contrasts. Yet the sombre spaces seemed to hang motionless, bounded by a shell of dry stone laid in small rough-hewn blocks with recessed bonding, making the starkest of wall planes. Thin forms of tracery or divided order would have disturbed these tensely held volumes, so every architectural detail was blunted, flattened, or thickened. Over the arcade, for instance, sustained on either side by low monolithic piers with scalloped capitals, only a single strong fillet marked off the flatness of the arch from the dry walling above. Within this grey cage (ill. 41), the fittings shone out with a violent, jewelled intensity. The pulpit, in red marble and gold mosaic (ill. 228), from a liturgical interruption of space became a sublime passage of brightness, and at the east end, where the dynamic progress of arcades, steps and flooring reached the Tractarian decorative climax, the flaming colours of Burne-Jones's Christ in the single lancet surmounting the reredos seemed to burst forth

61

40. (left) Holy Trinity Bingley, exterior.   41. (above) Holy Trinity Bingley, interior.

with splendour out of the dark vessel. It was among the consummate, most assured church interiors of the High Victorian movement; its destruction was an inestimable loss.

Of the several other projects that fell to Shaw in Yorkshire during the 1860s, two must here be mentioned, both at Leeds. By now, Aldam Heaton's business successes had reconciled him to his relatives and friends there. The caucus of Leeds potentates, among whom Dr Heaton was prominent, looked more favourably upon the Gothic cause than their less cultured rivals in Bradford. Naturally, they were cautious; Gilbert Scott, happily secured as architect to the Leeds Infirmary, represented to Dr Heaton the apogee of taste, a taste distinctly preferable to the Japanese style of drawing exhibited by Aldam at the Leeds Exhibition of 1865, or the curious 'brazen triptych' with its odd incised lettering and cramped flower designs which Aldam and Shaw put up in memory of Aldam's father at St George's Church in 1866.[65] But Scott and Shaw now united in a creditable piece of preservation. While visiting Leeds to see the Exhibition and sketch, Shaw found that demolition, long threatened, was at last impending for the double-naved Laudian Gothic church of St John's Briggate (ill. 42). Scott was sought out and wrote a report on the matter whose publication effectively saved St John's from destruction. Shaw now got the job of putting it into shape after long neglect.[66]

42. St John's Leeds, interior: a modern view
including changes made since Shaw's restoration.

It was a hard business. His clients were an obdurate committee of lawyers, the Trustees of Harrison's Charity, who wanted the work done cheaply and cannot have been pleased that it had to be done at all. They were all for moving the seventeenth-century chancel screens bodily westwards and dismantling the cresting, and for leaving the replastered panels in the ceiling bare, thus spoiling the great glories of the church. Shaw managed to avoid such peccadilloes, though he replaced the later seventeenth-century centre panels of the crestings with crosses, reduced the pew heights, and re-used the sounding board of the pulpit as the climax of a witty iron screen over a new font (ill. 225). Outside, a porch was well added, but Shaw erred in replacing the altar window with more conventional tracery.

Lawrence Weaver once suggested that the restoration of St John's Leeds was a turning point in Norman Shaw's career. 'The work there', he records, 'seemed to him to have a solid and reasonable character that put to shame the thin and hungry mediaevalisms of the new cheap Gothic churches which were rising round him on all sides'; therefore, he began to incorporate later elements.[67] This cannot be quite accurate. Willesley already betrays a whole-hearted devotion to the traditions of the seventeenth century as a supplement to the Gothic experience. But the right date of much of the vernacular which he imitated was probably unknown to Shaw, who was no scholar. He may never have realized that tile-hanging was a seventeenth-century device, to keep the wet off earlier, easily sodden walls, that before 1600 chimneys to the old farmhouses were often crude affairs, or that most of the lovely stacks of Cheshire, Essex and Kent

64

belong to the spread of the Dutch bricklaying tradition after that date. Certainly, the experience of St John's, its happy juxtaposition of Gothic masonry with grotesque joinery and plasterwork, must have reinforced in Shaw a sense of the continuity of Gothic and vernacular, if the latter were isolated from Ruskin's 'foul torrent' of academic Renaissance. His adherence to that was twenty years in coming, and even then it took a peculiarly seventeenth century form. A remarkable amount of Shaw's work falls unconsciously into one manifestation or another of the English seventeenth century tradition. This thought partially answers those who look upon an eclecticism which works by instinct rather than intellectual choice as mindless. It also means that we may have too emphatic a sense of the Victorian range of styles and the uncertainty of their choices. Though organized so differently, the seventeenth century too had many architectural styles, frequently conflicting at once; St John's Leeds, The Queen's House, Bolsover Castle, and Sparrowe's House Ipswich are, after all, works of the same years.

After this restoration came the Convalescent Hospital outside Leeds at Cookridge (ill. 43). Hospitals were the rage of the 1860s, and rightly so. A succession of events had concentrated attention upon the problem; the folk-heroism of Florence Nightingale, the ideas of John Roberton, and the scandal of the Netley Hospital had led to rapid reforms. Butterfield took up the problems of hospital planning at Winchester, Scott with equal ingenuity at Leeds, where the British Medical Association met to discuss hospital architecture at length in the summer of 1869.[68] By then, Cookridge had been started. The initiative came from a wealthy partner in Beckett's Bank, John Metcalfe Smith, an old friend of Aldam Heaton's who had supported him over the question of his marriage. Shaw set to work in 1867, and the hospital was constructed in 1868–9. The experience incited him to attempt two London hospital competitions during the building of Cookridge. The Metropolitan Asylum Board was holding a series of competitions to increase London's hospital accommodation, under the Poor Law Act of 1867, and one of these, for the Kensington Sick Asylum, Shaw actually won (ill. 44). But his design, for a site at North End, was eventually turned down, and a similar project for a fever hospital at Stockwell got nowhere.[69] Cookridge turned out to be Shaw's only medical work, except for a small extension to Coatham Convalescent Home in 1878.

Shaw set about Cookridge as though it were a regular hospital with the full dangers of infection. The basis of the plan is an excerpt from Scott's Infirmary, a central emphasized service area flanked by long lower wings for the wards and day rooms, one side for men, the other for women. 'In the absence of a very rapid renewal of all the air in a ward,' ran the contemporary theory of contagion, 'the exhalations from the skin and breath of the sick persons rapidly charge that air with such an amount of impurity that it becomes injurious even to persons in health, and fatally prejudicial to the recovery of the sick inmates of the hospital.'[70] Therefore, the wards occupy the whole of the upper parts of the wings from back to front, for the purpose of cross ventilation. This tended to make them cold, and in his Kensington and Stockwell projects (which had similar plans), Shaw evolved a system to combine centralized heating stoves, foul air extraction, and fireproof construction. At Cookridge this was not used, but the dayrooms beneath the wards had capacious half-ingles, comfortable settles, and plain Windsor chairs. There were other interesting technical points; the walls had a thick stone core with an exterior brick lining

43. Cookridge Hospital, with later addition (not by Shaw) to right.

44. Kensington Sick Asylum, perspective of competition design, 1868.

PROPOSED: SICK: ASYLUM: KENSINGTON: View of ends of Pavillions of Womens side, looking South.

to exclude damp, while the top lights of the tall mullioned windows opened on their centres by means of long rods, surely an early use of this technique.

While Scott produced for the Leeds Infirmary a fine version of his beloved foreign Gothic, Shaw at Cookridge employed a wholly different and yet still alien style. It is Kentish vernacular, unashamedly transferred to Yorkshire to cheer the city convalescents up among the bracken and pure suburban air. His desire for hospitals is to make matters light and happy, to avoid the Gothic dourness he was seeking at Bingley; the London schemes share the same elements. To get this, he willingly mixes the local stone with tile-hanging, a solecism he will not allow himself again in Yorkshire. In proportions, too, the design is one of the less happy Shaw made at this period, and cannot have been satisfactory even before the clumsy continuation of 1893 to the east. But after Leeds Infirmary, the cheeriness of Cookridge doubtless gave relief to many a Victorian convalescent, passing from one to the other.

CRAGSIDE

Finally, in culmination of the 1860s came Cragside, the chance of a new Leyswood to be built on a bolder and wilder site. Its genesis was strange. For one of the Palace of Westminster competitions, John Horsley painted a grand canvas some twelve feet high, showing 'Prince Hal taking the crown from his father's bedside.' The government did not want it, but a purchaser was found in Sir William Armstrong, patron and friend of Horsley and Cooke. Armstrong, the Northumbrian inventor and hydraulics engineer, had become involved in armaments at the time of Crimea, almost by accident; by 1869, his gunnery works by the Tyne at Elswick pullulated to orders from near and far, but its ageing founder hankered for a quieter country life. In Newcastle, Armstrong had a suburban house abutting the dramatic Jesmond Dene, which he had purchased and meant to keep as a park for the city. Here, a few years before, he had commissioned from John Dobson a 'Banqueting Hall', where he feasted the statesmen who were flocking to Elswick to purchase guns for the new ironclad navies, or entertained the local worthies as Newcastle's first citizen. The hall contained various statues and other works of art Armstrong had bought, but it was ill-lit, it had little unbroken wallspace, and *Prince Hal* would not fit. An extra gallery was mooted; Horsley, perhaps seconded by Lady Armstrong who at Willesley had been vouchsafed a taste of the new picturesque, proposed Shaw.[71]

At the end of September 1869, therefore, Shaw was summoned north. 'They are exceedingly kind', he reported to Agnes from Jesmond. 'I had a tremendous talk with Sir Wm about his gallery this morning, and think I am to have my own way. I dearly like my own way and not other people's!! . . . When he returned from Elswick at 5 he took me a long walk to shew me his farm and talked of guns and engines no end.' There was also the matter of the small hunting lodge that Armstrong had recently built in the hills outside Rothbury, which he talked of extending for his semi-retirement. Three days later, therefore, Shaw is writing from Cragside, sending 'fine old crusted kisses' and a paper cut-out of a man cocking a snook. More pertinently, he says: 'It will be very satisfactory working for Sir William as he knows right well what he is about', and mentions 'wonderful

45. (left) Cragside, a distant view taken in 1891.

46. (above) Cragside, entrance front.

hydraulic machines that do all sorts of things you can imagine.'[72] The estate, therefore, was splendidly equipped before a single alteration was made. But Shaw's work was soon in hand. Over the intervening weekend between these letters home, the story goes, while the guests were out on a shooting party, Shaw had sketched out the lines of the whole of the future fairy palace of Cragside.[73] And the addition to the Jesmond Dene Banqueting Hall was soon done; a robust, square gallery in no particular style, banked into the sharply rising hillside and lit from above. Between the old and new parts he engineered an organ loft for the entertainment of feasters, he revised the steep access from the road above, and he built a pretty lodge at the top which survives. It was an awkward job, well handled.

Cragside too is no absolutely unified masterpiece.[74] Whatever the initial master plan may have entailed, Armstrong's ideas altered and Shaw's conceptions and tastes changed. When their last additions were completed and Lethaby's milky marble chimneypiece was installed in the drawing room in 1885, the results were startlingly different from the original library and dining room added on in 1870. Even between 1870 and 1875, when Armstrong spurred his estate workmen ceaselessly on, there was no suggestion of a new house, but merely of additions at either end of the old hunting lodge, which is still visible both inside and out. That is why the plan of Cragside straggles so (ill. 47); only Flete shares such exhausting dispositions. For instance, in the interest of grandiloquence, drawing and dining rooms are separated by almost 175 feet, surely a splendid enough 'dinner route' for the potentates who adorned the Armstrongs' board. But to get from one to the other, the guest, having traversed the long picture gallery and descended six flights of stairs, must finally run the gauntlet of a cramped corridor forming the spine of the original lodge. Even Shaw's attempts to brighten this passage with a dado of tiles and an open book bay failed to dispel the pokiness of this central core.

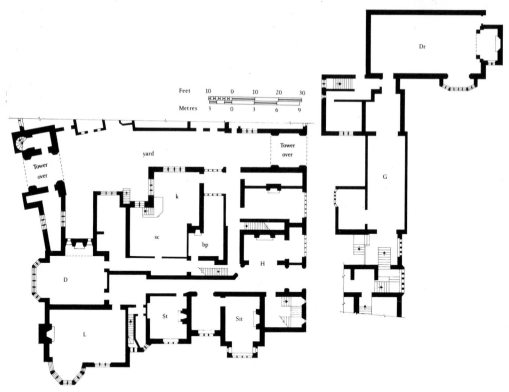

47. Cragside, ground plan and part of upper floor plan.

Yet the fascinations of Cragside are distinct from such things. Instead, they assail the spirit with that heady sense of stirring which stones so rarely parade strongly. When effort and will force this kind of triumph over nature's obstacles, beauty is little heeded. So neither the precipitous front to the glen, nor the blank entrance side, nor the jostle of roofs and towers speaks the language of elegance (ills. 45, 46); they are too affecting, too rhetorical, where not to use oratory would have been to waste breath and be shouted down by the rocks, declivities and waterfalls of the Northumbrian moorland. You may go below and, clinging to the scanty guardrails on the sleek bridge that Armstrong threw across the glen, be awed by the impassive walls of tightly dressed stone above you; you may stand inadequately before the door on the levelled forecourt; or you may clamber up the crag to the single chimney starting solitarily out of the rock, away from the house, and turn to look upon the medley of gable, tower and courtyard that go to make this new Haddon Hall. But your pleasures will hardly be analytic. To decide what was original, what of 1870, of 1872–5, or of 1883–4, seems pointless in the fast movements of impressionability.

All the starker, therefore, is the self-sufficient privacy of the three chief rooms of Cragside's interior, like inner chambers to which its master could retire from public acclamation. Library, dining room, and drawing room: to these, the only perfect survivors of all Shaw's schemes of interior furnishing, we should attend more carefully.

None of them impels an outward glance for any reason but curiosity. True, only gradually have the trees grown up to the height of the library windows, now so many portholes offering waterline views out of the vast vessel; for the full, liberating vision of the moors, one must ascend to the hutch round the attic nursery. Yet always the library has been still, self-contained, oblivious of the action raging around it (ill. 48). It essays only one grand effect, and that the least successful, an Egyptian onyx fireplace. Otherwise it depends upon exact, absorbing contrasts between the fittings: light wallpaper with a hint of relief against darker panelled ceiling, dado, and built-in bookcases; and this ponderous woodwork, itself in light oak, against the crisp blackness of the ebonized chairs. Plush of sofa and pile of carpet set off the lines of this nimbler furniture, whose cane seats and gold-embroidered back panels pick up the gold-grounded flowerpieces of the frieze. These elegant and lamentably unique chairs, made by Gillow, must be of Shaw's own designing. They are spiced with a mere touch of the Japanese taste, soon to dissolve so much of furniture design into the questionable spindliness of aestheticism.

Round the dining room (ill. 49) the high standards of craftsmanship continue. The chairs here are earlier, but Forsyth's intricate panelling and relief carvings, the massive sideboard and dining table, and the settles of the inglenook belong to the library's light oak range. Here however the tone is severe, set by heavy hooked voussoirs that fill the inglenook arch, a feature sketched at Fountains Abbey and used already by Nesfield at Combe Abbey. Between the settles glow two complex, burnished andirons, luring one to a kind of masculine episode within the inglenook, to the colourful play of stained glass and stonework and tile and oak, and the flashing of the fire upon all these fittings. The drama here is specially enclosed and exclusive, unconscious of the bare exterior, and performed only before the select audience of diners.

To travel the long distance from here to the drawing room (ill. 50) means passing through more than the twelve years or so that separates their date, and the change in style one learns to expect from Shaw in such a separation. It is the movement from ardent endeavour to the less attractive poise of achievement. One can fault little in the room; the proportions are perfect, the craftsmanship of the great chimneypiece and the detail, down to the lockcases, is first-class; the light texture of the walls surprises after the darkness of Cragside's other great rooms. Perhaps the top-lighting from the coved ceiling is too uniform—but then the purpose was to show pictures. It is a room to hold attention and respect but not love; right for receptions and balls, wrong for daily habitation. The chimneypiece, dwarfing all other fittings, imbues the atmosphere with a grand sensuality, as if the change from Old English to Renaissance, from darkness to light, has let loose from earlier restraint a current of opulence, self-indulgence, and physicality. On the basis of existing drawings, it seems safe to attribute to Lethaby this eclectic design, surely his finest youthful achievement: part François Premier, part derived from the frolicsome arabesque and strapwork patterns that Shaw and he had used at Flete, and carved upon choicest Italian marble in the most finished style by Farmer and Brindley. Again, the room is self-sufficient, this time almost self-satisfied. Mentally to contrast its snug inglenook with the sharper poise of library and dining room, or with the fantastical, braggart strength of the elevations brings more than half one's pleasure in it. The interior setpieces, in their different interpretations, aim at beauty, the outside at a wild sublimity:

71

48. Cragside, the library.

the old distinction in a single building. Cragside is a vivid, almost violent reading in Burke's aesthetic, and for domestic architecture its virtual epitaph.

This narrative of Shaw's early works ends with Burke, because the aesthetic writings of the English eighteenth century offer the best framework for their comprehension. Houses like Leyswood and Cragside belong to a remarkable and brief moment in English architecture, when the picturesque ideal had passed into something more passionate. Like many other houses, they meet not only rational demands, but demands stemming from the visual sensibility and the emotions. Picturesque architecture had from the start been devised to offer delights to the eye and heart. First, the eye. A hundred years had educated the gentleman's sensibility to the point where he could require as a right the highest complexity of landscape and architecture. A park by Capability Brown, in the earlier days of the picturesque movement, was a general expanse baldly related to the house, upon which an owner could contentedly gaze from his windows. Once he turned to face the structure itself, he was soon entering a plea against the considerable sacrifices previously made to symmetry, and untying the bonds which the eighteenth-century

49. Cragside, the dining room.

country house, with its basement or quadrant offices, had borne.[75] The movement we call picturesque in the strict sense and associate with Knight and Repton begins from the premise that a house must be seen in its setting, as well as the setting from the house. But still there are limits. A classical house had at the most four façades, and correspondingly few viewpoints and possibilities of integration with the landscape. Even so revolutionary and expert a composition as Thomas Hope's Deepdene, of the 1820s, was more or less axial, offering its set views. The Italianate style proved more helpful, but was naturally repetitious, so that by contrast the articulated Gothic of the 1840s and 50's seemed splendidly additive and supple for picturesque effects. Yet if the truth had been fully told, Gothic was far more compartmentalized and formal than its adherents admitted. Besides, they had more serious work to do than entertain the eye; they were savers of souls. Therefore, little by little, those of artistic sensitivity turned to the vernacular. When Shaw transfers this style to the bigger Victorian house, he is a descendant of the picturesque in a strict sense, not just a loose attributive one. Glen Andred, Leyswood, and Cragside are fused into the landscape as never before.

Any view, internal or external, must satisfy. As a child explores the ingles, bays and

73

50. Cragside, the drawing room.

attics of such a house, so the sophisticated visitor picks up new combinations of chimneys and groupings of gables as he approaches up the winding track at Leyswood or looks up from Armstrong's bridge at Cragside. The architect, Shaw's perspectives hint, must search even further; no mere circumference of a house can yield all these variations of effect, for viewpoints above must show a picture too. To get a glimpse such as only a bird could have of the yard at Leyswood or of the highest tower at Cragside, must please as much as any other view. These rocky sites seem sometimes swept by the searchlight of the eye, here and there encountering projections natural or built, serving only to put in relief the sure outlines of the whole conglomerate composition.

Beyond this, there is sentiment. To Cooke, to Temple, or to Armstrong, rattling home from the station after a hanging at the Academy, difficulties in the City, or troubles at the works, none of this would have meant much had they not identified their castle with home, and demanded topographical tokens of such an identity. The chimneys and inglenooks, front gable and front door, half-timber and tile-hanging, and the unique positioning of their homes, were symbols of their family, country, caste and property, in

74

fact a visible reminder of their independent existence.[*] It is hard to think that any other style of architecture before Shaw's had so perfectly expressed these things, had been so personal and yet so supple. In these houses the sentiment has been imbued with Shaw's own levity and wit, but it has also changed, in a strange manner, into passion.

It is hard to think of a more passionate decade in English architecture than the 1860s. The high intent of the Gothic Revival is still intact, and in this mongrel style, transfers itself to the houses of the bourgeoisie. The prophet of passion in the details of architecture is, of course, Ruskin. Cooke was a friend of Ruskin's, and Cooke and Shaw together heard him lecture during the building of Glen Andred.[76] To the Ruskin of the 1853 *Lectures on Architecture*, the various parts of the house are sacred, either for the delight they offer man's moral life, or for their symbolic value. In Shaw's early houses, such requirements are serious objectives. Each of the main rooms has the bow or bay that Ruskin stipulated, and some such windows are even provided with the bracketing and the capped, peaked roof which he held necessary. Again, the steep impenetrable roof enclosing the walls is to Ruskin, and no doubt to Shaw, earnest beneath the wit, not a mere token of shelter, but a symbol of the owner's hospitality. How much more sheltering, the lectures had said, to hear the expression 'beneath my roof' than 'within my walls'![77] Thus a moral vocabulary of the house had emerged, not yet trivialized by the stylistic proliferations and laxer tone of the late '70s and '80s. Building a house was still a serious business, involving the soul and the heart of a rich family man, as well as his pocket.

CHAPTER 3

The Country House

Socrate un jour faisant bâtir,
Chacun censurait son ouvrage :
L'un trouvait les dedans, pour ne lui point mentir,
Indignes d'un tel personnage :
L'autre blâmoit la face, et tous étoient d'avis
Que les appartements en étoient trop petits.

Quelle maison pour lui ! l'on y tournait à peine.
"Plût au ciel que de vrais amis,
Telle qu'elle est," dit-il, "elle pût être pleine !"

Le bon Socrate avoit raison
De trouver pour ceux-là trop grande sa maison.
Chacun se dit ami : mais fou qui s'y repose ;
Rien n'est plus commun que le nom,
Rien n'est plus rare que la chose.

La Fontaine, Fable XVII, Parole de Socrate.

OUTSIDE

To understand the styles of late Victorian country house building, we have also to understand the styles the Victorians themselves imitated. So to grasp the nature of 'Old English', we must briefly look back to the ancient types of English domestic architecture, especially to the history of brick building.[1] Brick, one must remember, was freely available in Britain only from the fifteenth century. Before that, the most durable form of walling was masonry; consequently the mediaeval churches and castles of England are mainly of stone. But in many parts of the country, the paucity of suitable building stone and lack of skilled masons, as opposed to carpenters, made masonry building impossible for all but the rich. Packed rubble, flintwork, or loosely dressed stone could be handled without difficulty and satisfied requirements in some areas but not in others. That is why, wherever there was poor stone but adequate wood, the sophisticated traditions of timber construction continued to flourish.

Between many of the houses which Shaw and his contemporaries admired there were differences in social rank and structural method which often transcended mere regional variation. On one side stood Penshurst, Haddon, and their Tudor and Jacobean successors, erected by masons and connected closely with the Church Gothic on which the revivalists had been nurtured; on the other, the pre-Gothic tradition of the carpentry guilds. This tradition was killed not by stylistic importation of Gothic or classic, but because timber was outmoded by a more malleable and efficient material: the brick. The

76

51. Pateley Bridge, watercolour perspective of unexecuted design for parsonage, 1865.

52. St Johns, Ilkley, view of entrance front taken *c*.1950, before alteration.

transition was fast. In the sixteenth century, many new timber-framed cottages and manors were being erected, but already brick chimneys were rising above the roofs or on the old exterior stone bases. By 1700, brick reigned supreme; brick chimneys and hearths, where there might before have been a hole in the roof, tile roofs instead of thatch or stone slating, brick walls for additions and reconstruction work, and (in some regions) tile-hanging to protect the lath and plaster walls from absorbing further wet. The improvement of communications, the decimation of the forests, and the demand for better planned housing all pointed to this simple, flexible product, moulded and cut to any shape, light, non-porous, rarely combustible, needing only a strong mortar for coursing, or proper pegging to be attached to wall or rafter. In some parts of England, therefore, the pure vernacular of timber-framing was transformed into a charming but mongrel pattern of architecture, whose origins lay in the forms of carpentry but whose development had been in the forms of brick. These houses, which were Nesfield and Shaw's first inspiration, were in fact themselves additive and historically complex.[2]

The stone houses of the Cotswolds and the north, on the other hand, belonged to an almost unbroken tradition of building since the middle ages. Continuity had made this tradition more austere, less flexible. But by the nineteenth century, stonework in major houses had come to mean only the basic, exterior skin. The masonry walls of the big Georgian and Victorian mansions were backed by brickwork; of brick too were the structural partition walls within. There was no question of abandoning stone in districts where stone was appropriate. Pugin, Salvin, and their associates (by dint of hard work and expense to their clients) had resuscitated much of the ancient art of setting out masonry, and later stone builders, ecclesiastical or secular, could stand on their shoulders. Shaw often did, which is why his stone houses often seem more continuous with the immediate architectural past than his brick ones (ills. 51 & 52). But stone was costly and

77

inappropriate for domestic work in much of the country and most cities. Plain brick was the dominant urban material. Thoroughly understood by the big London builders, it was adaptable, handsome and sanitary, and the skills to cut and lay it were there to command. In the recent past, it had been thought lowly, but by the time Shaw started practice the ecclesiologists had changed all that.

Pugin, says Phoebe Stanton, not only encouraged brickwork in the later part of his career but was particular about its usage.[3] He was probably the first to insist once more upon English bonding instead of the prevalent Flemish bond. In his Bishop's House at Birmingham, brick allowed him a new and daringly casual distribution of window and roof. Yet he was never so free when using brick in the country, it seems.[4] Butterfield, Street and White did what they could to improve on this in their country parsonages of the 1850s. These houses gained from a more careful scrutiny of the vernacular styles than Pugin had undertaken. But they do not attempt entire propriety of style; when a gable is half-hipped, it is as much to save space and cost as to give authenticity. For the walling, these architects had to rely on their own invention, and in brickwork they did particularly well. Firstly, they consolidated on Pugin by ridding the cheaper brick buildings of stone dressings. This is possibly Butterfield's contribution. It gave the houses an *ordonnance* and unity which many buildings of brick with lumpy stone dressings lack, and added a crispness often absent in the old vernacular, composed of brick, stone and timber elements. Secondly, they experimented with the texture of their brick walls by a selection of shapes, tones and types of brick, and explored these in combination. This is more than a matter of polychromy, though colour is the most striking feature of their innovation. Contrasting textures of brick were of course common in English building, both in late mediaeval practice and beyond. The old blue-glazed bricks, fired with their heads to the wood smoke, had long permitted simple chequer patterns in every tradition of rural brick building. Now for a short period, the advanced Goths played in their parsonages and churches with intensities of effect to supplement the old habits, using black, grey, yellow, red and white bricks from different areas and kilns, and redistributing them in coursing and arches as well as in the old non-structural patterns. If they, like Ruskin, were later to regret the plagiarism of these experiments by speculative builders, there was another result. When men reverted to simpler chromatic tones after 1860, a consensus emerged on the kind of brickwork colour most suitable, at least to London and the south of England—a range of reds, from the soft pinky hue of the weald to a richer, more flecked brown-red, typical of the Midlands. This was not the normal colour range of London stocks or of most previous London architecture. But it was this range that Nesfield, Shaw, and the architects of 'Queen Anne' took up. Its gradual adoption in English cities marked a step forward in their appearance.

The Gothic Revivalists, in an attempt to find good models for brick building, were forced to look abroad, not so much to France but to the Netherlands, Germany and Italy. If Pugin and Butterfield favoured Germany, Street looked more to Italy, openly disparaging such German brickwork tracery as he saw.[5] In northern Italy he found multicoloured brickwork, and fine cut and moulded bricks for dressings, plinths, copings and reveals. They began to appear in his secular work of the 1850s. Simultaneously, by exploring more subtly than Butterfield or White the interrelation of gables, he arrived at the better articulation which was to be a mark of Shaw's stylistic genius. By 1860, Street at, for instance, East Mersea Rectory, and his ex-assistant Webb at Red House had settled upon that calmer, less colourful brick walling which is the skeleton of the Old English style. What Nesfield and Shaw now did was to put flesh upon these bones, adding authenticity and piquancy of appearance without disregarding modern needs, as Devey's more radical attempts at the picturesque had been in danger of doing. We must now look at the origin and evolution of the style's main elements.

To begin with, walling. Shaw's principle of a uniform brick, laid in English bond, with a plinth of splayed bricks some three feet from the ground, was firmly established in the early 1860s. It derives directly from Street's practice. Bricks were to be had in most parts of the country and were rarely brought long distances. Shaw normally specified the best, but was not unduly concerned about their origin. On colour, he was more exacting than most of his contemporaries. In the country he plumped for a narrow band of pinks and reds; in London, after initial hesitation, he decided upon a similar range. This was in the face of advice from Scott and Stevenson to use respectively yellow or brown brick in London, in either case dressed with red brick.[6] Even minor polychromatic effects such as these were avoided by Shaw. In his cheaper houses in the country, he would take his red cutters right up to the window frames and finish off with a course of splayed bricks below and above. Where there was more money, dressings could be of rubbed brick in the less exposed urban settings, or of Bath stone in the country. At first, Shaw was anxious to retain some stone dressings and mullions for dignity and variety even in the smallest of his Old English jobs. They occur at the Bromley Lodge (ill. 15) but tend to drop out gradually. At Greenham Lodge (1879–83), the dressings obtrude strongly and make the house appear old-fashioned (ill. 80); after it, Shaw often cut them out even from his larger brick houses. Polychromy in the actual walling occurs only very rarely, and then in the light, traditional tones of blue: gentle hues on the headers at Willesley, a stronger diaper pattern on the school at Hammerwood (ill. 214).

When Nesfield used the Old English style in brick, his practice was superficially similar, but there are major differences. For cottages, he normally stuck to a coarser and probably cheaper type of brick than on the main house, while Shaw would use the same species on lodge, cottage and main house. His houses, more regularly than Shaw's, were of brick, and he was responsible in these for one important departure, recommended but not undertaken by Scott. The common size of a brick is about $9 \times 4\frac{1}{2} \times 2\frac{3}{4}$ inches; allowing for mortar, this gives a height of about one foot for four courses of brick. Anything bigger is exhausting for a bricklayer to handle and therefore less economical. At Cloverley, where bricks were produced on the site, Nesfield took the bold step of thinning the bricks from $2\frac{1}{2}$–$2\frac{3}{4}$ inches to 2–$2\frac{1}{4}$ inches. The precedent cited for this was early Tudor brickwork, where the bricks are not only thinner but longer, and separated by much thicker mortar joints. Nesfield imitated these joints too, so the total number of bricks may not have been greatly exceeded.[7] It became his standard practice to use thin brickwork on all his main houses, pointed with clean cement rather than ordinary mortar. Shaw took over this innovation, but only used it for very special jobs, a sign of its expense.[8] As he did not himself insist upon the thicker jointing practice, he could get nearly five courses to the foot with $2\frac{1}{8}$ inch bricks. They are found at the Farnham Bank, Lowther Lodge, New Zealand

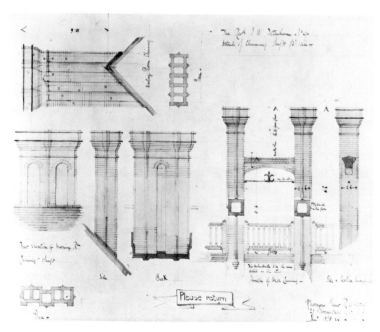

53. Bannow, working
drawing for chimneys, 1878.

Chambers, the first Alliance Assurance Offices, New Scotland Yard and Bryanston. Unbroken passages of the thin brickwork give a smart, sharp appearance beyond all expectation. Lutyens, the first architect to realize its potentials for texture, brought back the thicker jointing. In the interwar period, $2\frac{1}{8}$ inch brickwork became a cliché of Lutyens-influenced buildings, particularly the banks in town high streets. The bonding in this thinner brickwork is invariably English, but from surprisingly early on Shaw allows at times a reversion to Flemish bonding, and, in the north, to local bonding habits (three rows of stretchers and one of headers). At first this may mean a lesser job with incomplete specification, but by the 1880s the difference in bondwork is insignificant.

About chimneys (ills. 53–57), there was a general difficulty. Pugin had demanded exterior chimney-breasts as a form of functional display, but to push all fireplaces to outside walls was a wasteful practice. It dissipated warmth to the outside, and prevented each chimney from serving more than a single room on each floor, or possibly two if the flues were cleverly tracked.[9] In pointing to mediaeval precedent, the hearth-conscious Victorians forgot that when household fittings were of wood and the floors strewn with dry rushes, it was only prudent to relegate the hearth to an exterior wall, even in a stone-built house. Often, too, chimney-breasts had been added after the original house was built. This was common in vernacular architecture, where the hearth might first be built out from the wall of an existing timber-framed house in stone rubble or brick, and then later a proper set of high chimneys be added to take away the smoke. Out of loyalty to Pugin's tenets, the parsonage builders would essay at least one costly exterior chimney-breast even in their cheaper houses or schools. On these, they naturally made no attempt to exceed the plainest of forms in brick, though when stone was used an individual form of stack emerged.[10] But apart from the occasional delightful deformity, their chimney-breasts tended to be dull and their stacks limp.

54. Pierrepont, hall chimney.

55. Adcote, chimney.

56. Cragside, chimney.

57. Bryanston, chimney.

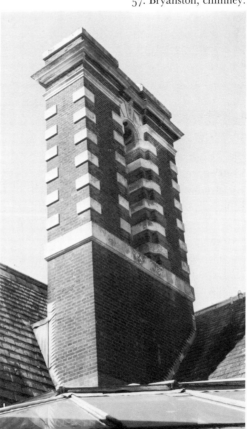

Though picturesque architects since Nash had been playing with the tall stacks of Tudor architecture, they normally borrowed only the main lines of their many profiles and stuck them on to incongruous points in their houses. It was Devey who refined this usage. Obsessed by chimneys, he sketched vernacular examples all over England and Europe, to study the change from the oblong or round type with simple caps into the mighty polygonal ribbed chimneys with oversailing courses, characteristic of the timber-houses of the north-west.[11] In his own practice, Devey preferred plain, wealden, square stacks, angled off at forty-five degrees to the line of the house, frequently in twos and threes touching at the caps. They are at their best when rising from the chimney breast. In his smallest Kentish cottages, Devey would start from a broad stone base, intersperse courses of bricks into the wall as height increased, and end up with his high and heavy brick angular stacks. The wider proportions of these chimneys are excellent, but one soon tires of this mannered, fake-additive practice. When his walling was of stone, Shaw himself used the trick occasionally, but more discreetly. Only in lavish commissions like Cragside (ill. 56) would a client run to elaborate chimneys of dressed masonry, so some transition between stonework and brickwork had to be arrived at. At first, as Devey did in the early Penshurst cottages, Shaw makes a frank break between stone base and brick stack, as at Gore Hill (1871–2), but the effect is coarse. In his Surrey houses of the 1870s, built of loose local stone, Shaw tends to limit his outside chimney-breasts, perhaps for this reason; the only such chimney at Pierrepont is tucked into an angle of the hall between half-timbering and lean-to roof (ill. 54). At Merrist Wood, the only other such case, the change is abrupt and unmarked, but occurs lower down and works well enough (ill. 68). Elsewhere, at Adcote and Bannow (ills. 53, 55), Shaw experiments with a gradual, smooth transition from breast to stack, introducing mixed brick and stone where the ribbing of the flues emerges. In his last Old English house, The Hallams, the brickwork bases themselves are spattered with patches of brown and green Bargate stone, but this is a wholly decorative effect (ill. 72).

Throughout his career, Shaw favoured the ribbed form of chimney in preference to the angle stack, because it gave an infinite number of profiles and plans. Since he sought to graft these heavy vertical excrescences into the house, rather than perch them upon it, their plans varied with their positions. At Bromley, the central stack of the lodge is part of the tying-down process in this intricate little composition, nearly square, but placed off the ridge so as to avoid crushing the cottage (ill. 15). At Willesley, the stacks are plainer and thinner, but still held very tight. Nesfield's stacks on the Crewe Hall cottages and his taller examples at Cloverley still keep the cut brick ribbing very close in, an excellent and disciplined effect in which he persisted. But for Shaw, acquaintance with the north-west's fabled chimneys meant liberation. From the time of Preen Manor (1870) onwards, he built his oversailing courses higher and made the surface of his stacks a whole brick's thickness in relief, reviving ranges of profiles and mouldings for this task.[12] Many of Shaw's exterior effects depend upon manipulation of the heights and profiles of these chimneys; points of stress and emphasis are determined by the verticals, while the planes of their longer sides reinforce or create axes (ill. 102). In the roof, Shaw learned to avoid putting the more complex chimneys upon the ridge, where they encumbered the line of the building. Instead, they would break through the slope of the tile roof; the greater their

82

height and mass, the lesser the 'slipping' effect (though this was not helped by the inevitable lead flashing at the join, which the old vernacular chimneys had not had).[13]

/ Nesfield and Shaw tackled the problem of the outside chimney-breast in two ways. In their smaller houses and cottages, they angled fireplaces across external corners, so that each chimney could serve at least two rooms per floor.\The other and more spectacular answer was the inglenook (ills. 94–96). Nesfield's Farnham Park (illustrated by Eastlake) and Shaw's Willesley (ill. 94) were the first, and few of either man's Old English country houses were subsequently without it. Since the ability to multiply outside chimney-breasts rested only with the rich, the inglenook connotes comfort and affluence far removed from the simple cottage hearth from which it is derived. It had its effect upon exterior design, for it pushed the whole chimney-breast bodily out, and usually required its own windows. Sometimes the room above might be the master bedroom, and a second ingle be provided.⁄ \Shaw normally gave the extrusion its own separate pitched roof, either letting the gable-end show or crowstepping the breast on either side of the stack. At Willesley, the original if ungainly effect of the peacock gable is an early attempt at this difficult manoeuvre (ill. 21); Shaw overhangs the upper storey, getting his inglenook chimney so far back as a result, that he is able to hip the roof back briefly over the plasterwork.

Shaw's Old English roofs and gables gradually retreat from the extreme vernacular stance implied by the Willesley inglenook gable. Until recently, the lines of roofs on large houses had been regularly blocked by parapets or coping, to the detriment of profile. Once these had gone, the roof could once more become an envelope enclosing the walls beneath⁄ The ecclesiologists took this practice further than the picturesque architects; once more it is their lead that Shaw follows, while borrowing from Devey in matters of detail. One or two examples of the treatment of gable ends will suffice. Here, the picturesque tradition favoured bargeboards, while Butterfield, Street and White finished off their roofs flush with the wall plane. But in the former case the boards were often mean and straggly, while in the latter the high pitch of the roof could make the gable-end abrupt. Shaw therefore reserved bargeboards for half-timbered gables, and built many houses, Glen Andred for instance, entirely without them. But he broadened out his gables considerably, and in order to display his roofing was not afraid to half-hip very wide gable ends (ill. 109). Half-hipping of minor gables was a favourite feature of the ecclesiological envelope, as it saved materials in the attics and gave buildings the blunt, tight profile sought in the 1850s. It is not part of Devey's normal vocabulary, but Butterfield used it often for his humbler rustic buildings. Shaw half-hipped cottages more often than houses, but always less timidly than his predecessors (Tongswood smithy, Ellern Mede). Early on, a hipped or half-hipped gable might occasionally return into the vertical under the apex of the roof to form a little 'gablet', a favourite trick of wealden vernacular roofing employed particularly by Nesfield, sometimes as a small plastered area, sometimes as a place for a dovecot. But soon enough, half-hipping and even hipping diminishes. Such tricks remained, to a degree, lowly and rustic; it may be significant that Butterfield's only known 'gablet' was on a boathouse.[14] Consequently they would not do for Shaw's richer clients, who got a straight gable treated in one of his various manners.

Another characteristic of gable ends is 'bellcast', the ancient feature whereby the pitch of an open-ended gable is slightly flattened at the end over the eaves, so as to throw

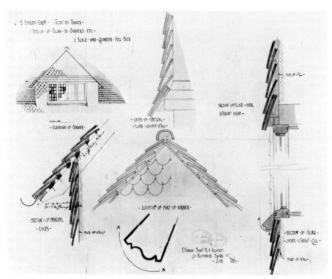

58. (left) Ashley Park, Walton-on-Thames, working drawing for tile-hanging on villas, 1881.

59. (below right) Knight's Croft, garden side, with Hubert Parry and family.

rain clear from the roof, as from a carefully shaped moulding.[15] Nesfield and Shaw use bellcast mainly with tile-hung gables where the roofing stops flush with the end wall. But it is most prominent on the bottom courses of the tile-hanging itself, in the form of a slight outward tilt which gradually becomes accentuated (ill. 58). For a really sophisticated use of bellcast, one must await Lutyens.

For roofing material, Shaw opted for picked clay tiles, which (following Scott) he believed to be cool in summer and warm in winter, and far superior to slates in appearance.[16] Even in town, he advocated Westmorland and other stone slates for public buildings, but Welsh slating never: 'in my mind it is associated with a very unpleasant and common aspect,' he wrote.[17] In this, Webb and he set the pace (though Webb in the north used pantiles, which Shaw never adopted). Despite Devey's fidelity to Kentish traditions, Hammerfield had a slated roof. The ecclesiologists varied their practice according to the district and availability of materials, and Nesfield still used slates at Cloverley. The new trend was followed unequivocally by the next generation of architects except Voysey, and brought about an improvement in the texture of domestic roofing which has been maintained. We have Shaw to thank for much of it.[18] But he could rarely obtain the local handmade tiles which make up so much of the charm of the old wealden roofs, and had to make do with manufactured tiles from the Midlands, just as we have to endure 'composition' tiles in their stead.

I have deliberately spoken of Shaw's roofs and gables as one. The roofs he uses are just interpenetrations of gables of different heights, sizes and pitches, extended backward or forward on a given elevation (ills. 75, 76, 88). Perhaps the subtlest gabled house of the preceding years was Butterfield's Milton Ernest Hall, which achieves interpenetration at the expense of fluency, each minor gable being curbed in breadth or depth and made subservient to the main ridge. By relaxing control over the minor gables and their ridges, and punctuating the composition with chimneys, Shaw not only articulates his houses but saves them from the fate of being two-sided, as the free-gabled house wholly subordinated to the main roof easily becomes.

Gables and walls might be tile-hung or they might be half-timbered, upon the basic walling material. Tile-hanging as a regular method of weatherproofing the upper storeys of timber-framed houses, reached its peak as late as the eighteenth century, and may still have been a living tradition among Kentish builders when Nesfield and Shaw discovered its charms.[19] Normally, the tiles are plain and rectangular, thinner than roof tiles, and either bedded solid in mortar or pegged upon battens across the wall face. Against the sides of the windows they finish close up without a break, but over them and at the base, as has been said, two or three courses are customarily tilted out to prevent dripping (ill. 58). Now and again, *cottage orné* builders had filled the apex of a gable or blank arch with a dash of tile-hanging, and Street and Scott follow the same principle now and again. Butterfield and White briefly used tile-hanging over a wide wall area of brickwork, Devey more authentically over lath and plaster in his Penshurst cottages.[20] With Shaw it became from the first a regular accompaniment to his out-of-town houses. In reports of 1868, Shaw seriously argued that tile-hanging gave a great increase in durability and warmth to the upper parts of the walls, which were built thinner.[21] But the decorative role came first. In Shaw's hospital designs, tile-hanging was used as much for warmth of appearance as for freedom from damp. Further, it allowed the effect of a slightly overhanging upper storey with the advantages of a solid brick wall; it kept down the thrust and sheerness of the walls, so that the diagonals and horizontals of the roof could dominate. Like their tile-hanging predecessors, Nesfield and Shaw had a *penchant* for the fishscale and other ornamental forms of tile which they had seen on their Sussex tour, but the rectangular type remained the norm (ill. 59). Nesfield went further and used ornamental slate-hanging on one of the Cloverley lodges and once or twice later. Shaw restricted it to a few instances on the sides of London dormers. Like Street, he could employ tile-hanging over block concrete to take off its raw appearance (ill. 130); he even agreed to the casting of concrete blocks in imitation of tile-hanging. The reason must be that until the late 1880s,

60. Farnham Bank, street front.

61. Spout Hall, Leek, perspective of street front, *c.*1871.

Shaw was still toying with the idea of the tile-hung house as the universal answer for bourgeois brick domestic architecture outside city centres. He was prepared to enforce it wherever brick building was the norm, whether in country districts, at suburban Bedford Park (where he compromises between Old English and the Queen Anne which city sophisticates demanded), or even in the three grand 'stockbroker' houses he built outside Liverpool—Mere Bank, Greenhill, and Allerton Beeches (ill. 69).

Half-timbering is the greatest stumbling block to the appreciation of Shaw's vernacular. \Pugin's legacy to today has been the insistence upon 'honesty'. Even if modern scruples about the abuse of structural principles can be overcome, surely Shaw's admiration for Pugin and his own early adherence to truth cannot be consistent with his use of sham half-timbering fronting structural brick walls? This is no case of lack of care or attention. Visits to houses like Ightham Mote, Speke Hall and Ockwells taught Nesfield and Shaw the secrets of timber-framing, and enabled them to improve upon the weakest element in previous revived half-timbering. The timber upper gables of Butterfield, besides masking brick walls, had hardly improved in appearance upon Wyatville's lodges at Chatsworth and other such buildings of the 1830s.[22] Such 'sticks of firewood' Shaw found 'starved, mean, and "modern" '.[23] So he applied study of the rough virile timbers of church belfries and roofs to the exterior framing and studs. He also insisted upon strong

86

bargeboards without the authentic but unvigorous piercing and fretting which Devey loved. After the incised pies upon bargeboard ends (ill. 60) are discontinued round about 1870, the wood is normally left plain, relieved by a few mouldings along the main lines. His studwork patterns, too, are conservative, settling on verticals and occasional diagonals in place of the fantastic structural shapes of Cheshire half-timbering.

Timber-framing began, of course, as a complete structural system. Originally, the main uprights were fitted into sockets in horizontal timbers along the ground, to prevent them from rotting. Then foundations of stone or a few courses of brick just above ground level gave better protection for the timbers and a drier floor—hence the plinth which Shaw regularly used in his houses. Jettying out the upper storey gave the early builders a safe means of adding height without putting too uneven a strain on the ground floor posts, and of throwing the rain clear of the foundation area. But once a brick or stone base was normal for the whole ground storey, any use of half-timbering above, whether structural or not, was arbitrary, and hardly likely to be cheaper. The advance in techniques, in fact, had made the historical approach irrelevant, however interpreted. To frame a building in timber throughout was from many aspects regressive; to frame only the upper storey or selected gables was already an admission that half-timbering was done for effect. Shaw's decision to treat half-timbering ornamentally merely ratified this. In the Willesley studio of 1869, he did experiment with timber construction in the old manner, direct on a brick plinth.[24] But there was no overhang here, whereas elsewhere it was this feature which made him sometimes so lavish with his timberwork. In such cases (e.g. the Farnham Bank and Spout Hall) the framework is only self-supporting, in other words it carries only the weight of its own gables and jetties (ills. 60, 61); the roof and chimneys have to be born by

62. Overbury, Post Office and Stores.

an ingenious system of internal brick walls and on occasions (notably at Farnham) rolled iron joists. Where less timberwork was used, less complicated measures were necessary. At Leyswood, the first of a number of country houses where the entrance gable alone was half-timbered (ill. 27), Mark Girouard reports that 'the timbers that met the eye were purely decorative 2 inch thick planks attached to a separate and invisible load-bearing timber frame.'[25] Many minor passages of timberwork on houses and cottages are tacked directly on to a brick wall behind, just like tile-hanging. And at Cragside, we have the astonishing (some may think scandalous) feature of half-timbering under the eaves along the entrance front pinned to great hooped iron stanchions carrying the roof and walls of the picture gallery behind.[26] The facing timbers at Cragside and other such houses were of seasoned oak, lightly coated with varnish and left a silver-grey colour, not tarred black.

The incidence of half-timbering in Shaw's work alters curiously. In his early wealden houses, though half-timbering and·tile-hanging would have been equally suitable, the timberwork played second fiddle. Then at Preen Manor, his first north-western house, the roles were switched. Although the walls were of ashlar, tile-hanging did not disappear, but the timberwork was played up (ill. 73). Iron girders trussed it to the structure, while wooden pins stood out an inch or two to draw attention to the pegging of the joints.[27] At Preen Manor, this showy work has now disappeared. But the pretty school Shaw built nearby survives, marred only by the cheap deal timbers that were sometimes prescribed to save cost. The technique, in fact, was effective only in expensive oak. Shaw was to go on using oaken half-timbering enthusiastically for his bigger houses, where clients could afford it. In the 1870s it appears freely, not just in the north-west but also in the series of stone-based Sussex and Surrey houses built for him by Frank Birch. The climax was Pierrepont, where expense was little object and all woodwork, inside as well as outside, was of oak (ill. 74). Then there is a sudden fall-off. Adcote has a single inconspicuous patch, and at Greenham the half-timbering on the rear elevation was much reduced on revision. After 1879, the year of the excellent Overbury Post Office (ill. 62), Shaw's half-timbering is confined to brick houses and makes much less play with overhang. This was the time when, with his pupils' help, he was moving towards a neater and softer texture to his houses. But once on the market, half-timbering was something wealthy clients were unwilling to forego. It had the right manorial ring; it was mediaeval and ancestral without being 'cottagey', as half-hipping and tile-hanging might be thought to be. Unlike Philip Webb, Shaw thought himself bound up to a point to indulge his clients' emotions.· So expanses of half-timbering went on appearing upon his Old English mansions after it had almost disappeared from his cheaper houses and cottages. Broadlands, Alcroft Grange, and Mere Bank are all biggish examples; and contrary to frequent assumption, it continued to the very end, at The Hallams (ills. 72, 76) and the garden front of Banstead Wood.[28]

The interstices of timber-framing could be roughcast, left in smooth plaster, or filled with brick nogging. Shaw veered between these possibilities. Plasterwork provided the possibility of the incised decoration which Nesfield and he favoured in the 1860s. The idea of such a geometrical decoration had been canvassed a decade earlier, notably by Ferrey, as appropriate to plaster or cement.[29] It had the advantages of being cheap (at Preen School, Shaw allowed ten shillings for stamped plaster in a coving under the gable

63. Willesley, detail of exterior coving.

64. Willesley, part of hall ceiling.

window) and could be impressed *in situ*.[30] Much of this decoration was only thinly incised, and may have vanished in later replasterings, but often it was never executed. Nesfield, who had a number of jobs in West Essex, where incised plasterwork was an old tradition, applied to them a mixture of *sgraffito* and relief ornament (ills. 32, 66).[31] In many of these works, the timbers themselves were covered. The only time that Shaw entirely encased timbers was also, appropriately, in East Anglia, when reconstructing the old village hall at Kelsale as a school. Probably he left the exterior much as he found it, with a smooth plaster finish without incised work. Roughcast, which Devey sometimes used, he favoured less. It occurs on the front of the 1866 Bromley cottages because the incised ornament he wanted was not carried out. By the time Shaw uses it on his very last domestic work, Sibleys Orchard of 1905, it had been brought into fashion by Voysey and Ernest Newton. In the country houses of the 1870s, roughcast is confined to small gable passages. So too is nogging, which Shaw used in passages at Grims Dyke (ill. 77) but little thereafter.[32]

Finally, a word on the doors and windows which punctuate the framework I have outlined. Both begin from the axiom that the ground floor must be more dignified than what is above. It was in the front doors that the Gothic element in Old English persisted longest. Well into the 1870s, a stout oak door boasting elaborate hinges and inset within a pointed arch hallowed the entrance to Shaw's country houses. Where there was a porch, it

65. Merrist Wood, windows
on garden side.

66. Lea Wood, window
(Nesfield, 1874–6).

67. The Knolls, window.

68. Merrist Wood, view of entrance front before alterations of 1917–8.

69. Allerton Beeches, entrance front.

70. Painshill, perspective of entrance front of proposed house (unexecuted), 1871.

71. Piccards Rough, ground floor plan and perspective of entrance front, drawn by Mervyn Macartney, 1878.

72. The Hallams, ground floor plan and perspective of garden fronts, drawn by Archibald Christie, 1894.

73. Preen Manor, perspective of entrance front, 1870.

74. Pierrepont, ground floor plan and perspective of entrance front, 1876.

would echo the arch in form and normally be dressed in stone. Pierrepont (ill. 74) and Ellern Mede (ill. 108) are among the first houses where the nature of the half-timbered gable above forces a square head upon the entrance. Thereafter, this form is the commoner, as it always had been for side and back doors. With ground floor windows too, Shaw began by insisting upon the formality of at least some stone-dressed windows containing iron casements. This was the treatment at Leyswood, and it persists in the bigger brick houses as well, of course, as the stone ones. But it was expensive and by no means obligatory. At Glen Andred, most of the large ground floor windows and the casements in them are of wood, in plain brick surrounds. Wood also became standard for upper storey windows, but these differed when set in half-timbering or tile-hanging. In half-timbering, the frames were originally left their natural colour, whereas those in tile-hanging were painted white, thus offering a contrast frequently lost today. By degrees, these more malleable wooden windows take over the whole of Shaw's smaller houses. In the 1870s, he allows himself greater freedom of fenestration in such houses than in his grander affairs.

75. Boldre Grange, front and garden elevations, 1872.

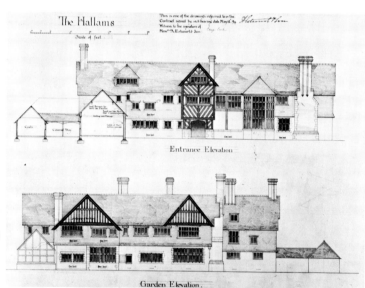

76. (right) The Hallams, front and garden elevations, 1894.

77. (far right) Grims Dyke, entrance front.

Merrist Wood, one of Shaw's cleverest mixtures of stone, brick, tile-hanging and half-timbering, depends greatly for its charm upon the way in which he manipulates windows (ill. 65). Though the walling is of stone, he avoids stone mullions even in so formal a feature as the bay of the hall, and in cavalier fashion cants out wooden windows here and there on a variety of brackets, to create more light within and to impede the upward progress of the elevation. The hall window is only just a bay, delicately splayed out from the wall so that it stays under the eaves; the others assume varying angles and positions. In Shaw's happy hands, bay windows take a life of their own which shows up earlier stodginess. They come in all shapes and sizes, single and double-storey, bowed, canted, polygonal, and straight-sided. He took particular delight in varying his ways of

roofing them over. Canted bays, for instance, were often awarded straight gable heads, an idea explored by Butterfield in half-timberwork, and passed on by Shaw in a refined form to Newton and Voysey. Hence it travelled fast to the fabled bypass semi-detached, so that it is hard to look at this motif in a fresh light; but it was rare before 1870. Other bays were flat-roofed and balustraded, or given a little lean-to. One pleasant idiosyncrasy is the bay with its own high polygonal capping, which could be set against the wall (Corner House) or, if two-storeyed, integrated into the roofline of the house (Glen Andred, Hopedene).

From about 1880, the thick wood casements in the wooden frames of upper storeys give way to thinner, lighter iron frames like those Shaw had always installed in stone-dressed windows. This gives a trimmer, more mechanical aspect to the later vernacular

78. Grims Dyke, view of the studio in W. S. Gilbert's time: the fireplace is by Ernest George and Peto, *c.*1890–1.

houses, but in no way presages the decline of the casement. The casement, it must be emphasized, was with rare exceptions the window type of the Old English style for the simple reason that it allowed easy vertical and horizontal extension. At its grandest, it became the great square-headed mullioned window, the lights ascending in decreasing height from transom to transom. Sometimes, every light of such a window was leaded, but the usual arrangement was to leave the bottom row clear, with alternate casements for opening, and one or two of the upper lights in a different vertical row movable on their centres for ventilation purposes. Leyswood's windows were, with Dickensian quaintness, diamond-leaded in part (ill. 27), but Shaw normally used square panes, authentically bound with saddle bars and wiring along the back. More complex patterns of latticework occur in the big houses and became a speciality of Aldam Heaton when he moved to London.[33] Casement openers with elegant spring fastenings are found at Willesley, Cragside, and Grims Dyke, but were soon replaced with a simpler type of handle.

This revulsion from plate glass is not novel. What is interesting is Shaw's refusal to follow the new fashion back into sash windows. Of the parsonage builders, White and Street had stood out for the propriety of casements, while Butterfield and Scott experimented with sashes but often did not use them.[34] Webb was the first architect for whom the sash window was virtually mandatory. When Shaw built the vicarage for Holy

96

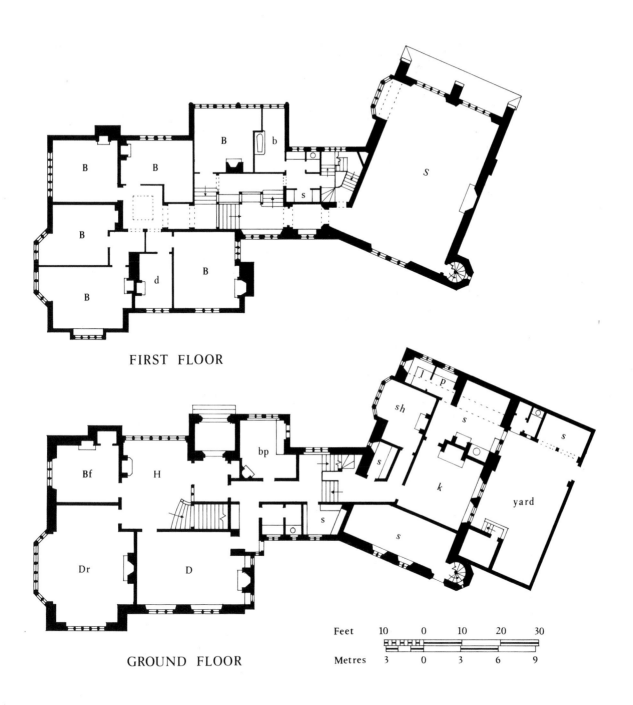

FIRST FLOOR

GROUND FLOOR

Feet 10 0 10 20 30

Metres 3 0 3 6 9

79. Grims Dyke, ground and first floor plans as built.

80. Greenham Lodge, entrance front.

Trinity, Bingley, a building markedly reminiscent of Butterfield, he too plumped for sashes. But they were suitable only where the frame was of greater height than width, whereas casements were infinitely adaptable. Under the eaves of old cottages, such windows often extended for some distance sideways. This was a device Shaw mimicked at Willesley, Leyswood, Wispers, and most spectacularly in an unbuilt design of 1871 for Leonard Micklem, where an unbroken row of twenty lights was to run along the corridors of ground and upper floors. Single rows of casements could even rise along with the stairs (on the back elevation of the Bromley lodge) or turn corners (Willesley and Leyswood).[35] Arguably, these horizontally extending casements under spreading eaves give the closest link between Shaw's style and the prairie houses of Frank Lloyd Wright. But these delightful tricks were gradually abandoned, to Lutyens' subsequent profit.

INSIDE

There is a legend, conceivably put about by Voysey, that when Norman Shaw went out to dinner, he would attire himself in a stiff white shirt with extra-long cuffs. At table, he would engage a rich neighbour in conversation and gradually lead the topic round to houses. Having admitted certain inadequacies in his own home, the gentleman would be

98

81. Greenham Lodge, the hall.

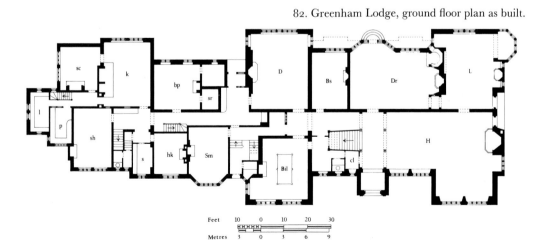

82. Greenham Lodge, ground floor plan as built.

83. (above) Adcote, entrance front.   84. (right) Adcote, the hall.

smartly confronted with the image of a new house speedily sketched upon the cuffs, and would have to have his wits about him to escape falling for a large and costly mansion designed by Mr Shaw.[36] Something of the kind no doubt happened once. There is, too, the story of the weekend visitors at Sir William Armstrong's hunting lodge returning from their shooting to find the whole of the future Cragside drawn out by its architect.[37]

Does Shaw's composition, therefore, precede his planning? The answer is emphatically not. In his day, few architects apart from Webb and Bodley strove to avoid designing and trying effects by the process of sketching; Pugin, who had insisted upon elevation following from plans, certainly drew perspectives of his works before they were more than roughly worked out, if not for himself, then for his client.[38] Elevation and plan ultimately always emerge together; the first rough sketches remind an experienced architect, as he groups and regroups his rooms, of the effects of mass and roofline to which they must in the end conform. Flexibility, I have suggested, is the reason for Shaw's choice of the Old English style, a flexibility of plan as well as of elevation. Add a bay here, shift a casement left or right, project the porch further, or change the proportions of the hall—problems insuperable for Palladian, difficult in picturesque Italianate or awkwardly articulated Gothic, easy for Old English, with its simple, additive vocabulary. Herein lies the secret of much of Shaw's fluency.

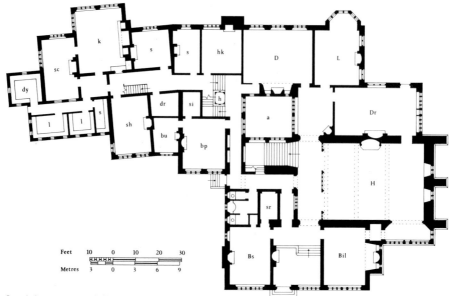

85. Adcote, ground floor plan.

Hence, too, the partly self-propagated myth of Shaw as an additive planner, combiner of crannies and rambling corridors into a magic architectural unity. Certainly, Shaw wished to emulate Mr Wickstead's drawing room at Canterbury in *David Copperfield*: 'It seemed to be all old nooks and corners; and in every nook and corner there was some queer little table, or cupboard, or bookcase, or seat, or something or other, that made me think there was not such another good corner in the room; until I looked at the next one, and found it equal to it, if not better.' Not just sentimental clients, but the ablest architects too fell for this recreated enchantment of Shaw's. John Belcher, recalls Beresford Pite, 'treasured up every feature and characteristic of his work; the crooked passages, the inviting window ravines and tumbling stairs, all had a fascination for Belcher when I first knew him, and we drank of the stream together.'[39] The R.A. perspectives, the asymmetry, the ample vernacular vocabulary, all conjure up a delightful and inefficient chaos. Shaw himself, it is recorded, 'was wont half-humorously to describe his method of planning by saying that he drew one room first and then the rest round it.'[40]

Yet in reality, Shaw's planning is the reverse of undisciplined. At least three widely differing plans were made for the Bournemouth Convent and explained by letter in exacting detail before any elevation was ever drawn up, and Shaw confidently expected major modifications beyond that. He asks Mother Etheldreda to give the plan 'your fullest consideration and deliberation, for upon it everything as regards the buildings in the future will depend, and if we make a false start we may fall into all sorts of troubles and blunders.'[41] For Alderbrook, six ground plans survive, in which Shaw puzzled over the unwieldy jigsaw of Victorian apartments for nine months, sometimes making radical, sometimes subtle changes, to integrate the building more efficiently (ills. 86 & 87). At the end of his career, Shaw showed an unholy enthusiasm for drawing up plans for Piccadilly Circus which he well knew had no hope of execution without mighty revision. Planning was a task which never bored him, however often it perplexed him. It was the real skill of architecture as he understood it, and in his lifetime as a planner he had no serious rival. Elevations, says Arthur Keen, he looked on as a relaxation to enjoy when the serious business of planning was done.[42]

There are complaints about Shaw's planning, but as frequently as not they are anachronistic. Victorian architects got into hot water with their customers over two main matters, the plans and the bills. On the occasions that it happened to Shaw, it was expense rather than incompetence that was the charge. From awkwardnesses of planning, Shaw liked to extricate himself with Houdini-like relish. 'The want of head room at Pierrepont alarms me', he writes to Frank Birch. 'I see nothing for it but getting 3 steps on the half landing and going down a step into the W.C. passage.'[43] Sometimes it was left to the builders: 'the flue must be got into this position somehow,' says a note on a detail of the Cragside dining room fireplace, and similar directions to get steps in occur on a couple of other drawings.[44] Such adventurous, casual competence would not have been approved by Webb. But as long as the result was good, this never worried Shaw. He spent a lifetime alternately playing the artist and the practical man, a position which he justified in some detail in *Architecture a Profession or an Art*. After all, the loudest 'professional' country house architect, Robert Kerr, turned out a blusterer who parted from his chief client on the worst of terms; maybe there was much to be said for the amateur approach.

All customers with enough pretensions to go to Shaw for a country house, whether the budget was to be big or small, would expect certain traditional features in common: drawing room, dining room, and one other reception room at least on the ground floor, with the string of 'offices' alongside.[45] The range of such houses is broad. The Victorian architect's dream client (in theory, if rarely in practice) was the grandee who decided to demolish and rebuild his ancestral home. That happened to Shaw only once, at Bryanston. Such occasions were rare after 1850; Shaw was only a 'middle-class architect' because everyone from his generation on had to be. There are only two other entirely new houses that cost over £20,000 in his *oeuvre*, both for shipowners, and both now demolished. At Leyswood, a new estate was formed and a number of ancillary buildings put up, factors which, with the trickiness of the site and the flamboyance of the scheme, explain how so huge a sum was spent on a house having only three very ordinary reception rooms on the ground floor. The other, Dawpool, was sited on a modest estate, replacing a previous, smaller building; it was very large and luxurious, and boasted every technological contrivance. Shaw's other well-known country houses follow a different pattern, whereby the old family or a new purchaser of a large estate recast the existing small house within a mansion commensurate with their income and the size of their property. Cragside, Adcote, Pierrepont and Greenham all encase an insignificant shooting lodge or farm. The remnants of the Elizabethan house were incorporated more openly at Flete; later on, Chesters and Haggerston Castle are again works of reconstruction.

These are the ten large country houses. After them, there is a drop in cost by a quarter to the next most expensive new ones: The Hallams (built in 1894–5 for a sum resented by its client,[46] but probably less costly in real terms than many Shaw houses of the

1870s), Alderbrook, Baldslow Place, Piccards Rough, Wispers, and Allerton Beeches. All these houses certainly cost over £10,000.[47] From here down to Dinah Mulock Craik's little Corner House, built for under £3,000, probably on the proceeds of *John Halifax, Gentleman*, there is a gradual diminution of expense which had to be reflected in plan and elevation without loss of dignity. The question was how to dispose the same series of rooms so as to make poor clients satisfied and the rich assured of their superiority.

The structure of the basic ground floor plan of these houses rests upon a simple, rational principle: build up the lines of communication around two axes cutting the hall of the house, and fit round them, as far as money would allow, a series of centrifugal but interlocked cells. Previous country house planning had either leant heavily upon symmetry, or adopted the corridor-and-suite system of Burn and the 'Scottish school', which reached horrendous complexity at Kerr's Bear Wood.[48] Two principal axes there had naturally been in hundreds of previous houses. Shaw's concern was to make use of them as corridors of communication without undue emphasis, particularly on the lateral axis. Therefore the reception rooms normally stand in close relation to the short, entrance axis, while the staircase hall runs across the main lateral one. The stairs themselves are usually placed off either axis (though they follow the lateral one at Boldre Grange and Broadlands, for instance) and are invisible from the main entrance. Stated thus, the positioning of main rooms off a short, broad line, and services off a longer, thinner line, suggests the L-shaped parsonage plan evolved by Butterfield and the other architects of ecclesiological persuasion. This is a far more important source for Shaw than anything Burn ever planned.[49]

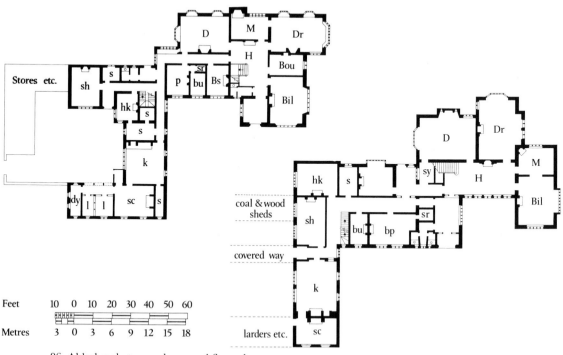

86. Alderbrook, two early ground floor plans.

87. Alderbrook, contract ground and first floor plans.

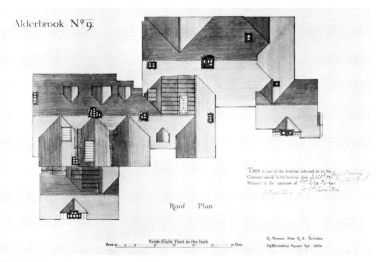

88. Alderbrook, contract roof plan.

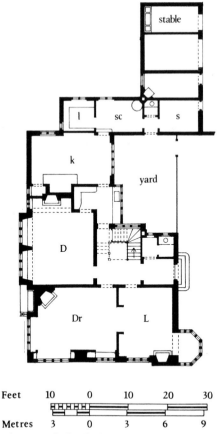

89. The Corner House, Shortlands, ground plan before additions of 1872.

At the aptly named Corner House (1868), the parsonage plan appears virtually intact (ill. 89). It is a compact little plan, instructive to compare with Webb's Red House not so far away, which Shaw did not in fact know.[50] To enliven the stodgy wall-and-window system of the ecclesiologists, Shaw increases the window space wherever possible and thickens up the reduced wall surface round the fireplaces. In one place, he turns the drawing room hearth across the corner of a room, in another he interlocks dining room and kitchen hearths to make an inglenook, and fits in a small cross wall for the serving lobby. On this scale, these massings of structure round the hearth appear more clearly than in the bigger houses. From them, by however tortuous a route, derive the hearth-centred houses of Frank Lloyd Wright and M. H. Baillie-Scott. They have a double function, both sustaining the top-heavy chimneys that Shaw insists upon even in his smallest houses, and providing a place which is not in immediate view of the doorway—that sense of 'corner house' in which contemporaries revelled. The bay in the book room, the fireplace across the corner in the drawing room (with 'Dorothy's Parlour' tucked in outside), and the settle seats in the dining room inglenook are all obscured from the opening door without the least addition to expense. In other ways, too, the Corner

House plan flouts formality, by doing away with back stairs and employing winders on the main staircase.[51]

As money is available, Shaw develops the small house plan into something more elongated and extruded. The first luxury is a single-storeyed bay, the second the thrusting out of whole areas under separate gables, and the third is the expanded hall. When it is just a bay here or an outside ingle there, the cardinal axes are not threatened, but as the houses begin to pull apart in different directions there is a danger that they will shift and break until the main spine becomes incoherent. It is Shaw's great achievement that this does not occur. A brief shift of either axis forward or backward is all he normally has to allow himself, and these breaks often serve their functions. At Houndswood, the double disconnection in the entrance hall marks off the servants' area from the family rooms on the lateral axis, and allows even in this small house for the door to be answered without disturbance, while the main axis is broken to cut off the draughts from the narrow porch (ill. 100). When the axial system is most seriously compromised, it is to maintain the separation of functions, especially front-door access. This happens in bigger houses like Adcote, where Shaw chose access round a central light well, and gave up his lateral axis behind the stairs (ill. 85). In the more modest plans, the disconnection stayed simple. But often it enabled Shaw to bring up the back stair from the kitchen area to the region of the butlers' pantry, or even to abut the two sets of stairs against the same wall, as at Boldre Grange.

Shaw's treatment of stairs cannot be separated from his planning of halls. At first, he made no attempt to provide a really grand hall. At Leyswood he called it an anteroom and gave it decent dimensions, a fireplace, and a recessed corner in which to sit, but it was an uncertain area, unfitted for social functions, and still only the departure point for the staircase, coyly tucked into one corner behind a screen (ill. 29). By degrees, this hall begins to dominate, and as it does so creates its own franker axis with the stairs. The staircase starts off as a unit on its own, beginning from one side of the hall and finding its light where it can. To get a good staircase light was another reason for dislocating the plan. Frequently, the staircase window rises over the back courtyard or a light well, since it is to provide light, not to see out of; often it is heavily leaded, even stained at Pierrepont, and when it is accessible it does not have opening casements. Like others, Shaw never lets his staircase intrude upon the garden front, where the sequence of reception rooms with bedrooms over is not to be interrupted. The simpler houses often have the showier staircase windows, turned to the front over a lavatory and closet next to the lobby; the grander ones, confident in the magnificence of their bays and ingles, accept more modest aspects. As the hall increases in size and grandeur, the stairs are often straitjacketed in panelling and the staircase window becomes only subsidiary. But it can still help to light the hall, or at least the screens passage. The very formality of a great hall encouraged Shaw to create an axis along the line of the main flight. It is very pronounced in the 1870s sequence of big houses with their regular procession of hall, passage and stairs, but it occurs even in the reduced anteroom halls of the 1880s, as at Holme Grange. Here and at Greenhill, Shaw starts encased stairs out of a one-storey hall back towards the entrance, a direction often necessary but ineffective in the high, narrow staircase halls of the 1870s, excellent when the same rectangular box is turned on its side.

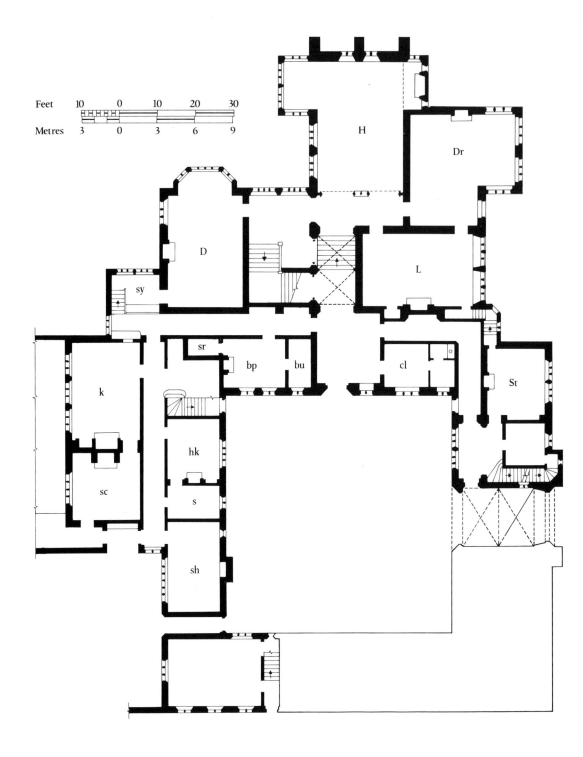

H

Dr

D

sy

L

sr

bp

bu

cl

St

k

hk

sc

s

sh

90. Unexecuted house for F. W. Fison, Ilkley, ground floor plan.

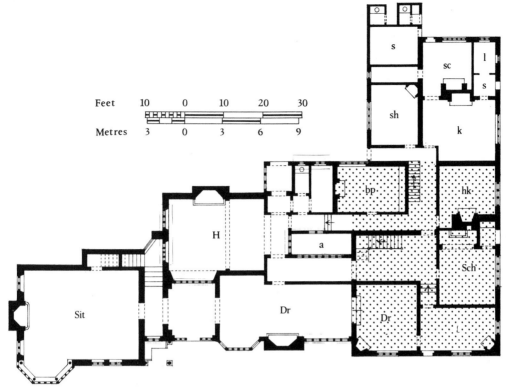

91. Upper House, Shamley Green, ground floor plan showing original house (shaded), with Shaw's extensions of 1874 and 1880: Shaw's further alterations of c.1888 and the various later additions are not shown.

These houses incorporate other tricks to vary the staircase. At Holme Grange, the steps spill out of the casing into the hallway, a technique which enabled architects to get in extra steps when short of space, but could only be sensibly used when the base of the stairs was isolated from too much traffic. When used with open stairs, as at Grims Dyke and Broadlands, the newel could, by another classical trick, be pulled out slightly into the hall and the bottom steps lengthened and curved. A much bolder practice that Grims Dyke (ill. 79) shares with Flete and Greenhill is the loosing of the staircase from its straitjacket, so that it turns at will in different directions until it unhurriedly lands at bedroom level. These staircases do not tumble but they twist, and require much room. At Flete, the stairs break through the back of a deep hall, and are designed to provide two views back to the entrance, one from high up over the well, the other from a half-landing at the front of the stairs lower down, so that the lady of the house may be well vantaged to view her guests and then descend to greet them (ill. 162). Many of the London houses with their first-floor reception rooms were specially adapted to this particular moment—the staircase greeting. Grims Dyke and Greenhill are in another category, the split-level house with one wing starting from the half-landing stage. In both these cases for entirely practical reasons, Shaw also 'offset' his plan, that is, he canted the wing away at an angle to the main house. At Greenhill, Shaw seems to have added on a new axis to a small existing building, recast the old part as smoking and billiard rooms, and split the stairs economically. At Grims Dyke, the house was aligned roughly parallel to the old dyke so as not to disturb it, but since Frederick Goodall wanted a pure north–south light for the high-ceilinged painting room which was to fill the east wing, Shaw canted it off at an angle at the end of a corridor on landing level. Both stairs and corridor follow the line of the rest of the house, and the upper staircase is spaciously turned back to give a vantage along the corridor. This device gives Grims Dyke the air of a larger house than it really is (ill. 77). It is in fact only middle-sized, and at a cost of some £7,000 was thought cheap.

Grims Dyke is virtually the only Old English house where the double axis is eliminated from the ground floor. It is also the first to experiment with two ideas which recur together—the 'offset' and the great hall. Offset plans were no novelty; Wyatville's Endsleigh may be their progenitor. Devey's big houses of the 1860s and '70s exploited the idea, but offsetting in his hands was a picturesque device which imperilled his already rather ramshackle planning, which depended upon alarming amounts of exterior walling.[52] Thrusting out rooms or bays to all points of the compass made for great heat loss and waste of materials. There is no doubt Shaw was guilty of this at Leyswood, but he soon got over it.[53] Instead, he came to use the conjunction of great hall and offset as means to exorbitance without too much waste. At Grims Dyke, the painting room imitates Horsley's studio at Willesley, with its plastered wagon roof, little gallery, and bay window tucked in the corner. But the scale is much increased; it is the centre of entertainment as well as of work (ill. 78). Soon in Shaw's houses the second characteristic will disappear, and the great hall will make its presence frankly known.

There had been great halls a-plenty before Shaw's time, many of them of limited practical use except as summer sitting rooms. 'It is as though the idea of the great hall came first, and a modern function had to be found for it afterwards', says Jill Franklin.[54] Nesfield created a fine if isolated example at Cloverley, but probably it was Shaw's restoration work at Ightham Mote in 1871–2 which brought him back to the idea. Soon after it, he adumbrated the development in an unexecuted plan for a large house at Ilkley for F. W. Fison, where a magnificent hall at half-landing level has the mature characteristics of bays on either side and end-buttressing; only the offset was missing (ill. 90). Then in 1874 came a more modest job, when Shaw was asked to extend Upper House in Surrey, and decided on the hall treatment (ill. 91). The Upper House hall was a mere dining room, twenty-five feet by eighteen feet, with a bay to one side looking onto a conservatory and an outside chimney-breast on the other. Shaw gave this room the full manorial treatment, extending it upwards to two storeys, and constructing his first secular open-timbered roof with lateral braces and a strong outside buttress at the end. The mediaevalism of this hall was so determinedly crude that the end was left open to the chilly entrance passage.

At Upper House the hall was not the main living room as it had been at Willesley. Nor was it regularly so; Shaw, once he had come back to the plan, used it in one of three ways, as an entrance hall, with the screens passage principle safeguarded but the double-storey effect lost (Wispers, Alderbrook, Burrows Cross), as a dining hall (Upper House, Merrist Wood, Adsdean), or as the grand ceremonial hall reserved for great festivities (Pierrepont, Adcote, Greenham). After 1880 the two latter types seem abandoned in favour of the picture gallery halls of Dawpool and Cragside, but Shaw has his last and

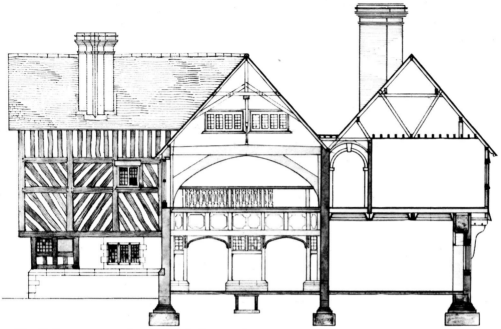

92. The Hallams, cross section through hall, etc., 1894.

most glorious fling with the mediaeval hall at The Hallams. There, it is a grand, dark, severe space of two storeys, functioning as both entrance and ceremonial hall, and integrated with the living rooms by girder work not only in the sections but within the very beams (ills. 72, 92). The Hallams shares with the other great halls of the '70s the device of making the gallery into an open first floor landing looking down into the hall from amidst the tie beams; and like Greenham (ills. 81, 82) it goes one further, by turning the main bedroom corridor along the side of the hall and opening internal windows between them, so that the hall is further embedded in the structure of the house. The wittiest, most picturesque trick of this kind is at Adcote. There, above the open landing at gallery level, Shaw reveals the corridor of the second bedroom storey, high up in the end of the hall. Faced with half-timberwork to match the hall rafters, and canted out slightly, its leaded lights provide a precipitous peep-show down to the hall two floors below (ill. 84).

The earliest of these greater halls, at Pierrepont, is at once the most manorial and the least integrated. Pierrepont's plan is odd, for it reverses the usual sequence of rooms (ill. 74). The dining room is pushed up against the entrance, the business room (with attached bathroom) faces the garden door, and the billiard room comes immediately opposite the drawing room. The hall itself, which is out on rather a limb, follows the Fison prototype closely. It has end bays facing both ways, and the seemingly functionless triple buttresses which had been used at Grims Dyke and which recur, perhaps with more need, at the end of the massive Adcote hall.[55]

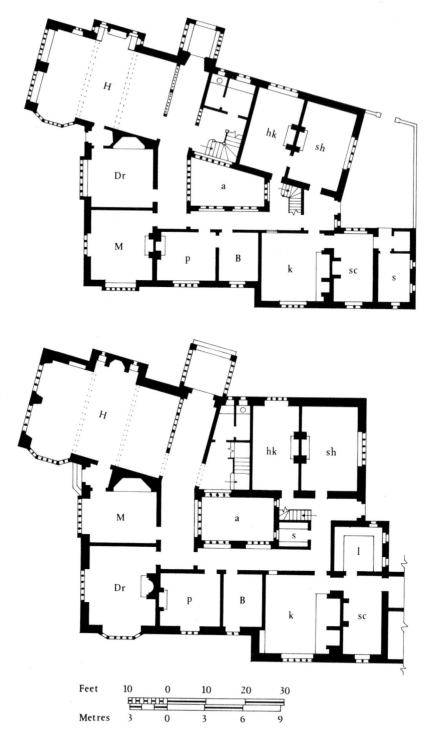

Feet 10 0 10 20 30

Metres 3 0 3 6 9

93. Merrist Wood, ground floor plan as first proposed (top), and as agreed for contract, omitting some late revisions (bottom).

Offsetting enjoys a briefer spell of popularity, confined as a mere picturesque device to the years 1874–7. In no case did Shaw have the justification of site he had at Grims Dyke. At Wispers, the first of the group of houses which exploits offsetting, the site is not level and the drawing room is pushed close to the edge of the escarpment, but this cannot explain why the kitchen wing is canted away. The old house did not determine the offset at Pierrepont and is unlikely to have done so at Adcote. Indeed it is very hard to know why Shaw did offset the service wing at Adcote (ill. 85). The motives of adding 'interest' to the front and giving novel shapes to the rooms do not arise there in the delicate slant of the back elevation away from a true line or the slight bend in the service corridor; in the early plans the old axis is retained. More often, Shaw produced a boldly offset plan to start with and modified it as he made the accommodation more compact. At Wispers, the first plan has a drawing room with three sides exposed to the outside, and the angle of the offset contrived rather clumsily. In revision, the offset remains, but the tricky angle is filled with the dining room inglenook and a store room. Piccards Rough started with an offset arrangement, Shaw's last except for Greenhill, but went on to a more conventional plan, again with a tighter grasp of the reception rooms (ill. 71). The only other house to employ offset is Merrist Wood. Its wonderful little plan shows Shaw reorganizing the units of his larger houses *in parvo*: offsetting, screens hall, light court and main stairs with its own well (ill. 93). Originally, he intended to cause his two axes to collide, letting one serve for the entrance front, the other for the garden, resolving the differences between hall and drawing room, and leaving the light court irregular, as at Pierrepont. It looks good, but the offices where the axes meet are cramped and skimped, so Shaw finally contents himself by offsetting only the hall and porch, and using the angle to give interest to his stairs. The hall, at thirty-two feet by twenty feet, only a little bigger than at Upper House, was the regular dining room.[56] Yet for all these hallmarks of Shaw's style, Merrist Wood is still weaned on the old L-shaped parsonage plan.

One advantage of the simple corridors was to facilitate upper floor planning (ill. 87). If the upper corridor was not superimposed upon the main corridor below, structure became complicated and costs increased. So long also as wall followed wall, the size of the upstairs rooms had to conform to those of the ground floor. Shaw's clients seem to have cared little for grand bedrooms, though the outlook was important in a place where a lady might spend much of the day. Therefore the commonest interruption of the upper floor pattern is by ordinary partition walls marking off bedroom and dressing room, sometimes with an outside lobby. Normally, upper storeys encroached only as far as the kitchen, not round the back yard. Nurseries or minor bedrooms in this part had aspects to front or back, not into the yard. In his organization of upper floors, Shaw was no more than up to date. One bathroom is all that the more modest country houses get, and all that Stevenson thought they needed.[57] One of Shaw's cheaper houses, Chigwell Hall, shows no bathroom at all; on this the client's susceptibilities and habits would be the deciding factor. His departures are more radical where there is money to spend and the principle of a good entrance hall and stairs has been established. Not only did Shaw have to cover these large voids without waste of upper space, but he had to get support too for the chimneys up over the roof. Some of the difficulty could be avoided by angle fireplaces and clever tracking of flues, but from the start it was inevitable that iron girders would be used.

The history of Shaw's girderwork needs technical investigation, for it has baffled and astonished later architects; it is the real justification for his claim to Blomfield that he was 'intended by nature to have been an Engineer.'[58] By Shaw's time, concealed iron girders had quite a history. It was the immense improvement in wrought iron, strong in tension where cast iron was fatally weak, which made their use possible. Smirke seems to have been the real pioneer when he put wrought iron girders into his King's Library ceiling at the British Museum, and his pupil Burn threw them quite liberally about his country houses; so Shaw and Nesfield will have learned the necessary techniques in apostolic succession.[59] But there was much anxiety and suspicion about the habit. Concealed iron girders were attacked as a dangerous hidden source of decay—a fair criticism if the girders were not properly sealed off and protected, as Burn and his pupils were careful to do. The Gothic Revival then confused the issue by insisting upon the truthful exhibition of materials, a troublesome stipulation in the case of iron, since exposed iron when in contact with other more combustible materials was far more likely to fail in a fire than concealed girders. Architects for a time paid lip service to the ideal by exposing the bottom flange of girders in ceilings; Scott did this at Kelham and in the St Pancras Hotel, Webb in the hall ceiling at Arisaig.[60] But Scott also used concealed iron stanchions for the framework of the Albert Memorial, and most architects, Webb included, went on using concealed girders for small jobs at least. Few however can have gone so far as Nesfield, who was already employing both girders and curved stanchions at Combe Abbey, and at Cloverley let girders run riot in the sections, using them sometimes just for an extra measure of security.[61] Shaw resisted girderwork until he faced the problems of the sections in the Farnham Bank, but from then on he relied on them with increasing confidence. Until Bessemer steel began to be applied for this task at all commonly, in the 1880s, he had to be content with the old rolled iron joists of limited bearing power; this frequently meant using a pair of girders bolted together.[62]

There were three main domestic uses to which Shaw put his girders. The first was for tying half-timbering or other types of overhang to the main lateral and transverse load-bearing walls of his building. The most spectacular example of this habit was the earliest, the Farnham Bank (ill. 60), where the cantilever was pronounced and the planning of the bank underneath at odds with James Knight's domestic rooms up above.[63] It occurs less often in country works than in the town, where strong overhang was a tradition of vernacular buildings; the double girders Shaw used at Swan House may be taken as typical, twelve inches deep, with five inch top and bottom flanges, one and a quarter inches thick, and bolted strongly together.[64] Secondly, girders could carry the chimney load while maintaining the interlocking character of the reception rooms. To do this, a girder often ran over an inglenook in order to distribute weight more evenly on the short cross walls. Sometimes, as at Cragside, Shaw was forced to spread the load further into the room, and have girders running across the room from over the fireplace, bedding into the opposite wall. Girders ran similarly across ceilings in the third use that Shaw gave them, as a device to liberate his upper plan from the constrictions of the main floor. This was purely a matter of expense, enabling stairs to arrive at a different point on the plan from that at which they began, and corridors and bedrooms to run across halls or rooms below, as at Lowther Lodge. Most of his girderwork involved these second two practices together, and allowed him to reduce the size of his upper rooms and shift fireplaces without fear by stiffening the whole structure. As town houses preoccupied him more, he began in the 1880s to thrust girders about without a second thought, round toplights and under outside walls, to get coherent circulation and distribution of space on each floor. At first, girders running across rooms would be concealed in deep timber casings parallel to the smaller floor joists, but as Shaw grew disenchanted with wood finishes, they were more frequently cased in plasterwork. The deep plaster ceilings of the later houses always hide girders. With the improvement of steel, these constructions become more technical and adopt odd angles; for instance, lattice girders brace the roofs at Bryanston. Throughout, Shaw seems to have worked out all his own engineering calculations, and so probably over-strengthened many of his structures.

Shaw's ironwork has been unjustly criticized as dishonest, which by contemporary standards it was not. Here, Ruskin's most intelligent discussion of iron is instructive. Metals, he says, may be used as a cement, but not as a support, 'nor does it make any difference, except as to sightliness, whether the metal bands or rods so employed be in the body of the wall or on its exterior, or set as stays and cross-bands; so only that the use of them be always and distinctly one which might be superseded by mere strength of cement.'[65] The dichotomy is, of course, facile, and does not correspond to Shaw's practice, which indissolubly combines binding and propping. But their philosophies are similar: the subordination of iron to the old materials and proportions must be complete, and the basic exterior supports must remain the same. The concealment of iron was a small and irrelevant issue. In London, to expose it in inhabited buildings was not only unsafe, but also after about 1870 strongly discouraged by officials.[66] Meanwhile at Paris, after a carpenters' strike in 1840, concealed iron girders became regular in the most ordinary of town houses to ease problems of floor planning.[67] So Shaw's was a sensible course towards liberation of plan and new forms in domestic architecture. When Morris, speaking of the girderwork of 180 Queen's Gate, said, 'If you *will* have railway architecture, why don't you show it?' he displayed ignorance of the conditions of design.[68] The main drawback to girderwork was expense. Certainly, if Shaw had allowed himself to be limited in planning, he would have had more money to spend on detail and furnishings. It was by rigid conformity to the old system of wall structures that Voysey was able to spend well on his interiors. But the matter was simply one of choice. Shaw's attitudes evolved. At first, he too was for the 'total' architect-designed interior. But as he was led deeper into the structurings of plan and elevation, he came to feel that his customers should be given leeway in choice of furnishings and fittings, and concentrated instead on the lay-out. This process, well under way by the mid-1870s, followed inevitably from the scale of practice which he undertook—one which only the firm attitude of Webb successfully resisted at this time.

In planning individual rooms, Shaw makes no particular changes from the dispositions he has inherited. The reception rooms conform closely to the suggestions Stevenson makes in his *House Architecture* (1880). Possibly Stevenson profited from Shaw's readiness to display his plans in a corner of his annual R.A. perspectives, as Shaw did from Stevenson's experiments in Queen Anne. Take, for instance, the dining room. Every major Shaw example measures at least 18 × 16 ft, ranging up to Greenham's 32 × 24 ft;

Stevenson's recommended 25 × 18 ft is a fair average. Most possess a connecting servery or sideboard recess just out of the room, face south, and have the main windows at the short end so as to cast sideways light upon the food. The last point is not regularly practised by Devey, Scott, or even Robert Kerr, so the agreement with Stevenson is of some significance.[69] The Old English country house dining room was usually panelled. If in oak, it was left a natural colour, if in deal, painted by preference a 'plain dark green'.[70]

A similar consensus arises between Shaw and Stevenson over drawing rooms, which are not planned as a single unified cell, but usually have two points of focus, the hearth and a bay, so as to allow for conversational groups. When, as at Pierrepont and Flete, Shaw experimented with a lengthier 'gallery' drawing room, it was in adaptation of rooms already existing. The drawing room bay is the critical window for aspect, and may determine the whole alignment of the house. Nesfield took extreme care at Babbacombe and Lea Wood to get the perfect view not just straight on to the window bay, but at an oblique angle which conformed to natural seating position. When he juggled with the plans of Alderbrook, the same problem troubled Shaw.[71]

For the billiard room, it was more predictable that Shaw should come to a solution like Stevenson's, of a room 24 × 18 ft or larger, toplit or with windows on two sides, closely connected with a W.C. or lavatory.[72] These conditions meant very variable positions. At Leyswood, it was first to be skied up in the attics but ended up next to the tower well away from the main house. The attic position prevailed too at Ellern Mede and Piccards Rough, but at Preen and Wispers billiards was relegated to the basement. Stevenson preferred somewhere near the dining room, and this often obtained. But toplighting pointed to the single-storey annexe, so that the billiard room, like the conservatory, was often an afterthought (Boldre Grange, Banstead Wood).

The billiard room lent itself particularly to the inglenook, as a raised area at one end where spectators might loll upon settles next to the hearth and comment upon the sport. From start to finish, inglenooks are the decorative *pièce de résistance* of the Shaw country house (ills. 94–96). Only rarely would Shaw allot more than one to a house; Cragside's two belong to different campaigns and styles, and Dawpool's have similar dissimilarities. At Boldre Grange there appear from the plans to be three, but the dining room example is only an unlighted recess; enclosure is the criterion for the full inglenook. The earliest inglenooks all come in dining rooms (at Willesley the Horsleys probably ate at first in their hall), and often that position is retained as late as the 1880s. Later ones frequently belong to the billiard room, where windows to the recess were not necessary, or less often to the drawing room (Piccards Rough and Greenham). The inglenook lent rooms a weight more acceptable in the ritualistic atmospheres of feeding and competition than in the brighter air of the drawing room. As his ideas developed, Shaw learned different ways to convey this weight. Over the hearth of the early inglenooks stood a rough stone chimneypiece, sometimes with a little carving, sometimes adorned with one of the sentimental texts beloved by picturesque architects, and made their own by Nesfield and Shaw.[73] Outside, in the less luxurious examples, ran a wooden beam supported on curved brackets, frequently with a ledge for pots and coving for embossed and stamped leather above. In 1857 Scott speaks of the successful revival of the craft of stamped leather;[74] but it cannot have been in great demand for some years, since Horsley could buy sixteenth-

94. Willesley, inglenook in hall.

95. Knight's Croft, fireplace in music room.

96. Greenham Lodge, inglenook in library.

century French leather for Willesley very cheaply, and Shaw prescribed old leather again for the Corner House inglenook coving.[75] Gradually, leather paper supplanted leather proper, but it remained Shaw's favourite frieze motif over panelling during the 1870s. It has now disappeared from nearly all the surviving inglenooks, so other features have to hint at the richness of colour. Inglenooks of the smartest sort at Cragside (ill. 44), Adcote, Flete and Dawpool (ill. 200) have or had stained glass in the lights. But the real centre of colour was the hearth, where inglenooks gave space to the full panoply of the ancestral home. Much of this apparatus was frankly ornamental and had long been so: 'The iron doggs bear the burthen of the fuel, while the brazen andirons stand only for state', says Fuller.[76]

The varying displays of multicoloured tiles backing the andirons and the rest of the panoply are specially memorable. When Shaw began practice, the days of Minton's monopoly of good architects were over, and De Morgan had yet to claim the inheritance. In the interim, Maw's majolica tiles were the prettiest for fireplace cheeks, lustre-painted and made by the 'hollow' method which gave the vaguest hint of relief. They derive from old Moresque patterns and come in several types, of which the commonest is a series of geometrical designs in blues and reds and greens.[77] These were much favoured by Nesfield and Shaw in the mid-1870s, and appear round the inglenook at Ellerdale Road. Occasionally such tile patterns escape the confines of the fireplace, and turn into glittering wall dados; not content to enliven the staircase and corridor at Cragside with them, Shaw panels church sanctuaries with Maw's tiles at Meerbrook, Youlgreave, Burghclere, Low Bentham, and St Swithun's, Bournemouth. Sometimes, fireplaces carry the scantily painted imitation-Delft tiles that came back into fashion about 1870 (Yateley Hall), or a rarer but similar oriental equivalent (Oakley House).[78] Some of these tiles could well be old ones, purchased from an art furnisher's emporium and re-used. On such a point as tiles, the client would usually decide; when Shaw had time, he would go down to the shop with his customer and select leather, tiles, grates or marble with him. Cooke's diary is full of these little expeditions for the perfecting of Glen Andred; to Murray Marks for Venetian leather, or Potter for heating apparatus.[79] In the busier 1870s and '80s the customer often had to go alone for tiles. By the end of the '70s, more discerning people would plump for De Morgan. His tiles are found at Adcote, Piccards Rough, Greenham, Knight's Croft, Flete, Jesmond Dene House and Bourn Hall, sometimes in flat patterns upon or next to the fireplace surround as well as on the normal canted cheeks. Mrs Mildmay of Flete, however, found him personally 'too affected'.[80] No Shaw house is known to have included De Morgan's work after 1885, as from this time the fireplace designs begin to omit tile cheeks.

As Shaw's style grew formal and classic, his inglenooks became sleeker and softer in texture without loss of weight. He was now after 'scale and character, and we timid mice generally fail in the former.' This remark is apropos of the Overbury Court billiard room of 1898–9, an excellent example of his later chimney pieces:

I think, (humanly speaking), that this is the last 'Ingle nook' I shall design . . . I don't want Overbury to have a commonplace looking thing, that might be anywhere. The inner fireplace ought to be quite simple, also large in scale so I am making it five feet

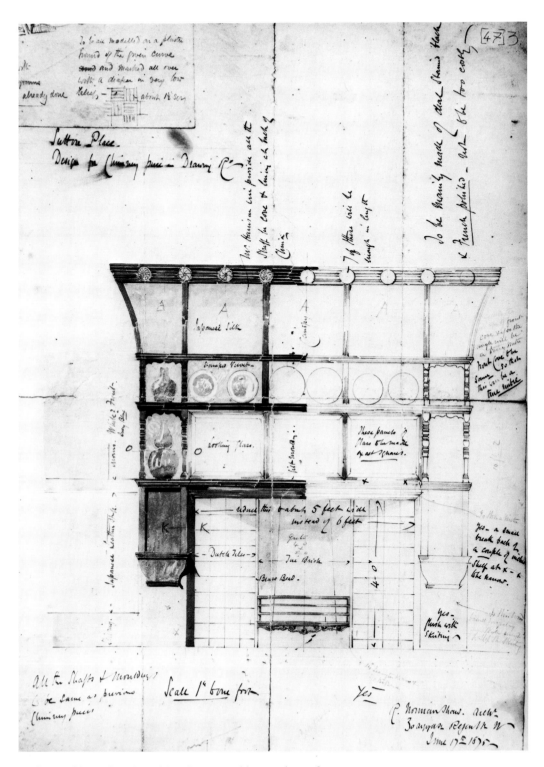

97. Sutton Place, elevation of drawing room chimney piece, 1875

119

98. Cragside, main staircase, with Joseph Swan's electric light fittings of 1880.

wide. This might be of stone, or preferably of a simple marble like 'Istrian'. In the Ingle nook I propose on each side a *real* comfortable seat—not a settle by any means, but a good width, deep and well stuffed, covered with leather I presume, as being most suitable for a billiard room, where folk smoke.[81]

In place therefore of the purposeful crudity of Willesley or Leyswood come rare marbles with massive bolection mouldings, and Ionic columns with exaggerated entasis. The prototype for these late marble inglenooks was in the dining room at Dawpool (ill. 200), so huge and rich that it now frames the entrance of a dance hall in Birkenhead. But the climax of the inglenook concept was not here but in the Dawpool picture gallery (ill. 199), where Shaw took the idea of the two-storey inglenook which he had foreshadowed partly in his own house, partly at Greenham, and applied it to his new toplit version of the hall. This great inglenook (which has now mostly found its way to Portmeirion) was all Shaw's—a bold mixture of Flemish and flamboyant Gothic detail enclosing a double-arched organ gallery above, and a dark nook below lit by windows in one of which Shaw was portrayed, holding a model of the house.[82] It is, of course, the idea which Lethaby developed and transformed in the Cragside drawing room chimneypiece (ill. 50). But neither the hall nor the inglenook stopped developing there, as we shall see with the reconstructions of Chesters, Haggerston and Addington.

Of the drawing room décor, more too can be said later, in connection with the town houses; there, the drawing room held undisputed pre-eminence over the dining room and was more affected by Morris's thoughts on the question of furnishing. For the present it is generally enough to say that Shaw followed orthodoxy in separating drawing room and dining room as far as possible not only physically, for ceremonial reasons, but also in tone, so as to give variety; this was evident at Cragside. But a word should be added on his characteristic drawing room fireplace of the 1870s. Like the rest of the room, it has gone classical from the first, however mildly so. Typically it is a high, narrow erection, stretching from floor to ceiling, perhaps coved out at the top, fitted always with several ledges besides the main mantel and often with small unobtrusive mirrors. This was sometimes called a 'dresser mantelpiece', and usually cluttered with *objets d'art*.[83] Almost all are gone today, replaced by better forms of heating; there can be little doubt that their grates were frequently too small, so that when the central heating systems failed they were soon found deficient. Stevenson advised double fireplaces, and these Shaw used in the elongated drawing room at Pierrepont, but in smaller houses they were impracticable.[84] One of his prettiest and most characteristic drawing room chimney pieces was designed when he was restoring Sutton Place in 1875 (ill. 97). It was a three-stage overmantel, stained black and french-polished to set off the pots that would be placed upon it and the inset mirror in its gilt frame. Below this came a thin line of Dutch tiles each side of the hearth; above, stamped yellow velvet with Japanese silk upon the coving. For the four-foot dado, Shaw suggests a hard-wearing Japanese leather paper, and then above it a light Morris paper with a fruit frieze along the top.[85] This was the typical scheme for many a drawing room: lighter, neater, more fully painted and papered. Other rooms would of course veer in accordance with their natural mood; a morning room would be as light as a drawing room, a library or business room darker and more severe. Each avocation and each hour had its place and its mood, to which Shaw had to be alive.

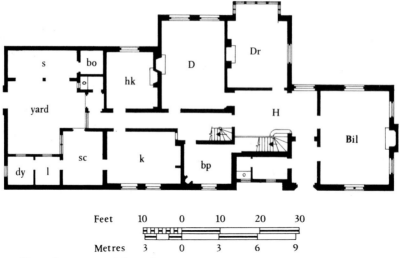

Feet 10 0 10 20 30

Metres 3 0 3 6 9

99. Harperbury, ground floor plan.

Feet 10 0 10 20 30

Metres 3 0 3 6 9

100. Houndswood, ground floor plan.

It is hard now to grasp the contrasts between individual rooms of the Shaw country houses. In most, only the ruins of a fragile interior remain, and in any case our eyes are accustomed to greater unity of interior decoration. It is in the smaller houses of the '70s, where Shaw affords less changing moods between the units of his design, that the sense of the whole seems happiest, and least affected by institutional use, additions, or destruction. So I shall end this chapter by mentioning four of these smaller houses.

Warm hills and woods have made Surrey *par excellence* the county of the Old English style. But north of London too, the less affluent bourgeois made his home in the flatter terrain of Essex and Hertfordshire. Here Shaw built four houses as good as much of his Surrey work: Harperbury and Houndswood at Radlett, Ellern Mede at Totteridge, and Chigwell Hall further east in Essex.

Harperbury and Houndswood stand up drives a little above the level of the lane that runs from Radlett to Colney Heath, on small neighbouring estates; in winter they are just visible to each other through the intervening belt of trees. They were built simultaneously in 1871–2 for two solicitors, Iltid Nicholl and John Oddie, of families long related and again united when Nicholl married Oddie's sister. Nicholl bought the whole estate in 1870, and put up Houndswood, the bigger house, while his brother-in-law built Harperbury, purchasing his part for a nominal sum. So the buildings correspond in style (ills. 101–4). But it is not quite the expected style; it is as near as Shaw ever allows 'Queen Anne' to engulf Old English, for to save expense these are buildings nearly all in brick and white-painted wood, with stone dressings for the first time eliminated from the windows. The houses are a joy for the joiner. Thick, deeply-grooved cornices run all the way round the eaves and under the overhang on the entrance front at Houndswood, and they even triangulate the Harperbury gables to make a kind of pediment. The windows, sometimes bracketed out, normally flush with the brickwork on the upper storey and a little recessed below, turn variously; inward-opening casements and drop-panels inwards and outwards abound, and there are one or two early sashes over the entrance at Harperbury. Only the plain chimneys escape the grasp of the bulky roof that Shaw clamps down on the Houndswood eaves, rendering economy expressive. At Harperbury, the clasp is a little relaxed and the gables gain some freedom, but again cannot vie with the stacks that point the axes above. In plan, the houses are Shaw's first essays in elongating the L-shape, and here too is the same sense of congruence with variety: flat-topped bays to both drawing rooms, the same turned and capped balusters for the stairs, but a porch, a full inner hall, an inglenook and a servants' hall for Mr. Nicholl, while Mr. Oddie makes do with a billiard room only, over and above the bare essentials (ills. 99 & 100). These unusual small houses are amongst Shaw's most attractive achievements.

The Radlett houses anticipate the joinery forms on which Shaw will ring the changes at Bedford Park; Chigwell Hall perfects them (ill. 105). Opposite Chigwell Church, Shaw must have seen the inn, 'an old building, with more gable-ends than a lazy man would care to count on a sunny day', as Dickens lovingly describes it at the start of *Barnaby Rudge*. Knowing the passage, Shaw will have been drawn to the gables as he pondered the house he was to build a few hundred yards away for Alfred Savill, brother of the Shaw Savill

101. (above left) Harperbury, part of entrance front.

102. (left) Harperbury, garden side and offices.

103. (above) Houndswood, garden sides.

104. (right) Houndswood, detail of external joinery.

105. Chigwell Hall, principal front.

partner Walter. The site was an open eminence, tailing off towards the road on the south and east, flatter and duller behind. Something compact was needful to crown the height and control the drive. So Shaw decided to go against tradition and bring the reception rooms round towards the drive, making it the show front, while the porch (ill. 106) was turned to the side. It is a lesson in composition. Three broad gables, evenly spaced against each other but unequally distributed over the windows of the main rooms beneath, are crowned by a hipped roof clear to view, with a chimney boldly right of centre. To counteract its stack, the drawing room to the right has a balconied bay, which turns attention round the corner to a second bay next to the entrance.[86] The Chigwell Hall plan, too, shows a masterly economy of means, cramming drawing room, morning room, dining room, business room, porch, hall and stairs, W.C. and lavatory, basement and back stairs, pantry and stores, into a square block 46 × 52 ft. without cramping or loss of light (ill. 107).

106. Chigwell Hall, entrance doorway and hood.

107. Chigwell Hall, ground floor plan.

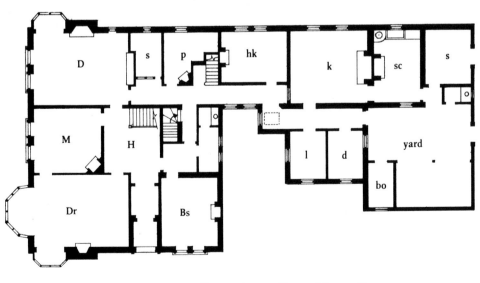

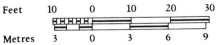

| Feet | 10 | 0 | 10 | 20 | 30 |
| Metres | 3 | 0 | 3 | 6 | 9 |

108. Ellern Mede, entrance front.

109. Ellern Mede, end view.

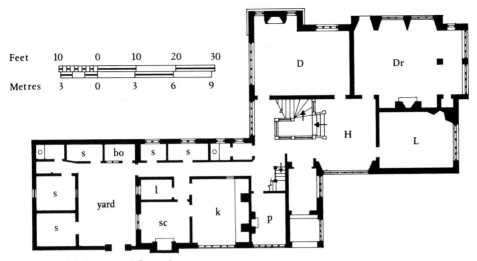

Feet

Metres

110. Ellern Mede, ground floor plan.

Last of this group, Ellern Mede (ills. 108–9) was built in 1876–7 for William Austin, a businessman who married an Academician's daughter. Standing on a plain restricted site near Totteridge, it belongs to the familiar elongated version of the L-plan (ill. 110). In contrast to the other three, Shaw deploys the full Old English range in a limited compass: half-timbering on the entrance gable, and a main block articulated well clear of the service wing and covered with a gargantuan tile-hung gable, which Shaw makes bold to half-hip at the end, giving the comical but pleasing effect of having bitten off more than he can chew. The roof is hardly dented with chimneys, but the dining room has an inglenook which earns the garden front a two-and-a-half-storey chimney-breast. Yet there is also to Ellern Mede a wayward lightness like that of Merrist Wood. The stairs have a free twist such as one would expect only in a larger house, while on the outside inscribed roughcast panels appear above the entrance, and a pretty assortment of bracketed windows mingle with the strings of mullioned casements.

These houses must stand token for the almost countless variety of Shaw's country house practice; they were the meat and drink of his mid-career.

CHAPTER 4

The Pattern of Practice

In our youth we think ourselves capable of building palaces for people, and when it comes to the point we find we have our hands full merely disposing of their excrement. Great resignation is required for this loathsome task, nevertheless it has to be done.

Goethe

QUEEN ANNE

In the early 1870s, Shaw shot rapidly from being an unpublicized architect of talent to the position of an established master. From 1870, the first spectacular perspectives of his country houses began to appear at the R.A. Exhibition. No sooner had they done so than buildings of his, no less novel, arose in the streets of London. These departures provided the world of architecture with the first accessible proofs of his genius.

Between 1863, the date of Eagle Wharf, and 1871, Shaw had no significant work in London.[1] In the interim, the strands had united which were to pull urban domestic architecture in a new direction, that of 'Queen Anne'. Everyone regrets (and regretted) the inaccuracy and vagueness of the name given to this bastard offspring. Queen Anne was born in 1871 at The Red House, Bayswater, to J. J. Stevenson, and his partner of the time, E. R. Robson, architect to the new London School Board.[2] Conception occurred well before then, during the 1860s, somewhere in the crowded, energetic, but often unfaithful office of Gilbert Scott, where Stevenson and Robson had been assistants. Scott himself was a partial progenitor; the undogmatic intelligence of his *Remarks on Secular and Domestic Architecture* (1857) is at odds with his own timid ventures in the field. The book plainly inspired some of the Nesfield and Shaw experiments, and must have struck Scott's associates, notably the young G. F. Bodley. But the overall direction in which Bodley and the junior pupils, G. G. Scott jnr., Basil Champneys, T. G. Jackson, Robson and Stevenson took their new domestic architecture was determined by a force outside the Scott office—Bodley's friend Philip Webb.

Webb's own Red House had taken the parsonage style to its limits. But he yearned for a more radical departure, retaining the feeling of Gothic without its trappings. In one or two projects of the 1860s, Webb played with tile-hanging and allowed his gables more freedom than he had done at Red House, but he could not conscientiously accept the Nesfield and Shaw initiative. Instead, he and in due course Bodley began to pursue with more purpose Butterfield's old enterprise of unifying Gothic with plain, modern building traditions. By accidents of commission, Webb's work was mainly in London, Bodley's in the provinces, but their ideas and intent coincided in town and country. They had no sense of one style for the one, another for the other.[3]

Reform of London's architecture was the more urgent demand. Charles Eastlake cried out for it in his *Hints on Household Taste* (1868), lamenting the lack of the picturesque in street architecture. Gothic had conspicuously failed to oust stucco Italianate, whose onward march, ever lumpy but ever practical, brought restlessness and reaction. People began to sympathize even with Ruskin's famous bugbears, the brick boxes of St Marylebone and Bloomsbury. 'Better far the monotony of Gower Street', urged Stevenson; 'if it is dull it is at least quiet and unobtrusive.'[4] John Petit, veteran apologist of continental Gothic, had proclaimed 'Queen Anne' a decade before, and a scramble now ensued to see what that might be.[5]

In the end it turned out to be the brick architecture of Webb and the Scott pupils, adapted to the London street and climate, and tricked out with archaeological trappings. For these, all at first agreed that the English Renaissance must supply the models; sometimes this meant genuine Queen Anne, sometimes houses of the kind now dubbed 'artisan mannerist', of seventy years before. The prototype London Board Schools were the first to blazon the new style abroad.[6] Bodley, Robson, Stevenson, Spiers and Champneys all designed examples, austere and Gothic still in their formal freedom, but devoid of period dressings and expressive of economy.

But for houses, there was a fast transition. Though the ornamentation of The Red House, Stevenson's own home in Bayswater, was modest, he began to look for motifs for his richer clients among artisan mannerist models, and beyond them to their origins in the street architecture of Germany and the Low Countries. From the work of Webb and Bodley was thus born 'Pont Street Dutch', the Queen Anne of Bayswater, Kensington and Chelsea, proliferating in Dutch gables, stunted pilasters, segment-headed sashes and brick mouldings. Soon, the London School Board was aspiring to this more ornamental and archaeological style. When Bodley erected its headquarters on the Embankment (1874), this was the vocabulary he used, however originally (ill. 176). The cause of a free brick style had suffered partial defeat.

When he began building in London, Shaw was willing enough to follow the new lead. At first he had reservations. Though he no longer, as at Eagle Wharf, wished to impose Old English upon the city street, the country vernacular had its authentic urban equivalent in the overhanging town houses of the seventeenth century. These the architects of proto-Queen Anne had ignored. In several of his earlier London buildings (New Zealand Chambers, Swan House, the first drawings for 196 Queen's Gate) Shaw is fighting a rearguard action on their behalf. On the other hand, such a style was hard to handle, expensive, and as we shall see difficult to get past the stringent metropolitan building regulations. For certain jobs, Queen Anne seemed the right answer, and something like it was already known to Shaw.

Nesfield, of course, had already experimented with something akin to Queen Anne during the 1860s, in his Kew Lodge and the designs for Kinmel (ills. 31 & 35).[7] Back in 1863 he had indeed produced a scheme, not apparently executed, for embellishing the front of Croxteth Hall in something much resembling the Queen Anne style. If there was no Kinmel among Shaw's works of the time, there had been a few tasks in which he had made use of a similar style, one which bears a distant but definite kinship to Webb's work of the 1860s and the developments of the Scott pupils. Asked in 1896 about the origin of

ELEVATION OF NEW ENTRANCE FRONT

111. Fowlers Park, revised elevation for new entrance front, 1864.

112. West Wickham House, garden side, showing Shaw's additions.

Queen Anne, Shaw remarked upon two very early jobs, at Bromley and Hawkhurst.[8] For the Bromley Palace estate, besides the Bailiff's Cottage, Shaw had made an all-brick terrace design of Queen Anne character, and appears to have added a storey to the main house; he could have been referring to either.[9] But the commission of 1864–5 for rebuilding Fowlers Park, a plain classic box, for the Gow Steuarts, Hawkhurst friends of the Horsleys, was more substantive. Lamentably, only a single bay of Shaw's new brick front to the house survives, but we have the drawings. The first idea was a poor one. On to a regular five-bay front with neat sashes in the upper floors, Shaw proposed to slap a mansard roof for the attic and four vast mullioned windows for the ground floor, like so many cuckoos in the Queen Anne nest. In the executed version, he comes to his senses (ill. 111). He divides up the front with pilaster strips, inserts high double sashes between them, each with its own painted wooden pediment, and gives the door a plain hood. The roof is now hipped and endowed with the splayed and pedimented dormer windows which will recur in several jobs of the 1870s. At Fowlers Park there are hints of much that is to come, not just in Queen Anne, but in the later urban style of Bolney House and 170 Queen's Gate.

Two other enlargement jobs in the country develop these ideas, germane to Shaw's approach to the town house. In 1869 another Steuart asked him to rebuild West Wickham House, a heavy stuccoed affair with a village street front, put up a few years before by W. M. Teulon. It still exists, demoralizingly mutilated by the insertion of shops along the street side. But much of the garden front remains, displaying a coved cornice and sashes, with only a hint of Old English in the half-hipping of the only major gable, over an untouched piece of stucco (ill. 112). The other work, Shaw's extension to Yateley Hall, Hampshire (1871) is a model of tact. Essentially the job was not so different from Willesley: additions on the right hand side of a house of true Queen Anne date. But instead of a defiant tile-hung gable, Shaw pushes the new drawing room out with three closely spaced sashes and carries the modillion cornice round. On the other side, overlooking the old moat, he repeats the same idea more irregularly for the stairs and dining room. It is a delightful job, done with evident affection. Houses like Yateley were to grow upon him year after year.

Shaw therefore had plenty of command of a plain brick and sash style when he started his London career in earnest in 1871. Yet initially, the experience may have seemed irrelevant; the first commissions were once again commercial. James Temple and the Shaw Savill Company were the instigators. They wanted an office building, they wanted further storage space, and the second requirement had priority. If Eagle Wharf displeases the purists, it is to this forgotten warehouse, long demolished, that they should turn (ill. 113). It stood on the corner of Lower Thames Street and Water Lane. The solution was rigidly plain, sane and assured; thick brick walls, their surface broken by the recessed window heads and deep vertical cut of the packing bays, while stone bands added horizontal accent. Within, the traditional iron columns maximized storage space, without fuss or architectural feature. It is a reminder that Shaw was capable of making a success of the most ordinary task, when need arose.

To New Zealand Chambers, the *succès de scandale* of the R.A. Exhibition of 1873, it is good to adopt the same rational approach. Had the plans of the new Shaw Savill office

133

113. (above) Warehouse, Lower Thames Street, perspective of street fronts, 1871.

114. (right) New Zealand Chambers, street front.

been shown on Shaw's R.A. perspective, they would have saved a good deal of misconception. The company had an enclosed site with a good frontage to Leadenhall Street, which they were anxious to keep for themselves. But they also wanted to make the most of their lettable office space, then as now more expensive in London than anywhere else in the world. Shaw therefore adopted and furthered the ideas of Edward I'Anson, the greatest contemporary expert on office planning.[10] On a site 165 feet deep, with three main storeys, a basement, and an attic, he managed to cram a compact, elegant suite for the company itself, and about 80 small offices, mainly in groups of twelve. This was done chiefly through the use of well-holes, lined with I'Anson's white-glazed tiles, and of cast-iron bearing shafts and partition walls. This was a well-tried system, but there were refinements. To get nineteen offices into the basement behind the shop cellars, Shaw converted the bottom of his well-holes into pitched roof lights illuminating each suite of offices at either end, and carried the walls of the well-holes throughout the basement on iron columns (ill. 115). This cannot have eliminated darkness, but at least it minimized it. He also insisted on a good ventilating system for the basement, with air flues carried up to the level of the top windows, and separate foul air extracts. In the ground front, the Shaw Savill general office was placed in the noisy, airy bays overlooking the street, whilst the directors, James Temple and Walter Savill, occupied a semi-circular room cantilevered out over the first well-hole behind the shops on rolled iron joists. Girderwork was also used for a quite different purpose, to pin the offices to the lavish front which Shaw devised to emulate and embarrass the neighbouring *palazzi*—dominating brick piers overhung by three great plastered tiers of oriels (ill. 114).

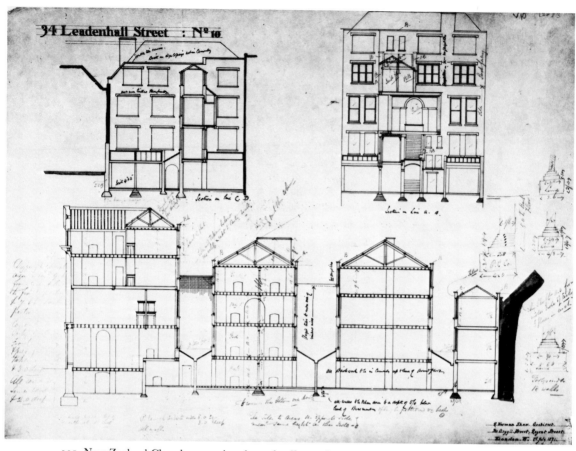

115. New Zealand Chambers, section through offices, 1871.

Bodley once said that Shaw 'got it all from a house in Ipswich.'[11] What this means is that the famous oriels, the most obvious stylistic device of New Zealand Chambers, are borrowed from Sparrowe's House in Ipswich, and that Shaw repeated them several times over in the next few years.[12] But there is more to them than that. Such a window, the English carpenter's quaint adaptation of the *Serliana* or Palladian window, can be found in variations on town houses all over the country. It gave a convenient window seat, a proudly classicizing equivalent to the old overhung oriel with views out into the street. One of the best versions appeared on a spectacular house very near Leadenhall Street in Bishopsgate, where the Elizabethan merchant Sir Paul Pindar lived and traded.[13] In Shaw's time it had sunk to an alehouse, but it was on this front that the proportions of New Zealand Chambers were remodelled. At a stroke, he was able to avail himself of a precedent at once mercantile and idiomatic to the urban vernacular.

Far from being a pure piece of associational sentiment, the oriel had its rationale. By extending its lights at either side, Shaw procured extra space and light for the offices. And by dividing the façade vertically into solid and void, he escaped the fault of the average shop and office, that of displaying a solid brick wall over a void below.[14] But now he ran up against the inexorable metropolitan building regulations. These, from of old, insisted that wooden windows should be set back from the wall plane, and at New Zealand Chambers they flagrantly projected right forward. To circumvent this, Shaw struck a brilliant first blow in a lifelong struggle against the regulations, by bringing his piers of narrow brickwork forward of the oriels and their ground floor counterparts, and pulling a deep cornice out over the top. These piers took virtually no weight; iron girders in the wall saw to that. But they fulfilled the eminently functional role of baffling the district surveyor. For where was the front wall? Was it before or behind? For the moment Shaw had won a cunning victory. But it would not be for long; the regulations were to prove the bane of attempts to revive an urban vernacular based on old models. Perhaps it was the district surveyor who vetoed the triple gables on top for which Shaw had hoped. Instead, he had to substitute rows of dormers perched uncomfortably upon the cornice, anomalously legal because they projected from the main roof slope. E. W. Godwin was one of the few critics to notice this change, when he went to check the building against the R.A. perspective.[15] He found New Zealand Chambers more impressive in reality than on paper, a judgement alas now impossible to test. Others were bewildered but enthralled by its novelties of structure and style, a reaction which persisted. The mischievous play of the front between thin, solid piers and wide, riotous voids led a critic, still confused forty years later, to classify many of the building's tendencies as Gothic.[16] But neither Gothic, nor Queen Anne, nor 'middle-class domestic' is the right label for New Zealand Chambers. Its associations are with ancient trade and civic pride. The fitting epithet was given by Muthesius—'bürgerlich', otherwise 'bourgeois'.[17]

In New Zealand Chambers, Shaw ignored the ideas of Webb and the School Board architects, who had hardly tackled the problems of offices. But at 18 Hyde Park Gate, the first house he built in London, their example was paramount. The commission was a modest one, once more emanating from E. W. Cooke, who before moving to Glen Andred had lived in Hyde Park Gate and still owned a house there. Early in 1871 he decided upon building an economical house to let on the site of his garden, and again turned to Shaw for help with the plans. The purpose of the house and the factor of collaboration may explain why Shaw stuck cautiously to the conventional terrace plan, and eschewed individuality. But the front (ill. 116) valuably indicates that his starting point for town houses was the work of Philip Webb. From Webb derive the use of cheap stock brick, the spacious tall sashes, the stone dressings burgeoning into *fleurs-de-lys*, and all the traces of Gothic characteristic of early Queen Anne but soon to be lost. It is an uncertain elevation, oddly proportioned and perhaps in part mutilated, but it has its elegance, not least in the brickwork strips and refined joinery.[18] Nothing could better illustrate the unsureness that still prevailed in the new London town house style in 1871, and continued to do so until Stevenson's 8 Palace Gate (1873) and Shaw's own 196 Queen's Gate (1874–5) set a more brazen tone.

None of the questions, therefore, had been resolved when in 1872 William Lowther M.P., a rich ex-diplomat, brought Shaw his most prestigious commission yet, for a monumental house on the one big freehold site obtainable in the area near the new Albert Memorial and Hall. Lowther Lodge occupied the equivalent of the great corner sites in Belgrave Square four decades before. Here, on the main west road out of London, Shaw

116. (left) 18
Hyde Park Gate,
street front.

117. (right)
Lowther Lodge,
ground and first
floor plans as
built.

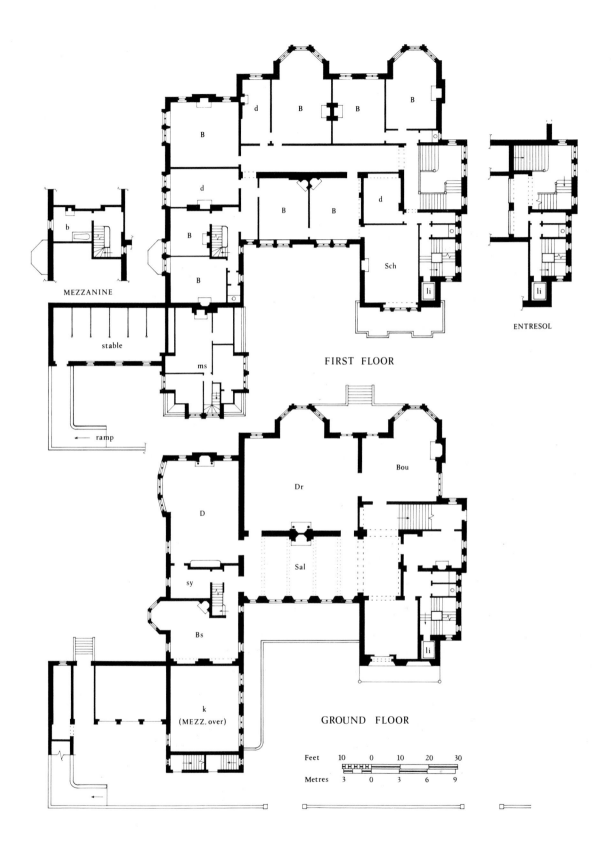

MEZZANINE

b

stable

ms

ramp

FIRST FLOOR

d

B

B

B

d

B

B

B

d

B

Sch

li

ENTRESOL

li

li

GROUND FLOOR

Dr

Bou

D

Sal

sy

Bs

li

k
(MEZZ. over)

Feet   10   0   10   20   30

Metres   3   0   3   6   9

could throw down a gauntlet to its stucco neighbours, in emulation of Stevenson's house, a politer but equally conspicuous challenge on the other side of Hyde Park. In his elevations, Shaw's main aim was to upgrade the emerging bourgeois style into something grave and ornamental enough for the grandest of lords and citizens. But the lavishness of scale which turned Lowther Lodge into a Queen Anne *palazzo* prevented it from being a model for later town houses in any more than the style of its outer husk. What the Lowthers wanted was the country house come to town; it is this which makes their building so difficult to place. There were other early Queen Anne houses on open sites, notably on the Holland Estate, but nothing with quite the ambition of Lowther Lodge or with its reticent but distinct arrogance of mood.

A first plan, had it been adhered to, would have marked this swagger out still further. A detached tower was to front Kensington Gore over an archway drive into the forecourt, no doubt reinterpreting the Leyswood or Cragside towers in the new style. The matured design, somewhat reduced, was built in 1873–5. It is hard to see how the exact style was arrived at. Though Lethaby thought Lowther Lodge showed 'very close study of Webb's ways', they are much less evident than at Hyde Park Gate.[19] For lack of precedent in the marriage of town and country styles, Shaw has been forced to innovate, sometimes even violently, reacting, for instance, in favour of casements and lead glazing, but thrusting them into sash-like frames. The plan too is forceful and direct (ill. 117); a broad open saloon at the front, giving access to the reception rooms behind and separated from the stairs and musicians' gallery by an arch of ponderous width (ill. 189). In such features there is more than a hint of Kinmel, building at the same time. Above, the main corridor perches between saloon wall and drawing room ceiling, sustained through the most

118. Lowther Lodge, entrance front.

arbitrary use to which Shaw had yet put his iron beams. The walls are of the new thin bricks, bonded upon rough brickwork as a facing, and instead of stone dressings appear gauged and cut brick details on a scale hitherto unattempted in the Queen Anne revival.[20] Below, deep vaulted basements stretching well under the forecourt and thick foundations helping to form the garden terrace, support the pile.

This tremendous power turns almost into tyranny in the elevations (ills. 118, 119), or so it must have seemed in the few years before Lowther Lodge was dwarfed by Albert Hall Mansions, its own architect's neighbouring creation. There is something of Giulio Romano in the front—a head-on collision of vertical and horizontal forces, extricated more to the onlooker's alarm than contentment. Shaw has started with the principles of the Old English style, the visible dominating roof and tall chimneys punctuating wall and ridge. This called for the front gables accommodating the second floor attics to be high and wide at either end. These he then breaks, at one end with an exposed chimneystack, at the other with a narrow Dutch gable-end, hips the roof on either side, and slate-hangs the return faces. The result of this is to give him the narrower vertical unit with which alone the thin tall board-school windows of the Queen Anne can be articulated, even in their normal pairs. Armed with this, he enlarges his dormers to pedimented minor gables, punches them through the main cornice to link first-floor and attic windows, and uses the corbelling-out as the brick cornice to the servants' wing and stable block to the left, which is again punctuated with the same ruthlessness. This extreme complication is augmented by yet more turbulence: the odd, open arcading perched upon the roof ends of the side wing; the brusque balcony over the entrance, standing upon what seems like part of the cornice which has become dislodged; the inverse L-shape of the back left-hand chimney;

119. Lowther Lodge, garden side.

and the continual re-echoing of each feature on a smaller scale in different, unexpected places. After this, the garden front, for all its sombreness, seems at first a relief, and then disquiet returns. For though the major part of the front maintains symmetry by virtue of one or two false lights in the dormers, the big bays fail to keep the centre of the roof between them. The right-hand gable and ridge chimney hold the real centre, and attention is forced to flicker between this proud façade and the deeper, uneven hipped composition constantly suggested by the roof. At Lowther Lodge, Shaw indulges his mischievous architectural ingenuity in its most mannered but least relaxing form.

THE R.A. DRAWINGS

By the time that Shaw showed his perspective of Lowther Lodge at the R.A. Exhibition of 1874, the treatment they received had already become customary; criticism from *The Builder*, admiration and subsequent publication from the *Building News*.[21] It was a pattern established when in 1870 he made his Academy debut with two views of Leyswood, the first drawings he had shown publicly for five years. Those who bothered to stop in the thoroughfare that was then the Architecture Room at Burlington House, to descry what merit they could among the cluster of close and high-hung drawings, never numbered many. Architects of course spent time there; more crucially, so did the critics of the building papers, who could fill their pages for the next twelve months with engravings of the new work that appeared at the R.A. The two principal antagonists quickly made up their minds, the *Building News* to worship and adore the works of Mr Norman Shaw with some reservations about Queen Anne, *The Builder*, under more prosaic but socially purposeful editorship, to pursue an intermittent campaign of growling against illogical features of structure in his work. It began with criticism of the Leyswood chimneys in *The Builder*, while the *Building News*, duly bowled over, illustrated the views early in 1871.[22] While Shaw pursued the habit, showing for a decade clever high and low-level pen perspectives of one, two or three of his creations each year, the *Building News* dutifully pressed its advocacy. Soon, E. W. Godwin was writing for its pages a first shrewd article upon Shaw's work.[23] In 1875, excited by the perspectives, the A.A. organized an outing to see the still unfinished rump of Lowther Lodge. Established art, too, paid its homage by electing Shaw an A.R.A. in 1872. It is hard to see why they gave this honour quite so early, but besides the persuasiveness of the perspectives, there were two well satisfied clients and Shaw's old master Street to champion him to the other academicians. By 1877, when he gained the full status of R.A., the risky choice had been abundantly and visibly justified in Chelsea, Kensington and Hampstead. Shaw had become the natural choice as the wealthy painter's architect.

Architectural publicity was both good and bad. If your buildings were original and pretty, any surveyor or 'spec.' builder who had the architectural press upon his Saturday morning breakfast table could and did filch from your inventions. This happened slowly. There was a ten-year lag, during which other architects, of gradually declining inventiveness, would try your ideas out, alter or amend them. This you might enjoy. But when the speculative nadir was reached, you would cry out like Ruskin against his own writings, not that you disbelieved them, but because on every journey through the suburbs you saw them used stupidly, 'as a physician would, in most cases, rather hear that his patient had thrown all his medicine out of the window, than that he had sent word to his apothecary to leave out two of its three ingredients.'[24] It is a factor to be remembered when Shaw radically changes style, and explains his shunning of publicity in the 1890s.

But in 1874, it was Ruskin and the ageing Goths who were doing the shuddering, and Shaw who could be delighted by the propagation of Old English amongst those who had access, direct or indirect, to Argyll Street. Waterhouse was the first acknowledged imitator; his Blackmoor, started in 1869, already quotes from Leyswood.[25] In the 1870s, successors began to abound. Ernest George's first big house, Rousdon, continued the obsession with the tall towers of Leyswood and Cragside; Street's own home in Surrey and his 'squarsonage' at Wigan showed him a convert to Old English; E. W. Godwin devised a personal version of the style for Beauvale Lodge (1871–3); and Scott or one of his pupils had picked up the idiom by 1871–2 for a little hospital outside Marlborough. After 1875 it is easier to catalogue the leading architects, led by Webb, who had not succumbed to some feature or other of Old English. Soon, many a young architect in these stylistically insecure years was anxiously awaiting Shaw's annual offering at the R.A. to see what he could purloin. 'Each recurring spring brought the question,' recollected Ingress Bell: 'What has Shaw got in the Academy?'[26]

In no sense were these drawings advertisements, as has sometimes been claimed. For a start, the general public took little notice of the shabby architecture room, as the building press was never tired of pointing out. In 1884, Shaw himself was commissioned to build a new octagonal architectural gallery for the R.A., which provided better spacing of drawings in a mere three of four tiers instead of the 'skying' which had previously befallen the less popular exhibits. But the room, a cul-de-sac, confirmed public apathy; nobody was ever seen in it. By 1902, when the *Architectural Review* printed a number of opinions on what might be done, Shaw was all for acknowledging that interest in architecture was bound to be specialized. Having faced the annual ordeal of hanging the room often enough, he took an austere line and lamented the days of *Vitruvius Britannicus* and the elder Pugin's books. 'Our present style of drawing has, I fear, grown up largely from a desire to make architecture more pictorial, and by this means to enlist the sympathies and admiration of those who would not understand it if they did.' Remembering thus the sins of his youth, he was for going back to the old style of elevation, 'with, of course, the well-dressed ladies and gentlemen and the hansom cabs . . . carefully omitted.'[27]

However much 'advertising-commercialism' there was in the style and appeal of Shaw's early drawings, it was unlikely to succeed. Hardly a single R.A. drawing ever led to an architectural commission. Friendship, recommendation, or experience of a particular building brought Shaw all the jobs for which the facts are known. When he was hungriest for work in the 1860s, he offered no drawings for exhibition, it seems. The R.A. perspectives of the 1870s are symptomatic of his good appetite and enjoyment of the feast. He is hardly banging his knife and fork upon the academical table; the next course was already coming quickly enough.

On the other hand, Shaw was certainly too ready to accept new jobs. Measuring himself by the standard of Street, he did not perceive the danger both for his health and for the quality of his work. A mania for work possessed contemporaries; it is a cardinal clue to the age. Mill, Carlyle, Ruskin, Keble, Smiles, Dickens were all in their different ways dinning the word into their readers' ears. An architect of impoverished background and Tractarian training could not hope to escape it. Webb alone was strong enough to submit so moral an urge to the discipline of concentration. Shaw, on the other hand, revealed much of his own straightforward sense of his duties when he said he wished that Webb had done more work in the world in which he had been placed, instead of withdrawing from it almost entirely.[28]

THE CUSTOMERS

Who then were these clients thronging the anteroom at Argyll Street, and how did they get there? Before 1870, we have the surprising spectacle of propertied middle-class people availing themselves more or less consciously of two artistic advisers who led them to Shaw, a professional painter, J. C. Horsley, and a merchant of modest means and artistic ambitions, Aldam Heaton. This was not an original arrangement. Fifty years before, we know that Smirke's R.A. friends West, Lawrence and Farington, often helped him to commissions.[29] Harking back to what used to be said about Butterfield's 'philistine' clients, some may suspect that these customers mistrusted their own judgment. If an adverse verdict is wanted, a happier one is that many fell victim to a powerful technique of persuasion; for Old English, and indeed all Shaw's styles, embody a rhetorical force directed towards the emotions. For the success of a speech, the orator's bearing had to conform with his periods and abet in the persuasion. Likewise, Shaw's behaviour was so charming and so meticulously correct, that few prospective clients could resist him. His uncondescending perfection of manner must, one suspects, have infuriated his rivals. Of whom else can Stevenson have been thinking when he wrote of the qualities which normally made for the selection of an architect: 'energy and business habits, the faculty of writing good letters, plausibility and pleasing manners, and especially that power of inspiring confidence which makes employers feel themselves safe in following their advice and entrusting their purses in their hands, and skill in getting work to do, which by no means implies the power of doing it'?[30] Naturally, it was Shaw's real power to do the work that was the bitterest gall and made every professional critic qualify his admiration.

Getting the tone right was of enormous importance. The previous generation of architects had been propriety itself; a collection of the letters of Street or Scott would make solid but dull reading. Their pupils rebelled against this respectfulness, even slavery, before the ignorance of clients, and the stiff legal relationship it entailed. Of course there had been many a friendship between architect and client, but Nesfield and Shaw's generation started out by wanting these exceptions to become the rule. The new familiarity implied a tacit contract between housebuilder and architect; the matter should be a partnership between the two, by which the former would be consulted upon each smallest point, from finger plates to foul tanks, if the latter's dignity and equality were respected. Even the reserved Webb charges his letters about Smeaton Manor with such man-to-man practicality and gruff wit that his client is forced, in sending his final payment, to address him without prefix. Webb replies: 'My dear Godman, I very willingly drop all formality in thanking you very sincerely for your quite kindly letter accompanying the cheque . . .'; as though with the climax of the whole house-building enterprise, a new plane of relationship had been attained.[31] Voysey's letters, too, exhibit the same progression to comradeship.[32]

It is helpful thus to compare Shaw's manner with others. Webb's famed independence, for instance, did not mean deciding everything without consultation, but the exercise of an absolute veto over any proposals against his principles. A more sharply aesthetic version of this attitude passed to his acolytes. To a woman client's complaint 'I cannot see, Mr Lethaby, that you have done a single thing that I asked you to do,' came the reply, 'Well, you see, my first duty as an artist is to please myself.'[33] By then, the golden age of partnership between middle-class housebuilders and their architects was on the wane, however much the stylish charm of Lutyens helped to prolong it.

Nesfield was as uncompromising with his clients as Webb, but more intimate and latterly more eccentric. There was a smattering of aristocrats among his employers, but the bulk of them were country gentry, proud old-fashioned characters as from a Meredith novel, endowed with land, money, and independence of outlook. Nesfield senior, one suspects, passed them on to his son as often as Heaton and Horsley proselytized for Shaw. The monster houses were paid for from commerce, of course, Cloverley from Liverpool banking money, Kinmel from copper mines in Anglesey. However Nesfield behaved towards such clients, towards those of at least one smaller house, the Walkers of Lea Wood, he was extraordinarily personal. His letters to Mrs Walker confide his hopes and ideas about himself as well as the house, burst into verse here and there, and even tease her husband.[34] Though this may be a special case, one suspects that Nesfield demanded intimacy as a matter of course. It is all rather like Burges's arcane relationship with the Marquis of Bute, except that at Cardiff Castle and Castell Coch Burges was employed more as a magician than a practical house-builder. Only rarely could Nesfield be persuaded to handle commissions involving any measure of public responsibility; a handful of church restorations, a grammar school at Newport, Essex, and a bank at Saffron Walden are virtually his only ventures outside domestic architecture.

Shaw needed no such strengths of relationship to sustain him. Others might seek the intimacies of artistic *bonhomie*, but after his marriage he enjoyed channelling his energies into lighter, gentle friendships with clients, builders and decorators in his calling. He was particularly adept, says his son, with the men on site, where architects often signally fail to inspire confidence.[35] With clients, correspondence was the key, and obviously something in which he took pride and pleasure. It was very rarely delegated and yet more rarely copied, so well did Shaw memorize his different jobs.[36] If he was on holiday, incoming letters were forwarded and answered from wherever he was. Reports too were treated as matters of personal responsibility, and written in his own hand. No collection of his letters survives entire, but we have 127 concerning the Quadrant, 117 to Mrs Johnston Foster over the new church at Richards Castle, 57 about Overbury Court, and 43 concerning the small restoration of a chapel at Bingley Parish Church.[37]

In such correspondence, the skill was to intuit what kind of relationship a client expected. J. A. Busfeild was an experienced landowner with a mind of his own which took him to Shaw instead of Messrs Healey, the architects restoring the rest of the Bingley church. He therefore remains 'Dear Sir' throughout the correspondence, and his wishes are acceded to when there are differences of opinion over the position of the seats and the builder to employ. Accordingly, Shaw leaves much of the supervision to Busfeild's watchful eye, not even making a single visit while work was in progress, as he unabashedly tells him, although three were planned.[38]

Mrs Johnston Foster, on the other hand, requires a partner, sometimes almost a parent, to guide her pious labours in building a memorial church to her husband. Shaw is therefore quickly to hand, admonishing her politely in his first letter *not* to pull down the dilapidated old church at Richards Castle. To this point he has to recur three years later, when the new church is nearly finished:

> I confess that your proposed programme for dismantling the old church . . . fills me with dismay. It really is courting opposition and objections, and before you have it half down you will have the county up in arms, protests thick and fast. A deputation from the 'Society for the protection of ancient monuments' will be down and you will be denounced as most likely the wickedest people to be found!—in *all* respects much worse than Mr Gladstone.

On other occasions during construction, peremptory demands arrived from Mrs Foster for different shafts to the arcade, and different tracery. Shaw's method is never to react angrily. One lengthy letter from on holiday must do for several such cases.

Dear Mrs Foster,

I am very glad to find that you did not think I had wilfully changed anything that had been decided on, for I should not like to feel that you could think I would do that, my great desire being to get the church in all respects what you, who are the builders, would like, and what you will have a real pleasure in looking at in the future. But the question is a difficult one, as all these things are more or less technicalities, and I am sure you would not like me to introduce features incongruous to the style, and which people who really understand these matters would afterwards smile at and point out as little ignorances, or to say the least incongruities. I am not at all a slave to any particular 'style', I never have been, but still there must be a certain limit to deviations. Your church all the way through belongs to what is called the 'Decorated' style, 14th century period. In the old church the Mitre window is 'Decorated', these square headed windows are emphatically 'Decorated' and so on. Well, that form of shaft and circular base and capital are very characteristic of this style, and octagonal shafts, bases and caps, are not. They are peculiar to the 15th century style, a 100 years later in style. You will find them, I think, in the nave arcade of the old church, but then that is 'Perpendicular', 15th centy., the same period as the west window.

As you have strong likes and dislikes with which, as I have said before, I should like to fall in, how would the enclosed do? I do *not* approve of them, but still if you like them better, I shall be quite ready to adopt them. I think the circular forms are in themselves so much more beautiful and they form such a pleasant variety when mixed with the straight hard lines which are more or less necessary. You see them in the finest Greek work, in fact in all the finest work, that is to say a mixture of curves with straight lines. I fear this is all very prosy, but I should like you fully to understand the principles that guide these things, for there *are* principles, that take a weary long time, and years of study to master. I mean, I don't want you to think that one thing is as *right* as another, and that it is only a whim of the architect. The East window I had drawn out was Geometrical, not Curvilinear, but I shall try and modify it, so as to make it even more geometrical, and shall then send you tracings and designs for the others. The square headed windows are going into the Chancel and some similar ones on south side, in Aisle—the Mitre window to go at West end of South aisle. I shall be here till Monday then home and at work as usual.

> Believe me to remain
> yours very faithfully
> R. Norman Shaw.

P.S. If possible, I should like your decision *here*, as then I could be moving things on a bit and so lose as little time as possible.

This bout continued a little longer. Mrs Foster still hankered after octagon shafts, so Shaw proposed in his next letter a joint visit to Westminster Abbey to compare examples. This was a trump card and she conceded, but after a fortnight she bounced back with a curious design for the west window with tracery like 'fly wire', which Shaw had to suppress. And so these amicable tussles went on, with Shaw invariably emerging the patient victor.[39]

The real contentions came later, when the bill turned out to be too much or the builder showed his incompetence. Such difficulties averaged about one per job. Shaw used a good firm of quantity surveyors, Franklin and Andrews of Ludgate Hill, but he was never a cheap architect and there was frequently a good surplus on the final bill over early estimates. If everything had gone well up to that point, a client would pay without demurring. That was the situation, for instance, when Shaw extended C. L. Norman's house at Bromley Common, and an estimate made only two months before was exceeded by over £1,000 through no fault of Shaw's. All he could do was explain why, wring his hands, and blithely hope the cloud would pass.

> The work is very splendid, as good as work can be, but it is very costly. Cubitts have been very good and civil in assisting to make up the account and have given way on some points, but the hard facts remain that all their prices are high. Everything in the shape of an extra work (and their name is legion) has had to be priced out on the same schedule from which their Contract was originally made. They have asked no more, and they would take no less, and to end all, they say they will not clear 10% on the whole. I am very sorry indeed to have to write to you thus, but I have no alternative. What annoys me most, and what I feel will annoy you, is that you were really misled by the Report I sent to you some 6 or 8 weeks ago.[40]

A more serious argument arose over The Hallams, when the client claimed he was being overcharged, but Shaw managed to vindicate himself.[41] Such quarrels usually stem from disagreements which have arisen earlier; Shaw's career was singularly free from them, because he regularly accounted for his actions, and normally took a client's point of view. He was particularly resourceful in cutting corners for the needy. At the Bournemouth Convent, Mother Etheldreda had difficulty in financing the main block, and was hardly persuaded to build it all at once. The builder made an estimate of £2,734 for the second stage; Shaw calmly told her, 'I have told Birch that he must do without this £34' and thus it was.[42]

Gawsworth Rectory can stand as an instance of Shaw's happy handling of his clients of the 1870s. The Hon. and Revd Henry Augustus Stanhope was a blithe bachelor clergyman of twenty-six. In 1872 he had just been instituted to the picturesque Cheshire parish of Gawsworth when he met Shaw, then building a lodge and repairing a dovecote at Madresfield for his relative Earl Beauchamp.[43] The Rectory, a beautiful late mediaeval house with a fine hall and half-timbered front, stood in bedraggled condition, having been grievously neglected by the previous incumbent. In December, Stanhope took Shaw up to stay at the house, and they decided upon a number of alterations. But before anything could be done, the diocesan surveyor was putting his oar in and insisting upon doing the minimum of dilapidations immediately to keep the house going. Shaw advised submission to his 'list of little pottering patches' though he opined the roof would leak just as much after as before. 'I should accept it, pay in the money, and then when the work was going on, you might get hold of the surveyor and (having given him 2 or 3 glasses of sherry) get him to sanction a re-adjusting of some of the money.' While the surveyor was at work, Shaw had the leisure to mature something for Stanhope. Of course, it turned out bigger than the latter had bargained for. 'Here is a plan for you, that will make you jump!' he writes on 6th January. But I see no way of doing it except by making a scheme, complete, so as to make the house habitable and comfortable and of this you can do as much or as little as you like.' An enlarged study was the first consideration: 'it would be dreadful work to have you boxed up in a little den in which you could hardly turn round.' Then a new stair was needed, which would mean clearing away the clumsy stair put into the hall, and generally restoring the latter; and that then led to an entirely new dining room with bedroom and dressing room over, 'but considering what a very seedy bit of building that existing dining room is, and also that there really can hardly be said to be a stair at all, I don't think the most fastidious cd accuse you of wild luxury.'

Stanhope capitulates to the logic of this salesmanship, and after a few months all is ready. 'Hooray! for the departure of all these surveyors &c. Now, of course you are Monarch of Gawsworth' writes Shaw on 1st May. At first he thinks of getting tenders from separate builders, but already he has up his sleeve 'just the very man to knock it off straight,' who turns out to be W. H. Lascelles of Bunhill Row, Finsbury. Already, Shaw has had his fill of country builders.

> I really don't think you can do better than this. You shall have an intelligent man to take care of the work, and you shall have thoroughly good work and material throughout. With local builders I cannot secure you this—I find their joiners' work invariably shaky and poor stuff (I except that poor man who did Lord Beauchamp's Lodge at Madresfield, but the poor animal couldn't have got fat on *that* work!!!!

Lascelles begins well, estimating the work at £700, and Shaw hopes to be able to reduce this a little. Then £700 becomes the absolute minimum; Stanhope now digs his heels in and the contract is signed in June for this sum. Lascelles sends a Scot called Bell up to superintend the work, and Stanhope continues in residence during the alterations. Shaw keeps him posted with a rattle of points, particularly on his favourite obsessions of stoves, drains, wells and pumps, and he tries to keep up his confidence in the builders. 'I have always found Lascelles singularly good at understanding the spirit of an agreement, a virtue that human nature in general and builders in particular don't seem to understand as a rule.' But alas! Bell turns out to be a dud, curmudgeonly and slow, perhaps a drunkard too, and in October when work is well on, Lascelles has to replace him. When the final bill is presented in February 1874, Stanhope has consented to £345 of extras, mainly for pumps, further alterations to the study, and various works to the bay and chimney of the hall. The whole cost including fees comes to something like £1,130, perhaps three times as much as he had initially meant to spend. Yet there is no loss of good nature; he has an excellent and comfortable house, still picturesque, tactfully but substantially added to at the back. 'You are a wonderful person to pay up!' enthuses Shaw,

> but it is pleasant to be out of debt. I only wish my visits were always as pleasant as those to Gawsworth have been . . . I fear you have had a sore experience of building and yet looking back at it, I really don't know that I could have done better than advised you to have Lascelles. Macclesfield I fear possesses but few attractions in the way of delightful builders, and my experience of bad country builders is that they are quite as slow as Bell with his failing, and give you very bad work into the bargain. So I hope in the course of time the bitterness of Bell will fade from your mind, and that you will come to like the work more and more.

Such jovial procedures had their drawbacks. They produced fine domestic architecture, but they were far from good enough for the collective client. The disinclination of Shaw, Nesfield, Devey, Webb and other of the accepted leaders of the '70s to submit to the rigours and impersonalities of commercial work widened the gap between 'professional' business architects and their 'artistic' counterparts. Shaw himself was reasonably accomplished with committees, but he got into difficulties in his last works partly because he was unfamiliar with the hard-headed priorities of businessmen. Frequently his own commercial commissions were supervised by a single director. With the most anonymous of all employments, government and municipal work, he had no conversance till he was fifty-five, at New Scotland Yard. Then he secured the job through contacts, not competition, and made haste to fasten upon the loyalties of the Commissioner as an individual·with whom he could work affably. Many of the problems he faced as assessor and architect in the Edwardian period might have been avoided had he evolved an alternative system for public jobs to the personal give-and-take on which his working method was based. Government officials and many businessmen, used to the subservience of the 'professionals', must have been puzzled by the jaunty notes they received from Shaw, which still breathe air into the turgid, official files. Sometimes they responded, often they did not.

When Shaw struck out into commerce in the 1870s, contact with the individual, Temple at the Shaw Savill Company, Robert and John Martin at Martin's Bank, was absolute; simultaneously, he had private work from the same clients on their estates. While extending Martin's Bank in Lombard Street (1874–6), Shaw undertook a new school for the family at Overbury, their pleasant Worcestershire village behind Bredon

Hill. It was the first of a long series of conservative estate works which he, and later Ernest Newton, built for the scattered parish. To Shaw, to Newton especially, and to the care of the Martins, Overbury owed the gradual, not-too-conscious growth which has made it amongst the most delectable of Cotswold villages. The school and adjacent cottages lack Shaw's usual mannerisms. They are quiet stone-built fabrics faithful to the local spirit, without overprecision of archaeology. Twenty years later, Shaw returned to the same mood when he built Overbury a village hall, in style equally self-effacing, but larger and longer in proportions, and more massively coursed in ashlar. In between came several other jobs, notably the pretty Post Office of 1879, more high-spirited than the rest, and breaking out unexpectedly into black and white work (ill. 62). Only after the village had been thoroughly put to rights, did R. B. Martin let Shaw loose on extending Overbury Court (1896–8).

Martin's was probably the Shaw Savill bank, and certainly the clearing bank for Barings, with which it was connected by family ties. With Barings, the pattern of personal contact was repeated. By the time that Shaw refronted Barings Bank in 1880–1, he had done small jobs for one partner, C. L. Norman, and was busy reconstructing Flete for another, H. B. Mildmay. There followed further work for Norman and a new Surrey house, Banstead Wood, for a third partner, F. H. Baring. Without the great 'Barings crisis' of 1890, there might have been more.

The bankers are one of two professionally homogeneous groups among Shaw's employers of the 1870s and '80s. At their centre stands Charles Loyd Norman (1833–89), a man of culture and attainments, friend of Lord Overstone and of George Grote, distant cousin of Wells of Redleaf, and son-in-law of Julia Margaret Cameron, the photographer. He is an excellent example of a Shaw client. The mid-Victorian surge in prosperity of the great banking enterprises pushed both the Martins and Normans into the ranks of the very rich at about this time. But they were new neither to wealth nor land. The Martins had owned the manor of Overbury since 1723, and the Normans too had been established nearer London at Bromley Common since the eighteenth century. Here they had two houses, 'The Rookery', a pleasant early Georgian affair, and Oakley, a converted farmhouse nearby. As the eldest of three sons, Norman enjoyed Oakley while his father was still alive. His first notion, therefore, was to build a huge family house to Shaw's plans on the Oakley site. This he would probably have done had his wife not died suddenly in 1873. Instead, he had to limit himself to getting Shaw to alter his London houses, first in Cromwell Road, then in Portland Place, and to extend Oakley modestly. Having remarried, when in 1882 he inherited 'The Rookery', he did not supplant it as he might have wished to do ten years before, but enlarged it according to his architect's revised tastes. Shaw was also employed in the 1880s by Charles Loyd's brother, F. H. Norman, partner in Martin's, to put on a service wing to Moor Place, Much Hadham.

Many of the features of this story are typical for Shaw's richer clients: the particular circumstance of marriage, an already existing estate with an inadequate house, and inherited wealth from at least one generation back, increasing through record profits of a family concern. This was not just a metropolitan phenomenon. Take, for instance, Shropshire. Here Shaw had three clients from the families of Midlands ironmasters; the Sparrows of Penn, the Staniers of Newcastle-under-Lyme, and the famous Darbys of

Coalbrookdale. W. H. Sparrow had in 1848 invested in the estate of Church Preen to add to his Staffordshire properties. When he died his youngest son Arthur, having an antiquarian bent, preferred the remoteness of Wenlock Edge to Wolverhampton. For him, therefore, Shaw rebuilt the dilapidated Priors House abutting the church as Preen Manor.[44] Arthur Sparrow was then forty-four, and his four children, all sons, were out of infancy; here was a case where house-building had to wait upon inheritance and had lost some of its practical point. The object of Preen was grand hospitality, to judge from its superb set of reception rooms and bedrooms, and Shaw's own occasional later visits.[45] The more remote your house was, the more satisfying your entertainment had to be, as the Shropshire clients well knew. At Adcote, Rebecca Darby must have wanted a great hall in her house for just these reasons. By birth she was a Christy, from a wealthy London firm of hatters, and perhaps did not care too much for provinciality.[46] She was also a widow, no doubt anxious through hospitality to marry her daughters off well. It was a vice which often beset Victorian widows to make this motive too obvious. One of Shaw's few unhappy experiences in house-building was The Clock House for Mrs Erskine Wemyss, whom he found brainless, difficult, and concerned only for her daughters' prospects.[47] (In reconstructing Upper House, the beautiful Mrs Guthrie perhaps had her own eligibility in mind rather than that of her children.[48]) To return to Shropshire, Francis Stanier, Shaw's third ironmaster customer there, more selflessly confined him to a school at High Hatton and a chapel at Peplow. Yet Shaw's work at Shavington Hall nearby once more followed the pattern of Preen and Adcote: reconstruction of a house from commercial profits by a second-generation landed family, this time of banking background, the Heywoods of Cloverley.[49]

The politically ambitious rarely went to Shaw for their country houses. He seems personally to have been a Tory, but was never identified with either party. His most obviously political houses were both for Liberals. Pandeli Ralli, of the Ralli Trading Company, native of Chios, Liberal M.P. for Wallingford, and bachelor, can have had only political reasons for purchasing and developing so huge and isolated an estate as Alderbrook. It was not near his constituency, but in those days that mattered little. Ralli's hospitality enticed Kitchener and other notables down to riotous house-parties that made locals fear for their daughters.[50] But this type of enterprise could easily go wrong. Charles Hodgson, an inheritor of brewing wealth, built The Hallams, also in the Surrey hills, to further his political aims, but failed to get into Parliament and was left with a remote and near-purposeless monster on his hands. Two other houses may also have had political motives which went awry. Bryanston was most likely erected by Lord Portman in hopes of a ministerial appointment which failed to materialize, leaving an even vaster redundance of empty bedchambers and stranger maids' rooms. And again, Nathaniel Clayton, unseated after corruption by his agent in a Northumbrian election, saw his ambitions crumble and with them the best reasons he could have had for enlarging Chesters.[51]

These three houses belong to the golden age of political house parties at the end of the century. Only Alderbrook in the country and Lowther Lodge in town served overtly political ends in the previous twenty years. Ralli also represents an anxiety on the part of rich outsiders to adopt the full rituals of upper-class behaviour. It was not unusual for such families to go to the most English of English architects. Webb altered the Ionides house on the Holland estate, and Devey was a regular Rothschild architect in the 1870s. Shaw worked now and again for lesser Jewish families who followed in the Rothschild wake. In 1877 he altered the town house of Nathan Montefiore, a prelude to his work for the predominantly Jewish Alliance Assurance Company.[52] Subsequently he built Holme Grange for Bartle Goldsmid, and a variety of small houses on Joseph Sassoon's Ashley Park estate. Nesfield, a despiser of 'Israelites', would not have considered such jobs.

Most of Shaw's house-building customers in town and country wanted capacious homes for their rising families. The lucky ones born to wealth built young, upon marriage; such were Charles Ebden of Baldslow Place, twenty-five at the time, and Douglas Horsfall of Mere Bank. Even more fortunate were those whose fathers built them houses. A double case of this occurs with the Tate dynasty of Liverpool. For Edwin Tate, who managed the London end of the sugar business, Shaw in 1881 designed Frognal Priory, Hampstead. So when his brother and sister were both to be married three years later, Shaw became architect to the two houses on adjacent estates in suburban Liverpool which Sir Henry Tate gave them as a wedding present: Allerton Beeches for Henry Tate junior, and Greenhill for the son-in-law, Colonel Thomas Gee.[53] Sidney Cooper R.A., the landscape artist, tried a similar ploy to keep his errant son Neville on the path of virtue, by presenting him in 1885 with a house design by Shaw for a lovely site outside Canterbury, not too far from his father's watchful eye. But when Alcroft Grange was built, it was improperly supervised, ending up with slates on the roof and matchstick half-timbering. Not only would it have horrified its architect, but it also quite failed in its moral purpose.[54]

Those who could build so young were the exceptions. Even the rich often waited upon inheritance, and the self-made men for whom Shaw sometimes designed were forced by circumstances to build for their retirement and their usually ungrateful posterity. There were four grandly *nouveau riche* businessmen among Shaw's clients: Temple of Leyswood, Armstrong of Cragside, Leyland of Princes Gate and Ismay of Dawpool, three shipowners and an armaments manufacturer. Armstrong had to wait till he was sixty before embarking on Cragside, but it is an index of the speed with which shipping fortunes were made that the other three all built before they were fifty. The architectural enterprises of all four were tarred with a natural exuberance and self-importance. F. R. Leyland, the Pre-Raphaelite patron and father-in-law of Val Prinsep is the most absorbing of them, a cold, ruthless, but cultivated man betraying little of his origins. He had begun in a lowly post in the Bibby Line in Liverpool, set up to cope with increased Mediterranean traffic after the repeal of the Corn Laws. Leyland had simply risen in the Bibby service, made himself indispensable, and bought out his masters in 1873. By this time, he inhabited the lovely Tudor mansion of Speke Hall. In 1876 he moved to London and began an internal reconstruction of the stucco house he took at 49 Princes Gate, at first under Thomas Jeckyll and Whistler. There followed the epic quarrel over the Peacock Room, which precipitated the nervous breakdown of the former and the disgrace of the latter. It was Norman Shaw who in 1879 picked up the pieces, at Murray Marks' suggestion. Jeckyll and Whistler had settled for the dining room; and for the grand stairs Leyland had imported the staircase from Northumberland House, recently demolished. To Shaw were left the first floor rooms, which he extended over the porch and converted into a grand triple drawing room round the stairs; five years later, he redecorated the morning room. There were no difficulties between Shaw and Leyland, who had crossed swords with many. In 1892, when Leyland with appropriate drama died on a Tube train between Mansion House and Blackfriars, Shaw was finishing the reconstruction of 'The Convent', one of the 'Kingsgate follies' close to Broadstairs, where he was to have retired. Shaw wrote thus to Murray Marks:

> Is it not too sad about poor Leyland? I have seen so much of him this last twelve months and he was looking forward to that house so much. You were to have hung the tapestry and done all sorts of things. He went to Binns and bought 3 chimney pieces, a big marble one, a bigger wooden one and a smaller marble one, and the day he died he went himself to Binns and said he would send a van on the Wednesday following to take them to Broadstairs. He never made the arrangement about the van, so I hear they are there still and are supposed to be waiting.[55]

THE PAINTERS' HOUSES

The artists, not the bankers, were the other real *nouveaux riches* among Shaw's clientèle. Previously, only exceptional painters like Reynolds and Turner had become very wealthy, but from about 1860 many started to make money hand over fist, from engraving rights as much as from the originals. It therefore became suddenly fashionable to build great studio houses, in contrast to the simple painting rooms which Mulready, Cope, Redgrave and others had tacked on to their homes. Webb was the real pioneer, but his four early artist-clients, William Morris, Spencer Stanhope, Val Prinsep and George Boyce all had substantial private means. Frederick Leighton was the first to show what could be done from artistic earnings alone, in the outlandish London house he built in 1864 to Aitchison's designs on the Holland estate, near Prinsep's. Of Shaw's painters, only Horsley was comfortably off before he began his career; Cooke and Goodall both built from their earnings, Cooke's outlay remaining within his capacities, while Goodall overextended himself and eventually had to sell up. These painters could remember Redleaf days, and had got their riches gradually. When Shaw added studios to Tom Webster's house in Cranbrook and Sidney Cooper's villa in Bayswater, he was working again for the same type of established R.A.

But there was another kind of painter who required his services when the London studio-house became a craze in the mid-1870s. The smart disciples of Whistler would fix on Chelsea to be near their master and try to emulate him by getting a house from Godwin. The younger genre-scene painters and portraitists, often from poor backgrounds and therefore more appetitive of academic honours, looked to Kensington and Hampstead, and to Shaw. Their houses, as Mark Girouard puts it, were 'bids for an established position rather than signs of it.'[56] The friends and rivals Marcus Stone and Luke Fildes were the first to go to Shaw, in 1875. It was bold of them; their new Melbury Road houses cost both well over £5,000 in building alone. But it is clear enough how it was done. Stone had a good line in book illustration, having drawn the pictures for *Our Mutual Friend*, and was just now illustrating Trollope's *The Way We Live Now*, while Fildes had scored a major hit at the R.A. in 1874 with a popular masterpiece, *Applicants for Admission*

120.
8 Melbury
Road, street
front.

121.
31 (formerly
11) Melbury
Road, street
front.

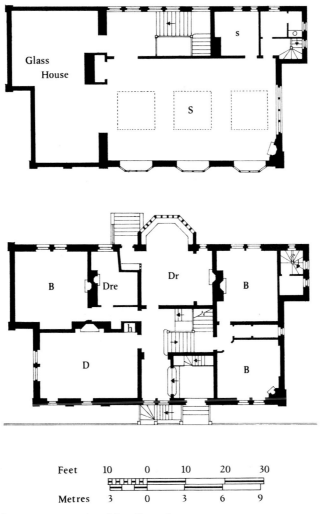

| Feet | 10 | 0 | 10 | 20 | 30 |
| Metres | 3 | 0 | 3 | 6 | 9 |

122. 8 Melbury Road, contract ground and first floor plans.

to a Casual Ward.[57] Since their houses seem to have consolidated their status, others keenly followed in their wake. First was West House on a confined site in Campden Hill, for G. H. Boughton, an American associate of the Cranbrook group; then came two Hampstead houses at either end of Fitzjohn's Avenue, Edwin Long's at the top and Frank Holl's at the bottom. Next, Kate Greenaway commissioned a studio house in Frognal, and soon Holl and Long came back to Shaw for more. In 1885 Holl built a small Surrey house, Burrows Cross, taken over after his death by B. W. Leader, for whom Shaw added a studio. The catalogue ends with the spectacular 42 Netherhall Gardens. Edwin Long was among the less talented painters for whom Shaw built, but he had character, his oriental scenes brought him fabulous returns, and he was bitten by the house-building bug.[58] Shaw and he had several tries at the plan of his first house before they were satisfied.

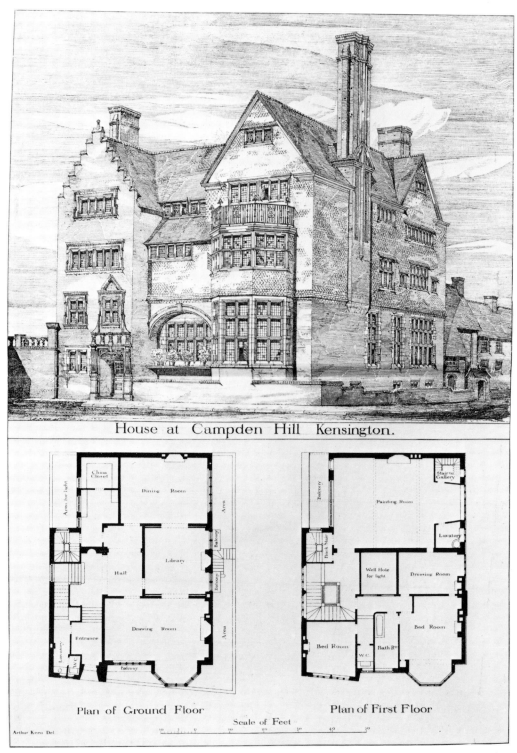

House at Campden Hill Kensington.

Plan of Ground Floor   Plan of First Floor

Scale of Feet

123. West House, Campden Hill Road, floor plans and perspective of street front, drawn by Arthur Keen and E. J. May, 1878.

But Long had settled there only eight years when he was bored with it and badgering Shaw for a new house in his back garden; the result was the last and grandest of the Queen Anne studio homes.[59]

The special requirements of the Victorian painter set these houses apart from the normal town house. The focus in each was the painting room, equivalent in status and sometimes in shape to the great hall of a country house. This room required extremely professional handling on two counts, those of access and of light. Academicians could be sticklers for propriety, so there were two kinds of access for which Shaw had to cater in the London studio. One was for models, who were 'not respectable'; a Victorian wife might tolerate a girl taking off her clothes for her husband, but she did not want to meet her on the staircase. So models used a back entrance, and were recompensed when the studio surmounted the house with a separate staircase, which often doubled with access to an easel room or painting store. Even in the country the separation of models' stairs was insisted upon by Horsley. The other access needed was ceremonial, for the preview of a picture before the R.A. show, when vast crowds might arrive, or for the occasions when the studio was decked out for entertainment, as Goodall and Boughton loved to do.[60]

With these requirements, Shaw combined the properly directed and accurately adjustable light sources demanded by his clients. In this they were probably more exacting than the Chelsea set. Vital for scene painters was the north and east light for which Shaw had turned the axis of Grims Dyke for Goodall (ill. 79). But Goodall's painting room, with its simple end and side lighting, boasted none of the refinements of its successors, the Fildes and Stone houses in Melbury Road (ills. 120–122). Though the plots here were open, a straggling plan like Grims Dyke was impermissible. Shaw followed Webb and Aitchison nearby in throwing the studios on the top of either house, but his tiers of north-facing windows occupied more of the upper halves of these elevations than before. Either studio was accompanied on the east by a glasshouse for outdoor effects and for finishing. The advantage of the north windows was to give high, slanting, even light which cast proper shadows, unlike roof-lighting. In Stone's house, where the studio monopolized the top floor, the centre oriel was raised shortly after the house was built especially to increase this high side light.[61] In Melbury Road, ground floor bedrooms were countenanced. At Boughton's West House, the site restricted the painting room to a mere half of the upper floor, but Shaw managed to get in big north and south windows, a gallery, high side light from a well-hole, and separate access for models, while the bedrooms are confined to first and second floors (ill. 123). For the Melbury Road elevations, he worked out a calmer, freer and plainer version of the Queen Anne articulation for which he had striven at Lowther Lodge, pairing up windows, elongating them still further, and dotting them about the façades. But at West House, an uncertainty appears; what style to adopt for the suburbs? Shaw equivocates between Old English and Queen Anne, and the solution he evolves for Boughton, his first frank mixture of the two in London, is unhappy. Artists normally plumped for Queen Anne; in his wish for some of the delights of Cranbrook days, Boughton foreshadowed the clients for whom Shaw would be designing at Bedford Park more accomplished compromises between the styles.

Whether because their sites were deep and narrow, or because the requirements of a Hampstead artist were different, Shaw allotted to the houses of Long and Holl a separate

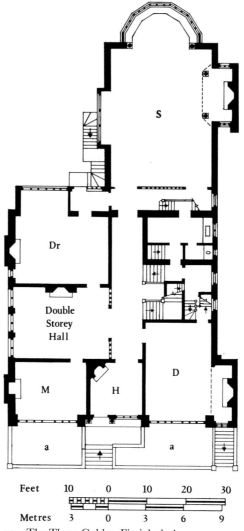

124. The Three Gables, Fitzjohn's Avenue,
contract ground floor plan.

ground floor studio. Long's house, 61 Fitzjohn's Avenue, survives as a maltreated and
divided Queen Anne rump, its massive studio projecting forwards to the road, now
deprived of its glasshouse. At Holl's, The Three Gables, the studio followed closely upon
this model, this time on the garden side, having the same square bay on the north,
restricted toplighting, polygonal bay on the east, and inglenook on the south side (ill.
124). Holl was a portraitist, and therefore had no glasshouse; he cared less for strength of
light than for gradations. He actually panelled his studio and had dark tones throughout
its decoration. *The Magazine of Art*, reporting this, adds that 'the modes of lighting it are
many and various, and permit Mr Holl to regulate, concentrate, or distribute his light, as
necessity demands.'[62] For the front, Shaw for the last time employed double oriels of the
Sparrowe's House type to liven up the three eponymous gables. The elevation drawings

Front Elevation

125. The Three Gables, Fitzjohn's Avenue, front elevation before revision, 1881.

(ill. 125) show them more crisply and originally handled than in the final executed version, which had less Queen Anne and more Old English detail, perhaps at Holl's request. Nevertheless, The Three Gables, with its deceptive double-pile appearance and off-centre ridge chimney gainsaying the main axis, was a happy and playful house.

The Kate Greenaway house (1884–5) and Edwin Long's second (1887–8) both returned to the Kensington idea of a top storey studio. No doubt this stemmed from site limitation (in Long's case a restriction self-imposed by building in his own garden). In every other way the houses are different to a point of parody of their clients. To Kate Greenaway, Shaw plainly could not resist allotting the pert charm of a tile-hung home, small but high, with a single simple gable and fetching bay window (ill. 126). That is all that one can see from Frognal, but the plan is delightfully clever (ill. 127). On the ground floor, a neat double drawing room and a dining room supply the wants of a maiden lady. Since she is her own housekeeper, Shaw abolishes back stairs, and divides the staircase at mezzanine level at the side of the house. One way, a short flight leads up to bedroom level, while in another, twenty-seven steep unbroken steps lead an unpretentious stairway up to the studio, an eyrie on top of the house. It is a plain, quite low room; it was a disappointment to Ruskin when he saw photographs.[63] But it is twisted across the axis of

159

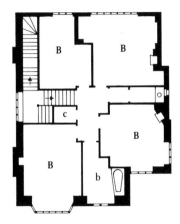
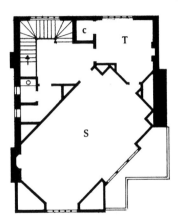

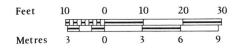

Feet 10 0 10 20 30

Metres 3 0 3 6 9

126. (left) 39 Frognal, street front.

127. (above) 39 Frognal, contract ground, first and studio floor plans.

the house to catch the precious north-eastern light. In this direction, Shaw gives the studio a good bay and a wooden balcony across the angle between front and side gable. Here on a fine day the little visitors might be sketched, before they were entertained in the tea room next door; or hence Kate could watch the toy-like children bowling their hoops down the quiet lane from Hampstead village.

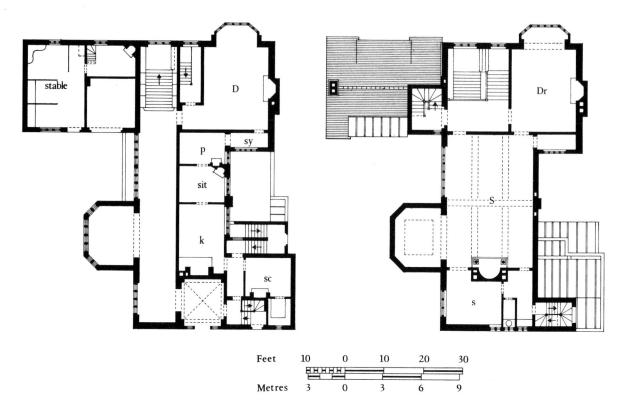

Feet	10	0	10	20	30
Metres	3	0	3	6	9

Edwin Long, since 1881 a full academician, demanded instead a grandeur worthy of his ageing dignity. Therefore at 42 Netherhall Gardens (ill. 128) everything had to be imposing, from the brazen entrance doors designed by the artist himself, 'filled with men in armour, horse and foot, doing all sorts of mysterious things,' to the entrance hall floor, 'paved with Carthaginian mosaics said to be over 2000 years old.'[64] The plan, one of Shaw's most deservedly famous, was in keeping; a long corridor from front to back at the side of the house, flanked on the left by only a single polygonal book bay, and on the right by service rooms without direct access to it. At its end, grand stairs ran up to a drawing room, as before with oriental décor, and a panelled studio nearly sixty feet in length, with a glasshouse over the book bay. The plain but monumental elevations of 42 Netherhall Gardens belong to the story of Shaw's stylistic transition of the late 1880s, and of his relationship with W. R. Lethaby (ill. 129).

BUILDERS

Every Victorian architect searched for the satisfactory block contractor.[65] Owing to the survival of the bulk of Shaw's drawings, we are well informed on his builders. In the 1870s, Frank C. Birch and W. H. Lascelles are the only two of importance; once he had found them, he avoided small local builders when he could. Open competition Shaw opposed, in case an insolvent builder cut corners and put in a low tender in a desperate attempt to get the job. Instead, he normally offered his clients the alternatives of limited competition

162

128. (left) 42 Netherhall Gardens, contract ground and first floor plans.

129. (right) 42 Netherhall Gardens, street front.

between good builders or of accepting a single, recommended contractor. The former system was open to the abuse of the cabal, but Shaw accepted it in or close to London, where there were plenty of good firms. In the countryside he preferred to use a trusted builder, with whose prices he was familiar. Thus Lascelles, a London man, often tendered for Shaw's houses and got many of his jobs by competition; Frank Birch, whose firm was at Farnham, appears to have acquired his country houses outside the competition system. When Birch failed and Lascelles retired in the early 1880s, Shaw tended instead to go for the 'tip-top' London men. For Barings in 1880 he proposes five builders, naturally of the very best, though he told the management to beware of 'fancy prices': William Cubitt & Co., Holland and Hannen, Trollope, Ashby and Horner, and Lascelles.[66] Ashby and Horner had built New Zealand Chambers and Martin's Bank, but did no known work for Shaw again. William Cubitt, who got the Barings contract, also built the first Alliance Assurance Office, the extensions to The Rookery, and 180 Queen's Gate. A little later, Holland and Hannen built Bryanston and remodelled Downside, Leatherhead; it was to them that Shaw's ill-fated pupil Harold Swainson went to learn more of building craft in the early 1890s.[67] The other important London contractor of the later period is the Shoreditch firm of John Grover and Son, who built New Scotland Yard in difficult circumstances to everyone's satisfaction, and did much work for Shaw in the early 1890s. For churches, Shaw was more willing to use local builders, scoring his best contracting success with James Heath of Endon, the builder of All Saints' Leek.

These grander builders of the 1880s and '90s lack the individuality of Birch and

Lascelles. Frank Birch came to Shaw's notice when he executed the complicated contract for James Knight's bank at Farnham. Over the ensuing twelve years, he turned out most of the Old English houses in Surrey, Sussex and Hampshire whose perspectives annually graced the R.A. walls. Boldre Grange, Wispers, Pierrepont, Merrist Wood and Piccards Rough were his, so too were the extensions to Upper House, the alterations at Sutton Place, and the cottage added to the Hammerwood estate. Then there is the Convent of Bethany at Bournemouth, and finally the time-consuming extensions to Flete as far away as Devonshire, which may have contributed to Birch's downfall.

The houses designed by Shaw for Birch to build are those in which Shaw develops and then discards the offset and hall plans. There is a kind of jealous family resemblance between them (Boldre Grange and Merrist Wood were indeed built for brothers). Many of them had interchangeable details. Harold Falkner, the Farnham architect, spent time with Birch and tried unsuccessfully to get into Shaw's office; happily he saved many of the detail drawings of these jobs. They show, for instance, bays at Pierrepont and Merrist Wood being made to the same detail, and the hall panelling at Merrist Wood following that of Upper House. Often the drawings have brief dialogues between Shaw and Birch, or his foreman; sometimes the decision on important points is left to Birch. Thus the Pierrepont entrance gable is noted: 'the barge boards cornice &c. to be all similar to Wispers—or Boldre Grange—or any of our best specimens', as though architect and builder belonged to one and the same firm.[68] Some surviving letters to Birch about Pierrepont maintain the tone of partnership. On the billiard room roof:

> I should let the lead run over into an iron eaves gutter. Surely it would be cheaper and I think better. The skylight must be a good looking fellow, to be the size shewn viz. 12/0 × 6/0 in the clear. I am afraid this will hardly give us air enough, and yet windows round the side are sure to leak. Couldn't we put a row of lights all along the upper part of outer wall (let them be extras of course), say 3 windows of 3 lights each, the cill about 9 feet from the floor? Say if you think this good and feasible, and I will draw it out. Then we could have 3 or 4 of these lights to swing in centres.[69]

Frank Birch was an honest, substantial country-town builder to whom an A.R.A.'s patronage was a rare honour. William Henry Lascelles was a much more original figure. He was a westcountryman who, on coming to London, worked first with Cubitt's and then with the Improved Industrial Dwellings Company of Sir Sydney Waterlow, the 'five per cent philanthropist'.[70] The I.I.D.C.'s working class flats were erected by Matthew Allen, but some role, perhaps that of technical experts, was played by the Bunhill Row firm of Waterlow, Draper and Webb. When Waterlow withdrew from this organization, Lascelles gradually took it over. By 1871 he was sole proprietor and an expert on labour-saving machinery, joinery and concrete construction.[71] At that date he is found contracting for the carpentry at Gore Hill, a small Shaw house in Sussex, having turned from low-cost housing to smarter work because of the threat from cheap Scandinavian joinery. In May 1873, Shaw could say that Lascelles 'does a great deal of work for me'.[72] This may mean mainly joiners' work; the unusual and beautifully made doors of Gore Hill recur at Boldre Grange, and Lascelles was certainly working at Flete a decade later, so perhaps a regular arrangement had been fixed with Birch. But from July 1873 at the latest, when he won Lowther Lodge against '9 swell London builders', Shaw employed Lascelles as a big general contractor.[73] He went on to build many of the early Queen Anne houses, 196 Queen's Gate, 8 and 31 Melbury Road, Shaw's own house, and 9–11 Chelsea Embankment. He tendered for most of the Shaw houses put out to competition, but the only country house he is known to have built was Hopedene (1873–4).

CONCRETE

Now comes an intriguing episode in Norman Shaw's career, his association with Lascelles in a series of designs for concrete cottages. To understand them one must go back a little. In the exploitation of concrete construction, the French were fastest off the mark.[74] English apathy began to be overcome in the 1860s when Tall introduced his system of standardized shuttering for monolithic construction, which church and commercial architects adopted with equal speed. In 1867, a concrete house erected on Tall's system by Arthur Blomfield was promptly discussed at the A.A. Next year Blomfield and William White were using a good measure of concrete to lessen the cost of churches in Oxford and Battersea respectively.[75] Both were friends of Street, so when Street got into difficulties over estimates for two boarding houses he hoped to build at Marlborough College in 1870, it was natural that as a last resort he too should turn to concrete. After experiments to test its impermeability, Street used a concrete made from broken flints in very thick walls enclosing lump chalk packing. He met the challenge of its uncouth appearance by tile-hanging the upper storeys all over, in the spirit of Shaw, and inserting regular white-painted wooden windows in the apertures.[76]

Now Shaw was still much in touch with Street. On the rare occasions when Street would admit that he was overwhelmed with work, Shaw far more often than Webb was the replacement. Marlborough is a case in point; for F. E. Thompson, one of the boarding house customers, Shaw designed a cottage (1877) and after Street's death another boys' house (1885). The most remarkable of several other instances is Bournemouth.[77] Here, Street had been architect to the Reverend Alexander Morden Bennett, the local High Church grandee, but shed some of the load in the early '70's, when work was contemplated on three new churches and a convent. Sedding secured one of the churches, St Clement's, which was paid for by Edmund Christy, brother of Rebecca Darby of Adcote; Shaw got the other jobs, all of which had to be financed and built in stages—St Michael's, St Swithun's, and the Convent of the Sisters of Bethany next to Sedding's church. And at the Convent, built by Frank Birch in 1874–6, Shaw uses concrete on very similar lines to Street's practice at Marlborough.

Working from first principles frequently fired Shaw's imagination; so it was in the Industrial Block of the Bournemouth Convent (ill. 130). It is the first building to snatch the Anglican sisterhoods out of stony Gothic cloisters and enfold them instead in the warmth of the new secular style. Yet this was done on severely limited funds, and in the harshness of concrete. Out of these difficulties emerges a masterly architectural composition. To start with, he takes a long, unbroken rectangle for his plan: 'I have denied myself all breaks and projections,' he tells Mother Etheldreda, 'and should steadily refrain from any tendency to burst out into architectural features. What you want

130. Convent of Bethany, Bournemouth, Industrial Block of 1874–6 before additions of 1878–80.

131. (right) Convent of Bethany, Bournemouth, Sisters' Wing as added in 1879–80.

is a simple massive unpretentious building at the minimum of cost.'[78] Next, he decides how best to break up the appearance of the concrete walls, which rise through three storeys. He therefore grasps the building in a monumentally broad gable enveloping the childrens' dormitories on the top; and he thrusts to the outside the eight main chimneys and their stacks, which must be in brick, so that they cut up into the attics like four regular sentinels on either side. The rest is sensible embellishment of the main lines. The dormitory windows become strips turning into the sides of the chimneys and puncturing their faces twice to form the washplaces, while on the first floor bigger windows and tile-hanging conceal the concrete. On the ground storey the rough pebble-dashed concrete stays crude and plain; in 1879, when he adds the Sisters' wing, he even exposes it on the staircase gable from ridge to ground (ill. 131). One end of the earlier building is left jauntily irregular, even half-timbered a little; the other is brick-faced, to cohere with Sedding's nearby school and parsonage. When in 1905 Shaw added a sober porch and an entrance wing linking lodge and convent, brick was again used and some of the bulky drama of the first block lost.

Lascelles, ingenious contractor that he was, went a different way about exploiting concrete. Monolithic concrete walls were cheap but inflexible and ungainly, and needed accurate and costly shuttering which had constantly to be moved and re-erected. Having faced some of these problems when working with Matthew Allen, Waterlow's contractor, Lascelles experimented instead with concrete bricks and slabs.[79] The slabs were his main brainchild, patented in 1875 and explained to a meeting of the R.I.B.A. in 1876. They

166

were made in a mould, of three parts coke breeze or clinker to one part of cement, and at first backed by iron rods. They were fireproof, they could be sawn, and they could be used for roofing or walling. The walling slabs were fixed with screws to thin upright posts spaced at three feet apart, usually of timber though Lascelles experimented with making these concrete too; together they formed a warm and secure wall of between one inch and one-and-three-quarter inches thick. The internal finishing was either to stain and varnish the posts, and to infill between them with lath and plaster, or in superior cottages to repeat the slab system on the inside and thus secure a hollow wall. Lascelles then had an artillery of concrete joists, rafters and window frames with which to complete his house, though he generally used the standard equivalents.

The opponents of this clever idea never claimed that it was ineffective. There were two initial lines of criticism, neither conclusive. Thomas Potter, an adherent of monolithic methods, argued that much skill and cost must go into the erection of the system, however cheap the casting might be. Lascelles answered that a single artisan could erect the framework. Potter also put the vaguer and more popular criticism, raised also at the R.I.B.A. and much aired since for this kind of innovation: if timber is used for the framing, 'the entire principle is wrong, for the concrete is not considered of any importance in a structural point of view, which is really its greatest feature, but is entirely subservient to an inferior material.'[80]

At the R.I.B.A., Lascelles exhibited the concrete mullions and transoms of Marcus Stone's studio oriels on to Melbury Road. They were the next step in Shaw's intermittent war with the London building regulations forbidding wood flush with or forward of window frames; they and the cornice were therefore wholly imitative of wooden mouldings. At about this time, when Lascelles was testing the slab system in a number of cottages near his home in Croydon, he asked Shaw for a set of concrete designs for it. Since the making of moulds and the variability of the designs must have been connected, no doubt Shaw was in on the experiment from the start. The results first broke upon a puzzled public at the Paris Exhibition of 1878, where Lascelles secured himself an excellent showing. Around the grounds of the Champs de Mars he erected two of the new cottages, wherein hung other of Shaw's designs for him and various of the R.A. perspectives. He also built a special stable for the Prince of Wales, and on the main street of the exhibition, the Rue des Nations, a special Shaw design for the English Jury House. This time it was made of his concrete bricks, and 'construite dans un style très-charmant et surtout très-aimé des anglais, le style du reine Anne.'[81]

Stay-at-homes did not have to repair to Paris or Croydon to see what Shaw and Lascelles were up to. In the summer of 1878, to coincide with the Exhibition, there appeared a thin blue volume entitled *Sketches for cottages and other buildings: designed to be constructed in the patent cement slab system of W. H. Lascelles, Bunhill Row, Finsbury, London E.C. From sketches and notes by R. Norman Shaw, R.A. drawn by Maurice B. Adams, A.R.I.B.A.* There, for all to see, was a series of Old English cottages just like those Shaw had been erecting for a decade, with half-timbering and tile-hanging, all to be put together from concrete slabs (ill. 134). The *Building News* was, for a change, insipid, but *The Builder* was triumphantly horrified. Here at last was its chance to lay into Shaw, and it did so with damning politeness. The designs were undeniably pretty:

132. Cottages in Sydenham Road, Croydon, ground floor plan and perspective from Ernest Newton, *Sketches for Country Residences* (1882).

133. 226 Sydenham Road, Croydon, detail of concrete ceiling.

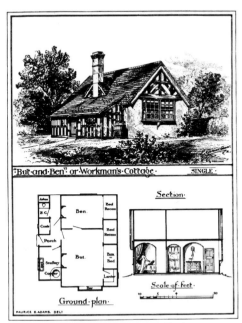

134. Concrete cottage erected at Paris Exhibition 1878, floor plan and perspective from R. Norman Shaw, *Sketches for Cottages* (1878).

We cannot but think, however, that even a better result might have been obtained had there been less of archaeology and more of architecture in these little buildings. . . . We fail to see the reason for thus imitating old rustic buildings in a modern material. . . . Our opinion is that here was a real chance for doing something new on the basis of a new material and method, which chance has been deliberately and almost perversely thrown away; for the very surfaces of the cement-slabs are made in what is called by the builder a 'fish-scale pattern', to imitate the effects of wall-tiling, and it is promised that the slabs may be stained with indelible red with the same object. All this dressing up of the new material in the old cloak is so much labour thrown away in making a sham. The object should be to find out how to treat the material picturesquely showing it as what it is.[82]

The visitor to Croydon who sees the two most important remaining cottages of the Lascelles/Shaw collaboration may well agree with *The Builder*'s verdict. The façade of 237–239 Sydenham Road adopts the tile-hanging that is the main design motif of the 1878 volume and has clumsy leaded windows reminiscent of some earlier *cottage orné*. 226–228 at first seems coarser, a crude parody of pargetting executed in concrete slabs dyed a strident claret. Yet this cottage, once set up as a showpiece for Lascelles' wares, impresses with the elasticity of the system. The front-to-back living room with concrete and iron joists over, and the dining room which has cement ceiling panels moulded with pretty flower patterns (ill. 133), surpass the rough and ready interiors of Lascelles' rivals in concrete. Nowhere is wood used for structural purposes, yet the joinery is exemplary throughout.[83]

Still, Lascelles and Shaw had fallen into a pit. If the Bournemouth Convent shows the genius Shaw could bring to a new idea, the concrete cottages warn of the danger of facility. How did he allow himself to err so blatantly? Without detracting from his responsibility, one can see he lacked time. 1877–8 was feverishly busy; palpably, *Sketches for Cottages*, without text, without explanation even of the process, is an accurate name for what has gone on. The drawings are all by Maurice B. Adams, from 'sketches and notes' of Shaw's, and under the plates, despite the signature of the master, is the tell-tale abbreviation 'dirext.', not 'invent.'. The simplest and best design, for 'Coffee and Entertainment Rooms, Bromley, Kent' was made and signed by Ernest Newton. Of the others, half are for cottages, the remainder for the gamut of respectable activities, including one 'seaside cottage residence' already entitled 'bungalow'.[84] At a guess they were dashed off smartly as rough notions by Shaw, developed by Newton and other pupils hungry for work, and worked over by Adams. The bungalow at least has a delightful vulgarity unexampled in Shaw's own buildings. Newton, who had an uncle near Croydon for whom he produced his first independent work in 1878, was probably the principal. In 1882 he issued a continuation to Shaw's book, *Sketches for Country Residences*, designed in the same format and adding sixteen further plates. By no means all of these are for concrete, or Newton's alone: Edward Prior, E. J. May and Adams all make contributions. Probably the same men had helped on the first volume before their independence. E. W. Godwin highlighted the vagueness of exact responsibility for the concrete cottages when he pointed out that one of the designs published in the *Building News* and shown in the second series as Newton's availed itself of Shaw's old plan for the Corner House. Newton replied that when the second book was in prospect,

170

Mr Shaw being at the time very busy, handed the work over to me, at the same time giving me permission to use any of his drawings I might wish to use in giving Mr Lascelles the sketches. The one that you published last week had a plan similar in nearly every respect to the house mentioned. The elevation was considerably varied, as far as I recollect. When you proposed to publish it I asked and obtained Mr Shaw's permission, he stipulating only that his name should not appear.[85]

There is one further piece of evidence in the second series. Here Newton signs a drawing for semi-detached houses in Sydenham Road, Croydon, almost equivalent in elevation but substantially different in plan to the show houses 226–228, attributed to Shaw in the *Builder* obituary (ill. 132).[86] The collaboration between a hectic Shaw, therefore, and an ambitious Lascelles, depended upon the pupils, and especially Newton, applying the Old English they had learned to a 'patent cement slab system' to which it was unfitted.

The Jury House on the Rue des Nations (ill. 135) can also be called fairly a lost opportunity. It was popular enough, earning itself a Gold Medal and the prospect of re-erection in an industrial museum on the site of the Tuileries. George Augustus Sala enthused over its 'Queen Anne-tics', imagining an appearance on its balcony by Addison, or the silhouette of Bolingbroke, Pope or Wycherley outlined through its windows.

It is the ghost of an Old English town house of the first years of the eighteenth century, with its red brickwork—showing the alternate courses of 'headers' and 'stretchers' of the 'English bond'—its white stone balcony, fluted pilasters, elaborately moulded panellings, and ornate cornices; but instead of being built of the old-fashioned bricks, it is entirely constructed of cubes of Mr Lascelles' patented red cement, which are truer, harder, and quite impervious to wet.[87]

No thought here, on the part of architect, builder or journalist, of how these exciting new bricks might be more originally employed!

Scale of Feet

Built entirely of Concrete bricks by W.H.Lascelles

135. Jury House, Paris Exhibition 1878, front elevation.

Concrete was not the limit of either Lascelles' or Shaw's contributions to Paris in 1878. Shaw designed the lay-out of the Minton ceramic display; Lascelles showed a range of bentwood conservatories and an area of patent dowelled oak flooring.[88] Upon this floor stood further efforts of collaboration: decorative 'art' furniture, designed by Shaw, executed by Lascelles, and ornamented by Mr J. Aldam Heaton. It was not enthusiastically received.

> We confess [said the *Furniture Gazette*] we do not admire the red Japanesque wardrobe; the bedstead is better, but as a whole, with the exception of a few good chairs upon Old English models, and one or two cabinets, nothing calls for a very eulogistic notice. The following list completes the exhibit. A wardrobe in vermilion and gold, a cabinet in green and gold, black chimneypiece, green armchairs, as supplied to the Princess Louise, Cromwell chairs in oak and leather, doors and architraves in green and gold, and another door and architraves in black walnut.[89]

In the mid-1870s, Shaw had been productive in furniture and fittings. There had always been two sides to his furniture: sturdy pieces in plain woods, descendants of the 1861 bookcase; and slim, polite, ebonized designs, orientalizing to start with but hankering soon after traditional models. In part, the types corresponded to the differences between fixtures and moveable furniture, in part, to the divergent atmospheres of dining and drawing rooms. Cragside boasts both, delicate chairs for the library, man-sized oak settles and sideboard for the dining room (ills. 48 & 49). Nesfield, famed in his day as a furniture designer, followed similar lines. Lamentably few pieces of his are left.[90] The built-in sideboard at Bank Hall (1873) and the settle at Llandyrnog Church (1877) are close to the heavy furniture of Cragside, while the wedding screen now at the Victoria and Albert Museum, given by Forsyth to Shaw, if designed by Nesfield, would show his approach to the delicate drawing room tradition. The distinction could be compromised, as in one surviving settle design of remarkable power Shaw made in the late 1860s (ill. 137), but by and large it held through most of the 1870s.[91]

Shaw conceived of resting-places from the smallest to the largest in terms of the masculine tradition, witness the charming zodiacal cradle he made for Alfred Waterhouse's son Julian in 1867, and Cragside's two massive oaken beds. The cradle (ill. 136), complete with lifting hood and treadle motion for rocking, is an ingenious curiosity, redolent of the early furniture of Webb in its heavy shapes and of Burges in its painting.[92] The beds are less esoteric though they still owe something to Burges—ponderous affairs in plain oak, with twisted end posts surmounted by carved owls. A similar bed, this time with the added attraction of a half-tester head, was shown by Shaw and Lascelles at an exhibition of their furniture in 1877. This took place in an annexe to the 1862 Exhibition Building run jointly with the Royal School of Art Needlework, where for two years afterwards Lascelles had some of his furniture on permanent display, along with some striking specimens of embroidery. The more massive pieces in the original exhibition were highly praised and hailed as pioneering by both the *Building News* and the *Furniture Gazette*.[93] Among them was a peculiar sideboard of which happily a photograph survives

136. Cradle designed for son of Alfred Waterhouse, 1867.

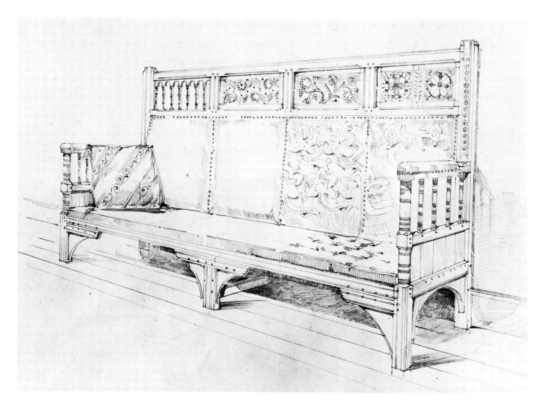

137. (above) Design for a settle,
c.1868.

138. (right) Sideboard by Shaw
and W. H. Lascelles, c.1876.

(ill. 138). Its rough structural base strikes abruptly against the great striated mouldings of the belly of the cabinet. Above, the flower panels are a pretty irrelevance and the two apologetic shelves fail to give height to the design, as though to see it properly it should be set into the wall with panels above and a heavy crowning cornice. It has close parallels in Shaw interiors round about 1880; the wooden half-inglenook head at Knight's Croft (ill. 95) and the massive sideboard at Adcote are most likely products of the Shaw/Lascelles partnership. But they are the last gasp of the masculine tradition. The Dawpool dining room has no such sideboard or settles. Indeed, not one Shaw design for furniture can confidently be dated after 1880.

The 1877 exhibition also included many examples of the slighter pieces. Though they were less well received, it was nevertheless these in the main that went to Paris in 1878. Shaw had designed such items long before, from the range of black furniture which he installed at Albion Road upon marriage to the superb ebonized chairs of the Cragside library with their delicate leather back patches. There is every reason to think that these were independent of the aesthetic furniture designs which E. W. Godwin was building up between 1867 and 1874, though Shaw certainly had at least one Godwin chair in his home.[94] But already among the Cragside set there is something more directly derivative, the corner chair, a type based on late seventeenth century models. 'Mr Shaw's chair', sketched by the young Lethaby on arrival in the office, was probably its original. The corner chair fascinated Shaw; various versions are scattered about his interiors. At Cragside they are painted, at Ellerdale Road and Dawpool they are plain, while Willesley had a deliberately crude and gawky set, stained a faint green, bereft of stiffeners, and with pierced back pieces and rustic rush seats (ill. 139).[95]

139. Corner chair designed by Shaw for Willesley.

By 1877, there were more of these 'sentimental reproductions of the past age'.[96] Some of them, and the pieces of red and green-stained furniture with lacquer panels and gilt tooling so equivocally greeted in 1878, may owe something to Aldam Heaton. Until 1876 Heaton remained in Yorkshire, but by now he 'posed in Leeds as an art furnishing authority', to borrow the words of the hostile *Cabinet Maker*.[97] His main business was at first with churches. One of his biggest early jobs was to carry out a complete scheme of hangings and embroidery, swept away long ago, for the extensions Shaw made to the church at Hebden Bridge (1874–6). At this time Heaton was often travelling down to London, having become involved in the launching of the Royal School of Art Needlework.[98] Meanwhile Shaw was looking round for a regular decorator for his ever-increasing practice, and appears to have persuaded his friend to set up in London as a secular designer and furnisher. His ready-made clientèle brought Heaton immediate success. Within a few years, he had worked at Adcote, Greenham, Flete, Dawpool, Frognal Priory and the Alliance Assurance Office, and was able to get Shaw to build him a large workshop in Bloomsbury.[99] Shaw integrated him into the working relationship with Lascelles, and the three exhibited not only at Paris, but also at the Building and Furniture Exhibitions of 1880 to 1882. The arrangement was never a commercial partnership or firm, as Shaw was careful to point out, and doubtless brought bigger returns to Heaton and Lascelles than to him.[100]

In default of survivors, the cool reception accorded to the 1878 pieces is hard to assess.[101] Queen Anne tendencies still disquieted the press, while the strength of the stains, Lascelles' own invention, combined with Heaton's lacquer patterns and gesso panels, may have given a disagreeable impression to the furniture trade, always suspicious of encroachment from an architectural direction. As far as Heaton was concerned, while he stuck to textiles and wallpapers he was strong, but with furniture there can be little doubt that he was out of his depth, as his later adventures showed.[102]

HOME AND HEALTH

On 20th October 1874, the day that his third and last child, William Campbell Shaw, was born, Shaw drew out the first elevations for a house for himself and his young family. In this, his most enjoyable task of the decade, Lascelles certainly and Heaton probably collaborated. Shaw had bought an ample plot, well out of town but close to Church Row and the village of Hampstead, where many an architect and artist already dwelt. It lay upon sloping terrain on a bend in the new Ellerdale Road, looking over an unimpeded view at the back towards Hampstead Church, where Shaw had been married and his brother lay buried. 6 Ellerdale Road was amongst the first of the great Hampstead houses. When it was building, no houses had yet risen upon Fitzjohn's Avenue, the lane that led down into town. Over the next twenty years the Shaws were to see London developing up the hill until it arrived at their door.

Architects' houses are often idiosyncratic; Shaw's was no exception. It was predictable that he would flout precedents when freed from his clients' demands. A certain looseness, too, was to be expected, since he hoped to add a wing on when time and money allowed. Queen Anne of course was an informal style, allowing openings exactly

140. 6 Ellerdale Road, street front.

141. 6 Ellerdale Road, the dining room.

where needed on the side elevations. But at Ellerdale Road Shaw transferred the informality from back and sides to the front (ill. 140), challenging the onlooker to find the true pattern behind the vertical fenestration. Can he have deliberately confused a basically symmetrical arrangement between gables? Or do the uneven central windows freely reflect the rising of the stairs? Neither is the right answer. The gables are trivial features of different height and placing, while of the windows in the middle only the biggest lights a staircase and several belong to rooms already represented in the bays. The front in fact is a topsy-turvy tease, and was even more so in the first drawings, when it was to be divided into vertical units by pilaster strips, and lacked the Ipswich oriels that liven up the asymmetry.

What the façade does show is that the house is vertically split between two camps, left and right. Despite the falling ground, the left has two principal storeys against the right's three; despite the better view west, the left hand rooms have an outside chimney-breast whereas the right hand ones' hearths all face inwards towards the centre of the house. These peculiarities are more obvious on examination of the plan (ill. 144). Shaw has faced both his reception rooms south towards the road, patiently reserving the garden view for future extension. Further, he has skimped his drawing room in favour of the dining room, the house's *pièce de resistance* (ill. 141). It is almost a cube, a storey and a half in height, which is why the levels are split. It has high panelling, quarry tiles round the carpet, and a massive inglenook to the west, the first to be used in town. The drawing room (ill. 142) also had half of one, with a little alcove towards the street, but that in the dining room is a new type of inglenook altogether, though laced as usual with Spanish leather and majolica tiles. Its beam is low; too low, since Lascelles's men made a mistake in the casing of the ceiling, and everything had to be pushed down.[103] Above, it accommodates the precious workroom or 'den', where Shaw's drawing was done. Though a mere ten feet by seven feet, the den was both a microcosm of the house and a miniature parody of the Victorian artist's gigantic studio. A little private stair led up to it with a porthole out along the length of Ellerdale Road. Within, Shaw sandwiched his drawing board between two corner windows on to different aspects of the garden. To his left, a small fireplace in the chimney-breast gave him warmth, and behind him, another window down into the dining room allowed him to survey or speak with his family below. It was in this den that the masterpieces of his maturity and old age were first conceived and drawn (ill. 238).

The changes of level at Ellerdale Road led to much juggling with the staircases. From the entrance hall, the stairs swung to the right with a graceful ease up to the reception rooms, while the back stairs bustled up from a lower level behind. Upwards from here, the stairs gave off from various levels to different parts of the house, especially after the long drawing room was added in 1885–6 (ill. 143). Front and back drawing rooms were then joined by an anteroom, four steps and a walnut screen. The house thus had an ideal reception room for entertainment. With its end chimneypiece, its bay opening out to the left, and the furniture thrust to the walls, it resembled a long and low version of one of the later Shaw halls. As at Cragside, the deliberate openness of this room as against the dens and alcoves of the old ones afforded one of the house's chief charms. Later again, Shaw thought of adding business and billiard rooms to the house, but this came to nothing. So too did plans to build another house next door in the corner of the

142. 6 Ellerdale Road, the front drawing room.

garden, no doubt destined for one of the family, but perhaps also intended to safeguard the architectural integrity of his surroundings.[104]

In the autumn of 1876, when his house was nearing completion, Shaw turned his attention to yet another subject—plumbing. Technical subjects had always had a special appeal for him; he loved to think and talk about them while leaving the artistic side to develop itself naturally. No pupil of Burn's was deficient in the mechanics of house-building and since then, Shaw had advanced much in every branch of the servicing of a house.[105] Now he made public a little of his ingenuity, to the consternation of the professionals, who liked to scoff at the impractical 'art architects' of Queen Anne and Old English.

Curiously, it seems to have been a fault of Burn's which stimulated Shaw's interest in drainage. Like other contemporaries, Burn used a primitive and ineffective form of trap to his W.C.'s, and sometimes carried the waste pipe down through partition walls. The liberal smattering of sewage which percolated the wall, if a pipe then leaked, produced both a stench and, when the wall was opened for rectification, a sight which neither a country gentleman nor an impressionable young architect would wish repeated.[106] Typically, the Prince of Wales had to come close to death in November 1871 before old axioms were seriously examined, but from then on progress was rapid. Suddenly, the sanitation experts began to agree that instead of closing up wastepipes in walls and

180

143. 6 Ellerdale Road, the back drawing room.

making them airtight at every point, the right policy was to get the pipes on to the outside walls and, more critically, to ventilate them. But the question remained—where and how?

At his house Shaw attempted a plain and easy answer. He installed simple valve closets of the Bramah type.[107] Beneath these, the waste pipe led as straight as possible into an open funnel on the outside wall. Hence the pipe descended directly to a further funnel at ground level, again open but protected by a grating, down into a trap a few inches below the surface, and into the main sewer. Simplicity itself! The two revolutionary features of the system were the lack of any kind of trap at all beneath the closet, and the complete disconnection of the downpipe at two points, so that the pipe was ventilated at either end. To Shaw's delight it worked admirably. He waited a year, then to test reactions he sent a lucid diagram and description of the system to the building press (ill. 145). 'I have no patent to protect, nor any interest of any kind at stake', he wrote. 'My only desire is to secure the simplest and most efficient means of effecting that which is admitted to be a difficulty and a source of danger.[108]

Response was large, mixed, but on the whole favourable. Many people very fairly wrote in to say that they had been using like systems for some years, but some had secured patents and few had put them forward for public benefit. The most cogent objections came from the 'trappists', who were horrified to see Shaw omit the conventional trap

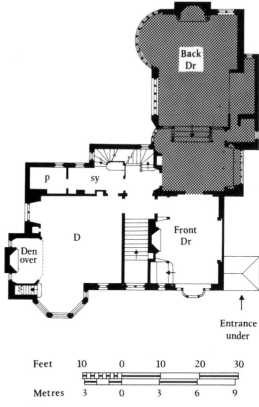

Feet   10   0   10   20   30

Metres   3   0   3   6   9

144. 6 Ellerdale Road, first floor plan, with addition of 1885–6 shaded.

beneath the pan of the W.C. They argued that in Shaw's system there was nothing to prevent the dreaded 'sewer gas', if under pressure from heavy rainfall, from pushing through the trap at the bottom, floating up the pipe, and penetrating into the house, especially if a Bramah closet (never very airtight) was used. Others feared that the bend in the pipe immediately below the pan would become coated with excrement and pollute the whole house, and many expected a pungent smell of 'gas or effluvium' from the open funnel near windows. Nearly every critic agreed that additional ventilation was needed, either by taking the wastepipe up to the top of the house and fitting it with a cowl, or by inserting a ventilated trap of modern type beneath the pan.[109]

To these objections Shaw supplied the best of answers—experience. Various experts hied to Ellerdale Road to test the system. One even burnt ozone paper in the bottom of the downpipe, succeeded in getting fumes all over the house, and triumphantly reported the system's failure to *The Builder*. 'Of course it was not for me to suggest tests or dictate in any way,' replied Shaw, 'but I could not help being quietly amused at the fact that these experiments, interesting though they were, were all performed on the *wrong side of the trap*.'[110] The following winter (1878–9), the soil-pipes came off with flying colours during severe frosts, which had been a source of anxiety to him.[111] The system in fact was a success.

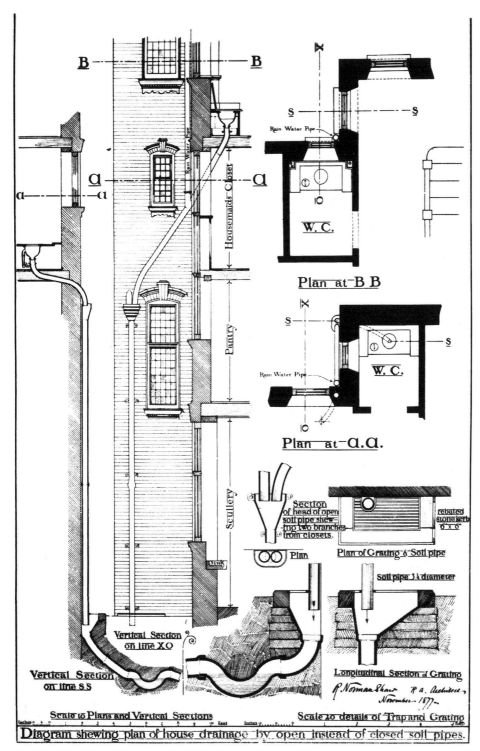

145. Diagram of open soil pipe system, as applied at 6 Ellerdale Road.

But though this was generally admitted, the 'open soil-pipe' was not taken up widely. One or two architects adopted it here and there, but not with consistency; it was left to Shaw to apply.[112] He used it at Cheyne House, George Matthey's house on the Chelsea Embankment (1875–6), and in every subsequent commission where he had the chance he had it installed by his regular plumbers, Wenham and Waters of Croydon. But it was much opposed by local sanitary boards. When Shaw was altering Rosemount, Matthey's Eastbourne house, they refused to allow it until Matthey threatened to report on the state of health of the town,[113] and there were further clashes. Eventually the 'trappists' won and had their views legislated upon. In 1928 the Ellerdale Road drains were proscribed and remodelled, but Robert Shaw records that everything was in perfect order. Only one change was made there after installation, and that was to narrow the diameter of the pipe to increase the force of the discharge.

> The original soil-pipe was 3 in. in diameter. I at once saw that it was too large, and in my practice I have always used a 2½ in. pipe. After the 3 in. pipe had been in use for some thirty years I had it removed and a 2 in. one put in its place with still more satisfactory results. When the original one was taken down, a section of the middle of it was cut out and brought straight into our dining room, where it stood for some days. It had no smell and was quite clean inside.
>
> I have often wondered at the manifest terror with which so many people regard soil-pipes. I assume that they are convinced (I believe erroneously) that a soil-pipe *must* necessarily be an evil-smelling and pestilential thing; they cannot disabuse their minds of this idea. If they could only realize the fact that a soil-pipe is used for the conveyance of slops and other foul matters at intervals, in an ordinary house for, say, ten minutes all told in the course of twenty-four hours, and that for the remainder of the day it is simply an air-pipe with a current of fresh air passing up it, I believe that their fears would rapidly disappear.[114]

The open soil-pipe was not Shaw's only innovation in drainage matters. In 1888 he reported at length to *The Builder* on a new type of drainpipe for culverts which he had invented.[115] It was 'egg-shaped in section, open all along the top, and with a rebated flange to receive covers', and was to replace the normal closed circular pipe. He commended it as cheap, better-jointed, better in section, and easy to lay and examine. It was not widely noticed but must still exist at many of his buildings.[116] There were other labour-saving inventions too. At much the same time, Robert Shaw says his father installed at 46 Berkeley Square one of the first small independent boilers that allowed water-heating and cooking to use different heat sources, and so saved the servants from sweltering during summer. One of these was made for Ellerdale Road. At home, too, Shaw introduced in the 1890s a kind of 'sanitary dustbin'. In those days, the scavengers would dig the refuse out of the huge open bins into their own baskets; portable dustbins were unknown. Instead, Shaw had a pair of metal bins made with covers, eighteen inches square. No doubt neither of these ideas was wholly new, but they were found worth commenting on at the time.[117]

At the end of 1876 the lease on Salvin's old premises in Argyll Street ran out, and Shaw moved east to Bloomsbury Square, on the very purlieus of his profession. Fashionable architecture of the 1850s and '60s had clustered round two centres: the shadow of All Saints' in Margaret Street, whither Nesfield betook himself for his last four years of practice, and further south, round Charing Cross, where Butterfield inhabited the Adelphi and Scott presided over his pupils in Spring Gardens. Webb and the Morris firm had broken east towards the inns of court, and now Shaw's move in the same direction inaugurated an architectural stampede. Soon, many a disciple was gathered round him in legal chambers or Bloomsbury attics, and the emulous followed fast.

The house Shaw took was no. 29, standing at the north end of the square's east side. If it survived today, we might see in this fine early eighteenth century house the source of much of Shaw's emerging classicism. But it fell a casualty to insurance in the 1930s, and instead we must rely on the glowing advocacy of the young Edwin Lutyens, writing to his beloved Emily in 1897 when they hoped to move there in their turn:

> Now darling, if I were a Duke, I should love to take my Emy to live in 29 Bloomsbury Square. The house is beautiful, large airey rooms, beautiful mantlepieces and staircase on the ground floor. You enter a square Hall and a beautiful staircase beyond. 3 rooms which the great Norman Shaw used as his offices!! during his busiest period!! such lovely doorways and cornices everywhere . . . such a beautiful staircase with a delicious wooden gallery upstairs overlooking it. It is like a country house like Milford House, but the architecture is good, so good, instead of being $\frac{1}{2}$ and $\frac{1}{2}$.[118]

Of this palace, Shaw took only the ground floor. Upstairs, the Aldam Heatons moved in. For occasional evening parties they overflowed down into his offices, and they finally ousted him altogether in 1893 when one of their two daughters was married.[119] One of the three downstairs rooms was a sanctum, complete with the master's corner chair; the bigger two doubtless housed the assistants.

In the cramped conditions of Argyll Street, Shaw's staff had always been small, never probably extending beyond two or three. After the partnership's dissolution, Nesfield and he had gone on sharing assistants while having their own articled pupils. Following Brydon's departure in 1869, there had been two such assistants: Richard Creed, a minor talent, and Edward John May, who came to Argyll Street after the expiration of his pupillage with the aged Decimus Burton.[120] Whether May, who maintained a devotion to Nesfield's memory, actually moved across to Bloomsbury Square we do not know. But he and Shaw's first own pupil, William West Neve, articled in 1870 and now free of his bonds, flitted in and out of the office in their first years of independence and became part of the happy circle or 'family' from which the Art Workers' Guild emerged. West Neve was the first of several pupils with backgrounds rooted in the Cranbrook group. Scion of a wealthy family well-known to the Horsleys, he was in Shaw's opinion 'not clever except as a conjurer' and built little.[121] Eventually he inherited money, which was partly spent on West Court, an exotic house built for himself on Bray Reach, Maidenhead, in a style approaching parody of Shaw's manner. E. J. May was a more considerable architect, an excellent draughtsman, and a charming and humorous man. As Shaw's trusted aide at Bedford Park, he designed the excellent vicarage and several other houses there. Up to this standard few of his later works seem to come; the smart R.A. perspectives of his work excite expectations often disappointed by brick and mortar, as Ernest Newton's do not. It was a bad habit which Shaw had set, best abandoned. Honestly to translate the dimensions, texture and details of an often unfinished building into the blandishments of architectural perspective required a struggle both for himself and for his pupils. Shaw began to shake himself free of the habit in the '80s, disillusioned by the whole perspectival manner of display. After this, he showed only public buildings in this form, and those all drawn without exaggeration.[122]

The two pupils who we know moved across to Bloomsbury were Ernest Newton and Edward Prior, articled in 1873 and 1874 respectively. Shaw loved and honoured these two dearly. When Lethaby joined them, this triumvirate of eminent, disparate talents became the natural founders and leaders of the Art Workers' Guild—Newton the modest, practical man, Prior the scholar and 'angular' intellectual, Lethaby the charismatic enthusiast and teacher. Before joining the office, Newton would have known Shaw's early work at Bromley, for he was brought up nearby and later built much in the district. A plan to article the boy to Ewan Christian miscarried and he found a place with Shaw. Here, as a natural learner, Newton found how to plan and compose well, and to draw prettily. For the genius and flair of the perspectives, Newton substituted elegance in measured drawings, evolving an exact range of mild, light washes like those of Devey, which foreshadow the texture of his own domestic work and become a popular instrument of draughtsmanship in the 1890s. Newton's peculiarity is to make modesty and reticence eloquent, to the discomfiture of critics seeking the original or the striking. His mature houses breathe an undramatic 'rightness' and 'fitness', to use the simple canons of the time.[123]

For Prior, 'perhaps the most gifted pupil of them all',[124] Shaw's affection mingled more with respect. Here was a man who differed much from Shaw and his friends, a specimen of the Victorian intellectual athlete, a forgotten type hymned by Clough. Fresh from his blue in the long jump and high jump at Cambridge, Edward Prior was deceptively bluff, but in practice learned and introverted. He could take off his trousers one day in the office because they were wet, or on another occasion he could tie up O'Neill, one of the dimmer pupils, in a brown paper parcel and leave him in the lobby; but he also produced distinctive, thoughtful, clotted plans for the second concrete cottage book. Later on came a series of daunting books and lectures on mediaeval art, in equally clotted prose, and a handful of designs of striking concentration and originality. Yet somehow, either out of generosity or from difficulties of temperament, Prior became an also-ran. He perhaps failed to be the Webb of his generation because Lethaby and Voysey managed to split and share the mantle, and he could not or would not spoil the award.

On moving to Bloomsbury Square, Shaw quickly brought in more pupils. The first was Arthur Keen, a competent, dedicated youth who venerated Shaw; he made a good career and became president of the A.A., but lived in the shadow of his contemporaries. Next, in 1877, came Frederick O'Neill, who after a brief and unsuccessful stay emigrated to America.[125] Then came the flood: in 1878 Mervyn Macartney and Edwin Hardy; in

1879 Philip Thicknesse, Reginald Barratt and Gerald Horsley. In the same period Frederic Miller and Frederick Harrison spent brief terms in the office. They were mainly gentleman pupils, sons of the 'professions' or of painters. Thicknesse, son of the Bishop of Peterborough, came straight from public school. Prior and Macartney, with legal and medical backgrounds respectively, were the only graduates trained by Shaw until Harold Swainson came down from Cambridge in 1890. But in the summer of 1879, when Newton and Prior were starting out on their own, Shaw, looking about for a chief clerk as Street had done twenty years before, lighted upon an unknown young man of lowly background then working in Derby, who had produced some impressive designs and drawings in the building press: William Richard Lethaby.[126] In some trepidation, Lethaby arrived at his famous office to command the expectant underlings. From the day he put pen to paper he justified Shaw's choice, was trusted utterly and revered by his fellows.

Shaw succeeded with his various pupils and was in turn loved by them because he read human nature well. Choice was of the essence; on one occasion he rejected an applicant on the grounds that his character was 'Laodicean'.[127] The pupils were selected from a lengthening waiting list (Harold Falkner, perhaps exaggerating, says that when he applied there were eighty on it).[128] But Shaw felt free to take sons of friends when he so wished. This was the way that Hardy, O'Neill, Horsley and, rather later, Archie Christie, son of the cabinet-maker Robert Christie, came to him. As a result, many talented men, of whom Lutyens was doubtless one, went on to study with Ernest George or John Belcher. Articles were for a five year term, and the standard premium was £300, though it could be negotiated lower or done without. No premium was paid nor were terms signed until after a trial of several weeks.[129] Of course the success of these gentleman pupils was by no means assured, and the casualty rate quite high. Edwin Hardy, a fine draughtsman who had transferred from painting to architecture, committed suicide in about 1890 after getting into financial difficulties. Frederick Harrison took to the stage, becoming secretary to Beerbohm Tree; Reginald Barratt, with Shaw's agreement, took up painting and went to Paris to study under Bouguereau; and Cyril Fitzroy, a pupil of 1882 whom Shaw thought very talented, after successes at the R.A. School and help with the foundation of the Art Workers' Guild, also went in for painting and ended up, to universal regret, as an inspector of government schools.[130]

Once the pupils had shown seriousness of purpose, Shaw would give them rein. On the superficial level, this could mean liberty to lark about in the office. After the austerities of their own training, Street's *alumni* were understandably given to allowing a little relaxation. Sedding and his men went in for a tug-of-war on one occasion, on another for an egg-and-spoon race happily won by the master; Shaw and Lethaby one dreary afternoon held a cricket match in the office with T-squares and an india rubber.[131] These were not typical Victorian incidents, for Bodley's office had a solemn atmosphere, and Leonard Stokes kept his pupils in fear of their irascible master. But the freedom young talents asked for and too rarely got was freedom of responsibility and design. To these higher liberties Shaw gradually conducted his pupils, if they were competent to attain them. Much of this must apply too to other offices, but in Shaw's case the wealth of extant evidence and the pupils' calibre make the procedure he adopted worth looking at.

The first things an articled pupil naturally had to be able to do were to learn to measure up buildings, and to draw plans acceptably and in the 'office style'—a concept not fully worked out until the days of Bloomsbury Square. For a normal building, the crucial set on which a pupil had to cut his teeth were the one-eighth inch scale plans and elevations for contract signature. The Shaw office brought the art of these drawings to as high a point as any comparable firm. Nesfield and Shaw themselves perfected the placing of boldly coloured one-eighth inch scale drawings upon the imperial-sized sheets of Whatman cartridge paper. The pupils took matters a stage further. They increased the scale of the lettering, bringing in a uniform round script of the kind that became standard in about 1875 in the *Building News* Design Club plates, and they introduced a variety of devices to give refinement of relief. Some ideas may have been due to E. W. Godwin and his circle, but others, such as the use of different tones of wash for different lights in a window instead of naturalistic shading of the whole, seem original. The lines were laid down by the time that Lethaby reached the office, but the finest results came during his reign, such as the drawings for Callerton Hall and Netherhall Gardens. Shaw was particular and proud of his office drawings. On one perfectly passable set (for 62 Cadogan Square) which boasts a strident red wash clearly not put in by him, he writes 'what hideous drawings! did anyone ever see such vulgar looking things? I am quite ashamed of them'.[132] These sheets took time and were made without complex artificial aids or copying methods. When the Post Office tiresomely demanded a duplicate set of drawings for the second Alliance Assurance building, Shaw predicted that the task would require 'two months' work for a good draughtsman'.[133]

After a year or two's experience in the office, Shaw usually sent his men along to the R.A. School, where even Lethaby did his time. Later, the pupils might go in the evenings to the A.A. Class of Design of their own accord. Next came the responsibility of co-ordinating information on one particular job. Any pupil naturally ran a number of errands to clients, builders and London sites, graded in importance according to experience. When drawing tasks became heavy, Shaw often retreated to Ellerdale Road for a day or two, and showered notes down on his office. The surviving letters to Arthur Keen convey his method and tone. In 1878:

> Please go to Chelsea as soon as you can. You will find Mr Franklin there about 10.30. Take the $\frac{1}{4}''$ scale plan in pencil and also the tracing you made. Tell Mr Franklin that as there is no basement to the stables the foundations will be a very small affair and so perhaps we might arrange to build up some few feet above ground line, but that above all things we want great speed used in that stable building, *as they want it up and covered in soon.*[134]

Some time next year, increasing his confidence:

> Will you go to Mr Leyland's, 49 Princes Gate . . . and measure tolerably carefully Porch and first floor over—Elevations. What we propose to do, is to make a gallery sort of place over existing Porch, and therefore we want an accurate plan of parapet of existing Porch, and outside line of cornice &c., and elevation of existing first floor windows &c.[135]

In October 1880, Shaw is freely discussing a design drawn out by Keen, perhaps from a builder's plan for Barings:

I can't make out these skylights. Instead of all that hipping and awkward cutting of glass &c. it seems to me that it would be so much simpler to have them both in one slope thus [gives drawing]. Is there any reason why it should not be so? It would be much simpler. These miserable little gutters next the wall shewn on your drawing would be stopped up in a week. Then as to the iron doors, I really do not understand at all. The floor outside is not to be on a different level from the floor inside on any *condition whatever*, and there is to be no raised cill to step over. This was discussed again and again, and the drawing which you sent up appears to me to be right. . . . If they have made a mistake they must alter it. If you don't see your way come up tomorrow and let us talk it over and you can go to Woodrow by N. L. Rail.[136]

Finally, in 1881, Keen has become 'manager' to the drawings for alteration of the R.A., and is directed to prepare much of the job; boring holes in walls to test their thickness, discussing the mysterious flues with academy luminaries and drawing out and taking the scheme to them while Shaw was in the south of France.[137]

In this year, Keen transferred to Newton's new office, for Shaw told him and his father he needed a change ('whilst he suits my purpose perfectly, he is not doing himself any good, and will soon begin to go backwards').[138] There were several further stages in responsibility to which the top pupils attained. The finishing school of architectural training was to act as a clerk of works. Shaw preferred not to use professional ones:

If you have a really good Builder you save the salary of the C. of Works, but of course you pay a little more for the work than if you had a scampy or ignorant man with a Clerk of Works to make him do his work well. So in point of expense it is as broad as it is long. All this I think points towards the good builder and *no* Clerk of work! and certainly as I said before, I have had my best work done in this way.[139]

Still, it was an excellent step in training, and sometimes necessary even with a good builder when the works were complex. Thus Ernest Newton served his term with Frank Birch at Flete, possibly at Pierrepont too, while Edward Prior went up to Ilkley to superintend St Margaret's, and Philip Thicknesse ended his time with Shaw as clerk of works on Dawpool. These jobs would frequently be followed by the 'setting-up' commissions, first small, then large, which Shaw sprinkled liberally among his best pupils. On Newton, after a couple of small jobs, he must have bestowed the London convent of the Sisters of Bethany, and on Prior the completion of the church restoration at Kelsale. Prior and Thicknesse found business notably close to their clerkships, Prior the building of Carr Manor in Leeds, Thicknesse a permanent partnership with W. E. Willink in Liverpool. Of the others, Shaw found E. J. May work and to spare at Bedford Park, where he was pleased to see him 'driving a devil of a trade';[140] Macartney early in his career was altering 8 Melbury Road and adding to Holmrook Hall; while Lethaby took the plum of these commissions, Lord John Manners' new mansion at Avon Tyrrell.[141] 'Scratch behind your drawing board and Providence will do the rest' was Shaw's maxim for his friends and pupils after this stage.[142]

All these steps in the training of Shaw's pupils help to illumine a question frequently asked—how much did Shaw let his pupils design for him? The answer has to be hedged around with caveats. First, laymen have constantly to recall that architects' offices neither are nor were studios, producing masterpieces by individuals for the general public—the narrow, modern category which obstinately lodges itself in the art-historical mind. No architect produces his work in a vacuum, no building even by Webb or Voysey was dictated from first to last by its designer. Then, the evidence of drawings can rarely be conclusive. Pupils sign them for masters as a matter of convention, whether or not they are copies or original drawings; it was part of the terms of pupilage so to do, and no one expected otherwise. For instance, there are two schemes of 1878–9 clearly by Newton, one for small additions to a church, the other an unknown cottage, to which Newton automatically puts Shaw's signature because the jobs came through him.[143] In the concrete cottages also, it is impossible to know the proportions in which collaboration occurred. Detail drawings are merely 'soft' evidence of pupils' designs, one-eighth inch scale sheets are no guide at all. Finally, the example of Lethaby is not representative. In fact he is the only person for whom there is really 'hard' evidence. It comes firstly in the shape of the many general statements made about his role by people who must have known. The classic formulation is Beresford Pite's: 'That he played with the opportunities that Shaw's practice afforded him most of us know. Mr Shaw had the largeness to let Lethaby loose on his buildings; that is generally appreciated, or was appreciated in his day. That Shaw loved and valued Lethaby and gave him liberty in dealing with his work was the real estimate of his quality.'[144] There is evidence, too, in many detail drawings, in Lethaby's sketch-books, and on the sheet in which Shaw draws out a rough revised front for the School of Art at Bedford Park for Lethaby to 'work up'.[145] This, be it noted, was not a building designed by himself but by Maurice B. Adams of the *Building News*, never more than a hanger-on at Bloomsbury Square. Shaw expected no jealousy or impatience among his collaborators, nor was he the object of it, because he gave as freely as he received, and himself wanted no particular credit. Within the office this was well understood. It was only to the sticklers for credits that he had to explain his guiding principle: 'a good deal of so called "professional etiquette" I hold in slight regard, in comparison with the far more important question of getting a really good building.'[146]

Before the late 1870s it is hard to discern any collaborative work. Then things begin to change. A series of drawings in Newton's hand hints at differences in exterior detail: roughcast panels clipped at the corners between timbers at Ellern Mede (ill. 108) and on the first designs for Greenham, a quaint roadside fountain at Overbury, and prettily plastered ancillary buildings at Piccards Rough. One would like to know more too of the light yellow-plastered elevations of Piccards Rough itself (ill. 71), a fitting answer at last to the problems posed for Old English by the friable, loosely coursed stone of south west Surrey. Might the idea not be Newton's? Indisputably, by the time he left the office his role in designing was a vital one and had to be filled. The chief clerks who follow him, Lethaby and Percy Ginham, therefore take over from an established tradition. More will be said of both of them, here I merely anticipate a conclusion. In Lethaby's time, the plans are invariably all Shaw's; critical details are frequently Lethaby's; and the elevations, which remain in doubt, must have resulted from intimate collaboration. When Ginham takes over from Lethaby in 1889, the intimacy continues and can by chance be better illustrated, but it extends more into planning and less into elevation and detail.

190

But it would be a mistake to think of Shaw's later practice as just an exercise in constant collaboration. Keen says that many jobs were scarcely seen in the office at all.[147] At the only place in which Shaw's extant letters touch on the point, he assures Mrs Foster that he is designing all the details of the Richards Castle church himself.[148] The same is undoubtedly true of the Quadrant. Even while he was running a busy office, only the chief clerks had a really free hand. Other tempting attributions are so many guesses; Gerald Horsley may have done detail work for the Leek church, Harold Swainson perhaps contributed to East Combe. There are various lodges, cottages and stables which one might give to one pupil or another, but the hard evidence is lacking. What is more to the point is that it was neither overcommitment nor failing interest that forced Shaw into habitual delegation, but something more devastating—illness.

CHAPTER 5

Turning Point

> Your present system of architecture is to get a rascal of an Architect to order a rascal of a Clerk-of-the-Works to order a parcel of rascally bricklayers to build you a beastially stupid building in the middle of the town poisoned with gas, and with an iron floor which will drop you all through it some frosty evening; wherein you will bring a puppet of a cockney lecturer in a dress coat and white tie to tell you smugly there's no God.
>
> Anon., probably Ruskin, noted by Lethaby in a sketchbook.

ILLNESS

Breaking-point came in the autumn of 1879, only a month or two after Lethaby had arrived in Bloomsbury Square. Shaw had come back from a family holiday in the country and was settling down to a lengthening list of commitments, when he fell seriously ill. This cannot have been unexpected. His delicacy had shown itself before, and both Prior and Robert Shaw say that he had been poorly since 1876.[1] But this had never really impeded work, whereas now there was nothing for it but prolonged confinement. By the end of the year Shaw seemed to be better. He was down at Flete early in December, and in January 1880 visited the new wing of the Bournemouth convent. Illness troubled him all through the year, but he was able to do most of his business. Hoping that a change would have the required effect, he took a month's holiday abroad in June and July. But by August the mysterious malady was back. The doctors sent him away again, but enforced idleness did him no good, and for a second autumn he was confined to Ellerdale Road, communicating with the office by means of a stream of messages to his pupils. By the end of 1880 there was a nasty hiatus in Bloomsbury Square. The only major new job that Shaw had been able to undertake was the refronting of Barings; after overcommitment in 1879, he may have refused all overtures in the following calendar year.[2]

1881 marked the crisis. In January, Shaw wrote to Arthur Keen's father, advising a change of work for his son:

> I have been so little at my office for some time now, hardly at all for the last three months, and now I contemplate going away bodily for 2 or 3 months more, so that really he is working at the greatest possible disadvantage and to one at his age, this is a real calamity as he is certain to fall into bad ways more or less. What he must do, is to get into an office where there is more *business*, and where he will see a greater variety of

work . . . It is a great bore being seedy as I am at present, to say nothing of the loss and inconvenience but I know nothing for it but resignation and patience![3]

They were qualities he still fully needed. Early in February Shaw and his wife packed up and set off for the Riviera, which the baffled doctors in the fashion of the time were now recommending. His friends hardly expected to see him again. It was a sombre year for architects of all ages. The elder statesmen disappeared with the deaths of Salvin and Burton, but they were accompanied to the grave by Burges and by Street, both much younger. W. A. Nesfield had died in 1880, his son abruptly retired soon after. Now it seemed that architecture would have to go forward without Shaw as well. He himself stayed composed, wavering between the beliefs that he would return and that he was doomed to exile and slow decline. 'This is in many respects a lovely place, such beautiful vegetation, and the weather is good. But neither weather nor vegetation seems to make much difference to me, and I am getting very heartily tired of it.'[4]

For the good of the office and his own peace of mind, he occupied himself with a number of new jobs in and near London, including the Alliance Assurance Office, The Three Gables, and Frognal Priory; Ernest Newton came back as needed to help the practice on. Shaw certainly lacked no energy; the first ebullient designs for the Alliance were flung off and dispatched to London as soon as he received the relevant sketches and site plan.[5] In May 1881 he returned for the English summer, a holiday in Malvern, and a modicum of painful work and travel. He was no better. On a visit to inspect the completed Knight's Croft, Hubert Parry's little house at Rustington, Parry found him 'very nice and simple in his ways, but looks very ill.'[6] The only answer, decided the doctors, was the dry heat of Egypt, and thither in mid-September Shaw reluctantly bent his steps. But he never arrived. Stopping at Aix-les-Bains en route, he took the baths and immediately rallied. The Egyptian arrangement was cancelled, the improvement continued at Aix, and on 24th October 1881 Norman Shaw returned to England to preside over a revitalized practice.[7]

What Shaw's ailment was we do not know, but the cause of the crisis is easy to find—overwork. In a sense he was lucky that his constitution could not take the strain; the alternative was to continue at full pace for a few more years, like Street, only to collapse and die. Up till now, Shaw had been catholic in accepting work. We know of no clients who were refused, and if there were such it was not because their jobs were small or of the wrong kind. The account books abound with small payments for odd jobs and sundries during the 1870s.[8] There was a dribble of church restorations, always time-consuming and unremunerative, and of small house alterations. All of these stopped smartly after 1880, unless they accompanied bigger jobs or were for old customers like the Martins. Meanwhile Shaw had been accepting more and more large-scale works, until by 1880 his income exceeded £4,000 per annum, just about twice what it had been in 1870. 1877–9 marks the climax of his early practice. At this time, Shaw had four of his largest country houses in nearly simultaneous erection. Adcote, unfinished till 1880, and Flete, where building stuttered on from 1878 to 1883, were continuous drains on his cares and energy, while no sooner had Pierrepont been completed in 1878 than Greenham Lodge was on the books. Then, the smaller houses he designed in this period were by and large bigger than their counterparts two and three years before; Alderbrook, Baldslow Place and Piccards Rough all cost appreciably more than Ellern Mede and Merrist Wood in a period of steady prices. Finally, Shaw got himself caught up at this moment in a number of unusual and time-consuming schemes which absorbed any energy remaining from his normal commitments. 'I have been so driven out of my mind lately with work, here, there, and everywhere,' he told Murray Marks at the end of 1877.[9] At that stage he had probably made most of his designs for Lascelles, the concrete cottages, the furniture, and the Jury House to be shown in Paris. But there were two other projects for which his responsibilities had hardly begun: Albert Hall Mansions and Bedford Park.

In the circumstances it is remarkable that neither was a humiliating failure. The briefs Shaw was given in either case were to produce designs and then slip gracefully back into normal practice. What happened was that the different problems absorbed him, time was somehow found for them, and what had started out as a peripheral involvement ended by being identified entirely with his name. The concepts of the high-rise flat or of a new structure for the middle-class suburb were not ideas that Shaw's type of mind could ever have originated. What he could do was to break down such things into hard, real terms, to translate original conceptions into remarkable buildings. His own originalities were invariably empirical.

Albert Hall Mansions

Much of Shaw's Edwardian career was to depend upon his ability to take schemes by the scruff of the neck and knock them fast and ruthlessly into shape. Albert Hall Mansions, his first experiment in this cavalier freelance architecture, foreshadowed in many ways future complexities of design procedure. The prehistory of the project is not easy to follow, but enough is known to prove that Shaw did not himself elect the disparity of scale between Lowther Lodge and its neighbour, Albert Hall Mansions.[10] The area round the Albert Hall was ripe for development, so ripe that not even the gardens of the Royal Horticultural Society could escape. When Shaw made his first plans for Lowther Lodge, he had drawn up an intriguing scheme for three detached blocks, probably separate residences rather than chambers or flats, for a thin strip of land on the east of the site running from Kensington Gore along the west side of Exhibition Road to the present corner with Prince Consort Road. This strip had been bought by William Lowther from the Royal Commission for the 1851 Exhibition, who owned nearly all the quadrilateral bounded by Kensington Gore, Queen's Gate, Exhibition Road, and Cromwell Road. Lowther did not pursue his scheme of speculation, and this side of the garden remained unbuilt upon into this century. But at the south end of his plot, J. J. Stevenson built Lowther Gardens in 1877–8. By this time, the Commission was hoping to recoup some of its losses on the 1862 Exhibition by estate development on the fine site facing the Park immediately west of Lowther Lodge.

The Commissioners' intention to develop so close by must have been made clear to Shaw and Lowther when they built. It is less likely that they had foreknowledge of the type of development which matured. When Henry Hunt, the Commissioners' surveyor, first raised the matter in 1875, there was still a possibility that single houses might be built, though Hunt advocated 'a large pile of buildings to be used for Residential Chambers something similar to the Belgrave Mansions on the Duke of Westminster's Estate.'[11] Whatever their expectations, there was no lack of communication. Lowther made no claim for compensation when Albert Hall Mansions was built, and as early as June 1875 Shaw had become consultant architect to the Commissioners. 196 Queen's Gate, built like all Shaw's houses on this street on the Commission's property, had perhaps convinced them that the crusade against stucco was a worthy one, and that its architect was a competent man of business. Possibly, too, there was pressure from above. There were fingers enough in the pie; the Queen would want something respectful to Albert's memory; Lowther would wish to keep up the tone of the neighbourhood and to have something as harmonious as possible with his house if he had really to put up with the height now talked of; the South Kensington Museum establishment had its view, certainly anti-stucco but by no means necessarily favourable to Shaw; and perhaps the Commissioners' Chairman, Earl Spencer, had his own ideas. All this is worth repeating because Albert Hall Mansions is the archetype of similar Edwardian situations. The decision taken as to Shaw's responsibilities is archetypal too; that he should prepare a façade design to which the speculator must then conform. This is not how Cubitt built Belgravia, nor were there many precedents in London of a special frontage for a key site, dictated by pressures of public responsibility and prestige rather than motives of mere commercial gain and exclusiveness. There is more than a whiff in all this of Haussmann's Paris.[12]

The eventual choice of a 'mansions' block, too, is redolent of Paris. Often building types, having made their debut in response to need, gain their own momentum and proliferate with less regard for real requirements. Hospitals and asylums, for all their value amidst the desperate state of sanitation, became the object of architectural fashion and political ambition in the 1860s, just as high-rise blocks achieved a similar history a hundred years later. Albert Hall Mansions belongs to such a craze, but a truncated one. There was, it seemed in the mid-1870s, a dearth in London's western areas of 'chambers' for wealthy bachelors, and of houses for well-off small families who did not want to buy and who perhaps spent little time in town. The easy answer to their wants was the apartment block, which had come a long way over the previous thirty years. But there were still very few fashionable flats. As yet, the speculators had not overcome the old British prejudice against lateral dwelling, an aversion fostered by the fondness of the philanthropic trusts for plain blocks of flats as a means of housing the deserving poor.[13] Flats for the fashionable classes demanded a grander lavishness than these, and were hardly attempted before 1870. The precedent that Hunt had in mind was Grosvenor Gardens (1865–8), which included one or two small blocks of flats interspersed amid its fashionable French-style town houses. These had evidently done well, but by 1875 competition was stiffer. Mr Hankey's great mansions in Queen Anne's Gate, higher than anything before and begun in 1874, were at first slow to catch on.[14] Most speculators wanted to see how this venture would let before following suit. So when Thomas Hussey, a Kensington builder, took the lease for the eligible site of Albert Hall Mansions, he at first suggested a row of high-class houses. Then in October 1876, persuaded perhaps by Hunt, he switched his proposal and brought forward a scheme for 'mansions'. Even so, it seemed

The·ALBERT·HALL·MANSIONS·COMPANY·Limited·

·KENSINGTON·

146. Albert Hall Mansions, scheme of 1877, with floor plans by C. H. Driver and C. H. Rew, and perspective of Shaw's proposed elevation.

for a time that Hussey and others like him had miscalculated the market. In November 1878 his solicitors, pressing for delay, reported that the new mansions in South Kensington were still empty, and that two out of three builders in this kind of venture were failing. The Commissioners, more indulgent than many authorities, obliged him; they did not want a bankrupt on their hands.[15]

At this stage, Shaw as well as Hussey favoured delay. The reason was simple; he was on the verge of taking over the whole job, in which he had now become immersed. When their collaboration started in 1876, Shaw had drawn out a general elevation to eighty feet to fit the block plan of Hussey's houses. When the scheme was changed to flats, the company which backed Hussey wanted more height, and in July 1877 their architect C. H. Driver submitted an elevation. This then went back to Shaw, who in October produced a compromise to the agreement of all parties (ill. 146). On its merits he was lukewarm, saying merely, 'I am quite prepared to "father" this design, for I have drawn it all myself and have taken a good deal of pains with it—it is a ponderous affair.'[16] There for the time the matter stuck, because of the building difficulties. The commissioners had other schemes in Queen's Gate which aborted too. Here in 1877–8 they had again

196

147. Albert Hall Mansions, street façade of front block.

asked Shaw to draw up elevations for two separate rows of speculative houses, but neither could be agreed upon with the developer. Like them, it looked as though Albert Hall Mansions, with its elegant inner court and communal dining hall and restaurant, might never be built.[17]

Then at the end of 1878, Hussey and Shaw came to an agreement. To escape failure, they divided the block plan into three distinct entities which could be built in separate stages, thus lowering the financial risks; and they altered the internal plan by introducing split-level flats with self-contained stairs which would appeal to the traditional English mentality. The new scheme abolished the communal dining facilities, and concentrated instead on high-class and high-rent family flats with reception rooms overlooking the park. It was put in outline to the Commissioners in March 1879 and gratefully accepted. In July, Shaw betook himself to Paris to study flats, in the company of Ernest Newton.[18] This was now a heavy job, and entirely his responsibility.

The expertise which Shaw and Newton acquired in Paris hardly affected the exterior; there was time yet before Shaw would admire the street architecture of the Third Republic. In fact his earlier Kensington Gore frontage, though less powerful an elevation,

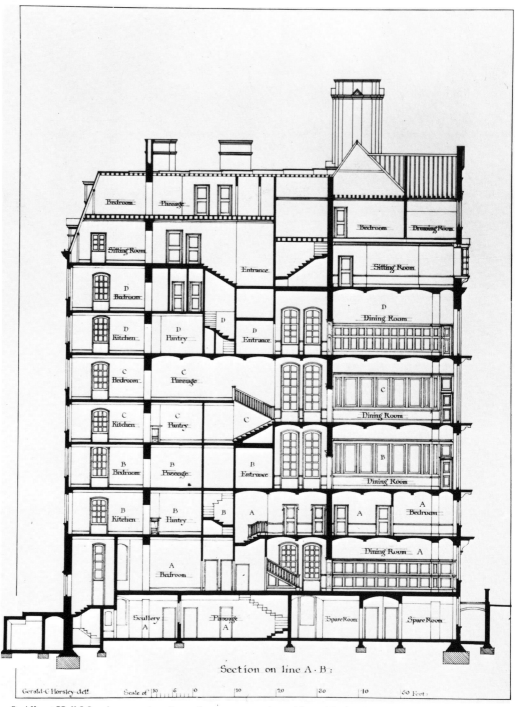

Section on line A·B:

Gerald·C·Horsley·delt.   Scale of   Scale labels   50 Feet.

148. Albert Hall Mansions, section through western portion of front block, 1879.

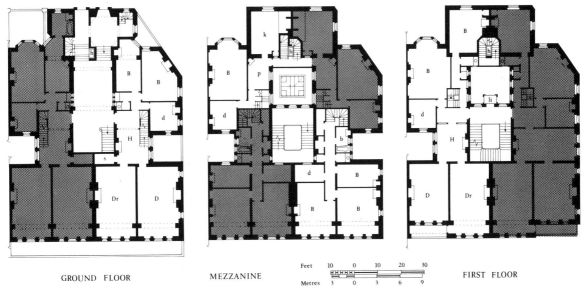

GROUND FLOOR   MEZZANINE

Feet   10   0   10   20   30

Metres   3   0   3   6   9

FIRST FLOOR

149. Albert Hall Mansions, ground, mezzanine and first floor plans showing western portion of front block, with the different flats indicated.

was better suited to the site. The 'ponderous' hundred foot height had been settled and could not be changed; now Hussey wanted to pile as much accommodation as he could into the front block. So Shaw dropped the through carriageway under the middle of the building, and brought the frontage well forward, with only the shallowest of front areas and of recessions in the upper storeys (ill. 147). With varying success, Shaw strove to lighten the solid aspect of this façade by means of balconies. Over the mezzanine level, a balcony runs the whole length of the front, to prevent the height from overpowering the passer-by. Thence upwards, the balconies in the recesses seem to step back the façade to roof level. Yet the upper balconies beneath the gables lie no further back, and Shaw even uses the licence the building regulations gave him above the main cornice, to thrust his attic windows forward of the line of frontage. The breaks he fills with pairs of another type of balcony, this time covered and arched in brick. As a device to tie the front together, these odd, bounding features are good, but their cavernous forms are too nervous to cohere with the patterns of plain brickwork and triple windows upon which Shaw elsewhere relies. Albert Hall Mansions is blatantly too large and strong, for all his efforts to conceal the fact.

A few peculiarities in the plans and sections of the front block (ills. 148, 149) must be pointed out.[19] From French planning Shaw borrowed the principle of a large public lobby and finely graduated stairs. His treatment of the staircase is far plainer and less curvaceous than the Parisian equivalent, eschewing winders.[20] Today, the spacious toplit entrance hall has been halved by a modern liftshaft. Originally, there was only a service lift from ground level, and the passenger lift did not begin until the first floor. Since the staircase does not 'arrive' at mezzanine level, which is devoted only to flats with entrances above and below, tenants must have been expected to climb not just one flight but two, and to take the lift on from there.[21]

The plan also avoids common corridors on the main floors, never an easy thing to manage. The entrance hall, front and back stairs, and large area make a thrice-repeated unit, but even then Shaw makes radical changes in each because of the shape of the ends of the site, so that the western unit here shown is an inexact guide to its neighbours. In section, there are no repeats at all; each flat takes its own plan from the shape of the one below, and passes on its idiosyncrasies to its neighbour above. Thus the ground floor flats (A) actually belong to three floors; the first floor flats (B) partition the mezzanine with those below but proceed no higher, and are therefore on two levels only; the second floor flats (C) restore the unity of levels by occupying only one storey at the front for two at the back, and so forth. At the top, the flats break out into gloomy corridors and small apartments without obvious service facilities, perhaps for bachelors who ate out, perhaps for servants.[22] The split-level planning with reception rooms of reduced height recurs on all but the top levels. Today, the single split-level survivor is no. 29, high up in the eastern unit; all the other flats have been subdivided and converted.

There are certainly faults in the planning of Albert Hall Mansions. The toplighting of the stairs is adequate but monotonous, so that an ascent is unrelieved and weary. There are many drab passages, internal lower down, public at the top. 'Objectionable' features can easily be found. On ground level, flat A has an unventilated W.C., anathema to the sanitary reformers, which with the housemaid's sink next to it borrows light from the toplit entrance hall; and the neighbouring bedroom appears poorly lit. The kitchens, well placed in proximity to the service lift and back stairs, are often remote from the dining rooms, especially in the ground floor flats. Nevertheless, Albert Hall Mansions ranks as Shaw's most intense study in concentrated planning, and the first of England's few great blocks of flats.

The successors to this front part of Albert Hall Mansions (1879–81), were less publicized. To fill out the 'grand piano' site, Hussey built two blocks on more conventional lines to the south. The plans of both are definitely Shaw's, though after his illness his involvement with the project may have diminished. The western block (1883–4) comprised three big flats on each floor, again cleverly planned to fit the curving site, but without any splitting of levels and with a lift descending to the ground floor. The eastern block (1885–6) occupied a yet more irregular piece of land, and here Shaw provided straightforward internal corridors. In both cases the elevations are of the simplest. How much of the interior detailing was Shaw's it is hard to say, even with the front block. C. H. Driver fades from the story after 1879, so perhaps his firm was paid off. Many of the fireplaces and other details are Shaw's, yet others are not. In the later blocks, there are features in the public areas which suggest another architect rather than mere builder's work. Probably Shaw provided a set of frequently re-used details, and in the 1880s Hussey went elsewhere for decorative work. The total sum Shaw earned from Albert Hall Mansions comes well below five per cent of the building cost. But Shaw was happy enough with the arrangements. At about the time he drew up plans for the front block, he was helping Hussey develop another site, by providing him with plans and simple elevations for three-storey flats in the Cromwell Road. These were to be built with

200

a plain corridor plan, but Shaw produced an alternative showing how the elevation could be used if preferred for houses, not flats. They were eventually erected in 1882–3, but in a vulgarized form.

BEDFORD PARK

Today's visitor to Bedford Park will scarcely sense himself, like the American artist Edwin Abbey, 'walking through a water-colour', or recognize a lineal descendant of the Rabelaisian Thelema in twentieth-century Turnham Green.[23] Many even with an eye for architecture must pass it by, noticing nothing special save the group of Tabard Inn, church and vicarage by the narrow, noisy Bath Road. The houses that radiate northwards from this nucleus merge quietly into the later suburbs which engulf them, and which borrow both the cut of their clothing and their length of dress; the same styles a little more debased, the same narrow plots and plot ratios, the same streets carry onwards towards Acton beyond the bounds of Jonathan Carr's original estate.

A closer look rather aggravates than appeases puzzlement. It is not just that the district has fallen on hard times; from the hardest it is now fast recovering. The houses, however charming, are sometimes ill-finished. Materials and workmanship defy prediction. Some of the brick detailing is good, but some seems crude and elephantine. The joinery, better equipped to withstand vulgarization, varies between the flat and broad and the starved; the balusters on the balconies appear here as plain sticks, there in the cheap, minimally turned forms beloved of every London builder, and only occasionally burgeon into the full-blooded bulbousness of true Queen Anne taste. At fifty feet, the roads are of little above average width for the day. The plots, a mere seventy-five feet deep with a fifty foot frontage and little space at the sides, are niggardly compared to other middle-class suburbs of the time.[24] The banishment of the basement, too, only confirms the best suburban practice of the previous twenty years. The front gardens are too cramped for anything but turfing, and must look for their shade and privacy to the limes and planes planted in the streets, or the old trees left when the estate was developed. Truly, the opaque and misty clouds of Abbey's watercolour seem sometimes to have wrapped themselves around the generation that sketched or wrote of the idyll that was Bedford Park.

A jaundiced judgment of Jonathan Carr's enterprise can be plausibly made out. Here was a cloth-merchant-cum-property-speculator-cum-dilettante, buying an estate at Turnham Green without the proper financial means to lay it out, securing house designs from one eminent architect, E. W. Godwin, and then transferring to another, Norman Shaw. While allowing their designs to be carried out without the proper care, Carr, it could be said, used the names of Godwin and Shaw and the pen of his art-critic brother to sell his speculation to a troop of like-minded men, second-rate artists and members of the professions with an ostentatious taste for culture and an ambition to rival better-off people in the West End. They, in response to the latest fashion, flocked to Bedford Park, where they embellished their villas with the sunflower, emblem of constancy, and with sentimental names such as 'Kirk Lees', 'Elm-dene' and 'Ye Denne'. They put on exhibitions at the Art School, they listened to extension lectures at the Club, they borrowed books from the Grosvenor Gallery, and generally found in their transmogrified existence there an answer to W. H. Mallock's testing question, 'Is life worth living?'[25] That is the view that an independent contemporary might have come to from a saunter round Bedford Park, and a brief perusal of that early bluffers' guide to art, Walter Hamilton's *The Aesthetic Movement in England* (1882).

But if Bedford Park gave the garden suburb a dubious pedigree, it was a genuine enough parent. Without Carr's flair for publicity, without Shaw's talents at planning, without the advent of the cultivated middle classes, the designers of Hampstead Garden Suburb would have made some very different choices thirty years later. There were originalities, too, not so much in the lay-out as in house-style and house-planning, and more critically, in the social structure of the suburb, which were vital for later developments. For these social changes, Carr's techniques of propaganda were essential. The church, the club, the inn, the stores and the tennis court were no longer erected by a squire to admonish the tenants of their grateful duties and loyalties, but built by a 'promoter' to service the leisure and the options of an independent community. Just like the poster of advertisement devised for the stations on the new line out to Turnham Green, these facilities 'sold' Bedford Park and were put up only after the first housebuilding campaign, to increase the value of the wares already on display. Again, the new houses were cheap, unornamented and small, renting from between £45 and £100 per annum, but they were decidedly charming. This is what made the artists and critics myopic to the defects. Here were houses where the cultured classes, leisured but without large income or many servants, could dwell in mutual daily intercourse, unembarrassed by the excesses of villadom. There was not a huge class of such people, but it was increasing; Comyns Carr and his cronies on *Harpers Magazine*, *The Magazine of Art* and so on saw to that. It was their accession to Bedford Park which made the community so strong and homogeneous. Others could design and publish cottages like these without a whimper of interest. But Jonathan Carr had his finger on the popular artistic magazines, and built consciously for their public. So curiously, from questionable beginnings, arose a project having more interest and relevance to the twentieth-century mind than any of Shaw's more ambitious achievements.

Shaw had no initial contact with the scheme, and nothing at all to do with the lay-out. He was not, nor were other high-ranking architects of his generation, a town-planner.[26] It was typical of Carr's methods that the lay-out should have been made by an unknown surveyor, and Godwin, its first architect, chosen on the basis of a pretty perspective of a country parsonage in the *Building News*.[27] What Godwin was asked to do (and this is important) was to produce a pair of house designs for re-use many times over. He was sacked soon enough, when William Woodward chose one of them to try and give 'high art' architecture a bloody nose. Woodward will reappear in our story. At the time he was just a pugnacious surveyor with the vice of writing too much and too often to the building press, but on this occasion there was much of substance in his criticism of Godwin's plans.[28] In reply, Carr meekly promised to do better. Doing better meant abandoning one of Godwin's designs, amending the other, relying less on his second-string architects (Coe and Robinson) and going early in 1877 for a set of new detached and semi-detached designs to Mr Norman Shaw.

A single pencil drawing is all that remains of Shaw's house designs for Bedford Park. Happily Maurice B. Adams, an enthusiast for Carr's scheme and very soon a resident, published them in the *Building News*. It is plain that Carr started by asking Shaw for precisely what he had from Godwin, a design for a semi-detached pair and a design for a detached house. The detached type, less in demand but several times used, stayed in currency until 1879, when Shaw produced a replacement. But to meet difficulties of planning and cost, Shaw made three attempts in 1877–8 to refine the more popular semi-detached type. His efforts proved successful and no further criticism was heard. By late 1877, Shaw had designed an experimental terrace block of three and four storeys, and the Bedford Park Club. Soon his responsibilities were extended to Carr's own house, the new church, and the stores, and to a general supervision over the whole estate. It was another case of a small brief expanding into a huge one.

The house designs were paid for direct; they were Carr's to do what he liked with, to be built with any modifications the individual tenant might desire, according to the resources of the ordinary builders and estate workmen employed. The plans had therefore to be simple and flexible, not just pretty, as Godwin's had been. In Shaw's three attempts at the semi-detached type, he tried to give a dignified lobby and entrance hall, a front drawing room of 18×14 ft. exclusive of bay, a dining room 16×13 ft., and a well-lighted kitchen. Obviously, compass for manoeuvre was small; the reception rooms had to go against the party wall and the kitchen at the back, so it was mainly the stairs and inner hall with which he played. The first scheme (A) was built only twice (ill. 150). It proved unsatisfactory because the drawing room bay was skimped for the sake of an independent small window next to it, and the upper stairs were separated from the lower ones, reducing the size of the first floor bedrooms. These faults vanished in the second semi-detached design (B), which has an attractive elevation, with roughcast coving and broad bays crowned by balconies (ill. 151). But there were now different problems. The flat-topped bays required an expensive iron joist over to support the wall above, and the carpentry was beyond the capabilities of Carr's joiners. Indeed, Carr was to explain in 1880 that he had had to abandon large bay windows and complicated joinery for just these reasons.[29] Because of cost, even the pretty white-painted fences planned for the estate were rarely carried out. The only Queen Anne woodwork decoration regularly executed on the later houses were the two-piece hoods over the doorways, designed by E. J. May.[30] Shaw's third semi-detached design (C), stuck to a similar plan but got over these problems by reducing the bay again (ill. 152). Instead, he carried it up on one side only into the roof, to increase the surface area of first floor and attic bedrooms. This eliminated the need for girders, reduced the external woodwork, and created a picturesque if lopsided design. The same principle of topheavy, multi-storey roughcast bays occurs also in the Woodstock Road terrace. An alternative all-brick elevation was sometimes adopted to go with design C, presumably to suit clients who preferred the Queen Anne style.

The detached designs, which were to fit corner sites, are independent of each other (ills. 153, 154). Shaw's 1877 plan (D) is uneconomic. He allows himself three outside chimney-breasts and puts in a small third reception room, while the exterior is given a complicated roof and tile-hung, to conform to Godwin's detached design. This tile-hanging soon disappeared. When the A.A. first visited Bedford Park in 1877, Carr told

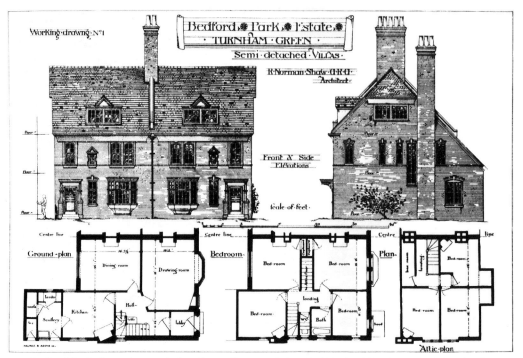

150. Bedford Park, floor plans and elevations of first semi-detached design (A), drawn by Maurice B. Adams, 1877.

151. Bedford Park, floor plans and elevations of second semi-detached design (B), drawn by Maurice B. Adams, 1877.

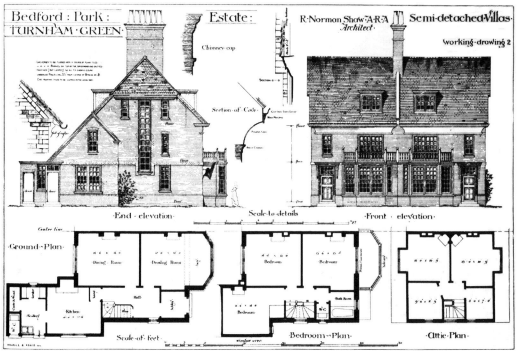

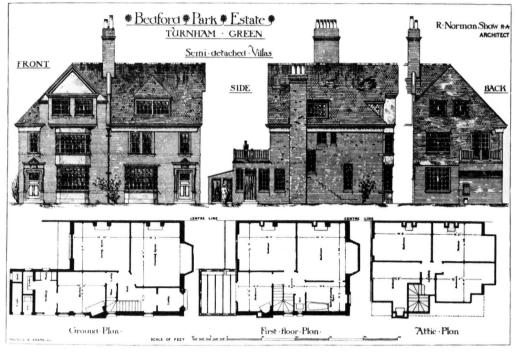

* Bedford * Park * Estate *

TURNHAM · GREEN

Semi-detached Villas

R·Norman·Shaw R·A·
ARCHITECT

FRONT

SIDE

BACK

CENTRE LINE

CENTRE LINE

Ground · Plan ·

SCALE OF FEET

First · floor · Plan ·

Attic · Plan

152. Bedford Park, floor plans and elevations of third semi-detached design (C), drawn by Maurice B. Adams, 1878.

them it was as cheap as brickwork because savings were made on pointing; those who returned in 1880 heard that moulded brick was now the preferred decoration because tile-hanging involved going over the work twice.[31] Duly, Shaw's second detached scheme (E) relies only on brickwork and is more plainly planned, with two good reception rooms and a preference for angle fireplaces.[32]

Since Shaw's hands were tied in the design of these small houses, they may not exactly represent his choice for domestic style in the suburbs. Besides the limitation of cost and skills, the precedence of Godwin directed him. Godwin began Bedford Park with the axiom that his *Building News* country parsonage was what was wanted, and therefore built small tile-hung houses. Shaw in his first detached design (D) felt bound to follow, and also hung the ends of his first semi-detached scheme (A). If left to himself from the start, he might have omitted the obvious mannerisms of Old English. The final results, using some cut and moulded brickwork, some roughcast gables, and some Queen Anne joinery, are compromises he may not have wished, and confuse the issue of two distinguishable styles.

In his last three projects for Bedford Park, Shaw took pains to make the elements of his design simpler for inexperienced builders to handle. It was trying to him, but the chance seemed unique and worth persevering in. He had to mix the aggregate of the styles so as to make a satisfactory cement for the whole suburb; hence his special effort at exploration in The Tower House, Stores and Church. By the time that these three were embarked upon, the Club was already up and functioning. Robert Shaw says it was

153. (left) Bedford Park, 36 The Avenue, built to first detached design (D).

154. (above) Bedford Park, 6 Bedford Road, built to second detached design (E).

designed by May, but it was at least published as Shaw's. It was a plain Queen Anne building on The Avenue overlooking the tennis courts and the site of Carr's garden, and incorporating assembly and committee rooms, and a billiard room for either sex. In its interior, the social and decorative climax of the estate, tapestry alternated with Japanese paper on the walls, and there was furniture by Godwin, Morris and Jackson, tiles by De Morgan, and a large mantelpiece exhibited at Paris by Aldam Heaton.[33] Together with The Tower House, the 'promoter's' home next door, the Club gave Bedford Park a much-needed second focus. Today this other centre has been forever lost, and the Club stands forlorn and mutilated. The southern end of The Avenue is closed on one side by flats erected when Carr eventually failed, and on the Club side by modern shops hemming in eighteenth century Bedford House—together barring the estate from an outlook to the green and the railway. To the north, more flats have replaced The Tower House itself, destroying one of Shaw's best designs and distorting the whole picture of the estate.

At The Tower House (ills. 155, 156), Shaw first began to yield to the temptation to make the independent house fully symmetrical. Street fronts of course often demanded symmetry; three of his Chelsea Embankment houses were regular, and in other façades like New Zealand Chambers or 196 Queen's Gate he deviated less or more from it. In the country house Shaw still felt symmetry to be an imposition, but what of the suburban house on a free site? In the five years since Lowther Lodge, Shaw had come a little to terms with classic formality; now at The Tower House he was ready to entertain more of it. The

206

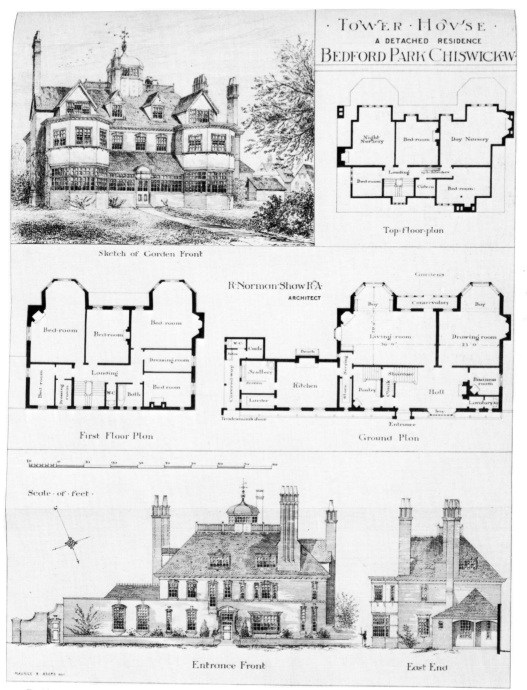

· TOWER · HOV'SE ·
A DETACHED RESIDENCE
BEDFORD PARK CHISWICK·W·

Sketch of Garden Front

Top·floor·plan

R·Norman·Shaw·R·A·
ARCHITECT

First Floor Plan

Ground Plan

Scale · of · feet ·

Entrance Front

East End

155. Bedford Park, The Tower House, floor plans and perspective of garden side, drawn by Maurice B. Adams, 1879.

156. Bedford Park, Bedford Road in 1881, with The Tower House in the background.

157. Bedford Park, Bath Road in 1881, with St Michael's Church and The Tabard.

front, only four feet back from the pavement in Bedford Road was still irregular, if plain. But to the garden side, visible from the Club roof and The Avenue, Shaw allotted a symmetrical elevation that was the chaste and pretty epitome of the Bedford Park ideal. All round the house he respected the cornice line, forcing most of the chimneys to rise from the roof with only two of the familiar breasts down the walls, confining the dormers, and stopping the eaves from running over. To mark the end of the war between roof and walls, he presented both with a resplendent award: to the walls, a white-painted pair of double-storey bays to living room and drawing room, flattened off under the cornice; to the roof, a belvedere looking forth to the rival cupola topping the church. The idea must come from Cromwell House, Highgate, or one of the other members of the 'artisan-mannerist' group of brick and wood houses of the 1630s that are the true English ancestors of Queen Anne.[34] The bland plan and hipped roof of The Tower House show Shaw looking more carefully now at such seventeenth-century houses, and paying a first conscious homage to their formality. The type was to haunt his mind for a decade.

The Tower House was finished in 1879, and in 1879–80 Shaw supplied the church on the north side of Bath Road and the 'hostelry' and stores on the other (ill. 157). The Tabard was a multifunctional building, comprising small public and private bars, a 'coffee and commercial room', a meeting room upstairs, and capacious stores 'conducted on the same principles as the "Civil Service" and other large co-operative establishments.'[35] Shaw's inspiration for the design was said to be Staple Inn, the group of gabled houses on the south side of Holborn.[36] If so, he articulated the seven gables quite differently, and brought the whole lengthy elevation under one massive roof vying with the church opposite. It was hard work fitting the needs of innkeeper and shopkeeper to a satisfactory elevation. Eventually the three separate shops coalesced into one big one, and access to the meeting room became tied up with the cut and moulded 'house fronts' in the centre.[37] These Shaw slightly recessed, extending the brickwork up into the first storey so as to pepper the middle of this merry piece of town-house vernacular with a dash of Queen Anne. Still, the building is too long to be well seen face on from the street, the gables too regular and unemphatic for a good side view. Once again, The Tabard seems to have been put up by Carr's workmen, whence the limp window and brickwork detailing familiar from the houses. The local residents consoled themselves with aesthetic paraphernalia: T. M. Rooke's inn sign, De Morgan tiles in bar and meeting room and Walter Crane reliefs.

Opposite stands the enigmatic St Michael's (ills. 157, 213). It was a puzzle to people then, it is still something of a puzzle now. How much is this a 'joke' church? How far would the devout Shaw dare to parody his employers in, of all places, a sacred edifice? He was toying at this time with informal styles for churches, in the little chapel at Peplow (ill. 215), and the parallel St Mark's Cobourg Road (ill. 209), perky buildings both. But St Michael's Bedford Park is a thing apart. Everywhere the image of the staid Victorian theatre thrusts itself forward: seven grand steps up to the chancel, where the action occurs, a 'proscenium' screen in three sections, and easeful benches down in the panelled nave, painted a sage green like all the woodwork (ill. 223).[38] But if the church is theatrical it is not dramatic, for in order to fit it to Tractarian worship, Shaw, with sly paradox, has imported into the setting the demure atmosphere of Nonconformity. In his pliant hands,

St Michael's becomes the comfortable auditorium where independent, clear-thinking folk can watch the enactment of the Lord's Supper without loss of self-respect, without over-involvement, without incongruity with their other social activities. At a blow, the tension and vehemence of the mid-Victorian church is laid low. St Michael's symptomatizes a new attitude towards church-going. It is less a parody than a bold and perceptive character study of a community.

Curiously, the stylistic peculiarity of the church began with Wren. At first Carr had wanted to re-use the oakwork from Wren's St Dionis Backchurch (just then being demolished) in the same position in his new church, and talked even of rebuilding its tower on the site.[39] In the event, pieces of the panelling, doorways, pews and organ-case from St Dionis went into The Tower House and the Club, but none appears to have been used in the church. However, echoes of a Wren church, updated, lingered in Shaw's design. Only in terms of such mongrel mixing of Gothic and Queen Anne for the details could contemporaries grapple with its eccentricity. Street, for instance, growled at the 'very novel and not very ecclesiastical style' adopted by his old pupil.[40] Some mirth was caused at the A.A. visit in 1880 by the inaccessible clerestory balconies in the interior, others objected to the oddity of the aisle roofs and to the exterior leadwork and balcony. But objections were on the whole subdued; the prancing pen of Woodward failed to perform its antics on this easy victim. The details are of course adapted to the skills and materials available, so that balconies proliferate but stone carving is minimized. Once more, the woodwork is uneven. The plain braces and trusses, carrying cross forms and riding six times unaltered through nave and chancel, constitute the best church roof Shaw ever designed; the green benches are charmingly revolutionary. But the two-stage cupola and porch hood are too clumsy and fussy for the church. Broadly speaking, the outside pleases less than the inside. The roof, prophetic of Lutyens' church at Hampstead Garden Suburb, unifying nave and aisles in a grand sweep and sinking the clerestory windows in deep reveals, is too hemmed in by Shaw's own porch, covings, parapets and balconies, and by Adams' later hall and south-east chapel, to reveal the fullness of its figure.

St Michael's and the Tabard mark the end of Shaw's work at Bedford Park. His relationship with Jonathan Carr, never perfect, was aggravated by the vexed questions of supervision and payment. He was probably never paid all he was owed, receiving a paltry £1,125 for all his work and expenses there. Years later, when Fred White brought Carr round to see Shaw, he took the unusual step of asking White not to repeat such a visit.[41] May and Adams, who had both settled at Bedford Park, took over his role, but May stayed only briefly. Like Shaw, he had 'tired of old Carr' by 1881 after designing the fine vicarage, and, though he built further houses there, he soon moved away.[42] Adams stayed on even after Carr failed in 1886, and designed further houses. It was his less than competent design for the Chiswick School of Art which provoked Shaw's last-known sally into design at Bedford Park, a freehand sketch emending Adams' elevation. This he sent to Lethaby to knock into shape, in order to prevent, as he put it, the imminence of bloodshed.[43]

158. Flete, east front.

FLETE

Flete can stand for the burdens a country house commission might bring. In its way it was a satisfactory job. Shaw was paid a clear thousand pounds more for his work there than his combined receipts from Albert Hall Mansions and Bedford Park, and went on to alter the town house of his client, H. B. Mildmay, in 1888. Mildmay was blessed with both ancient Devonian lineage and a partnership in Barings. He was the richest of Shaw's clients yet and determined to enjoy his affluence. Though he lost very heavily in the Barings crash of 1890, he escaped with Flete and the pick of his newly bought pictures intact.

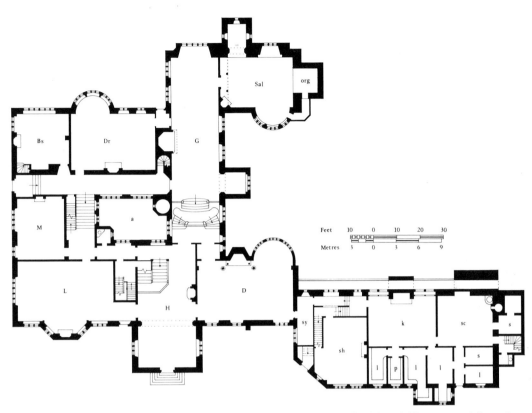

Feet 10 0 10 20 30

Metres 3 0 3 6 9

159. (left) Flete, kitchen wing.   160. (above) Flete, ground floor plan.

Flete was an old house, substantially rebuilt in about 1620 and since much altered and enlarged, most recently in a coarse Gothic of 1835 for J. C. Bulteel, Mildmay's father-in-law. It was just one of three good houses on the family estate; the others were Pamflete, an old farmhouse, and Mothecombe, the sweet Georgian dower house overlooking the mouth of the Erme and Bigbury Bay. Three spectacular miles of private drive built by Bulteel along the luxuriant Erme estuary linked and still link the three houses; in those days the road meandered many further miles on to Membland, home of Mildmay's partner and kinsman Lord Revelstoke, the head of Barings. But while Membland and Mothecombe look out to the sea, Flete itself, well inland, is only skirted to the east by the Erme and looks northwards to the granite crags of Dartmoor. Lavishly rich within, grey and dourly crenellated without, Shaw's Flete captures the privacy and pride with which this banking baron wished to endue his huge estate (ills. 158, 159).

Bulteel had sold the house and moved to Pamflete, but in 1876 Mildmay bought it back in a very dilapidated state. Next year he called in Shaw, and the Mildmays retired to Mothecombe pending reconstruction. They made the mistake of tackling the task piecemeal. At first Shaw's brief was to set the old plan to rights and put the entrance back into the centre of the western, Jacobean wing, flanked symmetrically by the library and dining room on either side of the forecourt. Though the 1835 additions had made a muddle of the plan, it was as much as Shaw could do to remove the dining room from the

213

middle of the house and locate it nearer the kitchens. The Mildmays seem to have insisted that the reconstruction should be planned and carried out in stages, that the block plan of the house should be exactly retained, that the battlemented style of the additions should be followed, and that the lines of the old reception rooms should be kept wherever possible.[44] Under these cramping conditions, Shaw was expected to rebuild Flete from top to toe. Gradually he got more liberty for himself, but the result was his least characteristic exterior and plan. From the latter at least he dissociated himself.[45] It conforms only to the traditional image of a Shaw plan (ill. 160): a collection of set-piece effects like the spectacular stairs (ill. 162), gallery and reception rooms, alternating with rambling corridors, steps up and down, and a battery of offices and chambers for all sorts and conditions of servant and appliance.

Planning and replanning took the scheme into 1879 before work began in earnest. Frank Birch was the builder, under Newton's direction; it was his last and most exacting work for Shaw, and may have ruined him. Then Shaw fell ill. This meant that the auxiliaries took over more extensively than ever before for the interior detailing. Heaton and Lascelles were both on the job, and at Flete one first sees Lethaby, himself a Devon man, coming into his own. He was on site in 1880, making notes on fittings and arrangements, preparing for Lascelles to panel the library ceiling and drawing out

161. (left) Flete, the gallery.

162. (right) Flete, main staircase.

details.[46] Soon he was designing doorways, fireplaces, lockcases, and finally in 1883 the beautiful organ-case for the reconstituted saloon, which marked the end of the work. Imps, Jack-in-the-Greens, strapwork, and all the frothier rustic motifs of Jacobean ornament adorn the friezes and ceilings of Flete, suggested maybe by the creatures that run amok amidst the benches and screens of the nearby village churches.[47] But Lethaby was already after something plainer and purer. It was apparently he who perfected the lengthy gallery along the western wing (ill. 161), by curling twelve steps down to ground level from the high entrance, and tucking round them a balustrade at the back, stuffed seats and two pots standing sentinel. This lost little feature bespeaks Victorian drawing room dalliance at its most tempting.

   Outside, since he was deprived of his favourite gables, Shaw may have been thinking back to Salvin, master of the castle style. At Flete, it fails quite to work. To be applied to buildings of rectangular outline, the style required smooth ashlar, but the estate stone here had to be laid in small rough-faced blocks dressed with Dartmoor granite. Windows Shaw dots around with his wonted proficiency. But all the chimney-breasts and stacks are expressly confined to the inner walls and hidden by parapets, except for one tough group serving kitchen and office wing. This lower north-west service wing, modelled on the gallery wing of Haddon Hall, is the exterior's most enjoyable part. On the main house, the

215

roof can rarely be glimpsed. Instead Shaw places topheavy towers on the north front and south-east corner. These towers promote uncertainty; does the house face north to the moors (its natural outlook), east to the Erme, south to the main area of garden, or west to the old forecourt? For each of these directions there is something but not enough to be said. Because of its position on the side of a slope, it cannot stand up free and four-square like its cleverer imitator, Lutyens' Castle Drogo. Flete's four sides never compose themselves compactly; one is constantly striving for a better view both into and out of the house.

CRISIS

Here therefore were three projects, conceived in difficulties and shot through with brilliance, but none transformed into the individual masterpiece each might have been. This was the more galling, in that Shaw knew he had, during this period, the skill to do anything he pleased. Adcote, conceived while he still had his health and build in ideal circumstances, is the proof of it. Concentration he never lost during his illness, energy was always available, and wit and charm were constant in his work and in his relations with those around him. Here for instance is a letter written to his twelve-year-old daughter from Pontresina, where he was supposed to be taking things easily for his health in July 1880:

> My dearest Betty,
>   I have been intending to write to you every day, but really we are so busy!! We are so glad to hear that Granny and all of you are so well, of course behaving nicely!! (especially Granny). I consider I have done a wonderful feat to day. I have been up Pitz Languard, 10715 feet high. We got up at 5 and were off by 6. Mother wouldn't go, and perhaps it was just as well, for there is no doubt it was a twister. I took a horse like a sensible pup as far as I could go, or nearly so, but after that we had about $2\frac{1}{2}$ hours of tremendous climb over stones ice and wide places covered with snow, the result being that my face is rather redder than most lobsters, my eyes bloodshot and my lips all cracked. But otherwise I am none the worse and shall soon be rested. As I went along I said 'Puff, I think old Betty would like this. Oh! puff! puff! This would, puff, suit old Betty to a T, puff, puff, the next time we come we'll bring our old Betty' and so on. But we stuck at it and it came to an end, four hours hard work, and when we got there it was astounding. We were up on this small place with just enough room to stand, just like a tea tray in the sky, with nothing all round but *thousands* of snowy peaks. You can see right over Switzerland to Mont Blanc and Monte Rosa. We saw some Chamois down in a valley about a mile below us. I certainly never saw anything so wonderful before, and I expect it will be a long time before I see anything so wonderful again for I shall not venture up any such places in a hurry. . . .[48]

But there were deeper currents. The unsatisfactory nature of these jobs and the time proverbially given by illness for reflection, brought to Shaw thoughts which had had no chance to lodge in his mind before. Coming back into full practice, he found his two old masters Salvin and Street dead, three of the ablest younger architects, Nesfield, Godwin and G. G. Scott junior, retiring, and his two dependable builders Lascelles and Birch leaving the trade. At fifty, Shaw was the acclaimed leader of a school, but it was a school of action not of thought. To each building type its own style, had claimed this school: for town houses the Queen Anne, for churches the Gothic, for country houses the Old English, and so on. Eclectic the nineteenth century must be, but let each type be as pure as its style would allow. The idea worked well enough in the hands of a versatile genius, but in lesser hands it was courting disaster, and as a theory it was riddled with holes. What style should be used for a new building type? How could the town house style claim to be pure when its bastard origins were so plain, its overlap with Old English in the suburbs so necessary? Why could no two proponents agree upon the simplest principles of application? Stevenson wanted to use his pet Queen Anne as a universal domestic style in town and country; Shaw hankered for an Old English town house style as an alternative to Queen Anne; Bodley and his partner Thomas Garner now favoured a refined Tudor or Jacobean in the country. Webb had some of the answers up his sleeve, but disdained to make them available through publication. There were in fact few propagandists or writers among the group. T. G. Jackson's concise *Modern Gothic Architecture* (1873) was a shrewd diatribe against pure Gothic and pure Classic, but suggested no new answers beyond the Queen Anne. And when Stevenson's *House Architecture* finally came out in 1880, it was no longer a battlecry but a speech congratulating the Queen Anne troops upon victory. On style, his negative arguments were excellent, but his positive ones carried no great weight.

Thus, for very lack of guiding principle, Shaw and his allies were hard put to defend themselves against the attacks of the Woodwards of their world. If they looked in their hearts, the origins of their movement lay in Ruskin. Ruskin himself was no longer available. A few harsh lectures of the 1860s touch upon architecture, but the sage, having retired to Brantwood and bouts of imbecility, would only preach his social gospel. The architectural system he despised; John Sedding, applying for advice, was bidden go and study sculpture and craftsmanship.[49] Ruskin's awkward precepts were now tinged with a maniacal intolerance, and could no more be soothed into acceptance and applicability among architects. To many minds, the future was shrouded in gloom.

One might be forgiven for thinking that Shaw escaped this pessimism, and that he cheerily soldiered on, deftly changing his style to suit new fashions as they emerged. Two documents alone prove the contrary: outspoken and painful letters of 1882 written to Sedding, his closest friend now among first-class architects. The first is partly missing.

. . . Come, I say old man, gently does it. You are coming it too waggish when you pretend to see any resemblance between the work of the present day and the 'Renaissance of the 15th & 16th Centuries of France Italy and Germany'. Their art was a perfectly imperceptible development from the work of the centuries which had preceded them. The difference between full blown 16th century work and 14th Centy work is not greater than between 14th & 12th. It was one long grand growth, and the links were *not* and never had been severed, and certainly no one can laugh at their work, or if they do laugh they are noodles. But with us it is very different. The "old links were (completely) severed" and to all intents and purposes a new style was revived, dug up, call it what you will. Every feature of that style was in direct antagonism to every tradition of work then existing, I think without excepting a single one, and for all practical purposes the style dug up might just as well have been Chinese or Egyptian and we have struggled on with that style from that day till this, between 40 & 50 years now. We have done it in perfect good faith, there can be no doubt, but that it is in any sense whatever a living art, I cannot see. Also I maintain that all the *best* of it is 'purely imitative'. Look at the enclosed photo, and say if it is not *copied* (and I use the word advisedly). I don't mean imitated, but clean copied from old work, general design and detail down to the smallest cusp. Is it possible that this can be *great* art? I fear not, and yet it is a good work of Bodley's, a man we both sincerely admire. You see your liberal views have distorted your vision, and prevent you from seeing these things clearly. Let me implore you to turn a conservative ere it is too late!!! You were brought up a good conservative I am sure, and what fiend perverted you I can't make out!! Oh! it is sad.

Sedding's reply is lost, but then comes the rejoinder.

... I am most sorry to find that my last letter had a depressing effect upon you (only I don't believe it!). What a lark! Now I am enjoying excellent spirits, thank you, never was in better, so pray let me beg of you to recover yours as soon as possible and be as jolly as ever. You state the case as clearly as possible, with a perspicacity (that's a good word!) all your own and what is better you *answer* your statement. Nothing could be more to the point than your sentence 'one sees that if good men copy they don't really enrich the world nor leave it better off for their work when they die'. And then you say 'I wish Bodley wouldn't copy. He is a real artist and he didn't copy like this in earlier days, and needn't and *oughtn't*'. Then you say afterwards, 'One sees that *bad* work dies. Good work never dies it is always fruitful of suggestion and always gives pleasure to the eye that knows what's what'. But then comes the question, what is good work? Can good 19th Centy work done by educated and intelligent mortals consist in a servile copy of 15th Centy? *Real* work of any kind whether good or indifferent must I contend be *living* work. Our art is like a language, it must be either living or dead. English is a living language now because we express all our wants in it. Latin is and has been for many centuries dead, it isn't used for anything now except as a study. But a couple of centuries ago (though it was really as dead then as now) it was very much used, no end of essays and odes were written in it, and nearly all dedicatory work was "done" in it. But that didn't make it alive and we now rather laugh at its use for these purposes as pompous and call it pedantic. The men who did all this Latin were able men and scholars, but such of them as we know at all now we do not know on account of their Latin but on account of their English, such as George Herbert and many others. You cannot say that these men enriched English literature by their classic imitations, and it seems that much the same will be said of us. Between them and us there is a vast difference. They did it from scholarly affectation, they might have written the vernacular had they liked to have done so, and often did. But unhappily our vernacular is not within the pale of art at all. I have never seen any rendering of plate glass and Portland Cement that one could call art. But I fear that the enemy might answer to that that that must be our fault. Then on the other hand it must be said for them, that their odes and things were *imitations*, not copies. What would have been said of them had they simply copied say an ode of Horace's, I really don't know! Their ideas were more or less their own and they put them into Latin. But what I complain of is, that there is absolutely no idea in such a thing as that screen. It is simply in general arrangement and design, and down to the minutest detail a *clean copy*.

Of course this is all very dreadful, and though we are talking at Bodley we are all in much the same boat, except Butterfield, who is in a boat of his own all by himself. It is bad enough to be in such a doleful plight, which may account for your bad spirits (though I believe your bad spirits arise from your evil conscience when you remember you are a liberal with a little 'l'), but I for one don't want to live and die in a fool's paradise. If I could get myself to believe that my half-timbered work and tall chimneys were in any way my own, I should sit up on my hind legs and purr away like our Tom cat John, but common honesty compels me to own that they are simply indifferent copies of old work. I find myself continually using the expression 'Just *like* a bit of *real* old work' when I see anything nice. One seems in a single sentence to get to the bottom of the whole thing, viz. 1st that old work was *real* and 2nd that ours is not real, but only like real. However you've never read all this, so I had better shut up. Pick up your spirits and go ahead.[50]

It is the last part that cuts deep. Sedding, from the extracts given, cannot have been seriously at odds with Shaw. Both agreed that copyism was the death of art, both yearned for originality based upon scholarship. On the evidence of his career, Sedding's little "l" liberalism can have meant not much more than a Ruskinian reformation of the conditions of practice so as to include more craftsmanship. The matter lay in a nutshell: how to be artistic and original without debasing the currency of those two much-abused words. The cant of old-fashioned revivalism was discredited; the cant of the 'plate glass and Portland cement' merchants and of the professionals of the R.I.B.A. was inflexible and destructive of all fine craftsmanship. Where then to look?

For all its restless inventiveness Shaw's cast of mind was conservative, as he here discloses. 'I fear there is much more of the mind of Jacob than of Abraham in *me*,' he admits to Agnes after eighteen years of marriage, 'and I enjoy looking back more than looking forward which of course is wrong, or anyway, not very noble.'[51] So he began to seek, personally and cautiously, a workmanlike interpretation of 'tradition' that signified abandoning neither past nor present. To Webb and Morris, tradition meant something much sharper and fresher, radical and social; imaginary perhaps, but vibrantly so and therefore potent, the tradition of *The Nature of Gothic* and *The Earthly Paradise*, reaching beneath the topsoil of mere style in art. Shaw's own interpretation was closer to the 'tradition' of Reynolds' *Discourses*, that trenchant statement of the principles underlying classicism in every art form. The artists who have made the most careful study of their predecessors, he used to quote from Reynolds, are soon doing the most original work themselves.[52] Elsewhere Reynolds says, 'Whoever would reform a nation, supposing a bad taste to prevail in it, will not accomplish his purpose by going directly against the stream of their prejudices. Mens' minds must be prepared to receive what is new to them. Reformation is a work of time.'[53] This was a gradualism which Shaw would be all the happier to embrace, recalling the fast changes and fashions of his early career. But it was broadly a gradualism of styles. Here Ruskin, in so many curious ways close to Reynolds, is once again a help: 'The forms of architecture already known are good enough for us, and for far better than us: and it will be time enough to think about changing them for better when we can use them as they are.'[54]

Shaw's changed attitudes are hard at first to discern. His 'half-timbered work and tall chimneys' could not be cast swiftly aside, for they too had gone to form a tradition, shallow though its author might think it. In churches, a Gothic tradition had been really replanted; in houses, the classic tradition, so rudely uprooted and lamely supplanted, had now to be reattained, but not roughly or suddenly, for the use of style had to bind old England to new England, past to present, and therefore needed special hallowing. By degrees, Shaw was to work more consistency and thought and less overt brillance into his practice. But in 1882 much was still dark. Morris, facing similar difficulties, spoke of 'making the best of it'.[55] Shaw, still in dimness of purpose, could only cry 'Pick up your spirits and go ahead'. At least he had his health again to do so.

CHAPTER 6

The Town House
and the Path to Classicism

Is all good structure in a winding stair?

George Herbert.

THE LONDON HOUSE

If you built a house in the smarter parts of Victorian London, you were unlikely to be the ground landlord; if you built in the country, you would almost certainly own the freehold of the site.[1] From this difference, much follows about the background to the Shaw town house. In that age of high profits, a landowner or his representative could expect excellent return upon his property if it lay in the path of fashionable development. Tradition allowed him to insist, even in the best districts, on a remarkably narrow street frontage, a large proportion of the surface area of each plot covered by building, and (from the 1850s) a good many storeys. As vital to his interests as his leaseholders were the builders and architects who developed his property. Upon them he relied for the regular progress in building which was essential to profit and made some speculation necessary even on the most exclusive of estates. Up till now he had also relied on them for conformity.

It was the problem of conformity that particularly lay before the fortunate owners of the high-class Chelsea and Kensington estates where Shaw worked in the 1870s and '80s. They could easily go on building 'first-class' housing speculatively, leaving the risks to builders and ensuring uniform lay-out just like other classes of development. But the Grosvenor Estate of Belgravia and its many outliers westwards had all but glutted the market for large stucco dwellings on the old London house plan. A new generation, too, saw a chance for better development. Four decades of architectural reform and innovation since Pugin, as many weekly papers devoted to building, and two international exhibitions had made men feel that they could and should have their own opinions on such questions. If they could afford it, they were entitled to individuality not just in their country dwellings but in their town houses too.

The landowner stood to gain by treating direct with rich individuals and allowing them to erect such houses. They would set the tone for the estate, they could afford expensive leases and high ground rents, and once settled in their own home they were unlikely to move away. But there were dangers. Architectural chaos, like traffic or trade, could lower the tone and lessen the value of an estate.[2] That is why sanctions were stringent on the smart estates against paraphernalia like professional plates and signboards. For the same reason, the façades of intended houses (as well as the credit of

221

their future inhabitants) were closely scrutinized by surveyors and management committees for conformity to the estate norm. When for instance George Vulliamy, the Metropolitan Board of Works surveyor, objected to the radical simplicity of the façades of Godwin's Tite Street houses on their Chelsea Embankment estate, he was as concerned with conformity as with aesthetics.[3]

There was therefore a perpetual wrangle between conformity and individualism. On this question there was no doubt where the architects of the new style stood. Queen Anne had begun by expressing individual planning in the Puginian spirit. As the style matured in the hands of Shaw and Ernest George, its range extended to capture something of the competitiveness and brio of the town houses of Amsterdam and Antwerp, so exactly fitting to the mood of Victorian mercantile rivalries.[4] The grossness in elevation of London's Cadogan Square or Harrington Gardens is not to be mistaken as naïve; where frontages were narrow and storeys rose high, old proportions had to be sacrificed and more boisterousness supplied.

To overcome the rampant individualism which might have resulted, the great estates seem to have had unofficial lists of approved architects. To these, intending lessees could go for their designs and be confident they would be approved. Quite how this system worked we do not know. On the Metropolitan Board of Works' Embankment estate, Shaw put up five separate houses, of which four were private commissions; Godwin built six, while Bodley & Garner, Spiers and Edis, all of whom could be trusted to design in an advanced Queen Anne manner, have one house each. Clearly, the Board made it plain whom it would and would not tolerate. On their Kensington estate, the Royal Commissioners for the 1851 Exhibition were for a time just as stringent; Shaw was their architect, and Shaw or someone comparable they expected an individual lessee to employ.

But like others, they were forced to admit speculation. In Queen's Gate, where stucco had already made headway when they adopted Shaw, they tried to make builders conform to a façade by him, abandoning individualism for the fruits of faster development.[5] The builders at first wanted none of it, but speculative Queen Anne was quick to come. The Cadogan and Hans Place Estate Company, developing Earl Cadogan's large Chelsea properties and facing similar problems, had Stevenson designing the whole of 42–58 Pont Street as early as 1876–8. Shaw's Albert Hall Mansions is merely one of many successors, however eccentric in conception. But once Queen Anne was extended to whole blocks, it soon began to decline. The style had been worked out to express sturdy individuality, and in reduplicated form easily became diluted and dull. The late 1870s are the brief heyday of the Queen Anne town house. Ernest George's Harrington Gardens façades of 1882–3, evolved no doubt through many a negotiation between builder, client and estate office, are the swansong of individualism. Subsequently, most estates reverted to a degree at least of conformity when they had brand new street fronts to compose.

When Shaw designed for subletting or direct speculation, he usually kept to the regular terrace house arrangement, with refinements, and suppressed individuality of planning. This happened at least three times, at 18 Hyde Park Gate, in the alternative house plans for 200–222 Cromwell Road, and at 9–11 Chelsea Embankment. The

163. (above left) 9–11 Chelsea Embankment, floor plans and perspective of street front, drawn by W. R. Lethaby, 1879.

164. (above right) Cadogan Square, perspective of street fronts, showing nos. 68 (right) and 72 (left) juxtaposed, 1878.

165. (left) Cadogan Square, part of west side in 1881, showing the present no. 68 (then 42) third from right, and no. 72 (then 46) second from left.

Embankment group (1878–80) was a speculation built by Lascelles for James Temple, in which Shaw uniquely had a small share.[6] The three houses (ill. 163) were intended to be let for eighty years or thereabouts to 'noblemen and gentlemen of the upper class', at a ground rent of £90 per annum and what seems the staggering purchase sum of £12,000 each. They had six storeys, stabling of their own, spacious double drawing rooms, and a fine prospect from reception rooms raised, as normally in the Embankment and Cadogan Square houses, well above ground level. Otherwise the planning diverged little from standard arrangements. The charm of these tall houses consists in the excellent effect Shaw obtains simply by reversing the plan of the middle house, thus binding the block into one at gable level while giving it interest beneath. The elevations are more disciplined variations upon the bayed façades of the two houses Shaw had just built in Cadogan Square, in 1877–8. One of these, no. 68, was built direct for a client, Laurence Harrison, but its near neighbour, no. 72, is a more individualistic example of speculation. Their different building histories manifest the confusion which could occur on the less strictly regulated estates. Here the Cadogan and Hans Place Estate Company made their own terms with clients and builders. The west side was partly built by Thomas Pink of Harlesden, and one would guess that either the company or Pink treated with Shaw for a block of contiguous houses. The plots were too narrow for well-proportioned fronts, so Shaw would have hoped for breadth by designing two or three elevations next to each other. In the event no. 70, an indifferent house built by Pink to A. J. Adams's designs, was interposed, and Shaw had to be content with the questionable device of illustrating 68 and 72 at the R.A. as though they were juxtaposed (ill. 164), as perhaps they were meant to be.[7] The plan of 72 probably followed Harrison's closely.[8] But though the gathered windows of these tall façades give this part of the square a much-needed tightness, much of the effect is lost on account of the lower, laxer neighbours (ill. 165). When Shaw added a third house in 1882, no. 62, he plumped for a calmer composition, recognizing a *fait accompli*. Cadogan Square was not a success for him as an exercise in façade treatments.

Almost more than in the country houses, it is with the plans of the commissioned town houses that Shaw's architecture really comes alive. For the single-fronted house, his archetype was J. P. Heseltine's 196 Queen's Gate, the first of the proper town plans (ill. 166). Many features of this he never improved on; he was content to reduplicate it nearly ten years later for Heseltine's friend H. F. Makins at 180 Queen's Gate. The street lacks a prepossessing prospect, the plots are not large, and Heseltine unlike his successors did not go for a corner site. So it was specially hard to produce light, large, and individual reception rooms. From the wilful lopsidedness of the façade (ill. 167) one could never surmise that the plan is an essay in classic clarity. Shaw took a hunk out of the small site to get light into the hall and first floor gallery, and thrust one chimney against the party wall. He then banished all possible ancillary rooms to other floors, and with a quaint device enveloped the whole back staircase in the grand and gradual turning of the main one. This gave him a spacious hall well away from the entrance, poised between library and dining room, and unencumbered by stairs. It became an axiom of Shaw's town house planning never to skimp either hall or stairs, but to allow them their separate orbits which might here and there coincide. The other improvement he made was to clarify the planning of the drawing room floor above. In fashionable circles where more than one

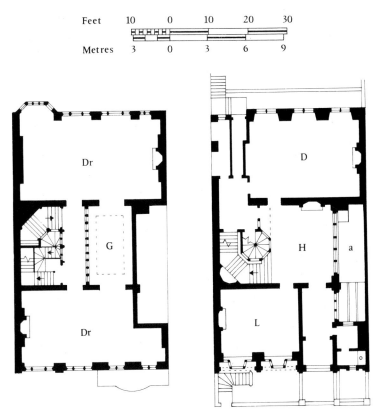

166. 196 Queen's Gate, ground and first floor plans.

reception room was the rule, it had become common to construct a small vestibule across the back of the landing between one drawing room and another.[9] Here Shaw abandoned the whole floor to this suite, widened the vestibule into a toplit gallery, and made the front and back rooms identical in shape to give his arrangement consequentiality. It was an idea he re-used at 62 Cadogan Square, and most spectacularly when he converted 49 Princes Gate for F. R. Leyland. Here the triple drawing room extended right round the stair well, the three parts separated by costly screens.

Several such tricks of the 196 Queen's Gate plan are to recur, but there is one awkwardness in the house which Shaw has yet to iron out. Because he enlarges the hall and clears the ground and first floor of clutter, he has to build more storeys. The house's six floors above ground occupy only a slightly greater height than its five storey neighbours, and the rooms are therefore low in proportion to their size. Hereafter, Shaw is unwilling to reduce room heights to make up for lateral space occupied by hall and stairs, and so his town houses frequently loom larger than their neighbours. To keep the height down, Shaw is compelled in Queen's Gate to put one of the family rooms (in Heseltine's case the library) in the noisy and exposed position next to the door on the ground floor. At Cadogan Square the plots stretched deeper, so he was able to add an extra good room on the main floors at the back and devote the frontage to his entrance hall without automatically incurring more height. Since he strove against putting too important a

167. 196 Queen's Gate, street front.

168. Farnley House, Chelsea Embankment, street front.

room in this position, his family rooms regularly extend up to the second floor. On the Chelsea Embankment, there were incentives in the shape of the river view and the possibility of flooding to put the major rooms on first and second floors. The effect in every case is to make the elevation more topheavy. One of the difficulties with the Cadogan Square frontages was to avoid crushing an unimportant ground storey with the weight of windows and bays above, inevitably narrowly tied together because of the small plot widths. Even at 185 Queen's Gate, where Shaw triumphs over his ground floor planning difficulties by running a low barrel-vaulted morning room uninterrupted along the street frontage, there is a tendency for the great bays above to crush the room's modest outside windows.

Reception rooms of varying heights and positions meant that floors had to be intelligently interlocked. Though 196 Queen's Gate opened out the two main floors, they were still rigidly interrelated. At this time, Shaw was breaking out into two-storey halls in the country. His studio houses also suggested how he could open up space and connect different levels, not only to give volume to constricted interiors but to achieve adventure

226

and event in what would otherwise be a mundane sequence of rooms. This could be done within a floor as well as between floors. One alternative Shaw devised to the double drawing room arrangements of 196 Queen's Gate was to connect the two rooms end to end by a few steps. Thus at Ellerdale Road, guests might advance down the narrower, higher part to a central screen, be seen, and descend to join the company by the hearth and bay below (ill. 143).

Such an arrangement had its perils. Whistler, in his cups after dining at West House, is said to have tumbled down some steps and cried, 'It must have been some damned teetotaller of an architect who designed this house!'[10] But Victorian gentry were used to having things carried for them, faced few hazards as long as they avoided inebriation and kept their eyes about them, and therefore worried little about the inconvenience of ups and downs. Journeying between storeys was just part of domestic life when the family rooms alone lay on at least two floors and sometimes more, and it might as well be made as adventurous as possible. The procession to dinner was the major exploit of the day, and in town had unique potentialities. A country house dinner route might mean assembly in the drawing room and a more or less stately advance across the hall into the dining room. But this would confine itself to a single floor, whereas in London it extended as a matter of course to two floors. This ritual suggested connections and aspects between the floors. 185 Queen's Gate, the last of Shaw's West End mansions, boasts the grandest of these dinner routes (ill. 173). The company passes out through the drawing room door, down the shallow steps of a massively broad staircase, and then turns transitorily past the morning room and across the double-storey hall. Here it re-emerges beneath the scrutiny of anyone peering out of the internal window of the room just left behind, and vanishes into the dining room.

At 185 Queen's Gate, a toplit hall supplied the light needed for the central corridor and spaces since the stairs were separated and encased, and opened up the interior to give it volume and power. The 'peep-show' window we have met before in country houses, as a means of overlooking public spaces from above. But in the town house it often has an idiosyncratic life of its own, from the example over the inglenook in Ellerdale Road to the tiny internal window between the different levels of morning and dining rooms at 68 Cadogan Square. There is a peep-show, too, from an internal oriel at Clock House down into the hall (ill. 170), half public and half private space. Here, its purpose was to light the corridor, sealed at either end by party walls, since the hall was not toplit and the light entered directly from windows high on its north side.

Of the private houses Shaw designed on the Embankment, Swan House claims pride of place for its setpiece drawing room and elegance of elevation; Clock House and Cheyne House excel in plan. The Metropolitan Board of Works Estate was developed approximately from west to east. Cheyne House, which occupies the irregular tongue of land at the corner of Royal Hospital Road and the Embankment, was the first house to be built (1875–6) and was shortly followed by its eastern neighbour, Swan House. The clients had their differences. George Matthey, the Government assayer, employed Shaw again at Eastbourne and remained his lifelong friend; Wickham Flower was a connoisseur who inclined to the Morris circle.[11] So either got a house after his own style of life. Cheyne House is excellently conceived and too rarely noticed. In contemporary Paris, the natural

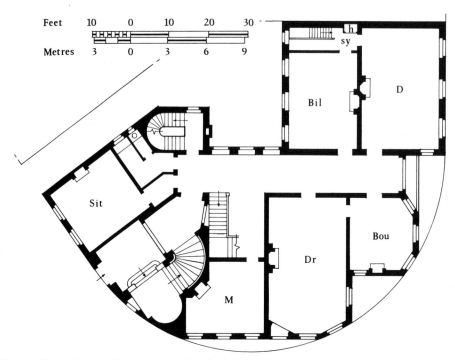

169. Cheyne House, Chelsea Embankment, first floor plan.

170. Clock House, Chelsea Embankment, basement, ground, first and second floor plans.

treatment for such a tongue-shaped corner site would have been to set a circular tower, probably for the stairs, at the apex of the plot, perhaps slightly set off from the main house, finished with a cupola to make a point of view, and flanked by regular elevations. This is not Shaw's method. The façade indeed is calm enough; the simple Queen Anne language of segmental windows with brick dressings, a cement coving at cornice level, and the occasional round window. In the wider sashes towards the Embankment, there is a touch of nearby Cheyne Walk, where Rossetti and the aged Carlyle lived (and perhaps, too, of Cheyne Walk's own paradigm, the Royal Hospital, which Carlyle had praised for its gentlemanly good manners). Cheyne House in fact is reticence itself compared to the extravagance of its neighbours.[12] But the plan is lively enough (ill. 169). From a casual entrance towards Royal Hospital Road, Shaw has turned the plan to face the river, and pushes dining room, boudoir and drawing room into buoyant positions at mezzanine level facing the Thames. The stairs divide into two parts. From the entrance hall, they rise to the flower balcony where the guest is received, and then start from the main corridor again. Above, rooms bridge over the courtyard access to connect the main house with the stables. Cheyne House is the only Embankment house to have escaped conversion, and its complex warren of servants' staircases, basements and sub-basements is still to be seen.

In the bowels of Clock House (ill. 170), a toplit passage ran through from amidst the same sort of warren to connect with the stable block. Besides covered access, this was the regular means to the control which the Victorian rich sought to exert over their servants' comings and goings. But oddly, the same connection recurs between the two blocks at bedroom level, by means of an isolated bridge passage. By an unusual arrangement,

GROUND FLOOR   SECOND FLOOR

BASEMENT   FIRST FLOOR

Feet 10 0 10 20 30

Metres 3 0 3 6 9

kitchen and servants' hall come beneath the stables, the back wall of which is carried on a series of girders in the kitchen roof. Clock House in fact marks new departures in Shaw's structural ironwork. The reception rooms are ruthlessly organized, with load-bearing walls striding over voids in the storey below, and the main upper corridor running across the centre of the great storey-and-a-half hall. Outside, Shaw even slings an exposed girder between the rear stable wall and the back of the main house, to take the weight of the isolated passage to the wash-house.

Though the rudiments of these great plans remain, their articulation has long been wrecked by conversion and the interiors irremediably changed. Now the Embankment houses hide little behind their 'elegantly fantastic' fronts.[13] In his first experiments with town house frontages, Shaw had thought of keeping quite a number of Old English and even Gothic elements, as an early design for the front of 196 Queen's Gate shows. But in the end, he had chosen there to connect the body of his front under a tall gable in the Flemish manner (ill. 167). This became the standard Queen Anne answer for the narrow terrace house, but was by no means so obvious at the time.[14] On the Embankment, nos. 9–11 follow the pattern but work differently because the three gables are straight and articulated as a group. On the wider plots allotted by the Metropolitan Board of Works for private houses, Shaw tried the gable-end idea once, on Farnley House (ill. 168). Here, he made the gable very wide and simple, broke it by a central chimney, and projected multi-storey bays at the side to give a sense of horizontality. Both of these Embankment compositions, and to a lesser degree Cheyne House, avail themselves of full bays to make the main storeys elegant and light. Swan House and Clock House rely on other means to

229

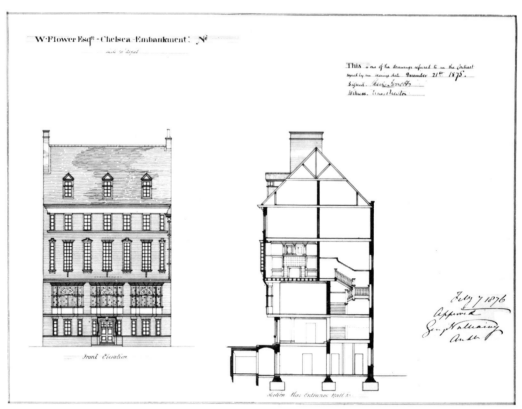

171. Swan House, Chelsea Embankment, front elevation and section, 1875.

the same end: the idea of the Old English town house, with upper storeys jettied out by means of overhanging oriels and bressumers. These had the added advantage of giving the frontages interest from the side, since the straight-on view is hindered by the river. In Clock House (ill. 172), Shaw allots three Dutch gables to the attic, and works upwards to them by way of Ipswich oriels, small bedroom balconies, and the adroitly placed clock, the only asymmetrical feature on the elevation. But it is no improvement on Swan House (ill. 171), the pearl of his town house elevations. This long-loved façade depends far more than is usual with Shaw upon precise proportion, making an exact square from ground level to cornice with the width. It takes its cue from its neighbour, as though Shaw had squeezed Cheyne House at the sides as it turned the corner, until every feature became elongated and extruded, and then had slapped on a battery of Ipswich oriels.[15] Yet the movement of each storey upwards and outwards is delicately done and anticipates the storey above. Entrancing is the play between the windows of the long second floor drawing room, from segment head to supporting bracket and back again, in a quiet echo of the heads and aprons of the Ipswich oriels below. After Swan House and Clock House, these strange thin windows were never re-used by Shaw, for all their originality; they had to await Lutyens for their revival.[16]

    The puzzle of the Swan House elevation is how it ever came to be erected. Even more blatantly than New Zealand Chambers, it transgresses the rules of the Metropolitan

230

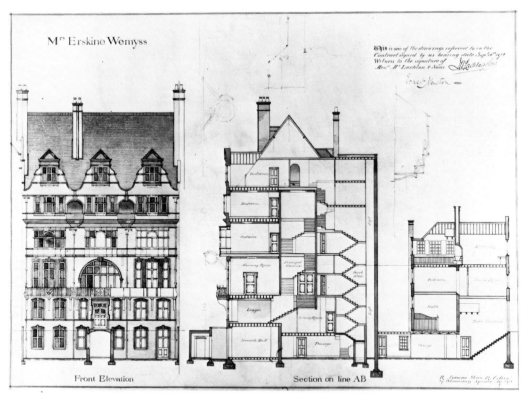

Front Elevation   Section on line AB

172. Clock House, Chelsea Embankment, front elevation and section, 1878.

Building Act over the setback of wooden window frames within reveals.[17] So that the building line may not be read as the line of the ground storey, but as that of the second and third floors, Shaw has carried a pier of projecting brickwork down to ground level at either end of the frontage, as at New Zealand Chambers. But still the elongated upper windows stand flagrantly forward of the brickwork. Yet Shaw had none of the trouble with the Board of Works that Godwin suffered with his Tite Street houses; Vulliamy passed the plans and there was no demurrer on the committee. It may be that the Board of Works, who on this estate were in the rare position of being both ground landlords and discretionary authorities for the building regulations, were prepared to experiment provided they were satisfied with the competence of architect and builder. All the same, Shaw had to apply to them to waive the section of the Act dealing with wooden windows for Cheyne House, Farnley House and Clock House.

By this time Shaw was constantly asking, in a spirit of rebellion, for exemption on this point. There was general agreement that the provisions of the 1855 Building Act dealing with wooden windows were out of date. When commenting on one such application, Vulliamy himself said:

> I do not attach much importance to this section of the Act. The object no doubt was to prevent the spread of fire from one building to another and this part of the Act might have been effectual if it had required the frames to be covered with brickwork. But this

231

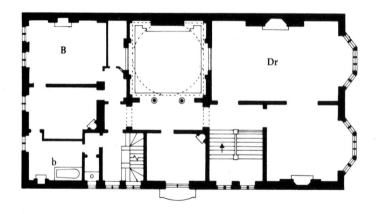

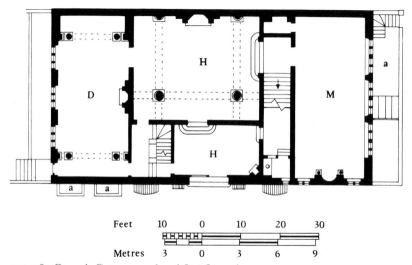

173. 185 Queen's Gate, ground and first floor plans.

is not done and all that can be required is that the frames should be kept $4\frac{1}{2}''$ from the front or outer surface of the wall. This is clearly of little avail to prevent buildings catching fire.[18]

Consequently, many district surveyors would wink at the habit of wooden windows flush with the walls such as Shaw often wanted. He only appears to have applied to the Board under pressure, and usually after completion. This is how he is writing to Arthur Keen about the matter, late in 1879:

I am afraid we cannot defy the District Surveyor any longer as he has got hold of the right end of the stick, so we must make application to the B of Works soon. You will find some duplicate tracings on cloth in my room somewhere, of the upper bay of Pink's house. That is one lot done. Then we want, Duplicate tracings on cloth of back bay of

232

drawing room 46 Cadogan Sq. This is exactly the same as back bay of Mr Harrison's, it is the same thing repeated, but you see they insist on a fresh permission. Duplicate tracings on cloth of window over porch at Mr Harrison's . . . then another set of tracings of same, for Pink's house, no. 46. Duplicate tracings in cloth of bay on stair at Mr Armitage's (Hardy will know), and duplicate tracing of front bay over porch and under balcony. Hardy will do these tracings of Armitage's. Duplicate tracings of Mrs Wemyss' bays.[19]

Though all four of these applications were granted, there were nevertheless signs of a hardening in the Board's attitude towards them. In each case Shaw had palliated his offence by coating the window frame with a layer of cement—a device to get round the Act, as Vulliamy saw. In 1881 he was refused leave to use a similar trick on overhanging bays in the attics of Albert Hall Mansions, and in another case two years later Vulliamy insisted that 'the Board should not strain its powers for the sake of improving the artistic effect of buildings'. The law, he said, must be observed until rescinded.[20] Once or twice Shaw had later applications for wooden windows passed, not always easily. But he had by no means abandoned his battle against the regulations and would use foul or fair means to undermine them when he thought them unnecessary. Sometimes he went right to the top. His friendship with W. E. Riley, the L.C.C.'s chief architect, smoothed many paths on the Quadrant's troublesome course. And when Shaw fell foul of the local authority over a Liverpool building, most probably Parr's Bank, he went to see Mervyn Macartney's father-in-law, C. T. Ritchie, happily then a Government Minister. The predicament having been explained, Ritchie advised Shaw to throw the correspondence in the wastepaper basket, and proceed; which he did, without interference.[21]

These regulations on woodwork were no trivial obstacle to Shaw. When the A.A. visited Bedford Park, thanksgivings are recorded that the estate fell outside Board of Works jurisdiction, as its appearance shows. The Act rendered Shaw's Old English town house type almost impossible, and forced him often to modify his Queen Anne detailing. In Cadogan Square, the rich wooden doorheads and brackets of nos. 68 and 72 shown in the R.A. perspective had to be redesigned and many windows altered (ills. 164, 165). Four years later, at no. 62, Shaw had begun to revert to stone-mullioned windows, which he preferred to adopt rather than abandon frames flush with the brickwork. This house, and 180 and 185 Queen's Gate, go, like the country houses, for stone surrounds on the lower storeys and woodwork in the smaller windows above. Sometimes it seems that the stonework may have been painted to give the windows uniformity of colour. The surprising effect of these changes, coinciding with a search for economy in elevation, is to reintroduce a Tudor note in these three late town houses. All were built on corner sites. The only survivor, 62 Cadogan Square, has an extremely subdued elevation but one of Shaw's most carefully matured plans.[22] 180 Queen's Gate, of 1883–4, has been a little overpraised because of the fine condition in which it was maintained until shortly before its all-too-recent demolition, and because of the Morris papers and furniture installed by the client, H. F. Makins. The plan was mainly a repeat of 196, and the undoubted power of the elevations makes all the more disquieting the way in which the weight fell unevenly upon the angle porch (ill. 175). In 1890, Shaw sought to improve upon the same theme for William Vivian at 185 Queen's Gate, and this time he managed better (ill. 174). Upon the

174. 185 Queen's Gate, street fronts.

175. 180 Queen's Gate, street fronts.

176. School Board Offices for London, Thames Embankment front, by G. F. Bodley, 1874.

two symmetrical, flattened façades, each detail had a protuberant forcefulness. Outside and in, Shaw pursued his eclecticism without apology. The Dutch gables, rusticated baroque voussoirs and mullioned bays had their respective counterparts in the varying character of the interiors (ills. 192, 193). Like all late Shaw, 185 Queen's Gate is an acquired taste and lacks the easy charm of Swan House. But in many ways it was its architect's greatest and most thoughtful town house. Its main rival must be its near neighbour and predecessor 170 Queen's Gate; but to understand that epoch-making house, we must look at the development of Shaw's style from the start of the 1880s.

COMMERCE AND RECONSTRUCTION IN THE '80s

There are steps back as well as resolute ones forward on Shaw's path to classicism. At first he was timid of exercising his revised opinions in entirely new buildings, but bolder in adding to old ones. The difference in policy shows in two commercial buildings which well mark his point of departure at the start of the decade, the first Alliance Assurance building, and the reconstruction of Barings Bank.

The Alliance block (1881–2) was designed during Shaw's period of illness, but shows no signs of it (ill. 177). Its position at the corner of St James's Street and Pall Mall gave it great prominence, and its derivatives can be seen on corner sites all over England. Yet it is hardly a typical Shaw building. New Zealand Chambers, his only previous complete office block, provided not a single hint for it. Instead he chose an ostentatious Queen

236

177. Alliance Assurance Offices, St James's Street and Pall Mall, street fronts.

Anne, more exactly modelled on Flemish originals than anything earlier, but with much too of the strong French tang of Bodley's School Board Offices (ill. 176). French also are the broad semicircular shop windows, still a rare method in England for articulating the ground storeys of commercial premises. I'Anson and others had used round-headed arcades in office buildings for the purpose of lighting shops well.[23] Cockerell, on the other hand, had used a high arched ground floor not to light shops but to articulate and proportion the storeys of his banks (an idea he probably borrowed from Percier and Fontaine's Rue de Rivoli). With Cockerell, the entresol floor level then came down to the springing of the arches, so that the arcade lit two internal floors. In Edwardian times, when Cockerell was once more appreciated, this device was to become standard; it was Shaw's refusal to sacrifice such a two-storey arcade that caused the final furore over the Quadrant. But in 1880 arched shop windows were uncommon, and the Alliance did much to popularize them. Shaw had tried them once before, in a Queen Anne design of 1877 for an abortive competition for a new front to Mercers Hall, with shops included. In both this and the Alliance building, the fanlights in the arches belong, as with I'Anson, to the shops still and not the entresol. Nevertheless, they show Shaw striving back by degrees to a more classical and evenly proportioned articulation for his elevations.

Both projects also share alternating stone and cut brick voussoirs to these arches, and the Alliance building extends the chromaticism to an all-over battle between pink brickwork and insistent bands of Portland stone. Though full constructional polychromy was a dying duck by now, stone and brick banding persisted through the 1870s, for

237

instance in the School Board Offices.[24] Shaw was now ready to explore these contrasts for a while in a few special buildings, reworking them once again in the Harrow Mission Church designs and at New Scotland Yard. The Alliance throws up ideas which Shaw will reconsider at New Scotland Yard, but cannot be counted such a success. Its striations are too strong and close for the disciplined fenestration, its scale overpowers its old neighbours, and the St James's Street gable, replacing two smaller gables in the first design, is arbitrary. Yet as usual there is much to admire and enjoy in the planning, especially the way in which light is procured for the basement with minimum loss of space for the chambers over.

The reconstruction and refronting of the Bishopsgate premises of Barings (1880–1) is a better guide than the Alliance to Shaw's new mood. Bankers at that time prided themselves on occupying premises which were rich but reticent, without the swagger of insurance companies and the like, yet in tune with the spirit of the City of London. The City was riddled with converted houses used as offices by the great mercantile firms. By and large, the new chambers and office blocks now rising were not occupied by companies of the top class. Rothschilds and Barings operated from old-fashioned buildings by Cubitts. Martins, five years before, had got Shaw not to reconstruct but quietly to extend their premises at the back. At Barings too, he was not asked to rebuild, but just to increase the accommodation, notably in the basement and main office, and design a new frontage (ill. 182). Hence the elevation was quite simple, without breaks or projections: a mere 'plain old fashioned red brick building'.[25] Only a few clues gave away the expense; the texture of the dressings, the modillion cornice, and the thin gauged brickwork. Among earlier buildings, its neat proportions recall Swan House, but it came close too to The Tower House in that Shaw was using modern Queen Anne details while feeling his way back to the style which really obtained in Queen Anne's day. Originally the roof was even hipped at the sides like that of a free-standing house, a perverse trick for a building with party walls, and deliberately meant to mark it out as other than mere commercial premises. This oddity and the witty distortion of detail prompted William Woodward to come forward once more and do battle in the *Building News* against Queen Anne. His 'quite too consummately utter' nonsense was easily put down by Brydon, who wrote a detailed reply to Woodward's 'ignorant squib.'[26] Shaw, then away ill, no doubt found it all very silly, but cannot have forgotten Woodward's behaviour. Auguries for future co-operation between the two were hardly encouraging.

The new front did not end Shaw's connection with Barings. In 1888–90 he built new basements and galleries to the banking hall. There was also much private work for the partners, and in 1890 he placed his son Robert in a job there, only a few months before the Barings crisis.[27] After that, of course, there could be no architectural jobs from the bank for a while. By the time recovery was complete, Lutyens was in the ascendant as bankers' architect.

The plain classical frontage which Shaw was able to offer the bankers accorded with the speedy change in taste for architecture between 1870 and 1880. It extended to their country houses as well. For this kind of client, rambling picturesqueness was already losing its appeal. If a new house was needed, Old English of a refined variety was still Shaw's formula; such was Francis Baring's Banstead Wood (1884–5). But from 1880, the

238

genuine Queen Anne house, even the formal Georgian house, were once more a social asset, and Shaw, instead of being asked to supplant, was in demand to alter, extend, or reconstruct. From now on, through his own will, such work became the preoccupation of his country house practice. C. L. Norman is a good weathercock; despite his desire ten years before for a grand new house, when he finally inherited in 1882 his decision was to alter The Rookery and respect its original style and 'Adam' wings. During and after this, Shaw was occupied with several taxing reconstruction and alteration jobs. Along with The Rookery, Walhampton House for J. P. Heseltine, Didlington Hall for W. A. Tyssen-Amherst, and Shavington Hall for A. P. Heywood-Lonsdale were the biggest, but there were other sizeable jobs: Exton Park (1882), Callerton Hall (1882–3), Low Bentham Rectory (1884), Greenlands (1884–5), Bourn Hall (1884–5) and Moor Place (1886–7). Shavington is an especial pointer to the change in taste, for Heywood-Lonsdale had Nesfield's Cloverley Hall in which he could have dwelt had he been so inclined. Already, less than twenty years after its construction, Cloverley was completely out of date.

Naturally there had been extension jobs and alteration before. But those which attracted Shaw's most loving care were half-timbered houses like Gawsworth Rectory and Ightham Mote. In contrast, Willesley and Fowlers Park were handled roughly, however effectively. The discreet extensions to Jupp's Painshill (1872) were a mere second best, Shaw's original notion having been to supply the estate with a new and highly picturesque house. Even the sympathetic treatment of Yateley Hall was only loosely archaeological. One ill-documented job of the late 1870s shows him beginning to respect as well as enjoy the brick houses of round about 1700: the alterations and extensions made in 1878 to The Grove, a genuine Queen Anne house above Caversham. The side wing here hints at a style later than one would suppose possible at the time; but a few details betray it as Shaw's work, the earliest example of his wholehearted return to the traditions of the eighteenth century.

By Victorian standards, earlier houses had several faults which Shaw had to rectify when he was called in to reconstruct. They were too small for modern families, their service wings were cramped and unspecialized, and last but not least they were often poorly built and drained. Besides any alterations to the main house, Shaw would offer, at least in his first designs, an extensive new service wing which had to marry with the old house.[28] At Walhampton (the only one of the big reconstruction jobs to survive) his best achievement is the symmetrical fitting of a front and hipped roof to the plethora of 'offices' he had to house (ill. 178). For this portion he adopted a 'lower' style and gave the windows segmental heads, not allowed elsewhere in the house. At The Rookery, nothing special having been the matter with the old house, the correspondence is obsessively centred on points about servicing: coal shoots, drying closets, flower places and all the domestic paraphernalia then thought requisite for up-to-date, dignified living within the modern home.

The best advertisement for the spirit in which these reconstructions and alterations were undertaken is Moor Place, Much Hadham. This is a delightful brick-built Palladian house of 1777, designed by Robert Mitchell, with a well-proportioned exterior and a pure interior in the up-to-date Adam manner. Frederick Norman bought the house in 1886 and asked Shaw to have a look to see what needed doing. It was really no more than a

178. Walhampton House, elevation of service wing, 1883.

surveyor's job, yet Shaw was willing to take it on. For the next four months he is hard at work putting house and stabling in order. During this period Shaw has a field day with the drains and W.C.'s, and writes long letters to Norman on the subject. He discovers with relish that the old brick drains run under the house,

> . . . that even the gullies for some wonderful reason instead of running away from the house turn round underneath it, and that the closet in yard goes the same way. It is a most eccentric and dangerous arrangement, as in the case of any leak anywhere, the soakage must saturate the ground clean under the house . . . I think you must face it, I really don't think you could go into a house with the knowledge that there are old drains ramifying all under the house more or less filled with putrid sewage. The bad state of the soil pipes is caused by the whole gas from the cesspool coming back uninterrupted, and eating away the lead. It is a horrid bore to find it so, but not unusual.[29]

By July 1887 the Normans were well esconced with a new drainage system. Only then was there any talk of adding a small service wing and conservatory. Shaw now went ahead with these, but this second campaign was as basic as the first, only this time the anxieties were water tanks and flues:

> The walls are not over well built and are I daresay full of holes!! . . . I am writing to Hunt and proposing to open the wall in one or two places, and see if it would be possible to slip in flue pipes. It would be madness to run any risks, for these old boys thought nothing of building good lumps of timber into their walls, and constantly stuck them into flues.[30]

The alterations to the old house were kept to a minimum, and the new wing was added with extreme unobtrusiveness, kept low, and toplit wherever possible. The extreme care Shaw took at Moor Place shows greater respect for Mitchell's architecture than for that of

240

the rather earlier houses he had reconstructed. Every year was turning him into more of a devotee of Georgian architecture.

Curiously, he wavered towards mid-Georgian detail in the bigger reconstruction jobs as well, even when the houses were of the earlier period. The Rookery, for instance, was another of the real Queen Anne brick houses, with a 'nice old-fashioned flavour about it which is exceedingly pleasant after the spick and span things we all do now a days.'[31] But it also had two small wings allegedly by Adam, and it was these as much as the original core of the house which gave Shaw the keynote for his rearrangement and addition. Deliberately, the new wings were made restful, the 'Adam' rooms were left intact, and all the fittings had to match. For a sitting room, he commended a 'fine old-fashioned' (again the same word) red paper: 'a red room would be magnificent and Sir Joshua's in black frames with light-coloured mounts would be most decorative!!!'[32] That was in the Adam spirit; and Jacksons plastered the boudoir and drawing room explicitly in the Adam style.

At Shavington Hall, a more considerable and formal house rebuilt in brick in 1679–85, Shaw tended under stronger restraint in the same direction. Though the exterior had not been much changed, it was not entirely satisfactory; Shaw's recorded comment is 'The house always struck me as dignified but dull; it just missed being a fine thing, one can hardly say why.'[33] But he kept his changes to a minimum, adding only a plain flat-topped porch and three round mezzanine windows in the western re-entrant angle to light the stairs (ill. 180). These roundels with their emphatic dripheads were obviously intended to give the design the tiniest touch of 'go', but they had authentic enough seventeenth century ancestry, at Hampton Court. Within, Shaw had more scope. The interior of Shavington had been altered drastically in the 1820s, so he had to derive his details mainly from the gallery and staircase. Yet his instinct was to push the period forward into the eighteenth century. The main room he created was the library, where he introduced a frankly Georgian screen of square Corinthian pillars on a dwarf wall. The ceilings veered between a true seventeenth century style, something richer and more rococo, and an 'Adam' character. But the most Georgian of features at Shavington is a pair of lodges at Tittenley crossroads, remarkably dated 1885 (ill. 181). These splendid square cottages, with their squat outline, central chimney, and white-painted Diocletian windows, foreshadow more vigorously many of the neat Neo-Georgian lodges of the Edwardian age.

However Georgian some details of these jobs may be, none could be called wholly Palladian. Even at Didlington, where Shaw entirely reclothed a house of no special character (ill. 179), he adhered to the same Free Classic in brick as had been suggested at Walhampton and The Rookery by the original portions. The long sash windows of Walhampton and of the Didlington 'museum', an opulent single-storey apartment destined for Tyssen-Amherst's collection of curiosities seem indeed, like some of Nesfield's work in the style, to be modelled on Wren's Hampton Court. Wren, in fact, was very likely Shaw's closest model for these brick reconstruction jobs. But the exteriors never submit to a pure period ideal. In each of these three jobs he employs the Venetian window, just as Wren often did, but always with exaggerated entasis on the columns. It is part of a trend irresistible for an architect brought up on the arch and gradually committing himself to trabeation, to use circular heads, arches and plans on every conceivable occasion. These

179. Didlington Hall, garden side after reconstruction, with the 'museum' to the right.

180. Shavington Hall, entrance front, 1679–85, with porch and *oculi* by Shaw, 1885–6.

181. Shavington Hall, one of the Tittenley lodges.

Venetian windows, the Diocletian lights on the lodges and the oculi on the main house at Shavington, the semicircular fanlights of The Rookery stables, and the round skylight in the service passage at Walhampton, will lead on to the domed halls of 170 Queen's Gate and Bryanston, and thence to the obsessively curving forms of Chesters. Virtually Shaw's only domestic works after 1885 in which arcuation is absent are the Old English houses. Now and again these still drop from the drawing board, but they are a dying breed. Some of the best are built towards the end: Burrows Cross in 1885, Kemnal in 1887, and The Hallams, a reversion to the fuller flights of the '70s, as late as 1894–5. But they are exceptions to the run of Shaw's practice. Effectively, the Old English style has a twenty-year run in his hands and no more.

'The Home and its Dwelling Rooms'

We now have the background to 170 Queen's Gate, built for Frederick Anthony White in 1887–8. The commission has a well-known pre-history. Shaw's four Queen's Gate customers were all on intimate terms. While the Makins and Vivian families intermarried, Fred White, a wealthy cement manufacturer and dilettante, decided to rival his friend Heseltine with a house of his own. Heseltine was an acquaintance not only of Shaw's but of Whistler and the Morris circle; and White, according to his own account, went first to Philip Webb. In an interview, Webb made it plain that he would want to manage the whole thing from start to finish and would brook no interference, whereas White had ideas of his own. The upshot, as he told Lethaby, was that he went instead to Mr Norman Shaw.[34] What he omitted to say is that he had drawn out and may have taken to his interview with Webb a precise pair of elevations for his new house, a rudimentary plan, and several other sketches of his own.[35] They show that the elevations of 170 Queen's Gate, though not the plan, had already been designed by Fred White in a fair approximation to what was built. White, therefore, appears at first sight to have struck the decisive blow for what was to be labelled Neo-Georgian out of the strength of his personal

243

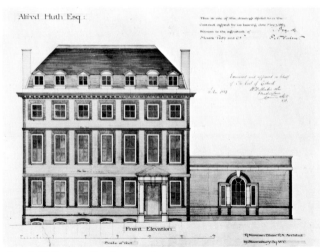

Alfred Huth Esq:

Front Elevation

182. (left) Barings Bank, street front.

183. (above) Bolney House, Ennismore Gardens, front elevation, 1883.

184. (below) 170 Queen's Gate, street fronts.

taste. And this surprising verdict upon White's importance and Shaw's pliancy in the matter seems corroborated by the latter's remark, well remembered in the White family, '*You* call it *my* house, but *I* call it *yours*.'[36]

But there is more to the matter. It is really a case of an agreeable client catalysing Shaw's designing powers and prodding him faster along a path he was already following. To appreciate this, the country house reconstructions and the kindred galleries and refreshment rooms Shaw added to the Royal Academy in 1883–4 are a help. The vital link is a long-forgotten town house which lamentably disappeared without proper record not long after the last war: Bolney House (1883–5), a commission in Ennismore Gardens, not so far from Queen's Gate. The client was yet another collector and connoisseur, Alfred Huth, son of the Hanseatic merchant and bibliophile, Henry Huth.[37] It was a reserved and absolutely regular design, broken only by the single-storey extension to the right, fifty feet by thirty, rather like Tyssen-Amherst's museum at Didlington, and designed to house the famed Huth collection of *incunabula*.

Can it be that White, who was a habitual picker-up of hints from other houses and will have known Huth, cast his eye over Bolney House before producing his own designs? There are precise similarities (ills. 183, 184); on each, seven bays and three storeys for the main front, with an attic in the hipped roof, a rich cornice like that at Barings, and a low extension to the right. The Bolney House roof was mansarded and the entrance affectedly off-centre, but these differences, like the proportions of the windows, show Shaw trying to improve in Queen's Gate upon the uncertainties of his earlier house. Huth, therefore, was the first patron to have an uncompromisingly 'Georgian' house from Shaw. But of course it was far from out of the blue. Since the first Queen Anne of Webb and Bodley, the town house had been pressing towards purity and symmetry.[38]

The true novelty of Bolney House and 170 Queen's Gate was the return to house architecture of the plain façade with undeviatingly regular sash windows, massive cornice, and no bays. When Shaw had previously used such a cornice, at Barings, we have seen that he chose to hip the roof back at the sides, a feature for which he was criticized because the building was engaged by party walls. Now he was trying the same trick with houses. Bolney House was detached all round and so presented no difficulty; but 170 Queen's Gate is engaged to the rear, so the hip back from the side opens up a clumsy space again. The moral was that this new model of formal hipped town house could contribute no answer to the problems of the terrace house, enclosed on a street front. Indeed, Shaw never designed a house for such a situation after his Embankment and Cadogan Square ones.

In the planning of 170 Queen's Gate (ill. 185), Huth's house was of no account. Apart from the grand library, it had been simply arranged, with regulation double drawing rooms upstairs. To keep some freedom in face of the dictates of symmetry, Shaw had been even more liberal than before with girderwork. But by the time of Fred White's house, more urgent measures still were needed; regularity was beginning to reach beyond the exterior and insinuate itself in each individual floor plan. So iron joists are now doubled or slung across at an angle, bedded deep in the plasterwork of the ceiling and encased round the whole of the upper hall.[39] They will reach their apogee at Bryanston and Chesters.

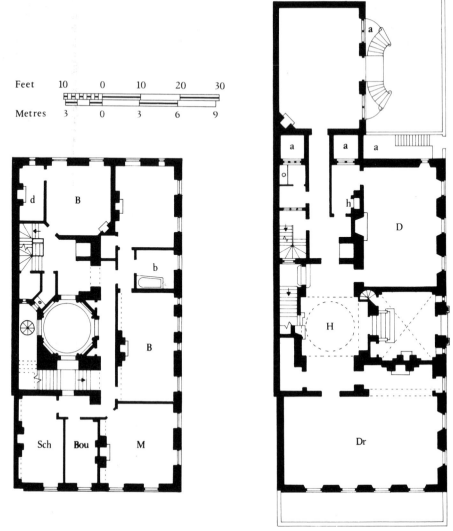

185. 170 Queen's Gate, ground and first floor plans.

What marks out the plan of 170 Queen's Gate is its sophisticated and entirely conscious derivation from the models of the English Renaissance, the houses then ascribed to Inigo Jones and his circle. At Bryanston (ill. 241), Shaw will vastly extend the main feature of the 'double-pile' plan, the long corridor running through a central hall from end to end of the house, and will incorporate virtual quotations from Coleshill, then believed to be by Jones.[40] But for Fred White, Shaw has made a skilful précis, curtailing the great hall and corridor into an extended inner hall and short passage to the billiard room. The hall (ill. 186) is lit by a saucer dome over the first floor landing, and behind it Shaw has pushed the stairs, also toplit but by separate skylights. These lights all come well below roof level, so that what appears as a pure hipped roof to the front conceals a U-shaped building with a central area. Staircase lighting from above such as this was a celebrated

246

186. 170 Queen's Gate, the hall.

feature of John Webb's Ashburnham House, which once again was often thought by the Victorians to be by Jones, and certainly supplied the model for the rich plaster ceiling of White's drawing room. In other details the house is equally derivative, an amalgam of borrowed archaeological motifs.[41] In line with this deliberate homage to seventeenth century classicism, Shaw keeps the three main reception rooms downstairs and reserves the first floor for more private apartments.[42] From now on, upper class social life would gradually re-establish itself at ground level.

After the first sketches, White went on helping in the design of the house. Shaw and he were in constant consultation both at home and abroad. For instance, White selected the sash bars, while the unequal glazing patterns in the tall ground floor windows (three lights above and four below, instead of the standard square lights, four above and four below as Shaw had suggested) were also his idea, agreed upon only after trial windows had been compared side by side. The green Italian shutters, too, could be due to White, or perhaps to Lethaby, whose personality is stamped upon the rain water heads and down pipes. 170 Queen's Gate, 42 Netherhall Gardens and New Scotland Yard were the last jobs on which Lethaby worked before he left the office in 1889, and the contract drawings are certainly from his hand.[43] Yet the idea of once again using Portland cement for the projecting parts of the façade, to avoid the building regulations, could only have been Shaw's. Not only is the modillion cornice made of the cement concrete from which White got his wealth, but the quoins are a mere skin-deep layer of cement backed by brickwork. By now one might think Lethaby would have been unhappy to countenance so flagrant a disregard for propriety. Shaw had the knowledge to grapple properly with the challenges of concrete, but here chose not to. From that point of view, 170 Queen's Gate and the later church at Swanscombe, built by the very gates of the Bazley White cement factory, were lost opportunities.

Shaw's new delight in round shapes in arches and domes, and the archaeology of the Fred White interiors (ills. 187, 188)—plain plastered ceilings and walls, marble floors, old mantelpieces bought from Duveen, and standard small Georgian-type fireplaces—raise the question of how Shaw conceived the finishings of his interiors in town.

To begin with, Shaw fitted his town house interiors to the same traditional oppositions as his country houses. Broadly, the contrast between woodwork and fabrics divided the domains of the sexes, marking off the virility of dining, business and billiard rooms from the cheerier lightness of the ladies' retiring places, drawing room, boudoir or bedroom. Where an area belonged equally to men and women, the males tended to win out, but there could be a struggle. Such a case was the saloon at Lowther Lodge, Shaw's first big urban interior (ill. 189). Important here was the strong personality of Alice Lowther, who had her own large ground floor room and painted the tiles in the saloon fireplace. Shaw could not expunge the Queen Anne detail of his exterior and endue the room with the weight of some baronial hall; it had to be loosely classic, and this upset the vocabulary he had used at Cragside to give such spaces severity. So he kept the proportions and details grand, with a wide arch, double doors with lugged surrounds, and a floor to ceiling chimney-piece. He wainscoted the walls too, but only to dado height, and then painted the panelling and allowed a busy paper over. These features freshen and lighten the room, but are at distinct odds with the mighty walnut ceiling.

187. 170 Queen's
Gate, the drawing
room.

188. 170 Queen's
Gate, the dining
room.

189. Lowther Lodge, the saloon.

The original interiors of 196 Queen's Gate, of which photographs survive (ills. 190, 191), had no comparable areas where the tune being called was uncertain. If the dining room at the back is still dark and severe, the front drawing room, with its Venetian blinds, leaded windows, flowered fabrics and patterned paper is the image of the early 'artistic' interior, to modern taste too busy, but still sympathetic. But the contrasts were harder to contrive than in the country. Without the full range of Old English detail and the deep inglenook space, the dining room has to rely upon its ceiling and dark furniture (much of it probably part of the Shaw/Lascelles collaboration) to convey the wonted assertiveness. Inside the restrictions that exterior style and spatial limitation set the town house, little could be done for the old dining room mood. Something else was needed; lightness and clarity all the way through.

In town, the rich interiors of the Leyland drawing rooms at Princes Gate were the last really dark domestic rooms which Shaw designed. Contrast with these the crisp decor of 185 Queen's Gate, or the relaxed elegance of no. 170. Gone are the strong papers, the ribbing of the ceiling, and the strongly patterned stuffs. At 170, the drawing room carpet is patterned only round the border, the curtains are plain, and the wall coolly monotone (ill.

250

190. (above) 196 Queen's Gate, the dining room.

191. (below) 196 Queen's Gate, the drawing room.

187). Inner and outer hall, billiard room and dining room, all maintain the chastity. Even in the upstairs morning room, the dark patterned paper, Lethabitic chimneypiece and crowded fittings are still 'little more than a background—a background to those daily scenes from the drama of household life which are acted within the dwelling rooms.'[44] At 185, Shaw has pressed this idea further and given each room an architectural character which will render furniture, paper, curtains and carpet subordinate (ills. 192, 193). In a sense it is a more highly decorated house than 170; there are more 'features', like the fireplaces with detached columns and the ornate morning room ceiling, but they dictate reticence elsewhere. Indeed, William Vivian seems to have responded by clearing away the usual late Victorian clutter and making do with little standing furniture.

The change in taste, in fact, is inextricable from the reaction against clutter. In the 1870s only Philip Webb saw that the way to austerity in interior design was to be rid of inessentials. That was not a doctrine which appealed either to Burges, always a crammer, or to the young Nesfield and Shaw. Nor, to judge from early interiors of the Morris firm, was it Morris's own. Only because Webb kept such a tight hold on his jobs and often worked for friends could he keep his interiors comparatively clear. As a self-confessed collector, Shaw was never able to practise personal restraint, always having a jumble of clocks and furniture filling up space at Ellerdale Road. But from about the time he built for himself, he began to appreciate cleanliness and simplicity of wall surface, and to dislike violently patterned wallpapers. Perhaps the experience of building for painters, who would not want strong patterns in their studios, stimulated the change. In Melbury Road, both Fildes and Stone had unusual decorative schemes. In his drawing room, Stone had silk stuff on the ceiling and plain soft tones on the walls, while his studio walls were hung with tapestry and a huge carpet covered the whole floor.[45] Fildes too had a wall-to-wall carpet and undemonstrative colours in his studio. In addition, Stone's dining room possessed what is described as the reproduction of an Adam mantelpiece, which sounds similar to the small fireplace in Heseltine's. Full archaeologizing in details had already hit the Queen Anne revival by 1876 at the latest. In many ways indeed, it makes nonsense to speak of the new town house gradually feeling its way back to the eighteenth century. A glance at Cubitt's interiors, or the kinds of fireplace which Stevenson used, shows that there was complete continuity with Georgian tradition in the detailing of the London town house. It is just that architects like Shaw who had pledged their faith elsewhere had to find their own ways of accepting the tradition, and in so doing came up with some revitalizing ideas.

The decorative history of 6 Ellerdale Road (ills. 141–3), helpfully recorded by Robert Shaw, points up the changes in his father's taste. When the dining room was built in 1876, high panelling in the country tradition was still used, but it was painted white all over and had a yellow paper above. This was surely an innovation for Victorian dining room décor; the white walls of his Albion Road house against which Shaw had set black furniture ten years before belonged probably to the drawing room. Later (and this is the stage for which most photographs survive) the Ellerdale Road panelling was painted green and a green paper hung to match. This lasted until quite near the end of Shaw's life, when he replaced the green paper with cheap modern tapestry from Maples. Shaw had certainly designed special spaces for tapestry, in the dining room at Dawpool (ill. 200), the

192. (above) 185 Queen's Gate, the morning room.

193. (below) 185 Queen's Gate, the dining room.

194. 10 Chelsea Embankment, a dressing room.

museum at Didlington, and again on the end wall of Fred White's drawing room. During the Edwardian period tapestry was much in vogue as a wall-covering, and Shaw praised its excellence as a reticent background.[46]

The other reception room at Ellerdale Road dating from 1876, the front drawing room, was originally painted white all over. Though the woodwork always stayed white, Shaw changed the walls first to a green patterned paper, later to a formal red paper with vertical bands. On the other hand the back drawing room always kept its reticent 'background' wallpaper of 1885 under Shaw's favourite peony frieze.[47] Here, what little structural woodwork there was was white like the plasterwork. The mature scheme Shaw adopted for deal woodwork was to paint large areas in one shade or another of green, or in unpanelled rooms to pick out details in white. One other little fact of interest is recorded about Ellerdale Road. The ceilings in the entrance hall and front drawing room consisted only of coats of rough grey plaster floated on carefully, and covered by a white paper. The

254

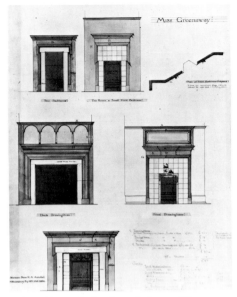

195. The 'Flete' fireplace, with De Morgan tiles, from J. Aldam Heaton, *Catalogue of Work* (1887).

196. 39 Frognal, fireplace designs, 1884.

usual finishing coat of white plaster was omitted because Shaw believed this gave a ceiling a hard look.[48]

The advent of Aldam Heaton to London meant that Shaw had a competent decorator to rely on for his interiors. Heaton evolved a series of wallpapers and other designs for furnishings and for about a decade executed most of Shaw's work in this line. Much of Shaw's collaboration with him must have worked by rote. An easy way of seeing this is by looking at their fireplaces. Aldam Heaton's first catalogue illustrates a set of classicizing fireplaces which had been evolved by Shaw over a series of jobs and in 1887 could still be ordered: the 'Adcote', the 'Flete' (ill. 195), the 'Shaw', and so forth.[49] The surrounds are normally of white-painted deal, frequently lugged and enclosing a border of tiles. Smarter types like the 'Flete' may incorporate a thin sliver of marble within the frame, and the egg and dart pattern henceforward so recurrent in late Victorian work. Gradually Shaw and Lethaby extended this range, marble supplanting tiles in popularity. Another set of standard surrounds appears on a drawing for Kate Greenaway, each one marked with the number of the relevant Elsley grate (ill. 196). Elsleys had by this time become Shaw's standard cast iron firm, and he designed fireplaces for both them and the Coalbrookdale Company.[50]

If one of this range of choices was too impersonal, there were various alternatives. At Dawpool, Shaw himself designed the dining room and picture gallery fireplaces, but more often in the 1880s he seems to have called in Lethaby for this sort of work. The times when he could let Lethaby 'loose' on entire interiors were rare; usually it was only practicable to put him to work on such setpieces. Certain examples were the fine chimneypieces at Cragside (ill. 50), Greenhill, and 185 Queen's Gate (ill. 193). But it was standard practice for a client to go outside the range of his architect's designs altogether. Stone's dining room mantelpiece, made in *carton pierre* by Jacksons, and Leyland's three 'off the cuff' chimneypieces bought at Binns for The Convent just before he died, have already been mentioned.[51] The fashion for re-using antiques, always present among the rich, was also on the increase. Shaw himself used for his own front drawing room the discarded framework of a memorial tablet taken out of a church because it wasn't Gothic.[52] Then came Leyland's importation of the Northumberland House staircase to 49 Princes Gate. By the turn of the century the thing had become a none-too-healthy craze.

Shaw loved grubbing around West End dealers' shops by himself or with clients and friends, searching for appropriate fittings. His son remembers an early visit to Joseph Duveen's in Soho, to see some German panelling.

> In the yard we found the future Lady Duveen peeling potatoes, and two of their sons making mud-pies in the gutter. Soon after that Mr Duveen opened a shop in Bond Street, and built a large house on the edge of Hampstead Heath. He appreciated fine things, but was quite prepared to deal in ugly ones. One day Mr Shaw happened to see in the shop a hideous piece of furniture and said in a bantering way: 'That is a neat thing you have there,' to which Mr Duveen replied: 'That is not for you nor any of your friends, that is for some rich American with no taste.'[53]

But a more lasting connection was also made through these visits. As Heaton's work became too fussy for Shaw's taste, he was supplanted by a new decorative collaborator, Robert Christie (1831–1924). Christie was a cabinetmaker and dealer with a shop in George Street near Portman Square; he was a Scot, an eccentric, and probably illiterate. But Shaw trusted him for furnishings and decoration, regularly employed him from the mid-1880s, and took his son Archie into the office. Indeed there was nothing to do *but* trust Christie, who had his own canny way of doing things. At Richards Castle, he was asked to supply carpeting:

> That wonderful old Christie, hearing or knowing by instinct what you wanted about the Communicants kneeling mat has been ransacking London and has found a rug with what I believe to be the very same border in colour and design as the two carpets you have.[54]

Later on, Christie had the whole business of the decoration and refurnishing of Overbury Court in hand:

> I drew out a small scheme for Christie's book cases, so as to introduce the new window. It will come nice and quiet and he *says* he has them all in hand. What a queer old thing it is! I went down this morning to hurry him up about patterns of colour for doorways at Village Hall and paper for upper part of walls. He altogether declines to be 'hurried up'; but I saw, certainly one of the most admirable pieces of furniture I have ever seen in my life, for you, and made out of an old wash stand! which he found in an attic at Overbury! It is quite beautiful. I don't think there can be much of the wash stand left, but that is a detail. The result is beautiful down to the green velvet lining, it is absolutely perfect. Yes, he is a funny old person. Also he has become possessed of some *old* Japanese prints, which I should much like you to see. They are Japanese 'old masters', lovely in colour and full of interest. Unhappily they are not cheap, but *good* art

is not often cheap, at least not now a days. Of course they are totally different from the thing we now call a "Japanese print".[55]

Shaw's letters about Overbury supply the proof, if proof is needed, that he was concerned to the last with the detailed decoration of his houses. This involvement, though, was absolutely confined to the permanent structure. Here are some extracts which convey his preoccupation with method and a plain but rich appearance.

I enclose you a design . . . for the Chimney piece for the old Entrance Hall . . . I would suggest plain *stone* for the great bulk of it, with little bits of black marble in the frieze and black marble slips round the opening, all very simple with *no* carving, just masons' work.

I have been thinking a great deal of the Dining room, and enclose for your consideration a tracing of one wall, where the fireplace comes. Would it not be good to have all this plain walnut, no stain or polish on it, just clean from the tool? After all, nothing looks so well, or is so good as the real wood. When done, it is done for ever. We often deceive ourselves I am sure. The deal of course sounds so much cheaper but then the painting is quite overlooked, and very often, as you know, painting comes to a very considerable item. I should make the cornice of walnut, not plaster or deal.

I should say Collins could do all the painting in bed rooms just as well as Christie, and much cheaper. Are you having them painted in oil or flatted? This is a subtle question. I do not believe in flatting. Of course it is much easier and presents a respectable appearance no matter how bad and rubbishy the work (the woodwork) is. Flatting hides up all defects, at least you do not *see* them, but plain oil painting can only be done successfully, on *good* work. Then it lasts six times as long. You can wash it, and do all sorts of things to it, that you cannot do to "flatted" work. Of course it is a little shiny at first, but this goes off very soon. All painters like flatted work. In answer to Mrs Martin's query, 'Would not the gallery of the upper set of rooms look well with a bright paper, instead of painting the walls a dull buff colour', I confess I should lean to paint, but *not* a dull buff. I should like nearly white, not dead white but a soft ivory colour. This with a few prints on it in black frames would look very nice and light, and clean, at least I fancy so.

You will never be able to make up your mind about the red for the corridor, from patterns. Why not go in faith for that which we *know* is right and always looks well viz. plain *Venetian* red, pure and simple, and again no tricks. I should paint all the 'Architecture' cornice &c. of the corridor plain white, in oil, and then put on an ordinary lining paper and distemper it pure Venetian red, it is sure to look well. You see, you must allow for the shade that some parts are in, and bright light in others. You can never see that in a pattern, and as a rule, a thing that looks well in the hand rarely looks well on the wall. See the everlasting traps we fall into with wall papers, judging from scraps. But all this is very prosy, and I am sure Mrs Martin is listening to you with a resigned aspect, and saying 'Really we don't need Mr Shaw to tell us all this twaddle!' and no more you do, for you have heard it all before.[56]

In 1904, Shaw produced a résumé of his latter opinions on domestic interiors in an essay called 'The Home and its Dwelling Rooms'.[57] It is a disappointing document, couched in the wan aesthetic prose of the artistic magazines of the day. There are one or two points of interest. He enthuses on tapestry, bewails the degeneration of houses into confused museums (surely a self-criticism), and warns of the difficulty of hanging pictures well when windows are set picturesquely. Most emphatically, he condemns pattern in wallpapers, obtrusive at all times, distracting when ill. All that is needed, says Shaw, is a dozen patterns or so of 'tone wallpaper' made in fifteen to twenty shades of colour, to be chosen to suit the lighting of each room. 'The present-day belief that good design consists of pattern, pattern repeated *ad nauseam*, is an outrage on good taste. A wall-paper should be a *background pure and simple.*' Modern teaching has encouraged pattern because of the authority of William Morris, 'a great man who somehow delighted in glaring wall-papers.'

This belittling of Morris is no accident. Morris was ready to criticize Shaw's architecture on Ruskinian lines, and had spoken with a degree of banter of his 'elegantly fantastic Queen Anne houses at Chelsea'.[58] In public, Shaw acknowledged Morris's greatness but always qualified it; in private he tended to be much more critical. The price of Morris work galled him especially, though he was willing to recommend it. At Overbury, he advised the Martins to put plain lining paper on the walls of their best bedroom to start with, and then after a year or two, to 'put on a Morris paper, not at 10d a roll, but 18/6d! as provided by that rampant (but defunct) socialist for well-to-do people.'[59] On stained glass his praise was equally tempered. Enthusing over Holy Trinity, Sloane Street, he could ask Sedding to call Morris in.[60] Yet in 1895 he was advising Ilkley against Morris glass in these terms: 'Morris is no good. His work is sometimes splendid (not always) but he is so full of cranks and general stubbornness that it is nearly impossible to do anything like what is called "business" with him. Being an advanced Socialist he cannot do with much less than from 100% to 250% clear profit in his work, and so his work is dear!!!'[61] Thus also Robert Shaw: 'In those days there was much talk among socialists of unearned increment. Mr Shaw used to say that Morris was a noticeable instance of this.'

Reginald Blomfield, who knew and appreciated both men, gives a summary of their relationship which cannot be bettered: 'The fact was that the temperaments of Morris and Shaw were radically different, and never could have come to terms. Morris was impetuous and fanciful, he was not called "Topsy" by his friends without reason; Shaw was a cool clear-headed Scot, of first-rate ability, with immense power of concentration, with no strong instincts for poetry.'[62] Though Shaw (just like Blomfield) did misunderstand the active sincerity of Morris' socialism, it was not the real stumbling block. He looked at socialism with the ordinary contemporary suspicion; but it was not automatic anathema, and he was quick to prick the bubble of a pupil's father who complained his son was 'going sketching with a socialist', meaning the harmless Lethaby.[63]

It was the gradual divergence of their artistic aims and tastes which must have made for the antipathy between Morris and Shaw. In the 1860s their aims were common and they knew each other, if not well. We have Shaw's word that he did not know Red House when he made his first domestic designs, and he seems never to have employed Morris directly, unless the Cragside windows are an exception. Heaton Butler and Bayne were his regular firm for stained glass; for something special he usually commended Burne-Jones, who in the latter days was remote from the firm's activities. On the domestic side, only Swan House and 180 Queen's Gate were decorated by the Morris firm, both in a taste somewhat different from Shaw's. Morris papers he sometimes but not often commended to his clients; Heaton's he used more often. Perhaps Shaw and Morris's friends got on tolerably well before Heaton's furious quarrel with Rossetti, and were then estranged.[64] But suspicion of their posing and facetiousness had always lurked. John Clayton, least humourless of men, told Shaw once how on an early visit to one of the Pre-Raphaelite dens, he found various old master reproductions hung upside down on the walls and asked why. 'But we had no idea that they were hung wrongly,' they cried. 'This is most interesting. Here is a man who can tell us which way these things ought to be hung.'[65] This kind of antic was what made the earnestness of the later socialism difficult for so many to believe in.

On the substantive question of interior decoration, Morris and Shaw slowly parted company. In about 1880, Morris gave his most informative lecture on the subject, 'Making the Best of It'.[66] It is packed with little insights on interiors. He advises smaller windows which do not come too low, and a division of the floor surface between carpets and liberal areas of bare boarding. These ideas coincide with Shaw's country house practice of the 1870s. But for the wall, Morris wants a strong horizontal division: either a narrow frieze, if the main wall is to be hung with stuffs or panelled, or a high dado rising to four feet or so, if painting or papering is intended. These are Gothic or Old English prescriptions which Shaw was slowly discarding. Henceforward, Shaw would keep a dado down low, and panel or paint the whole wall from skirting to cornice without interruption. He would also plaster his ceilings, while Morris was still recommending exposed beams. Morris' advice on colour is again quite close to what is known of Shaw's colour schemes. But the lecture soon dissolves into an elaborate set of rules on pattern design without reference to its location. This was exactly what Shaw was coming to mistrust and why he discarded not only Morris but Heaton. Indisputably, the Morris firm had failed to maintain its impetus beyond the mid-1870s. 1874 was the critical year, when Webb and the other partners, seeing that its work was really done, wished to disband the firm. Afterwards, though Morris himself went on turning out new patterns of individual brilliance, his commitment to whole schemes of interior decoration was much diminished. By 1885, the firm's interiors were looking old-fashioned. But there is more than fashion to it; Webb, Burne-Jones and even Morris were otherwise preoccupied, and the lesser lights failed to inject the needed new blood. The initiative was passing to Heaton, Crane, Day and other designers happy to work in the Renaissance tradition. At the turn of the century, Shaw felt that the example of the later Morris had led to the self-absorbed glaring pattern designing of *art nouveau* and the 'spook school'.[67] It was indeed true that only a few men like Walton and Voysey could produce quiet enough wallpapers to avoid clashing with their understated domestic interiors.

If Shaw so mistrusted Morris and his vision, how could he work so well with Lethaby, a fervent Morris admirer? Firstly, Shaw's antipathy extended to neither Burne-Jones, a life-long hero, nor Philip Webb, Lethaby's real mentor.[68] Sydney Barnsley once described

197. Dawpool, garden side.

a visit to Shaw at which the latter spoke of his life-long friendship with Webb and produced treasured photographs which Webb had given him fifty years before. And when Shaw died, Webb wrote to Lethaby 'I had thought that the old and trustworthy friend Norman Shaw would have held on as long as myself. But no! He has done good and serious work and could have done more if he had lived longer.'[69] Secondly, when Lethaby entered Shaw's office, he was young and provincial. It was probably some time before he met Webb, who had small effect upon his work until nearly 1890. At first Lethaby designed in a florid Renaissance style which began at Flete and reached its culmination in the Cragside chimney-piece. His early taste was catholic and eclectic, to judge from his sketchbooks and a number of unusual detail designs for Shaw which seem to be his: the pulpit and bold Byzantine font for All Saints' Leek (ill. 237), and the intarsia decoration for Leyland's morning room at Princes Gate. But there is nothing in them even faintly reminiscent of Webb.

Even after Lethaby had set up on his own, Webb's hold over him was primarily moral and spiritual. For every hint of Webb's work in Avon Tyrrell and Melsetter, there is one of Shaw's as well. Avon Tyrrell, Lethaby's 'setting-up' present from Shaw, follows approximately upon the orthodox Shaw country house plan of the 1880s. Melsetter too may hark back to Shaw's remodelling of the old stone and roughcast manor house at High Callerton, Northumberland, carried out with an austere observance of locality of which Webb might have been proud.

There must have been some differences of opinion between Shaw and Lethaby on the subject of style. But though Shaw's move towards archaeology of interior detail may have been irksome to the younger man, the new restraint and purity were valuable for his own future, however differently he would interpret it. It is well recorded that Shaw admitted 'that he never pierced the heart of Lethaby! At the end of 20 years he was no nearer knowing him than at the beginning.'[70] Nevertheless, he had boundless respect for him, summed up in the famous rejoinder to a friend who referred to him as Shaw's pupil: 'No, on the contrary it is I who am Lethaby's pupil'.[71] Even better tribute to their relationship was that when Tyssen-Amherst insulted Lethaby on a visit to the office in Shaw's absence, saying he would not be put off with a mere minion, Shaw wrote straight away telling him he could take himself and his work elsewhere, and the matter was patched up only after delay and difficulty.[72] In fact, Lethaby's privileges and opportunities in Shaw's office were such that minor differences of opinion mattered very little.

Two Commissions

It must not be thought that now the comelier classic was before his eyes, Shaw would entirely desert his ancient favourites. Old English, if rarer, was still about in the 1880s; pure Gothic was once more his undisputed choice for churches, after some wavering at the time of Bedford Park; and before he abandoned the Haddon Hall tradition he had used for Flete and his earlier stone-built houses of the north, this too had its final fling: Dawpool.

In Dawpool's short heyday, the house stood firm and grim upon the dank bluffs of the western Wirral, overlooking the sandbanks of the Dee. The note of Kingsley's melancholy poem overhangs the region:

> They rowed her in across the rolling foam,
> The cruel, crawling foam
> The cruel, hungry foam
> To her grave beside the sea;
> But still the boatmen hear her call the cattle home,
> Across the sands o' Dee.

Seemingly the same spirit pervaded the site of Dawpool too. Few trees came at all near the door; even a flower garden was forbidden. Instead, the mass of the immense mansion, palliated only by dark ivy patches clasping at the ruddy sandstone walling, started out from barren heath, amidst outcrop, gravel, furze, heather and bracken. To judge from photographs (ill. 197), the mood of Thomas Ismay's house was alternately fearsome and ghostly, lowering in shadow and rainfall, bleaching balefully in sunlight, in accord with the rich but chilly red of the Wirral sandstone from which it was fashioned. Next to the gates and stables of Dawpool lies the small village centre of Thurstaston; here, as the

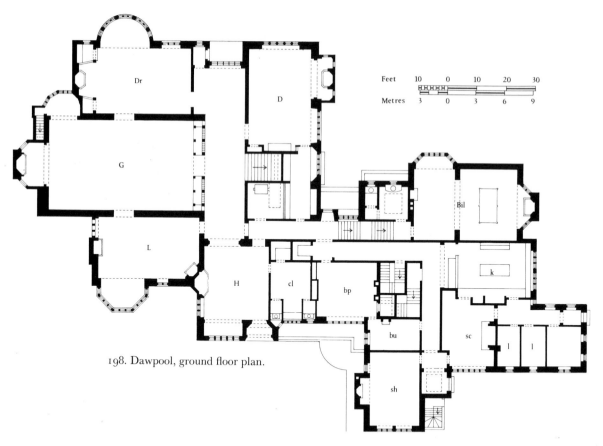

198. Dawpool, ground floor plan.

contours descend to the shaded group of old hall, church, and churchyard where the Ismays lie, the traveller from the drabness of Birkenhead's flat hinterland finds first promise of rural gentleness. All the starker, therefore, must it have been to emerge from this oasis and take the winding drive up to the monster perched upon heathland above. Yet it was return to reality of a kind. Dawpool's bracing strength and sobriety hint at the other nearby estuary and mighty city from whose fortunes those of the Wirral are inextricable. Upon Liverpool, upon the Mersey from which the house was hidden, and upon the sea towards which it tentatively turned, the shipping wealth of Ismay and the existence of Dawpool depended utterly.

These determinants of site and character forced Dawpool into a framework of stylistic severity for which in 1882 Shaw's classic was as yet unready. Liverpool's classic traditions of architecture could for the moment only impress, not yet inspire him. Besides, Thomas and Margaret Ismay travelled to Adcote in January 1882 to decide upon their architect, and may have asked for something of the kind, only grander.[73] Ismay was a true *nouveau-riche*. His father was a shipwright from Cumberland, and he had been in the Liverpool shipbroking business since the age of nine. He had owned his own company since he was twenty, and in 1870 amalgamated with his old firm to form Ismay, Imrie & Co., specializing in American traffic. Their White Star line soon had the lion's share of the transatlantic crossing market, which prospered until after Ismay's death, but had a less happy later history, culminating in the Titanic disaster. Perhaps Ismay employed Shaw because of his shipping connections, though a contact through Leyland is more likely. It

262

can be no coincidence that during the years of the building of Dawpool, an agreement was made whereby the White Star Line provided ships and crew for the New Zealand trade for the Shaw Savill Company, then going through an awkward period.[74] Ismay's commercial enterprises were to stand Shaw himself in good stead, too.

Even more clearly than Cragside, Dawpool exhibited the symptoms of new riches. Ismay had none of Armstrong's technological enthusiasm, but had made his fortune himself and wished to express the philosophy of 'only the best will do'. Technically therefore, there is little that is new in Dawpool. The underground railway for coal transportation in the basement, if unprecedented in Shaw's houses, had long been used by others.[75] An odder decision was to dispense with nails anywhere in the building, and lavishly rely on brass screws alone, a policy verifiable in the stables today. Indeed, Dawpool seems to have represented a further tightening up in Shaw's exacting standards of building strength. The four lowest tenders were all passed over, to local annoyance;[76] and villagers recall the difficulty the demolition squads encountered when Dawpool came down in the '20s—dynamite had to be copiously used.

So the ostentatiousness of the house lay in solid strength rather than ornament. Of decoration there was plenty, but everywhere tempered by sternness. The plan (ill. 198), in many ways a perfection of the country house type Shaw had been evolving for so long, appears through its logic unrelaxed, as though by driving an unremitting corridor through the centre of the house he had dispelled his earlier charm. Previously, he had controlled his tendency to grandeur in domestic work well; at Dawpool, it returned and brought with it frigidity. The new classicizing features like the elliptical picture gallery ceiling and billiard room fireplace must have overpowered the pretty decorative detailing. Top-lighting for large rooms is always apt to give a stale effect, and thus in photographs at least (ill. 199), the picture gallery has a deadness that undermines the fine proportions. It is a fault partially corrected in the Cragside drawing room, but even that lacks the airy vigour of the Adcote and Greenham halls. Uncertainties likewise invaded the other rooms. The dining room (ill. 200), ponderous still in style, had to rely now for its charms, not on furniture or carving, but on the soft furnishings and tapestries supplied by Heaton. In outline it was a stark room, reminiscent of those pictures by Orchardson in which the grandee and his bored wife dine in desperate solitude. All through, Dawpool was over-reliant on its setpiece effects, the part Tudor and part Classic inglenooks in dining room, picture gallery and billiard room.

Dawpool, then, was stringent and slightly cold within, grandly overpowering without. This was the problem that Shaw would face henceforward with his buildings; how to make them as lovely as they were strong and clever. Prettiness he had tried as an aesthetic and found wanting, though he would go back to it now and again. It was not what Ismay wanted, and the house was after all built entirely to his wants, not even to his family's. A telling extract in a letter of Shaw's, written when the Ismays left the house in 1907, shows how far such palaces were just the brief playthings of their builders, and with what indifference Shaw could view the fate of his own creations:

Poor old Dawpool! I am sorry. Perhaps it can be turned into a sanatorium or a small pox hospital! I remember Mrs Ismay saying to me more than 10 years ago, that even then it had more than answered its purpose, for it had interested and amused Mr Ismay

199. Dawpool, the picture gallery.

every day of his life for 15 years! 'Sich is life, vich likeways is the hend of all things', as Mrs Gamp said.[77]

To an extent, it was the problem of the nation as well as that of an ageing and more serious-minded architect. The sluggish British were waking up to their eminence, and realizing that they might owe it more responsibility than mere lip-service; it might demand a style of living that was weightier than before. Life in the late Victorian decades may have become perceptibly lighter in artistic and intellectual circles. But the rituals of official and high social life were becoming more sharply divisive, as consciousness grew that a way of life stood for something over and above self, or family, or even class. Dawpool does not stand for the full imperial spirit, but its self-consciousness points in that direction. Shaw was continuing to succeed because his own artistic development kept pace with the national mood to an extraordinary degree. It happened to others as well, but Shaw's changing styles epitomize the matter with special aptness. This mood could be

200. Dawpool, dining room fireplace.

consciously accepted or rejected. Even in architecture, imperialist attitudes towards the styles were making themselves known. Architects would become split into two camps, and Shaw was to find himself part of the established order while his pupils were among the dissidents.

The idiosyncrasy of Shaw's status as a half-private and half-public figure was highlighted when a mark of official approval was at last granted, and he was made architect for the new Metropolitan Police Central Offices on the site of Scotland Yard, in December 1886.[78] The obscure way in which Shaw slipped into the commission marks both his acceptability to government figures, and the hole-in-the-corner manner in which such big businesses could still be handled at this date. Later, when he became advisory architect to the Quadrant, there was to-ing and fro-ing of an unofficial kind, but he was at least picked by a committee of architects. For New Scotland Yard, the architect was decided peremptorily by the Tory Home Secretary, Henry Matthews. Afterwards, Matthews claimed he had gone to 'high artistic authorities' in London.[79] Whoever these were, one may doubt whether they weighed more than the opinion of Matthews' cabinet colleague W. H. Smith, who had commissioned Shaw to reconstruct parts of his country house, Greenlands, Hambleden, in 1884–5, during a prolonged spell of opposition. Greenlands was the least remarkable of Shaw's reconstruction jobs; but Smith, only Shaw's third M.P. client, did not forget his architect.

New Scotland Yard is an example of the relative enlightenment of Tory policy towards official architecture, compared to the Liberal record. The coincidence which had united Disraeli's Young England movement with Pugin's social and architectural ideals may have been modified but went on right through the century. The Foreign Office débacle was caused by a Whig, and the Law Courts was hampered by the non-co-operation shown to Street by Gladstone's Works Commissioner. The latest Liberal muddle, the Admiralty Offices competition of 1884, had put both parties off competition, but their attitudes to the new police building were instructively different. Sir William Harcourt, Matthews' predecessor as Home Secretary and later the intransigent parliamentary opponent of New Scotland Yard, had pressed for a Royal Engineer as architect, against the Receiver of Police, Alfred Pennefather, who wanted to employ John Dixon Butler, the police surveyor, with an 'architect of standing' supervising the job.[80] When Matthews took over the Home Office, he sent for Shaw and probably promised him the whole job. But so as not to offend Pennefather, his first task was to report on the efficient draft plans which Dixon Butler had prepared.

The final four-square plan of New Scotland Yard, with the large central court, adheres closely to Dixon Butler's preliminary draft. In arranging the various branches of the constabulary, Shaw naturally felt glad to follow his advice. In the absence of police records it is hard to say how far they collaborated on the building; less, certainly, than on the extension, but probably quite intensively. Although Shaw had been foisted upon them, Pennefather and Butler were easily won over to his notions. The main recommendation of Shaw's report, and the chief change he made in planning, was to remove the corridors from the centres of the four sides, widen them, and push them against the internal court, in order to obviate fanlights over the doors and all the other forms of borrowed light which were so popular in government offices.[81] This allowed him to reduce the court a little, but the consequence was probably to heighten the building.

The site, however fine, imposed difficulties and limitations from the first. The Government had agreed to buy it cheap in the summer of 1886, after urgent representations from Pennefather. It had an unhappy history. First it was to be occupied by a National Opera House, but the company financing the operations had bankrupted; then it was to be used for residential chambers, but this company too had failed. To combat the waterlogged soil, both enterprises had put in concrete footings which had then been covered in, and no reliable record remained of the whereabouts or quality of these foundations. So difficult was the soil, that the whole first year of building was taken up in putting in new foundations, which had to go down in places to a depth of thirty-five feet because of the lack of firm ground. Steam pumps were constantly taking away the water, and the digging was like an archaeological excavation, with the same need for interpretation. In the event, many of the Opera House foundations were re-used.

These delays allowed Shaw to mature the scheme considerably. In April 1887 he sent

201. (above) New Scotland Yard, perspective of first design showing Embankment front, drawn by Gerald Horsley, 1887.

202. (right) New Scotland Yard, perspective showing part of revised design, drawn by Gerald Horsley, 1890.

203. New Scotland Yard, Embankment and south fronts.

a perspective drawn by Gerald Horsley to the R.A. Exhibition, showing the building as first designed. It now looks disappointing (ill. 201): a relaxed block, a good deal lower than the final version, broken only by the 'pendentive towers' at the corners, the gables which now earmark the sides being absent. There are one or two picturesque details which Shaw later omitted; slate-hung sides to the dormers, fussy designs to the stacks, and shutters with heart-shaped cut-outs, no doubt the idea of one of the pupils.[82] There is something of both Barings and the Alliance Assurance in the design, which shows Shaw in a distinct mood of understatement. By the end of the year it had been superseded by the need for more accommodation, and he set about revamping the whole thing.

For a change, New Scotland Yard shows Shaw puzzling over elevational design more than planning. The offices he had to house were many and their grouping involved some clever touches of disconnection in the plan. The accurate tracking of the concrete flues, often from outside walls, to the four great chimney stacks was a particularly complex job involving tricky (and often exposed) girderwork, for which Percy Ginham did most of the work.[83] But the plan was simple in outline. The great need was to make the building bulk and tell in its magnificent position over the Thames. Over this Shaw and Lethaby must have pored for weeks on end. They were both helped and hampered by an

268

enthusiastic agreement made at the start between Matthews and Sir Edward DuCane, Director of H.M. Prisons, to experiment with granite quarried by Dartmoor convicts, and, in the upper part, Portland stone, which could again be acquired cost free because of government ownership of quarries. This would certainly not have been Shaw's notion. In an early letter we find him fighting a rearguard action for his beloved brickwork:

> I confess that at present my feeling would be to try the effect of the introduction of a certain amount of red brick in this upper part, mixed of course with the Portland stone. It is a serious question whether a building with a grey granite base, a white stone upper part and a slate roof might not look very cold, and whether it would not materially gain by the introduction of a warm material like red brick.[84]

Happily this plea was heard. Brick, still very rare in prominent public buildings, had been introduced by Street in areas of the Law Courts; Shaw may have followed his lead in confining the Portland stone to the strong cornice, to the gable aedicule and doorways, and to a banding of the building. This banding allowed him to grade the transition from the granite base to the brickwork upper storeys, in fact to give this polychrome layering the logic it had lacked in the Alliance Assurance building.

In no Shaw building is there a greater sense of a mind working from first principles. In its rational compromises between classic and Gothic spirits, New Scotland Yard is the most Webb-like design he ever produced. For precise models we are in ignorance; Albert Richardson thought the details derived from a Renaissance building in Copenhagen, while Beresford Pite speaks of Shaw transporting to the Embankment 'a Dutch-cheese warehouse from the banks of the Dort'.[85] There was, probably, a Netherlandish model for the outlines of the composition. The drawings reveal greater and greater restraint in the outline as the scheme progressed, and a purifying of the detail. Originally, pedimented niches were to be placed against the chimneys, but these were dropped when the external details were finally redesigned during 1889. The source for the revision is quite clear: John Belcher's Institute of Chartered Accountants, designed in 1888 and now being built.

The intermediary between Shaw and Belcher was Mervyn Macartney, Shaw's most classically inclined pupil. He records that the two first met on the site of the Institute of Chartered Accountants, with which Shaw was 'immensely taken', and that he afterwards championed Belcher's admission to the R.A.[86] Belcher had long admired Shaw's work, and from this time his links with Shaw's entourage tightened.[87] Lethaby's friendship with Beresford Pite, who had been with Belcher since 1881 and who is often suspected of having designed the detail at the Institute, must also have helped. The two had similar relationships with their masters, so much so that one wonders if the Belcher/Pite partnership was modelled on Shaw's with Lethaby. Shaw and Belcher were certainly of mutual profit to each other. Belcher's American journey of 1899, of importance for his architecture, came about because Shaw passed on to him the assessorship of the Phoebe Hearst University in California.[88] And Belcher championed Shaw through the travails of the Quadrant and the King Edward Memorial in Liverpool.

At New Scotland Yard, Shaw is the first and cleverest imitator of Belcher's baroque, having lighted upon his blocked columns and boldly broken pediments as the things to give braggadoccio to a set of previously insipid classical details. If there is a major fault in the detailing of the building, it is that the windows, placed upon the surface with such frank irregularity, do not cohere with the style of these final details; it may indeed have been too late to have them altered. The new style of detailing was of enormous importance to Shaw. Instead of a revised view of the building as a whole, the drawing he sent to the R.A. show in 1890 was a Horsley perspective emphasizing the great rusticated entrance doorway (ill. 202). His subsequent designs almost run over with the same blocked windows, aedicules and doorways. Shaw saw such details as neither French nor Genoese (as some have thought the Institute of Chartered Accountants), nor even as links with Hawksmoor and Vanbrugh's English baroque, but as authentic elements of the English classicism of Jones and Wren.[89] Archaeologically he was quite correct; but his practice was more licentious than his sources.

When New Scotland Yard began to emerge from its cocoon of scaffolding in 1890 (ill. 203), it provided the politicians with a puzzle. Triumphant, swaggering classical details could be recognized, but the shape and form of the building were a mystery; there was nothing remotely like it. Some attack could therefore be predicted. The most obvious handle would have been to censure the Government for incompetence, but unfortunately for Sir William Harcourt this was not possible. The whole job was free of dissension; Shaw, Pennefather, Butler and the excellent clerk of works, George Eraut, had all worked in harmony. The contractors, John Grover and Son, had made a fine job of the work during a period of difficulty for the building trade; there were not even any extras, the superstructure being finished for the contract sum of £93,770. So Harcourt, who is said to have thought that Dixon Butler was responsible for the design, could only attack the building on grounds of taste.[90] He launched two parliamentary attacks, one in 1890 when the scaffolding was still not down, and another much later, in 1898. The first, a vague and indefinite criticism by Harcourt and Cavendish-Bentinck, was important because it drew Shaw, at the Home Office's urgent request for ammunition with which the attack could be returned, to articulate his motives and ambitions in the design. His statements are typically uninformative and modest, and rely heavily on the old adage of there being no disputing about tastes. Here is the gist of them:

> That this work is in some respects a new departure from the regulation public building there can be no doubt, but a question arises how far a departure is not merely allowable but desirable . . . My aim has been to have less of what I should call 'style', and more of what I should call 'character'. Style gives what we have already got many examples of, viz. dull copies of Italian palaces, mediaeval buildings &c. and they are generally found to be unsuited to their purpose, ill lit, and from an artistic point of view, dead, and so failures.[91]

> In the old days it was very different. A style was then a living art, the result of character. Now with us it is a mere re-production and for many years we have all recoiled from it and have been trying to get more individuality and character into our buildings, often failing lamentably, but surely on the whole better and more interesting than that dead old stuff.

> The regulation modern building has generally a show front, or fronts, but round the corner or in any part supposed to be not much seen it is made plain and common, if

270

not hideous. I dwell on New Scotland Yard being a genuine building, in which we have no sham or shew fronts, all is of the same quality and in the court it is the same. In order to secure this, a quality that I consider essential to good building, I have reduced the ornamental features to a minimum, relying on the bulk and outline to give the desired character. Had I sacrificed what I believe to be a sound principle I might have put more ornament on the shew fronts, and so possibly have made it more attractive to a certain class of mind. But after all the whole matter is a question of taste, on which I fear people never can and never will agree, certainly not for some time.[92]

In an interview Shaw gave to *Murrays Magazine* on this subject, he let a little more out. He had aimed, it was reported, at 'solidity and sternness to give simplicity . . . His view of the Metropolitan Police is that it is an essentially stern, and not at all frivolous body.'[93] That was a better clue; but for the time the attack passed without serious comment. When Harcourt returned to the charge in 1898, on the general subject of public building, his language was more virulent. Most modern buildings, he said, recalled Byron's view of certain poetry, that 'the most recent was the least decent'. In this he included the Houses of Parliament, the Foreign Office, the Law Courts and the Admiralty, and added: 'I do not know whether the building which has been erected for the accommodation of the police at Westminster Bridge can be regarded as a decoration to the metropolis, but it is rather inferior, in my opinion, in architectural beauty to the premises of Messrs. Crosse and Blackwell, which face it on the other side of the river.'[94] In the subsequent protests to *The Times* condemning Harcourt's remarks, one writer leapt to the defence of the famous jam factory, but others did better. An impressive list of signatories wrote in, endorsing the view that 'of the public buildings erected by Government in London during the present generation it is the one of which London may be most justly proud.'[95] The list is worth giving; Jackson, Alma-Tadema, Blomfield, Butterfield, Onslow Ford, Belcher, Brock, Webb, Sargent, Lethaby (!), Thornycroft, Crane, Bentley, Frampton, Armstead, J. C. Horsley, Dicksee, Prinsep, Boughton, Crofts, MacWhirter, Riviere, Ouless, George, Fulleylove, Cave, Micklethwaite, Philip Norman, Ricardo and Champneys.

Besides the old rival Philip Webb, the interesting person on this list is the eighty-seven-year-old Butterfield.[96] His inclusion was possible because, as he probably saw, Shaw was harking back as much as forward. The roots of New Scotland Yard lay in Ruskinian Gothic. With this building Shaw had resumed, however differently, the heroic scale and passion of Bingley. If only through the person of Lethaby, the long-laid ghost of Ruskin had surely returned to haunt Shaw. Beresford Pite was the only critic perceptive enough to pick this up, pointing out how the pendentive towers bulging at the corners follow Ruskin's plea for the swollen outline.[97] But much more is Ruskinian than that. The Edinburgh *Lectures on Architecture* had been strong for pendentive turrets. The *Lamp of Power* had urged 'the choice of a form approaching a square to the main outline', indeed if possible a hollow square like that of the Doge's Palace.[98] No building had been so bravely four-square as New Scotland Yard since the Oxford Museum. The colouring, rising from a heavy granite base to lighter materials, white Portland stone and cheerful brick above, answered Ruskin's plea for associational geology, mass giving way to lightness and brightness as it rises. Finally, the very conception of New Scotland Yard is imbued with the spirit of *architecture parlante*, so dear to Ruskin's heart. Its smooth, unscaleable surface speaks of a fortress built 'against infection and the hand of war'; indeed Shaw had been required to make the building safe against riot, with the extra irony that it was the labour of convicts in the hewing of Dartmoor granite that had made it unassailable. The turrets placed at the corners speak of Scottish military architecture, passing on to posterity the name of New Scotland Yard. And by a last curious stroke of wit, unmistakeable on the drawings but toned down for the onlooker from below, the turrets are capped with a spiked helmet form. A 'pickel-haube', Pite calls it,[99] but to uneducated eyes it speaks unambiguously of the old London policeman's helmet. Square in metropolitan might, flanked by four guardians of the Queen's peace, New Scotland Yard keeps its stalwart watch upon London's riverside.

CHAPTER 7

The Churches

Quit thy state,
All equal are within the church's gate.

Motto from George Herbert, Cheltenham Parish Church
Competition, 1863.

FRAMEWORK

FROM his early days at St Mary Magdalene, Munster Square, Shaw had a personal commitment to the Tractarian Movement within the Church of England. The loyalty lasted for the rest of his life, and separated him from agnostics such as Webb, Godwin and Lethaby, however little was said of it. His family embraced piety more fervently than he. Agnes and Robert took their devotions very seriously, and his daughter Elizabeth Helen joined the Sisterhood of Bethany.[1] Shaw himself felt a responsibility towards church work. He would often make donations to church building funds, sometimes waived fees, and twice worked for missions.[2] Broadly, therefore, he shared the ideals of Butterfield, Street, Pearson, Brooks and Bodley, the great church designers of their time.

Yet Shaw never gained widespread popularity as a church architect. Certainly, there is no dearth of ecclesiastical work in his career. He designed at least eighteen complete churches, of which sixteen were built, and performed roughly the same number of restorations.[3] But though Shaw's merits as a church architect were appreciated, few of his churches were conspicuous or well-known. Muthesius was full of enthusiasm for them in *Die Neuere Kirchliche Baukunst*, but his essay was never translated.[4] English writers of the time tend to nod politely towards the churches, only to redirect attention back to the houses. Houses were, of course, far more numerous. Once his career was established, the same proportions of domestic to ecclesiastical jobs tended to go on. When Shaw deliberately altered the pattern in 1881, church restoration was indeed one of the areas of practice he eliminated; but as many trivial secular jobs also disappeared.

To an extent, Shaw did not feel at home with church work. Perhaps the monopoly that Street and his peers held blocked him from getting all the church commissions he had at first hoped for, and blunted his spirits. Certainly, these men had imposed a severity, not to say pomposity, upon the whole business of ecclesiastical architecture alien to both the spirit of Pugin and the tenor of the early Nesfield/Shaw practice. Nesfield never built a whole new church, though he reconstructed a few; he was not, so far as is known, 'High Church', preferring to work for private patrons. Shaw usually got on well with the clergy. But his levity would not always have been appreciated by the earnest parsons of the day.

273

Later on at least, his diffidence in the field sprang from an honest belief that his talents lay elsewhere. Thus to Sedding:

> Why you should *pretend* (yes sir, pretend) to care anything about the Ch at Bedford Park I can't conceive, but I'll send it to you all the same, and I'll send you another which I was to have built for the Harrow Mission, but which has been modified. And you needn't say any mortal thing about either, or as little as possible. You know I am not a Church man, I am a house man, and soil pipes are my speciality.[5]

At the end of his life, commending Gerald Horsley to Fred White for the chancel panelling at Swanscombe, Shaw writes

> I *do* think you could do ever so much better with a man more used to that sort of work. I always feel, in all sincerity, that church decorative work is *not* my metier. I am not quite at home in it . . . I date from the 'Gothic' of 50 years ago, and the modern man does much better. Bodley's work is, to me, absolutely perfect.[6]

Such professions of inability jar harshly for anyone who has seen Bingley, Meerbrook, Leek or Richards Castle. They stretch back to before the sapping period of illness. In a note on a first design for St Michael's Bournemouth, written hurriedly for the *Building News* in 1873, Shaw writes: 'I really have nothing to say about the Bournemouth Church. It is to be a very simple, commonplace thing, trusting to its size and proportion for any dignity it may have, which won't be much.'[7] An insignificant remark, perhaps; but it ties in with his visible frustration with contemporary taste as manifested in the later churches of Scott, Butterfield and even Street. In Gothic work, his admiration thenceforward would be directed to Bodley, Sedding and G. G. Scott junior.

There is a legend that in his palmiest period Shaw had a card printed saying he was too busy to oblige Lord So-and-so, and would cross out 'Lord' and insert 'Mr' where appropriate; and that pupils would add 'but advises clients that Mr Ernest George's office is at . . .'[8] Neither the snobbery nor the commendation lends the story authenticity; disappointed house-seekers, if they wanted advice, were pointed towards his pupils. But for church work, Shaw would have firmly advised his friends Bodley and Sedding. For Bodley there is abundant praise besides the quotation above. When he was elected A.R.A. in 1882, Shaw characterized Bodley thus to Luke Fildes: 'he is a *long* way the most accomplished artist on our little list—stiff a little, not the sort of man to poke in the ribs and call "old cockywax", but a most able architect and I am glad for the Academy's sake that he is no longer an outsider.'[9] Then, in 1891 he is 'Mr Bodley, whom many of us consider our greatest architect', and in 1903 'beyond all doubt the most accomplished and refined architect in Europe'.[10] Every church of Shaw's after 1875 follows some of his ideas or details. Between Sedding, a more intimate friend, and Shaw there was mutual admiration. In some ways Shaw may have overesteemed him. Having marked the elegance of St Clement's Bournemouth, so much lovelier than Shaw's own two churches in the town, he may have passed one or two jobs over to Sedding during the latter's lean period in the 1870s.[11] But however good Sedding's work may have been, he was not necessarily the more original as a church architect. Holy Trinity Sloane Street, which Shaw admired extravagantly, profits much from study of the Harrow Mission Church drawings he had lent Sedding, and the boot seems rarely to have been on the other foot.[12] On the other hand, Shaw learnt from G. G. Scott junior, the third reformer of late Victorian church architecture, much more than he gave. This brilliant architect's retreat from practice after 1883 because of a breakdown removed one of the ablest exponents of Queen Anne as well as of refined Gothic. Shaw had been acquainted with him, not apparently intimately, but well enough to understand his aims and follow some of them himself.[13]

Shaw learnt his early lessons about church-building from Pugin and from Street. At first, he attempts to apply their teaching; soon, he is unlearning what is inessential and getting a mature idea of what a church was to be. The first-generation ecclesiologists had made much of status and clarity. A church must look like a church, not a temple; it should have different parts, according to the distinct activities which the liturgy said should take place there and to the hierarchies of priest, acolyte and layman. Decoration too, Pugin and his followers thought, should belong to the centres of activity: font, pulpit, sanctuary and of course high altar, focal point of both architectural clarity and ornament. Externally, aisles, nave and chancel were all to have their separate roofs and be unmistakeably what they were.

These prescriptions achieved two very different results. On the one hand, men applied themselves avidly in Pugin's wake to each craft in the art of church-building: metalwork, stained glass, encaustic tiling, woodwork and architectural sculpture. From these roots grew the intense originality of High Victorian decorative design. The crafts were then combined, sometimes congruously, sometimes incongruously, but always in a conscious spirit of opposition, as though each medium and material was eager to be the protagonist. Then on the other hand, architects strove for arbitrary disconnections in the structuring of their designs, for disparate rhythms, asymmetries, and interruptions, to emphasize the parts. Butterfield and Street, the greatest exponents of this abruptness, knew already that it could never be a complete aesthetic ideal but must be tempered by some other articulation. One means, for instance, was height. Ruskin had asked for church towers like 'the tower of Babylon, which looketh towards Damascus';[14] many of the tall towers of the High Victorian movement respond to the call, overtopping a medley of roof planes and pitches, and drawing the churches together by sheer height. At All Saints' Margaret Street, Butterfield had used height inside as well as out to give cogency to his cramped and cluttered site.[15] In contrast, Street preferred horizontality as a means of harmonizing his disconnected parts. In his office, Shaw learnt the effects that could be got by keeping a church profile long and low, a rare lesson.

By such devices, the High Victorian church architects managed to prevent their exteriors from dissolution. But in the interior, the different portions grew if anything further apart under Street and Butterfield. Merely raising the altar so as to put it in conspicuous view of the rest of the church could not supply the structural unity which an emphatic chancel arch contradicted. From 1860, Street began subordinating parts of his double-aisled churches to others, in the interests of unity. First he narrowed the aisles (at Oxford), then he made them into mere passages (at Clifton). But though this improved the aspect of the nave, the chancel in either case was still tacked on as self-consciously as ever, and relied upon different proportions.

275

Shaw's early church designs all accept the need for a structurally separate chancel, a principle upon which the ecclesiological theorists stayed adamant. Instead, he concentrated upon what to do with the tower. Following Butterfield and Street, he had the alternatives of presenting the tower as a separate entity at the west end barely joined to the main vessel, or of building it up to a fine central position over the choir. The second type was a way of exploiting the disconnections. Shaw's obsession with the centralized, integrated tower runs from Bingley to Swanscombe, but the other idea is almost as long-lived; a west tower off the main axis appears in his Ruskinian church project of the early 1860s (ills. 38–9), and returns in the designs for Port Elizabeth and Richards Castle.[16]

As with Street, the central towers of Shaw's early churches go to make magnificent exteriors, but compound interior problems. Whereas Street sought to combat this with massing and strength of design, Shaw from the first was anxious for a quieter system that depended on proportion. By using a central tower at Holy Trinity Bingley (ill. 40), he was accepting the fact of discontinuity, but inside the church, he tried to minimize it. Since the nave was broad and high, the chancel narrower and lower, he had to juggle with vessels of opposing dimensions. So he put in a strong eastern tower arch to obscure the low sanctuary roof and create an effect of recession in echo of the chancel arch (ill. 41). By rejecting Street's solution of an apsidal east end and setting an abnormally large lancet alone on the east wall, he drew the chancel into the proportional system of the body of the church. This is Shaw at his most brilliant. But even at Bingley, nave and chancel remained from some angles incompatible bodies, so that these efforts were so many sops.

The same problems arose at Shaw's other most valuable early church, Meerbrook in rural Staffordshire (1868–73). It is the best of a group of commissions for gradual reconstruction or major restoration of small country churches which came to Argyll Street during the years of the Shaw–Nesfield partnership.[17] All, whether undertaken by Nesfield or Shaw, are alike: quiet, competent, more original in detail than in conception, and closer to Butterfield than to Street. Instead of Street's plate tracery, all favour the wirier bar tracery of Butterfield, always more adaptable to integrated stained glass scenes.[18] The basis for the Meerbrook church, with its low, buttressed, and pyramidally capped tower over the choir (ill. 204), is Butterfield's Milton, itself a derivation from Pugin's Ramsgate church.[19] Like many of Shaw's churches it was built in stages, the chancel first by gift, then the nave by public subscription. The chancel is endowed with a set of crowded fittings typical of the churches in the group; oak stalls of sharp outline, lively ironwork hinges, an extruded organ case, and marble reredos of irregular details flanked by a colourful tile dado. Above is one of Heaton Butler and Bayne's best windows, probably drawn out by Shaw. The Japanese taste, well subordinated in these fittings, comes out strongly in a masterly frontal in blues and greens, the first recorded piece to be worked by the ladies of the future Leek Embroidery Society (ill. 224).[20]

Despite the good proportions of the little Meerbrook chancel, the nave is too long and thin, and remains a separate vessel.[21] But what else was possible with a central tower and strong chancel arch? With this system, there was always going to be a problem. At Meerbrook, Shaw was already looking for other ways to co-ordinate nave and chancel, and therefore gave his two end walls similar three-light windows. But these could only be the same size and shape at a cost. The steps up to sanctuary floor level and the reduced

S·E·VIEW OF THE CHURCH OF S·MATTHEW MEERBROOK NEAR LEEK SHEWING CONDLYFFE MEMORIAL CHANCEL

204. Meerbrook Church, perspective of exterior as originally proposed, *c*.1868.

height and length of the chancel meant that the east window loomed larger in its wall and finished lower than the west window, intruding into the reredos space. Not only did this create proportional problems, it was also liturgically illogical. Large west windows, preferably unstained, were needed for the congregation's convenience (especially in a church without a clerestory), whereas east windows could be dispensed with if absolutely necessary.

One means of overcoming these obstacles to articulation without breaking ecclesiological rules about the supremacy of the east end was hit upon at this time by J. L. Pearson. At St Peter's Vauxhall (1863–5) he relied on French mediaeval precedent to get rid of the chancel arch in favour of a through-vaulted system with clerestory and apse. Shaw never vaulted any of his churches completely, but one building of his that

The English Church: LYONS.

LONGITUDINAL SECTION.

CROSS SECTION.

GROUND PLAN.

PLAN OF CLERESTORY.

W.W.Neve, delt.

205. English Church, Lyons, plans and sections, drawn by W. W. Neve, c.1869.

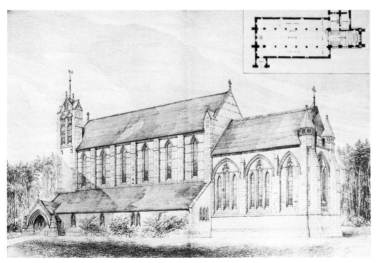

206. St Michael's Bournemouth, perspective of exterior, first design, 1873.

207. St Michael's Bournemouth, perspective of exterior, revised design, 1874.

followed not long after shows him alert to what Pearson had done.[22] It is the English Church at Lyons (1867–9), built in a Cistercian lancet style based as much upon his travels in Yorkshire as those in France. Because of an eccentric site, the Lyons church contributed nothing to the ordinary problems of design, but it had the virtue of releasing all Shaw's resourcefulness of planning (ill. 205). Faced by a confined rectangle with light available from the street side only, he designed a unified nave and chancel (without east window), and a low north aisle breaking up in the middle into a transept. By curtailing his space, already so small, into two uneven areas, Shaw left nave and chancel free and well-lit by a clerestory, and allotted to the separate parts of his aisle an inside porch, an organ, and a vestry. He was even able, by a device inevitably to be questioned by purists, to hide a bell turret behind the tall gable of his façade. As a *tour-de-force* in crowding the maximum of accommodation on a small site, the Lyons Church had no peer in the Gothic Revival.

In the early 1870s, Shaw's church designing passes through an unambitious phase. The lancet style predominates, at Boxmoor, Cottingley, Hebden Bridge, in the aisle designed for Kiltegan, and the more important Bournemouth churches. He may have been making conscious efforts to suppress his individuality, as if in compensating austerity for his Old English extravaganzas. If so, he was not wholly successful. The first design for St Michael's Bournemouth has intriguing touches, especially the dash of half-timbering over the east window, a hint of an incipient wish to amalgamate house and church styles (ill. 206).[23] On revision, Shaw purified the detail and went back to the idea of a central tower, so that had the whole church been built, it would have looked like a reworking of Bingley to fit the coupled lancet style (ill. 207). In the event, only nave and aisles were built at first, and appear a little old-fashioned, though ably proportioned. When the chancel was added in 1882–3 neither tower-arch nor tower was attempted; building by stages like this did not suit Shaw's personality. At St Michael's, he made scant progress with the problems of integration. West and east end are less well related than in many a

279

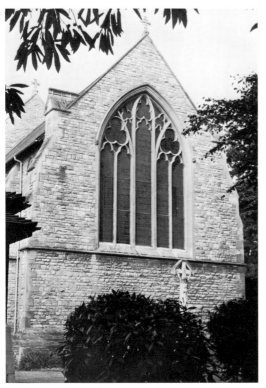

208. St Swithun's Bournemouth, east end.

209. St Mark's Cobourg Road, interior.

210. All Saints'
Swanscombe,
interior.

contemporary church by Brooks or Butterfield; the temptation of the central tower had again intervened.

At about this point, Bodley became the catalyst. From 1875, Shaw was busy with the confusing church of St Swithun's Bournemouth (ill. 208). It was built in the reverse order from St Michael's, chancel first (1876–7) and nave long after (1891–2) to a design like that of Holy Trinity Latimer Road. In the intervening years there were several interesting schemes for adding the nave, in which Shaw wavered between aisled and aisleless versions, but all aborted. Though the chancel at St Swithun's remains loyal to lancets and bar tracery, new features are creeping in. High-shouldered buttresses intervene between the lancets and finish flush with the east wall. This idiosyncratic profile is roughly that of Bodley's St Salvador's Dundee (1868–74), and the whole system had been further developed in his St Augustine's Pendlebury (1874–6), a church of prophetic importance.[24] At Pendlebury, Bodley at a stroke had abandoned Early English, the chancel arch, and the integration of a tower in the design of the main church. Instead, he presented a single uninterrupted vessel in which detail was subordinate and east and west ends of equal architectural value.

Immediately, Shaw was a convert. The first full result of his change of heart was St Margaret's Ilkley, designed in 1876–7. Though not the finest of Shaw's church-building achievements, it is the most original, and the prototype of his major churches afterwards. Pendlebury had plainly reinspired him to build a church which should be vigorous and personal. A letter concerning his earliest intentions survives:

> I send you a preliminary plan of the new church, and a tracing of the sort of thing I would suggest. I am so sick of the everlasting modern church, with its orthodox pitched roof and its feeble spire, and I do think it would come in so badly in your valley that I long to do something that I hope would come in better. I should like to keep it all simple, but as large in *mass* as possible. Let us save as much money as possible in the items of plinths and cornices and string courses but let us have the walls as high and as thick as we can afford, and let the tower be as bulky as possible, and no very extravagant height. After all there is plenty of room for it in the valley, it won't choke you up much.
>
> I shall be very anxious to hear what you think of this general scheme. I am sure it is *mass* that tells and not mouldings or architecture. Then you would find it very splendid in effect if you had very few windows in the aisles, and the great preponderance of light coming from the clerestory and from a large west window. I should like to get the windows interesting in their tracery, if I could, as I know grim plain lancets are not much approved of by some of your members.[25]

In fact the site was not *in* a valley like Bingley, where the tower drew in the surrounding hills to a focus, but on the side of slopes leading up out of the town to the moors, and originally within the grounds of the town's Hydro. 'Ilkley as a rapidly rising watering place, is just one of those spots where the demand for accommodation at church, vastly exceeds the means of supply . . . The majority of tourists here are of the poorer sort, and cannot help us much. The richer ones are almost entirely Bradford Noncon-formists.'[26] Therefore the church had to be large; 819 sittings for the stream of consumptive visitors attending the Hydro, coughing the coaldust out of their chests into the clean moorland air, and thanking their maker with alacrity that they were still alive to do so. In Ilkley's expansion, Shaw was briefly caught up. He had planned a grand house at Crossbeck for the local millowner Frederick Fison; another was probably projected here for Aldam Heaton's associate Charles Hastings, and a third house, called St John's, he actually built near the new church for Heaton's brother-in-law, J. W. Atkinson (ill. 52). But the prosperity of Ilkley soon waned, so St Margaret's has always been too big.

At Ilkley, Shaw was intent upon combining Bodley's new vision of the open vessel with his own favourite, the church with central tower. Shortly after Pendlebury, Bodley himself attempted this exacting task at Hoar Cross, but his method was height and extravagance of detail, whereas Shaw opted for length and plainness. Of his early design a crude sketch survives, revealing a massive low central tower such as Leek and Swanscombe were to have. But at Ilkley it never came off; the tower was reputedly abandoned for fear that the structure, 'built in slippery, spongy sort of ground', might not take it.[27] Even without it, there was a settlement and brief scare over the nave piers in 1879. Once the tower was abandoned, Shaw avoided any big alternative and substituted a stepped bellcote.

In fact the long, low profile of the church (ill. 211) is deceptive. The walls are almost as high as at Pendlebury, and the windows start well above the normal level. At the east end, expanses of blank masonry appear beneath the chancel windows because of the fast downward slope of the site. By accident or design, Shaw procured similar strong inclines for four of his later churches: north-east at Ilkley, south-east at Leek, less emphatically south-east at Richards Castle, less profitably south-west at Swanscombe. They give the key to his methods. The proud height of a Pendlebury fitted level ground, but declivities needed horizontal accent to draw the church into the land and make it 'racy of the soil', as the Arts and Crafts critics were to say. The course which Shaw chose at Ilkley to deal with the slope he repeated more or less in later churches. He put a heating chamber and vestries under the chancel, so giving it a height which made it as important as the nave, instead of leaving it the poky adjunct that chancels of small length and height had previously been. He then kept nave and chancel roofs at a single level and at the very low pitch which G. G. Scott junior had just pioneered at St Agnes' Kennington. He also reinforced their interdependence by endowing east and west ends with a wide window at the same level. Windows like these had not been seen in parish churches of the Gothic Revival before; they were of ten lights, flowing with tracery worthy of a cathedral. Inside, the floor level began well above what was customary, and the ascent to the altar was made gradual. As a result, the nave became light and spacious, and a new freedom of movement opened up between east and west ends, unimpeded by the high chancel arch.

All this half works, but only half; the real revelation of this new church type's potentialities was left to Leek. The low pitches of transept and porch roofs are uncomfortable, while the aisle roofs are rarely visible, so that from many angles St Margaret's is a church that is all windows and walls and no roof, never a happy phenomenon. The interior (ill. 212), with its octagon piers, Perpendicular details and functionless chancel arch, does not quite hang together. Shaw was to find that Perpendicular is the hardest of Gothic styles to make interesting without a wealth of colour and fittings, for which Ilkley at first had no money. Though fittings came later, some of them to his designs, the interior remained bland.

211. St Margaret's Ilkley, exterior from north-west.

212. St Margaret's Ilkley, interior.

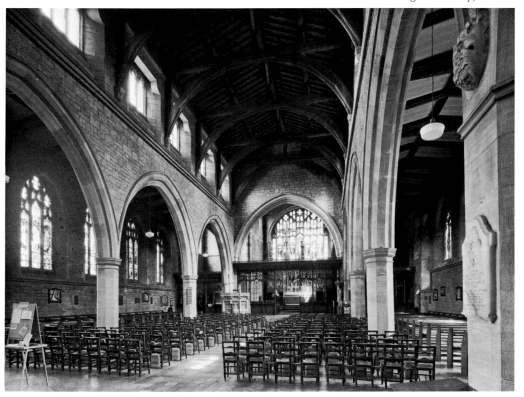

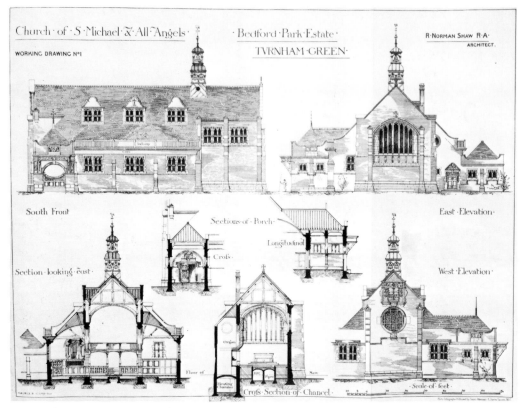

213. St Michael's Bedford Park, elevations and sections, drawn by Maurice B. Adams, 1879.

Of the five churches Shaw designed between Ilkley and its first descendant, All Saints' Leek, none has special affinity with this new type. Subsequently, a pair of foreign church projects carries on the earlier tradition of his ecclesiastical designing. But to Shaw, these seven cannot have meant as much as Bingley, Ilkley, or Leek. To the late 1870s belongs a special group of two churches and a chapel which were the first Shaw built in brick.[28] St Michael's Bedford Park (1878–9) we have already looked at. It attempts like Peplow Chapel (1877–9) to amalgamate house and church styles, and like St Mark's Cobourg Road (1877–8 etc.) to inject some vigour into the London town church. Yet the three have little in common save novelty. The charming Epiphany Chapel, Peplow (ill. 215), was built as a proprietary chapel by Francis Stanier of Peplow Hall. At first he seems to have been shown a drawing of the mission chapel Shaw had just erected at Cottingley, near Bingley, in a run-of-the-mill lancet style; but either Stanier or Shaw decided they could do better.[29] Instead, Shaw tossed off a witty brick design. Its exterior shares more with the several schools Shaw had built in the early 1870s than with any of his previous churches. In Sussex, the two schools of New Groombridge and Hammerwood (ill. 214) had served also at first as mission churches for their districts, so their east elevations were ecclesiastical and broke out into modest tracery. This is what Shaw did again at Peplow. Under an unbroken roof with ample eaves, he threw together a Gothic east end and an

214. (above)
Hammerwood,
school-chapel,
exterior from south-
east.

215. (right) Peplow
Chapel, exterior
from south.

Old English west end of timber-framing perched on a plinth and filled in with nogging, leaded lights, and tile-hanging.[30] To the sides, the framing and square windows persist, and the whole is topped by the most rustic of bellcotes. Peplow is the kind of chapel often built at the turn of the century. It has no obvious prototype in Butterfield or Street, and no immediate successor. But it can be doubted whether Shaw thought much about it.

St Mark's Cobourg Road, Walworth, on the other hand, was a more deeply considered design than its appearance can now suggest. Its conception was odd, its history has been complex, and it is now redundant. When Samuel Wilberforce became Bishop of Winchester in 1869, one of his first acts was to appeal for new churches in South London. Upon his death, his friend Adelaide Thrupp procured Shaw as architect for one of these projected churches, St Mark's; she gave all the money for the original building campaign, but not enough to finish the church. Shaw's design proposed a 'hall church': a wide double-aisled nave, chancel and short chancel aisles, with the possibility of an eventual south-west tower. The oddity was that nave and aisles were to be vaulted to equal height, using groined vaults of wood. His source for these was both recent and close: St Agnes' Kennington (1874–7) by G. G. Scott junior, most original of the new South London churches. For Ilkley, Shaw had borrowed almost verbatim the buttressing and low pitch of the transepts of St Agnes, a subject of heated controversy at the time.[31] Now he went further, and imitated not only Scott's proposed wooden vaulting but the way in which he had encased his aisles and the base of his free-standing octagon piers with a dado of green-painted panelling. This was an innovation in the spirit of Wren, meant to humanize the bare brick walls of such town churches. At St Mark's (ill. 209), the drab-painted vaulting springs gracefully from the piers and creates a spacious auditorium quite different from the nave of St Agnes'. But the panelling is less happy. By one of Shaw's bewildering quirks of disloyalty to the Puginian ideal, it is all made of cement, though moulded and painted to look like woodwork. Against the fine red of the brickwork, especially on the piers, it looks contrived and confusing. For comfort, panelling (or pseudo-panelling) needed the plastered walls it was to get at Bedford Park. To judge the church as a whole is hard, since Shaw's designs were never completed. Like Bedford Park, it was an experiment but also a dead end.

Of Shaw's four minor church projects of the 1880s less need be said. Only one, New Groombridge, was for England; the other three were destined for foreign parts, Port Elizabeth, San Remo and Lisbon, as part of the prolific output of Anglican church building abroad. Though unambitious in the main, and showing signs of Shaw's quietening down, all take enough advantage of the new articulation to get rid of the chancel arch and have an unbroken roof running from end to end. This had been the chief advance at Bedford Park. New Groombridge is a comfortable Decorated design, with little to mark it out as Shaw's except a rugged roof frame and hutch belfry as concessions to the Sussex vernacular.[32] The foreign churches were relatively austere affairs in the lancet style, no doubt calculated to keep out glare and heat. Only the church at San Remo (1883) was actually built.[33] It is an ultra-English composition for an ultra-English resort, quite plain, with only the grey-brown masonry, flattened pantile roof, and round west window to remind one of the Riviera, but with a surprisingly spacious interior. Towards

216. All Saints' Port Elizabeth, South Africa, floor plan and perspective of proposed church (unexecuted), drawn by W. R. Lethaby, *c*.1883.

the end of the decade, Shaw entered a design for a competition for an English church at Lisbon, which 'ended in the usual way!!!'[34] At first the differences from San Remo are striking, for Shaw intended round-arched arcade and windows, and for the east end his only apse. There were also to be four square piers in the body of the church, giving the nave narrow passage aisles. But though he conceded more to foreign style and indulged his new-found fondness for the half-circle, the proportions, the use of a narthex, and the modesty of the project all recall San Remo. The third and most celebrated of these foreign projects, a mission church for Port Elizabeth in South Africa, also belongs with San Remo despite its startling first appearance. It may have been the first of the group, since Shaw was working on another church in Port Elizabeth in 1880.[35] In any case, it was never built. Fundamentally, the design (ill. 216) shows a long aisleless building with the hallmark of San Remo upon its lancets and continuous roofline. It would have had nothing like the scale hinted by Lethaby's perspectives. A south-west tower over the porch, tinged with polychromy and stepped back in stages, obscures the simplicity. Also, the blank arches Shaw habitually threw between his chancel buttresses have now turned into deep window embrasures to keep the African sun off the lancets and allow a kind of outside passage aisle beneath. In an alternative version of the design, these arches have been supplied with spirited shades which block out the lancets and endow the church with a veneer of stylelessness.

With the foreign church designs ended a series of projects eccentric by nature or location, which could not help to realize Shaw's dream of articulating the free-standing

287

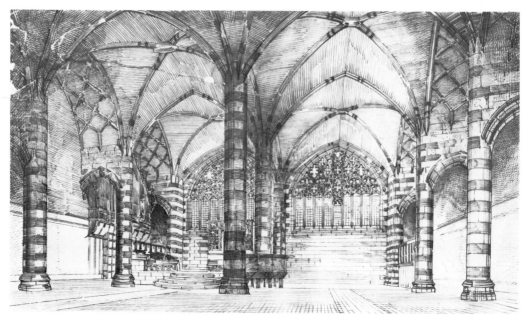

217. Holy Trinity Latimer Road (Harrow Mission Church), interior perspective of double-naved design, *c*.1885–6.

218. Holy Trinity Latimer Road (Harrow Mission Church), interior as built.

English parish church. That was superbly achieved at All Saints' Leek, the great church of his maturity, a building worth looking at *in toto* and so reserved for the end of this chapter. It was one of four churches of the major group which follow along the lines he set at Ilkley. Of these, Leek, Richards Castle and Swanscombe are parish churches of the classic type, but the fourth, Holy Trinity Latimer Road, was another unorthodox commission. Yet it was this church which allowed him to see how simple the articulation for which he had so painfully striven at Leek might be, and to refrain from pursuing it so ardently to the end. Neither Richards Castle nor Swanscombe sustains the tension of Leek, and this slackening is undoubtedly due to Holy Trinity.

Despite its peculiarities, the church belongs firmly to the tale of Shaw's devotion to Bodley. The Harrow Mission had acquired land in Latimer Road, West London, and in 1883 asked Shaw for a simple mission room for the west end of their enclosed site. This was duly erected. For the rest of the plot, where they wanted a church with the maximum accommodation, Shaw suggested a wide continuous structure with one aisle on the north and two on the south, making a rectangle with the mission room. Two years later, he worked out the plan properly. The new plan comprised a double nave, flanked by passage aisles with internal piers, which were to be banded in brick and stone and left without capitals. These and the piers down the centre were to carry vaults like those of St Mark's Cobourg Road, while the side passages were to be arched transversely and ribbed. This idea had been borrowed by Bodley from Albi Cathedral for Pendlebury. But Shaw extended it in two ways, by applying it to a double-nave design and by abolishing the side windows over the passages. Instead, since properties abutted at the sides, he intended to illuminate the building from either end, with pairs of majestic nine-light windows like those at Ilkley and Leek (ill. 217). On the same precedents, he relegated the vestries to the basement, this time to a London area, not a natural slope.

This *tour-de-force* of a design had to be cut down. It was expensive, and the double nave would have looked lopsided in a single-altared Anglican church. So in his 1886 revision, Shaw reduced the superficial area and threw the church into one vast vessel, under the mighty curve of a boarded roof tied three times across to the tops of external buttresses (ill. 218). To hold this daring structure together, steel girders were encased within the ties and formed the framework of the roof principals. The result was more like Pendlebury than before, but a Pendlebury in which the illogicality of Bodley's internal buttressing and passage aisles had been purged. Yet curiously, the sides of the building were now unengaged on this reduced site, so Shaw could have had windows here. Evidently he knew that this would have detracted from his airy tunnel, braced by the extravagant, identical thirteen-light windows at either end, and so himself sacrificed a measure of logic to gain the perfectly articulated horizontal space he had long sought.

People sometimes assume that Lethaby's was the decisive role in this church. As so often, it is more likely that the idea and development of the building were Shaw's, while Lethaby was 'let loose' on the interior. How else does one explain the dependence on Shaw's hero Bodley, or the lending of the double-naved design to Sedding without a word of their mutual friend Lethaby's role?[36] The reredos was certainly Lethaby's, so too in all likelihood were the organ, font, stalls and pulpit erected, together with the original idea of a basilican cancellum around the open sanctuary, as a satisfactory way to demarcate the chancel. All that remains of these brilliant designs in the building as converted today is the tracery. In this, Lethaby has woven half-glimpses of other windows, like so many fraying strands, into the broadest and proudest reticulated windows of Shaw's late churches.

After this, Shaw felt free in his church architecture to seek something quieter and more rarified. Without abrogating grandeur, personality, or coherence, the Richards Castle and Swanscombe churches uphold the earnest ideals of Pugin and Carpenter once again, as though the wheel has turned full circle and Shaw is content to see himself as a disciple of the Gothic of 'fifty years ago'. As Richards Castle was drawing to its consecration, he wrote thus to Mrs Foster from Ramsgate:

> There is a charming little church here (Roman Catholic), built by the great Pugin, some 45 years ago, for himself. He designed and *paid* for the whole thing, and it is beautiful, so full of interest all through. Hideous stained glass, but in spite of that serious drawback, a most delightful and interesting work, and done *so* long ago. I am afraid we have not advanced much. Such a work makes one feel small, *very* small.[37]

In either interior, he ceases to strain for special or unusual effect; as long as the clarity of previous work can be emulated, he is happy. The great end windows remain on a level, but are reduced to five lights. At Richards Castle, although there is no central tower to require it, the chancel arch makes an unobtrusive return. As though provenance or originality of ornament was of no matter, some of the details look to have been lifted bodily from Parker's *Glossary*, some from other sources. For Richards Castle Shaw borrows tracery patterns from the old parish church, and one, a square-headed chancel window, recurs at Swanscombe. These are spiritual interiors in which rhetoric is out of place. When Shaw for a moment gives his Richards Castle design more 'go', by ornamenting the vestry doors with ballflower, it intrudes discourteously upon the surfaces of blank walling.

In these church exteriors, Shaw fights an odd battle against his own panache. Richards Castle (ill. 219) tops a soft, isolated hill-site, the best Shaw ever had for a church. Here was the place for some show of height, so he opted for a detached tower, bulking square and unbroken like the disconnected belltower at the old church nearby, but positioned at the south west over the porch, as in the Port Elizabeth design. Up to this porch he drove a yew hedge: 'It will (very soon) enclose the whole thing and will draw it all together and all help to make the church itself part of the country, and not (as so many are) like a thing stuck down on a flat deal board.'[38] He also chose, for the first time in his practice, the normal change between chancel and nave roof heights. Yet then he thrust the organ chamber up into the junction, to remind the quiet body of the church by discordance of its massive, alien tower.[39] This south elevation and the bald unbuttressed west end conflict sharply with the conventional mood of the east and north sides. Swanscombe is a less gentle and comely church (ills. 210, 220). Here, a gritty flint texture and grim crossing tower in the manner of Leek are groomed to fit the cheerless industrial surroundings. Yet Swanscombe takes the process of reticence a stage further. Every exterior detail is simplified and flattened once more, but to different effect than in the idiosyncratic High Victorian flattening. New invention in itself, Shaw felt, had become wrong for his final church; better, the knowledge that sure strength and proportion could be attained. But it is a personal, puzzling decision, and the casual visitor

219. All Saints' Richards Castle, exterior from south-east.

220. All Saints' Swanscombe, exterior from north-west.

221. Youlgreave Church, interior as restored in 1869–71.

222. Low Bentham Church, interior as restored in 1876–8, before installation of organ case in 1886.

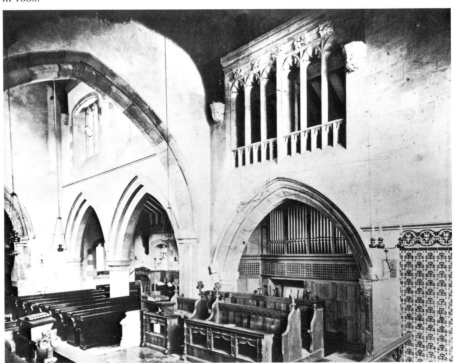

who comes across this church, bereft of its intended south aisle, squeezed between road and railway at Galley Hill amidst an ocean of white dust from the cement works, must find its lengthy profile forlorn and eccentric enough.

FITTINGS

Shaw's anxiety to design a church which should be single and uniform could not exclusively preoccupy him. He never scorned detail work in his churches. True, he delegated more and invented less as his interest in the overall frame became more singleminded, and so came eventually to mistrust his talent in the field. But from early on, a wealth of fittings not just in new churches but also in his various restorations shows the slow evolution of his ideas on church decoration.

He began work when stridency in churches was already upon the wane. Take, for example, floors. Pugin had roused the potteries to recognition of encaustic tiling's artistic possibilities. Hall floors in his houses, church naves, chancels and sanctuaries had been covered with Minton's strong stencilled tiles. The High Victorian church designers followed in his footsteps and extended the range. Yet from the first, Shaw saw the church floor as a force for unity, adhered to red tiling right through the nave, and carried it beyond where possible. Though conventions of church design required something livelier near the altar, he was grudging on this score. At Bingley, there were strips of brighter tiling in the sanctuary, but stencilled patterns round only the altar itself, on the footpace.[40] Often, he stuck to an end-to-end scheme of austere red quarry tiles, of which some 34,000 were used at Leek. The place for coloured tiles, he felt, was on the sanctuary wall, where they several times appeared in the 1870s (ill. 221). Later, a different kind of threat to his red floors materialized. At churches like Hoar Cross, Bodley set a fashion for cool marble floors in the chancel, and in deference Shaw at first designed one for the Richards Castle chancel. But he could not be persuaded; he complained that it had 'a tendency to lead to smartness. . . . Let us throw this marble floor to the winds, or leave it for Restaurants and Theatre entrances where smartness seems to be more appreciated, and where perhaps it is more appropriate.'[41] And so the red tile floor reigned from the start to the finish of Shaw's church-building and restoration career.

Of the fittings that broke into the floor surface, liturgy decided which would be most often noticed and therefore most carefully designed. This was natural enough, but did not answer to Shaw's priorities when he designed a church. Persuading Mrs Foster to have oak seats rather than deal, Shaw writes:

> This is quite one of the things that I must advise you to accept as when once done it can never be undone. If once we have deal seats they must remain for ever, even if you don't like the look of them and think them shabby. It is like the stone facing of the walls, which will look nice 500 years hence!! as the seats will. I care nothing, or at all events, little, about Pulpit, Font, Reredos!! Altar Standards and heaps of things that can be added afterwards; as for instance the organ! which we cannot have for a year or so, but the seats we *must* have for the consecration.[42]

This was shrewd. At Bingley, the reredos and font followed by gift close on completion of

223. St Michael's Bedford Park, bench, 1879.

the church, while the poor deal pews always remained. Rather than run this risk, Butterfield seated All Saints' Margaret Street with chairs, and Shaw did the same at Leek. On pews, Shaw did not claim to be an expert, recognizing Butterfield as 'an infinitely higher authority than I can pretend to be'.[43] Longstone has nave pews of distinctive chamfered profile, typical of the church-work of Nesfield and Shaw in the early 1870s. From these Shaw proceeded to something more adventurous—benches. He first used them instead of proper pews to complement a number of seventeenth century fittings in his restoration at Edburton, and put them to bolder use at Kelsale and at Bedford Park (ill. 223).[44] But often, nave seats were neglected in favour of ampler chancel stalls. At Bingley, the stalls and also the altar table had all the sturdy merit of Shaw's early secular oak furniture. Later altar tables, though none is quite so fine, remained open and pierced at the front so as not to look like chests. A series of stalls of the early 1870s carry carved ends and abrupt poppyheads with 'pies' or leaf carving; examples can be found at Youlgreave (ill. 221), Meerbrook, Bingley parish church, Tarring Neville, Longstone and Low Bentham (ill. 222). Nesfield's rare church furniture, though similar, tends to more extravagance, while Shaw keeps some hold on simplicity and authenticity. At Youlgreave, the stalls are in an elaborately archaeological Perpendicular style still remarkable for their date, 1870.[45]

For Bingley parish church, Shaw provided not only seats but a rich screen to partition the north chancel chapel from the chancel. Over it he took much pains, gaining a certain malicious pleasure in making it just that bit better and richer than the equivalent southern parclose screen designed by the 'tiresome and disagreeable' Messrs Healey of Bradford, who were restoring the body of the church.[46] This kind of archaeological affair, splendidly pierced and carved, was most appropriate for a side chapel, since chancel screens tended to destroy the openness for which Shaw was struggling. On the whole he was content to rely on a dwarf chancel screen wall, sometimes itself quite elaborate (Hebden Bridge). By the late 1870s he had evolved an alternative, a 'veil of the temple' screen, filling the apex of the chancel arch but hardly interrupting the view through the lower part over the dwarf wall. St Mark's Cobourg Road (ill. 209) has the only known executed version still intact, but Shaw hoped to use the same idea at San Remo and Port Elizabeth.[47] These were in wood, but he toyed with iron screens as well. An early example

294

was in the Rhydd Court Chapel; at one stage a metal screen by Shaw was destined for St Luke's Leek.[48] As late as 1897, when asked to design a screen for Ilkley, he commended gilt iron, 'a big fellow mainly composed of vertical bars, pretty close, twisted and dodged of course and reaching up to the springing of the chancel arch, and extending right across the church'.[49] This would have avoided cutting up the space with anything as solid as the mullions, canopy and cresting of a wooden screen. It is a sign of Shaw's loss of grip in this sphere that he gave in to pressure and agreed to design a conventional wooden screen for Ilkley in partnership with Ginham. It was the only part of a scheme he then drew up for decorating the chancel which was carried out. His apologia for the reversal is quite out of key with the logic of the design: 'I know you will call out about seeing the East window, but that is all gammon. The East window is *there*, and there will be quite points of view from which you will be able to see it, and if you didn't I am not sure but what it is better if only suggested.'[50]

This was not the end of his work for Ilkley. Ten years later the church asked for a font canopy. Shaw struggled unavailingly to think the matter through and sketch several schemes, but to his self-disgust could approve his own efforts no more than those of his fellow-helpers. Eventually, in 1910–11, a design was carried out in partnership with H. S. Chorley, but the Ilkley font canopy (ill. 226) is a pathetic last effort for the designer of the superb Bingley fittings.[51] Shaw had the grace to realize this: hence his recommendation of Gerald Horsley, on the strength of his work at Leek, for the Swanscombe chancel panelling.[52] Horsley did no better; the truth was that the writing was on the wall for Gothic detailing by 1900. After Bodley's death, only a few personal idiosyncrasies continued with any real success.

At Ilkley the font itself may have been designed by Prior. It is the kind of contribution that Shaw would allow his clerk-of-works, and does not match his known fonts. The first of these was for St John's Leeds, where Forsyth carried out a well-detailed octagonal bowl quite like many of Butterfield's. It too originally stood under a free-

224. Meerbrook Church, altar frontal, 1870.

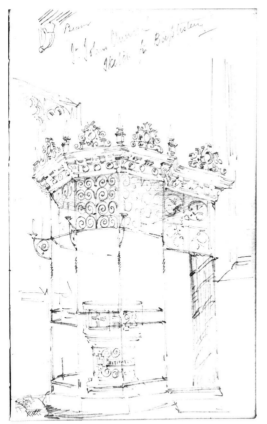

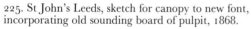

225. St John's Leeds, sketch for canopy to new font, incorporating old sounding board of pulpit, 1868.

226. St Margaret's Ilkley, font (1879) and canopy (1911).

standing canopy, of open ironwork topped by the discarded sounding board of the pulpit (ill. 225). Before Lethaby took hold of his church fittings, Shaw usually followed the Leeds pattern in fonts, with a clustered stem surmounted by a plain octagonal bowl. There are good specimens at Peplow and in the prettily restored church at Upper Langwith. The Holy Trinity Latimer Road font is an updated version of this type. Sometimes, it is abandoned in the interests of a tall cover. At Holy Trinity Bingley, the font (ill. 227) was gauged to the primitive feeling of the other fittings: a scalloped bowl in grey Boulton Woods stone upon clustered colonnettes. On top, a great pierced canopy, added in 1873, hung from a coved wooden bracket upon the west wall, and descended from a pelican figure to fit the complex shape of the bowl. Longstone has a fine font with relief panels and moderately high pierced cover, on analogy with Holy Trinity Bingley. For Bingley parish church too, Shaw or one of the pupils designed a new font and tall cover in 1882, but it is an unoriginal business.

When he could, Shaw placed these fonts on the main axis of the church below the west window. Early ecclesiological theorists had thought that they should stand in the south-west position, near the door, since the faithful 'entered' the church through the font. In this view, the symbolic sense of a liturgical prop should always overrule mere

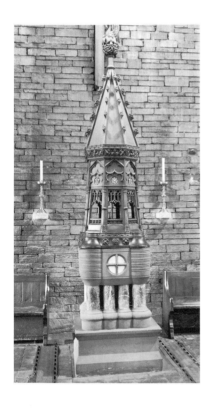

227. (above left) Holy Trinity Bingley, font and cover.

228. (above right) Holy Trinity Bingley, pulpit.

229. (left) All Saints' Swanscombe, reading desk.

230. (right) Boldre Church, pulpit.

aesthetics. Shaw quarrelled intuitively with such rulings, thinking that architectural cohesion and grandeur had their spiritual functions too. That at least seems the philosophy of All Saints' Leek. Here and in other of his mature churches, he set his pulpit and lectern aside in parallel, to act as solid twin mid-points defining the clear passage from end to end of the church, and enclosing the open relation between reredos and font. This may be why Shaw reacted against thin brass eagle lecterns, of which there is no certain example to his design. If given the job, he plumped for a wooden reading desk with solid top. Youlgreave and Longstone have them, Meerbrook may have had one with a socket attaching it to the dwarf screen. At Leek it becomes massive, vying in size and dignity with the pulpit. Shaw's last and finest work of this kind was the huge reading desk for Swanscombe (ill. 229), an integral, immovable part of the church. It was designed in a seventeenth century manner, made by Farmer and Brindley, and adorned with silver brackets by Krall, 'the balmy German'.[53]

With pulpits, Shaw's practice varied. For all their brilliance with fonts, seats and reredoses, Butterfield and Street never perfected the pulpit. Street often chose bulbous stone pulpits, and Shaw's at Meerbrook is of the type. Shaw never surpassed the dynamic, flat Devonshire marble slab of the Bingley pulpit, touched with mosaic and canted slightly inwards from the cross axis of the church. Set off against the plainest of grey columns and ledges, it looks like the most exotic Arts and Crafts work of thirty years later, but twice as tough. Since Devonshire marble was to be had there, he tried its effects more modestly in his restoration at Longstone.[54] Normally something plainer had to do. Only three later stone pulpits are known, none a great success. At Boldre Church (1876), a polygonal pulpit (ill. 230) veers between different dates of Gothic but is enlivened by pretty leaf carving; and at Hebden Bridge (1876) and Ilkley (1880–1) broad and richly carved vessels with oblique-angled sides nestle up around the pier. Better are the linenfold pulpits of Shepshed, Low Bentham, Youlgreave and Peplow, on stone bases with the upper woodwork parts open. By a charming variation, the top half at Upper Langwith is filled with stamped and gilt leather patterns of fruit, suggestive of Heaton's work. Lethaby animated the type for Leek and Holy Trinity Latimer Road, simplifying the linenfold and making the designs sharp, wiry and compact. When Shaw was again left to himself, he chose a similar pattern for the Richards Castle and Swanscombe pulpits, but neither has the panache of Lethaby's two efforts of the 1880s.

Likewise, Lethaby revived and extended the scope of Shaw's organ cases in the 1880s. Organs, we know, had intrigued Shaw ever since his 'Rampagenous' designs of 1858. It took him some time to recover from them. The organ pipes at both the Rhydd Court Chapel (1865) and Holy Trinity Bingley (1870) were not only canted out rather lamely but fitted up closely under arches. This habit he was later to deprecate, telling Fred White 'they seem to me to suggest a set of false teeth'.[55] By the early 1870s, Nesfield and he had escaped the spell of Burges and had learnt much from seventeenth century organ cases. They decided to avoid arches, project the pipes well into the chancel, and keep them compact by enclosing them in a plain wooden case with shutters over a coving. Shaw's excellent examples at Meerbrook and Longstone are less elaborate than Nesfield's at Kings Walden and Radwinter. No case from the later 1870s survives; one, altered now, was at Hebden Bridge. But soon organ designing was as much part of his domestic as his ecclesiastical work. Flete had one, so did Dawpool, Didlington, Downside and Chesters, while grand church organs were installed at Low Bentham (1886) and Holy Trinity Latimer Road (1887–8).[56] The secular organs affected the church designs. Lethaby had a *penchant* for carved, fretted, and gilded pipe shades, first used on the organ at Flete. They were soon universal, and an integral part of the Low Bentham design. Teak, the material at Low Bentham, probably began in earlier secular cases. It occurs again at Chesters (1893) and Thurstaston (1905), where the Dawpool instrument was apparently reinstalled in the church with a magnificent new case. Both these organs bear on the shutters Burgundian-style paintings by Robert Christie and his sons. They have excellent compact cases exhibiting none of the falling off from Lethaby's work of other late Shaw fittings. In respects they are preferable to the organ at Holy Trinity Latimer Road (ill. 218), which thrust up into the roof with a rough gesture.

The catalogue of fittings reaches its climax with the reredos. Always foremost in the Tractarian church, the reredos gathered size and stature as the obstacles in its way were removed. Thus with Shaw it evolved along with his ideas on articulation. However large the Bingley reredos appears (ill. 41), it would have been lost before the vast east windows and wide chancels of his later churches. In contrast, it started higher because of the intensive raising of the sanctuary steps, and emerged from a darker background. Hence its High Victorian coloration and texture, mixing red marble and gold mosaic, flat patterning and high relief. It was not Shaw's first such reredos; another smaller one survives in the remnants of the Rhydd Court Chapel, and there was a reredos with gold mosaic by Salviati at St John's Leeds. The type continues at Meerbrook, Youlgreave and Burghclere, where the colour and detail are gentler because of tiled sanctuary dados.[57] Later in the 1870s, Shaw twice designed conventional Caen stone reredoses with carved figure scenes in Street's later manner, at St Swithun's Bournemouth and Low Bentham (where the sculptor was Earp); both again rely for colour upon the surrounding tiled dado. One suspects that with so many half-built churches on his hands at this period, he was experimenting with hangings often enough. At Bingley, every possible fitting was firmly built in. But as fear of Protestant riot receded along with High Victorian taste, there was no reason why fabrics should not serve their turn in church decoration. Bodley took the lead in introducing dossals and hangings round the altar. Unhappily, schemes such as these are impermanent and easily swept away, and so it is that Shaw's most remarkable chancel interior of the 1870s, at Hebden Bridge, has disappeared. Here Aldam Heaton organized a scheme with a crewel sanctuary carpet, green serge backing to the east wall relieved by strips of embroidered red cloth, an eight-foot dossal to the altar, and matching frontals. Even the painted side walls have been obliterated; only the pulpit, dwarf screen, and Heaton Butler and Bayne's series of Anglo-Japanese windows remain.

The Ilkley church-type required a new kind of reredos. Ilkley itself could not afford such a thing until 1897, by which time Shaw could supply the answer from experience: a triptych 'at least ten feet wide and with shutters (which might be added at some future time), opening out to a width of say twenty feet'.[58] The first opportunity Shaw got was at Leek, and with Lethaby's help he seized it. For some time Bodley and his school had wanted to revive the painted polyptych. Isolated attempts had been made before, but still in the mid-1880s most new reredoses were sculpted and carved, because of the dearth of

231. All Saints' Richards Castle, reredos, painted by C. E. Buckeridge.

good painters.[59] Burne-Jones apart, English religious painting had made dim progress. The ecclesiastical decoration firms like Clayton and Bell and Bodley's own favourites Burlison and Grylls monopolized the trade, but rarely threw up individuals to rank with carvers of the stature of Forsyth, Earp or Shaw's later favourite, H. Barnes of Farmer and Brindley. Bodley therefore divided his painted reredoses into small panels and kept the scale of the figures down. Not so Shaw. For Leek, Lethaby and he designed a rich frame which stretched right across the chancel (ill. 234). It was well carried out by Farmer and Brindley, but the large figures by F. Hamilton Jackson were a sad come-down, even before the recent bad retouching. It was not all Jackson's fault; the frame and gold leaf background were too archaeological for a modern painter to fight against successfully. Moreover, the contrasts were at first too bare from afar.[60]

To remedy these faults, Lethaby and Shaw had one more attempt each, Lethaby with Jackson at Holy Trinity Latimer Road, Shaw with the young C. E. Buckeridge at Richards Castle. Both are improvements upon Leek. Lethaby tried a one-panel reredos

300

with a Crucifixion scene, and gave the frame a fretted Spanish surround set cleverly against the parting tracery above. Even if the flanking hangings left the reredos isolated, it was a memorable ensemble in an awkward situation (ill. 218). In effect, Lethaby had relieved his painter's difficulties by updating the frame. Shaw on the other hand took the more conservative path of keeping the Leek framework (though some Spanish details seem to have stuck) and adapting the style of painting. His was the less difficult task, since at Richards Castle he had a narrower chancel with only a five-light window. He could easily fill his space with the reredos, though he was careful to have the east wall stencilled to go with it. Shaw picked Charles Edgar Buckeridge, a Burlison and Grylls pupil, on the strength of his work for Bodley, particularly at Scarborough, where he had finished off the Morris scheme of decoration.[61] In his experience, he told Mrs Foster, 'hitherto the painting has always been the weakest part, modern-looking stuff and uninteresting', whereas from Buckeridge he looked for 'one of the finest things that has been done in modern times'.[62] But he had to do his bit in checking Mrs Foster's fondness for the Italian style, in place of Buckeridge's Burgundian leanings. His trump card was a visit from Bodley.

> Mr Bodley was looking at the reredos, I mean at the sketch and said 'That is a very fine thing, is it going to be done?' Buckeridge said yes, the centre part only, and that is modified and changed into the Italian manner. Bodley said 'I am sorry for that as it will entirely destroy the character it promises to have, and will be inharmonious with the building.' He put his finger on the angels on the shutters, and said they were exceptionally good. He returned to the sketch again and again and expressed great regret that it was proposed to alter it, as he thought it would be an unusually fine thing. All this is the more remarkable coming from him, as he is a very reticent man, not prone to chat, but it interested him I suppose. I should feel so very happy if you would let us try and do our very best over this. . . . Do please let us revert to the earlier and purer character of painting, not by any means to the flat bulbous German people, but to the Van Eyck school, with its lovely diapery and delicacy.[63]

This plea triumphed. The result is splendid (ill. 231), if the weak faces are excepted. It is a pity that this painstaking style of painting has as yet not been at all reappraised, for there are some fine things to it. Buckeridge, who died young, was one of its best-reputed masters, and his Richards Castle reredos merits comparison with any English ecclesiastical art of the 1890s, conservative or progressive.

The reredos, of course, was not to be isolated from its natural companions, the east window and its glass. Shaw was always championing 'a definite programme' for decoration as opposed to casual gifts of fittings, and in this area it was vital. 'The reredos and the east window ought to be one big grand composition,' he told the Vicar of Ilkley in 1897.[64] So often had he preached on the integration of decorative schemes for chancels, that by then he was prepared to abate his charges to get matters properly organized:

> If you saw your way to this, a really *worthy* thing terminating the east wall of your church, I should be only took delighted to design it for you, and superintend its execution for *nothing*. It would be a labour of love. On the other hand, if you want me to

do a commonplace piece of trade, a regulation reredos on a wooden screen such as scores we have seen, I should desire to charge you 10%, or perhaps 15%! Oh! I should be exceedingly dear, and you would do well not to employ me. A reredos such as I speak of would cost from £300 to £500. You might easily make it cost more but it would not cost less. No good firm of wood carvers would on any account bate any of their charges, and you must only go to the *very* best. Ecclesiastical trade carvers are rather to be avoided, only the clergy go to them!! The parcloses certainly ought to form part of the design. I can only beg and pray of you to allow no cheap or inferior work to find its way into your church. It is that odious thirst for cheapness that ruins everything now a days.[65]

The rub of this, as vicars well knew, was that the architect might cost nothing, but his scheme would cost the earth. So no matter how much Shaw warned of the 'dismal failures' at St John's Leeds, where 'I talked about the windows till I was hoarse, and made something less than nothing of it', or of the bickerings at Bingley parish church, where the donor of the east window's attitude was ' "Oh! I am not going to have a reredos sticking up, and hiding at least a foot, perhaps 2 feet, of *my* beautiful window" ', he was rarely heeded.[66] Only at Hebden Bridge was a systematic stained glass scheme carried through, and only at Holy Trinity Bingley was there a really striking match between east window and reredos. There were half successes; at neither Ilkley nor Leek was anything too incongruous put in. But even this incidence was low. There were disadvantages too at Richards Castle and Swanscombe, where the lack of glass in the great windows lends an unintended austerity. Only in the west window, where an even spread of light helped the congregation's reading, did Shaw positively frown on stained glass; yet this was among the first to be filled at Ilkley.

Part of the trouble, as Shaw admitted in 1907 to Frederick Radcliffe, was 'in a whisper, that stained glass is one of the arts that appears to me to have made wonderfully little progress in the last 20 or 30 years.'[67] He might have said that it had retrogressed. In his early days there was a wealth of talent. It is odd that Clayton and Bell, favourites of Scott and Street, did only the excellent small panels in the Rhydd Court Chapel for Shaw, considering his intimacy with John Clayton. Burne-Jones was Shaw's regular choice for special commissions, but after the Bingley east window there is nothing comparable in the work of the Morris firm for his churches. Ilkley and Leek are full of late glass by Morris and by Powell, all at best of negative excellence. But Heaton Butler and Bayne had the closest association with Shaw. In the 1860s they evolved a delicate style of colouring and draughtsmanship which only began to break up round about 1880, at the time of the inexplicable degeneration of English stained glass. Shaw had worked with them as early as 1868, when with Henry Holiday, a regular Heaton Butler and Bayne designer, he helped with the memorial window to John Horsley's brother-in-law I. K. Brunel at Westminster Abbey. It is the best piece of Victorian stained glass in the abbey, and augured well for his future in glass design. Heaton Butler and Bayne went on to make the very pretty east windows at Meerbrook, Longstone and Peplow, the outline of all of which must have been furnished by Shaw, so exactly do they fit their context.[68] At Longstone, he went on to design other windows by the firm, one of 1897, and two as late as 1908. None is really characterful; they have much of the effeminacy and little of the refinement of other contemporary glass. Shaw could only tell the donors 'they are really *very good* specimens as work goes, but the art is a terrible one, not as bad as architecture, but getting on that way.'[69] There are several further good Heaton Butler and Bayne windows in Shaw churches or restorations, and he went on recommending them despite his reservations. Fred White employed Christopher Whall for a window at Swanscombe, but Shaw could 'make nothing' of his fashionably spiky design;[70] and neither C. E. Kempe nor Ninian Comper came under his consideration. Burlison and Grylls, who had made what Shaw thought a good job of the south transept of Westminster Abbey, were an obvious choice as Bodley's regular firm. Although he never appears to have worked with them, he did commission from them a memorial window to his daughter-in-law.[71] He also commended them to both Mrs Foster and Mrs Ismay. In memory of her husband, Mrs Ismay wished to give the east window of the new Liverpool Cathedral. She thought at first of asking the aged G. F. Watts for a scheme, but Shaw advised her against it. He expatiated on this both to her and, after Watts' death, to Frederick Radcliffe:

> You are not the first man that has been worried a good deal by stained glass. As you know, Burne Jones and Watts are both dead! The former would have done superb work for you, I don't think Watts would, but that must ever be a matter of opinion. If you go to various men, and get a window here, and a window there, even supposing them to be good, all of them to be good, the result might be that your church would look like a pattern card. We have seen this often, and the result is devilish. I could tell you of a score of examples but they would only make your blood run cold. If you have 49 angels all of the same family, the result may not be exciting, or particularly interesting, but on the other hand it would not be maddening! It would be negative, it might even be pleasant! After all, what you want in a window is splodges of splendid colour. The *story* is mainly a second class affair, as the medium is not suited for anything much beyond a general effect. You may get an agreeable sensation, just as you do from an oriental carpet, and so on!!
>
> You are on the horns of a dilemma. If you had a Watts, who cd and would give you (possibly) a fine St Michael or St Gabriel in a picture, the chances are dead against it being presentable in glass. A good many people (painters) have tried it from Sir Joshua Reynolds downwards, and have generally, I may say always, failed. Then the other horn is, that when you get pleasant colour, and 'silvery glass' that you so much despise the chances are you get a considerable amount of insipidity! and that gets *your* monkey up! Can you tell us any place where you have seen it done? Westminster Abbey and St Paul's are pretty considerable cautions especially the latter. Of course a lot of the old glass is superb—Chartres, and some better still I think at Canterbury, but about both there is a strong flavour of the Turkey Carpet. There is another church at Chartres, St Pierre I think, that knocks you down flat, but it is simply the colour, the magnificent splodges. I have not the faintest recollection of one single subject, or saint, but the memory of the effect will never die out of my mind.[72]

Today I sign the contract for building the All Saints Church, Compton, Leek. May God in his great wisdom and mercy help me to complete the same to his glory and my honour and everybodys satisfaction. Amen.

Thus begins the building diary of James Heath of Endon, contractor for the church, pious convert from Methodism, and brother to George Heath, the Staffordshire 'Moorland Poet'.[73] It is a uniquely fine and apposite commentary to the construction of a great Victorian church (ill. 232). To build a church to seat 750 for the town round which your life was centred, renowned for its civic pride; to carry out the orders of an architect of national fame: this could be the crown of a provincial mason's career. Local eyes would be upon those who erected the most ambitious Leek building within living memory. Local materials would be insisted upon throughout, not just the red stones from the Peak or the roofing tiles, but the very mortar limes as well; all of these Heath would be especially equipped to know.[74] The skills needed to build any Gothic church were great, for such a daring one as All Saints they were enormous. Shaw constantly extended his builders, and Heath perhaps most of all. 'Any want of care or foresight might have led to grave disasters,' he afterwards testified, 'but owing mainly to his thoughtful intelligence, un-remitting zeal and assiduity in conducting the work, we have had no troubles of any sort.'[75] Heath's prayer in fact had been fulfilled. In despite of the tens of shoddy jerry-builders, the speculators and even the great London firms, Victorian architects stood on the backs of middling men like James Heath, who had an absolute and undeviating commitment to the job they undertook. They shirked nothing and they spared nothing. Heath lost three workmen; one was imprisoned for desertion, two he dismissed, the one for boozing, the other for sitting too long on the closet.[76] What price was such stern punishment, when so magnificent and sacred an undertaking (his own monument, as Shaw told him to see it) was at stake?

The Architect payes us his second visite and is well pleased with the work he is a very grand man indead I admire and respect him more than I can say he very much hopes the Committee will finish the church.

Leek was a hierarchical society with a long memory. The great families were the Wardles, the Sleighs and the Challinors, all interrelated and High Anglican by persuasion. Their business was in silk mills and in dyes. Morris had come to Leek to learn from Thomas Wardle about dyeing; in the 1870s the Leek Embroidery Society, finest of the provincial bodies that took up art needlework, arose around the Wardles. Shaw had first impinged upon Leek through an old friendship between John Horsley and the Sleighs. There had been talk of him doing work nearby at Cheddleton, where the Scotts and Morris restored the church. Instead he found himself through the Sleighs rebuilding Meerbrook, on the other side of the town, for the last of another great local family, the Condlyffes. For Hugh Sleigh, he then rebuilt Spout Hall in St Edward's Street, Leek, a high half-timbered house (ill. 61) which affected the style of the local architectural dynasty, the Sugdens. Shaw and Sedding also worked for the Challinor family at St

232. All Saints' Leek under construction.

Luke's Leek. So it is not surprising that the chief subscriber for All Saints was Joseph Challinor with £3,500, or that Miss Condlyffe's executors and Hugh Sleigh (who paid for the triptych and the whole of Gerald Horsley's chancel decorations) were also big contributors. These men were the backbone of the committee and believed in paying well for good architecture. Under this firm directorate, determined to push on whatever the deficiency of subscriptions, and under the authority of Shaw, who appeared occasionally to preside over the works like some genial god possessed of all wisdom and all thoroughness, James Heath felt himself automatically both secure and full of awe.

We are dressing big template for iron girders. We set out templates for 4 big arches nave arcade. I do hope we may be able to get them up quick and safely God help us . . . I am very very busy. I feel almost overpowered with the weight of responsibility. God help me. Amen . . . I recd a letter from R. N. Shaw in which he expresses a fear of the tower through this exceedingly wet weather and the tremendous weights being put on.

305

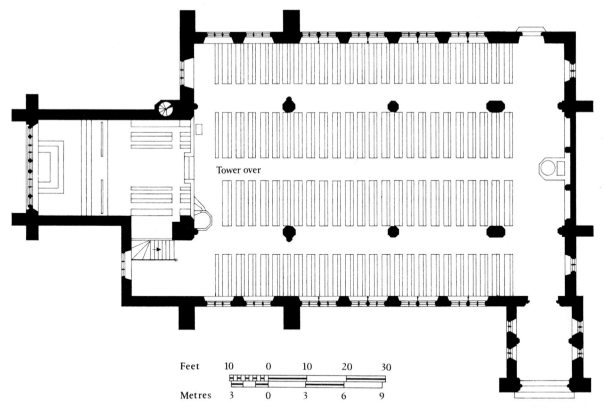

Feet 10 0 10 20 30

Metres 3 0 3 6 9

233. (above left) All Saints' Leek, exterior from north-west.

235. (above) All Saints' Leek, floor plan.

234. (below left) All Saints' Leek, interior.

It was an extraordinary church. What Shaw had done was to take the Ilkley design and then, to improve the outside aspect of his chancel, thrust the crossing tower not upon the choir, as had been the intention there, but upon the last bay of a very broad nave (ill. 235). To keep the whole width clear of visual impediment, the western tower arch is widened right out compared to its eastern brother, the chancel arch, and springs from a point high above the capitals of the nave piers (ill. 234). The piers propping this arch are themselves free-standing, since the aisles continue for the whole length of the nave, so making a much better exterior than the transepts which orthodoxy would have prescribed at this point. Therefore Shaw had to build up big flying buttresses through and over the roofs of these clasping aisles at all four weighty corners of the tower. This utterly logical but daring system relied upon girders and tie-rods as a legitimate extension to Gothic construction. The roof beams, for instance, have iron flitch plates, while between the outer and inner walls of the belfry Heath laid an old steel pitrope he had bought from a colliery.[77] Many of these devices were temporary, since the greatest danger in all span structures is during construction. Open tie-rods ran across the tower arches and were only removed several years later; when sawn off, at least one cracked like a revolver shot. There were certainly mishaps. Quite early on, one of the vestry arches fell in. 'God help me. It is dreadful. Never had such a Sunday before' wrote Heath. And in November 1886 two of

307

the centres near the south west tower pier bent under the strain, so that Shaw and Heath were under great anxiety until Lethaby visited Leek and pronounced all well.

Outside, the aspect of this low central tower between nave and chancel, enhanced by the small square-headed windows of clerestory and aisles, is of ruthlessness; the image of some strange slow-moving creature of mechanized warfare, stranded by chance upon the streets of Leek (ill. 233). But within, the nave and tower arches, crowding and swaying in uneven height and rhythm, are stilled by the perfect perspective from west to east and the congruence between end windows, so that the body of the church basks in a generous peace.

Myself, son and the Foreman are setting out the templets for north and south chancel windows. The tracery is very fine indeed. Mr W. L. Sugden sayes Mr Leathby is the finest architectural draughtsman in the world.

The fittings of All Saints' Leek herald Lethaby's undoubted arrival as a designer of genius. Up till now most of his work had been subordinate to his master's, but here he designed a set of fittings and details of tremendous prestige for the burgeoning Arts and Crafts movement. Some were perforce still reliant on Shaw's style. In overall form, the nine-light end windows do not differ from Ilkley, but in place of dry Perpendicular tracery, they arch out into nervous, delicate patterns. The east one, said to derive from the south transept at Ashbourne, hints at overlapping windows, the west one in contrast divides into two complete forms separated by a centre light. Other of the fittings (ills. 236, 237) are fully Lethaby's own. The font, for instance, translates Butterfield's octagonal type into glistening black marble and foreshadows the Byzantinism soon to come into fashion.[78] At the pulpit, Lethaby breathes life upon Shaw's staid efforts at linenfold panelling, emphasizing and piercing the verticals, and simplifying the old sagging panels. As a final tribute to his power, Shaw left to Lethaby and his friend Hamilton Jackson the details of the reredos at the climax of the church. The later decoration of All Saints testifies too to the spell of Lethaby, not to Shaw's own taste. The Morris windows and the schemes of decoration for the chancel and south aisle by Lethaby's friends Gerald Horsley and Edgar Platt are done in the Arts and Crafts spirit.

We have our architect R. N. Shaw over to day and we have a good half day at the church and I am very happy to say he is greatly pleased with the result of our work now it is done he said to me it is the best and most satisfactory piece of work I have ever had done and we have to thank you Mr Heath for it and together we will yet build a cathedral together. Thank God for such kind and encourageing gentlemen.

All Saints' Leek was built under ideal circumstances at a time when Shaw's office was not overloaded. No other church he built to subscriptions so lacked administrative problems. He could therefore think and design strenuously, combine old with new, complication with simplicity, with an ease he was usually denied. It is the proper church on which to judge Shaw as an ecclesiastical architect, and the clearest of all his buildings from which to understand his particular application of the age-old belief that originality should derive from tradition. In the whole structure, hardly a moulding could be called new or inventive. Yet each portion is steeped in the effort of architect, builder, and town to sustain a unified, original, and communal expression of worship, in the spirit of the old cathedral builders. But look as Shaw might with envy upon Bodley's £70,000 Hoar Cross nearby, there was to be no cathedral for either Heath or him. The nearest he got was Liverpool, where he did the next best thing. As will be seen, Shaw picked the man who was to give that city its magnificent monument upon St James's Mount, swansong of the great Gothic church-building movement which Shaw served so long, and so well.

236. All Saints' Leek, pulpit.

237. All Saints' Leek, font.

CHAPTER 8

The 1890s

'Solid, masculine, and unaffected'—those memorable words of
Inigo Jones, which epitomize the best traditions of English art.
Reginald Blomfield, *A Short History of Renaissance Architecture in
England* (1900), conclusion.

EMINENCE

DURING the 1890s, a personality cult grew around Norman Shaw. At sixty, he was to
many minds England's pre-eminent architect. The impact of his domestic style of the
1870s and '80s appeared ineradicable. Among the younger architects of talent, a select
few had been his pupils; others had been disappointed in that expectation and had gone
off to the next best office—Ernest George's or John Belcher's.[1] Many had sought his help
in the furtherance of their careers, amongst them the youthful Edwin Lutyens.[2]

The example of Lutyens must stand by itself for the overwhelming impression Shaw
made upon that whole generation. Lutyens' style of personality, not just of design, was
consciously modelled upon Shaw. He had had ample chance to study him. They first met
when Lutyens was still adolescent, and we have a description of the event. In about 1888,
Shaw was engaged on his third campaign of alterations at Upper House in Surrey for Mrs
Guthrie, now remarried. Her husband had got to know Lutyens' father, the painter:

> He had taken a fancy to the old Bohemian, and being a generous man he thought
> that to give him employment was the best way of helping the family, for whom life
> seemed a struggle. Ned the son, with his shock of hair and fantastic sense of humour,
> should be put in the way of entering some profession. He had ability and even an
> unusual originality that demanded a worthwhile outlet. That had been demonstrated
> when he had been shown Norman Shaw's drawing for an addition to our house. With
> extraordinary dexterity he had taken a pencil and with a stroke or two indicated where
> a great improvement could be made to the design. When the architect was shown this
> suggestion, he looked at my stepfather with a puzzled air.
>
> 'Whom in the world have you been consulting?' he asked, inclined to be rather
> annoyed. When he heard it was a lad of eighteen whose hobby was building daub-and-
> wattle cowsheds and other constructions, for which he got orders from farmers around,
> he said, "Send him to me; that lad is worth training; he has ideas!"—then, after a
> pause—"Still, it was pretty good cheek, don't you agree with me, sir?" . . .
>
> Next time Mr Norman Shaw was due to come, Ned was told to hold himself in
> readiness in case the great man should ask to see him. So there was the young miscreant.

238. Shaw at work in the 'den' at Ellerdale Road, c.1905.

To do justice to the occasion, he had heavily anointed his hair, which now lay in streaks instead of standing on end; his garments had been borrowed for the occasion from a friend, whose figure did not remotely tally with Ned's, and his feet were encased in the Vicar's Sunday boots. These hurt him, and a limp was the consequence. He remembered the Vicar's instructions and wore, besides the clerical boots, an air of holy submission.

Mr Shaw looked at him askance. So this was the youngster who had dared 'improve' on the design of one of architecture's pillars! After a little conversation the P.R.A. of the future was telling Norman Shaw R.A. of his experiments in the type of building suited to agricultural enterprise; just mud-encased on wooden piles, roofed with heather, resistant to wind and weather, warm in winter, cool in summer, conforming with the surroundings in accordance with what he called "my fixed principles"—this made Shaw smile—and those were, that anything that was put up by man should harmonize with what Nature, who had been there first, should dictate. Materials should be drawn from those obtainable in the area and foreign elements strictly eliminated. 'Very interesting, my boy, but not always feasible,' interrupted the great man. 'All right for cowsheds, but human beings demand something a little more in keeping with the age in which we live, and if you had my experience you would find that the newly-rich, who after all are the patrons of today, demand replicas of

311

something they have seen in other countries they have visited. Why, they must even have marble for their tombstones, instead of the beautiful mellow stuff that is to be found in most districts of England.'

Still, on the whole, Ned made a good impression. After Shaw's departure Ned released himself from the bondage of the unnatural garments he had worn and gave the company a good imitation of the successful professional man.[3]

At about this time, Lutyens began his training with Ernest George, not Shaw. But in the early 1890s Shaw and he were hand in glove more than once. When for instance Shaw remodelled Framfield Place in his now-customary discreet classic, he handed the dining room over to Lutyens, who in contrast panelled it, mischievously parodying Shaw's Old English of the 1870s.[4] And at The Hallams, close to Upper House, Lutyens looked once more over Shaw's drawings and made some suggestions.[5] Shaw must have been impressed with him, for he never made such arrangements with other young men who had not been in his office. But the relationship did not last. In 1897 when planning his marriage and his move to 29 Bloomsbury Square, Lutyens suggested that Emily Lytton might visit Shaw: 'I should like to see him too but perhaps he would not wish this.'[6] Possibly, Shaw tired of the pushy young man. When in 1901 a partnership with Lutyens or Newton was offered to him for the second Alliance Assurance building, he unhesitatingly plumped for Newton.[7] But the image of Shaw haunted Lutyens. His ambition in life was to emulate and surpass him; he even dreamt about him.[8] The facility of design, the whimsy, and the social ease he showed towards his clients were all hallmarks of Shaw's manner. Of Lutyens' equal or even greater talent there was no question. But over his professional integrity there has always been doubt, as if the qualities which made Shaw respected were purposely and histrionically used to further Lutyens' ambition. The appetite for work became rapacity; the charming humour turned into witty but eventually tiresome japes. Lutyens of course belonged to a more socially insecure age, so the verdict is a shade harsh. But though their temperaments were at many points close, Lutyens never lived down a lifelong insecurity, while Shaw was a happy man.

Lutyens was one of many who looked to Shaw for patronage and support. His blessing was constantly asked and too often given. Commissions, assessorships and honours of one kind and another were continually on offer; old jobs were exhumed, revisited, and illustrated now in the building press, and journalists even sought him out for interview. One such went to see Shaw in his new chambers at 10 Hart Street, just round the corner from Bloomsbury Square, where he moved in 1893 for the last years of official practice. An aura of distinction had settled upon the master, who received the man in a small neat room, furnished with a few ornaments on the mantelpiece and a cabinet of his own design.

There is nothing typical of the man of T-squares and drawing boards about Norman Shaw. The sleeves of his coat are not shiny, nor is there an atom of that superior 'don't-care-if-I-do-appear-shabby' look about the Royal Academician. In fact he has the aspect of a Cabinet Minister, even though he possesses a supremely gentle and courteous bearing unknown to gentlemen who rule the political destinies of the moment.

He sees his architecture as a reaction from the acutest Gothic taste, says the reporter, and will say little except to denigrate it. To a question as to his best work, comes the reply:

> Best work! Best work! I have no best! I have never yet been satisfied. I have never yet conceived a work which has not fallen miserably short of my conception. I am always striving to do something good, but when I think of what I *have* done, when I see how much I could improve *that* now, how much I should like to alter *that*—and *that*—and *that*, it makes me shudder and I am miserable; therefore I have no best![9]

Being so self-critical, Shaw chose largely to ignore his fame. To the end of his life he eschewed all the posturing of public eminence and clung to his belief in dealing with matters great or small practically and personally. But though embarrassed by the panegyrics, he was amused and flattered as well. Thus, after one such article, he writes to Fred White: 'Have you seen my obituary notice? I don't think I really could have the cheek to send you a copy, it is so excessively flowery. When I really do die, there will be nothing left to say, and in my own little heart I think much of this would have been better to have been left unsaid.'[10] But more was to come. One paper tipped him for P.R.A. in succession to Leighton; another, in support, named Shaw 'incomparably the greatest Architect that England has produced since the time of Wren'.[11] Of his popularity among the artistically aware, Patrick Abercrombie recalls:

> In the household in which I was brought up the three magic syllables 'Normanshaw' were repeated as often and were given as unquestioned veneration as that accorded to the syllables Williammorris, Robertbrowning and Burnejones. So deep indeed was my father's veneration of Norman Shaw that when he contemplated building a house, on a scale at least as large as some of the lesser buildings illustrated, he dared not approach the great man but must needs be content with an obscurer person 'who worked in the manner of Norman Shaw'! It was a source of snobbish grief to us children to have to qualify the authorship of our house as 'by an architect of the school of . . .', though I am now sure that many people to whom that confession was made, knew not either the master, his family or his imitators.[12]

Beyond Britain, Queen Anne and Old English were by now identified almost exclusively with Shaw's name. Several parts of the empire, especially Australia, had happily adapted to their capacities and materials the various features of his styles.[13] In part, these experiments were anticipated in or imitated from the United States, where Shaw made the greatest mark. But the connection between Shaw's own work and the American 'Shingle Style' is far from simple.

Across the Atlantic, Old English had struck in the mid-1870s like an answer to the prayer of those trying at that precise moment to refine what was to be known as the Shingle Style.[14] Many an American architect, responding to the pleas of Emerson and Thoreau for a simpler, more traditional life-style, was working back to the wooden architecture of the settlers' first farmhouses. The earlier houses of this revival, coarse and confused in style, showed that European (and especially English) sophistication was still needed. But few Americans knew modern British buildings at first hand. An exception was John Sturgis, back in Boston in 1870 after four years' study in England, and possibly the harbinger of changes soon to come.[15] Others had to rely upon the *American Architect and Building News*, which often published English work, usually in the shape of R.A. drawings already illustrated in the British periodicals.

Thus the picturesque Shaw country house perspectives, when they began to appear, sounded a special chord in American hearts. Feverishly, one facet after another of his published work was borrowed: the offset plan, the tile-hung gable, the chimneys, the inglenook, and so on, until every mannerism of the Shaw country house was enveloped in the Shingle Style. Even the names came in for imitation; Shaw's Cragside, Northumberland, became Peabody and Stearns' Kragsyde, Manchester-by-the-Sea. Fortunately though, the originals and their derivatives were far apart. So since little was known of the techniques and materials involved in Old English, American architects had to improvise, select and interpret. Every stylistic element had to be sifted for its practicability in the context of a different climate, different living habits, and different materials. After the first craze, many were gradually discarded, until by 1890 few American houses much resembled the English originals which had offered such fruitful hints for refinement, softening, and articulation. The final results, in the hands of architects like Wilson Eyre, W. R. Emerson and J. C. Stevens, were often superb and free. That is why Frank Lloyd Wright could begin his country house career without the hand of precedent tapping too heavily upon his shoulder.

Even in the 1870s, only one architect ever looked like taking over the Old English system wholesale. This, surprisingly, was H. H. Richardson. Richardson was never impervious to British ideas. Intermediaries like Sturgis, or his young pupil Stanford White, who is always held responsible for most of Richardson's work in this idiom, may have been a help, but the fact remains that Richardson's own houses and furniture designs were reflecting the new English style well before anyone else's. As early as 1874, his Watts-Sherman house not only incorporated the first and most accurate renderings of most of the Shaw devices, but also aimed at fidelity of overall effect. Soon after came the Blake and Rush Cheney projects, on similar lines.[16] How Richardson and White could digest the style so fully without visiting Britain, before the *American Architect and Building News* had started to show Shaw's work, is a mystery; perhaps Sturgis is the answer. Still, even so loyal an imitation as the Watts-Sherman house diverged from its models very deliberately. By what was to be a standard practice in later American borrowings from the style, tile-hanging was translated into shingles, half-timbering into cement panels; while within, the pies and the woodwork lost their Japanese nuances and became experiments with the motifs of that Cairene and Hispano-Moresque art so beloved by Richardson.[17] Even Stanford White's inglenook, which would have been America's first, had it been carried out, was to have taken a quite different form from its models. And soon, Richardson and White had tired of Old English and were moving on to less derivative things, while others followed on.

So distance from Europe was to be a boon for the future originality of American architecture. Yet it also led to misapprehensions and confusions which persist to this day. For a start, all the credit and all the odium (and there was much of either) for the exciting new import were attached willynilly to Shaw. Little was heard in the States of Godwin or of Stevenson, and nothing at all of those proud innovators and reluctant publicists, Devey,

Nesfield and Webb. The 'long shadow' of Norman Shaw was left hovering over the Shingle Style, from the sheer chance that he allowed his skill and assurance as a perspective artist to be manifested each year on the walls of the Academy, and so speedily wafted therefrom across the Atlantic. More seriously, because of the divide, America never grasped the distinction between Old English and Queen Anne. It was a difference confused enough at home because of the poor terminology and because the styles could merge here and there, as at Bedford Park, but it could usually be discerned in principle. In the United States, however, the whole gamut of reformed English building styles was dubbed Queen Anne, despite the fact that the English 'Queen Anne' city style travelled far less well than its sister. For instance, R. S. Peabody of Peabody and Stearns, one of the first imitators of Old English after Richardson and White, was also in the forefront of proponents of Queen Anne in the *American Architect and Building News*. Anything his firm did in the next few years was connected popularly with Shaw. Soon enough, Shaw and his contemporaries were believed to have plotted a Queen Anne takeover of American architecture, and associated with much with which they had not the remotest connection. Thus in 1883, Montgomery Schuyler, very fairly imagining that Queen Anne ought to have something to do with the monarch in question, but less fairly judging Shaw from so-called Queen Anne work in New York City, was lambasting him as the 'chief evangelist of this strange revival', who had 'bedevilled the weaker of his brethren' into architectural 'mischief' of one kind or another.[18] Probably, poor Shaw never knew the full range of influence so confidently attributed to him. Had he done so, it is hard to know whether he would have been more amused or appalled.

Still, he cannot have been unaware of this high tide of popularity (or notoriety). From the sheer weight of exhortation his self-esteem grew. Gradually he rose to the role of importance which others had allotted him. By 1890 the purely architectural adjustments had begun, and Shaw started to see himself as the classic tradition's prodigal son. In the field of public authority and responsibility, self-assurance took a little longer. New Scotland Yard's success must have encouraged him. Then in 1891–2 arose an issue which pitched Shaw personally into the public controversies of architecture: his quarrel with the R.I.B.A. over registration. These were the experiences which gave him the confidence for his late surge of civic architecture.

R.A. OR R.I.B.A.?

At the time of the registration controversy, Shaw was not a member of the 'Institute' (as the R.I.B.A. was familiarly called). In the 1860s he had become an associate at the instigation of Street, who believed in paper-reading and debate as a means of improving architecture. Then, the Institute served a useful role as a forum, though its discussions were often dominated by dogmatists. The standard had fallen off since, not least because many of the leading architects had ceased to belong. Shaw's case may be typical. He went to a couple of dull meetings and fell asleep at the second.[19] Then Professor Donaldson, one of the Institute's leading lights, called on Shaw to ask him to read a paper, in accordance with the by-laws. Shaw was out, but Nesfield, another unenthusiastic associate, was at home:

315

'What paper?' asked Nesfield.

'What paper!' replied the Professor, in mock horror—'What paper; don't you know that all Members of the Institute are *expected* to read a paper?'

Poor Nesfield protested that he had never read a paper in his life, and Donaldson retorted that it was an excellent time to begin.

Nesfield, taking Donaldson seriously, consulted Norman Shaw, who likewise affirmed that he had never written a paper in his life and never intended to.

'What's to be done?' queried Nesfield.

'Resign', laconically came from Shaw, and their resignations were posted the same night.[20]

With hindsight, Shaw's action appears thoughtless. But he may have acted out of a misguided sense of loyalties. The proper place for architectural aspirations, he always believed, was not the R.I.B.A. but the R.A. There he had made his first mark. From the time of his elevation to A.R.A., Shaw stood by the Academy unswervingly. He always attended and often spoke at Council and Assembly meetings; he staunchly supported the presidential policies of Leighton, whom he saw as architecture's ally within the Academy[21]; he frequently hung and always helped choose the architectural room at the annual exhibition; and he extended the galleries and built the restaurant. For a short time he held the post of Treasurer, abandoning it with embarrassment at having broken the long history of architectural succession in this office.[22]

But his chief work was for the R.A. Architecture School. Whereas the R.I.B.A. had no school for architectural training, the Academy had old-established evening classes. These, having been revitalized by the indefatigable Street and further reformed by the Drawing Master, Richard Phené Spiers, were still attended by articled pupils from most of the leading London offices. From 1878 Shaw taught with regularity and devotion in the school, wittily, gently, possibly a little leniently. Reginald Blomfield remembered him as 'the only one of the visitors to whom we attended seriously', but knew others who thought otherwise.[23] Though Shaw constantly urged the development of the school, he failed. The Academicians were too inert and conservative to achieve much collectively. Many were just ageing, individualistic painters, who liked the R.A. as a club, had their own preoccupations, and cared little for architecture. Until T. G. Jackson joined, even the few architectural A.R.A.'s gave scant help. Bodley, whom Shaw admired, would infuriate him by writing poetry during Council meetings;[24] Arthur Blomfield, whom he did not, straddled the fence between Institute and Academy.[25] The system of articles, too, militated against reform. As long as they remained, no pupil could devote much more time to training, as Shaw himself was forced to admit when an addition to the syllabus was canvassed in 1890. 'By the time they have worked in their respective offices from 9.30 to 5.30, and then three days a week from 6 till 8 in the schools, getting home about 9, you could hardly expect them to throw themselves with much ardour into the study of "descriptive geometry applied to scientific masonry".'[26] In these circumstances the A.A. School, more autonomous, more flexible, and less reliant upon the individual 'big guns' for instruction, gained ground. By 1900 the R.A. School no longer mattered much. Shaw had out of loyalty put his eggs in the wrong basket.

316

The R.A.'s stagnation as a force for education was plainer in 1890 that it had been twenty years before; but the future of the R.I.B.A. was by no means clear. Since so many able men had defected, the Institute had fallen into the hands of men like Robert Kerr, Macvicar Anderson, and Shaw's old foe William Woodward. They, partly on practical grounds, partly out of self-interest, were bent on turning architecture into an 'examinable profession', like law or medicine. They did not hope to 'close' it immediately. But they insisted that when the time came, the R.I.B.A., fortified by royal charter as the official national representative of architects, must itself be the examining body and define the qualifications for compulsory registration. That is why they fought the first Registration Bill, which came before Parliament in 1886. It was so collectively opposed that it got nowhere, but it squarely raised the question: 'Architecture—a Profession or an Art?' It was some time since a matter of principle had so thoroughly divided Victorian architectural thinking.[27]

Though the majority of well-known London architects were still members of the R.I.B.A., most were infrequent attenders, and many become disquieted with its policies in the 1880s. Both from within and without, opposition began to mount. Shaw was known to be unhappy with the R.I.B.A., so any general resistance would be at least referred to him. A resuscitated registration bill of 1888 was brought to his notice by Jackson, who for many years had observed architecture's progress towards a closed profession.[28] Shaw agreed to sign any letter of protest but forecast that the bill would fail of its own accord, as it did. But Jackson had sown the seeds of dissent. When yet another bill was introduced in 1891, 'this time Norman Shaw took it up hot'.[29] This bill, championed by the new Society of Architects, was again opposed by the Institute as premature, and duly disposed of for lack of parliamentary time. But Shaw and Jackson were not to be deprived of expressing their views. They wrote to *The Times*, they 'memorialized' the Institute, and having triumphed over the bill, they issued a volume of controversial essays entitled *Architecture a Profession or an Art*.

The initiative in this campaign was Shaw's. It was he who convened the first meeting at Macartney's house to oppose the bill, and who encouraged the outright attack on the R.I.B.A. Five of the seven memorialists who resigned from the Institute over the affair were his pupils. To Reginald Blomfield, a sixth, he wrote, 'I was very glad to hear that you had sent in your resignation to the R.I.B.A. and I have no doubt you feel happier and more independent. . . . It must be war now and no quarter.' As the idea of the book took shape, he became no less virulent: 'Of course you have read that wishy-washy twaddle of Anderson's in yesterday's *Times*. Don't you think that *now* is the time to have a shy at them?'[30] While Jackson organized the literary side of the book, Shaw went about getting the right reviewers in the periodicals. Broadly, these were more favourable than the building press. The most interesting review appeared in *Nineteenth Century* from the august pen of Lord Grimthorpe, the ancient controversialist. 'The worst of Lord Grim,' predicted Shaw to Blomfield, 'is that he will bang us about the head as much as our enemies . . . It is past his powers to be anything but brutal.'[31] He was right. Grimthorpe invoked a plague on both houses, decreed that professional and artistic architects were equally incompetent, and proposed litigation, not registration, as the proper tool to protect the public.[32] As often before, Grimthorpe had shown an uncanny skill in mixing sense with his nonsense.

By any critical standard, the book was dreary and repetitious. As glaringly as the registrationists' plans for a closed profession, its woolly 'prize-essay style' and abstraction laid bare the poverty of Victorian architectural education. This was the issue that needed thrashing out, but few of the essayists fully grasped it. Instead, they reiterate their twin themes, that architecture is art and that art is sacred and unexaminable. Rarely do they see the difficulties to their approach. What is artistic ability? How is it to be tested, if not by examination? What shape should architectural education take? The answers to these questions are often vapid. Lethaby's essay leans upon Ruskin and Morris without, as yet, any lessening of their impractical idealism; Basil Champneys admits he knows no alternative to articles; J. R. Clayton commends French training but does not explain why it works. Despite Reginald Blomfield's assault upon the R.I.B.A. exam, 'framed with careful reference to a dead level of mediocrity', the essayists cannot deny that at least some branches of architecture may be examinable. By denigrating these branches, they show that they speak for only the most fortunate and talented part of their profession. Outside the London ambience which the memorialists knew lay the uninspired and often incompetent preponderance of architecture. Jackson does indeed point out that nine-tenths of building is not designed by architects at all, and therefore argues that registration will give no significant safeguard.[33] But he forgets that the authors of nine-tenths of that one-tenth have to concentrate upon economy, not upon art; and here a minimum standard would have been helpful. It was too easy for successful London men to deride attempts to limit their freedom, not knowing the conditions and standards of run-of-the-mill provincial practice. Unconsciously, they were substituting for professional freemasonry another insidious élitism of their own.

Amidst these mediocre efforts Shaw's own essay, 'The Fallacy that the Architect who makes Design his first Consideration, must be unpractical', passes muster as a modest venture into polemic. He puts it that the architect's aim should be to build beautifully, that this involves more than good construction, and that business habits are a separate issue. It is printed as the first chapter, marking Shaw as ringleader of the protest.

Now that the rift had become visible, it was hard to close it quickly. There were several appeals to Shaw to come into the Institute and bring his friends with him, notably from Brydon, one of the memorialists who did not resign.[34] But he remained unmoved. Shaw's differences with the R.I.B.A. were never made up, indeed they became worse over the ensuing twenty years. On occasions the rancour broke out over competitions, because he disputed the Institute's claim to be an impartial, arbitrating body. He also refused the olive branch twice tendered to him in the shape of the R.I.B.A. Gold Medal. On the first occasion (only the second time that it had been declined in R.I.B.A. history), the wits said Ruskin had refused it because he wasn't an architect, Shaw because he was. Later on, he received a curt note saying he was to get the Gold Medal; he took umbrage and again refused, complaining to Ernest George (then P.R.I.B.A.) that this was not the way to treat people. If gently approached, says his son, he would probably have accepted this time. But his intransigence remained to the end; he was bitter when his ally Bodley accepted the Medal.[35]

318

This confused campaign did at least raise the issues of architectural training. After the debates of 1891–3, the intelligent men in either party knew they had to get together if standards were to improve. Others too were anxious about England's poor technical training. Not long afterwards followed the appointment of Lethaby to Sidney Webb's new Technical Education Board at the London County Council, and the first practical steps were thought out. In 1906, Aston Webb arranged a reconciliation between the Institute and the lapsed memorialists, whereby the Board of Architectural Education was set up and proper schools encouraged. So for a time registration was dropped for lack of urgency. It came eventually in 1931, in a very different climate to that in which the registrationists of the 1890s had tried to foist their values on the whole profession.[36]

SHAW AND THE ARTS AND CRAFTS MOVEMENT

For the initiate, *Architecture a Profession or an Art* meant something further. It was the first open token of disagreement between Shaw and the band of pupils who had founded the Art Workers' Guild. Superficially they did not disagree; they were in the same cause. But between Shaw's essay and those of Newton, Prior, Lethaby, and Horsley loomed a void. Throughout his essay, Shaw saw the architect as an isolated designer of masterpieces in the mould of Inigo Jones or Wren, whereas the others spoke at every stage of the interdependence of the crafts. Four of the thirteen contributors helped found the Art Workers' Guild, and others belonged to it. So the book often threatens to become pure propaganda for their movement; in Gerald Horsley's essay the threat matures. Shaw and his friends Bodley, Clayton and W. B. Richmond try to redress the balance, but the contributors frequently resemble a tug-of-war team in which the captain's style and directions are persistently flouted.

It had been just a decade since the Shaw pupils founded the St George's Art Society for their own private amusement. In 1884 this turned into the Art Workers' Guild, initiated on the day Weir Schultz arrived to take a place in the office.[37] The Guild was more serious and broadly based, but in its early days it was dominated by the pupils. Shaw took an indulgent, fatherly interest, but did not attend the meetings, whereas Sedding joined his own pupils and became an active member. Then came the leap of 1886–7, when the group sought wider publicity and membership. They started the Architectural Illustration Society, which published their work regularly in *The Architect*, and they encouraged the new Arts and Crafts Exhibition Society, covering craft interests. Other developments followed. Kenton and Co., a short-lived furniture firm involving Macartney, Lethaby and Reginald Blomfield, was founded in 1890; and a year later appeared Lethaby's first book, the arcane *Architecture, Mysticism and Myth*, popularly christened 'Cosmos'.[38]

There were of course other groups and individuals who contributed to the early history of the Arts and Crafts Movement. But its distinct profile as early as 1892 was broadly due to Shaw's pupils and followers. It was they who had succeeded in widening and diversifying the movement, in comparison with earlier guilds. Like them, they wished to carry out the precepts of Ruskin and Morris and reintegrate architecture with the crafts. But the grouping of the Art Workers' Guild was loose, its role passive and coordinating, and its stylistic dogmas few. They could, for instance, absorb an interloper like Reginald Blomfield, who already thought Gothic Revivalism mere play-acting, and found virtues in the most formal classic imaginable. They agreed no more firmly on the political orientation which their movement, if it was to be taken seriously, must eventually adopt. The socialists in their ranks were outweighed by the Tories; Macartney's father-in-law was a Conservative minister, Blomfield was a diehard church-Tory, and Prior embraced Ruskin's nostalgic Toryism 'of the old school, Sir Walter Scott's and Homer's'.[39] Lethaby, the undisputed mentor of the group, lent the movement its socialist tinge through his acquaintance with Morris and friendship with Philip Webb. While Morris had now virtually abandoned art for politics, Webb went quietly on with his practice. Slowly he replaced Shaw as 'master' in the eyes of Lethaby and other of the old pupils. Still, they continued to value Shaw's support, to respect and often follow his work, and to love the man. There was never any real break, even at the expense of consistency. Prior, for instance, combined an ultra-vernacular approach towards architecture with fervent admiration for Bryanston.[40]

We can only guess at Shaw's private opinion on the merits of a movement which originated in his office and was often erroneously associated with him. He was eager to encourage initiative, genuinely pleased by the successes of his pupils, and appreciative of their architecture. He lent drawings and photographs for the Architectural Illustration Society, and a silver biscuit box he had designed for the R.A. was shown at the Arts and Crafts Exhibition of 1890.[41] He cannot have cared much for their furniture, metalwork and jewelry, for he rarely used distinctly 'arts and crafts' fittings in his houses or churches after Lethaby left him. In architecture proper he was still susceptible to new stimulus, but infrequently now outside the range of classicism. His admiration for the work of Voysey as well as of Newton can be seen in his last domestic job, the little additions at Sibleys Orchard (1905). But as a penitent hates most his own past sins, Shaw now deprecated anything undisciplined or eccentric in house architecture. In 1904 he could say, 'There is a great "straining after the picturesque" but this is the natural outcome of the state of things. In every thing now a days there is a tremendous exaggeration. It is of no use mentioning things, as it pervades everything, and in our art finds its last expression in "l'art nouveau" work, that simply reduces me to tears.'[42] Compared to the extravagances of the Century Guild or the Glasgow School, there was little overtly *art nouveau* work in anything his pupils designed. Webb and Shaw were formidably agreed in opposition to it, so their disciples rarely tried it. Yet Shaw could praise the exotic jewelry of Harry Wilson, one of the most idiosyncratic artists of the movement.[43]

If Shaw approved some of the movement's products, he did not hold with its Ruskinian design philosophy. In *Architecture a Profession or an Art*, the agreement upon the high artistic status of the architect just papers over the cracks between contributors. For how did the Arts and Crafts Movement intend to apply the philosophy to intrinsically architectural problems? Experienced architects had been grappling with this for years. In the applied arts, Morris had been able to introduce only a few of Ruskin's ideas on worker participation in production and design. The guilds of the 1890s included, by contrast, a broader range of activities. Their members aimed both to learn craft skills and to teach the craftsmen who already had them how to use them more coherently and therefore more artistically. It was, in fact, a fraternal programme of 'give and take'. This programme, always in the forefront of the minds of Lethaby and the other really committed members of the Art Workers' Guild, was foreshadowed in their essays on the registration controversy. It became definite in the *Arts and Crafts Essays* of 1893, and got off the ground in 1896 when the Central School of Arts and Crafts was founded. Yet even then, this radical remedy did little for architecture itself. The crafts method produced fine furniture and metalwork, and embellished many good houses with original ornament. But it did not help the architect with little money, a limited brief, or a niggardly client. To have followed rigorously the prescriptions for this kind of artistic architecture would have meant reducing still more the small proportion of architect-designed buildings. The conditions of the Victorian city simply did not allow the procedures of building by leisurely day-work with which Lethaby and Prior so earnestly toyed. One of the failures of the Arts and Crafts Movement was that in an era when government and public at last grasped at the chance of making Britain's cities worthy of empire, it had neither a style nor a method for civic architecture to rival Edwardian baroque. Even the Central School of Arts and Crafts building itself turned out a compromise and muddle, instead of the advertisement it might have been. This lack of urban accomplishment and commitment was a sad shortcoming.[44]

Besides all this, much of the movement must have given Shaw and his remaining contemporaries a sense of *déjà-vu*. He had himself participated in the revival of the crafts in the 1850s and '60s, from which Morris's work sprang. It had produced fine work but likewise failed to solve the problems of building. When Shaw clambered up on the gable at Willesley to stick bottle bottoms into the plaster, it was, he now realized, icing on the cake. It was good that such things should be attended to, but the prerequisite was a thoroughly well-built structure. To get this, it was better to bypass local craftsmen, go instead to a good professional builder, create an atmosphere of mutual trust and understanding, and supervise his efforts stringently. Webb and Voysey did this as a matter of course, and the other Arts and Crafts architects were forced by circumstances to follow. As a result, they devolved less responsibility, not more. We have seen that Shaw trusted pupils and builders, devolving more decisions in the building process than his craft-orientated contemporaries, who assumed abnormal powers of interior and detail design.[45] The paradox shows how hard it was under contemporary conditions to apply the full Arts and Crafts programme to architecture, even amongst those most committed to Ruskin's ideals. Shaw had dallied with Ruskin long enough in youth and still felt his potency. His mature verdict on Ruskin was: 'Every word I believe to be fallacious, but I read it with pleasure and lay it down with regret.'[46] As he spoke, he must have been thinking of Ruskin's long stranglehold on English architectural ideals.

HOME AND HABITS

These divergences never touched Shaw's personal relations with his old pupils. If they made him a little isolated, that was part of a natural process. His attitudes at sixty were bound to look old-fashioned; the surprise is that he had novelties yet to spring. By the time of his move to Hart Street, he was already running down the scope of his practice. Those jobs that he did accept being often on the largest scale, his annual income from architecture hardly declined at first; indeed in 1894, when Lord Portman paid him the balance on Bryanston, it hit its highest point at just over £8,000. Since the mid-1870s, Shaw had normally netted between £3,000 and £6,000 per annum. On top, the unearned income from his savings, mainly in colonial and railway shares, soared from £30 in 1869 to well over £2,000 in the 1890s. The purchase of the Ellerdale Road site and the building of the house cost nearly £6,500 in the 1870s, and the new drawing room wing over £3,000 in the next decade, when his children were all at school or at home.[47] In the 1890s there were no comparable payments to be met. So by keeping the Hart Street office going, Shaw was to an extent indulging himself. At the end of 1896 he closed it down, but it made small difference. Before, several works had been built without much office help, the drawings having been done in the 'den' at Hampstead. From 1897, this simply became the source of all jobs. The result of 'retirement' was that Shaw was obliged neither to pose as a practising architect, nor to travel much into town. For help and draughtsmanship he relied on one man alone, Percy Norman Ginham.

Ginham had started out as the Bloomsbury Square office boy in 1879. He graduated to a post as assistant, succeeded Lethaby as chief clerk, and ran the Hart Street office for the three and a half years of its existence. After it closed, he carried on a modest practice next door at 11 Hart Street, but spent much of his time helping Shaw. Ginham obviously preferred a subordinate role, so in 1902 he procured a post in the L.C.C. Architect's Department. He was among the design team for the Central School, having for a time assisted Lethaby by teaching there.[48] Shaw felt a special affection and trust for him, and characterized him thus:

> He is an excellent all round draughtsman and designs with skill and nice taste, never with affectation or vulgarity. But I have always thought that his especial excellence consists in the exceeding great care and accuracy with which he works out difficult problems in arrangement and construction. Whilst he was with me I gave him many of these, such as complicated stairs, intricate arrangement of flues, and many other difficult 'bits', and I never on any one occasion found a single error or oversight. Amongst the scores of draughtsmen I have come in contact with, I have never found one to be so absolutely relied on.[49]

Many of the later office drawings are Ginham's: elegant sheets drawn in Lethaby's manner, but sharper, neater, and less imaginative.[50] Several pencil designs drawn up by him suggest that in small projects Shaw gave him as free a hand as Lethaby, if not more.[51] But the fall-off in decorative detail in Shaw's work of the 1890s shows how hard it was for him to replace Lethaby. Whether Shaw used Ginham much after he joined the L.C.C. is hard to know; there is no trace of him helping with the Quadrant. His own work is obscure.[52] Like many talents, Ginham disappeared completely into the anonymity of the L.C.C. He retired prematurely after some sort of breakdown in 1915. His background may have made him shrink from the kind of public exposure which the more privileged pupils could easily handle.

Ellerdale Road, where Shaw could now spend more of his time, offered a simple domestic background, little changed since his period of illness. Neither Agnes nor he had ever been gregarious, and this changed little after the children grew up. For such a smart house there were few special occasions; the high point was a grand party in May 1893, perhaps celebrating the formal completion of the house by the addition of a ground floor bay towards the garden. This was not the end of Shaw's building plans. By the turn of the century he was dissatisfied with the house. In March 1901 it was actually put up for sale, though no offers are known; at the same time Shaw was thinking of adding a little wing in the south-east corner, perhaps to make it more saleable.[53] At about this date he did work for a time on an entirely new house-project for himself, rather smaller than Ellerdale Road, for Lindfield Gardens, Hampstead. The surviving drawings, though rudimentary, give an idea of what this house would have been like.[54] It was to have kept to the free-gabled style, probably mixing roughcast with brick in the elevations. Inside, it would have had the spatial ingenuity of Ellerdale Road without the haphazardness. In this last major domestic project, all the old originality is still there.

But there were plenty of reasons for staying put. One was health. The month-long holidays which the Shaws took to Europe staved off repetition of the 1880 crisis for a long time. But Agnes developed a strain of neuralgia which plagued her for the rest of her life. Shaw's own constitution stood up tolerably well until 1899, when he had pleurisy. After that, he was unwell more often than not, so there were no more trips abroad after 1902. There were anxieties, too, about Robert, the elder son. All three children had remained close to the family, but none more so than Bobbie. Bessie, the eldest, stayed at home till 1896, when at the age of twenty-eight she decided to join the Sisterhood of Bethany. Willie, the youngest, born in 1874, went to Uppingham, and then after a short period abroad was apprenticed to a mechanical engineering firm. He soon transferred to civil engineering and joined the London and North-Western Railway. Willie was the only one of the three to marry. At first there was some parental opposition to his choice, soon overcome. But he had the misfortune to lose his wife after five years of marriage. Consequently their three small infants spent much of their childhood in the grandparental home at Ellerdale Road.[55] Robert Shaw, on the other hand, wished to follow his father into architecture, but was dissuaded; he was physically frail and nervous to the point of disability. Instead, he joined Barings as a clerk after leaving Haileybury, staying there till 1914 despite the collapse of the wrist muscles to his right hand early in his career. To compensate for these disappointments his father tried to keep him informed on all he was doing and to discuss architecture with him. In return, Robert noted down his father's opinions and *obiter dicta*, kept a check list of his drawings and accounts, and after his death compiled the autograph volume that is the source of most of the personal information we have on Shaw's life.[56]

Most of the observations and habits recorded by Robert pertain to this later period of his father's life, when dignity had relaxed any remnants of his earlier awkwardness, and calmed his wit into a maturer humour. By now, Shaw's bearing breathed confidence and success (ill. 238). His hair, which thinned little, had turned an even white. His face through all the changes of fashion remained clean-shaven, soft and fastidious, with a high line of cheekbone and a prominence of vein upon his forehead. He spoke with a gentle drawl, and his talk, says an obituarist, 'was flavoured with a certain amount of honeyed sarcasm, often very amusing, and having more of banter in it than real acerbity'.[57] Life at

Ellerdale Road was neither lax nor aesthetic. The household was still a little Scottish and stiff, reminiscent of old Mrs Shaw. High standards of behaviour were expected. Religion was taken seriously; meals were frugal; the routine was exact. On work days, Shaw left Hampstead for the office after the eight o'clock breakfast, making his professional calls by preference on the way in or back. He had only biscuits and a glass of milk at lunch, arrived home at about six and ate dinner soon after. He then slept for an hour, wrote letters for another hour or so, and went to bed shortly after ten. From such a simple, watertight routine, the fertility and concentration of the eminent Victorians often stemmed. It relied upon the collaboration of all, from cook to clerk-of-works, to avoid interruptions. Everybody had to do their bit as well as Shaw did his.

But Shaw was never the archetype of the Victorian *paterfamilias*, emotionally remote, daunting, and moralizing. For example, he was happy to let his children watch him draw, since his work gave him such pleasure. Robert Shaw: 'I only know of one story which suggests the contrary; and that was when my Sister was watching him drawing a wreath, and seeing it flow so easily from his pencil, she said: "How lovely to get your living by doing such beautiful things," and he replied: "Ah, but to get your living by it takes away the pleasure".' But whatever the occasional frustration, his gifts were spontaneous, and this meant he could be spontaneous in private life as well. His method of dispensing discipline, for instance, when his grandchildren became too rowdy in the dining room and he was busy at some project in the den, was to throw things down at them from above.[58] His intimacy with Agnes lost none of its style. Thus he confides to Murray Marks about a hatstand he had designed:

> I have told the maker to put a sort of trellis of strong wire for the bottom tray, so as to prevent umbrellas from slipping, which in my case, at home, is an astounding curse. I always carefully put the point of my umbrella into one of my wife's goloshes so as to prevent its tumbling down. I hear her grumbling sometimes, complaining of damp feet and declaring there are holes in her goloshes, but up to this time she does not suspect the cause!![59]

The levity became more needful as their healths declined. Here he is writing on their wedding anniversary in 1902, amidst the throes of the Liverpool Cathedral competition:

> *My sweet old Mugwump!* Do you think it is in the least likely that I should forget it? Only *I* maintain it was the 17th. Dear me, it is a long time ago and many things have happened since. We have been *very* happy, long may it go on!! anyway, for some years. And really we are hardly a day older. Possibly we may look it!! but we don't feel it, apart from tum-tums and fatigue, I don't think I *feel* much older. And you may remember that this time 35 years ago the tum-tum was not much to boast of. Today, *this* day, it is miles better than it was then, with cold veal cutlets in it![60]

Shaw's letters seem to have become, if anything, racier and more zestful as the years passed, whether to private or professional correspondents. His handwriting itself developed into a larger, faster-flowing line, produced at speed, elegant but not self-conscious. A typewriter was never introduced at Ellerdale Road, all letters and reports being written in longhand to the end. Some of them must have seemed eccentric to the officials who handled them, for Shaw still believed in writing as a personality to a personality. Towards individual clients he of course felt the same. Many of these were among his closest friends; Robert Shaw names Lord Armstrong, T. H. Ismay, H. D. Horsfall, R. B. Martin, George Matthey, C. L. Norman, Arthur Sparrow, Edwin Tate and Fred White as particular intimates. He can have seen few of them as frequently as he wrote to them. The exceptions were Edwin Tate, who lived nearby, and John Clayton, another Hampstead resident, an old friend with a splendid sense of humour and tastes that had changed in a similar way to Shaw's own.[61] Most of his other friends were architects, collectors, or dealers. One exception was the young Liverpool lawyer Frederick Radcliffe, who dealt with the Ismays' affairs. To him Shaw wrote a series of letters that pullulate with life, as thus in 1907 on the subject of pianolas:

> I am so glad you like your piano player. We stick to ours, at least I do, 'like a pitch plaster to a pine plank'. It really is an immense solace and comfort. When I get tired, here, of doing what I call work?? I dash into the drawing room and tackle a long Sonata of Beethoven's. It is most refreshing and *interesting* and I believe does one good. Of course I don't understand it a bit! but that is a detail. I don't play the Sonata to company, but to *myself*.
>
> When you are next in town, (and I expect you are often in town) you must squeeze out an hour, if you will, and let me hear you play. When our tube is open we shall only be about 10 mins from Euston! but the shaft, Oh! that shaft! 225 feet deep. What a smash there will be someday. . . .[62]

Music was a favourite diversion of the family. In the drawing room a recess had been planned for an organ, which never materialized. Instead, they had to be content with a grand piano (as well as the pianola). There were plenty of books as well, but Shaw was not a great reader. His tastes remained early Victorian: Dickens, Thackeray, Tennyson, the Ingoldsby Legends, Carlyle's *Heroes and Hero-Worship*. He read virtually no science or history, and only a little theology.[63] As for architecture, he certainly kept an eagle eye on the periodicals, but it is hard to say how deeply he had read. His library, lost without trace, contained valuable books, but many must have been collectors' items or source books of details. Shaw was usually ready to tackle anything contemporary which was plain and straightforward, and being himself a good stylist, could judge what was well written and what was not. This was one reason why he admired Reginald Blomfield, whose review of Lethaby and 'my dear' Swainson's book on Santa Sophia he found so much more readable than the original.[64]

After designing, Shaw's only major interest was collecting. At Ellerdale Road he accumulated a motley assortment of Nanking porcelain, Rhodian ware, metalwork, and Japanese prints. There were, too, all sorts of odd pieces of furniture, few of real beauty. Such bric-à-brac gathered apace in rich Victorian households, often disfiguring the rooms.[65] But from 1890, it was all overshadowed by a more consuming passion—clocks. Until then, Shaw had had a number of timepieces scattered about, but now he began to buy. He owned 92 at the turn of the century and 170 in 1910. Albert Richardson says that Shaw possessed about 75 grandfather clocks, but that is wrong.[66] His real *penchant* was for smaller ones. Bracket clocks, table clocks, skeleton clocks, and lantern clocks littered the tables and sideboards at his home and must have tried the family's patience to the limits of cacophony; fortunately, few of them worked. Shaw delighted most in the mechanisms. Nothing pleased him more than to buy old clock movements, examine them, and if they were worthy, send them round to H. Knowles Brown's shop in Hampstead High Street for repair, or design new cases for them to be made by Robert Christie.[67] Most of them came from Percy Webster, a dealer in Great Portland Street. Webster introduced him to William Edwards Miller, a small-time portraitist and well-known clock collector, and the hobby brought the three families close together. After Shaw's death, most but not all of the clocks were sold.[68] Of the 114 items in the 1913 sale, over half were foreign. They included a number of unusual early German clocks, particularly by Augsburg makers, perhaps picked up during holidays abroad. But the products of the classic English clock-making school, reliable in workmanship, plain and rich in appearance, were peculiarly calculated to appeal to Shaw's late taste. It is irresistible to compare the bracket clock cases he was handling every day with the plain, polished panelling in mahogany, oak, or walnut, of his later interiors. In the work of Tompion or the Knibbs, Shaw could contemplate an ideal of his own: a stately frame encasing perfect mechanical servicing in a relationship which was formal, proper and proud, and never baldly functional.

JOBS OF THE '90s

Having graduated to the status of public figure. Shaw took pains to avoid publicity for his new work of the '90s. So it can be hard to understand what he was about. Hand in hand with his new anonymity came the occasional stentorian outburst of style, bellowing for the full classic manner of an earlier century. Because none of this work was published, it took the architectural world some time to discover what was going on. When they did find out, they were puzzled. The Northern A.A., making a pilgrimage to the unfinished extensions at Haggerston Castle in 1896, could perceive only scale and costliness.[69] Their southern counterparts visited Bryanston three years later, and were no more impressed.[70] Ingress Bell, commemorating Shaw's retirement, found the monumental classic of Chesters a 'trial of faith'.[71] How, he asked, would Shaw defend it? Hermann Muthesius, also perplexed, voiced the possibility that after years of greatness, Shaw's elasticity had at last failed him. But with a German's eye for generalities, he rejected this explanation for something broader and more telling, in which Shaw played only a part: the renewal of conservatism in every walk of English life at the expense of liberalism.[72]

Nothing could be more cogent than this invocation of the *Zeitgeist* for an understanding of Bryanston, the broadside with which Shaw opened his campaign of the '90s for a colossal architecture. In 1886, just before inheriting the huge family estates in London, the second Viscount Portman had parted from the Liberals and joined the Unionists. He already had a house here in Dorset, one of James Wyatt's smaller but finer classical mansions, of 1778. We do not know what the matter with it was. One story says that the house was waterlogged, and since none of the papers has survived, there is nothing to go on but stories. At this stage in Shaw's career, he would not have agreed to demolition without good reason. As it is, mantelpieces taken or copied from the old Bryanston are scattered through the new house. What, with hindsight, astonishes is that a

239. Bryanston, entrance front.

hereditary peer of moderately enlightened views should in 1889 have been willing to spend over £200,000 on an ampler, more monumental seat. Where none had previously existed, vast houses were commonly constructed for another twenty years yet. But already it was peculiar for an aristocrat bodily to replace his house with something double the size. To do so was to believe that his tenure, line and status were secure, that he ought to be seen to live publicly, and that those overlooking his life comprised not just his tenantry or constituents, but all his countrymen and indeed more than his countrymen. The classic of Bryanston aspired to international recognition in a way that Gothic palaces, the Duke of Westminster's Eaton Hall for instance, did not.[73] With Norman Shaw's house, the Portmans joined the great club of European aristocracy, not knowing that its days were numbered.

Bryanston has its own impeccable international pedigree. In the summers of 1888 and 1889 Shaw was in France, the second time 'partly on business'.[74] Probably, he visited the Loire. The basis of Bryanston's garden front (ill. 240), lower and recessed side wings strung out along a line with the two-storey central block, seems to be a borrowing from Menars, Gabriel's château for Mme de Pompadour.[75] Menars, though a friendlier and less formal house than Bryanston, also has very red brick walls, strong stone dressings, and much rusticated detail. From another French house, Vaux-le-Vicomte, Shaw took ideas for the terrace work beneath this front.[76] There are English antecedents too: Coleshill for the plan, the shape, and the detail of much of the centre block; Stoke Edith for the chimneys, roofs, and quoins; Cobham Hall for the voluptuous balusters on the main stairs. Shaw attended, too, to the Georgian architecture of nearby Blandford Forum, in an effort to give local tone to this eclectic monster.

The plan of Bryanston (ill. 241) carries on the selectiveness. A house of this size needed four wings, and by English classic custom Shaw should have projected one at each corner. The contours on the garden side prevented this, which is why he adopted the Menars idea. But on the entrance side he brought traditional east and west wings forward

327

240. Bryanston, garden side.

to make a U-shaped court. This gave him his four wings with more compactness of plan than the old houses had had, and he now took advantage of it. Disregarding pictorial effect, he drove the corridor which his double-pile central block suggested right through from one wing's end to the other without a break, some hundred yards in all. In its course, the only event he allowed was a high inner hall (ill. 242). Here he released his pent-up energies, sweeping back an entablature across the tunnel of the corridor, and topping the hall with four wide rusticated arches. These support the skylight and reveal the windows lighting the upper corridors, high in the ends of the central block. The first floor passages,

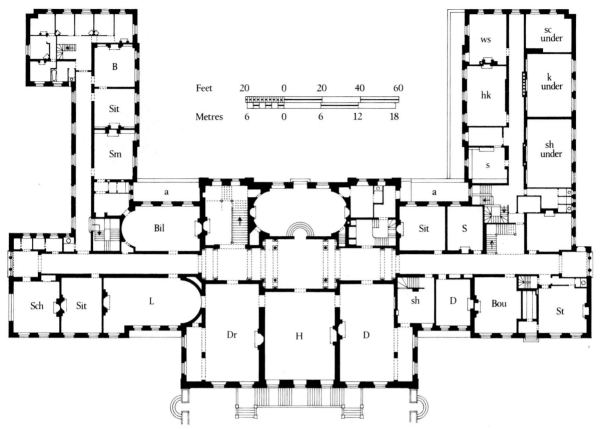

241. Bryanston, contract ground floor plan.

with their half-open and half-closed spaces surrounding the central well, succeed exactly as the ground floor fails; where they abound in gradations of light, the long corridor just progresses drearily away from or into the light source. In the Portmans' time, the inner hall was often curtailed by the closure of doors at either end to break up the corridor, but even so it must have been a cheerless place except as a point of departure. The great symmetrical reception rooms (ill. 243) enhance the bleakness, despite their good proportions. Nearly all go for a careful but dead 'period' detail, based on the previous Bryanston, and conceived as a polite background for pictures and soft furnishings.[77]

But few houses so much reward a scramble in the backrooms and attics. There can be seen the vast effort it took to make a late Victorian mansion, replete with the latest appliances, absolutely symmetrical. It was here, 'behind stairs', that Shaw put in the work, and the details of Bryanston's construction and technology matter more than those of the reception rooms. By all accounts Portman gave Shaw the proverbial *carte blanche* as to cost. Over 6,000,000 bricks, 58,000 cubic feet of stone, and 6,480 cwt of iron and steel girders were used.[78] The walls, some three feet thick, were built with an inside lining of

242. Bryanston, the central hall.

243. Bryanston, part of the drawing room.

'sawdust compressed bricks' with tar between, and a facing of the finest two-inch bricks that Holland and Hannen could find.[79] The new classicism extended to the central heating system, connected to a series of radiators in which the pipes became thick fluted cast-iron columns; a bank of thirty runs along the basement corridor.[80] Steel runs riot in the sections, and the roofs rely on sets of lattice girders to support the chimneys. At first, Shaw thought of cutting out the centre of the roof towards the entrance front, presumably to allow more light to his inner hall. In the event, he decided against interrupting his hipped roof, and took the attic storey corridor round three sides of the skylight over the inner hall. Still, the slightly greater width of the central block on the garden front than on the entrance side involved him in an unorthodox juggling operation with his eaves levels and valleys.

The entrance front (ill. 239) is the real architectural success of Bryanston. Towards the garden, the proportions cannot redeem the enormous scale; the detail repeats too often, so the composition flags. But on the other side the enclosing wings prevent monotony. Shaw throws in a measure of verticality by breaking the centre into three sections (falsely repeating the staircase windows on the right across floors on the left) and crowning the roof with a pair of looped chimneys. The stone banding of these chimneys and the window surrounds, though excessive on old photographs, has toned down now and lost much of its stridency. Dressings like these were never conceived of as intruding upon classic calm, but as integral to English late seventeenth-century tradition.[81] Because they stand out from the brickwork, they give a superficially foreign look to Bryanston and recall the texture of Nesfield's Kinmel, built twenty years before. But the details here are purer, and the similarities due really to either architect's admiration for Wren and his school.

Bryanston, though built only eighty years ago, is the most unimaginably remote of all Shaw's works. We do not know whether he regarded it (as one might be tempted to hope) as a Waterloo, never again to be attempted, or as the first triumph of a new colossal classic. It was by accounts marred by difficulties. Portman was something of an autocrat, happy alternately to wield the blue pencil on matured drawings, and to demand that all should be ready and finished for his convenience. There was a prolonged building strike during work, and Shaw was not allowed to construct the garden or approaches in accordance with more than the barest outline of his ideas.[82] This was a pity, since he had never to our knowledge laid out a garden in full, and others close to him were busy at this time reviving the traditions of formal gardening.[83] One of the best Bryanston stories is of Lady Portman standing at her bedroom window with a handkerchief, as minions moved about in the grounds with flagposts. When they reached a spot she judged appropriate for a tree, she would drop the handkerchief and they would stick in a post. True or false, it has the right ring, for it encapsulates the wilfully tight social hierarchies which the new Bryanston stood for even more fervently than the old, and which had so short a lease of life. Like Dawpool, Bryanston's span was less than forty years. It became a school in 1928, and some hundreds of boys now dwell in the house that Norman Shaw designed for two, living and sleeping perhaps more comfortably than its original begetters.

No architect could hope for, or even want, a bigger private commission than Bryanston. The only new country house Shaw built after this was The Hallams, a surprise return to the vernacular, but now explored for spatial possibilities, not picturesque effects. In 1899, at his own Banstead Wood, he added a garden front veering wittily between symmetry and asymmetry. Both show him as supple as ever with his old style, but they were the last times he used it fully.[84] The other big domestic jobs he now accepted were all for additions to classical houses, at Chesters (1891–3), Haggerston Castle (1893–7), Overbury Court (1896–8) and Addington Park (1899–1900).

Chesters was the first of two faraway Northumbrian jobs which it is odd to see Shaw still undertaking. The old house, a sturdy stone mansion of 1771, was set in low-lying country, next to the course of Hadrian's Wall and right beside the Roman camp of Chesters, which was part of the estate. It had belonged to the famous antiquary and Newcastle town-clerk John Clayton, who died in 1890 aged ninety-eight. He had begun what were according to contemporary lights careful excavations of the camp. In these he was enthusiastically succeeded by his heir, Nathaniel Clayton, who also called in Shaw to augment the house, and began ambitious estate works including stud stables and a room to house the archaeological finds.[85] At Chesters, the classical past was immediate and inescapable, since the house looked directly across to the camp. It brought Shaw face to face not with the traditions of modern classic, but with the authentic presence of Rome itself.

The boldness with which Shaw applied himself to rivalling the antique made Blomfield judge Chesters Shaw's finest country house.[86] But the formal problems of monumental addition without wrecking the scale of the old house were big, and he did not quite overcome them. At Bryanston, Shaw had the central block at his disposal when he set about organizing the wings; at Chesters, they had to be fitted on to an existing house. He had managed the entrance side well before, and so used the same projecting wings (ill. 244). But this time they protrude too far and box the old front into a mean entrance courtyard. On the east, he hid his vast servants' wing behind trees and bushes.[87] This

244. Chesters, entrance front during construction.

made it possible to avoid full wings on the garden side. Instead he thrust three vast rooms, each thirty-three by twenty-two feet, at angles to the ends of the old house, and connected them with a pair of sweeping segments. The gentler curve, which faces south towards the camp over formal terraces, is frankly additive (ill. 246), as the brief wings remain lower than the old part and have their own more rugged style. To the west, where Shaw had a whole new side to himself, he built up a tighter and blanker segment between drawing room and billiard room, and threw a colonnade round the centre in a gesture of Vitruvian extravagance (ill. 245).

This splendid device originated the 'butterfly' plan, which in more fanciful forms underlay many Arts and Crafts houses.[88] With Shaw it received a colossal expression (ill. 247) which imitators could not or would not follow. The mixture of axes complicated the circulation, lighting and girderwork. Semicircular and segmental spaces and arches abound in the interior, as if Shaw, having freed himself from the yoke of the rectangle, wanted to give rein to the curve in every dimension and aspect of the house. The climax of Chesters is the library, a sixty-foot-long saloon along the south side of the house, panelled in walnut and furnished with an organ. If in this room Shaw is in complete control, that is not always the case elsewhere. The entrance hall is abrupt and may never have been finished; at a late point in the project, the stairs were moved and access to the library altered, which may have upset matters. Although there is nothing in the nature of

332

245. Chesters, screen front during construction.

246. Chesters, garden side.

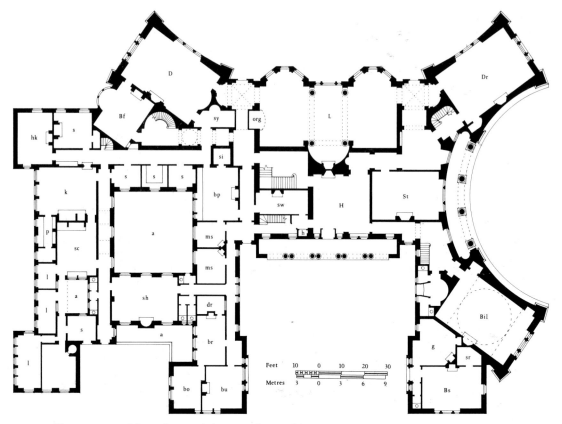

247. Chesters, ground floor plan, omitting some late revisions.

pastiche, the décor is bland to the point often of dullness. Shaw still missed someone like Lethaby to liven up these interiors. Lutyens, who would have been a good choice, visited Chesters in 1901 and summed it all up thus: 'It was lovely and loveable in great and many respects, but there are mistakes which I could not help thinking I should have avoided. An *enormous* house and all details left go lucky beyond a point. But the planning of it all is a masterpiece and the big library is quite delicious.'[89]

After Chesters, Shaw and his contractor Walter Scott turned to the farthest tip of Northumberland, and the remote Haggerston estate of C. J. Leyland, a few miles from Berwick. Neither house nor drawings survive. There was a ruinous fire in 1911, after which Leyland rebuilt even more lavishly than before, retaining the basis of Shaw's plan but adding a storey in places. This house had no better luck, and after it had failed to sell, it was nearly all demolished in 1931. Today all that remains of Haggerston Castle is Shaw's forlorn watertower to the north of the main site. It is enough to give the monumental scale, and from photographs and a plan more can be deduced. It is another version of the Chesters story; huge additions to a Georgian house, with a different planning solution and greater external simplicity. The Haggerston elevations (ill. 248), just big blocks of dressed stone broken up by a minimum of features, belied the swagger and complexity of the interiors, where as usual Shaw was up to all his ingenuity. He kept

248. Haggerston Castle, east front and watertower.

249. Haggerston Castle, the hall.

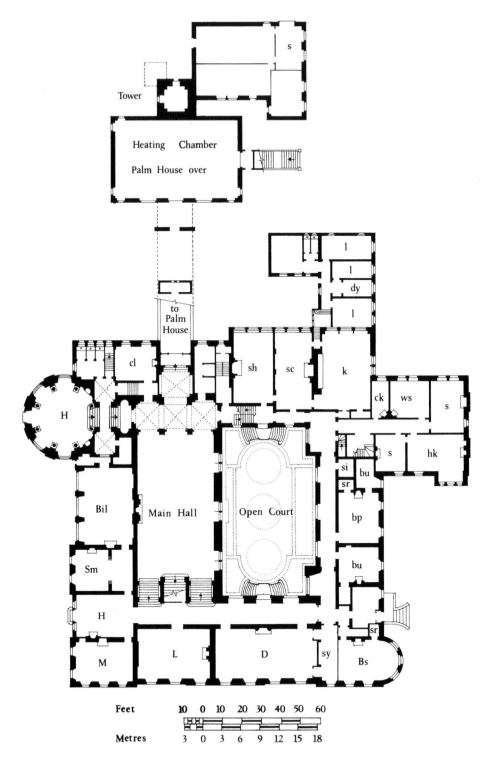

the old south-facing front, reconstructing behind it the main reception rooms, while at the back he added three sides round an internal courtyard, more than doubling the size of the house. Then into the middle he introduced a great hall (ill. 249), 84 × 40 ft., entered from a circular vestibule in the north-west corner, and axial with the winter garden and watertower to the north. The higher level of this hall meant that it could be sealed off by a flight of steps from the family rooms to its south, and gave it its own access and circulation for ceremonial occasions. Its ornaments, notably the fireplace, took Shaw's experiments with banded columns and voussoirs a stage beyond classic orthodoxy. But so too, in a way, did the plan (ill. 250). At Bryanston, he had been obsessed with symmetry of plan at all costs. That is still the preoccupation at Chesters, though already the circulation has been complicated to improve the rooms at the expense of the corridors. Haggerston is a further step backwards, towards the combination of clarity of plan with asymmetry of means which Shaw had already mastered at Dawpool. The signs are that at the end of his domestic career he was beginning to think Bryanston a mistake.

There is little more to say of Shaw's country house practice. Neither of his last two reconstruction jobs, Overbury Court and Addington Park, broke new ground. At both, his attention went into getting the best workmanship and proudest decorative effect in the interiors. At Overbury the elevations of the additions were almost brutally plain, and at Addington the exterior of the house became higher, harsher, and colder.[90] Addington was the bigger job; the reconstruction for a South African diamond magnate of Robert Mylne's Palladian villa, inhabited until recently by the Archbishops of Canterbury. Shaw concentrated upon an enclosed two-storey hall, the last he ever built. It confirms in a way what he had done at Haggerston, for it neatly combines the old screens-and-gallery type with a feeling for classic, cubic proportions. Its climax is a coved fireplace niche lined in variegated marbles (ill. 251). Elsewhere, the décor frequently peters out into mere 'period' frigidity.

251. Addington Park, hall fireplace.

Having therefore started the 1890s with a burst of fireworks, Shaw sobered down his elevations without renouncing interior pomp. The change, though uneven, was nearly complete by the time the main work at Chesters was finished in 1893. Some of the cheaper London buildings show it even earlier. In a group of little-known works of the early 1890s, Shaw stretched this necessity into self-conscious virtue. Two of these stemmed from 'church extension' in South London. This area worried the late Victorian episcopate. The East End was a fashionable target for philanthropy, but the slums of Camberwell, Southwark and Bermondsey were equally bereft of church accommodation, and were administered from far-off Winchester. By an episcopal reform of 1877, much of South London was transferred to the Rochester diocese; and then in 1905 the bishopric of Southwark was set up so that these problems could be tackled thoroughly. By then missions, chiefly from the universities, had proliferated.[91] In 1888 Trinity College Cambridge asked Shaw for a mission hall for Church Street, Camberwell, not far from St Mark's Cobourg Road. It was erected in two stages, in 1890–1 and 1894–5. He followed the pattern of his Harrow Mission Room and took continuous lights along either side of the roof. But because of the width of the room, he elected to expose his ironwork (ill. 254) and carry stanchions right across it, writing proudly on the drawing: 'My notion is to shew the rib'.[92] Round the mission room, he fitted the rest of the accommodation upon a confined site, the small frontage having three separate entrances. For this he chose a square and uncharacteristically flat elevation, of a kind he had avoided for nearly twenty years, in brick with simple stone dressings and mullions. There is something of Voysey about it, and indeed Voysey is recorded to have had some connection or other with the building.[93] But it was meant to attract no attention whatsoever.

At the Bishop's House, in Kennington Park Place nearby, Shaw exercised the same self-denial in another style. The house was designed as the new metropolitan seat of the Bishop of Rochester, then Randall Davidson, but he was transferred to Winchester before he could live in it. Davidson wanted the house to be palatial, a fit centre for the permanent South London diocese already in the offing. Hence the choice of Norman Shaw as architect, and the liberal planning brief: a good suite of reception rooms, space for secretaries, a chapel, and an examination room for testing candidates for the ministry.

252. East Combe, garden and side elevations, 1891.

Garden Elevation.

Side.

R. Norman Shaw RA.
29 Bloomsbury Square.

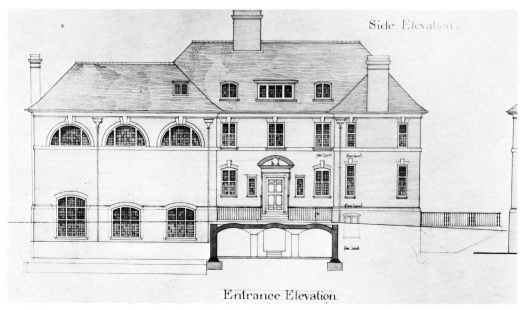

253. Bishop's House, entrance elevation, 1894.

The site was generous and allowed Shaw a free-standing town house, but he did not let himself go. Instead, he produced his most authentically late-seventeenth-century house design, an austerer and rougher version of 170 Queen's Gate. The Bishop's House (ill. 253) combines the now familiar double-pile plan with another seventeenth century domestic type, in which the end bays project slightly forward at front and back. This was known to Shaw from houses like Groombridge Place. The exception is the north-west corner, where the chapel and examination room have an autonomous position. But these cannot be easily seen, as the house gracelessly turns not its front but its side to the street and park opposite, and is shielded by a high wall. The details are deliberately coarse: crude, narrow transomed windows, emphatic keystones, and a massive eaves cornice.[94] Yet once more, it is another story within. The chapel had, before it was dismantled, the pure flavour of Wren. A grander version of the house, at first projected, was to have an apsidal drawing room and generous curving staircase. In execution Shaw had to sacrifice much of this and re-use the domical inner hall of 170 Queen's Gate, but he managed in many places to keep the bounding elegance of his beloved segments and semicircles. Such shapes were invading even his late vernacular works. In a third South London job of this period, a large tile-hung house of 1891–2 in Sydenham called East Combe, round arches turned up in the entrance porch and garden side verandah (ill. 252). East Combe has disappeared without proper record. It must have been an interesting work, for Shaw was using the chance of a suburban house to impart a little of his new formality to the ever-popular vernacular.

For the most charming example of the new facelessness, untouched by period bombast, one must turn away from domestic work to look at a police station. New Scotland Yard had cemented a friendship between Pennefather, the Receiver of Police,

254. (left) Trinity College Mission, interior of hall.

255. (right) Kentish Town Police Station, street front.

and Shaw. Just after its completion, the authorities began to press for proper divisional headquarters for the Metropolitan Police all over London. The Police Surveyor, Dixon Butler, designed a number of stations, but Shaw was brought in by Pennefather to supplement him and do two of the jobs. He rebuilt the station in Walton Street, Chelsea, and designed an entirely new one for Holmes Road, Kentish Town. The Walton Street Station, built in the roughest of stocks, with crude rusticated detail, heavy sashes, and weighty cornice, like some pub of the 1840s, was perhaps a reconstruction, with the old front partly retained. Yet one witty reminder at least of its authorship breaks through the anonymity; Shaw has stuck a semi-circular look-out post on one corner of the building, to show that the architect of the New Scotland Yard *tourelles* has passed by and left his signature.

If the Walton Street station façade was new, it may have taken its lead from the neighbouring houses;[95] at Kentish Town this was certainly so. Holmes Road lies in the sturdiest of stock brick neighbourhoods. Shaw just meant his new station to carry an undistinguished street on with the most discreet of architectural stimuli. It is a charmingly judged and gradually matured elevation (ill. 255). Architecturally there is much to point

340

to: the sparing use of keystones, dressings and lintels against absolutely plain stocks; or the narrow pairs of upper windows, articulated against the rhythm of the ground storey. But the Kentish Town Police Station, like New Scotland Yard, transcends pure architecture by delineating character and mood. Time and again, the presentation of a new type or personality brought out the best in Shaw; this time it was the British Policeman. It is a friendly building, up to a point inviting, anxious not to emphasize or inflict idiosyncrasies; it is provided, like the neighbouring houses to which it so nearly conforms, with a garden neatly but unostentatiously kept; it is plain, square, austere, and solid, even a little stolid, certainly unpretentious, and entirely without deceit. But it is not to be slighted or undervalued. The citizen about his lawful business can choose to enter at the front door, but there is another and less pleasant arch under whose harsher, emphasized voussoirs he may be forced to pass if he transgresses. No Londoner of the 1890s, when Newgate prison still stood, could mistake its import; it reminded him that the Metropolitan Police had teeth to show if they so required.

The police liked their latest character study less than New Scotland Yard. Unpredictably, it was an expensive building, and Pennefather had to put up with Home

Office grumbles. 'Mr Shaw goes in for rather greater strength in construction than we should adopt and he has allowed the men a greater cubic capacity, but these are *good* points, even if they cost a little extra money,' he argued.[96] In the event, he was right. The value of the experiment was proved in the divisional police stations Dixon Butler built over the next twenty years. The façades and probably also the planning of several derived from the Kentish Town station, as though Shaw's ideal had been taken over by the police as their own self-image. At the end of his official career, Shaw had still not stopped creating prototypes.

Imagination is nowhere so plainly the key to Shaw's architecture as in the Kentish Town Police Station. In many ways it was the closest he ever got to the self-effacing architectural expression of Philip Webb. But its greater vividness and impishness show, for a change, to his own advantage. It is not so much, as Mark Girouard has charmingly suggested, that Webb did not help himself often enough to strawberries and cream, as that his architecture is rigidly teetotal.[97] Shaw too often helped himself to the bottle, but with a new draught he could be magnificent, not least when it was beer and not brandy.

CHAPTER 9

Improving the Cities

A Londres, on ne s'occupe que de satisfaire le mieux possible les
besoins de la circulation.

Napoleon III.

LONDON

VICTORIAN London, it is well known, was a city without effective government. At the time
of the Queen's accession, few troubled about the administrative anarchy of the world's
largest conurbation. But by the Golden Jubilee, when the population had risen from two
to five million, anxiety had become general and obsessive. First, medical wisdom had
proved an appalling chain of connection linking maladministration, lack of centralized
sewage schemes, and high mortality. Then the broader drawbacks of urban chaos started
to thrust themselves disagreeably upon public attention; for every convert to social
improvement made by Dickens or Doré among the leisured classes, there must have been
ten from the stench of horse dung and human effluent, or from the poison of smut-laden
fogs. To tackle all this, the Metropolitan Board of Works was set up in 1855. Despite
limited powers, it acted speedily; by 1865, London's main sewerage system was complete,
and the Board was at work constructing hospitals and organizing a proper fire brigade.
But as endeavours to right the most pressing wrongs got under way, less pragmatic
sentiments began to make themselves heard. Such improvements as there were had been
made in a practical, cheeseparing spirit. Could not something more ambitious be
achieved?

By degrees, the Board did enlarge its capacities, and was soon biting off the awkward
mouthful of new streets. Nash's Regent Street, laid out so long ago as 1820, had been the
last achievement of note, made possible only because it ran through Crown property.
Pennethorne, his successor at the Office of Works, had managed to cut New Oxford Street
through the heart of one of London's most notorious slums, but even there had a hard time
of it with the landlords.[1] Elsewhere, the writ of property ran unquestioned. Apart from the
difficulties of compulsory purchase, the Board had no powers to rehouse the working
classes that their new roads displaced.[2] So old street lines were extensively followed for
Shaftesbury Avenue (1877–86) and Charing Cross Road, its successor. All the same, there
were major delays which excited criticism. The Board could proceed only by dint of
perseverance or by taking unique opportunities, as for example when the demolition of
Northumberland House allowed a road to be driven through virtually a single property to
their new embankment. But architecturally, Northumberland Avenue was a missed

opportunity, unambitious and stodgy along its whole length. As for the rest of these new roads, the result was an acknowledged muddle.

The critics of London's development pointed to Paris and the authoritarian achievements of Napoleon III. The difference was vividly revealed to visitors to the later International Exhibitions, the major forum for cultural exchange in the second half of the century. After 1851, Britain had a dismal record in mounting exhibitions, while France went from strength to strength, with first-rate shows in 1867, 1878, 1889 and 1900. To the regular attender, one side-effect was to demonstrate the dramatic transformation of Paris, as the rebuilding policies of Haussmann were completed under the Third Republic. An Englishman could scoff at France's political chaos; he might even reasonably despise French contemporary architecture as inferior. But he could not escape the conclusion that as an imperial city, Paris presented an appearance far superior to his own.

Further, during the last decade of the century, the old English inferiority complex about French pre-eminence in the arts reasserted itself for architecture. It was precipitated by the collapse of the Gothic Revival and the sheepish return to classicism, rather than by any startling achievements by France's architects. Men who had spent themselves moving, however profitably, from one style to another, could now see the intransigent Beaux-Arts training as a virtue productive of uniformity and discipline.[3] Young architects began to listen at last to Richard Phené Spiers, Master at the R.A. Schools and therefore a crucial figure in English architectural training. He was the only English architect of consequence to have been trained in Paris, and knew Gilbert and the great J. L. Pascal. Spiers warmly advocated French achievements and methods. In 1906, after his retirement from the R.A. schools, Pascal himself came over from Paris and made him a presentation. The gesture symbolized closer relations between French and English architecture than at any time over the previous century.[4]

Pascal's followers were prominent at the 1900 Exhibition, an event too often dismissed by historians seeking the long-term hints in architecture. Here, the spacious group of Petit Palais and Grand Palais, together with the ceremonial Pont Alexandre III, struck a note of gay facility such as even Garnier's Opéra had never quite achieved. Under the riotous stone skin of these buildings was a rational, ferrous framework; the spirit of the *dix-huitième* was back, but encompassing the legacy of Labrouste. The show was a particular hit with the English. Shaw, for instance, had visited Paris frequently since 1878 and was present in 1900.[5] By now he was an enthusiast for French culture, equally familiar with the Parisian furniture dealers and with the frescoes of Puvis de Chavannes. He did not ignore the lessons of the show.

So when, amidst a burst of chauvinism, Edward VII assumed the throne, English architects were looking to Paris for precedents of planning and architecture, so that they might latterly invest their capital with a dignity worthy of empire. A rash of urban planning broke out, the civic and nationalist equivalent to the radical garden city movement that was being fathered at the same time. The most immediate scheme was the Queen Victoria Memorial, the *rondpoint* which Aston Webb constructed in front of Buckingham Palace in 1900–1.[6] Over the next ten years, this became part of a typical Beaux-Arts layout stretching from the refronted palace itself to the Admiralty Arch at the other end of the Mall. During the period that this improvement was in the making, there appeared a plethora of official and unofficial schemes for metropolitan London. Never since the Great Fire had the capital been so avidly replanned. Yet once again the fruits were small. In a series of bruising battles, many schemes were defeated or seriously dented by the forces of property and commerce. In each case, public interest was intensely engaged; the conflicts were rough and the upshot often unexpected. One of the major surprises was the frequency with which the septuagenarian Norman Shaw contrived to be involved in the hurly-burly.

When Shaw first committed himself to such a scheme, he had no experience of planning beyond Bedford Park; he was an innocent, and it showed. In 1898, a consortium of politicians, stockbrokers and gentry hatched a high-class speculative scheme to extend the Victoria Embankment beyond the Houses of Parliament to Lambeth Bridge and redevelop the area round Smith Square. It was not a well devised plan, and in the teeth of opposition from the new London County Council, which had plans of its own for an Embankment extension, they asked Shaw to revise it. Unwisely he consented, and Lutyens came in as his partner.[7] In the modified version of the Westminster Improvement Scheme, less of the surrounding property was touched and the new Embankment Road was widened, as Shaw took pains to point out in a letter to *The Times*.[8] But the scheme remained ill-conceived, ill-planned, and purely speculative, as informed critics reaffirmed.[9] Luckily, the L.C.C.'s disapproval gave it the kiss of death and it failed in Parliament. But it had the excellent effect of achieving a virtual consensus against private schemes of redevelopment in metropolitan London. They were heard of no more during the Edwardian period; it has been left to the post-war era to resurrect them in their most vicious form. The fate of the Westminster Improvement Scheme may also have convinced Shaw that the right approach to London's planning problems lay in alliance with the L.C.C.

The L.C.C. from its inception in 1889 as London's first real organ of government was an administrative success. Combining the valuable spadework of the old Metropolitan Board of Works, whose headquarters and staff it inherited, with new plenary powers of its own, it could draw on two separate types of support. On one side stood dignitaries who hankered for London's transformation into the imperial capital that Britain merited. On the other were Fabians and radicals like Sidney and Beatrice Webb and John Burns, who fought for a just, efficient, and more or less egalitarian system of local government, and hoped great things of the L.C.C. For a time, both groups were amicably prepared to put their backs into the cumbersome business of administration; the initial enthusiasm lasted up until the First World War, and to some extent beyond.

In no section of the Council did the dichotomy reveal itself so plainly as in the Architect's Department. In a renowned series of early urban housing estates, the young men of the Department produced some of Britain's most radical and moving architecture. Yet there was also a steady flow of Beaux-Arts-inspired works from their office, ranging from the new metropolitan planning schemes to the Central School of Arts and Crafts itself. For the latter type of job, impetus came often from above or from the outside. The task of harmonizing these divergent forces fell to the L.C.C. Architect himself, who from 1899 was W. E. Riley. The Architect signed all the jobs, but in practice the designing was mostly done by underlings. Riley's real talent was the ability to delegate and to resolve difficulties.

In about 1900, when Shaw let it be known quietly that he would in his retirement help freely with urban improvement, he stood in unique, Janus-headed relation to the L.C.C., precisely because he could unite the conservative and radical elements on which they depended. Within the Architect's Department, the vernacular side of his work was revered, though the young assistants had more time for Webb than for Shaw, whom they thought of personally as a 'child of the aristocracy'.[10] Lethaby, who had been appointed to the L.C.C.'s Technical Education Board, was often in conference with the Department over design policy, while at least two of Shaw's pupils, Ginham and George Weald, held posts there.[11] At the same time, Shaw stood in a position of useful public eminence, and Riley must have known that in any matters of controversy over L.C.C. schemes, his new and more conservative opinions would come to the fore.

The first occasion upon which Shaw was drawn in to help the L.C.C. demonstrated the naïveté of all parties in the matter of central city improvements. After the Strand/Aldwych fiasco, they all retrenched and decided how better to order these things. But the harm was done; London's first street of the Edwardian era was another acknowledged failure, 'a ragged and ill-considered thoroughfare'.[12] The question of a new street (subsequently Kingsway) to link Waterloo Bridge with Holborn and improve London's execrable north-south communications, stood high on the list of priorities of the new L.C.C. in 1889. But it was deferred for one reason or another till 1898. One difficulty was to accommodate its junction with the Strand to the alignment of the bridge and the position of two churches, St Clement Danes and St Mary le Strand.[13] The 1898 solution, agreed in consultation with the R.I.B.A., was to split the street so as to form a sizeable triangle round St Mary le Strand. By 1899 this triangle had changed to a segment, with the divided road taking the lines of the present Aldwych, which was to be developed before the northern part of the scheme. Many architects, hoping for a finger in improvement pie, fiddled with this plan. In 1899–1900 the *Architectural Review* put forward suggestions for the planning of the new street, among them those of Shaw, who had been in on the founding of this new paper.[14] Like several others, he was against the segmental road. Instead, he proposed a bifurcation to enclose a square: the west branch was to divide in two so that its upper part could run across the Strand at high level to meet Waterloo Bridge, while the lower part descended to the Strand.

So Shaw was keenly interested in the project. Yet when asked in 1900 to submit competition designs for the elevations of both sides of the segmental road agreed upon, he refused on grounds of retirement. Curiously, the request came from the R.I.B.A. This may be enough to explain his refusal, but Shaw also disliked competitions and believed, as he told the L.C.C. later, that they should be used to give younger men a chance.[15] The history of this one was a bungle. At the start of the year, the L.C.C. Improvements Committee had ambitiously agreed to a competition between eight architects for suggestions for treatment of the Strand/Aldwych façades. Their decision was premature. For one thing, several of the firms who held sites along the new street had their own plans for rebuilding, notably the Gaiety Theatre and Restaurant, who had hired Ernest Runtz to design a new theatre for the prominent site on its western horn, looking along the Strand. No agreement had been made about the relation between such designs and the results of the competition. More seriously, the Improvements Committee had failed to persuade the Estates and Sites Committee to decide whether to place the much-needed new County Hall in the middle of the segment facing towards the Strand. The competitors were given vague instructions on this point; afterwards, it was the continuing indecision on the matter which put all the entries into cold storage. Nor were they given assurances that the winner would be employed, or that the entries would be professionally assessed. This brought down the wrath of the R.I.B.A. on the L.C.C., who had to agree to a few concessions. But when Riley, in consultation with Brydon, produced a possible list of competitors, half to be chosen by the L.C.C. and half by the R.I.B.A., it was not surprising that others besides Shaw refused. The final list, agreed in June 1900, consisted of Reginald Blomfield, William Flockhart, Ernest George, H. T. Hare, Mervyn Macartney, E. T. Mountford, Ernest Runtz (evidently chosen out of courtesy, having designed nothing of distinction) and Leonard Stokes.

In October, therefore, when the designs were in, the Improvements Committee looked around for an assessor to recommend the three best sets of drawings, and chose Shaw. In accepting, he declined a fee: 'I think, as a good citizen (and an Architect!) one ought to be prepared to put one's services at the disposal of a body engaged in the congenial occupation of beautifying the Architecture of the City where one dwells, and I am both prepared and anxious to do so.'[16] This tenor of civic service he maintained in all his work for the L.C.C.; next year, after the business of the Gaiety had been settled, 'when thanked by a leading member of the Improvements Committee, who professed a desire to do something for London, Mr Norman Shaw merely replied, "Do you think you are the only people who want to do something for London?"'[17]

Shaw by this time had some experience as an assessor. He had been in demand since Alfred Waterhouse, widely regarded as the doyen of assessors, had reduced his commitments in this line (having blotted his copybook in Shaw's eyes by choosing Aston Webb's design for the Victoria and Albert Museum in 1891).[18] To Shaw's own first assessorship had attached delicate circumstances, when he intervened and sorted out a muddled competition for the Bromley School Board in 1889. His willingness to serve had not been to the liking of the R.I.B.A., and in this it established a pattern. In 1895, Lethaby secured Shaw's services for the Passmore Edwards Settlement in Bloomsbury (later known as the Mary Ward Settlement); this was an interesting little limited affair, in which some of the best Arts and Crafts architects and some of the young L.C.C. men competed. His award went to an outstanding design by Dunbar Smith and Cecil Brewer, but there was no real anonymity about the business.[19] Then again next year, architects Shaw knew were chosen in the two limited competitions he assessed: Gerald Horsley for St Paul's Girls' School, J. F. Doyle for the Royal Insurance Building, Liverpool. And in 1897, on his decision, his friend Belcher won the Colchester Town Hall competition. In none of these cases was the victor unworthy; the designs of Smith and Brewer and of Belcher were particularly fine. But though there was little question of Shaw's probity or competence, he may have looked malleable. Also, at St Paul's and the Royal Insurance, he had been unabashed in closely following the development of the designs after the competition.[20] At Liverpool he even altered the winning design openly and with Doyle's consent, and was paid for it. This kind of practice infuriated the R.I.B.A., who thought it unethical. It might have been, in other architects' hands; but Shaw, as a virtuous individual, could not see it that way. His view was simple:

347

256. Aldwych, western horn, with Gaiety Theatre on corner and Restaurant behind.

I have always felt that the object of a competition is to get the very best building that can be had, and that any means (short of injustice) towards the attainment of this end is not merely legitimate but desirable. A good deal of so-called 'professional etiquette' I hold in slight regard, in comparison with the far more important question of getting a really good building.[21]

So by choosing so unorthodox an assessor for Strand/Aldwych, the L.C.C. were unwittingly adding to their risks. Officially Shaw shared the duty with Riley, but the report seems his own. He hailed the designs for their restraint, enthused upon the English Renaissance (the style more or less followed by most competitors), and plumped for the entries of Hare, Flockhart, and Macartney, in that order. He also praised the amended block plan of Leonard Stokes, the only outstanding feature of the competition, which was ruled out of court by the conditions. And he emphasized, as Riley had done from the start, that these could only be treated as preliminary studies, 'as the governing conditions of plan, which are so helpful in designing elevations, are necessarily absent at this stage'.[22]

This was far from the end. Poor Runtz was unplaced, but wanted to begin on his Gaiety designs. He had to wait until December to discover that Hare was to be associated with him in the elevations. Like most of the competitors, Hare had taken his cue in part from nearby, and incorporated in his design a number of fine bridges over streets, in homage to the bridges Chambers used on the Thames front of Somerset House. This was not at all the kind of thing that Runtz had conceived, and the two were soon at loggerheads. Next, the L.C.C. turned down Walter Emden's terracotta frontage for a restaurant on another part of the site, and had to agree to pay the difference between the cost of terracotta and of Portland stone, the material they now stipulated. Finally, at the end of April 1901, Runtz sent in his revised designs for the Gaiety, and they were terrible. There was only one thing to be done. Mindful of his continued offers of help, Riley sent them up in despair to Norman Shaw.

Shaw's report on Runtz's Gaiety Theatre and Restaurant design was at once kindly and devastating.

> I must candidly confess that this is to me a most uncongenial task, and nothing would induce me to undertake it were it not in the hope that possibly some good may ultimately arise. I know of few things more disagreeable than criticizing a brother Architect's work, knowing only too well how weak and vulnerable one's own work is.
>
> I have examined this design again and again at intervals for some days, and I deeply regret having to state that the more I examine it the less I see that is good in it, and consider it quite impossible for the Council to sanction it in its present form. To give an official approval to such a design would not merely be fatal to the starting of this very important Improvement, but it would have the inevitable result of throwing back all advance in Street Architecture for an indefinite period. Everywhere this would be quoted as evidence (and strong evidence too) of what the Council's standard in Architecture is. A standard that would be pronounced so low as to be more than disheartening.[23]

The upshot of this was that Runtz went to Ellerdale Road of his own volition, but very much on his guard. Like others, he was immediately won over. 'If you will permit me to take you by the hand [said Shaw] I will do my best to pioneer you through your difficulties, as you are not being properly treated.'[24] So Runtz agreed to be guided by Shaw, who made some sketch designs following his precedent as far as possible, while Runtz worked them up. Together they presented them to the Improvements Committee, who fell upon their necks with gratitude.

How much of the Gaiety design was Shaw's is hard to tell. He had a complete plan to adhere to, and had no wish to minimize Runtz's part, so the shape of the building with its domed corner was entirely fixed. Certainly, the block as it appeared before its mutilation (ill. 256) was unlike any of his other works; and Robert Shaw, who dissociates his father from any part in the restaurant, specifically says that the high aedicule in its gable was not his idea.[25] The chief problem in the design was that the Gaiety Restaurant, facing towards the Strand, wanted to build high, but the Theatre, which occupied the corner site, did not need all this height and stood in danger of looking stunted. Shaw's main contribution was, without obliterating the change of levels to add extra height to the theatre by suggesting an open loggia right round its summit, passing through the domed tower in the corner. In this, despite his panegyric in the assessors' report on the virtues of English Renaissance, he has concealed his inexperience of theatre design with borrowings from Charles Garnier. The paired columns of the loggia come from the Opéra, the neat disconnection between corner turret and side walls from the Cercle de la Librairie. To end a corner composition with a dome was a familiar Parisian trick of the Second Empire, perfected by Garnier.[26] But on the prominent Strand/Aldwych corner, so French a dome, perhaps a piece of still-unsublimated Runtz, jarred somewhat with the austere façades.

Such is the story of Shaw's first collaboration with the L.C.C. Once they had found so authoritative a champion, they were happy to go on using him as a bulwark against the R.I.B.A. The next occasion was Vauxhall Bridge, which the L.C.C. Engineer, Maurice Fitzmaurice, brought forward for the Bridges Committee to consider in November 1902. The idea of reconstructing the bridge in concrete and granite had been dropped only after the abutments and four river piers had been built, and Fitzmaurice was given the tricky task of designing a steel girder bridge upon them. The R.I.B.A., jealous at being deprived of another project which they had hoped to control, howled with rage when they saw his lame attempt.[27] The Bridges Committee referred the superstructure to Riley, who produced his own design but at the same time took the matter to Shaw. Riley's version kept Fitzmaurice's segmental arches, but took the metal superstructure through on a horizontal line from end to end; on the northern approach were to be pylons and bronze statuary, as on the Pont Alexandre III.[28] Shaw was unhappy with this. Having studied London's bridges, he thought the equal arches and level parapet of Waterloo Bridge not so fine as London Bridge, where the parapet rose towards the centre.[29] So while accepting Riley's idea for the approaches, he commended for the superstructure, 'a beam of simple, graceful camber from one abutment to the other, resting at intervals upon the piers. The footway on the bridge at each end would be screened by girders sufficiently deep to protect passers by. It would gradually rise towards the centre and there merge into a high grille.'[30] Possibly thinking of the allegorical figures on the piers of another Paris bridge, the Pont Mirabeau (1896–7), Shaw also submitted a design for cast relief figure panels for the upper parts of the piers, to be executed on a gold ground, and he wanted part of the grille gilded. But though Riley and the Committee concurred, economy and compromise prevailed. Fitzmaurice got his segmental arches, Shaw got his camber, and the approach statuary and relief panels dropped out, leaving the bridge with eight rarely noticed statues against its piers.

During the business of Vauxhall Bridge, a new pressure group made its début in the highly politicized world of Edwardian architecture. This was the Architectural Vigilance Society, a short-lived body 'formed for the purpose of promoting and assisting in the architectural improvement of London, by advice and suggestion'.[31] The eminence of their committee gave their views weight, but they successfully eluded publicity, ironically, seeing that their Secretary was the editor of *The Builder*, H. H. Statham.[32] Intelligent alike as an architectural and musical critic, Statham was to lend Shaw's Quadrant designs all the support he could muster, through both the Architectural Vigilance Society and *The Builder*, which he restored to pre-eminence in the building press. Shaw and he became closely acquainted in these years, and it may be that the Society's support was deliberately courted.[33]

Statham recollected in an obituary that Shaw several times altered designs without lending his name to them: 'On this point, in fact, he was chivalrously sensitive, and in some cases in which he is almost certainly known to have given advice or sketches he would never allow this to be stated.'[34] Soon, his reputation for helping out the L.C.C. became something of a joke. It elicited from the younger generation the following heartfelt parody of Gilbert's verse in *Iolanthe* on his famous namesake, Captain Shaw of the Metropolitan Fire Brigade:

> A word to thee, designer great,
> Thy efforts we appreciate
> The L.C.C. to regulate.
> But fees at least you need not shirk;
> 'Tis thus we're fleeced of public work
> On which you feast as private 'perk'.
> O Norman Shaw, give heed to our petition.
> Why should you choose to thus abuse
> Your well as-shawed position?[35]

What else besides the Gaiety and Vauxhall Bridge was the author thinking of? There are one or two possible candidates. One unconnected with the L.C.C. was Waring and Gillow's new store in Oxford Street. Its architect was Frank Atkinson, once the right-hand man of J. F. Doyle of Liverpool, and therefore known to Shaw. Atkinson chose a 'riotous Hampton Court baroque';[36] but, as a single drawing at the R.A. betrays, at some stage of difficulty with the frontage he took it along to Shaw. Whatever Shaw did on this occasion, he seems to have kept the fat out of the fire.

The confidence with which Shaw could be relied upon is illustrated by some remarks of Lethaby's to Sydney Cockerell in 1905, at a time when the L.C.C.'s new County Hall was at last in the offing:

> As to L.C.C. I wish it were possible to get a Frenchman but that is impossible. I hardly see any way out: a comp. means the swashbuckler gang and the swashbucklest being taken. Probably the best thing obtainable now wd be the *L.C.C. Office* with Shaw as *Consulting* Archt. . . . The Shaw business wd work probably more or less, because after the main bulks were kept simple (which he wd do in two days) the office cd carry it out.[37]

When the County Hall project finally did materialize, Shaw ended up not as consulting architect but, once again, as assessor. After three vain efforts to dislodge themselves from Spring Gardens, the L.C.C. agreed in April 1905 to purchase the great site on the south side of Westminster Bridge for their headquarters. Shaw and Beresford Pite testified before the Lords Committee on the urgency of acquiring all the site, and preparations began in Summer 1906 for a grand open competition. Riley asked for Shaw to serve with him, and together they set out the regulations. But they were more cautious than they had been in 1900, as Shaw was toughened by recent experiences with Liverpool Cathedral. There were to be two stages, with ten to fifteen designs going on from the preliminaries to compete with eight selected architects, among whom Shaw was keen to include some younger names. The sequence of events conforms to the familiar pattern, however: a struggle with the R.I.B.A., a confused competition, and continuing involvement on Shaw's part with the winning entry to save it from rejection or mutilation, thus provoking new jealousy. But this time the R.I.B.A. could not shout so loud. The conditions allowed the competitors to elect a third assessor in the second stage, and the entrants chose Aston Webb, one of the Institute's luminaries. Instead, the R.I.B.A. had to be content with complaining about the fees, and about the condition allowing Riley to be joint architect as well as assessor, so that he could assist the winner. Shaw cunningly cited Liverpool Cathedral back at them:

> You are perfectly at liberty to tell them that the appointment of an Assessor as joint Arch't has precedent amongst their own body, and good precedent too. At Liverpool Mr Bodley walks off, not with one tenth of the commission, but with *one half*! and Mr Bodley is a Member of the Institute, and one of their big guns, a Gold Medallist. All this, they know as well as I do, but you must not send them a copy of my letter. Their ways make me rather sick![38]

The actual competition went off quite smoothly. To inspect the 1,199 drawings of the 99 preliminary competitors was 'a daily mental exhaustion and a physical effort of some moment which will readily be seen when it is realised that a single walk round the hanging represented over a third of a mile'.[39] The second stage was less taxing but more awkward, since Webb had to be convinced that there was no favouritism in awarding the job to Ralph Knott, a young and unknown pupil of his. In fact, Knott's design flavoured more of Shaw than of Aston Webb. It had a corridor plan, a little of the English baroque and a lot more that was French in the detailing, and a high roof with tall stacks not unlike Shaw's recent Quadrant design. Towards the main entrance in Belvedere Road, Knott proposed a concave crescent partly hidden by the Council Chamber, which was to be detached from the main building. But the assessors did not like this feature. Over the lengthy period between the end of the competition in early 1908 and the laying of the foundation stone in March 1912, they made many alternative suggestions, seemingly at Shaw's initiative.[40] They persuaded Knott to integrate the Council Chamber in the main building, transfer the crescent to a magnificent position on the river side, and carry an engaged giant order round it instead of the open double colonnade which he had then proposed across the front of the crescent. These are improvements integral to the familiar appearance of County Hall today (ill. 257).

On the opposite side of the river, Shaw was still active too, this time with the troublesome extension to New Scotland Yard. Almost immediately the first building had been finished, the Metropolitan Police were engulfed in new work and clamouring for more space. But Shaw's building was impossible to enlarge. The Home Office, displeased at the prospect of new expenditure, tried to suppress the idea of an extension, but Pennefather submitted that it would fulfil police needs for years if done on the right scale. What could not be denied was the need for a new district police station near Parliament, and in December 1896 it was agreed that Dixon Butler should build this in Cannon Row, opposite the south-west end of New Scotland Yard. Pennefather insisted that Shaw should be consulting architect for Cannon Row and 'on all questions relating to the treatment and design of the building to be erected at the Embankment end.'[41] The fee was

352

257. County Hall, river front, by Ralph Knott, 1911–33.

fixed at 300 guineas, for which he was to design elevations. There was then a long delay while the sites were acquired.

When Pennefather sent in the scheme for approval in March 1899, Shaw as usual had gone further than expected. He had replanned Dixon Butler's extension scheme, and designed elevations for both this and Cannon Row (ill. 258), with the Embankment front answering the main block, and the gateway, connecting bridge, and high gable on the end of the police station, all on the lines of what was eventually built. Finding that this would cost some £100,000, the Home Office upbraided Pennefather for premature and extravagant action, and went broody. All foundation work stopped, and only Cannon Row was allowed to go ahead.

In 1900, bored with the three-year delay, Shaw asked for his fee. 'I never can bear things dragging on for an unlimited period; one loses all interest and forgets so much', he told Pennefather, who speedily informed the authorities how much free help he had given in solving problems.[42] At this point the project took a fresh lease of life and the big difficulty presented itself: how to lay the foundations of the southern part of the extension, which were to come over the open end of the District Railway tunnel where it debouched into Westminster Station. John Wolfe-Barry, the engineer of Tower Bridge, was called in. Shaw had lively discussions with him, and proposed a hollow steel wall instead of a brick one at the back of the extension, which he claimed would be more economical both on space and on money.[43] He was overruled, and Barry decided to roof the tunnel instead with a system of huge girders, as any future demolition contractor will find to his cost. Further delays ensued because of other priorities. The foundations were finished only in 1902–3, and the superstructure built in 1905–6. By then, Shaw must have been even more exasperated. But he had a final unpaid blitz on the design in 1904, altering many aspects and securing gates by Reginald Blomfield from an Arts and Crafts Exhibition for the

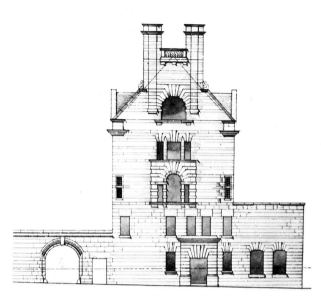

258. Cannon Row Police Station, end elevation, 1898.

259. New Scotland Yard, extension building and bridge.

street entrance between the blocks. He told Blomfield: 'You see this is all very cunning. To those who say to me, "I don't think much of your new gates", I shall say, "They are not mine, they are Blomfield's", and when others say, "What splendid iron gates you have done, you have covered yourself with glory this time", I shall put my hands in my pockets and smile blandly.'[44]

Despite the magnificence of gates, gables and most of all bridge, and despite some cunning planning, it is hard to disagree with those who believe the extension block a mistake.[45] For one splendour, the four-square free-standing fortress, Shaw has substituted another, the formal, high-flanked avenue (ill. 259). Alas, the street is now too ill-kept and unfrequented for many to savour this pleasure. Instead, the traveller along the Embankment or over Westminster Bridge is confronted with the extension's abrupt ending, detracting as much from the symmetry of approach to the avenue as from the independence of the original block. But to replace it now would be folly, as any substitute would obliterate the existing glory and, by necessity of height and proximity, fail to restore the old one.

From 1904, the worry of the Quadrant fell heavily upon Shaw, and his health by degrees was breaking down. Yet he still found the vitality to go on coping with existing tasks and even grapple with new ones. In a fascinating interview he gave in 1906, he could throw out a far from casual pair of suggestions of his own for the improvement of London on Beaux-Arts principles:

> We have such a knack of half-doing things. Take the district of Regents Park—Portland Place opening up into Park Crescent, and then Park Square and the Broad Walk. Make one fine road of it. Cut it through those stupid gardens, in which you never find anybody but two or three nursemaids and a few happy but indifferent

children; put up a fine monument at the end of Primrose Hill; and you would there have a magnificent thoroughfare which would run the Champs Elysées close.

Again:

There is another place that represents a wasted opportunity, and that is the line through Bloomsbury Square, Russell Square, Upper Bedford Place, Tavistock Square, and Endsleigh Gardens to Euston. Look at a map, and you will see what a splendid district that would be if a road were cut through it—a road with sculpture, fine trees, and places where people could sit down. Why, it would be magnificent. To begin with, the scale is majestic, and scale is what you want. Inevitably the improvement of the road would lead to an improvement of the houses. They would be refronted on a good design; they would have high roofs and big chimneys; and that would all help in the important matter of scale. And remember that the cost of both these improvements would be trifling. The line is there already. Every house in Russell Square could be refronted at moderate cost. The Place des Vosges, in Paris, is nothing like as large as Russell Square, yet, with its high buildings and symmetrical outline, it has an impressiveness in which Russell Square is sadly lacking.[46]

As an 'optimist of optimists' Shaw doubtless hoped to fulfil these grandiose ideas, just as he trusted in the entire success of the Quadrant. They were no mere shots in the dark. The avenue from Bloomsbury Square to Euston was an idea generated from discussions between Shaw and T. H. Ismay, a director of the London and North-Western Railway, on the subject of Euston Station. Euston at the turn of the century had degenerated from the splendours of P. C. Hardwick's Arch and Booking Hall into a 'ramshackle, disjointed, temporary-looking place', a mere collection of platforms and buildings.[47] Ismay died in 1899 before Shaw could put any ideas on its reconstruction to paper, and the project dropped. So his son must have been surprised when Shaw insisted on redeeming the promise, and sent him a full matured 'suggestion' for the station in about 1906. On this (ill. 260), the station itself is shown as an unpretentious building with a good entrance hall, and end approaches to the platforms from a long 60 ft. by 60 ft. concourse modelled on those of the northern Parisian stations which Shaw so much admired.[48] In front of the station, he wanted to widen the street for cab traffic, and to rebuild the whole rectangle of housing between it and Euston Square with a huge hotel flanked by blocks of flats. This hotel was to have the advantages of overlooking gardens free from dust and dirt, of fresh centralized planning round a circular entrance lounge, and of a generous crescent towards the station, in the middle of which (preservationists will note) the Euston Arch was to stand unscathed. All this ambitious development had a simple motive. Shaw wrote in his report: 'I should never dream of suggesting the thing at all except on the lines of a good paying concern. Money enough in all conscience has been wasted by Railway directors on architecture, or what they are pleased to call architecture, but I won't go into this branch of the subject, as I should be on delicate ground.'[49] This was a snook cocked at St Pancras nearby. But what Shaw realized in neither his report nor his planning was that the age of the automobile had dawned. Railway profits in the 1860s and the 1900s were things apart; Euston had to await the era of state control for its rebuilding.

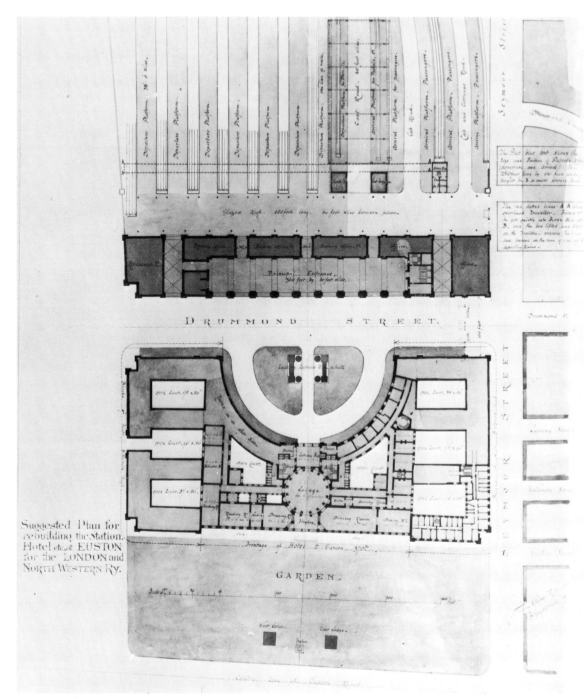

260. Euston Station and Square, proposed rebuilding plan, c.1906.

In Liverpool, Shaw's work for the Ismays was crowned with more success. Before the building of Dawpool in 1882–4, he had never so far as we know visited the city. Even now, the traveller with the slightest tinge of the sea in his blood or the most tenuous love for architecture cannot fail, on arriving at Lime Street, to be caught by Liverpool's tremendous brio, and above all by the grandeur of St George's Hall. Shaw had causes enough besides Dawpool for return visits, and time to dwell upon the splendours of Merseyside. Greenhill, Allerton Beeches, Mere Bank, and the taut little vicarage of St Agnes' Sefton Park all followed in the years 1883–6. Yet all were suburban house commissions in which he could pay no homage to the monumental spirit of central Liverpool.

After a decade's pause the chance came, and he leapt at it. Ismay Imrie and Co. needed new headquarters for their Oceanic Steam Navigation Company, which ran the White Star Line. They acquired a fine site near the waterfront, at the bottom of James Street. In 1894 Thomas Ismay asked Shaw for a design, which he agreed to make on the same principles as Dawpool, with J. F. Doyle acting as superintendent architect. Perhaps Doyle did more this time, but as in all the partnerships of his late years, Shaw took the brunt of the design work. For the exterior (ill. 261), he unapologetically reworked the New Scotland Yard elevations, applied to a corner site rather than a freestanding block, and with some minor faults eliminated. Besides his desire to get the thing right, Shaw also wanted a proud and hardy building with which to convey the mood of Merseyside. New Scotland Yard's granite and brick, appropriate in London only for the police, fitted the gritty independence of Liverpool's whole character. In both the White Star Offices and the later Parr's Bank, Shaw chose flamboyant colour contrasts at odds with the Portland stone sobriety of his last schemes for the capital.

It was on the interior of the White Star Offices that Shaw bestowed new thought. They were to be on an open plan with partitions, a type he had not designed since New Zealand Chambers. The course which he took was to support the floors on cross girders, with upright iron stanchions running as pillars through the storeys, in the immemorial tradition of warehousing. In London office buildings it had become imperative to cover such ironwork; but Liverpool's building regulations, in accordance with the city's steelier and more commercial character, were laxer. So Shaw took his chance to give a lesson on the functional design of office interiors. He boxed in neither his stanchions nor his girders, but constructed the ground floor office (ill. 262) so as to bring out their character by emphasizing the rivet heads and joining the cross girders with a series of jack-arches lined with fireproof bricks. The modicum of classical infilling on the brackets and along the longitudinal girders does not detract from this weird interior, since Shaw's purpose was to harmonize his raw girderwork with the dignified details of counters and arches, not to banish the one at the expense of the other.

There is a distinct naval nuance about the White Star interior. Soon enough it was followed by the real thing. In 1897 Ismay, unhappy with the proposed interior decorations of one of his new liners, asked Shaw to take it on. Here was an even better chance to experiment at blending modernity with comfort and dignity. The *Oceanic* was

261. (left) White Star Offices, Liverpool, street fronts.

262. (below) White Star Offices, Liverpool, ground floor office.

263. Royal Insurance Building, Liverpool, perspective of J. F. Doyle's design, drawn by C. W. English, 1896.

something special. It was the first ship built to order for the White Star Line by Harland and Wolff of Belfast, and by a novel arrangement the cabins were placed amidships to lessen vibration.[50] Unfortunately it was chartered as a merchant cruiser in 1914, soon ran ashore, and was lost.[51] Shaw treated it as a major commission, was well paid for his pains, and took Robert up to Liverpool to see her off on her maiden voyage in September 1899.[52] Then, only a few weeks later, Ismay suffered a fatal series of heart attacks, and Shaw was designing his tomb for Thurstaston churchyard (ill. 290).

One other spin-off from the White Star Offices was Shaw's part in Liverpool's Royal Insurance Building. Among his directorships Ismay counted one in this ambitious company, which in 1895 had held a local competition to supplement their offices. Content with neither its results nor extent, they plumped for a second competition for an entirely new and far more lavish building. Shaw was asked to participate, but became assessor instead. The competitors were three London men, Belcher, Collcutt and Mountford, against the four locals who had done best the first time around: J. F. Doyle, F. W. Holme, W. A. Thomas, and Woolfall and Eccles. When the entries came in, Shaw was baffled and on the whole disappointed. No. 4 had a splendid and extravagant exterior, no. 2 had a creditable one in almost exactly the same style, but all the entries were poorly planned as regards the lighting of the ground floor office. He decided that no. 2 was probably Belcher's. Opening the envelopes, he was electrified; Belcher's was no. 7, which he had dismissed as 'a most fanciful, showy and theatrical design, just like the architecture you see on a drop scene!'[53] No. 2 was Mountford, and no. 4, the outright winner, came from Doyle, his partner down the road.[54] Though this was embarrassing and provoked the usual complaints and suggestions, it gave Shaw an opportunity to improve the design, as he conceived his duty to be. Doyle's ground floor office needed clearing of a clutter of columns and piers, the lighting wanted improvement, and the upper corridors required

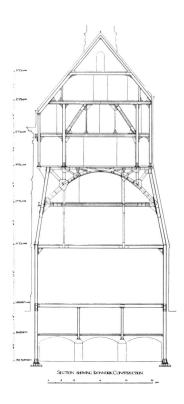

SECTION SHOWING IRONWORK CONSTRUCTION.

had to be moved out of the middle of the building. It was probably for achieving the first two aims that the directors paid Shaw a commission of one per cent.

But here the puzzle of the Royal Insurance Building begins. Its structure comprises what, so far as is known, is Britain's 'first steel frame'.[55] Quite when a steel frame becomes complete is a matter of opinion. The Royal Insurance frame (ill. 265), though complete horizontally and vertically, is not of the orthodox 'post and beam' type soon to become widespread, as it has enormous arch braces at second floor level. Since Shaw omits this striking construction from his report, since Doyle's competition design for the general office included columns that Shaw pronounced 'all unnecessary', and since we are told that the steel frame was specifically devised to meet the directors' wish for an unobstructed office (ill. 264), it looks as if he himself suggested it when the paraphernalia were cleared away. This is supported by one or two sentences in his report.[56] Also, there is the oddity that the architecture rises well above Doyle's level elsewhere, skilfully compounding Belcher's Institute of Chartered Accountants with Shaw's own manner. The angle turrets, gable and aedicule of the short Dale Street elevation should have warned Shaw that this (ill. 263) was a design by someone who knew the White Star Offices before they were published. Possibly, the competition entry may in part be due to one of the able 'ghosts of the profession' whose names were bandied about architectural offices in the nineties. One would like to know more about the design, if only because it became the most important source after the Buxton crescent for Shaw's Quadrant elevations.

360

264. (far left) Royal Insurance Building, Liverpool, ground floor office.

265. (left) Royal Insurance Building, Liverpool, section showing steel frame.

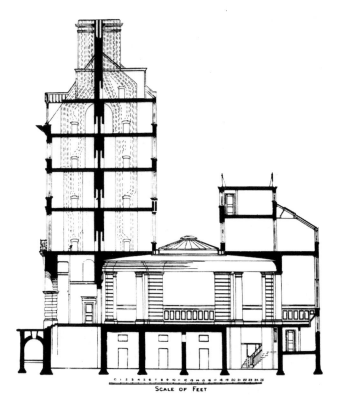

266. (right) Parr's Bank, Liverpool, section through offices.

SCALE OF FEET

His final building for Liverpool, Parr's Bank (1899–1900) once more follows from abnormal principles. It is a structural *tour-de-force* which makes nonsense of an obituarist's claim that Shaw hardly troubled himself with the engineering of his buildings.[57] For their Liverpool head office, the directors of this great North Western bank wanted something altogether exceptional. Shaw willingly undertook it, this time together with Philip Thicknesse, who had gone into a local partnership with W. E. Willink. Once again there is every reason to suspect that the planning and principal elevations are Shaw's work. The project was to include plenty of lettable office space. Significantly enough after the Royal Insurance, one of the main conditions was a banking hall free from obstruction. Sceptical of the lighting available for a rectangular hall stretching from front to back of an enclosed site, if the offices were to be built on top, Shaw opted for a circular hall with counters to match, toplit by a shallow dome (ill. 268). The lettable space was then divided into front and back blocks, so that the plan resembled some of his late houses with their concealed toplit spaces in the centre. But here the banking hall had to be so large that it cut right into the office blocks in front and behind, and entailed massive girderwork to prevent its fragile roof being crushed by the weight of building above (ill. 266). In a discerning article, Halsey Ricardo explains the construction of Parr's Bank. The bulk of the girders, he says, is bedded in brickwork at second floor level, while the first floor is hung from their underside, so as to avoid putting stress upon the banking hall. To one side, the main stairs are built round one of a pair of stanchions thrust upwards at an angle to truss the great

361

267. Parr's Bank, Liverpool, street front.

268. Parr's Bank, Liverpool, banking hall.

horizontal girders. But Ricardo criticizes the way that the banking hall ceiling is patterned with moulded cofferings irrelevant to the position of the beams.[58] This was more typical of the old Shaw than the structural purity of the White Star Offices.

The exterior is as much of an oddity (ill. 267). For anyone building in Castle Street, the paradigm was Cockerell's splendid and sober Bank of England, a few yards along and opposite. Shaw took notice of it, but in 1899 was not yet ready to follow it, being still bent on expressing Liverpool's monumentality in colour. Therefore the base of Parr's Bank, like the White Star and Royal Insurance, was still of Kemnay granite, superbly disposed and cut; so far did Cockerell's discipline extend. But above, Shaw branched out, with green and cream bands of marble veneer alternating, against red terracotta window frames.[59] The taste could be dubbed Ruskinian, were it not for the ruthless classicism of the elevation. The aim, Robert Shaw tells us, was to provide a washable surface. It is an interesting idea, but not entirely successful, as the building clashes both in scale and texture with the rest of Castle Street. C. H. Reilly, once a protégé and soon an antagonist of Shaw's, has the last word on Parr's Bank.

> The passage of time . . . does not reconcile its strange materials with the street. They are too insistent, and, to be frank, too coarse. The red terracotta dressings to the windows have alone involved this. You cannot get mouldings of the quality, say, of those of the Bank of England and in such material. In the business-like reserve of this street, Mr Shaw's building looks to me as some handsome but overdressed woman might look who had strayed there by mistake. The fact that her clothes are slightly soiled, as the marble facing already is, does not really add to her respectability.[60]

Shaw had more to do for Liverpool, however. In 1903 he helped to save the Anglican Cathedral competition from disaster. As justice has not been done him, it is worth going into the matter.

It was imperative that the second Liverpool Cathedral competition should succeed. In the first, held in 1886, William Emerson came out the winner, but a lack of funds and enthusiasm shelved his project.[61] By 1901 a new bishop, F. J. Chavasse, had got matters moving again, and with the change of site to the red sandstone bluffs over St James's Cemetery high up above the city, Emerson's design was ruled out. At this time, feeling ran high among Anglican architects that they could and must achieve something better than Truro, their only new cathedral of the last century, and that the right road might at last lie away from Gothic. With the acknowledged success of Bentley's Westminster Cathedral, Catholicism had stolen a march on them. Was not Liverpool, where popery was so strong, the right place for a cathedral builder's revenge?

When, therefore, the stipulation of a Gothic style for competition entries was announced, cries of protest were heard in the *Architectural Review*, amongst them one from Norman Shaw.

> The proposal to restrict the style of the new cathedral to so-called Gothic appears to me to be simply deplorable. And in a modern city like Liverpool, filled with an exceptionally large number of Renaissance buildings, some of them exceptionally good, and proud in the possession of certainly one of the finest, if not *the* finest, modern classic building in the world, the decision seems to be incomprehensible.

He had some advice for the committee:

> Let them abandon this worn-out competition system, a system which has produced ten failures for one success. Let them select some well-known architect whose name alone would inspire confidence . . . Let them put the designing of their cathedral unreservedly into his hands, impressing on him that he is to do his very best. Give him an entirely free hand, and a year in which to prepare his design, and let no Committee meddle with him or offer him counsel, which would be sure to be wrong.
>
> This is very much what has recently been done at Westminster in the case of the new Roman Catholic Cathedral . . . And see what the result is! Beyond all doubt the finest church that has been built for centuries. Superb in its scale and character, and full of the most devouring interest, it is impossible to overrate the magnificence of this design. It is like a revelation after the feeble Gothic stuff on which we have been mainly

fed for the last half-century. Why should not a similar success be achieved in Liverpool?[62]

Hyperbole apart, most other architects agreed with Shaw. One dissentient, however, was Bodley, who quoted from Coleridge and sighed for the days of Gothic supremacy. So when the Executive Committee removed the Gothic restriction, they logically enough asked Bodley and Shaw to be their assessors of the two-stage open competition, as the respective leaders of the Gothic and Classic schools. With some weariness, no doubt, Shaw accepted. In July 1902 he was up in Liverpool judging the first stage.

We have had a good day's work and have broken the back of the whole thing, and really tomorrow will almost finish it. It is very disappointing, really a very poor show, a few men strong, but the overwhelming number just twaddle. We have had *all* the names covered over, but in spite of that we know many and of course some of these are embarrassing. Bodley is all right and quite pleasant—awfully lame. I should say that he is in rather a serious state, but he says nothing about it.[63]

All this was ominous. The trouble was that for the preliminary stage, the Committee had asked only for sketches and evidence of ability to design a cathedral. The result was predictable:

One competitor sent a single plan, rather suggestive of the Albert Hall, the entire area being closely seated. In his report he said he had never built any buildings, and that he had been unable to prepare a design, as he had been ill. Another competitor submitted a large chalk drawing of a figure; a third, two photos of a brass lectern, and so on. There were many similar, and many designs equally little to the point.[64]

One wonders if the experimental concrete-roofed design sent in under Harry Wilson's name by six Bentley-inspired Arts and Crafts men, and the less radical one by C. R. Mackintosh under Honeyman and Keppie's, were classed by Shaw among the 'embarrassments' or the 'twaddle'. At any rate, they got nowhere. The five finalists included only one firm well known at that date, Paley and Austin. The others were Charles Nicholson, Walter Tapper, Malcolm Stark and Giles Gilbert Scott. All five were Gothic; so Bodley prevailed. The best classic entry, in the assessors' opinion, was from an unknown one-time assistant of Belcher's, Charles Reilly.

Bodley and Shaw then rested for nine months. But they had to reassure the committee when a rumour went round that they were changing the site. They also chose the exact orientation, and Shaw worked out the rough lines of the crypt to guide the finalists; 'but I don't want to get myself into hot water', he told Frederick Radcliffe.[65] He also gave some advice to Mrs Ismay, who wanted to give the east window of the cathedral.[66] Then on 5–6 May 1903, the assessors judged the matured drawings of the finalists, and chose No. 1.

No. 1 was the work of Giles Gilbert Scott, son of G. G. Scott junior, twenty-three years of age, without a building to his credit, and a Roman Catholic. For all these reasons the Executive Committee understandably dithered, and for a fortnight it veered between rash decisions and no decision at all. Unfortunately, its seventeen members, among whom were Shaw's friends Frederick Radcliffe and H. D. Horsfall, were divided. An earlier attempt to make W. D. Caroe, an architect with strong Liverpool connections, first an assessor and then, when that miscarried, a finalist, had put Horsfall and one or two others on their guard. Shaw, whose information came mainly from Horsfall, always maintained that there was a concerted attempt to ditch Scott, but this may not quite have been the case.[67] At any rate, a motion that no design was acceptable was passed on 15 May, the reason given being that Scott's seating plan showed inadequate accommodation. An alternative proposal made by Radcliffe and emanating from Shaw to have Bodley associated with Scott was narrowly rejected. On the former motion the assessors were not consulted, and when Shaw read of it in the papers he was greatly vexed. He at once set to work to show that the accommodation was sufficient, and on the nineteenth wrote to the Committee's Chairman, Sir William Forwood, with some calculations. In reply Forwood made the blunder of suggesting, however informally, that Bodley might do the whole job. Back came the answer:

> Your suggestion that I should approach Mr Bodley with the view of ascertaining whether he will undertake to design your cathedral, has filled me with dismay, as Mr Bodley in conjunction with myself, did his duty most loyally, and awarded the prize as he thought right. How then in common honesty can he connive at the ousting of Mr Scott and secure that prize for himself? I do not for one moment believe that he will do it, and I on my part can lend no help to such a proceeding.[68]

In a follow-up letter to Forwood he pointed out the grave imputations cast on the competence of the assessors by the decision that Scott's seating was inadequate, on which the papers were commenting. The consequence of Shaw's stance, and of the less forceful but honourable behaviour of Bodley, was that on 26 May the Committee reverted to the Shaw/Radcliffe proposal, and Bodley and Scott were appointed joint architects.

Public reaction was predictably unfavourable, and an outcry ensued against poor Bodley in ignorance of the circumstances. But Shaw, having himself picked Scott's design out in the preliminary stage and seen him through his difficulties, clung to the Committee's decision. To Mrs Ismay he wrote:

> There can be no doubt that Scott is an extraordinarily gifted fellow. He is just 24! And when he has a man of Bodley's knowledge and refinement at his elbow, the result of their labours is certain to be a great success. It will be St George's Hall over again; I think Elmes was about 24 or 25 when he gained the Competition. That seems to be Liverpool's way.[69]

His interest in the Cathedral's fortunes continued. Soon he was exhorting the Committee to start, and in March 1907 he had this to say about the partnership he had promoted:

> I wonder if old Bodley is doing his duty by you. I doubt it!!! for there was some beastly detail in the large drawing Scott exhibited a year ago. Now he was put there for the purpose of correcting Scott's detail. Detail is a question to a large extent of experience, rather than genius. I believe Scott has the genius, but Bodley has the experience. That tracery was detestable, and as ignorant as a pig, and there was a discharging arch over the transept window, so hopelessly out of scale, that it made me lie down on my stomach and squeal![70]

Shaw's suspicions in part were justified. Bodley had made many interventions, but now that he had Washington Cathedral to design as well, they were less frequent and less helpful. The arrangement had worked partly because Scott had been articled to Temple Moore, and at the time of the design was an assistant to Thomas Garner, the two closest disciples of Bodley among English architects. But it had become frayed; at the time of Bodley's death late in 1907, Scott was on the point of resigning.[71] Instead, he set about a radical revision and transformed a merely adequate design into something masterful, as Shaw had prophesied. Shaw knew all about the change, continued to encourage Scott, and through Radcliffe stimulated the Committee to approve it. But these were just incidental tasks. Shaw had saved the last masterpiece of the English Gothic Revival from disaster.

After the competition, Shaw may never have seen Liverpool again. Failing health lessened his mobility; from 1900 he was always an 'uncertain quantity'. Three times he got as far as Buxton on holiday, but after a visit to Dover in May 1907 he stayed in London till he died. That is why he confined his architectural attention to the capital, since he could not make regular journeys elsewhere. There are only two major exceptions to this policy: the large extensions to Bradford Town Hall, and his last vain fling over the King Edward Memorial, Liverpool.

The Bradford job must have been sweet revenge. In December 1902, the proud citizens of Bradford who had rejected his Exchange design forty years before, humbly requested the eminent R.A. to advise them on their extensions and state his terms. The existing Town Hall was by Lockwood and Mawson, the same local architects who had outfaced Shaw over the Exchange. They had won the later Town Hall competition with another controversial entry, heavily reliant upon Burges and Gilbert Scott. But it little behoved Shaw to be vindictive about the building; its style was Gothic, the spirit of central Bradford was Gothic, and to Gothic he had to conform. One of the heaviest tasks was already half done. The City Architect, F. E. P. Edwards, was an ex-Liverpool Corporation man and friend of W. E. Willink who had recently transferred to Bradford. He was a capable planner and had already got the distribution of the departments on the triangular site into good shape. Dodging bouts of ill health, Shaw visited Bradford in February 1903 and sent in a report next month. Apart from a homily on the need for diligent refinement of the plan, he had only one important suggestion to make: an additional storey over the proposed extensions, and a pair of extra storeys in the old part.

> The whole building must *not* look as if it had had additions made to it entirely regardless of the existing building, and no pains must be spared to give the Town Hall, when enlarged, *the appearance of one complete building under one roof.* The words 'one roof' are to me most suggestive. We talk glibly enough of being 'under the same roof' but few of us realize what an important factor in design a really fine roof is![72]

The Bradford Council opted only for an extra storey over the extension. As a result, Shaw was left with a disjunction between old and new parts. Otherwise, the elevations of this too-little regarded work can hardly be overpraised; they rank among Shaw's most spectacular and witty Edwardian successes (ills. 269–270). Towards Town Hall Street, he allowed himself next to the original building a seven-bay front of quite conscious stylistic

367

269. Bradford Town Hall, Town Hall Street front to extension building.

270. Bradford Town Hall, corner of extension building.

271. Bradford Town Hall, council chamber.

absurdity. At the base, an open granite arcade mixes the Romanesque with the shop-arch style of the first Alliance Assurance building. Above comes a row of windows in homage to Lockwood and Mawson, of purest 1860s Gothic; then a tall Queen Anne series with balconies of the *dix-huitième*; next, a small set of mullioned lights; and on top, a pair of attic storeys finished off with late French Gothic gables. Plainly, Shaw is recapitulating his progress, and showing off how to fit styles together. The demonstration does not stop there. Across the corner, Shaw summons up his remaining loyalties to the Gothic and gives Bradford a mighty reminiscence of the heroic style of Adcote, with smooth masonry, a broad gable, and massive mullioned bays to the council's double-storey dining hall within.

Inside the Town Hall extensions, it is harder to disentangle the contributions of Shaw and Edwards. The dining hall is steeped in the old Shaw, having high arches in the roof, a musicians' gallery with peep-hole, and a sculpted chimney-breast. The reception rooms nearby also seem to be his. But what of the Council Chamber (ill. 271), with its Soanic arches and toplighting, and its Gimson plasterwork in the ceiling? Though Shaw

370

kept up with the Bradford project after 1903, he does not seem to have gone there again. Building took place only in 1905–9. By the time work was over, Edwards had transferred to Sheffield, where he was to give the Town Hall extensions on the lines of Shaw's designs for Bradford. His successor, Reginald Kirkby, completed the job, and also conferred with Shaw to produce an unexecuted scheme for replanning the old entrance hall and principal staircase.[73]

THE QUADRANT

Back in London, the overwhelming obsession of Shaw from September 1904 was the Quadrant, which preoccupied him from then until nearly the time of his death. For a foretaste of this drama, one previous commission will introduce the reader, as it did Shaw, to some of the principals with whom he had soon to grapple. That is the second Alliance Assurance building, opposite the earlier one at the bottom of St James's Street. It occupies a superb site next to the Thatched House Club, on the corner with Cleveland Row, and looks straight down Pall Mall.

Insurance had been booming towards the turn of the century and the Alliance directors wanted to expand out of their former premises. They approached Shaw in July 1901 and offered him a choice of partner, suggesting Lutyens, William Woodward, their own man N. S. Joseph, or Newton. Shaw selected Newton, and set to work at the design. The situation was a delicate and complicated one. The site was Crown property, administered by the archaic-sounding Office of Woods and Forests under a powerful Commissioner, J. F. F. Horner. The lease of the property, which expired in 1903, was shared between a wine merchant called Wallace and a Mr Lidyard. At the date of expiry, the lessees had intended to erect a block of flats to the designs of William Woodward, which was why he was suggested as a possible partner of Shaw's when the Alliance managed to take over the lease instead. One of the conditions of this change was that the company should rehouse Wallace at the back of the property. Another was that they must rebuild the Post Office which, as a sublessee of Lidyard, occupied the northern portion of the site next to the Thatched House Club; for this they had to co-operate with Henry Tanner of the Office of Works. So Shaw had to deal simultaneously with the company, the Commissioner of Woods and Forests, the two lessees and the Office of Works, besides getting the relevant permissions from the District Surveyor and the L.C.C. To make matters worse, there was active interference from St James's Palace on the opposite side of Cleveland Row. In 1899, when rebuilding was first canvassed, the Prince of Wales and the Duke of York decreed that the height must be kept down, and had the Office of Woods and Forests instructed accordingly. Now that Edward was king, he was no less tenacious of the 'ancient lights' of St James's Palace. Fifty-two feet, Horner advised Shaw, was the absolute maximum height to the cornice; and the use of ground floor arches, with their commercial overtones, was strongly deprecated so near the palace.

In the negotiations he went through with the 'Woods and Forests', Shaw found Horner easy to deal with, but his secretary Hellard 'not so amiable or yielding'.[74] But the real obstacle at first, the Palace apart, was their architect Arthur Green. Green's attitude typifies the resentment with which the 'professionals' viewed Shaw's late incursions into

what they thought was their territory. Shaw, he reports to Horner, is an 'Art Architect' who 'appears to have been resuscitated by the Alliance Assurance Company', and has now produced a design of haphazard contrasts, just as he did in his earlier buildings—and he cites the unhappy juxtaposition of Lowther Lodge and Albert Hall Mansions.[75] In Green's report, there is much bias in favour of Woodward and the old proposals. The reason is not far to seek. William Woodward was one of a band of architects, more familiar now than then, who concentrated upon central London development on sites of high property value, preferably for flats or hotels. They worked by promoting a tight nexus of acquaintance, and were active wherever there was appreciable redevelopment. Edwardian London was ill equipped to control them, except through the feeble powers of the L.C.C. On Crown land in the West End they anticipated a field day; many of the leases were soon to fall in, and 88 St James's Street was one of them. Woodward had Arthur Green in his pocket, and both were understandably vexed when their scheme fell through.

Shaw grasped little of all this at the time. He had difficulties enough with royalty, an unofficial but invincible opponent. In vain did he point out that the neighbouring Thatched House Club would stand nearly thirty feet above the new block, and that a low front would make an unworthy termination to the vista along Pall Mall. He had to give up his arches on the Cleveland Row side, stick to Portland stone fronts without the admixture of brick he had intended, and adhere to the fifty-two foot limit. The only concessions were on the front, where he was allowed to keep his arches and to have a small pedimented

272. (far left) Alliance Assurance Offices, 88 St James's Street, main street front.

273. (left) Bank of England Branch Office, Liverpool, main street front, by C. R. Cockerell, 1845–8.

274. (right) Alliance Assurance Offices, 88 St James's Street, main office.

gable over the cornice. 'Half a loaf is better than no bread,' he reported back to the Company.[76]

Perhaps it was at this stage that Shaw began to think of his old teacher Cockerell, and of the Liverpool branch of the Bank of England in Castle Street, where he had just been building. The stout and square proportions of the two buildings with their abbreviated central pediments present an unspecific but irresistible likeness (ills. 272–3). Their differences illuminate the unorthodoxy of Shaw's classicism. Though Cockerell's composition is constructed of contrary motions and forces, he manages to juggle them into equipoise, so that the strife is eventually unmasked as just the old gentlemanly game of playing with the orders. No Edwardian building is like that, least of all Shaw's. His squatter proportions are intuited, not calculated, and look strange and aggressive besides Cockerell's calm amplitude. The exemplary transition from three bays to five above, and the abruptness of the lifted pediment, suddenly stick out brutally. In the attics there protrudes a naked contrast between leaded lights in the roof and massive hooked voussoirs in the centre. This is true mannerism, not in the scholarly sense that some of Cockerell's buildings are mannerist—evocations of the spirit of Giulio Romano or of Vignola; but the mannerism of a man who is exploring classic articulation after his own lights, and who wants to bend it here and push it there, retaining discipline without rigid adherence to the old proportions, and so sometimes succeeding, sometimes not.

As an independent composition, the second Alliance Assurance building succeeds; in its environment, as Shaw predicted, it is too stumpy and does not. He came through the

373

headaches of planning well enough, and produced a fine-looking ground floor office and boardroom for the Company (ill. 274). For the office, Newton may have taken over much of the detailing.[77] But Shaw's chief feat in the commission was to cope resiliently with the many authorities. Though at the time he had no inkling of this, he had made a distinct impression of competence upon the sticky Woods and Forests officials.

Well before construction on the Alliance building began in 1904, these same officials had been laying plans for the rebuilding of Regent Street.[78] It was to begin with the southern end which swept round into Piccadilly Circus in Nash's famous Quadrant, where the leases on Crown property were soon to fall in. Already, some reconstruction work had started in Lower Regent Street, where the road widens out into Waterloo Place. Here the Office of Woods and Forests insisted upon severe classic frontages to chime in with the tone of the Athenaeum and the United Service Club. Almost from Edward VII's accession, they were forced to decide about the sites further up beyond the Circus. In May 1902, a consortium called the P & R Syndicate came forward with a plan to rebuild the premises of St James's Hall, a concert hall situated right behind the centre of the Quadrant's south side, between Air Street and Vigo Street. Their architects were William Woodward and E. A. Grüning, and they wanted to know whether they would have to keep the Regent Street façade, as they wished to build much higher. By the beginning of 1903, Walter Emden had changed places with Grüning, and at the end of the year Woodward and he were anxious to proceed, as the syndicate had £700,000 tied up in the project and now wished to erect a massive and luxurious hotel. But as yet they had no word from the Woods and Forests.

From the Crown point of view, the rebuilding of Regent Street was an inevitability. First, it must be remembered that Nash's architecture was not yet prized; it was, as so often, the plan of reconstruction that made people think about and look at what they had previously taken for granted. Indeed Nash was one of the great bogeys of the Gothic Revival for his unscholarly detail, slapdash construction, and habit of hiding brick behind a coating of stucco keyed and painted to resemble stone. Regent Street was a particular butt. Even its best buildings came under fire. Ruskin, for instance, commented that the portico pillars of Cockerell's Hanover Chapel 'look as if they were standing on a pile of pewter collecting-plates'.[79] From Ruskin derived the ethic which made many, and not just architects, criticize the 'dishonesty' of the Nash school. Though Ruskin was dead, one of his architectural doctrines which had escaped unburied and lingered on into the new classic revival was the reprehensibility of stucco. Edwardian architects who had never been nurtured on Gothic were willing to clad a brick wall or a new-fangled steel frame with a Portland stone facing or even with a mere coat of roughcast, yet still looked on stucco as cheap and fraudulent.

Another point: the shops of Regent Street, though fashionable, were small and ill-constructed, and their owners wished to move into something more expansive, even at the price of higher rents (which they could well afford). The clamour for rebuilding Regent Street better and bigger came more from them than from the Crown or from the idealists for improving London. Many of the shopkeepers and owners had rebuilding plans of their own, including the 'Imperial' and 'Gambrinus' restaurants on the north side of the Quadrant, and Swan and Edgar on the critical corner with Piccadilly Circus. So the P & R

Syndicate were not alone, though they were unusual in being outsiders. This raises a third point that hurried reconstruction on. Already, the purity of Nash's Regent Street had been violated, if the charming medley of styles and buildings along its length, by no means all by Nash, could be held chaste. The first loss occurred in 1848, when his successor Pennethorne removed the famous colonnades on both sides of the Quadrant sector from Piccadilly Circus to Vigo Street. They had served, so it was said, only to obstruct light from the shops and accommodate vagrants who wished to relieve themselves; Macartney tells the story that the police only allowed the Ritz Hotel a colonnade fifty years later on the supposition of an 'improvement in the public manners' during Victoria's reign.[80] Pennethorne's balconies and decorative panels were an excellent substitute. But his shopfronts had been in places mauled out of recognition, and were objects of the fashionable accusation that the building above seemed to 'stand upon glass'. Further, several buildings had entirely disappeared; St Philip's Chapel, Robinson and Cleaver's, and most tragically the Hanover Chapel itself, demolished despite protest in 1896. On one of these sites, the Crown had erred in allowing a first massive and high new building, 184–6 Regent Street, built in 1899.

If this mistake prompted the Woods and Forests to think of an overall scheme of rebuilding, only the realities of the Syndicate's proposal plus some prodding from the Treasury stirred them to action. This was their architect Arthur Green's great chance, and he leapt at it. In Autumn 1903, Woodward and he were putting their heads together to see how the huge Hotel, which would occupy the whole site between Piccadilly and Regent Street, could fit into an overall design for the Quadrant. They could not entirely agree, as Woodward wanted a monumental eighty foot height to the parapet. Green told him: 'You have all along understood from me that the Quadrant must be reproduced in stone on the same lines as at present perhaps with some further up to date embellishments, and probably some projecting pavilions which might give a storey or so above the present parapet, and beyond this I think it might be possible to have one storey in stonework set back from the parapet.'[81] This does not sound very appetizing, nor did it prove to be. Green's designs for both sides of the Quadrant, completed in February 1904, were full of domes, mansards and towers, all higgledy-piggledy. But prophetically, the shopkeepers' desire for display was fully catered for by oblong blank glass spaces between narrow piers, giving the objectionable appearance of heavy masonry bearing down upon glass. Foreseeing the difficulty of any other answer, Green gave in at the beginning.

Perhaps under pressure, the Treasury insisted that the designs for the new hotel and Quadrant be submitted to a Committee under the President of the R.I.B.A. But by the time the Advisory Committee, consisting of Aston Webb, John Belcher and the official government architect Sir John Taylor, had been set up in July, Arthur Green had suddenly died, and there was no heir apparent to the job. They found themselves, therefore, in the unexpected position not of counsellors but of kingmakers, especially since they could none of them stomach Green's design. In a report to the Treasury of August 1904, they recommended the appointment of an advisory architect outside the Office of Woods and Forests. Their choice fell upon Norman Shaw, J. Macvicar Anderson and H. T. Hare, in that order. A month later Webb reported that Shaw, who was away on holiday at Buxton, had accepted and would charge a nominal fee of 100 guineas.

275. Regent Street Quadrant, perspective view of design as revised in 1906, drawn by C. W. English.

276. Buxton, The Crescent, by John Carr, 1779–84.

The dates and details of these transactions matter, because once again Shaw had quietly sidled into a job of political prestige under the Tories. At this time, Balfour's government had still a year and a bit to run before it was ousted in the Liberal landslide of January 1906, a sad event for Shaw's Quadrant scheme. Austen Chamberlain held the Treasury purse strings, but his predecessor a year before had been C. T. Ritchie, whom Shaw knew as Mervyn Macartney's father-in-law. Macartney himself is often to be found on the sidelines of the scheme, explaining and supporting its aims; at one point he is actually suggested as someone who might help his old, overworked master with the details. When this was put to Shaw, Macartney's name was not mentioned, and he refused, thinking that Woodward or one of his acolytes was intended as a colleague; the misunderstanding pained Macartney and was not cleared up until later. Robert Shaw, who tells this story, says nothing of Ritchie, but mentions Lord Windsor (later the Earl of Plymouth), a noted patron of architecture who was at this time Commissioner of Works and later chief subscriber to the memorial erected to Shaw at New Scotland Yard.[82] In any case, the decision plainly descended from the higher echelons of politics via the architects of the Advisory Committee. Another advantage in Shaw will have been pressed by Horner and Hellard at the Woods and Forests. Not only did they know him from his work at the Alliance Assurance, but the same partnership would be soon in evidence again. One of the briefs for the job was the replanning of Piccadilly Circus, which had been a muddle ever since Shaftesbury Avenue was thrown into it in the 1880s. On the best site in the Circus stood the County Fire Office, which was attached to the north-east end of the Quadrant and looked proudly down Lower Regent Street. The company had just been bought out by the Alliance Assurance, who like their neighbours planned to rebuild—once again under Norman Shaw.

Shaw, hearing in advance of the proposal, must have let it be known that he would accept. Why else should he have been, of all significant places, at Buxton when the news came? And within five weeks he had submitted to the Advisory Committee preliminary but very careful designs for the Circus plan, the County Fire Office, and the south side of the Quadrant. It should be understood, however, that his appointment was not unambiguous. The Office of Woods at least had imagined that he would merely revise Green's elevations, and that his work was just to serve for guidelines. So by the end of 1904 they were ready to pay him off. But the Committee, in a fit of enthusiasm for what they had seen, immediately petitioned the Treasury to prolong Shaw's appointment as architect to the Quadrant and Piccadilly Circus, and extend it to all the elevations of the new hotel. This meant that he became responsible for the Piccadilly façades of both Swan and Edgar and the hotel, apart from the Quadrant, the Fire Office, and the rest of the Circus. Only when this arrangement was approved in February 1905 did Shaw assume control. As was his wont, he had begun in a comparatively small way and widened his range.

He now had several separate problems of different urgency and feasibility on his hands. The first job was the Quadrant, more specifically the south side, where the concavity of the curve created its own special conditions. The design he showed the Committee late in October 1904 was closely modelled on John Carr's crescent at Buxton (ill. 276). It had ground floor arches, a giant engaged order above, the cornice at sixty-five

277. Regent Street Quadrant, details of plan, elevation and section as revised in 1906, drawn by C. W. English.

feet as Green had insisted, and high chimneys in a steeply pitched roof. Though refined over the next three years (ills. 275, 277), it differs little from what was built. The clusters of engaged and half-blocked columns were reduced from three to two, the cornice was simplified, and the roof redesigned in an attempt to get more accommodation in for the hotel, but the main lines are to all intents and purposes the same. What the Committee appreciated was that they were inspecting a masterpiece, of enormous costliness and ambition perhaps, but yet a masterpiece. The sheer scale and virility of the composition make the Buxton prototype pale into genteel febrility. By infusing the tight baroque blocked rustication of the Institute of Chartered Accountants and the Royal Insurance Building into a concave elevation, Shaw has given his design shadow, strength, and plasticity without loss of the large horizontal and vertical accents that fix and fortify its lines. And he has rejected the crude breaks and projections that marred Green's elevations, by boldly bridging over the streets in close imitation of Hare's scheme for the Aldwych. From the point of view of pure design, there are only two clear failings. One is that Shaw never managed in his late projects quite to articulate the join between an arcuated ground storey and a trabeated system above, so that the springing of the arches in the Quadrant elevation seems at odds with the huge columns superimposed over the piers. This becomes a serious fault on the Piccadilly front. The other is a related criticism, put by Statham and the purists. Neither columns nor arches carry the real load of the walls, which falls further back upon a series of girders distributing it upon the party walls between the shops. The design in fact is a vast decorative façade. It satisfied the Advisory

378

Committee, who abhorred the appearance of masonry bearing down upon plate glass, but it represented the realities of construction in a less honest way.

Practically, there were many cogent objections which would in time be heard. But in October 1904 Horner's small voice pleading for more plate glass was lost in the paean of praise from the experts. The main task was to square the hotel company's architects. At first they were inclined to be friendly, but in December their design for the hotel, a monster with a protuberance of domes towards Piccadilly, was peremptorily rejected by the Advisory Committee. This event hastened the rush to get Shaw to design the Piccadilly fronts of the hotel, but whittled Woodward and Emden's autonomy away still further and made them peevish. In a letter to Horner they sounded the first warning. Shaw's wide piers on the Quadrant had reduced the number of shops they hoped to get in by three and lowered the commercial value, they said. Now, they were suddenly expected to conform to his elevations on both sides, and their clients were losing £3,500 a month through the delay.[83] A further anxiety was that Horner had at the King's command stipulated a seventy foot limit to the Piccadilly cornice height, as well as the sixty-five foot height to Regent Street. This meant further loss of accommodation.

In consultation with Woodward and Emden, Shaw did his best to right these complaints. His first design for the Piccadilly front of the hotel, of early March 1905, presents an unlovely, unbroken street façade with Dutch gables at either end and variant ideas for squeezing the maximum accommodation into the attics. A few days later, he revised the elevation so as to compensate the hotel on this side with the innovation of wide, unarched shop fronts and gilt rivet heads (ill. 278). Had he tried this idea on the Quadrant side, it would have avoided a great hue and cry, but spoilt his composition. On the Piccadilly side, he was still uncertain. The high front much reduced the daylight for the shops opposite, and might be opposed by the L.C.C. So in early April, working under pressure because of the urgency, Shaw decided to turn the whole scheme back to front, open out the light well in the centre, have the high part of the hotel with its back to the Quadrant, keep the Dutch gables as a pair of wings coming forward to the street, and join them with an open colonnade (ill. 279). By this act of effrontery he was able to get most of the accommodation away from the frontages, and have a cornice level of a hundred feet to the high part while keeping to the sixty-five feet limit in Regent Street. Admittedly, the entablature to the Piccadilly colonnade rose to seventy-five feet, but the neighbours could hardly quarrel with that, since it was open. Much replanning of the hotel must have followed, but by mid-May its architects were placated. Shaw wrote to Hellard: 'I think I may say that you will not hear any more from Messrs. Woodward & Emden about their objections to your action, or their grievances! It has taken some trouble, and a good deal of talk, to bring them to this desirable frame of mind, but they have arrived at it at last.'[84]

Once again in his difficulties, Shaw had turned to the tradition of Liverpool classic. As surely as the Alliance Assurance leans upon Cockerell's Bank of England, so the Piccadilly Hotel screen derives from the open colonnade Elmes threw across the rear elevation of Shaw's beloved St George's Hall. Both were extravagant, festal gestures, but on this occasion Shaw hardly integrated the stern language of Elmes with his own racier rhetoric. He emulated the hot-bloodedness of the Liverpool colonnade only at the expense of the proprieties that must go with classic grandiloquence. Even without the

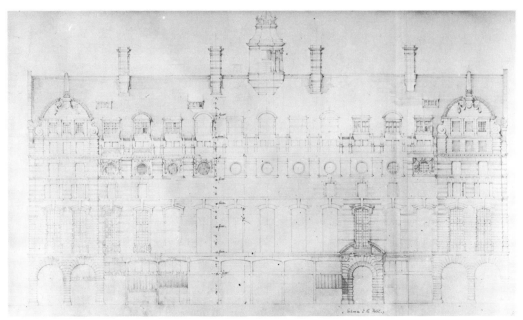

278. Piccadilly Hotel, design with steel shop fronts for elevation to Piccadilly, 1905.

279. Piccadilly Hotel, perspective of design for Piccadilly street front as revised in 1906, drawn by C. W. English.

280. Piccadilly Hotel, uncompleted street front to Piccadilly as built.

mutilation that was to follow, the baroque gables and lanterns of his original design would have looked perilously out of place above so strong an entablature. Also, Shaw had now returned to arches for the shops, and the difficulty of relating them to the pattern of the storeys above was compounded by the vast void in the middle. The battle he had so brilliantly won in Regent Street, to bring relief to a high street façade, he lost in Piccadilly. But the task was redoubtable, given the cornice levels stipulated for the streets, the accommodation required by the hotel, and the need for light wells.

Confident of the whole project's success, and pleased that his weight with the L.C.C. had secured their agreement to the bridging of Air Street, Shaw set out at the beginning of June for a refresher visit to Buxton. From then until the turn of the year he was maturing the Quadrant design, getting on with the details of the hotel, 'so that they may have no shadow of a ground for complaint',[85] and the less urgent task of organizing a plan for Piccadilly Circus. On this score, he had no illusions that any plans he prepared might be immediately carried out. His efforts were closer to guidelines for the Woods and Forests to show to the L.C.C., the County Fire people, and other interested parties, so that gradually a plan for the whole Circus could be arrived at. Seventy years on, one can only smile indulgently at the supposition that there would ever be a harmony of interests on Piccadilly Circus.

The first design Shaw made for the Circus, in October 1904 straight after his appointment, was a pure trial run—a kind of ideal solution with the maximum gain for Crown properties (ill. 281). There were two main ideas. One was a proposal to set back the County Fire Office, which Shaw hoped to redesign entirely himself, away from the line of the northern end of the Quadrant. It was to stand above a flight of steps right in the mouth of Glasshouse and Sherwood Streets, which would debouch into the rebuilt Circus under bridges on either side. The other idea was to move the ill-sited Shaftesbury Memorial into the new open area in front of the Fire Office, and build a large free-standing block, seventy-five by forty-five feet, on its site opposite the end of Swan and Edgar. The new block divided the Circus into two, making the main axis north-south, and masked the entrances to Shaftesbury Avenue and Coventry Street, where for the moment Shaw proposed little rebuilding. The Advisory Committee and the Woods and Forests liked this scheme, but it was too difficult. The Crown had no powers of compulsory purchase and could not acquire properties owned by the Central London Railway; nor could they push back so far into Glasshouse Street, where some of their lessees had recently rebuilt. Hellard also anticipated difficulties with the L.C.C. over any central block, so that was dropped forthwith. In a first revision of February 1905, Shaw left the County Fire Office where it was, but with an extended frontage and an arch to its right bridging the end of Glasshouse and Sherwood Streets, where the properties needed setting back. The Shaftesbury Memorial was also left in its position.

In the haste over the hotel, he had to wait till the autumn before getting seriously back to the Circus. By then, the Treasury had intimated that they opposed the purchase of properties in Glasshouse and Sherwood Streets; if the L.C.C. wanted to make street improvements, that was up to them. Therefore Shaw would have to wrestle with the Fire Office's very awkward site as it was. In October, he sent in a radically revised scheme (ill. 282). The whole axis was turned the other way, and to mask the unworthy eastern end, he

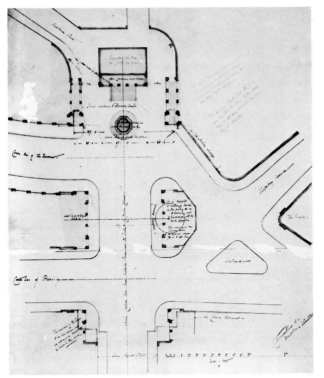

281. Piccadilly Circus, plan of October 1904.

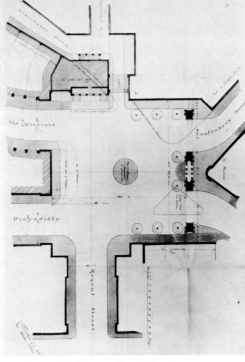

282. Piccadilly Circus, plan of October 1905.

283. Piccadilly Circus, plan as revised in March 1906.

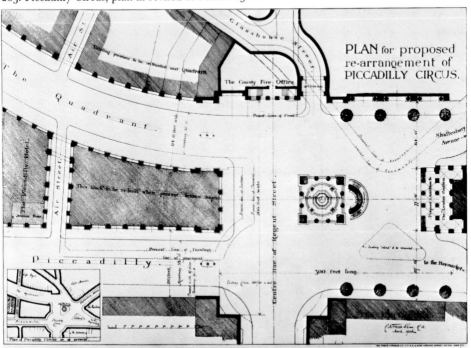

PLAN for proposed
re-arrangement of
PICCADILLY CIRCUS.

proposed pylons before the street entrances and a fountain in front of the London Pavilion. On the northern side (the Monico site), the frontage was set back drastically to the line of the end of the Quadrant; here and in front of the Criterion opposite, Shaw wanted trees to create a Parisian air. Over the next month or two, despite the Treasury's sulkiness, he continued to play with this scheme, tinkering with the Fire Office and indulging his new-found passion for open screens and colonnades. With Hyde Park Corner in mind, he tried several colonnaded schemes for the street entrances. But his most lavish idea was for a vast, open, semicircular end for the Circus side of Swan and Edgar. 'This ought to be stately, and a superb shop, as shops go. I should not propose to take that rounded end higher than the first floor (if as high) . . . I think you might say that you would lose no ground here, or anyway, no money, for the value of such a site ought to be enormous. Surely quite a fancy price might be asked.'[86] This front was a point long at issue in Shaw's mind, not finally settled in favour of the square end for another four years. 'I drew it first as a square end, then I drew in a semicircular end, then before sending the drawing to the Academy in 1906 (and when it was all done and tinted), I washed out the circular end and re-drew the square.'[87]

The scheme for the Circus sent to the R.A. (ill. 283) was, in fact, Shaw's final solution, a cheaper modification of the plans worked out the previous autumn, and informally given the L.C.C.'s blessing by Riley. It abolished all the pylons and screens in favour of an extra colonnade in front of the London Pavilion, the masking of north and south sides by trees, and a square enclosure for the Shaftesbury Memorial in the middle of the Circus. When the plan, together with beautiful drawings by C. W. English of the Quadrant and the Piccadilly façade of the Hotel, was exhibited in 1906, they received the rare and unanimous acclamation of the whole architectural press. It was the first time that the public had been properly told about the enterprise, and they were astonished by its grandeur and scale. But by then, Shaw's triumph was turning steadily into tragedy.

Trouble began in earnest in January 1906, when a bank which had premises on the west of the hotel, across the alley called Piccadilly Place, complained of loss of light. Emden, the shiftier of the hotel company's architects, blamed it on Shaw; Shaw replied that the Woodward and Emden design presented the same difficulties, and that they should have sorted this out before. This was the signal for a whole brigade of the hotel's neighbours to cry out. In February, Denman's on the south-east corner of the site brought an action against Westminster City Council; in July, Spink and Son in Air Street asked for an injunction against the hotel company for loss of light; and in November the Metropolitan Police followed suit, since their station in Vine Street was likely to be overshadowed. Three of these cases mattered little to Shaw, merely reinforcing the point he had made to Hellard on the first occasion: 'Surely such cute business men ought to have foreseen any difficulty in carrying it out . . . If they are not *business men*, then I really don't know what they are.'[88] But the Denman's case was a real disaster.

Not then knowing their mind, the Woods and Forests had allowed Messrs Denman to rebuild their premises on the corner of Piccadilly and Air Street in 1903. The L.C.C. then announced a road-widening scheme for Piccadilly to coincide with the building of the hotel. This would, it was thought, compel Denman's to fall in with the company's plans, destroy their recently erected building, and move into the right-hand wing of the hotel.

But Denman's refused to treat, and in February 1906 they were granted an injunction to the effect that they needed only to give up the few feet of their property strictly wanted for road-widening. When the widening took place, they intended to rebuild their old front further back; this, to general consternation, they finally did in 1911. It is still there on the corner with Air Street, in the place where Shaw's right hand wing and gable should have stood.

On learning of this, the dumbfounded architects cast desperately around for a solution. A pay-off was the real answer, but it was rapidly emerging that money was in ever shorter supply for the hotel company. Woodward's attitude was simple and characteristic: move the eastern pavilion bodily westward, curtailing the colonnade and destroying the proportions of the whole front. This also deprived the hotel of many rooms, but so anxious was the company to proceed now that foundations were being dug, that they pressed on for a week or two with this idea, to the fury of Shaw and the Woods and Forests. Legal letters had to be exchanged before this was stopped. Unfortunately Shaw did little better. With more time, he might have gone back to square one and redesigned the whole Piccadilly elevation on the basis of the foundations already laid. Instead, he produced early in March an ingenious but makeshift idea, dependent on the all-too-prevalent hope that Denman's would accept the wing once the hotel was built, and complete the design. This involved tucking a few extra rooms behind either end of the colonnade, to compensate the hotel company for the loss of the wing. These he thought 'would give a little interest to the composition, and from my point of view would not be any drawback'.[89] But to get the insertions accepted, he had to enlarge them further and make gabled pavilions facing each other across the back of the colonnade. It is these which so much destroy the clarity. Shaw's philosophy of the building as erected (ill. 280) was that 'anyone could see that circumstances prevented the other Pavilion from being built, and that in time it might be built'.[90] Paradoxically, he was guilty both of over-optimism and of the resignation that comes with the onset of exhaustion.

Only one more thing was needed to complete the discomfiture. That was the concerted attack on the Quadrant which began while the designs were on show at the R.A. in April–May 1906. This event, and the gaping hole in Regent Street, convinced the shopkeepers that the Crown meant business, and they did not like what they saw. The cry soon went up that Shaw's design, however fine as architecture, meant loss of display space and consequent loss of revenue. Once this was abroad, it was seized upon by the fast-failing hotel company and used as another source of excuse. The shopkeepers were happy to press the company's case, knowing it would affect their own, but they had no intention of helping beyond a certain point. The hotel's only real ally, Swan and Edgar, employed Emden as their architect and numbered among their directors G. M. Chamberlin, the chairman of the hotel company. They knew they would be next on the block once the hotel was finished, for Shaw had already made designs for two of their fronts and would soon be engaged on the Piccadilly side. They therefore sponsored a petition amongst the Regent Street shopkeepers, which arrived on Horner's desk at the beginning of July.

The battle over the shopfronts that now ensued has an importance out of proportion to its results, because it marked the first occasion in the history of London improvement when tenants efficiently united against their landlord to throw out a development that was being thrust upon them. Many schemes had come to grief before through the power of proprietors or the intervention of authority; others had failed because of bad financing or some species of architectural débacle. But the concerted, democratic action of lessees was a new and bewildering phenomenon. It would hardly have succeeded had the Tories not been ousted at the turn of the year. Where Lord Windsor stood as Shaw's stalwart supporter, come good or ill, Reginald McKenna and Walter Runciman, who had to answer the pointed questions now asked in the House, were lukewarm. For a time they were willing to shoulder the scheme, but they had nothing to do with its inception and would not seriously lament its mutilation.

It was a bitter campaign and it lacked facts. Whether the shopkeepers really did stand to lose from Shaw's twenty-one foot shopfronts under arches is unclear. A writer in the *Daily Telegraph* (the shopkeepers' mainstay) may have put his finger on it when he argued that Regent Street had declined into a middle-class, cut-price shopping street over the previous decade, in favour of Sloane Street and Brompton Road. 'The doom of Regent Street as a fashionable shopping centre was sealed when it took to selling cheap articles to attract chance customers,' one shopkeeper even said.[91] The indignant response was that casual trade, the only trade that could seriously depend upon shop windows, was essential for good shops and high rents; but very likely the thought of any further advantage going to Knightsbridge struck fear into the hearts of Regent Street proprietors, who one and all denied any decline. Shaw himself believed that extending the plate glass was not only bad architecturally but would actually lower the values. In one of a series of press interviews, he put the matter trenchantly:

> Where the shoe pinches is that I have solid stone piers that cover the whole front. The shopkeeper wants an iron stanchion 12 in. wide, covered with a slip of granite or a sheet of looking-glass! He likes one large window down to the pavement stuffed full of things, generally so crowded together that to my mind, they show badly, and the general aspect is beyond all doubt vulgar and ostentatious.[92]

And he quoted approvingly a shopkeeper he knew in Mount Street who thought as he did.

There was authority on both sides. The shopkeepers pleaded that there was nothing like these arches in modern commercial architecture the world over, and that the old arcaded shopping streets of Paris (an inexact parallel) were dead. Their opponents pointed to the arches of Debenham and Freebody in Wigmore Street, and to Gorringe's near Victoria, for the setback of glass from the front of the piers. Shaw was careful to lean upon the Advisory Committee, who did sterling work on his behalf; Aston Webb, for instance, wrote an article in *Nineteenth Century* in praise of the design.[93] But nothing could alter the fact that nearly every shopkeeper in Regent Street had signed the petition against the 'Drapers' Newgate'; Shaw's old friend Arthur Liberty alone stood up for him, bravely but vainly. And although the unpredictable Woodward supported the design in public, he too was constantly pushing for a change in the hotel shopfronts. It was the history and fate of these, the first shops in the projected Quadrant, that so greatly weakened the Crown's resolve.

On the finished Quadrant design, the shopfronts were scheduled to start some two feet back from the pier faces. Shaw did not want absolute uniformity of fascia but planned that the ends of each front should cant forward slightly, so that the main glass line should be only some fifteen inches behind the piers. This was not enough for the shopkeepers or the hotel. At about the time the petition was delivered, the Advisory Committee found out that Woodward was cutting away the stone much closer to the front of the piers. 'Did Shaw approve?' they telegraphed up to Ellerdale Road. 'Certainly not, most dishonourable,' was the reply.[94] Woodward had to take the blame for this. Next, new models for shopfronts were made and put up, and a meeting of all parties took place on site in early August, at which it was agreed to have a fifteen inch setback and a straight front. A trivial point, one might think; but everyone knew how critical it was that these shops should let. The hotel directors were most aware of this, but by the time the shops were ready in December 1906 they also needed every penny they could get. Therefore the rents were fixed high, and the shopkeepers had a perfect excuse for boycotting them. For a few months the company concealed the embarrassment by getting Swan and Edgar to support them and put goods in the windows. But by April 1907 the secret was out; the shops would not let. This was the signal for renewed campaign by the shopkeepers, and now the tide of publicity turned in their favour. Horner had to ask Shaw to try one more time at new shopfronts, but nothing much could be done; while the arches remained, the shopkeepers had the whip hand. They just sat and did nothing, knowing that their leases would run out in 1919, and sooner or later the Crown would have to treat. At the end of the year, only one shop had been taken and the hotel company was on its last legs. At their Annual General Meeting, Chamberlin diffused an air of good will and confidence in the light of the near completion of the hotel, and claimed that they did not care for letting the shops until the work was over. The truth was far otherwise, as Horner well knew from a desperate series of interviews with Chamberlin. The Piccadilly Hotel opened in May 1908 and promptly bankrupted in August. Liberty had always said they were over-capitalized,[95] and they were certainly clumsy, inefficient and grasping. But the stringency of their landlords and the coolness of their fellow lessees materially hastened the collapse.

Formally, the Woods and Forests never faltered during this whole period. When Horner was replaced by George Leveson-Gower in 1908, the shopkeepers renewed their petition but were summarily rebuffed. Soon after, Swan and Edgar sent in a design for their own Quadrant front, as they wished to rebuild on the right terms. It embodied the worst suggestion yet, plate glass *in front of* the piers, and the Advisory Committee contemptuously rejected it.[96] But the moral victory was the shopkeepers'; they knew they could win now. Instead of a busy campaign of rebuilding, there was no activity on the Quadrant, where the hotel front stood as a huge displeasing rump, with bulkheads and excrescences visible behind (ill. 284), exciting the contempt of the admirers of Nash, now beginning to make themselves known. Shaw was willing to make changes almost anywhere except the arches. The circular windows, for instance, he had always thought 'rather strong meat for the ordinary Philistine',[97] and they were omitted from the revised design. But this was not enough. By the time a further four years had passed, the supporters of his design had defected in droves.

By now, to all intents and purposes, Shaw had reverted to the advisory role, a process which began with the renewed adverse publicity of April 1907. In July he was paid his fee, having completed his official brief. The drawings he handed over comprised a careful

387

284. Regent Street Quadrant, showing the Piccadilly Hotel frontage as it appeared in 1910.

285. Regent Street Quadrant from Piccadilly Circus, showing the rebuilding as completed by Reginald Blomfield.

plan for the junction of the Quadrant with the rest of Regent Street at Vigo Street, slight revisions of the Circus plan, elevations for the north side of the Quadrant with its different problems of planning and articulation, and designs for the other fronts of Swan and Edgar (where he proposed modest pavilions and high attics in the Beaux-Arts manner, not so different from what was built, and trabeated shopfronts to Piccadilly). He wrote to Hellard: 'I have done the whole thing as far as it can be done at present . . . . I think I may say that a large instalment of the scheme has been achieved. That the rest will all follow in due course I have not a shadow of a doubt.'[98] That, at least, was becoming daily more implausible.

From now on the initiative passed to John Murray, Arthur Green's successor as Woods and Forests' architect. He had been a considerable help to Shaw and a strong supporter of his scheme. Late in 1908, with Shaw's approval, Murray made a reduced scheme for the Circus along the lines of what had been done, with revised elevations to Swan and Edgar and the County Fire Office, which Shaw still hoped to design once the site was settled. The Woods and Forests were hopeful that they could get agreement on this, their final attempt at replanning the Circus, and contacted Riley at County Hall. But the L.C.C. had schemes of their own, and in May 1909 submitted an astonishingly extravagant plan, far more impractical than anything yet suggested. This was to bite off the whole of the end of Swan and Edgar to a depth of seventy feet, add a compensating area of land to the front of the London Pavilion, and thus make the axis of Piccadilly Circus (or Piccadilly Square) central about Lower Regent Street. It would have entailed substantial loss of Crown land and further trouble with Swan and Edgar. Shaw was asked to report on the rival schemes, and here put forward his last suggestions for the Circus. The L.C.C. plan he entirely rejected, pointing out its effect on the Quadrant: 'It would entirely destroy the grand sweep of the curve, and this of course is its great glory, and I fear would give it an awkward, broken backed look.' As to the Pavilion end of the square, 'if it did no other harm, it would relegate the whole of the Criterion to a sort of side street, and considering the general excellence of the design, and the position it has occupied for many years, this would be most unjust'. Murray's scheme he had fathered and scarcely commented on, but he felt its lack of ambition. He was now for removing the Shaftesbury Memorial to one of the parks, bringing back his semicircular end to Swan and Edgar in order to join the Quadrant with Piccadilly, and setting back the County Fire Office as he had first desired.

> In the designs I made about three years ago, I feel that we all approached this rather timidly, and with a subdued admiration for the existing building, which it hardly merits. I suppose it shines by contrast with the excessively mean Architecture of the Quadrant, but it can in no sense be said to be great. It is respectable and somewhat dull, and that is about all that can be said for it.[99]

Shaw closed his report with a last peroration on the need for ambition and purpose in such a project. But it was not to be. His stance was unrealistic; the Crown could not, after several meetings, come to terms with the L.C.C., and by April 1910 everyone knew that the chances of replanning the Circus had receded into the future. Yet Shaw worked on at ideas for the County Fire Office. Murray published his ideas in October as an Edward

VII Memorial Square, but even this scaled-down version had no hopes of proceeding. There was stalemate here as well, and eventually the *coup de grâce* occurred; the Crown capitulated over the Quadrant.

In March 1911 *The Builder* for the first time sympathized with the shopkeepers, and in May, Denman's triumphantly set back their shop. Next January, Henry Tanner junior submitted the first Quadrant rebuilding scheme for nearly four years, for Messrs Hope at 84–88 Regent Street. The drawings were deliberately alien to the spirit of the official design. The Woods and Forests wished to support Shaw but could not go on like this for ever, so Hellard wrote to him for a new initiative incorporating the larger windows and smaller piers of Tanner's design. By now he was eighty and 'well nigh played out'.[100] For a fortnight he valiantly strove, against strong disinclination, to save the project from disaster and modify these elevations. His letters express a grand, Michelangelesque pain, each sentence costing him effort; 'I am, I am afraid, getting somewhat indifferent to architectural matters, but I have not yet arrived at the stage of absolute indifference, and to see a design with which I took so much pains thus vulgarized, troubles me.'[101] After a fruitless attempt to compensate for the loss of arches on Tanner's drawing, he gave up. On 1st March 1912 he sent in his famous resignation letter:

Dear Mr Leveson-Gower,

I have pored over the Quadrant till I am worn out, and now I am compelled most reluctantly to ask you to allow me to retire. The question really lies in very small compass. At one time the design might be said to be mine, and I was prepared to stand or fall by its merits or demerits. But now all is changed. To fully understand this it is necessary to go into some detail. From the first I was anxious to give the street more or less of a monumental character. As an architect I dwelt much on the piers and arches on pavement level to carry the upper part, but they are gone bodily. The arrangement of windows between the columns on first, second, and third floors I had hoped would have given some distinct character, but they have gone, and very commonplace windows inserted giving the whole front the aspect of a block of flats. Even the pillars themselves have been mutilated by the omission of the blocks on the lower part. I hope I do not exaggerate, but with all these alterations it can be no longer said to be my design at all, and practically a new design would be required, of which all the odium would attach to me. I cannot say I should like that, nor do I think that I should be exposed to it. In addition to all this, I have grave doubts whether I should be justified in pursuing this course. The original design had the approval of the Committee appointed by the Treasury, consisting of Sir John Taylor, Sir Aston Webb and Mr John Belcher. Every detail had their careful examination and approval, and for me to set all this aside and to make a fresh scheme to fall in with the views of some shopkeepers might I fear be misunderstood, and subject me to merited censure.

Believe me to remain,
Yours very truly,
R. Norman Shaw.[102]

Eight months later he was dead. In the intervening time, the preservationists had raised the hue and cry, a decade too late; writers like Roger Fry bombarded *The Times* with letters deploring these 'sacrifices to art'. A scramble to supplant Shaw also ensued. *The Builder,* on the sponsorship of Swan and Edgar and others, held a competition for revised Quadrant designs, won by the unknown firm of Richardson and Gill;[103] Belcher submitted to the Woods and Forests a clever scheme of compromise worked out by J. J. Joass. But the real initiative passed to a new Advisory Committee consisting of the Earl of Plymouth (Lord Windsor), Reginald Blomfield, Sir Henry Tanner and John Murray. Still no progress was made, and after the outbreak of war yet another committee, Blomfield, Aston Webb and Ernest Newton, took over the job and set about redesigning the Quadrant. Blomfield bore the brunt of the work and produced the intelligent, scholarly compromise we have today (ill. 285). He made the best of it, but hardly rose to the illustrious power of Shaw's design. Complete reconstruction began only in 1923, when the leases had mainly run out.

The morals to be drawn from the Quadrant's failure are many, and of contemporary relevance. The tragedy was that it both deprived London of Nash's great street scenario and broke the reputation and the remaining morale of the man whom many had believed to be England's finest architect. Naïveté, overconfidence, ambition for art, and plain obsolescence had contributed to his fall; commercial meanness, mismanagement, ignorance and fear of the future had done more. Shaw had been brought up to despise the tradition of façade design practised by Nash, and more recently by the French; now he had tried it himself and failed. Perhaps Pugin was right after all.

An entertaining and damning epitaph on Shaw's role in the wreck of Regent Street was supplied by Trystan Edwards in his *Good and Bad Manners in Architecture* (1924). Like many clever polemics, it is unfair on detailed points, but carries emotional conviction. 'How did it come about,' he asks, 'that without public protest of any kind this particular bull, such a matchless prize bull, was allowed to play havoc in this particular china shop?' Was he a lofty idealist, or a commercial pragmatist?

> The fact is Norman Shaw had not the faintest idea that the old Regent Street had any special architectural merit at all. To him it was just 'the sham classic of Nash' and he had no compunction whatever in smashing up the delicate stucco forms so lacking in that hardness and heaviness which to him were the hall-marks of good building. . . . It is clear that so far from experiencing any pangs of regret at the disappearance of Nash's work, so expressive of urbanity and mature accomplishment, he was itching to substitute for this his own rustic interpretation of the theme, his steep roofs and dormers and row of aggressively tall chimneys.

And in all this Edwards sees the wraith of the dead Ruskin, inveighing still against stucco:

> Often I lie awake at night and imagine that I can hear an odious grating sound, and that I can see a still more odious sight, of ugly little teeth, crooked, self-righteous little teeth—the Ruskinian rats are gnawing, nibbling, and picking away at masterpiece after masterpiece of our national civic art.[104]

Edwards knew the history of the project only scantily. How else could he criticize Shaw's substitution of re-entrant angles for Nash's curves at the corners of Piccadilly and Lower Regent Street, when the old circus and its proportions had already been

286. Portland House, Lloyds Avenue, street front.

destroyed? Nor could he know, for instance, that the pressure for height came from the hotel company. The charges that stick are that Shaw wantonly disregarded the 'commercial ideal', and refused to provide a light design over plate glass to satisfy the shopkeepers. But when Edwards blames him for not coming forward at the start to dissociate himself from the Crown's destructive proceedings, he betrays wilful anachronism. Not only Shaw, but everybody, cared little for Nash right at the start; the first whimper of sympathy was heard in the *Daily Telegraph* in April 1905, and the preservationists took another two years to wake up properly. There was, of course, a great deal of humbug and pretention in the old antipathy to stucco. But in every architectural style there is humbug and pretention: in Nash's neat but often gimcrack façades, in Shaw's imperial elevations, in Edwards' plea for stucco streets of the future, and not least in the 'styleless' style to which they have all given way.

THE QUIETUS

After the Piccadilly Hotel façades, Shaw had just one more building to erect, yet still a surprise in store, though frustratingly little is known about it. Portland House was built as the City headquarters of the Associated Portland Cement Manufacturers, a wider grouping of which Fred White's firm at Swanscombe was now part. It stands in Lloyds Avenue, complete with Shaw's name on the front and the date, 1908. Superficially, it looks just a modest, disciplined classical front (ill. 286), based on the Parr's Bank

392

elevation, but built in mannerly Portland stone instead of the marble and terracotta facings Shaw had used at Liverpool. But the structure is a revelation. 'Reinforced concrete ought to do a lot for us. What do you say to have a turn on those lines? I am sure we are doing no good at present.'[105] Thus wrote Shaw to Lethaby at about this time. Lethaby had had his 'turn' at concrete (not reinforced) in his church at Brockhampton; here is Shaw having his. Portland House, it has recently been discovered, is one of the first major English office blocks in reinforced concrete.[106] It is easy to see why Shaw should have hankered for this material. He had spent thirty years and more chafing under the limitations of planning, using more and more iron and steel for freedom. At Parr's Bank he had reached the absolute limit in concealed girderwork. Now, with a not dissimilar plan, he could use a more supple material for the same job.

The reinforcement is in the up-to-date Kahn system, using small trussed bars with angled 'wings'. The structure has now been completely changed in a recent remodelling, but it depended originally on reinforced piers at regular intervals with an infill of brickwork in decreasing thickness at greater height. The central dome, high over the hallway, was of concrete, with plaster pendentives and arches, and the treads of the stairs were also reinforced. It is all a far cry from the concrete experiments of the 1870s with Lascelles. Presumably, Shaw must have had a good deal of technical help with the structure. But it would have been entirely characteristic if he had worked it out himself; there is no reason to think his role in the design subsidiary. Nothing could better illustrate than this last novelty the justice of his claim to Reginald Blomfield: 'I was intended by nature to have been an Engineer, but somehow I missed my tip and became a *so-called* Architect!!'[107]

The 'so-called Architect' had no more to build now, but one or two things still to do. However, nothing would come right. In 1907 the Acton Council asked him to assess their new Municipal Buildings. Five years before, Shaw had acted in another London Borough competition, for the Chelsea Baths, but he had earned himself little praise and nothing had come of the result. This time it was worse. An absurdly low cost limit had led to disagreement over an earlier competition, and the R.I.B.A. not only refused to appoint an assessor for another but asked their members to boycott it. When Shaw agreed to act, the Chairman of the Committee was delighted, saying 'it is something as if the Lord Mayor had refused to appoint a person to open a bazaar and the King himself consented to do so'.[108] Shaw was doubtless provoked by the Institute's boycott, and incensed when they sent him a warning not to act. But this time they were wise. Though Acton scraped together forty competitors, the cost limit made it a poor showing. When the design he placed first was shown to exceed the limit, his credit quickly failed with the Council, and he was sharply criticized in the building press. All in all, this assessorship was his least happy one. Heterodoxy was out of date; the R.I.B.A. had prevailed.[109]

Another task was Shaw's appearance before a Select Committee of the House of Lords in Autumn 1907 to testify on ways of making small internal alterations to Parliament. The opinions of one who knew and loved each corner of the building intimately, 'more intimately fifty years ago than I do now', were of particular value.[110] They were also opinions of detail on many questions of past and present taste. But they were not to be acted upon. After toying with the idea of a higher roof to the front, he agreed to think about raising the level slightly round one of the internal courts. He duly surveyed the building and made a sketch-plan for minor space-saving alterations and for adding a number of rooms looking into the Commons Inner Court. But the Commissioner of Works found his ideas oversimplified and beyond the brief of the Committee, so they were dropped.

All these experiences show gradual signs of failing, which was now to be expected. Since 1899 when Shaw had contracted pleurisy, his health had been well broken once more and was never again to be relied on.[111] These taxing Edwardian commissions led, especially in winter, to a trail of broken appointments and petty delays which distressed him. Almost every private letter betrays physical suffering and the despondency that goes with it. The common cold and influenza were regular, but jaundice was the main foe. He had three separate attacks in 1902, and it kept recurring, accompanied by eruptions of the skin. Agnes' neuralgia was now rampant as well. 'You see, we are an amusing old couple. Neither of these ailments are fatal but they are entirely incapacitating.'[112] When regular injections finally threw off the jaundice in 1909–11, in its place came 'a most awful trouble, "Punctiform Hydrophobia". One of my legs has a huge patch like a large beet root in aspect and colour, too hideous for words, and it gets worse! It is some form of insane Eczema of the most fiendish character. However, I suppose I must grin and bear it.'[113] But little by little the incapacity of old age began to tell and depress Shaw. His repeatedly unsuccessful trials in 1907–10 at providing Ilkley with a font canopy, for instance, much discouraged him.[114] And from about 1909 the cool clear writing begins to deteriorate. That year, not seeing why an Academician should occupy a sinecure, he finally persuaded the R.A. to put him on the list of retired members, a very rare event.[115]

One incident in November 1907 did much to cheer him. Campbell-Bannerman offered him a belated baronetcy, which Shaw declined. He told Radcliffe: 'Of course, I look on it as a *very great honour offered to architecture*, and it is agreeable that it was offered through me, but beyond that I don't go. I am sure it would have been a bore, I am not built that way. It did not smile much, if at all, on my wife.'[116] And to the Prime Minister, he merely said, 'We are exceedingly quiet people, living what would be called a retired life, and we venture to think it would not be wise to change all this, at my time of life.'[117] Still, he was genuinely proud of the offer, and wrote round to tell his friends the news at length and in much the same terms.

To the last, Shaw kept up his now often garrulous correspondence. Most of the old friends were dead, but he had made as many younger ones and could still serve them. In 1906 he commended both Lethaby and Prior for the surveyorship of Westminster Abbey; in 1910 both Statham and Harry Wilson for the Slade Professorship at Oxford; next year Ernest Newton finally became an A.R.A. through his help. To C.H.B. and Marjorie Quennell, a young architect and his wife already collecting material which would form the basis of their *History of Everyday Things in England*, he wrote in 1910 a letter explaining his conversion from the Gothic.

> It was always supposed that 'Gothic' was to develop, and there was any amount of tall talk as to what it was to do, but it didn't do anything. It was like a cut flower, pretty enough to look at, but fading away before your eyes, and if we don't take care, the English Renaissance that we now have will do the same, so unlike the French. They

went on all the last century doing work that was founded on their old work, and magnificent work it was; and this was the result of gentle development, new features and arrangements growing from the old stock. In fact their Architecture was alive, ours dead, a mighty difference, and arriving of course from their having a School, and we have none.

It was all rather pathetic. 'We remember,' say the Quennells, 'that it was a little saddening at the time to receive the letter and realize how the high hopes had faded.'[118]

But the light was not quite quenched. There was a final flare-up in 1910–11. Shaw to Radcliffe, 4th November 1910:

You must be very quarrelsome people in Liverpool. There is a fierce warfare going on now about the placing of the King's Memorial at the end of St George's Hall, and the worshipful the Lord Mayor requested my presence at the Athenaeum on Wednesday last to meet Sir Aston Webb, John Belcher, Blomfield and Thornycroft to discuss the question and advise him. Of course we did not agree!! There is no doubt but that that would be a grand place for it, the question is how to do it!! I have my little view, and I have no doubt I am wrong, but I rather like to stick to what I am pleased to call 'my views'. We settled that there should be a good sized model made, with the power of altering it by moveable pieces, and that we should see it here and then that it should go down to L'pool and encounter the storm of abuse that it will raise.

Then, on 25th January 1911, at greater length:

I made a sketch plan of my idea, and I liked it!! The 'experts' were divided. Some liked it entirely, others half and half, and some *not at all*!! The feeling that actuates me most deeply is the gross injustice that is being done to the original architect Elmes, and to his successor Professor Cockerell. There cannot be a shadow of a doubt that Elmes designed his building to enter at the south end under the Portico, and that Cockerell desired the same. Many schemes were made for steps approaching this Portico, possibly not perfect, but all leaning one way, viz. to enter there into the square entrance with stairs on each side, leading to the side corridors, the courts and the upper floors. All this was a *design*, and a fine one too. They fiddle about during Cockerell's life, and wait till he had been dead 6 years and then they build a wall 15 feet high straight across, give up all idea of entering by the portico, and in fact reduce it to a piece of scenery, a thing stuck up to be looked at, practically inaccessible, a great and dignified entrance at which no one goes in. The other day your Lord Mayor said he had only been once in by that door, and he had been 55 years in Liverpool.

No, this gross injustice and want of appreciation sticks in my gizzard. I ask myself what Elmes wd say, and what Cockerell wd have said, and I weep!! Both of these men were as much superior to your tinpot Liverpool professors and so called architects, as light is superior to darkness. Oh! don't talk to me.

The scheme I have ventured to suggest would, I think, go a long way towards wiping out this injustice, and would I feel sure have pleased Elmes and Cockerell, and I maintain it is also logically correct. Could anything be conceived more absurd than the present arrangement, where you enter at a side door in a back street, into the corridor

287. St George's Hall, Liverpool, exterior by H. L. Elmes, 1842–51, view showing the end portico and wall to St John's Lane.

sideways, cross the corridor, and find yourself in the large hall, from which you find your way to the place you want to go to anyhow! I taxed some of the objectors with this, and the reply was, that it was a silly stupid ill considered *plan*, but a splendid design that must not be tampered with. . . . To sum up: my first and abiding feeling is to try and do justice to Elmes & Cockerell, and this gives the opportunity. It was a mean trick to wait till old Cockerell's death to put up that wall, and I resent that much. As to the King's statue, I do think that would be a very fine place for it, and I maintain that the whole arrangement would give great *interest* to that front. I said this at our meeting and some of the enemy rejoined 'Oh! yes we agree with you, it would give great interest, but how about that wall that gives such dignity to the whole design?'

'I said no word to indicate a doubt
But I put my thumb unto my nose and spread my fingers out.'

Of course there may be a finer site for the Monument in L'pool but of course on that I cannot express an opinion as I do not know your city well enough.

Goscombe John told the meeting that he had shewn the model to Sir Alma Tadema, and that he (Tadema) had expressed the utmost enthusiasm for my modest little suggestion. I don't know how far this is considered 'private'. Personally, I would

396

rather have Tadema's opinion than all the Architects in Liverpool with the whole Bench of Bishops thrown in . . .

I have not been out since the day I managed to drive down to the Grand Hotel to see the other 'experts'. I declined to go to lunch. When I got there, I found about a dozen who had been feeding up to the nines, with champagne and all sorts of foreign drams running out of the corners of their mouths. I regretted missing that guzzle, but of course it was impossible.

I fear this letter will not carry much conviction even to you, and none at all to your local duffers, but I do think it is scandalous to have a transcendently fine building disfigured by that wall. Just ask the objectors, if you have a chance, if they really think Elmes and Cockerell would be pleased by the present arrangement. If they say 'Yes', then I'll shut up.

The 'tinpot professors' were C. H. Reilly and S. D. Adshead, who resented any intrusion upon their rule over Liverpool's architecture. In 1904 Reilly had secured the Chair in Architecture at Liverpool University, following his classic design for the Cathedral competition, and fortified by a reference from Shaw.[119] He had breathed vitality into the School there, but he now saw himself and his School as sole guardians of Liverpool's classic heritage, especially St George's Hall. In his interpretation of the Beaux-Arts tradition, there was no room for this proposed improvement. His autobiography gives a partial view of the controversy without mentioning Shaw, so it is well to set some of the facts straight.

Sir William Goscombe John had been the first to suggest a new approach through the end wall, to supplement his intended equestrian statue of King Edward. Both the professors and the London experts were opposed to his design, with its double dog-leg flight of lateral steps up to the portico. Some of the experts also disliked Shaw's first scheme, for flights of straight steps on either side of the statue, but they let it go forward for his later emendation. But as he had predicted, howls of protest were soon heard in Liverpool. Reilly whipped up opposition, produced an old unsigned drawing showing the blank wall shielding the podium which the scheme would supplant, and claimed it as Cockerell's. This raised a battle royal between the *Liverpool Daily Post* on behalf of the locals and the *Liverpool Courier* which supported the scheme. For months there was heated argument, very much on 'town versus gown' lines, or, as Reilly saw it, municipal Fabians against corporation crustaceans. Since Shaw was one of the last survivors who had sat at the feet of Cockerell, his opinion of the wall, though not necessarily more accurate, was bound to weigh with the Memorial Committee, who accepted his assurances that it was not genuine.

But the job was not easy. The portico faced into a hill on St John's Lane and was seen from a slight angle (ill. 287); any flight of steps that failed to manage the change in levels well could easily look ridiculous. And every day, work was becoming harder. To Radcliffe he wrote:

I am now suffering from an awful ailment, viz. the demoralization arising from illness. It is rather new to me and is I assure you quite terrible, I feel so utterly helpless. I am entirely rolled up in surgical lint and cotton wool, with one mile of surgical bandages all over me. I really can't say if it is mending or not, one place gets better and another worse. I think the 'professors', did they know, would say, 'Ah! we see the finger of God in this—Sarve him right, we hope he may get worse.'[120]

Then in August he had to admit, 'I have behaved shamefully and disgracefully to these good Town Hall steps folk but somehow I *can't* work, it is no use, I can't. This is the demoralization of illness, and it is awful.'[121] Somehow, he managed to settle a single flight of steps with the intended memorial statue on one side and space for another on the opposite flank. This was agreed upon, though the professors quickly claimed that if the memorial had to be here it was what they had suggested all along. Their agitations successfully held things up. By the time of Shaw's death, nothing had been done and other sites were being investigated. It was the final failure.

In February 1912, Edward Prior was appointed Slade Professor at Cambridge. Shaw wrote to congratulate him: 'We are rejoiced indeed, it is the best piece of news I have had for many a day. My wife sends special congrats to Mrs Prior and to *you*, she has a flush of joy in her whole manner this morning. We shall hear in good time when your work begins and when you will begin to wake them up.'[122] At much the same time, he wrote also to Newton. 'I have been wondering how you are. I trust you have quite got over the bad trouble you had in the summer: that was a caution. . . . I have been much interested in Blomfield's French Renaissance. If I could write like that I should dash out into the street and stand on my head.'[123] On 1st and 4th March he sent his letters of resignation from the Quadrant. From then on Robert Shaw records a slow decline. On 18th April he went out for his last walk, on 29th August he gave Robert his gold watch, on 10th October he came downstairs for the last time. Two weeks later his brain began to give way, and on Sunday 17th November, 1912, at just before nine in the evening, he died.[124]

At the funeral on the following Thursday there was a good attendance: among architects Aston Webb, George, Jackson, Newton, Stokes, Horsley, Burnet, Lethaby, Macartney, Ricardo, Warren, May, Joass and Curtis Green; among artists Sir Edward Poynter and many R.A.s. He was interred in the family vault in Hampstead churchyard looking over towards Ellerdale Road, beneath the High Victorian tombstone he had erected for his brother half a century before (ill. 288). This was not what he had wanted. A year or two before he had seen published drawings of a tomb in Fairford churchyard and wanted to design a substitute on these lines, but illness had intervened. Instead, Ernest Newton took up the idea at the family's request, and the simple table tomb, executed by Laurence Turner, was soon erected and the old inscriptions transferred (ill. 289).[125]

The obituaries were full, but strangely cool for the dominant figure in English architecture. Five years or a decade before, they would have been ampler and less critical. In 1912, despite his ceaseless activity, Shaw risked being forgotten. There was no memorial service. The building press produced no long assessment of his architecture. The only commemorations were a brief exhibition of his drawings in 1913, and a plaque, designed by Lethaby and worked by Hamo Thornycroft, which was set on the wall of New Scotland Yard in July 1914 (ill. 291). There was some sorrow at his departure, but none of the sobbing that would be heard upon the death of Philip Webb.[126]

288. Shaw family tomb, Hampstead churchyard, c.1865.

289. Shaw family tomb, Hampstead churchyard, as replaced by Ernest Newton, 1913.

290. T. H. Ismay's tomb, Thurstaston churchyard.

291. Memorial medallion to Shaw on New Scotland Yard, designed by W. R. Lethaby and Hamo Thornycroft, 1913.

Catalogue
of Executed Work

THIS catalogue comprises a complete list of Shaw's known buildings but excludes unexecuted projects. It is mainly organized chronologically so as to give a conspectus of his development, but common sense has dictated that estate works, groups of buildings, additions to previous works etc. should be treated together. Thus for instance I have grouped together all the commissions connected with Holy Trinity Bingley (6A–E), but have kept apart the separate restoration at All Saints' Bingley (19). For topographical clarity, I append a gazetteer by catalogue number, arranged according to current administrative districts, with the London commissions broken down by borough. I have attributed a small number of estate buildings to Shaw without source, but have not done this when in any doubt. At the end of the main catalogue will be found a list taken from Robert Shaw's abstract of accounts, of minor works of entirely unknown nature for which his father was paid.

It remains to explain the principles of the subheadings in the main catalogue (for abbreviations see p. xix.

The buildings are referred to by their original names, with modern equivalents (where applicable) given below. House numbers follow modern street-numbering, except in the case of demolished works. Postal rather than administrative addresses are given in this section, but works in outer London boroughs are referred to as being in London.

The *dates* given, unless specified, refer to the dates of execution as far as they are known. But the order of the catalogue depends upon Shaw's first known connection with each project.

Under *contractor* I have given the name of the builder, where available, together with his place of work if outside the town or area concerned. I have added information, if known, on important subcontractors, decorators, and craftsmen, and the name of the clerk of works.

Materials are normally confined to those used for exterior walling, with occasional additions. I have omitted this category for restoration work.

Drawings refer to the whereabouts of original drawings, not of illustrations.

The full *cost* is given in the rare cases where a true figure is available; an accepted builder's tender is given too where known. More frequently I have had to give the figure of Shaw's receipts from Robert Shaw's abstract of accounts, which should amount to 5% of total cost. This however is usually a conservative figure and should be treated, like the tenders, with the utmost caution.

The *references* are to publications containing valuable visual or historical material. I have not given modern critical literature except where genuinely helpful.

I have added brief comments after these headings to explain the nature or quality of the work further, especially the church restorations and the buildings not fully discussed in the main text. Important later alterations or extensions are mentioned here, if known, and any demolition recorded. Total demolition is signified by an obelus (†) in the margin.

Acknowledgments are to those for whose help on a particular building I am grateful.

1. Presbytery, Drogenbos, nr. Brussels, Belgium (†)
New house
d: 1860
r: drawing exh. at Architectural Exhibition, 1860; *B* 5.5.1860; *BN* 11.5.1860; *CEAJ* 1.6.1860; *E* 21 (1860) p. 177
Described as 'about to be executed'; if so, now dem. The present presbytery is of 1885–6.

2. Warehouse, Gould Square, Coopers Row, London E.C.3 (†)
New wine-vaults, storage space, etc.
d: 1862
cl: Duncan Irvine
ctr: Myers & Sons
m: brick
dr: R.A.
c: t of £6298
r: *B* 31.5.1862 (t)
Irregular Gothic elevation, cast-iron columns and girders to interior.

3. Beechwood, (? Kent) (ill. 14)
New gardener's cottage
d: 1862
m: brick, st/drs, t/h
dr: R.A.
As yet unidentified.

4. Eagle Wharf, Narrow Street, London E.14 (†) (ills. 18, 19)
New warehouse etc., next to Gin Alley
d: des. 1862, exec. 1863
cl: James William Temple & Co.
ctr: Alfred Savill of Chigwell
m: brick, st/drs, t/h
dr: R.A.
r: *Marble Halls* (V & A Exhibition Catalogue, 1973) p. 104
Probably only the part on the S side of street was built. Now all dem.

5. Bromley Palace Estate, Bromley, London
cl: Coles Child (1814–73)

A. Bailiff's Cottage, Widmore Road (†) (ills. 15, 16)
  d: 1863–4
  m: brick, st/drs, t/h, ½tmb
  dr: R.A.
  c: acc. bk, £20 9s, 1863

B. 4–6 Page Heath Lane, Widmore
  d: des. 1865–6
  m: brick, roughcast, t/h
  dr: R.A.
  Probably built by Child's workmen with bricks from the estate brickyards. The R.A. has drawings for two other cottage schemes, one in Queen Anne style, both possibly built and dem. Shaw may also have added an attic storey and chimneys at the rear of Bromley Palace. For his Town Hall project of 1863 see p. 30 and ill. 17.
  ack: Miss Plincke (Bromley Library); Mrs Mattholie

6. Holy Trinity Church, Bingley, Yorkshire
New church, schools, vicarage etc.

A. Church (†) (ills. 40, 41, 227, 228)
  d: des. 1864, main church built 1866–8; tower and steeple revised 1869, exec. 1880–2
  ctrs: J. & W. Foster, 1866–8; Joseph Foulds & Bros., 1880–2
  m: Gilstead stone etc.
  dr: R.A.; R.I.B.A.
  c: acc. bk, £245 12s, 1867–9
  r: ICBS file 6267; *B* 9.6.1866 & 14.11.1868; *Keighley News* 26.5.1866, 3 & 17.6.1881, 7.1.1882, 25.11.1882, & 9.8.1884; Parish Centenary Booklet 1968; *CL* 27.12.1973
  Dem. 1974. Shaw's fittings, now mainly in store at York, included font and pulpit of 1868, reredos and organ-case of 1869–70, and font cover of 1873.

B. Drill Hall (†)
  d: 1867
  m: stone
  dr: R.A.
  A plain shed, presumably exec. and now dem.

C. Schools
  d: des. 1870 etc., exec. 1871–2 and 1879
  m: local stone
  dr: R.A.
  c: acc. bk, £30 14s, 1872
  r: Parish Centenary Booklet 1968
  Plain stone buildings, next to and in character with church. Much extended.

D. Vicarage
  d: 1873–4
  ctrs: Samuel Johnson, and John Ives & Sons; c/w Richard Hartley
  m: local stone
  dr: R.A.
  c. £2355 14s; acc. bk, £138 14s 6d, 1874
  r: Eccl. Comms. file 35983
  A good house, out of the run of Shaw's normal style. Now divided into two, and called White Lodge.

E. Cottingley Chapel, nr. Bingley (†)
  d: des. 1873, exec. 1876
  m: local stone
  dr: R.A.
  c: acc. bk, £25, 1875
  r: Parish Centenary Booklet 1968
  Small plain Gothic chapel in outlying area of parish, now dem. Some cottages in Cottingley have been attributed to Shaw, but not convincingly.

7. Willesley, near Cranbrook, Kent (ills. 20, 21, 22, 63, 64, 94)
Additions to house, and new stables
d: 1864–5 (main work), 1868–9 (studio and stables)
cl: John Callcott Horsley, R.A. (1817–1903)
ctr: G. Cramp of Cranbrook
m: brick, t/h, some ½tmb
dr: one sketch in skb. only, for studio entrance
r: drawing exh. at the Architectural Exhibition, 1865; *B* 13.5.1865; J. C. Horsley, *Recollections of a Royal Academician* (1903) pp. 338–43; *CL* 30.8.1973
Now the Willesley Arms Hotel, and altered in parts.

8. Shops, North Gate, Huddersfield, Yorkshire (†)
d: 1864
m: stone, some t/h
dr: R.A.
This project for two shops was probably executed but dem.

9. Fowlers Park, Hawkhurst, Kent (†) (ill. 111)
Rebuilding, with new front
d: 1864–6
cl: James Gow Steuart (1808–70)
m: brick

dr: R.A.
c: acc. bk, £185 4s., 1865–6
Dem. except for one bay, c.1950.

10. The Rhydd Court, Guarlford, Worcestershire
Connecting link between house and chapel, and completion of chapel during illness of its architect, Charles Hansom
d: 1865–6
cl: Sir Edmund Antony Harley Lechmere (1826–94)
m: brick for link building
dr: R.A.
c: acc. bk, £53 12s., 1866
r: *Malvern Advertiser* 6.8.1864 and 20.1.1866
The work included organ-case, seats, and screen, now gone, and the reredos, still *in situ*.

11. St John's Church, New Briggate, Leeds, Yorkshire (ills. 42, 225)
Church restoration
d: 1866–8
cl: Trustees of Harrison's Charity
ctrs: John Garland & Sons (masons); J. & W. Pearson Bros. (joiners); c/w Isaac Newton
dr: R.I.B.A.; Leeds City Archives; one in church
c: £3906 4s; acc. bk, £235 2s., 1867–9
r: Leeds City Archives DB 209/22, 30 & 31; *E* 27 (1866) p. 242 and 29 (1868) pp. 263–4 & 313; *Leeds Mercury* 1.2.1868; *BN* 7.2.1868; *Thoresby Society Publications* 24 (1919) pp. 190–226; *St John's Church Leeds, 1634–1934*, passim
Work included a new churchyard wall, S porch, font, reredos with Salviati mosaics, and east window. The N vestry was dem., the pulpit moved and sounding board reused as font canopy; the pew doors removed and made into chancel panelling; the choir seating made from old fragments; the reading desk and Founder's Tomb moved; the walls bared of plaster; and the floor repaved. Much of this work was undone or altered in 1884–98.

12. Draycott Villa, Kings Road, Fulham, London S.W.6 (†)
Additions and alterations to house
d: 1866
cl: Capt. Arthur Palliser
ctr: Oliver Pitts

m: brick, rendered
dr: R.A.
c: acc. bk, £28 5s, 1867
r: C. J. Feret, *History of Fulham* (1900) Vol. 2
  p. 68
Work consisted of a new two-bay entrance
  front and extensions to the dining room.
  Later lived in by Holman Hunt, and dem.
  *c.*1903–4.

13. Field Green House, Sandhurst,
  Hawkhurst, Kent
Minor alterations to house
d: des. 1866 etc., exec. 1869
cl: Lt. Col. D'Aguilar
dr: sketches in sketchbook (rough)
c: acc. bk, £23 3s, 1870
Extent unknown.

14. Glen Andred, Groombridge, Sussex (ills.
  23, 24)
New house, lodge and stables
d: 1866–8
cl: Edward William Cooke, R.A. (1811–80)
ctr: George Punnett of Tonbridge
m: brick, t/h
c: acc. bk, £281 1s 10d, 1866–9
r: Diaries of Cooke and two letters from Shaw
  at National Maritime Museum;
  Goldsmiths' Company Archives, Guildhall
  Library; *BN* 3.6.1881; *Mariner's Mirror* 53
  (1967) pp. 111–3; *CL* 6.9.1973
House now divided into two parts, but in
  good condition.
ack: C. R. Cooke

15. Leyswood, Groombridge, Sussex (ills.
  25–29)
New house, stables, lodge, dairy etc.
d: des. 1866 etc., revised and exec. 1868–9
  with later additions including dairy (1871)
  and doors to gateway (1873)
cl: James William Temple (1821–98)
ctr: George Punnett of Tonbridge
m: brick, st/drs, t/h, some ½tmb
dr: R.A.; R.I.B.A.
c: acc. bk, £550, 1869–72; £484 15s 8d, 1875
r: drawing exh. at R.A., 1870, & reprd. in
  BN 31.3.1871; Goldsmiths' Company
  Archives, Guildhall Library; C. L.
  Eastlake, *A History of the Gothic Revival*
  (1872) pp. 342–4; *DEH* 1 pp. 115–8; *CL*
  6.9.1973
Shaw's outbuildings include the lodge at the

end of the drive, the walled garden, and the
dairy (dem.), but not the stud stables away
from the house. A project to bridge the
drive was not exec. Most of the house was
dem. *c.*1955.
ack: Ian Simpson

16. Farnham Bank, Castle Street, Farnham,
  Surrey (†) (ill. 60)
New bank with house over.
d: des. 1866 etc., exec. 1867–9
cl: James Knight (1838–96)
ctr: Frank Birch; carving etc. by Forsyth
m: 2″ bricks, st/drs, ½tmb, some t/h
dr: R.I.B.A.; R.A.
c: acc. bk, £567 14s, 1868–70
r: letters etc. with R.I.B.A. drawings from
  Harold Falkner; Falkner in *CL* 15.3.1941
A work of great elaboration and
  overwhelming scale, dem. in 1933.
  Materials, including chimneys, re-used in
  various Farnham buildings.

17. Cookridge Convalescent Hospital,
  Cookridge, Leeds, Yorkshire (ill. 43)
New hospital and lodge
d: des. 1867, exec. 1868–9
cl: John Metcalfe Smith (1828–70)
ctrs: several, by separate contract
m: stone from site, brick, t/h
dr: R.A.
c: about £13,000; acc. bk, £412 6s, 1868–9
r: *In Memoriam J.M.S.: The Cookridge
  Convalescent Hospital, Leeds* (1871)
Eastern extension of 1893 not by Shaw, and
  another large southern extension (modern).
  Now called Cookridge Hospital.

18. English Church, Quai d'Albret, Lyons,
  France (†) (ill. 205)
d: 1867–9
cl: Charles Seymour Haden (the consul)
m: local stone
dr: R.A.; R.I.B.A.
c: acc. bk, £172 10s 11d, 1868–74
r: *B* 8.6.1867; drawings shown at R.A., 1872,
  and reprd. in *BN* 10.1.1873
Dem. *c.*1965.

19. All Saints' Church, Bingley, Yorkshire
Restoration of Ryshworth Chapel
d: des. 1867 etc., exec. 1869–71

cl: Johnson Atkinson Busfeild (1814–82)
ctrs: Joseph Foulds & Bros. (masons); J. &
   W. Pearson Bros. of Leeds (joiners)
dr: R.A.
c: acc. bk, £26 5s, 1872
r: 43 letters from Shaw and other documents
   at the church; *Keighley News* 7.10.1871; *B*
   14.10.1871
The work included a new screen and new
   stalls. The organ now occupies this chapel
   and the stalls are dispersed. The rest of the
   church was restored at the same time by
   T. H. and F. Healey of Bradford. In
   1881–2 Shaw supplied the church with a
   new font and cover.

20. Meerbrook Church, Staffordshire (ills.
   204, 224)
Rebuilding of church in two stages
d: chancel 1868–70, nave des. 1872, exec.
   1873
cl: for chancel, Elisabeth Condlyffe (1813–78)
   per Hugh Sleigh; for nave, public
   subscription
ctrs: for masonry, J. & J. Barlow, 1869, Paul
   Bailey, 1873; for joinery, W. & J. Nixon
   both times
m: local stone
dr: R.A.
c: acc. bk, £112, 1871–4
r: ICBS file 7496; *BN* 16.10.1868 &
   7.11.1873; *B* 29.11.1873; *Staffordshire
   Advertiser* 22.10.1870 & 1.11.1873
Of the fittings, the E window is by HBB,
   1870; the reredos made by J. & J. Hall,
   1871; the pulpit and font by Edward Ash,
   1873. Altar cloth designed by Shaw, 1870,
   and worked under superintendence of Mrs
   Wardle with help of Mrs Bodley and Mrs
   Sleigh. Other fittings also by Shaw. In 1887
   Shaw got James Heath to alter the window
   cills slightly.
ack: Staffordshire County Planning Office

21. The Corner House, 114 Shortlands Road,
   Beckenham, London (ill. 89)
New house with some later additions
d: 1868–9, with addition of 1872
cl: George Lillie Craik and Mrs Craik (Dinah
   Mulock)
ctr: Samuel Simpson
m: brick, t/h
dr: R.A.; R.I.B.A. (at R.A.)
c: acc. bk, £133 14s 6d, 1869; £25, 1875
r: *BN* 31.5.1872 & 7.6.1872; Mary Howitt,
   An Autobiography (1884) Vol. 2 pp. 172–4

22. Kelsale, Suffolk

A. Altering old 'Town House' into a school
   d: des. 1868 etc., exec. 1869–70
   cl: Revd. George Irving Davies
   ctrs: Thomas Denny and William Kerridge
      of Kelsale
   m: brick, plaster
   dr: R.A.; sketchbook
   c: acc. bk, £30, 1872
   r: *B* 19.11.1870
   At present unoccupied. The work
      involved clearing and restoring the fine
      old roof. The bellcote that Shaw put on
      has recently been removed.

B. Restoration of St Peter's Church, chancel
   only
   d: sketches 1868, plan 1873, work done
      1876–7
   cl: Revd. George Irving Davies
   dr: R.A.; sketchbook
   c: acc. bk, £104 14s, 1877–9
   r: ICBS file 7943
   Shaw intended to restore the whole church,
      but the nave was left to E. S. Prior, who
      reseated and restored it in 1882–3. Shaw
      confined himself to chancel, chancel
      aisle, and vestries. Some of the glass may
      be by HBB.

23. Sissinghurst Place, Sissinghurst Kent
New office wing and stable block for house
   of 1842
d: 1868–9
cl: Adml. Wallace Houston (d.1891)
ctr: William Carr
m: brick, t/h
dr: R.A.
c: acc. bk, £50, 1870
The main house was reconstructed by George
   & Peto in 1894, but burnt in 1948, so that
   only Shaw's part survives.

24. Boxmoor Church, Hertfordshire
Rebuilding in two stages of previous church of
   1829
d: des. 1868–70, nave exec. 1873–4, chancel a
   little earlier
ctr: Nash & Matthews (1873–4)
m: Bath stone
dr: R.A.
c: acc. bk, £228 18s 6d, 1868–74
r: *Hemel Hempstead Gazette* 2.8 and 11.11.1899;
   Kelly's Directory to Essex, Herts and
   Middlesex (1890) p. 758

406

Enlarged by extra bay to nave by T. F.
Woodman in 1893. Stripped of almost all
its original interior features, but probably
never a very interesting design.

25. Youlgreave Church, Derbyshire (ill. 221)
Church restoration
d: 1869–71
ctr: J. & W. Pearson of Leeds
dr: R.A.
c: £3888 5s; acc. bk, £188 19s 3d, 1870–2
r: papers at church; *Derbyshire Times*
16.7.1870; *A* 30.7.1886 (ill.)
A thorough restoration of the structure, with
new pews, stalls, lectern, pulpit, and
reredos, etc. A screen was projected but not
executed.

26. Whitwell-on-the-Hill, Yorkshire.
New school
d: des. 1869, revised 1870 (twice), much
simplified and exec. 1875
cl: Sir Edmund Antony Harley Lechmere
(1826–94)
ctr: Seth Tinsley
m: stone
dr: R.A.
c: acc. bk, £50, 1875
The design built is of minimal interest
compared to earlier schemes. Shaw also
designed in 1868–9 a large 'cottage' at
Whitwell for Lechmere, but it was not
built.

27. West Wickham House, High Street, West
Wickham, London (ill. 112)
Remodelling of a house of 1856 by W. M.
Teulon, and new stables
d: des. 1869, exec. 1870–1
cl: William McAndrew Steuart
ctr: Samuel Simpson
m: brick
dr: R.A.
c: acc. bk, £400, 1871–2
r: Sale Catalogue, 1875
Now very much altered on main front, and
stables dem., but the garden front still
identifiable.

28. Jesmond Dene Banqueting Hall, Jesmond
Dene, Newcastle
Additions, including a secondary hall, new
stairs from entrance, and new lodge

d: 1869–70
cl: Sir William Armstrong (1810–1900)
m: stone
dr: R.A.
c: *see* Cragside
r: J. C. Horsley, *Recollections of a Royal
Academician* (1903) pp. 256–7
Likely to be dem. except for lodge (1975).

29. Cragside, Rothbury, Northumberland
Works for Sir William Armstrong
(1810–1900)

A. Enlargement of shooting lodge into a large
country house, by stages (ills. 45–50, 56,
98)
d: des. 1869 etc. Library and dining room
etc. exec. 1870–2; entrance front and the
three towers 1872–5; drawing room
wing, 1883–5.
ctrs: estate workmen; carving by Forsyth,
1870–2
m: dressed freestone from estate, some
½tmb with roughcast
dr: R.A., R.I.B.A.; and one of tower in
possession of Mr J. C. H. Templer
c: acc. bk., £1612 18s 10d, 1870–6
(including work at Jesmond); £507 13s
8d, 1884–6
r: drawings exh. at R.A., 1872, and reprd.
in *BN* 10.5.1872 & 8.11.1872; and at R.A.
1883, and reprd. in *A* 7.7.1883; *CL*
14.4.1900; D. D. Dixon, *Upper Coquetdale*
(1903) pp. 430–442; Mark Girouard in
CL 18 and 25.12.1969 and *The Victorian
Country House* (1971) pp. 141–6; D.
Dougan, *The Great Gun-Maker* (1971)
pp. 119–122
Intact with furniture and fittings, some by
Shaw. The billiard room and some other
rooms on the E side are not his.

B. Addycombe Cottages, Rothbury
d: 1874–5
ctrs: estate workmen
m: local stone with some ½tmb
Attrib. Two blocks of cottages planned with
front to back living rooms and entrance
to upper flats from the backs. Apparently
Shaw's only estate work for Armstrong.

30. Church Preen, Shropshire
cl: Arthur Sparrow (1826–98)
ctr: Samuel Simpson
c: acc. bk, £788 11s 11d, 1870–2

A. Preen Manor (†) (ill. 73)
Rebuilding of house
d: des. 1869 etc., exec. 1870–1
m: local stone, brick chimneys, ½tmb, some
t/h
dr: V & A; R.A.
r: drawing exh. at R.A., 1871, & reprd. in
BN 11.8.1871; Arthur Sparrow, *History
of Church Preen* (1898) pp. 66–9
Almost wholly dem., but house on site
incorporates fragments and fine walled
garden partly survives.

B. Church Preen School
d: 1870
m: local stone, brick, ½tmb
dr: R.A.
Pleasant and attractive village school.

31. Hillside, Groombridge, Kent
New house with stable, and possibly one
cottage
d: 1870–1, with addition of bay to front,
1874
cl: William Cotton Oswell (1818–93)
ctr: George Punnett of Tonbridge
m: brick, t/h, some ½tmb
dr: R.A.
c: acc. bk, £120, 1871
r: E. W. Cooke's diary, National Maritime
Museum; W. E. Oswell, *William Cotton
Oswell* (1900) Vol. 2 pp. 104–7

32. Grims Dyke, Old Redding, Harrow
Weald, London (ills. 77–79)
New house, with lodge and possibly also
stables
d: 1870–2
cl: Frederick Goodall, R.A. (1822–1904)
ctrs: house, Jackson & Shaw; lodge,
Frederick Harler
m: brick, st/drs, t/h, ½tmb
dr: R.A.; R.I.B.A.
c: acc. bk, £300, 1870–2
r: drawings exh. at R.A., 1872, & reprd. in
BN 6.9.1872; *Architecture* 2 (1897)
pp. 355–368; *A.A. Notes* 14 (1899)
p. 106; F. Goodall, *Reminiscences* (1902)
pp. 279–282
Billiard room added by Arthur Cawston
c.1885, and studio chimneypiece and
other additions by Ernest George and
Peto for W. S. Gilbert c.1890–1.

33. Ightham Mote, Kent
Restoration of hall and its lobby, with new
panelling, doors and fireplace
d: des. 1870–1, exec. 1872
cl: Charles Selby-Bigge (1834–89)
dr: R.A.
r: *CL* 23.3.1907
A discreet renovation.

34. Jesmond Dene House, Jesmond,
Newcastle
Gradual additions to house towards the Dene
d: rear wing 1870–1; rooms towards front
1875; billiard room 1885
cl: Capt. Andrew Noble (1831–1915)
ctr: T. & J. Phillipson, 1870–1
m: dressed stone
dr: R.A.
c: acc. bk, £164 17s 6d, 1872; £100, 1886
Now much altered internally. The house was
greatly enlarged by F. W. Rich in 1896–7,
when the original part was demolished and
rebuilt. Similarities to Cragside are
deliberate, as Noble was Armstrong's right-
hand man.

35. Harperbury (now Harper House), Harper
Lane, Radlett, Herts (ills. 99, 101, 102)
New house (cf. Houndswood), and
outbuildings
d: 1871–2
cl: John Oddie
ctr: Manley & Rogers
m: brick, t/h
dr: R.A.
c: acc. bk, £156 6s, 1872

36. Houndswood, Harper Lane, Radlett,
Herts (ills. 100, 103, 104)
New house (cf. Harperbury) lodge and stables
d: 1871–2
cl: Iltid A. Nicholl (1837–99)
ctr: Manley & Rogers
m: brick, t/h
dr: R.A.
c: acc. bk, £303 1s 3d, 1872; t of £4917
r: G.L.C. Record Office, B/HIG/6 (tenders)
Small extension, 1900.

37. 18 Hyde Park Gate, London S.W.7 (ill.116)
New house, for subletting
d: 1871
cl: Edward William Cooke, R.A. (1811–80)

ctr: Manley & Rogers
m: stock brick, st/drs
c: £2029; acc. bk, £100, 1871
r: Diaries of Cooke and one letter of Shaw's at the National Maritime Museum; *Survey of London* XXXVIII p. 36

38. Lower Thames Street, London E.C.3 (†) (ill. 113)
New warehouse at corner with Water Lane
d: 1871
cl: Shaw Savill & Co.
ctr: Browne & Robinson
m: brick, st/drs
dr: R.A.
c: acc. bk, £386 10s 6d, 1871–2

39. New Zealand Chambers, 34–5 Leadenhall Street, London E.C.3 (†) (ills. 114, 115)
New shipping offices with lettable space
d: 1871–3
cl: Shaw Savill & Co.
ctr: Ashby & Horner; carving by Forsyth
m: 2″ bricks, cement coving, Portland stone base
dr: R.I.B.A.; R.A.
c: acc. bk. £715 15s, 1872–4
r: drawing exh. at R.A., 1873, and reprd. in *BN* 5.9.1873; *DEB*
Destroyed by bombing, 1941.

40. New Groombridge Schools, Groombridge, Sussex
New school and mission room, with later addition
d: 1871–2; classroom added, 1887
ctr: John Morris of East Grinstead, 1871–2; Aaron Moon, 1887
m: brick, ½tmb, t/h
dr: R.A.
c: £1120 2s 3d; acc. bk, £50 12s 6d, 1872
r: Goldsmiths Company Archives, Guildhall Library; *A* 22.6.1872
Built for combined church and school use. Mainly dem., except for the master's house.

41. 66 Wigmore Street, London W.1
New warehouse, factory and showroom behind the old frontage
d: 1871–2
cl: Messrs. Benham & Sons
c: acc. bk, £193 7s, 1872

r: MBW Minutes of Proceedings, 7.7.1871
Much altered, but still surviving and of some structural interest. One showcase for the display of Benham's wares remains.

42. Spout Hall, 66–68 St Edwards Street, Leek, Staffordshire (ill. 61)
Two new shops with houses above
d: 1871–3
cl: Hugh Sleigh
m: stone, ½tmb, brick chimney
dr: R.A.
c: acc, bk £44 only, 1875
A simpler version of the Farnham Bank composition
ack: Leek Public Library

43. Hughley Church, Shropshire
Restoration of roof
d: 1871–2
cl: Earl of Bradford (1819–98)
dr: R.A.
c: acc. bk, £70 8s, 1873

44. Bourton Cottage (Bourton Manor), Bourton, Shropshire
Extensive additions to house
d: des. 1871, revised and exec. 1874
cl: Lord Wenlock (1818–80)
m: stone, t/h, ½tmb, roughcast
dr: R.A.
c: acc. bk, £236 12s, 1874–5
Almost separate from main part of house. Poorly redecorated internally, *c.*1900.

45. Gorehill, Petworth, Sussex
New house
d: 1871–2
cl: Henry Upton (1817–1902)
ctrs: George Pulling and W. H. Lascelles
m: Pulborough stone, brick chimneys, ½tmb
dr: R.A.
c: acc. bk, £200, 1872–3
A medium-sized house with some limp exterior detail but good interior features, notably joinery.
ack: Sir Leslie Fry

46. Eldersfield Lawn School, Eldersfield, Worcestershire
New school
d: 1871–2

cl: Sir Edmund Antony Harley Lechmere
  (1826–94)
ctr: James Griffiths
m: local stone
dr: Worcester County Record Office (with
  specification)
Simple building with bellcote, now extended.

47. Madresfield Court, Madresfield,
  Worcestershire
Estate works
cl: Earl Beauchamp (1830–91)
c: acc. bk, £44 12s 6d, 1872

A. North lodge
  d: 1871–2
  m: stone base, brick chimney, ½tmb
  dr: R.A.

B. Restoration of dovecote
  d: 1872
  m: brick, st/drs
  dr: R.A.
Another lodge is sometimes wrongly
  attributed to Shaw.

48. Longstone Church, Great Longstone,
  Derbyshire
Thorough restoration
d: des. 1871 etc., exec. 1872–3 with later
  additions
cl: George Thomas Wright
ctr: Joseph Brown & Co. of Matlock Bridge;
  woodcarving by James Knox, ironwork by
  James Leaver
dr: R.A., and with Wright family
c: acc. bk, £123 2s 6d, 1872–4
r: Papers including reports and 9 letters from
  Shaw with Wright family; ICBS file 7464;
  High Peak News 25.5.1872; *B* 4.12.1897;
  J. N. Tarn, *Journal of Derbyshire
  Archaeological Society*, forthcoming article
Work included rebuilding top of tower,
  stripping and replastering all walls, and
  recasting chancel with new windows and
  vestry. New seats and woodwork
  throughout, also font (with cover), pulpit,
  and organ. East and N aisle windows by
  HBB, with whom Shaw designed two other
  S aisle windows, in 1897 and 1907–8.
ack: Mrs V. Wright

49. Tarring Neville Church, Sussex
Small-scale restoration of chancel

d: 1871–2
dr: R.A.
r: *A* 11.11.1887, with illustration of a more
  elaborate scheme
Work comprised new E lancets, roof, and
  stalls.

50. Yateley Hall, Yateley, Hampshire
Addition of staircase and new south wing
d: 1871–2
cl: M. de Winton Corry
m: brick
c: acc. bk, £74 12s 6d, 1871–2

51. Hammerwood House, Sussex
Estate works
cl: Oswald Augustus Smith (1826–1902)

A. School and mission room (ill. 214)
  d: 1872
  ctr: John Morris of East Grinstead
  m: brick, t/h, ½tmb
  dr: R.A.
  c: acc. bk, £96 3s 6d, 1872–3
  Originally a very attractive building, with
    diapered brickwork and traceried
    window to mission room. Now converted
    into cottages and denuded of its *flèche*.

B. Bower Cottages
  d: 1874
  ctr: Frank Birch of Farnham
  m: brick, t/h
  dr: R.I.B.A. (at R.A.)
  c: acc. bk, £27 17s 6d, 1875
  A double cottage to E of school

52. Painshill, Cobham, Surrey
New servants' wing, and some alterations to
  house
d: 1872
cl: Charles John Leaf
ctr: Abraham Newland
m: brick, stuccoed
dr: R.A.
c: acc. bk, £348 19s 6d, 1872–3
The wing is plain, and the alterations to
  Jupp's house of 1778 are insignificant.
  Payment must include costs of drawing up
  plans for a large half-timbered house,
  illustrated in *A* 2.7.1886 and wrongly
  attributed to a site near Oxted by Robert
  Shaw and Blomfield (ill. 70).

53. Boldre Grange, Boldre, Hampshire (ill. 75)

New house, with stables

d: des. 1872 etc., exec. 1873–4, billiard room added 1879

cl: John Lane Shrubb (1840–84)

ctr: Frank Birch of Farnham

m: brick, st/drs, ½tmb

dr: R.I.B.A.; R.A.

c: acc. bk, £403 17s 8d, 1873–5; £111 15s, 1879.

r: drawing exh. at R.A., 1874, & reprd. in *A* 22.8.1874

Good and original house, with excellent interior joinery. Now converted internally into separate dwellings and much altered. Also connected, a stone pulpit designed by Shaw for Boldre Church, 1876, in memory of Revd. Charles Shrubb; *B* 8.4.1876 (ill. 230).

54. Lowther Lodge, Kensington Gore, London S.W.7 (ills. 117–119, 189)

New house

d: des. 1872 etc., exec. 1873–5

cl: William Lowther, M.P. (1821–1912)

ctr: W. H. Lascelles; c/w W. James

m: 2″ bricks, moulded brick drs, some slate-hanging

dr: R.A.; R.I.B.A.; Royal Geographical Society

c: acc. bk, £1124, 1873–7

r: drawing exh. at R.A., 1874, & reprd. in *BN* 25.6.1875; *BN* 5.2.1875; *The King* 3.5.1902; *DEH* 1.120–2 and 2.142–3; *Survey of London* XXXVIII pp. 327–331

Billiard room added in SW corner after 1882, and large extensions to E in 1928–30, after the house had been taken over by the Royal Geographical Society.

55. Ditton House, Thames Ditton, Surrey (†)

New stables, and possibly alterations to house

d: des. 1872, exec. 1873

cl: William Wentworth Fitzwilliam Hume Dick (d.1892)

ctr: W. Callingham

m: brick

dr: R.A.

c: acc. bk, £57 7s 6d, 1873

Shaw also designed an unexecuted chapel for Dick for Kiltegan Church, Ireland, *c.* 1871 (R.A. drawings).

56. St Michael's Church, Bournemouth, Hants (ills. 206, 207)

New church, built in stages

d: des. 1872–3, revised design exec. by stages, nave and aisles 1874–6, chancel 1882–3

cl: Revd. Alexander Morden Bennett

ctr: Samuel Clarke, 1874–6, E. Abley, 1882–3

m: local stone

dr: R.A.

c: acc. bk, £321 13s 4d, 1875; £137 5s 8d, 1883

r: drawing of first design exh. at R.A., 1873, and reprd. in *BN* 23.5.1873; ICBS file 7646; *BN* 30.5.1873; *Bournemouth Observer* 26.1.1876; *A* 20.8.1886 (illustrating revised design)

No known fittings are Shaw's, though some aisle windows are by HBB. Chancel poorly decorated by R. G. Pinder; SE tower designed by J. O. Scott, 1899–1901; S chancel chapel by T. G. Jackson, 1919–20; W narthex by W. D. Caroe, 1930.

57. Gawsworth Rectory, Gawsworth, Cheshire

New dining room and stairs, and alteration and restoration of rest of the house

d: 1873–4

cl: Hon. & Revd. Henry Augustus Stanhope (1845–1933)

ctr: W. H. Lascelles

m: brick, ½tmb

dr: R.A.

c: *c.*£1100; acc. bk, £61 8s 6d, 1874

r: 16 letters from Shaw and other papers at R.I.B.A.

58. Compton, Angles Road, Streatham, London S.W.16 (†)

Addition to house

d: 1873

cl: George H. Best

c: acc. bk, £51 18s, 1873

r: MBW Minutes of Proceedings, 3.1.1873

Demolished

59. 2 Cromwell Houses, 23 Cromwell Road, London S.W.7.

Alterations internally, especially to dining room.

d: 1873

cl: Charles Loyd Norman (1833–89)

dr: R.A.

c: acc. bk, £218 14s 6d, 1874

No trace now remaining.

60. Hopedene, Holmbury St Mary, Surrey
New house and lodge
d: 1873–4
cl: Hensleigh Wedgwood (1803–91)
ctr: W. H. Lascelles; c/w Allan Clark
m: brick, t/h, ½tmb
c: acc. bk, £267 10s 5d, 1873–4
r: drawing exh. at R.A., 1874, and reprd. in
   BN 8.5.1874
A good house, extended (not by Shaw) in
   1878–9, and again by Percy Ginham, who
   added the transverse nursery wing in 1902.
   Converted into separate dwellings and
   much altered.
ack: W. Garner, A. C. Cross.

61. Meanwood Towers, Stonegate Road,
   Leeds, Yorkshire
Some decoration, including panelling, to
   house by E. W. Pugin after the latter's
   bankruptcy
d: 1873
cl: Thomas Stewart Kennedy
dr: R.A.
c: acc. bk, £66 3s 6d, 1873–4
Not now discernible.

62. Burghclere Church, Hants
New chancel and spire and general
   restoration of church of 1838
d: des. 1873, exec. 1874–5
cl: Revd. George Raymond Portal
ctr: William G. Adey of Newbury
m: stone
dr: R.A.
c: acc. bk, £134 2s, 1875–6
r: *Newbury Weekly News* 16.5.1875; *B* 5.6.1875
Shaw's role was only supervisory and some of
   the detail seems to have been left to Adey.
   But the reredos (now altered) and the
   sanctuary dado are his, as is the general
   design. The spire has now been removed.
ack: Sir Godfrey Nicholson, Bt.

63. Tongswood Estate, Hawkhurst, Kent
New smithy cottage, on main road
d: 1873–4
cl: William Cotterill
m: brick, t/h
dr: R.A.
c: acc. bk, £24 14s 6d, 1875
Now called The Old Forge, with the smithy
   incorporated into the cottage. Tongswood
   is now St Ronan's School.

64. St John's Gate, Clerkenwell, London
   E.C.1
Restoration and additions to old gatehouse
d: main restoration 1873–4, adjoining house
   built 1876
cl: Sir Edmund Antony Harley Lechmere
   (1826–94)
ctr: A. Braid & Co., 1876
m: brick for house
dr: R.A. (Gate only)
c: acc. bk, £116 5s 6d, 1878
r: *B* 1.7.1876 (t); *B* 22.11.1912
Shaw restored the gateway and added a room
   on the W side at the top, then later built
   the house to the NE. Much of his discreet
   work to the gatehouse was obscured by
   J. O. Scott's additions of 1903.

65. Convent of Sisters of Bethany, St
   Clement's Road, Bournemouth, Hants (ills.
   130, 131)
New convent, built by stages
d: Original part (Orphanage) des. 1873, exec.
   1874–5; Porter's lodge, Sister's wing, and
   some back additions 1878–80; small
   addition over link building 1903–4, and
   new porch, 1905
cl: Etheldreda Anna Benett (1824–1913)
ctr: Frank Birch of Farnham (1874–80)
m: mass concrete, brick, t/h some st/drs
c: acc. bk, £300, 1874–5
r: 9 letters from Shaw and many documents
   at Convent
Later additions include an Infirmary of 1897
and W. G. Newton's link building and chapel
of 1928–9.
ack: Sister Felicity, S.S.B.

66. 49 (formerly 46) Gloucester Square,
   London W.2
Decoration of the dining room, etc.
d: 1874
cl: Henry Lucas
dr: R.A.
c: acc. bk, £150, 1874–5

67. Meadowside, 58 Holden Road, Finchley,
   London N.12 (†)
New house, near Woodside Park station
d: 1874
cl: William Morgan Brown
ctr: Henry Cooper
m: brick, t/h
dr: R.A.

c: acc. bk, £65 3s 7d, 1874
A smallish house, dem. 1967 without record.

68. Brooms Farmhouse, West Dean, West
    Sussex
New farmhouse
d: 1874
cl: Frederick Bower
m: squared flints, brick drs, t/h, some ½tmb
dr: R.A.
A pretty and remote house.

69. Martins Bank, 68 Lombard Street,
    London E.C.3 (†)
Alterations, and addition of new offices at
    rear to face Change Alley
d: 1874–6, with some extra work, 1880
cl: Messrs. Martin & Co.
ctr: Ashby & Horner, c/w C. Leach
m: brick
dr: R.A.; R.I.B.A. (at R.A.)
c: acc. bk, £937 5s, 1875–6; £228 4s 6d, 1881
r: 5 letters of Shaw's and other papers in
    archives of Barclay's Bank; *A* 19.9.1874 (t)
Further additions by Ernest Newton, 1913–1
    The whole bank was dem. and rebuilt by
    Herbert Baker in the 1930s, and the only
    relic of Shaw's copious work is the
    grasshopper symbol on the wall in Change
    Alley.
ack: Miss K. Bryon

70. 196 Queen's Gate, London S.W.7 (ills.
    166, 167, 190, 191)
New house
d: 1874–6, and some redecoration *c.*1880
cl: John Postle Heseltine (1843–1929)
ctr: W. H. Lascelles
m: brick, moulded and cut brick drs.
dr: R.I.B.A.; R.A. (at R.I.B.A.)
c: acc. bk, £575, 1875–7
r: drawing exh. at R.A., 1875, & reprd. in
    BN 4.6.1875; *DEB*; *Survey of London*
    XXXVIII pp. 331–3
Converted into flats in late 1920s, when the
    planning was destroyed and ground floor
    elevation altered.

71. Upper House, near Shamley Green,
    Surrey (ill. 91)
Three campaigns of additions to small house
d: hall, drawing room, and offices to N,
    1874; sitting room to W and bedroom

over, 1880; new staircase and possibly
    further additions, *c.*1887–8
cl: Mrs Elinor Guthrie, later Mrs Arbuthnot
    (d.1911)
ctr: Frank Birch of Farnham, 1874
m: brick, ½tmb, t/h
dr: R.A.
c: acc. bk, £203 16s, 1875
r: *B* 22.11.1912; V. Stuart Wortley, *Grow Old
    Along With Me* (1952) pp. 31–2
Further additions and later alterations make
    this house difficult to disentangle, but some
    of Shaw's interiors survive.

72. St James' Church, Hebden Bridge,
    Yorkshire
New chancel to church of 1833 and
    restoration of nave
d: 1874–6
cl: Revd. G. Sowden
ctr: J. H. Thorp of Leeds; J. Aldam Heaton,
    decorator
m: stone
dr: R.A.
c: acc. bk, £162 16s 9d, 1876–7
r: *BA* 21.4.1876 & 9.6.1876; *B* 30.12.1876
Shaw also produced plans to rebuild the nave.
    Work included a new organ, pulpit, dwarf
    screen, etc., and many hangings, as well as
    a complete set of HBB windows. Later
    alterations have left only the structure,
    pulpit and windows intact.

73. 6 Ellerdale Road, London N.W.3 (ills.
    140–144)
New house for himself, built by stages
d: des. 1874 etc.; main part exec. 1875–6;
    drawing room wing 1885–6, bay added to
    back on ground floor 1893
ctr: W. H. Lascelles, 1875–6; c/w Allan Clark
m: brick, some t/h
dr: R.A.; R.I.B.A.
c: £4719 9s 9d, 1875–6; £2892 17s 4d 1885–7
    (figures from Robert Shaw partly including
    some of cost of land)
r: Robert Shaw *passim*; *B* 25.3.1876; *BA*
    19.11.1880 and in Vol. 35 (1891) *passim*;
    DEB; *BN* 4.1.1901; *The King* 11.10.1902;
    W. Shaw Sparrow (ed.), *The Modern Home*
    (1906) pp. 105–6 and *The British Home of
    To-day* (1904) (photographs)
Further alterations contemplated but not
    exec., 1901. The house was sold in 1935
    and serious alterations made, including the

curtailing of the back drawing room, removal of front drawing room, and changing in position of entrance door.

74. Wispers, nr. Stedham, Sussex
New house and stables
d: 1874–6
cl: Alexander Scrimgeour
ctr: Frank Birch of Farnham
m: local stone, ½tmb
dr: R.I.B.A.; R.A.
c: acc. bk, £574 11s 6d, 1875–7
r: drawing exh. at R.A., 1876, and reprd. in *BN* 2.6.1876
Much extended *c*.1920, but perhaps always a disappointing house compared to the R.A. perspective. Fine site. Now St Cuthman's School.

75. 42a Chepstow Villas, London W.11
New studio in garden of villa, facing Denbigh Road
d: 1874–5
cl: Thomas Sidney Cooper, R.A. (1803–1902)
ctr: W. H. Lascelles
m: brick
c: acc. bk, £50, 1875
r: MBW Minutes of Proceedings 26.2.1875; T. S. Cooper, *My Life* (1890) Vol. 2, pp. 83–4
Pleasant stock brick building, single-storey, still in good condition.

76. Sutton Place, Surrey (ill. 97)
Restoration of fabric, and minor alterations
d: 1875–6
cl: Frederick Harrison (1799–1881)
ctr: Frank Birch of Farnham
m: Blashfield's terracotta for window frames
dr: R.I.B.A.
c: acc. bk, £63, 1876
r: odd papers at R.I.B.A.; Frederic Harrison, *Annals of an Old Manor House* (1893) pp. 118, 129, etc.
Tactful restoration, now indiscernible. Shaw's redecoration of some of the smaller rooms has been swept away.

77. Cheyne House, 18 Chelsea Embankment, London S.W.3 (ill. 169)
New house and stables
d: 1875–7

cl: George Matthey
ctr: Charles Jarrett of Croydon
m: brick, st/drs
dr: R.A.; R.I.B.A.; G.L.C. Record Office
c: acc. bk, £853 4s 6d, 1876–8
r: *B* 29.7.1876
Now a nurses' home, with the planning mainly intact. An extension not shown on the drawings, towards Royal Hospital Road, is attributable to Shaw.

78. Swan House, 17 Chelsea Embankment, London S.W.3 (ill. 171)
New house and stables
d: 1875–7
cl: Wickham Flower
ctr: Charles Jarrett of Croydon; some interior decoration by Morris & Co.
m: brick
dr: R.A.; V & A; G.L.C. Record Office
c: acc. bk, £421 12s, 1876–9
r: drawing exh. at R.A., 1877, & reprd. in *BN* 15.6.1877; *DEB*; *Marble Halls* (V & A Exhibition Catalogue, 1973) pp. 86–7
Damaged in the war, and since gutted internally. The stables facing Royal Hospital Road have undergone alterations.

79. Webster House, High Street, Cranbrook, Kent
Addition of corridor and new room at rear
d: 1875–6
cl: Thomas Webster, R.A. (1800–86)
m: brick, t/h
dr: R.A.
c: acc. bk, £25, 1875
Small addition of some charm, but poorly built. Incised plasterwork ceiling like that at Willesley.

80. 8 Melbury Road, London W.14 (ills. 120, 122)
New house
d: 1875–6
cl: Marcus Stone (1840–1921)
ctr: W. H. Lascelles
m: brick, concrete oriels
dr: R.A.
c: acc. bk, £231 18s, 1876–7
r: *BN* 38 (1880) pp. 525, 558, & 584; *BA* 19.5.1882; M. B. Adams, *Artists' Homes* (1883); *Art Annual* 1896 pp. 26–31; *DEB*; *Survey of London* XXXVII pp. 143–4; *CL* 16.11.1972

Central oriel raised by Macartney in about
1881–2. Converted into flats and gutted
internally c.1950.

81. 31 (formerly 11) Melbury Road, London
W.14 (ill. 121)
New house
d: 1875–7
cl: S. Luke Fildes (1843–1927)
ctr: W. H. Lascelles
m: brick
dr: R.A.; R.I.B.A. (at R.A.)
c: acc. bk, £226 10s, 1876
r: letters from Shaw in V & A Library; *BN*
38 (1880) pp. 702, 706–7, & 746–7; M. B.
Adams, *Artists' Homes* (1883); *Art Annual*
1895 pp. 29–31; *DEB;* L. V. Fildes, *Luke
Fildes, R.A.* (1968), *passim; CL* 16.11.1972;
Survey of London XXXVII pp. 148–9
Studio windows altered 1881 and winter
studio added 1885. Now in flats, but with
some interiors surviving. Front wall
damaged in war and not fully rebuilt.

82. St Swithun's Church, Bournemouth,
Hants (ill. 208)
New church, built in stages
d: des. 1875 etc; chancel exec. 1876; nave
revised 1878, c.1880 and again in 1888, and
exec. 1891–2
ctr: Hale of Salisbury, 1876; reredos carved
by Earp
m: stone
dr: R.A.; and some at church
c: acc. bk, £150, 1877; £313 10s 6d, 1891–5
r: *B* 3.6.1876 & 27.1.1877; *Bournemouth
Observer* 30.12.1876
Apart from the reredos, none of the present
fittings is certainly Shaw's, though the
chancel screen might be attrib. Alterations
and additions have been made on the N
side, including a new vestry.

83. Chigwell Hall, Chigwell, Essex (ills.
105–7)
New house
d: 1875–6
cl: Alfred Savill (d.1905)
ctr: probably Savill's workmen
m: brick, t/h
dr: R.A.
c: acc. bk, £200, 1876–8
Now institutionalized, much altered internally,
and with poor additions on S side.

84. Pierrepont, Frensham, Surrey (ills. 54, 74)
New house, incorporating old core
d: des. 1875 etc., exec. 1876–8
cl: Richard Henry Combe (1829–1900)
ctr: Frank Birch of Farnham; woodcarving by
Knox of Lambeth
m: Churt stone, brick chimneys, ½tmb, some
t/h
dr: R.I.B.A.; R.A.
c: acc. bk, £1374 13s 1d, 1876–9
r: drawing exh. at R.A., 1876, and reprd. in
BN 26.5.1876; *CL* 10.10.1903
Extended eastwards, but probably not to
Shaw's designs. Stables of 1888 are by
H. T. Keates of Petersfield (*BN*
18.10.1889), and there is no evidence for
estate buildings by Shaw, though he made
a lay-out plan for outbuildings in 1878.
Now a school, but with remaining interior
features.

85. Low Bentham, Yorkshire

A. Restoration of church, with new chancel
(ill. 222)
d: des. 1875 etc., exec. 1876–8, with later
fittings
cl: Mrs Alfred Foster
ctrs: William Cumberland (masons); J. H.
Thorp of Leeds (joiners); reredos carved
by Earp; ironwork by Leaver; organ-
case carved by Knox of Lambeth
m: local stone
dr: R.A.
c: acc. bk, £199 19s 8d, 1876–8
r: *BA* 3.5.1878 & 23.5.1890
Virtually a complete rebuilding. Full set of
fittings, including seats, stalls, pulpit, and
stone reredos. Organ-case by Shaw and
Lethaby, 1886; font by Lethaby, c.1890.
Several HBB windows, the W one
designed by Henry Holiday.

B. Rebuilding of Rectory
d: 1884–5
cl: Revd. Walker Joy
ctrs: William Cumberland (masons); J. H.
Thorp (joiners)
m: stone, some roughcast
dr: R.A.
c: acc. bk, £150, 1887
Discreet house built round an old core.
Now the local Grammar School, with
some extensions.

86. Adcote, nr. Little Ness, Shropshire (ills. 55, 83–5)
New house round old core, stables, and two lodges
d: des. 1875 etc., exec. 1876–81
cl: Mrs Rebecca Darby (1820–1909)
ctr: Hale & Son of Salisbury; J. Aldam Heaton, decorator
m: estate stone, brick chimneys, some ½tmb
dr: V & A; R.A.; R.I.B.A.
c: £29,792 (builders' bill, 1881); acc. bk, £1530 7s 2d, 1877–81
r: *B* 11.11.1876 (t); drawing exh. at R.A., 1878, & reprd. in *BN* 20.12.1878; *CL* 25.12.1909 & 22.10.1970; Mark Girouard, *The Victorian Country House* (1971) pp. 158–60; bills in possession of Lady Labouchere
Justly recognized as Shaw's maturest house of the 1870s. Now a school, and in good state inside as well as out.

87. Merrist Wood, Worplesdon, Surrey (ills. 65, 68, 93)
New house, pair of lodges, and probably also stables
d: des. 1875 etc., exec. 1876–7
cl: Charles Peyto Shrubb (1837–99)
ctr: Frank Birch of Farnham
m: Bargate stone, brick chimneys, ½tmb, t/h
dr: R.I.B.A.; R.A.
c: acc. bk, £403 3s 6d, 1877–8
r: drawings exh. at R.A., 1877, & reprd. in *BN* 25.5 & 29.6.1877; E. Willmott, *English House Design* (1911) pp. 166–71
Stables built to a different design than that of drawings. The house was enlarged to the E in 1917–18, when the internal planning was also much altered. Hall now partitioned, and few surviving interiors. Now an Agricultural College.

88. Oakley House, Bromley Common, London
Additions at N end of house
d: 1875–6
cl: Charles Loyd Norman (1833–89)
ctr: William Smith & Co.
m: brick
dr: R.A.
c: acc. bk, £222 2s 3s, 1876
A very plain stock brick two-storey addition to the dower house of The Rookery. In 1872 Shaw had designed a completely new house for the site, for which Norman paid him £200.

89. 395 Oxford Street, London W.1 (†)
New shop and shop-front
d: 1875–6
cl: Messrs. Marks & Co.
ctr: W. H. Lascelles
m: brick, white woodwork etc.
dr: R.A.
r: G. C. Williamson, *Murray Marks and his Friends* (1919) pp. 12–14
An important landmark of the Queen Anne revival, but long dem.

90. Overbury, Worcestershire
Estate works
cls: Robert Martin (1807–98) and Richard Biddulph Martin (1838–1916)

A. Two cottages near school
d: 1875 (insc.)
m: stone
Attrib.

B. School
d: des. 1875, exec. 1876–7
ctr: Charles Ancill of Overbury
m: stone
dr: R.A.
c: acc. bk £58 9s 10d, 1877
In a restrained Gothic, with bellcote. Small addition by Ernest Newton, 1905, and a more recent one.

C. Conversion of cottage opposite gates to Overbury Court into a lodge
d: 1877–8
m: stone, ½tmb
dr: R.A.
Rebuilding, with small extension.

D. Roadside fountain
d: 1878–9
m: stone, timber
dr: R.A.
Probably designed by Newton. Now a bus shelter.

E. New Post Office and Stores (ill. 62)
d: 1879
m: stone, ½tmb
dr: R.A.
Charming village shop. Extended at rear by Newton, 1905
The R.A. Collection contains one further cottage design of 21.12.1878, probably not built.

F. Restoration of church
   d: 1879–80
   ctr: Thomas Collins of Tewkesbury
   dr: R.A. (plan only)
   r: Charles Glynn, notes on Overbury in
      Worcester County Record Office
      899:38 acc. 2367
   Conservative restoration of fabric. New
      seats in part of nave, stalls, and bases to
      font and pulpit.

G. New gates to Overbury Court
   d: 1887
   dr: R.A.
   Stone piers and simple iron gates.

H. The Manor House, Conderton
   Reconstruction work, mostly internal
   d: 1888
   m: stone etc.
   dr: 1 sheet at Overbury Court, showing
      approaches
   c: acc. bk, £117 13s, 1888 ('Conderton
      etc.')
   Discreet alterations, partly intact.

J. Silver Rill, Overbury Hill
   Alterations and additions to large cottage
   d: 1891
   ctr: Thomas Collins
   r: 2 letters from Shaw, at Overbury Court
   Now much altered and reduced.

K. New village hall
   d: 1895–6
   ctr: Charles Ancill
   m: stone ashlar
   dr: R.A.
   r: various letters from Shaw at Overbury
      Court
   Sizeable, dignified building facing cricket
   pitch.

L. Engine and Dynamo House
   d: 1898
   ctr: Collins & Godfrey of Tewkesbury
   m: stone
   r: two letters from Shaw at Overbury
      Court
   Small building down lane to S of Court,
   altered.

M. Overbury Court
   Major extensions and alterations
   d: small alterations, 1887; new wing
      1897–1900
   ctrs: Collins & Godfrey; Robert Christie,

decorator; Farmer & Brindley, carvers
   (all 1897)
m: local stone, Bath st/drs
dr: R.I.B.A.; Overbury Court
c: acc. bk, £921 16s 6d, 1898–1900
r: about 50 letters from Shaw to R. B.
   Martin at Overbury Court
Plain stone exterior, rich but simple
   interiors. One HBB window on stairs.
   Later alterations to house by Newton,
   Herbert Baker, and Victor Heal. Heal's
   work entailed demolishing nearly all the
   Shaw wing, but some of the work
   remains.
ack: Edward Holland-Martin

91. St Margaret's Church, Ilkley, Yorkshire
   (ills. 211, 212, 226)
New church
d: des. 1875–7 etc., exec. 1878–9; later
   additions
ctrs: B. Whitaker & Sons of Horsforth
   (masons); J. H. Thorp of Leeds (joiners);
   c/w Edward Prior; J. Aldam Heaton,
   decorator; ironwork by Leaver
m: Bradford and Ilkley stone
dr: V & A; R.I.B.A.; R.A.
c: acc. bk, £580 0s 5d, 1878–80
r: 31 letters from Shaw and other papers at
   church; ICBS file 8112; drawing exh. at
   R.A., 1877, & reprd. in *BN* 18.5.1877; *BA*
   12.9.1879
See pp. 281–283. Fittings from Shaw or his
   circle include the font (? by Prior), 1879;
   the pulpit, 1881; main screen, centre
   section only, 1898–9 (Shaw & Ginham);
   font cover, 1911 (Shaw, Chorley, &
   Davidson). Reredos sketched out by Shaw
   & Ginham, 1897–8, but not exec. Most
   other fittings are later. Stained glass mixed,
   some by Powell's.
ack: Revd. T. H. Levesley

92. Adsdean, Funtington, Sussex
Alterations and additions, including new
   entrance wing and stables
d: 1876–7
cl: Robert Belford Wallis Wilson
m: flint, stone and brick drs.
dr: R.A.
c: acc. bk, £264 11s 6d, 1877–8
Much of original house now dem., and
   interiors altered in part by Ernest George,
   1899–1900. The Shaw hall and stables etc.
   survive intact, though now in separate
   occupation.

93. Ellern Mede, Totteridge, London (ills. 108–110)
New house, and possibly small stable
d: 1876–7
cl: William Austin (1820–1909)
ctr: William Brass
m: brick, t/h, some ½tmb
dr: R.A.
c: t of £4078; acc. bk, £220, 1877–8
r: *B* 1.7.1876 (t)
Wrongly called Denham by Robert Shaw and Blomfield. Stables extended. House with some good interior features still.

94. Albert Hall Mansions, Kensington Gore, London S.W.7
Three new blocks of flats, erected in succession
cls: Royal Commissioners for 1851 Exhibition and Thomas Hussey
ctr: Thomas Hussey
m: brick, slate roofs
dr: R.A.
c: acc. bk, £3310 10s, 1879–90
r: S. Perks, *Residential Flats* (1905) pp. 126–9; *Survey of London* XXXVIII pp. 342–5

A. Front Block (ills. 146–9)
  d: elevations for front, to fit plans by Driver & Rew, 1876–7; new plans and elevations exec. 1879–81
  r: Commissioners for 1851 Exhibition, minutes and files, with 5 letters from Shaw; MBW Minutes of Proceedings 13.5.1881; *BN* 9.3. & 13.4.1877, 4 & 25.1.1878, 8.7 & 21.10.1881; W. Shaw Sparrow, *Flats, Urban Houses and Cottage Homes* (1907) pp. 26–7; *DEH* 2 pp. 158–9

B. Western block
  d: des. 1882, exec. 1883–4

C. Eastern block
  d: des. 1884, exec. 1885–6

95. 61 Fitzjohn's Avenue, London N.W.3
New house and studio
d: des. 1876–7 etc., exec. 1878–90
cl: Edwin Long, A.R.A. (1829–91)
ctr: A. Braid & Co.
m: brick
dr: R.A.
c: acc. bk, £378 5s, 1878–81
r: *B* 8.12.1877 (t); *A* 15.11.1879

Poorly converted into flats, 1947, and planning mostly lost.

96. 18 Portman Square, London W.1 (†)
Internal alterations
d: 1876–7
cl: Nathaniel Montefiore (d.1883)
ctr: W. H. Lascelles
c: acc. bk, £170, 1877
r: *BN* 23.3.1877
Extent of work unknown. Dem.

97. High Hatton and Peplow, Shropshire
Estate works
cl: Francis Stanier (1838–1900)
c: acc. bk, £132 7s, 1879

A. High Hatton school
  d: 1876 (insc.)
  m: stone
  r: RNS to Arthur Keen, 13.10.1879: 'Will you look out the Hatton plans and send them to Francis Stanier'.
Attrib. on basis of above and family tradition, but not a remarkable building and conceivably not Shaw's.

B. Epiphany Chapel, Peplow (ill. 215)
  d: 1877–9
  ctr: Richard Price of Coleham
  m: brick, ½tmb, some t/h
  r: *Newport and Market Drayton Advertiser* 25.1.1879
Screen, pulpit and font are all Shaw's, and the E window is by HBB. Chancel redecorated, 1903.
ack: Mrs D. Stanier

98. Piccards Rough, Guildford, Surrey
House and villas
cl: Thomas Wilde Powell (1818–97)

A. Piccards Rough (ill. 71)
  New house, stables and two cottages
  d: des. 1877 etc., exec. 1878–9
  ctr: Frank Birch of Farnham; ironwork by Leaver
  m: local stone, plaster and roughcast, some ½tmb
  dr: R.I.B.A.; R.A.
  c: acc. bk, £650, 1878–80
  r: *A* 11.2.1887 (illustration)
Excellent house, lamentably converted by demolition of centre in 1958.

B. 1–4 Rectory Place, Portsmouth Road
Group of two large semi-detached houses
d: 1882–3
m: brick, t/h
Ernest Newton added to no. 1 in 1911. A
pretty group.

C. Hitherbury, 97 Portsmouth Road
Detached villa on sloping site
d: 1882–3
m: brick, t/h
Cleverly contrived composition. 'It was
disgracefully remodelled in 1965–6,
hardly a detail surviving unmauled'
(Pevsner/Nairn, *Surrey* (2nd ed. 1971)
p. 293).
c: acc. bk, 'villas at Guildford', £395 15s,
1882–4

The group of stables and cottages further S
facing the end of Sandy Lane and dated
1881, is probably not Shaw's but by a
pupil.

99. Flete, Devonshire (ills. 158–162)
Reconstruction of house, by stages, and new
wing
d: des. 1877 etc., exec. 1878–83
cl: Henry Bingham Mildmay (1828–1905)
ctr: Frank Birch of Farnham, c/w Ernest
Newton; J. Aldam Heaton, decorator
m: estate stone, Dartmoor granite drs.
dr: R.A.; R.I.B.A.
c: acc. bk, £5670, 1878–83
r: diaries of Mrs Mildmay; *A* 18.1.1889; *BA*
18.12.1891; *CL* 20.11.1915
See pp. 211–216. Much altered internally, but
some interiors survive. Now Mutual
Households Association.

100. Charlton House, Charlton, London S.E.7
Addition of billiard room, and restoration of
house
d: 1877–8
cl: Sir Spencer Maryon-Wilson (1829–97)
m: brick
dr: R.A.
c: acc. bk, £884 os 6d, 1877–9
r: *Transactions of the Hampstead Antiquarian and
Historical Society* 1900 p. 68
The cost suggests a thorough restoration,
probably mainly structural. The billiard
room was a small single-storey addition to
the south, later incorporated into a public
library and entirely destroyed inside. Some
of the panelling and many of the fireplace
tile cheeks in the main house seem to be
Shaw's.

101. West House, 118 Campden Hill Road,
London W.8 (ill. 123)
New house
d: 1877–8
cl: George Henry Boughton, R.A.
(1833–1905)
ctr: A. Braid & Co. of Chelsea
m: brick, cut brick and stone dressings, some
t/h
c: acc. bk, £227 18s, 1877–9
r: MBW Minutes of Proceedings 4.5.1877;
drawing exh. at R.A., 1878, & reprd. in
BN 26.8.1878; *Survey of London* XXXVII
pp. 82–3
See pp. 155–156. Now in flats, and much
altered internally; also some external
alterations.

102. Upper Langwith, Derbyshire
Restoration of church, with new W end and
chancel
d: 1877
cl: Revd. A. Blythe
ctr: Richard Langley
m: stone
dr: R.A., also some notes in sketchbook
c: acc. bk, £80, 1878
A sympathetic small restoration, with new
bellcote, font, pulpit, etc.

103. Bedford Park, Turnham Green, London
W.4
Estate work
d: 1877–80
cl: Jonathan T. Carr (1845–1915)
c: acc. bk, £1125, 1877–80
r: *BN* 9.3, 9.11 & 21.12.1877, & 30.1.1880; *B*
31.1.1880; Moncure Conway, *Harper's
Monthly Magazine* 62 (1881) pp. 481–90 and
Autobiography (1904) Vol. 2 pp. 339–41; W.
Hamilton, *The Aesthetic Movement in England*
(1882) pp. 111–123; *Architectural Record* 5
(1896) pp. 326 & 648–62; *DEB*; *CL* 7 &
14.12.1967; Walter Creese, *The Search for
Environment* (1966) pp. 87–107; Ian
Fletcher, *Romantic Mythologies* (1967)
pp. 169–207
Shaw's work may be divided up into house
types and individual buildings, as listed
below.

A. First semi-detached house type (ill. 150)
d: des. 1877
m: brick, optional t/h at sides
dr: R.A. (at R.I.B.A.)
r: *BN* 9.11.1877

Designed with alternative roof lines for attic storey. Only two examples built: 19–21 and 20–22 The Avenue, both with gabled ends.

B. Second semi-detached house type (ill. 151)
d: des. 1877
m: brick, optional t/h at sides
r: *BN* 9 & 16.11.1877
Designed, as A, with alternative roof lines. Examples in Woodstock Road, e.g. 3–5 & 7–9 (hipped roof), 11–13 (gabled roof).

C. Third semi-detached house type (ill. 152)
d: des. 1878
m: brick, optional roughcast on bays
r: *BN* 19.4.1878
Copious examples with varying elevations, e.g. 23–25 The Avenue (one roughcast bay), 1–3 Blenheim Road (double roughcast bays), 14–16 Queen Anne's Gardens (no roughcast bays). Alternative all-brick elevation with Dutch gables: e.g. 24–26 The Avenue, 3–5 Queen Anne's Grove.

D. First detached house type (ill. 153)
d: 1877
m: brick, t/h
r: *BN* 23.11.1877
Several examples, often with variations, e.g. 36 The Avenue, 20 Woodstock Road, 3 Queen Anne's Gardens.

E. Second detached house type (ill. 154)
d: des. 1879
m: brick
r: *BN* 18.4.1879
Many examples, often with variations, e.g. 17 Blenheim Road, 1 Bedford Road.

F. Terrace of six houses, 24–34 Woodstock Road
d: des. 1877–8
m: brick, roughcast
r: *BN* 11.1.1878
Asymmetrical terrace with varying height.

G. Bedford Park Club, The Avenue
d: 1878, with addition of 1879 at rear
m: brick
r: *BN* 3.5.1878 & 30.1.1880
Attrib. by Robert Shaw to E. J. May, perhaps because May made a later addition: see *BN* 29.5.1885. Now the C.A.V. Social Club, and gutted internally.

H. The Tower House, Bedford Road (†) (ills. 155–6)
d: 1879
m: brick, some roughcast
ctr: built by daywork by estate builders
dr: V & A
r: *BN* 31.10.1879; *A* 18.5.1894; T. A. Greeves, *Bedford Park Festival Programme 1968*
Dem. *c*.1931.

J. The Tabard Inn and Stores, Bath Road (ill. 157)
d: 1879–80
m: brick, t/h, roughcast
dr: R.A. (at R.I.B.A.); V & A
r: *BN* 2.1.1880; *B* 31.1.1880; *DEB*; *Marble Halls* (V & A Exhibition Catalogue, 1973) p. 186
Damaged by fire in 1960s, but well restored. Planning of the inn much altered.

K. St Michael's Church, Bath Road (ills. 157, 213)
d: des. 1878; nave, S aisle and chancel exec. 1879–82; N aisle and hall added 1887
ctr: Goddard & Sons of Farnham; brick carving by Walter Smith of Lambeth; panelling by Holland & Sons
m: brick, st/drs
dr: V & A; R.A. (at R.I.B.A.)
r: Eccl. Comms. file 80148; ICBS file 8306; *BN* 36 (1879) *passim*, & 30.4.1880; *B* 31.1.1880; *BN* 11.11.1881 (†)
Maurice B. Adams was responsible for the addition of aisle and hall, the former entirely to Shaw's design. He also added a SE chapel later on. Fittings by Shaw include benches, screen and altar, but many are later additions.

104. Edburton Church, Sussex
Restoration
d: des. 1877–8, exec. 1878–80
cl: Revd. C. H. Wilkie
c: acc. bk, £70 7s 6d, 1881
r: some notes in sketchbook; ICBS file 8325
Thorough structural repairs, with some new roofs. Fittings include benches and stalls after C17th character of pulpit and sanctuary rail. E window HBB, 1880.

105. 68 (formerly 42) Cadogan Square, London S.W.3 (ills. 164–5)

New house
d: 1877–8
cl: Laurence Harrison
ctr: Thomas Pink & Son of Harlesden
m: brick
dr: V & A
c: acc. bk, £500, 1878–81
r: drawing of nos. 68 & 72 exh. at R.A., 1878, & reprd. in *BN* 27.6.1879; MBW Minutes of Proceedings 31.5.1878 & 9.1.1880; *DEH* 2 p. 150
See 106 below. Now converted into flats.

106. 72 (formerly 46) Cadogan Square, London S.W.3 (ills. 164–5)
New house
d: 1877–9
cl: Thomas Pink (for subletting)
ctr: Thomas Pink & Son
m: brick
dr: V & A (one sheet only, inscribed in error as for no. 68)
c: acc. bk, £50 only, 1878
r: as 105
Built by arrangement with Pink, and possibly not planned by Shaw. Alterations at rear, 1914. Now in flats, with porch removed, and entrance via no. 70, which is by A. J. Adams.

107. Bannow, Quarry Hill, St Leonards, Sussex (ill. 53)
New house
d: 1877–9
cl: Revd. John William Tottenham
m: stone, brick chimneys, ½tmb, t/h
dr: R.A.
c: acc. bk, £464 17s, 1878–81
r: *BA* 15.7.1887
Little-known but pleasant house on hillside site, in full country house manner. Now called Hazelton, and with many interior alterations, but other surviving features.

108. St Mark's Church, Cobourg Road, London S.E.5 (ill. 209)
New church and schoolroom, built by stages, but not completed

A. Church
d: des. 1877–8, chancel and part of nave exec. 1879–80, S chancel aisle added 1883–4
cl: Adelaide Thrupp (d. 1908)
ctrs: Browne & Robinson, 1879–80;

Richard Conder 1883–4; pulpit and lectern carved by Baker Wigram
m: brick, wood vaults, cement panelling
dr: R.A.
c: acc. bk, £446 15s, 1880–4
r: ICBS file 8298; *BN* 18.6.1880; *B* 23.6.1883 (t); T. F. Bumpus, *London Churches Ancient and Modern* (1883) pp. 217–8; *Transactions of the Ecclesiological Society* 2 (1951) pp. 249–51
Pulpit, lectern, altar furniture and chancel screen all by Shaw. The nave was cleverly finished off by Victor Heal, 1931–2. Badly damaged by bombs and now redundant, with all fittings except screen removed.

B. Schoolroom
d: 1883–4, extended 1892
ctrs: Richard Conder, 1883–4; T. W. Haylock, 1892
m: brick, st/drs
dr: R.A.
c: see above; also, acc. bk, £116 15s, 1893
The adjacent vicarage is probably by someone from the Shaw office.

109. Exhibition Buildings, Paris International Exhibition, 1878 (†)

A. Jury House, Rue des Nations (ill. 135)
cl: British Commission for 1878 Exhibition
ctr: W. H. Lascelles
m: stained concrete bricks
r: *BN* 14.6.1878 (illustration); *Les Merveilles de l'Exposition de 1878* pp. 112–3; G. A. Sala, *Paris Herself Again* (1880) pp. 148–151
Wrongly identified by Pevsner in *RIBAJ* 64 (1957) p. 174. A scheme to re-erect the building in an Industrial Museum after the Exhibition closed seems to have aborted.

B. Two concrete cottages in grounds of Exhibition, near the Seine (ill. 134)
cl & ctr: W. H. Lascelles
m: slab concrete
r: *A* 30.3.1878; *Official Catalogue of British Section* p. 251; Shaw, *Sketches for Cottages* (1878) nos. 1 & 9
A one-storey house at the entrance to the English Court may also have been Shaw's.

110. Concrete cottages, Croydon, London (ills. 132–3)

d: 1878 etc.
cl & ctr: W. H. Lascelles
m: slab concrete
r: *B* 14.8.1875; *BN* 19.7.1878; Shaw,
Sketches for Cottages etc.; Ernest Newton,
Sketches for Country Residences (1882) no.
33; *Concrete* 3 (1908–9) pp. 296–8 & 6
(1972) pp. 28–9; *B* 22.11.1912
The exact scope of Shaw's work here is
unclear, but the earliest cottages may not
be his. *The Builder* speaks of seven houses
in Gladstone and Sydenham Roads,
amongst which must be included the
surviving nos. 226–8 and 237–9
Sydenham Road. The remarkable no.
226 appears to date from about 1881.
ack: Miss Helen Brooks

111. Caversham Grove, Surley Row, Emmer
Green, Reading, Berks
Additions to house, on S side
d: 1878–80
cl: Frederick George Saunders
m: brick
c: acc. bk, £178 4s 6d, 1880–1
r: some notes in sketchbook; Sale Catalogue,
1915
Now High Down Comprehensive School, and
much extended and altered internally.

112. Farnley House, 15 Chelsea
Embankment, London S.W.3 (ill. 168)
New house and stables
d: 1878–9
cl: William James Armitage
m: brick
dr: G.L.C. Record Office; R.A.
c: acc. bk, £569 17s 6d, 1878–80
r: MBW Minutes of Proceedings 9.1.1880
The least-known of Shaw's Embankment
houses, and interesting in plan (now much
altered). Chimneystack to front reduced.
Now called Delahay House.

113. St Michael's Church, Blackheath Park,
London S.E.3
New vestry
d: des. 1878, exec. 1879
ctr: Samuel J. Jerrard
m: stone
dr: R.A.
r: W. G. Newton, *The Work of Ernest Newton,
R.A.* (1925) p. 209
Drawings signed for Shaw, but more properly
attrib. to Newton.

114. Coatham Convalescent Home, Coatham,
Yorkshire (†)
Addition of Childrens' Department to main
building
d: 1878
cl: Revd. John Postlethwaite
r: *Kelly's Yorkshire Directory 1879*; *BN* 3.1.1890
Street had added a chapel in 1870–1. Dem.
*c.*1956.

115. Greenham Lodge, Greenham, Berkshire
(ills. 80–82, 96)
New house, lodge, stables, convalescent home
and cottages.

A. House, lodge, and stables
d: des. 1878 etc.; main part of house and
lodge exec. 1879–81; kitchen wing and
stables exec. 1882–3
cl: Lloyd Baxendale (1822–82)
ctr: Samuel Elliott of Newbury
m: brick, st/drs, some ½tmb
dr: R.A.; R.I.B.A. (at R.A.)
c: acc. bk, £1970, 1879–84
r: *A* 4.1.1889 (ill.); W. Shaw Sparrow, *The
British Home of To-day* (1904) (ill.)
In a severer style than most of Shaw's brick
houses, and probably based on Shaw
House near Newbury. Kitchen wing
built round core of old house. Good
interiors, with some alterations. Now a
USAF Officers' Mess.

B. St Andrew's Home, Greenham Common
South
d: 1886
cl: Mrs Baxendale
ctr: Samuel Elliott
m: brick, t/h
dr: R.A.
c: acc. bk, £100, 1886
Built as a 'rest home' for sick employees of
Pickfords. Now converted into a house
and called Brackenhurst.

C. 1–3 Norman Cottages
d: 1891
cl: Lloyd Harry Baxendale (1857–1937)
m: brick, t/h
dr: R.A.
Pleasant pair of cottages, possibly planned
by Ginham. Reputedly named after
Norman Shaw.

116. St Johns, Queens Road, Ilkley, Yorkshire
(ill. 52)

New house
d: 1878–9
cl: John William Atkinson (1825–89)
ctr: ? B. Whitaker & Sons of Horsforth
m: local stone
c: acc. bk, £387 6s, 1878–82
r: *Ilkley Gazette* 14.6.1929
Built for the brother-in-law of Aldam Heaton, who probably did decorative work. This house and St Margaret's Church had a mortar mill in common. Now divided into flats and very much altered externally and internally.

117. Clock House, 8 Chelsea Embankment, London S.W.3 (ills. 170 & 172)
New house and stables
d: 1878–80
cl: Mrs Erskine Wemyss
ctr: J. McLachlan of Clapham
m: Fareham brick
dr: R.A.; R.I.B.A. (at R.A.)
c: *c.*£13,500; acc. bk, £784 1s 6d, 1879–81
r: *A* 7.9.1878 (t); *B* 27.12.1879 (ill.); MBW Minutes of Proceedings 9.1.1880
Planning now much altered, and upper storeys mutilated.

118. 9–11 Chelsea Embankment, London S.W.3 (ills. 163, 194)
Group of three houses, built speculatively
d: 1878–80
cl: James William Temple (1821–98)
ctr: W. H. Lascelles
m: brick
dr: R.A.
c: t of £21,945; acc. bk, £561 10s 6d, 1879–81
r: *A* 7.9.1878 (t); *BN* 12.8.1881 (ill.); *DEH* 2 p. 153
Now divided into flats.

119. The Knolls, Plantation Road, Leighton Linslade, Bedfordshire (ill. 67)
Small new country house and lodge
d: 1879–80
cl: Frederick Bassett
ctr: Albert Kimberley
m: brick, ½tmb, t/h
dr: R.A.
c: acc. bk, £255, 1880–1
Well-composed exterior, but disappointing interior. Now a Sports Club and offices, with some internal alterations.

120. Searles Estate, Fletching, Sussex
d: 1879–80
cl: Sir Spencer Maryon-Wilson (1829–97)
c: acc. bk, £386 10s 9d, 1880

A. Alterations to house (†)
   dr: R.A.
   Shaw added bays and probably changed the internal planning of this strange Gothic house of *c.*1845, dem. *c.*1950.
   ack: Mrs Helen Kastrati; Sir Hubert Maryon-Wilson

B. Shop and cottage, Fletching village
   m: brick, ½tmb, some t/h
   dr: R.A.
   Pleasant group, now Tower Cottage and St Andrew's Cottage. Shop front altered and bow put in.
   ack: Mrs I. Salimbeni

121. 49 Princes Gate, London S.W.7
Interior redecoration, mainly of first floor
d: 1879–80 (first floor drawing rooms); 1885 (morning room)
cl: Frederick Richards Leyland (1831–92)
dr: R.A.; R.I.B.A. (at R.A.)
c: acc. bk, £198 15s, 1880; £52 10s, 1886
r: *A* 17.12.1886 & 26.1.1894; *Harpers Monthly Magazine*, December 1890, pp. 81–99; *Art Journal* 1892 pp. 129–138, 249–252; Sale Catalogue, 17.6.1892; G. C. Williamson, *Murray Marks and his Friends* (1919) pp. 84–97
Mostly now dismantled or destroyed, and house now in flats.

122. Broadlands, Sunninghill, Berkshire (†)
New house
d: 1879–80
cl: A. William Quilter (1808–88)
ctr: Perry & Co.
m: brick, ½tmb, some t/h
dr: R.A.
c: acc. bk, £446 15s 6d, 1879–81
r: drawings exh. at R.A., 1880, & reprd. in *BN* 7.5 & 25.6.1880; *DEH* 2 pp. 120–1; *CL* 10.11.1934 (ill.)
The stable-block of 1882 is not Shaw's, but by J. T. Christopher & E. White. In 1898 W. W. Neve added a large hall; *BN* 9.3.1900. House demolished *c.*1933 and replaced by new house by Minoprio & Spenceley. Broadlands Farm Cottage, the nearby Keeper's Cottage, and the walled garden could all be Shaw's.

123. Alderbrook, nr. Cranleigh, Surrey (†)
(ills. 86–88)
New house, stables, lodge, and estate cottages
d: des. 1879, exec. 1880–2
cl: Pandeli Ralli, M.P. (1845–1928)
ctr: Charles Fish
m: brick, t/h, some ½tmb
dr: R.A.
c: acc. bk, £791 19s, 1881–2
r: B 1.5.1880 (t); DEH 2 p. 123
Large country house, dem. c.1955. Survivors
  include the stables (altered), walled garden
  and cottage, and S lodge. Elaborate
  gardens now in decay.
ack: Mr P. van den Bergh

124. Baldslow Place, Baldslow, Sussex
New house, stables, lodge, and cottage with
  vineries
d: des. 1879 etc.; house exec. 1880–1, vineries
  1880, stables 1881, lodge 1882
cl: Charles John Ebden (1853–1936)
ctr: house, A. Braid & Co.; vineries, James
  Stubberfield
m: brick, t/h, some ½tmb
dr: R.A.
c: acc. bk, £717 17s 6d, 1881–2
Good country house, now Claremont School,
  and extended, but with surviving interior
  features. Vineries and cottage now Harrow
  Lodge.

125. Barings Bank, 8 Bishopsgate, London
  E.C.2 (†) (ill. 182)
New front to street, and various internal
  alterations
d: des. 1879 etc.; new front block and some
  internal changes and new vaults, 1880–1;
  new basement rooms and galleries to
  banking hall, 1888–91
cl: Baring Bros.
ctr: William Cubitt & Co.
m: 2″ bricks, stone dressings
dr: R.A.; some at Bank
c: acc. bk, £1041 7s, 1881–2; £10 10s, 1903
r: 6 letters of Shaw and other papers at the
  Bank; MBW Minutes of Proceedings
  4.6.1880; BN 40 (1881) passim and
  8.7.1881
Barings was later extended to the N by Gerald
  Horsley in 1913, and altered internally by
  various architects including Lutyens. Dem.
  1974 for road-widening.
ack: Mr Tom Ingram

126. Knight's Croft, Rustington, Sussex (ills.
  59, 95)
New house and small stable
d: 1880–1
cl: C. Hubert Parry (1848–1918)
ctr: Leggatt & Buckly of Littlehampton
m: brick, t/h
c: acc. bk, £178 3s 6d, 1882
r: diaries of Sir Hubert Parry; C. A. Graves,
  Hubert Parry (1926) Vol. 1 pp. 190 &
  209–10
Delightful small house. Now much
  encroached upon, and divided into flats,
  but with excellent interiors, notably Parry's
  music room.
ack: Lord Ponsonby of Shulbrede; Mrs
  Magnus Osborn

127. Rosemount, Eastbourne, Sussex (†)
Alterations and additions to house
d: 1880–1
cl: George Matthey (d.1913)
dr: R.A.
c: acc. bk, £153 1s, 1882
Alterations to a large early Victorian house in
  the centre of Eastbourne. Dem. c.1930 and
  replaced by Victoria Mansions, Victoria
  Place.

128. Holme Grange, Holme Green, Berkshire
New house and stables
d: stables 1881, house 1882–3
cl: Bartle Goldsmid
ctrs: Thomas Wescott, stables; Richard
  Conder, house
m: brick, t/h
dr: R.A.
c: acc. bk, £313, 1883–4
Pleasant and relaxed country house, now a
  school, and with some additions. Stables
  now separate dwellings.

129. Alliance Assurance Offices, 1–2 St
  James's Street, London S.W.1 (ill. 177)
New office block and chambers over
d: 1881–3
cl: Alliance Assurance Company
ctr: William Cubitt & Co.; J. Aldam Heaton,
  decorator
m: 2″ bricks, st/drs
dr: R.A.
c: acc. bk, £1340 9s 6d, 1882–3
r: Guildhall Library MS 12,162 c/1 (Building
  Committee Minutes); drawing exh. at

R.A., 1882, and reprd. in *BN* 26.5.1882;
DEB
Now altered internally.

130. Frognal Priory, Frognal, Hampstead,
London N.W.3 (†)
New house, with later added attic storey
d: 1881–2
cl: Edwin Tate (d.1928)
ctr: Charles Fish; J. Aldam Heaton,
decorator
m: brick, t/h
dr: R.A.
c: acc. bk, £439 15s, 1882–3
r: drawing exh. at R.A., 1882, & reprd. in *BN*
22.12.1882; *BN* 26.6.1885 (ill.)
Split-level house on a secluded site and
therefore with some country house
attributes. Dem. in 1930s.

131. The Three Gables, 6 Fitzjohn's Avenue,
London N.W.3 (†) (ills. 124–5)
New house with studio and stables
d: 1881–2
cl: Frank Holl, A.R.A. (1845–88)
ctr: W. Tongue of Plumstead
m: brick, some t/h
dr: R.A.
c: acc. bk, £453 16s 1d, 1881–3
r: drawing exh. at R.A., 1882, & reprd. in
BN 8.9.1882; *Magazine of Art* 1885
pp. 144–150; *DEB*
Demolished for Tavistock Clinic, *c*.1965.

132. Royal Academy, Burlington House,
London W.1
Alterations and additions to premises,
including new galleries, refreshment rooms
and staircase etc.
d: des. 1881 etc., exec. 1882–5
cl: Council of the Royal Academy
ctr: George Shaw; c/w William Oldrieve
c: £37,305 13s 6d; acc. bk, £1952 18s 6d,
1882–6
r: R.A. Building Accounts Book; *B* 4.8.1883
(t) & 2.5.1885; Sidney C. Hutchison, *The
History of the Royal Academy* (1968) p. 141;
Survey of London XXXII pp. 421 & 428
For details, see *Survey*. A large job, including a
new octagonal gallery for architecture. The
setpiece was the large refreshment room,
recently restored.

133. Ashley Park Estate, Walton-on-Thames,
Surrey
Villas on estate

A. Riverdene and Cranesdene, 1 & 3
Oatlands Drive, Weybridge (ill. 58)
d: 1881–2
ctr: Martin, Wells & Co. of Aldershot
m: brick, t/h
dr: R.A.
Good small houses, refined versions of the
Bedford Park detached model (103E).
No. 1 altered internally after fire, but
both in good condition externally.

B. Bracken House, Hersham Road, Walton-
on-Thames (†)
d: 1882
ctr: Martin, Wells & Co. of Aldershot
m: brick, t/h, ½tmb
dr: R.A.
Larger house, dem. *c*.1967.
A & B: cl: Joseph S. Sassoon (1855–1918)
c: acc. bk, £275 3s, 1882–3
r: *BN* 24.3.1882

C. Another house (†)
d: 1884–5
cl: Mrs Sassoon
m: brick, roughcast
dr: R.A.
c: acc. bk, £226 19s 3d, 1885
An interesting design, with sash windows,
and roughcast all over; possibly
Lethaby's. Dem.

These villas were reputedly all built for
lesser members of the Sassoon family, as
outliers to the Tudor house of Ashley
Park. This has now been dem., and the
whole vicinity very thoroughly built over.

134. 62 (formerly 36) Cadogan Square,
London S.W.3
New house on corner site
d: 1881–3
cl: Edward Howley Palmer
ctr: William Brass
m: brick
dr: R.A.
c: acc. bk, £472 9s, 1882–4
r: drawing exh. at R.A., 1883 & reprd. in *BN*
11.5.1883
Now converted into flats and altered
internally.

135. Chipstead Church, Surrey
New N aisle
d: des. 1881 etc, exec. 1882
cl: John Garratt Cattley of Shabden House

ctr: William Carruthers
m: flint, local st/drs
dr: R.A.
c: acc. bk, £57 7s, 1883
A plain addition, but with good new W
    elevation, now much decayed. One
    drawing signed jointly with Stanley F.
    Monier Williams. A lychgate was designed,
    but is different from the existing one.

136. High Callerton, Northumberland
Additions and alterations to Callerton Hall,
    and new adjoining cottages (1–3 High
    Callerton)
d: 1882–3
cl: Robert Maddison Warwick (b.1853)
ctr: Nicholas W. Maugham
m: stone, roughcast
dr: R.A.
c: acc. bk, £128 4s, 1884
The addition included a new service wing and
    archway. Much replanning internally, now
    altered, but exterior survives well. Cottages
    plain and substantial.

137. Exton Park, Rutland
Small alterations to new house, and plans for
    restoring and rebuilding old one
d: 1882–3
cl: Earl of Gainsborough (1850–1926)
ctr: F. Halliday of Greetham
m: stone
dr: R.A.; Exton Park
c: acc. bk, £101 1s, 1883
The executed work consisted of minor
    extensions to the servants' wing, mostly
    dem. c.1968. But Shaw also planned a
    complete restoration of the old Tudor
    house, then ruinous.
ack: Earl of Gainsborough

138. Dawpool, Thurstaston, Cheshire
Various works

A. New house (†) and stables (ills. 197–200)
    d: house, 1882–6, stables 1892
    cl: Thomas Henry Ismay (1837–99)
    ctr: Holme & Nicol, c/w Philip Thicknesse;
        J. Aldam Heaton, decorator
    m: local stone
    dr: V & A; R.A.; R.I.B.A.
    c: c.£53,000; acc. bk, £2309 15s 6d, 1886
    r: *BA* 17 (1882) pp. 39, 49 & 79; drawings
        exh. at R.A., 1884 & reprd. in *A*
        25.10.1884; *CL* 18.2.1911; Wilton J.

Oldham, *The Ismay Line* (1961) pp. 65–8
Designed with J. F. Doyle, whose role
    appears to have been small. Shaw made
    various internal alterations, e.g. a new
    drawing room fireplace in 1887–8. Sold
    in 1907 and dem. c.1927, with interior
    features variously disposed:
Dining room chimneypiece: Kingsland
    Dance Hall, Birkenhead
Dining room panelling etc.: Abbotsford,
    Oldfield Road, Heswall
Doors: Imperial Hotel, Llandudno
Picture gallery chimneypiece: Portmeirion
Mantelpiece (old): Wishing Gate, Mount
    Road, Bebington
Other features in houses on site

B. 2–3 Dawpool Cottages, and East Warren
    lodge
Attrib., undated.

C. Thurstaston Church, various works
    Tomb of T. H. Ismay in churchyard,
        c.1900 (ill. 290), and later plaque to
        Margaret Alice Ismay (1869–1901). See
        Lawrence Weaver, *Memorials and
        Monuments* (1915) pp. 368–9.
    Lychgate, c.1900. Attrib.
        cl: Mrs Ismay (d.1907)
    Organ case, 1905. Shutters painted by
        workshop of Robert Christie. See C.
        Nicholson & C. Spooner, *Recent English
        Ecclesiastical Architecture* (n.d.) p. 103.
        cl: daughters of T. H. Ismay
ack: Wilton J. Oldham

139. Walton House, Walton Street, London
    S.W.3
New house and studio
d: 1882–4
cl: Edward Sherrard Kennedy
ctr: Richard Conder
m: brick, some t/h
dr: R.A.;
c: acc. bk, £173, 1885
r: MBW Minutes of Proceedings, 20.6 &
    15.10.1884
Unpretentious brick house at angle to road.
    Much altered from the first design. Now
    in flats.

140. 200–222 Cromwell Road, London S.W.5
Large block of flats and houses, speculative
d: 1882–3
cl & ctr: Thomas Hussey
m: brick
dr: R.A.

r: MBW Minutes of Proceedings, 10.12.1886;
Survey of London XXXVIII p. 343
The drawings show alternative plans for
houses and flats to the same façade,
designed *c.*1880. In execution, 200 & 222
became houses, while between them
202–220 were planned as flats. In 1886–7
Hussey added a porch in the centre,
possibly to stimulate letting. Interiors much
as Albert Hall Mansions, second and third
block.

141. The Rookery, Bromley Common, Kent(†)
Reconstruction of house with new wings, and
stables
d: des. 1882 etc., exec. 1883–4
cl: Charles Loyd Norman (1839–89)
ctr: William Cubitt & Co; plasterwork by G.
Jackson & Sons
m: brick, st/drs
dr: R.A.
c: *c.*£25,614; acc. bk, £1021 16s, 1884–5
r: Accounts and 9 letters from Shaw in Kent
County Record Office U310, A159; CL
21.9.1967 (pp. 661–2); Bromley Library, *A
Short Account of the Rookery Estate*
Gutted by fire, 1946, and dem. afterwards. A
few interior features survive at West
Farleigh Hall, Kent.
ack: General C. W. Norman

142. Bolney House, Ennismore Gardens,
London S.W.7 (†) (ill. 183)
New house and adjoining library
d: 1883–5
cl: Alfred Henry Huth (1850–1910)
ctr: Perry & Co.
m: brick, st/drs
dr: R.A.
c: acc. bk, £634 5s 6d, 1884–6
r: MBW Minutes of Proceedings, 29.6.1883
Dem. *c.*1955.

143. Trevanion, Totteridge, London
New small country house
d: 1883–4
cl: R. J. Mackay
ctr: Martin, Wells & Co. of Aldershot
m: brick, t/h
dr: R.A.
c: acc. bk, £164 1s, 1884.
An unremarkable house, possibly not having
its original name. Drawings include one for
a lodge, perhaps dem.; this was published
in M. B. Adams, *Modern Cottage Architecture*
(1904) pl. 18. House now divided. Badly
damaged by fire, 1975

144. All Saints' Church, Corso
dell'Imperatrice, San Remo, Italy
New church
d: 1883 (foundation stone)
ctr: G. Castaldi
m: local stone, pantiles
dr: R.A.
Probably designed somewhat before 1883.
Plain exterior but well-proportioned
interior. Pulpit possibly Shaw's, but no
other fittings. Reredos of 1910 by H. & A.
De Wispelaere of Bruges.

145. 27 Charlotte Street (now Bloomsbury
Street), London W.C.1 (†)
New warehouse and workshop, behind street
d: 1883–4
cl: John Aldam Heaton (1830–97)
ctr: probably Richard Conder
c: t of £2695
r: *B* 3.11.1883 (t)
Workshop premises for Aldam Heaton's firm,
behind NW corner of crossing with Great
Russell Street. Dem. *c.*1910.

146. Didlington Hall, Didlington, Norfolk (†)
(ill. 179)
Reconstruction of house and addition of
museum
d: des. 1883 etc., exec. 1884–5
cl: William Tyssen-Amherst
ctr: William Hubbard of East Dereham
m: brick, st/drs
dr: R.A.
c: acc. bk, £1823 10s, 1884–7
r: *B* 11.7.1885
Entirely dem. 1951.

147. Harrow Mission, Latimer Road, London
W.11
New mission room, church, and house
cl: Harrow Mission

A. Mission Room
d: 1883–4
ctr: Lawrance & Sons
m: brick
dr: R.A.
c: acc. bk, £142 5s 1d, 1885
r: B 24.11.1883 (t)

B. Holy Trinity Church (ills. 217, 218)
d: first design 1885–6, revised design built
1887–9

ctrs: Thomas Rider & Sons; steelwork,
    Homan & Rodgers
m: brick
dr: R.A.; R.I.B.A.
c: acc. bk, £333 16s, 1887–9
r: *A* 18 & 25.10.1889; Peter Howell,
    Victorian Churches (1968) pp. 40–1
Fittings, including stalls, organ and reredos,
    all contemporary. Now redundant, with
    divided interior.

C. Clergy house and club room
d: des. 1895, exec. 1896–7
ctr: John Ginn & Son
m: brick, st/drs
dr: R.A.
All premises now given over to a youth
    club, and much altered internally.

148. Greenhill, Allerton Road, Allerton
    Liverpool (†)
New house
d: 1883–4
cl: Thomas Gee (d.1923)
ctr: Thomas Urmson
m: brick, t/h, some ½tmb
dr: R.A.
c: acc. bk, £365 11s 6d, 1884–6
r: *AAJ* 71 (1955–6) pp. 20–21
Neighbour to 149, and dem. *c.*1930.

149. Allerton Beeches, Allerton Road,
    Allerton, Liverpool (†) (ill. 69)
New house and stables
d: 1883–4
cl: Henry Tate junior (1853–1902)
ctr: Thomas Urmson
m: brick, t/h, some ½tmb
dr: R.A.
c: acc. bk, £558 4s 6d, 1884–6
r: *AAJ* 71 (1955–6) pp. 20–21
Neighbour to 148, and dem. *c.*1930 except for
    stables, which have been converted into
    houses.
ack: J. F. F. Rathbone

150. Walhampton House, nr. Lymington,
    Hampshire (ill. 178)
Remodelling of house with new E wing
d: des. 1883 etc., exec. 1884–5
cl: John Postle Heseltine (1843–1929)
ctr: Thomas Rashley
m: brick, st/drs
dr: R.A.

c: acc. bk, £679 6s, 1884–5
r: *BA* 17.12.1886 (ill.)
Good surviving interiors. The older parts of
    the house were rebuilt by T. H. Mawson in
    1912–14. Now a school.
ack: N. Plumley

151. 180 Queen's Gate, London S.W.7 (†) (ill.
    175)
New house
d: des. 1883 etc., exec. 1884–5
cl: Henry Francis Makins
ctr: William Cubitt & Co.; decorators,
    Morris & Co.
m: brick, st/drs
dr: R.A.
c: acc. bk, £735 6s 6d, 1885–6
r: Royal Commission for 1851 Exhibition file
    46; *A* 22.4.1887 (ill.); *CL* 30.8.1956; *Survey
    of London XXXVIII* pp. 333–4
Dem. for Imperial College, 1971.

152. St Thomas' Church, New Groombridge,
    Sussex
New church
d: 1883–4
ctr: John Paine of Crowborough
m: stone
c: c.£2000; acc. bk, £90, 1884
r: ICBS file 8833; Goldsmiths' Company
    Archives, Guildhall Library; *BN* 27.7.1883
No fittings known to be Shaw's, and many of
    later date.

153. Greenlands, Hambleden,
    Buckinghamshire
Alterations, and additions on N side
d: 1884–5
cl: Rt. Hon. William Henry Smith, M.P.
    (1825–91)
ctr: Samuel Elliott of Newbury
m: brick and stone, some stuccoed
dr: R.A.
c: acc. bk, £617 7s 3d, 1885
r: Sir Herbert Maxwell, *The Life and Times of
    W. H. Smith* (1893) Vol. 2 pp. 127, 131
Additions included a smoking room and
    dining room, both altered, and much
    replanning of service wing. Further
    enlargements to house, 1894 and 1905.
    Nothing of importance internally is now
    Shaw's.

154. Banstead Wood, Banstead, Surrey
New house, also lodge and stables (attrib.)

d: main part of house 1884–6; garden front altered 1899
cl: Francis Henry Baring (1850–1915)
m: brick (some 2″), ½tmb, some t/h
c: acc. bk, £1769 5s, 1884–7
dr: Goodhart-Rendel collection, R.I.B.A. (see below)
r: *A.A. Notes* 1 (1887) pp. 85–6; *A* 71 (1904) *passim* (ill.)
Large country house, badly damaged by fire, 1938, and partly rebuilt by H. S. Goodhart-Rendel for use as hospital offices. His drawings show plans before and after rebuilding. He remodelled all fronts in a convincing pastiche of Shaw's style, eliminating ½tmb in favour of t/h throughout. Partly empty; no surviving interiors.

155. 39 (once 50) Frognal, Hampstead, London N.W.3 (ills. 126–7, 196)
New house
d: 1884–5
cl: Kate Greenaway (1846–1901)
ctr: Thomas Rider & Son
m: brick, t/h
dr: R.A.
c: acc. bk, £150, 1885
r: *BA* 8.5.1885; M. H. Spielmann & G. S. Layard, *Kate Greenaway* (1905) pp. 142–4
Now in flats, but with studio largely intact.

156. Bourn Hall, Bourn, Cambridgeshire
Additions to house, new wing to stables, and lodge
d: 1884–5
cl: John James Briscoe (1835–1910)
m: brick, st/drs
dr: R.A.
c: acc. bk, £431 12s, 1884–6
r: Royal Commission on Historical Monuments, *West Cambridgeshire* (1967) p. 20
Dining room added towards garden, and other changes in planning made to this Tudor brick house. A projected large new service wing was not built, and the lodge is smaller than intended at first. In excellent condition.
ack: Peter F. King

157. All Saints' Church, Compton, Leek, Staffordshire (ills. 232–7)
New church

d: des. 1884 etc., exec. 1885–7, and some later fittings
ctr: James Heath of Endon; carving by Farmer & Brindley
m: various local stones (see p. 456 n. 74)
dr: V & A; R.A.
c: acc. bk, £456 10s, 1886–8
r: many papers at church, including 3 letters from Shaw and builder's diary; ICBS file 8989; *Leek Times* 1.8.1885 & 30.7.1887; *A* 3.1.1890 (ill.)
Many fittings by Shaw and his office staff; reredos by Lethaby and painted by F. Hamilton Jackson, pulpit and font probably also Lethaby's. Many later fittings and decoration of chancel by Gerald Horsley, and other additions.
ack: Revd. J. Dilnot

158. Upcot House, Marlborough, Wiltshire
New boarding house and master's residence for Marlborough College
d: 1885–6
cl: Francis Edward Thompson
ctr: Benjamin Hillier
m: brick, t/h, some ½tmb
dr: R.A.
c: acc. bk, £77 12s 6d, 1886
The house includes an attached dormitory, apparently remodelled from an older building, and entirely rebuilt later by W. G. Newton. Building probably not supervised by Shaw, and now derelict. In 1877 Shaw had designed a cottage for Thompson, but this has not been found.
ack: Mr E. G. H. Kempson

159. Burrows Cross, nr. Gomshall, Surrey
New house and lodge, with later addition
d: 1885–6 (original part), 1889 (addition)
cl: Frank Holl, R.A. (1845–88) for original part; Benjamin Williams Leader, R.A. (1831–1923) for addition
ctr: Samuel Elliott of Newbury
m: brick, t/h
dr: R.A.
c: acc. bk, £253 18s 6d, 1886; £161 13s, 1889
r: *Art Annual* 1901 pp. 25–30
Built as small country retreat for Holl, and extended on either side of entrance after his death by Leader, who wanted a bigger studio. Now divided, but with some interior features remaining.

160. Shavington Hall, Shropshire

A. Alterations to house (†) (ill. 180)
  d: 1885–6
  cl: Arthur Pemberton Heywood-Lonsdale
    (1835–97)
  c: acc. bk, £1226 3s, 1886–7
  r: *CL* 3 & 10.8.1918
  Some later alterations by Ernest Newton, in
    1903. Misnamed Warrington Hall in
    Blomfield. Dem. c.1960.

B. Two lodges at Tittenley, insc. 1885. Attrib.
  (ill. 181).

C. Double cottage in the hamlet. Brick, t/h.
  Attrib.

161. Alcroft Grange, Hackington,
  Canterbury, Kent
New house
d: 1885 or later
cl: Thomas Sidney Cooper, R.A. (1803–1902)
  for Neville Cooper
m: brick, ½tmb, slate roofs
dr: R.A.
c: acc. bk, £50 only, 1889
Design clearly given to Cooper, and executed
  afterwards without proper supervision, as
  the details show. Now divided, and with
  some fair interior features surviving.
ack: Canterbury Public Library

162. St Agnes' Vicarage and Church Hall,
  Buckingham Avenue, Liverpool.
New vicarage and hall
d: des. 1885 etc., exec. 1886–7
cl: Mrs R. Horsfall and Howard Douglas
  Horsfall (1856–1936)
m: brick, st/drs
dr: R.A.
c: acc. bk, £230 11s, 1886–8; £4276
r: Eccl. Comms. file 63475; *AR* 1 (1896–7)
  pp. 268–9; *DEB*; Reports for Department
  of Architecture, University of Liverpool, by
  (a) E. P. Jones & M. V. Beswick, 1960; (b)
  J. B. Dutton, 1962
Simple house with small chapel upstairs. Hall
  attached to vicarage at one end, and
  church at other end.

163. Mere Bank, 56 Ullet Road, Liverpool (†)
New house and small stable
d: 1886–7

cl: Howard Douglas Horsfall (1856–1936)
m: brick, t/h, ½tmb
d: acc. bk, £499 8s, 1886–8
r: Report for Department of Architecture,
  University of Liverpool by Chapman,
  Morrow, Walton & Tankard, 1962
Large suburban house in full vernacular
  manner. Dem. c.1964.

164. Kemnal, Grayswood Road, Haslemere,
  Surrey
Small new house
d: des. 1886 etc., exec. 1887–8
cl: Mrs Harrison
ctr: Samuel Elliott of Newbury
m: brick, t/h
dr: R.A.
c: acc. bk, £76 8s, 1888
r: *Academy Architecture* 43 (1913) pp. 66–7
Pleasant house, possibly for the mother of
  Shaw's pupil Frederick Harrison. Well
  extended in similar style to the east.
  Grounds now much built upon, and
  approaches changed; some internal
  alterations.

165. New Scotland Yard, Victoria
  Embankment, London S.W.1
New central offices and later extensions for
  the Metropolitan Police
cl: H.M. Government
m: 2″ bricks, granite, st/drs, Westmorland
  slate roofs

A. Original building (now Norman Shaw
  North) (ills. 201–3)
  d: des. 1886 etc.; foundations exec. 1887–8,
    superstructure 1888–90
  ctr: John Grover & Son, c/w George Eraut
  dr: R.A.; R.I.B.A.; some with
    Metropolitan Police
  c: £104, 855; acc. bk, £6008 14s 6d,
    1888–92
  r: P.R.O. MEPOL 5/265, HO 45/9765/B
    841 & B841A, & HO 45/9630/A23696,
    with 15 letters from Shaw; drawings exh.
    at R.A., 1887 & 1890, the second reprd.
    in *BN* 2.5.1890; *B* 29.3, 3.5 &
    15.11.1890; *BN* 29.4.1887; *BJAR* 6 &
    20.4.1898; *A.A. Notes* 4 (1889–90) p. 114
    & 8 (1894) pp. 129–131; Hansard 343
    (1890) cols. 1282–3, 24.4.1890 & cols.
    1814–15, 1.5.1890, & 55 (1898) cols.
    114–16, 17.3.1898; *The Times* 3.5.1890 &
    30.3.1898; *Murrays Magazine*, July 1890

pp. 7–18; R. Blomfield, *Magazine of Art* 1894 pp. 330–4; Susan Beattie, *Architectural History* 15 (1972) pp. 68–81

The work included the boiler house, engine room and chimney to the NW. Now converted as an extension to Parliament, and much altered internally.

B. Extension building (now Norman Shaw South), bridge, and Cannon Row Police Station (ills. 258–9)

d: planned 1897 etc.; Police Station built 1900–2; foundations of extension 1901–3, superstructure built 1905–7

ctr: John Mowlem & Son, c/w J. S. Ham

dr: R.A.; and some with Metropolitan Police

c: *c.*£73,000; acc. bk, £302 10s, 1900

r: P.R.O. HO 45/9996/A47240 & 45/11742/10840, & MEPOL 2/417; *BN* 10.11.1899 & 21.2.1902 (ills. of Cannon Row), & 25.1.1907; *B* 20.7.1907; *BA* 21.12.1906; *A.A. Notes* 21 (1906) p. 135; Susan Beattie, *Architectural History* 15 (1972) pp. 68–81

Shaw was helped greatly on Cannon Row and partly on the extension by J. Dixon Butler and the Police Surveyor's Department. Engineering by Sir J. Wolfe Barry; E gates by Reginald Blomfield, made by Elsley, who exec. ironwork etc. in both blocks. Carving by Daymond & Son.

166. Moor Place, Much Hadham, Hertfordshire

Alterations to house with small new service wing, and some alterations and extensions to stables

d: des. 1886 etc; alterations 1887, extensions 1888–9

cl: Frederick Henry Norman (1839–1916)

ctr: G. Thurgood (1887); Thomas Hunt (1888–9)

m: brick, st/drs

dr: R.I.B.A.; and one at house

c: acc. bk, £242 12s, 1887–9

r: 33 letters from Shaw at house

Ernest Newton added a tactful wing at the opposite end to Shaw's, 1906–7. House in excellent condition, but service wing much altered internally.

ack: Mark Norman

167. 42 Netherhall Gardens, Hampstead, London N.W.3 (†) (ills. 128–9)

New house

d: 1887–8

cl: Edwin Long, R.A. (1829–91)

ctr: William Downs of Walworth

m: brick, st/drs, some t/h

dr: R.I.B.A.; R.A. (at R.I.B.A.)

c: acc. bk, £400, 1888–9

r: MBW Minutes of Proceedings 17.6.1887; *The Graphic* 9.6.1888; *A* 7 & 14.3.1890 (ills.); *DEB*; Sale Catalogue, November 1921 (Swiss Cottage Library)

The elevations of this large house are commonly attrib. to Lethaby. Entrance doors des. by Edwin Long. Later lived in by Edward Elgar, and dem. *c.*1937.

168. 170 Queen's Gate, London S.W.7 (ills. 184–8)

New house

d: 1888–90

cl: Frederick Anthony White

ctr: William Downs of Walworth

m: brick, cement dressings

dr: R.A. (F. A. White bequest)

c: acc. bk, £695 1s, 1888–90

r: MBW Minutes of Proceedings, 10.7 & 26.10.1888; *A* 2 & 9.1.1891 (ills.); *Architecture* 1 (1896) pp. 167–72; *The King* 12.4.1902; *B* 4.1.1902; *DEB*; Sale Catalogue, 1924; W. R. Lethaby, *Philip Webb and his Work* (1935) p. 116; *Survey of London* XXXVIII pp. 334–8

Now part of Imperial College, but with planning intact and some interior features.

ack: Mrs Helen Pingree, Julian Raikes, Jeremy White

169. Henley Hall, nr. Ludlow, Shropshire

Alterations to house

d: remodelling planned 1888, smaller additions and alterations exec. 1892

cl: John Baddeley Wood (1849–1911)

m: brick

dr: R.A.

c: acc. bk, £30, 1894

Projected refronting of house etc. of 1888 not carried out, but in 1892 Shaw added a billiard room on the SW side. Major alterations and extensions to house, 1907.

ack: Capt. J. M. G. Lumsden

170. Trinity College Mission Hall, 95 New Church Road, London S.E.5 (ill. 254)

New hall, rooms, and caretaker's flat

d: des. 1888 etc., basement exec. 1890–1,
    superstructure 1894–5
cl: Trinity College Cambridge Mission
ctr: Higgs & Hill
m: brick, st/drs
dr: R.A.
c: c.£15,000; acc. bk, £476 10s, 1891–5
r: Parish Magazines of St George's, Wells
    Way
C. F. A. Voysey's account books record a
    payment in connection with this building
    for unspecified work. Various later
    alterations probably including the bellcote.
ack: Revd. Michael Vonberg

171. Downside, nr. Leatherhead, Surrey
Alterations and additions to house
d: des. 1888 etc., exec. 1889–90
cl: Alfred Tate
ctr: Holland & Hannen
m: stone
dr: R.A.
c: acc. bk, £368 2s 4d, 1889–90
r: *CL* 17.9.1898 (ills.)
Work included a new ballroom and service
    wing, and remodelling of hall with new
    organ and large bay window, to Victorian
    Italianate house. Ballroom wing dem., but
    hall remains (without organ).

172. 46 Berkeley Square, London W.1
Alterations, and new small wing behind house
d: 1889–90
cl: Henry Bingham Mildmay (1828–1905)
m: brick, st/drs
dr: R.A.
Careful alterations to main house, and
    sensitive addition in garden behind, with
    first floor bay canted out on columns. This
    was dem. c.1972.

173. All Saints' Church, Richards Castle,
    Shropshire (ills. 219, 231)
New church
d: des. 1889 etc., exec. 1890–3
cl: Mrs H. Johnston Foster
ctrs: J. Thompson of Peterborough; carving
    by Farmer & Brindley, furnishings by
    Robert Christie and others; reredos painted
    by C. E. Buckeridge
m: local stone
dr: R.A.
c: £11,181 18s 6d; acc. bk, £601 14s 7d,
    1891–3

r: many papers and 118 letters from Shaw in
    possession of Lord Inchiquin; H.
    Muthesius, *Die Neuere Kirchliche Baukunst in
    England* (1901)
Many interior fittings by Shaw, i.e. pulpit,
    reredos frame, altar, stalls, and organ.
    Cartoon of reredos exh. at R.A., 1892.
ack: Lord Inchiquin

174. Bryanston, nr. Blandford, Dorset (ills. 57,
    239–43)
Very large new country house, and stables
d: 1889–94
cl: 2nd Viscount Portman (1829–1919)
ctr: Holland & Hannen
m: 2″ bricks, st/drs
dr: R.A.; R.I.B.A.
c: acc. bk, £11,141 9s 4d, 1890–4; c.£200,000
r: *B* 5 & 12.8.1899 & 2.8.1902; *A.A. Notes* 14
    (1899) p. 130
Now Bryanston School, and with many rooms
    altered, but plan mostly intact. Stables
    converted.
ack: Mrs Marjorie Portman, Mr E. T.
    Williams

175. Bristol House, Portsmouth Road,
    Roehampton, London S.W.15 (†)
Unspecified alterations
d: 1889
cl: Thomas Dickson Galpin
c: acc. bk, £140 17s, 1889
House dem. c.1903, when Bristol Gardens was
    laid out.
ack: Wandsworth Central Libraries.

176. 185 Queen's Gate, London S.W.7 (†)
    (ills. 173, 174, 192, 193)
New house
d: des. 1889 etc., exec. 1890–1
cl: William Vivian
ctr: John Grover & Son
m: brick, st/drs
dr: R.A.
c: acc. bk, £669 11s, 1890–1
r: *BA* 18.9.1891; *A* 22.1.1892; *Magazine of Art*
    1892 pp. 125–7; *B* 4.12.1897; *DEB; Survey
    of London* Vol. XXXVIII pp. 338–40
Redecorated by William Reynolds Stephens,
    1904. Destroyed by bombing, c.1940.

177. Framfield Place, Framfield, Sussex
Estate work
d: 1890–2
cl: Francis Hugh Baxendale (1862–1918)
c: acc. bk, £342 1s, 1892

432

A. Framfield Place
   Alterations and addition to house of c.1830
   m: brick, stuccoed
   dr: R.A.
   Work included remodelling of hall, and
     adding of nursery wing and billiard
     room. The drawing room was decorated
     by Lutyens at or very shortly after this
     date in a parody version of Shaw's Old
     English manner. Interiors in good
     condition.

B. Bailiff's Cottage
   m: brick, t/h
   dr: R.A.
     Now Hailwell House, and radically altered
       and enlarged.
   ack: Major W. J. Baxendale

178. Chesters, nr. Humshaugh,
   Northumberland (ills. 244–7)
Complete remodelling of house, with new
   stables
d: des. 1890, exec. 1891–4
cl: Nathaniel George Clayton (1833–95)
ctr: Walter G. Scott of Newcastle
m: dressed stone
dr: R.I.B.A.; R.A.
c: acc. bk, £2500, 1891–4
r: *ABJ* 27.7.1910; *CL* 17.2.1912; *Newcastle
   Daily Chronicle* 6.9.1895; *Newcastle Daily
   Journal* 6.9.1895
Organ in library with panels painted by
   Robert Christie. Service wing dem., but
   rest of house with fine surviving interiors.
   Stables attrib., and possibly also Chesters
   Museum and lodge.
ack: Mrs Benson

179. The Convent, Kingsgate, Broadstairs,
   Kent
Remodelling and extension of house
d: 1891–2
cl: Frederick Richards Leyland (1831–92)
ctr: W. & J. Denne
m: flint, st/drs
dr: R.A.
c: acc. bk, £526 5s, 1891–2
Original house was part of Lord Holland's
   Kingsgate follies, in Gothic style, but much
   updated before Shaw's remodelling. Good
   surviving interiors, but some possibly a little
   later. Stables and walled garden probably
   not parts of Shaw's campaign. Now Port
   Regis School, Convent Road.

180. East Combe, 44 West (later Westwood)
   Hill, Sydenham, London, S.E.26 (†) (ill. 252)
New house and stables
d: 1891–2
cl: James Paddon
ctr: John Grover & Son
m: brick, st/drs, t/h
dr: R.A.
c: acc. bk, £720 15s, 1891–5
r: L.C.C. Minutes of Proceedings, 27.10.1891
An important suburban house with extensive
   stabling etc. Probably dem. *c.*1965.

181. Kentish Town Police Station, Holmes
   Road, London N.W.5 (ill. 255)
New divisional police station
d: des. 1891 etc., exec. 1894–6
cl: Metropolitan Police
ctr: W. J. Mitchell
m: brick, st/drs
dr: R.A.; Metropolitan Police
c: acc. bk, £645 18s 6d, 1894–6
r: P.R.O. HO 45/9673/A46538; *B* 27.1.1894
   (†); L.C.C. Minutes of Proceedings
   10.4.1894
Slight external alterations to front; internal
   planning much changed and stable block
   dem.

182. Hampstead Mission Room, Hollybush
   Vale, London N.W.3
Small church hall
d: 1892
cl: Hampstead Parish Church
ctr: Higgs & Hill
m: brick
dr: R.A.
r: *Hampstead & Highgate Express* 17.12.1892
Much altered and extended, and now called
   Moreland Hall.

183. Haggerston Castle, nr. Beal,
   Northumberland (†) (ills. 248–50)
Remodelling and enlargement of house, and
   new adjacent watertower
d: 1892–7
cl: Christopher John Leyland (1849–1926)
ctr: Walter G. Scott of Newcastle
m: dressed stone
c: acc. bk, £5600, 1893–8
r: *BN* 19.6.1896; *BJ* 24.6.1896; *A* 19.6.1896;
   B 23.7.1915
Badly damaged by fire in 1911, and rebuilt by
   J. B. Dunn with added exterior colonnades
   and interior redecoration. Dem. 1931 and

more recently, but watertower survives.
ack: Mrs G. L. Y. Radcliffe

184. All Saints' Church, Galley Hill,
Swanscombe, Kent (ills. 210, 220, 229)
New church
d: des. 1893, exec. 1894–5
cl: Frederick Anthony White, Leedham
White, and John Bazley White
ctr: Thomas Boyce of Bloomsbury; carving by
Farmer & Brindley
dr: R.A.
m: knapped flint, st/drs
c: £5321 17s 11d; acc. bk, £267 16s, 1893–5
r: 10 letters of Shaw at R.A.; papers
including specification and one letter of
Shaw with Major Jeremy White; Eccl.
Comms. file 62801; *BN* 3.1.1896; H.
Muthesius, *Die Neuere Kirchliche Baukunst in
England* (1901) figs. 15 & 16; *Victorian
Church Art* (V & A Exhibition Catalogue,
1971) p. 134
S aisle of design never built. Fittings by Shaw
include stalls and pulpit, font, Bishop's
chair, and reading desk (1897). Organ case,
chancel panelling and reredos by Gerald
Horsley, 1912. Some other antique fittings
given by White family and since removed.
Since 1971 a Catholic church.
ack: Jeremy White

185. Bishop's House, 5 Kennington Park
Place, London S.E.11 (ill. 253)
New house and chapel
d: 1894–6
cl: Ecclesiastical Commissioners via Randall
Davidson, Bishop of Rochester
ctr: Higgs & Hill, c/w George Eraut
m: brick, st/drs
dr: R.A.
c: acc. bk, £523 16s 6d, 1895–6; £10,434 18s 8d
r: Eccl. Comms. files 5799/4 & 5; *A.A. Notes*
19 (1904) pp. 64–5; *BJAR* 15.10.1902;
G. K. A. Bell, *Randall Davidson* (1938)
p. 210
Front wall and gates form part of Shaw's
design. Chapel now gutted internally and
some interior alterations made.

186. The Hallams, nr. Shamley Green, Surrey
(ills. 72, 76, 92)
New country house and stables
d: 1894–5
cl: Charles Durant Hodgson (1850–1920)

ctr: Albert Estcourt & Sons of Gloucester
m: brick, st/drs, t/h, some ½tmb
dr: R.A.
c: acc. bk, £798 0s 10d, 1894–6
r: *BN* 3.1.1896; *DEH* 2 pp. 209–12
Fine and virtually unaltered house, with doors
of 1820 from Arundel Castle. Notes by
Lutyens on one of the drawings. Wing
added to stables.
ack: R. B. C. Hodgson; Margaret Pettersson

187. Walton Street Police Station, Walton
Street, London S.W.3
New divisional police station
d: 1894–5
cl: Metropolitan Police
ctr: John Grover & Son
m: stock brick, st/drs
c: acc. bk, £318 15s 6d, 1894–5
r: P.R.O. HO/46/9673/A46538/84; *B*
2.6.1894 (t)
Perhaps a rebuilding, and certainly an
uncharacteristic work. No longer a
divisional station, and much altered
internally.

188. 1 South Villas, Campden Hill Road,
London W.8
New iron and glass covered way and porch
d: 1894–5
cl: Francis Elmer Speed
r: L.C.C. Minutes of Proceedings, 11.12.1894
Apparently removed.

189. Hindhead Free Church, Hindhead,
Surrey
Plan for church
d: des. 1895, exec. 1896
cl & ctr: John Grover & Son
r: *B* 22.11.1912
Elevations of church were by Percy Ginham
who also designed the manse in 1900–1.
The plan was reused for further free
churches built by Grover at Hammer
(1903) and Beacon Hill (adapted, 1904–5).
ack: Revd. F. M. Hodgess Roper

190. White Star Offices, 30 James Street,
Liverpool (ills. 261–2)
New offices, designed with J. F. Doyle
d: 1895–8
cl: Messrs. Ismay, Imrie & Co.
ctr: J. Henshaw & Sons; c/w Allen Lloyd

m: granite, 2″ brick, st/drs, exposed steel stanchions
dr: R.A.
c: acc. bk, £1952 8s 6d, 1896–9
r: *B* 8.5.1897; *AR* 8 (1900) pp. 99–102; *DEB*; Wilton J. Oldham, *The Ismay Line* (1961) pp. 25, 130.
Some interior alterations, including the covering of most of the girders and stanchions. Ground floor office much changed.

191. Royal Insurance Offices, Dale Street, Liverpool (ills. 263–5)
Alterations and improvements to competition designs by J. F. Doyle
d: des. 1896 etc., exec. 1897–1902
cl: Royal Insurance Company
c: acc. bk, £527 12s, 1897; £819 2s 8d, 1904
r: papers at Royal Insurance Offices; J. N. Hetherington, *The Royal Insurance Company's Building, Liverpool* (1904)

192. Parr's Bank, 22 Castle Street, Liverpool (ills. 266–8)
New bank and lettable offices, designed with Willink & Thicknesse
d: 1898–1901
cl: Messrs. Parr of Warrington
ctr: Jones & Son of Warrington
m: granite, Piastraccio and Cipollino marbles, terracotta window frames
c: acc. bk, £870 16s 0d, 1898–1902
r: *Liverpool Daily Post* 30.9.1899; *AR* 10 (1901) pp. 146–155
Now National Westminster Bank, and much altered internally, especially in upper storeys. Banking hall intact in plan, but counters etc. changed.

193. Addington Park, Addington, London (ill. 251)
Internal reconstruction of house
d: 1898–1900
cl: Frederick Alexander English
ctr: John Thompson & Co.; carving, Farmer & Brindley
dr: R.A.
c: c.£70,000; acc. bk, £598 10s 6d, 1898–1902
r: W. Shaw Sparrow, *The British Home of To-Day* (1904), (ill.); *B* 22.11.1912
The payments suggest that not all the work was Shaw's, and the drawings show only

reconstruction and decoration of the hall. An extra storey was added to the house in this campaign.

194. Gaiety Theatre and Restaurant, Aldwych, London W.C.2 (ill. 256)
Alterations and improvements to design of façades by Ernest Runtz
d: des. 1901, exec. 1902–3
cl: London County Council
c: acc. bk, 10 guineas, 1905
r: L.C.C. Improvements Committee Minutes and Papers, 1901–2, *passim*; *BN* 9.8.1901; *BJAR* 4.9.1901; *BJ* 27.11.1912
The theatre façades have been entirely dem., but the Strand side of the Restaurant elevation still remains.

195. Alliance Assurance Offices, 88 St James's Street, London S.W.1 (ills. 272, 274)
New offices with lettable space over, and Post Office to north; designed with Ernest Newton
d: des. 1901 etc., exec. 1904–5
cl: Alliance Assurance Company
ctr: Trollope & Sons and Colls & Sons
m: Portland stone
dr: R.A.; R.I.B.A.; Crown Estate files
c: c.£57,000; acc. bk, £1686 8s 1d, 1903–11
r: documents with Sun Alliance Company, including 10 letters from Shaw; Crown Estates Office, files 15145 & 15320, with 15 letters from Shaw; *B* 19.5.1906; *AR* 21 (1907) pp. 46–51; W. G. Newton, *The Work of Ernest Newton* (1925) pp. 78–9; *Survey of London* XXX pp. 485–6
Some internal alterations, but generally in good condition.

196. Bradford Town Hall Extensions, Bradford, Yorkshire (ills. 269–71)
Large extensions to original building, designed with F. E. P. Edwards, and later, Reginald G. Kirkby
d: des. 1902 etc., exec. 1905–9
cl: Bradford Corporation
ctr: Michael Booth & Sons; carving by H. M. Millar, plasterwork by Ernest Gimson
m: dressed stone
dr: R.A.
c: acc. bk, £884 5s, 1905–11
r: documents at Bradford Town Hall, including 8 letters from Shaw (Box 153); *Yorkshire Post* 22 & 29.7.1905 and 29.9.1909; *An Account of the Town Hall Extension* (1911); *BN* 14.9.1906

Plans by Shaw and Kirkby to remodel the old
  entrance hall were not exec., this being
  done to other designs in 1914. In good
  condition.

197. Vauxhall Bridge, London
Contributions to design of new bridge in
  collaboration with L.C.C., W. E. Riley
  architect, Maurice Fitzmaurice engineer.
d: des. 1903, exec. 1904–6
cl: London County Council
dr: R.A.
r: L.C.C. Bridges Committee Minutes and
  Papers 1903, *passim*; *BN* 22.11.1912; *Survey
  of London* XXVI pp. 79–80
Balustrade removed and other alterations, 1973.

198. Regent Street Quadrant, Piccadilly and
  Piccadilly Circus rebuilding scheme (ills.
  275, 277–285)
Plans for rebuilding Crown properties in these
  streets, and designs for façades. Piccadilly
  Hotel only exec., in partnership with
  William Woodward & Walter Emden
d: des. 1904–11; Hotel exec. 1905–8
cl: H.M. Office of Woods & Forests
ctr (Hotel): Perry & Co.; carvers, Farmer &
  Brindley
m: Portland stone
dr: R.A.; R.I.B.A. (at R.A.)
c: acc. bk, £1605 (Hotel) and £2020
  (Quadrant), 1905–7
r: Crown Estates Office files 15276, 15382,
  15458, 15480 & 15492 (Hotel); 15325,
  15419, 15468, 15530, 15578 & 15794

(Quadrant & Circus); *B* 5.5.1906,
  16.2.1907, 27.3.1909 & 5.5.1911; *BN*
  26.5.1905, 4.5.1906, 15.6.1906 & 28.9.1906;
  BJAR 20.6.1906; *CL* 30.12.1922;
  A. Trystan Edwards, *Good and Bad Manners
  in Architecture* (1924) pp. 44–90; *Survey
  of London* XXXI pp. 87–95
The rest of the Quadrant, Swan & Edgar,
  and the County Fire Office were rebuilt,
  mainly to the amended designs of Reginald
  Blomfield, in 1920–3.

199. Sibleys Orchard, Chambersbury Lane,
  Leverstock Green, Hertfordshire
Extension to small house
d: 1905–6
cl: Percy Webster
m: brick, roughcast
dr: R.I.B.A.
Altered internally, but with exterior surviving
  well.

200. Portland House, 8 Lloyds Avenue,
  London E.C.3 (ill. 286)
New office building
d: 1907–8
cl: Associated Portland Cement
  Manufacturers Ltd.
m: reinforced concrete; Portland stone facing
dr: R.I.B.A.
c: acc. bk, £245, 1907–8
r: *B* 22.11.1912; *Concrete* 6 (1972) pp. 30–4
Gutted internally, 1971–2.
ack: J. H. H. Williams

2. Miscellaneous Jobs, Recorded in Robert Shaw's Abstract of his Father's Account Books

Date	Description or Client	Receipts
1866	'Proposed Hotel at Douglas'	£38 19s 1d
1867	W. D. Hertz, Bradford	£87
1867	Wedgwood & Sons	£22 12s 5d
1868–9	W. P. Pattison, Holmesdale House, Nutfield	£79 13s 6d
1870	Haslemere Church (probably help with J. W. Penfold's rebuilding)	£50
1871	J. P. Ellames, Manor House, Little Marlow	£40 2s 9d
1872	Miss Ogle, 80 Coleshill Street	£52 13s 2d
1872	W. H. Wall, Pembury	£64 13s
1873	Miss Hall, Ravenswood, West Wickham	£48 12s 6d
1874	Bishop McDougall, The College, Ely	£52 1s 0d
1875–6	G. H. Best, Builth (?)	£108 1s 6d
1875	Ottawa, 'Terraces and steps'	£20
1876	Miss Courtenay, 34 Brompton Square	£40
1876	Pickford & Co., Gresham Street	£74 6s

1876	A. G. Thorold, 3 Grosvenor Gardens	£66 6s
1877–9	C. L. Norman, 90 Portland Place	£275 3s
1879	R. B. Martin, Chislehurst (possibly for Overbury)	£100
1892	D. Sinclair, Eliot Bank, Sydenham	£80

N.B. The addresses here given do not necessarily imply that the work was carried out at that place, though that seems usually to be the case.

3. Short Gazetteer of Executed Buildings, by Administrative District

Italics indicate demolished buildings

APPENDIX:

Pupils and Assistants

This brief and possibly not exhaustive list covers the known architectural assistants and articled pupils who worked in the Shaw office, but not the purely administrative clerks. No list of works is attempted, but a few references are given; the main works of Brydon, Horsley, Keen, Macartney, May, Newton and Prior can be found in the building press. Note the absence of Reginald Blomfield and Halsey Ricardo, frequently but erroneously assumed to have been Shaw pupils.

SYDNEY HOWARD BARNSLEY (d.1926). Brother of Ernest Barnsley, Sedding's pupil. Briefly in the office from 1885. Travelled with Schultz to Greece, 1887. Short practice as a London architect, c.1890, then in 1892 went with his brother to Gloucestershire, where they set up a craft workshop.

REGINALD BARRATT (1861–1917). Son of a London doctor. Articled in 1879, but transferred to painting, with Shaw's agreement, and studied with Lefebvre and Bouguereau. Painted scenes of oriental life and architecture. *BN* 14.2.1917; *Who Was Who 1916–28*.

JOHN MCKEAN BRYDON (1840–1901). Scottish. First with J. & J. Hay of Liverpool, then c.1856 with David Bryce of Edinburgh, and managing assistant in Glasgow to Campbell Douglas and J.J. Stevenson, c.1863–6. Chief assistant to Nesfield & Shaw, 1867–9. Began career as a furniture designer, helping to found firm of Wallace and Cottier. Large and successful architectural practice, 1869–1901. *BN* 7.2.1890; *BJAR* 12.3.1895 & 5.6.1901; *B* 1 & 8.6.1901; *DNB*.

ARCHIBALD HASWELL CHRISTIE (d.1945). Younger son of the dealer and decorator Robert Christie. Went to Shaw's office in mid-1890s 'to learn to draw the orders' (Robert Shaw). Good draughtsman. Educational work with Lethaby at Royal College of Art; L.C.C. Art Inspector to Technical Education Board, 1902. Settled near Cromer.

RICHARD CREED (1846–1914). Articled in Worcester, and then assistant to Nesfield and Shaw, dates uncertain. Began practice c.1874, but not an interesting architect. *B* 15.5.1914; *BN* 15.5.1914.

CYRIL DUNCOMBE FITZROY (1861–1939). Articled 1882, but on completion in 1885 changed to painting, to Shaw's regret (Robert Shaw). With Gerald Horsley in Italy, 1886. Reputedly very talented, but became Inspector of Government Schools.

PERCY NORMAN GINHAM (1865–?). Office boy c.1880, then articled, and finally principal assistant c.1890–6. Continued to help Shaw c.1896–9, while running small independent practice. Entered L.C.C. Architect's Department, 1902, left owing to neurasthenia, 1915.

EDWIN GEORGE HARDY (1859–?). Son of the painter F. D. Hardy. Started as a painter, but in Shaw's office c.1879–82. Abroad with Barratt, 1884 (sketchbooks at R.I.B.A.). 'He seemed very capable at first, but got into some financial trouble, and I believe committed suicide early in the nineties' (Robert Shaw).

FREDERICK HARRISON (d.1926). Articled c.1879. Soon left, and eventually took up the theatre. Became Beerbohm Tree's first secretary, and then lessee of the Haymarket Theatre (Robert Shaw).

GERALD CALLCOTT HORSLEY (1862–1917). Youngest son of J. C. Horsley. Articled 1879, and stayed on as assistant. Fine draughtsman. In Italy and France, 1886, and again abroad, 1887–8. Moderately successful practice, 1889–1917. President of A.A., 1911–3. *B* 13.7.1917; *RIBAJ* 24 (1917) p. 221; *Who Was Who 1916–28*; Blomfield pp. 95–6.

ARTHUR KEEN (1861–1938). Articled c.1878, and assistant to Newton c.1882–4. Sizeable practice of good quality, c.1890–1920.

President of A.A., 1910–11. Documents at R.I.B.A.; *ABJ* 10.8.1910.

WILLIAM RICHARD LETHABY (1857–1931). Articled in his native Devon to Alexander Lauder, then with Richard Waite of Duffield, 1878–9. Chief assistant to Shaw, 1879–89. Small architectural practice from 1889. On L.C.C. Technical Education Board, 1894, and first Principal of Central School, 1896. For his career see *RIBAJ* 39 (1932) pp. 293–302; Blomfield pp. 97–105; and the monographs by R. W. S. Weir (1938) and A. R. N. Roberts (1957).

MERVYN EDWARD MACARTNEY (1853–1932). Son of Irish doctor. At Oxford 1873–7, articled 1878. Large and interesting architectural practice, 1882–1932. Editor of *Architectural Review*; Surveyor to St Paul's Cathedral, 1906–31; knighted 1930. *BJAE* 11.8.1909; *Who's Who in Architecture* (1914); *AJ* 2.11.1932; *ABN* 4.11.1932; *Who Was Who 1929–40*; Blomfield pp. 90–2.

EDWARD JOHN MAY (1853–1941). Articled to Decimus Burton, 1869, and on completion, assistant to Nesfield and Shaw. Abroad on sketching tour, 1876; fine draughtsman. Began career with houses etc. at Bedford Park. Large and varied domestic practice. 1880–1929. Sketchbooks at R.I.B.A.; *Who's Who in Architecture* (1914); *RIBAJ* 48 (1941) p. 124.

FREDERIC MILLER. Articled *c*.1878, but nothing is known of him.

WILLIAM WEST NEVE (1852–1942). From Cranbrook. Articled 1870, and then assistant. Small architectural practice from 1877. Went to live at West Court, Bray, 1899. *B* 12.2.1943.

ERNEST NEWTON (1856–1922). Educated at Uppingham. Articled 1873, and then chief assistant, 1876–9. Very big and successful high-quality practice, 1879–1922. President of R.I.B.A., 1914–17. For his career see W. G. Newton, *The Work of Ernest Newton* (1925).

FREDERICK O'NEILL. Probably son of the painter G. B. O'Neill. Articled 1877. 'He was not clever in any way and soon disappeared. I think he went to America' (Robert Shaw).

EDWARD SCHRODER PRIOR (1852–1932). Son of a chancery barrister. Educated at Harrow and Cambridge; articled 1874, and then assistant. Restricted but always fascinating practice, 1880–1916. *ABN* 26.8.1932; *Who Was Who 1929–40*; Blomfield pp. 88–90.

ROBERT WEIR SCHULTZ (1861–1951). Scottish, and articled to Rowand Anderson in Glasgow. Assistant to Shaw *c*.1884–6, and then with Ernest George and Peto. Travelled in Greece 1887–8 and 1890. Sizeable practice, 1891–1939. Changed name to R. Schultz Weir, *c*.1914. *Who's Who in Architecture* (1914); *B* 11.5.1951.

HAROLD SWAINSON (1868–1894). Educated at Haileybury and Cambridge; a scholar. In office *c*.1890–2, and studied also with Holland and Hannen. Went with Lethaby to Istanbul, and then with Somers Clarke to Egypt, where he died at Luxor. Sketchbook at R.I.B.A.; *A* 4.1.1895; *Alumni Cantabrigienses 1752–1900* Vol. 6 p. 90.

PHILIP COLDWELL THICKNESSE (1860–1920). Son of Bishop Thicknesse of Peterborough; educated at Marlborough. Articled 1879. Varied practice in Liverpool, in partnership with W. E. Willink from 1884. *AJ* 10.3.1920; *Town and Country Planning* 9 (1941) p. 98.

CHRISTOPHER GEORGE WEALD (d.1959). Office boy *c*.1890, and then assistant. Officer in L.C.C. Architect's Department from 1899, where he spent his whole career. *B* 28.3.1959.

Notes to Text

Notes to Preface

1. H. Bolitho, A Batsford Century (1943) p. 37.
2. See AR 89 (1941) pp. 41–6.

Notes to Chapter 1

1. Phoebe Stanton, Pugin (1971) p. 189.
2. B 25.9.1852 gives an account of Pugin's funeral. For Nesfield and Shaw's 'accidental' presence see Spiers in RIBAJ 2 (1895) p. 607.
3. Family information in this and later chapters comes mostly from Robert Norman Shaw's manuscript notes on his father, henceforward 'Robert Shaw'. I have also used a family tree in the possession of Mr Bryan Shaw.
4. Inventory of personal estate of William Shaw, 5th February 1834, in Scottish Record Office.
5. 'Fools and their money are soon parted' was a favourite expression of hers when given something (Robert Shaw).
6. Edward Prior in DNB article.
7. Speculation as to Shaw's first master is probably fruitless, but one possibility must be T. H. King, for whom see p. 9.
8. He was recommended by Burn for the R.A. School on 26th April 1849 (R.A. Admissions Book).
9. For Burn, see Proceedings of the R.I.B.A. (1869–70) pp. 121–9, B 3.6.1882, and the forthcoming article by David Walker in Six Victorian Architects. Architecture 1 (1896) p. 5 records some complimentary comments made by Shaw about him.
10. The only account of W. A. Nesfield's life is in DNB, which is based on J. L. Roget, A History of the 'Old Water-Colour' Society (1891) Vol. 1 pp. 522–3 and Vol. 2 pp. 82–4.
11. Gardener's Magazine 1840 pp. 50–6 describes the villas in an article of 1838; their exact date is not clear.
12. A list of country houses where the elder Nesfield worked would have to include Alnwick, Alton Towers, Arundel, Bylaugh, Castle Howard, Drayton (Northants.), Eaton Hall, Grimston, Harewood, Hengrave, Holkham, Kinmel, Somerleyton, Stoke Edith, Teddesley Hay, Treberfydd, Watcombe, Witley, and Worsley Hall.
13. Many of W. A. Nesfield's charming letters are preserved in the Kew Archives.
14. For W. E. Nesfield's early career see Spiers in A.A. Notes 10 (1895) pp. 47–9 and RIBAJ 2 (1895) pp. 605–11.
15. BN 15.9.1905. For Colling, see also RIBAJ 9 (1902) p. 188.
16. J. M. Brydon records the meeting with Shaw in AR 1 (1897) p. 236.
17. RIBAJ 2 (1895) pp. 605–11 and B 22.11.1912 mention the Houses of Parliament escapade. The R.I.B.A. albums show that Nesfield had already visited St Augustine's Ramsgate in May 1852 and went again in July 1853.
18. They lived first at 2 Hill Road, then from 1849 at 8 Albion Road (later Harben Road).
19. Robert Shaw, who speaks of Stuart's influence upon Shaw.
20. Robert Shaw.
21. From an essay in Description and History of the Church of St Mary Magdalene, Munster Square (1902), ed. Tom E. Sedgwick, pp. 6–9.
22. Record book, R.A.
23. Illustrated London News 31.12.1853. Significantly, Colling drew architectural subjects for the I.L.N. between 1849 and 1855.
24. E 18 (1857) p. 28.
25. Shaw's sketches are in loose sheets at the R.A., Nesfield's in the R.I.B.A. albums.
26. Thus E. J. May in one of his sketchbooks, August 1876: 'To quote the epitaph in Scott's office, "Here lies one of an earnest band who spoilt half the churches in the land".'

27. Letter to Elizabeth and Janet Shaw, 14.1.1855.

28. Information on this tour comes from Robert Shaw and from Shaw's letters to his family.

29. His itinerary, reconstructed from letters and surviving drawings, ran roughly thus: Rouen, Evreux, Beauvais, Gisors (18.7.1854), Amiens (25–27.7). Nesfield then returns home, Shaw goes north and meets his family in Brussels (early August), whence he proceeds to Vilvorde, Malines (10–12.8), Antwerp (19–22.8), Ghent (23.8), and also visits Bruges and Tournai.

   In October 1854 Shaw and his family are in Paris, and travel thence via the Rhône and Côte d'Azur into Italy, stopping at Genoa. In November–January they are in Florence.

   He is then at Prato, Pistoia, Lucca (16–17.1.1855), Pisa (22.1) and Leghorn; takes the boat via Civitavecchia to Naples (31.1) and comes north to Rome (21.3). This section was travelled with J. T. Christopher, who proved an uncongenial companion.

   Mrs Shaw, Jessie and the Temple cousins were in Rome with him in April 1855. They then return to Florence, while he visits Perugia, Assisi, Foligno, etc. He probably rejoins them and they travel north, seeing Verona, Padua and Venice and going on to Innsbruck. In late May 1855 they split, and Mrs Shaw and Jessie settle at Cannstatt for nearly a year.

   Alone, Shaw visits Augsburg, Nordlingen, Nuremberg (28.5–8.6), Regensburg (23–27.6), Ulm, Esslingen, calls in at Cannstatt briefly, proceeds to Heilbronn, Heidelberg, Strasbourg (12.7), Freiburg im Breisgau (18.7) and thence to Cannstatt, where he takes a month's holiday.

   He sets out again, meeting David Macgibbon at Nuremberg (22.8). Together they go to Bamberg, Erfurt (1–7.9), Weimar, Naumberg, Merseburg, Halle, Leipzig, Altenburg, Magdeburg (12.9), Halberstadt (14.9), Hildesheim, Lübeck (27.9), Schwerin, Berlin (2.10), Dresden, Prague (15.10), Vienna, Venice and Padua. From here Macgibbon proceeds to Ferrara, while Shaw turns west to Vicenza, Verona (7–9.11), Brescia and Milan (10.11). After seeing Pavia, he turns back north to Cannstatt via Como, Constanz and Ulm (20.11).

   Finally, in February 1856 Shaw is back in France. His route is Braisne, Strasbourg (13–14.2), Metz, Toul (26–28.2), Chalons sur Marne, Reims, Paris (28.3), Chartres, Le Mans (9–18.4), Alençon, Séez, and Angers; and then in uncertain order, Tours, Bourges (1.5), Sémur, Auxerre, Sens and Troyes. By then his family have moved to Heidelberg, and after joining them, Shaw returns to England.

30. RNS to Elizabeth and Janet Shaw, 22.1.1855.

31. See p. 20.

32. Robert Shaw says he missed Vézelay because Murray then omitted it. This was just before Viollet-le-Duc published drawings of it in his *Dictionnaire*.

33. Extracts in this and the following paragraphs are from letters of Shaw to his family. This one is a mild example of what Pevsner has christened 'St Peter-baiting', a fashionable sport in the 1850s.

34. RNS to Fred White, 19.9.1905.

35. For Harding (who lived in St John's Wood), see J. L. Roget, *A History of the 'Old Water-Colour' Society* (1891) Vol. 1 pp. 500–14 and Vol. 2 pp. 177–89. Nesfield's experiments are recorded in the R.I.B.A. albums, e.g. an engraving marked 'ye first time of trying Sept. 1856'.

36. John Clayton, like James Forsyth, was then working with Salvin on the restoration of Wells Cathedral, which is perhaps how Shaw got to know him.

37. See G. G. Scott, *Remarks on Secular and Domestic Architecture* (1857).

38. See James Forsyth in *A.A. Notes* 16 (1901) pp. 109–111, and John Hebb in *RIBAJ* 10 (1903) pp. 396–400, the main list of Nesfield's works.

39. For the visit to Viollet-le-Duc, see *B* 7.4.1888. There are drawings copied from or by him, principally for Amiens and Vézelay, in the Nesfield R.I.B.A. albums. Was it Viollet-le-Duc who drew Nesfield's attention to the *armoire* at Bayeux, drawn out in *Specimens*?

40. Nesfield's itinerary is given in Spiers, *A.A. Notes* 10 (1895) pp. 47–9 and *RIBAJ* 2

(1895) pp. 605–11, and by Hebb in *RIBAJ* 10 (1903) pp. 396–400.

41. RNS to C. F. Hayward, 1.3.1859, in 'Fabs' file, R.I.B.A. Drawings Collection.
42. Frank C. Bowen, *The Flag of the Southern Cross* (1939) pp. 16–17.
43. *E* 19 (1858) p. 46 and *BN* 5.2.1858.
44. Information on Street's office comes from Robert Shaw, from Paul Joyce, and from correspondence between Robert Shaw and Miss Sedding seen by John Betjeman. A noted Prayer Book in the possession of Anthony Symondson, given by J. D. Sedding to Shaw after Edmund Sedding's death, corroborates the affection between the clerks in the office and the preoccupation with music.
45. Robert Shaw.
46. For Street, see H. R. Hitchcock in *Society of Architectural Historians' Journal* Vol. 19 No. 4 (1960) pp. 145–71, and S. Muthesius, *The High Victorian Movement in Architecture* (1972) Chs. 3 & 5.
47. *Architecture* 1 (1896) p. 39; from a longer extract in A. E. Street's biography of his father.
48. Reginald Blomfield, *Richard Norman Shaw R.A.* (1940) p. 16, henceforward 'Blomfield'.
49. Sketchbooks at R.I.B.A. and loose sheets at R.A.
50. *RIBAJ* 2 (1895) p. 610. For Harding and sketching paper see *DNB*, and *Foreign Art Quarterly Review* 2 (1863) p. 411.
51. *RIBAJ* 10 (1903) p. 397 mentions Nesfield's association with the Fabs, for which see the file in R.I.B.A. Drawings Collection. Nesfield's friendships with Albert Moore, Whistler and Caldecott are mentioned in *A.A. Notes* 16 (1901) pp. 109–111. Other close friends among painters were Simeon Solomon and Thomas Armstrong.
52. For Burges see Charles Handley-Read in *Victorian Architecture* (1963), ed. P. Ferriday, and in *Burlington Magazine* 105 (1963) pp. 496–509.
53. For Nesfield's early works see the list in *RIBAJ* 10 (1903) pp. 398–400. For Combe Abbey, see the drawings in the V & A and the photographs in *CL* 4 and 11.12.1909.
54. John Baron, *Scudamore Organs* (1862) p. 17. The rare first edition is of 1858.
55. *BN* 25.3.1859.
56. *BN* 6.5.1859 and 13.4.1860.

57. The present presbytery at Drogenbos dates from 1885–6 and no records could be found of what preceded it. At Bruges, many of the headstones have been removed.
58. For Forsyth, see the brief obituary in *BN* 11.2.1910, and his article on Nesfield in *A.A. Notes* 16 (1901) pp. 109–111. He had a son called James Nesfield Forsyth.
59. Leaver did much later work for Shaw, including the charming hinges at Low Bentham and Piccards Rough inscribed with childish figures and the words 'James Leaver made me'. According to the Post Office Directory for 1866, Leaver and Shaw were working together in that year only in some capacity as 'iron tank manufacturers', using James Temple's Billiter Street offices.
60. See the letter from Alphonse Warington in *B* 27.4.1861.

NOTES TO CHAPTER 2

1. For William Wells' life and character, see the scanty accounts in *Gentleman's Magazine* 29 (1848) p. 87, and *Art Journal* 9 (1847) p. 335. For his pictures, see Christie's Sale Catalogues, 12–13.5.1848, 21–22.1.1857 and 27.4.1860. Constable disliked him: see R. B. Beckett, *John Constable's Correspondence with C. R. Leslie Vol. III*, Suffolk Records Society VIII (1965), esp. pp. 94–9.
2. *The Diaries of Joseph Farington* (1922–8) esp. Vols. 6 & 7, *passim*.
3. J. C. Horsley, *Recollections of a Royal Academician* (1903) pp. 55ff., and Frederick Goodall, *Reminiscences* (1902). At Penshurst Place is a painting by Landseer, Lee and Goodall showing many of the painters under the '1000-year' Sidney oak. Peel, the Princess Victoria, and the King of Saxony were among visitors to Redleaf.
4. See his long article on Redleaf in *Gardener's Magazine* 15 (1839) pp. 353–79, and photographs of the grounds in AR 82 (1937) pp. 203–6. Wells' gardener, Joseph Wells, was no relation, but father of H. G. Wells! See *An Experiment in Autobiography* (1934).
5. He designed in the 1830s The Grove, Penshurst, and Burrswood, Groombridge: John Newman, *West Kent and the Weald* (1969) pp. 299 and 441. Mrs Allibone has

now discovered that the clients of The Grove knew the Devey family well.

6. For Devey and his friends, see Mark Girouard, *The Victorian Country House* (1971) p. 103. His cottages are discussed in *CL* 23.12.1899, his work at Hammerfield is illustrated in *CL* 16.2.1901, and his work in and around Penshurst considered in Newman, *op. cit.*, pp. 440–2. Recently, Jill Allibone has found much that is new from Devey's R.I.B.A. drawings.

7. Nesfield albums at R.I.B.A.; information from Jill Allibone.

8. Shaw and Nesfield R.I.B.A. sketchbooks.

9. Extracts from Nesfield's sketchbook, *ibid.*

10. Though Eagle Wharf was never published, C. L. Eastlake hints that he knew it in *A History of the Gothic Revival* (1872) p. 339.

11. The Town Hall was built to designs by T. C. Sorby, and has long been demolished.

12. For Hook, see below, n. 22. *A.A. Notes* 16 (1901) p. 105 mentions Birket Foster's house, now demolished.

13. C. W. Cope, *Reminiscences* (1891) p. 232. See also the entries in *DNB*, and Christopher Wood, *Dictionary of Victorian Painters* (1971).

14. J. C. Horsley, *Recollections of a Royal Academician* (1903), esp. pp. 338–342. For Horsley's personality, see also L. T. C. Rolt, *Isambard Kingdom Brunel* (1957) pp. 279–81.

15. Horsley, *op. cit.*, p. 341, and *B* 13.5.1865.

16. Personal information in this paragraph comes from Rose Horsley's diaries, 1865–9; for permission to use them I am grateful to Mrs Nancy Strode. James Knight is also mentioned in the diary, but he is more probably the artist than the client of Shaw's Farnham Bank.

17. Cooke designed some garden buildings at Biddulph Grange.

18. E. W. Cooke's diaries at National Maritime Museum, 1864–5.

19. Ruskin, *The Two Paths*, 5.140.

20. Goldsmiths' Company archives, Guildhall Library.

21. Information in this paragraph from E. W. Cooke's diaries, 1866, *passim*.

22. 'Hooksville' and 'Cookesville' are mentioned in John Munday's excellent account of Cooke in *Mariner's Mirror* 53 (1967) pp. 99–113. For Hook's Silverbeck, see F. G. Stephens, *James Clarke Hook*

(1888) and Allan J. Hook, *James Clarke Hook* (1932) Vol. 2 pp. 171–2.

23. *B* 7.5.1870.

24. The first perspective is illustrated in C. L. Eastlake, *A History of the Gothic Revival* (1872). The second, showing Glen Andred in the background, was shown at the R.A. in 1870 and published in *BN* 31.3.1871.

25. G. G. Scott, *Remarks on Secular and Domestic Architecture* (1857) pp. 159–60.

26. For Combe Abbey see *CL* 4 and 11.12.1909.

27. For photographs and analysis of the Regent's Park and Kew lodges, see R. P. Spiers, *The Magazine of Art* 22 (1898) pp. 83–88.

28. Lady Cowper-Temple, *Memorials* (1888) pp. 63–5.

29. See *A.A. Notes* 16 (1901) pp. 109–111. There is a good article on the Regent's Park gardens in *Gardeners' Chronicle* 17.9.1864.

30. For a full assessment of Nesfield's architectural work see J. M. Brydon, *AR* 1 (1897) pp. 235–247 and 283–296, supplemented in *AR* 2 (1897) pp. 24–32.

31. See pp. 131–3.

32. RNS to E. W. Cooke, 9.3.1866.

33. Nesfield sketchbook, R.I.B.A.

34. See Simeon Solomon in Cecil Y. Lang, *The Swinburne Letters* Vol. 2, 1869–75 (1959) pp. 32–4.

35. For the history of blue and white, see G. C. Williamson, *Murray Marks and his Friends* (1919) pp. 31–50.

36. Robert Shaw.

37. Williamson, *op. cit.*, pp. 12–13, 45 and 84–89.

38. Robert Shaw.

39. That is why the name of Ruskin could sometimes be used in its support. Ruskin's opponents on aesthetic matters like Pater and Lady Dilke had little in common with the designers of the Aesthetic Movement.

40. See e.g. Nesfield's R.I.B.A. sketchbooks, notably a chest from Chichester and a settle finial from Winchester. Street often used 'pies', on mediaeval precedent.

41. *AR* 1 (1897) p. 235.

42. Glen Andred: Cooke's diaries, 20.8.1866 and 20.9.1867. Cloverley: notes on V & A drawing of 21.9.1867. Kew Lodge: papers in Kew Archives, esp. 'Gates' Volume, 1847–1913, pp. 231 ff.

43. See n.42. The papers show that a double

443

lodge with central entrance was originally intended. The cornice was to carry plaques in a framework of ware from the Etruria Works, which Shaw specially visited in December 1866; cf. the contemporary lodge at Kinmel Park.

44. *RIBAJ* 10 (1903) p. 397.
45. Simeon Solomon in Cecil Y. Lang, *The Swinburne Letters Vol. 2*, 1869–75 (1959) pp. 32–3.
46. One R.I.B.A. sketchbook includes an odd page of moralizing prose, with pages apparently describing the horrors of debauchery excised.
47. Nesfield to Mrs Walker of Lea Wood, 9.11.1877, letter in author's possession.
48. Robert Shaw.
49. Letter in possession of Mrs Nancy Strode.
50. Robert Shaw, with supplementary information from Miss M. C. Shaw.
51. RNS to Agnes Shaw, 16.7.1885.
52. Robert Shaw.
53. Information from diaries of Dr. J. D. Heaton, in possession of Brian and Dorothy Payne of Horsforth. For Ellen Heaton, see Virginia Surtees, *Sublime and Instructive* (1972) pp. 143–254.
54. *The Artist* 19 (1897) pp. 121–7.
55. Ruskin's *Modern Manufacture and Design*, reprinted in *The Two Paths*, was given at Bradford on 1.3.1859.
56. For Woodbank, Harden Grange and Oakwood see *AR* 144 (1968) pp. 35–8, and for Waterhouse's Mechanics Institute, *Keighley News* 19.11.1864. Shaw may also have entered the abortive Keighley Town Hall competition of 1865 (Keighley Public Library).
57. *Bradford Observer* 28.4.1864. This paper announces the lecture (14.4.1864) as being given 'at the solicitation of a friend of Mr Ruskin'. The committee secretaries were Heaton, Harris and John Mitchell. *Traffic* was published in *The Crown of Wild Olive* and has recently been reprinted in J. D. Rosenberg, *The Genius of John Ruskin* (1963) pp. 273–95.
58. Some of Webb's drawings survive in the R.I.B.A. collection.
59. The follow-up to the competition is best pursued in *Bradford Observer* 19 and 26.5 and 2.6.1864. See also *B* 28.5 and 18.6.1864.
60. See Shaw's report on his designs in the R.A. Collection.

61. *BN* 15 and 22.4.1864. Mr Power faded into oblivion.
62. ICBS file 6267.
63. Goodhart-Rendel, in his index of Victorian churches.
64. For the sequence of events leading to demolition see *CL* 27.12.1973.
65. Dr Heaton's diary describes this job in unflattering terms.
66. *St John's Church Leeds 1634–1934* pp. 16–21.
67. *CL* 18.2.1911.
68. On Netley and Windsor, see Paul Thompson, *William Butterfield* (1971) pp. 112–7. On the pavilion plan see A. D. King, *Medical History* 10 (1966) pp. 360–373.
69. See *B* 14.11.1868, and Shaw's illustrated reports on his competition designs at the R.A.
70. *BN* 26.2.1869.
71. J. C. Horsley, *Recollections of a Royal Academician* (1903) pp. 256–7. There is no satisfactory biography of Armstrong, but see D. Dougan, *The Great Gun-Maker* (1971).
72. RNS to Agnes Shaw, 24 and 27.9.1869.
73. Blomfield p. 20.
74. This account of Cragside is designed not to overlap too much with Mark Girouard's excellent articles in *CL* 18 and 25.12.1969, abridged in *The Victorian Country House* (1971) pp. 141–6. The best early description is in D. D. Dixon, *Upper Coquetdale* (1903) pp. 430–442.
75. See, for instance, Reynolds's thirteenth Discourse on Art (1786).
76. E. W. Cooke's diary, 7.6.1867.
77. Ruskin, *Lectures on Architecture and Painting* 1.16.

NOTES TO CHAPTER 3

1. See Alec Clifton-Taylor, *The Pattern of English Building* (1962 and later edns.), and Jane A. Wight, *Brick Building in England from the Middle Ages to 1550* (1972).
2. For Victorian and Edwardian analysis of these buildings, see S. O. Addy, *The Evolution of the English House* (1898), and for regional variations, the excellent *Old Cottages and Farmhouses* series: *Kent and Sussex* (1900) by E. Guy Dawber and W. Galsworthy Davie, *Shropshire Herefordshire and Cheshire* (1904) by J. Parkinson and E. A. Ould, and *Surrey* (1908) by W. Curtis Green and W. Galsworthy Davie. A more specialized pioneering study is Ralph

Nevill, *Old Cottage and Domestic Architecture of South West Surrey* (1889).

3. Phoebe Stanton, *Pugin* (1971) pp. 160–3.
4. The cottages attributed to Pugin at Albury, Surrey, reject local village tradition in favour of piquant Tudor devices like pepperpot stacks and emphatic diapering. Can they really be his?
5. See G. E. Street, *Brick and Marble in the Middle Ages* (1855), *passim*, and Paul Thompson, *William Butterfield* (1971) pp. 145–69 and 226–50.
6. G. G. Scott, *Remarks on Secular and Domestic Architecture* (1857) p. 179; J. J. Stevenson, *House Architecture* (1880) Vol. 1 p. 349.
7. Lawrence Weaver, *Houses and Gardens of E. L. Lutyens* (1913) pp. xxi–xxii, gives Cloverley categorical primacy in the revival of thin brickwork. The thicker pointing there and at Lowther Lodge is scarcely noticeable. Possibly, the use of pale red thin bricks was suggested by Nesfield and Shaw's visit to Ockwells in 1864: see Wight, *op. cit.*, p. 229.
8. Edmund Beckett, *A Book on Building* (1876 edn.) p. 81: 'It is a very absurd waste of money to have special bricks made smaller than the usual size, as some architects do'.
9. J. J. Stevenson, *op. cit.*, Vol. 2 p. 50.
10. Benjamin Woodward's stacks on the Oxford Museum are a good example.
11. See the albums of Devey sketches at the R.I.B.A. Drawings Collection.
12. On thickness of chimneys, see W. Curtis Green and W. Galsworthy Davie, *Old Cottages and Farmhouses in Surrey* (1908) p. 55.
13. E. Guy Dawber and W. Galsworthy Davie, *Old Cottages and Farmhouses in Kent and Sussex* (1900) pp. 16–7.
14. Mark Girouard, *The Victorian Country House* (1971) pl. 186 illustrates Butterfield's Milton Ernest boathouse; but the same book, pls. 309–12, shows E. W. Godwin's Beauvale Lodge (1871–3) abounding in gablets, a possible sign of genuine Japanese architectural influence, as John O'Callaghan suggested to me.
15. This is sometimes called 'sprocketing'.
16. Stockwell Hospital and Kensington Asylum Competition Reports at R.A.; cf. G. G. Scott, *Remarks on Secular and Domestic Architecture* (1857) p. 140.
17. Report on competition in Bromley School Board Minutes, 28.10.1889.
18. Alcroft Grange is Shaw's only rural building to be slated, one of many proofs that it was not supervised by him.
19. Dawber & Davie, *op. cit.*, p. 23.
20. Butterfield's only certain use of this extended tile-hanging is Alfington school, Devon (1849–50): Paul Thompson, *William Butterfield* (1971) p. 203 pl. 120.
21. Stockwell Hospital and Kensington Asylum Reports at R.A.
22. Derek Linstrum, *Sir Jeffrey Wyatville* (1972) pp. 96–7 illustrates the Edensor lodges at Chatsworth.
23. RNS to Mrs Johnston Foster, undated.
24. At much the same date Pearson was experimenting with genuine timber construction direct on a brick plinth at Roundwick.
25. *CL* 6.9.1973.
26. Drawing of 19.4.1873 at R.I.B.A.
27. Drawing of 26.12.1870 at V & A; see also Blomfield p. 23.
28. By 1911, Jill Franklin points out to me, R. A. Briggs in *The Essentials of a Country House* says that structural half-timbering is virtually impossible because of by-laws.
29. See Ferrey's lecture in *Proceedings of R.I.B.A.* (1856–7) pp. 151–5, and G. G. Scott, *Remarks on Secular and Domestic Architecture* (1857) pp. 108, 132 and 139.
30. Drawing of 7.1.1870 at R.A.
31. See the church porch (1869) and cottages (1874–5) at Radwinter, the Rose and Crown Inn front, Saffron Walden (1872–4) and the Newport Grammar School (1875–6).
32. There are many precedents for nogging: Devey used it at Hammerfield, Street at his East Grinstead Convent.
33. See his first catalogue (1887).
34. See the examples in S. Muthesius, *The High Victorian Movement in Architecture* (1972) and Paul Thompson, *William Butterfield* (1971).
35. Some of the early corner-turning casements may be based on the Amberley farmhouse sketched by Shaw and Nesfield on their 1862 tour.
36. John Betjeman heard this story from Voysey's lips.
37. Blomfield p. 20.
38. See e.g. the drawings for Garendon: Phoebe Stanton, *Pugin* (1971) figs. 160 and 163.
39. *RIBAJ* 22.1.1915.

40. *B* 22.11.1912.
41. RNS to Mother Etheldreda, 19.3.1874.
42. *AR* 32 (1912) p. 301.
43. RNS to Frank Birch, 20.4.1876.
44. Drawing of 26.7.1870 at R.I.B.A.
45. For the rest of this chapter I have drawn deeply from Jill Franklin's Ph.D. thesis, *The Planning of the Victorian Country House* (University of London, 1973), as well as from Mark Girouard, *The Victorian Country House* (1971).
46. Robert Shaw records a quarrel over costs at The Hallams, referred to by Blomfield p. 86.
47. Figures mainly calculated on the basis of Shaw's 5% commission, from an abstract of his account books. But Jill Franklin warns that the true costs are usually higher than they look.
48. Girouard, *op. cit.*, fig. 21. See also Burn's Buchanan House (Girouard fig. 2) and the discussions in Robert Kerr, *The Gentleman's House* (1864).
49. For the parsonage plan see S. Muthesius, *The High Victorian Movement in Architecture* (1972) fig. 47 (White's Little Baddow) and Paul Thompson, *William Butterfield* (1971) fig. 21 p. 108 (Butterfield's Alvechurch).
50. See a remark in *The Studio* 7 (1896) p. 98.
51. The success of this plan is acknowledged by the fact that James MacLaren appears to have plagiarized it not long after. See *BN* 17.5.1872, Shaw's protest in *BN* 31.5.1872, and later correspondence. The plan was re-used for one of the concrete cottage designs later on: see *BN* 25.2 & 4.3.1881.
52. For Endsleigh, see Derek Linstrum, *Sir Jeffrey Wyatville* (1971) p. 89. Coombe Warren was Devey's first important house to employ offset; for a later one, Goldings, see Girouard, *op. cit.*, fig. 7.
53. The revisions and additions to the original Leyswood plan already consolidate the accommodation and make the arrangements more logical.
54. Franklin, *op. cit.*, p. 101.
55. Whether these buttresses are really functionless is debatable, as Shaw had unusual methods of tying and propping the ends of his open spans.
56. Only later was it converted to a living room. Blomfield's fig. 4 and Girouard's pl. 52, borrowed from the photograph in Ernest Willmott, *English House Design* (1911), are misleading.
57. J. J. Stevenson, *House Architecture* (1880) Vol. 2 pp. 75–6.
58. Blomfield p. 109.
59. For Smirke see J. M. Crook, *The British Museum* (1972) pp. 171–2. For Burn, see *Catalogue of the R.I.B.A. Drawings Collection, B*, (1972) pp. 124 and 129, for examples at Fonthill Abbey and Buchanan House. For the change from cast to wrought iron, see W. K. V. Gale, *Iron and Steel* (1969) Chs. 4–6.
60. A lecture on iron by J. A. Picton in *Transactions of the R.I.B.A.* (1879–80) pp. 149–161 with ensuing discussion is specially helpful; p. 187, Street condemns the Albert Memorial box girders, and admires Matthew Digby Wyatt's 'public retiring places' as the best examples of iron architecture. See also W. H. White in *Transactions of the R.I.B.A.* (1877–8) p. 33. For Kelham, see Mark Girouard, *The Victorian Country House* (1971) p. 14; for St Pancras Hotel, Nicholas Taylor, *Monuments of Commerce* (1968) pl. 36, and for Arisaig, drawing by Webb in R.I.B.A. Drawings Collection.
61. See Nesfield's drawings at the V & A. At Combe, the exposed stanchions were for a conservatory.
62. It is hard to know exactly when steel became regularly available for concealed girderwork. The *Notes on Building Construction arranged to meet the syllabus of the Science and Art Department at South Kensington* (4 vols., various dates), give some helpful technical details.
63. The sections at Farnham bewildered an experienced architect like Harold Falkner: see his notes with the R.I.B.A. drawings.
64. Drawing of 14.1.1876 at V & A.
65. Ruskin, *Seven Lamps of Architecture* 2.10.
66. The Metropolitan Building Act of 1855 did not prohibit exposed iron but left its use to the discretion of the district surveyors. For strong safety evidence against exposed iron see the Minutes of Evidence to the Select Committee on the abortive Metropolitan Buildings and Management Bill, 1874.
67. W. H. White, *Transactions of the R.I.B.A.* (1877–8) p. 33.
68. *CL* 30.8.1956.
69. J. J. Stevenson, *House Architecture* (1880)

70. Vol. 2 p. 56.
70. RNS to Henry Stanhope of Gawsworth, 30.8.1873.
71. For Babbacombe, see Nesfield's drawings at the R.I.B.A.; for Lea Wood, Nesfield to Mrs Walker, 2.4.1876 (author's possession); for Alderbrook, drawing of August 1879 at R.A.
72. Stevenson, *op. cit.*, Vol. 2 pp. 62–3.
73. 'East and West Home's Best' wins hands down on number of appearances. Pierrepont has: 'Here's to the Ingle where true hearts mingle' and 'It is not the quantity of the meats but the cheerfulness of the guests that makes the feast'.
74. G. G. Scott, *Remarks on Secular and Domestic Architecture* (1857) p. 81.
75. J. C. Horsley, *Recollections of a Royal Academician* (1903) p. 341; and for Corner House, undated drawing at R.A.
76. Fuller, *Worthies* ix.R.
77. For the originals see Arthur Lane, *Guide to Collection of Tiles, V & A Museum* (1939) pls. 44e & f. A more unusual type occurs in the Leyswood smoking room and at Nesfield's Bank Hall. Michael Darby tells me that Owen Jones had used this type of tile some years before.
78. For these types see Julian Barnard, *Victorian Ceramic Tiles* (1972).
79. E. W. Cooke's diaries at National Maritime Museum, 1867–8, *passim*.
80. Mrs Mildmay, diaries, in possession of Mrs Mildmay White.
81. RNS to R. B. Martin, 5.12.1898.
82. *CL* 18.2.1911.
83. E. W. Godwin's comments on mantelpieces in *A* 3.6.1876 are illuminating.
84. J. J. Stevenson, *House Architecture* (1880) Vol. 2 p. 58.
85. Drawing of 17.6.1875 at R.I.B.A.
86. Shaw plays the same trick with an off-centre stack at The Three Gables (1881–2), and with windows along the garden front at Banstead Wood (1899). The rear elevation of Nesfield's nearby Loughton Hall (1878) is closely related.

NOTES TO CHAPTER 4

1. The sole exception is the extension at Draycott Villa, Fulham, of 1866.
2. For the origins of Queen Anne, see Mark Girouard in *The Listener* 22 and 29.4.1971, and for Stevenson, the same writer in *The Connoisseur* November 1973 pp. 166–174 and February 1974 pp. 106–112.
3. The crucial early houses of Queen Anne are: Webb's 91–101 Worship Street (1863), 1 Holland Park Road (1865–6), 1 Palace Green (1868), 19 Lincolns Inn Fields (1868), and 35 Glebe Place (1869); Bodley's Scarborough Vicarage (1864), Valley End Vicarage (1868), Cefn-bryn-Talch (1868) and houses at Malvern (1869); Jackson's Send Rectory (1863); G. G. Scott junior's Garboldisham (1869 etc.).
4. J. J. Stevenson, *House Architecture* (1880) Vol. 1 p. 183.
5. For Petit see *B* 25.5.1861, and for Stevenson's original paper on Queen Anne, *BN* 26.6.1874.
6. See E. R. Robson, *School Architecture* (1874).
7. See p. 45.
8. *The Studio* 7 (1896) p. 26.
9. The Bromley terrace design, if built, has been demolished. It may have connections with the almshouses in Monkwell Street, City, sketched by Shaw in 1862. Evidence for the added storey at Bromley Palace comes from photographs in the Bromley Public Library.
10. For I'Anson's techniques, see his article in *Transactions of the R.I.B.A.* 21.11.1864, and N. Taylor, *Monuments of Commerce* (1968) pp. 35–43.
11. Notes on Bodley from Cecil Hare's family, communicated by Peter Howell.
12. The full form of the oriels appears at Swan House and Clock House on the Embankment, and at 6 Ellerdale Road and The Three Gables in Hampstead. Sedding used a close equivalent in the early 1870s for his vicarage at St Clement's Bournemouth.
13. The house front was later taken down and is now in the V & A.
14. For one of many objections to this practice, see C. L. Eastlake, *Hints on Household Taste* (1878 edn.) pp. 35–43.
15. *BN* 24.10.1873.
16. *The Times* 19.11.1912.
17. *DEH* 1.120 uses the phrase 'das bürgerliche Barock'.
18. The contractors, Manley and Rogers, were building Harperbury and Hounds-

wood at the same time.

19. W. R. Lethaby, *Philip Webb and his Work* (1935) p. 75.
20. *BN* 23.3.1877 mentions that Lascelles executed the whole of the arches and cut brickwork for Lowther Lodge and 196 Queens Gate on a special brick-cutting machine he devised.
21. *B* 16.5.1874 and *BN* 25.6.1875.
22. See *B* 7.5.1870 and *BN* 20.5.1870 & 31.3.1871. For subsequent criticism, see e.g. *B* 16.5.1874, 6.5.1876 & 5.5.1883.
23. *BN* 24.10.1873.
24. Ruskin, *The Stones of Venice* Vol. 2, preface to 1874 edition.
25. On Blackmoor see *CL* 29.8 and 5.9.1974.
26. *B* 4.4.1896.
27. *AR* 12 (1902) pp. 124–6.
28. Robert Shaw.
29. J. Mordaunt Crook, *The British Museum* (1972) p. 79.
30. J. J. Stevenson, *House Architecture* (1880) Vol. 1 p. 105.
31. *Architectural History* 1 (1958) p. 55 (letter of 10.12.1879).
32. See the correspondence published by John Brandon-Jones in *ABN* 3.6.1949.
33. Robert Shaw.
34. Letters in author's possession.
35. Robert Shaw.
36. Robert Shaw says the only recorded copy was of a stiff letter sent to Mrs Erskine Wemyss of Clock House.
37. See the selection in *Architectural History* 18 (1975) pp. 60–85.
38. Shaw seems to have visited some of his works quite rarely. On minor neglect, he told Fred White: 'I hesitate to say that I have not got my price from neglecting my work, I do not know what it is, but it is certainly not a brace of pheasants' (Robert Shaw).
39. RNS to Mrs Johnston Foster, 8.6.1889 & 29.7.1892 (old church), 22.7.1890 (shafts), 24.10 & 10.11.1890 (tracery).
40. RNS to C. L. Norman, 29.12.1884.
41. Robert Shaw.
42. RNS to Mother Etheldreda, 8.9.1874.
43. The following account is derived from papers and letters of 1872–4 in the R.I.B.A. Drawings Collection.
44. For the earlier state of Preen, see A. Sparrow, *History of Church Preen* (1898).
45. Sparrow remained Shaw's lifelong friend, and Shaw stayed there at least once while building Richards Castle church.
46. But possibly the driving force was her brother Edmund Christy, for whom Sedding built a house and St Clement's Church in Bournemouth: see p. 165. The builders for both Adcote and Shaw's St Swithun's Bournemouth were Hale and Son of Salisbury.
47. Robert Shaw.
48. If so, she succeeded. See Violet Stuart-Wortley, *Grow Old Along With Me* (1952).
49. Arthur Heywood-Lonsdale was heir to J. P. Heywood of Cloverley. This is the only recorded case of a commission coming to Shaw through the Nesfield connection, and could suggest that Shaw got to know the family at the time Cloverley was built.
50. Local lore recorded in C. G. Timmis' Cambridge B.A. thesis on *The Domestic Revival in Surrey* (1973), which contains other interesting facts on Surrey clients of the period.
51. *Newcastle Daily Journal* and *Newcastle Daily Chronicle* 6.9.1895.
52. Small works like this often preceded bigger ones. Thus in 1876 Shaw did some work for Pickford and Co., before re-building Greenham Lodge for their proprietors the Baxendales (Account book).
53. *AAJ* 71 (1955–6) pp. 20–21.
54. Local lore.
55. RNS to Murray Marks, 16.1.1892. For further reading on Leyland, see Clement Jones, *Pioneer Shipowners* (1935) pp. 115–124, and for his artistic connections and collection, *Art Journal* 1892 pp. 129–138. Some accounts of the Peacock Room, notably that by E. R. and J. Pennell, *The Life of James McNeill Whistler* (1908) Vol. 1 pp. 202–9, suggest that Shaw's work at 49 Princes Gate was contemporary with Jeckyll's, but that is not the case.
56. *CL* 16.11.1972, in an article on the Holland Estate artists' houses; see also the sequel on Godwin's Chelsea houses in *CL* 23.11.1972.
57. This was the first picture to be illustrated in *The Graphic*. Fildes' later great hit, *The Doctor* (1891), was painted from a full-scale replica of a crofter's cottage erected in his studio.

58. The Long painting best recalled is *The Babylonian Marriage Market* (1875).
59. A full list of Shaw's studio houses should include also the addition to Compton, Streatham (1872–3) for George H. Best, now demolished, and Walton House, Chelsea (1882–4) for E. S. Kennedy. Both were probably rich amateur painters.
60. For Boughton's house-warming, see W. Crane, *An Artist's Reminiscences* (1907) p. 200.
61. *BA* 19.5.1882; the architect was Macartney.
62. *The Magazine of Art* 1885 pp. 144–150.
63. M. H. Spielmann and G. S. Layard, *Kate Greenaway* (1905) pp. 142–4.
64. Blomfield p. 44; Sale Catalogue, November 1921.
65. Devey was one of the few mid-Victorian architects who set his face against block contractors, but even he had to rely upon them a lot; W. H. Lascelles, for instance, built Killarney.
66. RNS to Barings, 9.2.1880.
67. Robert Shaw.
68. Drawing of June 187[6?] at R.I.B.A.
69. RNS to Frank Birch, 20.12.1876.
70. For Waterlow and Matthew Allen see G. Smalley, *Sir Sydney H. Waterlow* (1909) pp. 61–66, and J. N. Tarn, *Five Per Cent Philanthropy* (1973) pp. 50–7.
71. *BN* 30.10.1885 briefly summarizes his career. For an account of a visit to Lascelles' works by the A.A., see *BN* 23.3.1877.
72. RNS to Revd. H. A. Stanhope, 21.5.1873.
73. RNS to Revd. H. A. Stanhope, 7.7.1873.
74. Peter Collins, *Concrete* (1959), gives an outline history of the material, but for early British developments needs much supplementing.
75. Collins, *op. cit.*, Ch. 2, and *B* 18.1.1868. Blomfield used concrete at St Barnabas' Oxford, White at St Mark's Battersea. For the latter see *BN* 23.7.1875.
76. For Street's boarding houses at Marlborough see *BN* 25.6.1875 and 23.7.1875. All Street's work at the school is unorthodox in one way or another.
77. Other cases: Shaw's work at The Rhydd Court, Whitwell, Eldersfield Lawn, and St John's Gate for Sir E. A. H. Lechmere,

for whom Street designed the church at Whitwell; and his addition to Coatham Convalescent Home, where Street had built a chapel.
78. RNS to Mother Etheldreda, 15.12.1873.
79. I am grateful to Miss Helen Brooks for much help in connection with Lascelles; see her article in *Concrete* 6 (1972) pp. 28–9, and Collins, *op. cit.*, pp. 42–3. For early accounts of his work see *B* 14.8.1875, 15.4.1876 and 30.12.1876, and *Concrete* 3 (1908–9) pp. 296–8. *Transactions of the R.I.B.A.* 1875–6 pp. 185–7 and 226–7 gives a verbatim account of Lascelles's part in the meeting there.
80. Thomas Potter, *Concrete* (1877) pp. 28–9.
81. *Les Merveilles de l'Exposition de 1878* pp. 112–3. For a photograph of the house see *The Aesthetic Movement* (Camden Arts Centre Exhibition Catalogue, 1973) p. 24. Pevsner in *RIBAJ* 64 (1957) p. 174 misidentifies the house.
82. *B* 31.8.1878. For other notices of the book, amongst the earliest of Batsford imprints, see *BN* 19.7.1878 and *A* 24.8.1878.
83. See the description in *Concrete* 6 (1972) pp. 28–9.
84. Robert Thorne tells me this is an early use of the term.
85. *BN* 4.3.1881; for the earlier plagiarism of this plan see p. 446 n.51.
86. *B* 22.11.1912.
87. G. A. Sala, *Paris Herself Again in 1878–9* (1880) Vol. 2 pp. 148–151.
88. Sala, *op. cit.*, Vol. 1 p. 197; *A* 30.3.1878.
89. *FG* 7.9.1878.
90. For an illustration of a piece of Nesfield furniture see *BN* 16.10.1891, showing a sideboard from Farnham Park very like that at Bank Hall.
91. Clive Wainwright, who has guided me much in this section, points out the originality of this design in the light of settles by, for instance, H. H. Richardson.
92. The cradle is sometimes misdated to 1861, but 1867 is right.
93. *BN* 23.3.1877 and *FG* 24.3.1877; the sideboard is illustrated in *BN* 5.1.1877, the half-tester bed in *FG* 31.3.1877.
94. See pl. 141. Elizabeth Aslin discusses Godwin's furniture in *V & A Museum Bulletin* 3 (1967) pp. 145–154.
95. The Willesley chairs are now at High

Hall, Dorset.

96. *BN* 23.3.1877.

97. *Cabinet Maker* 8 (1887–8) pp. 57–9.

98. *The Artist* 19 (1897) pp. 121–7, in a good account of Heaton's London career.

99. For Heaton's London 'atelier' see *BN* 19.10.1894.

100. See Shaw's letter in *BN* 30.3.1877. The contrary impression is given in Elizabeth Aslin, *The Aesthetic Movement* (1969) pp. 68 and 77. For the work of Shaw, Lascelles and Heaton at the Building and Furniture Exhibitions, see *B* 9.4.1881 and 25.3.1882; *BN* 16.4.1880 and 8.4.1881; *A* 1.4.1882; *BA* 12.5.1882; *FG* 13.8.1881 and 20.5.1882; and *Cabinet Maker, Guide to Furniture Exhibitions* 1881 pp. 7–8 and 1882 p. 9. All these reviews suggest that Heaton's role at this time was still small. Shaw's work included designs for G. S. Lucraft and Co. and the Coalbrookdale Iron Company as well as for Lascelles.

101. Possible survivors in the light furniture range are a battered sideboard with some gilding at Adcote, and one or two later pieces at Cragside and Bourn Hall.

102. See Heaton's catalogues of work of 1887 and 1894, the latter including much derivative Neo-Georgian furniture.

103. Robert Shaw.

104. See the undated drawings for 6a Ellerdale Road at the R.A.

105. Cragside is a good example, with its plunge baths in the basement, Tobin tubes for foul-air extraction, complex heating system, and unusually tracked flues.

106. Robert Shaw says he had one such experience while with Burn.

107. Bramah closets were getting old-fashioned by the 1890s but Shaw still stuck to them. 'I cannot get myself to believe entirely in these wash-out or wash-down closets. They are good enough for hotels and public lavatories, but they are *not* clean, especially the wash-out, and they are very noisy, and the flush is not nearly so good as in the valve closet, though it makes more noise about it.' RNS to R. B. Martin, 12.9.1898.

108. *B* 12.1.1878 and *BN* 25.1.1878 are the original publications. The diagram and text were reprinted as a pamphlet.

109. For comments see *B* 36 (1878) and *BN* 34

110. (1878) *passim*. Shaw's main reply is in *B* 9.2.1878.

111. *B* 23.2.1878.

112. *B* 8 and 15.2.1879.

113. Ewan Christian used it once with success: *Transactions of the R.I.B.A.* 1880–1 p. 710.

114. Robert Shaw.

115. *B* 20.11.1909.

116. *B* 30.6.1888.

117. Examples of both the open soil pipe and the drainpipe survived at New Scotland Yard until 1974.

118. Robert Shaw reports both these inventions.

119. E. L. Lutyens to Emily Lytton, 14.7.1897.

120. RNS to Mrs Foster, 10.8.1893.

121. For Creed see *BN* 15.5.1914; for May, *RIBAJ* 48 (1941) p. 124 and *Who's Who in Architecture* (1914).

122. Robert Shaw.

123. After 1879, the perspectives sent to the R.A. were drawn by the pupils. Dawpool was the last domestic work Shaw showed there (1884) and for this, plans, elevations and sections were provided to supplement Lethaby's four views.

124. For Newton's early career and his debt to Shaw, see W. G. Newton, *The Work of Ernest Newton R.A.* (1925) pp. 3–4.

125. Robert Shaw, no doubt reflecting his father's opinion. For excellent vignettes of Prior and the other pupils see Blomfield pp. 87–96.

126. Robert Shaw, who gives dates and details for several of the pupils.

127. Robert W. S. Weir, *William Richard Lethaby* (1938) pp. 3–4.

128. Robert Shaw.

129. *AR* 135 (1964) p. 240.

130. Robert Shaw.

131. *Ibid.*

132. A. R. N. Roberts, *William Richard Lethaby* (1957) p. 14. For the Sedding stories, see the notes by Sir Charles Nicholson in the V & A library.

133. Drawing of November 1881 at R.A.

134. RNS to R. Lewis, 24.3.1904.

135. RNS to Arthur Keen, 17.3.1878.

136. RNS to Arthur Keen, undated.

137. RNS to Arthur Keen, 27.10.1880.

138. RNS to Arthur Keen, 15.1.1881 and 9.4.1881.

139. RNS to Mr Keen, 28.1.1881.

140. RNS to Mrs Foster, 22.10.1889.

140. RNS to E. J. May, 2.7.1882.
141. Robert W. S. Weir, *William Richard Lethaby* (1938) pp. 12–13 says that Avon Tyrrell came to Lethaby via Shaw.
142. *BJ* 4.2.1896, in a profile of James Weir.
143. These are the vestry to St Michael's Blackheath Park (1879), included in W. G. Newton's list of his father's work, and an R.I.B.A. drawing of 11.6.1878 for an unknown cottage for a Mr Robert Warton.
144. *RIBAJ* 39 (1932) p. 306.
145. Drawing of 1881 at R.I.B.A.
146. RNS to G. L. Gomme (County Hall), 24.4.1907.
147. *AR* 32 (1912) p. 301.
148. 'I am drawing all the details for your work myself, and so it takes me some time, but I would rather make time and do them myself.' RNS to Mrs Foster, 24.10.1890.

Notes to Chapter 5

1. *DNB* article.
2. Alderbrook, Baldslow Place, Broadlands and The Knolls were all undertaken in 1879; Rosemount and Knight's Croft in 1880; the Alliance Assurance office, Holme Grange, The Three Gables and Frognal Priory do not seem to antedate 1881.
3. RNS to Mr Keen, 28.1.1881.
4. RNS to Arthur Keen, 15.4.1881.
5. *AR* 32 (1912) p. 301.
6. C. H. H. Parry's diary, 25.6.1881, kindly communicated by Lord Ponsonby.
7. Robert Shaw.
8. See p. 437.
9. RNS to Murray Marks, 12.12.1877.
10. See the excellent account in *Survey of London* XXXVIII pp. 342–5.
11. Royal Commission for 1851 Exhibition, file 100, 5.3.1875.
12. The only true precedent appears to be Grosvenor Gardens, overlooking the grounds of Buckingham Palace, built speculatively in the late 1860s to the designs of Thomas Cundy III, after a limited competition for Grosvenor Place had aborted. Grosvenor Gardens is in quite a few particulars relevant to Albert Hall Mansions.
13. For the smarter flat, see Sydney Perks, *Residential Flats* (1905); and for working-class flats, J. N. Tarn, *Five Per Cent Philanthropy* (1973).
14. A larger second block was added to the original by E. R. Robson in 1888.
15. Royal Commission for 1851 Exhibition, file 100, 18.11.1878.
16. RNS to General Scott, 2.11.1877.
17. The other schemes were for a terrace of houses to be built by John J. Chappell (1877), and for another terrace on the future site of 180–5 Queen's Gate. Royal Commission for 1851 Exhibition, files 99 and 100.
18. Robert Shaw.
19. Blomfield omits the essential mezzanine level.
20. Perks, *op. cit.*, pp. 126–9, admires the stairs but says they occupy more space than would be allowed in his day; and p. 40, puts English dislike of winders down to difficulty with carpets.
21. The drawings show no passenger lift, but the evidence for one is conclusive; see Perks, *op. cit.*
22. The planning of these levels was much varied in execution.
23. 'Our Inglewood Mondays had the attraction of being attended by the artists and literary people whose residence made Bedford Park a village such as Rabelais dreamed of in Thélème.' Moncure D. Conway, *Autobiography* (1904) Vol. 2 pp. 339–41, which also gives Abbey's remark. For maturer views, see W. Creese, *The Search for Environment* (1966) pp. 87–107, the excellent articles by T. Affleck Greeves in *CL* 7.12 and 14.12.1967, and Ian Fletcher, *Romantic Mythologies* (1967) pp. 169–207.
24. Compare, e.g., the generous plots on the Norham Manor Estate of North Oxford, begun *c*.1867.
25. See *Harpers Monthly Magazine* 62 (1881) pp. 481–90, and Walter Hamilton, *The Aesthetic Movement in England* (1882) pp. 111–23.
26. 'I am afraid I really do not know what all this "Town Planning" is about. It seems to me to be a kind of epidemic which has broken out all over the world. I sincerely hope it may have good results.' RNS to Frederick Hellard, 24.8.1910.
27. *BN* 2.2.1877.
28. *BN* 5 and 19.1.1877. Among other harsh critics of Bedford Park was J. P. Seddon:

see *BN* 6 and 20.2 and 5.3.1880.

29. *BN* 30.1.1880.
30. *B* 25.3.1882.
31. For the visits see *BN* 9.3.1877 and 30.1.1880.
32. This design, more fully worked out, was re-used for villas on the Ashley Park Estate, Walton-on-Thames.
33. *BN* 30.1.1880.
34. Bodley and Garner used a similar belvedere on their contemporary River House, Chelsea Embankment (1879).
35. *BN* 2.1.1880.
36. *B* 31.1.1880.
37. None of the existing drawings or lithographs shows exactly what was built. On the first (June 1879), Shaw has written 'Please do not let the "Building News" get hold of this in its present state'.
38. The present green appears a little blue for accuracy.
39. Eccl. Comms. file 80148, letter from Carr of 6.11.1877.
40. ICBS file 8306.
41. Robert Shaw.
42. 'So you have tired of old Carr. . . . I expect you have made at least twice as much out of the place as I have. Very glad to think it and to hear that you are driving such a devil of a trade.' RNS to E. J. May, 2.7.1882.
43. Drawing at R.I.B.A., illustrated in R. Macleod, *Style and Society* (1971) fig. 4.1.
44. *CL* 20.11.1915.
45. Robert Shaw.
46. See his sketchbooks at the R.I.B.A.
47. Sedding, who built a lodge at Flete, restored the neighbouring churches of Holbeton and Ermington for the Mildmays with a wealth of such motifs.
48. RNS to Elizabeth Shaw, 6.7.1880.
49. Cook and Wedderburn, *The Works of John Ruskin* Vol. 36 p. 199, letter of 27.5.1876.
50. RNS to J. D. Sedding, 5 and 20.11.1882.
51. RNS to Agnes Shaw, 16.7.1885.
52. Robert Shaw.
53. Reynolds, *Discourses on Art* no. 7.
54. Ruskin, *The Seven Lamps of Architecture* 7.5.
55. Lecture title, *c.*1880.

NOTES TO CHAPTER 6

1. The classic exposition of London development is John Summerson, *Georgian London* (1945 and later edns.). For later periods see especially Hermione Hobhouse, *Thomas Cubitt* (1971), and the *Survey of London* Vols. XXXVII and XXXVIII.

2. An unforeseen danger was that individualistic houses would prove less adaptable to changing taste and conversion. That is partly why Cadogan Square, Chelsea Embankment, and Queen's Gate have failed to keep the prestige of Belgravia.

3. See Mark Girouard on Godwin's Chelsea houses in *CL* 23.11.1972.

4. Shaw took a significant holiday in Belgium and Holland in 1873, and much later could still commend Antwerp as a model for town houses (*The Tribune* 19.11.1906). Ernest George's debt to the Low Countries and North Germany is obvious.

5. See p. 451 n.17, and the account of the estate in *Survey of London* Vol. XXXVIII.

6. Robert Shaw.

7. A. J. Adams also illustrated in the building press a pair of juxtaposed houses, of which no. 70 is one.

8. Several exterior details for these houses were interchangeable: see the letter to Keen quoted on pp. 232–3.

9. See e.g. Hobhouse, *op. cit.*, fig. 9.

10. Robert Shaw adds quaintly: 'As a matter of fact his words were not accurate.' The trouble with the story is that the plan of West House is without steps in the relevant place.

11. Philip Webb later restored and added to Great Tangley Manor for Wickham Flower. See also G. C. Williamson, *Murray Marks and his Friends* (1919) pp. 167–8.

12. In a letter in the possession of John Brandon-Jones, Philip Webb disparages the new Embankment houses and contrasts them with the sobriety of Cheyne Walk.

13. William Morris's term for them: see p. 258.

14. J. J. Stevenson, for instance, was against setting single gable ends to the street because of difficulties with gutters, chimneys, and party walls: see his *House Architecture* (1880) Vol. 1 pp. 260–5.

15. Once again, the Ipswich oriels were an afterthought, not present on the first drawings.

16. See Lutyens' The Pleasaunce at Overstrand, and his house at Varengeville.

17. See Metropolitan Building Act 1855 Sec-

tions 14 and 56.

18. MBW, Presented Papers to Board, 4.6.1880 (49), on Barings.

19. RNS to Arthur Keen, n.d. The houses concerned are 68 and 72 Cadogan Square (renumbered), Farnley House and Clock House.

20. MBW, Presented Papers to Board, 13.5.1881 (55) and 29.6.1883 (86), on Albert Hall Mansions and Bolney House.

21. Robert Shaw.

22. Robert Shaw singles out the plan of this house for special mention.

23. N. Taylor, *Monuments of Commerce* (1968).

24. Compare also Street's St Mary Magdalene, Paddington and the rear elevations of the Law Courts.

25. MBW, Presented Papers to Board 4.6.1880 (49), no doubt reflecting the words of Shaw's application.

26. *BN* 40 (1881) *passim*.

27. Shaw had his own views on the firm. 'Things seem to be settling a bit in Bishopsgate. The general opinion is that Lord Revelstoke will have to retire from the firm, and that that very disagreeable Charles Baring will come back.' RNS to Agnes Shaw, *c.* Nov. 1890.

28. Bourn Hall is a case where a large service wing was designed but not accepted.

29. RNS to Frederick Norman, 27.1.1887.

30. RNS to Frederick Norman, 27.10.1888.

31. RNS to C. L. Norman, 25.4.1885.

32. RNS to C. L. Norman, 2.7.1884.

33. *CL* 3.8.1918.

34. W. R. Lethaby, *Philip Webb and his Work* (1935) pp. 115–16. Lethaby became White's friend as a result of his work on 170 Queen's Gate.

35. These survive with similar sketches for the Swanscombe Church, at the R.A.

36. Information from Mr Edward Raikes.

37. Henry Huth's country house was E. M. Barry's gargantuan Wykehurst, and at Bolney House, Alfred was reacting strongly against his father's taste.

38. Among comparable examples are Bodley and Garner's River House (1879) and Batterbury and Huxley's estate houses in Hampstead Hill Gardens (1879 etc.).

39. 170 Queen's Gate was by accounts badly built, a danger with girderwork, which might encourage a builder to skimp elsewhere in the construction.

40. There were few reliable sources for such houses before 1890, but in the 1880s many were illustrated in the building press. It was much easier to be a classicist after 1890, with help from books like J. A. Gotch, *Architecture of the Renaissance in England* (1894), R. Blomfield, *History of Renaissance Architecture in England* (1894) and Belcher and Macartney, *Later Renaissance Architecture in England* (1897–1901).

41. E.g. marble floor in entrance hall from Squerries Court; other plaques and inlays from Halstead Place and houses in the City; and some features from houses in the Millbank area (*B* 4.1.1902).

42. There was an upstairs morning room, but in fact the single-storey extension meant for a billiard room seems always to have been used as a morning room.

43. Lethaby did some out-of-office detail work after this date, e.g. on 185 Queen's Gate.

44. RNS in W. Shaw Sparrow (ed.), *The British Home of To-day* (1904).

45. *Art Annual* 1896 pp. 30–1.

46. *The British Home of To-day*, ibid.

47. This frieze, based on an old piece of silver, seems first to occur at Lowther Lodge, but reappears, e.g. at Bannow.

48. Robert Shaw.

49. These are illustrated in Heaton's rare first catalogue of 1887. The second catalogue of 1893 is less interesting.

50. *Furniture Gazette* 20.5.1882; L. Weaver, *The House and its Equipment* (1912) pp. 28–9.

51. See pp. 153, 252.

52. Robert Shaw, who is probably wrong in suggesting the church was Youlgreave.

53. Robert Shaw. For J. J. Duveen, see S. N. Behrman, *Duveen* (1952).

54. RNS to Mrs Foster, 3.10.1892.

55. RNS to R. B. Martin, 24.9.1898.

56. RNS to R. B. Martin, 11.7, 15.8, and 20.12.1898, and 9.2.1901.

57. Printed in W. Shaw Sparrow (ed.), *The British Home of To-Day* (1904).

58. *Collected Works of William Morris* Vol. 22 (1914) p. 329, from *The Revival of Architecture* (1888).

59. RNS to R. B. Martin, 24.9.1898.

60. See John Betjeman, *A Plea for Holy Trinity Church Sloane Street* (1974).

61. RNS to Canon Irton Smith, 27.7.1895.

62. Blomfield p. 13.

63. R. W. S. Weir, *William Richard Lethaby*

64. Helen Rossetti Angeli, *Pre-Raphaelite Twilight* (1954) pp. 87–8.
65. Robert Shaw.
66. Reprinted in *Collected Works of William Morris* Vol. 22 (1914) pp. 81–118.
67. Voysey's term for Mackintosh and his acolytes.
68. 'I am afraid I am a somewhat unreliable authority on pictures. Like many people, in fact like *most* people! "I know what I like—!" and I know I like Burne-Jones very much indeed.' RNS to Mrs Foster, 1.6.1892.
69. John Brandon-Jones in *RIBAJ* 64 (1954) p. 177.
70. R. W. S. Weir, *William Richard Lethaby* (1938) p. 8.
71. Weir, *op. cit.*, p. 6.
72. Robert Shaw.
73. Wilton J. Oldham, *The Ismay Line* (1961) p. 67.
74. Oldham, *op. cit.*, p. 71.
75. E.g. Salvin's Harlaxton, Barry's Cliveden, Vulliamy's Westonbirt.
76. *BA* 17 (1882) pp. 39, 49 and 79.
77. RNS to Frederick Radcliffe, 30.11.1907.
78. In this account I have tried to avoid too much overlap with Susan Beattie's excellent article in *Architectural History* 15 (1972) pp. 68–81.
79. *Hansard* 343 (1890) cols. 1814–5, 1.5.1890.
80. HO 45/9765/B841A/1 and 45/9630/A23696/12.
81. Report of RNS, *c.* December 1886, in MEPOL 5/262.
82. These heart-shapes occur on Shaw's office drawings often enough, but only occasionally on the buildings themselves.
83. Robert Shaw.
84. RNS to A. R. Pennefather, 7.1.1887.
85. *A.A. Notes* 8 (1894) pp. 129–31.
86. *RIBAJ* 21 (1913) p. 50.
87. In 1890–1 Belcher designed Mark Ash, Abinger for the son-in-law of Aldam Heaton, who had furnished the Institute of Chartered Accountants. See also Pite's comments in *RIBAJ* 22 (1915) p. 126. For Belcher's career see A. Service in *AR* 148 (1970) pp. 282–90.
88. *RIBAJ* 21 (1913) p. 75.
89. 'I hope a further study of the tracing of the design for the Entrance door at Overbury may have so far softened your heart as to allow me to have those blocks on the jambs

of which I confess I am very fond, in conjunction with Inigo Jones, Wren and a few others.' RNS to R. B. Martin, 2.2.1898. An earlier reviver of this usage was J. M. Brydon, whose Chelsea Town Hall (1887) was an important landmark in the return to formal classicism.
90. Blomfield p. 57 for Harcourt's confusion.
91. After the Foreign Office was completed, Robert Shaw says, 'Mr Shaw's cook went to look at it, and came home and said it was a magnificent building, and that there was not a plain piece about it. Mr Shaw said that the latter statement was quite correct.'
92. RNS to Mr Stuart Wortley, 1.5.1890.
93. *Murrays Magazine* July 1890 pp. 7–8.
94. *Hansard* 4th Series 55 (1898) cols. 114–6, 17.3.1898.
95. *The Times* 30.3.1898.
96. One of Shaw's last acts was to join a successful protest against the proposed demolition of Butterfield's Balliol College Chapel, thereby repaying the debt.
97. *A.A. Notes* 8 (1894) pp. 129–31.
98. Ruskin, *The Seven Lamps of Architecture* 3.9.
99. *A.A. Notes, ibid.*

NOTES TO CHAPTER 7

1. Robert Shaw. Elizabeth Helen Shaw went to Newton's Lloyd Square Convent, Clerkenwell, in 1897.
2. Shaw refused a fee for the Hampstead Mission Room of 1892, but was paid for his work for the Trinity College and Harrow Missions.
3. At the time of writing, twelve of Shaw's churches are still in use: Meerbrook, Boxmoor, St Michael's and St Swithun's Bournemouth, St Margaret's Ilkley, Peplow, St Michael's Bedford Park, All Saints' San Remo, All Saints' Leek, New Groombridge, Richards Castle, and All Saints' Swanscombe (now Roman Catholic). Holy Trinity Bingley and the English Church at Lyons have been demolished; St Mark's Cobourg Road is a warehouse; Holy Trinity Latimer Road is a youth club.
4. H. Muthesius, *Die Neuere Kirchliche Baukunst in England* (1901) pp. 32–34.
5. RNS to J. D. Sedding, 11.11.1886. Sedding wanted the Bedford Park and Har-

row Mission drawings for a lecture on church planning at the A.A., in which he exhibited them and praised them highly: see *BA* 3.12.1886.

6. RNS to Fred White, 19.9.1905.
7. *BN* 30.5.1873.
8. Told by Harold Falkner in *CL* 15.3.1941.
9. RNS to Luke Fildes, 21.1.1882.
10. RNS to Mrs Foster, 5.3.1891; RNS to Sir William Forwood, 27.5.1903.
11. Besides the Bournemouth churches, there are three possible other connections. 1. St Luke's Leek. Here at one stage Shaw was going to erect a metal screen, but Sedding extended the chancel and may have designed the executed wooden screen. 2. Wheatcroft, Scarborough: a house of 1878 by Sedding in the Shaw manner for G. Alderson Smith, donor of the Bingley organ case and brother of J. Metcalfe Smith of Cookridge Hospital. 3. Flete. This has a lodge by Sedding, who restored the nearby churches of Holbeton and Ermington at H. B. Mildmay's expense.
12. For Shaw's admiration of Holy Trinity see p. 258.
13. Besides St Agnes' Kennington, Shaw will have known of G. G. Scott junior's designs for Milverton (1873–8, and very similar to Sedding's St Clement's Bournemouth), and All Hallows' Southwark (1876–8).
14. Ruskin, *Lectures on Architecture* 1.19 and *Stones of Venice* 1.19.12.
15. Shaw admired the conception and proportions of All Saints' Margaret Street, but not its scheme of colouring (Robert Shaw).
16. The only west tower on the main axis in Shaw's church designs occurs in a draft of 1878 for the nave of St Swithun's Bournemouth.
17. The group comprises Shaw's reconstructions at Meerbrook and Boxmoor and restorations at Youlgreave and Longstone; and Nesfield's reconstructions at Kings Walden, Radwinter and Farnham Royal.
18. This may be why Shaw preferred Heaton Butler and Bayne to Clayton and Bell, who excelled in smaller-scale stained glass.
19. Nesfield drew St Augustine's Ramsgate in 1854 and sketched Milton a few years later: see his R.I.B.A. sketchbooks.
20. The silk parts of this frontal, the prototype for Shaw's later design for a frontal at All Saints' and St Edward's, Leek, were in the hands of Mrs Bodley, perhaps the architect's mother: see *Staffordshire Advertiser* 22.10.1870. These three frontals are the only known extant examples of needlework designed by Shaw. For the Leek Embroidery Society, not formally founded till 1879, see *Studio* 1 (1893) pp. 136–140.
21. The V & A lithograph (ill. 204) shows that a shorter nave was originally intended.
22. Apart from Lyons, Shaw's only executed vaults were the wooden nave vault at St Mark's Cobourg Road and the small stone vaults of the Meerbrook tower and the Bingley sanctuary. Parts of the Bradford Exchange were to be vaulted, as was the intended aisle at Kiltegan and the double-nave design for Holy Trinity Latimer Road, where the material proposed may again have been wood.
23. Nesfield appears to have been the first to use half-timbering in church work, in his Radwinter porch (1868–70); but Ted Hubbard reports that John Douglas designed half-timbered church porches at the same time or very soon after, as at Dodleston (1869–70) and Tattenhall (?1869–70). Douglas did not begin to use half-timbering for his churches to any greater extent until he remodelled Whitegate (1874–5).
24. For St Salvador's Dundee, see A. Symondson in *Bulletin of the Scottish Georgian Society* 1 (1972) pp. 10–21.
25. RNS to F. W. Fison, 22.1.1876.
26. Revd. W. Danks in ICBS file 8112.
27. RNS to Canon Irton Smith, 25.1.1896.
28. Of later churches, only Holy Trinity Latimer Road was in brick.
29. The R.A. drawing of the Cottingley chapel was sent to Stanier in April 1877.
30. The Peplow Chapel may have been inadequately supervised, as the structural detailing is weak.
31. See *BN* 29 (1875) *passim*, especially the letters from Sedding defending Scott's design.
32. Disagreements between J. W. Temple and the Rector of Withyham may have jaded Shaw's enthusiasm for this project. He was repeatedly late with plans, and the design is not of great merit.
33. No receipts for San Remo are recorded. The church may be partly designed as a thank-offering on recovery from illness.
34. Note on undated drawing at R.A. for Lisbon Church.

35. *BN* 30.8.1895, and information from R. R. Langham-Carter.

36. RNS to J. D. Sedding, 11.11.1886, quoted on p. 274.

37. RNS to Mrs Foster, 18.10.1892.

38. RNS to Mrs Foster, 4.9.1891.

39. In the first design, vetoed by Mrs Foster on grounds of expense, Shaw proposed an aisle with its own pitched roof, and kept an unbroken roof line for nave and chancel. In revision, he united nave and aisle roofs with a change of pitch, but to maintain interest on this 'show' side, threw in the organ chamber and lower chancel roof.

40. Nesfield and Shaw sometimes used small triangular tiles arranged asymmetrically on their early floors; an example is the corridor connecting The Rhydd Court and its chapel. Usually the standard quarry tiles were 6 in. square, but could vary from $4\frac{1}{2}$ in. (Radwinter, Overbury) to 9 in. (Ilkley). Red quarries were the usual material for flooring the service corridors of Shaw's houses.

41. RNS to Mrs Foster, 20.11.1891.

42. RNS to Mrs Foster, 30.6.1891.

43. RNS to Mrs Foster, 18.10.1892.

44. Benches do not seem to have been common before this, but Peter Howell points out a design for them in *Instrumenta Ecclesiastica* pl. XLVII.

45. At Youlgreave and Bingley Parish Church, the carvers were Pearsons of Leeds; at Longstone and Low Bentham, Shaw used the well-known James Knox of Lambeth. Nesfield's best church furniture is at Radwinter, Kings Walden, Calverhall and Llandyrnog, and some of it may be due to Forsyth.

46. RNS to J. A. Busfeild, 30.5.1871, and *passim*.

47. Drawings at R.A. T. F. Bumpus, *London Churches Ancient and Modern* (1883) p. 218 says that the St Mark's screen derives from one at St Ninian's Perth.

48. J. Sleigh, *A History of the Ancient Parish of Leek* (1883) p. 101. The extant open metal screen at St Swithun's Bournemouth may also be Shaw's.

49. RNS to Canon Irton Smith, 21.9.1897.

50. RNS to Canon Irton Smith, 24.12.1897.

51. It is partly based on the mediaeval font canopy at Trunch.
See p. 274.

53. RNS to Fred White, 18.6.1897. The reading desk was exhibited in the Victorian Church Art Exhibition at the V & A, 1971–2: see the Catalogue, p. 134. Since then, the silver brackets have been stolen.

54. This pulpit may have been given by the Duke of Devonshire.

55. RNS to Fred White, 12.7.1911.

56. At Low Bentham the organ was given by the Rector, Walker Joy, who was an amateur enthusiast and became Shaw's expert on organs. But Shaw came badly unstuck with Joy over Richards Castle, where he proved unreliable.

57. Burghclere's simple reredos of this type has been altered by the insertion of figure panels.

58. RNS to Canon Irton Smith, 16.8.1897.

59. The most important early painted reredoses were Rossetti's at Llandaff Cathedral (for Seddon), Burne-Jones's at St Paul's Brighton (for Bodley) and Leighton's at Lyndhurst (for White). Street and Bodley both used painted polyptychs here and there in the 1870s.

60. See RNS to Hugh Sleigh, 30.6.1888. The fault was righted when Gerald Horsley decorated the chancel.

61. Andrew Saint, *Oxoniensia* 38 (1973) pp. 363–4.

62. RNS to Mrs Foster, 5.3.1891.

63. RNS to Mrs Foster, 4.9.1891.

64. RNS to Canon Irton Smith, 16.8.1897.

65. *Ibid.*

66. *Ibid.*

67. RNS to Frederick Radcliffe, 30.11.1907.

68. Other Shaw churches or restorations including some Heaton Butler and Bayne stained glass: Holy Trinity Bingley, Hebden Bridge, St Michael's Bournemouth, Low Bentham, Overbury, Edburton, and Kelsale. St Luke's Leek has a south aisle window of 1884 which has been attributed to the firm in conjunction with Shaw, and an east window of this date at Kingston, Kent, may be theirs also. The chancel windows by Heaton Butler and Bayne at Haslemere could be due in part to Shaw, who was paid a small sum for work here at the time of his friend J. W. Penfold's rebuilding, 1870.

69. RNS to Miss Wright, 27.5.1908.

70. RNS to Fred White, 22.10.1902.

71. Robert Shaw. It is in St Chad's Ladybarn,

72. RNS to Frederick Radcliffe, 5.3.1905.

73. The diary is kept now at All Saints' Leek.

74. Kniveden stone was used for the walling, Red Hollington for windows and arches, Ladderedge for piers and copings, Red Roche for bases, weatherings and string mouldings. Trial walls were built before the church was begun. Only local stones and limes were permitted: see *Leek Times* 30.7.1887.

75. Memorandum from Shaw in building minutes, 15.10.1887.

76. See the article on Heath's diary by M. J. C. Fisher in *Six Towns Magazine*, March 1969.

77. *Ibid.*

78. J. F. Bentley's Westminster Cathedral design owed much to Lethaby's pioneering interest in Byzantine architecture, which sent Weir Schultz and Sydney Barnsley to Greece in the late 1880s. The Leek font, if not totally Byzantine, is one of the earlier examples of this tendency in late Victorian art.

NOTES TO CHAPTER 8

1. See C. H. Reilly, *Scaffolding in the Sky* (1938) p. 48 for debates on the merits of respective offices. Among disappointed applicants for a place with Shaw was Harold Falkner: *AR* 135 (1964) p.240.

2. Another man helped by Shaw was Charles Nicholson, as he makes clear in his manuscript notes at the V & A.

3. Violet Stuart-Wortley, *Grow Old Along with Me* (1952) pp. 31–2.

4. Lutyens' work at Framfield antedates his marriage in 1897 and may be presumed contemporary with Shaw's. His letters also show that he knew the Combes of Pierrepont, the Claytons of Chesters, and the Shrubbs of Boldre Grange.

5. There are pencil notes marked E.L.L. on Shaw's plans for The Hallams at the R.A.

6. Lutyens to Emily Lytton, 22.7.1897.

7. See p. 371.

8. Lutyens to Emily Lytton, 21.9.1897.

9. *BJ* 19.2.1895.

10. RNS to Fred White, 5.2.1896.

11. *BJ* 4.11.1896, following the *Daily Chronicle*. Lutyens and Voysey have been variously recorded as holding the same opinion.

12. *Town and Country Planning* 9 (1941) pp. 97–8.

13. David Saunders in *Architecture in Australia* (August 1969) pp. 655–662 discusses 'Queen Anne and the Balcony Style'. One Australian house decorated in advanced English taste was Urrbrae, Fullarton, near Adelaide, for which Aldam Heaton sent out exotic furnishings in about 1892–4. I am much indebted to John Bonython and Sir Edward Morgan for information about this house.

14. The fullest account is Vincent Scully, *The Shingle Style and the Stick Style* (1971 edn.), mostly based on the British and American periodicals. For Shaw and the Shingle Style see especially pp. 10–18. See also W. Knight Sturges in *Society of Architectural Historians' Journal* 9.4 (1950) pp. 15–20.

15. I am grateful to Margaret Floyd for telling me about Sturgis and his English connections.

16. These houses are discussed by Henry-Russell Hitchcock, *The Architecture of H. H. Richardson and His Times* (1961 edn.) pp. 156–63.

17. A point noticed by Clive Wainwright.

18. Montgomery Schuyler, *Concerning Queen Anne* in *American Architecture and Other Writings* (ed. Jordy and Coe) Vol. 2 (1961) pp. 453–487.

19. Robert Shaw.

20. R. Phené Spiers in an interview, *BJ* 16.4.1895. The date of their resignation was 1869.

21. RNS to Fred White, 5.2.1896. Shaw designed the grave slabs of both Leighton and Millais at St Paul's Cathedral, at the request of the R.A.

22. Sidney C. Hutchison, *The History of the Royal Academy* (1968) pp. 137, 141 and 231. See also RNS to the R.A. Council, 18.3.1882, and to Leighton, 29.3.1882.

23. Blomfield p. 21.

24. Robert Shaw.

25. On Arthur Blomfield, see RNS to J. D. Sedding, 1.5.1888: 'I hope you admired our new architectural member's work, a slate-coloured church of the seediest character, and some other deplorable things.' Of the other architectural R.A.'s, Alfred Waterhouse supported the R.I.B.A., and J. L. Pearson was relatively inactive.

26. RNS to Frederic Eaton, 9.11.1890.

27. For the background to this controversy,

see Barrington Kaye, *The Development of the Architectural Profession in Britain* (1960) pp. 135–43, and C. M. Butler, *The Society of Architects* (1925) pp. 50–55. The issues are well discussed by R. Macleod, *Style and Society* (1971) Chs. 6–8.

28. T. G. Jackson, *Modern Gothic Architecture* (1873) Chs. 5 & 6.
29. T. G. Jackson, *Recollections* (1950) pp. 223–7, a lucid contemporary account of the argument.
30. Letters of RNS of 6.9.1891 and 6.11.1891, quoted in Reginald Blomfield, *Memoirs of an Architect* (1932) pp. 62–3.
31. RNS to Reginald Blomfield, 15.11.1892, quoted in Blomfield, *Memoirs*, ibid.
32. *Nineteenth Century* 33 (1893) pp. 65–82.
33. Macartney's essay develops this theme by suggesting that byelaws are the proper means to control over incompetence in architecture.
34. *A* 27.11.1891 reprints this and several other letters to *The Times*.
35. This paragraph comes mostly from Robert Shaw.
36. For later developments, see Barrington Kaye, *op. cit.*
37. R. Schultz Weir, *William Richard Lethaby* (1938) p. 6. For a general history, see H. J. L. J. Massé, *The Art Workers' Guild 1884–1934* (1935), especially E. S. Prior's essay, pp. 6–14.
38. Blomfield p. 103.
39. Ruskin, *Praeterita* 1.1.
40. See his *DNB* article on Shaw.
41. RNS to Frederic Eaton, 2.9.1890. This is Shaw's only known piece of silver.
42. RNS to Mother Etheldreda, 25.7.1904.
43. See Shaw's reference for Wilson's application for the Slade Professorship at Oxford, 14.3.1910 (Bodleian MS. Top. Oxon. c.178).
44. That is why a city building of real genius like Mackintosh's Glasgow School of Art comes as such a shock and contrast.
45. See pp. 187–91.
46. Robert Shaw.
47. These figures are drawn from Robert Shaw's abstract of his father's account books.
48. R. Schultz Weir, *William Richard Lethaby* (1938).
49. L.C.C. Establishments Committee, Presented Papers, 19.6.1902 (13).
50. Ginham won an R.I.B.A. Medal for some fine measured drawings of St George's Bloomsbury.
51. See the design drawings at the R.A. for Norman Cottages, Greenham, and the Bailiff's Cottage, Framfield.
52. In 1902 Ginham exhibited an addition to Shaw's Hopedene at the R.A. His other known work also involves Shaw. After New Scotland Yard, Shaw several times re-employed its builder John Grover, a wealthy congregationalist with brickyards and building estates in the developing area round Hindhead. Grover asked Shaw for a church plan which he could build at his own expense in several places in the district. Of the three examples constructed, the first was the Hindhead Free Church (1895–6), built to elevations by Ginham. It is a dull rock-faced building but has an excellent set of Arts and Crafts benches. The later churches built to the plan, at Hammer (1903) and Beacon Hill (1904–5), though attributed in *B* 22.11.1912, have no necessary connection with either Shaw or Ginham.
53. Drawings at the R.A.
54. Drawings at the R.A.
55. I am grateful to Miss Marjorie Shaw and Mr Bryan Shaw for the personal information in this paragraph.
56. Robert Shaw threw away many ancillary papers and much private correspondence at the time of the paper shortage in the Second World War, but preserved the essential documents.
57. *The Times* 19.11.1912.
58. Information from Miss Marjorie Shaw.
59. G. C. Williamson, *Murray Marks and His Friends* (1919) pp. 178–9.
60. RNS to Agnes Shaw, 16.7.1902.
61. Robert Shaw mentions several anecdotes connected with Clayton.
62. RNS to Frederick Radcliffe, 11.3.1907.
63. All this information from Robert Shaw.
64. RNS to Reginald Blomfield, 14.5.1903, quoted in Blomfield p. 109.
65. Robert Shaw says that a brass altar candlestick was his father's favourite piece. It stood alone on a small table so that he could get regular pleasure from the way it passed from a triangular base to a circular baluster.
66. *AR* 140 (1966) p. 199.
67. Five charming letters from Shaw to H. Knowles Brown, who tended all his clocks,

68. See the auction catalogue, Christie Manson and Woods, 10.4.1913.
69. *BJ* 24.6.1896.
70. *A.A. Notes* 14 (1899) p. 130.
71. *B* 4.4.1896.
72. *DEH* vol. 1, p. 129. In a memorable passage in *DEB* pp. 24–25, Muthesius compares Shaw's transition to the different styles of Goethe's early and late poetry.
73. Nearer equivalents are Charles Barry's Trentham or Cliveden.
74. RNS to Mrs Foster from Boulogne, 20.8.1889.
75. A master from Bryanston School first spotted this convincing parallel while on holiday in France. For other helpful points on Bryanston, I am indebted to Alan Powers and Mr E. M. Williams.
76. E. S. Prior's *DNB* article on Shaw.
77. An exception was the billiard room, where Shaw contrived toplighting which missed out the floor above. This was the only major structural loss when the house was converted into a school.
78. Copy of a memorandum, held by Mr E. M. Williams of Blandford.
79. E. J. May's sketchbook at R.I.B.A., records of a visit to Bryanston, 27.5.1892.
80. Were these radiators (supplied by Wenham and Waters of Croydon) made to Shaw's design? Other examples within his practice occur at Trinity College Mission, Framfield Place, and Bishop's House; outside it, at the Connaught Hotel, the restored chapel at Ightham Mote, and Lutyens' early house at Crooksbury.
81. See p. 270. Brydon's Chelsea Town Hall of 1887 used brick and stone rustication like this in a pure classic design, and may have some connection with Bryanston.
82. *DNB* article on Shaw.
83. See J. D. Sedding, *Garden Craft Old and New* (1891), and for an opposing view, Reginald Blomfield and F. I. Thomas, *The Formal Garden in England* (1892). The subject was often discussed at Art Workers' Guild meetings of the period.
84. East Combe of 1891–2 is another semi-vernacular commission, for which see p. 339; after that there is the addition to Sibleys Orchard of 1905–6.
85. The little Chesters Museum, with its broad Tuscan eaves and Gibbs surrounds, could well be Shaw's or Ginham's.
86. Blomfield pp. 29–30.
87. Now demolished, with little visual loss to the house.
88. For instance, Prior's Home Place, Holt, Lutyens' Papillon Hall, and Schultz's How Green. For a full analysis, see Jill Franklin in *AR* 157 (1975) pp. 220–5.
89. Lutyens to his wife, 23.4.1901.
90. There is no evidence that Shaw worked outside the hall at Addington, but in default of other information the rest of the work, including an additional storey, must be presumed his.
91. Pembroke College Cambridge had a mission in Barlow Street, Southwark, with interesting buildings by Prior.
92. Drawing at the R.A., undated.
93. Voysey's account books at the R.I.B.A. mention a small payment but do not specify the work.
94. Schomberg House, Pall Mall, could have suggested some of these details.
95. These have now been rebuilt.
96. HO 45/9673/A46538/33, records at P.R.O.
97. Mark Girouard, *The Victorian Country House* (1971) p. 171.

Notes to Chapter 9

1. For details of Victorian street planning in London, see Percy J. Edwards, *History of London Street Improvements 1855–1897* (1898).
2. J. N. Tarn, *Five Per Cent Philanthropy* (1973) discusses how the MBW made over hidden subsidies to the philanthropic housing trusts to cope with this situation.
3. The reforms for which Viollet-le-Duc campaigned did loosen up the nature of French architectural training after 1870, but the basis of the *atelier* system remained.
4. *BN* 11.10.1916; see also Lethaby's obituary of Spiers in *RIBAJ* 23 (1916) pp. 334–5. Pascal was a fellow juror with Shaw for the first half of the 1898 University of California competition at Antwerp. For a profile of Pascal, whose *atelier* pupils included Charles Mewès, Arthur Davis, and J. J. Burnet, see *BJAE* 1.12.1909. For a French viewpoint on

London architecture see the regular *Lettres de Londres* in *La Construction Moderne* 16 (1900–1).

5. For remarks by Shaw on Paris see his evidence to the Lords Select Committee in *A* 4.10.1907.

6. Shaw's views on the Queen Victoria Memorial competition are to be found in *BJAR* 17.4.1901.

7. *B* 19.2.1898. This is the only evidence for Lutyens' involvement, which cannot have been great.

8. *The Times* 12.3.1898.

9. These included E. P. Warren and the Art Workers' Guild.

10. D. G. Jones in *AAJ* 70 (1954) p. 98, in an article on the early L.C.C. Architect's Department reflecting Owen Fleming's opinions.

11. George Weald, like Ginham, had been Shaw's office boy and was an assistant in the 1890s. He had a long career with the L.C.C.

12. Shaw's later opinion, quoted in W. R. Lethaby, *Philip Webb and his Work* (1935) p. 77.

13. Shaw had been part of a delegation of 1889 to the L.C.C. which successfully appealed for the saving of St Mary le Strand.

14. *AR* 7 (1900) pp. 118–121. Shaw was a passive member of the *Architectural Review's* first Editorial Committee, but the editorship soon passed to Macartney.

15. L.C.C. Establishment Committee Minutes, 26.7.1906 (7).

16. RNS to Riley, 16.10.1900, in L.C.C. Improvements Committee Presented Papers, 17.10.1900 (37).

17. *BJAR* 4.9.1901.

18. Robert Shaw says his father predicted that Waterhouse would choose Webb's design, and was disappointed that Macartney's entry got no further. For an account of the competition see *Survey of London* XXXVIII pp. 118–9. Shaw was asked to compete but declined.

19. Owen Fleming, who was involved, suggests in *RIBAJ* 42 (1935) p. 738 that the competition was to some extent a put-up job, but this is not quite right. Shaw was allowed to pick several of the competitors (Horsley, Newton, Prior, Ricardo, W. Stirling and F. W. Troup), and any of them as winners would have been equally

acceptable.

20. For St Paul's, see a letter of Shaw to Dendy Watney at Mercers' Hall; for the Royal Insurance Building, pp. 359–60.

21. RNS to G. L. Gomme, 24.4.1907, in L.C.C. Establishments Committee Presented Papers.

22. Joint report of Riley and Shaw, 23.10.1900, in L.C.C. Improvements Committee Presented Papers.

23. Report of RNS, 7.5.1901, in L.C.C. Improvements Committee Presented Papers.

24. *ABJ* 27.11.1912 (as recalled by Runtz).

25. He may, however, be wrong, as it seems very unlike Runtz.

26. Garnier, like Shaw, was often consulted and gave free advice on replanning problems in Paris.

27. See particularly the letter of Sidney R. J. Smith, the Tate Gallery architect, in L.C.C. Bridges Committee Presented Papers, 28.11.1902. The question of Vauxhall Bridge had been in the air since the demolition of the old bridge in 1898, when the R.I.B.A. had held a small 'ideas competition'.

28. Riley's report in L.C.C. Bridges Committee Presented Papers, 11.2.1903.

29. Robert Shaw.

30. Riley's report, *ibid.*, commenting on Shaw's design.

31. Letter in L.C.C. Bridges Committee Presented Papers, 25.3.1903.

32. The Society's committee consisted of Lord Windsor, Sir Edward Poynter, W. B. Richmond, Brock, Frampton, Aston Webb, Belcher, Sir Benjamin Baker, Caroe, Beresford Pite, H. T. Hare and M. H. Spielmann.

33. Shaw wrote a reference for Statham for the Slade Professorship at Oxford in 1910.

34. *ABJ* 27.11.1912.

35. *ABN* 166 (1941) p. 69, as reported by E.G., probably Edwin Gunn.

36. N. Pevsner, *London I, Cities of London and Westminster* (1957) p. 534.

37. Letter of 9.11.1905, communicated by Godfrey Rubens.

38. RNS to G. L. Gomme, 27.4.1907, in L.C.C. Establishments Committee Presented Papers.

39. Assessors' report, 3.10.1907, in L.C.C. Establishments Committee Presented

Papers.

40. This is suggested by the tone of the Committee Minutes and confirmed by the mention of the improvement to the front as Shaw's in several of his obituaries, e.g. *BN* 22.11.1912. The open colonnade which Knott had proposed in front of his crescent may have been related to Shaw's schemes for Euston and Piccadilly Circus.

41. HO 45/9996/A47240/38.

42. HO 45/9996/A47240/80.

43. Robert Shaw.

44. RNS to Reginald Blomfield, 30.12.1904, quoted in Blomfield p. 111.

45. There is no reason to show that Shaw himself thought it a mistake.

46. *The Tribune* 19.10.1906.

47. Draft of letter to J. B. Ismay, at R.A.

48. The Gare de l'Est is a more probable model than the Gare St Lazare or the Gare du Nord, which Robert Shaw cites.

49. Draft of letter to J. B. Ismay, at R.A.

50. William Forwood, *Recollections of a Busy Life* (1911) p. 184.

51. Wilton J. Oldham, *The Ismay Line* (1961) p. 130; Ray Anderson, *White Star Line* (1964) pp. 84–6. The only known photographs, in *A* 5 & 19.1.1900, do not suggest anything very special about the Oceanic interior.

52. RNS to Agnes Shaw, 2.9.1899, and abstract of Robert Shaw's diaries.

53. Assessors' report at Royal Insurance Building.

54. Robert Shaw records his father's surprise at the result of this competition.

55. This honour is often ascribed to the Ritz Hotel.

56. 'I think such a very serious problem [sc. the lighting] must be very seriously faced and as I think I see how it can be done quite easily I should have much pleasure in explaining the scheme should you desire me to do so. Then as regards the obstruction by pillars, in this [scheme] there would be no real difficulty in doing away with [the pillars and get]ting an entirely unbroken area . . . I should like a thin floor, and a moderately flat ceiling, in this case this can be done perfectly, and as a matter of fact I did it in a City Bank 20 years ago.' Assessor's report, with missing words restored in brackets. The bank thus referred to must be Barings.

57. *The Times* 19.11.1912.

58. *AR* 10 (1901) pp. 146–55.

59. In his interview in *The Tribune* 19.10.1906, Shaw claimed that he 'hated and loathed' terracotta for its unyielding texture, and only used it once, when restoring windows at Sutton Place. Parr's Bank seems the only other exception.

60. C. H. Reilly, *Some Liverpool Streets and Buildings* (1921) pp. 34–5.

61. *The Book of Liverpool Cathedral*. ed. Vere Cotton (1964) p.1. For the following account I am grateful for use of the Radcliffe papers and Liverpool Cathedral Executive Committee Minutes and Papers, deposited in Liverpool City Library.

62. *AR* 10 (1901) pp. 170–1. For Shaw's admiring visit to Westminster Cathedral in the company of Bentley and Lethaby, see W. de l'Hôpital, *Westminster Cathedral and its Architect* (1920) Vol. 1 pp. 88 and 308.

63. RNS to Agnes Shaw, 15.7.1902.

64. Bodley and Shaw, letter in *The Times* 17.10.1902, in reply to criticism.

65. RNS to Frederick Radcliffe, 26.8.1902.

66. See p. 000.

67. H. D. Horsfall had a reputation for precipitate judgment.

68. RNS to Sir William Forwood, 23.5.1903.

69. RNS to Mrs Ismay, 31.5.1903.

70. RNS to Frederick Radcliffe, 11.3.1907.

71. *The Book of Liverpool Cathedral* (1964) pp. 21–22.

72. Shaw's report, 5.3.1903.

73. An alternative scheme for this part was carried out by William Williamson in 1913–4.

74. RNS to R. Lewis, 8.11.1901.

75. Arthur Green's report of October 1901 in CEO 15145.

76. RNS to R. Lewis, 7.8.1901.

77. However, *AR* 21 (1907) pp. 46–51 says that the flute key action to the lamps in the main office was Shaw's idea.

78. For an excellent account of the Quadrant rebuilding, see *Survey of London* XXXI pp. 87–95, and for the background, Hermione Hobhouse, *A History of Regent Street* (1975). There is an invaluable but typically personal account in Blomfield pp. 59–71. The following discussion, except where noted, is based on Crown Estates Office files.

79. Quoted by Macartney in *B* 16.2.1907.
80. Macartney, *ibid*. The County Fire Office arcade was a well-known pick-up spot for homosexuals.
81. Arthur Green to Woodward, 20.10.1903, in CEO 15276.
82. Lord Windsor had already commissioned huge country and town houses for himself (Hewell Grange by Thomas Garner and 54 Mount Street by Fairfax Wade), was President of the Ruskin Union, and sat on the Architectural Vigilance Society's committee.
83. Woodward and Emden to Horner, 22.3.1905, in CEO 15382.
84. RNS to Hellard, 13.5.1905.
85. RNS to Horner, 8.8.1905.
86. RNS to Hellard, 14.11.1905.
87. RNS to Hellard, 13.12.1909.
88. RNS to Hellard, 26.1.1906.
89. RNS to Hellard, 13.3.1906.
90. RNS to Hellard, 9.3.1906.
91. *Daily Telegraph* 9.4.1907.
92. *Daily Mail* 11.6.1906.
93. *Nineteenth Century*, July 1906 pp. 165–8.
94. Robert Shaw.
95. Robert Shaw.
96. The Advisory Committee now consisted of Aston Webb, Belcher, Sir Henry Tanner, and Ernest George.
97. RNS to Hellard, 26.2.1910.
98. RNS to Hellard, 9.8.1907.
99. Shaw's report, June 1909, in CEO 15530.
100. RNS to G. Leveson-Gower, 16.2.1912.
101. RNS to Hellard, 15.2.1912
102. RNS to G. Leveson-Gower, 1.3.1912. This is the version as sent; Blomfield pp. 63–4 gives a draft.
103. Richardson in *AR* 140 (1966) pp. 202–3 and 205 n. 31 perpetrates two falsehoods about his connection with Regent Street. Shaw never approached him as a partner, as he suggests, nor is there any evidence that he was helped by anybody in the design, let alone the little-known furniture expert Ingleson Goodison.
104. A. Trystan Edwards, *Good and Bad Manners in Architecture* (1946 edn.) pp. 81–7.
105. W. R. Lethaby, *Philip Webb and his Work* (1935) p. 77. The date of this letter is probably 1910, not 1900.
106. See J. H. H. Williams' illuminating article in *Concrete* 6 (1972) pp. 30–4.
107. RNS to Reginald Blomfield, 14.5.1903, quoted in Blomfield p. 109.
108. *BN* 1.11.1907.
109. There was one further assessorship, apparently uneventful, for the Southport Homoeopathic Hospital, won by H. Percy Adams and Charles Holden: *BN* 11.12.1908.
110. *A* 4.10.1907.
111. Information in this paragraph mainly from Robert Shaw.
112. RNS to R. B. Martin, 28.12.1904.
113. RNS to Frederick Radcliffe, 25.1.1911.
114. See his letters on the subject at Ilkley, 1907–11.
115. The *Daily Mail* commemorated this event with a *gauche* poem, 6.1.1910.
116. RNS to Frederick Radcliffe, 30.11.1907.
117. Robert Shaw preserves a copy of this draft.
118. C. H. B. and Marjorie Quennell, *A History of Everyday Things in England* Part III (1938) p. 154.
119. C. H. Reilly, *Scaffolding in the Sky* (1938) p. 65; and for his views on the King Edward Memorial, pp. 138–9.
120. RNS to Frederick Radcliffe, 11.2.1911.
121. RNS to Frederick Radcliffe, 30.8.1911.
122. RNS to Edward Prior, 21.2.1912 (communicated by Lynne Walker).
123. Quoted in W. G. Newton, *The Work of Ernest Newton, R.A.* (1925) p. 4.
124. Robert Shaw. The death certificate gives as causes: 'senile decay, gall stones 8 years, exhaustion 6 months'.
125. Robert Shaw.
126. *Charles Canning Winmill*, by his daughter, (1946) pp. 53–4.

Notes on Sources

A. SELECT BIBLIOGRAPHY

THIS is a brief list of articles and books that incorporate original information or valuable insights on Shaw and his work. The last three items are not published, but are included out of several such items on merit.

BN 24.10.1873 (article by E. W. Godwin)
BN 3.1.1890 (brief profile)
BJ 19.2.1895 (interview)
The Studio 7 (1896) pp. 21–30 and 98–109 (articles)
Architecture 1 (1896) pp. 2–18 (article)
B 4.4.1896 (brief article by Ingress Bell)
DEH Vol. 1 pp. 109–33 (critique by Muthesius)
The Tribune 19.10.1906 (long interview)
B 1.1.1910 (critique by H. H. Statham)
AR 32 (1912) pp. 299–308 (article by Arthur Keen), and contemporary obituaries in A, ABJ, B, BA, BN, RIBAJ, and The Times
  Robert Shaw's notes on his father, mainly of 1930s, in the possession of the Shaw family
  W. R. Lethaby, Philip Webb and his Work (1935) pp. 74–6 (brief sketch)
  Reginald Blomfield, Richard Norman Shaw R.A. (1940) (biography)
  Nikolaus Pevsner, AR 89 (1941) pp. 41–6 (critique of Blomfield, revised and reprinted in Victorian Architecture, ed. P. Ferriday, (1963) pp. 237–46)
  W. Knight Sturges, Society of Architectural Historians' Journal 9.4 (1950) pp. 15–20 (article on American influence)
  John Brandon-Jones, AAJ 71 (1955–6) pp. 15–19 (article on Webb and Shaw)
  H. R. Hitchcock, Architectural Nineteenth and Twentieth Centuries (1958) pp. 206–20
  J. M. Welbank, R.I.B.A. Silver Medal Essay, 1961 (biographical essay)
  David C. Low, Cambridge B.A. thesis, 1973 (thesis on Shaw's churches)
  N. Halbritter, A.A. thesis, 1974 (thesis on Shaw's town houses)

B: DRAWINGS AND LETTERS

THE bulk of Shaw's surviving drawings is at the Royal Academy, where they were deposited a few years ago. There is also a large collection at the R.I.B.A., consisting mainly of drawings given by Agnes Shaw and of working drawings for houses built by Frank Birch. A smaller number was given by Shaw during his lifetime to the Spiers collection at the V & A.

Besides these, there are five extant sketchbooks. The earliest, including his sketches of the Houses of Parliament, is at the R.A. The two sketchbooks at the R.I.B.A. mainly relate to Shaw's English tours of 1859–63. There are two further working sketchbooks in the Shaw family, one of 1868–9, the other, incomplete, of 1876–8.

The accompanying list, obviously incomplete, gives the present provenance, by owner or institution, of the main collections of Shaw letters quoted or referred to in the text or catalogue. I have not included collections of less than five letters, except where they bear upon others.

Provenance	Number	Topic or Recipient
Crown Estates Office	142	Quadrant rebuilding (127); second Alliance Assurance Office (15)
Lord Inchiquin	118	Richards Castle Church
Edward Holland-Martin	52	Overbury Court, etc.
R.I.B.A.	47	Arthur Keen (21), Gawsworth Rectory (16), Frank Birch (4), others (6)
All Saints' Bingley	43	Restoration of Ryshworth Chapel
Bryan Shaw	37	Continental Tour (19), Family (18), also two draft letters
Mark Norman	33	Moor Place alterations
Church Commissioners	32	Bishop's House (also other brief notes on various churches here and in ICBS files)
St Margaret's Ilkley	31	Building and furnishing church
Royal Academy	29	R.A. business etc. (19); Fred White (10), mainly about Swanscombe Church (3 further letters still with White family)
V & A	22	Luke Fildes (12), Murray Marks (5), J. D. Sedding (4), other (1)
Liverpool City Library (from Cathedral Archives etc.)	20	Frederick Radcliffe (14), Sir William Forwood (4), Mrs Ismay (2)
P.R.O.	16	New Scotland Yard
Sun Alliance Company	10	Second Alliance Assurance Office
Convent of Bethany	10	Building convent etc.
Kent Record Office	9	The Rookery, Bromley Common
Mrs V. Wright	9	Longstone Church (stained glass)
G.L.C. Record Office	8	Strand/Aldwych Improvements (4); County Hall (4)
Barings Bank	c.6	Alterations to bank
Royal Commission for 1851 Exhibition	5	Albert Hall Mansions
Barclays Bank	5	Martins Bank alterations
National Maritime Museum	5	E. W. Cooke (4); Miss Cooke (1)
Leeds City Archives	5	St John's Leeds restoration

Index

All figures in italic are references to illustration numbers

469

471

472

478